M000087474

Special Edition Using Oracle 11*i*

By
BOSS Corporation,
Jim Crum

With

Satyakanth Abbaraju
Don Bieger
Karen Brownfield
Don Castro
Telisa Seiter Conlin
Ken Conway
Darren Cooper
Don Driggs
Bill Dunham
Don Grons
Pat Keeley
Stephen King
Patti Kingsmore
Kris Saha
Bill Stratton
Jyh Yi (GE) Wang
John Wells
George Wilson

Special contributions by

Project Partners, LLC
With
Randy Egger
Martha Anne McKillip
John Pilkington
Sheila Reardon
John Sasali

que®

201 W. 103rd Street
Indianapolis, Indiana 46290

Contents at a Glance

Special Edition Using Oracle 11i

International Standard Book Number: 0-7897-2670-X

Library of Congress Catalog Card Number: 2001094301

Printed in the United States of America

First Printing: September 2001

03 02 01 4 3 2 1

Trademarks

All terms mentioned in this book that are known to be trademarks or service marks have been appropriately capitalized. Que cannot attest to the accuracy of this information. Use of a term in this book should not be regarded as affecting the validity of any trademark or service mark.

Oracle® is a registered trademark of Oracle Corporation. The publisher gratefully acknowledges Oracle's kind permission to use its trademarks in this publication. Fastforward, Jinitiator, Oracle, Oracle Alert, Oracle Alliance, Oracle Application Object Library, OracleBRONZE, OracleSILVER, OracleGOLD, Oracle Consulting Services, Oracle Financials, Oraclemetals, Oracle MetaLink, Oracle Method, Oracle Workflow, Oracle7, Oracle8, Oracle8i, PL/SQL, SmartClient, SQL*Forms, SQL*Loader, and SQL*Plus are trademarks, registered trademarks, or service marks of Oracle Corporation. Oracle Corporation is not the publisher of this book and is not responsible for it under any aspect of press law.

Warning and Disclaimer

Every effort has been made to make this book as complete and as accurate as possible, but no warranty or fitness is implied. The information provided is on an "as is" basis. The authors and the publisher shall have neither liability nor responsibility to any person or entity with respect to any loss or damages arising from the information contained in this book or from the use of the Web site.

Associate Publisher
Dean Miller

Acquisitions Editor
Michelle Newcomb

Development Editors
Sarah Robbins
Sean Dixon
Maureen McDaniel

Managing Editor
Thomas F. Hayes

Senior Editor
Susan Ross Moore

Production Editors
Amy Jay
Megan Wade

Indexer
Sharon Shock

Technical Editors
Mike Bartoletti
Nancy Beck
Rob Berry
Karen Brownfield
Don Castro
Don Driggs
Alyssa Francini
Brett Green
Don Grons
Patti Kingsmore
Martha McKillip
Randy Sanders
Pat Schaffer
Chuck Steedley
Bill Stratton

Software Specialist
Michael Hunter

Team Coordinator
Cindy Teeters

Interior Designer
Ruth Harvey

Cover Designers
Dan Armstrong
Ruth Harvey

Contents

About the Authors

BOSS Corporation is an Oracle Applications services company. BOSS is an acronym that stands for Better Organization Service Solutions. The consulting organization was formed in July 1995 and has focused exclusively on providing Enterprise Resource Planning (ERP) solutions, applications implementation project services, and database administration services for the Oracle Applications.

BOSS Corporation headquarters is located near Atlanta, Georgia, but our consultants provide services throughout the United States or globally as our clients require. Regional offices are located near Dallas, Raleigh, and Chicago.

The company is proud of the quality of its consultants. It uses a combination of its own employees and associates to provide the correct skills at the right time to meet the needs of its clients.

BOSS Corporation offers many services to customers using the Oracle Applications. These services include the following:

- Expert assistance for financial applications implementations and upgrades (GL, AP, PO, FA, AR, and PA)
- Expert assistance for distribution applications implementations and upgrades (PO, INV, AR, and OM)
- Expert assistance for manufacturing applications implementations and upgrades (MRP, MPS, OM, INV, BOM, ENG, CST, CPP, and WIP)
- Expert assistance for human resources management system (HRMS) applications implementations and upgrades (HR, PAY, OAB, OTM, and OTA)
- Project management and planning for Oracle Applications implementations
- Database administration services for installation, upgrade, and tuning of the Oracle Applications
- Remote database administration services
- Technical services to convert legacy data, create interfaces, and extend or modify the basic functionality of the Oracle Applications

See the advertisements at the back of this book for more details about BOSS Corporation.

You can contact the authors at the following address:

BOSS Corporation
6455 East Johns Crossing, Suite 404
Duluth, GA 30097

Tel: (770) 622-5500

Fax: (770) 622-5400

E-mail: `authors@bosscorporation.com`

The company maintains a Web site with free Oracle Applications tips and techniques at `http://www.bosscorporation.com`.

Project Partners, LLC is a systems integration and consulting company, specializing in the implementation of Oracle Project Accounting and related Oracle financial applications. Founded in 1997 by Randy Egger, former Chief Architect of Oracle Projects (Project Accounting), Project Partners was formed in response to the growing needs of companies as they shift their operations toward a project orientation.

Headquartered in Half Moon Bay, California, Project Partners has worked with more than 50 clients worldwide, offering functional and technical expertise to client companies who are undergoing full implementations or implementation audits, or who require gap analysis, conversions, or upgrades. We offer clients project management, change management, and systems training using our in-depth knowledge of Oracle Projects, Oracle Financials, Self-Service technology, and other Projects-related applications. Our technical team has years of practical experience in the customization of forms and reports, as well as the effective use of client extension technologies. We have successfully created many legacy interfaces, as well as third-party software integrations. With substantial implementation experience in the fields of engineering, entertainment, advertising, construction, telecommunications, government, military, and service companies, Project Partners' consultants are recognized as experts in Oracle Projects. Our industry experience includes multinational corporations and foreign national firms, as well as U.S.-based companies. Using Oracle's Activity Management Gateway (AMG), Project Partners has also developed a proprietary product—Project Loader—to integrate third-party and legacy systems with Oracle Projects for both one-time conversions and ongoing seamless data sharing. Project Partners offers a wide array of services for client companies, including the following:

- Full implementation of Oracle Projects and related financial applications
- Implementation audits
- Gap analysis
- Education and training programs
- Client extensions
- Legacy system interfaces
- Third-party software interfaces
- Custom database/forms coding solutions
- Custom report design and implementation

What our clients say about Project Partners, LLC:

"Project Partners is the right choice if you have a projects-oriented organization. Rafael, facing a complex implementation challenge, has found Project Partners to be the most reliable resource. They will always help you find the best solutions, functionally and technically, based on their broad experience and in-depth knowledge."

—Dina Rotem, Projects and Financial ERP Director, Rafael, Israel.

"ABS operates globally and required all of the new multinational and intercompany functionality provided in Oracle Projects 11i. Our implementation utilized multicurrency costs and billing, inter-project billing, project allocations, and significant integration using the Activity Management Gateway.

Choosing Project Partners has proven to be a critical element of our success. Project Partners leverages the experience and knowledge of their entire organization staff to ensure that solutions are well considered and rationally implemented. They are genuinely interested in the Oracle product and are committed to ensuring a smooth hand-off to their clients."

—Tom Kirk, Manager, Projects Implementation Team, American Bureau of Shipping

You can contact us at the following address:

Project Partners, LLC
520 Purissima Street
P.O. Box 373
Half Moon Bay, CA 94019
Tel: (650) 712-6200
Fax: (650) 726-7975
E-mail: `www.projectp.com`

Jim Crum is the Chief Operating Officer and one of the original founders of BOSS Corporation. Previously, he was Practice Manager for consulting services at Oracle Corporation. Jim has more than eight years of functional experience with the Oracle Applications and fifteen years of technical experience with the Oracle database and tools. While at Oracle Corporation, Jim was a certified trainer in the Application Implementation Method (AIM). In addition, Jim has been employed as Director of MIS, Division Financial Director, Plant Controller, and Manufacturing Manager for several large international corporations. Jim has a B.A. degree from DePauw University. Jim is active in the local chapter of the Oracle Applications User Group (OAUG), and he edits the *Tips and Techniques* newsletter for the Atlanta OAUG.

Satyakanth Abbaraju is an Oracle ERP Specialist with BOSS Corporation, with more than three years of extensive experience in Oracle financials and Oracle Process Manufacturing applications. Satyakanth has a Bachelor's degree in commerce and is a member of the Institute of Chartered Accountants of India. He also has more than nine years of industry experience in various capacities as a user, a manager, a consultant, and an auditor in several manufacturing and service industries. Prior to becoming an applications consultant for Oracle's ERP products, he worked as an Accounts Manager and MIS Manager and practiced as a Chartered Accountant in India. He was a key functional member of the team that converted Oracle GEMMS to Oracle Process Manufacturing Release 11.

Don Bieger is an Oracle ERP Specialist with BOSS Corporation, who has more than four years of extensive experience with Oracle Financial applications. Don has a Bachelor's degree in business and holds a CPA designation. Don has more than eight years experience in various accounting and financial roles in a range of industries, including Internet communications, nonprofit, and manufacturing. In the last three years, he has also performed delivery of consulting services for Ernst and Young, LLP in the Oracle ERP field across several industry sectors.

Karen Brownfield is an Oracle ERP Specialist with BOSS Corporation. Karen has ten years of extensive experience in Oracle financials and twenty-five years experience in managing, maintaining, and configuring other software applications in various industries including process manufacturing, entertainment, government contracting, and hospitality. Karen has served on the Oracle Applications User Group Board of Directors for eight years in various positions, including president, VP-Enhancements, conference chair, and member of multiple committees. Karen has presented several papers at OAUG and other regional conferences and has developed and taught Workflow classes at clients and for the Financial Boot Camp at her former employer.

Don Castro is a BOSS Corporation HRMS Specialist. In 1996, working at American Color Graphics, Don implemented Oracle HRMS that was accessed by seven locations throughout the U.S. and one location in Canada. As an Oracle Corporation Principal Consultant from 1997 to 2000, working with public-sector organizations, he implemented Oracle HRMS applications to replace legacy payroll and HR systems. Prior to employment at Oracle, Don was a programmer, systems analyst, and MIS manager, mostly in the printing industry. Don has earned a B.S. in business administration from the University at Buffalo.

Telisa Seiter Conlin is an Oracle ERP Specialist with BOSS Corporation with more than six years of experience in Oracle Financial Applications. Prior to becoming an Oracle Financials ERP Consultant, Telisa was a tax accountant. Telisa is a Certified Public Accountant and has both an M.S. degree in taxation and an MBA from the University of Tulsa.

Ken Conway is Executive Vice President of BOSS Corporation. He has fourteen years of consulting and highly technical software experience. He has been involved in the management, design, development, and installation of projects involving both custom and package software. Ken has managed many implementations of Oracle Human Resources and Oracle Payroll, including several of the first successful implementations that have gone into production in the United States. He was also involved in the Oracle BETA program during the early releases of the Oracle HR and Payroll products. Ken has been very active in the Oracle Global Human Resources Information Systems (HRIS) Special Interest Group (SIG). He has made several presentations to the HRIS SIG and to OAUG regarding creative solutions using the Oracle HRMS product suite. He is also an active member of the Society for Human Resource Management (SHRM). Ken has earned an MBA degree from the University of Houston at Clear Lake and a B.S. degree in computer science from Sam Houston State University. He achieved both degrees in only four years.

Darren Cooper is an Oracle ERP Specialist with BOSS Corporation. He has more than four years of functional Oracle manufacturing and distribution experience. He has a B.S. degree in accounting from Oral Roberts University and more than four years of industry experience, primarily in purchasing and inventory. Previously, he was a Senior Consultant with Oracle Corporation providing consulting services to Oracle's international clients in

France, Belgium, China, and West Africa. His experience includes multiple full life cycle implementations, as well as post-production support involving several Oracle applications. He is currently engaged as the functional team lead for an Oracle Purchasing and Inventory implementation.

Don Driggs is an Oracle ERP Specialist with BOSS Corporation. Don has more than seventeen years of experience assisting enterprises in their use of financial software, four of them with Oracle applications. Don has led numerous projects to implement and upgrade ERP applications. As a financial systems manager, Don has worked in retail, mining, and manufacturing organizations delivering internal system development, support, and end-user training. As a consultant, Don has led the implementation of the financial applications in several public-sector organizations and presented training sessions at OAUG conferences. Don received his B.S. degree in accounting from Brigham Young University.

Bill Dunham holds the position of Vice President, Practice Director, for BOSS Corporation. Previously, he was Managing Principal and Practice Manager for consulting services at Oracle Corporation. Thirteen years of Bill's seventeen-year career have focused on Oracle Applications, products, and technology. He has more than nine years of functional experience with various Oracle Applications and thirteen years of technical experience with the Oracle database and tools. Bill has functioned as Systems Programmer, Application Developer, Database Administrator, Technical Team Lead, Project Manager, and Director of Information Technology for several public sector, manufacturing, and consulting organizations. While an employee at Oracle Corporation, Bill led a variety of projects. These include custom development projects for clients and multimillion-dollar Oracle Application implementation projects for clients and Oracle Corporation. Bill has a B.S. degree in computer science from High Point University and an MBA from Wake Forest University's Babcock School of Management. Bill has presented papers at local and regional Oracle Application and Technology User Groups and is cofounder of the Piedmont/Triad Oracle Users Group. Bill has authored articles for *OAUG INSIGHT* magazine and OAUG conferences. Bill's papers have been presented at the OAUG conferences in Philadelphia, Hawaii, Geneva, Atlanta, and San Diego. Bill also participated on OAUG discussion panels in Philadelphia, Hawaii, Atlanta, and San Diego.

Randy Egger, as president and founder of Project Partners, LLC, has a large vision for project-centric companies. Randy orchestrates complex business solutions for Project Partners' clients worldwide. Its primary business is the implementation of the Oracle Projects Application suite and its integration with third-party software. During Randy's 12 years of employment at Oracle Corporation, his primary responsibilities centered around the formation of project accounting systems. Randy worked with many companies in diverse industries and disciplines as he developed a core understanding of two operational worlds: financial accounting and project management. In 1988, he designed and developed an internal system that helped manage Oracle's consulting organization. Two years later, he moved into Application Product Development where, as Chief Architect, he spearheaded Oracle's Project Accounting application, now called Oracle Projects. Randy is the "Father of Oracle Projects" and widely regarded as the expert source for Oracle Projects.

Don Grons is a BOSS Vice President, Practice Director with thirty-five years of balanced experience. He has twenty years of practical business experience within the manufacturing and distribution industries. He has comprehensive knowledge of manufacturing, materials management, and financial integrated systems. He has held positions as plant manager, materials manager, and production and inventory control manager at various manufacturing companies. Don also has an additional fifteen years of applications software consulting, education, training, courseware development, and implementation experience—of which eight years was as a member of Oracle's Consulting and Education Practices. He is an active member of APICS, the Education Society for Resource Management, and is a member of OAUG. He has made numerous presentations at the OAUG conferences. Don has earned a B.S. degree in business administration (BSBA) from John Carroll University in Cleveland, Ohio.

Patricia Keeley is an Oracle HRMS Specialist for BOSS Corporation. Pat has been providing Oracle HRMS functional consulting services to clients for six years. Pat has authored two white papers for the Oracle Applications Users Group: "Making Oracle's Involuntary Deductions Work for You" and "Creating Easy-to-Use Adjustment and Refund Elements." During her previous employment with one of North America's largest retail organizations, she served as a payroll manager and human resource systems business analyst.

Stephen King is an Oracle ERP Specialist with BOSS Corporation, who has more than five years of extensive experience in Oracle Financial and Manufacturing applications. Stephen has a Bachelor's degree in business and holds a CPA designation from the Australian Society of Certified Practicing Accountants. He has also earned an M.B.A. from the University of Southern Queensland in Australia. Stephen has more than eight years industry experience in various accounting and financial roles with Australian-based manufacturing organizations. In the last three years, he has also performed delivery of consulting and support services for both Oracle Corporation and PricewaterhouseCoopers in the Oracle ERP field for several industry sectors.

Patti Kingsmore is a BOSS Corporation functional Oracle HRMS Specialist. She has established an expertise in projects that reengineer a client's business requirements to an Oracle systems solution. Her range of experience includes human resources, payroll, accounting, consulting, education, and functional and technical implementation of Oracle Applications software. She began her career with the Oracle Applications in 1996. As a former employee of Oracle, she has also implemented several of the financials modules and was an instructor. Patti has implemented several releases of the Oracle Human Resources Suite of Applications and has experience with higher education, government, and corporate entities. She is currently implementing Oracle Advanced Benefits, Human Resources, and Payroll. Patti earned a B.S. degree in accounting from South Carolina College, the Honors College at the University of South Carolina.

Martha Anne McKillip is a Managing Principal Consultant with Project Partners, LLC, with more than ten years of experience providing training, consulting, development, and technical assistance with Oracle tools, applications, and databases. She has focused the last five years specifically on working with Oracle Projects, Project Manufacturing, and related applications. Martha has extensive career experience in several specific areas: development, documentation, education, training, technical support, database and systems administration, project leadership, and project management. With an emphasis on her strong technical background, Martha has provided numerous business process solutions involving client extensions, custom code, form modifications, and custom reports. She frequently designs, codes, and tests interfaces between Oracle Projects and external third-party or legacy systems. Martha has a deep understanding of the use of AMG for data conversions and the specific differences between MRC and multi-organization environments.

John Pilkington, a Managing Principal Consultant for Project Partners, LLC, writes from his long experience in the implementation and management of Oracle Projects and financial applications. He has managed full product implementations, performed gap analysis, and designed and implemented upgrade and conversion strategies as well as training and integration with other financial systems. John has provided recommendations and solutions for business process change or product implementation as it pertains to current business practices. John has more than twenty years of experience in private industry accounting for both public and nonpublic companies. He has worked heavily in the construction and consulting industries with an emphasis on public and commercial contracts. John has held a variety of interesting financial positions, including corporate controller.

Sheila Reardon is a Senior Consultant with Project Partners and has been consulting with enterprise project management systems and financial applications for more than eight years. She has focused on project billing; job costing; and methods of capturing time and expense, including full life cycle implementation experience. Sheila has supported all phases of implementations, including planning, needs analysis, installation, customization, integration, and training. Sheila's skill set includes providing both technical and functional support. She has conducted and developed training classes for consultants and clients, including the necessary training materials, class format, and tutorials. She also offers functional R11*i* experience using Oracle Projects and Self Service Time, including the integration of ABT's Results Management Suite 5 with Oracle Projects.

Kris Saha is an Oracle ERP Specialist with BOSS Corporation. Previously, he was a Managing Principal for consulting services at Oracle Corporation. Five years of his career in IT, which has spanned more than ten years, has been in implementing Oracle Applications. He has functional experience with several Oracle Applications and has worked on Oracle projects in the USA, Europe, the Middle East, and Africa. His experience includes multiple full life cycle implementations as well as post-production support with various Oracle applications. He has a B.A. degree from Calcutta University in India.

John Sasali, a Managing Principal Consultant for Project Partners, LLC, offers a wealth of Oracle Projects and related Oracle financials experience to his clients. He was among the first users of Oracle Projects and has spent the ensuing years implementing this application for clients worldwide. His engagements often include full product implementation, gap analysis, upgrade and conversion strategies, integration with legacy systems or third-party software, and user training. With more than ten years of experience, John is frequently called upon to provide recommendations and solutions for business process changes during product implementations as they pertain to current business practices within the client company. His hands-on style and approach is very much appreciated as he offers business solutions for both North American and international implementations within widely diverse industries.

Bill Stratton is a BOSS Corporation HRMS Specialist with more than twenty-five years of experience designing and managing computer solutions to business problems. He has managed traditional computer projects involving General Ledger, Accounts Payable, Fixed Assets, Human Resources, and Payroll. Currently, Bill is actively involved in the Oracle HR/Payroll practice at BOSS. He was instrumental in the successful implementation of two of the first completed installations of Oracle US Payroll and is also active in the HR/Payroll Special Interest Group (SIG) within the OAUG. He has presented numerous papers at OAUG conferences, including the recent training sessions for Advanced Benefits. Bill earned a B.S. degree in computer science from Virginia Polytechnic Institute and State University.

Jyh Yi Wang achieved a Bachelor of Business degree in marketing from the University of Georgia's Terry College of Business. She is currently responsible for the development, design, and support for all aspects of marketing at BOSS Corporation. Jyh Yi is an active member of the OAUG.

John Wells has more than eight years of experience in implementing Oracle financial and manufacturing applications in both a functional and technical capacity. Prior to joining BOSS Corporation as an ERP consultant, John served as a Senior Financial Applications Consultant for Oracle Corporation. There he had the opportunity to serve as a primary team member of Oracle's FastForward implementation team. John has also served as a senior business analyst for Carolina Power and Light as well as financial systems administrator for Revlon, Inc. John holds B.S. degrees in both business administration and systems information from North Carolina Wesleyan College. He also holds an Oracle Education Masters in Application Administration.

George Wilson is an Oracle ERP Specialist with BOSS Corporation, with more than six years of experience in Oracle Financials and extensive knowledge of General Ledger systems and financial reporting. George has an M.S. degree in business administration from Northeastern University. He has more than twenty years of industry experience in various capacities as a user, manager, consultant, team leader, and project manager in several manufacturing and service industries. Prior to his Oracle Applications experience, George worked as a consultant and project manager on other application products and as a financial analyst and accounting manager in the computer industry. He was a key member of the team that developed the Oracle implementation toolkit for a large consulting firm.

Dedication

We dedicate this book to the fantastic clients, consultants, and friends of BOSS Corporation. Your support, enthusiasm, and friendship have made this endeavor especially rewarding.

Most importantly, we say thank you very much to the spouses and families of the authors and technical editors. We know you gave up countless weekends and evenings so we could work on our assigned chapters. We couldn't have created this book without your support.

Also, thank you Jyh Yi Wang for production support and development of BOSS Corporation material at the back of the book. Thanks to Philip Duffie of the BOSS Corporation IT department for producing the screen shots for this edition. Thank you to Michelle Newcomb and the editorial team at Que for all the support, hard work, and guidance needed to publish this book by September 2001.

Project Partners, LLC created Chapter 15 for this book. We would like to give special thanks for the contributions to this effort by their authors and some of their seasoned team members: Patrick Lavey, Randy Martin, Zach Connors, Paul Grice, Serge Pellicelli, Bakta Salla, and Rob Merryman. We greatly appreciate their valuable contributions.

Finally, thank you to all the readers who purchased the first version of our book Special Edition Using Oracle Applications. Your wonderful comments, enthusiastic support, and patronage made the whole effort one of the most worthwhile experiences of our lives.

Jim Crum—July 2001

Tell Us What You Think!

As the reader of this book, *you* are our most important critic and commentator. We value your opinion and want to know what we're doing right, what we could do better, what areas you'd like to see us publish in, and any other words of wisdom you're willing to pass our way.

As an associate publisher for Que, I welcome your comments. You can fax, e-mail, or write me directly to let me know what you did or didn't like about this book—as well as what we can do to make our books stronger.

Please note that I cannot help you with technical problems related to the topic of this book, and that due to the high volume of mail I receive, I might not be able to reply to every message.

When you write, please be sure to include this book's title and authors as well as your name and phone or fax number. I will carefully review your comments and share them with the authors and editors who worked on the book.

Fax: 317-581-4666

E-mail: `feedback@quepublishing.com`

Mail: Associate Publisher
Que
201 West 103rd Street
Indianapolis, IN 46290 USA

PART I

INTRODUCING THE ORACLE APPLICATIONS

CHAPTER 1

Reviewing ERP and Oracle Corporation

In this chapter

Enterprise Resource Planning (ERP) systems evolved from the Material Requirements Planning (MRP) systems of the late 1970s. In the 1980s, businesses implemented systems for Total Quality Management (TQM), Just in Time (JIT) manufacturing, and MRP II. In the 1990s the big initiatives were Business Process Reengineering (BPR, Enterprise Resource Planning (ERP), and Year 2000 (Y2K) compliance. Today, a business can implement a large and integrated suite of application software modules for most common business practices. Several leading software companies sell and support full-featured accounting, distribution, procurement, manufacturing, customer relationship, and human resource systems.

This book is about implementing and using the Release 11*i* version of Oracle Corporation's ERP Applications. Part I introduces ERP systems and the Oracle ERP Applications. Part II will help you implement the applications, and Part III will help you configure and use the core financial, distribution, manufacturing, and human resources applications. Part IV offers information about implementing software with partners, vendors, and consultants.

INTRODUCTION

The Oracle suite of ERP applications is a big and complex subject. If you purchased the Oracle Corporation manuals for the core financial, distribution, and manufacturing applications, they might easily occupy 15 feet of your bookshelf space and cost several thousand dollars. The product documentation is good, and if you use the detailed reference material enough, you can find almost all the answers for even complex business situations. However, the documentation and its topic are so large and complex, many users find the documentation difficult. We hope this book will serve as a more practical reference material between the high-level overviews and the detailed reference manuals provided by Oracle. Our goal is to present enough information and concepts about the Oracle applications to enable you to manage your software implementation project, configure the system, and run some functional tests in a complete conference room pilot.

Due to space requirements, we can only present so much detail on each application and business process. For specific report, screen level, field level, and technical information, you will want to consult the online help, the User Guides for each application, and the Technical Reference Manuals. Researching a concept or specific topic takes practice. Start with the material in this book, and then drill down into the Oracle reference manuals and online help when necessary.

During the writing of this book, we had several types of readers in mind. Generally, we present material that is suitable for the intermediate or advanced user, and we assume that you already know your individual business processes, the basic Oracle vocabulary, and navigation techniques. Some readers who might find this book useful include the following:

- The implementation team project manager who must determine the scope of the project and understand the concepts and issues to be resolved for each application will want to read most chapters in this book. Start with Part II, "Implementing the Oracle Applications," to learn the details of package software implementation. Then skim through the chapters of your most important applications in Part III, "Configuring and

Using the Oracle Applications," as you build your implementation team, set your project scope, and identify issues. Read the three chapters on this book's Web site to understand the importance of Oracle Support, consultants, and vendors of compatible software. Finally, use the checklist in Appendix C, "Implementation Checklist," to start planning and establish project control.

- If you are on a software implementation team and you are assigned to configure and test an application module, you will want to study the individual chapter in Part III about that application. You will obtain an understanding of how each application is configured and the main transactions the application can perform. You will also want to read the other chapters that bracket your core business functions to understand the integration points and process flow. For example, if you are implementing the Payables module, consider reading the chapters for Purchasing (Chapter 16) and General Ledger (Chapter 11) to see how Payables integrates with the other applications.
- A database administrator or a technical person can gain interesting insights into the issues and concerns of functional users by reading chapters in Part III about specific applications. Use these chapters to put your technical reference material into a business perspective and map the functional areas of the business to the internal database objects.
- If you are contemplating purchase of the Oracle ERP software, consider reading Chapter 4, "Understanding What Affects the Degree of Effort and Cost," about how much things cost and how much effort an ERP implementation takes. Use the chapters in Part III about individual modules to prepare questions for your Oracle sales representative. Understand the compatible software of other software vendors in the chapter titled "Finding Additional Compatible Solutions" on this book's Web site. Also on the Web site, check out the chapter titled "Working with Support."
- A functional consultant who is an expert in three or four applications could extend his skills to include another application, by reading a chapter or two in Part III.
- If you want to become a project manager, consider reading the chapters in Part II. Then consider becoming a functional expert in three or more application modules in Part III.
- If you are a power user of one or two applications and your job description is about to change, consider reading the chapters in Part III about the applications that describe your new responsibilities.

This book is organized into four parts. This is a reference manual, and you will not read it cover to cover. Just try to get familiar with the structure of the book so you will know what topics are available and how to access them quickly from the table of contents or the index. Each part has a specific purpose as follows:

- Part I, "Introducing the Oracle Applications," introduces the organization of this book, discusses the topic of Enterprise Resource Planning, and gives a high-level overview of Oracle Corporation and the Oracle software.
- Part II presents project management techniques and implementation methods for packaged software and ERP systems. Oracle has an Application Implementation Method

called AIM and other consulting firms have developed similar work plans and templates. We discuss the phases of a software project, key activities, and deliverables of the project team.

- In Part III, you will read about each of the core financial, distribution, manufacturing, and human resources applications. Each chapter is generally divided into a section on configuration parameters and another section on major transactions and using the application.
- Finally, Part IV, "Appendixes," has two appendixes about the careers of people that work with ERP systems, and a final appendix has an implementation checklist.

UNDERSTANDING ERP CONCEPTS

ERP is software system that is often referred to as the backbone for the entire business. However, these systems are more than just a bony skeleton. These systems have lots of brains (process logic), muscle (business transactions), and heart (business policy). The software communicates (as a nervous system) across business functions.

Also, the medical analogy is appropriate because these systems grow and evolve over time. For example, ERP systems can get soft and flabby if left unattended. The freshly implemented system is not stable like your legacy system. It can be more like a young adolescent with raging hormones, limited experience, and a contrary disposition. As with an adolescent child, your users might not like your ERP system until it matures.

Oracle ERP software is online transaction processing (OLTP) software, and many manual or automatic transactions start coordinated and automatic transactions in other modules. For example, when the clerk at the shipping dock records the transaction that goods have shipped to a customer, integrated changes are made in the order management, billing, and inventory systems, and new transactions for revenue recognition and cost of goods sold are started.

ERP systems attempt to replicate your business structure, processes, policies, and procedures. Because each business is different, you can't just install the programs on a computer and start business operations immediately. First, you must determine the basic nature of your business and compare that with the functionality of the software. By carefully setting thousands of configuration parameters, you can often achieve a system that meets 90%–100% of your business needs.

Configuring an ERP system can be tricky because many of the parameters interact with each other, and you need to understand how the software works before you actually have a chance to use it. For example, your strategy for configuring your enterprise organization structure can have significant impact on the way you prepare financial statements, manage inventories, fulfill customer orders, procure materials, manage compensation and benefits, secure your data, and so forth. Your company might be centralized for fulfillment of customer orders and decentralized for procurement and inventory management. In this example, to configure your system properly, you will want to resolve the centralized/decentralized issues within each application.

Understanding the Attributes of ERP Systems

The Oracle ERP systems have the functionality to support industry standards and best practices. The recommendations of the American Production and Inventory Control Society (APICS) and Generally Accepted Accounting Practices (GAAP) are well supported by the Oracle software. Look for the following characteristics:

- These systems are composed of many modules called applications. The core Oracle Applications support broad business functions, such as financial, distribution, manufacturing, and human resource transactions. For example, the financial applications are General Ledger, Accounts Payable, Accounts Receivable, and Fixed Assets. You can license only the applications you need.
- The applications are integrated and work together to pass individual transactions through an entire business process. The modularization approach gives flexibility, and the modules interact by passing data through program interfaces. A single manual transaction in one application can initiate transactions in other applications.
- ERP systems are complex, and the more applications you use, the more complexity you have. Thousands of configuration parameters interact with each other and change the logic of the programs to fit your unique business situation. It can take months to set up and learn how the programs operate. The documentation is voluminous.
- The flexibility of these systems is the upside of the complexity problem. Oracle has thousands of customers in hundreds of industries all over the world using the applications in their own special way. Manufacturing companies, utilities, service companies, governments, and others have all been able to configure the applications to meet their specific business needs.
- ERP systems often use powerful data storage mechanisms such as the Oracle Relational Database Management System (RDBMS). The database gives the transaction system the performance and scalability to process thousands of transactions per hour and store the data for years. A large ERP database can be more than 300GB in size.
- ERP software vendors are highly competitive. Each has loaded its software with every conceivable function point and business process. Typically, interfaces among vendors are proprietary solutions and must be implemented as custom extensions.
- These systems can be a mixture of online and batch processes. Many functions support a manual interactive process and an automated batch process. For example, you can apply cash receipts to your Oracle Receivables by keying the data into a form, or you can configure the system to use the AutoLockbox program to process a data file from your bank.

ERP Advantages Drive Implementation Projects

Companies implement ERP systems for many tangible, intangible, and strategic reasons. Many companies don't even try to calculate a total return on investment from an ERP system because there are so many intangible and strategic benefits. If you understand what you want from the new software, you might be able to obtain some of the following benefits:

- Reduce the amount invested in inventory.
- Improve worker productivity.
- Reduce processing costs per business transaction.
- Reduce the time it takes to perform a financial close and prepare financial statements.
- Reduce procurement costs.
- Install systems with vendor-supported maintenance.
- Improve the scalability of business systems to support future growth.
- Upgrade systems to support global accounting transactions (for example, Euro currency requirements).
- Obtain better reporting and information about your business.
- Replace a hodgepodge of old systems, and install new or improved business processes.
- Improve fiscal controls.
- Integrate and standardize processes among your business units and trading partners in your supply chain.
- Improve system performance, reliability, and fault tolerance.
- Reduce the costs of Information Technology.
- Improve order management, customer service, and on-time delivery.

ERP Disadvantages Must Be Overcome

However, ERP systems are not without their share of problems. ERP systems can be difficult to implement and operate. Although the odds of success have improved in the past five years, you should carefully consider the following issues as you work with ERP applications:

- Everyone in your organization from the database administrator to the receiving clerk to the CEO needs new skills to work with the new technology and business processes.
- Most companies must hire outside consultants to help accelerate and improve the implementation.
- In the early 1990s, almost half of the MRP/ERP implementation projects could be called failures. Many of these early projects were either abandoned or were finished late and over budget. An industry of software implementation specialists was created to assist businesses with implementation projects.
- Many large and costly implementation projects have produced little or no return on investment for their owners other than to solve the Y2K problem. Several companies

have actually observed a reduction in productivity in the first six to twelve months after starting their new systems.

- Many companies are surprised to discover the ERP implementation wasn't just a software replacement project, but the start of a continuous process of change, evolution, and improvement.
- Many implementation team members have discovered after the ERP project is over that their old jobs either no longer exist or are dull and insignificant.
- Package software can force you to make certain choices about how your business will operate, and you might introduce some constraints on your traditional business processes.
- In the mid-1990s when customers evaluated software packages, they often selected the one with the most features. A competitive war among the ERP software vendors caused feature bloat as every possible feature and function of virtually every industry was added. The systems became a lot more flexible and capable, but many companies found themselves spending good money to turn off features or scale down systems and processes they did not need. Many users had to spend money to work around features that added overhead to their businesses.

Application Service Providers

In the past two years, the Application Service Providers (ASP) business model has been steadily growing as an optional way to implement and operate your ERP applications. Oracle Corporation calls this the Business On-Line (BOL) service model. The BOL model establishes a service provider to host your ERP applications in a centralized data center over an Internet/intranet connection for a monthly fee. In October 1999, Oracle launched this service and expected it to become a significant part of its future growth. I suspect that Oracle is disappointed that BOL has not performed better as an improved way to outsource the Information Technology business function, but it takes many years to develop and implement these new kinds of business computing models. While BOL probably will never create billions of dollars in new revenue for Oracle, it still might become a viable alternative for several customers.

Important considerations under this model are similar to the issues and concerns you would have with any outsourcing arrangement:

- You want to make sure the application implementation meets the needs of your business.
- The support expertise of the service provider must exceed the expectations of the users.
- Data center management must be better than your own data center.
- The ASP must provide an acceptable level of security and performance.
- The costs of the service must be reasonable.

When you evaluate the economics of the BOL model, compare the monthly charge per user of the BOL system to the initial investment in software, hardware, support, implementation services, and the continuing costs of operating your own systems. If you have 100 users at a monthly subscription cost of $500/user, your BOL costs might be $50,000/month and might grow or shrink proportionately as your business changes. Compare that monthly charge with a $2 million up-front investment in hardware, software, and consulting, and add annual direct operating costs of $300,000+ for system administrator, support, and data center costs. Typically you must sign a multiyear deal for the BOL services, but you would pay by the month.

Consider the following advantages and disadvantages when you evaluate Oracle and other companies as an Application Service Provider.

ADVANTAGES OF BUSINESS ON-LINE

The advantages of the BOL model come from your relationship with Oracle Corporation or the hosting company and your ability to avoid the initial costs of starting up the system. Consider the following benefits of BOL:

- You know who is responsible with the single vendor solution for system operations, configuration, administration, and performance.
- This architecture moves complexity off the desktop and on to the managed server located in a professionally managed data center.
- You avoid a large, up-front investment in hardware, software, and implementation costs.
- You avoid the cost of support (which can be 20+% of the software costs).
- You don't have to find and retain talented technical staff to run these systems.

DISADVANTAGES OF BUSINESS ON-LINE

The disadvantages of the BOL model come from your relationship with Oracle Corporation or the hosting company and the loss of control and flexibility you need to meet current and future business requirements. Evaluate the following issues before considering the Business On-Line service:

- The solution is proprietary. If you want to rent the ERP and e-commerce applications, you must get them from Oracle or an Oracle partner.
- Oracle is still an unproven outsourcer. Hosting ERP applications is still a relatively new business for it. If it can't make its normal growth rate and profit margins, it might not sustain the business as you expect.
- You are locked into Oracle, and it will be hard to switch vendors because you would have to switch applications, too.
- You will be restricted to the types of customizations and extensions available. Are there additional pieces of software you need to run your business?
- There will be little price competition or flexibility after you commit.
- You will be locked in to a long-term contract with limited flexibility to change or terminate.
- Application performance issues might be a concern.
- Consider the ASP capability to implement and administer the applications.

- When you use an ASP, security concerns must be resolved. You must be sure your business data remains private and secure.
- The ASP business model is unproven. (If it doesn't work out, where are you in three years?)

ORACLE IS A LEADING-EDGE TECHNOLOGY COMPANY

Oracle Corporation is a very successful, high-technology company. The database, programming tools, applications, services, support, and educational products from the company use modern computer hardware and software capabilities. Oracle advertises itself as the second largest software company in the world. Through its actions and alliances with other high-technology companies, Oracle influences the working and computing environment for millions of users.

Oracle Corporation customers should understand and react to the attributes of their favorite database and ERP applications vendor. For example, in the software industry, a system might be rushed to market for competitive reasons. If the support and the quality of the product are not quite ready for release, you must deal with those problems while enjoying the improved features and performance. The following attributes of Oracle's business model might affect your ability to use the software.

RAPID GROWTH

Oracle competes aggressively and tries to grow its business rapidly. The sales force has always been considered high-powered and aggressive. Annual revenue growth for the past five years is about 35%, and ERP Applications and Services is a significant part of fiscal 2001's total revenue of approximately $12 billion. The company strategy is aligned to take advantage of the growth in Internet technology and products.

NEW PRODUCTS AND CAPABILITIES

To sustain revenue growth rates of 30%–40%, Oracle has introduced new products and services every year throughout its history. Often, the products improve dramatically over the capability of earlier versions, and the company regularly produces better-than order-of-magnitude improvements in the software performance. In 1995, 50GB was considered to be a huge Oracle ERP applications database. Now, 50GB is common, and large companies are consolidating global data centers into ERP instances ten times larger.

CONSTANT CHANGE

The technology sector is always changing, and Oracle Corporation has been the root cause of a lot of that change. Occasionally, companies such as Oracle can introduce new products and features faster than their customers can implement them. You must stay reasonably current with new releases and upgrades to the products you license.

COMPETITIVE NATURE

The ERP software vendors compete aggressively when governments or large companies replace legacy systems. Oracle has been at the forefront of the stampede to sell loads of software, services, and education to the Fortune 1000 companies. The competitive marketing effort to sell software can sometimes affect the technology. For example, even though Oracle now says the client/server architecture was a flawed design, its message was quite different when it was trying to beat the competition with release 10.6 of the ERP Applications. As someone who uses packaged software to run your business, you should realize that occasionally software vendors adjust their products to meet competitive pressures. You must be prepared to deal with that change.

EXPERIMENTAL DISPOSITION

Occasionally, products and services have been marketed and promoted before they are ready to see the light of day. More than once to close a big deal, features have been added without adequate testing. Products have been announced as "in the pipeline" simply because the competition had a similar product, feature, or service. Many long-time Oracle customers have fallen for the promise of "its in the next release"—some more than once.

Tip

If you are running a business on production software, no matter how badly you want to use the new technology, consider waiting about six months from the production release date before upgrading any Oracle software. New software is often late and, for production systems, shouldn't be considered real until it is actually shipping with production status. It will take about six months to work out the kinks and get the support staff trained. Let the implementation sites with nonproduction systems find the bugs in the new release. These rules of thumb were formulated 14 years ago when Oracle was releasing version 5.0 of the database and tools, and these rules are still appropriate today.

DISCOURAGES CUSTOMIZATION OF ITS APPLICATIONS

Oracle has declared war on complexity and has a philosophy to discourage customization of the applications by its customers or consultants. Larry Ellison, Oracle's CEO, and Jeremy Burton, a Senior VP of Marketing, advise their customers that the software will support 80% of customer needs out of the box. Oracle management tells customers that users have to change their business to conform to the processes in the software. This concept of "you can have any color as long as it's red" is not being received well by many customers. The vast majority of customers know that Larry Ellison is not naive, but, to customers with real businesses to run, Ellison's position seems irrational. Customers cannot understand how Oracle can sell a very expensive product that doesn't produce, by its own admission, 100% customer satisfaction, and then take the position that it is unacceptable for the customer to modify the product to remove the problem.

UNDERSTANDING THE ORACLE CORPORATION IMPACT ON YOU—THE CUSTOMER

Organizations allocate money and resources to change and maintain their computerized business systems in two ways, continuously and periodically. I call a company that keeps its systems and skills relatively current with the latest technology a type one Oracle customer. I label the company that undertakes large technology projects periodically and spends only small amounts between projects a type two Oracle customer.

Your organization's spending patterns may be somewhere in between these two extremes. However, if you understand which type of customer you are, you will begin to know your relationship with Oracle Corporation.

UNDERSTANDING THE IMPACT OF ORACLE ON TYPE ONE CUSTOMERS

Type one customers invest in computer systems continuously and think of information technology as a strategic business activity. New or continuously improving systems give them a competitive edge or are strategic to the definition of the business. These companies tend to pick which technology is currently important to their business and proactively allocate budget dollars and work assignments to those activities. These companies can tolerate quite a bit of change and have a goal of continuous improvement. Change is evolutionary at the type one company.

Oracle sales and the type one customer might get along very well. The customer will be a showcase site for the latest technology and might provide enthusiastic references for the latest release of the software. The sales representative can arrange for the type one customer to participate in informal beta testing programs so the customer can experiment with the next release of the software.

Type one companies will try to employ technically aggressive people. They will set up continuing education programs to bring the targeted skills in-house. These companies might establish the position of internal consultant to go between the information technology department and the business units. The technical people at these companies think of their users as their customers. Everyone is comfortable with continuous change and the occasional disruptions caused by new software.

The type one company will attempt every upgrade and major release of the software. It will read each statement of direction published by Oracle and eagerly anticipate using the new features and functionality. It will participate in the user group's committees to suggest ways to improve the software to Oracle Corporation. It will complain loudly when the software is late or poor in quality and affects its business.

The type one company allocates available budgets continuously across desirable technologies. Because these companies don't have unlimited funds, they pick the most important investment areas and leave the rest. Their attitude might be "last year we did ERP, and this year we will do the Internet." Because they are always improving and changing the systems to fit their needs, the type one companies might be heavily customized. These companies develop techniques for dealing with the disruptions caused by patches and new software releases.

Working with Oracle Support is a critical function at the type one company. There will be problems with new software, and problem diagnosis is an important skill to have. If you are a type one company, consider upgrading the support services that you buy.

UNDERSTANDING THE ORACLE IMPACT ON TYPE TWO CUSTOMERS

Type two customers invest in computer systems periodically and like to establish quiet periods of stability and low cost of operations between large spending projects. Type two customers often adopt a strategy of skipping every other generation of computer technology to maximize the return on investment from the previous spending program. These companies tend to think of information technology as a necessary but burdensome expense to be controlled and minimized. For example, these companies might be thankful they stayed away from that "horribly expensive client/server mess," and now, they are ideally positioned to replace their aging systems with a model based on the Internet. Or, these companies are thankful they implemented great new ERP systems in the previous two years, but they are pretty sure their company doesn't have to adopt the latest new business model, and can rest comfortably for the next year on a stable but less-than-current release of the Oracle Applications. There are probably a lot more type two than type one customers.

Type two customers are only in phase with the standard Oracle marketing program when they are in their heavy spending cycle and will lose contact with Oracle sales during their stability cycle. Larry Ellison, the Oracle CEO and industry visionary, had a message for business in late 1999 that the Internet changes everything and you must throw away everything in IT to survive. The type two customers that just finished a big ERP implementation project will not feel the need to follow Mr. Ellison's leadership. These companies are happy to wait until late 2001 or early 2002 to make their upgrade to release 11*i*.

Type two companies implement systems with relatively large, periodic projects. Change is revolutionary at these companies. Typically, change happens when the cost of doing nothing is greater than the cost of the project. When the project is completed, change activity diminishes, and stability and cost management become important.

The type two company will disband its implementation or upgrade team and send the key project team members back to their operating departments. If the project was successful, the project team members often will have added responsibility and career enhancement. They might become the power users and might be the key people who now know how the business is supposed to operate with the new software and business processes.

An employee of a type two company who really wants to work for a type one company will often leave the company when the implementation project finishes. Other companies that are about to start implementations, consulting firms, and Oracle Corporation itself will happily hire these former implementation team members who don't want to go back to their old jobs after a year of hard work on an ERP project.

Upgrades and new software releases are troublesome for the type two company because they can destabilize the production systems, and everyone who should test the new release is busy with their primary responsibility to run the business.

When you upgrade, you must almost always pay more money to someone. It is wise to plan for these expenses and set management's expectations that it can't be avoided. Oracle Corporation doesn't always get your money unless you buy more products, use its services, or attend its education classes. However, the upgrade will utilize new technology, and you must change the system to accommodate the new release. For example, the R10.6 upgrade sold a lot of disks. The upgrade to R10.7SC required lots of desktop memory and many customers had to buy 17-inch monitors for their users. The R11*i* upgrade implements a three-tier hardware architecture. Depending on your level of customization, these upgrades might require you to engage outside consulting help. Paying for Oracle support gets you the upgrade software, but you must set the type two company management's expectations for other expenses to fully maintain the Oracle ERP system.

Tip

It is very important to stay reasonably current on major releases of the ERP applications, the operating system, and the database. If you get too far behind, you might find yourself forced into an upgrade project without the funding, people, or support from senior management. You can plan to skip release 11 and stay on release 10.7 of the applications until release 11*i* is stable, but you must plan to upgrade to something before the support on release 10.7 runs out in December 2002.

At the type two company, use of Oracle Support is mostly for maintenance, access to required patches, and a way to prepay for the next release of the software. The main desire is to avoid destabilizing the production systems and avoid all the testing to certify new patches and upgrades. If the type two company upgraded to premium support during the implementation of the system, it can consider capturing a cost reduction by falling back to the basic pricing plan after the project is completed.

SUMMARY

Enterprise Resource Planning systems are complex, configurable, flexible, and tightly integrated. You can purchase additional software to extend your ERP system from non-Oracle vendors. You can achieve substantial strategic, tangible, and intangible advantages to your business by implementing these systems, but you must overcome the disadvantages.

Oracle Corporation is a really great technology company, and it has highly functional and popular software. This book is generally quite positive about the Oracle ERP software, and most Oracle customers are quite satisfied. However, ERP systems and their vendors can dramatically affect your business, and when appropriate, we will try to alert you to risks, problems, solutions, and opportunities.

Most companies are not 100% type one or type two in their orientation toward Oracle technology. However, it helps to know the predisposition of your management. Your company's orientation might affect the way you view the rest of this book.

The next chapter investigates the specific features and capabilities of the Oracle ERP applications.

CHAPTER 2

Introducing the Oracle Applications

In this chapter

In this chapter, I introduce the Oracle Applications. If you are an experienced user, you can proceed directly to the chapters that interest you. If you are new to the subject, however, read this chapter to understand what kinds of business functions are available and how the Oracle Applications might meet your business requirements.

The Oracle Enterprise Resource Planning (ERP) applications are really an integrated suite of modules identified by major business function. The applications discussed in this book are online transaction processing (OLTP) applications. For example, the Receivables application is designed to bill customers, collect cash, and keep track of what amounts are owed to your company. Most functions are designed to enable you to continuously interact with the system and perform the transactions of your business. Most reports are designed to list what transactions were made, control your processes, and show what balances remain after the transaction is made.

The customer base of Oracle Applications users numbers over 8,000 sites in more than 60 countries. More than 10,000 users attend one of the Oracle Applications User Group (OAUG) or Oracle AppsWorld conferences each year. The business grows about 40% per year.

The breadth and depth of the Applications is too great for any one book or any one user to deal with completely. For example, if you ordered a complete set of user guides, technical reference manuals, installation manuals, and upgrade manuals for all the applications, you could easily fill 15 feet of bookshelf space. If you install all the applications discussed in this book, your database might have over 20,000 objects in it. It would take you several years to understand it all, and by that time, Oracle will have released new versions and your business will have changed.

Because this is a big and complex set of modules, one of our biggest challenges when writing this book was to present the right amount of information about each topic and to limit the scope so that it would all fit in one desktop reference manual. To meet that challenge, we made some hard choices, and many topics you might find interesting had to be cut. For example, the process manufacturing (OPM) and customer relationship management (CRM)applications are real software, but they are going through rapid and radical changes as Oracle develops these new modules. Also, in the space allowed, we found we couldn't cover the many tightly focused applications for everything from grants and quality to salesman compensation. For this book, we pruned the topics we could reasonably cover to four broad, core areas:

- Financial applications
- Manufacturing applications
- Supply chain management applications
- Human resource management systems

As this chapter is being written in June 2001, the vast majority of the installed Oracle customer base is contemplating an upgrade to version 11*i* of the Oracle Applications. Upgrade considerations are the top priority for most Oracle ERP customers, and discussion about 11*i* is starting to have an urgency like the Y2K activity in 1999. Oracle has changed the technical architecture of 11*i* to a three-tier, Internet-computing model, and because of the popularity of the Internet during the past three years, 11*i* is being treated as a major point release of the ERP software by Oracle customers. I will discuss 11*i* concepts near the end of this chapter.

FINANCIAL APPLICATIONS

The financial applications of the Oracle ERP suite of applications are the General Ledger and the subledgers. The financial applications discussed in this book include the following (the common shorthand abbreviation is shown in parentheses):

- General Ledger (GL)
- Accounts Payable (AP)
- Accounts Receivable (AR)
- Fixed Assets (FA)
- Projects (PA)

In addition, the Inventory (INV), and Purchasing (PO) applications can make journal entries into the General Ledger, but these applications are more properly classified as manufacturing or distribution applications.

The General Ledger provides the capability for multiple sets of books and supports complex enterprise organizations. The General Ledger hosts the subledgers and provides the definition of the chart of accounts structure, a fiscal calendar, and a currency. Because the GL and FA applications can support multiple sets of books and the other financial applications can support multiple organizations, you can set up separate and fully functional accounting systems for each of your business organizations.

GENERAL LEDGER

The General Ledger (GL) application is the foundation for a full-featured accounting system. The GL receives journal entries from the Oracle subledgers and has an open interface for incoming journal entries from non-Oracle systems. We discuss this application in detail in Chapter 11, "Using Oracle General Ledger." Although not strictly part of the GL application, the Application Desktop Integrator (ADI for GL enables you to perform reporting, journal entry, and budgeting functions while using an Excel spreadsheet interface. The GL application provides you with the following major business functions:

- The capability to create, change, approve, reverse, and post manual and electronic actual, statistical, and budget journal entries
- The capability to create and update budgets
- The capability to establish budgetary control and online funds checking
- Accounting for multiple companies
- Consolidation of multiple sets of books
- Financial reporting writing through the Financial Statement Generator (FSG) and the Application Desktop Interface (ADI)

- Fiscal calendar and chart of accounts maintenance
- Currency transactions, conversion, translation, and revaluation

PAYABLES

Use Oracle Payables (AP) to control and process your payments for purchases of goods and services, employee expense reports, taxes, rents, and so forth. The release 11*i* version of this application provides two user workbench environments for invoice and payment processing. The manual invoice entry screens can be set up for high-speed data entry. The AP application is a subledger to the GL, and it is tightly integrated and shares data with the purchasing application. There are 20 general application steps and 27 specific AP steps to set up and configure the AP application in 11*i*, and we discuss the following features of AP in Chapter 12, "Using Oracle Payables":

- The capability to set up and maintain supplier records
- Electronic and manual invoice entry
- Expense report processing
- The capability to create and maintain invoice holds and payment schedules
- Cash disbursements for checks and electronic transfers
- Accounting distributions
- Two-, three-, and four-way invoice matching and validation with purchase orders and receipts
- Sales tax and VAT processing
- Expense and disbursements journal entries to GL
- Foreign currency transactions
- Bank transaction reconciliation

RECEIVABLES

Use the Oracle Receivables (AR) application to recognize revenue, process cash receipts, and collect money that is owed to you. A user workbench is provided for each of these three functions. In addition, there are manual and automatic versions of programs to support billing and cash receipt transactions. The AR application is a subledger to the GL, and it is closely integrated and shares data with the Order Management (OM) application. There are 53 setup steps to configure the release 11*i* AR application. You will find a discussion of these functions in Chapter 13, "Using Oracle Receivables":

- The capability to set up and maintain customer records
- The capability to process cash receipt transactions
- The capability to support collection activities with call history, statements, and dunning letters
- The capability to create and maintain revenue and adjustment transactions

- Accounting distributions
- Revenue and cash receipt journal entries to GL
- Foreign currency transactions
- The capability to archive and purge

FIXED ASSETS

The Fixed Assets (FA) application can be set up to maintain asset records and process transactions using three workbenches for assets, mass additions, and tax. FA is a subledger to the GL. There are 32 setup steps to configure the release 11*i* FA application, and I discuss this application in Chapter 14, "Using Oracle Assets":

- The capability to create, maintain, and retire fixed asset records
- Asset physical inventory
- The capability to compute and maintain depreciation calculations
- Depreciation and asset transaction journal entries to GL
- Tax accounting
- Capital budgeting
- Asset listings and construction in progress reports

PROJECTS

The Oracle Projects solution provides a suite of highly integrated applications enabling your organization the capability to capitalize on global opportunities, and I discuss this application in Chapter 15, "Using Oracle Projects." Oracle Projects (formerly known as Project Accounting) enables your organization to set up projects and tasks and assign related expenditures. Costs can be burdened and translated to Revenue, Billing, and Capital items when required. One of the major benefits of using Oracle Projects is the capability for a project-oriented business to manage its projects with a proactive approach. Projects offers detailed online and standard reporting, including the following features:

- Defines projects and tasks (WBS) and enables the control of posting transactions to projects
- Cost and revenue budget entry and maintenance, tracks budget versions
- Records transactions in detail and tracks expenditures via Timecards, Expense Reports, Usages, Commitments, and Supplier Invoices; Interfaces these transactions between Oracle Applications
- Allocation functionality from costs within the Projects application (input/output) or General Ledger accounts (input)
- Capital project maintenance, CIP transactions, and the capability to interface assets to Oracle Assets
- Tracks customer contracts as Agreements, which are funded by projects

- Revenue and Invoice Generation with various methods, including Time and Materials, Cost Plus, and Percent Complete; fully integrated with the General Ledger (Revenue) and Accounts Receivable (Invoices) modules
- Multi-currency support for your customer invoices and expenditures
- Cross Charging, Inter Company, and Inter Project Billing
- Detailed audit trail when data is interfaced between Oracle Applications
- Reports cost and revenue

MANUFACTURING APPLICATIONS

The Oracle manufacturing applications are used to define and value the items you produce. In addition, these applications help you plan, schedule, track progress, and manage the production process. These applications are closely integrated with the financial and supply-chain applications. These applications are at the center of your supply chain and are almost always implemented with the Oracle financial and supply-chain applications. The manufacturing applications include the following:

- Bills of Material (BOM) and Engineering (ENG)
- Work in Process (WIP)
- Cost Management (CST)
- Material Requirements Planning (MRP), Master Production Scheduling (MPS), and Capacity Planning (CPP)

BILLS OF MATERIAL AND ENGINEERING

The Bills of Material (BOM) and Engineering (ENG) applications maintain and control the specifications of your product structure and process information for products. Although these applications are relatively easy to configure, the Bills and Routings are at the heart of the planning, scheduling, and costing processes. You will want to make sure this foundation data is complete and accurate. In release 11*i*, there are 19 tasks to configure BOM and 9 steps to set up the ENG application. We discuss these functions of BOM and ENG in detail in Chapter 19, "Using Oracle Engineering and Bills of Material":

- The capability to create and maintain bills of material
- The capability to create and maintain manufacturing process routings
- Flow manufacturing specifications
- The capability to configure to order definition and maintenance
- Scheduling and lead-time definition and maintenance
- Engineering change orders
- Engineering prototypes

Work In Process

The Work In Process (WIP) application supports the actual manufacturing process on the shop floor. In your factory, WIP can support combinations of discrete, repetitive, assemble to order, and work order–less manufacturing methods. There are 11 configuration tasks to set up the WIP Application. We discuss this application in Chapter 22, "Using Oracle Work in Process." The following are the main features of WIP:

- The capability to create and maintain discrete jobs
- Flow manufacturing
- The capability to create and maintain repetitive schedules
- Material control and management
- Shop floor control and transactions
- Resource management
- Job status controls
- Costing, valuation, and variances from standard
- Shop floor scheduling
- Outside processing

Cost Management

The Cost Management (CST) application provides a full absorption-cost accounting system for use by the Inventory, Work in Process, Purchasing, and Order Entry applications. CST calculates the values and variances of each transaction and keeps a current, perpetual valuation for each item inventory balance. There are 11 setup steps you should evaluate to set up CST. You will find more details about the following topics in Chapter 20, "Using Oracle Cost Management":

- Standard, average, and activity-based costing
- The capability to create and maintain item costs by cost element and sub-element
- Bill of material cost rollup by cost type
- Inventory transaction costing
- Work in Process costing (perpetual balances and transactions)
- Revaluation for cost changes
- Valuation of perpetual inventory balances
- Project and flow manufacturing
- WIP and INV transaction and variance journal entries to GL

PLANNING

The Material Requirements Planning (MRP), Master Production Scheduling (MPS), and Capacity Planning (CPP) applications support the manufacturing planning process. The planning process attempts to balance the supply and demand for item components and products in your supply chain of vendors, factories, inventories, and customers. See Chapter 21, "Using Oracle Planning Applications," for information on these topics:

- Forecasting and management of product demand
- The capability to simulate supply and demand scenarios
- The capability to create and maintain master demand and production schedules
- The capability to generate and maintain material requirements plans
- Supply-chain planning
- The capability to create and maintain aggregate production plans
- Rough-cut capacity planning
- Planner workbench
- Demand classes
- Time fence control and planning
- Repetitive planning
- Two-level master scheduling for key subassemblies and configure to order final assemblies
- Kanban planning

SUPPLY-CHAIN MANAGEMENT APPLICATIONS

The supply-chain management applications are used for procurement, inventory, and customer fulfillment processes:

- Purchasing (PO)
- Order Management (OM)
- Inventory (INV)

PURCHASING

The Purchasing (PO) application is used to buy and receive all sorts of goods and services to supply the needs of your business and customers. The planning applications can make integrated requisitions for required items, and manual requisitions can procure other items, supplies, or services. The PO application is tightly integrated with Accounts Payable, Material Requirements Planning, and Inventory. There are 40 setup tasks to accomplish when you configure the PO application. We discuss these features of PO in Chapter 16, "Using Oracle Purchasing":

- The capability to create and maintain purchase requisitions
- The capability to create, source, and maintain purchase orders

- The capability to create and maintain requests for proposals and requests for quotations
- Document approval and control
- Receiving and inspection
- Returns to vendors
- Accrued receipts transactions and price variance journal entries to GL

Order Management

The Order Management (OM) application is the cornerstone of the customer fulfillment and customer service process. In the planning process, OM is the primary source of demand for your goods and services. This application is tightly integrated with AR to recognize revenue for shipments and control the extension of credit to your customers. There are 30 setup steps to consider when you configure the OM application. See Chapter 18, "Using Oracle Order Management," for information on these topics:

- The capability to create and maintain sales orders
- The capability to create and maintain pricing and customer discounts
- The capability to plan, pick, pack, and ship deliveries for order fulfillment
- The capability to return material authorization
- The capability to interface shipped transactions to Oracle AR
- The capability to control orders with multiple holds and credit check from Oracle AR

Inventory

The Inventory (INV) application is an important application for the manufacturing and supply-chain management activities of the ERP system. The INV application is closely integrated with the GL, PO, MRP, BOM, WIP, CST, OM, and AR applications, and there are 58 setup tasks to perform when configuring a release 11*i* INV module for your business. Chapter 17, "Using Oracle Inventory," has a discussion of these features of the INV application:

- Item master and inventory organization structure definition
- Inventory transactions for customer returns, inspection, transfers among subinventories, transfers among organizations, and miscellaneous transactions
- Lot and serial number control
- The capability to maintain perpetual quantity balances and on-hand availability
- Available to promise (ATP) calculations for sales order schedules
- Value of transactions journal entry to GL
- ABC Analysis
- Multiple item category groups and catalogs
- Cycle counting and physical inventory controls
- Min-max planning and purchase requisitioning for resupply

Human Resources Applications

This book discusses the Human Resource (HR), Payroll (PAY), and Advanced Benefits (OAB) applications of Oracle release 11*i*. These applications were developed after the Financial and Manufacturing applications, and they are now achieving the stability and robust functionality of a mature set of products. The HRMS applications are complex and somewhat difficult to implement because of their technology and your business requirements for extreme flexibility and accuracy. Your organization has a unique culture, and the relationships with its people are governed by a combination of company policies, laws, regulations, and industry dynamics. These Oracle applications provide a core system to support the basic elements, but you might have to customize them to meet your unique requirements.

Human Resources Management Systems

The Human Resources (HR) application enables you to build an information model to represent your business organizations, pay and benefit policies, and people in a system that can be used to support the payroll process and manage the human resources business functions. We discuss this application and the following features in Chapters 23, "Implementing Oracle Human Resources and Oracle Payroll," and 24, "Using Oracle Human Resources":

- The capability to create and maintain employee (and applicant) records by date through the full cycle of hiring, employment, and termination
- The capability to create and maintain employer and other organizations for the enterprise organization model
- The capability to maintain jobs and positions
- The capability to maintain and manage pay grades
- The capability to create and maintain elements for compensation and benefits
- The capability to administrate salaries, budgets, and labor costs
- The capability to manage benefit programs
- Labor costs journal entry to GL
- Recruitment, selection, and hiring
- Reporting required by the government
- Career path management and competency tracking
- Assessments and appraisals
- The capability to match people and enterprise requirements
- Absence and paid time-off administration
- Event administration

Payroll

The Payroll (PAY) application is much more than just paying people for hours worked or services performed. This application builds on the information model of the HR application to support the key management and administrative processes of compensating your people.

We discuss the implementation, configuration, and operation of the following Payroll application functions in Chapters 23 and 25, "Using Oracle Payroll":

- Absence and attendance
- Compensation
- Benefits
- Wage attachments
- Taxes
- Tax and wage reporting
- Worker's compensation administration
- Payroll runtime processing, corrections, and adjustments

ADVANCED BENEFITS

Oracle delivered two new Benefits models with 11*i*—Standard and Advanced. In addition to these new models, the existing Basic Benefits model that users are currently using with 10.7 and 11.x will still work in 11*i*. See Chapter 26, "Using Oracle Advanced Benefits," for a discussion of these three models and a description of the differences. In Chapter 26, I also outline various implementation strategies that you can follow, whether you are doing a fresh install of 11*i*, or you plan to upgrade your current version to 11*i*. Other items discussed in this chapter include

- Description of the various compensation objects in Standard and Advanced Benefits
- Participant and dependent eligibility profiles
- Life events
- Variable rate profiles
- Standard rates
- Flex credits
- Imputed income calculation example
- A walkthrough of a sample benefit program setup

OTHER APPLICATION FEATURES

In addition to the individual applications modules, there are four major topics you will want to understand:

- Workflow
- Multi-org
- System administration
- Software of the many vendors who provide additional compatible solutions

These additional topics add many features and capabilities to the Oracle ERP system, and in release 11*i* of the applications, these features are an integral part of your system.

WORKFLOW

The Workflow application helps you manage business processes. For example, in the GL application, there is an Approve Journal Entry process using an approval hierarchy and limits that can be implemented. The Workflow system uses the approval hierarchy and money limits to route journal entries to the appropriate user before posting. If you need to modify the Workflow definitions embedded within the applications, you can do so, but if you want to write new Workflow process definitions, you must license the Workflow application software from Oracle.

You can provide additional logic and process steps based on your business requirements. Workflow is a technical solution to a functional business process, and to implement Workflow, you will want to use both technical and functional resources. In 11*i* there are 13 steps to configure Workflow.

Workflow consists of four major systems, and you will find detailed information in Chapter 28, "Using Oracle Workflow":

- Use the Workflow builder to create or modify workflow process definitions.
- The Workflow engine executes the process definitions and interacts with the Applications.
- The notifications system communicates with users by sending and receiving messages.
- The monitoring tool enables you to observe Workflow processes.

MULTI-ORG

The multi-org functions within the Oracle applications enable you to define a complex enterprise business model with many organizations. The multi-org model is important because it can affect how the business units interact with each other and how transactions flow through the enterprise. AR, OM, AP, PO, and PA are the key applications discussed in this book that can use multi-org capabilities. The GL and FA applications implement an enterprise organization model through multiple sets of books. The manufacturing and human resources applications also implement an organization model but without using multi-org. There are 20 steps to configuring and setting up the multi-org functions, and we discuss the features of multi-org in detail in Chapter 29, "Understanding Multi-Org."

The main features of multi-org include the following:

- Organization security and limited access through partitioned data tables.
- Intercompany AR invoice processing and accounting.
- Intercompany AP invoice processing and accounting.
- Many business units can use the same database instance.
- Support for nine types of organizations, including set of books, legal entity, business group, balancing entity, operating unit, inventory organization, HR organization, project organization, and asset organizations.

- Flexible purchasing and receiving by different legal entities.
- Flexible selling and shipping by different legal entities.

System Administration

The system administration functions of the applications enable you to implement security, change user preferences, and set up batch jobs. Although a user might be able to perform many of these functions, not all users will be comfortable with the technical aspects of managing printers, menus, and concurrent processing. These functions are different from the administration tasks performed by a database administrator (DBA). Because there are important technical and security requirements for the system administration functions, realize that most users should not have access to this part of the system and consider carefully how you assign staff to these functions.

There are 11 setup tasks you should consider early in your implementation project, and we discuss system administration in detail in Chapter 27, "Administering the Oracle Applications." The system administration functions include the capability to do the following:

- Define security and access for the ERP applications.
- Create and maintain profile options and preferences.
- Extend the online HTML help for local policies and procedures.
- Manage concurrent processing of batch programs.
- Customize menus and interactive navigation paths for users.
- Set up and maintain printers.

Other Software

When Oracle added approximately 30 Application Program Interfaces (APIs) to the first releases of release 10.x of the applications in 1994, it started a small industry of software companies that built extensions and enhancements to the core functionality provided by Oracle. Today, many software vendors partner with Oracle Corporation to add functionality to the core ERP Applications. You need to know about these companies because many times your business requirements will be best served through a combination of Oracle Corporation and another vendor's software.

Note

Implementing "best of breed" software from many vendors is hard to do, and the compatibility among mixed vendor solutions varies in robustness from one vendor to the next. Although Oracle does have certification standards for software and vendors to belong to its partner program, don't assume this certification translates to automatic or even easy implementation. A mixed vendor implementation still produces issues with support, process flow, documentation, and no matter what anybody says, it is never seamless. Do not underestimate the integration costs.

If you spent your entire software budget with Oracle Corporation and if you have no gaps in functionality, you can skip to the next chapter. But, if you have some money left and business requirements beyond the functionality you get from Oracle, consider the other vendors discussed in the chapter titled "Finding Additional Compatible Solutions" on this book's Web site. These vendors are grouped into the following major categories:

- Administration Utilities
- Asset Management
- Data Collection and Bar Codes
- Document Management and Workflow
- Electronic Commerce and Electronic Data Interchange
- Implementation and Interface Tools
- Maintenance Management
- Planning and Supply-Chain Management
- Printing and Output Enhancement
- Quality Management
- Reporting Enhancements and Business Intelligence
- Taxation
- Warehouse and Distribution Management

11*i* Architecture Concepts

The Oracle 11*i* Applications use the three-tiered Internet computing architecture. This architecture distributes services among many nodes on a network to support the processing load. The three tiers of the architecture include:

- The database tier is an Oracle 8*i* database.
- The application tier manages the Oracle ERP Applications and eliminates the need to install application software on each desktop.
- The desktop tier provides a plug-in for a browser-based user interface over a network.

The application tier operates effectively over a Wide Area Network (WAN) and provides the following services to the ERP system:

- Forms Server
- Reports Server
- HTTP Server
- Concurrent Processing Server
- Discoverer Server
- Administration Server

In addition, many Oracle 11*i* Applications use Oracle Workflow running on the Application tier through a connection to the HTTP Server with program logic controlled through stored procedures written in PL/SQL and Java.

SUMMARY

Therefore, the Oracle ERP Applications are a suite of modules that can provide your organization with robust transaction processing capability for accounting, distribution, manufacturing, and human resources business requirements. This chapter contains information about the high-level capabilities of the applications. If you are interested in application implementation techniques, please continue reading in Part II, "Implementing the Oracle Applications." If you need to understand more details about a specific business function, you will find a chapter on each application in Part III, "Configuring and Using the Oracle Applications."

PART II

Implementing the Oracle Applications

CHAPTER 3

SOFTWARE IMPLEMENTATION METHODS

In this chapter

In this section of the book, we discuss techniques for implementing the Oracle Applications. This chapter discusses general strategies and differences of various implementation methods. In other chapters in this section, you will read about the following topics:

- Factors affecting how much your project will cost and how much effort it will take
- Techniques for project management and control
- Planning project tasks and scope definitions
- Analysis techniques for your business and technical systems
- Designing ERP solutions for your business
- Techniques to enable the system
- Managing change, transitioning from old to new systems, and supporting users after your systems "go live"

USING ORACLE'S APPLICATION IMPLEMENTATION METHOD

Oracle Corporation formalized an Application Implementation Method (AIM) in 1994 to support its rapidly growing consulting organization and the first shipments of release 10 of the Applications. Prior to AIM, Oracle consultants used something called Application Implementation Plan (AIP) for release 9 implementation projects. Because AIP was really nothing more than a huge list of project tasks and loosely defined activities, AIM was a big improvement. AIM provided the Oracle consultant with an integrated set of templates, procedures, PowerPoint presentations, spreadsheets, and project plans for implementing the applications. AIM was such a success, Oracle created a subset of the templates, called it AIM Advantage, and made it available as a product to customers and other consulting firms. Since its initial release, AIM has been revised and improved several times with new templates and methods.

AIM IS A SIX-PHASE METHOD

Because the Oracle ERP Applications are software modules you buy from a vendor, you will use different implementation methods than the techniques you use for custom developed systems that you get from your information technology department. AIM has six major phases:

- **Definition phase**—During this phase, you plan the project, determine business objectives, and verify the feasibility of the project for given time, resource, and budget limits.
- **Operations Analysis phase**—Includes documents business requirements, gaps in the software (which can lead to customizations), and system architecture requirements. Results of the analysis should provide a proposal for future business processes, a technical architecture model, an application architecture model, workarounds for application gaps, performance testing models, and a transition strategy to migrate to the new systems. Another task that can begin in this phase is mapping of legacy data to Oracle

Application APIs or open interfaces—data conversion. If you know what data is going to be converted, and know what API it needs, then begin this task. The sooner you can start data conversion, the better!

- **Solution Design phase**—Used to create designs for solutions that meet future business requirements and processes. The design of your future organization comes alive during this phase as customizations and module configurations are finalized.
- **Build phase**—During this phase of AIM, coding and testing of customizations, enhancements, interfaces, and data conversions happens. In addition, one or more conference room pilots test the integrated enterprise system. The results of the build phase should be a working, tested business system solution.
- **Transition phase**—During this phase, the project team delivers the finished solution to the enterprise. End-user training and support, management of change, and data conversions are major activities of this phase.
- **Production phase**—Starts when the system goes live. Technical people work to stabilize and maintain the system under full transaction loads. Users and the implementation team begin a series of refinements to minimize unfavorable impacts and realize the business objectives identified in the definition phase.

Note

AIM tends to create large and robust project plans that are suitable for complex enterprises. Because large and robust also means costly, we discuss a modified and more reasonable version of implementation methods later in Part II, "Implementing the Oracle Applications," of the book. The basic phases, activities, and tasks are suitable for most implementations.

Defined Deliverables

AIM has a defined set of project tasks, and each task has one or more deliverable results. Each deliverable document has a template with some form and content, and there is a standard style to give a consistent look and feel to the templates. If you do a good job of completing the deliverables, you will have a well-documented project library.

Tip

Many of the deliverable documents build on each other to produce a solution. For example, analysis documents drive design, build, transition, and production project activities. Try not to skip deliverables if they are required by other project activities.

Also, you should retain these documents for future use. Organizations pay a lot of money to consulting firms to develop these deliverables, only to find the consultants are the ones who benefit, not the organization.

ADVANTAGES OF AIM

AIM was a great thing when it was first released in 1994. Oracle consultants took to it like a drowning man grabs for a life preserver. Since that time, Oracle has improved the product several times, and thousands of consultants have learned basic packaged software implementation techniques. Consider using AIM to gain these advantages:

- The method is usually successful and reduces the risk of an ERP project.
- AIM is a good roadmap for inexperienced customers and consultants.
- Complex projects are supported.
- Communication among project team resources is improved through the project library, presentations, and integrated activities.
- The documentation is a good source of reference for future upgrades and customizations.
- The templates look professional.
- AIM is based on the familiar MS Office suite of products.

DISADVANTAGES OF AIM

It is hard to say much that is bad about AIM. On balance, the advantages outweigh the disadvantages. However, like any tool, you can misuse it and get less than great results. Consider the following before automatically selecting this method for your project:

- AIM produces a relatively high-cost project plan.
- Several activities are appropriate only for complex projects. It takes a skilled practitioner to know how to scale AIM down for the less-demanding situation.
- Like any tool, you must learn how to use AIM techniques. You can't get great results if you try to skip the learning curve. Early in the project, you must learn how to use the method and approve the deliverables.
- Many AIM deliverables are required and not flexible because they are needed for downstream activities.
- Skipping or poor execution of a required deliverable can throw off dependent project activities.
- AIM does not help you find bugs in the software, diagnose problems with the software, or learn how to work with Oracle support.

UNDERSTANDING RAPID IMPLEMENTATIONS

In the late 1990s as Y2K approached, customers demanded and consulting firms discovered faster ways to implement packaged software applications. The rapid implementation became possible for certain types of customers. The events that converged in the late 1990s to provide faster implementations include the following:

- Many smaller companies couldn't afford the big ERP project. If the software vendors and consulting firms were going to sell to the "middle market" companies, they had to develop more efficient methods.
- Many dot.coms needed a financial infrastructure; ERP applications filled the need, and rapid implementation methods provided the way.
- The functionality of the software improved a lot, many gaps were eliminated, and more companies could implement with fewer customizations.
- After the big, complex companies implemented their ERP systems, the typical implementation became less difficult.
- The number of skilled consultants and project managers increased significantly.
- Other software vendors started packaging preprogrammed integration points to the Oracle ERP modules.

Note

A rapid implementation of five basic financial applications using preconfigured modules and predefined business processes for 30–50 users can still take three or four months. When you add the manufacturing applications, rapid means six months.

DESCRIPTION OF RAPID IMPLEMENTATION TECHNIQUES

Rapid implementations focus on delivering a predefined set of functionality. A key set of business processes is installed in a standard way to accelerate the implementation schedule. These projects benefit from the use of preconfigured modules and predefined business processes. You get to reuse the analysis and integration testing from other implementations, and you agree to ignore all gaps by modifying your business to fit the software. Typically, the enterprise will be allowed some control over key decisions such as the structure of the chart of accounts. Fixed budgets are set for training, production support, and data conversions (a limited amount of data).

Note

There is an important difference between the terms *preconfigured module* and *vanilla implementation*. In a vanilla implementation, you analyze and choose your configuration parameters to use any or all of the software functionality without customization. In the preconfigured method, you gain speed by accepting a basic configuration and predefined business processes.

Tip

Faster implementations usually mean lower costs. If you use an experienced team of consultants, the critical factor to the speed of your implementation is probably the ability of your organization to absorb change.

ADVANTAGES

For certain customers, the rapid implementation of preconfigured modules and predefined business processes, has several advantages:

- The business can start to realize ERP benefits quickly; it's basically a turnkey approach.
- The Oracle customer will have to spend less staff time on project. This can be a big plus if the project team members can't get away from their regular job assignments.
- There might be fewer business disruptions during the implementation project.
- Decisions are made quickly.
- Rapidly implemented projects can cost less.

DISADVANTAGES

When using this project method, the disadvantages often outweigh the advantages for some customers. If you are inexperienced with the Oracle software, you might be unable to predict the changes that a rapid implementation will have on important aspects of your business. Consider the following items:

- You will not have the time to customize or make interfaces to the ERP software to support your business processes the way you need them.
- If end users cannot or will not receive changes at the rapid implementation pace, your business processes might become unstable or uncoordinated.
- Certain aspects of your corporate strategy might have to change to fit the predefined processes. Consider the effects of the software on your customers, employees, and vendors. For example, are you prepared to change your product pricing formulas and salesman compensation programs? Can you visualize how your factory will run with the new software?
- Even when the implementation project ends, end users and technical people will not understand the full capabilities of the system, or how to work with Oracle Support.
- These techniques are only appropriate for small groups of users (20–80 users).
- The rapid implementation might require a core group of senior people to participate and to make decisions quickly.
- This project method might require higher up-front costs over the phased implementation.
- To implement effectively, you must have good understanding of your business processes and the software capability.
- The information technology department might not have the skills to support the production software, and possibly the hardware, when the system is ready to go live.
- There might be more business disruptions after the system goes live.

Note

Typically, these rapid implements require rework–or additional consulting expertise after the transition to production–possibly leading to higher project costs. Evaluate the rapid approach thoroughly to determine whether it's appropriate for your organization. These implementations usually are inflexible and have limited functionality, access to legacy information, and user training.

UNDERSTANDING THE PROGRAM OFFICE

The program office method can be used in very complex situations to coordinate, control, and manage many parallel implementation projects. Using this method, the program office staff performs certain implementation tasks at an enterprise level and then issues requirements to the subprojects at each site. For example, the program office often creates a global chart of accounts and requires each business unit to translate and convert the various legacy general ledgers to the new corporate standard chart.

Typically, the program office is interested in the definition of all Key Flexfields, the definition of some of the Descriptive Flexfields, implementation of corporate policy, audit requirements, intercompany transactions, and the centralized business processes. The program office might also control the budget and master schedule for all the subprojects. Often, the program office allows local autonomy to the individual site projects for testing, end-user training, data conversions, interfaces, customizations, and configuration of system parameters that support local functions or never cross organization boundaries.

Also, the program office project team monitors the local activities and deliverables of the individual subprojects. The goal of this activity is to facilitate the flow of coding and knowledge among the subprojects. For example, if one site develops a customization, the program office knows which of the other subprojects have the same requirement and are interested in the work. The program office makes the customization available to the other sites through a centralized library of project deliverables.

ADVANTAGES

The advantages of the program office method come primarily in project efficiency and control. Often, the centralized project team can accomplish centralized tasks and give the results to the subprojects. Consider the following:

- The program office method can reduce total implementation costs by 20%–30%.
- The program office can consolidate buying power for enterprisewide software licenses.
- Enterprise configuration parameters are established in a uniform way.
- Many project tasks are performed only one time.

- Corporate policies and procedures can be consistently established and enforced by the new software configuration.
- The business rules for intercompany transactions are clearly defined and rationalized.
- Removes organization barriers and improves intercompany communications.
- Senior management can become involved in important aspects of the ERP software.
- Facilitation of project-related decisions might be made faster, as well as the resolution of issues.

DISADVANTAGES

The disadvantages of program office techniques are related to the top-down nature of the method and include the following items:

- Sometimes, the program office compromises on the lowest common denominator for a configuration decision. Many sites perceive a gap relative to their specific local requirements and the enterprise configuration. The subprojects spend time and money to customize the applications or work around the gap created by the program office.
- The implementation team members in subprojects often resent the controls and decisions of the centralized authority.
- Because each site has an active implementation subproject, staff requirements and costs are still very large.
- The analysis phase of the program office can take a very long time.
- Program office project team members must travel a lot.

Note

Consider creating a program monitoring team consisting of executives from each subproject, or subsidiary organization. This small team will help monitor progress of all projects, as well as keep executive management, the president or CEO, and the board of directors informed on progress. Having these people engaged will provide additional support to the projects for activities such as time and resource commitments, as well as supply advice and consul to everyone involved with the projects.

UNDERSTANDING PHASED IMPLEMENTATIONS

Phased implementations seek to break up the work of an ERP implementation project. This technique can make the system more manageable and reduce risks, and costs in some cases, to the enterprise. In the mid-1990s, 4 or 5 was about the maximum number of application modules that could be launched into production at one time. If you bought 12 or 13 applications, there would be a financial phase that would be followed by phases for the distribution and manufacturing applications. As implementation techniques improved and Y2K pressures grew in the late 1990s, more and more companies started launching most of their applications at the same time. This method became known as the big-bang approach. Now, each company selects a phased or big-bang approach based on its individual requirements.

Another approach to phasing can be employed by companies with business units at multiple sites. With this technique, one business unit is used as a template, and all applications are completely implemented in an initial phase lasting 10–14 months. Then, other sites implement the applications in cookie-cutter fashion. The cookie-cutter phases are focused on end-user training and the differences that a site has from the prototype site. The cookie-cutter phase can be as short as 9–12 weeks, and these phases can be conducted at several sites simultaneously.

For your reference, we participated in an efficient project where 13 applications were implemented big bang–style in July at the Chicago site after about 8 months work. A site in Malaysia went live in October. The Ireland site started up in November. After a holiday break, the Atlanta business unit went live in February, and the final site in China started using the applications in April. Implementing thirteen application modules at five sites in four countries in sixteen months was pretty impressive.

Advantages

There are several advantages to the phased implementation over the all-at-once approach:

- The enterprise is in control of how much change it must absorb at one time.
- Each phase or organization success can be considered a win for the project team; therefore, management's confidence in the team's ability to succeed is high for subsequent phases.
- Typically, a phased implementation has less risk than the big-bang approach because problems can be isolated and complexity is reduced.
- Phases can be scheduled so new software is not going live during the busy season of the business.
- Lessons learned, project materials, and deliverables from early phases can be applied to later phases to improve performance.
- Because the user population and transaction volume grow at a slower rate, the technical infrastructure can be developed more precisely over a longer period.
- The core implementation team doesn't have to do all the work when using the cookie-cutter approach. Power users from the first sites can assist with subsequent implementations. Key users at unimplemented sites can observe and learn about the production software from the already implemented locations.
- The big-bang approach takes more training and coordination during the transition phase as the new systems are about to be launched. With the big-bang method, it is hard to predict which groups of users will have problems with the new software and what affect those problems will have on the integrated system.

Disadvantages

The phased implementation technique has a few disadvantages compared with the big-bang method:

- Phased implementations can cost more and take longer to complete.
- Returns on the investment in ERP software are slower to develop.

- Oracle can release new software while the company is between phases. An upgrade might become required before a new phase can start.
- The phased approach might require creation of temporary interfaces between the Oracle system and the legacy system. As the system is completed, these temporary interfaces cost money and are typically thrown away.
- If any of the sites goes poorly, word will quickly spread, and the project team will have a credibility problem and a rough time when it starts work on the next site.

CASE STUDIES ILLUSTRATING IMPLEMENTATION TECHNIQUES

Some practical examples from the real world might help to illustrate some of the principles and techniques of various software implementation methods. These case studies are composites from about 60 implementation projects we have observed during the past 9 years.

BIG COMPANIES

We have observed both extremely efficient and almost totally dysfunctional big company implementations of the ERP software. Each big company project is unique and has special needs. To meet those needs, the big company project manager can construct a customized project plan and implementation method to fit the situation. Phased implementations work well at big companies because it is hard to coordinate many complicated modules or handle the logistics of many sites. Sometimes the financial applications are implemented in the first phase followed by phases for distribution, manufacturing, and payroll applications. Sometimes all the applications are implemented at one site, and each site becomes a subsequent cookie-cutter implementation project.

Big companies often have a horrible time resolving issues and deciding on configuration parameters because there is so much money involved and each of many sites might want to control decisions about what it considers its critical success factors. For example, we once saw a large company argue for over two months about the chart of accounts structure, while eight consultants from two consulting firms tried to referee among the feuding operating units. Another large company labored for more than six months to unify a master customer list for a centralized receivables and decentralized order entry system.

Transition activities at large companies need special attention. Training end users can be a logistical challenge and can require considerable planning. For example, if you have 800 users to train and each user needs an average of three classes of two hours each and you have one month, how many classrooms and instructors do you need? Another example is that loading data from a legacy system can be a problem. If you have one million customers to load into Oracle receivables at the rate of 5,000/hour and the database administrator allows you to load 20 hours per day, you have a 10-day task. Can you imagine trying to load customers and train users on the same system during the week before going live? Now, combine those two nontrivial tasks with a hundred other transition activities.

Because they spend huge amounts of money on their ERP systems, many big companies try to optimize the systems and capture specific returns on the investment. However, sometimes companies can be incredibly insensitive and uncoordinated as they try to make money from their ERP software. For example, one business announced at the beginning of a project that the accounts payable department would be cut from 50–17 employees as soon as the system went live. Another company decided to centralize about 30 accounting sites into one shared service center and advised about 60 accountants that they would lose their jobs in about a year. Several of the 60 employees were offered positions on the ERP implementation team. Both of these projects encountered considerable delay and resistance by the affected users.

SMALL COMPANIES

Small companies sometimes have a hard time staffing their project implementation teams. However, at the end of the project, the implementation team members become very qualified power users of the system. Often, the team members retain their primary job responsibilities during the project and can only work on the new system part-time. This part-time status typically has employees assigned to the project at 50%—in other words, 20 hours per week on the project and the other 20+ hours on their jobs. This situation doesn't work, and the 50% that is neglected is the project.

I managed one project in which the organization had six developers assigned the project 50% and normal maintenance duties 50%. I asked the client to provide us with three developers at 100% of the time, with the other three remaining on legacy maintenance activity. The next issue we faced was helping the organization determine which three developers to choose.

Small companies have other problems when creating an implementation team. Occasionally, the small company tries to put clerical employees on the team and they have problems with issue resolution or some of the ERP concepts. In another case, one small company didn't create the position of project manager. Each department worked on its own modules and ignored the integration points, testing, and requirements of other users. When Y2K deadlines forced the system startup, results were disastrous with a cost impact that doubled the cost of the entire project.

Project team members at small companies sometimes have a hard time relating to the cost of the implementation. We once worked with a company where the project manager (who was also the database administrator) advised me within the first hour of our meeting that he thought consulting charges of $3/minute were outrageous, and he couldn't rationalize how we could possibly make such a contribution. We agreed a consultant could not contribute $3 in value each and every minute to his project. However, when I told him we would be able to save him $10,000/week and make the difference between success and failure, he realized we should get to work.

Because the small company might be relatively simple to implement and the technical staff might be inexperienced with the database and software, it is possible that the technical staff will be on the critical path of the project. If the database administrator can't learn how to handle the production database by the time the users are ready to go live, you might need to hire some temporary help to enable the users to keep to the schedule. In addition, we often see small companies with just a single database administrator who might be working 60 or more hours per week. They feel they can afford to have more DBAs as employees, but they don't know how to establish the right ratio of support staff to user requirements. These companies can burn out a DBA quickly and then have to deal with the problem of replacing an important skill.

GREEN FIELD COMPANIES

The green field company is just starting operations. They literally start with a green field, build a factory, hire some workers, and start production. In these companies, a small core group of key managers start everything. Typically this group is very busy because they are involved in all aspects of constructing buildings, setting up production lines, hiring and training workers, and so forth. However, the green field company has many advantages over other ERP implementations, and these factors can easily result in an implementation that is 25% more efficient. Even if you are an established company, consider the following to learn some of the dynamics behind how an implementation project progresses:

- Everyone is new to the company. Politics and departmental boundaries are nonexistent. Everyone's agenda is aligned toward getting the systems into production.
- Tolerance for change is high. Everything changes every week, and it is exciting, positive change. When things change, there is a sense of accomplishment. Employees expect problems, deal with them, and move on.
- Users are easy to train. They have no habits to unlearn, and they are eager to understand the systems of their new employer. User expectations of the new systems are low.
- There is no legacy system, and that means there are few data conversions and almost no interfaces. There are no spreadsheets, personal databases, and other isolated islands of computer processing on user desktops. In fact, the only other systems in the whole business might be a remote financial system at a parent company and some shop floor control systems.
- There are no favorite reports that have to be replicated in the new systems.

PUBLIC SECTOR

The public sector implementation project can have some unusual dynamics. These projects can be large and complex with significant numbers of users, transaction volumes, interfaces to control agencies, and requirements for server performance. Business processes are different in the public sector. Oracle provides the capability to configure the software and documentation for these customers, and some consultants specialize in the unique needs of the public sector.

In addition, the public sector project can have a different perspective from the commercially driven implementation. These projects are funded and therefore take on the characteristics of a fixed-price project and typically require an agreement not to exceed a proposed dollar amount. Also, change management techniques are important to the public sector project. Procedures and business processes can be difficult to change, and there are many issues to be resolved. Issues and configuration decisions might be addressed differently by the public sector project team. Communication is important as everyone tries to figure out how the new relationships and processes will work. Usually many barriers exist within public sector organizations, primarily due to the silo nature of their operating units.

Many public sector organizations experience difficulty in hiring qualified resources. Public sector implementations are very different from commercial implementations because you deal with very different organization cultures and structures. Specifically within HR and Payroll, many configurations of resource structures and payment schedules exist.

Some public sector organizations have set work hours, such as 7 a.m.–3 p.m. five days per week. Many traveling consultants work 4–10 hours per day. This time in the evening when clients are not around can become very productive for a consultant. It can also become a problem because clients tend to leave at 3 p.m. whether you're in a meeting or they are sitting at their desks. On some projects, we have had clients get up and walk out of meetings at 3 p.m., with no questions asked or next steps discussed.

Often, the legacy system is in terrible shape. The data conversions and interfaces to and from the legacy systems might be difficult or involve significant programming. We were once asked to convert a 50,000-record file that held both vendor and customer information in the same record layout because it was really just names and addresses. About 70% of the required fields by Oracle Payables and Oracle Receivables weren't in the file. In another situation, the agency had no funding for laser printers and expected the ERP system to print reports on old daisy wheel printers. We calculated that some daily reports would not finish printing in less than 8 hours.

The ASP

The ASP module is not for every organization and seems to have dwindled some in popularity the past year, although Gartner Group indicates the worldwide ASP market will reach $25 billion by the year 2005. There are also predictions of many, many failures in the ASP market. This can be a very costly alternative to hosting your own applications.

Giving management and control to an ASP can be a double-edged sword. Basically, you trust the ASP to follow good security, data backup, and data recovery procedures, upgrades, maintenance, and support (service-level agreements). These are all the things organizations have tried to achieve over the years—so make sure the ASP has these and more in place.

The ASP approach is a quick and easy way to get your organization up and running with Oracle Applications. The approach is a simple concept and one with which most of us are familiar. This approach is not applicable to all organizations, but it does have its benefits. Research this option well to determine whether this is attractive to your organization.

The ASP approach has its advantages, such as decreased customer maintenance, decreased hardware costs, and an overall implementation that is typically much less expensive. The opportunity to secure the Oracle Applications while forgoing significant infrastructure, software, and personnel can be very attractive to organizations. There is certainly a lower total cost of ownership that we've seen estimated at between 30% and 70%.

Some disadvantages are speed and security of the applications, use of preconfigured application modules, uptime guarantees, and future transition of hosting your own applications. There are many things to consider when selecting an ASP, and we can't possibly cover them all in this chapter.

When considering an ASP approach, here are some other things to consider: service level agreements, documented disaster recovery procedures, statements of data security, scalability scenarios, and proven technical maintenance and support. Also, equally important is the financial stability of the ASP you are selecting.

SUMMARY

There are different techniques that you can use to implement your Oracle ERP Applications. The Application Implementation Method developed by Oracle is a good place to start when you evaluate the methods you will use. However, each technique has its strengths and weaknesses and might be more or less appropriate for your enterprise. Your best solution might be a hybrid approach based on your unique needs.

In the remainder of this section of the book, we will discuss the principal activities and deliverables associated with each major phase of an implementation project.

CHAPTER 4

Understanding What Affects the Degree of Effort and Cost

In this chapter

Packaged software implementation is expensive. However, progress is being made to lower the costs. In the past seven years, consulting firms and Oracle have developed many techniques to control costs, project scope, and complexity. The cost, scope, and risk of an ERP project are directly proportional to the following items:

- The degree of business complexity
- The number of applications to be implemented
- The amount of extensions to the package software
- The nature of the business processes

There are trade-offs that you must make when implementing packaged ERP software. You can implement your software rapidly, cheaply, or fully featured. Usually, you cannot capture all three benefits at the same time. Because they do less, rapid implementations are often less expensive than full-featured, customized implementations. If the rapid implementation must also be full-featured and customized, the amount of implementation work is the same as the slower-paced, full-featured implementation. There will be a large, coordinated, and expensive project team to accomplish both projects.

The project method you pick affects the costs and the skills required on the project. Oracle uses several methods including the following:

- Application Implementation Method (AIM)
- Program Office
- Rapidly Preconfigured Modules (RPM)
- Fast Forward
- Business Models

Other consulting firms have a wide assortment of work plans, templates, methods, and techniques to reduce cost and minimize the risks of these projects.

Tip

Remember, Oracle provides services to sell software. If you choose a low-cost implementation method, make sure the technique will actually work in your company. For example, the preconfigured module method might produce an inexpensive implementation, but if you require several interfaces to non-Oracle systems, you might not meet your business requirements.

To understand cost drivers, BOSS Corporation analyzed a complex project to determine what factors controlled the cost. The work plan for this project was over 1,500 consulting workdays and 4,000 client workdays. The method chosen for the project was similar to Oracle AIM. The people at BOSS looked at each task in the work plan, the cost factors controlling the task, and the number of planned days to complete the task. Then, they weighted the results to determine which factors contributed the most to implemented cost. Because multiple factors might contribute to the cost of a single task, results add to more than 100%. Table 4.1 shows factors affecting the total cost.

Table 4.1 Factors Affecting Total Cost

Factor	Impact
Applications to be implemented	45%
Business complexity	40%
Customizations, interfaces, data conversion	31%
Business processes and reengineering	13%

Using the Number and Type of Applications to Estimate Costs

The number of applications to be implemented is the main cost driver for an ERP project. Implementation of each application is a miniproject within the main implementation project. A full suite of twelve manufacturing applications takes more work than a financial suite of a General Ledger plus three or four subledgers. The process analysis, setup, testing, training, and so forth, must be done for each application.

In addition, when you implement more applications, you have more function points to interface, more interdepartmental relationships, and longer business processes. For example, a simple Payables implementation can involve more effort (and be more rewarding) if you implement it as part of a procurement system with purchasing and receiving. When you involve many business functions and processes, project management, issue resolution, and coordination take more effort.

Understanding the Relative Complexity of Each Application

Some of the Oracle Applications are more difficult to implement than others, and you might have business conditions that will emphasize one of the more difficult applications. For example, if you have a million customers and generate 100,000 billing lines a day through the AR module, you will want to have a much more robust implementation effort than the typical AR project.

Table 4.2 shows typical relative weights for each application with GL and INV set to a degree of difficulty of 100. When you calculate your project work plan, allow more time and resources for the more complex applications and adjust the relative difficulty for your business requirements.

TABLE 4.2 RELATIVE DEGREES OF DIFFICULTY

Application Name	Difficulty Index
General Ledger	100
Payables	80
Purchasing	120
Receivables	90
Fixed Assets	80
Projects	200
Order Management	170
Inventory	100
Bill of Material	80
Engineering	50
Master Production Scheduling	90
Material Requirements Planning	150
Capacity Planning	30
Work in Process	100
Cost Management	120
Human Resources	No Estimate
Payroll	No Estimate
Advanced Benefits	No Estimate

Tip

The HR/PAY applications are very complex and often use a different method for implementation. A complex payroll implementation can take more than five times the effort of a General Ledger. The Advanced Benefits Application is too new to estimate.

The Order Management estimate in Table 4.2 is the value for the old Order Entry Application. Because Order Management is a completely new application, your situation might vary. Many companies are spending large amounts of effort to debug, patch, and stabilize the functionality of Order Management.

BUSINESS SYSTEMS COMPLEXITY

The complexity of your business directly affects the effort and cost of the application's implementation. Complexity is the second most important cost driver of your ERP project. The type of industry, regulations, technology, integration, and company culture might dictate reduced flexibility and business requirements that can increase costs. Global companies with many sites using different currencies, languages, and systems have special requirements that affect costs and effort.

Counting the Number of Users and Sites

The number of users and sites is often a good proxy to indicate complexity. The number of users involved in the project can impact the project in several ways. Costs for security, training, and support for each user are directly proportional to the number of users. However, added users often bring additional requirements and agendas for what the new system must do. These requirements often result in extensions and customizations to the applications. A project with more end users is more costly than a project for a smaller group.

For projects with multiple sites, a program office method can coordinate common tasks across all sites. In a five-site implementation, the program office methods save about 20% of the costs in comparison to five separate projects.

In addition, multisite projects have technical architecture complexities that must match the application's architecture and business processes. The centralized/decentralized business model might constrain the implementation. For example, a multisite company with centralized payables and decentralized purchasing has a more complex implementation.

Understanding the Agendas of Users

Increasing the number of users and sites adds cost by increasing the number of agendas and issues to be addressed. Many users might not appreciate the software because their leaders were not on the software selection team. When the project leadership is from a specific group (MIS, accounting, or manufacturing) or from a specific site (headquarters, shared services, or plant X), the project inherits the attributes of the leadership.

Accountants seem to be more structured and therefore have an easier agenda during implementation than HR, Order Management, or Procurement users. Perhaps the financial applications have been around longer and have a better fit rate for most business processes because there is less variation from company to company in accounting systems as opposed to fulfillment, HR, or procurement systems.

Also, the political process of the organization can dramatically affect costs because the issue-resolution mechanism is affected. Package software can often redistribute workloads and information flows in an organization, and those users on the wrong side of the redistribution can use the political process to delay, change scope, or place additional requirements on the implementation.

Excellent executive sponsorship is the classic way to resolve issues, minimize the political process, and ensure end-user cooperation with the change to new systems and procedures. If you can involve executives at a high level, you can reduce the costs of the project. Also, form a project team that can make efficient decisions and represent the full constituency of end users to resolve potential stumbling blocks.

Considering Other Types of Complexity

Complexity can also be brought to the project by requirements of trading partners, government regulations, industry practices, and so forth. You might simply have to activate more function points in the application to meet the minimum requirements of your business. Your trading partners might expect supply-chain management practices. You might want to activate lot and serial number tracking for raw materials and finished goods. Your industry might have intricate pricing mechanisms. When you know your business well, the trick to estimating the cost of complexity is to understand what the applications support and how to fill the gaps.

Understanding the Effect of Complexity on the Simple Project

Complexity affects the simple ERP project too because Oracle has built the applications to service large organizations in many industries. The pressure to compete with SAP, PeopleSoft, and others forces features and functions into the applications that you might never use. However, you must cope with extensive documentation, configuration parameters, testing, patches, and so forth, for these features that might be irrelevant to your requirements.

Minimizing Customizations and Extensions to Lower Costs

The third significant area of expense and effort is customizations and extensions to the applications. There are 10 common types of customizations. Remember, to meet a business requirement or fill a gap, you might require several of these elemental customizations to meet a single business requirement:

- Modify a copy of an Oracle form
- Create a new form
- Modify a copy of an Oracle report
- Create a new report
- Modify an existing Oracle workflow
- Create a new program, package, workflow, or procedure
- Convert legacy or external data for import into an Oracle application
- Interface to external systems
- Create different menus
- Create tables, indexes, and other database objects to support other customizations

Tip

Many extensions have a system lifetime cost as well as an implementation cost. You will have the opportunity to revisit your extensions on virtually every upgrade or patch application to make sure they continue to work with the changes coming in from Oracle.

At the beginning of the project, prepare a list of each type of possible customization or extension by application, and use that list to control the scope of the project. As the project progresses, ask the steering committee to approve additions to the list.

Each customization should be evaluated by degree of difficulty:

- Very easy
- Easy
- Moderately difficult
- Complex

Also, each customization will have various work components: analyze, design, build, test, document, train, and so forth. Make sure you have the skills on the project team to accomplish each component and task. Estimate the effort for each work component for each customization. In addition, estimate the potentially significant life-cycle maintenance costs for your customization to understand the cost of upgrading your code when Oracle releases new software.

AUTOMATING DATA CONVERSION WORK

Conversion of legacy data is a popular and potentially expensive implementation activity. If there is an Application Program Interface (API) for the incoming data, the task might be rated easy and built in three to five days by an experienced consultant. If there is no API, you might have to reverse-engineer the applications and spend time mapping data elements. Conversions without an API are complex to build and have higher risks associated with them.

Tip

There are APIs for almost all the major data entities. If there is not an API, evaluate carefully the cost of analyzing, programming, and testing the conversion against the value of the converted data.

Another factor affecting the difficulty of data conversions is the cleanliness and consistency of the legacy data. Some very old legacy systems don't even have the minimum data fields to map to the required fields in Oracle. For example, one organization with very old and proprietary systems had vendors, customers, and employees in the same legacy data file because the data was little more than names, addresses, and phone numbers. If you must create required Oracle fields with program logic during data conversions, plan for highly complex analysis, programming, and testing activities.

Tip

It might be less expensive to clean and enhance the legacy data before converting to Oracle. A partial load combined with interactive query and field updates through Oracle forms can actually take longer than manually entering all the data through a data entry form.

Another popular data conversion technique uses a spreadsheet to organize the data from the legacy system. If you import the data into a spreadsheet, users can often clean up many records before the data are loaded into and validated by the Oracle interface programs. When the records are in spreadsheet format, you can rearrange the columns and export them as comma-separated values for easy insertion into the interface tables by the SQL*Loader utility.

Tip

Consider a combination of automatic and manual techniques to load a data set one time. For example, if 5,000 customers load correctly and 100 are rejected by the API validation routines, simply enter the rejected 100 records manually. Don't spend a lot of time modifying the load programs to handle the special cases that make up only a small percentage of the transactions.

INTERFACES

Interfaces can represent incoming or outgoing data from Oracle's perspective. Outgoing interfaces are like reports with a data format. Incoming interfaces are a lot like one-time legacy data conversions, except they occur many times and must be 100% reliable, well documented, self-balancing, and operable by users. You still have to map the foreign data elements to the Oracle data, write a loader program, prevalidate the incoming data, and run the Oracle interface programs.

REPORTS

Reporting and information processing are consistent problems for Oracle Applications projects. Users and executive sponsors expect the new database systems to give them valuable information about the business. However, the applications are mostly transaction processing systems, and stock reports are usually transaction listings, registers, journal entries, account balance listings, and so forth. Users and executive sponsors might expect more from the project.

Oracle provides a report developer, a browser, a financial statement generator, and desktop integration tools to help with reporting requirements. Other third-party vendors also have several query and output format utilities. Using these tools might provide production of a custom report in two to four days, but an ERP implementation easily might have 50 to 100+ reports. Reporting requirements can easily add 100 to 400 workdays to a moderately sized project, and you should develop a strategy early in the project to manage these costs. Relying on end users to learn a reporting tool is usually a risky strategy because only about 20% of end users will learn the tool and almost all end users will have difficulty understanding how the Oracle Applications store the data. Many ERP projects don't address reporting requirements early enough in the work plan, and you might have to meet business requirements with expensive resources late in the project.

Business Processes

Your business processes are the fourth significant contributors to effort and cost. The executive sponsor might support a no-customizations (vanilla) implementation or changing the business to do it the Oracle way. Oracle Applications are designed to accommodate several business models, and a reasonable vanilla configuration might be an improvement over the legacy systems and processes.

Tip

If you have a simple project, the key to controlling costs is to manage the ability of the organization to absorb the changes the new software will bring.

For the more complex business, a large part of the implementation process involves making decisions about configuration parameters that might then constrain other choices. When the constraints outnumber the available choices, an extension or workaround might be required, and costs increase. For example, the GL chart of accounts structure determines how much information is stored in the General Ledger, and this drives other requirements for a reporting strategy. Companies have implemented an account structure of from four to eleven segments. The longer structures might meet business requirements for reporting and budgeting, but they can cause difficulties or added complexity when configuring and operating the subledgers.

Documenting and Understanding Processes

The implementation team must work with the applications on at least three levels: unit transactions inside one application, interfaces between applications, and enterprise integration. A clear understanding of processes facilitates the work of the implementation team because the applications often redistribute work and information throughout the organization. For example, Oracle developed the receiving function as part of the purchasing application. If the legacy system has receiving as part of the inventory, planning, or logistics process, there might be some adjustment or realignment of responsibilities in your organization. If the implementation team has a novice understanding of the new applications and the legacy processes are also not well understood, the implementation will be inefficient.

Flexible or Rigid Business Requirements and Processes

What is the organization's ability to absorb change? When the business is flexible, a workaround is usually cheaper to implement than customizing the applications. Are the business processes rigid because of regulations or corporate policies? Does the implementation team have the authority to make changes? Can policies be revised? Consider how the organization uses information and whether the standard reports can replace the familiar legacy reports.

OTHER PROJECTS IN PROCESS

Often, an organization has several systems projects in process at the same time. In the mid-1990s, some companies tried to implement radically reengineered processes or ISO9000 certification at the same time as an ERP project. Other projects can often change the scope, affect the resources, or complicate the ERP implementation.

NON-ORACLE APPLICATIONS

Integrating "best of breed" or non-Oracle applications into a suite of applications to service the enterprise is hard. Everything from interfaces to training requires extra effort. Legacy systems that will remain live might have a different data model. Data elements must be mapped, cleaned, documented, and tracked for the life of the system. APIs require support from the MIS department. The upgrade and patch cycle must be continually managed and tested. Finding and maintaining a compatible combination of release levels for the Oracle Applications, the non-Oracle applications, the database, the operating system, the desktops, and so forth, can be quite challenging and force you to upgrade your schedules.

REENGINEERING AND BEST PRACTICES

Reengineered processes are theoretical, conceptual, and hard to understand in the context of the new ERP software. The user doesn't understand either system. When reengineering risk is transferred to the ERP implementation, the scope and risk of the ERP project increases. The decision-making process in combined projects is slower, and more time is spent in testing, pilots, and training.

ISO9000

Often, ISO9000 certification becomes a mission-critical application required for industry, corporate survival, or regulatory compliance. Documenting new procedures can take a lot of time because they are not well understood, and implementation team members might be required to serve both the ERP and the ISO9000 projects.

MERGER AND ACQUISITION ACTIVITY

Mergers and acquisitions can cause uncertainty and system integration issues for the implementation team. I know of one company that worked for about 14 months to implement Oracle at three sites and was then acquired by a firm that was implementing SAP. After 6 more months of creating interfaces and moving the work around the new organization, the acquired company started converting to SAP. You can't avoid merger and acquisitions activity when it happens, but be aware of the impact on implementation costs.

CAPABILITY OF THE PROJECT TEAM

The capability of the project team is important to the success and cost of the project, and you need an advanced level of business, technical, and project management experience. Cross-functional capability among project team members is a plus and can improve issue resolution. Try to staff the project team with the current or future leaders of the company. Sponsors are important to controlling costs, maintaining scope, and creating a sense of urgency and purpose. The project team should be able to communicate with the rest of the organization and fully represent their constituents. Get temporary outside help in areas where the project team needs experience.

Tip

Experienced consultants are important. I know of one large company that spent approximately an extra 25% ($1–2 million) because its chosen consulting firm was large but had little Oracle Applications experience.

DEVELOPING THE ABILITY TO RESOLVE ISSUES

The decision-making process in some organizations can increase costs. Once, a client and two large consulting firms tied up four consultants and eight client team members for three months as they debated the structure of the chart of accounts. The real agenda was that a recently acquired business didn't want a lot of information to be stored in the GL where the parent could run reports and comparative analysis. Definition of the issue is 90% of the resolution.

Issues should be logged, tracked, and escalated when they become critical to progress. Issues can be functional, technical, procedural, managerial, political, and so forth. An issue will have one of three characteristics:

- The item will change the scope of the project.
- The item will require a decision that must come from outside the project team or through a team consensus.
- A task on the critical path of the project is late and is affecting completion of other tasks.

Tip

Only a few items in the Oracle Applications cannot be changed (or are very expensive to change) after the initial setup. If the issue is caused by a lack of familiarity with Oracle Applications, try to resolve the problem by considering the pros and cons of three or four alternatives suggested by an expert. Don't get paralyzed. You can usually make changes during the conference room pilot.

Items that are difficult or expensive to change after the initial setup are usually configuration definitions used across many modules. For example, the key accounting flexfield, fiscal calendar, and inventory item definition are widely used in many modules and become the foundation for transaction data when you start your system. To change these items, you have to deal with the impact on the historical transactions maintained by the system.

Key issues in many organizations usually revolve around the following areas:

- The structure of the key accounting flexfield, the item definition, the PO approval hierarchy, and several key flexfields in HR
- Centralized versus decentralized business processes and the technical architecture model
- The reporting strategy and information flow
- Installation and testing of new releases of the software
- Change management and impact on end users
- Application function points and the degree to which they fit your business requirements
- System performance, space requirements, and bugs
- Implementation of the multi-org setup

IMPROVING AND MANAGING TOLERANCE FOR CHANGE

The ability of your organization to absorb change will affect your costs and degree of implementation effort. Improving flexibility of policy and procedure and your ability to match the Oracle Applications design model are important considerations. The impact of external constraints from trading partners, governments, industry practices, labor contracts, corporate headquarters, and so forth, will cause requirements that force extensions to the basic Oracle Applications.

Tip

Change happens when the cost of doing nothing is greater than the cost of the change. New organizations or those with very old legacy systems often have the least resistance to change because the cost of change is very low for new companies and the cost of doing nothing might be very high for old systems.

UNDERSTANDING THE PERSONALITY OF THE ORGANIZATION

The culture and personality of your organization can affect the cost of the implementation project. Three different companies are described in this section. Six to nine months after startup, there was little difference in the satisfaction level of users, and all three companies were continuing to improve in the way they used Oracle Applications.

One company was very respectful of each user's requirements and formed a large implementation team to make sure everyone was represented. Issues were resolved well in advance of the go-live date. Everything possible was done to meet each user's expectations for the new software. Much effort was spent to communicate progress and project status to users outside the project team. At the end of the project, the project team members became users. This project was very expensive, and many users were still not satisfied at startup.

At the other extreme, another company formed a very small team and empowered it to decide for a vast constituency of users. Expectations were set early in the project that the software couldn't be and didn't have to be perfect. Major issues and proof of concepts were resolved in a conference room pilot, and a pact was made with users to address concerns and minor issues in a cleanup phase of the project. On transition, users took ownership rapidly and resolved many issues. This project was very efficient, but did not meet all the business expectations at startup.

A third company announced at the beginning of the project that the implementation would be part of a major company restructuring. The Accounts Payable function would be cut from over 50 employees to less than 20 when it was consolidated into a shared service center. Similar staff changes would be made in finance as the monthly closing and reporting processes became centralized. Two competing consulting firms were used to manage the ERP project and the restructuring project. The project team was partially staffed with employees whose jobs would be eliminated by the new software. This project had extra costs as team members and consulting firms worked through personal agendas before dealing with issues.

These three examples demonstrate a wide variety of approaches to implementing the Oracle Applications with about the same results. Although all these projects are considered successful, the cost and effort required of the implementations were higher than expected or the results were less than expected. Your organization and ERP implementation project will have its own internal dynamics that affect the cost effort to implement the Oracle Applications.

SUMMARY

The effort and cost of an Oracle ERP Applications implementation project are driven by many factors, including the following:

- The complexity and culture of your organization
- The number of application modules
- The complexity of your business processes
- The amount of customizations required
- Other projects happening at the same time
- The capability of your implementation team
- The ability of your organization to absorb change

You can significantly reduce the cost and effort of your project by understanding the complexity and dynamics of your specific organization. You must consider these dynamics when you construct your project work plan. The plan that works for one company might not work well at all for another organization. If you can modify or take advantage of the dynamics of your organization and minimize the number and magnitude of customizations, you might save quite a bit of money.

CHAPTER 5

PROJECT MANAGEMENT AND CONTROL

In this chapter

The Oracle Applications implementation project is a significant piece of work and requires formal project management techniques. You might not require or use all of the practices discussed in this chapter, but you should choose carefully when you decide to eliminate a particular technique. Generally, an ERP Applications implementation plan should allow 7%–10% for project management and control activities. Although these activities might seem to be overhead to the project, they pay for themselves. If you eliminate these activities, you lose more time in the long run.

Ideally, projects must be carried out within specified schedules, resources, dollars, and other constraints dictated by the client and project. Successful project management has become more about using effective communications, flexibility, integrity, trust, problem solving, leadership, and customer satisfaction than Gantt charts and work breakdown structures. Our approach to project management is moderate, yet effective and efficient. We constantly look for ways to improve our project management methods.

Understanding Project Team Roles

Following are some typical teams that might exist on your project. Three teams are listed: Steering Committee, Project Management, and Core Team, each providing a different level of commitment and direction to the project.

The Steering Committee

The Steering Committee provides the overall ownership and sponsorship of the project. It oversees the project from a management, financial, and mentoring perspective with little or no day-to-day involvement with the project. Following are some key responsibilities of the committee:

- Provides executive ownership and sponsorship
- Provides overall project management and control responsibility
- Provides additional guidance, leadership, and support to project management and team members
- Provides participation and commitment to regularly scheduled meetings
- Identifies, selects, and supports the project sponsor, project manager, and core team members
- Reviews, evaluates, and responds to escalated issues

The Project Management Team

The Project Management team provides the overall management and control of the project. It oversees the project from an activity and task management perspective and sometimes is heavily involved with day-to-day activities of the project. Following are some key responsibilities of the team:

- Provides overall management and control of project deliverables and resources
- Provides guidance, leadership, and support to team members
- Reviews, evaluates, and responds to escalated issues
- Provides participation and commitment to regularly scheduled meetings

THE CORE TEAM

The Core team provides the functional and technical leadership to execute the daily activities and tasks associated with the project. These team members are considered the subject-matter experts in their fields and are key to a successful project. Initially, the Core team consists of key users assigned to the project team, as well as consultants. The Core team grows as the project progresses, getting more and more users involved with CRP testing and training. Following are some key responsibilities of the team:

- Provides functional and technical leadership and guidance throughout the project
- Provides installation, setup, maintenance, and support of applications
- Performs business operations analysis and design
- Provides solutions to gaps, analysis, and design effort
- Provides system interface design and development
- Provides application configuration and setup for each module being implemented
- Participates in initial system installation and configuration
- Participates in CRPs and testing
- Provides roll-out assistance and production transition support

DEVELOPING ISSUE-RESOLUTION TECHNIQUES

The ability to identify and resolve issues is an important one for the project team and a critical success factor for the project.

Tip

Definition of the issue is probably 90% of the requirement for solving the problem. If you are having trouble resolving an issue, look at how you have defined the problem.

We know a consulting firm that defines an issue as follows: "An issue is any project-related concern and controversy that needs to be documented so that risks (if any) can be addressed, resolved, and managed." Because it can cover almost any topic, this general definition works well and creates an open communication capability among the project team members.

For Oracle ERP software implementation projects, we usually use a narrower definition of an issue to focus on the tasks at hand, and we try to identify significant issues so everyone knows that issue resolution is high-value and high-priority. We believe an issue will have at least one of three characteristics:

- The item will change the scope of the project.
- The item will require a decision that must come from outside the project team or through a team consensus.
- A task on the critical path of the project is late and is affecting completion of other tasks.

Tip

The common task of creating a Technical Assistance Request (TAR) with Oracle Support is likely *not* an issue by itself unless it meets one of the previous three criteria. Projects are all about solving problems, and the TAR is just another problem to deal with. Just get the support from Oracle, close the TAR, and move on to the next item on the work plan.

Issues should be recorded in a log. The log can be a simple word processing or spreadsheet document, or the log can be a relational database schema with forms and reports. All of the project team should have access to the issues log and the status reports. Key information you want to capture about an issue includes the following:

- The functional application or project area that is affected, as in GL.
- An issue identifier, such as an issue number. This can be a unique sequential number, as in 1, 2, 3, and so on.
- Date issue is first identified.
- Owner responsible to resolve the problem.
- The type of issue (scheduling, function gap, decision, configuration parameter choice, scope change, and so forth).
- Priority (high, medium, low, or red, yellow, green).
- Status (open, closed, hold, cancelled).
- Resolution date requirement.
- Comments and description. Some issues can lead into TAR; this section can be used to capture TAR or patch-related information.

Note

Oracle Metalink offers good TAR management reports that provide statistics that can prove helpful in times of need. Visit the Web site at `http://metalink.oracle.com`.

IMPLEMENTING STATUS REPORTING FOR YOUR PROJECT

The project team owes periodic status reports to the project sponsors and management. If the project is big enough to have subproject teams, status reports can promote communication throughout a large team. Typically, status reports should be issued weekly or every two weeks.

Tip

Evaluating status reports from multiple sources is much easier if the format is the same, so use a consistent format or consolidate the reports.

Status reports can have several of the following sections. Not all are necessary, and they can vary per project requirements:

- The executive overview section summarizes the project or subproject for the reader who is not involved with the details of the project. This section should be free of technical jargon and written in laymen terms. If you include an unresolved problem or issue in this section, you are asking the reader to get involved.
- There should be a section that provides a high-level overview of the tasks completed by each team. This can be a bulleted list by team member. This provides general information to document who is doing what.
- The specific progress made from the previous report should be listed. Often, this is a list of completed deliverables and resolved issues from the planned work section of the previous report.
- List the assignments, milestones, and planned work that will happen before the next report is created.
- You should provide a summary section identifying the total quantity of issues outstanding, new or opened, and closed. This summary can be helpful in many ways to the project management team in determining issue resolution and follow-up.
- You should list detail information on important issues, and issues where the resolution date is past due.
- You should provide a summary section on the total quantity of TARs outstanding, new or opened, and closed. This can be helpful to the project management team, as can a report to Oracle Support.

CREATING MEETING MINUTES

Oracle software implementation projects produce lots of formal and informal meetings as the project team works through requirements, new business processes, configuration parameters, pilot activities, issues, and so forth. Meeting minutes are a way to formalize and document the decisions, issues, action items, responsibilities, and progress of the project.

Tip

A very wise project manager once told me, "If it's not written down, it was never said and never agreed to."

Meeting minutes are also a great way to communicate between project teams, levels of project administration, and company management not directly involved with the day-to-day details of the project. Each meeting should have a scribe to take notes and publish the minutes. It is a good idea to establish a template so important details are not missed. The template can be set up to do the following:

- Name the meeting: Steering Committee Meeting or Project Management Meeting, and so on
- Note the date, start and end times, and location
- List who called the meeting, who led it, and who was the note taker
- List the attendees, as well as those scheduled to attended and who did not and the distribution for the minutes
- Attach a copy of the agenda and any handouts
- Report issues and discussion, assign a unique item number to each minute for easy reference during subsequent meetings
- Report any agreements, action items, due dates, and who is responsible for future progress

Tip

If you openly and faithfully publish meeting minutes, status reports, and other project deliverables to all concerned and everyone on the distribution list is engaged in the project, you might be able to implement the "Silence = Acceptance" rule. If you achieve this level of communication, the project team should operate efficiently.

IDENTIFYING RED FLAGS

Red flags are telling warnings that might indicate the project would have trouble meeting its goals. One, two, or several of these warnings might not prevent the project from succeeding, but too many of these problems indicate a higher-than-normal degree of risk for the project. Consider objectively testing your project for these warning signals every few months or when major milestones are delivered. These warnings can be grouped in three ways:

- User red flags
- Communications red flags
- Project management red flags

User red flags indicate the degree of interest and involvement of the end users or their project team representatives. Ultimately, each successful project will transfer ownership of the new software and business processes to the end users. The following items might indicate how graceful that transfer will be:

- The user is frequently unavailable or not onsite.
- The user is not fully involved with the project.

- The user is assigned to the project 50% of the time, and to her real job 50%, but the project 50% suffers or gets little to no time.
- The user is not part of or represented by the project team.
- The user lacks full functional knowledge of the new (or old) system.
- There is an intense political atmosphere between users, a user and the MIS staff, or the client and a consultant.
- The user is looking for a quick fix and signs off too quickly on configuration parameters, design, or issue resolution.
- The user can't make up her mind.
- The user is uncomfortable with change in general. Any deviation from the current routine is resisted.
- The user wants to cut corners to make deadlines.

Communications red flags show the openness and honesty of the project. Good communications inspires trust and acceptance of the new software and business processes. An effective communications plan will eliminate surprises and facilitate the transition to the new systems. Look for these red flags:

- Project staff and users do not meet to discuss day-to-day requirements, configuration, process, and design issues.
- There are communication gaps at the user-to-user, user-to-manager, manager-to-staff, or staff-to-staff levels of the project hierarchy.
- The scope of the project is poorly defined, and user expectations are different from what the project team can deliver.
- Project leadership has not clearly explained the reasons and goals for the project. Participants do not fully understand why the project is necessary.
- All participants (project manager, user, sponsor, DBA, programmer, consultant, and so forth) are not defined clearly at the beginning of the project.

Project management red flags show the degree of control and organization of the project. A well-run package software implementation project will have several distinct phases, including plan, analysis, design, build and test, transition, and production. These red flags might appear at any time:

- No formal definition of requirements has been made for the business.
- There is no provision in the work plan for development of conversion programs, security systems, testing, revisions, project management time, and so forth.
- There is excessive overtime on the project.
- The project manager has no to-do or issues list for the project. The manager does not have a work plan in sufficient detail.

- The project manager cannot give a definitive answer when asked what is done, what is not done, and which tasks are assigned to which team members.
- The project manager does not know how the project's actual expenses and stage of completion compare to the budget and the planned schedule.

Tip

Straight from project management 101: "What goes unmeasured, goes unmanaged and uncontrolled."

- There has been no sign-off on the plan, functional requirements, design, conversion results, or system test.
- Configuration or setup has begun prior to the sign-off on the analysis, requirements, and gap issues.
- There was no design audit performed prior to starting to build the systems.
- Project resources are double-booked between projects or between the project and their regular jobs.
- There is a sharp change in number of staff available to the project. There might be a good reason for adding resources to a project, but it is hard for the newcomers to get up to speed. If resources are transferred to other work, the software implementation project might fall behind schedule or be unable to make good progress.

MAINTAINING THE PROJECT PLAN

There should be a complete project plan, and you should measure progress against each task in the plan. Project plans should be made of phases, activities, and tasks. In some cases the identification of subtasks is required. The project plan should include the following:

- WBS ID# or a unique identifier for each task in the project plan. WBS stands for *work breakdown structure*.
- The task list, or task description, shows the work to be done and defines the scope of the project. Tasks can be grouped into phases, and transitions between phases can be marked by milestones. Each major milestone can also be consider a checkpoint to replan remaining project tasks.
- The duration of each task has two components. The first component shows the amount of work effort in some unit of time that is required to complete a task. Because we often work on many tasks simultaneously, the second aspect of duration shows the scheduled dates between the start of work and the completion date of each task. For example, if resources aren't exclusively devoted to an activity, a four-day task might be in-progress for two weeks.
- The dependencies of each task and the work schedules of the project resources establish the critical path for the project. Determine which tasks have other activities that must precede the startup of the task to understand the dependencies of each task.

- The resource assignments schedule shows who is responsible for completing each task. Multiple resources can be assigned to a task. With multiple resources assigned to a task, you might consider assigning one resource to the task lead.
- Clear roles and responsibilities should be defined on the project plan.
- Consider having a percent complete indicator for each task.

Tip

As a rule of thumb, if the amount of effort for a task is more than four days' duration, divide the task into subtasks for better control. For example, a twelve-day task to create a legacy system interface could be scheduled as subtasks to analyze, design, code, test, document, and so forth.

As the project progresses, it is important to record progress compared to the plan. The simplest way to determine progress is to periodically estimate the percentage of completion of each task. Coordinate the completion estimate with the status report, and you will be able to determine whether you are ahead of or behind schedule and whether you have enough resources.

Tip

It doesn't matter whether you use a sophisticated project management tool such as ABT's ProjectWorkbench or Microsoft Excel; the most important thing is that you have a project plan.

Other elaborate ways are available in which we've tracked project progress. Large projects typically have administrative staff that gathers project timesheets each week and applies progress directly to the project plan.

Another simple approach to monitoring and measuring progress is by taking tasks directly out of the project plan and pasting them into a timesheet template for each team member. As each member makes progress on a task, he records his time and submits it to the project administrator at the end of the week. In turn, the project administrator applies each team member's time to the project plan. This can be an effective way to monitor and manage project progress to plan.

Another approach is to track an estimated percentage complete as follows: 0% means the task is not yet started; 25% means the task has started and requirements are understood; 50% means the task is well underway by the developer/functional team member; 75% means the task is fundamentally complete and only minor items remain; and finally 100% means the task is complete.

MAINTAINING CONTROL OF THE PROJECT SCOPE

The project scope is usually not fixed in the early phases (planning, analysis, and design) of the software implementation. The project scope provides the framework for the implementation and is vital to its success. However, by the time the schedule reaches the building, testing, and transition phases, you should have a precise understanding of what the project will accomplish. When the budget and implementation schedule become firm, you will want to implement change control procedures. Whoever supplies the budget and resources to the project must be involved in the project change process. For this reason, most successful projects establish a cross-functional steering committee to authorize changes in project scope that are consistent with similar changes in budget, resources, and schedule.

Tip

Because programming, or at least substantial discussion, will be involved, pay particular attention to functionality gaps in the packaged software. These gaps can radically change the scope of the project work plan.

Consider preparation of a gap analysis document to control and communicate potential changes to the steering committee and other project participants. This gap analysis document should include comments for the following topics:

- Describe the business requirement and the gap in the packaged software.
- List the people who support the proposed changes.
- List the applications that will be affected.
- Describe the current practices in the legacy system.
- Describe the proposed practices as they will be supported by the Oracle Applications.
- List the consequences of doing nothing to show the impact of the gap.
- Discuss possible workarounds or alternative processes that might fill the gap.
- Describe the extension that must be made to the Oracle applications.
- List the benefits to be obtained if the extension is authorized. If possible, assign a monetary value to quantify the benefit.
- List the costs that will be incurred to create the extension. Don't forget to include the cost of ongoing maintenance and upgrade considerations.
- Estimate the level of effort required to fill the gap and describe the impact on the project schedule.
- Describe changes (if any) that must be made to Oracle's code.
- Draw a conclusion, with a recommended course of action, and explain why various alternatives are not recommended.

Tip

Project change control typically includes the modifications or deviations to project Scope, Time, or Budget.

MANAGING THE CRITICAL PATH

When tasks are blocked by other activities that must finish before the task can start, you have a critical path to the project. The critical path will control the software implementation schedule. If you can understand and manage the critical sequence of events, you can improve the performance and efficiency of the project team. Because each project has a different set of dynamics, you must determine and manage your own project's critical path.

Tip

If a resource is on the critical path of a project because you matched the best skills with each task, consider assigning some tasks to other team members. This technique is a growth opportunity for the team, and it is possible to shorten a project schedule by as much as 20% by managing the critical path through alternative resource assignments.

Tip

If possible, try to keep the technical resources off the critical path and make alternative plans when this happens. Because the new technology might introduce difficult-to-understand or unpredictable delays, avoid schedule slippage by making sure the technical tasks and issues are managed well.

ESTABLISHING QUALITY CONTROL PROCEDURES

Many Oracle Applications implementation projects are large enough to benefit from formal quality control procedures. Usually, these procedures introduce a semi-independent third party to audit the project implementation team. The auditor will typically look at the following items:

- Work should be progressing satisfactorily according to the plan and schedule. Tasks should be assigned to team members with the skills to complete the activity. Team members should not be consistently scheduled beyond normal working hours. The plan should be complete.
- Project controls, communications procedures, and issue-resolution techniques should be in place.
- The quality of deliverables should be adequate.
- Red flags and risks should appear to be under control.

Tip

Even if your project doesn't establish formal quality control procedures, it will likely benefit from a constructive review you can conduct yourself.

Other quality considerations include the use of administration tools, such as MS Word and Excel, as well as other Oracle Development tools such as Developer and Designer. Consistency will improve the quality of your project and its deliverables.

Consider establishing quality review sessions, which could consist of the following:

- Reviewing deliverables for errors, inconsistencies, and incompleteness prior to promotion to next step
- Evaluating the technical and functional aspects of deliverable
- Checking whether QA review document is attached to all deliverables
- Scheduling technical peer reviews to evaluate technical aspects and feasibility of proposed solutions

TAR Tracking, Resolution, and Logging

Working effectively with Oracle Support is a critical success factor for most implementation projects. A Technical Assistance Request (TAR) is created by Oracle for each problem, and it does a pretty good job of documenting the problem, the status, and the resolution. To effectively manage Oracle Support as a critical project resource, you need to be able to monitor its work. Often, you will solve the same problem in several instances as the project progresses, and we suggest you construct a log of all activity so that you can re-create the solutions you get from Oracle Support. For additional techniques for working with Oracle Support, see the chapter titled "Working with Support" on this book's Web site.

Tip

Even if you implemented the applications years ago and your system has stabilized, consider keeping a TAR log so that you will have a history of system problems.

Understanding the Impact of Other Projects

ISO9000 projects, business process reengineering, mergers, acquisitions, and other package software projects can have an impact on your Oracle software implementation. These projects often cannot be avoided, but they introduce complications that you must manage:

- Other projects compete for scarce resources that you will need for your Oracle software implementation.
- Issues become more frequent, and their resolution becomes more complex. You might have to negotiate and compromise to resolve issues.
- The external projects might not have the same implementation schedule as your project. There might be extra tasks and one-time interfaces required to synchronize each project's requirements.

- Reengineering projects often require additional analysis and prototyping of various scenarios for an Oracle software project. If the reengineering project team members are not expert in the Oracle software, reengineering projects can introduce gaps when a perfectly good Oracle-based solution already exists.

Note

The only other thing more important than implementing Oracle Applications in your organization is keeping your business running.

- ISO9000 certifications often create additional documentation requirements for the Oracle software project. This documentation is often time-consuming to create because the people writing the documentation don't quite understand yet how the Oracle software works. Also, keep in mind that some of the deliverables created during the implementation could be used to support ISO documentation requirements.
- Mergers and acquisitions create restructuring pressures that can affect the users' desire to cooperate with project teams who bring process change and career uncertainty.

SUMMARY

Effective project management and control is a critical success factor for your implementation project that can require 7%–10% of the project budget. The management and control activities are not simply overhead to the project. The effort you make to effectively manage the project is required to avoid the consequences of several kinds of project risks. For example, we know of one company with nonexistent project management, and three months before startup it had many red flags and unresolved issues. Its management techniques consisted of several department heads meeting as a committee without an adequate leader, plan, or implementation method. After delaying their software startup several times, they decided to launch the systems even if they weren't ready. Within three weeks, they were shutting down factories, and they were unable to make shipments because the inventory, planning, and fulfillment applications were configured improperly and were not integrated. This company fixed many of the problems within six months, but the cost to the company was over two million dollars, damaged customer relationships, unhappy employees, and so forth. It spent more money recovering from the problems than it spent for all of the hardware, the software, and 18 months of prelaunch consulting.

CHAPTER 6

Getting Started

In this chapter

Each Oracle Applications implementation project must start somewhere. The start is a mix of strategy, high-level analysis, planning, and organizing. This chapter shows you how to build a good foundation for your project.

Forming the Project Team

The project team is a mix of project manager, project leader(s), application consultants (technical and functional), business analyst(s), developer(s), and database and system administrator(s). The size and complexity of the project determines the number of each of the resources. Team building starts with the minimum resources required, and a complete team may be formed in phases as the project progresses.

Typically, the team starts with a project manager and project sponsor who will interact, negotiate, and finalize the project requirements with an implementation consultant. This is the project conceptualization phase. As the project progresses, the project manager, project leader(s), business analysts, application consultants, database administrators, and developers are drawn into the team depending on the input required from each of these skills. These additional team members can provide valuable insight to business and team requirements.

An understanding of the activities involved to get started, as discussed further in this section, provides a fair idea as to the composition and building of the project team.

Sponsor

The sponsor provides the business case and funding for the project. Some enterprise resource planning (ERP) projects appear to have many sponsors because the entire enterprise is involved. Ideally, sponsorship should be focused, involved, and established at the highest level of the organization as possible. If multiple sponsors are involved, they should form a steering committee to resolve issues, provide funding, set priorities, and coordinate high-level project direction.

Project Manager

The project manager is the formal head of the project team. In a large project where resources are formed into many groups, each group may be headed by a project leader who will discharge the role of project manager at this group level, and the project manager manages the total project based on input from project leader(s). In a small project, a project leader may be the project manager.

The project manager determines the scope and plan of the project, coordinates the activities and resources, monitors the progress, resolves issues, and implements decisions for the sponsor or steering committee.

The attributes of the project manager include the following:

- The project manager should have knowledge of the functionality of the software. She can always take the help of application consultants for finer details. The project manager should also have an understanding of integration issues with other modules and systems.

- She will be able to coordinate the resources, recognize and resolve issues on time, negotiate compromise, and make decisions. The project manager should be respected throughout the organization.
- The project manager will have good knowledge of management and communication tools for efficient execution, monitoring, and reporting. She will have good oral and written communication skills.
- She will have a good knowledge of the implementation methods to be used.

The responsibilities of the project manager are as follows:

- Studies the requirements and works to meet the needs of the business and users.
- Determines direct processes, workarounds, and customization requirements for the new systems.
- Finalizes the training schedules.
- Usually defines the scope of the project and possibly drafts the implementation contract with consultants.
- Continuously monitors the changes required during the project and manages any changes in scope.
- Selects and adapts the implementation methods for the project.
- Initiates the project and forms the project team.
- Coordinates the resources and activities and monitors progress and prepares status reports.
- Represents the project team and interacts with the sponsor on behalf of the team. When there are issues, the project manager brings them to the attention of the sponsor and makes decisions for resolving the issues.

Applications Consultant

An applications consultant is experienced with the software and determines the functionality, gaps, and related issues. Applications consultants are usually categorized as either functional or technical consultants—although some talented individuals can perform in both classifications. An applications consultant may also be expected to have a reasonable knowledge of related third-party items such as operating systems, networking, bar code systems, electronic commerce, peripherals, desktop software, and so forth.

The applications consultant may give training and also guide the customization team according to the specifications given by the project manager.

Because each module of the applications suite serves a specialized set of business functions and no one consultant can know the full range of the Oracle Applications, it is likely that several applications consultants will be on a project with many applications.

A functional consultant is an applications consultant who works on the business aspect of the project and is expected to have the following attributes:

- Good understanding of the scope of the project and implementation method to be followed
- Good knowledge of software functionality including data setup and training
- Good knowledge of the business functions of the user
- Good knowledge of security issues controls and audit requirements
- Understanding of integration issues with other software
- Skills to prepare high-level and functional design specifications
- Good knowledge of Oracle Support procedures and capabilities
- Good understanding and ability to use all sorts of documentation and help materials to research and assimilate information
- Reasonable knowledge of technology and tools to be used in customization or product extensions

A technical consultant is an applications consultant who works with the technology and systems architecture of the project and is expected to have the following characteristics:

- Good understanding of the scope of the project and implementation method to be followed
- Good knowledge of product technology and installation
- Good knowledge of technology and tools to be used in customization or software extensions coupled with programming skills
- Good knowledge of related third-party products such as operating systems and networking
- Good knowledge of integration issues with other products
- Good understanding of the security implementation
- Skills to prepare detailed designs and technical specifications
- Familiarity with online and reference documentation sources
- Reasonable understanding of the product functionality and business functions of the users

The responsibilities of the applications consultant are as follows:

- The applications consultant gives necessary input to the project manager during the project planning stage.
- The functional consultant identifies process mapping, gaps, and customization requirements.
- The functional consultant makes resource estimates and a detailed activity plan based on the gaps and customization requirements identified.
- The applications consultant collects test data from users and ensures that it is as close to reality as possible. The consultant sets up the modules with the test data.

- The technical consultant prepares the detailed design for customization and in most cases leads the group carrying out any custom development.
- The technical consultant tracks and resolves bugs in custom-developed code or extensions.
- For any bugs in the applications products, the consultant initiates a technical assistance request (TAR) with Oracle Support.

TECHNICAL STAFF

The technical members of a project team include the database administrator (DBA), applications administrator, Unix administrator, technical consultant (discussed previously), developers, and support staff. The following paragraphs briefly discuss the roles of each technical member.

Note

Remember, this discussion is about technical roles. Small projects often assign multiple roles to one or two key technical individuals.

DATABASE ADMINISTRATOR

The role of DBA in an Oracle Applications implementation project is very important. Typically, there may be three or more instances of the database. The most common instances are for production, testing, and training. In addition, there may be other instances for development, demonstration, conference room pilots, and so forth. A full implementation of Oracle financial and manufacturing applications can create more than 20,000 database objects in each instance that must be maintained and monitored by the DBA.

The typical DBA performs these tasks for normal system maintenance:

- Becomes a point of contact with Oracle Support.
- Allocates space and data storage needs for the database objects and plans future disk space requirements.
- Plans hardware capacity requirements for the database and Web servers.
- Installs, upgrades, and maintains the Oracle database, tools, and applications software.
- Maintains the fault tolerance of the database (backup, restore, import, export, and so forth).
- Manages activity of the control files, rollback segments, and online redo logs.
- Administers the SQL*Net software.
- Starts up and shuts down databases.
- Documents system administration procedures and policies.

The DBA is also responsible for the performance of the system:

- Monitors and optimizes performance of the database.
- Evaluates and adjusts database initialization parameters.

- Controls fragmentation in the tablespaces.
- Evaluates hardware performance.
- Distributes the physical data storage to maximize hardware I/O and minimize disk hot spots.
- Tunes the allocation of available memory.

Also, the DBA provides security and controls access to the database:

- Enrolls new database users and controls access with passwords.
- Provides system uptime.
- Establishes system fault tolerance and backup/recovery capability.
- Maintains archived data.
- Disables access for terminated database users.
- Controls access to database objects.

APPLICATIONS SYSTEM ADMINISTRATOR

The Oracle Applications system administrator maintains the setups in the SYSADMIN module. The Oracle Applications system administrator typically performs these tasks:

- Secures access to the Oracle Applications via user accounts, menus, passwords, and environment variables.
- Defines and assigns alternate menus, responsibilities, report groups, and report sets.
- Registers custom programs.
- Defines and sets profile options at the system, application, and responsibility levels; advises users how to set individual profile options at the user level.
- Becomes a point of contact with Oracle Support to define problems and order patches.
- Configures, starts up, and shuts down the concurrent managers.
- Defines and assigns printers and printer styles.
- Assists with periodic processing (archive and purges).
- Evaluates system online response time.
- Administers alerts and workflow definitions.
- Diagnoses and repairs interface problems.

OPERATING SYSTEM (UNIX OR NT) ADMINISTRATOR

The operating system administrator maintains the Unix or NT operating system. The typical operating system administrator performs these tasks:

- Manages and plans disk space usage.
- Adjusts kernel parameters for tuning and sizing the system.

- Becomes a point of contact for the hardware vendor's support organization.
- Backs up and restores the system.
- Establishes the disaster recovery plan.
- Plans and manages the system architecture of servers, network, desktop devices, and peripherals.
- Monitors system loads and evaluates hardware performance and bottlenecks.
- Sets up user accounts and computing environment on the operating system.
- Disables accounts of terminated users.
- Installs peripheral equipment and networked devices.
- Schedules periodic system jobs.
- Writes utility scripts to automate system processes.

Development Staff

The development members of the project team create enhancements, do the coding, and perform all the programming jobs in the project. The typical development staff performs these project tasks and takes on the following responsibilities:

- Develops the custom forms and reports and modifies existing forms and reports.
- Writes concurrent programs using PL/SQL or Unix shell scripts.
- Writes custom database triggers, packages, or procedures.
- Develops custom alerts and workflow procedures.
- Converts legacy data.
- Builds interfaces to third-party systems.
- Writes detailed technical documentation.
- Loads data from legacy systems for Oracle Applications initial balances.

Support Staff

The support staff members are involved with many activities necessary for the project to start up and progress smoothly. The typical support staff performs these project tasks:

- Communication with users.
- Change management.
- End-user training in large projects.
- Help desk and end-user support.
- Timekeeping and tracking progress against the schedule.
- Record keeping and preparation of meeting minutes and status reports.
- Travel coordination.

Starting Quickly

Many activities can get an implementation project off to a quick start. When you rapidly establish high visibility with the users and sponsors, you create a good feeling about the changes that are about to happen.

Set Up a "War Room"

Establish an environment for the project team to work efficiently. The project team needs personal computers, network connections, printers, a white board, phones, e-mail addresses, Internet connections, office supplies, file cabinets, bookshelves, and so forth. Try to get the project team away from their regular jobs and involved in the new activities.

Tip

To improve communication, consider asking the technical people to establish their work areas near the functional team members.

List High-Level Business Requirements

List all the major business functions and processes to be performed by the proposed software implementation. Also, indicate the areas where third-party products will integrate.

This listing should be grouped by business function and performing department. Show the flow of transactions and data through the entire functional cycle. Show the relationships between different functions of the cycle and relationships with other functional cycles or business processes as well.

This document forms the basis for and helps in preparing the mapping document. The business requirement listing and the mapping document allow the project team to identify gaps and draw the customization specifications. Also, you might identify special skills you will need on the project team.

Organize Documents on a Server

Establish a documentation directory structure for the project team on the network server. Create the directory and sub-directories to mirror the phases and tasks in your project work plan. Use the directory to store work-in-progress and signed-off versions of documents. Establish procedures at the start of the project to manage source and executable code changes and document versions. When you use this procedure, you create a centralized library of project work that becomes a resource for all to use. Avoid fragmentation of your documents, and don't allow project team members to store the official copies of project deliverables on their personal computers.

Tip

Very large, complex, or formally run projects may implement document management and version control software.

Gather Business Volumes and Frequencies

Make a list of all transactions of the business and note the frequency and volume of each event. This analysis should cover all the business functions listed in the high-level listing of business requirements. Identify the number of users you will have for each business function. Make sure that the hardware vendor and the Oracle sales support staff use this information to help you determine the size and architecture of the hardware.

Collect Samples of Inputs and Outputs from the Existing Business Processes

For each of the transactions listed previously, prepare a list of input parameters and gather samples of output data and reports. After taking sample outputs from existing systems, check with the users to identify any changes or discrepancies. Determine the distribution of each report.

Selecting and Scheduling the Modules

The modules that are least dependent on others and need minimum information from other modules should be implemented first. Traditionally, the following order is accepted as most suitable for ERP implementations. This order is not a hard-and-fast rule, and it is possible that a unique business process of your enterprise may require a different sequence. First, implement the financial and supply chain modules. They are General Ledger (GL), Receivables (AR), Human Resources (HR), Payables (AP), Inventory (INV), Purchasing (PO), Projects (PA) and Order Management (OM) in order of least dependencies. You may prefer that OM be done with manufacturing modules. Then, implement the manufacturing modules: Inventory, Bills of Material (BOM), Work in Process (WIP), Engineering (ENG), and Order Management. Finally, implement Payroll (PAY) and Planning in any order. Assets (FA) may be implemented at any time after GL.

Many companies adopt a strategy to their ERP implementation called the "Big Bang Approach." This method involves implementing all the modules at the same time. Despite the fact that all the modules start at once, they must still resolve issues and dependencies in order of the implementation dependencies discussed previously. The most important factor in the Big Bang Approach is to estimate and coordinate the resources and users simultaneously and have adequate backup measures for any technical obstacles. This approach is suitable for projects where

- The modules involved are simple and fall in one functional business cycle—for example, GL, AP, and AR.
- The implementation sites and end users are not scattered over a wide geographical area. For a successful Big Bang implementation, it should be easy to coordinate all sites and users together.

UNDERSTANDING TYPICAL TASKS, DELIVERABLES, AND MILESTONES

The planning and strategy phase of an implementation project has several key tasks and deliverables. Typically, you want to develop a work environment and plan an activity framework for the project. However, until you are close to completing the analysis phase, you will not have a complete definition of the scope of the project. Try to perform these tasks simultaneously with the activities of the analysis phase of the project and keep the planning deliverables open and flexible. Your consultants should be able to provide templates and master copies of most of the documents you will need to get started.

GET ORGANIZED

One of the first tasks to do (and arguably the most important) is to have all the paperwork in place before attempting to start the project. Following is a typical list of necessary documents:

- A terminology and scope document to determine the boundaries of the implementation project
- An implementation method document including formats for reporting, progress monitoring, communication of issues, minutes of meetings, deliverables, sign-off documents for each deliverable, change requests, and issue tracking (maintaining open and closed issues)
- List of requirements for all the proposed team members, possibly in the form of a resume
- Details of the sponsors, team members, and users who will interact with the project team; know how decisions will be made and who will make them
- Checklists for the hardware and software features and capabilities
- List of the details necessary to contact Oracle Support
- A tentative project work plan
- A time and progress tracking and reporting document to show cost and progress against plan
- An education plan for the project team
- Documents, formats, and checklists to be used for analysis and user responses
- List of quality and acceptance criteria for the software and for each project deliverable
- Documentation about legacy systems, third-party software, and interface requirements
- Details of any other projects, ongoing or recently completed, that are likely to impact this Oracle Applications implementation project

CREATE THE PROJECT WORK PLAN

See Appendix C, "An Oracle Applications Implementation Checklist," for a list of project activities. Your organization may have additional requirements, or your project may be able to avoid performing some of the tasks. If you skip a task, make sure that it is really optional for your organization and not a critical success factor. Many projects try to skip tasks at the beginning of the project and then end up performing them at the last minute during the transition phase when it is discovered that the activity really wasn't optional. For example, if during the analysis phase you skip the tedious task of business requirements analysis of legacy system reports, after training, users could possibly present you with a list of real or imagined showstopper reports that they must have before the system can go live. This example is one of the single most common reasons why projects miss their planned "go live" date.

How Much Time Is Needed?

Every organization has different implementation requirements, and you need to understand what will control the critical path for your organization. Although many factors contribute to the time and expense of a software implementation, the controlling factor for how long it takes is usually your organization's ability to accept and absorb the changes in procedures, processes, and technology.

Generally, rapid implementations may be more successful than slow implementations. In a slow implementation, business requirements tend to change during the project, and scope is more difficult to control. Keep it simple, and you will implement faster.

Create an Education Plan

Education is different from end-user training. Education is for the project implementation team. Even though your project team may be made up of employees who are end users, they need more than training in how to use the modules. The team should receive education about how the modules are configured, how the applications work together, and all available features of the applications.

Tip

If you have a large project with more than 100 days of education, contact education sales at Oracle Corporation. It can do much of the planning and coordinating for you.

Consider including the following in your training plan:

- Construct a worksheet with the course name, location, phone, start date, course content, and student prerequisites.
- Determine who on the project team will represent which skill sets.
- Match the team member skill sets with the course content and produce a schedule.
- If you have more than four students for a class, calculate your break-even point for onsite classes.
- Immediately after class ask students to record open issues and questions raised by the education.
- Record course attendance by student and course name.

- Document the student's evaluation of the course and evaluate comprehension and retention of the material.
- If you attempt onsite education, make sure that you have a technical environment with the right software installed, printers, working concurrent managers, student workstations, and so forth. Also, create a good classroom environment by providing a white board, markers, a flip chart, written login procedures, overhead projector, a keyboard mapping template, and so forth.
- Establish an education coordinator to communicate and execute the plan.

Tip

Oracle Education has occasionally canceled classes with a small number of registrants. Try to remain flexible and plan alternative classes and schedules. Monitor future scheduled class registrations to determine the odds that a class will actually be held.

CREATE A PROJECT ENVIRONMENT AND INFRASTRUCTURE PLAN

Prepare a plan and a checklist for the hardware and software environment. It should typically include the hardware makes and models, configuration, quantities, and install locations. The plan should also include the software including operating systems, database, Oracle Applications, programming tools, word processors, spreadsheets, project management, and presentation software with their versions and installation particulars. When you document the purposes for each piece of the project environment, you will know that everything is in place before the project begins.

COMMUNICATE YOUR PROJECT STRATEGY

The implementation strategy must be communicated to the entire project team, including the sponsor and steering committee. This communication is ideally done in the form of a kick-off presentation. Answer the following questions to determine the details and agenda of the meeting:

- Determine the members to whom the presentation will be made. The list should ideally include all the members of the project team. If you plan to make more than one presentation to address specific requirements, group the members accordingly for respective presentations.
- Determine the level of detail necessary to address the audience. Consider the complexity of the project, the experience of the members of the team, the purpose of the presentation, and the time allotted. You should not only identify the final project goal in a single statement but also determine goals for major project phases. Present measurable targets and milestones for each phase. List critical success factors for each work phase.
- Include an organization chart of the project team. Identify the team members, team leaders, and project leaders, and their roles and responsibilities.
- Make sure to briefly mention the progress already made by any team members in terms of groundwork, study, infrastructure, and other arrangements.

- Determine who will make the presentation. It may not necessarily be the project manager. The presentation must be made by a person who understands the varying interests in the project and of the members present, and who can communicate the appropriate level of detail. Your consultants should be able to help, especially if they are providing most of the work plans and implementation methods.

Pay attention to following points before making the presentation:

- Plan the presentation; many details relevant to the current project or phase must be gathered and incorporated into the kick-off meeting.
- If any members of the audience need exposure to information about this project or phase and its background, do this in advance.
- Plan the content and level of detail of the presentation in consultation with the sponsor and users. If users are to be at the presentation, they may want a work session or demonstration as well. Consider planning for work sessions separately.

Develop a Quality Plan

The quality plan forms the procedural framework to control how the project will be executed, delivered, and accepted. It typically establishes the systems to be followed during the normal course of the project as well as during abnormal situations that may arise from time to time. Your quality plan should include the details for the following topics:

- Team hierarchy with members' general roles and responsibilities
- Monitoring and reporting the status and progress
- Issue tracking and control, including procedures for escalating and addressing issues and support problems
- Change control and scope management
- Testing and software review criteria and procedures
- Acceptance criteria for deliverables in each phase
- Configuration management and version control
- Programming standards for customization work

Document the Scope and Objectives of the Project

The scope of your project is the outer boundary for the activities. It defines what is included in the project and how much work will be done. The objectives of your project are all that are intended to be achieved within the scope.

The scope is important because your project plan, project activities, and all cost estimates are dependent on the scope determined. If any change is proposed in the project activities, you should study its impact on the scope of the project. For any change or addition of project activity, scope control and change control procedures should be established and followed.

Also, establish a procedure for issue tracking and resolution. This procedure is necessary because many issues will come up during the project that are within the scope but must be resolved. A final record of all open and closed issues should be maintained. Your quality plan will tell you how to resolve issues and acceptance criteria when there are open issues.

The objectives to be achieved by the implementation project should be identified, listed, and briefly explained in a Scope and Objectives document. Define the objectives in terms of the major business requirements to be satisfied by the current project including the following:

- Implementation of the different modules of the Oracle Applications
- New business systems that will come into operation as a result of the implementation
- Major changes in business process with intended improvement in efficiency or savings
- Training objectives
- Data migration objectives

Another important aspect of scope documentation is risk management. Clearly document all the risks perceived at this stage of the project and how or to what extent they will be addressed by the project plan. Also establish guidelines for managing other risks that may arise during the course of the project.

DEVELOP A STAFFING PLAN

Create a twofold staffing plan. One part should include the staffing requirement from the implementation consultant(s), and the other part should include the staffing requirement from the sponsor. Each of the two parts should include the following:

- The composition of the project team in terms of smaller groups such as steering committee, functional teams, development teams, documentation and training teams, and so on
- A detailed estimate of staffing requirements for each phase and activity
- A list of skills required for each role of the project team.
- The timing of staff deployment, where all activities do not begin and end at the same time
- Additional resource requirements for each staff member in terms of hardware, communications, and other supplies
- Procedures to monitor resource utilization and effectiveness

SUMMARY

You can accomplish many startup activities between the time you sign the contract for Oracle software and when it is installed on your new computer system. You can select the people for the project team and establish their roles; set up a project environment so the team will be organized, comfortable, and efficient; perform a high-level analysis of future business requirements and transaction volumes; start planning and coordinating the work; develop education, staffing, and quality plans; and determine the scope and objectives for the project.

In Chapter 7, "Analyzing the Project," you will begin to study the detailed work of implementing the Oracle software.

CHAPTER 7

Analyzing the Project

In this chapter

PROJECT ANALYSIS OVERVIEW

The analysis phase of the project should define the business and system requirements of your organization and the Oracle Applications. Current business processes, policies, and procedures are documented. This stage can define the need for interfaces to external systems, customizations, or enhancements to the applications. Typically, these external system interfaces and customizations already exist and are required as part of the future business model. During this phase, the project team will assess the fit of the applications to the business processes.

Often, you will want to perform the analysis from two perspectives. From your business perspective, document the special things your business does very well and your critical success factors. From the Oracle applications perspective, review the functions and capabilities of the applications and make a detailed study of how well those functions fit your business. If you employ outside consultants, they should be able to bring the applications perspective to your business. If you send your project team to classes at Oracle Education, they can compare existing business practices to the course material.

The analysis phase of an Oracle applications implementation project accomplishes several things:

- Establishes the scope and boundaries of the project
- Determines the technical and information infrastructure for the new systems
- Acquaints the project team with the new business processes and software functions
- Determines the degree of fit and gap for business requirements
- Develops a reporting and information strategy
- Educates outside consultants about business requirements and critical success factors for the project

BUSINESS PROCESS ANALYSIS

A study of your business processes has four main activities:

- Understanding the current business processes
- Defining the business requirements for the new software
- Assessing the fit and identify gaps
- Developing a vision of future business processes

UNDERSTANDING THE BUSINESS

The basic processes embedded in the logic of the Oracle Applications might be different from your legacy system processes. The implementation team members must develop an understanding of how the new enterprise-wide systems will work in that context. This analysis starts with an understanding of the current business processes. If you assemble a team of functional business analysts from many areas of your company and use outside consultants, you will want to spend time to make sure everyone acquires the same view of the essential business transactions, practices, policies, controls, data flows, interfaces, reports, performance indicators, and so forth.

Draw pictures. Resolve issues. Document and communicate the results. However, because this activity represents the systems you will be leaving, don't spend too much time on it. Your new system doesn't have to copy the old system. You can meet your business requirements using the new software and techniques. This is an opportunity for your organization to be thinking outside the box. You might even want them to think that there is no box because it's time to be creative. Your goals are to establish a baseline to know the business requirements and to create a structure to discover weaknesses or gaps in the new software.

Discovering and Documenting the Business Requirements

Many years ago, we were helping a credit manager implement Oracle Receivables. After only two interviews of four hours, we started to discuss how to configure the applications and what software features would be used. The credit manager asked how we could determine the business requirements and their special needs so quickly. She was amazed that we could be making such good progress after just a few hours when it took her several weeks to train a new recruit for the credit department. There were several good reasons for our progress:

- We had a questionnaire to organize the topic.
- The Oracle Receivables software was a good fit for this customer.
- The client was open to changing most of its processes to match the standard Oracle application process flow.
- An experienced consultant concentrated on parts of the process where this client had special business requirements. For example, because it was in the construction supply business, it placed many liens on properties where it delivered products, and Oracle Receivables had no equivalent function.
- Almost no time was lost on the process steps where the Oracle application could be set up in a standard way.

It helps to be organized when you look for business requirements. If you prepared a Request for Proposal or if you have working papers from the competitive evaluations from when you purchased the software, you could use that information to start a requirements evaluation. If you use a consultant to help with the implementation, he should have a questionnaire. If you have to discover requirements from scratch, consider running a conference room pilot to evaluate each function of the applications and make a detailed map from your legacy system to the Oracle Applications.

DISCOVERING THE DEGREE OF FIT

The degree of fit for an applications module is determined by several factors. The relationships in your supply chain, the complexity and size of the business, the regulatory environment, and the ability for your organization to accept change are all factors you will want to consider. If your business closely follows Generally Accepted Accounting Practices (GAAP) and the teachings of the American Production and Inventory Control Society (APICS), you might have a good fit.

One of the key deliverables of the analysis phase of an implementation project is the Gap Analysis document. This document should show the differences between your current business practices and the Oracle Applications. You can resolve gaps by customizing the Applications, by configuring the Applications, or by changing your business processes and requirements. When the Gap Analysis is completed, you should have a pretty good idea of the project scope, and you can finalize the project cost, schedule, and work plan.

Each organization will have different gaps between its business processes and the capability of the Oracle applications. Look for three kinds of gaps: integration, data conversion, and functionality. Sometimes, these gaps can be very strange. For example, a functionality gap was discovered many years ago when an agricultural supply company was considering implementing the Oracle Receivables module. This company shipped its products to customers in the spring during planting season and required the farmers to pay 30 days after the harvest. Because the dates for both planting and harvesting were different for each customer and could not be predicted by any formula at the time of shipment, something as basic and simple as the terms and aging formulas in Oracle Receivables were a major problem. Because of this gap, the customer actually discontinued the project to implement Oracle Receivables.

To understand the impact on the project implementation schedule, you should categorize gaps by priority and requirement. The priority classification indicates when the gap must be resolved (for example, on the go-live date, by the end of the first fiscal quarter, and so forth). The requirement to fill the gap can be categorized by an ABC analysis. For example, all "A" requirement gaps could be considered show stoppers unless some kind of extension or workaround is available when the software is turned over to the users. Gaps with lower requirements might be post-launch requirements (for example, year-end processing) or "nice to have" requirements that don't enhance mission-critical activities.

Tip

If the ABC analysis of gaps turns up many "C" status items, consider creating a Phase II for the implementation project to resolve these issues after the system is active. Because users might have a fuzzy idea of how the Oracle Applications really work at this point in the project, when you assign these gaps to Phase II, you might gain enough delay time for the user to realize the gap was really a training issue.

Developing a Vision of How the Future Business Process Will Work

During the analysis phase of the applications implementation, you evaluate the changes the new software will make to your business. Consider the interdepartmental relationships and how the implementation of the applications will change the way work is done. Hopefully, many process steps will be automated after you convert to the Oracle Applications, but some work might move from one department to another. When work moves in the process sequence, you might have to consider headcount staffing allowances and how your business units cooperate with each other.

For example, the back-office functions of the payables and receivables departments in accounting are often the beneficiaries of improved processes after the applications are implemented. However, this improvement often comes at the expense of new process steps that will be performed in the purchasing and order entry departments.

Because implementation projects are expensive, many companies require a return-on-investment commitment from the operating units before they will buy the software. When you understand how the Oracle Applications will work in your business, you can start to determine how you will capture the return on investment and deliver the performance improvement that your project sponsorship expects. At this point in the project, you might realize some expected returns will not materialize unless you also accomplish some business process reengineering or some specialized end-user training.

Many features and functions of the Oracle Applications cannot be utilized without configuration of some of the setup parameters. When you determine which future business processes you will use and how they should work, you then will be able to select the proper settings for the configuration parameters. If you don't have a unified and integrated design of how the ERP system will work, you might have to make several conference room pilot tests. Also, your risk can be increased that you might configure something incorrectly or miss a point of integration.

Tip

Because the applications are a series of integrated modules, adopt a broad definition for basic business functions that span the boundaries of several Oracle Applications and the departments within your organization. For example, it is much better for the project team to implement the procurement process as a whole instead of implementing the planning (MRP), purchasing (PO), receiving (PO), and payables (AP) processes individually.

Create future process flow diagrams or business scenarios to communicate to the users outside the project implementation team how the new system will work. These documents provide a picture of what the business does, who performs the process steps, and the sequence of process steps. Typically, these documents are not concerned with where, how, or why the process is performed. You can use future process flow diagrams to organize a conference room pilot and help train users.

Tip

Process flow diagrams are not like the old data flow diagrams that define the logic and flow of a computer program. Figure 7.1 shows a sample process flow diagram. Focus on the verbs that describe what business work is to be done and the sequence of steps or tasks that will define the business process.

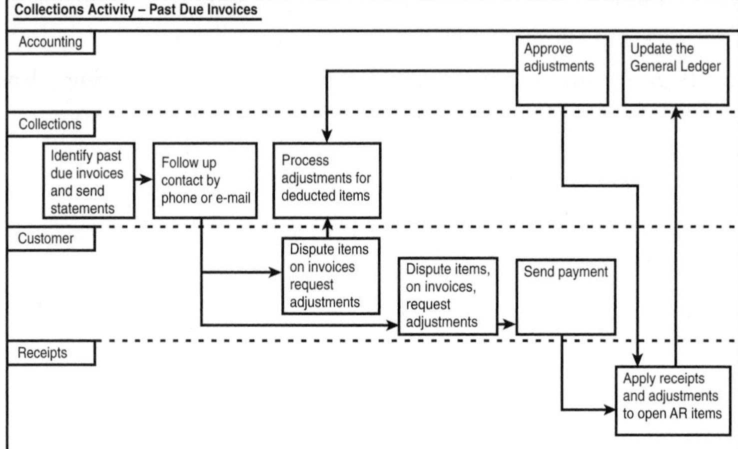

Figure 7.1
Process flow diagrams show what happens, who is involved, and the sequence of events.

DETERMINING YOUR REPORTING NEEDS

The analysis phase of the project should determine the information flow and reporting requirements for the new software. Reporting is a continuing problem with Oracle Applications implementations because these information requirements can easily change the scope of the project. Without the familiar reports and system outputs of the legacy system, end users and sponsors feel a sense of loss, and change in the organization becomes difficult. If users don't see their familiar reports, you might have a gap list with many items on it.

Tip

Develop a strategy to deal with reporting issues early in the project. When reporting, information and managerial requirements are known, determine who will be responsible for these requirements and what tools will be used. Communicate your strategy to all concerned.

The Oracle Applications are an On-Line Transaction Processing (OLTP) system that uses the powerful Oracle Relational Database Management System (RDBMS). Many users and project sponsors assume that storing transaction information in the database automatically creates all kinds of interesting reports. This assumption often causes problems because the act of storing the transaction data in the database doesn't actually create the report, and the Oracle database structure is too complicated for an end user to access the data without help. If the project sponsor expects to perform data mining or gain new knowledge about the business transactions in the Oracle database, that requirement is a sizable gap for the OLTP applications, and you will want to develop a separate strategy for that requirement.

Concerning OLTP outputs, you can classify reports in the six ways shown in the following list. The list includes the report group category and several general examples that you might find in your legacy system and your new Oracle software. You should map existing legacy system reports to the equivalent reports that Oracle provides with the software:

- **Transaction Reports**—Check registers, journal entry listings, depreciation details, WIP transactions, cost revaluation details, and so forth
- **Special Forms**—Checks, invoices, statements, purchase orders, bills of lading, packing slip, and so forth
- **Control Reports**—Financial statements, aged trial balances, AP open items, inventory valuation reports, asset listings, and so forth
- **System Configuration Listings**—Listings of customers, vendors, items, codes, cross validation rules, allocation formulas, and so forth
- **System Operation and Management Reports**—Job execution logs, menu listings, and so forth
- **Executive Information Inquiries**—Sales history by product (or time, customer, or region), key performance statistics, balanced score card, margin analysis, and so forth

Tip

Mapping legacy reports is time-consuming and often thought to be a thankless task. However, it must be done to help ensure end-user satisfaction. This task is better done during the analysis phase than during user training.

Many implementation teams have a hard time reconciling the reports that ship with the Oracle applications and the expectations of the users and executives. For example, many users want the Order Management and Receivables Applications in Oracle to also support the business's requirements for sales history reporting and planning. Although these applications have much interesting data stored away in the database, their primary mission is to ship products, track what is owed, and collect cash. That primary mission does not extend to answering questions such as, "How many of part number 1234 did we ship last month?"

The legacy software that is being replaced will likely have all kinds of interesting reports that users and management will not want to lose. You can deal with this situation in several ways:

- Educate the users about new processes and reports that support those processes. Determine which legacy reports will not be needed because processes are changing.
- Verify which reports are used frequently and map their content by data element to the Oracle reports.

- Use the software change as an excuse to eliminate redundant, unused, and inconsistent reports.
- Classify the important legacy reports as business requirements, and if the equivalent function is not supported in the Oracle application, add the requirements to the project work plan and scope. Deal with the requirements early in the project.

INFRASTRUCTURE ANALYSIS

Most implementation projects acquirex and install the server hardware and the Oracle applications early in the project. Often, in simple organizations, you can easily specify and acquire the infrastructure your systems will need from the information you received when you were evaluating the purchase of the applications. However, you should still consider studying the infrastructure. The infrastructure analysis helps determine the system requirements.

For example, most Oracle Applications implementations require the purchase of additional disks within the first year of operation. It is very easy to underestimate the requirement for disk space, and you don't want to go back to your source of funding too many times.

Larger organizations will want to make sure the servers can handle the transaction volume and that response time will be adequate. Try to understand the loads your business will place on the new system. Often, it is easy to add more memory and processors to a piece of hardware, but you want to avoid exceeding the maximum configuration of your hardware and performing a "box swap" within the first two years of the system's life. Give your business some room to grow, and estimate your margin of safety.

Consider completing an Oracle Applications transaction volume spreadsheet. These volumes help determine the long-term growth of the applications and can assist with ordering hardware.

Sizing spreadsheets are used to estimate the amount of disk space, CPU, and memory that is required to install Oracle Applications. True sizing of the Oracle Applications will not take place until application setups are completed, legacy data has beenx converted, and testing is complete.

PHYSICAL ARCHITECTURE

You must determine the physical architecture and structure ofx the system to serve users. Determine the volumes, frequencies, and sources of key business transactions to estimate requirements for disk space and interfaces. Map where users and functions are located to determine network, desktop, support, and education requirements. A good technical architecture baseline deliverable should include your strategy and configuration for the following:

- Processor Configuration
- Memory
- Disk Space
- Redundancy Requirements

- Disk I/O Balance Plan
- Network
- Shop Floor Data Collection
- Printers
- Operating System
- Desktop Computerxs

DEVELOPING A HIGH-LEVEL APPLICATION MODEL

During the analysis phase, you should develop a model of how your business willx operate with the new software. This document can be considered the strategic vision for your organization's business applications. Many organizations have never had this type of document. This document can be broken down into a multiyear, multiphase plan for your organization. Each phase can be decomposed into smaller projects and organization resource requirements.

You also want to understand the function points and interfaces among Oracle modules, external systems, and third-party products. A brief conference room pilot can help clarify how much change your business will have to absorb when it starts using the new software.

Tip

Many companies adopt the "vanilla" implementation approach to save customization costs. "Vanilla" is a code word among project sponsors to mean they don't want to complicate (or pay for) the implementation project with customizations. To these sponsors, "vanilla" means to configure and use the software exactly as intended by Oracle Corporation; even if it changes thex business. However, some sponsors only give lip service to really operating their business exactly as provided by the Oracle Applications. You need to get high-level sponsorship for the future processes, interfaces, transaction flows, controls, procedures, and so forth. If you skip this step, you run the risk of discovering all kinds of showstoppers and reports just as you are about to enter the transition phase of the project.

DATABASE INSTANCES

Determine the number, purpose, and locations of thex physical Oracle database instances you will need in order to implement your system. You might determine there are different degrees of fault tolerance and performance requirements for each instance. For example, you probably won't have the same configuration parameters for a pilot database that you use in the production database. Some installations try to put all the instances on one database server, and other sites establish different machines for production and test instances.

Consider diagramming all your instances for your team's general comprehension. Also consider creating an installation log for each instance that documents the init.ora parameters, physical disk location of .dbf files, and other pertinent information. These documents can become invaluable to the project team and DBA.

Common instances you might considexr creating during your implementation include the following:

- **Vision**—Oracle 11*i* ships a fully configured demonstration database with the software. Many implementation projects use this instance, at first, to perform business scenario tests, for validation of certainx functionality, and occasionally use it during the first conference room pilot.

Note

The Vision application that is provided with the Oracle software is a sales tool. Features and functionality within this application vary and might not reflect a true production instance. Use this instance wisely and do not make any functionality commitments until you have a real application instance configured.

- **Pilot**—Implementation teams likex to stage conference room pilots to try out various business scenarios and evaluate configuration choices. This instance might be refreshed from a prior backup after each pilot is complete.
- **Test**—Many customers rigorouslyx analyze and test every patch and program change before making the change to the production database.
- **Development**—This databasex instance is often established so the high-risk activities of programmers and consultants won't affect other project activities. Many clients restrict their outside consultants and contractors to this instance.

Tip

Copy your production-related CBO statistics to your development environment. This way your developers have the latest database statistics without having to copy all of the data. They can use production-related statistics to develop efficient running reports, and so forth, in development.

- **Training**—A training database can be established and periodically refreshed for inexperienced users. Some users relax and learn more when they can experiment and explore an instance where they can't hurtx anything. Typically, this instance contains organization-related information and is not a copy of the Vision instance.
- **Production**—This instance is the online transaction processing database. It will be fully configured with security, faultx tolerance, and tuned performance parameters and architecture.
- **Data warehouse**—Some companiesx make nightly copies of the production database to a different machine. This database instance can be refreshed each evening, or at a time that is most convenient to its users. This instance can be used for ad-hoc reporting, reporting development, or quality assurance.

Tip

Remember that every instance you create requires some degree of configuration, administration, and maintenance. If you have many instances, you will need a mechanism to track the configuration setup and patch level of each instance. Also, if you regularly copy your production database to a development instance to give programmers a realistic set of data, will you have to establish new passwords, responsibilities, and so forth, each time you make a copy?

Also, for your development instance, if you're using Payroll and have sensitive data, such as Social Security numbers or annual salary amounts, that are copied from your production instance, consider writing scripts to mask the data values. This will ensure that privacy and confidentially are retained.

This also brings up another subject–having separate instances for separate application teams. For example, the HR/Payroll team might want to have its own instance of the applications for data conversion, whereas the Financial team might want its own to test the functional aspects of the project.

Note

The basic architecture of the Oracle Applications is designed for only one physical production instance of the database. You can put multiple organizations and multiple sets of books within one instance of the applications. However, if you have the requirement to establish several production instances of the application database, please realize you are setting up a difficult architecture; you should consider every possible alternative before implementing the complexity of multiple production instances.

DETERMINING IT DEPARTMENT STAFFING

Another part of infrastructure analysisx and planning relates to the structure of the information technology department. The new software and hardware will require new skills. There's an old saying, "When you retool your business, retool IT." Determine changes that might be made in job descriptions, roles, and responsibilities. Analyze your inventory of skills for new requirements and obsolescence problems. During a rapid implementation project, it is conceivable that some of the application modules might be ready for production status before the technical skills are in place to support a production system. Usually, you will want to avoid situations where the technical staff is on the critical path of the project.

Tip

As soon as the decision to go with Oracle Applications and technology is known, determine how your IT staff will be trained. Consider having pilot projects that will either enhance the skills of your staff, or have them mentored by a Senior Level Consultant during the early stages of the implementation, which ultimately makes the IT staff responsible for the customizations. This mentoring approach will pay huge dividends in many areas, such as time, cost, and knowledge, later during production cutover and maintenance.

Tip

Consider hiring experienced Oracle Applications and technology people. The market for good, experienced people is very tight, but if you find good people, hang on to them. Continue to train and develop these people because the more they learn while working for you, the more you will benefit. It doesn't make sense not to train and develop your staff. You should train these people so their skillsx are very marketable–you want them to benefit.

CUSTOMIZATIONS

The analysis phase of the project is concerned with identifying customizations to the Applications. After you understand the business requirements and have a gap list, you can begin to address the customizations you will require. Perform a high-level analysis of each customization before you finalize the project scope and work plan. If you decide to extend the Oracle applications, you will want to add and track tasks for design, build, unit test, integration test, CRPs, and document to the project work plan. Because customizations change the scope, cost, and schedule for the implementation, your steering committee and project sponsor should be aware of all customizations.

Create a master customizations list, which can be used and read by all team members. The project managers or technical team members can use this list to monitor progress; it can be very useful for everyone involved with the project. This list contains information such as in what Oracle Application the customization resides, a laymen-terms description of the customization, and rough estimates for design, build, unit test, integration test, CRP, and document. These estimates can be applied directly to the project plan or can be tracked by individual (technical team members) customization assignments.

Note

Customization is a general term to refer to almost any enhancement or extension that you make to the Oracle applications. Some customizations are ill-advised because they might impact your ability to obtain support from Oracle Corporation, and they require much work during upgrade projects. Other customizations are a normal part of Oracle Applications implementations and include reports and interfaces.

LEGACY DATA AND CONVERSION

During the analysis phase of the project, you should understand and develop a strategy for each major data entity you are going to load into the new applications. Also, consider the shared entities, such as customers and vendors, from all perspectives. For example, the purchasing and payables departments often have a completely different view of vendor data, but this data is shared by both departments when using Oracle Applications. Understand both departments' vendor data requirements prior to data conversion.

First, determine what to convert from the legacy system. Look at the table of contents of the reference manuals and find nouns that name objects in your business. These are the entities you will want to estimate. For example, in the table of contents for the Receivables user's guide, you will find transactions (invoices and memos), customers, receipts, and so forth. The following is a list of major business entities you might want to convert during your applications implementation project:

- GL Balances
- GL Transactions
- Customers
- Vendors
- Items
- Inventory Balances

Note

When converting Inventory Balances, you might want to consider doing this manually versus programmatically. Manual conversion could take place during your physical inventory process just prior to going live. You basically start out with a "zero" on-hand balance; then, you enter the actual on-hand balance, you accept the variance, and your data is converted. This also reinforces learning the Oracle physical inventory process.

- AP Open Items
- AR Open Items
- Open Purchase Orders
- Open Purchase Order Requisitions
- Open Sales Orders
- WIP Balances
- Bills of Material
- Routings
- AP History
- AR History
- Inventory Transaction History
- Employees
- Year-to-Date Payroll Balances
- Budgets for Project Accounting
- PA Projects and Tasks

Next, determine a strategy for conversion of each entity for planning purposes. You can choose to manually enter 1,200 vendors because that can be accomplished with clerical labor in under 10 days. However, loading 50,000 items with more than 150 attributes for each item is clearly something that should be programmed and converted from legacy data.

Consider whether the data from the legacy system is clean, consistent, and worth loading. For example, if you reorganized your entire department structure in the General Ledger a year ago, it might make no sense to load five years of legacy GL balances because there is no comparison between the current year and the prior year balances.

Tip

Inconsistent data is hard to load programmatically, and you should try to avoid putting lots of logic into your conversion programs. You'll spend more time writing programs to convert convoluted data than it takes to actually convert the data!

Tip

Some data is not worth the trouble to convert. Consider developing alternative strategies. Some companies have left their legacy systems available to users after startup—either mirroring the legacy application as a custom/registered Oracle Application with inquiry access only, or archiving legacy data to a simpler database structure than the Oracle applications.

If there is an Oracle Applications Program Interface (API) for the entity you must convert, that is the conversion technique you will want to use. Usually, the API will have a set of tables and an import program to process the legacy system data you put in the interface tables. Most APIs have a report to tell you about data that fails validation. APIs are not end-user tools, however. It usually takes a functional analyst, and an experienced technical analyst, to map each data element in the legacy data to the Oracle interface structure. Also, you need a programmer, or the technical analyst, to load the data into the Oracle interfaces and clear invalid records.

If you must synchronize a major data element in a foreign system and an Oracle application, you have a special problem that is more of a continuous interface than a data conversion task. For example, if you have a non-Oracle order entry system and must share customers with Oracle AR, you will have a customer master file for each system, and you will want to make sure that every customer in each application is replicated in the other. In this example, you might use the customer API in AR to avoid duplicate data entry by programming a recurring conversion for new order entry customers. These recurring data conversions require more analysis, programming, testing, and documentation than the one-time data loads.

Tip

Evaluate the major data elements in the foreign systems, and see if they can be stored as a descriptive flexfield somewhere in the Oracle Applications. The foreign element can possibly be converted fully to a new descriptive flexfield, which eliminates the need for an interface.

UNDERSTANDING TYPICAL TASKS, DELIVERABLES, AND MILESTONES OF THE ANALYSIS PHASE

You should prepare several documents during the analysis phase of the project. These tasks and deliverables will provide a foundation for the rest of the project implementation activity. These project deliverables document the current processes and requirements, the new processes, the system architecture, the degree of fit, the data conversion strategy, and the system interface strategy. You will use these documents to support your configuration choices, conference room pilots, test plans, customization designs, and end-user training.

DETERMINING EXISTING BUSINESS SCENARIOS

Document how your business currently operates. Work with broad processes such as procurement and customer fulfillment instead of narrow applications such as purchasing and order entry. You want to focus on how your organization operates, and not the modules it is using. For each application, consider producing a document to show the following baseline items:

Tip

Define or use a standard process diagram template. Make sure all team users who are creating these diagrams use the same template and process objects. This consistency will increase the usability and readability of the diagrams throughout the organization. Note that these templates usually are reviewed and approved by project management prior to their use. Consider having "template review sessions" with your team, or team leads, prior to their execution.

- Identify and document the business scenarios or "as is" business processes.
- Draw diagrams of business process flows to show what happens in the business, the sequence of events, integration among unit transactions, interdepartmental relationships, intercompany activity, and system interfaces.
- Use questionnaires to document and analyze each business function.
- Analyze the information, requirements, and format of special forms. Collect special forms for future reference.
- Analyze information on management, transaction, and control reports.
- Document security requirements.
- Document legal and regulatory requirements.
- Determine the process inconsistencies and differences among all your business units.

DETERMINING THE EXISTING COMPUTER SYSTEM ARCHITECTURE

A good technical architecture baseline document will establish the boundaries and capabilities of the legacy system. Typically, users will expect new user interfaces, reports, procedures, and capabilities of the new systems. However, users will also expect the new systems to replace each and every function and feature of the outgoing systems. You will want to map existing capabilities to the functions of the Oracle Applications to establish a baseline and to manage user and management expectations from that basic set of requirements.

Note

Many organizations will have some, but usually not all, of their technical architecture documented. Even though they have this documentation, it is usually very old or in need of update. Consider using this documentation as a starting point to document the existing architecture. This deliverable is best completed by the information systems technical team members, and not a consultant.

Consider the following items as you establish your technical architecture baseline:

- Document each existing application.
- Catalog databases.
- Understand existing interfaces.
- Inventory key hardware.
- Evaluate the existing network.
- Document expected changes.
- Note areas of improvement.

DETERMINING THE BUSINESS TRANSACTION VOLUMES AND FREQUENCIES

Almost every Oracle Applications installation must buy additional disk space sooner than expected. In addition, you will want to determine what history and basic data you will load into the new system and what techniques you will use to enter startup data. For example, if you have more than about 2,500 customers or vendors, you will want to consider loading them with a program instead of manually. We know of one client that loaded one million customer records into its AR system at the rate of about 5,000 per hour. At 20 hours per day, this volume required a 10-day task, lots of coordination with other systems, and lots of system resources right before the system went live. Consider producing a document to show the volumes and frequencies of each of your significant transactions. Use this information to calculate disk space requirements, balance I/O across the disk array, and evaluate expected system loads.

Tip

This information can be used to purchase an implementation technical architecture early in the project or before the project starts. Many hardware providers can provide business transaction questionnaires to assist with server sizing and selection. Also note that some hardware vendors provide free seminars for your System Administrator or Technical staff members prior to hardware selection. Take advantage of these free services prior to sizing and purchasing new hardware.

Agreeing on Detailed Business Requirements

For each future business process or scenario, document the business requirements. Define each step of the process, who is involved, and what information they use to execute each transaction. Understand corporate policies, controls, audit requirements, and management involvement with the process. Document external influences from customers, vendors, and government agencies.

Tip

Also, consider business calendars or seasonal activities for the project implementation schedule. (For example, consider waiting until the busy season is over before launching the new systems.)

Understand the transactional, technical, cultural, informational, and managerial needs of the business in these areas:

- Business goals
- Key performance drivers
- Objectives and policies
- Definitions
- Seasonal influences
- Transaction event sequences

Every Oracle applications implementation is different and will have several critical success factors that will define the project. Even if the project sponsor proclaims your project to be a "vanilla" implementation, make sure you understand which application functions you must activate. For example, if you are in an industry that requires lot or serial number control and tracking for your products, the Oracle applications can likely meet that requirement. However, you should document the need and make sure that the person who loads your item master understands what must be done.

ANALYZING TRANSACTION REQUIREMENTS

Determine which transactions are required. During the analysis phase, users might ask for every feature and function provided by Oracle Applications. However, does it really make sense to activate the AutoLockbox transactions for cash receipts on fewer than 2,000 invoices per month? You will want to determine the setup and processing overhead of activating an automatic Oracle process. Many customers disable standard Oracle application features to avoid adding overhead to their business.

Tip

Remember, the features you activate in Oracle Applications during setup will have to be maintained in the future. Evaluate the form, fit, and function of each setup option prior to making the commitment to During activate.

PERFORMANCE AND EQUIPMENT REQUIREMENTS

Consider documenting appropriate system response time in During the technical architecture deliverables if you have significant transaction volumes. For example, if you are trying to create 10,000 invoices an hour in your AR system, you will want to understand the performance issues. Response time requirements can impact the physical technical architecture of the servers, desktops, user interface, network, and so forth. Consider disk space requirements for your transaction volume. For example, will the administrators be able to support a database that is growing at a rate of 5% a month?

SECURITY REQUIREMENTS

You might have strict security requirements for your Oracle applications. You should understand who has access to which menu choices for screens. You should determine whether certain reports are sensitive and which users can run which reports. If you will use multi-org functionality, you will want to understand how partitioning the data will affect your reports and what kinds of responsibilities you will need to support.

Tip

Create a security matrix to document who has access to what applications. Also, consider creating a new user account process. Document the process of adding new employees/users to your network, OS, and Oracle Applications. This can be a workflow or e-mail process; regardless, develop a method of adding and maintaining new users.

REPORTING AND EXECUTIVE INFORMATION REQUIREMENTS

Reporting requirements are often the most neglected critical success factor for an implementation project, and you should develop a strategy for reporting after you have analyzed the requirements. Your worst nightmare is to skip this analysis and discover show-stopper requirements for 50 or more reports a month before going live. If it takes two to three days to create a report, it is almost impossible to avoid postponing the launch schedule when this happens. Determine your reporting scope and strategy in a document in the project analysis phase. Make sure gaps in reporting requirements are linked to the primary gap analysis document.

Tip

Consider developing Oracle Application views to replace the design and development of new reports. This can be an easier approach, and in the long run more manageable and cost effective than written reports. You can access these views using the Oracle Discoverer or another end-user query tool.

AUDIT AND CONTROL REQUIREMENTS

Most large companies have established audit and control requirements, and you will have a hard time changing these policies during your implementation project. You will want to create a document if you have to work around the Oracle Applications to satisfy these policies. Examples of requirements in this area include the following:

- Auditors might need specialized reports. Consider your internal auditors, public accountants, and government auditors. Typically, these reports are not daily operating reports, and you might have to search for them.
- Most companies establish separation of duties when cash is involved. If you have a very small payables or credit department, you will have to devise a process, security, and work assignments to satisfy this requirement.
- Many companies require special approvals for certain types of expenditures, and you might have requirements for the purchasing approval hierarchy. Also, you might have to modify an Oracle Workflow process to fit new approval hierarchy requirements.

Tip

Visit with other companies in your industry. Hearing from them firsthand will benefit you and your organization in many ways. Also, don't be afraid to ask them for help. They might be willing to provide setup information or details of their approach on an industry-related customization. Don't reinvent the wheel!

DETERMINING YOUR FUTURE BUSINESS PROCESSES

When you know your business requirements and process flows, you can create a map of each function to an Oracle Applications function to see how it fits. If there are gaps in the function map, you will have to start planning for user process changes or customization of the software.

A business process reengineering (BPR) project can be disruptive to an Oracle Applications implementation project. If you include BPR in your project, make sure the reengineering team is well-integrated with the applications and uses the new systems as the baseline for change. Consider the Oracle capabilities before designing a reengineered process.

Tip

Implementation team members with little Oracle Applications experience often have a hard time visualizing how Oracle Applications will work in a given business situation. An experienced consultant can often add a lot of value and help determine the degree of fit among your requirements and the applications.

Consider estimating the degree of fit as 25%, 50%, 75%, or 100%. These rough guidelines will help provide an overall estimate of fit. If you determine the fit to be less than 80%, you might want to revisit each customization less than 100% and determine whether it's truly a custom requirement or if a business process can change. Do not settle for "because we have always done it that way!"

Tip

Some processes in the business often will change during the Oracle implementation project. Make sure to design new processes from the new software's natural process flow. Often, a legacy process is reengineered, and the improvement becomes part of the requirements for the new system. Unfortunately, the great new change is made late in the applications project, and the Oracle process might be entirely different. When this situation occurs, customization to the basic Oracle code could be required to make the reengineered solution successful, and you must deal with changes in scope late in the implementation project.

DETERMINING THE DEGREE OF FIT

Make sure to itemize and publish to everyone a document of where your business requirements and processes are different from the basic functionality provided by the Oracle applications. Consider using the requirements mapping document to identify and document all requirements, gaps, and level of fit. Consolidating all of these into a single document will provide one source of all known requirements and gaps. Make sure to capture gaps in an issue log entry, and assign a project team member and a resolution date to each. Update the project work plan to create tasks to design, build, test, and document customizations or a workaround for each gap.

Tip

Prepare the gap analysis document in plain language, and describe the gap in terms of the current user process. Many steering committee members, sponsors, and department heads won't be able to help resolve issues that are presented from a technical or Oracle Applications perspective—write in laymen terms!

TRANSITIONING YOUR ORGANIZATION

When you transition from your legacy systems to the Oracle ERP software, you will have many diverse tasks including end-user training, data conversion, change management, and so forth. During the analysis phase of the project, you can prepare a document to outline a transition strategy. This document will be updated as new roles and responsibilities are defined throughout the implementation. Consider documenting new roles required to support the business scenarios defined earlier in the project, as well as who will need to be trained in Oracle Applications, the business scenarios, and any specific support requirements.

Tip

The transition strategy is one of the most important deliverables of the implementation. It is not the implementation that is difficult–it is the transition of your organization from your old legacy applications to the new Oracle Applications.

ANALYZING AND DEVELOPING A DATA CONVERSION STRATEGY

For each entity to be converted, publish an analysis to support the conversion strategy. Consider doing the following in your document:

- Document the record layout of the legacy data.
- Determine who owns and is responsible for the source data.
- Determine whether the conversion will be manual or programmed. Estimate the time required for each technique.
- Determine whether there are problems with the legacy data.

Tip

Ask some basic questions about your data. Where does data reside in the legacy system and not in Oracle Applications? Where does Oracle Applications have mandatory data requirements where there is no legacy data?

- If the conversion is programmed, map the source data to the required Oracle API.
- Determine when the conversion will take place for each CRP and for final cut-over to production.
- Determine balancing, reconciliation, and validation tests.

ANALYZING AND DEVELOPING AN APPLICATION INTEGRATION STRATEGY

Often, Oracle Applications will interface with non-Oracle systems. For each interface point, determine how the system will operate. Integration can be single-directional or bidirectional. For example, you might want to send billing data to a non-Oracle sales history system (outbound interface). You might bring in cash receipts transactions from your bank (inbound interface to an Oracle API). You might need to synchronize all kinds of shipping, receiving, and billing transactions with a non-Oracle warehouse management system. By the end of the analysis phase of the project, you should know which interfaces are part of your implementation project and how much effort will be required to build, test, and document each interface program.

Tip

Consider creating a high-level interface diagram, which can be easily referenced by the project team. This document can be invaluable throughout the project. Remember to use a consistent format or template when creating this deliverable.

Tip

Make sure each integration point is identified in your integration and CRP testing tasks. The integration to third-party products should be easily identified in your testing scenarios and scripts.

SUMMARY

The analysis phase of an Oracle Applications implementation project is the foundation for almost all project activities that come later in the implementation. Most of the deliverables of the analysis phase are "living documents" in that they will be included in deliverables for other activities. This functional and technical analysis is vital to the success of your project. If you skip parts of analysis, you will have to perform those parts at a later and less-convenient time, and at higher cost. This phase of the project determines your project scope and will have a major influence on the total cost of the project.

The analysis deliverables are like a road map to guide you from your legacy system to your new Oracle Applications. Implementing an ERP system such as Oracle Applications can be fun, but confusing. However the analysis helps keep you from getting lost. When you have a good map and refer to it often throughout the trip, you improve your odds of success. To improve the chances of delivering your project on time and within budget, make sure you do well in the analysis phase of the project.

Note

This is a time to reshape your organization and implement those ideas and processes that have always been missing. Think outside the box–or that there is no box at all. Oracle Applications provide general best practices; it is up to you and your team to be creative and define the best practices for your organization.

CHAPTER 8

Converting Analysis into Solutions

In this chapter

In the previous chapter, I told you about discovering your business processes and the typical project tasks, deliverables, and milestones of the analysis phase of an implementation project. This chapter discusses how you convert that analysis into solutions and overcome the gaps between the Oracle Applications and your organization. These solutions can be customizations, setups, or specific configurations of the Oracle Applications during the implementation. This chapter provides a framework for designing solutions that utilize the Oracle Applications and technology to fulfill your organization's business requirements.

The primary purposes of this phase are to develop the design documents for the solutions that fill the gaps between the Oracle Applications and your business requirements, and develop supporting application setup documents. Many other deliverables in this phase complement the business requirements and setup documents. You will design your technical and application architecture, create data conversion scripts and programs, develop initial testing and training documents, and prepare your organization for transition to the production environment.

Each business requirement solution may have several alternatives developed that should be further reviewed and discussed with the project team members. The alternatives presented could range from doing nothing to building a very complex customization. The pros and cons, as well as the cost and benefit, for each alternative should be evaluated. Selection of the most cost-effective alternative might not necessarily prove to be the best choice for your organization. The project team members need to examine the solutions and select the one most suitable and cost effective for your organization. As these solutions are created, your team will begin to design the end-user documentation. This documentation will be reviewed and revised appropriately as the solutions are approved and finalized.

While you are converting your business analysis gaps into solutions, keep in mind the organizational changes and reengineering of business processes. These changes should be considered in the future business model and included in the scope of the overall implementation project. Downstream project activities and resources may be affected by these business changes. I recommend that you bring all new processes, policies, and procedures into the scope of the project as soon as possible to set proper expectations with your project team and management.

During this phase of the project, the application and technical architecture is designed and documented by technical team members. The technical architecture is designed to support the standard Oracle Applications, custom solutions, additional applications, and third-party products. The technical team will also design and document the performance testing approach and programs.

Converting the business analysis into solutions is an iterative process. Many tasks in converting the analysis into solutions and enabling the system (discussed in Chapter 9, "Enabling the System") overlap. These overlapping tasks will appear seamless to the project team as they progress from project phase to phase, continually building on the preceding tasks. This is an exciting time for all team members as the business requirements and solutions begin to shape the future business model of your organization.

DESIGNING CUSTOMIZATIONS

Designing customizations is one of the main objectives of this phase. Your team's focus will be to produce design documents for Oracle Application customizations that meet the functional requirements of the business—functionally, technically, and financially. You will design customizations to fill the gaps between the Oracle Applications, legacy systems, third-party applications, and your organization's business requirements. The overall customization approach is defined in the customization strategy prepared earlier in the project. Each design specification must be created in a way so that it promotes and supports the future maintenance and support of the system. These design documents must also take into consideration the application setups and test plans for each Oracle Application module. You also need to consider your organization's security, database, and network requirements because these create additional constraints on the design of your customizations.

Customizations to the Oracle Applications can be categorized in three ways:

- Extensions
- Modifications
- Interfaces

Some project activities that can be considered customizations are the following:

- Creating a new report or form
- Renaming or modifying a copy of a standard Oracle report or form
- Creating a one-time interface to convert legacy data
- Creating a recurring inbound or outbound interface to a non-Oracle application
- Creating an Oracle Application Alert
- Renaming or modifying a copy of an Oracle Workflow
- Creating a database trigger, package, or program to perform or automate some business function

PROJECT DESIGN AND BUILD STANDARDS

Design and build standards ensure that all project team members follow a consistent method of delivering work products to the team and end users. Normally, project team members discuss what standards they want to develop and establish prior to beginning any design work. It is highly recommended that you review the following documents before establishing your own standards. These documents have evolved over the years and are full of helpful information:

- *Oracle Applications Developer's Guide*
- *Oracle Applications System Administrator's Guide*
- *Oracle Applications User's Guide*
- *Oracle Applications Flexfields Guide*

- *Application Object Library/Workflow Technical Reference Manual*
- *Oracle Workflow Guide*
- *Oracle Applications User Interface Standards for Forms-Based Products*
- *Installing Oracle Applications, Release 11*i
- *Oracle Forms Developer and Reports Developer Release 6i: Guidelines for Building Applications*

Many other standards need to be considered prior to any deliverables being designed or developed. Make sure to establish an application short name and custom working directory for your customizations. Establish an acronym (such as CUST) or use the first four letters of your company's name for the short name for your customizations.

The short name will become a prefix on all your custom work. It will be used internally within the application as well as operating system files. For example, BOSS could be the application short name for BOSS Corporation custom development. This helps to ensure that your customizations won't get mixed up with Oracle Applications code. Register your custom application within the Oracle Applications. When your custom application has been registered, it then becomes accessible to you like any other Oracle Application module. You will begin to see it listed in Lists of Values throughout the Applications. After the custom application has been created, you have the ability to mix it with the standard Oracle modules. You can mix and match custom and standard menus and forms, creating an extraordinary customized application. Also, make sure that each new custom object that is created gets registered within your newly defined application. Doing this secures your work during future upgrades, allowing for a smoother and more successful transition to new releases of Oracle Applications.

Tip

One of the principle ways you can help your customization survive an upgrade or a maintenance patch is to keep your code separate from that distributed by Oracle Corporation. You should establish your own unique names, directories, and registered applications for your customizations. Never mix your own customizations (even menus) with Oracle code because that risks that an upgrade or a patch program will overwrite your work.

SOURCE CODE: SQL, PL/SQL, AND PROGRAMMING LANGUAGES

As you begin to develop new code, make sure that there are common programming standards for source code. Specifically, for program file headers, consider capturing information such as filename, description of the program, how the program is used, any notes that would be of importance, and a complete history of the changes, including the developer's name, date, and reason for making the change.

Note

I know of one very large and heavily customized organization that cross-referenced standard header information for more than 4,600 customizations from more than 100 sites in Oracle database tables. Even with that information, it would take months of analysis to prepare for an upgrade.

Also make sure that any helpful comments embedded within your source code follow a common standard. I recommend that you use comments liberally and generously throughout the code to assist your development staff in the future. It is best to encapsulate comments in a box of dashes (-) or pound signs (#) to help them stand out within the code. You should have comments before each step in a program, before each procedure in a program, and wherever they can assist in understanding complex program logic or algorithms.

Oracle Tools

For Oracle Forms, Oracle Reports, SQL, PL/SQL, and database trigger coding standards, follow the published standards in *Oracle Forms Developer* and *Reports Developer Release 6i: Guidelines for Building Applications* and *Oracle Applications Developer's Guide*. These products have evolved over the years and have developed natural layout conventions that can be found in the aforementioned books. You have no reason to invent your own coding standards because these have been proven successful and are widely accepted within the Oracle community.

Designing New Tables

When new tables are designed for your customizations, make sure to create them in an exclusive "custom only" Oracle user account. Create the user account with the same name as the application short name previously discussed. Create all new tables with the application short name prefix, so that the custom tables are easily identified and recognized by your development team. For example, a BOSS custom table would be identified as follows: BOSS_LOOKUPS, where BOSS is the application short name, and LOOKUPS is the table name for the custom application lookups.

Source Naming Conventions

Another mechanism for keeping objects organized within your custom working directories is the use of naming conventions. Consider using a standard approach for naming objects, such as BOSSGLU10.sql. Where BOSS is the application short name, GL is for the Oracle General Ledger module, U is a unique identifier for Update, which is the type of transaction being performed within the object, and 10 is a unique sequence number for the customization. The .sql suffix is the standard Oracle extension that indicates the code as being an SQL*Plus or PL/SQL program.

Tip

Consider developing a one-page, high-level document that contains an example of the naming convention standard, with a description of each segment and possible values. Distribute this to your team and have them tape it up in their offices. This helps promote the standards, by making the standards readily accessible for reference.

You may want to use similar naming conventions for all your project deliverables to help keep objects organized and understood by all team members. For example, in BOSSGS021.doc, BOSS represents the short name, GS stands for a Getting Started phase deliverable, 2 represents the second deliverable of the phase, and 1 represents the first revision of the document. The .doc is the standard extension for MS Word documents. Be creative in designing your naming convention, but be consistent.

Custom Installation Routines

The creation of installation scripts is more important than the code itself. Develop scripts for your custom objects to install them with minimal steps and re-execute without errors or failure due to duplicate data. The installation scripts also must be transferable to other hardware platforms and operating systems. Generate scripts for creating your database objects, generating seed data, and creating grants and synonyms. Scripts can be created to do just about anything needed to support your customizations. Be sure that these objects are included as part of your unit and integration testing. To help put things into perspective, what if a disaster occurred and your custom application was wiped out? How would you recover? Your immediate response would be let's restore from our backups. Well, there are no backups; the tapes can't be read by your tape drive. Now what? Inevitably, you will need a way to re-create your custom application from scratch. Having these installation scripts will be invaluable in this situation. Take the time and effort required to design, develop, and test these installation scripts!

The Solution/Conceptual Design Document

This design document summarizes your business requirements that are not addressed by a specific application module and recommends one or more solution(s) for each requirement. The document is created as one of the last tasks in the Analyzing the Project phase of the implementation (see Chapter 7, "Analyzing the Project") but is reviewed in detail prior to beginning the next step of design tasks assigned to your team. It serves as a confirmation that your project team understands your business requirements and documents the solution and assumptions that are the foundation for the level of effort estimates.

A description of each business requirement should be contained in this document, along with the specific requirements and your recommended solution. Your solutions may include workarounds in the application, use of standard features, extensions to the database, creating flexfields, customizations to the applications, or business procedural changes.

Upon completion of this design document, it is followed by two more documents, the functional/high-level design and technical/low-level design. These documents are discussed in the following sections, and when all three have been completed, they are considered a complete design package for your customizations.

Tip

Suggest to end users the possibility of an application workaround or use of standard functionality prior to committing to a customization. Many times there may be an acceptable way to fulfill the users' requirements by using standard application functionality. Also, explain to your users that customizations add complexity to the implementation, as well as ongoing maintenance and future upgrades. Often, users are focused on their needs and don't see the additional burden placed on their organizations by customizations.

Because a customization will likely represent a change in scope for the project, an estimate for the amount of time and resources for each recommended solution should be provided to the steering committee. Each solution should have a specific list of the customizations that are going to be created. These modules include new or modified reports, forms, and programs; conversion scripts; and database tables. You should determine the degree of difficulty to create the customization and make an estimate of the cost to create and maintain the customization.

The estimates provided need to cover all work associated with the customization until the end of the project. The estimates should include functional and technical designs, creation of the custom object, associated test scripts, and installation routines. Also take into consideration how many resources will be needed to complete the customization based on your estimates. See the section "Estimating Customizations" later in the chapter for more details on providing realistic estimates.

THE HIGH-LEVEL/FUNCTIONAL DESIGN DOCUMENT

This design document is developed in layman terms and is normally written by the functional project team members. It is used as a bridging document between the end users' business requirements and the technical team design documents.

The document begins with a narrative essay that presents the requirement in layman terms and expands on the solution design document created earlier in the project. The next section of the document should cover the business needs to justify why this customization is being produced. You can also provide additional information such as the major features, end-user procedures, and any supporting assumptions that will help your technical team understand the customization. The addition of business scenarios, which are based on real business transactions, will help the project team further understand the requirements of the customization.

The functional design document is straightforward, but important and should be designed for every customization. This document should be reviewed and approved by your project team and end users prior to being presented to your technical staff. This project deliverable should have an acceptance certificate created and signed by the end users. Changes after the acceptance certificate should require a change order to bring them into the scope of the project.

THE LOW-LEVEL/TECHNICAL DESIGN DOCUMENT

The technical design documents are complex in nature and are not meant to be reviewed with your end users. These documents are very technical and provide a level of detail required only by the technical team. This document defines the components required to support and implement the customizations. It serves as the bridge between the functional design document discussed earlier and the actual code that will be required to support the business requirement. Both documents should be considered a complete detailed design.

The technical design document provides all the details necessary to maintain and support a customization. It contains information on the specific module names, objects that describe the customization, navigation logic on how to enter the application to execute the customization, and how to leave the applications. There should also be information that represents the relationship of database objects being used within the customization and any special logic that will help the development team understand how the customization is set up and meant to be used in a production environment. There can also be pseudo code that supports the program logic for SQL, PL/SQL, or any of the Pro languages. Overall, this document is meant to be the all-inclusive guide to a customization. Your development team needs to spend time developing code and this document to have a successful customization. To put things in perspective, if a customization works fine and there are no problems, that is excellent. However, if it doesn't, and there is minimal supporting documentation, it is going to be difficult to research and resurrect the problem. The final words on the subject—a customization is not complete without supporting detailed design documentation!

Each of the design documents should go through a peer review by the more experienced team members to ensure that quality and efficient deliverables are being developed. The peer review is a good place to enforce coding standards. A good-quality control process helps further enhance your team's ability to deliver good work products. These quality reviews should be constructive and a learning experience for all team members involved.

ESTIMATING CUSTOMIZATIONS

Providing cost and time estimates for customizations is always difficult. This section can be used to help devise a way to estimate your project customizations or other uncertain activities.

Tip

It is helpful to have a skilled developer help with the estimate at this point. This technical person can help identify alternative ways to perform the customization and verify the difficulty factor of each technique.

The following is an estimating model that has been used on many Oracle projects. This formula provides a method for project planning that is easy to use and produces a realistic estimate. You must remember that this is only an estimate.

Figure 8.1 shows a time-estimating model that helps provide more realistic estimates. The result field is TIME, which represents the estimated time it's going to take to complete all phases of the customization. Additional information on this model can be found in PERT/CPM estimating and project management books. This is a standard model for estimating uncertain activities and tasks.

Tip

Create a spreadsheet of the estimating model for your project team members to use. Place it in a working directory, or have them create a shortcut on their desktop so that they can easily access and execute the estimating model. This model is not the answer to all estimating, but an approach that provides more realistic estimates.

The variable fields you ask your team members to provide estimates for are *To*, which represents your optimistic time estimate, *Tm*, your most likely time estimate, and *Tp*, your pessimistic time estimate. If a wide range of estimates is provided, then there is a high degree of uncertainty of the business requirements.

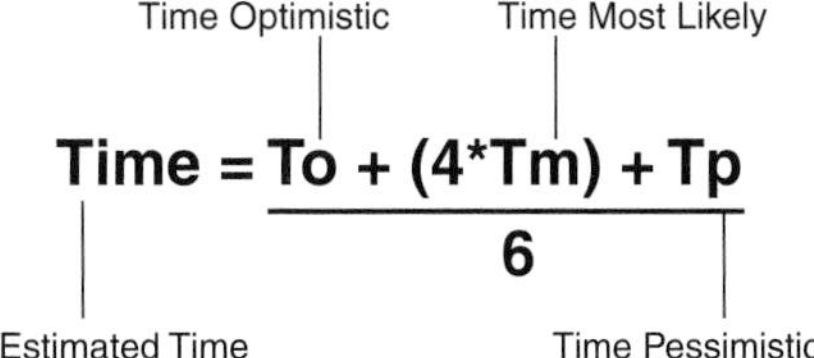

Figure 8.1
An estimating formula.

When providing estimates, consider many different factors that may affect your time to completion. Understand the business objectives behind what you are estimating. Also, consider the primary resources assigned to the project. An inexperienced developer may work at half the speed of an experienced developer. Or, the use of certain tools such as Oracle Designer, may speed up a development effort. Understanding the experience level of an organization's resources is critical to estimating. Many organizations provide estimates without taking into consideration the available skills, tools, or technology. If your estimate is for a significant amount of time or cost, consider decomposing the main task into subtasks such as analyze, design, build, document, and so forth. Don't be afraid to use estimates from prior projects. You may require additional time or resources based on the experience you've gained from completing the first customization. But, it's a safe bet to use an existing estimate.

Note

The application developers are critical to this phase of the project. Estimates for a customization can make or break a project. If you find the time is going to push your project past the target date, add another developer to shorten the duration. If these tasks are associated with the critical path of a project, then adding resources may be your only alternative.

Many professionals are too confident in their estimates and assume that no unexpected events will occur and the task or project will progress smoothly. Consider adding contingency time to your estimates, which will act as a cushion for unexpected events. Many developers just estimate the coding time required. Make sure your technical people include the time for documentation, training, and integration testing in their estimates.

MANAGING THE PHASE

As you progress from phase to phase of your project, you will validate the accuracy and completeness of the documentation and information developed in the previous phases. One of the first things that needs to be defined is the design and build standards and guidelines that will be used by your project team. Standards should be defined for each kind of object that is going to be designed to support the solutions earlier defined. For example, if no new forms are being developed, then there is no need to have a standard created for forms. After the standards have been defined, your development staff can begin to focus on creating the design documents. If there are many customizations, the module design and build process can use up a great deal of the time and budget of a project.

It is important to schedule the right technical resources and provide time for functional team members and end users to participate in testing. Many tasks between this phase and the Enabling the System phase will overlap, and you will find your team working on tasks in each phase simultaneously. Your work breakdown structure should allow plenty of time so that resources can be assigned to individual modules to manage and control their assignments properly.

Having a good technical team lead can provide solid technical leadership and management of the lesser experienced staff. The technical lead must assume the responsibility and accountability for creating good-quality work products that will be maintained by your organization for years to come. A systematic approach to quality control is essential to the success of a project.

Note

If you are implementing Oracle Applications in phases, keep in mind that you will then be supporting legacy and new systems simultaneously. You will need to think about reporting consolidation or building additional interfaces to support both applications. Now is the time to rethink your approach, or to estimate and design the reporting procedures and interfaces.

When scheduling your resources to develop design documents, take into consideration the number of available and qualified team members. Also take into consideration the productivity of the work environment. Don't put your design and development staff in a high-traffic area. These people like to be heads down on activities and have a quiet place to work.

When developing schedules and the project plan you need to consider which tasks can be conducted in parallel. Take into consideration the diversity of your group when creating your estimates. Don't assign a task that has been estimated for an experienced developer to a lesser experienced individual. If you do, re-estimate your plan.

During this phase of the project, some project team members may be phased out due to budget considerations or unplanned events. Make sure that all supporting documentation is transferred to other project team members or is saved in the project repository before team members are released from the project.

Phase Success Factors

The following are some critical success factors to consider during this phase of a project:

- Implementation of standard practices for design and build of customizations
- Clear definition of business objectives
- Involvement of key executives, functional experts, and technical staff from all areas of the business
- Knowledge of key features and capabilities of the application and technology
- Complete traceability of design to specific business requirements
- Management of designs within the scope and objectives of the project
- Ensuring that proper resources and time commitments can be met
- Management and control of scope changes via a change control system
- Ensuring that there is sufficient data for performance testing of the database, application, and system
- Development of a comprehensive strategy for transitioning the organization to the new application
- Development of a contingency plan to support all transition and retransition activities

Revisiting Business Requirements

As you continue with the design of application customizations, you will continue to develop new business requirements. To help support these requirements and transition your user community later in the project, you need to create training material and user procedures that support the customizations and standard functionality of the application. Some organizations like to create process narratives that are based on the business processes that support their daily operations. These narratives lay the groundwork necessary for developing user procedures, user training material, and system and acceptance testing.

Tip

If you experience a constant change in requirements from your users during the design effort, implement a review and sign-off procedure for each design to keep control of the project scope.

DESIGNING THE TECHNICAL ARCHITECTURE

During this phase, the technical architecture begins to take shape. Detailed design documents for the application and database architectures are developed. Documents for the detailed network, hardware, and software needed to support the application's deployment in the future are designed. Identify all applications involved, including legacy and ancillary systems. This document will become invaluable later in the project and will provide management with "the big picture" of all applications being implemented.

The degree of detail needed to support the preceding documents depends on the scope of the project and required architecture. If the architecture is a localized implementation with one installation of the applications, a system administrator or technical architect can perform these tasks. The system administrator can configure and install the technical foundation for the new system without additional work.

If the architecture is at the enterprise level, designing below this level may be difficult without understanding the localized issues. In this case, architects will design only at the enterprise level and leave the detail architecture to the local system administrator or technical architect.

Tip

Consider developing a one-page, high-level design document using a business drawing tool. Design the document using objects that represent the hardware, network, and applications architecture being implemented. Also include customizations and third-party applications. Include a list of software that will reside on each server. Consider shading or coloring these objects to represent the phase or time frame in which they will be implemented. Try to keep this to one page and make sure that project team members and management receive a copy.

The application architect(s) should develop a detailed application plan identifying key setups, logical databases, and the modules to be installed. The technical architect works closely with the application architect to design the hardware, and networking needs to support the applications and ensure the business and technical architecture needs are met.

The technical architect role is critical to the success of the project. Some organizations are hesitant to use external technical architects if they feel their groups' abilities are adequate. It really shouldn't matter whether the technical architect is a consultant or employee. What matters most is that the architecture be the best for your organization.

DATA CONVERSION

One of the first tasks that must be performed is the creation of a conversion environment. This environment will be used to prepare conversion design documents during the build and testing tasks in the subsequent phases of the project. Next, perform a data element mapping exercise where legacy data sources are mapped to the Oracle Application tables and columns. Depending on the Oracle Application module, you will have access to open interfaces and application program interfaces in which legacy data can be mapped.

Note

Establish regularly scheduled meetings with the data conversion team and your end-user community; once or twice a week should be sufficient. This meeting will keep all team members abreast of progress and issues. Your team will have many informal meetings with the end users to discuss mapping details. Also, make sure that you have legacy application technical expertise available to help with the conversion mapping exercise. Many legacy application data elements are not intuitive, and it will take someone with the proper expertise to decipher the information.

On completing the mapping exercise, the conversion programs and scripts to convert data should be created. If you plan to use an automated conversion approach or tools, you may need to develop traditional code to perform the data conversion. Regardless of the approach, business rules need to be created to support the conversion effort. In addition to creating programs and supporting business rules, you should develop test plans to ensure that all data is converted successfully. Simple programs can be written to ensure that data has been converted successfully and the integrity has remained intact.

You may determine that manual conversion of data is the best approach for your organization. Depending on the amount and complexity of the data, you will still need a conversion plan. It is best to create a plan that your conversion staff can follow to help them understand the data dependency requirements of the application. When planning your data conversion tasks, take into consideration changes caused by discovering new application requirements found while creating your design documents. For example, you would not want to enter an employee into Oracle HR until her manager's data has been entered. This is a simple example of how a manual data conversion plan will save time and money.

Data conversion design documents can be created by individuals with both technical and functional experience and good knowledge of the integration required for performing this exercise.

INITIAL PROJECT DOCUMENTATION

During this phase of the project, you create the initial designs for the custom user guide and reference manual, as well as the technical manual and system guide. The need and time to develop these documents is often underestimated, which leads to poor or no documentation being developed. The following sections discuss the need for training and transitioning your organization to the production environment.

TRAINING DOCUMENTATION

Design the initial training material during this phase after the future process modules have been reviewed and finalized. The end-user training material should be developed based on user roles and aligned closely with your business scenarios created earlier in the project. When designing the training documentation, keep in mind how training will be delivered. The following is a list of things to think about as you are designing your training material:

- What size classes are acceptable?
- Will you use onsite trainers to assist?
- Will it be a train-the-trainer approach?
- How much training will the instructors need prior to delivering the classes?
- Will classes be held in multiple sites at the same time?
- Will you need multiple training database instances?

As you design your documentation, take into consideration new policies and procedures that have been defined during the implementation. Also keep in mind that as new employees are hired into your organization, these people will need to be trained. Get them trained as part of their orientation to your organization.

Note

Good training material and delivery have a direct impact on the continued success of your implementation!

TRANSITIONING TO PRODUCTION

During the transition to production, you will need a support infrastructure as well as contingency and transition plans. The production support team will act as the help desk for all application, database, and network issues during the transition. The roles and responsibilities of this team must be identified early in the project so that the team is trained and educated properly to supply adequate support.

DESIGNING THE TRANSITION AND CONTINGENCY PLANS

The development of a detailed transition and contingency plan includes the tasks associated with transitioning the organization to production. These documents are inspired by documents created earlier in the project, such as the education and training plan, performance testing strategy, and the transition strategy. The transition plan should include a series of specific tasks to assist the project team and end users. These tasks should promote and facilitate the planning and estimating activities required to guide your team through the transition to production.

Many organizations overlook the need for contingency plans prior to implementing. There is, at times, a false sense of security in implementing a solid ERP application such as Oracle. There have been many successes, as well as many failures. The design of a contingency plan should provide alternatives to your organization if the transition to production is unsuccessful.

Tip

Consider playing a "what-if" game to determine things that might go wrong. For example, consider this question, "What if the concurrent managers place too great a load on the system and fall behind in transaction processing?" As soon as the question is asked, solutions and alternatives come to mind. The key to a good transition is to ask the questions and develop answers before they are needed.

The plan should cover all circumstances that would require its execution. The contingency plan should also include a list of implementation steps that, if failed, could be used to understand specifically what went wrong and how the team should react. It might be possible that a specific implementation step could cause the transition to stop; although, if a resolution or solution is documented, the project could resume after the problem is fixed. The plan should also include steps to retransition to the production system after the problems are resolved.

Preliminary Application Setup Documents

These documents are perhaps the most important to be created during the project. After the business models have been developed and the final requirements determined, the application setup documents must be defined. These setup documents are detailed plans of how to set up each Oracle Application module. A typical application document should include information on data conversion, system, application, and data administration tasks. Do not underestimate the time required to develop these documents. You will need to review these documents with your end users on a regular basis and test the values in a SETUP only database instance of the applications prior to your final version.

In release 11*i*, Oracle has created the Implementation Wizard as a tool to facilitate configuration and documentation of setup parameters. The wizard understands process hierarchies and common data elements among related modules. For example, the AP and PO applications share many data elements, and the wizard can reduce the setup effort required by eliminating redundant steps when you implement both modules. The wizard also understands interdependent setup tasks. Finally, you can use the wizard as a project management tool to assign tasks, set objectives, and monitor project team performance against setup steps. The wizard isn't wondrous enough to advise you how to set up the applications, but it can organize and sequence the task.

Tip

If disk capacity allows, create a separate instance for testing the values in conjunction with designing your setup document. This database instance should be for setups only, and as soon as your documents have all been created, the SETUP instance can be removed. This provides a safe and static place for application setups to be tested and documented.

Another setup task is to design a form for capturing the application sign-on profiles for your end users. This document should capture information such as the user's name, application sign-on name, role or title, responsibility, and department or group assignment. It is also good to add the network and operating system logons. Many times this information is not shared between your system administrator and applications administrator. Putting this information together in one document helps manage, control, and organize the process.

PREPARING FOR SYSTEM TEST

At this stage in the project, you need to be developing a test strategy that encompasses all testing tasks. This document should include an overview of your testing approach, the test scripts to be created, a testing plan that includes resources and responsibilities, and a step-by-step review of the issue resolution process. The objective of the testing strategy is to provide overall direction and guidelines for testing all aspects of the system. This includes developing an overall approach to the testing effort, organizing and scheduling testing resources and the execution of test scripts, installing and configuring the test environment and tools as needed, and establishing the issues management process.

Tip

Create a separate application database instance for business system testing. This database instance should be for testing the application only. This provides a safe, clean, and static place for testing the application.

You should develop the testing strategy based on the characteristics of the customizations. You need to take into consideration how many custom modules are being developed, how much data is being converted, any system performance concerns, the number of interfaces, the scope and types of testing to be performed, and the level of importance of the system to the business.

To facilitate testing, develop a master test plan that consolidates all detailed test scripts into a complete checklist for testing the applications. Develop detailed scripts for each type of testing to be performed. The test scripts should include unit, link, integration and system testing. Unit tests may include checklists for the developers to check off as they execute the tests, making sure that they have performed specific activities and tasks. Integration, link, and system tests should include testing scenarios, with action steps to lead testers through the testing effort. These tests are sometimes called application thread tests because they weave themselves through a complete set of business scenarios from initial to final transactions.

When developing your business system tests, take advantage of the previously created project documentation. There is no sense developing this documentation from scratch. There are future process modules, which can lead you through the application, that can be used as direct input into the business system tests. As the project progresses there should be a continuous reuse of project deliverables. Each test will build on the previous, or if it is an initial document, you may still be able to use sections of other documents to create the draft. Most of the design documents, and the testing strategy should be completed by the end of this phase.

The business system tests are created to test, monitor, and document specific test scenarios executed within the applications. Each test scenario needs to include specific action steps, identify who is responsible for executing the steps, and identify the expected and actual results. As previously mentioned, make sure that testing is performed in an instance of the application that has sufficient and clean test data. It is important that you test in an instance that will yield valid results. These tests should be executed with data that will properly exercise the application functionality. If these tests are inadequately prepared, your team may be faced with a credibility problem. The users may think that it is the application, not your tests. Be sure to spend significant time and resources in the preparation and execution of your system tests.

The preparation for business system testing is normally underestimated by inexperienced project implementation teams. Adequate preparation includes carefully planning to thoroughly and efficiently test the application. You need to determine the number of resources, locations, organizations, and the deployment schedule prior to developing your test plans. Developing your test plans should be a carefully planned and organized effort. Good test plans yield good results.

In conclusion, consider the following thoughts as you progress with your implementation. If you want to improve the productivity and quality of the documentation, it may be best to outsource the development of these documents to a technical writer or other writing professionals. Take the design and development of your project documentation seriously because the implementation, maintenance, and ongoing support of your applications will rely heavily upon it. Also, don't underestimate the time required to develop these documents; most likely it will take longer than you think.

Performance Testing Preparation

When designing the performance testing approach, you need a test database and a method for populating the instance. You need to identify special loading programs and testing transactions to load and test the application. Often, organizations use a simplistic approach to stressing the applications using minimal data. As part of performance testing, be sure to use valid volumes of data when stress testing the applications, the database, and the technical architecture. Involve your users in this effort; they can add tremendous value and credibility to your testing. You also should develop performance monitoring scripts or take advantage of tools offered by Oracle such as Enterprise Manager. Establish a baseline for acceptable performance and measure how well the system does against that baseline after the systems go live.

Note

If you experience inconsistent problems with performance testing, you may want to revisit the database, network, and server sizing estimates created earlier in the project or provided to you by your vendors. You may be experiencing symptoms of poor capacity planning. Revisit the transaction volumes and frequency numbers, as well as determine whether the concurrent user estimates are accurate.

You do not need to test every transaction in the application; that would be time consuming and not worth the effort. You want to develop test models that will adequately test performance of the application. Your technical team can design and develop these test scripts with the assistance of your functional team members. They will work together to determine specific test scripts that simulate business transactions.

They also need to determine the amount of data and number of transactions to be tested. Normally, there is very little data in the testing instance, so you'll want to make sure that you have enough data to adequately stress test the database and system. Take advantage of the data conversion instance where data has already been loaded, or programs to load data into your performance testing instance. You can easily copy the data conversion instance to a performance testing instance to give your team the volume of data necessary for proper testing.

Note

If you have purchased a testing tool and don't have the expertise on staff, you may want to consider contracting or hiring someone with the product expertise to design your test scripts. Many times, testing can be flawed due to inexperience or inadequately trained project team members.

Automated testing tools can also be used for performance testing. The technical team will need to develop test scripts and configure the testing tools to simulate your user environment. Many testing tools are available that can simulate large environments and yield excellent testing results for adequate sizing, tuning, and configuration of your servers and network. You may want to consider contacting your hardware vendor to assist with performance testing, by providing information and benchmarks.

DESIGNING THE SUPPORT ORGANIZATION

Some organizations have already defined a support team, mostly referred to as the help desk, which provides support and could take on additional responsibilities of supporting the Oracle Applications. If you are lucky enough to have a dedicated and disciplined help desk, then continue to use it. You may want to review its procedures and determine whether there are any areas for improvement. You need to create a method to document, manage, and control support problems, whether you use previously defined procedures or design new ones.

Tip

As you design your help desk procedures, contact your software or hardware vendors to get ideas on how they handle support problems. The more ideas you can obtain, the better support service you can provide to your end users. Don't be afraid to ask questions and seek advice from your vendors.

Your help desk team needs to have in-depth knowledge of the Oracle Applications and your business to properly support your organization while in production. In some cases, it may be best to take some of your project staff and convert them into the help desk after the implementation. Most likely, these team members have been away from their original job duties while working with the project team and could move nicely into a support role.

Note

You also might consider purchasing a help desk software product that can integrate with your in-house e-mail product, and therefore integrate your help desk with the entire organization. For remote users, this can be a helpful and efficient way to communicate.

When the support organization and procedures are defined, remember, you need to communicate this information to your end users. Some organizations like to provide end users with this information as they participate in training. Consider designing a business card with contact information and general procedures, or develop a Web page with the help desk policies and procedures. Help desk information can be disseminated to the user community in many ways. You need to determine which approach is most effective in your organization.

SUMMARY

As you progress from phase to phase, additional requirements may be found. Consider their business value and determine whether they should be included in the scope of the project. You may also consider holding the requirement for another phase or project. Often, these requirements are superficial and once put on the shelf, never come off.

Being a part of an implementation is exciting and a learning exercise for you and your team members. Having the opportunity to design the way your business will operate in the future does not happen often. During this phase of the implementation, take advantage of the opportunities presented to you and your team to design the most efficient and effective organization possible.

CHAPTER 9

Enabling the System

In this chapter

The next phase of your implementation project is to prepare the system and your company for a change to the new software applications. The primary objective of this phase is to "code and test" customizations, conversions of data, interfaces, and modifications that have been identified and determined to be in scope for your project. If there are no customizations, data conversion, interfaces, or modifications, this phase is still important because of the business system test, or the conference room pilot (CRP). The CRP validates solutions and simulates your production environment and configuration. Other key tasks during this phase are the development and execution of performance test scripts, unit tests, and integration tests. Each of these tasks is vital to the success of this phase as well as the overall project.

This phase may overlap the Converting Analysis into Solutions phase of the project (see Chapter 8, "Converting Analysis into Solutions"). You don't want developers waiting around until the analysts have completed all the design documents for every customization before building the customizations. This overlapping schedule approach saves time and money. In many cases, you will have several developers on your project, each with his own skills and work pace. Don't feel as if each developer has to be synchronized, task by task, on the project. As long as the team is managed appropriately, customizations have been approved by the steering committee, and milestones are being met, let them work at their own pace and construct successful customizations to the applications.

This phase of the project should also be used to validate any documentation associated with tasks mentioned previously. Make sure that you receive supporting documentation for each customization that is within the scope of your project. Often, organizations are left without supporting documentation and must bring resources back to finish; make sure that documentation is reviewed at the same time.

Also during this phase, refine and update the documentation for any policies and procedures that were developed during the early phases of the project.

CUSTOMIZATIONS

A customization is a change made to a standard Oracle Application object that resolves a gap between the standard Oracle Application functionality and the requirements of the users and your business. Customizations to the Oracle Applications may be categorized in three ways:

- Extensions
- Modifications
- Interfaces

When making customizations to the Oracle Applications software, you must take the responsibility to maintain and support the code, and take into consideration what may happen during and after an upgrade to application software. Some activities that can be considered customizations include the following:

- Creating a new report or form
- Renaming or modifying a copy of an Oracle Application report or form

- Creating a one-time interface to convert legacy data for beginning balances or initial transactions
- Creating inbound or outbound interfaces to non-Oracle applications
- Creating new application alerts and workflows
- Creating any database object, including new tables, indexes, triggers, functions, packages, and procedures
- Renaming or modifying a copy of an Oracle Workflow

Requirements for customizations are normally found during the Analyzing the Project phase of an implementation (see Chapter 7, "Analyzing the Project"). Some customizations are known prior to the beginning of a project and are normally documented within the scope of the overall project. It is inevitable that requirements for customizations will change as the project team learns more about the application modules being implemented. Often, customizations are removed, and new ones are added. Make sure to update your project work plan when customizations are removed from the original scope of the project. You should document changes at this stage of the project with a change request form or a control log. The time for the original customizations should be substituted with new customizations or removed entirely from the scope of the project. Don't forget about these in the heat of trying to get other project tasks completed. For every customization, there is money that might be needed downstream in the project for more critical tasks or post-production support.

If you get into a situation where you have several large customizations, consider beginning work on them as soon as possible after the analysis and design are complete. Starting early on the biggest jobs will help expedite the build and test efforts. On the other hand, some implementation teams like to knock out all the easy customizations first. This all depends on the preferences of your project team and the needs of your management. You could also create a subproject for certain customizations. A subproject can be created to ensure more control over specific customizations. A subproject creates more finite management and control, and requires the assistance of a technical team lead to ensure milestones are met.

Modifications

Modifications are considered to be minor changes to forms, reports, and programs to resolve application gaps between customer requirements and Oracle Application functionality. The project team should consider application workarounds before undergoing a custom modification or new development. Some modifications may be classified as a configuration versus customization. Configuring an application module during setup is far less expensive than a customization.

Progressing from the Simple to Complex

When building customizations, start out small with some simple code or changes that will provide a fast return on investment. This technique will provide quick and positive feedback to your project team and management. You will build confidence in your team and in its ability to deliver good-quality work products.

CREATING AND TESTING CUSTOMIZATIONS

The actual creation effort for a customization should be a heads-down activity for developers. They should have frequent build reviews with the functional users to ensure progress is being made in the right direction. Often, developers go off and develop a form and report that looks nothing like what the user requested. This should not happen!

The testing effort should take place as an iterative process during the Enabling the System phase. As developers construct a customization, they should constantly be testing. This can be considered a unit test or a "desk check," where, while working at their desks they perform iterative tests, testing and retesting what they are building. The build and testing effort should not be distinct. Developers should consider performing desk checks and unit and link testing. Unit testing can be considered the second step of testing, whereas the desk check is first. Unit testing is designed to confirm the results of the gap analysis performed earlier in the project. It ensures that the solution or approach suggested meets each business requirement identified by the project team. Unit testing is also known as the developers' formal and final testing of their assigned customizations.

The expectation is to finish the test with the customization being solid under verifiable conditions with testing being performed under normal and abnormal operations. In addition, the unit testing should evaluate the initial, standalone measurement of performance. The developer or tester should show that the customization allows correct use and excludes incorrect use. When the testing is completed, the developer or tester can submit the customization to the next stage of testing.

The testing effort should be performed for each custom module until all have been thoroughly tested and are ready for system testing. Please review the section "Testing Strategies" found later in this chapter for additional discussion about unit, integration, and system testing.

After custom modules are complete, they should be moved from the development environment to a system test environment where they can be executed to ensure that all components work properly and to make sure the migration between instances worked correctly.

Migration of the customization depends on the type of change or new code that you are installing. Most organizations have a production load procedure where an objective team member moves custom objects from development to production.

DOCUMENTING THE CUSTOMIZATIONS

The documentation you create to support the customizations is indispensable to the ongoing maintenance and support of the application. If you include test plans and scenarios in the documentation, you will be able to easily execute those tests again during an upgrade project. Documentation should be constantly updated as the application is being tested and revised. All associated documents, such as the technical reference and users guide should be finalized only after all testing has been completed. This documentation can be easily converted into HTML and placed on your project's intranet Web site, or used to develop online help text for supporting your application.

Tip

Many excellent developers do not have good communications skills and try to avoid documentation activities. Consider developing the documentation at the same time you develop the functional specification for the customization. If you move documentation to the front of the development process, when testing validates that the program functions as documented, then you are done.

Consider using the Oracle manuals as a template for documenting customizations. For complex customizations, documentation should consist of a user's guide, a technical reference manual, and system management guide. The following documents can be created to support your customizations:

- **User's guide**—A road map of how to use the module or customization within the application.
- **Technical reference manual**—Can be used to support customizations after the implementation team has disbanded. This document describes technically how the customization was constructed, including tables, views, and code. The document also identifies what support tools are required. This document can be generated from the high-level and detail design documents developed in the earlier phases of the project. This also contains information on how to re-create the customization in case of code being lost, database corruption, or any other emergency.
- **System management guide**—Will be used by your system administrator, database administrator and applications administrator to support your customizations from a technical standpoint.

The user's reference manual/guide should be created to support the user and describe the features and functionality of the customization. Pay close attention to details because this document will support the customizations well after the implementation project is over.

The system management and technical reference guides discuss the technical aspects of the customization and what is required to install and maintain them. The technical documentation discusses how to execute the installation scripts required to support the customization, also the specific details of objects contained within. Keep in mind that all these documents can be derived from early documentation developed during the analysis phase of the project.

Tip

Don't skimp on documentation. If you need to hire a technical writer to develop all your documentation, do it. These documents will be the only representation of customizations that are created beyond the code itself.

Also, as previously mentioned, the use of installation routines can become critical to support each customization. These installation routines support the initial install as well as any future installations or upgrades. They also provide the capability to quickly recover after a system crash. The routines or documentation should be accessible to all personnel who are required to support or maintain the customizations in the production environment.

BUILDING CUSTOM REPORTS

If you understand the Oracle Applications data schema and the SQL language, building custom reports for Oracle Applications is relatively straightforward for a technical programmer with Developer 2000 or *6i* skills. However, building custom reports against the Applications database is not an end-user task. Reports can use PL/SQL to perform computations, implement conditional control, format data, and restrict output. Reports can be enhanced in appearance with the graphical layout editor and can be displayed via the output viewer to see exactly how your report will look when printed. There are no layout restrictions using Oracle Reports; report objects can be positioned anywhere you want.

DATA CONVERSION, INTERFACES, AND APIS

Data conversion should be considered as early in the project as possible. The conversion of legacy data can be complex and tedious depending on the cleanliness and integrity of the legacy data. Also, depending on the age of your legacy application, you may find that your newer staff is not familiar with the schema, file layout, or technology. Make an assessment of skills needed for data conversion and begin mapping your legacy application to the Oracle Application open interfaces as soon as you can.

During this phase of the project, the actual data conversion programs are developed. Determine which entities must be converted, such as customers or inventory items. Within the legacy applications, determine what data needs to be converted and what does not. It may not be a business requirement to carry closed invoice data, as well as the payments for each closed invoice, forward into your new Oracle Application.

Tip

Try to anticipate the level of data cleansing that will be required before converting data to Oracle Applications. If you have cleaner data coming into the Oracle Applications, you will have a better conversion. Data cleansing can be time consuming and requires someone with in-depth knowledge of the source application to lead the effort.

DETERMINING ORDER OF APPLICATIONS TO CONVERT

Determine the order in which the legacy application modules will be converted. All legacy module dependencies should be understood and taken into consideration prior to converting. For example, customer data needs to be converted prior to invoice data. Also decide how the data will be converted, whether manually or programmatically. Develop a simple mapping document to map each legacy application to the matching Oracle Application. This helps maintain the scope of what will be converted, and in what Oracle Application it will be converted.

MANUAL, PROGRAMMATIC, OR AUTOMATED DATA CONVERSION?

You will no doubt have some type of manual data conversion or cleanup on your data conversion project. If all data is converted successfully and there is no manual effort, you're way ahead of the game!

A benefit of manual data conversion is that data validation within the application is used for all data entered. One drawback of the manual process is that it is time consuming and might not be feasible if your data set is large. Take into consideration how long it will take for the manual transaction to be entered into the Oracle Applications and multiply that times the number of records that need to be converted. This will give you a rough idea of how long it will take to manually execute data conversion. Certainly, you can add resources, and your time goes down, but the cost and mistakes go up. Think about this alternative carefully.

The programmatic approach is one of the fastest ways to fulfill data conversion requirements. It does require that programs be written from scratch to load the database directly. There is good and bad with this approach as well. The good thing is that it speeds up data conversion time when the conversion actually takes place. Therefore, automated conversion is good to use with a lot of data. Based on the volume of data to be converted, a decision needs to be made on whether to choose manual over programmatic. There will be more time spent on writing the code to populate the tables than actually converting the data itself; therefore, this method can be more expensive. Data conversion scripts and programs can be written with tools such as SQL*Plus, Pro*C, Shell scripts, and PL/SQL.

To supplement or replace these programmatic conversion programs, an automated approach can be used by using a tool from a third-party vendor. These automation tools offer reusable preconfigured templates containing validation, mapping, and transformation rules and documentation providing an integrated, faster solution. These templates are available for many Oracle Applications including Manufacturing, Financials, Human Resources, and E-commerce. If you want to find out more about third-party conversion tool vendors, see the chapter titled "Finding Additional Compatible Solutions" on this book's Web site.

Although they are a more expensive solution, use of these commercially available conversion products may significantly improve the resource and time requirements of data conversion.

WRITING AND TESTING DATA CONVERSION PROGRAMS

Conversion programs that are written should be integrated into unit testing when test scripts are created. Some organizations that don't look at the conversion programs as part of testing find out the hard way when data has not been converted successfully or the integrity of the data has been jeopardized. I know of one company that failed to load about 20% of its item master before launching its new systems. The incomplete bills of material and MRP calculations were very expensive to correct.

Upon completing data conversion, the integrity of the data should be tested within each application. Also, validation tests should be executed to test the application with all this new data loaded. This performance test should cover all application modules and be included in the application integration testing.

Based on whether you are implementing in multiple phases or multiple organizations, you may need to perform and execute all data conversion tasks at different times. Coordination of this effort is important and should be scheduled according to all project implementation schedules.

DATA CONVERSION SIZING

Sizing of the application database seems to always be an issue when you are converting legacy data. There are estimating spreadsheets that are used early on in the project, or sometimes used by Oracle to recommend disk capacity.

Determine the number of records per object that will be converted. It's also helpful to indicate whether the object will be a one-time conversion or periodic.

As legacy data is converted, more of the allocated disk space is being consumed. Make sure that you have plenty of room to grow after all legacy data has been converted. Plan to revisit the disk capacity requirements for your production server during the Enabling the System phase. This gives you time to react to any unplanned disk capacity issues prior to the start of production business transaction processing.

USING THE OPEN INTERFACES

Open interfaces are provided with the Oracle Applications. They are primarily used to integrate with custom or non-Oracle applications. However, these interfaces are also used for importing historical data from legacy applications and from spreadsheets.

The following application modules have open interfaces available for use, and each has detailed information contained within the Oracle Open Interface manuals for Financials, Manufacturing, and Distribution applications:

- Oracle Assets
- Oracle General Ledger
- Oracle Inventory
- Oracle Order Management
- Oracle Payables
- Oracle Purchasing
- Oracle Receivables

The open interface documentation indicates which fields are mandatory and optional. It identifies key fields and whether a column should be null. The documents are helpful and should be used as a guide when converting data.

Tip

Make sure that you have the most recent version of the Oracle documentation on open interfaces when you start development. Occasionally, the specifications will change, and you can save a lot of testing time by developing from the information in the correct manuals.

Internally, Oracle Applications use many of the open interfaces for daily processing. These interface programs are scheduled in the Concurrent manager. The open interfaces validate the integrity of data and ensure that all business rules are met. The primary function of the open interfaces is to import data from Oracle and non-Oracle applications.

ORACLE HR APIS

The Oracle HR module has many application program interfaces or APIs that support such functions as creation of employees, creating grade rates, and payment methods. These APIs may be used to convert data, or pass transactions to the Oracle HR application. APIs pull data versus push, pulling data from a file in which you have defined, whereas the open interfaces receive, or are pushed data, from a source file. Unfortunately, APIs are not found in the Financial applications, so Financial users must continue to focus on using the open interfaces.

An advantage of APIs is that they validate data and enforce business rules that have been established by the application suite. Unfortunately, APIs can't be used directly by an end user and must be used within PL/SQL programs.

MANAGING THE PHASE

During this phase, one of the keys to success is having a strong technical team lead to manage and control the work effort. The team lead must continue to motivate and keep the team focused on tasks and achieving milestones. This person must have strong Oracle Applications and technology experience.

Managing the shift from phase to phase is difficult, more so from Solutions to Enabling the System. Normally, during this phase, you shift from functional activities to technical tasks. It's best to keep a strong functional team member on the duration of the project for the continuity of staff. Most implementation teams do not want to rotate the team members on and off the project. So, it's best to leave at least one strong functional staff member who can assist with issues and questions relating to the project. While the technical tasks are in process, the functional implementation team members can perform unit testing of customizations, validate configuration parameters, create documentation, create training materials, and perform an integrated conference room pilot during this phase of the project.

PHASE SUCCESS FACTORS

The following are some critical success factors to consider during this phase of a project:

- Obtain a clear understanding of the requirements of the project.
- Ensure accurate and comprehensive functional and technical design documentation.
- Encourage the involvement of user management.
- Assess the skills of the technical team early. If they are not what you need or are not performing at the expected level, obtain the proper skills!

PHASE MILESTONES

Activities considered milestones in this phase are the creation of a development environment, final data conversion mapping, documentation to support customizations, and a final version of each testing document. Upon successfully completing these activities, the project should be able to move onto the next phase. The following presents an overview of each milestone:

- **Development environment**—One of the most important milestones of this project phase is having a development environment readily available for the technical staff. From a technical perspective, having a separate application user where all custom objects reside is just as important but obviously can't be done without an application instance. As the project progresses, the use of modular code becomes a time-saver, as well as keeps code smaller and more organized for easier quality checks. Finally, the last technical milestone would be to have all the installation scripts and routines readily available in case of an emergency or in case the customizations need to be re-created for some reason.
- **Data conversion mapping documents and conversion programs**—Within data conversion there are a couple of milestones. The final data conversion mapping documents are of most importance. After these documents are created, then development staff can begin working on the conversion programs, which are considered the next milestone.

  After the conversion programs have been written and informal testing has been completed, unit testing of all the data that has been converted needs to take place. This helps enforce integrity constraints and ensures proper programming techniques and quality. When all data has been converted into the test or development environment, the data must be validated to its source. This validation can primarily be a user task, but most likely some technical assistance will be required—especially if large data sets are involved.
- **Documentation**—Documentation is one of the most important aspects of a project and is always one of the most difficult tasks to complete. A first milestone within documentation responsibilities is having the user's guide and reference manuals completed for the customizations. The following task of creating technical reference material, help desk and system administrator documentation comes next. The help desk documentation can be a boiled-down version of the system administrator document, or a complete guide. Certainly, this requirement depends on the knowledge and experience of the help desk operators.
- **Testing**—Testing milestones start with unit testing of customizations, data conversion, interfaces, or modifications as they are being developed by the applications development staff. Linking or integrating a customization into the application can be considered the next milestone for testing. This testing brings together the customization and the application into an integrated solution. System testing follows the integration testing and is the execution of thread and non-thread application tests throughout the application. Performance testing is the last testing to take place due to the overall objective it's trying to accomplish.

SETTING UP NEW HARDWARE

Each Oracle Applications implementation project must ensure that the development environment is ready on time. A development team must have the resources needed to be successful. If the hardware is not installed prior to the development team's arrival, this can become costly, in dollars, as well as lost personnel. Many projects try to time the arrival of technical staff as soon as the customizations have been identified and accepted. Not having the computing resources, such as workstations, connectivity to the network, access to the application and database server, and in some cases access to the IS Operations area, can cause major delays in this phase of the project.

Tip

Make sure that at least one development environment is set up and tested well before the technical staff starts on the project. Also, obtain technical team members' names prior to their arrival. Have the network, operating system, and application logins or accounts established for them when they walk in the door. Once on board, these folks should hit the ground running!

INSTALLING THE APPLICATIONS

At this point in the project, a test or development environment has been established for the technical staff to use all by themselves. Often, the technical staff will need to unit test a customization that may be integrated with an object within the application. It is best to have a separate instance of the application that will not affect the rest of the project team. Although some organizations like to copy the Vision Applications instance for use by the development staff, this procedure can be risky because the Vision Application doesn't contain the same configuration or functionality as the application that you are implementing. The Vision instance is primarily an Oracle sales tool used for application demos to prospective clients. The Vision applications are a copy of the Oracle Applications that can be installed prior to your implementation. Many organizations use Vision as their temporary playground prior to having a Test or Development application instance available.

OPTIMAL FLEXIBLE ARCHITECTURE STANDARD

The Optimal Flexible Architecture (OFA) concept was created several years ago by Oracle employees who decided to add some organization to the installation and support of Oracle Applications. OFA is the method for installing and organizing Oracle products on an application or database server or client. You will want to use OFA methods to organize the customizations to the applications as well.

The OFA-compliant directory structure provides a mechanism for organizing all Oracle Applications, standard or custom, under one top directory usually called $APPL_TOP. Each Oracle Application has a default top directory name and location, such as $FA_TOP. The directory architecture provides subdirectories under each application's top directory to store programs, forms, reports, shell scripts, data, and so on.

For example, the standard naming convention for the Oracle Fixed Assets home directory is FA_TOP. Customizations to Fixed Assets would reside in CUST_FA_TOP, where CUST would represent the directory for all Fixed Asset customizations with all the appropriate, or needed, subdirectories.

Many organizations use prefixes like CUST, or a short name for their organization, such as BOSS_FA_TOP, for BOSS Corporation Fixed Assets customizations. Be creative and consistent when establishing a customization prefix.

DELIVERABLES

Some major deliverables found in this phase of the implementation are the programs, reports, test scripts, and documentation required to support each customization. Many deliverables throughout this phase will be used during the remaining phases of the project. Some deliverables can be consolidated with others based on content, time, and need. The following paragraphs describe several key deliverables that should be considered during this phase.

For all custom objects, project team members need to create technical reference manuals, user's guides, and help desk documentation. Users will appreciate having this documentation for future reference, follow-up, and guidance during upgrades and installations.

Development of conversion programs and supporting documentation is essential to a project's success. Documenting the conversion programs, as well as which conversion programs have been tested and accepted by the end-user community, will be needed prior to executing them in production.

You need to document all installation routines for customizations. Often, these routines are not clearly documented, and when it comes time to install these objects into production, it is performed incorrectly. These routines include all shell scripts, SQL, SQL*Loader, and keystroke files that are required to install and configure customizations into the production environment. These are also good reference documents for production support, maintenance, and upgrades.

Unit, integration, and system testing of customizations are other vital steps to a successful project. Developing unit test documents for each customization will support the objects as they are transitioned into production. Your development or testing team will develop and execute these tests to ensure that quality and coding standards are met. The creation of an integration test document is written as part of the detailed design and is usually performed by several developers or test team members. These tests focus on all external application interfaces and help document associated programs and unit and link tests for the customizations.

System testing is written specifically for the business process flow and is performed by key project team members and end users. Because of the amount and complexity of these tests, additional end users are brought in to assist with the effort. The testing is performed after all unit and integration tests have passed. A combination of customizations, integration, and standard functionality is tested during these tests.

Another key deliverable found throughout the implementation, and most important during this phase, is the acceptance certificate. You may decide that on completion of each deliverable an acceptance certificate be signed by your end users. This certificate documents their acceptance and verification of your development team's work. Be sure you clearly communicated what is being signed and that acceptance means the requirement has been filled and that later changes mean a change in scope.

A deliverable sometimes overlooked and considered one of the most important, is the end-user training material. These documents are normally created by your application owners or end users. Some organizations hire technical writers or someone specifically for developing this type of documentation. This documentation is essential during the transition and production phases of your project.

TESTING STRATEGIES

The testing environment you create needs to support each type of testing that is planned, such as unit, integration, system, and acceptance testing. This environment should be unique and only accessible and used by the testing team. You don't want other team members using the testing instance as, or in conjunction with, the development instance.

Consider making the testing instance a standalone instance in which the data is only being changed by the testing team and no one else. The integrity of the testing data is vital to successful testing and if corrupted could invalidate all applications testing, cause inaccurate results, and create unnecessary tension within the project team.

Some testing concepts were discussed earlier in the chapter and will be solidified in the next few paragraphs. The primary emphasis during the testing activities involves testing all customizations as they move through unit testing in development to integration testing with the other application modules.

The use of test scripts is vital to the management and control of testing customizations. Test scripts guide users through the business systems testing effort as well as act as a tracking document for test success or failure. Each test script needs to be executed multiple times, preferably by different users, to be successfully tested.

On success or failure, certain activities should occur. If the test is a success, then document it appropriately and move onto the next steps or test. If the customization fails, then document the failure and notify the applications developer or team member responsible for the customization. Often, failures have a simple solution and can be resolved quickly by another team member. After the issues are thought to be resolved, re-execute the test and stay in this test loop until all testing is successful.

CONFERENCE ROOM PILOT

The APICS dictionary describes prototyping as "a product model constructed for testing and evaluation to see how the product performs before releasing the product to manufacture."

A Conference Room Pilot (CRP) is exactly that, a prototyping of the software functionality before releasing the product to the end user.

Each customization should be prototyped and executed during a series of detailed pilots or a module walk-through. Each pilot should be designed to target a specific stage, event, or business process of the implementation and determine success or failure as the outcome.

Some organizations may want to have separate module walk-through and prototyping sessions for departmental customizations. The execution of a CRP is conducted by the entire team to validate the interoperability of business processes. I call the final conference room pilot the dress rehearsal for the new system because all players should be involved using real-world business transactions to test the system.

This effort allows all decisions to benefit the entire organization and not just one department.

SOME ALTERNATIVES TO CUSTOMIZATIONS

Due to the cost and complexity of customizations, alternatives should be considered. Instead of building a new multirow form, maybe consider customizing a standard folder to fulfill your end user's requirements. Think of ways to utilize standard features of Oracle Applications such as folders, flexfields, and the custom library.

FOLDERS

A folder is a special block within an Oracle Application form that resembles an Excel spreadsheet. Folder block field and record layout can be customized to retrieve a subset of records or display records in a different format.

Tip

When saving folders, be creative with their names. Users often name folders something that doesn't relate to what the folder does. If the folder is set up to query all open purchase orders, then save the folder as "Open Purchase Orders," not MyFolder. Each folder should be saved with a name that represents the layout of the fields or query criteria selected. If your organization uses many folders, you may want to consider developing a naming convention. If users recognize a public folder because its name is intuitive, it will be used.

On installation of the Oracle Applications, a default folder block is available. This folder can be modified and saved as a new customized folder. The customized default folder is easily distinguished from the original folder because its name appears next to the Open Folder button on the form.

The Folder Tools button is enabled when you navigate to a folder block. By selecting the button, a tools palette will be displayed. The following buttons are available for customizing a folder:

- **Open Folder**—Allows you to select another folder to open
- **Save Folder**—Allows you to save a modified folder
- **Create New Folder**—Provides capability to create a folder
- **Delete Folder**—Provides capability to select a folder to delete
- **Widen Field**—Increases field width
- **Shrink Field**—Decreases field width

- **Show Field**—Shows an undisplayed field
- **Hide Field**—Hides a displayed field
- **Move Left**—Moves field to the left
- **Move Right**—Moves field to the right
- **Move Up**—Moves field up one character height
- **Move Down**—Moves field down one character height

FOLDER QUERIES

Folders can be further enhanced by defining queries. You can customize a folder to retrieve only the records you want to see. Altering the query criteria of the folder and saving the folder can do this. When in a multirecord block, you can alter the sorting order of the records retrieved.

Defining a query is simple and is created as follows:

1. Navigate to the appropriate application folder.
2. Execute query by using Query find or query-by-example (QBE).
3. Select Save As on the Folder menu if you want to save this version of the folder.
4. Provide a name for the folder. Associating it with the query criteria provides an easy understanding of what the folder provides.
5. Select an Autoquery Option Group—Always, Never, or Ask Each Time:
    - If Always is selected, the query automatically is executed each time the folder is opened.
    - If Never is selected, the query is not executed when the folder is opened.
    - If Ask Each Time is selected, the query prompt appears each time the folder is opened.
6. Select OK. The folder is now created.

Note

On saving a folder, the query criteria is saved at the same time as the default query. If data is initially retrieved on opening the folder, each subsequent query is executed on this initial subset of data. If you want to enter a new query on all data, you need to reset or remove the default query within the folder before proceeding with another query.

Occasionally, you may want to view the query criteria for a specific folder. By selecting the Choose View Query from the Folder menu, a window called Folder Contents appears.

This window may display the WHERE clause that is used for criteria to retrieve the records displayed for the selected folder. If the window is empty, then there is no SQL WHERE clause defined, and all records will be retrieved.

There may also be times when the query must be reset. In this case, choose the Reset Query option from the Folder menu. After this is selected, the WHERE clause is cleared from the current folder. Executing this only resets the WHERE clause and not the folder name or layout. On resetting the query, perform another query and choose the Save option on the Folder menu to save the current folder with the query criteria.

SORTING IN A FOLDER

As mentioned earlier, sorting the retrieved records in a multirecord folder is simple and can be done by selecting the Show Order By option from the Folder menu. After this is selected, sort buttons appear directly below the first three fields of the folder block.

The sort buttons may be clicked for different settings, such as ascending, descending, and unsorted. Depending on which sort is selected, the folder displays the records accordingly. The sort is applied to the records from left to right when the records are retrieved. After the sorting options are selected, choose the Run option from the Query menu to execute the query to see the changes.

Folders are a powerful and inexpensive way to customize Oracle Applications. Power users who have been trained and educated on foldering capabilities primarily create folders. Folders were created with end users in mind. With a little practice and patience, you can create folders to improve your use of Oracle Applications.

FLEXFIELDS

Flexfields are user-defined data-entry fields that are available throughout the Oracle Applications. They can be used to customize Oracle Applications without programming. The two types of flexfields are key and descriptive.

When designing a key or descriptive flexfield, take your time and create a design acceptable to all personnel affected. Organizations sometimes rush through this effort only to find that they are capturing too much information or not enough. First, create a team to design and develop your flexfield structure and values. This is time well spent and will keep all concerned parties informed and part of the definition and decision-making process. Second, design the structure such that it is flexible enough for future growth or easy expansion.

Because flexfields do not require programming, they allow you to perform significant customizations to the Oracle Applications relatively easily. These "flexfield customizations" are extensions to the applications guaranteed by Oracle to be preserved through an upgrade. The use of key and descriptive flexfields versus customizations saves time and money and allows for a smoother and more efficient upgrade in the future.

KEY FLEXFIELDS

Key flexfields are commonly used when multisegment values such as account numbers and inventory part numbers are required. They are made up of segments that have a value and a meaning. Key flexfields are usually stored in the *SEGMENTx* columns of an Oracle Applications database table. Key flexfields are referred to as an intelligent field that organizations can use to capture information represented as codes.

DESCRIPTIVE FLEXFIELDS

Descriptive flexfields are used to capture additional information in generic fields. If the Oracle Applications do not provide a field, a descriptive flexfield can provide the capability to expand application forms to capture additional information organizations may need. A descriptive flexfield is represented by a two-character unnamed field enclosed by brackets, or as some like to say, "it looks like a two-fisted beer mug."

As you're reading this, you may be wondering why descriptive flexfields are being mentioned in the Enabling the System phase. When organizations must customize a form to capture additional information on a row, or about a certain subject, they should first try to use a descriptive flexfield. Organizations can customize descriptive flexfields to include many locally defined fields. These fields are also referred to as segments and appear in the descriptive flexfield window. Descriptive flexfields are usually stored in the *attribute* columns of an Oracle Application database table.

Each segment of a descriptive flexfield has a name and associated value. The values used within the descriptive flexfield can be independent or dependent on other descriptive segment values. Descriptive flexfields are widely used by organizations and continue to be an excellent way to extend the usability of Oracle Applications.

USING THE CUSTOM LIBRARY

Use of the Custom library allows extensions of Oracle Application modules without modifying module code. The Custom Library is a PL/SQL library for use throughout Oracle Applications. The Custom library can be used for customizations such as zooms, enforcing business rules, and disabling application form fields. The Custom library is available for use only by Oracle Application customers.

Procedure shells also are available for developing your own custom code. The code is written inside these shells where logic is associated with a specific form and block in which the code is to run. These procedure shells add a layer of flexibility in the use of the Custom library. There is no predefined logic in the Custom library other than the procedure shells.

The Custom library also supports application events. These events are executed throughout Oracle Applications, and custom code can be written in conjunction with them to perform various types of transactions. There are two different kinds of applications events: generic and product-specific. Generic events are available to all Oracle Application forms. The generic events are as follows:

- WHEN-FORM-NAVIGATE
- WHEN-NEW-FORM-INSTANCE
- WHEN-NEW-BLOCK-INSTANCE
- WHEN-NEW-RECORD-INSTANCE
- WHEN-NEW-ITEM-INSTANCE
- WHEN-VALIDATE-RECORD

- SPECIAL*n* (*n* represents number)
- ZOOM
- EXPORT
- KEY-F*n* (where *n* is a number between 1 and 8)

The Custom library can be used in five cases:

- Zooming to open another form and possibly pass parameters to the new form
- Logic for generic events to augment the logic provided by the Oracle Applications
- Logic for product-specific events to augment or replace Oracle logic
- Custom entries for the special menu
- Setting visual attributes to make some fields appear different at runtime

Each case must be coded differently. Zooms are fairly simple and straightforward. They typically consist of opening an Oracle Application form and passing parameter values to the form via Zoom logic. This can be an effective way to execute inquiry forms from an application module. An example could be to Zoom to an Inventory form from the Order Management screen to inquire about the on-hand balance for a particular product.

Generic and specific events actually extend Oracle Applications through the use of events such as WHEN-NEW-FORM-INSTANCE, WHEN-VALIDATE-RECORD, or WHEN-NEW-BLOCK-INSTANCE. See the complete list of events presented earlier. The product-specific events can augment or replace applications logic for certain products or business rules. Be cautious when using this type of event because the expected results may vary due to the complexities of the Oracle Applications code. Be sure to thoroughly test all your customizations.

BUILDING CODE WITH THE CUSTOM LIBRARY

The Custom library can be found in the `$AU_TOP/res/plsql` directory. After designing and developing your own code, you must replace the default Custom library. After your code has been written, you must compile and generate the library using Oracle Forms on the applications server (not the development machine) and place it into the `$AU_TOP/resource` directory. Active Oracle Applications users need to exit the applications and log back in to execute the newly written code.

Tip

Oracle Forms always uses a . plx (complied code) for a library over the .pll. The .plx file is created when you generate a library using the Forms generator COMPILE_ALL parameter set to 'YES', not when you compile and save using Designer. The best thing to do is delete the .plx file to allow your code to run from the .pll or create your own .plx file using the Forms generator. However, using the .plx file produces better performance than the .pll file.

The Custom package within the Custom library cannot be changed. Packages added to the Custom library must be added after the Custom package and must begin with an alphabetical letter after "C". Oracle recommends that custom packages begin with "USER_" for the code to remain sequenced appropriately.

Recommendations and Coding Standards for the Custom Library

These are some supporting comments, considerations, restrictions, and recommendations when using the Custom library.

When adding code to the Custom library, keep in mind that Oracle Applications may run in many environments. The following are some considerations and restrictions you should understand when using the Custom library or any additional libraries:

- You cannot use any SQL in the library.
- PL/SQL package variables do not change between calls to the Custom library. This also has no bearing on which form actually makes the call.
- PL/SQL code contained within the Startup code (Package but not in a function or procedure) is executed only once when the Custom library is initially called.
- The `custom.pll` file can't exceed 64KB.
- Global variables contained within Oracle Forms are visible to all running forms.

Tip

When you need to know the names of blocks, fields, or particular items within Oracle Applications, use the Examine feature from within the appropriate application form by going to the Help, Tools menu option.

The use of coding standards within the Custom library is important. The Developer/2000 and 6*i* products must support all code. The only exception is that you cannot call APPCORE routines from the Custom library or from within any Zoom, or other event. Almost all APPCORE routines begin with the "APP" prefix. Starting with 11*i* you can attach the APPCORE2 library to the Custom library. APPCORE2 duplicates most of the APPCORE functions.

After an upgrade, the following items should be considered regarding customizations to the Custom library. If there are problems with forms operating with a version of the Custom library that has changed, the Custom code can be turned off temporarily by executing the menu choice Help, Tools, Custom Code, Off until the problem has been resolved. The Oracle Applications code can be evaluated while the Custom code is turned off. Earlier versions of Oracle Applications require the Custom library shipped with the applications to be replaced versus the capability to turn it on/off via the menu option.

Prior to upgrading Oracle Applications, make a backup copy of your current Custom library. If a backup is not made, you will lose all changes made to the Custom library because the upgrade will install a new version of the Custom library. After the upgrade, all custom logic should be tested to ensure that the code still operates as intended.

PERFORMANCE TESTING

The Oracle ERP Applications can consume large amounts of server, network, desktop, and disk resources, and some customers experience slow response times when a full business load is placed on the system. If there is any doubt about the capability of the infrastructure to handle the load, performance testing is normally conducted during this phase of a project, and this testing can help to avoid response-time problems. Many implementation projects make the decision to not perform performance testing tasks. This decision may cause the project schedule to slip due to inaccurate and insufficient computing resources.

Performance testing should happen early enough in the project to allow for timely resolution. Testing results should be analyzed and documented. System administrators and DBAs need to perform as much technical environment testing as possible. They need to make sure that the test environment is stable and operating at an acceptable level, so that there is no delay with system or integration testing. Delays or false starts cause frustration on the application team and erode the credibility of your technical staff.

The technical team should test all transaction programs, test scripts, data conversions, and the database itself, in a test instance of the database. The testing time taken at this stage of the project may save a great deal of user time, money, and frustration in the future. Performance testing often defines some type of problem or system bottleneck.

Tuning and retuning happens on a regular basis during heavy transaction volume testing. Certain test parameters or a specific configuration may require multiple tests to be performed to properly tune for realistic results. Tuning needs to be proactive instead of reactive. If the database is being monitored proactively, there's a good chance that problems can be found prior to the users even noticing.

After performance testing has been completed, a formal report can be generated and presented to management as needed. All the code and scripts written will be useful in the future, so put them in a safe place; you'll need them. Developing a toolbox of performance monitoring code and scripts is an excellent investment in time for DBAs. Having the right tools available in a crisis can make the difference between success and failure.

The test environment can be used as a baseline environment for future testing of enhancements, reports, and so on. Try to keep the environment static so that the baseline performance numbers you generated do not constantly need to be refreshed. Following are some of the tasks your DBA and system administrator may perform during or prior to this phase:

- Preparation of hardware, software, and network
- Installation of performance monitoring tools
- Installation and configuration of a test environment
- Installation and configuration of test scripts and transaction programs

Performance Testing Tools

Many performance testing products are on the market today. Some vendors offer automated software that provides a complete testing solution for Oracle Applications. These products have the capability to predict system performance, verify functionality, and test scalability. These products can also manage the entire testing process. See the chapter titled "Finding Additional Compatible Solutions," on this book's Web site, for a list of vendors and their product offerings.

Additional Reference Material

This section covers additional documentation and products that can assist you in this phase as well as the entire project. Most of this documentation and reference material is not free. You must contact Oracle Documentation Sales, or your Oracle Sales representative for additional information.

Technical Reference Manuals

Oracle Applications Technical reference manuals, or TRMs, are available for all Oracle Applications modules. This documentation provides the entire Oracle Applications database schema with all tables, columns, indexes, and views. This documentation is available on the 11*i* disks, but the TRMs are propriety information and are covered by your software license with Oracle Corporation.

Understanding the Position of Oracle Support

Oracle will support customizations that follow the standards identified within the Oracle Applications Coding Standards document. Following Oracle guidelines and standards is the most logical and safest approach. Play it safe and follow Oracle's recommendations. If you want to read more about Oracle Support, see the chapter titled "Working with Support" on this book's Web site.

Summary

Customizations are a common occurrence during Oracle Applications implementations. Many organizations indicate they would like to execute a "vanilla" implementation, installing the Oracle Applications with *no* customizations. This hardly ends up being the case. Because customizations will exist in varying areas of the application, from Alerts to designing your own Oracle Payables check, they will exist in some form for all implementations.

With this in mind, the use of design and build standards is critical during Oracle Applications implementations. If your organization doesn't employ these practices today, consider acquiring consultants or hiring staff that can bring a method or discipline to your organization. You can also review Chapter 8 for additional thoughts and ideas about creating your own customization standards and methods.

After all customizations have been created and documented and your project team has been dismantled and members returned to their real jobs, someone needs to maintain the system. The next chapter, Chapter 10, "Launching Your New Systems," will help you understand how to manage and control your production environment.

CHAPTER 10

Launching Your New Systems

In this chapter

This chapter is about managing change, transitioning from old to new systems, and supporting your production applications. These activities facilitate the first use of the ERP software by your users. Typical activities include training users, converting beginning balances and historical data from the legacy system, and migrating proven solutions from a pilot database to a production system.

MANAGING CHANGE

Managing change is one of the most important things you can do to improve the success of your software implementation. The capability of the organization to absorb change is a key factor to the critical path and the total cost of the project. The critical path is the series of tasks that must be completed in sequence and on schedule for the project to finish on time. Because each activity on the critical path must finish without delay, you must manage the changes caused by those activities to stay on schedule. Many information technology professionals, project sponsors, and project managers view an Oracle ERP project as a technical activity involving new computers, a sophisticated database management system, and complex application software.

In reality, implementing a big ERP system is about half technological issues and half organizational and human issues. It is easy to focus on the technology and overlook the nontechnical side of the project. Try to avoid that mistake.

The impact of these complex software packages will be felt throughout your company. The dynamics of your project may require action by the project team to accomplish the following:

- Manage changes in the organizational structure
- Facilitate the alteration of business processes
- Gain concurrence on process modifications
- Neutralize barriers to change
- Promote adoption of the system in various functional departments and geographical sites

COMMUNICATING

Communication is a key activity throughout the ERP project, and you should not wait until the transition phase to begin communicating. ERP systems force a lot of adjustment on an organization, and everyone must understand what is happening, when the changes will happen, who will make them happen, and why they must happen. Consider the following techniques to establish interest, trust, and confidence in the new systems:

- Stage demonstrations for the steering committee and key users. Target certain key employees for communication and try to reach beyond just the interested users.
- Make sure you tell everyone about the boundaries and scope of your project.
- Get the users involved with resolution of issues and make sure concerns are addressed. If there were employees who wanted to participate and were excluded from the implementation team, consider trying to involve them during testing.

- Publish your project materials to the entire organization. Set up a Web page with links to the project schedule, deliverables, status reports, issue logs, meeting minutes, and so forth. Set up e-mail distribution lists and use them to push these materials to the people who need to see them but who are too busy to pull them from the Web page. Also, consider adding general interest articles to your company newsletter to advertise the project. You must sell the project internally to get key employees to buy in to your activities.
- Be enthusiastic, open, honest, and available.
- Schedule regular steering committee meetings and make these managers work on the project. If everything is going well and they have nothing to do, invent some minor issues to keep the members interested and participating. Don't let the steering committee become an uninformed rubber stamp that just approves project activities.
- Listen to what the users are telling you and understand their agenda and concerns.
- Interface with other software projects and company programs that are causing change at the same time as your project.

ESTABLISHING USER AND MANAGEMENT EXPECTATIONS

Accurately setting user and management expectations is quite important to your successful project. If you are expected to deliver a perfectly working system that meets every desire business ever had, you will have a difficult transition. On the other hand, if your users and management understand that the complexity of these integrated systems might cause problems and if they take responsibility to resolve problems as a normal business activity, the transition to the new ERP systems will be much smoother. Frequent and honest communication is the best way to set the expectations of your constituents.

Tip

Many ERP projects have difficulty because the organization was not prepared to accept change or they were expecting something different or better. Deal with erroneous expectations as soon as you become aware of them–this improves the acceptance of the new software.

RESOLVING ISSUES AND CONCERNS

If you do a good job of resolving issues at each stage of the project, the transition phase will be easy and uneventful. If you don't address issues and concerns, you will have to resolve "show stopper" items at the most inconvenient time (during transition), you might lose control of the schedule, and you might have to delay the start of the system.

There are several ways to resolve issues. Try making a master log entry for every issue to make sure all concerns are tracked. Publish the log regularly. Assign each issue to a responsible person for resolution and determine the due date. If the due date is missed, it is possible you don't have a critical resolution factor. Perhaps the responsible person doesn't have the authority or political consensus to close the item. Don't be afraid to escalate issues to the ERP project steering committee or to the sponsor.

Also, act on items that are out of the scope of your project but that your organization wants to put into scope. A common example is an immature reporting strategy. For example, if your company really wants data warehouse-like reporting from the online transaction processing system, you must deal with expectations that you cannot meet with a basic Oracle ERP system.

HOW MUCH TRAINING IS APPROPRIATE?

Training users is a significant change-management activity. Training provides information about change and sets new expectations for acceptable behavior. Training requirements are different in every organization. Small groups of users might be trained on the job just a few days before the production systems go live. Larger groups of users with many integrated applications require formal, cross-functional classroom training led by instructors.

Tip

Budget carefully for training because this activity can require significant amounts of money and time. One rule of thumb is to allow between 10%–15% of the total project budget for training activities.

Consider special-needs training for certain users of the system. For example, the high-level manager who approves a purchase order only once a week will have radically different training needs than the help desk staff who must support that manager. Consider the audience to be trained and the appropriate level of detail to present. The technical staff of database administrators, system administrators, and support staff often have special training needs, and these people must achieve a high level of proficiency before the system goes live.

TRANSITIONING TO NEW SYSTEMS

The success of your final conference room pilot—the dress rehearsal—usually dictates when it is safe to migrate to the transition phase of the project. If the pilot raises issues from key users about business process steps, missing reports, format of business forms, system response time, and so forth, you are not ready for transition.

Everyone has heard stories of failed implementations and blown budgets. If you are going to have problems, they will show up in the transition phase. An honest reappraisal of your risks and preparedness is worthwhile at this point. Listen carefully to what the users are saying as they become familiar with the new software.

This phase of the implementation should involve user training and a fairly mechanical process to migrate your legacy data and proven solutions to a production database. If you are still programming customizations, chasing bugs, formulating company policy, selecting configuration parameters, debating the best business process flow, and so forth, you are still building the system. Because these activities can disrupt the transition phase, you must proceed carefully if they are still occurring.

Preparing for the Transition

Just like during any other phase of the implementation project, you should plan and prepare for the transition from legacy systems to your new Oracle ERP applications. You might have significant tasks if you have large numbers of users to train or large volumes of data to convert from the legacy system. Consider the following items as you create your transition plan:

- Define the goals of the implementation project team for the transition phase. Identify the goals of each group of users.
- Define the scope of the transition activities. For example, identify how much legacy data will be converted by the time the system goes to production status.
- Determine the sequence of events. Create a script of tasks, responsibilities, dependencies, and due dates. Since it is easy to overload your project team and your launch date is important, make sure the due dates are realistic and coordinated with work schedules.
- Identify who will perform the user training.
- Double-check the commitment and level of participation of your senior management. Will management help you to establish new job roles, create new business processes, activate new business requirements, deal with out-of-scope situations, and support user training schedules and content?
- Define the criteria you will use to accept the quality of training materials, configuration of the production instance, customization documentation, and conversion accuracy.
- Determine who will install the production software, who will configure each application, who will maintain the production system, when production maintenance officially will start, and when users should access the new system for the first time.
- Determine the activities needed to shut down and disable the legacy system.
- Identify how the user support infrastructure will work. Determine special support requirements for the first three months after the go-live date. Communicate problem resolution procedures to the users.
- Consider whether parts of the legacy system should run parallel for a number of days. For example, you might schedule full parallel runs for several payrolls.
- Perform an analysis to determine the point of no return to your legacy system. Identify your contingency options and procedures.
- Describe the detailed criteria to determine your organization's readiness to switch systems. Some companies simply hold a go/no-go vote and some users vote for production status because of political pressure or ignorance of what is about to happen. Detailed criteria are important to determine your true readiness status and are your true indicators that the users are ready to operate the software.
- Determine how you and the organization will respond to users' requests to change the scope of the system.

CONFIGURING THE PRODUCTION SYSTEM

You must manually install and configure your production version of the Oracle ERP Applications. Because the configuration steps for each application must be accomplished in sequence and the forms under the setup menu use a lot of logic and perform required validation, you must reenter the configuration for each application. This manual process is required, even though you might have several working systems for pilot, test, and training, because you cannot create a production version by copying pieces of other systems.

Because this manual configuration process takes several days for the full implementation team and the schedule is tight during the transition phase, consider making a backup copy of the system after the configuration is complete. This backup copy might be valuable if problems are encountered during data conversion or when production transaction processing starts. Also, you might want to take a backup of the system, immediately before the first transactions start.

TRAINING YOUR USERS

The primary question a user has when entering a training program is "How do I do my job with this new software?" You want to be able to answer that question. Of course, since your ERP implementation may have fundamentally reengineered the user's responsibilities and business process, you might have to deal with the fundamental definition of the user's job. For this reason, the more sophisticated training activities use a role-based, process-oriented approach. If you are presenting new concepts or significant change to clerical users, ask a responsible functional leader to participate and endorse the new systems as part of the training.

Tip

Ease of use and training should be top priorities for an ERP project, because integrated applications reach new users who may be unfamiliar with ERP systems.

During user training, you must respond to changes in the workload caused by the new ERP systems. Depending on the capabilities of your legacy systems, some users may experience an increase in effort required to accomplish their key business function. For example, users of Oracle Order Management and Purchasing Applications often complain of extra data-entry requirements when they first see the new software. If the instructors can explain how the expanded data entry enables new or more powerful business functions, the users can balance their complaints with appreciation for new features such as advanced scheduling or pay on receipt processing.

The users doing the additional work will still be unhappy, but they will be less unhappy than if you just blame the Oracle system for the increased workload. Try to explain the Oracle system requirements in a way that shows how they enable your business goals and meet your requirements.

Consider the following activities and items as you train users:

- If you have many users to train, prepare a dedicated training environment. Create a separate installation of the applications to isolate training from data conversion and keep untrained users away from the production system.
- Many companies adopt a "train the trainer" strategy when they start the ERP project because that phrase sounds clever and easy to execute. This approach assumes the project team or power users will become trained in the software during the course of the project, and they will be able to perform the user training for little or no cost. Since there are special skills required to be an effective trainer, consider the effectiveness of this strategy when you determine who will be instructors, and consider training the trainers in how to train.
- Review user procedures, policies, and requirements. If you are changing any business processes, be prepared to show the users how each step of their current process will be transformed in the new system.
- If appropriate, use actual business scenarios and transactions in instructor demonstrations and user laboratories. You may have extra setup requirements to use actual scenarios. For example, if you want to train the AP three-way match process, you must create several purchase orders and make receipt transactions before the class starts.
- One hour of formal classroom training can require a day of preparation by a skilled instructor. A full day of instructor lead training might take a week to prepare training materials and set up data for examples and exercises.
- Prepare training aids such as quick reference cards, keyboard templates, help desk procedures, and lists of common navigation paths for users to take away from class.
- If users must retain classroom material for more than a few days before they use it in production, assign exercises to be performed between the time the class ends and the system goes live. Provide a test database for the users to practice their new skills on their own.
- Prepare an instructor and classroom schedule. Make sure classrooms are fully equipped, and that the response time of the training system is appropriate.
- Consider how some classes may be prerequisites for other training. Some users with broad business roles may require seven to ten classes. Consider providing cross-functional classes for some users with more theory and less detail than you provide to the daily users.
- Take attendance and determine how you will handle absenteeism. If you don't address absenteeism during transition, the effects will show up rapidly after the system starts business transactions.
- Collect and review feedback from the training sessions. You don't have to measure the popularity of the instructor, but you want to determine at the earliest possible time whether the users will be able to operate the system. Some organizations use a formal student survey at the end of each class. You should also talk to a sample of users to get extended feedback.

- Plan for continued training. Save materials, class notes, and the training database instance. These items may become valuable during a software upgrade or as new users are added to the system. After the system has been operational for a few months, consider providing both advanced user classes to explore underutilized features and remedial classes to improve productivity.

CONVERTING AND LOADING DATA

In the previous project phases, you analyzed, created, documented, and tested data conversion programs and scripts. During the transition phase, you perform the data conversion into the production database. Since the Oracle database generates relationships and distinct primary keys each time data is loaded, the conversion load process must be repeated on each database, and you cannot simply copy or export/import the data from the test database. For each data entity such as customers, items, general ledger balances, and so forth, perform the following tasks:

- Extract data from legacy systems. Make sure you know which data are time-sensitive and observe proper transaction cut-off procedures.
- Run conversion programs, spreadsheets, and scripts to clean, validate, load, convert, and audit the legacy data.
- Check on the actual volume of data. Verify row counts, records processed, and records that did not validate.
- Repair invalid records and reload them.
- Begin maintenance of data by responsible users.
- Perform data entry on entities to be converted manually.
- Verify and reconcile balances. For example, the trial balance in the Oracle General Ledger should be the same as on the legacy system. When the change in systems forces a complex reconciliation, such as when the chart of accounts changes, involve the users to ensure that all is satisfactory.

DEALING WITH THE NEW RELEASE

Since your implementation project might take longer than eight or nine months, Oracle may release a new version of the ERP software while your project is in progress and before you launch your systems.

Tip

Consider carefully your desire to install the new software release if you are in the transition phase. What you are really contemplating is an upgrade, and that action is a project within itself. To avoid invalidating your testing, training, configuration, customization, and documentation, you must freeze the system at some point and launch your new systems from a known and stable configuration.

Preparing to Support Production Users

In the transition phase, you determine and set up your production support infrastructure. Every organization is different and has procedures for user support. Small companies might simply establish a buddy system among implementation team power users and novice users. Larger companies may have already established a help desk organization to take over support from the implementation team. Consider the following activities to establish your support infrastructure:

- Make sure points of contact with Oracle support are well established.
- Transfer the library of project deliverables and documentation from the implementation team to the support group.
- As required, create special responsibilities within the Oracle Applications for support staff.
- Perform additional functional, cross-functional, and business process training for support personnel.
- Consider obtaining extra copies of Oracle reference manuals, technical reference manuals, and user guides.
- Train everyone to use the online help. In release 11*i* it is in Web page format, it is context-sensitive, and it is quite good.
- Implement an online system to track issues and problems.
- Establish a procedure for users to make change requests.
- Create a test database instance as a copy of the production instance. Use this instance as a staging area to test patches from Oracle Support before applying them to your production database.
- Establish a bug reporting and tracking procedure.
- If you have multiple sites, distribute all procedures and support materials to all locations.

Supporting Production Operations

When you put a full transaction load on the applications, the system achieves production status. Due to the nature of the business process, not all applications start transacting immediately. For example, the first payables check run may be a full week after purchasing goes live and the first fiscal close of the general ledger may be five weeks after the revenue and inventory transactions begin.

Production support involves auditing, maintaining, tuning, and improving the systems. The production launch date is not the end of the ERP project activities, and post-launch tasks can easily continue for a year or more.

Auditing the Production Systems

Go back to the documentation you created during the planning and analysis phases of the implementation project. Verify that you are meeting the goals and business requirements that you identified at the beginning of your project.

Determine your return on investment (ROI) for the new software. This calculation takes several months or even more than a year because you have to measure results and convert the change in your key performance indicators to hard currency. However, make sure you save key statistics from the legacy system as you shut it down so that you have something to compare. For example, if one of your project goals was to improve inventory turnover 30%, you need to know how the old system was performing to make a valid comparison with the Oracle software.

Tip

Consider conducting a formal user satisfaction survey or at least interviews with key users. Try to quantify a baseline satisfaction level and measure improvements against the baseline. Take the survey about four months after the systems go live, and use the results to start the continuous improvement activities for the system.

MAINTAINING THE PRODUCTION SYSTEMS

Within a few hours of launching the system, you must begin system maintenance and administration activities.

Make sure transactions are not hung up in the interfaces. For example, two days after start up in July 1998, I saw a new user make a simple keystroke error and enter a July 1988 date in the Ship Confirm window of Order Entry. The invoicing interface would not process the shipment because July 1988 was not in the fiscal calendar. Most interfaces produce a validation report or have a window to show unprocessed transactions and you should look for invalid transactions.

Tip

Some interfaces require a technical person to correct the data in the transaction interface table with Structured Query Language (SQL).

Activate database and hardware fault-tolerant systems for backup, archive, and restoration of production data. Verify that the fault-tolerance systems and procedures are actually working. If required, implement changes to your disaster-recovery procedures.

Activate daily, weekly, or monthly postings of the AP, AR, PO, INV, PAY, PA, and FA subledgers to the general ledger. Balance and reconcile the subledgers to the general ledger. Activate and monitor interfaces to and from non-Oracle computer systems.

Apply patches after appropriate testing and check regularly for invalid database objects. You should keep your Oracle system reasonably current to gain the most from your service from Oracle support. You must balance the production system' s need for stability with the need to fix problems and remain close to the current release level of the software.

Note

Invalid database objects are not the same as invalid data. An invalid database object may be a piece of a program logic that is used by a window or report. If a patch causes an object to be out of date or inconsistent with the rest of the system, the object may be marked invalid and the program will produce cryptic error messages that are hard for users to understand. Your database administrator can easily fix invalid objects.

TUNING PRODUCTION SYSTEMS

Since you may find your database is growing at more than 5% per month, you must quickly start production database administration procedures to manage disk space usage, eliminate disk hot spots, and control fragmentation. Compare your actual disk space usage with the estimates you made during the analysis phase and analyze the variances.

Tuning is a continuous process because the system is dynamic. Evaluate the following areas to improve performance:

- Look for hot spots (areas of high read/write activity) on the disk array. If you have excessive disk I/O on several disks, consider redistributing some database objects. Make your hot spot surveys at various times during the day, week, and month to evaluate the system under maximum and normal loads.
- Determine whether you need performance patches from Oracle Support. New releases are often tuned with patches after Oracle can observe real-world performance dynamics. Also, if you have an unusual data distribution or transaction volume, you may be able to obtain technical assistance from Oracle support that will patch your specific requirements.
- Analyze usage patterns and distribute the work schedule for the concurrent manager(s) so those batch jobs don't block interactive user activities.
- Look for the top-ten resource hogs on your system. A hog may be either a single program that runs for a long time once a day or a program that runs for just a few minutes but runs hundreds of times per day. Once you have identified potential problems, you can determine which strategy you should use to minimize the load on the system.
- Analyze memory usage per real user. Sometimes users will develop the habit of opening windows for each responsibility or business function, and Oracle systems will allocate memory and a connection for each window.
- Verify that your network is performing acceptably. In release 11*i*, network costs are lower than in previous releases, but you might have to analyze your routers and network configuration after you see the real loads.
- Analyze how well your processors and the server operating systems are handling the transaction loads throughout the business day. The application servers will have different capabilities than the database server. You want to determine where the system is constrained, which is where you must perform tuning.

BEGINNING CONTINUOUS IMPROVEMENT

The launch of an ERP system can be disruptive to the business. For example, inventory turnover can go down and some users may have a loss of productivity. Typically, users must work with the system for a time to fine-tune everything from min-max reorder points to interdepartmental agreements about workloads and process steps. It can take from four months to over a year for users to take ownership of the new system.

Tip

After several months, review how the users are using each function of the system and compare their actual practices to the business processes you trained them to use. You might find some radical differences when you see the real-world effects of the ERP system, and that can be a good starting point for further innovation or a return to standard practice.

If you deferred any customizations into the "nice to have but not a show stopper" category, you can start work on these business requirements after the system and business stabilizes. These items could be a new report or any process change to repair the disruptions caused by the new software. The users will remember all of the scope issues from the first project and your promises to revisit each issue will come back to haunt you. Consider a proactive approach to meeting your pledges.

Evaluate profile options for each user role and responsibility. Some of the profile options affect security and user productivity. These options should be evaluated periodically as new users are added to the system and as experienced users become more common.

Since ERP systems are primarily transaction-processing systems, they do not handle certain tasks well. The best ERP implementations come from a series of continuous improvements. This process enables the system to evolve into a stable and integrated platform for enterprise computing. These improvements are designed to extend ERP beyond the basic transactions of the initial implementation. Consider the following projects to enhance your new ERP system:

- Archive the transaction data in a data warehouse and take a new approach to reporting business information.
- Implement customer relationship management applications.
- Automate computer operations for the database and application servers.
- Create a business information and analysis system.
- Add sales force automation applications as a front end to ERP.
- Extend your supply chain with e-commerce.
- Begin using Internet/intranet-based self-service applications for customers, suppliers, and employees.

- Activate automatic versions of transactions that were implemented in manual mode. Examples include AutoLockbox in AR, Pay on Receipt in AP, and workflow enabled functions.
- Prepare for the next upgrade of the Oracle Applications.

You must decide whether you will develop these extensions yourself, buy the software from Oracle, or purchase from third-party vendors such as those described in the chapter titled "Finding Additional Compatible Solutions" on this book's Web site. The latter approach might buy you more functionality, but integrating products to work together can be a challenge.

Summary

In this chapter, you have learned all of the details and tasks necessary to launch your new systems into production. Although Oracle software projects have a large technical requirement, an ERP project must incorporate the human and organizational requirements to be successful. You must properly set your users' expectations of the software and resolve their issues and concerns.

During the transition phase of the project, you train users, convert and load data, and develop the user support infrastructure. For many months to a year after the system goes live, you audit, maintain, tune, and improve the system as the users take ownership. At that point, the new software becomes the backbone of your enterprise and the key platform for growth and improvement.

PART III

Configuring and Using the Oracle Applications

CHAPTER 11

USING ORACLE GENERAL LEDGER

In this chapter

INTRODUCTION

Oracle General Ledger (GL) performs the accounting and budgeting functions in the Oracle Applications suite. It is the central module of Oracle Applications because it owns the set of books that forms the basis for all other Financials modules. Receivables, Payables, Inventory, and Assets are the main subledgers of GL. GL shares the setup information with subledgers.

GL only receives transaction information and does not send any transaction information to other modules. The main transactions in GL are Accounting (including Multi-Company and Multi-Currency), Budgeting, and Encumbrance Accounting. The main setups are Chart of Accounts (Accounting Flexfield Structure), Calendar, Currencies, Set of Books, Currency Conversion Rates, Journal Sources, Journal Categories, Encumbrance, System Controls, Profile Options, Budgets, and Accounting Periods.

RELATIONSHIP TO OTHER ORACLE APPLICATIONS

GL has relationships to most of the modules in the Oracle Applications suite. The Inventory, Purchasing, Order Entry, Payables, Receivables, Assets, Projects and Cost Management modules share the setup information from GL, and the accounting transactions from these modules are imported into GL. GL depends on the Applications Object Library (AOL) for responsibilities, menus, profile options, and other related setups. Figure 11.1 shows how various modules are related to GL. In each module, the information it shares is indicated. Arrows show the direction in which this information flows and to which modules the information flows.

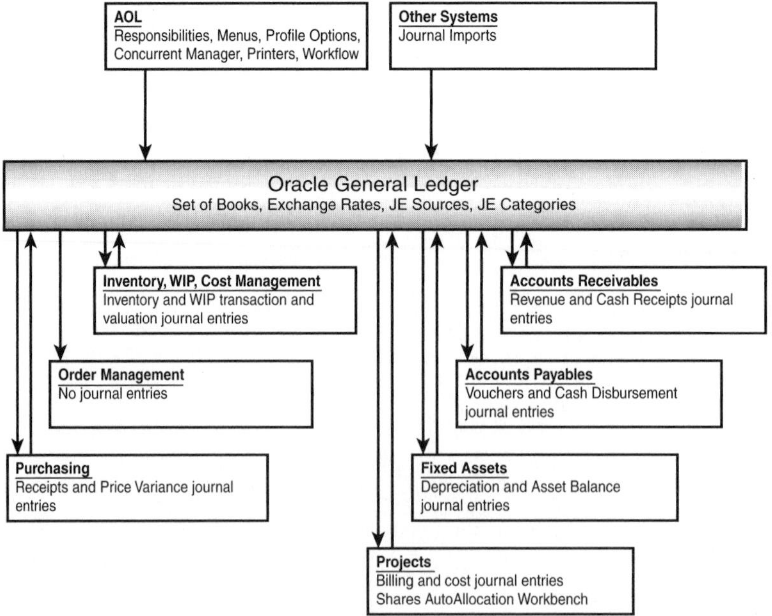

Figure 11.1
General Ledger relationships to other applications.

Discovering New Features in Release 11*i*

The following sections describe some of the important new features in Release 11*i* of GL. These features include AutoAllocation Workbench; Automatic Journal Reversing and Journal Scheduling; and enhancements to the Global Consolidation System (GCS), Intercompany Accounting, Global Intercompany System (abbreviated GIS and formerly called CENTRA) and subledger integration and drill down.

AutoAllocation Workbench

In prior releases, to perform an allocation based on a previous allocation (step-down), users had to generate the first allocation and post it prior to generating the second allocation. Allocations had to be generated by selecting the allocations from a form.

In Release 11*i* the AutoAllocation Workbench can be used to create step-down and parallel allocation sets. The allocation sets can combine Mass Allocations, Mass Budget Allocations, and Recurring Journal batches. In a step-down allocation set, allocations can be sequenced and are dependent on the successful completion of the prior allocation. Step-down allocations can be used to distribute revenue and expenses through multiple levels of an organization. Additionally, AutoAllocation Workbench is now available to Oracle Projects users and can be used to allocate project amounts.

Parallel allocations are different in that each allocation is independent in a set and can be executed at the same time. Allocations and recurring journals can now be scheduled to be generated at a specific date and time as a concurrent process. In Release 11*i*, Workflow is used to monitor and track each allocation through posting.

Figure 11.2 presents some of the new functionality in AutoAllocation Workbench, such as the step-down, schedule, and view status capabilities.

Automatic Journal Reversal

In Release 11*i* journals can be automatically reversed by journal category. The effective date or period of the reversing journal can be selected.

General Ledger provides the following options for the automatic reversal of journals:

- Can generate when a new period is opened
- Can manually launch separate reversal programs
- Can automatically post all reversing journals

Global Consolidation System

In Release 11 the Global Consolidation System provided a tool to make the complex consolidation process easier to manage. Within GCS is the Consolidation Workbench. This is the central control for tracking the status of all the consolidations. The Consolidation Workbench provides the means to perform the various consolidations, keep you informed of the status of each, and indicate whether transactions have been made to the subsidiary after the consolidation has taken place with the parent.

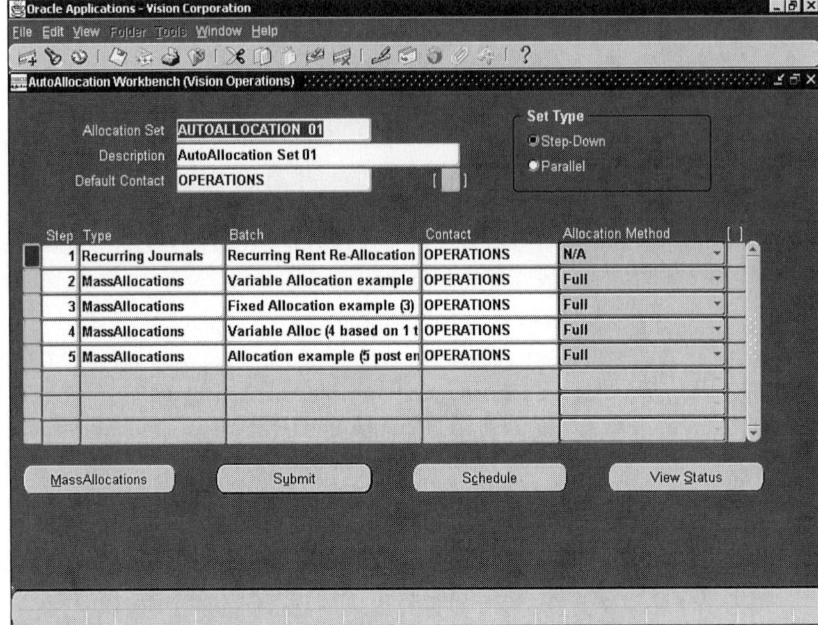

Figure 11.2
The AutoAllocation Workbench.

In Release 11*i* automatic intercompany eliminations have been added to the Global Consolidation System. This feature provides the capability to define elimination sets for a logical grouping of subsidiaries, such as Europe. You can specify your subsidiary's intercompany accounts to be eliminated, the source accounts, and an elimination company and target accounts for the elimination entries. Intercompany accounts defined in an elimination set can include parent values for one or more segments. The elimination can then automatically loop through each child of the parent, generating an elimination for that child in the elimination company, much like a Mass Allocation. Eliminations can be performed on a period-to-date, quarter-to-date, or year-to-date basis. Threshold rules can be used to determine whether an out-of-balance elimination journal should post. Net credit and debit differences in an elimination journal can be posted to alternative accounts. The Consolidation Workbench is used to track the status of each elimination set in the consolidation process.

Tip

Elimination sets can't be executed across sets of books. To perform an elimination, all subsidiaries must be consolidated to a parent set of books. Then, the elimination set can be generated in the parent set of books.

Intercompany Accounting and Balancing

In prior GL releases, I/C entries between a given company and all other companies were netted together and any given company could not determine the individual balances owed to it or that it owed to other companies. In Release 11*i*, GL provides the capability to determine the balance relationships between pairs of trading companies.

The intercompany segment has been added as an additional qualifier to the Accounting Flexfield. It shares the same value set as the balancing segment. The intercompany segment is used when GL generates intercompany transactions that are defined by journal entry source and category in the Intercompany Accounts form or by GIS AutoAccounting Rules. The balancing segment value of the trading entity populates the intercompany segment, providing the capability to track offsetting intercompany transactions.

In Release 11*i* GL intercompany accounting has enhanced the definition of due to and due from accounts for each journal source and category by adding trading company or entity. Additionally, the user can define a default clearing company against which all trading entities can balance.

Global Intercompany System

The Global Intercompany System, formerly called Centralized Transaction Approval (CENTRA), manages intercompany transactions between multiple subsidiaries across different sets of books and even application instances. It helps prevent out-of-balance intercompany transactions. The sender subsidiary enters and submits a GIS intercompany transaction to a receiver subsidiary for review and approval. The transactions can't be posted unless they are approved. Parent subsidiaries can alternately automatically approve selected intercompany transactions.

In Release 11*i* AutoAccounting can be used to generate both the sender and receiver clearing (intercompany) accounts and the receiver distribution accounts based on the charge type and sending subsidiary. The new intercompany segment is used to track the trading subsidiary. Notifications can be sent to trading subsidiaries via e-mail, the Internet, or Oracle General Ledger. Threshold amounts for notification can be defined for each subsidiary.

An open interface for intercompany transactions has been added in Release 11*i*. This feature allows input of intercompany transactions from external sources and use of the AutoAccounting rules defined in GIS.

Tip

New Global Intercompany System functionality can be backported to Release 11 by applying a patch. This makes the new functionality available in General Ledger Release 11 without upgrading to Release 11*i*.

SUBLEDGER DRILL-DOWN

General Ledger inquiry and drill-down to the subledgers has been significantly enhanced in Release 11*i*. In Release 11, the user could drill from GL to Oracle Receivables and Oracle Payables from the GL Account Inquiry form. This functionality has been expanded in Release 11*i* to provide drill-down from GL account balances and journal entries to Oracle Projects, Oracle Assets, Oracle Purchasing, Oracle Inventory, and Oracle Work in Process. You can now access subledger details from either the Account Inquiry form or the Journal Entry form by drilling into the View Accounting Lines form. Additionally, the user can now view all lines of a journal entry created by a subledger when drilling down from a particular account inquiry. Two new views or windows have been added to the GL inquiry functionality: T Accounts and Summary Activity Format. Figure 11.3 shows the application drill-down window. Figures 11.4 and 11.5 display the new T Accounts and Activity Summary formats, respectively, that are available in Release 11*i*.

The following is a brief discussion of other new features and enhancements available in GL Release 11*i*.

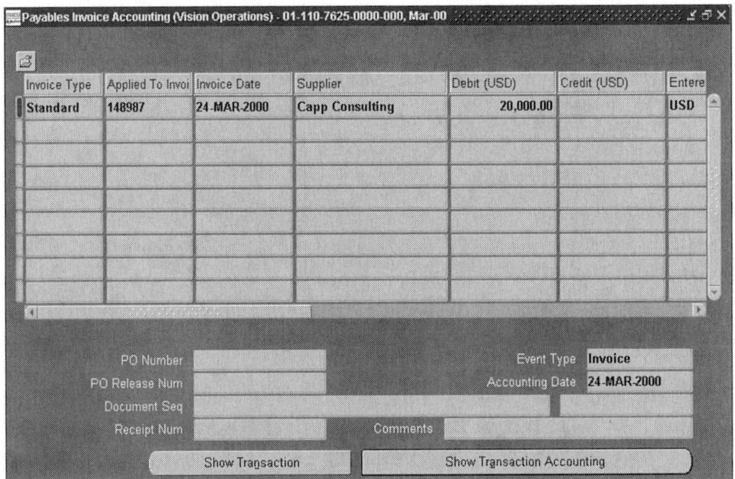

Figure 11.3
The Application drill-down window.

FLEXFIELD POP-UP WINDOW

The Flexfield:Open Key Window profile option has been added to control whether the Accounting Flexfield window pops up automatically when a user enters that field on any form. If this option is set to Yes, the window will pop up. However, if it's set to No, the user must click the List of Values icon to open the window.

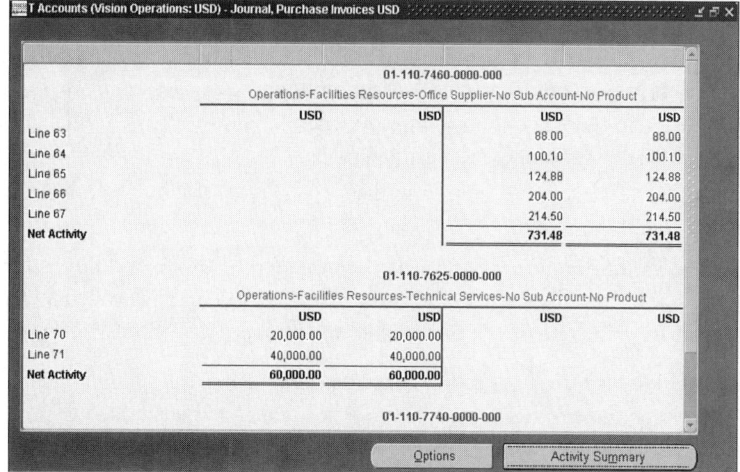

Figure 11.4
T Accounts.

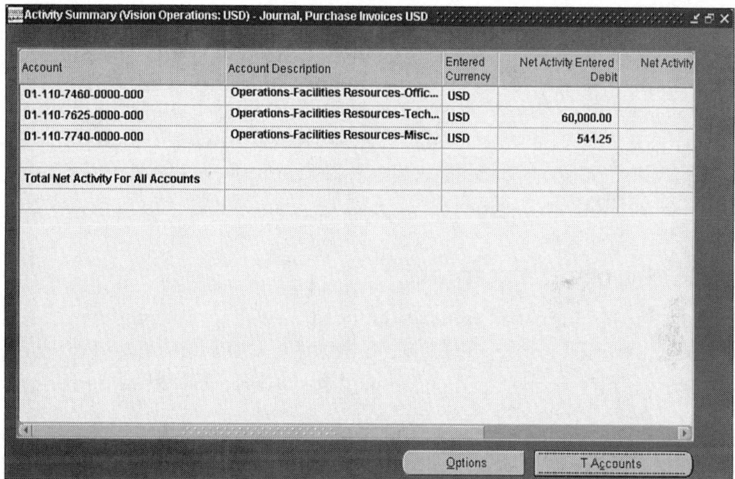

Figure 11.5
Activity Summary.

PART III CH 11

SEGMENT VALUE INHERITANCE

This feature facilitates chart of accounts maintenance by replicating changes to segment value attributes or properties to the account code combinations that contain that segment value. For instance, when you disable a particular account segment value, such as a prepaid account, you can optionally disable every account code combination containing that prepaid account.

CALENDAR AUDITING

A new program has been provided to audit the maintenance of the accounting calendar. Every time the accounting calendar is maintained, the system prompts execution of this program. The report contains common calendar setup errors, such as the omission of dates within the calendar and overlapping periods.

MULTICURRENCY

A Rounding Differences account has been added to the Set of Books form. Rounding differences resulting from the conversion of a foreign currency journal can be posted to this account. In prior releases, it was posted to the largest amount in the journal.

The Daily Rates form has been enhanced to allow entry for a range of dates. The date range can even cross periods. In Release 11, an interface table had been added to provide this functionality.

REVALUATION

Two new profile options have been added to facilitate the revaluation process. When the profile option GL:Revaluation AutoQuery Last Run Range is set to Yes, the Revalue Balances form uses the account range from the last execution of the program.

You can specify whether you want to revalue Income Statement accounts on a period-to-date or year-to-date basis using the GL: Income Statement Accounts Revaluation Rules profile option. If you select the PTD option, the results of revaluation will be in compliance with SFAS #52 standards.

MULTIPLE REPORTING CURRENCIES

To facilitate the Temporal translation method and compliance with SFAS #52, MRC creates revaluation journal entries in each reporting sets of books based on the primary set of books. This process directs the revaluation gain/loss accounting to the proper accounts.

Multiple Reporting Currencies (MRC) upgrade utilities have been provided to synchronize beginning balances between primary and reporting sets of books for both the General Ledger and subledgers.

Within MRC, drill-down has been enhanced to drill from the account balances and journal entries in the reporting set of books to those residing in the primary set of books.

A new feature has been added to MRC to facilitate the reversal of journals in the reporting set of books, when the original entry does not exist in the reporting set of books, but does in the primary set of books. This situation can occur after the General Ledger Reporting Balance Initialization Utility has been run.

FINANCIAL STATEMENT GENERATOR

The Financial Statement Generator (FSG) reports can now be created with no limitation on the number of columns on the report. FSG dynamically determines the width of the report based on either the widest column or the total width of the report.

An absolute value function has been added to the row set definition to display all amounts as positive for any specified row.

Euro Enhancements

Foreign currency journals can now be generated by Mass Allocation or Recurring Journals using the fixed conversion factor when a fixed relationship exists between the foreign currency and the functional currency.

Closing Journals

In Release 11*i* Oracle General Ledger provides two optional closing journals that address statutory reporting requirements for Greece, Italy, Portugal, Spain, Columbia, and Mexico, as well as other countries. The Income Statement Closing Journal closes revenue and expense accounts to the retained earnings account. The Balance Sheet Closing Journal, on the other hand, closes asset and liability accounts to a specified account.

Process Navigator Close Process

The Process Navigator is a new tool in Oracle Applications Release 11*i* that provides a graphical view of the business processes inherent in the applications. This view can be customized to fit your needs and business processes. With the Process Navigator, the user can move directly to a form to accomplish a task.

Resolving Issues and Gaps

The decisions made during the implementation will affect the use of GL modules for years to come. Some configuration and modification decisions cannot be reversed without a significant additional investment of time and money, and some customizations or corrective actions might cause you to lose your technical support from Oracle. All these factors are critical for an implementation and should be given due consideration at the very beginning of implementation.

The most important issue in setting up the General Ledger is defining the Accounting Flexfield. Important questions to resolve include the following:

- How many segments should we use?
- What length should they be?
- Should we use parent values, summary accounts, and rollup groups?
- How will we validate the various account code combinations?

There always seem to be two opposing criteria in defining the Accounting Flexfield - Reporting Needs versus Data Entry Constraints. Remember, the segments of the Accounting Flexfield should mirror the dimensions of your organization.

Summary Accounts

Summary accounts maintain summarized balances. You can use them for online inquiries and rapid reporting. See the discussion on summary accounts and summary templates later in this chapter in the section "Set of Books Setup." You can assign budgetary control options to summary accounts to perform summary-level budgetary control.

Rollup Groups

A *rollup group* is used to identify a group of parent values. Rollup groups enable the use of summary accounts, so if you need summary accounts, chances are you will need rollup groups. Refer to the discussion on rollup groups later in this chapter in the section "Set of Books Setup."

Parent Values

Parent Values allow for a hierarchical organization of your segment values. They are useful in producing financial statements and in developing recurring journals. However, no balances are maintained online for them.

Other issues in implementing Oracle GL include how much data history will be converted and whether balances or transactions will be converted. Most organizations convert transactions from the most recent year-end to the go-live date and convert balances for any prior periods that are needed. The most important thing to remember in this regard is that Oracle Financial Statements can only report on balances that have been converted.

Gaps

Most companies find relatively few gaps in the General Ledger. In the past, they typically were in the intercompany accounting, allocation, and reporting areas, but these have been greatly improved in the latest releases.

Parent Accounts

Parent Accounts allow for a hierarchical organization of your segment values. They are useful in producing financial statements and in developing recurring journals. However, no balances are maintained online for them.

"Other issues in implementing Oracle GL include how much data history will be converted, and will we convert balances or transactions. Most organizations convert transactions from the most recent year-end to the go-live date and convert balances for any prior periods that are needed. The most important thing to remember in this regard is Oracle Financial Statements can only report on balances that have been converted."

Proposed Enhancements

Following are some enhancements that have been asked for by users at large and are being considered for future releases. Many of the long outstanding proposed enhancements have been addressed in Release 11*i*.

ABILITY TO PRINT RANGE OF JOURNALS BY USER

Currently, users can print and select one or all posted journals using GL standard Journal Entry reports. This feature would add the ability to select all journals for a specific user or location.

CHANGE ACCOUNT TYPE

Many times a new natural account is established with the wrong account type. This is common when the account type defaults to expense if another type is not selected. This feature would add the ability to change the type from asset to liability, or vice versa, within balance sheet accounts or to change the type from revenue to expense, or vice versa, within income statement accounts. The limitation to not allow changes across balance sheet and income statement accounts helps minimize data integrity issues involved with restating retained earnings.

MULTIPLE SORTING OPTIONS FOR ACCOUNT ANALYSIS REPORTS

The account analysis reports are some of the most widely used reports within GL. Often users want to see these reports sorted in different ways to provide different subtotals for analysis.

Tip

Many of the enhancements developed for new releases are made available to users of earlier releases. This includes many of the features related to GIS and Intercompany that have been made available in Release 11. These are called *backports* and are made available to licensed users by the application of patches. To see a list of current backports, check Oracle's MetaLink Web site at `http://metalink.oracle.com`.

CONFIGURING THE GL APPLICATION

The following section lists all the setup tasks for a GL implementation and briefly describes each task. The tasks should be performed in the order discussed here.

RESOLVING CRITICAL SETUP ISSUES

In addition to understanding the factors discussed previously, you should identify and understand some key issues underlying a GL implementation. The issues vary depending on the business scenario and requirements. The following are some common issues that apply in all circumstances.

DETERMINING THE STRUCTURE OF THE KEY ACCOUNTING FLEXFIELD

The Accounting Flexfield (AFF) structure forms an important component of the set of books and can't be easily changed after transactions are entered. As you design the Accounting Flexfield, you should thoroughly consider your financial reporting requirements, data-entry constraints, and interfaces from non-Oracle applications, as well as the transaction flow between the various Oracle modules. An understanding of various features, such as rollup groups, summary accounts, cross-validation rules, and set of books requirements, will help you design a practical AFF structure. Determine at this stage whether a common AFF structure can serve your business requirements. If there is a need for multiple AFF structures, you must create multiple sets of books.

DETERMINING THE SETS OF BOOKS FOR YOUR ENTERPRISE

This configuration task depends directly on the requirements of the AFF structure, currency, and calendar. If the business requires more than one combination of these three components, you need multiple sets of books. See Chapter 29, "Understanding Multi-Org," to understand the role and importance of a set of books in a multiple-organization structure of Oracle Applications. You must understand the consolidation and reporting features with multiple sets of books and their limitations to determine the best configuration for your implementation.

Tip

Use of a common AFF structure across the organization simplifies the consolidation definition and process, as well as consolidated reporting. If a common AFF structure is used, typically only a difference in functional currency dictates the need for another set of books.

Tip

When considering the design of the AFF structure, use the General Ledger as a financial reporting tool–not as a warehouse reporting tool.

REQUIRED SETUP TASKS

Table 11.1 shows the tasks to set up the GL Application in the order they should be performed. Try not to skip tasks or perform them out of sequence because many tasks use predecessor tasks for data validation, and you might receive error messages.

TABLE 11.1 GL SETUP TASKS

Setup Task Name	Required?
Define Responsibilities	Yes
Define Value Sets	Yes
Define Flexfield Structure	Yes
Define Segment Values	Yes
Define Rollup Groups	No
Define Security Rules	No
Define Cross-Validation Rules	No
Enter Account Code Combinations	No
Define Intercompany Accounts	No
Enter Additional Suspense Accounts	No

Table 11.1 Continued

Setup Task Name	Required?
Define Summary Accounts	No
Define Calendar Period Types	Yes
Define Calendar Periods	Yes
Define Transaction Calendar	No
Define Currencies	Yes
Define Daily Conversion Rate Types	Yes
Enter Daily Conversion Rates	No
Define a Set of Books	Yes
Assign Set of Books to a Responsibility	Yes
Set Up Journal Approval	No
Define Historical Rates	No
Define Shorthand Aliases	No
Define Journal Sources	Yes
Define Journal Categories	Yes
Define Statistical Units of Measure	No
Define Journal Reversal Criteria	No
Define Budgetary Control Groups	No
Define Encumbrance Types	No
Set Up Automatic Posting	No
Index Accounting Flexfield Segments	No
Define System Controls	Yes
Define Profile Options	Yes
Define and Assign Document Sequences	No
Open and Close Accounting Periods	Yes
Set Up Budgets	No
Configure the Desktop Integrator	No
Set Up the Global Consolidation System	No
Set Up the Global Intercompany System	No
Administer System Issues	No
Define Concurrent Program Controls	No
Use the Optimizer to Improve Performance	No
Set System Storage Parameters	No

UNDERSTANDING EACH SETUP TASK

This section discusses the details of each setup task in the order they should be performed. They are categorized broadly into two parts: set of books setup and GL setup. The first category is necessary for the functioning of any module of Oracle Applications. The second category is directly related to the functioning of GL. Before carrying out these two sets of setups, though, you must define one responsibility to use for setup tasks.

DEFINING RESPONSIBILITIES

The responsibility definition is done in the Oracle Applications System Administration module. GL has six predefined responsibilities. Copy one of these predefined responsibilities to create a new responsibility with different capabilities.

Choose a responsibility that has access to set up functions, such as General Ledger Controller, to carry out the following setups.

SET OF BOOKS SETUP

A set of books is a combination of Currency, Calendar, and Chart of Accounts or Accounting Flexfield structures. One set of books can be shared by many organizations, and if so, they must share the same Currency, Calendar, and AFF structure.

This section discusses the setup of a set of books that is necessary to use any module of Oracle Financials. The setups specific to the operation of GL are discussed in the next section.

CHART OF ACCOUNTS Defining a Chart of Accounts involves first defining an AFF structure and entering Account Code Combinations (ACC) for that structure. Perform the following steps.

DEFINING VALUE SETS A *value set* contains the definition and rules that will be assigned to a flexfield segment. The values that can be entered in a segment, their validation, and other properties are determined by the value set assigned to it. You must understand each segment in the AFF with respect to the values that go into it, the validations to be performed, and other general properties. Then, define a value set for each combination of these requirements.

Two types of values can exist within a value set: *parent* and *child*. A parent value is one that has one or more child values associated with it. A child value is one that lies in a range of values belonging to a parent value. A child value can belong to more than one parent value. A child value, however, cannot be a dependent value; that is, the actual value of the child must not depend on the value of another segment.

You create parent-child relationships by defining a range of child values that belong to a parent value. You can use parent-child relationships for reporting and other application purposes. Parent value sets are used to create rollup groups.

Tip

Using a value set in multiple segments reduces maintenance. Similarly, using a value set in multiple AFF structures improves the consolidation process. Change in the value set affects all the flexfields it is assigned to. In such a case, quickly create a new value set by copying from the existing value set and updating its properties as required.

DEFINING A FLEXFIELD STRUCTURE The AFF structure is the GL's definition of the chart of accounts. Define an AFF for use in a set of books definition, define segments for each flexfield structure, and assign a value set to each segment. You must designate one segment as the natural account segment and another segment as the balancing segment. If you choose to use the new functionality of the intercompany segment, you must designate one segment as the intercompany segment and use the same value set as is used for the balancing segment. Next, you enable and freeze the structure after the flexfield definition is complete, and freeze the rollup groups after segment values have been defined in the next step. Then, you enable dynamic inserts (see the following section, "Defining Segment Values") or enter segment values before using them in account code combinations.

Note

If you choose to use the intercompany segment and are upgrading from a previous release of Oracle Applications, this decision might dictate a new implementation as opposed to a standard upgrade.

Note

Changes cannot be made in a frozen flexfield definition. Uncheck the frozen box, make changes as necessary, and freeze it again.

DEFINING SEGMENT VALUES This task determines the scope within which the values entered in this segment will be validated. These values must be entered before they can be used in account code combinations.

DEFINING ROLLUP GROUPS A rollup group is used to identify a group of parent values for reporting or other application purposes. Rollup groups are used to create summary templates. You can assign key flexfield segment values to rollup groups using the Segment Values window.

Rollup groups are separate from parent-child relationships. You can assign any parent value to a given rollup group, regardless of that parent value's place in a parent-child hierarchy you might create.

DEFINING SECURITY RULES Security rules enable you to restrict data entry, online inquiry, and the running of reports for unauthorized values. Each rule is defined for a specific segment. Rules come into effect only when attached to a responsibility. The rules are defined to exclude or include the absolute values restricted by the rule. When a rule is defined, by default, GL excludes all values except those specifically included. Therefore, each rule must have at least one Include rule element. Attach these rules to responsibilities in the Assign Security Rules window.

Tip

Exclude elements override include elements. If a rule does not appear to be working at first, remember users must change responsibilities or log off and log on for security rules to take effect after you assign them to a responsibility.

DEFINING CROSS-VALIDATION RULES *Cross-Validation rules* enable you to restrict creation of account code combinations, as opposed to security rules, which restrict access to values entered for individual segments. Account code combinations already in existence are not affected by new rules, so always define these rules before you create or enter account code combinations. The cross-validation rules are for the entire AFF structure and not assigned to any responsibility. When a cross-validation rule is defined for an AFF, by default, GL excludes all combinations except those specifically included. Start with a general include element. Then, exclude the ranges that should be restricted.

Tip

Keep your cross-validation rules simple. It is better to develop rules just two segments at a time. This enables clearer messages to be written when the rule is violated and enables easier understanding and troubleshooting if problems occur with the rules.

Tip

There is a System Administration report, called the Cross-Validation Rules Violation report, which reports account code combinations that violate cross-validation rules. This report can be used to disable these invalid account code combinations.

DYNAMIC INSERTION The use of dynamic insertion is a key issue to be determined at the beginning of your implementation. Manually entering a long list of account combinations is difficult because any missing combinations give rise to errors in data entry. On the other hand, having the dynamic insertion enabled always results in some unwanted account combinations, which might be due to errors in data entry. To minimize the creation of unwanted account code combinations with dynamic insertion, define and use cross-validation rules.

DEFINING AN ACCOUNTING CALENDAR Defining an Accounting Calendar involves defining calendar period types and periods for the calendar.

Tip

If time prevents the creation of cross-validation rules, having dynamic insertion enabled initially when keying in or migrating initial data into GL is easy. After a period of time, prune the list and determine a policy on usage of account code combinations. You should disable dynamic insertion at this stage unless the business requirement determines otherwise. Any code combination to be used subsequently should first be defined.

DEFINING CALENDAR PERIOD TYPES GL has three predefined period types: Month, Quarter, and Year. Use the predefined types, or define new types. For best use, the name of a new period type should give the best possible indication of its nature or purpose. The type definition indicates the number of periods per year and the year type (Calendar or Fiscal).

DEFINING CALENDAR PERIODS Define your calendar by creating a name, and define the periods within the calendar. The periods in the calendar must be of a predefined or user-defined type. Adjusting periods can overlap, but nonadjusting periods cannot overlap.

Note

Carefully consider the following restrictions before choosing the earliest period:

- After opening the first period, prior periods cannot be opened.
- Foreign currency translation cannot be performed in the first period opened. Open the period prior to the first period that needs to be translated.

DEFINING CURRENCIES GL comes predefined with all the currencies of ISO member countries. Enable a currency before using it in a set of books. The currency used in a set of books is called its *functional* currency. USD is the only currency enabled by default. You must enable other currencies and enter conversion rates before using them in foreign currency transactions. Additional currencies can be defined as required. Consider things such as the functional currency, precision required for accounting, foreign currency transactions, use of multiple currencies in the organization (which requires multiple sets of books), dual-currency accounting, method, and frequency of foreign currency translations.

DEFINING CONVERSION RATE TYPES GL comes with three predefined rate types: Corporate, Spot, and User. Additional rate types can be defined as required.

When currency rates must be entered at the time of transactions, use the User rate type. If rates must be stored in GL and validated, use Corporate, Spot, or another newly defined rate type. Enter these rates using the Daily Rates window.

ENTERING CONVERSION RATES Use the Daily Rates window to define exchange conversion rates for combinations of foreign currency and date. The daily rates can be for corporate, spot, or other newly defined rate types.

CREATING THE SET OF BOOKS FROM AN AFF, CURRENCY, AND CALENDAR A set of books is a combination of the following three components:

- Currency
- Calendar
- Chart of Accounts (AFF)

The set of books is the foundation of not only the GL but also of all other modules of Oracle Applications that share any kind of accounting information. You must define at least one set of books for an organization.

Define a set of books and select a Currency, Calendar, and AFF structure for it. To complete the definition of the set of books, specify the following accounts:

- **Retained earnings account**—Necessary for GL to post the net balance of all revenue and expense accounts at the beginning of each fiscal year.
- **Suspense account**—Necessary if Suspense Posting is enabled. In such cases, GL automatically balances the unbalanced journals by posting the difference to the suspense account.
- **Intercompany account**—No longer is necessary. If intercompany balancing is enabled, the system reminds you to enter intercompany accounts using the Intercompany Accounts form.
- **Translation adjustment account**—Necessary to perform currency translation.
- **Reserve for encumbrance account**—Required if budgetary control is enabled or if encumbrance accounting is to be used. If this is entered, GL posts the difference of out-of-balance encumbrance journals to this account.

Note

Encumbrance journals need not be balanced like actual accounting journals.

ASSIGNING THE SET OF BOOKS TO RESPONSIBILITIES (OR SITE) You assign the set of books to a responsibility by specifying the set of books in the responsibility's profile option. This is the set of books you will operate on when you log in as this responsibility. The set of books of a responsibility can be changed only by assigning value to its profile option, and it cannot be changed by selecting online.

ENTERING ACCOUNT CODE COMBINATIONS The Account Code Combination is a combination of segment values for the AFF that can be used in transactions. Enter all the possible ACCs that will be used in transactions. Typically, if historical data is being converted, ACCs can be generated automatically by using dynamic insertion.

Note

If dynamic insertion is enabled, GL automatically creates the new ACCs as they are entered in transactions. The Applications Desktop Integrator (ADI) can be used to create account code combinations by entering journal entries with zero amounts.

When new ACCs are entered manually, do the following:

- **Make sure the Enabled option is selected**—Without this, the account cannot be used in transactions.
- **Select the Allow Posting option**—Without this, the GL will not post any transactions to the account. There might be accounts (such as parent accounts) to which you do not want to post entries directly, in which case you can leave the Allow Posting option unselected.
- **Make sure the Allow Posting option is enabled for each segment value of the ACC that is not a parent value.**
- **Enter an optional end date**—Do this only in future periods when you want this account not to be used in any transactions.

Tip

When preparing an exhaustive list of ACCs, it is good to start with a study of existing account codes in the system. Taking that study as a base, modifications can be made to suit the business requirements. This exercise many times leads to a completely different account coding, but it is easy to start with because the users are familiar with the existing account coding. Make sure you have a segment value blocking strategy that supports your financial reports, account hierarchy, budget organizations, summary accounts, and rollup groups.

DEFINING INTERCOMPANY ACCOUNTS Intercompany (I/C) accounts can be defined for each combination of journal source, journal category, and company. You should define I/C accounts to indicate you want to balance I/C journal entries from specific journal sources and journal categories by company to different I/C accounts. A default I/C account can be specified using the source and category "other" and a company of "All Other." See Figure 11.6 for an example.

GL posts a balancing I/C amount to an intercompany account only if the following are true:

- The source of the journal entry matches the source in this definition.
- The category in the journal entry matches the category in this definition.
- The type of balancing entry (debit or credit) matches the debit/credit value specified in this definition.

If the intercompany segment has been designated, when GL creates an intercompany journal line, it populates this segment with the offsetting trading company.

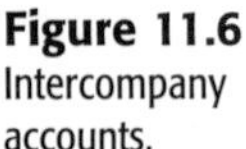

Figure 11.6
Intercompany accounts.

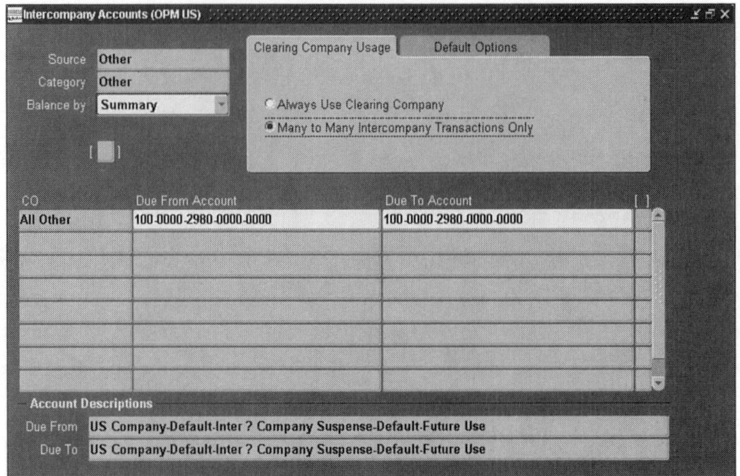

DEFINING ADDITIONAL SUSPENSE ACCOUNTS Additional suspense accounts can be defined for each combination of journal sources and journal categories. If Suspense Posting is enabled in a set of books definition, GL automatically posts the difference of unbalanced journals and ACC errors to the suspense accounts.

DEFINING SUMMARY ACCOUNTS A *summary account* is an accounting flexfield combination that is the sum of the balances in other accounting flexfield combinations. Create summary accounts for your set of books using the Summary Accounts window. Enter a name, a description, an earliest period, and a template for the summary accounts. GL uses summary templates to generate summary accounts. You denote in the template whether each segment is a Detail, Total, or rollup group by using the letters "D", "T" or the rollup group name, respectively. This designation determines whether GL creates and maintains a detail summary account for each segment value, one summary account that sums the balances of all detail segment values, or a summary of values for each parent value assigned to the rollup group.

Note

The status field displays Adding while GL is generating summary accounts by running a concurrent process. The field displays Current when the process is complete and the account is active. Similarly, the status field displays Deleting while GL is running a concurrent process to delete summary accounts.

You delete and re-create summary accounts when either modifying the contents of a rollup group or moving existing child segment values between parent values.

Summary accounts are updated immediately on posting an entry to the corresponding detail accounts. Therefore, querying and reporting are possible with summary accounts and also save time.

GL Setup

The following section discusses the GL specific setups. These setups are necessary to use the GL functions.

Setting Up Journal Approval Setting up journal approval involves a number of steps, including the following: setting two profile options related to journal approval, configuring Oracle Workflow, enabling journal approval for each set of books, setting up journal sources for journal approval, entering employees, creating an approval hierarchy, and defining approver authorization limits. This setup enables a workflow process for journal approval by journal source. If journal approval is enabled for a particular source, that journal must be approved by a manager with the appropriate authorization levels.

Defining Daily and Period Rates You use the Daily Rates window to define daily foreign currency exchange rates. These rates are used when entering a foreign currency journal and specifying a conversion rate type of Spot or Corporate. You use the Period Rates window to assign period end and period average rates. Period rates are used primarily for translation and calculating gain/loss on revaluation.

Defining Historical Rates Use the Historical Rates window to assign historical exchange conversion rates or amounts to accounts. These rates override the use of period rates. Historical rates often are used for translating equity accounts.

Defining Shorthand Aliases *Shorthand aliases* are simple names to identify an account combination and considerably ease data entry. For example, "Cash" can be used to identify a complex five-segment account combination "1.10.21.30.400". An alias can represent the value for one or several segments or an entire account. When entering account combinations in transactions, invoke the account pop-up window. The shorthand window appears, enabling you to enter aliases. You can also skip the shorthand window to go ahead and enter the actual account combination.

Defining Journal Entry Sources GL uses journal source definitions to identify the origins of journal entry transactions. Transactions can be grouped by sources for reporting and analysis. GL comes with more than 20 predefined sources. You can define additional sources as necessary. By default, all manually entered journals are assigned a source of manual, and this source can't be changed. Remember, I/C accounts and suspense accounts can be defined for each combination of journal sources and categories.

Defining Journal Entry Categories GL enables you to group or categorize transactions by their purposes—such as accrual, payments, receipts, and so forth—by using journal categories. GL comes with more than 35 predefined categories. You can define additional categories as necessary for your business requirements. Also, I/C accounts and suspense accounts can be defined for each combination of journal sources and categories.

Tip

In Release 11*i* you can set a default category by user. If your user default is not appropriate, you must specify a category for that transaction. Categories help in reporting. In addition, categorization enables you to make good use of additional suspense accounts and I/C accounts.

Tip

Where assigning a transaction to a specific category is not possible, have several general categories and assign the transaction to one of these.

Tip

It might be sufficient to use predefined categories for most purposes and avoid managing a mass of categories. However, if your specific purpose requires a new name for better categorization, don't hesitate to define a new category; just keep the list easy to handle.

DEFINING STATISTICAL UNITS OF MEASURE Statistical units of measure enable you to additionally track nonmonetary measures for specific natural account segments. Examples of statistical units of measure are Hours for consulting, Students for training programs, and so on. The use of statistical units of measure is explained later in this chapter in the section titled "Understanding Statistical Entries."

DEFINING JOURNAL REVERSAL CRITERIA Use the Journal Reversal Criteria window to establish journal reversal criteria, including reversal method, period, and date by journal category (see Figure 11.7). You can optionally choose to mark each journal category for Autoreverse and Autopost. The profile option, GL:Launch AutoReverse after Period Open, can be set to generate reversing journals when a period is open. This setup procedure can be used to automatically generate and post reversing journals defined by journal category either at the beginning of a period or by running a concurrent process.

DEFINING BUDGETARY CONTROL GROUPS Defining budgetary control groups involves defining budgetary control rules by grouping the journal sources and journal categories with similar rules. You can establish any of the following:

- Advisory or absolute control
- Tolerance percentage or amount
- Override amount

An *absolute* control is where the transaction will not pass budgetary approval if it exceeds the tolerance specified. An *advisory* control is one where the system warns of the transaction but allows it to pass. These sets of rules can be specified for specific combinations of journal sources and journal categories.

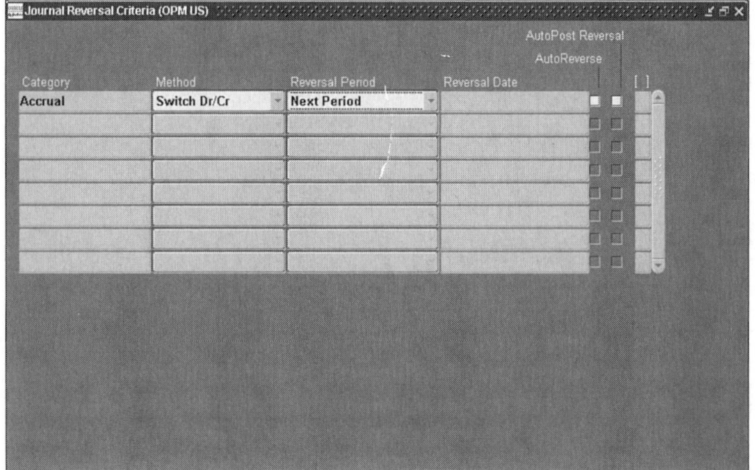

Figure 11.7
Journal reversal criteria.

Finally, use profile options to assign different budgetary control groups to different users.

If budgetary control is used, GL checks and reserves funds prior to posting journals. Funds available by definition is equal to budget less encumbrances less actuals. Requisitions and Purchase Orders create encumbrances, whereas Payables reverses them when it records the actual expenditures. These modules together create and manage the funds available and encumbrance balances.

Tip

For strict budgetary control, always first include a general combination of Other journal sources and Other as the journal category to be absolute with no tolerance. This implies that for all the journal source/category combinations that are not specifically allowed, transactions will not pass if they exceed the budget, with 0% tolerance.

DEFINING ENCUMBRANCE TYPES GL comes with two predefined encumbrance types: Commitment and Obligation. Enable these types before using budgetary control. You can define additional types as required. These names are for easy identification, and you can track total encumbrances under different names. For example, in a business function such as purchasing, encumbrances can be tracked by a different type at each stage of the process.

DEFINING AUTOMATIC POSTING OPTIONS The AutoPost setup enables you to schedule automatic posting of journals by sources, balance types (Actual, Budget, Encumbrance, or ALL), and periods. Choose a priority between 1 (highest) and 99 (lowest) for each of the criteria. Finally, submit the automatic posting concurrent request to run on a periodic basis by selecting the Resubmit parameter of the Run Options window.

SETTING THE PROFILE OPTIONS Profile options can be set at the Site (lowest priority), Application (second lowest priority), Responsibility (second highest priority), and User (highest priority) levels. The options default from a lower priority level to a higher priority level unless another option is specified at the higher priority level. Table 11.2 indicates which options can be set or updated at each of the levels. The system administrator can set these profile options for each of the levels specified.

TABLE 11.2 GL PROFILE OPTIONS*

Profile Option	User	Resp.	App	Site
ADI: Allow sysadmin to view all output	View	Yes	Yes	Yes
ADI: Use function security	View	Yes	Yes	Yes
Budgetary Control Group	View	Yes	Yes	Yes
Currency: Allow direct EMU and non-EMU user rates	Yes	Yes	Yes	Yes
Currency: Mixed currency precision	Yes	Yes	Yes	Yes
Daily Rates Window: Enforce inverse relationship	View	Yes	Yes	Yes
Dual Currency	View	Yes	Yes	Yes
Dual Currency default rate type	View	Yes	Yes	Yes
FSG: Accounting Flexfield	No	No	Yes	Yes
FSG: Allow portrait print style	Yes	Yes	Yes	Yes
FSG: Enforce segment value security	No	Yes	Yes	Yes
FSG: Expand parent value	Yes	Yes	Yes	Yes
FSG: Message detail	Yes	Yes	Yes	Yes
FSG: String comparison mode	Yes	Yes	Yes	Yes
GL: AutoAllocation rollback allowed	Yes	Yes	Yes	Yes
GL: Debug log directory	No	No	Yes	Yes
GL: Income statement accounts revaluation rule	View	Yes	Yes	Yes
GL: Journal review required	Yes	Yes	Yes	Yes
GL: Launch AutoReverse after open period	View	Yes	Yes	Yes
GL: Owners equity translation rule	View	Yes	Yes	Yes

Table 11.2 Continued

Profile Option	User	Resp.	App	Site
GL: Number of purge workers	Yes	Yes	Yes	Yes
GL Revaluation: Autoquery last run ranges	View	Yes	Yes	Yes
GL Set of Books ID	No	View	View	View
GL Set of Books name	No	Yes	Yes	Yes
GL Summarization: Number of deleted workers	No	Yes	Yes	Yes
GL Summarization: Accounts processed at time per	No	Yes	Yes	Yes
GL Summarization: Rows deleted per commit	No	Yes	Yes	Yes
GL Summarization: Maintenance index selection	No	Yes	Yes	Yes
GL/MRC: Balance Sheet conversion type	View	Yes	Yes	Yes
GL/MRC: Historical amount segment	View	Yes	Yes	Yes
GL/MRC: Historical rate segment	View	Yes	Yes	Yes
GL/MRC: Income statement conversion type	View	Yes	Yes	Yes
GL/MRC: Post reporting journals automatically	View	Yes	Yes	Yes
GL/MRC: Reporting book using overriding historical	View	Yes	Yes	Yes
Intercompany: Subsidiary	No	Yes	Yes	Yes
Intercompany: Use automatic transaction numbering	No	No	Yes	Yes
Intercompany: Protect receiver natural account	No	Yes	Yes	Yes
Journals: Allow multiple exchange rates	Yes	Yes	Yes	Yes
Journals: Allow non-business day transactions	View	Yes	Yes	Yes
Journals: Allow preparer approval	View	Yes	Yes	Yes
Journals: Allow posting during entry	View	Yes	Yes	Yes

TABLE 11.2 CONTINUED

Profile Option	User	Resp.	App	Site
Journals: Default category	Yes	Yes	Yes	Yes
Journals: Display inverse rate	Yes	Yes	Yes	Yes
Journals: Enable prior period notification	View	Yes	Yes	Yes
Journals: Find approver method	No	Yes	Yes	Yes
Journals: Mix statistical and monetary	Yes	Yes	Yes	Yes
Journals: Override Reversal Method	View	Yes	Yes	Yes
MRC: Reporting set of books	View	Yes	Yes	Yes
Use performance module	No	No	Yes	Yes
GL AHE: Saving allowed	View	Yes	Yes	Yes
GLDI: AHE privileges	View	Yes	Yes	Yes
GLDI: Analysis Wizard privileges	View	Yes	Yes	Yes
GLDI: AutoCopy enforcement level	View	Yes	Yes	Yes
GLDI: Enforce Budget Wizard security	View	Yes	Yes	Yes
GLDI: Budget Wizard privileges	View	Yes	Yes	Yes
GLDI: Journal Wizard privileges	View	Yes	Yes	Yes
GLDI: Journal Source	View	Yes	Yes	Yes
GLDI: Report Wizard privileges	View	Yes	Yes	Yes
GLDI: Allow drill-down across books	View	Yes	Yes	Yes
GLDI: Balance by accounting date	View	Yes	Yes	Yes
GLDI: Converted entry threshold	View	Yes	Yes	Yes
GLDI: Create Group ID	View	Yes	Yes	Yes

TABLE 11.2 CONTINUED

Profile Option	User	Resp.	App	Site
GLDI: Force full validation	View	Yes	Yes	Yes
GLDI: Force journal to balance	View	Yes	Yes	Yes
GLDI: Maximum effective ranges for drill-down	View	Yes	Yes	Yes

**View = allowed to view only*
Yes = allowed to update
No = not allowed to view or update

The user can access only the following profile options and only at the User level:

- Budgetary control group (View only)
- Currency: Allow direct EMU and non-EMU user rates
- Currency: Mixed currency precision
- Daily Rates Window: Enforce inverse relationship during entry (View only)
- Dual currency (View only)
- Dual currency default rate type (View only)
- FSG: Allow portrait print style
- FSG: Expand parent value
- FSG: Message detail
- FSG: String comparison mode
- GL: AutoAllocation rollback allowed
- GL: Income statement accounts revaluation rule (View only)
- GL: Journal review required
- GL: Launch AutoReverse after open period (View only)
- GL: Number of purge workers
- GL: Owners equity translation rule (View only)
- GL: Revaluation autoquery last run ranges (View only)
- GL/MRC: Balance sheet conversion type (View only)
- GL/MRC: Historical amount segment (View only)

- GL/MRC: Historical rate segment (View only)
- GL/MRC: Income statement conversion type (View only)
- GL/MRC: Post reporting journals automatically (View only)
- GL/MRC: Reporting book using overriding historical rates/amounts (View only)
- Journals: Allow multiple exchange rates
- Journals: Allow non-business day transactions (View only)
- Journals: Allow preparer approval (View only)
- Journals: Allow posting during entry
- Journals: Display inverse rate
- Journals: Default category
- Journals: Enable prior period notification (View only)
- Journals: Mix statistical and monetary
- Journals: Override reversal method (View only)
- MRC: Reporting set of books (View only)

All the ADI (GLDI) profile options are View only at the user level.

DEFINING AND ASSIGNING DOCUMENT SEQUENCES You can choose automatic or manual document sequence numbering. The automatic numbering option numbers journal entries in ascending order, starting with a specified initial value. This can be used with all journals. You can also choose to inform the user by displaying a message of the document number generated. The manual numbering option requires you to enter a document number at the time of creating a journal entry and as such can be used only with journals created manually—not with those created automatically.

Use the Document Sequences window to define the document sequence numbering option for each of the documents including journal entries.

Assign each document sequence to an application and a journal category. Optionally, you can assign each sequence to a set of books and a journal creation method. To assign a document sequence to a set of books, enable the set of books segment in the Document Flexfield.

The Sequential Numbering profile option must be set to one of the following three values:

- **Always used**—In this case, GL requires sequential numbering for journal entries.
- **Partially used**—In this case, GL allows sequential numbering for journal entries.
- **Not used**—In this case, GL does not allow sequential numbering for journal entries.

GL provides Journals by Document Number Report, which lists the journals with Number, Status, Creation Date, Batch Name, Header Name, Category, Posting Status, Posted Date, Currency Debits, and Credits. Typically, document sequencing is required in Europe and is not used widely within the United States.

SETTING UP THE GLOBAL CONSOLIDATION SYSTEM The design and purpose of GCS is to enable the user to consolidate information by posting journals from all your companies residing in different sets of books into ultimately one parent set of books and then perform eliminations within the parent set of books so that you can produce consolidated reports using FSGs. This process can be multistaged and involve more than one parent set of books. The user can create mapping sets and elimination sets to perform multiple consolidations, such as a European consolidation, an Asian consolidation, and then a global consolidation—performing eliminations at each consolidation.

First, the user must create mapping rules, which map one set of books and the chart of accounts to another set of books and chart of accounts. This must be done for each set of books that needs to be consolidated. A mapping set usually contains multiple mappings of various sets of books to one set of books and represents one consolidation. Each segment in the parent set of books must be mapped. The mapping process is greatly simplified if the charts are the same in each set of books, requiring only a copy of each segment. Other segment rules can be used, such as assign single value or rollup rules. Additionally, account rules can be used that map a single account or range of accounts in the subsidiary to one parent account.

Second, elimination sets need to be defined if you choose to perform your eliminations automatically. An elimination set can contain multiple elimination journals and represent an elimination for one consolidation. An elimination journal defines source accounts (the accounts to be eliminated) and target accounts (the elimination entry) that optionally can be posted to an elimination company. The source accounts can contain parent values for one or more segments. See Figures 11.8 and 11.9 for examples. The elimination journal loops through each child of the parent value, creating an elimination entry for each. Eliminations can be performed only within a set of books.

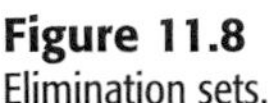

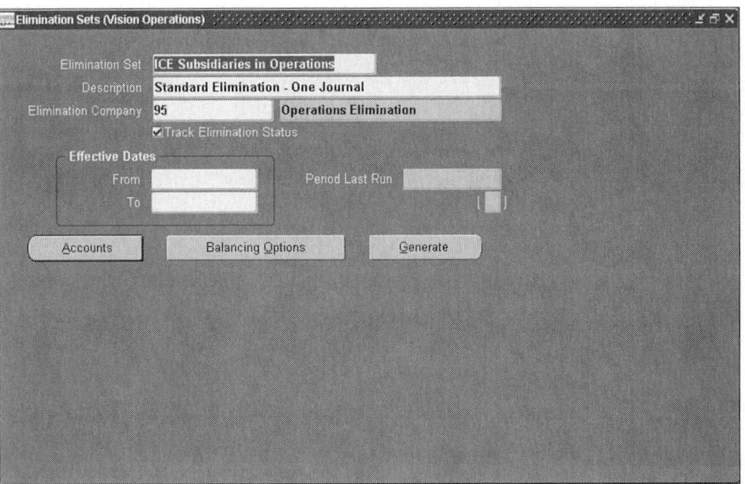

Figure 11.8
Elimination sets.

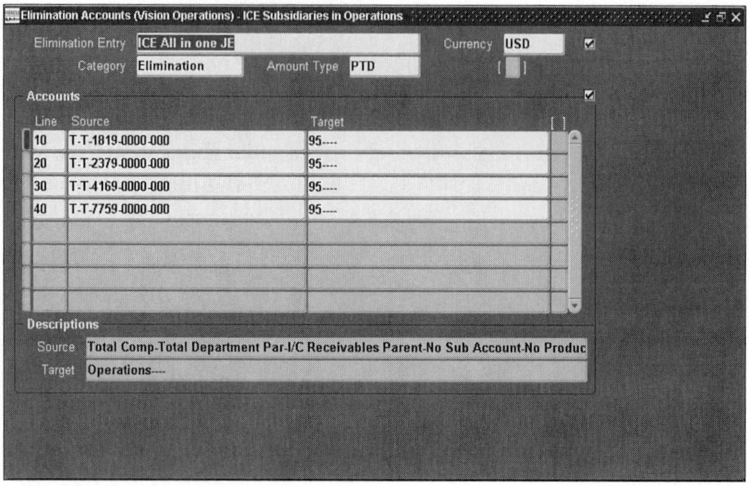

Figure 11.9
Elimination accounts.

Elimination Accounts (Vision Operations) - ICE Subsidiaries in Operations

Elimination Entry: ICE All in one JE — Currency: USD
Category: Elimination — Amount Type: PTD

Accounts

Line	Source	Target
10	T-T-1819-0000-000	95----
20	T-T-2379-0000-000	95----
30	T-T-4169-0000-000	95----
40	T-T-7759-0000-000	95----

Descriptions
Source: Total Comp-Total Department Par-I/C Receivables Parent-No Sub Account-No Produc
Target: Operations----

SETTING UP THE GLOBAL INTERCOMPANY SYSTEM Setting up GIS involves the setup and definition of the following major items:

- Subsidiaries
- Profile Options
- Clearing Accounts
- Transaction Types
- AutoAccounting Rules

A subsidiary must be set up for each trading entity and associated with a company or balancing segment value. Each subsidiary name must be unique, and subsidiaries can have different charts of accounts, calendars, and currencies, residing in different sets of books and instances. The Intercompany: Subsidiary profile option must be set for each GIS responsibility associating that responsibility with a GIS subsidiary.

You next define clearing (intercompany) accounts that can be used by GIS, specifying the natural account segment values using only the Clearing Account form. This must be done for each set of books and GIS responsibility.

A transaction type needs to be defined for each type of intercompany transaction that will take place between trading subsidiaries. You can optionally specify whether AutoApproval is allowed for each transaction type.

For each transaction type, you can define autoaccounting rules for the sending subsidiary clearing account, receiving subsidiary clearing account, and receiving subsidiary distribution accounts based on the sending subsidiary.

ADDITIONAL SETUPS

The following sections explain some setups to be completed outside GL.

Configuring the Desktop Integrator Applications Desktop Integrator (ADI) is a spreadsheet-based extension to Oracle General Ledger that offers full cycle accounting within the comfort and familiarity of an Excel spreadsheet. ADI combines a spreadsheet's ease of use with the power of General Ledger to provide true desktop integration during every phase of your accounting cycle. ADI comes with an installer that automatically installs the ADI and chosen components on your personal computer. ADI includes the Budget Wizard, Journal Wizard, Report Wizard, Analysis Wizard, and Request Center.

The Budget Wizard enables you to automatically build a budget spreadsheet based on budgets and budget organizations set up in GL. Using the Budget Wizard, you can do the following:

- Download existing budget and actual balances from GL, or create new budgets.
- Enter new budget balances manually.
- Use budget rules.
- Use spreadsheet formulas and models.
- Graph your budgets, and compare budgets and actual balances.
- Save the budget on your PC, and work on it locally.
- Automatically upload your budgets into GL.

The Journal Wizard enables you to easily build journal entry worksheets. You can enter journals directly into Excel using the spreadsheet's calculation capabilities and formulas. Then, you can automatically upload journal entries into Oracle GL. ADI validates data against the accounts, security rules, and information defined in GL.

The Report Wizard provides a spreadsheet-based interface to GL's Financial Statement Generator (FSG) and the capability to use the FSG reusable components. You can define reports entirely in a spreadsheet, using a combination of spreadsheet and assistance windows, or in configurable property sheets.

FSG reports can be output directly to an Excel spreadsheet using ADI. The Analysis Wizard provides the capability to drill from an amount on an ADI-generated FSG report to the detail balances and then to journal details. In ADI release 6.0 and later, the Analysis Wizard enables drilling down to AP and AR subledger details.

The Request Center is used to request reports and monitor concurrent requests. It provides instant status notification by flashing a message on your PC's screen. You can use it to simultaneously monitor any concurrent program submitted by any Oracle Application against any database. From the Request Center, you can request GL standard reports and FSG reports. The requested reports can be output to text, Excel, or the Web.

Processing Transactions

GL is the central repository of accounting information, and it receives transactions from financial and manufacturing subledgers. When in the GL, the accounting information can be inquired, adjusted, converted, revalued, translated, consolidated, and reported on.

This section discusses GL transaction processing in nine areas dealing with the following topics, respectively:

- Open/Closed periods
- Actual journals
- Budget journals
- Encumbrance transactions
- Consolidation and Elimination entries
- Year-end activities
- Archive and Purge
- Understanding the Global Accounting Engine

OPEN/CLOSED PERIODS

Calendar periods can have one of five statuses: Never Opened, Future Enterable, Open, Closed, or Permanently Closed. These are explained in the following:

- **Never Opened**—If a period is Never Opened, journals cannot be entered.
- **Future Enterable**—If a period is Future Enterable, journals can be entered but cannot be posted. A fixed number of Future Enterable periods can be defined from the Set of Books window. Often, setting up recurring invoices in Payables dictates the number of required Future Enterable periods. To post journals, open periods using the Open and Close Periods window.
- **Open**—If a period is Open, journals can be entered and posted. You open or close periods using the Open and Close Periods window.
- **Closed**—If a period is Closed, journals can neither be entered nor posted. A period must be opened again to enter or post journals. You open or close periods using the Open and Close Periods window.
- **Permanently Closed**—If a period is Permanently Closed, it cannot be reopened, so do not permanently close a period unless you are sure you won't want to reopen it.

PROCESSING ACTUAL JOURNALS

Actual journals refer to actual accounting journal entries as compared to budget or encumbrance entries, which are discussed in later sections.

Journals can be created in several ways by any of the following methods:

- Direct entry using Enter Journals window
- Importing using Journal Import window
- Creating reversals for existing entries
- Creating recurring journals using defined formulas

- Creating MassAllocations using defined formulas
- Creating Eliminations using defined Elimination Sets

Each of these is discussed here.

ENTERING JOURNALS ONLINE

Journals have three levels of information: Batch, Header, and Lines. Each journal has several account distribution lines, and optionally, several related journals can be grouped into a batch. Journals can be posted individually or by batch. Use the Reverse Journal button in the Enter Journal window to quickly create a reversal entry for the current journal or for all journals in the batch. Use the Post button to quickly post a journal or a batch. Set the profile option Journals: Allow Posting During Journal Entry to Yes if you want to use the online posting feature.

BATCH LEVEL INFORMATION Following are some important points related to entering journal batch information:

- All information entered at this level is optional.
- GL enters a default name and the latest open period if nothing is entered, and it creates one batch for every new journal entered. Enter new information and override the defaults where needed.
- Optionally, enter a control total. The batch will not be posted unless the total of all the journals in that batch agrees with the control total entered.

HEADER LEVEL INFORMATION Following are some important points related to entering journal header information:

- All journals within a batch must have the same period.
- GL enters a default name and functional currency if nothing is entered. You can enter new information or override the defaults.
- Optionally, enter a journal control total. This works for a journal in the same way batch control total works for a batch.
- Optionally, enter a Journal Description for the journal, which defaults to each line description.
- Optionally, enter reference information for the journal, which will be printed in reports.
- The Document Ordering Sequence can be configured to automatically generate a document number for each journal.
- To default a category for all journals, set up the profile option Journals: Default Category. This can now be set at the user level.
- Customize the Enter Journals folder by selecting columns to display and their display properties. Also consider making multiple versions of the folder.

LINE LEVEL INFORMATION Following are some important points related to entering journal line information:

- All Lines within a journal must have the same currency and category.
- The journal must be balanced in terms of total debits and total credits of all the lines unless Suspense Posting is allowed or the journal has a currency of STAT.

IMPORT JOURNALS

Subledgers and ADI send information into the GL_INTERFACE table. The Journal Import program imports entries into GL_JE_BATCHES, GL_JE_HEADERS, and GL_JE_LINES. The Journal Import program can be run automatically from these subledgers or manually from GL. The only exception is Fixed Assets, which directly populates the GL_JE_BATCHES, GL_JE_HEADERS, and GL_JE_LINES tables directly without the need to run Journal Import.

The subledger to GL transfers can be made in two ways: Detail or Summary. Detail transfer creates journal entry lines for all transactions against each account within a category. Summary transfer creates only totals for transactions against each account within a category.

Tip

If you are going to post journals in detail, make sure your Database Administrator understands this requirement and provides space in the database.

Journals can be imported from other legacy systems as well. To do this, populate the GL_INTERFACE table. For details of columns in this table, their contents and validations, refer to the *Oracle General Ledger Technical Reference Manual* and the *Open Interfaces Manual.*

REVERSING JOURNALS

The primary use of Reversing Journals is to reverse an accrual, a revaluation, an encumbrance, or an error. GL automatically creates a journal entry by reversing the amounts of the preexisting journal entry. The Reversible option must be Yes to be able to reverse a journal. You can choose the fiscal period that will receive the reversing entry. Create reversing journals in one of the following ways:

- Use the Reverse Batch button from the More Actions screen in the Batch zone of the Enter Journals window to create a reversing entry for the preexisting journal batch. An unposted reversal batch is created for each journal in the original batch.
- Use the Reverse Journal button from the More Actions screen in the Journals window or from the More Details screen in the Enter Journals window to create a reversing entry for the preexisting journal entry. An unposted reversal batch is created for each such reversal entry.

- Use the Reverse Journals window to reverse journals with a predefined reversal period. Select the journals to be reversed, and click the Reverse button. Journals not having a predefined reversal period do not appear in this list for selection.
- Reverse journals can now be automatically generated and posted. See the section "Automatic Journal Reversal," earlier in this chapter.

RECURRING JOURNALS

With the Recurring Journal Entries function of GL, journal entries can be created using fixed amounts and accounts. Multiple journals can be created with the same or similar information.

The following types of recurring journals can be created in GL:

- **Skeleton journals**—Here you enter accounts only. This creates journals without amounts, which are entered using the Enter Journals window.
- **Standard journals**—Here the amounts and accounts are entered as constants, and journals are created with the same account and amount information. Use the Enter Journals window to modify specific journals.
- **Formula journals**—Here the amounts vary based on the formula defined. Each generation uses the specified account balances to calculate the journal line amounts. Use the Enter Journals window to modify specific journals.

Create recurring journals in two steps as follows.

DEFINING RECURRING FORMULA Use the Define Recurring Journal Formula window to create skeleton templates, standard templates, or formulas. Reuse these templates to generate journals multiple times.

GENERATING RECURRING JOURNAL ENTRIES Use the Generate Recurring Journals window to generate unposted journal entries based on the templates or formula defined as previously mentioned. The window lists defined recurring templates or formulas. Select the batches to generate from this list. The generation of recurring journals can be scheduled as concurrent processes.

MASSALLOCATIONS

Use MassAllocations to create multiple entries from a single source account by using a formula. The source account can either be a summary account or contain parent values. First, you must define a formula for MassAllocation and then generate MassAllocation entries using the formula.

DEFINING MASSALLOCATION FORMULA Use the Define MassAllocations window to create MassAllocation definitions. GL prompts to start a concurrent program to validate the MassAllocation. Without successful validation, formulas cannot be generated.

When working with actual balances, you can select Full Balance or Entered Currency to allocate. The first option allocates both functional currency and converted functional currency amounts, resulting in functional currency entries. The second option only posts the entered currency, ignoring the converted functional currency amount. This option results in transactions of the entered currency.

Tip

When working with encumbrance balances, always use full balance because GL always keeps track of budgeting in functional currency, and all encumbrance entries should be in functional currency.

GENERATING MASSALLOCATION ENTRIES Use the Generate MassAllocation Journals window to generate journals from the MassAllocation formula defined in the previous step. MassAllocations can be generated for a range of periods. To generate for one period, enter the same period in the From and To fields. In Release 11*i* to accomplish a multistep allocation, step-down and parallel allocation sets have been added. These allocation sets can optionally contain recurring journals. Allocations and recurring journals can now be scheduled and submitted through a concurrent process.

MassAllocations can be run in Full and Incremental modes. In Full mode, the allocations are run once. In Incremental mode, the allocation is made for the differential amount where there is a change in the original balances.

USING THE DESKTOP INTEGRATOR WIZARD FOR ENTRIES

Applications Desktop Integrator (ADI) comes with a Journal Wizard to enter journals in a worksheet. You can use all the spreadsheet features for easy entry and formulas to calculate journal amounts.

ADI validates entries in the worksheet against accounts, rules, and reference information in GL.

MASSALLOCATIONS VERSUS RECURRING JOURNALS

There are some overlapping functions in MassAllocations and recurring journals and some possible business scenarios where either can be used. A few simple differences can determine how to use these features for a specific purpose:

- The recurring journal definition allows skeleton entries; MassAllocation does not. However, both feature formula and standard entries.
- The MassAllocation definition allows use of Foreign Currency. Recurring journals allow use of Foreign Currency, when a fixed relationship exists between the foreign and functional currency.
- The MassAllocation definition allows the use of parent values, whereas the recurring journal definition does not. Both allow the use of summary accounts.

- The recurring journals definition allows one formula per line; MassAllocations can have one formula for many lines.
- Formulas in recurring journals can be of any type, but MassAllocation formulas must be in A×B/C format only.

UNDERSTANDING STATISTICAL ENTRIES

Statistical Journal Entries can be accomplished in two ways. The first way is by simply using STAT for the currency field and entering the journal normally as with other currencies.

The second method is to combine statistical amounts with normal amounts. To use this technique, define the Statistical Units of Measure for any natural account segment value. Set up the Journals: Mix Statistical and Monetary profile option. When entering a journal, you can additionally enter the statistical quantity.

UNDERSTANDING INTERCOMPANY ENTRIES

Intercompany entries are those journal entries that record transactions between companies in the same enterprise. GL keeps the records balanced for each company by automatically creating offset entries to I/C account you have defined for the journal source and category. Where no I/C account is defined for the journal source and category combination, GL posts the entry to the I/C balancing account specified with a Source of Other. GL uses the value of the company segment of the AFF to determine the companies and the balancing accounts between them.

If GIS has been set up, the user can sign on with a GIS responsibility and enter GIS intercompany transactions. The sending subsidiary enters and submits a GIS intercompany transaction to a receiving subsidiary for review and approval. If the transaction requires a foreign currency, GIS automatically converts the currency to the target set of books. Certain predefined transactions from a parent subsidiary can be automatically approved. When approved, both subsidiaries run the Program - Intercompany Transfer to transfer the intercompany journals to their operating sets of books.

UNDERSTANDING CURRENCY PROCESSING

Transactions can be entered in either the functional currency (from a set of books) or a foreign currency. GL automatically converts the amounts in foreign currency journals to functional currency equivalents using daily exchange rates. GL also saves and maintains both of the amounts for all transactions.

GL provides three standard reports showing foreign currency exchange rates:

- **Daily Conversion Rates Listing**—Lists daily rates for specific currency and accounting period.
- **Historical Rates Listing**—Lists defined historical translation rates and amounts.
- **Periodic Rates Listing**—Lists defined exchange rates for any accounting period, including the period-average and period-end translation rates and revaluation rates.

GL also provides few standard reports dealing with foreign currency account balances. For these, refer to the section titled "Understanding Reports," later in this chapter.

POSTING THE JOURNALS

Journal entries can be posted into GL individually or by batch. The Post Journals window lists the batches and displays batch information including the Post Status and Batch Status. Select the batches to be posted and post them. The Enter Journals window has a More Options zone where you can post individual journals or a journal batch.

GL balances unbalanced journals if Suspense Posting is enabled for the set of books.

GL automatically balances I/C journals if I/C balancing is enabled. GL Posting automatically generates journal lines to balance debits and credits for each balancing segment value using the specified I/C account.

Posting will not be successful, when any of the following occurs:

- A control total is used and the actual batch total does not match the control total entered.
- An attempt is made to post to unopened periods.
- Unbalanced journals exist and Suspense Posting is not allowed.

REVALUATION

When transactions are entered in a foreign currency, the currency exchange rates might change by the date the amounts are paid or realized. Revaluation reflects these changes in conversion rates. Revalue account balances to update functional currency equivalents. The most commonly revalued accounts are receivables and payables. GL posts the change in converted balances to an Unrealized Gain or Loss Account.

Revalue the necessary accounts in the following steps:

1. Define an Unrealized Gain/Loss Account for posting the gain or loss resulting from revaluation.
2. Define a Revaluation Rate (use the Period Rates window). Enter either a Period-End Rate or the Revaluation Rate. GL calculates the other automatically.
3. Run a revaluation concurrent request. This creates an unposted revaluation journal batch. After reporting, restore original balances by reversing this batch of journals.
4. When a foreign currency transaction amount is paid or received, the functional currency value of the foreign currency amount is recomputed, and the difference between this amount and the original transaction amount is posted to the Realized Gain or Loss Account.

TRANSLATION

GL allows reporting of functional currency transactions in another currency using *translation*. Translation does not affect functional currency balances, nor does it create journals. The translated values are stored by GL and used for reporting. To consolidate a set of books with a different functional currency than the parent company, translation must be run in that set of books to convert to the currency of the parent company.

Translate actual or budget balances to foreign currencies for online inquiries, reports, and consolidations. GL translates balance sheet accounts using a period-end rate, and income and expense accounts using a period average rate. GL posts the difference on translation to a translation adjustment account specified in the set of books. When different rates are used to translate different accounts resulting in an out-of-balance Balance Sheet, GL posts the discrepancy to a cumulative translation adjustment account (CTA). Define a CTA account as an owner's equity account or an income account. An income account typically is used for countries experiencing hyper-inflation. Run the Translated Trial Balance to verify translated balances.

CONSOLIDATION AND ELIMINATION

When multiple sets of books are being used in GL, they can be consolidated for reporting. You must define a parent set of books into which the regular sets of books will be consolidated. GL enables you to define consolidation rules to map each set of books to the parent set of books. Run consolidation and journal import to create a consolidation batch in the parent set of books. Enable the consolidation audit trail to show any errors in consolidation so that the consolidation can be run again after corrections.

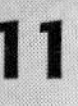

After posting consolidating journals, generate elimination journals using Elimination Sets. Post elimination journals and review results on consolidated reports. The Consolidation Workbench can be used to track the status of the consolidation and elimination process, as shown in Figure 11.10.

Tip

Consolidation can be used to consolidate sets of books with different charts of accounts, currencies, and calendars. When consolidating from subsidiary sets of books with a currency different from a parent set of books, simply revalue and translate balances as needed before transferring the consolidation data.

Tip

FSGs can be used for preliminary consolidated reporting, when all sets of books contain the same chart of accounts. In either the column set or the row set–usually the column set–a set of books and currency can be specified. This enables an FSG report to report across multiple sets of books.

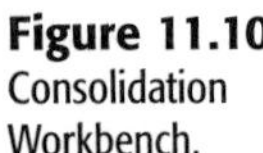

Figure 11.10
Consolidation Workbench.

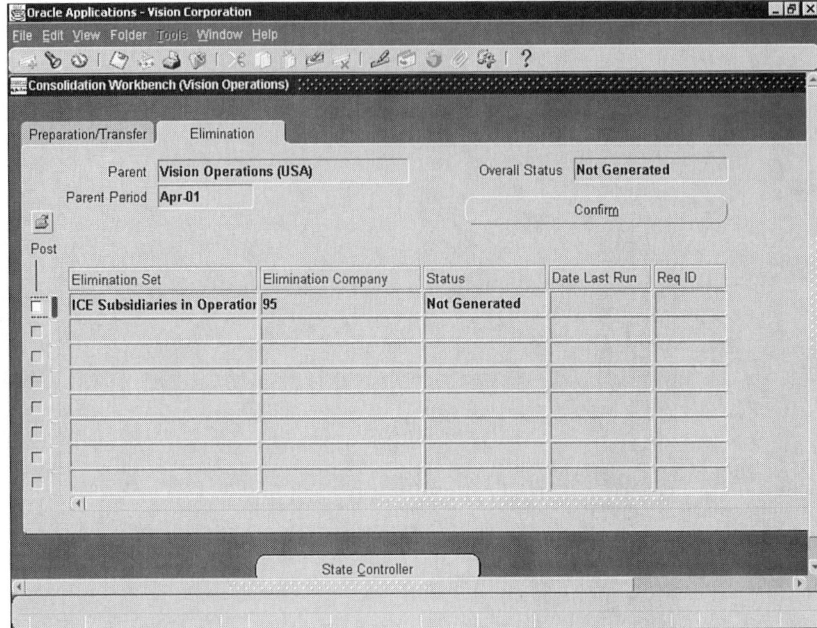

PROCESSING BUDGET JOURNALS AND TRANSACTIONS

Budget Journals are journal entries that are identified by journal type Budget. Simple budget journals can be entered the same way as Actual journal entries as discussed previously, using the Enter Journals window. Budget Journals are used as a means of entering budgets when Budgetary control is enabled. GL also provides some special techniques to manage budgets, which are discussed in this section.

BUDGETING AND ENCUMBRANCES

Budgeting for the public sector in GL implies the process starting from defining budgets, entering budget amounts, defining budgetary controls, and letting GL perform funds checks and control transactions based on availability of funds against the budget for these transactions.

Encumbrance simply is burdening or reserving funds for specific transactions. GL automatically creates encumbrances when budgetary control is enabled. You can also enter encumbrances manually like journal entries. These two topics are discussed in this section on budgeting and the following section on encumbrances.

UNDERSTANDING THE GL BUDGETING PROCESS

Budgetary control in GL or in Oracle Financials is optional and only certain types of organizations use these financial techniques. You can use budgetary control by checking the

Enable Budgetary Control option in a set of books definition. To begin the budgetary control process, it is necessary to decide the degree of control by way of the following options:

- Detail or Summary
- Absolute or Advisory
- The Budgetary Control Group rules
- Limits/budget amounts

Budgetary control requires three components to be set up: periods, accounts (including the degree of control), and amounts. A budget definition has periods to which the budget applies. This is defined using the Define Budget window. Accounts are defined using the Define Budget Organization window. Amounts can be entered in different ways, including entry of budget amounts and journals, Upload, MassBudgets, Formulas, Transfer, and ADI.

Finally, when you freeze Budgets and Budget Organizations, you prevent any updates to the budget. If changes must be made, you must open or unfreeze the budget.

When the preceding setup is in place, the budgetary control activity takes place online. GL allows only those journals to be posted that pass the funds check (assuming absolute control). GL, in integration with subledgers, tracks encumbrances for all the transactions and updates budgets/encumbrances online. GL prevents overspending by online notification of funds availability. You can build a budget hierarchy to control allocation of budget amount. You have the flexibility to enter Master/Detail budgets to suit the actual budgeting needs of the business.

Determining Degree of Control

GL gives you the flexibility to implement budgetary control at several levels. Following is a brief description of each method.

Control Level

- **Detail Level**—This is for budgetary control at the individual account level.
- **Summary Level**—This is for budgetary control at the summary account level. Specify the options for the summary template.

Funds Check Level

- **Absolute**—This is to prevent transactions that exceed the available funds.
- **Advisory**—This is to allow completion of transactions that exceed available funds, but with a warning message.
- **None**—Use this level if you do not select Automatic Encumbrance accounting.

OTHER CONTROL LEVELS

- **Amount Types and Boundaries**—Amount type determines the cumulative balance used for the funds checking interval and boundary determines the end point of the time interval. The expenditure can be controlled against a specified period, quarter, year, or project.
- **Budgetary Control Groups**—Journal sources and categories implement this control. Group your transactions and define rules for budgetary control groups. Specify tolerances for each rule, to which deviation can be allowed. Also, where there are insufficient funds, selectively enter an override amount to allow transactions exceeding the budget limits.

DEFINING A BUDGET

You can create, modify, open, or freeze a budget using the Define Budget window. The Budget Periods and Status are the most important parameters in this window and have direct impact on budgetary control.

You can also create new budgets using AutoCopy from existing budgets. However, the following restrictions apply:

- A new budget must have same beginning and ending periods as the source budget.
- A new budget must span same number of years as the source budget.
- A new budget cannot have any open years.

Open budgets are available for updates and frozen budgets are not. The Current budget is one in which the current date falls and is the default in the inquiry window. Open budget periods only when you need to use them. Open budget periods cannot be closed but are Frozen. Use the Open Next Year button to open the next budget period. Check the Require Budget Journals option to create an audit trail. Use this option only with Budgetary Control enabled.

The first period budget cannot be changed after a budget is defined. Also, the last period cannot go beyond the last calendar period of the fiscal year.

You can create a master/detail budget hierarchy using the master budget assignment. Several detail budgets can belong to a master budget. By assigning a master budget to several detail budgets, you can control the combined limit at the master budget level. This control provides flexibility between detail budgets.

Tip

> You do not need to create a budget for each year. Use the same budget year after year to ease the maintenance of FSGs and other features that reference a budget.

DEFINING BUDGET ORGANIZATIONS GL uses budget organizations to specify budget accounts. You define budgetary control options by a range of accounts. You use common business-related budget areas such as company, department, or cost center to define the Budget Organizations.

Use the Define Budget Organization window to create a new Budget Organization or to modify an existing Budget Organization. GL defaults the natural account segment name for the ordering segment and sorts accounts by this segment in ascending order when entering budget amounts or journals or querying accounts. You can optionally enable password protection for the Budget Organization using the Set Password button.

Enter the segment display sequence. This sequence is the order in which the account flexfield segments are displayed in the budget entry windows.

Use the Maintain button to start the concurrent process to add newly created or delete recently disabled accounts for a budget organization falling within the account ranges associated with a Budget Organization.

You can use the Delete button to delete the Budget Organization, and this action automatically deletes all the account assignments to this Budget Organization.

Use the Assignments window to review, delete, or assign accounts and budgetary control options to the Budget Organization. Enter them manually in the Account Assignments window. Alternatively, assign ranges manually in the Account Ranges window and use the Maintain button in the Define Budget Organization window to add all the available accounts within the assigned range.

Against each account in the Account Assignments window, specify a Budget Entry Method for the account/range from any of the following:

- Enter Budget Amounts
- Enter Budget Journals
- Upload Budgets
- Generate MassBudget Journals
- Transfer Budget Journals

Specify the budgetary control option (absolute or advisory). This assignment will imply detail-level budgetary control. Alternatively, specify None, and specify absolute or advisory in the summary template, which will imply a summary-level budgetary control. If budgetary control is not enabled, all budget entry methods can be used.

Choose the Automatic Encumbrance option for GL to create encumbrances for Payables and Purchasing transactions to this account.

Entering Budget Amounts

Use the Enter Budget Amounts window to manually enter and post budget amounts directly to balances. This action replaces any existing balance against the account. Use the Budget Rules button from this window to automatically distribute or calculate budget amounts for all budget periods specified. Budget rules give you flexibility to derive budget amounts in one of the following ways:

- Dividing the total evenly among periods
- Repeating a fixed amount in every period

- Computing an amount from actual or budget balances for every period
- Dividing a total by ratio

However, budget rules apply to a specific period range and can be applied for up to thirteen periods at a time.

Where an audit trail is necessary or Budgetary control is enabled, use the Enter Budget Journals window. Use the Worksheet mode, the Single Row mode, or the Journal mode for entering budget journals. You can also use the ADI Journal Wizard to enter budget journal transactions.

You can use Budget Formulas (discussed next) to create recurring entries for accruals or complex allocations and post calculated budget amounts to balances.

You can use MassBudgeting to create multiple allocation entries from a single formula.

Finally, you can use the Budget Transfer feature to transfer budget amounts from one account to another within the same budget. Use the Budget Transfer window to transfer fixed amounts or percentages of budget amounts. There are, however, the following restrictions that apply to Budget Transfer:

- Accounts must not be frozen.
- Accounts must be denominated in the same currency.
- Accounts must have amounts entered for the same unfrozen budget.

You can post budget journals (created by Enter Budget Journals, MassBudgeting, Budget Transfer, and Consolidations) like actual accounting journals.

You can make manual corrections to wrong budget amounts posted by Budget Upload, Budget Formulas, or Budget Carry Forward using the Enter Budget Amounts window. You can make corrections in budget journals created by Enter Budget Journals, MassBudgeting, Budget Transfer, and Consolidations using the Enter Journals window. If the journals have already been posted, enter correcting journals using the Enter Journals window.

DEFINING BUDGET FORMULAS You can create recurring budget amounts based on other budget amounts or on actual results using Budget Formulas. Use the Define Budget Formula window to create new budget formulas or to modify existing budget formulas. Budget formulas can also be created by AutoCopy from already existing formulas. Use the Lines button on the Define Budget Formula window to enter formula lines.

You can generate budget amounts from defined formulas using the Calculate Budget Amounts window. Check the batches for which amounts are to be calculated, and click the Calculate button. GL calculates these amounts and replaces existing values for specified accounts.

DEFINING MASSBUDGETS You can allocate budget amounts across a group of balancing segment values using MassBudgets. Use the Define MassBudgets window to define a

MassBudget formula. This process is similar to MassAllocation formula definition. Use the Generate MassBudget Journals window to generate budget amounts from formulas defined. MassBudgets, similar to MassAllocations, can be run in Full or Incremental mode.

Using Desktop Integrator Wizard for Budgets The Budget Wizard enables you to prepare and work on budgets in a spreadsheet environment. Budgets, budget organizations, budget rules, and formulas defined in GL can be used in the spreadsheet. Create new budgets or download budgets from GL and modify them. You can see the familiar spreadsheet analysis and graphs before automatically uploading the budget to GL.

Tip

Using the Budget Wizard, you can download actuals for multiple periods into a spreadsheet and use this as a basis for a new budget.

Freezing the Budget Freeze a budget by specifying Frozen in the Status field of the Define Budget window. No updating is possible on frozen budgets. To make an update, unfreeze the budget by specifying Open in the Status field.

Processing Encumbrances

Encumbrance implies burdening and reserving the funds. When budgetary control is enabled in the set of books, GL automatically creates encumbrance entries for Purchasing and Payables. Enabling Budgetary Control in a set of books is different from defining Budgetary Controls, as discussed in the earlier section.

Encumbrances can also be created in GL by manual entry of journals, MassAllocation, or journal import. If you do not want to use automatic encumbrances, Budgetary Control need not be enabled in a set of books unless Budgetary Controls are to be defined and implemented.

Encumbrance Types

GL has two predefined encumbrance types: Commitment and Obligation. The former implies that the funds have been reserved or committed for the transaction (for example, a requisition). The latter implies that a liability has been incurred and budgeted funds are permanently reduced (for example, a purchase). You can define additional encumbrance types.

An encumbrance type is necessary to do the following:

- Enter encumbrances manually.
- Define an encumbrance allocation.
- Import encumbrances using Journal Import.

Automatic encumbrance entries created by GL for Purchasing and Payables use the predefined encumbrance types.

ENTERING ENCUMBRANCES

Enter encumbrances in one of the following ways:

- Manual entries
- MassAllocation
- Journal Import
- Automatic entries from Purchasing and Payables

You can enter encumbrances manually using the Journals - Encumbrance window. These entries can be deleted before they are posted. For corrections after posting, correcting journal entries must be entered. GL validates entries online and creates a balancing entry to the Reserve for Encumbrance account (defined in a set of books). Encumbrance journals can only be created in the functional currency for the set of books. Both posted and unposted encumbrance entries can be reversed.

You can define MassAllocations for encumbrances just like for actual accounting journals and specify Encumbrance for Balance Type. Create unposted encumbrance entries using the Generate MassAllocation Journals window. Post these entries to update budget balances.

GL is fully integrated with Purchasing (PO) and Payables (AP) modules for encumbrances. Encumbrances are created and reversed as necessary when transactions are entered in PO and AP. For example, a commitment type encumbrance might become an obligation type on completion of the transaction. In such a case, the former entry is reversed, and the latter is created automatically by PO or AP.

Encumbrances created by manual entry, MassAllocation, or Journal Import can be relieved by reversing entries. Post the reverse entries to relieve encumbrances. You can specify a current or future period into which the encumbrance is to be reversed.

Funds availability can be determined by comparing actual balances against budget and encumbrance balances.

PROCESSING YEAR-END

In the public sector budget and encumbrance balances for any account can be carried forward to a new budget period using predefined rules. GL updates the new balances directly and does not create a journal entry.

Use the Year-End Carry Forward window to process the carry forward. Before doing a carry forward, do all of the following:

- Post all unposted journals.
- Close the last period of the fiscal year.
- Open the first period of next fiscal year.
- Open the next budget year.
- Open the next encumbrance year.

UNDERSTANDING THE GLOBAL ACCOUNTING ENGINE

The Global Accounting Engine (GAE) is a relatively new addition to Oracle Applications. It is intended to aid in creating journal entries, adjusting existing balances, and posting entries to GL directly, avoiding the Transfer to GL program that exists in each subledger application.

Following are some important features of GAE:

- Define accounting rules per set of books.
- Post different accounting rules to different sets of books.
- Maintain legal and fiscal audit trail requirements.
- Reconcile a subledger accounting system with the General Ledger.
- Audit and control period and fiscal year closing procedures.
- Define journals rather than using hard-coded categories. These journals must be numbered sequentially to comply with legal requirements.
- Assign sequential numbers to the defined journals across applications.
- Create all accounting entries within subledgers, including miscellaneous entries and intraorganization entries. No adjusting entries are necessary in General Ledger.
- Secure subledger accounting entries. You can either secure accounts individually or secure the procedure to create accounting entries. To secure subledger accounting entries, use control accounts to define accounts. A control account is only accessible from the subledgers. Securing your entries ensures a valid audit trail is maintained. The secured posting makes sure that you are only given access to a range of steps involved in the posting cycle.
- Print legal subledger accounting reports.
- Define your own accounting entries and the accounts involved.
- Use an online drill-down to original documents in the subledgers.

Following are some new features and enhancements for GAE available in Release 11*i*:

- You can update account balances directly with a balance calculation concurrent program. This program can be run for range of account combinations or a specific customer or supplier. GAE updates account balances for all periods up to the current open period.
- You can purge and archive accounting information by period from your online tables based on meeting certain requirements.
- You can use cutoff rules to enforce whether transactions can be entered and translated from subledgers, such as AP and AR.
- The Transfer to GL program provides a daily summary for control accounts from subledger entries.
- You can assign unique sequence numbers to GAE entries and optionally to GL entries using the Legal Sequencing program when the GL period is closed.

SETUP STEPS

The following components must be set up before GAE can be used:

- Create Posting Manager defaults.
- Compile the GAE program. Use the Translator Program window to enter all the parameters before compiling. Also, you need to meet certain prerequisites on the GL side, such as defining the set of books, defining and assigning sequences, and defining and assigning categories.
- Set up control accounts. These are accounts whose balances are accessed by subledger programs. GAE automatically creates detailed balances for control account balances. Look in the GAE installation manual for more details on creating control accounts or changing status of existing accounts to control account.
- If Oracle Inventory is being used, set up additional accounts for Inventory Costing.

HOW THE ENGINE WORKS

The GAE has the following main components:

- **Journal Entries window**—This form enables you to make journal entries and adjust current account balances. You can enter, query, and update adjusting subledger entries. You can also delete untranslated adjusting entries.
- **Journal Entry Lines window**—This enables you to view GAE-translated transactions.
- **Closing subledgers**—Be sure to translate all subledger transactions before trying to close a subledger. If there are untranslated entries, the program will not close the subledger. This essentially involves closing your accounting period and creating balances for accounting period transactions.
- **Submit Posting Manager**—This program posts or transfers the subledger entries to GL.

REVIEWING GAE REPORTS

- **Daily Journal Book - Line Descriptions**—Lists all accounting entries for your set of books by sequence name and period. The report prints the amounts in functional currency.
- **Daily Journal Book - Header Descriptions**—Lists all accounting entries for your set of books by sequence name and period. The report prints the amounts in functional currency.
- **Account Ledger by Account/Accounting Flexfield**—Lists all accounting entry lines per account and period.
- **Supplier/Customer Subledger by Account/Accounting Flexfield**—Lists the activity per control account in your subledger for a chosen period or periods. This report reconciles to your balances in the Supplier/Customer Balance by Account/Account report.
- **Supplier/Customer Balance by Account/Accounting Flexfield**—Lists information about balances and period activities by account and supplier/customer for one or more accounting periods. This report enables you to justify your balances in General Ledger, Receivables, and Payables.

Understanding Reports

Each transaction in GL can be traced back to the source using standard reports. GL also provides a report utility tool called Financial Statement Generator to define custom reports for specific financial purposes.

Table 11.3 lists some important GL standard reports, with a brief description of each of their purposes.

Table 11.3 GL Standard Reports

Report Name	Description
Account Analysis Report	Lists the accumulated balances of a range of accounts and all journal lines that affect that range. Details listed for each journal line include source, batch name, and description.
Account Analysis with Payables Detail Report	This report is the same as the Account Analysis Report, and the details listed for each journal line additionally include vendor name and invoice number.
Budget Trial Balance Report	Lists the GL account budget balances and activity for a specified period or range of periods in a specific currency.
Detail Trial Balance Report	Lists the GL account balances and activity for all GL account code combinations for specified balancing segments.
Encumbrance Trial Balance Report	Lists the encumbrance balances and activity for GL accounts in detail.
Expanded Trial Balance Report	Lists the beginning, ending, and net balances, as well as period activity, for a set of accounts.
Foreign Account Analysis Report	Lists the accumulated foreign balances of a range of accounts and all journal lines that affect that range. Details listed for each journal line include source, batch name, and description.
Foreign Account Analysis Report with Payables Detail	This report is the same as the Foreign Account Report, and the details listed for each journal line additionally include vendor name and invoice number.
Foreign Currency Detail Trial Balance Report	Lists the GL account balances and activity entered in a foreign currency in detail.
Foreign Currency General Ledger Report	Lists beginning and ending account balances and all journal lines affecting each account balance entered in a foreign currency.
Foreign Currency Summary Trial Balance Report	Lists the GL balances and activity entered in a foreign currency.
General Ledger Report	Lists beginning and ending account balances and all journal lines affecting each account balance in functional currency. Details listed for each journal line include source and category.

TABLE 11.3 CONTINUED

Report Name	Description
Summary 1 Trial Balance Report	Lists the GL account balances and activity for each natural account segment value by balancing segment.
Summary 2 Trial Balance Report	Lists the GL account balances and activity for a combination of account segment values and secondary segment values.
Translation Trial Balance Report	Lists the translated account balances and period activity for a specific foreign currency.

Table 11.4 lists new GL standard reports, added in Release 11*i* with brief descriptions of their purposes.

TABLE 11.4 NEW GL STANDARD REPORTS

Report Name	Description
Inactive Accounts Listing	Lists disabled and expired accounts as of a specific date
Inherit Segment Value Attributes Execution Report	Lists each account affected by running the Inherit Segment Values Attributes program
Calendar Validation Execution Report	Lists errors in your calendar when calendar maintenance is performed
GIS Import Execution Report	Indicates status of GIS Intercompany Transaction Import process and lists any errors in the data

UNDERSTANDING THE FINANCIAL STATEMENT GENERATOR

Financial Statement Generator is GL's report-designing tool. Use FSG to design custom financial statements. You can generate the reports using the Run Financial Reports window or GL's standard report submission, and you can run reports individually, in a single set, or in multiple sets.

The FSG report definition is modular, and the defined components can be reused in more than one report. Use the following items to design simple reports using FSG:

- Identify the rows and columns in your report.
- Define rows, row sets, columns, and column sets in FSG by configuring the attributes of the rows and columns and grouping the rows and columns into sets of rows and columns.
- Define a report by simply giving it a name and assigning it a row set and a column set.

DEFINING A ROW SET

Use the Row Set window to define row sets and their formats and contents. A row set normally contains the line items, accounts, and calculation row for totals. You can also create new row sets by copying from existing row sets.

Click the Define Rows button on this window to go to the Rows window and add lines to the row set. Create or modify the rows, specify their format options, assign accounts, or define calculations. If the Override Column Calculations option is selected, the row calculations take precedence over column calculations. When the similar option is checked in both row set and column set and there is a clash of priorities, refer to the Row Set Vs Column Set Override Summary matrix on pages 4–113 of the *Oracle GL User Guide* to determine which takes precedence in the given circumstances.

Select the Display Row option to display the row in a report. You might not want to display rows you have defined for any calculations or for future use.

For each row, you can assign accounts or define calculations, but you can't do both in the same row.

Tip

You can designate a different set of books to different rows. However, these different sets of books must share the same chart of accounts and calendar periods (currency can differ). If no set of books is designated, the row set can be used by any set of books.

Tip

Normally, row numbers (sequence) can be used in calculations. You can also name the rows and use the names in calculation formulas.

DEFINING ROW ORDERS

GL enables you to modify the order of detail rows in a report in different ways. Choose the ranking method, and then choose to display segment values, segment value descriptions, or both. With the Row Expand option often used in a row set definition, a row order can be used to display segment values and descriptions for only one segment.

Tip

A row order can be used with a row expand function on a range of accounts to provide the natural account value and description for every account in the range. This feature can be used to change a summary financial statement into a detailed financial statement.

DEFINING A COLUMN SET

Use the Column Set window to define sets of columns and their formats and contents. A column set typically contains the headings, subheadings, currency assignments, amount types, and calculation columns for totals. You can also create new column sets by copying from existing column sets.

Click the Define Columns button on this window to go to the Columns window and add columns for the column set. Here you create or modify the columns, specify their balance control options, and define calculations and exceptions. If the Override Row Calculations option is selected, the column calculations take precedence over row calculations. When the similar override option is checked in both row set and column set and there is a clash in priorities, refer to the Row Set Vs Column Set Override Summary matrix on pages 4–113 of the *Oracle GL User Guide* to determine which takes precedence in the given circumstances.

Select the Display Column option to display the column in a report. You might not want to display columns you have defined for any calculations or for future use.

The Column Amount Type field defines the contents of a column. Choose from predefined amount types that reflect balances or calculated amounts; actuals, budgets, or encumbrances; and single or multiple period amounts. The Column Control Value must be entered where the amount type refers to budget or encumbrance.

If one column of a column set has a level of detail, every column in that set must have a level of detail.

Click the Exceptions button of the Columns window to enter exception flags. You can designate a one-character flag for the exception conditions listed and give a description. The description will not print in the reports.

You can create column sets—as previously described—column by column or create a column set graphically, by clicking the Build Column Set button. Create headings for existing columns by clicking the Create Heading button from the Column Set window.

Tip

The amounts displayed in the column default to the functional currency from the set of books. To display the entered currency in foreign currency transactions, enter a column control value. Then, you can override the currency when defining or requesting the report.

Tip

Normally, column numbers (sequence) can be used in calculations. You can also name the columns and use the names in calculation formulas.

DEFINING A CONTENT SET

Use a content set definition to do the following:

- Override segment values and display options in row sets.
- Print multiple reports in a specific order.

Use the Content Set window to do the following:

- Create or modify content sets.
- Override row set values and display options for account segments.
- Print segment ranges in separate reports. Use this functionality to print department or cost center reports.

As in the case of row sets and column sets, content sets also can be created by AutoCopy from the existing content sets.

DEFINING REPORT DISPLAY GROUPS AND SETS

The display of ranges of rows and columns in a report can be controlled by using Display Groups and Display Sets. Define Display Groups to identify the ranges of rows and columns whose display you want to control in a report. You can enter the name of either a row or column set to control display range, but you can't enter both.

Define a Display Set, which is a combination of display groups as defined previously. When the display groups included pertain to row and column ranges from different sequences, both columns and rows are controlled. However, when they pertain to the same sequence, only the intersection of the row and column is controlled.

USING THE DESKTOP INTEGRATOR WIZARD FOR REPORTS

The Application Desktop Integrator Report Wizard provides you with a familiar spreadsheet-based interface to GL's FSG. Reports can be easily designed in a worksheet with reusable report objects from FSG. When the reports are designed, submit them for processing and view reports in the spreadsheet. Use the Analysis Wizard to drill from an amount on the report to detail account balances, journal detail, and AP and AR subledger details.

Report templates can be saved on your personal computer, and you can inherit this formatting using the Report Wizard.

SUMMARY

The Oracle General Ledger Application is the foundation for financial transactions in the Oracle Applications. GL has close ties with the subledger applications: Payables, Receivables, Projects, Inventory, Assets, and Purchasing. You can define almost any financial organizational structure for your enterprise through multiple sets of books and the Key Accounting Flexfield structure. The GL Application can handle transactions in multiple currencies and has many features for those organizations that operate in many countries. Also, GL provides budgeting and reporting capability.

CHAPTER 12

Using Oracle Payables

In this chapter

Oracle Payables is the final link in supply-chain management. The primary purpose of Payables is to enable you to perform the tasks required by this last stage of the procurement cycle. The primary task is paying suppliers for goods and services received. Oracle Payables enables you to pay suppliers using every form of payment, including automatic checks, manual payments, wire transfers, bank drafts, and electronic funds transfers.

A good payables system ensures that suppliers are paid on time, but not earlier than necessary. It also gives you the ability to manage close supplier relationships and make informed price comparisons. Oracle Payables permits you to maximize supplier discounts, prevent duplicate payments, and pay for only the goods and services you order and receive.

RELATIONSHIP TO OTHER ORACLE APPLICATIONS

Oracle Payables is only part of the total procurement cycle. Its full benefit can only be realized when it is integrated with the other applications.

Integration with Oracle Purchasing ensures that you pay only for goods that have been received and are of acceptable quality. It also ensures that purchases are properly approved and that you do not pay more than the price quoted by the supplier.

Integration with Cash Management enables you to reconcile all payments with your bank statements automatically or manually, as well as forecast cash requirements.

Integration with Assets enables you to manage all capital assets purchased, and integration with Human Resources ensures that employee expenses are paid efficiently.

Figure 12.1 shows how the other applications are related to Payables. For each application, the information shared is indicated, and the arrows show the direction in which this information flows.

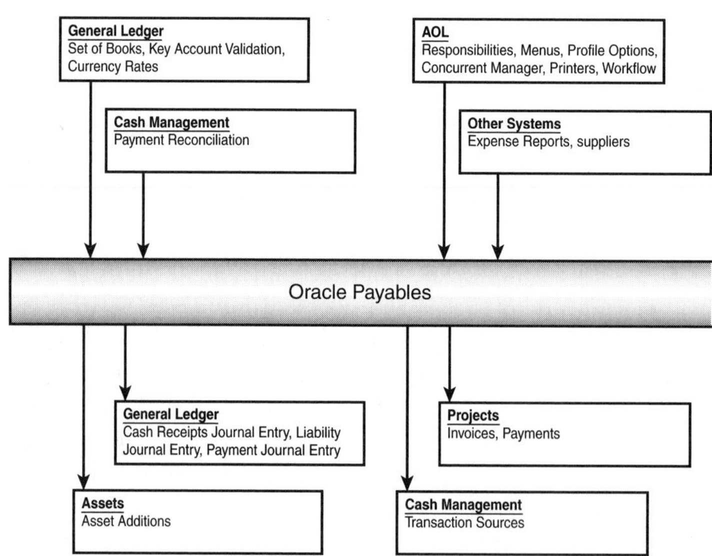

Figure 12.1
AP relationships to other applications.

NEW FEATURES IN RELEASE 11*i*

The following section describes some of the important features of Payables in Release 11*i*. These features include change in the accounting architecture related to the accounting model: functional enhancements to the handling of prepayments, easier reconciliation for the end user, and support for calculation of gain or loss at different levels.

ACCOUNTING HANDLED IN THE AP SUBLEDGER

The accounting for Oracle Payables documents is now visible in the subledger. The architecture of the Payables transactions tables has been modified to allow for accounting based on particular accounting events. The Payables Accounting Process (formerly Transfer to GL Program) enables users to view accounting entries before the entries are transferred to the General Ledger (GL). Three new tables are used in the new 11*i* architecture to hold the accounting entries created in Oracle Payables—AP_Accounting_Events_All, _AP_Ae_Headers_All, and _AP AE_Lines_All.

INVOICE GATEWAY

You can process large volumes of invoices in the Invoice Gateway window and customize the forms to the users' preferences by using the Oracle folder forms technology to make data entry more efficient. The Invoice Gateway validates your invoice records and creates invoices with distributions in the Payables system using the Payables Open Interface Import. If the invoices fail the validation during the import, Payables produces a report listing the invalid or missing information. The rejected invoices can be corrected and resubmitted for import. Figure 12.2 shows the Invoice Gateway window. You can review the rejected invoices by clicking the Rejected Invoices button located in the lower-right corner of the window. These are the same rejected records that appear on the Payables Open Interface Report. Click the Create Invoices button to submit an import, which validates the records and creates invoices from them.

ACCOUNTING EVENTS

The 11*i* accounting model tracks transactions based on accounting events. Eleven accounting events are divided into two categories, Invoices and Payments. The accounting event controls the accounting that is created for a transaction and how the accounting appears in the subledger.

VIEWING THE ACCOUNTING LINES WINDOW

This new window enables you to view the accounting lines before transferring to the General Ledger. Prior releases of Oracle required the use of the Account Analysis Report or the drill-down feature in the Account Inquiry screen of the GL. Figure 12.3 illustrates the benefit of visualizing the net effect of transactions before posting to the ledger. You can view all existing accounting entries for the invoice or payment in your query. If your organization uses Multiple Reporting Currencies, you can click the Alternate Currency button to view the accouting using an alternate currency.

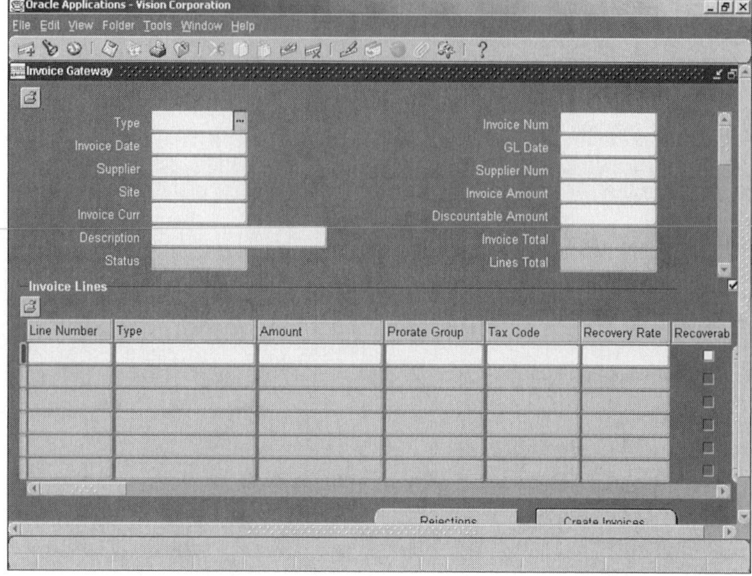

Figure 12.2
Customize your invoice gateway folder forms to hide features you don't use. This prevents you from entering values that can cause rejection during the import process.

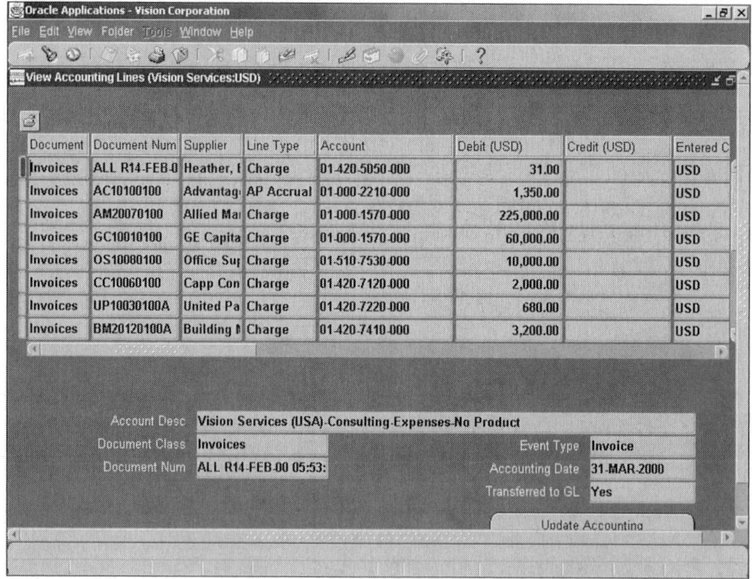

Figure 12.3
The View Accounting Lines window enables you to view the Payables Transaction in the form of a balanced accounting entry. This feature allows you to visualize the transactions' effects on the ledger without having to post journals before reviewing.

THE T ACCOUNTS WINDOW

Anyone who has taken a semester of Accounting will welcome the new T Accounts window. This feature enables the user to view the accounting entries in graphical T account format. The form can be customized to the preference of the user based on several available options. You can view the account information in Summary or Detail and print the displayed information.

Recoverable Taxes

You can ensure that you are recovering all allowable taxes by automatically accounting for recoverable and partially recoverable taxes. You also can reclaim or recover tax based on a variable recovery rate.

Record Refunds

Refunds received from suppliers and employees can be linked to the associated invoices, expense reports, credit memos, and debit memos. The link provides an easy audit trail because the transactions appear in the supplier transaction history and are reflected in the supplier balance. This enhances the clerk's ability to handle the vendor discrepancies.

VAT on Expense Reports

Supporting VAT information can now be captured for expense receipts. You can update VAT information on expense reports that have been imported.

MLS Support

Values for lookups can now be entered in other languages your site uses. The Print Invoice Notice, Prepayment Remittance Notice, and Invalid PO Supplier Notice can now print in the language set at the supplier site.

Rounding Account for Liability and Cash Clearing

Liabilty and Cash clearing accounts are fully relieved as Payables resolves and rounds differences to a rounding account.

Charge Allocations Replaces the Proration Feature

Charge amounts can be fully allocated across all eligible distributions. The Charge Allocations window can be used to associate multiple taxes and specific tax amounts with an Item line and to adjust allocations.

Invoice Matching to Receipts

Now you can accurately account for the cost of your material items by matching the invoice to receipts as opposed to the PO distribution lines in prior releases. Exchange-rate variances are likely to be smaller because the time between the receipt and the invoice is less than the time between the purchase order and the invoice.

Enhanced Accounting for Calculation of Currency Gain or Loss

The calculation of gain or loss can now be executed at the desired level. The calculation can be done at the payment level or the payment-line level. The change was instituted for people in countries who need to be able to account for gain or loss at the time of payment clearing.

IMPROVEMENT OF FUTURE DATED PAYMENT AND PREPAYMENT FUNCTIONALITY

The entry of a prepayment into Oracle payables is accounted for as an invoice. The maturity of a future dated payment can now be accounted for in a clean manner.

SUMMARIZED ACCOUNTING ENTRIES

A single accounting entry is created to the liability, cash clearing, cash, and discount as opposed to a transaction corresponding to each invoice distribution. This improvement is intended to make the reconciliation process less cumbersome to the users.

CONFIGURING THE APPLICATION

Oracle Payables is a very flexible application that can be tailored to meet your business needs using the standard functionality. Planning early in the process ensures that the decisions made during configuration will not hamper the long-term effectiveness of Oracle Payables.

Oracle Payables is easy to set up and easy to change to fit your changing business requirements. The following sections discuss the issues that are most critical to successfully configuring Oracle Payables.

RESOLVING CRITICAL SETUP ISSUES

If you are implementing more than one Oracle application, you must review the systemwide setup tasks, such as configuring concurrent managers and printers, setting up responsibilities, and assigning users to these responsibilities. You also must review the cross-product dependencies of setup tasks and reduce redundant ones.

You must decide whether you need to use the Oracle Applications Multiple Organization Support feature that enables the use of more than one set of books for one Payables installation.

REQUIRED SETUP TASKS

Table 12.1 shows the tasks required to set up the Payables application. The tasks are listed in the order they should be performed. Many tasks have predecessor tasks for data validation, so they should be performed in the proper order.

TABLE 12.1 ORACLE PAYABLES SETUP TASKS

Setup Task Name	Required?
Install or Upgrade Payables	Yes
Create User Sign-ons	Yes
Define Chart of Accounts	Yes
Define Period Types and Accounting Calendar	Yes
Enable Currencies	Optional

Table 12.1 Continued

Setup Task Name	Required?
Define Set of Books	Yes
Assign Set of Books to a Responsibility	Yes
Enter Conversion Rate Types and Rates	Optional
Select Primary Set of Books	Yes
Define Payment Terms	Yes
Define Purchase Order Matching Tolerances	Optional
Define Tax Authority Type Suppliers	Conditionally
Define Tax Name and Tax Withholding Groups	Optional
Define Invoice Approval Codes	Yes
Define Distribution Sets	Optional
Define Payables Lookups	Yes
Define Payment Interest Rates	Optional
Create Templates for Entering Expense Reports	Optional
Enter Employee Lookups	Optional
Enter Locations	Yes
Enter Employees	Conditionally
Define Reporting Entities	Conditionally Required
Define 1099 Income Tax Regions	Conditionally Required
Define Inventory Organizations	Conditionally required
Define Financials Options	Yes
Define Payables Options	Yes
Define Payment Programs	Yes
Define Payment Formats	Optional
Update Country and Territory Information	Optional
Define Bank Accounts	Yes
Define Suppliers	Yes
Assign Reporting Set of Books	Optional
Open Accounting Period	Yes
Define Request Sets	Optional
Define Reporting Formats	Optional
Set Up Printer Styles and Drivers	Yes

TABLE 12.1 CONTINUED

Setup Task Name	Required?
Define Special Calendars	Optional
Implement Budgetary Control	Optional
Implement Sequential Numbering	Optional
Define Descriptive Flexfields	Optional
Define Tax Recovery Rules	Optional
Define Witholding Tax Certificates and Exceptions	Optional
Set Up Credit Card Program	Optional
Set Profile Options	Optional

UNDERSTANDING EACH SETUP TASK

The setup tasks are where you shape the application's standard features to meet your business's particular requirements. Many setup steps affect other setups, not only in Payables but in Purchasing and Cash Management as well. You need to analyze the interdependencies of theses setup steps as you are preparing to configure Payables.

The following sections discuss the details of each setup task in the order they should be performed. The tasks are arranged into two loose categories; the first is concerned with tasks related to general applications installation and the creation of the set of books. If Oracle General Ledger is being used, the creation of the set of books and related tasks is performed during the configuration of General Ledger. The second category is regarding Payables' specific setups.

FIRST STEPS

The Payables application must be installed or upgraded to release 11.5. Next, you must use the System Administrator responsibility to create application user sign-ons and passwords. After the user is created, select the General Ledger Superuser and Payables Superuser to complete the remainder of the setups. The Application Developer responsibility can be helpful during the initial setup process because it enables you to perform cross-functional setup steps during the implementation.

CREATING A SET OF BOOKS

A *set of books* determines the functional currency, account structure, and accounting calendar for each company or group of companies. If you need to report on your account balances in multiple currencies, you should set up one additional set of books for each reporting currency. Your primary set of books should use your functional currency. Each reporting set of books should use one of your reporting currencies.

If you choose to enable budgetary control, encumbrances will be created automatically for your transactions in General Ledger, Oracle Purchasing, and Oracle Payables:

- **Defining Chart of Accounts**—If you are using General Ledger, the chart of accounts is defined there. If not, you need to define a chart of accounts. The chart of accounts is an integral part of the implementation. Take the time during your initial design to ensure the chart will meet the needs of your organization to avoid headaches down the road.
- **Accounting period types and the Accounting calendar**—If you are using General Ledger, the accounting period types and calendar are defined there. If not, you must define period types and an accounting calendar.
- **Currencies**—If you are not using General Ledger, you must enable the currencies you plan to use.
- **Choosing a set of books**—In Payables, you must select a primary set of books. After choosing the primary set of books, if needed, use the Application Developer responsibility to set the GL Set of Books ID profile option to updateable. Then, use the System Administrator responsibility to set the GL Set of Books profile option. For a single set of books installation, set the options at Application level for Oracle Payables. For a multiple set of books installation, set the option for each unique combination of organization and responsibility. The responsibility you select when you log on determines the set of books you transact in. The set of books will appear on all standard reports generated in Payables.

ENTERING PAYMENT TERMS

You can define an unlimited number of payment terms that you assign to an invoice to automatically create scheduled payments. You can define payment terms with more than one payment line to create multiple scheduled payment lines and multiple levels of discounts. Each payment terms line and each corresponding scheduled payment has a due date or a discount date based on either a specific day of a month, such as the 20th of the month, or a number of days added to your terms date, such as 30 days after the terms date. Each payment terms line also defines the due or discount amount on a scheduled payment. When you define payment terms, you specify payment amounts either by percentages or by fixed amounts.

After you define your payment terms, you can select default system payment terms that Payables automatically assigns to the suppliers and supplier sites you enter. The payment terms for a supplier site default to the invoices you enter for the site. Oracle provides a predefined payment term called Prepayment Immediate that Payables automatically assigns to all prepayments you enter.

DEFINING MATCHING TOLERANCES

Payables enables you to define both percentage-based and amount-based tolerances. Matching tolerances determine whether Payables places matching holds on an invoice. When you submit Approval for an invoice you have matched to a purchase order, Payables checks that the invoice matches the purchase order within the matching tolerances you define.

Tip

If you update the payment terms on an invoice, Payables recalculates the scheduled payment for the invoice. You must reenter any manual adjustments you made to the previous scheduled payment. For example, if you update the payment priority on a particular scheduled payment and then change the payment terms, Payables recalculates the scheduled payment using the same payment priority defaults as before, and you must redo your updates.

If you enter a zero for a percentage tolerance and enable the check box for that tolerance, Payables treats the tolerance as infinite and will never apply a hold to the invoice. You must enter a very small percentage if you want a low tolerance. If you do not have a purchasing system installed, enter the tolerances in the Tax Region only.

TAX AUTHORITY TYPE SUPPLIERS

To use automatic withholding tax, you need to define the Tax Authority type suppliers used by automatic withholding tax.

DEFINING TAX NAMES AND GROUPS

You define the tax names you use on invoices to record invoice taxes you pay to your suppliers and to your tax authorities. Each tax name has a tax type, tax rate, and account to which you charge tax amounts. If you assign tax names to expense or asset accounts, Payables automatically enters the appropriate tax name when you enter an account. During Approval, Payables uses the Tax Name to validate that tax distributions are correct.

The Withholding Tax type tax names can have multiple rates, effective date ranges, tax amounts limits, and taxable amount limits. You can also link a tax authority supplier to a Withholding Tax type tax name so you can create invoices to pay taxes you withheld from your suppliers.

To have Payables calculate the invoice sales tax and automatically create tax distributions when you enter a Sales type tax name during invoice entry, enable automatic tax calculation. Payables uses the tax rate of the tax name to calculate the sales tax. Do not define special tax names for distributions that include tax. Simply check the Includes Tax Distribution check box when you enter the distribution, and Payables adjusts the calculation.

DEFINING INVOICE APPROVAL CODES

You can define hold codes that you assign to an invoice during entry to place the invoice on hold; you can define release codes you use to remove the holds you place on invoices. You cannot pay an invoice that has a hold applied to it. You can define as many invoice hold codes and approval codes as you need.

You can also determine whether to allow posting for the hold codes you define. If you assign a posting hold code to an invoice, you cannot post the invoice until you remove the hold.

Defining Distribution Sets

If you are not matching an invoice to a purchase order, you can use a distribution set to automatically enter distributions. You can assign a default distribution set to a supplier site so Payables will use it for every invoice entered for that supplier site. You can also assign a distribution set to the invoice when you enter it.

Use *full* distribution sets to create distributions with set percentage amounts or *skeleton* distribution sets to create distributions with no amounts. If you enable and use a descriptive flexfield with your distribution set lines, the data in the flexfield is copied to the invoice distributions created by the distribution set.

Note

Distributions created by distribution sets are always exclusive of tax even if you use Automatic Tax Calculation and have checked the Includes Tax check box at the supplier site.

Defining Lookups for AP and Vendors

You can create and maintain Lookups for the following items:

- **AWT Certificate Type**—Used to define withholding tax certificates.
- **AWT Rate Type**—Used to define Withholding Tax type tax names.
- **FOB**—Used as the supplier default for all new purchase orders.
- **Freight Terms**—Used as the supplier default for all new purchase orders.
- **Bank Branch Type**—Payables predefines the following values: ABA, CHIPS, OTHER, and SWIFT.
- **Card Brand**—Four basic card brands are included: American Express, Diner's Club, Mastercard, and Visa.
- **Minority Group**—Used to classify suppliers for reporting.
- **Pay Group**—Used to initiate payment batches.
- **Disbursement Type**—Used to define payment documents.
- **Don't Pay Reason**—Used to modify payment batches.
- **EDI Payment Format**—The following are predefined: CCD, CCP, CTP, CTX, PPD, and PPP.
- **EDI Payment Method**—The following are predefined: ACH, BACS, BOP, FEW, FWT, SWT, and ZZZ.
- **EDI Remittance Method**—The following are predefined: Do not route, EDI to third party, EDI to payee, EDI to payee's bank, and EDI to payer's bank.
- **EDI Transaction Handling**—The following names are predefined: C, D, I, U, and Z.
- **Source**—Used to submit Payables Invoice Import and Payables Open Interface Import.

- **Tax Type**—Used to define tax names.
- **Supplier Type**—Used for supplier reporting.

Payables displays Lookups in the list of values for fields that require these codes. You can create as many Lookups for each item as you require. You also can update the description and inactive date of a Lookup at any time, but you cannot change the type or name after you enter and save it.

DEFINING PAYMENT PROGRAMS AND FORMATS

You can define payment formats for the four payment methods Payables uses. You can define as many payment formats as you require for each payment method, but each payment format must be unique for that payment method.

You must choose a Build Payments program and a Format Payments program for each payment format. You can choose any payment program you have defined in the Payment Programs window or any standard program Payables provides. Each Format Payments program provided by Payables includes a remittance advice program, and you can control how many invoices to include on your remittance Advice.

Payables predefines one program for building payments and many standard programs for formatting payments. Payables also predefines a program for creating a separate remittance advice for payments. You can select these predefined programs when you define a payment format, or you can use these programs as templates for creating your own custom payment programs.

DEFINING PAYMENT INTEREST RATES

In the Payment Interest Rates window, you must define the interest rates Payables will use to calculate and pay the interest on overdue invoices. Payables calculates interest only on overdue invoices if you enable the Allow Interest Invoices Payables option and enable the Allow Interest Invoices option for the supplier site of an invoice. The formula compounds monthly, up to a maximum of 365 days interest. You can add or change a rate at any time. Payables uses the interest rate that is valid on your payment date to calculate and pay interest on overdue invoices. You can specify the effective dates for each rate you define, but the effective date of rates cannot overlap.

DEFINING BANK ACCOUNTS

You must define banks and bank accounts to create payments. Payables uses this bank information when you create electronic payments for your suppliers. You must create at least one payment document before you can use a bank account to create payments.

When you define payment documents, you can select only payment formats that use the same currency as the bank account currency. If the bank account is a multiple-currency bank account, you can select foreign-currency payment formats or multiple-currency payment formats. You should use manual payment reconciliation for a multiple-currency bank account to avoid a large number of exceptions that would occur with automatic payment reconciliation.

DEFINING EXPENSE REPORT TYPES

You must define expense report templates for the various types of expense reports you use in your company. You can define default values for expense items, and you can then select those items from a list of values when you enter expense reports. During Invoice Import, Payables uses the expense item information to create invoice distributions.

If you use Oracle Web Employees, you can define expense templates and expense items that your employees can use to enter their own expense reports using a standard Web browser. Employees can enter project-related expense reports via Self-Service Expenses.

DEFINING EMPLOYEE LOOKUPS

If you define your employees in Payables rather than Oracle Human Resources, you can also define Employee Lookups in Payables.

DEFINING LOCATIONS

In Oracle Human Resources, you set up each physical site where your employees work as a separate location. You can also enter the addresses of external organizations you want to maintain in your system. When you are setting up internal or external organizations, you select from a list of these locations. This approach enables you to enter information about each location only once, saving data entry time. It provides for central maintenance of locations to ensure consistency of address standards.

DEFINING EMPLOYEES

You can enter, maintain, and view basic personal information and addresses for employees. You can also enter work assignment information, which includes organization, job, position, work location, and supervisor's name.

Note

You cannot use this form if Oracle Human Resources is fully installed at your site. You must use the HR Person form, which maintains a date-tracked history of any changes you make to employee records.

DEFINING REPORTING ENTITIES

A *reporting entity* is any person or organization that has a unique Tax Identification Number (TIN).

You can submit the following 1099 reports for a specific reporting entity:

1096 Form

1099 Forms

1099 Invoice Exceptions Report

1099 Supplier Exceptions Report

1099 Payments Report

1099 Tape

For each reporting entity, you need to assign one or more balancing segment values. Payables sums up the paid invoice distributions that have these company balancing segment values in their accounts.

DEFINING INCOME TAX REGIONS

You must define tax regions if you are using 1099 Combined Filing Program reporting in the United States. If you enable the Combined Filing Payables option, when you submit the 1099 Tape, Payables produces K records for all tax regions (or states) participating in the Combined Filing Program that have qualifying payments. Payables also produces B records for suppliers with 1099 payment amounts that equal or exceed the tax region's reporting limit in qualifying states.

Payables has predefined the region abbreviations and the descriptions for all U.S. states, the District of Columbia, and some U.S. territories. Payables has also predefined the region codes for those tax regions participating in the Internal Revenue Service's current Combined Filing Program. You must enter a region code for all tax regions that you want to use for the Combined Filing Program reporting and that Payables has not already defined. You must define your income tax regions so that they conform to the IRS codes. Use the 1099 Supplier Exceptions Report to identify any 1099 suppliers with state abbreviations that do not conform to the income tax regions defined here. Payables uses the tax region from the invoice distributions to determine to which tax authority Payables should report the payments when you submit your 1099 reports.

DEFINING INVENTORY ORGANIZATIONS

If you are using Oracle Inventory or Oracle Purchasing, you must define at least one Inventory Organization before you define Financials Options.

DEFINING FINANCIALS OPTIONS

Oracle Payables, Oracle Purchasing, and Oracle Assets share Financials Options. Depending on your application, you might not be required to enter all fields.

You need to define these options and defaults only once for each operating unit; you can update them at any time. If you change an option and it is used as a default value elsewhere in the system, it will be used as a default only for subsequent transactions.

You are required to enter defaults for the Accounting Financials Options in the Accounting region. If you are not using Oracle Purchasing, you do not need to enter defaults in the Supplier-Purchasing region. In addition, if you are not using Oracle Human Resources, you are not required to enter defaults in the Human Resources region. If your organization does not need to record a VAT registration number, you don't need to enter defaults in the Tax region. Most of the Supplier-Payables Financials Options are used as defaults for entering suppliers.

Defining Payables Options

The Control options and defaults are used throughout Payables to simplify supplier entry, invoice entry, and automatic payment processing. You define these options and defaults only once for each operating unit, but you can update them at any time to change controls and defaults for future transactions. Figure 12.4 displays the Accounting region of the Payables Options window. Notice the first of the two options in the Cash Clearing region—Allow Reconciliation Accounting. If this is enabled, Cash Management is used to clear and reconcile payments.

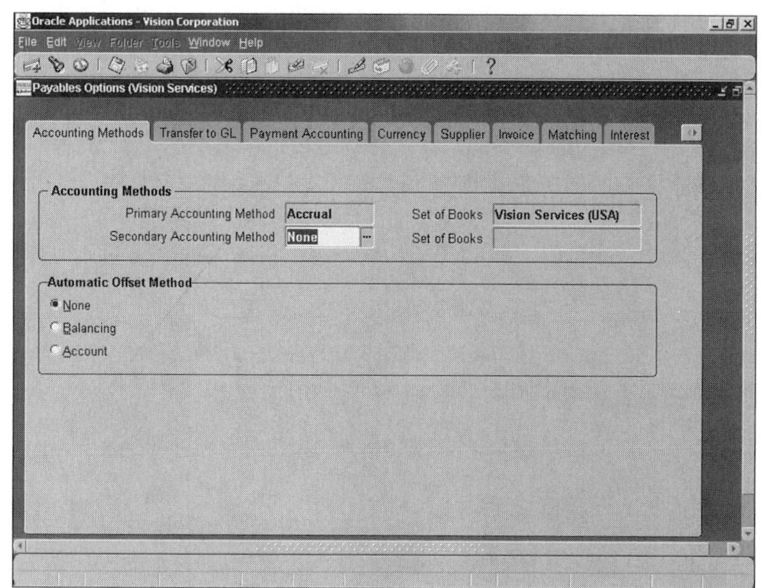

Figure 12.4
The Accounting region of the Payables Options window includes a setup area called Journal Entry Creation. This setup controls defaults for the submission of the payable transfer to General Ledger process, for how it creates entries in the gl_interface.

Defining AP Periods and Period Types

Oracle Payables provides you with the Period Types of Month, Quarter, and Year. You can set up additional types if necessary. Use these types when you define the Payables calendar. The periods define the number of periods in the calendar year.

The possible period statuses are as follows:

- **Never Opened**—First status of a new period. Must be changed to Future or Open for transactions.
- **Future**—Invoice entry allowed.
- **Open**—All transactions allowed.
- **Closed**—Transactions not allowed. Can be reopened.
- **Permanently** Closed—Cannot be reopened.

OPEN PERIODS IN THE AP CALENDAR

Payables periods are separate from General Ledger periods. For example, you can close the January period in AP before you close the January period in General Ledger.

Payables provides for invoice entry, payment entry, and payment voiding in open accounting periods. You can enter invoices in Future accounting periods, but you cannot post any invoices in Future accounting periods until the status is changed to Open. The period statuses available in Payables are Never Opened, Future, Open, Closed, and Permanently Closed.

When you update a period status to Closed, Payables automatically checks whether you have any unposted transactions in that period. If you have any unposted transactions in a period you are trying to close, Payables prevents you from closing the period and automatically submits the Unposted Invoice Sweep report. You can use this report to view all your unposted transactions for the period. You can submit the Unposted Invoice Sweep program if you want to move all unposted transactions from one period to another. Then, you close your period. The form to control the status of an accounting period is found under the Accounting Section of the menu. This is a change from previous releases, in which it resided in the Setup section of the menu.

DEFINING REPORT SETS

Defining report sets enables you to submit the same set of reports regularly using the same request. You can use the Request Set window or Request Set Wizard to create report sets.

DEFINING REPORT FORMATS

The Payables Account Analysis Report replaces the Expense Distribution Detail report from prior releases. The report does not require a setup form and was created to assist with the reconciliation of accounts to the General Ledger. It can be submitted for an account date range and for a full account segment range.

The Invoice Aging Report requires you to set up the Aging Periods. The Invoice Aging window is used to define the format of the Invoice Aging Report.

When printing tax forms, it is important to ensure that your report formats meet IRS standards. Payables provides 1096 and 1099 forms, but you might have to work with your DBA or system administrator to ensure you have the proper print setup string and form alignment.

DEFINING SPECIAL CALENDARS

You can create special calendars to define periods that Payables will use for automatic withholding tax, recurring invoices, and the Key Indicators Report. The periods defined using the Special Calendars are separate from the periods defined for the AP Accounting Periods. The Key Indicators Report provides valuable information for tracking performance, such as number or invoices and payments for a given period of time as defined in the special calendar.

DEFINING BUDGETARY CONTROL

You enable Use PO Encumbrance in the Financials Options window. This enables you to check funds before you save a transaction, and you can have Payables automatically create encumbrance entries to reserve funds for your transactions. If you use *absolute* budgetary control, Payables places an Insufficient Funds hold on any invoice that fails funds checking. On the other hand, if you use *advisory* budgetary control, Payables allows the invoice to pass Approval, even if it fails funds checking. During Approval, Payables creates encumbrance entries to reserve funds against the budgets you define in Oracle General Ledger.

DEFINING SEQUENTIAL NUMBERING

You can assign sequential voucher numbers to each invoice and payment to ensure that you have a unique number for each document. For example, you might get two invoices with identical invoice numbers from two different suppliers. If you assign each a voucher number, you can locate each invoice based on its unique voucher number.

If you use sequential voucher numbers, you can confirm that no document has been lost or unposted. The voucher number retains audit records even if invoices or payments are deleted. An audit trail is maintained so you can trace a journal entry back to the original document if you post detail journal entries in your general ledger.

Note

Do not use voucher numbers that exceed nine digits because Payables cannot process vouchers that exceed nine digits.

DEFINING DESCRIPTIVE FLEXFIELDS

To define your descriptive flexfield, you define the segments, descriptive information, and value set information for each segment in a structure. You also determine the appearance of your descriptive flexfield window, including the size of the window, number and order of the segments, and segment descriptions and default values. The maximum number of segments possible within a single structure depends on which descriptive flexfield you are defining.

After you define or change your flexfield, you must freeze your flexfield definition and save your changes. When you do, Oracle Applications automatically compiles your flexfield to improve online performance.

After you freeze your flexfield definition and save your changes, Oracle Applications submits a concurrent request to generate a database view of the table that contains your flexfield segment columns. You can use these views for custom reporting at your site.

Tip

You should plan your descriptive flexfield structures carefully–including all your segment information, such as segment order and field lengths–before you set up your segments. You can define your descriptive flexfields any way you want, but changing your structures after you have entered data can create data inconsistencies that could have a significant impact on the performance of your application or require a complex conversion program.

SETTING THE PROFILE OPTIONS

You set values for profile options in Oracle Financials to specify how Payables controls access to and processes data. In addition to the Payables profile options, Payables uses profile options from other Oracle Financials applications to control features, such as Budgetary Control and Sequential Numbering, which affect more than one application.

Many of these user profile options are set, using the System Administrator responsibility, at one or more of the following levels: Site, Application, Responsibility, and User. Use the Personal Profile Options window to view or set your profile options at the user level.

PROCESSING TRANSACTIONS

Transactions refer to the process of creating, approving, and maintaining invoices, credit memos, adjustments, and payments. The following sections describe how to work with the various types of transactions.

SETTING UP AND MODIFYING VENDORS

You might want to use a naming convention that minimizes the risk of separate entries of the same supplier with slightly different spellings of the same name. If you inadvertently add a duplicate supplier, use the Supplier Merge requests to merge both suppliers into a single supplier record. You can update the purchase orders and invoices to refer to the merged supplier. If you enable the Automatic Supplier Numbering option in the Financials Options window, Payables automatically enters a sequential supplier number for you. You specify the beginning number when automatic Supplier Numbering is enabled. If you did not enable this option, you must enter a unique supplier number for each supplier.

The following information can be entered for each supplier. The available windows can be accessed by clicking the Alternative region shown in Figure 12.5. This information is defaulted into each supplier site created:

Bank Information

Classification Information

Control Information

Electronic Data Information

Invoice Tax

Payment Information

Purchasing Information

Receiving Information

Tax Information

Witholding Tax Information

After entering the preceding supplier information, you must enter the supplier site name and address. The site name will not appear on documents you send to the supplier. It is for your reference when you select a supplier site from a list of values during transaction entry. You can enter any additional supplier site information you want to record for each supplier site. Most of the information set at the Supplier level can also be set at the Supplier Site level. Contact information is set at the site level. If supplier information has automatically defaulted to the new supplier site, you can override these defaults. At least one Pay Site must be set up for a supplier before entering invoices.

If you want to prevent invoice or purchase order entry for this supplier after a certain date, enter an inactive date.

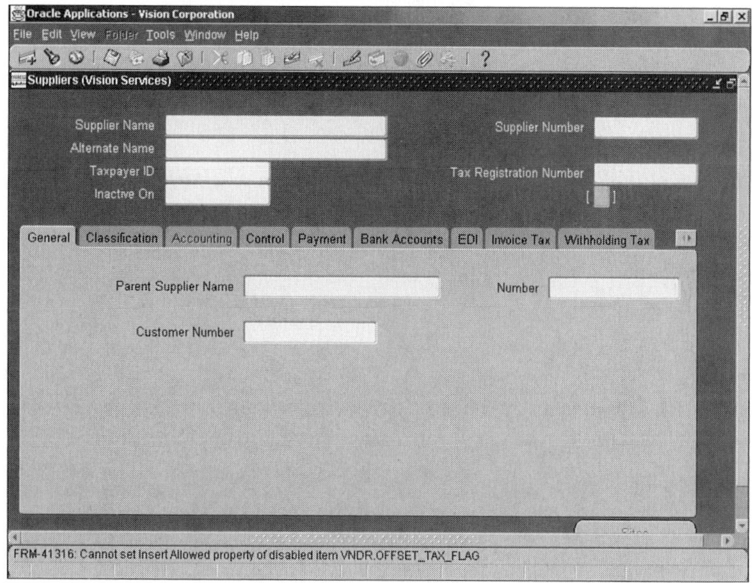

Figure 12.5 Before entering suppliers, verify that the suppliers have not already been entered into the system. You can use the Suppliers Report and Supplier Audit Report to aid the process. This prevents you from having to use the Supplier Merge function later.

ENTERING INVOICES

Before payments can be made to a supplier, the supplier's invoice must be entered. Invoices can be manually entered or entered through Payable Open Interface. The new Invoice Gateway enables you to enter high volumes of invoices in a timely manner. If invoices are entered manually, they can be entered individually or as part of a batch.

You can use batches in the following ways:

- You can enter invoice defaults at the batch level that override both system and supplier site defaults for all invoices in the batch.
- You can maximize accuracy by tracking variances between the control invoice count and total and the actual invoice count and total resulting from the invoices entered in your batch.
- You can easily locate a batch online and review the name of the person who created the batch and the date it was created.

There is much information that can be entered for each invoice; some of this information is required, and some is optional. Invoices can be matched to purchase orders or entered without matching to a purchase order. Payables supports eight types of invoices. The data requirements might be a little different for each one. The Invoice Type is the first field entered in the Invoices window (see Figure 12.6).

Following are the eight types of invoices:

- **Standard**—This is the typical invoice from a supplier.
- **Credit Memo**—This invoice represents a credit for goods or services.
- **Debit Memo**—This is used to notify a supplier of a credit you recorded.
- **Expense Report**—This is an internally generated invoice to record business-related expenses incurred by an employee.
- **PO Default**—When you match the invoice to a specific PO number, information is defaulted from the PO.
- **QuickMatch**—This is used when you want to automatically match all PO shipment lines to an invoice.
- **Mixed**—Mixed invoices can perform both positive and negative matching to purchase orders and other invoices.
- **Prepayment**—This invoice is used for advanced payments. They can be entered for suppliers or employees. The two types of prepayments are temporary and permanent.

Payables offers full integration with Oracle Purchasing and with other purchasing systems. Payables automatically creates distributions lines for you when you enter an invoice and match it to a purchase order. If you have set up matching tolerances, Payables validates that the match is within the tolerances defined.

Payables supports two-way, three-way, and four-way matching. *Two-way* matching is matching the invoice to an approved purchase order, whereas *three-way* matching is matching the invoice to an approved PO and receipt. Finally, *four-way* matching ensures that the invoice is for goods that are on an approved PO, have been received, and have been accepted.

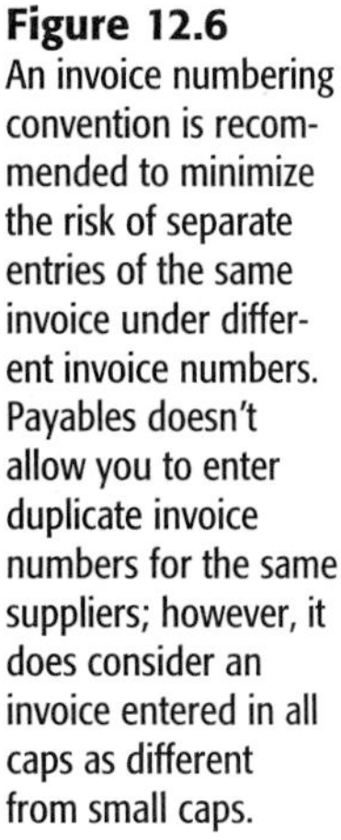

Figure 12.6
An invoice numbering convention is recommended to minimize the risk of separate entries of the same invoice under different invoice numbers. Payables doesn't allow you to enter duplicate invoice numbers for the same suppliers; however, it does consider an invoice entered in all caps as different from small caps.

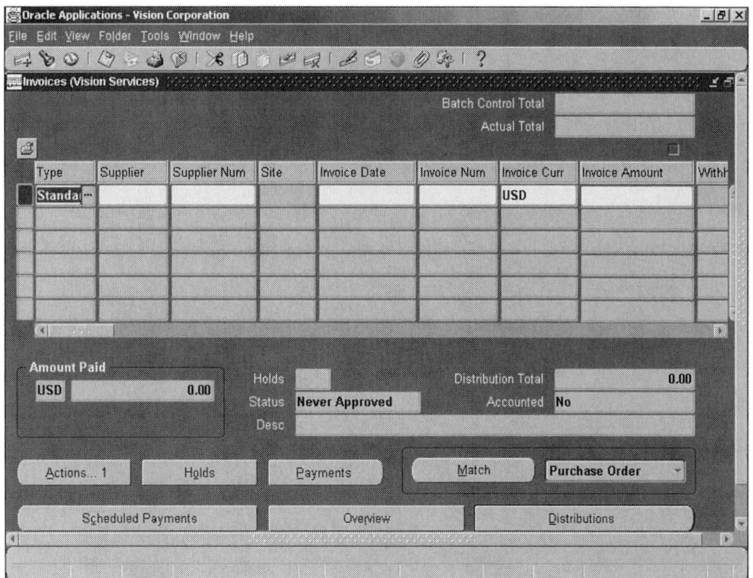

USING EXPENSE REPORTS

You can use the Expense Reports window to enter, review, and modify expense reports for your employees. You also can review and modify expense reports that are entered in Oracle Projects or Web Employees and then transferred to Payables. If you have paid advances to an employee, you can apply advances to expense reports to reduce the amount you pay. You can also apply a hold to an expense report to prevent payment and apply advances and holds to expense reports that are from any source.

You must submit the Payables Invoice Import program to have Payables automatically create invoices from the expense reports before you can pay expense reports. You can then use Payables to pay the invoices and create journal entries for posting to your general ledger. If expense reports have been purged during the Payables Invoice Import, you can no longer view them in the Expense Reports window. If reports have not been purged, you can view them in the Expense Reports window, but you cannot make changes.

IMPORTING INVOICES

Invoice Import creates Payables invoices from expense reports entered in Payables, Oracle Web Employees, or Oracle Projects. You can then use Payables to pay these invoices and create journal entries for general ledger posting.

When you import invoices, Payables records the source of the imported invoices and the imported invoice details. Payables Invoice Import verifies all your expense report and invoice information to ensure it creates valid, fully distributed invoices that are ready for approval and payment. If the expense report fails validation, Payables Invoice Import does not create an invoice and reports the exception on the Payables Invoice Import Exceptions Report. When you submit Payables Invoice Import, Payables automatically prints the Payables Invoice Import Exceptions Report, which displays detailed information on all exceptions.

Tip

If you are importing invoices from an external system, note that beginning with Payables release 12, you will be able to import external invoices only through the Payables Open Interface Import process. While using Release 11*i*, you should plan to migrate any existing processes from the Payables Invoice Import Interface Tables to the Payables Open Interface Tables. If you are implementing any new Payables Invoice Import processes, you should use only the Payables Open Interface Tables and the Payables Open Interface Import process.

If you enable the Automatically Create Employee as Supplier Payables option, Payables automatically creates suppliers and supplier sites for employees who are not already suppliers. Otherwise, you must manually enter the employee as a supplier before submitting Payables Invoice Import.

To purge expense reports from the Payables Invoice Import Interface Tables, enter the date criteria you want Payables to use. Payables deletes all records for expense reports that were entered before this date and have already been imported. Payables does not import an invoice or expense report more than once.

Defining and Creating Recurring Invoices

Recurring invoices are great for periodic business expenses such as rent, where you do not receive invoices. To create a recurring invoice, you must first create a template. The template enables you to specify the intervals in which the invoices will be created, create as many as two nonstandard invoice amounts such as deposits or balloon payments, and create invoices that increase or decrease from period to period by a fixed percentage.

Approving Invoices

Before you can pay or post an invoice, the invoice must pass the Approval process. This can be done online by using the Invoice Actions window or the Approve button in the Invoice Batches window, or it can be done by submitting the Payables Approval program from the Submit Request window.

Approval validates the matching, tax, period status, exchange rate, and distribution information for invoices entered and automatically applies holds to exception invoices. If an invoice has a hold, you can release the hold by correcting the exception that caused the hold to be applied and then resubmitting Approval. You can correct the exceptions either by updating the invoice or the purchase order or by changing your Invoice Tolerances. Payables automatically releases the hold when the exception is no longer an issue. You can manually release certain invoice holds even if you have not resolved the error condition. Authorized users can always correct an invoice, even if you have approved, paid, or created journal entries for the invoice.

You can check for unapproved invoices by submitting the Invoice Register for Unapproved Invoices Only or by viewing the invoice online.

Payables and Oracle Alert are fully integrated to enable you to notify approvers and purchasing agents when an invoice is placed on hold. Exception reporting in Alert is accomplished using either e-mail or printed reports.

You can automate your approval cycle by scheduling the Approval process to run at specific intervals, such as once a day at 5 p.m. You define your submission options for the Payables Approval program in the Submit Request window.

ADJUSTING INVOICE PAYMENT SCHEDULES

If an invoice is not fully paid, you can make any adjustments you need to the scheduled payments. You can add new scheduled payments and alter unpaid scheduled payments. You can defer payment by adjusting due dates on schedules or by applying holds to selected scheduled payments.

Note

Payables recalculates and replaces scheduled payments if you adjust the invoice Payment Terms or if the Scheduled Payment Recalculation Payables option is enabled and you submit Approval for the invoice. If you manually adjust scheduled payments and Payables subsequently recalculates the scheduled payments, you need to reenter your changes.

ADJUSTING DISTRIBUTIONS

If you have not yet created accounting entries for an invoice distribution, you can update most of the Invoice distribution details, including Description, GL Date, Income Tax Type, Withholding Tax Group, and Income Tax Region. If the Invoice is paid, enable the Allow Adjustments to Paid Invoice Payables option. Some invoice values, such as the GL Date, are used as defaults when you create new invoice distributions. If you change an invoice GL Date, it does not affect the existing GL Dates for the invoice distributions. If you want to change invoice distribution GL Dates, you must change them in the Distributions window.

You can cancel an invoice if it has not been paid. When an invoice is canceled, no more changes can be made to it. If the invoice has never been submitted for approval, you can simply delete it.

Adjusting Purchase Order Matched Invoices

You can reverse matched distributions or create new distributions by matching to new purchase order shipments or distributions of either the same purchase order or another purchase order. If you add or reverse invoice distributions, you must also change the scheduled payment amounts to match the new invoice total; otherwise, Payables places holds on the invoice.

If you have enabled the Allow Flexfield Override Payables option and have not yet posted the invoice, you can change the account fields to a purchase order–matched invoice distribution. You can always adjust the GL Date and Income Tax Type.

You use a price correction to adjust for a change in the invoiced unit price of previously matched purchase order shipments or distributions. You do not have to change the quantity billed.

Entering Notes

Attachments can be created in the Enter Invoices window and viewed in either the Enter Invoices or Invoices Overview window. Attachments enables you to link almost any data type to your invoices. Examples are spreadsheets, documents, or images.

Writing Off Accruals

The Accrual Write-Off Report provides the supporting detail for the journal entries you create to write off accrual transactions. When you have identified through research all transactions that should be removed from the Accrual Reconciliation Report, you use the Accrual Write-Off window to remove those transactions from the report (see Figure 12.7).

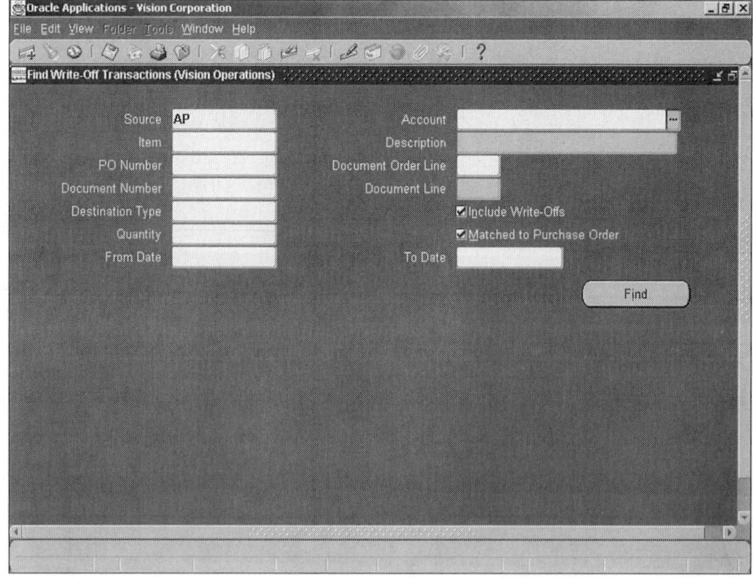

Figure 12.7
In the Find Write-Off Transactions window, enter AP as the source and enter any other search criteria. Then, click the Find button.

Note

The Accrual Reconciliation Report is a barometer to ensure you are being invoiced for the items you received. The Accrual Write-off Process is a necessary exercise to keep the Accrual Reconciliation Report current and manageable. Efficient use of this process enables the parameters of the Accrual Reconciliation Report to limit the size of the report. It is vitally important to understand the value of these reports and avoid the costly write-offs associated with not managing them properly.

ENTERING PREPAYMENTS

A *prepayment* is a type of invoice used to pay an advance payment to a supplier or an employee. For example, you might need to pay an employee an advance for travel expenses. You can later apply the prepayment to one or more invoices or expense reports you receive from the supplier or employee to offset the amount paid to him.

You can enter either a Temporary or Permanent type prepayment. *Temporary* prepayments can be applied to invoices or expense reports you receive, whereas *Permanent* prepayments cannot be applied to invoices. For example, you use a Temporary prepayment to pay a catering deposit. When the caterer's invoice arrives, you apply the prepayment to the invoice to reduce the amount you pay. You would use a Permanent prepayment to pay a lease deposit for which you do not expect to be invoiced. Prepayments can be changed from Permanent to Temporary if they need to be applied to an invoice.

Prepayments must be approved and fully paid before they can be applied to an invoice. You cannot partially pay a prepayment. The Settlement date controls when a prepayment is available for use. During Invoice entry, Payables notifies you if you have outstanding Temporary prepayments for that supplier or employee. You can also review the Prepayment Status Report to check the status of all Temporary prepayments.

When a prepayment is applied to an invoice, Payables automatically creates a negative distribution and a negative scheduled payment for the prepayment in the amount of the applied prepayment. Payables also reduces the amount available for prepayment by the amount applied. You can either select an invoice and apply a prepayment to it or select a prepayment and apply it to an invoice.

You apply prepayments, or employee advances, to expense reports during expense report entry (see Figure 12.8). Unless you specify a specific advance to apply, Payables applies all outstanding, available advances—starting with the oldest—up to the amount of the expense report.

If you mistakenly apply a prepayment to an invoice, you can unapply it. Unapplied and unpaid prepayments can be cancelled; however, prepayments that have been paid and applied to an invoice must be unapplied and the payment cancelled before the prepayment can be cancelled.

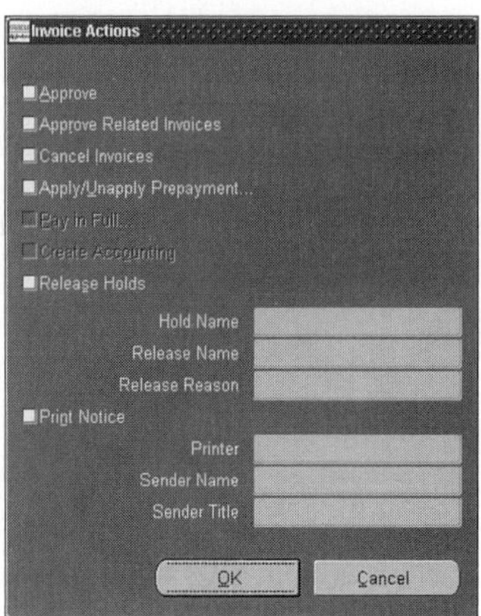

Figure 12.8
The prepayment functionality in 11*i* has enhanced the accounting created by associated transactions. The prepayment application event relieves the liability account for the amount of the applied prepayment, and it credits the prepaid expense account for the amount applied.

MAKING PAYMENTS

The next step after entering and approving invoices is to pay the invoices in an efficient and timely manner. Payments can be made to suppliers by any of the following means:

- Automated checks
- QuickCheck
- Manual payments
- Wire transfers
- EDI
- Electronic Funds Transfers (EFT)

AUTOMATED CHECKS

Automatic checks are computer-generated payments to pay a supplier for one or more invoices. Automatic checks use the payment terms and due date to select invoices for a payment batch. You follow a series of steps to create your payment batch payments, and you initiate each step from the Payment Batch Actions window. The following sequence of steps must be followed to create a payment batch:

1. Invoice Selection
2. Payment Build
3. Modification
4. Format and Print
5. Confirmation

Note All payment batch windows display amounts in the payment currency.

SELECTING ITEMS FOR PAYMENT The following are the steps to follow for selecting items for payment:

1. Enter a unique batch name.
2. Define your invoice selection criteria in the Payment Batches window. Payables selects all approved invoices that match your invoice selection criteria.
3. Enter or change the default bank account.
4. Select a payment document.
5. Enter or change the payment date.
6. Optionally, select a Pay Group.
7. Verify the pay-through date.

Payables selects all invoices due for payment based on the preceding entered criteria. Payables then selects invoices with a discount or due date on or before the pay-through date. Figure 12.9 illustrates the beginning of a Quick payment type. You use a Quick payment type for a single computer-generated payment.

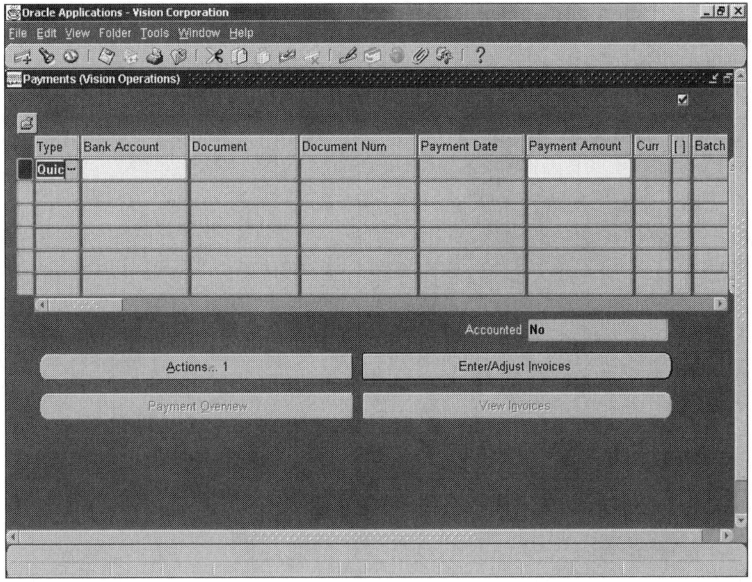

Figure 12.9 For payments originating outside the Payables system, you use a Manual Payment type to record the transaction. You can also record zero-dollar payments, if you have allowed them in the bank account setup. The zero-dollar payments might be necessary to remove certain invoices of the AP trial balance.

Note

If you want to save this payment batch as a template for future payment batches, check Template.

PAYMENT BUILD When Payables builds payments, it determines which invoices will be paid with each payment document. Payables automatically builds payments when you initiate invoice selection. Payables also automatically builds payments after you modify a payment batch. You do not have to perform this task unless the build process does not complete successfully.

Select Actions to open the Payment Batch Actions window. Depending on whether you want to be able to review and modify the payment batch before formatting, complete one of the following two options:

- If you want to format the payments without modifying them, select Format Payments to have Payables automatically select and perform the required prerequisite actions, which are Select Invoices and Build Payments. Payables then formats the payments. After formatting is complete, continue with Printing Payment Batch Checks, or if you are creating electronic payments, proceed with Confirming Payment Batches.
- If you want to review and modify the invoices selected in the payment batch before you format payments, select Select Invoices to have Payables select invoices and build payments.

After the build process is complete, you have the option to proceed with Modifying Payment Batches or Formatting Payments.

MODIFYING THE SELECTION After selecting invoices and building payments, you have the opportunity to review and modify the payment batch. You can prevent payment of a particular invoice, modify the payment amount of an invoice, or add an invoice that Payables did not originally select. After you complete your modifications, you can review your changes on a new Preliminary Payment Register. You can continue with the next step in the process, or you can modify the payment batch as many times as necessary.

Note

If invoices include withholding tax, you cannot adjust the payment amount or the discount amount.

FORMATTING PAYMENTS When Payables formats payments, it creates an output file that is used to print the checks, or if you are making electronic payments without the EDI Gateway, you can deliver the output file to your bank for processing. The output file is stored in the Payables output directory. Its name is created by appending a period and the concurrent manager request number to your AOL user ID (for example, `SYSADMIN.12345`). If you are making electronic payments with Oracle e-Commerce Gateway, the Remittance Advice Outbound Extract creates a flat file in your e-Commerce Gateway output directory.

Payables uses the printer you assigned to your payment program as the default printer. If you have not assigned a printer to your payment program, Payables uses the printer assigned as your default printer in your Printer profile option.

After printing is complete, the next step is confirming payment batches.

CONFIRMING PAYMENTS Confirming is the final step in processing a payment batch. This step updates the payment history of invoices paid and associates payment document numbers with the invoices and invoice payments. You cannot close a period or use the same payment document for any other payments until you confirm the payment batch.

You must record the status of every payment document during confirmation. The four statuses are Setup, Printed, Skipped, and Spoiled. Setup is used to designate check stock that is wasted as part of the process of aligning checks in the printer; usually this is a preset number. The Printed status designates successfully printed checks, whereas Skipped is used to designate check numbers that were skipped over or not used on a check. Lastly, Spoiled refers to checks that were damaged as part of the printing process.

If you are using check overflow, you should record the status of all the checks as Printed. Check overflow occurs when you have more invoices paid on a single check than can fit on the remittance stub and Payables voids all checks except the one on the last remittance stub for that supplier site.

From the Confirm window, you can record the status of the payments and, if necessary, restart the payment batch or cancel the remainder.

RESETTING A PAYMENT BATCH Troubleshooting begins with identifying the current status of your payment batch so you can determine the best course of action. You can review the payment batch status in the Payment Batches window.

Most payment batch problems are due to a printer malfunction during check printing, causing skipped or spoiled checks. If you have printer problems during check printing, you still confirm the results using the Confirm Payment Batch window.

To record a partial payment batch and restart check printing, record the checks as either Setup, Skipped, or Printed and then select Restart Payment Batch.

To record a partial payment batch and cancel the remainder, record the checks as either Setup, Skipped, Spoiled, or Printed and then select Cancel Remainder.

Tip

Do not record a damaged check as Spoiled. That results in an adjustment to the check numbering sequence, causing incorrect payment information to be recorded.

If a concurrent program does not execute successfully, you can resubmit the program by using the Payment Batch Actions window.

You can tell whether a payment batch program did not complete successfully by looking at the Concurrent Requests Summary. Unsuccessful batch programs display one of the following statuses in the Payment Batches window:

- Selecting
- Building
- Modifying
- Rebuilding
- Formatting
- Confirming
- Restarting
- Canceling

When you cancel a payment batch, Payables updates the status of each invoice selected in the batch to Unpaid. In addition, canceling a payment batch makes the payment batch's payment document available for another use.

PROCESSING A QUICKCHECK

QuickCheck enables you to select an invoice and immediately create a computer-generated payment. QuickCheck also enables you select an invoice regardless of the payment terms and due date.

The following restrictions apply to Quick Payments:

- You can only pay as many invoices as you defined for the remittance advice of the payment document.
- You can only select invoices that have the same supplier site as the payment supplier site entered for the check.
- If you want to pay multiple invoices, none can be a "Pay Alone" invoice.
- You must pay in the same currency as the invoice. You can enter and pay a foreign currency invoice only if your Allow Multiple Currencies Payables option is enabled and you have defined a multicurrency or foreign currency denominated bank account.
- You cannot stop a Quick Payment after it has been formatted.

ENTERING MANUAL PAYMENTS

Manual Payments enable you to record payments that were created outside of Oracle Payables. For example, using a typed check or wire transfer, within Payables you can record the payment and update the invoices you paid. The invoice(s) you paid must be approved, uncancelled, without holds, and have the same currency as the payment.

With a manual payment, you can override some payment controls. You can record a single payment for multiple Pay Alone invoices. You can also pay an invoice for a supplier that has the Hold All Payments option enabled.

Wire Transfers

Wire transfers are accounted for in the same manner as manual payments. Within Payables, you can record that the payment was made as a wire transfer and update the invoices you paid.

EDI

You follow nearly the same steps as in creating checks in a payment batch when creating an electronic payment file. Oracle EDI Gateway formats the payment file in the outbound payment format and transfers it to your bank. The EDI translator is used to transmit the formatted payment data to your bank for disbursement.

EFT

You follow nearly the same steps as in creating checks in a payment batch to create an electronic funds transfer (EFT) payment file the Oracle e-Commerce Gateway can deliver to your bank. Instead of printing the checks, though, you transmit an electronic copy of the formatted payments to your bank. Your bank then disburses the payments directly into each supplier's bank account.

Changing Payment Distributions

An invalid payment distribution might be created if Automatic Offsets is enabled and you pay an invoice or prepayment from a pooled bank account. Payment distributions containing an invalid distribution can be corrected in the Invalid GL Accounts window.

Future Dated Payments

You can control your cash flow by instructing your bank to disburse funds to your supplier's bank on specific dates. Future dated payments can help you to use the benefits of supplier discounts and efficiently forecast future outflows of cash.

Processing Stop and Void Payments

Recording a stop payment status in Payables does not initiate a stop payment with the bank. You must call your bank to initiate a stop payment on a payment document. You can then void the payment to reverse the accounting and payment records. Otherwise, you can release the stop payment to reset the invoice status to Negotiable to allow it to be picked up in a subsequent payment batch. You can review all current stop payments in the Stopped Payments Report.

The following restrictions apply to Stop Payments:

- You must first unapply any prepayments that have been applied to an invoice before you can initiate a stop payment on the payment document that paid the prepayment.
- You cannot initiate a stop payment on a Quick Payment that has been formatted.

When you void a payment, Payables automatically reverses the payment and its distributions. Payables reverses any realized gains or losses on foreign-currency invoices recorded as paid by the payment. The action taken on the invoices paid by the voided payment can be selected at the time the payment is voided. You can choose to place the invoices on hold, cancel the invoices, or do nothing with the invoices, leaving them available for payment.

Tip

You should keep voided checks in your possession for audit purposes. You cannot reverse a void on a void payment, so have the document in your possession before recording it as a void.

The following restrictions apply to voided payments:

- When you void a payment, you cannot cancel a related invoice if it was partially paid by a second payment. Instead, when you select Cancel Invoice, the system applies an Invoice Cancel hold to the invoice for your reference. You can release the hold manually in the Invoice Holds window.
- If you attempt to cancel an invoice that has been partially paid by another payment by using the Cancel Invoice Action—instead of canceling the invoice—Payables applies an Invoice Cancel hold to the invoice. This hold is manually releasable.
- You cannot void a payment the bank has already cleared.
- You cannot void payment on a payment document that pays a prepayment you have applied to an invoice. You must first unapply any prepayments, and you can then void the payment.

RECONCILING CASH

With Oracle Cash Management, you can reconcile payments created in Payables to your bank statements. When you reconcile payments using Oracle Cash Management, Cash Management updates the status of Payables payments to Reconciled. If you enable the Account for Payments When Payment Clears Payables option, Payables creates reconciliation accounting entries for the delay in the bank clearing of payments from the time of issuance to the time of reconciliation. It also creates entries for any differences between the original payment amount and the cleared payment amount due to exchange rate fluctuations, bank charges, or bank errors of unreconciled payments. Oracle Payables transfers these entries created by Oracle Cash Management to your general ledger when you post payments within Payables.

Note

You can reconcile foreign-currency payments that have no exchange rates. However, Payables does not create reconciliation accounting entries. If you enter the exchange rate in the GL Daily Rates table and then submit the AutoRate program, Payables automatically creates the reconciliation accounting entries for payments that were reconciled without exchange rates.

Balancing the Subledger to the General Ledger

To ensure that your Trial Balance accurately reflects your accounts payable liability, you should reconcile your posted invoices and payments to your Accounts Payable Trial Balance. For a given period, add the current period's posted invoices (total invoice amount from the Posted Invoice Register) and subtract the current period's posted payments (total cash plus discounts taken from the Posted Payments Register) from the prior period's Accounts Payable Trial Balance. This amount should equal the balance for the current period's Accounts Payable Trial Balance. This can all be summed up in the following equation:

> Prior Period Accounts Payable Trial Balance + Current Period Posted Invoice Register - Current Period Posted Payment Register = Current Period Accounts Payable Trial Balance

Using Open Interfaces in This Application

You can use the Payables Open Interface Import program to create invoices from invoice data imported into the Payables Open Interface Tables. You can populate the Payables Open Interface Tables with invoice data from the following sources:

- Supplier EDI invoices (ASC X12 810/EDIFACT INVOIC) transferred through Oracle EDI Gateway
- Invoices from other accounting systems loaded with a custom SQL*Loader program
- Credit card transactions transferred using the Credit Card Invoice Interface Summary

The Invoice ID field grayed out in Figure 12.10 is automatically populated by the Payables system.

Note

In Payables Release 11*i*, you still use Payables Invoice Import to import expense report data from the Payables Invoice Interface tables.

If you are importing EDI invoices through the Oracle EDI Gateway, you can submit the EDI Invoice Inbound Set. This report set submits both the EDI Gateway program and the Payables Open Interface Import Program. The EDI Gateway program populates the Open Interface Tables, and the Payables Open Interface Import program transfers the invoice data from the interface tables into the transaction invoice tables.

While trying to import invoices, you might encounter errors caused by incorrect data or program failure. If a problem exists at the invoice level, invoice line level, or distribution level, the invoice is rejected. The Payables Open Interface Report lists all invoices that were not imported correctly, regardless of whether the problem occurred at the invoice, line, or distribution level.

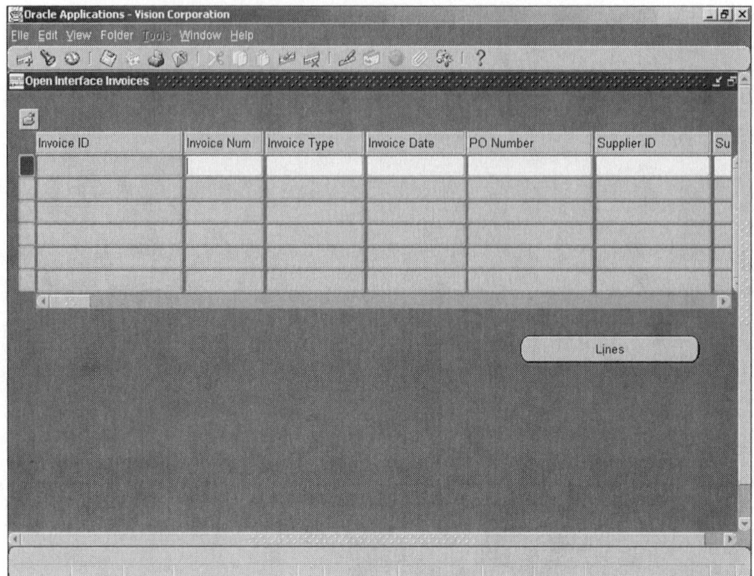

Figure 12.10
If you do not enable the Create Employee As Supplier Payables option, the employee will need to be manually entered as a Supplier in the Supplier window before importing expense reports in the Open Interface.

You can correct the data either by using the Open Interface Invoices window or by submitting Purge Payables Open Interface. When the interface tables are purged, you can reimport corrected data for the rejected records. If there is a failure with either the EDI Gateway Program or the Payables Open Interface Program, you can query the program in the Concurrent Requests Summary and read about any errors in the log file.

You can use the Payables Open Interface Purge Program to purge records from the Payables Open Interface tables (AP_INVOICES_INTERFACE and AP_INVOICE_LINES_ INTERFACE). You can choose to purge only invoices you have successfully imported; alternatively, you can choose to purge all records in the table that match the Source and Group parameters entered.

POSTING TO THE GENERAL LEDGER

Payables Transfer to the General Ledger has the option to summarize the accounting entries in the subledger and transfer to the General Ledger Interface Table. The Accounting information is visible within the Payable Application. As already noted, Payables Transfer to General Ledger is a new process designed to transfer and optionally summarize the accounting entries in the Payables subledger to the general ledger interface.

The process works by transferring accounting data in a selected date range and in a selected journal category. The accounting entries are assigned a journal category at the time they are created. This category can be viewed in the accounting inquiry windows. Three journal categories are available: Purchase Invoices, Payments, and Reconciled Payments. All the invoice accounting events are created with a journal category of Purchase Invoices. All the payment accounting events, except for the payment clearing and payment unclearing events, are created with a journal category of Payments. The payment clearing and unclearing events are created with the journal category of Reconciled Payments. The list of values displayed is the list of the three types of Payables journal categories.

The Validate Accounts Parameters checks the accounting entries against the current account status in the General Ledger. If invalid accounts are found, the entries are not transferred. If this option is not used, Journal Import automatically validates the accounts.

The Transfer to GL Interface options are In Detail, Summarize by Accounting Date, and Summarize by Accounting Period. The Journal Import process takes the data in the GL Interface table and creates unposted journal entry batches, headers, and lines in Oracle General Ledger. From there, the journal entries can be posted to update the account balances.

The drill-down capabilities of the subledger enable the transferring of all accounting entries in summary while retaining the ability to view the accounting information when inquiring on the accounts. When viewing a journal with the source of Oracle Payables, Drill-Down to Oracle Payables can be clicked. A window has been created for the drill-down, and the window title and the information displayed vary depending on which journal category is being reviewed. The three window titles are Payables Invoice Accounting (from the Purchase Invoices category), Payables Payment Accounting (from the Payments category), and Payables Reconciled Payment Accounting (from the Reconciled Payments category). The windows use the standard Oracle folder functionality so they can be easily modified to meet the inquiry needs.

Creating Mass Additions to Oracle Assets

You run the Mass Additions Create program to create mass additions for Oracle Assets from invoice line distributions in Payables. The AP transfer to GL must be run before the mass additions process can take place. After you create mass additions, you can review them in the Prepare Mass Additions window in Oracle Assets.

Using Oracle Alert

Payables supplies you with several predefined alerts. These alerts can be used as they are or customized. These alerts notify the appropriate person of invoice price holds and invoice receipt holds. If you install Oracle Alert, you can also create your own alerts to notify the appropriate people of specific exceptions or about key indicators occurring in the Payables database. All predefined alerts are initially disabled, so you must enable the alerts you want to use.

Laser-Printed Checks

Payables provides the Evergreen Check Laser Format program and corresponding Evergreen Long (Laser) Format to support your check laser-printing needs. This format can be customized with variable fonts, MICR encoding, scanned signatures, and so on, as necessary. Just associate the customized payment format with a payment document for a bank account to begin printing laser checks. If you are not using one of the standard formats, you must adjust the setup strings of the print drivers to line up your payment forms.

USING ORACLE CASH MANAGEMENT

The Cash Management application enables you to control the cash cycle for your business. Cash Management is integrated with General Ledger, Payables, Receivables, Purchasing, and Order Entry. However, this section discusses Cash Management as it pertains to Payables. Cash Management covers basically two distinct areas: bank statement reconciliation and cash forecasting. *Bank statement reconciliation* is the method of determining whether the bank balances kept in Oracle Financials match the balances per the bank's records. *Cash forecasting* enables you to project what your balance will be at some point in the future.

BANK RECONCILIATION

Cash Management enables you to reconcile the payments created in Oracle Payables against your bank statements. When you reconcile your payments, the system automatically creates accounting entries to the Cash, Cash Clearing, Realized Gains and Losses, Bank Charges, and Bank Errors accounts you specified in the Bank setup.

Two major process steps must be followed when reconciling bank statements:

- **Load bank statements**—You need to enter the detailed information from each bank statement, including bank account information, deposits received by the bank, and checks cleared. You can enter bank statements manually or load electronic statements that you receive directly from your bank.
- **Reconcile bank statements**—When you have entered detailed bank statement information into Cash Management, you must reconcile that information with your system transactions. Cash Management provides two methods to do your reconciliations:
    - **Automatic**—Bank statement details are automatically matched and reconciled with system transactions. This method is ideally suited for bank accounts that have a high volume of transactions.
    - **Manual**—This method requires you to manually match bank statement details with accounting transactions. The method is ideally suited to reconciling bank accounts that have a small volume of monthly transactions. You can also use the manual reconciliation method to reconcile any bank statement details that could not be reconciled automatically.

AUTORECONCILIATION

You can use the AutoReconciliation program to reconcile any bank statement in Oracle Cash Management. These three versions of the program are available:

- **AutoReconciliation**—Use this program to reconcile any bank statement that has already been entered.
- **Bank Statement Import**—Use this program to electronically import a bank statement after loading the bank file with your SQL*Loader program.
- **Bank Statement Import and AutoReconciliation**—Use this program to import and reconcile a bank statement in the same run.

After you run the program, you can review the AutoReconciliation Execution Report to identify any reconciliation errors that need to be corrected. This report is produced automatically, or you can run it whenever necessary. You can also review reconciliation errors online.

After you automatically reconcile a bank statement and correct any reconciliation errors, you can run the Bank Statement Detail Report or use the View Bank Statements window to review reconciled and unreconciled statement lines. If lines remain unreconciled, you can update the bank statement and rerun AutoReconciliation or reconcile the statement lines manually.

USING CASH FORECASTING

Cash forecasting attempts to forecast a future cash position by taking the current position and adding future inflows and subtracting future outflows.

Cash forecasting enables you to generate a cash forecast that automatically includes cash flows from other Oracle applications and external sources, as well as Payables.

Cash Management enables you to view cash forecast information online in a spreadsheet format, with the forecast periods in columns and the sources in rows. The Cash Forecast Report uses Oracle Report eXchange to export cash forecast data to a spreadsheet application. You can also print the Cash Forecast Report to review your forecasts.

RELEASE 11*i* FEATURES

The following sections describe the cash management features new to release 11*i*.

CASH FORECASTING INTEGRATION WITH ORACLE PROJECTS

Oracle Cash Management integrates with Oracle Projects so you can analyze cash flows and currency exposures by project. Oracle Projects cash flow sources include budgets; billing events; and expenditures covering usages, labor, and miscellaneous transactions. Other project cash flow sources include customer invoices, supplier invoices, sales orders, purchase orders, purchase requisitions, and expense reports.

CASH FORECASTING INTEGRATION WITH ORACLE SALES

Oracle Cash Management can automatically generate cash forecasts based on sales opportunities. The selection criteria include sales stage, channel, win probability, and status. You easily can define the expected cash activity date by specifying a lead time that is added to your opportunities' close dates.

CASH FORECASTING INTEGRATION WITH ORACLE TREASURY

Oracle Cash Management can automatically generate cash forecasts based on treasury transactions, including money market and foreign exchange deals and other exposures.

BANK RECONCILIATION INTEGRATION WITH ORACLE PAYROLL

Oracle Cash Management can reconcile bank statements with payroll payments, automatically or manually. The AutoReconciliation process automatically reconciles your bank statements with your payroll transactions using the check number and amount. You can also manually reconcile your entire statement or just those exceptions that could not be reconciled automatically.

RECONCILIATION OF VOIDED AND REVERSED TRANSACTIONS

Oracle Cash Management provides easier reconciliation of voided payments and reversed receipts. You can reconcile an original receipt and its reversal in any order and exclude receipts that are reversed due to user error as available transactions for reconciliation. Optionally, you can exclude voided payments as available transactions for reconciliation.

GENERAL LEDGER RECONCILIATION REPORT

Oracle Cash Management's General Ledger Reconciliation Report helps you reconcile your General Ledger cash accounts with your bank statement balances. The report compares a bank statement balance, adjusted for unreconciled and error statement lines, with the General Ledger cash account balance.

ENHANCED VALUE DATE SUPPORT

Oracle Cash Management adds value date support for payments from Oracle Payables to the existing support for receipts from Oracle Receivables. You can enter the anticipated value date when recording payments. Oracle Cash Management updates the actual value date during reconciliation. You can also optionally postpone reconciliation until the value date. With value date support, you can calculate a more accurate short-term cash forecast.

CONFIGURING ORACLE CASH MANAGEMENT

Table 12.2 shows the tasks required to set up the Cash Management application. The tasks are listed in the order they should be performed. Many tasks have predecessor tasks for data validation, so they should be performed in the proper order.

TABLE 12.2 ORACLE CASH MANAGEMENT CONFIGURATION TASKS

Task Name	Required
Set Profile Options	Yes
Define System Parameters	Yes
Define Bank Transaction Codes	Optional
Set Up Bank Statement Open Interface	Optional
Set Up Reconciliation Open Interface	Optional
Set Up Forecasting Open Interface	Optional
Define Cash Forecasting Templates	Conditional
Set Up Sequential Document Numbering	Optional
Define Request Sets	Optional
Define Descriptive Flexfields	Optional

Setting Profile Options

You set values for profile options in Oracle Financials to specify how Cash Management controls access to and process data. Many of these user profile options are set—using the System Administrator responsibility—at one or more of the following levels: Site, Application, Responsibility, and User. Use the Personal Profile Options window to view or set your profile options at the User level.

Configuring System Parameters

System parameters determine defaults and controls such as which set of books Cash Management uses, the default options for manual reconciliation windows, and the control settings for the AutoReconciliation program.

Configuring Bank Transaction Codes

To electronically load bank statements or use the AutoReconciliation feature, you must set up the transaction codes your bank will use to identify the various transaction types on its statement. You need to do this for each bank account from which you will be importing statements. You can make codes inactive and even delete codes that have not been used.

You easily can view the bank transaction codes you have created here by submitting the Bank Transaction Codes Listing.

Setting Up Bank Statement Open Interface

Before you can reconcile to your bank statement, you must enter the bank statement information into Cash Management. If your bank provides bank statements in a defined format, such as BAI or SWIFT940, you can use the Bank Statement Open Interface to load this file into Cash Management.

You must first create an import program to map the structure of the bank statement file to the Cash Management bank statement open interface tables. You need a separate program for each unique file structure, and import programs are usually written using SQL*Loader. The Bank Statement Open Interface consists of two bank statement open interface tables. The first table is the Bank Statement Headers Interface Table that contains the bank statement header information, named `ce_statement_headers_int_all`. The second table is the Bank Statement Lines Interface Table that contains the bank statement transaction lines, named `ce_statement_lines_interface`.

Setting Up Reconciliation Open Interface

You can reconcile receipts and payments that originate in applications other than Receivables, Payables, and General Ledger. The Cash Management Reconciliation Open Interface enables you to manually or automatically reconcile transactions imported through the open interface to bank statement lines in Cash Management.

SETTING UP FORECASTING OPEN INTERFACE

Two source transaction types exist for cash forecasting. The first source type is the Open Interface Inflow, which is used for cash receipts. The second, the Open Interface Outflow, is used for disbursements. The Forecasting Open Interface collects these externally generated cash flow amounts and includes them in the cash forecasts.

DEFINING CASH FORECASTING TEMPLATES

Cash forecasting templates enable you to format the incoming cash flow data to fit your needs. Among other things, you can specify the number and type of rows for the forecast data and columns for the periods for your forecast.

SEQUENTIAL DOCUMENT NUMBERING

Cash Management supports Oracle Applications' Document Sequences feature. With this feature enabled, you can assign sequential document numbers to your bank statements.

DEFINING REQUEST SETS

Defining report sets enables you to submit the same set of reports regularly using the same request. Use the Request Set window or Request Set Wizard to create report sets.

DEFINING DESCRIPTIVE FLEXFIELDS

To define your descriptive flexfield, you define the segments, descriptive information, and value set information for each segment in a structure. You also determine the appearance of your descriptive flexfield window. The maximum number of segments possible within a single structure depends on which descriptive flexfield you are defining.

PROCESSING CASH MANAGEMENT TRANSACTIONS

Bank statement transactions are identified by transaction codes. As you define each code, you select a transaction type. This transaction type determines how Payables matches and accounts for transactions having that code. The types are as follows:

- **Payment**—Checks, wire transfers, EFT
- **Receipt**—Receipts
- **Miscellaneous Payment**—Nonsupplier-related payments
- **Miscellaneous Receipt**—Noncustomer-related receipts
- **Stopped**—Stopped or voided payments in Payables
- **Rejected**—Rejected receipts, except for NSF
- **NSF**—Nonsufficient funds

Cash Management–generated journal entries are transferred to the General Ledger from Payables or Receivables.

REVIEWING CASH MANAGEMENT REPORTS

You can run the following Cash Management reports from the Submit Request window.

STATEMENT REPORTS

- Bank Statement Detail Report
- Bank Statement Summary Report
- Bank Statements by Document Number Report

TRANSACTION REPORTS

- Cash Forecast Report
- Cash Forecast Execution Report
- AutoReconciliation Execution Report
- GL Reconciliation Report
- Transactions Available for Reconciliation Report
- Cash in Transit Report

ARCHIVING AND PURGING TRANSACTIONS

You can archive and purge the information from both your bank statement open interface tables and bank statement tables. You can configure Cash Management to automatically archive and purge records from the bank statement open interface tables during Bank Statement Import. The information is archived and purged only after successful transfer from the open interface tables to the bank statement tables.

SUMMARY

Oracle Payables, along with Oracle Cash Management, is continuously evolving to support the growing trend toward conducting business over the Web and via electronic commerce. It also supports the increasing requirements for more multinational features. The new accounting model in Payable 11*i* has dramatically changed the way the accounting works in the subledger. The improved architecture required to support the new accounting model opens the door for continued enhancements in future releases. The Payables architecture will allow the accounting data to be visible to the end user, thereby increasing the efficiency of the month-end close process.

CHAPTER 13

Using Oracle Receivables

In this chapter

INTRODUCTION

Oracle Receivables (AR) is a subsidiary ledger to the Oracle General Ledger. The main processes in AR focus on billing, cash receipts, and collections transactions. The main setup tasks involve customers, AutoAccounting, AutoInvoicing, sales tax, transactions, and receipts. AR can use the multi-org partitioning features.

RELATIONSHIP TO OTHER APPLICATIONS

AR has close relationships to other Oracle Applications. Figure 13.1 shows that AR is dependent on GL, INV, AOL, OM, PA, and possibly external systems for validation, input, shared objects, and so forth. AR provides outputs and services to General Ledger, Cash Management, and Order Management. It also shares some setup values with AP.

Figure 13.1
Oracle Receivables has relationships with many other Oracle applications.

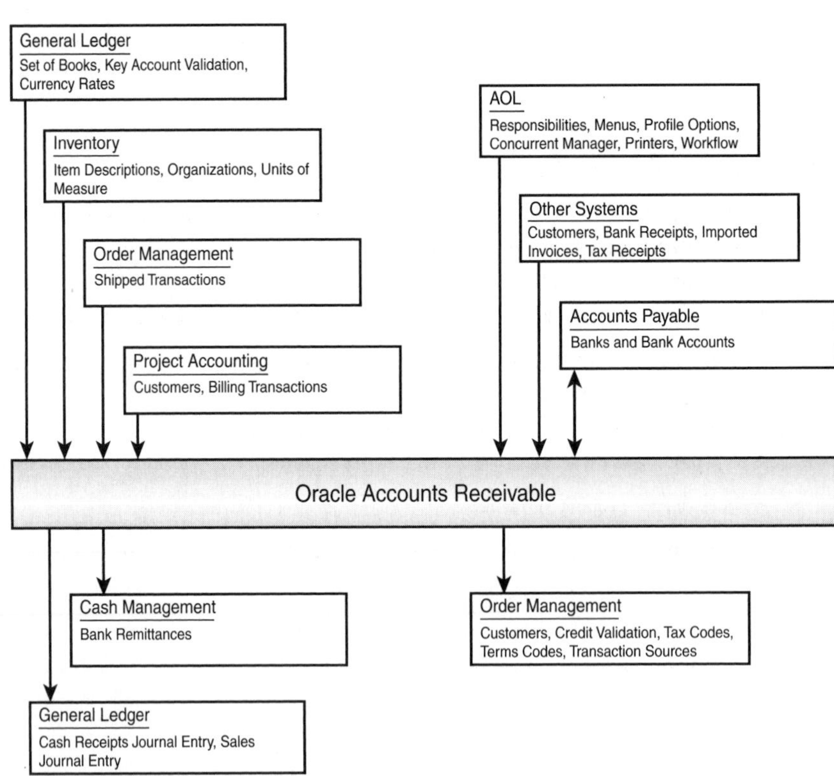

DISCOVERING NEW FEATURES IN RELEASE 11*i*

Established users and consultants who are familiar with Release 10.7 or 11.0 should have no trouble with the features and functions of Release 11.5, or 11*i* as it is commonly known. Nevertheless, nearly 100 new tables have been added to the database to enhance customer records, taxation policies, and multiple language support. This section discusses some new features and some significant enhancements in Release 11*i*.

USING *i*RECEIVABLES

This Self-Service application allows your customers using a standard Web browser to do the following:

- Print transactions
- Review account balances
- Dispute bills

All transactions and data are protected by the application's standard security. This means that only users you define will have access to this data.

USING CREDIT CARD PROCESSING

Oracle Receivables can now accept credit card payments for open debit items provided you are using Oracle Payment Server. You can enter the transactions manually or import them using AutoInvoice. In addition, you can use Automatic Receipts to close the transactions and create the remittance. These remittances will initiate the transfer of funds to your bank.

Before you can use Automatic Receipts, however, you must create a receipt program (use Oracle Reports to do this) and register it to the application. Then, you navigate to the Automatic Receipts Program form and enter the name of this automatic receipt program. Next, you enter the type of program you are defining. Four types can be defined, namely these:

- **Print Created Receipts**—This program creates a batch of automatic receipts.
- **Transmit Created Receipts**—This program formats the output of automatic receipts you created for a magnetic medium.
- **Print Bank Remittance**—This program prints a batch of remittances.
- **Transmit Bank Remittance**—This program formats the output of bank remittance batches you created for a magnetic medium.

Finally, you enter the name of the receipt program. This is the name you used to register the program. If you create a custom program, its name cannot exceed eight characters.

Tip

Because you can use both a format and transmit receipts program with a single receipt format, give both of them the same name. Even if the program type is different, you can use the same name.

Oracle *i*Payment handles the requests for credit card authorization and capture. You can secure confidential financial information in the Receivables forms by hiding either the first or last four digits of the account number with the AR: Mask Bank Account Numbers profile option.

USING THE CREDIT MEMO REQUEST WORKFLOW

This workflow enables customers to request a credit memo via *i*Receivables. When the customer requests a credit, the workflow forwards the request for approval based on your management structure or approval limits.

Once approved, the workflow creates the credit memo based on the information submitted and then notifies the requestor of the approval. The workflow also notifies the requestor if the credit is denied.

You can use the supplied workflow or modify it to suit your needs.

USING AUTOACCOUNTING ENHANCEMENTS

You can now use the customer bill-to address to derive account numbers for Revenue, Freight, Tax, AutoInvoice Clearing, Unearned Revenue, and Unbilled Receivable transactions. This gives you more flexibility in letting the AR system determine the account numbers you want.

USING AUTOINVOICE EXCEPTION-HANDLING ENHANCEMENTS

You can use two new forms to review and correct invalid records in the AutoInvoice interface table. Those transactions that pass validation during the AutoInvoice import are transferred to Receivables tables, but those transactions that fail validation are known as *exceptions* and their records remain in the AutoInvoice interface table.

Use the Interface Lines and Interface Exceptions forms to correct the invalid data. The Interface Exceptions form displays the interface ID, exception type, error message, and invalid values associated with each error. After selecting the transaction you want to edit, click the Details button and you will be able to edit the transaction in error. An example of this form is shown in Figure 13.2.

The Interface Lines form displays Line or Charges record types and indicates which records contain errors. You can edit data in this window as well as drill down to see more detailed information.

These two windows enable you to correct error transactions that previously required outside programming.

USING BILLS OF EXCHANGE ENHANCEMENTS

You can use enhanced transaction numbering to link Bills of Exchange to their associated invoices and debit memos. This enhancement more clearly distinguishes Bills of Exchange from other receivables transactions and enables better management and tracking.

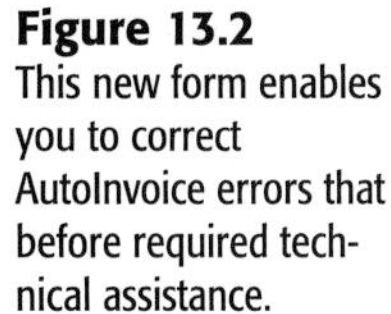

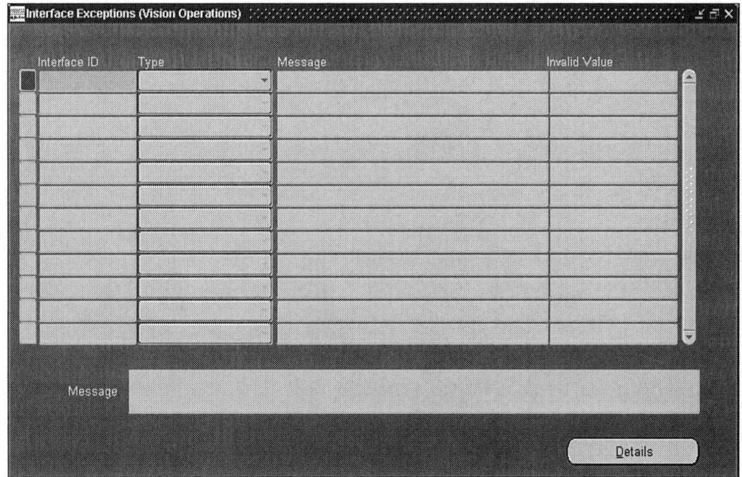

Figure 13.2
This new form enables you to correct AutoInvoice errors that before required technical assistance.

You can view receipts at risk and Bills of Exchange in the Receipts form. You can also specify whether to include or exclude Bills of Exchange when the system calculates customer balances in the Collections workbench.

RESOLVING COMMON ISSUES AND GAPS

The AR application generally works well in its role as a subsidiary ledger, a billing system, a perpetual record of open amounts due from customers, and a cash collection system. However, many customers have expectations or business requirements of the AR application that exceed the design. The following topics are often identified by implementation teams as implementation issues or gaps in functionality.

AR IS NOT A SALES HISTORY REPORTING SYSTEM

Many companies have built sales history reporting systems into their legacy billing systems. The AR Application stores information about product shipments, customers, invoice details, sales allowances, and so forth. However, many of these data items are only used to print the invoice. Project sponsors are often surprised when certain key management billing reports are not available. The primary mission of AR is to recognize revenue and collect cash. Although AR can print product information on an invoice, there are no revenue reports by product, by customer, by accounting period, and so forth.

If you also have Oracle Order Management, General Ledger, and Inventory, the Margin Analysis Report can help resolve this gap. The Margin Analysis system is really two programs: a report and a data collection module. The data collection module can gather revenue, cost, accounting period, customer, and sales representative information into a temporary table called cst_margin_temp. You can then generate fairly simple reports from the temporary table with a data browser or an end-user reporting tool.

Tip

If your sales history reporting needs are significant, consider reviewing the separate Sales Analyzer application. This application is like a data warehouse product and runs in a separate database from the AR application.

AR Is Not a Point of Sales System

Even though AR can handle miscellaneous receipts, you shouldn't consider it a system that interacts with customers at the sales register or customer service window. It doesn't produce sales receipts or lend itself to inventory support.

AR Is a Subsidiary Ledger to the General Ledger

The AR application creates journal entries for revenue and cash receipts. AR maintains perpetual balances for many balance sheet accounts. Make sure all receivable activities are transacted in the AR system and allow the AR application to update the General Ledger.

AR Might Impact Your Customers

Any system that directly touches your customers automatically could be classified as strategic. Know your business processes and policies before setting up AR. Consider carefully the content of invoices, statements, and dunning letters. Many AR users customize these documents to meet their business requirements. Look at these documents early in your implementation project.

Because Order Management provides billing data and customer/banking information is the foundation for cash receipts, make sure you map and understand each data element coming into the AR application. Make sure the billing, credit authorization, and collection systems can support the variety of deals that will be made with your customers.

The customer merge utility is useful in managing mergers and acquisitions among your customers and handling duplicate customer records. It should be tested before you use it to make sure you understand and agree with what it does.

The Remit-To Strategy Is Not Always Geographical

AutoInvoice selects a remit-to address on invoices it creates by looking at the country code and postal codes of the Bill-To address. The logic of the program tries to pick the geographically closest address to the Bill-To customer. However, many AR users have a customer-driven strategy for selecting the remit to address and believe the remit to address should always be the same for a customer.

The Due Date Is Used in Aging Calculations

Many companies make deals with their customers so that each transaction has its own terms. For example, "Buy this software by the end of the quarter and take 90 days to pay." AR supports overriding the default terms code at the transaction level. However, the management of these companies usually wants to measure their aged invoices by the transaction date, and a report showing an 89-day old invoice in the current column is a problem.

Tip

AR is a collection system, and any invoice not yet due must be shown in the current column so the collector and dunning system won't erroneously ask the customer for payment.

Performance and Access Issues

AutoInvoice is usually the critical performance issue for AR. AutoInvoice is a batch program that converts rows in the ra_interface_lines_all table into validated invoices. System performance is dependent on many factors, but the largest and most efficient Release 10.7 and 11.0 systems have achieved between 10,000 and 20,000 invoice lines per hour.

Oracle Support has performance patches to help customers with high volumes. Because AutoInvoice performs extensive validation, efficient access to configuration data, QuickCodes, and customer data is critical for high throughput. In addition, indexes on the flexfield columns of the ra_interface_lines_all table are important so that rows can be rapidly grouped into complete invoices.

Configuring the Application

The following section of this chapter describes the setup tasks and sequence required to configure the AR application. The tasks should be performed in the sequence listed.

Resolving Critical Setup Issues

Customers, billing, collections, and cash receipt transactions are the essence of the AR Application. If you get these items right, the AR Application should do well for your business.

Determining How to Set Up Customers

The customer definition is critical, to the smooth operation of the AR Application. Customers are grouped by profile classes. A customer can have many addresses, and an address can have multiple business purposes. However, a customer can only have one name, and that name must be unique. Consider the setup carefully. If you have the same customer trading with you under more than one name, you set up multiple customers for the same customer entity, and you might have to develop techniques or even extensions to relate or combine them for reporting, credit checking, collections, and cash applications. If you have many customers with the same name that actually represent separate entities, you must develop a naming convention to differentiate the customer records.

With Release 11*i* you can identify customers as organizations or persons. Although you can continue to classify all customers as organizations, you can use features in the persons classification to better personalize your correspondence. This feature also simplifies customer searches.

If you have distinct groups of customers, consider how to set up the profile classes. Profile classes are groups of customer attributes, such as payment terms, finance charges, statement cycles, dunning letters, and more, that can be assigned to customers with similar attributes. Attributes can be overridden at the customer level, but that might involve lots of maintenance. In all but the simplest customer setups, it is best to develop a matrix of key profile options to determine how many profile classes will be needed and the procedures for applying them to individual customers.

In multi-org implementations, the customer is shared by all organizations, but the customer details (addresses, business purposes, contacts, and phones) are specific to each operating unit. Transactions with customers are partitioned by operating unit. Therefore, if you have decentralized customer fulfillment processes in many operating units and centralized credit, collection, and cash receipts, functions, you might have to coordinate how you create customer records.

GENERATING GL ACCOUNT DISTRIBUTIONS

Because AR is a subsidiary ledger to the General Ledger, ,it is important for the AutoAccounting setup to generate revenue, tax, receivable, freight, and other account distributions for transactions. AutoAccounting provides some degree of control over the value that will be assigned to each segment of the Key Accounting Flexfield for each distribution line of each transaction.

AutoAccounting can use account distributions from the definitions for transaction types, sales representatives, standard memo lines, tax codes, and new with 11*i* customer bill-to sites. If you have specific business requirements to distribute revenue to the GL accounts, you might have to evaluate how to set up transaction types, sales representatives, or standard memo lines to accomplish the distribution.

Note

The revenue account distribution is determined by the AutoAccounting function in AR. However, when Order Management (OM) sends shipped transactions to Inventory, Flexbuilder in Release 10 and the Workflow Account Generator in Releases 11 and 11*i* determine the cost of goods sold account distribution. You will want to ensure that distributions for revenues and costs of, goods sold are matched.

USING MANUAL OR AUTOMATIC RECEIPTS

Your invoice transaction volume and, customer payment patterns determine whether it makes sense to set up AutoLockbox processing. If receipt transaction volume is less than 2,000–3,000 invoices per month, you will probably use the manual or QuickCash processes. If you can't justify the overhead of AutoLockbox processing, don't set it up.

UNDERSTANDING TAXATION

Sales Tax and VAT calculations are made with a fairly complex logic. There are tax codes and rates, geographical locations, exemptions, and exceptions. Various combinations, of transaction types, customers, and items can be defined to affect the result of the tax calculation. If you have taxable transactions, products, or customers, you will want to develop an implementation strategy to make sure the application is set up to handle the wide variety of taxation requirements. If you collect tax, make sure you test these calculations completely.

SETUP TASKS

Table 13.1 shows the tasks required to set up the AR Application in the order that they should be performed. Try not to skip tasks or perform them out of sequence because many tasks use predecessor tasks for data validation and you might receive error messages.

Note

Some tasks are not required for proper system operation in manual mode. However, if you want to use some of the automated functions, such as AutoLockbox, you might be required to perform additional setup tasks. Also, if you are implementing many applications, some tasks are best set up in other applications. For example, defining the sets of books is commonly the responsibility of the GL implementation team.

TABLE 13.1 AR SETUP TASKS

Setup Task Name	Required?	Primary
Define Sets of Books	Yes	GL
Use the Account Generator	Yes	Sysadmin
Define the Transaction Flexfield Structure	No	AR
Define Item Flexfield	Yes	PO
Define Territory Flexfields	Yes	AR
Define Organizations	Yes	PO
Define the Sales Tax Location Flexfield Structure	Yes	AR
Define AutoCash Rule Sets	No	AR
Define Receivable Lookups	No	AR
Define Demand Class Lookups	No	Inv
Define AutoInvoice Line Ordering Rules	No	AR
Define AutoInvoice Grouping Rules	No	AR
Define Application Rule Sets	No	AR
Define System Options	Yes	AR
Set Up Flexible Address Formats	No	AR
Maintain Countries and Territories	No	AR

TABLE 13.1 CONTINUED

Setup Task Name	Required?	Primary
Define Payment Terms	Yes	AR
Assign Reporting Set of Books	No	GL
Define Accounting Rules	No	AR
Maintain Accounting Periods	Yes	AR
Define AutoAccounting	Yes	AR
Set Up Cash Basis Accounting	No	AR
Define Transaction Types	Yes	AR
Define Transaction Sources	Yes	AR
Define Collectors	Yes	AR
Define Adjustment Approval Limits	Yes	AR
Define Remittance Banks	Yes	AR, AP, or CE
Define Distribution Sets	No	AR
Define Receivables Activities	Yes	AR
Define Receipt Classes	Yes	AR
Define Payment Methods	Yes	AR
Define Receipt Sources	Yes	AR
Define Aging Buckets	No	AR
Define Statement Cycles	No	AR
Define Statement Messages	No	AR
Define Dunning Letters	No	AR
Define Dunning Letter Sets	No	AR
Define Territories	No	AR
Define Salespersons	Yes	AR
Define Profile Options	Yes	Sysadmin
Define Customer Profile Classes	Yes	AR
Define Customers	Yes	AR
Define Remit-To Addresses	No	AR
Define Customer Relationships	No	AR
Define Lockboxes	No	AR
Define the Transmission Format	No	AR
Define Receipt Programs	No	AR
Define Unit of Measure Classes	No	PO

Table 13.1 Continued

Setup Task Name	Required?	Primary
Define Units of Measure	No	PO
Define Standard Memo Lines	No	AR
Set Up Cross Currency Receipts	No	AR
Set Up Tax	Yes	AR
Set Up Tax Vendor Extension Document Sequences	No No	ARDefine Sysadmin

Understanding Each Setup Task

This section discusses the details of each setup task in the order they should be performed. If you are a multi-org installation, you must perform all these steps for each operating unit unless otherwise noted.

Creating a Set of Books

The Receivables Application is a subsidiary ledger of the Oracle General Ledger and must be attached to a set of books definition from the General Ledger. The set of books defines the Chart of Accounts, the Fiscal Calendar, and the Functional Currency of the AR application. When you define a set of books, use the set up process described in Chapter 11, "Using Oracle General Ledger." These tasks are the following:

- Define the Key Accounting Flexfield structure, segments, segment values, and code combinations.
- Define the Fiscal Calendar period types and periods.
- Enable Currencies and define rate types and conversion rates.
- Create the set of books by assigning a name to a combination of the Key Accounting Flexfield, a Calendar, and a Currency.
- Assign the set of books to the site or individual responsibilities.

Repeat these steps for each set of books.

Setting Up the Account Generator

The Workflow Account Generator was introduced in Release 11. It determines the correct balancing segment value in the account distribution when AR generates finance charge transactions or currency exchange rate gains and losses. This setup step is required even if you will never charge finance charges or recognize currency gains or losses.

Repeat this step for each set of books.

Note

The Workflow Account Generator in Releases 11 and 11*i* replaces Flexbuilder in Release 10 of AR. Determining the balancing segment in finance charge and currency gain/loss transactions is the only place in AR where the Account Generator or Flexbuilder is used. All other account distributions are defined by the AutoAccounting setup.

Oracle AR provides a default Account Generator Workflow process to derive the balancing segment. If this default process does not meet your requirements, you must use the Oracle Workflow Builder to create a new process.

Tip

You can copy the default AR process to a different name and then make modifications to the copy (see Chapter 28, "Using Oracle Workflow"). If you develop an alternative process, make sure to test it in a development database by running the GL Interface Program.

If you change the Account Generator process, you must implement the process in AR for it to take effect. Follow this procedure to assign your newly named process:

1. Go to the Account Generator Process Window.
2. Choose the appropriate Key Accounting Flexfield and structure for AR from the lists of values.
3. Specify the workflow item type as "Replace Balancing Segment."
4. Specify the name of your new Account Generator Process.

Note

There is a profile option in Release 11*i* called Account Generator: Purge Runtime Data. It should be set to Yes unless you are debugging an Account Generator Process.

CREATING TRANSACTION FLEXFIELDS

The AutoInvoice program uses the Transaction Flexfield to uniquely identify incoming transactions to be invoiced through the ra_interface_lines table. If you are processing large volumes of transaction lines through AutoInvoice, the Transaction Flexfield is important for tuning because the validation portions of AutoInvoice must efficiently access rows in the ra_interface_lines table. Consider creating indexes on the segments to improve AutoInvoice performance.

If you do not plan to use AutoInvoice, you can skip this step.

Tip

If you are experiencing performance problems with AutoInvoice, be sure to check Metalink for notes and patches on this subject. If you process more than 1,000 records at a time and you are at patchset level 11.5.AR.B or lower, you must apply patch 1567536 or Mini-pack AR.C to correct a problem with incomplete GL Distribution records.

If Oracle OM is the source of your incoming transactions, the Transaction Flexfield is contained in the columns interface_line_attribute1–interface_line_attribute10.

Tip

You should create indexes on the Transaction Flexfield. This will enable you to query on the invoice headers and lines, as well as improve the performance of the AutoInvoice program.

Tip

If Oracle OM is the transaction source, use the *Manufacturing, Distribution, Sales, and Service Open Interfaces Manual* to determine how to set up the Transaction Flexfield. The documentation is found in the Order Entry/Shipping section of the manual. There is no documentation in the AR manuals.

If you are importing transactions from a non-Oracle system, the Transaction Flexfield should uniquely represent one interface line. You can use as many interface_line_attribute columns as available to achieve a unique combination.

DEFINING THE SYSTEM ITEM AND TERRITORY FLEXFIELDS

The Item Flexfield is required to transact and report item information. Usually, the Item Flexfield is defined in the Inventory application, and you should see Chapter 17, "Using Oracle Inventory," for a detailed description of this process.

Tip

After you have defined the Item Flexfield, there are several profile options that should be configured. These include the OM: Item Flexfield and the AR: Item Flexfield Mode profile options.

THE TERRITORY FLEXFIELD

Defining the Territory Flexfield is optional in AR. Territories are used in reports, and you should review the standard reports to see whether you have a business requirement to define the Territory Flexfield. You can refer to territories with salespersons, invoices, commitments, and customer purposes.

These flexfields are defined once per database installation.

DEFINING ORGANIZATIONS

Organizations are often defined in another application (usually Inventory), and these definitions are shared with AR so you won't have to perform this task if it has already been done. If organizations have not been previously defined, follow these steps:

1. Define at least one organization. This step is required so that you can use the shared Inventory forms and tables without having Inventory fully installed.
2. Define the organization parameters for the organization. You need a three-character short code for the organization name and the account distribution defaults for item transactions.
3. Configure the profile option called OE: Item Validation Organization
4. Finally and optionally, you can define items to be used by AR transactions.

Define organizations for each business group.

CREATING THE SALES TAX LOCATION FLEXFIELD

AR provides six seeded Sales Tax Location Flexfield definitions for various combinations of city, county, state, province, and country. If none of these definitions is acceptable for your requirements, you can define a Location Flexfield by defining value sets, a structure, and segments as with any other key flexfield.

Note

If you are implementing Value Added Taxation (VAT), Oracle recommends the Country Flexfield structure. If you are implementing Sales Tax in the United States, Oracle recommends the State.County.City flexfield structure.

The Tax Account and Exemption qualifiers for the Flexfield should be set to the correct level for your business requirements. Double-check these levels for all classes of customers and taxing authorities. Usually, the State.County.City flexfield structure predefined by AR is adequate for United States–based sales tax calculations. However, assigning taxation boundaries on state, county, and city geographical boundaries or postal codes is not perfect. There are third-party vendor solutions that will compensate when geography doesn't work for every one of your customers.

In the Tax setup step, you define tax codes, locations, rates, and other information for each segment of the flexfield. AR uses these locations to validate the customer shipping address. Optionally, you can use the Tax Rate Interface program to load large quantities of locations.

The Sales Tax Location Flexfield is defined once per database installation.

DEFINING AUTOCASH RULE SETS

AutoCash rule sets are used to determine the sequence of cash application methods. If you are not using AutoCash or QuickCash, this setup step is optional. Assign an AutoCash rule set to one or several customer profile classes.

Note

Consider using the Apply to Oldest Invoice as one of the sequences in your AutoCash rule sets. This minimizes the number of receipts that remain unapplied or on-account after you run AutoCash or QuickCash.

The system also uses AutoCash rule sets when applying receipts imported using AutoLockbox.

To define an AutoCash rule set, do the following:

- Name and describe the rule set in the AutoCash Rule Set form.
- Enter the type of discount option (earned, earned and unearned, or none).
- Indicate whether disputed items are to be included in calculating the customer balance.
- Indicate whether finance charges are to be included when calculating the customer balance.
- Define the automatic matching rule.
- Mark Unapplied or On-account if you use the oldest-invoice-first rule. This selection determines processing for remaining amounts if none of the rules in this rule set apply.
- Determine whether you will allow application of partial receipts.
- Use a sequence number to set the order of each rule in the rule set. Lower-numbered rules are applied first.
- Select a rule from the available rules (apply to oldest first, clear the account, clear past due items, clear past due items by payment term, and match with invoice).

DEFINING RECEIVABLE LOOKUPS

Oracle AR defines more than 30 Receivable Lookups (or QuickCodes, as they were known in earlier releases) that you can update. Generally, you add values to expand the validation and available choices in a List of Values (QuickPick). QuickCodes can be grouped as follows:

- **Customer codes**—Include address categories, business purpose codes, customer categories, customer class codes, demand classes, FOB codes, freight carriers, customer contact job titles and business titles, communication types, and document types.
- **Customer profile**—Include account statuses, credit rating codes, and customer risk codes.
- **Transaction**—Include adjustment reasons, approval types, batch status codes, Canadian province codes, credit memo and invoice reason codes, tax classifications, tax exemption reasons, tax type codes, statement message and text usage types, and special instruction values.
- **Collections**—Include collector actions, collector follow-up action codes, customer response codes, call outcome codes, and line type codes for aging buckets.
- **Receipt**—Include mandatory field prompt and reverse payment reason codes.

DEFINING DEMAND CLASS LOOKUPS

You can use Demand Class Lookups to track and consume scheduled demand and supply. You can assign demand classes to customers.

DEFINING AUTOINVOICE LINE ORDERING

Line-ordering rules can be used to affect the way the AutoInvoice program sequences invoice lines. The line ordering rules are a component of the AutoInvoice grouping rules. To create a line ordering rule, do the following:

- Name a rule in the line-ordering rules form.
- Enter effective dates and an optional description.
- Enter the priority of the transaction attribute in the sequence field. Lower numbers receive first priority.
- Enter the transaction attribute for this priority. Commonly used attributes are sales order and sales order line number, waybill number, and various components of the Transaction Flexfield.
- Indicate whether the attribute values should be processed in ascending or descending order.

DEFINING AUTOINVOICE GROUPING RULES

Definition of AutoInvoice grouping rules is an optional setup step and can be used to control how the AutoInvoice program assigns invoice numbers to imported invoice transactions. Several mandatory rules come seeded with the Oracle Applications. For example, only one currency or Bill-To customer is allowed for each invoice.

AutoInvoice uses a four-level hierarchy to determine the sequence for applying grouping rules to imported transactions:

- The rule attached to the transaction source
- The rule attached to the Bill-To site for the transaction
- The rule attached to the customer profile class for the Bill-To customer
- The rule specified as the default in the AR system options setup

You can assign an invoice line ordering rule to each grouping rule.

DEFINING APPLICATION RULE SETS

You use Application Rule Sets to control how Receivables will reduce the balance due of open debit items when you apply payments. The seeded rule sets are

- **Line First – Tax After**—This rule set first applies the payment to the open line amount, with any remaining amounts being applied to the tax. Additional amounts are then applied to freight and finance charges. This is the default.

- **Line First – Tax Prorate**—This rule set applies proportionate amounts to the open line item and tax amounts for each line. Additional amounts are then applied to freight and finance charges.
- **Prorate All**—This rule set applies proportionate amounts to all open amounts associated with a debit item, including the line, tax, freight, and finance charges.

You can define additional rule sets in the Application Rule Sets form.

Defining System Options

This step is critical to defining how your AR application will work. It identifies the accounting method you will use (Accrual or Cash), the set of books, accounting flexfields, taxation method, location flexfield, customer address validation, and more.

Tip

If you do not want to validate your customer addresses–in other words, validate ZIP codes to cities and counties–then use the Country - No Validation Sales Tax Location Flexfield structure.

Tip

Only use the Cash Basis Accounting method if your accounting policy is to recognize revenue upon cash receipt.

Defining Flexible Address Formats

The standard AR address format is composed of a country, four lines of address, city, state, postal code, province, and county. If this format is adequate for your purposes, setting up flexible formats is optional.

In addition, AR provides address formats for Japanese, Northern European, Southern European, South American, and UK/Asia/Australia. You can define additional formats by defining other descriptive flexfield structures. The name of the descriptive Flexfield is Address.

Defining Countries and Territories

You should use this step if you want to assign address styles created in the previous step to other countries. You can identify those countries that are part of the EU by entering a VAT Member State Code.

Note

The territories mentioned here are not related to the territories enabled by the Territory Flexfield.

Tip

The AR responsibilities can't create new countries. To create a new country, you must use the System Administrator responsibility.

DEFINING PAYMENT TERMS

Payment terms determine the payment schedule and discount information for customer transactions. You can define simple terms, such as Net 30, as well as complicated discount or installment terms. Payment terms can be defaulted to invoices from the customer record or the transaction type. AR provides two seeded payment terms: 30 NET and IMMEDIATE. See Figure 13.3 for an example of the 30 NET Payment Terms.

ASSIGNING REPORTING SET OF BOOKS

Perform this step only if you are using Multiple Reporting Currencies (MRC) functionality. The MRC functionality enables you to maintain transactions and balances in multiple currencies, so you can generate reports in each of your currencies.

DEFINING ACCOUNTING RULES

Accounting rules are used to determine how to recognize revenue in multiple accounting periods. This setup task is optional, but if you use accounting rules, associate them with an invoicing rule. Invoicing rules determine when to record the receivable (in arrears or in advance).

If the accounting basis is cash, accounting and invoicing rules do not apply, and AutoInvoice rejects imported transactions with these kinds of rules.

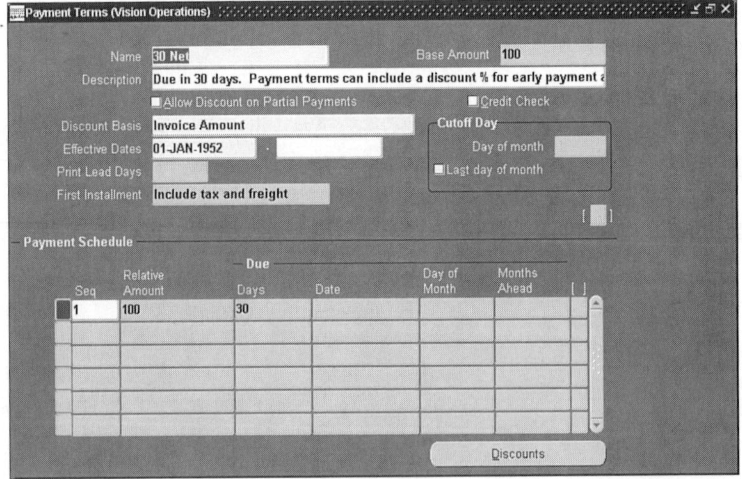

Figure 13.3 By manipulating data in this form, you can create just about any type of payment terms imaginable.

Note

If you are using rules and importing transactions from OM and you use a different accounting period type than Month, update the period field for the IMMEDIATE accounting rule to match your accounting period type.

MAINTAINING ACCOUNTING PERIODS

Before using AR, change the status of accounting periods in the AR calendar. Available period statuses are Not Open, Future Transactions Allowed, Open, Close Pending, and Closed. Periods with a Future Transactions Allowed status can receive transactions but cannot post those transactions. Open periods can write journal entries and post transactions. Not Open, Close Pending, and Closed periods cannot make journal entries, postings, or transactions.

A Close Pending or a Closed period can be reopened. The AR application checks for and prevents closure of a period with unposted transactions.

SETTING UP AUTOACCOUNTING

AutoAccounting structures are used to determine how AR creates the GL accounting flexfield combinations for the revenue, receivable, freight, tax, unbilled receivable, unearned revenue, finance charges, and AutoInvoice clearing accounts. AutoAccounting enables you to use variables or constants to determine the values used in each of the segments of the account code combinations.

You use table names or constant values or a combination of the two to tell AR how to derive each segment of the account code combination for all your transactions. Some of the table names the variables use to determine the account code combinations are transaction types, sales reps, standard lines, tax codes (on tax lines), and customer bill-to sites. The standard lines choice also gets account codes from the inventory item definition. Figure 13.4 shows a potential setup for the revenue account.

AutoAccounting (Vision Operations)

Type Revenue

Segments

Segment	Table Name	Constant
Company		01
Department	Salesreps	
Account	Transaction Types	
Sub-Account		0000
Product	Standard Lines	

Figure 13.4
AutoAccounting gives you a lot of flexibility in building your account distributions.

For example, if your GL Key Accounting Flexfield was defined as Company, Department, Account, Sub-Account, and Product you could set up AutoAccounting to derive a revenue account as follows:

- The Company and Sub-Account are constants.
- The Department is defined by who made the sale (Salesreps).
- The Account is defined by the Transaction Types.
- The Product is defined by what was sold (Standard Lines).

Tip

If you base some of the segment values on salesrep definitions, consider making the salesrep mandatory when you set up miscellaneous AR system options. Also, please realize if multiple salesreps are assigned to a transaction, multiple account distributions are generated for the transaction.

DEFINING CASH BASIS ACCOUNTING

If your system option is set to cash basis accounting, this step is required. Otherwise, you should skip this step.

Cash basis accounting recognizes revenue when cash is actually received. If you sell to customers on credit but choose cash basis accounting, AR provides a system for creating invoices and tracking amounts due without making the accounting entries until cash is received.

If you choose this method, you must run a script to make the GL Transfer and Journal Entry reports incompatible with each other.

Tip

The following is the script to run if you are using cash management:

```
$ cd $AR_TOP/install/sql
$ sqlplus <AOL username>/<AOL password>
SQL> @arsedpcf.sql
```

DEFINING TRANSACTION TYPES

Use the transaction type definition to assign a payment term, revenue account, tax account, freight account, and creation sign to your AR transactions. In addition, the transaction type determines whether a transaction will update customer balances and create GL transactions. You can define transaction types for the following types of transactions:

- Credit memos
- Invoices, debit memos, and chargebacks
- Commitments (Deposits and Guarantees)

AR comes with two transaction types already defined: Manual Invoice and Credit Memo. See Figure 13.5 for a snapshot of a transaction type.

Figure 13.5
Transactions types define the nature of your invoices, credit and debit memos, and all your AR transactions.

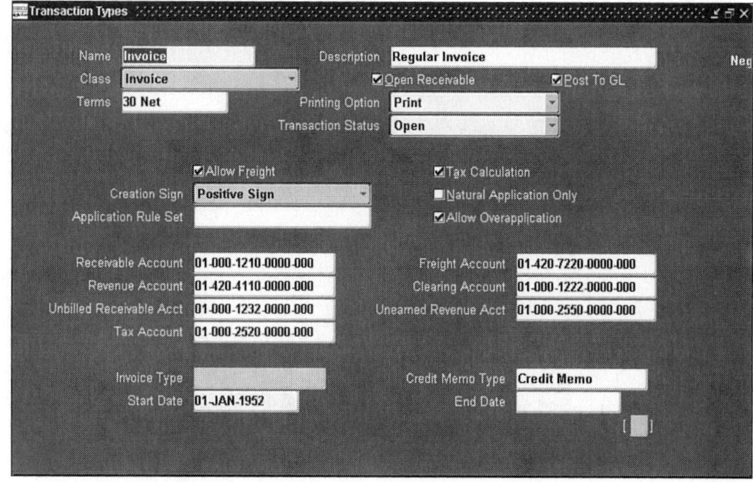

Tip

Use transaction types to default as much information as possible on the invoice transactions. This minimizes the data entry and time required to create transactions and reduce the chance for errors.

If any AutoAccounting structures depend on transaction type, AR uses the Accounting Flexfield values you enter here. You can devise an elaborate series of transaction types to support multi-company, intercompany, and other account distribution requirements.

Tip

Before setting up a complex transaction type naming convention, consider how the transaction source system will generate the transaction type names. If the transaction source is Oracle OM, you might make the order entry process more complex.

Tip

If you define a transaction type of VOID with the open receivables and post-to GL fields set to No, you can easily cancel a transaction with no activity against it by changing the transaction type to VOID.

The Natural Application and Allow Overapplication fields add controls to determine how applications can affect the balance remaining on a transaction. For example, if Allow Overapplication is set to No and Natural Application is set to Yes, AR only enables you to make an application that brings the balance remaining on the original transaction closer to zero. These fields can improve control of the cash applications function but might be restrictive based on certain payment practices of your customers.

Defining Transaction Sources

Transaction batches can be either manual or imported. Transaction source definitions are used to control transaction processing, transaction batch numbering, a default transaction type, and validation options for imported transactions. To properly define a transaction source for an imported transaction, you must understand precisely what data elements the import-processing program is placing in each of the columns of the open interface table.

> **Tip**
>
> Much of the AutoInvoice validation logic is defined in the Other Information tab. When you choose ID, your import program must supply the internal AR identifiers for the validation item. If you specify VALUE, AR uses the common values or names to look up the validation. Oracle OE generally uses IDs, and non-Oracle transaction sources generally use values.

> **Tip**
>
> If your implementation also includes Oracle OM and Inventory, use the shipment date as the transaction General Ledger date. This setup ensures that the revenue and cost of sales entries will be made in the same accounting period as required by generally accepted accounting principles (GAAP).

Defining Collectors

Collectors are used by credit profile classes and are assigned to customers when the credit profile class is assigned. Several key reports can be sorted or grouped by collector, and the collector name and phone number can be printed on dunning letters.

Setting Adjustment Approval Limits

Adjustment limits are used in the Receipts, Adjustments, and Approve Adjustments windows. You can assign a control limit for each user for each currency. Adjustments can occur for many reasons, including write-offs, tax corrections, and so on. Adjustments that exceed your limit must be approved by a user who is defined with the appropriate limits. Workflow sends a notification to users with the appropriate limits indicating that adjustments are pending their review.

You can create different approval limits based on the document type. The document types available are Adjustments, Credit Memo, and (new with version 11.5.3 and higher) Receipt Write-Off.

Defining Remittance Banks

Banks have a shared definition with the Payables application and can be defined in either application. Define all banks and accounts that receive deposits from remittances. Each bank account refers to one currency, but you can enable multiple currency receipts in the account. In this case, because receipt and bank account currencies could differ, use manual payment reconciliation to avoid the exceptions that automatic reconciliation creates.

DEFINING DISTRIBUTION SETS

Distribution sets default the entry of accounting flexfield values for miscellaneous receipt transactions with a predefined accounting distribution. Distribution sets can be assigned to receivable activities with a type of miscellaneous cash. These values can be changed and additional distribution entries entered if desired when entering a miscellaneous cash transaction.

Tip

The total of the distribution lines must equal 100% before you can save your work.

DEFINING RECEIVABLE ACTIVITIES

Use Receivable Activities to link accounting information to adjustments, finance charges, and miscellaneous cash transactions.

After you define a receivable activity, you cannot change its type, and it will appear in a list of values in the Receipts and Adjustment windows. The definition provides default accounting information and distributions to go with the activity. There are four kinds of activity types: adjustment, bank error, finance charges, and miscellaneous cash. The activity type determines whether you use a distribution set or an accounting flexfield value.

DEFINING RECEIPT CLASSES

Use a receipt class definition to specify the processing steps for manual or automatic receipts. Manual receipts must be either entered manually in the Receipts or Quick Cash windows or imported using AutoLockbox.

Automatic receipt definitions specify a remittance and clearance method and whether the definition requires confirmation. The processing steps include confirmation, remittance, and reconciliation. If you define a class to confirm and reconcile, you must also remit. If you choose No for all three steps, AR automatically creates your receipt as reconciled.

If you choose to require confirmation, also choose a remittance method to determine the accounts that AR uses for automatic receipts. Available methods are standard, factoring, standard and factoring, and no remittance. Figure 13.6 illustrates the definition of a manual receipt class.

DEFINING PAYMENT METHODS

Use payment methods to identify the nature of the payment—for example, cash, check, or credit card. Payment methods also determine the accounting for receipt entries and determine a customer's remittance bank information. This task is a required setup step. AR requires a payment method to create automatic receipts through the Receipt Batches window. You can choose from five receipt rules: one per customer, one per customer and due date, one per site, one per invoice, and one per site and due date.

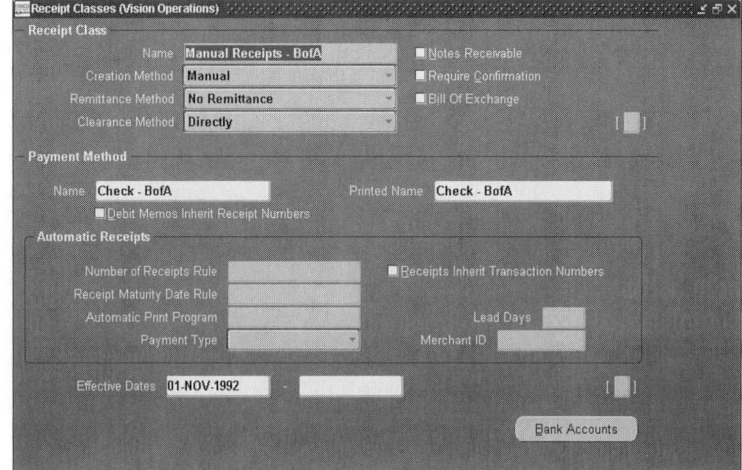

Figure 13.6
Receipt Classes and Payment Methods define the nature of your receipts and how you process them.

Payment methods are assigned to receipt classes and in fact are defined on the Receipt Class form. By clicking the Bank Accounts button, you associate a bank account to the payment method. Figure 13.6, previously in this chapter, also illustrates the definition of a payment method.

Tip

You can use multiple payment methods with the same receipt class. This might make sense if you have multiple payment methods but want your data-entry people to use consistent default information in the receipt batches.

Defining Receipt Sources

Receipt batch sources are used to provide default values for the receipt class, payment method, and remittance bank account yields when you create a receipt batch. You can create receipt sources with the type value of manual. AR provides an automatic receipt source. You can set the last number of field on the automatic receipt source provided.

Defining Aging Buckets

Define aging buckets so that the statement report and the aging reports can group open invoices by age. Common aging buckets for a company with 30-day terms might be named Current, 1–30, 31–60, 61–90, and Over 90. You can define four types of aging buckets: 4-bucket aging, 7-bucket aging, credit snapshot, and statement aging. Oracle provides a seeded bucket for each type:

- Current buckets display transaction values when the due date is equal to or less than the current date.
- Past Due buckets display transaction values when days past due falls into the day range specified.

- A Dispute Only bucket shows transaction values that are marked in dispute. You can have only one Dispute Only or Pending Adjustment entry per bucket definition.
- A Pending Adjustment Only bucket shows transaction values that are marked pending adjustment.
- A Dispute and Pending Adjustments bucket shows both disputed and pending transactions. Because you define only one dispute or pending entry per bucket definition, it is not necessary to specify day ranges.
- Future buckets show transactions due in the future as specified by the day range.

DEFINING STATEMENT CYCLES

Define a statement cycle to determine and control how statements are sent to customers. You choose a statement cycle when you print statement reports. You can default statement cycles to customers by assigning statement cycles to your customer profiles. If you are using multi-org, you must define statement cycles for each operating unit using the AR application.

DEFINING STATEMENT MESSAGES

Statement messages are optional and when used print at the bottom of the delivered statements. There are two types of standard messages: holiday and promotional. You can control when a message prints by assigning start and end dates. 255 characters is the maximum length of the standard message text.

DEFINING DUNNING LETTERS

If you send letters to your customers to advise them of past-due items or if you want AR to automatically calculate and bill finance charges, you should define dunning letters and sets. AR provides three predefined dunning letters and ten user-defined dunning letters. The predefined dunning letter files reside in the $AR_TOP/srw directory. There is a body and footer text file for each dunning letter definition. You can also create your own dunning letters within the application.

Tip

> If you want to add to or edit your dunning letters, consider using the user-defined letters. The predefined letters must be written in a .txt file and delivered to a DBA or programmer analyst for insertion to the `$AR_TOP` directory. The user-defined letters are built in to the application and require no intervention by the technical staff.

The dunning letter is composed of the remit to address, the customer name and address, the text from the letter body file, a list of past-due invoices, and the text from the letter footer file.

DEFINING DUNNING LETTER SETS

You can create sets of dunning letters to show a progression of urgency and severity to the series of letters. Proceed carefully with automatic communications to your customers. Before designing a series of letters, consider customer setup data, transaction data, profile options, and system parameters to determine how the letter-writing program will process receipt grace days, items in dispute, finance charges, on-account receipts, and unapplied receipts. Dunning letter sets are assigned to groups of customers by assigning a set to a customer profile class. Like all values in the customer profile, this assignment can be overridden, if necessary, on the customer record.

DEFINING TERRITORIES

AR enables you to assign a territory flexfield value to salespeople, invoices, and customer business purposes. However, there are no reports or transactions processed by territory in the basic AR system. You must write your own reports to effectively use territory categorization of customers and transactions.

DEFINING SALESPERSONS

Definition of salespeople is a required setup task. If AutoAccounting depends on the salesperson, consider making salesrep mandatory in the system options setup because the General Ledger accounts that you enter in the salesperson definition are used for revenue transactions. If you don't need to credit sales, use the seeded entry of No Sales Credit.

Note

> If you use Oracle Order Management and AutoAccounting uses salespersons, note there are two levels of salesperson credit on the sales order. The order header salesperson is used to determine the receivables account distribution. The order line sales credits distribution is used to determine revenue account distribution.

Installations using multi-org define receipt salespersons for each operating unit.

SETTING THE PROFILE OPTIONS

Setting Profile options is a required and important task. Many AR programs use profile options to determine fundamental logic in the way that they process transactions. Table 13.2 shows the profile options in AR that can affect user and system productivity.

Tip

> Don't skip a profile option simply because it is optional. Some of the profile options can improve your corporate controls over cash and enhance user productivity.

Another group of profile options helps you establish corporate controls and implement policy. These profile options are shown in Table 13.3.

TABLE 13.2 AR USER/SYSTEM PRODUCTIVITY PROFILE OPTIONS

Profile Option Name	Required?	Level*	Comment
AR: Automatic Contact Numbering	Yes	SARU	Default is Yes
AR: Close Periods - Run Effectiveness Report	Yes	SARU	
AR: Customer Merge Commit Size	No	SAR	Default is 1
AR: Customers - Enter Alternate Fields	No	SAR	Default is Yes
AR: Debug Level for PostBatch	No	SARU	Default is 3
AR: Default Exchange Rate Type	No	SAR	
AR: Item Flexfield Mode	No	SARU	Default is segments
AR: Receipt Batch Source	Yes	SARU	Can be set by the user
AR: Sort Customer Reports by Alternate Fields	No	SAR	
AR: Transaction Batch Source	Yes	SARU	
AR: Transaction Flexfield QuickPick Attribute	No	SARU	interface_header_ Attribute1
AR: Use Invoice Accounting for Credit Memos	Yes	SARU	Default is Yes
Default Country	No	SARU	
Journals: Display Inverse Rate	No	SARU	Default is No

**Levels can be Site, Application, Responsibility, or User. The system administrator sets most profile options.*

TABLE 13.3 AR CORPORATE CONTROL PROFILE OPTIONS

Profile Option Name	Required?	Level*	Comment
AR: Allow Update of Existing Sales Credits	No	SARU	Default is Yes
AR: Change Customer on Transaction	Yes	SARU	Default is Yes
AR: Change Customer Name	Yes	SARU	Default is Yes
AR: Create Bank Charges	No	SAR	Default is Yes
AR: Cross Currency Rate Type	Yes	SAR	Default is Corporate
AR: Document Number Generation Level	No	SARU	Default is When Saved

TABLE 13.3 CONTINUED

Profile Option Name	Required?	Level*	Comment
AR: Enable Debug Message Output	No	SARU	Default is No
AR: Enable SQL Trace	No	SARU	Default is No
AR: GL Transfer Balance Test	Yes	SARU	Default is Yes
AR: Invoices with Unconfirmed Receipts	Yes	SARU	Default is None
AR: Mask Bank Account Numbers	No	SAR	Default is Mask-First Four Digits Visible
AR: Override Adjustment Activity Account Option	Yes	SARU	Default is Yes
AR: Update Due Date	Yes	SARU	
AR: View Customer Bank	No	SARU	
Enable Transaction Codes only used in public sector AR	No	SAR	Default is No
HZ: Generate Contact Number	No	SARU	
HZ: Generate Party Number	No	SARU	
HZ: Generate Party Site Number	No	SARU	
HZ: Internal Party	No	SARU	
Sequential Numbering	No	SAR	
OE: Item Flexfield	No	S	Default is System Items
OE: Item Validation Organization	Yes	S	

**Levels can be Site, Application, Responsibility, or User. The system administrator sets most profile options.*

Another group of profile options controls how the collections and cash receipts functions work. These options are listed in Table 13.4.

TABLE 13.4 AR PROFILE OPTIONS FOR COLLECTIONS AND CASH RECEIPTS

Profile Option Name	Required?	Level*	Comment
AR: Alternate Name Search	No	SAR	Default is Yes
AR: Application GL Date Default	No	SAR	Default is Later of Receipt or Invoice Date
AR: Allow Overapplication in	Yes	SARU	
AR: Cash – Allow Actions	Yes	SARU	Default is Yes

TABLE 13.4 CONTINUED

Profile Option Name	Required?	Level*	Comment
AR: Cash – Default Amount Applied	Yes	SARU	Default is Unapplied Amount
AR: Commit Between Validation	No	SARU	
AR: Dunning Letter Remit To Address Label Size	No	SAR	
AR: Enable Cross Currency	No	SAU	Default is No
AR: Include Receipts at Risk In Customer Balance	Yes	SARU	
AR: Zengin Character Set	No	S	

**Levels can be Site, Application, Responsibility, or User. The system administrator sets most profile options.*

There is one profile option that influences the invoicing function. It is shown in Table 13.5.

TABLE 13.5 AR PROFILE OPTIONS FOR INVOICING

Profile Option Name	Required?	Level*	Comment
AR: Show Billing Number	No	SAR	
AR: Enable Credit Card Preprocessor	No	SARU	

**Levels can be Site, Application, Responsibility, or User. The system administrator sets most profile options.*

Finally, there are several important profile options that affect the way the system handles taxation. These options are listed in Table 13.6.

TABLE 13.6 AR PROFILE OPTIONS FOR TAXATION

Profile Option Name	Required?	Level*	Comment
Tax: Allow Ad Hoc Changes	Yes	SARU	Default is Yes
Tax: Allow Manual Tax Lines	Yes	SARU	Default is Yes
Tax: Allow Override of Customer Exemptions	Yes	SARU	Default is No
Tax: Allow Override of Tax Code	Yes	SARU	Default is Yes
Tax: Calculate Tax on Credit Memos	No	SAR	Default is No
Tax: Inventory Item for Freight	No	SARU	Can be set by the user
Tax: Invoice Freight as Revenue	No	SARU	Can be set by the user

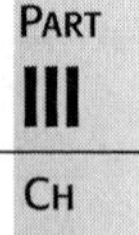

TABLE 13.6 CONTINUED

Profile Option Name	Required?	Level*	Comment
Tax: Use Tax PL/SQL Vendor	No	SARU	Can be set by the user
Tax: Use Tax Vendor	No	SAR	Default is Yes
Tax: Vertex Case Sensitive	No	SAR	Default is Yes
Tax: Vertex Secondary Taxes	No	SAR	Default is Use Secondary Taxes

**Levels can be Site, Application, Responsibility, or User. The system administrator sets most profile options.*

DEFINING CUSTOMER PROFILE CLASSES

Customer profile classes enable you to default many of the values necessary to maintain your customers when you have customers with similar characteristics. The values you can default fall into seven major categories. They are

- **Credit parameters**—Enable you to record a default collector and credit limit tolerance percentage. You can also activate new order credit checking or order hold by Oracle OM.
- **Terms parameters**—Enable you to record a default payment term for customers with this profile class. If the override box is checked, you will be able to change the terms code during transaction entry. Discounts for prompt payment and receipts can be adjusted by entries in the Grace Days fields.
- **Receipt parameters**—Control the number of clearing days, the AutoCash rule set, the Match Receipt rule, the Remaining Amount rule, and the Include Disputed Items for customers with this profile class.
- **Statement parameters**—Determine whether customers receive statements and what statement cycle is used.
- **Finance Charge parameters**—Determine whether customer accounts are charged interest on outstanding balances.
- **Dunning parameters**—Determine whether the customer receives dunning letters when invoices, debit memos, and chargebacks in the account become past due. If you check the Send Letters box, you can also enter a Dunning Letter Set for this customer class.
- **Invoicing parameters**—Control how tax is printed on the invoice and which grouping rule is used for customers in this class. If you don't specify a Tax Printing value, AR uses the value from the System Options, or if that value is not set, AR defaults to the Total Tax Only value. Detail or summary consolidated invoice billing can also be specified.

Figure 13.7 shows an example of a customer profile class.

Finally, customer profile classes are currency-sensitive. Use the profile class amounts region of the form to enter the currency, currency rates and limits, minimum invoice balance for finance charges, minimum dunning amount, and credit limit.

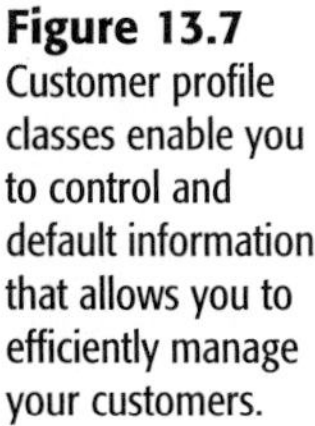

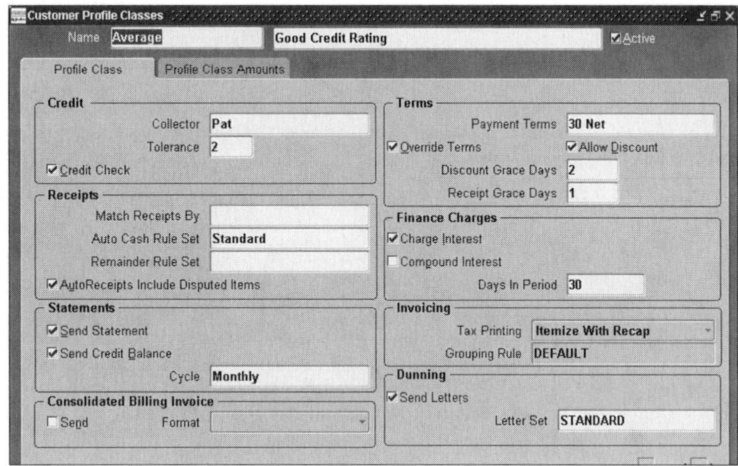

Figure 13.7
Customer profile classes enable you to control and default information that allows you to efficiently manage your customers.

On the customer record you can override any of the values supplied by the customer profile. Furthermore, if you need to change a customer profile, you have the option to update the changed value on all customers who are assigned to that profile. This step is required, but AR provides a default profile class.

DEFINING CUSTOMERS

Customer data may be entered into the AR application manually or through the customer application program interface (API). The API is discussed later in this chapter in the section called "Converting Data for Major Entities." If you have more than about 2000 customers to enter into AR, consider using the API to load them programmatically.

However, if you have a smaller number of customers to enter, navigate to the Customer or Customer Summary window to begin manually defining a set of customer records. Customers are a major data entity in the ERP applications, and there are five major areas to fully define a customer:

- **General**—This area includes the customer name, customer number, and a few global fields that set defaults for the rest of the customer records that might represent your customer's different addresses or business purposes.
- **Addresses**—You can have multiple addresses for each customer record. In the address record, you have the opportunity to override customer profile options that you attached to the customer at the general level.
- **Business purposes**—You can have multiple business purposes for each customer address. For example, an address may be both a Bill-To and a Ship-To customer site. However, it might not be a site that receives dunning notices. The business purposes recognized by the system include: Bill-To, Ship-To, Statements, Dunning, Legal, and Marketing. Other seeded values are available, as well, and if those aren't adequate, you can use the SITE_USE_CODE Lookup Code to define additional business purposes.

Also on the business purpose record(s), you have the opportunity to set default values for carrier, demand class, fob term, freight terms, inventory location, order type, payment terms, price list, sales territory, ship partial indicator, and tax code.

- **Contacts**—You can have multiple contacts for each customer and also multiple contacts for each customer address. You may assign a contact to a specific business purpose.
- **Telephone numbers**—You can assign one primary phone number to the customer, and you may have multiple phone numbers for each contact.

Figure 13.8 shows an example of a customer record. Note that all the tabs you see at the Customer Address are overrides to information on similar tabs at the Customer Header level.

The data storage structures for defining customers are quite flexible and can handle a wide variety of organizational and corporate relationships. However, most common problems that users have with the way AR handles customers are caused by the way AR uses the customer name. AR requires the name of the customer to be unique in the same way most legacy systems have a unique customer number. The unique name facilitates easy inquiry, but can cause problems for customers with many sites. In Release 11*i* of AR you can activate an alternate names feature by setting the profile option AR: Customers - Enter Alternate Fields to Yes. That feature gives you an alternate name on both the customer record and the customer address record. However, you will still want to test the system to make sure you have access to the alternate name whenever your business requirements dictate.

Tip

Use the online help as you enter customer data to get a precise definition of each field's purpose. This is one of the fastest and surest ways to understand field level requirements.

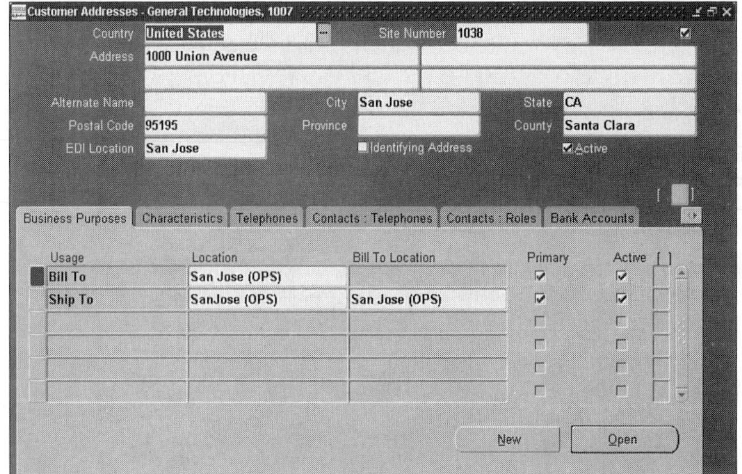

Figure 13.8
Business Purposes is one of the many tabs that define your customers.

In addition, there are other data records you can create to further define your customers. You can add these three items from the Customers or Customer Summary window:

- **Relationships**—If you define relationships among any of your customers, you are defining a one-way or reciprocal relationship to control payments and commitments. For example, you can define a one-way relationship where a parent customer could pay the invoices you send to a child customer.
- **Banks**—You can assign bank accounts to customers. If you are using the Automatic Receipts function, this feature facilitates transfer of funds from the customer bank accounts to your remittance bank account.
- **Payment Methods**—If you are using the Automatic Receipts function, you can attach payment methods to the customer. The payment methods define the processing steps for the Automatic Receipts function.

Tip

Customer entry is a tempting place to take a false shortcut because most fields are not required. The AR application provides lots of customer-related fields so that you can set up defaults to speed up transaction processing. If you leave the optional customer fields blank, you will have to supply the data on each transaction, and that tends to be inefficient. If you set up customers completely, the transaction processing system will usually work more efficiently for you.

DEFINING REMIT-TO ADDRESSES

Remit-to addresses print on invoices, statements, and dunning letters and designate where customers should send payments. Each remit-to address is associated with a state, country, and postal code combination. The Bill-To address is used to determine the remit-to address.

Tip

Make sure to declare a default remit-to address by selecting DEFAULT from the list of values in the State field. If you do this, when you set up new customers in the future, you won't have to check whether the Bill-To address fits an already defined state, country, and postal code combination.

Because a geographical association is the only way AR can determine the remit-to address, many companies make an extension to allow assignment of remit-to addresses to a customer. Briefly, the specification for the extension is as follows:

- Define a descriptive flexfield on the business purpose for the customer. Make it conditional to be required when the business purpose is Bill-To.
- Load the desired remit-to address into the descriptive flexfield for each customer.

- Write a post processor program to run in a report set behind the AutoInvoice program. The postprocessor program should replace the remit-to address ID selected by AutoInvoice with the one stored on the Bill-To business purpose flexfield. Remember, this data is org-specific in multi-org implementations. The remit-to addresses are stored along with the customer addresses in the ra_addresses table (where customer_id = -1).

Installations using multi-org define remit-to Addresses for each operating unit.

Defining Customer Relationships

Defining customer relationships allows you to receive cash from one customer and apply it to the transactions of another customer. Applications of receipts can be restricted to related customers only when you set the system option Allow Payment of Unrelated Invoices to No. If you choose this option, consider defining customer relationships to allow application of receipts to related customer invoices. Relationships can be one-way (a parent can pay a child's invoice) or reciprocal.

Note

The application-level profile option OE: Customer Relationships controls whether relationships are enforced when entering sales orders. Set it to Yes to make sure only related customer addresses are available in Bill-To and Ship-To fields.

Defining Lockboxes

Defining lockboxes enables you to import receipts from a bank file. If you want to enable the lockbox features, you must define at least one lockbox. The lockbox definition controls the receipt batch size, the GL date, the currency exchange rate type, the receipt method, the billing location requirement, the match receipts by method, the AutoAssociate technique, and unapplied amounts.

Defining the Transmission Format

If you use the AutoLockbox program to process receipts, define the transmission data file format. The format definition controls the import of receipt information from the bank into AR. AR provides two standard formats that can be modified to conform to your bank's format. The two formats are SQL*Loader control files and are named ardeft.ctl and arconv.ctl. The ardeft.ctl file processes a standard Bank Administration Institute (BAI) file.

Defining the Receipt Program

If you use automatic receipts, define the receipt programs that will be used to send documents to customers and remittance banks. AR provides sample receipt and remittance document programs. You might want to copy the sample programs as a template for your own. If you create your own program, its name must be eight characters or less.

DEFINING UNIT OF MEASURE CLASSES AND UNITS OF MEASURE

Unit of Measure Classes and Units of Measure definitions are described in Chapter 17. See that chapter for a complete discussion of Units of Measure.

Note

AR does not perform unit of measure conversions and the price is not affected if the unit of measure is changed.

DEFINING MEMO LINES

Standard memo lines are predefined lines for invoices, debit memos, and on-account credits. There are four types of lines:

- Line
- Freight
- Tax
- Miscellaneous charges

If AutoAccounting structures use standard memo lines, the revenue, freight, AutoInvoice clearing, tax, unbilled receivable, unearned revenue, and receivable account segments can come from this definition.

You can optionally enter a standard invoicing rule, accounting rule, tax code, unit list price, and unit of measure for each standard memo line.

DEFINING CROSS-CURRENCY RECEIPTS

If you need to apply receipts of one currency to transactions in another currency, set the profile option AR: Enable Cross Currency to Yes. Be sure to define a cross-currency rounding account in the System Options form and a suspense account in the General Ledger.

DEFINING TAXES

You began your tax setup in the System Options step when you identified your Tax Method. In this step, you set up your tax codes and rates. Defining taxes can also include defining tax locations, tax exceptions, tax exemptions, and tax groups.

AR supports two types of tax methods: VAT and Sales Tax. Generally, you do not try to enable both taxation types in the same organization. Both tax types require you to create tax codes and rates. Tax codes can be assigned to customers at all levels of address and Bill-To or Ship-To business purposes. A tax code can also be assigned to products and standard memo lines.

If your system option tax method is VAT, you define a code and rate for each tax authority. For an example of the setup of a tax code, see Figure 13.9.

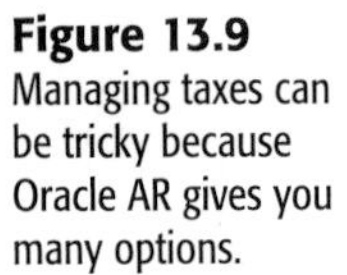

Figure 13.9
Managing taxes can be tricky because Oracle AR gives you many options.

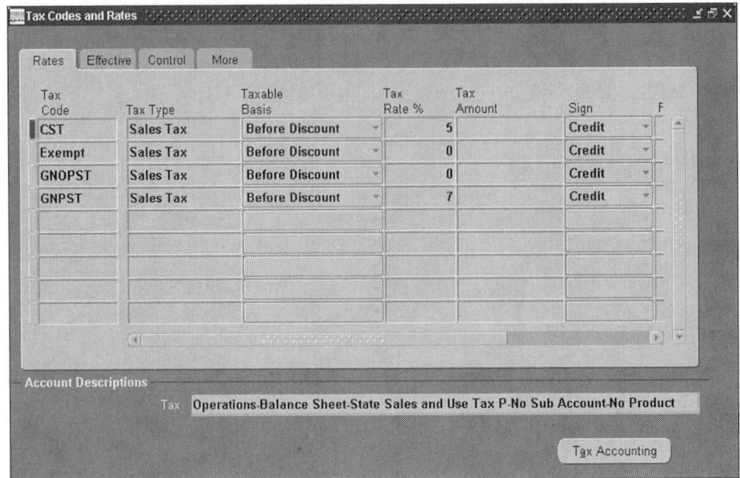

If your system option tax method is Sales Tax, enter a tax code for each location. Usually, this is based on the destination of your shipments or location of your services. In the U.S., a typical location is a state and possibly includes county and city combinations as well.

Tip

To control the tax calculation, many users set up tax codes of Exempt, Intercompany, or International with a tax rate of 0%. Assign these tax codes to customers with no tax liability.

Define tax locations if your sales are subject to tax by many taxing authorities and you want the system to calculate the tax due based on postal codes. You can enter multiple tax rates and postal code ranges for each location as long as the effective date and postal code ranges don't overlap.

For each tax code and tax location, you can assign a tax account.

Define tax exemptions if you need to partially or fully exempt customers or items from your taxation rules. To enable exemptions, you must set the Allow Exemptions for customer or items to Yes in the Tax Defaults tab of the system options.

You define tax groups to group multiple, conditional taxes in one name. Tax groups enable you to calculate each applicable tax in countries where multiple taxes are collected. For example, some countries have a national tax and a provincial tax. The rules and rates for the national tax might be standard for all shipments but not so with provincial taxes.

Finally, define tax rate exceptions only if you have special tax rates that apply to specific tax authorities. You can define tax rate exceptions only to a location-based tax; therefore, your location flexfield structure must be defined as State.County.City to use tax rate exceptions.

Note

Another way to exempt a customer or item from all taxes is to assign the customer or item to a tax code with a zero tax rate.

DEFINING DOCUMENT SEQUENCES

Although Oracle AR enables you to assign sequential numbers to your transactions, you must use document sequences if you want to use sequential numbering for your receipts. To enable document sequence numbering, set the sequential numbering profile option to either Always or Partially Used. Then define and assign categories and sequences for each activity that you use.

Define document sequences for each set of books.

CONVERTING DATA FOR MAJOR ENTITIES

Before processing transactions, you can choose to load three major data entities from legacy systems. AR has open interfaces to accomplish these tasks. Because each open interface requires programming, the effort to manually enter the data might be less than the effort to extract data from legacy systems, map data elements to the AR interface tables, load data into the interfaces, and balance the transactions. The major entities are as follows:

- Customers
- Open Balances
- Transaction History

CREATING OR MODIFYING CUSTOMERS

AR provides an open interface program to help convert customer records from other systems. The open interface program can process a one-time conversion of legacy data, or it can be used to maintain and synchronize the Oracle AR customers with another system. If you have more than 2,500–3,000 customers, consider automatic conversion to load customer data. If you have fewer customers, consider entering them manually in the Enter Customers form.

Tip

You should complete the setup tasks for the AR application before loading the customers. The open interface program uses the setup data to validate incoming customer data.

If you choose to convert customer data using the open interface program, use the following process:

1. Load your data into the five customer interface tables.
2. Run the customer interface program from the Submit Requests window.
3. Analyze the Customer Transfer Report to resolve problems of records that did not load.

The customer interface tables include the following:

- ra_customer_interface
- ra_contact_phones_interface
- ra_customer_banks_interface
- ra_customer_profiles_interface
- ra_cust_pay_method_interface

The automated customer interface validates many of the columns in the interface tables and does not import records that do not pass the validation described in the customer interface table description documentation.

If you enter customers manually, only the customer name, the customer number, and an address are required. However, the customer definition provides defaults for many transactions and enables you the specific control to adjust the system behavior and activate AR functions by customer, so be sure to complete your setups before processing your customer loads.

Tip

Entering a complete customer record when you create the customer might seem like a lot of work, but it is more efficient than creating the record with minimum information and making several updates.

Note

If you implement Oracle Order Management, the customer definition is shared between AR and OM. Consider the effect of each field on the OM application.

CREATING OPEN BALANCES

Open balances can be created from legacy system data with the AutoInvoice program. To use this interface, you must insert rows into the ra_interface_lines_all table and then run the AutoInvoice program. The programmer must consider the AutoInvoice setup to properly map legacy data to the interface table columns. Many columns are validated against setup data and AutoInvoice produces errors if validations fail. Refer to the AutoInvoice validation table and column descriptions to determine the proper values for the interface table.

You can choose to let AutoAccounting determine the accounting for the transactions you convert, or you can create the accounting transactions by inserting the related records into the ra_interface_distributions_all table. If you choose to let AutoAccounting determine the account number and if you use salesreps as one of the table names in AutoAccounting, you must also insert records into the ra_interface_salescredits_all table for each invoice line.

Other conversion techniques include the following:

- Many companies define special transaction types specifically for the one-time conversion of their open invoices, credit memos, and debit memos.

- Because the actual invoice was created and printed and revenue was recognized on the legacy system, many companies do not convert line-item details. Because AR is only concerned with the amount receivable for the total invoice, a single line invoice for the invoice total is adequate for open balances. There are no revenue, tax, or balance sheet issues, and converting a total amount is enough to activate AR's collection and cash receipt functions.
- AR creates a sales journal for the revenue, tax, and receivable amounts when you load open items. Generally, this sales journal is not needed or desirable because the legacy system already updated the General Ledger when the item was originally created. Consider creating the open items in an accounting period earlier than the first live transactions. In this way, you can easily identify and reverse (or delete) the unnecessary sales journal entry.

Tip

Make sure you coordinate with the owners of the GL accounting calendar to open the accounting periods you need for data conversion. When the first GL period is opened, it is not possible to open earlier periods.

CREATING TRANSACTION HISTORY

Conversion of transaction history (closed items) is an optional implementation task and should be justified by business requirements. Closed items are created just as open items, discussed previously. Then AutoCash is used to simulate receipt history and close the items.

PROCESSING TRANSACTIONS

AR uses three workbenches to organize transaction processing:

- Use the Transactions workbench to create and maintain invoices, debit memos, credit memos, on-account credits, chargebacks, and commitments.
- Use the Receipts workbench to create batches and enter, apply, correct and delete receipts. You also use this workbench to create adjustments and chargebacks.
- Use the Collections workbench to assist credit and collection activity. You can view customer account balances, place credit holds, place items in dispute, record call history, and view dunning history.

CREATING INVOICE TRANSACTIONS

Invoices in AR can be created manually or automatically. The AR system can process invoices from many sources, including Oracle and non-Oracle Order Management and customer order fulfillment systems.

MANUALLY CREATING INVOICES OR MEMOS

To manually enter an invoice or a receivable transaction, use the Transactions window and create a batch of transactions or a single invoice or memo. First, enter the transaction header information, including date, currency, transaction type, Bill-To customer, terms, salesperson, remit to address, and header freight information. Next, enter line-item details, including items, quantity, tax code, line freight, and price. Note that most of this information can be defaulted from the Transaction Source and Customer record. See Figure 13.10 for an example of a transaction.

Figure 13.10
All the information in this invoice was defaulted from either the Source or the Bill-To.

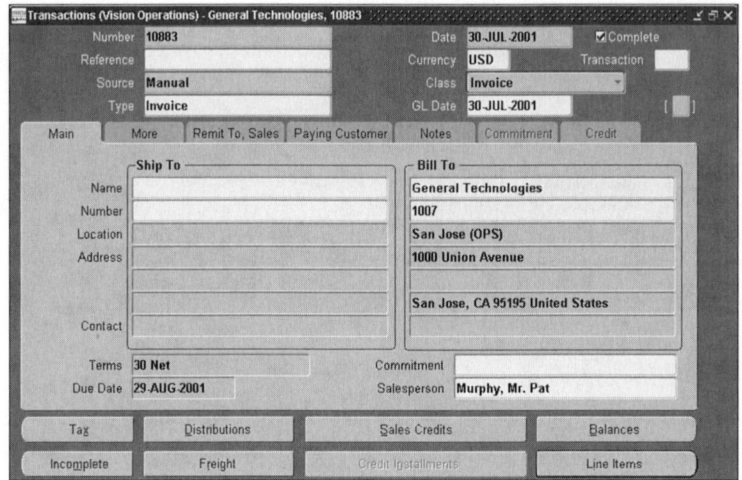

When you complete the transaction, AR performs a validation to make sure the transaction conforms to the requirements of that transaction type. For example, the GL date must be in an open or future enterable period, taxes must be correct, freight lines must have account distributions, and the sign of the transaction must agree with the creation sign of the transaction type. When the transaction is marked complete, AR updates the customer balance and creates a transaction to be passed to the GL.

RUNNING AUTOINVOICE FOR BATCHES OF IMPORTED TRANSACTIONS

The AutoInvoice program can be used to create large batches of invoices without data entry. The AutoInvoice program processes data in three tables:

- ra_interface_lines_all
- ra_interface_sales_credits
- ra_interface_distributions

Using a tool such as SQL*Loader you must load the invoice data into these tables. The table and column descriptions for the interface tables in the Oracle documentation show the requirements and validation for each column. If you are using Oracle's Order Management module, a few setup steps activate the interface.

AutoInvoice processes the data and inserts successful transactions into the following eight tables:

- ra_batches_all
- ra_customer_trx_all
- ra_customer_trx_lines_all
- ra_cust_trx_gl_dist_all
- ra_cust_trx_line_salesreps_all
- ar_payment_schedules_all
- ar_receivable_applications_all
- ar_adjustments_all

PROCESSING RECEIPT TRANSACTIONS

In Release 11*i*, you can use the Receipts Workbench to apply cash receipt transactions and update your customers' open balance items. Because customers often pay amounts other than the full open item balance, the Receipts Workbench is able to make transactions for adjustments, chargebacks, manual receipts, and automatic receipts.

APPLYING RECEIPTS MANUALLY

You can apply cash receipts including bills of exchange to open AR items, including invoices, debit memos, credit memos, chargebacks, deposits, guarantees, and on-account credits. To apply receipts, use the receipts or receipts summary window and a receipt type of Cash. Enter information about the receipt, including receipt number, currency, amount, GL date, and payment method. Identify the customer by entering a transaction number or customer name and Bill-To location. See Figure 13.11 for an example of the Receipts form.

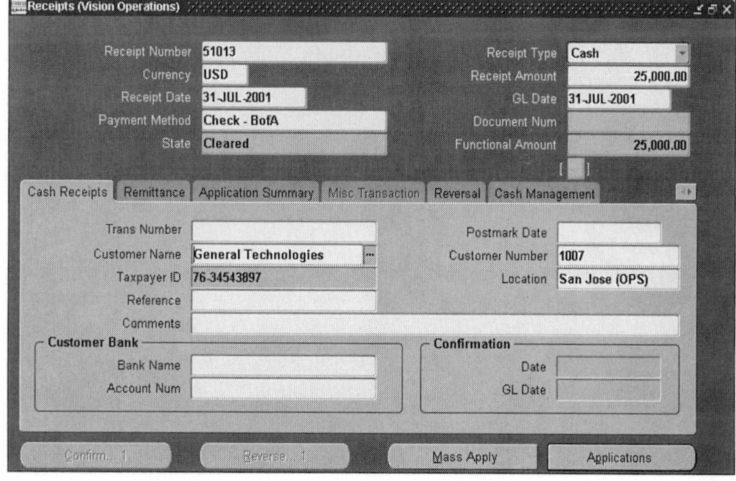

Figure 13.11
This is the information necessary to process a receipt.

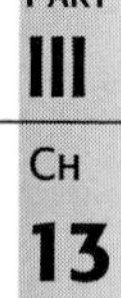

Because the payment method determines the default bank account, verify that this account is correct or select an alternative account assigned to that payment method.

If the customer is paying many open items, use mass-apply techniques. If you choose Apply, AR marks for application open items until the full amount of the receipt is consumed. If you choose Preview, AR displays a list of open items, and you can mark which transactions are to be closed.

Tip

Sort the list of open items to match the customer remittance details. Many customer AP systems print the remittance advice in document number order or date order.

To quickly apply cash, you can also use the Post QuickCash routine if you can define rules that identify how the cash should be applied to a customer's account. This can speed up the entry of your cash application. The rules are defined in the AutoCash rules setup.

If the customer is paying one or just a few open items, choose applications in the receipts window and select the transaction from the list of values window. Repeat for all transactions. To place an amount on account, enter On Account in the transaction number field.

AR uses the transaction type of the debit item and several user profile options to control the application process. If the transaction type does not allow overapplication, you cannot enter a transaction that would reverse the sign of the debit item. If the transaction type specifies natural application only, you must enter transactions that always progress the open item balance toward zero.

Processing Lockbox Transactions Automatically

If you can get a data file of lockbox activity from your bank, you can use AutoLockbox to eliminate manual data entry for cash receipt transactions. The AutoLockbox process involves three steps:

1. Use a SQL*Loader script to import the bank data file.
2. Run the AutoLockbox validation program. Validated data is transferred to the QuickCash tables.
3. Submit the Post QuickCash process to actually update the customer balances and open items.

Tip

Evaluate your cash application process carefully before implementing AutoLockbox. If your customers make lots of deductions or if manual cash applications only take an hour a day (2,000–3,000 invoices per month), you might not save enough work to make this process worth automating.

CREATING CHARGEBACKS

You can create chargeback transactions during receipt processing. A chargeback is a new debit item that you can assign to a customer when you close an old debit item. This transaction is effective when the customer pays an invoice short, you want to clear the original invoice, but you believe the customer still owes the full amount in the account.

To create a chargeback while entering receipts, choose chargebacks, enter the transaction type, amount, and change the account distribution provided by the transaction type if necessary. Complete the chargeback by adding a due date, a reason, and comments.

CREATING ADJUSTMENTS

You can create manual adjustments to invoices, debits, chargebacks, on-account credits, deposits, and guarantees in your customer accounts. Adjustments are subject to approval. Subject to approval limits, you can approve adjustments that you create.

An adjustment can have one of the following four approval statuses:

- **Approved status**—Is complete, and the debit or credit item is updated.
- **More research status**—Is a hold status waiting on new information.
- **Rejected status**—Closes the item without updating the debit or credit item.
- **Pending approval status**—Indicates the adjustment is outside the approval limits of its creator and must be processed by a user with greater authority.

Note

If the transaction type of the item to be adjusted does not permit overapplication, you cannot create an adjustment that will reverse the sign of the debit item.

You can apply an adjustment to an entire invoice or select an adjustment type for the line, miscellaneous charges, freight, or tax. To create an adjustment during receipts processing, choose adjustments, enter an activity, choose an adjustment type, and enter an amount. To complete the adjustment, enter the GL date, enter the adjustment date, and adjust the account distribution if necessary.

Also, you can create automatic adjustments when you run the AutoAdjustment program. You can specify selection criteria to limit adjustments to a specific remaining amount, due date, customer, or transaction type.

PERFORMING COLLECTION ACTIVITIES

The third major activity of the AR application is to support collection efforts. AR uses the Collections workbench to organize and assist collection activities. You can record calls and customer contacts, produce customer contact documents, and analyze a customer's account with inquiry screens and reports. See Figure 13.12 for an example of the Customer Calls form.

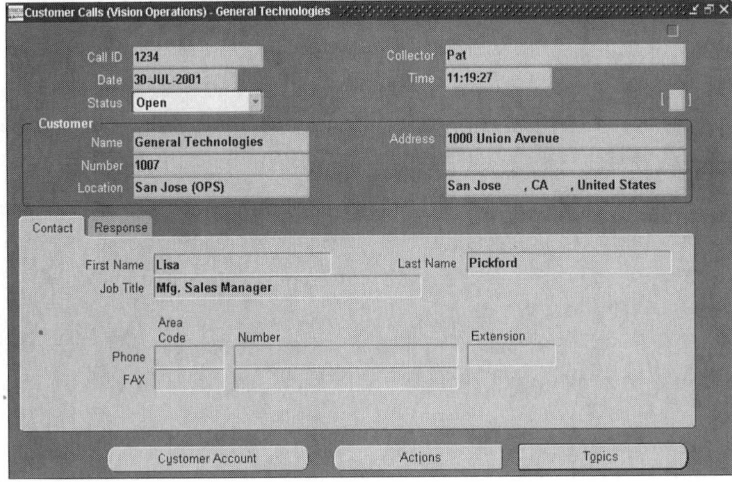

Figure 13.12 There are many ways to manage the contacts you make with your customers.

Recording Calls

When you contact a customer about scheduling a payment for any open item, you can record the details of the conversation in the Customer Calls form. For example, this form can document items in dispute or promises to pay past-due items.

Tip

It is a good idea to record customer contacts and phone numbers in the customer master record. This information assists you when contacting the customer.

For each call, enter the collector, the customer name, the contact, the customer's response, the outcome of the call, and additional notes. If the customer makes a commitment to pay, enter the promise information to improve the accuracy of cash forecast reports. Finally, enter a call action to schedule future collection actions.

Tip

You define Receivable Lookups to standardize and help you enter customer responses. You also can define lookups to identify collector actions, follow-up actions, customer responses, and call outcomes.

Analyzing a Customer Account

You can review open balances and activity of a specific account in several ways. There is an Account Summary window that quickly shows the total amount overdue. For more details, you can drill down in the Account Details window which shows all past due items. In the Customer Accounts window, you can view account balances by aging bucket and drill down to view detailed items in each aging bucket.

In addition, there are several reports of interest:

- **Past Due Invoice report**—Shows information about past due invoices, debit memos, deposits, chargebacks, and guarantees. This report does not include on-account or unapplied cash. Review the On Account/Unapplied Payments Balance report for these items.
- **Account Status report**—Lists all open items and the total balance due in your functional currency.
- **Customer Credit Snapshot report**—Shows key customer setup values, open-item aging, credit history, a 12-month summary, and recent transactions.
- **Aged Trial Balance listings**—Show account details of open items and can be run by range of customers, by amount, by collector, and by salesperson. Four- and seven-bucket aging reports are available.

PLACING AN ACCOUNT ON CREDIT HOLD

If you are also using the Oracle Order Management application, you can place a customer account on credit hold. When an account is on hold, you can still create transactions for that customer in AR, but you prevent creation of new sales order and shipping transactions for that customer. Place or release a credit hold from the Customer Accounts window. If you place and release a lot of credit holds, use the Credit Hold report to summarize the customers on credit hold, the balances due and past-due by currency, contact information, and days on hold.

CREATING STATEMENTS

AR can produce specific statements for each customer billing location. Each customer can be assigned a statement cycle in his credit profile. The statement cycle controls when a statement will be produced. You can print a statement, a draft statement, or reprint a statement from the Print Statements window.

Note

Because the statement is designed for a preprinted form, AR creates the formatted output file but does not route it to the printer immediately. You must issue the printer command for your computer's operating system when proper forms are in the printer.

Tip

Many Oracle users are using print output format programs to laser print or fax statements and avoid the need for preprinted forms.

CREATING DUNNING LETTERS

Some AR users send dunning letters in addition to, or instead of, statements to advise customers of past-due items. When you submit the Dunning Letter Generate program, AR prints dunning letters using dunning letter sets, customers, and collectors that meet the selection criteria.

BALANCING THE AR APPLICATION INTERNALLY

Use the following six reports to collect the reconciliation totals. Make sure all of these reports are created for a consistent set of dates:

- Use an Aging report to determine beginning and ending balances.
- Use the Transaction Register to obtain the total of transactions.
- Run the Adjustment Register report to obtain the sum of adjustments for the period.
- Check out the Invoice Exceptions report to get the sum of invoice exceptions.
- Use the Applied Receipts Register to obtain the total of receipts.
- Run the Unapplied Receipts Register to determine the amount of unapplied receipts.

Use this formula to verify that your AR balances are correct:

> Period Beginning Balance + Transactions + or – adjustments – Invoice Exceptions – Applied Receipts – Unapplied Receipts = Period Ending Balance

BALANCING THE SUBSIDIARY LEDGER TO THE GENERAL LEDGER

The AR application is a subsidiary ledger to the Oracle General Ledger application. You can reconcile and balance the two applications by verifying reports and constructing a progression of transaction totals from the beginning balances of an accounting period to the ending balances. All transactions in AR are date-stamped with a GL Date.

Tip

A sound practice to use when entering transactions is to ensure that the GL date and the invoice date are the same. The same holds true in processing receipts. Make sure the receipt date and the GL date are the same. If you must handle exceptions to this rule, keep good documentation to enable you to reconcile your AR and GL balances.

Tip

Make sure the AR reports you use to reconcile to the General Ledger are all run for the correct accounting period dates. Use the Detail By Account option to conveniently group amounts for reconciliation purposes.

Use the Sales Journal and Receipt Journal reports to verify the General Ledger transfer process. Look at the Unposted Items Report to determine whether AR is holding transactions that cannot be sent to the General Ledger.

USING OPEN INTERFACES IN THIS AR

The AR application has six major Application Program Interfaces (API):

- Inbound billing transactions
- Inbound customer records
- Inbound bank receipts
- Outbound update to the General Ledger
- Inbound sales tax rates
- The Tax Vendor Extension

Many of these Application Program Interfaces require some programming to use them. Typically, an inbound interface consists of a SQL*Loader program to load the external data into one or more database tables that mirror the record layout of the external data. Also, a PL/SQL program is used to validate the external data, clean up the external data, and migrate it to the Oracle Applications open interface tables. In addition, you can also program one or more operating system scripts and reports to control the interface, provide a user interface to the interface, and provide an audit trail of records processed.

INCOMING TRANSACTIONS TO BE INVOICED

AR uses three tables to store data for processing by the AutoInvoice program:

- ra_interface_lines
- ra_interface_salescredits
- ra_interface_distributions

The ra_interface_lines table uses the Line Transaction Flexfield as its primary key to uniquely identify each invoice line. If you are using Oracle Order Management as the source of the incoming transaction, the Transaction Flexfield uses the first 10 interface_ line_attribute columns.

Tip

This setup is documented in the Order Management chapter of a reference manual titled *Oracle Manufacturing, Distribution, Sales and Service Open Interfaces Manual*. This manual is also found in the file mfgopen.pdf on the Release 11*i* documentation disk.

If you are processing many rows through this interface, it is a good idea to create indexes on the columns of the Transaction Flexfield and the corresponding columns in the ra_customer_trx_lines and ra_customer_trx tables to improve performance.

IMPORTING AND MAINTAINING CUSTOMER RECORDS

The Customer API can be used to initially load a large quantity of customers on system startup, or it can create and update customer records as a slave to a non-Oracle customer master. To use the customer API, load data into five interface tables:

- ra_customer_interface
- ra_contact_phones_interface
- ra_customer_banks_interface
- ra_customer_profiles_interface
- ra_cust_pay_method_interface

When you submit the customer interface program, the data in these tables is validated and transferred to the customer tables as if it had been entered by a data-entry function. Each time the customer interface API is run, AR creates the Customer Interface Transfer report to document records processed and show validation errors.

Note

The interface does not create location combinations for foreign locations (when the country code is not the same as the country code defined in your system options).

IMPORTING BANK RECEIPTS

If your bank can produce a data file of lockbox cash receipts, the AutoLockbox API processes receipt data that you load into the ar_payments_interface table. Each row in this table can accommodate payments for eight invoices and amounts. An overflow record type is available if your customer is paying more than eight transactions.

Note

AutoLockbox does not process miscellaneous or non-invoice cash receipts.

Each time the AutoLockbox API runs, you automatically receive the AutoLockbox Execution Report. This report shows invalid transactions as follows:

- The receivable item does not match the currency of the receipt.
- The receivable item belongs to an unrelated customer.
- The receivable item is not an invoice, debit memo, chargeback, credit memo, deposit, or on-account credit.
- The receivable item is a duplicate or is invalid for this customer.
- The receivable item has already been selected for automatic receipt.
- The installment number or the receivable item is invalid.

Updating the General Ledger

The General Ledger interface is an outbound interface from AR to transfer Sales and Cash journal entry data from the AR subsidiary ledger to the General Ledger. This API places the journal entry data into the gl_interface table in the General Ledger. If you are using the Oracle General Ledger, no programming is necessary to implement this interface.

Tip

You can choose to run journal import as part of the transfer of AR data to the gl_interface table. The journal entry name contains the word "Receivables" and the concurrent process request ID number for the transfer job.

Importing Sales Tax Rate Data

The Sales Tax Rate interface is an API to load locations and tax rates into AR. Because there are about 60,000 different sales tax rates in the United States, if you have many customers in a wide variety of tax locations, you might want to buy a subscription service to get data file updates to maintain current tax data. This API processes data stored in the ar_tax_interface table and AR provides two SQL*Loader control files, aravp.ctl and arvertex.ctl, to help with the loading process.

You can run the interface in one of three modes:

- Load all data in the ar_tax_interface table.
- Load changed data only.
- Review mode prints the report without actually loading any data from the API.

Using the Tax Vendor Extension

The tax vendor extension is an interface to allow integration with an external tax calculation program. The tax extension program is called whenever AR computes a tax in any of the following windows, programs, or workbenches:

- OM Sales Order Workbench
- OM Sales Acknowledgement Report
- AR AutoInvoice
- AR Transaction Workbench
- AR Copy Transactions
- AR Credit Memos Window
- AR Adjustments Window

The tax extension passes the AR data to the vendor programs and returns a tax rate or tax amount from the vendor's program. AR is then able to use the returned information to construct the appropriate tax lines and accounting information.

Note

If you are implementing the tax extension in the U.S., select State.County.City or State.City for your Sales Tax Location Flexfield structure.

UNDERSTANDING KEY REPORTS

The AR application provides over 100 reports to assist with accounting, collections, execution, printing documents, listings, tax reporting, and miscellaneous activities. In addition, because they have a variety of run parameters and sort sequences, many reports serve multiple purposes.

Accounting reports (see Table 13.7) assist with recording the history of transactions, balancing the AR subsidiary ledger internally, and recording entries into the General Ledger.

TABLE 13.7 ACCOUNTING REPORTS

Report Name	Description
Adjustment Approval Report	Use this report to see information about transaction adjustments.
Adjustment Register	Review approved adjustments with this report. This is one of the reports used to balance the system.
Aging - By Account Report	This is a variation of the aging reports to show open items in summary or detail by accounting flexfield value. This is one of the reports used to balance the system.
Applied Receipts Register	This report shows all activity of a receipt. This is one of the reports used to balance the system.
AR Reconciliation Report	This report summarizes receivable activities and compares them to the ending balance.
Automatic Receipt Batch Management	This report is used to review the status of Automatic Receipt Batches.
Automatic Receipts Awaiting Confirmation	This report lists automatic receipts that have been formatted and have been assigned a payment method with a receipt class with Require Confirmation.
Bad Debt Provision Report	This report can calculate a bad debt exposure from the percent collectable value in the customer profile class.
Bank Risk Report	If a receipt has been factored but the collection risk has not been eliminated, it can be included on this report.
Billing and Receipt History	Use this report to see a detailed list of transactions for a date range.
Billing History Report	This report shows a summary of transactions in an account.
Commitment Balance Report	This is a summary listing of information about commitments.

TABLE 13.7 CONTINUED

Report Name	Description
Cross Currency Exchange Gain/Loss Report	If you have set up AR to use cross-currency settlements, use this report to review detailed information about these transactions.
Customer Balance Revaluation	This shows customers with negative balances for use in some countries where these balances must be adjusted.
Customer Open Balance Letter	Use this letter to inform customers of open balances. The letter includes an introductory paragraph and individual transactions.
Discount Projection Report	This report calculates and estimates your potential exposure when customers take discounts.
Invoice Exception Report	This report shows transactions where Open Receivables is equal to No. These transactions do not appear on an aging report but are on the transaction register.
Invoices Posted to Suspense Report	This is a listing of invoices where the revenue account is a suspense account.
Journal Entries Report	Use this report to reconcile the AR subledger to the General Ledger.
Journal with GL Details Report	Use this report to show journal entries for specific transactions in AR.
Miscellaneous Transaction Report	List miscellaneous receipts activity with this report.
Notes Receivable Report	This reports general information about notes receivable.
Open Items Revaluation Report	Use this report to calculate and revalue open items for currency exchange fluctuations.
Other Applications Report	This report shows information for invoices against guarantees, invoices against deposits, and credit memos for these transactions.
Projected Gains/Losses Report	Use this report to calculate potential gains and losses for currency revaluation.
Receipt Analysis - Days Late	This is a report to show customer payment patterns.
Receipt Register	This is a listing of receipts for a date range.
Receipts Awaiting Bank Clearance	This report includes automatic and manual receipts that have been remitted but have not cleared the bank, and the receipt class requires clearance.
Receipts Awaiting Remittance	This is a listing of receipts that have been confirmed, and the receipt class requires remittance.
Receipts Journal Report	This report lists the details of the receipts that have been included in a journal entry.
Remittance Batch Management	This is a listing to show the status of Remittance Batches.

TABLE 13.7 CONTINUED

Report Name	Description
Reversed Notes Receivable	Use this report to see information about reversed notes receivable.
Reversed Receipts Report	This report lists information about receipt reversals.
Sales Journal by Customer Report	This report lists all transactions by customer.
Sales Journal by GL Account	This report is similar to the transaction register by GL account. Use this report when you balance the AR aging to the General Ledger.
Transaction Reconciliation Report	This is a report to show GL journal entry lines created from specific AR transactions.
Transaction Register	Use this register to verify that postable items are included in the sales journal. This is one of the key reports used to balance the system.
Transactions Check Report	Use this report to audit and verify your transaction data.
Unapplied Receipts Register	This report lists the details of on-account and unapplied receipts.
Unposted Items Report	Use this report to see items not posted to the General Ledger for a date range.

COLLECTION REPORTS

Collection reports (see Table 13.8) assist with the collection, tracking, and management of open items.

TABLE 13.8 COLLECTION REPORTS

Report Name	Description
Account Status Report	For each customer, this report lists all open debit and credit items in the functional currency.
Actual Receipt Report	This report shows receipt activity by bank accounts and receipt dates. This report helps to reconcile receipts.
Aging - 4 and 7 Bucket Reports	The bucket reports are really a series of reports. The series shows open items in either four or seven aging buckets. The report can be sorted by customer, transaction type, balance due, or salesperson.
Call Actions Report	This report shows a detailed list of actions entered by collectors in the Customer Calls window. Review this report to see which actions require follow-up.
Collection Effectiveness Indicators	Use this report to track customer payment history and patterns.

TABLE 13.8 CONTINUED

Report Name	Description
Collection Key Indicators	This report shows collector effectiveness. The report shows the number of calls, information about customer responses, and the outcome of the calls.
Collections by Collector Report	Use this report to tabulate payment applications for each collector.
Collections Receipt Forecast Report	This report projects the collector's estimates of cash collections into a cash receipts forecast.
Collector Call History	Use this report to see collector call information for a date range.
Collector's Follow Up Report	This report lists items that require follow-up action.
Credit Hold Report	Use this report to review customer accounts with a credit hold status.
Customer Credit Snapshot Report	This report shows a customer's credit history.
Customer Follow Up History Report	This report is used to review the history of collection calls to a customer.
Disputed Invoice Report	This report lists information and totals for debits you place in disputed status.
Invoices Awaiting Automatic Receipt	Use this report to list transactions assigned to an automatic payment method.
Past-Due Invoice Report	This is a listing of past-due open items by customer.
Receipt Analysis - Days Late Report	This report shows an analysis of the timing of customer payments and terms.
Receipt Forecast Report	This report identifies dates on which you can expect to receive payment for debit items.
Receipt Promises Report	This is another report to show information from the Customer Calls window.

EXECUTION REPORTS

Execution reports (see Table 13.9) show transactions, validation results, and activity made by the batch transaction processing programs.

TABLE 13.9 EXECUTION REPORTS

Report Name	Description
Archive Detail and Summary	These reports are created automatically when you perform archive activities.
AutoAdjustment Reports	These reports list the effect of running AutoAdjustment. You can run and review the preview report before running Create Adjustments.

TABLE 13.9 CONTINUED

Report Name	Description
AutoInvoice Reports	When you run AutoInvoice, these reports are created automatically to show the effect of the batch process.
Automatic Clearing Receipts Execution	These reports are created each time you run the automatic clearing process.
Automatic Receipts and Remittances Execution	This report is generated when automatic receipts or remittances are created, approved, or formatted.
Lockbox Execution Report	This report is created automatically whenever you run the AutoLockbox process.
Posting Execution Report	Use this report to review transactions that are transferred to the General Ledger.

INVOICE PRINT REPORTS

Invoice Print reports (see Table 13.10) are used to prepare the documents to send to your customers' accounts payable department.

TABLE 13.10 INVOICE PRINT REPORTS

Report Name	Description
Invoice Print Preview Report	Use this report to preview items that will print.
Print Invoice Reports	Use this report to print a batch of invoices, memos, chargebacks, deposits, guarantees, invoices against deposits, invoices against guarantees, on-account credits, and adjustments.

LISTING REPORTS

Listing reports (see Table 13.11) show the way your system is configured and document the various codes, profiles, lists of values, rules, and so forth.

TABLE 13.11 LISTING REPORTS

Report Name	Description
Accounting Rules Listing	This is a report to document accounting rules.
AutoCash Rules Listing	Use this report to document the sequence of AutoCash rules assigned to an AutoCash rule set.
Customer Listing	The customer detail listing produces a very long report and lists the configuration for each customer site.
Customer Profiles Report	This report shows the profile information for each customer or customer site.

Table 13.11 Continued

Report Name	Description
Customer Relationships Listing	Use this report to document all active and inactive relationships that have been defined among customers.
Duplicate Customer Report	This report locates possible redundant customer records.
European Sales Listing	This report shows sales to customers in the European Union.
Incomplete Invoices Report	This report locates and reports invoices with an incomplete status. These invoices do not update the General Ledger or receivable balances.
Ordering and Grouping Rules Listing	This report lists rules used by AutoInvoice to sort and group billing transactions.
Payment Terms Listing	This is a listing of term codes in the system.
Receipts Without Sites Report	Use this report to review all receipts that do not have an address assigned to them. The address is required to determine on which Bill-To site's statement the receipt should appear.
Standard Memo Lines Listing	This report documents anything you enter in the Standard Memo Lines window.
Tax Group Listing	This report lists information concerning tax groups.
Transaction Batch Sources Listing	This report shows all batch sources that are defined for the system.
Transaction Types Listing	This report shows the details of what you enter in the Transaction Types window.

Tax Reports

Tax reports (see Table 13.12) assist with the reporting, collection, and payment of tax collections.

Table 13.12 Tax Reports

Report Name	Description
Canadian GST/PST Tax Report	This report supports the reporting requirements of Canadian taxes.
Country Specific VAT Reporting	Specialized reports are available when you install Belgium, Chinese, Czech, German, Hungarian, Italian, Korean, Norwegian, Polish, Portuguese, Spanish, Swiss, Taiwan, or Thai localizations.
Customers with Invoices at 0 and no	Use this report to VAT Registration Number locate customers who are not paying VAT but have not documented their exemption.

Table 13.11 Continued

Report Name	Description
Financial Tax Register	This report extracts data from the Tax Reporting Ledger and creates custom tax reports.
Sales Tax Listing	This report lists the details of each sales tax location.
Tax Code Listing	This report lists the details of each tax code in the system.
Tax Exceptions Listing	This report documents what you enter in the Item Tax Rate Exceptions window.
Tax Exempt Customer Report	This report documents customers marked tax-exempt in their configuration.
Tax Exempt Product Listing	This report documents products marked tax exempt.
Tax Interface Report	This report is automatically generated when you run the Sales Tax Rate Interface program.
Tax Received Report	This report shows in each currency the amount of tax received for each item.
Tax Only: Open Invoices Report	Use this report to locate open invoices where the balance open is equal to the amount of the tax.
US Sales Tax Report	This report shows tax liabilities by taxing authority for invoices, credits memos, and adjustments. This report is the basis for a tax return.
VAT Exception Report	This is a report to list various AR transactions that meet VAT exception conditions.
VAT Reconciliation Report	Use this report to support periodic VAT returns.
VAT Register Report	This report is used to show VAT tax liability.

Miscellaneous Reports

Miscellaneous reports (see Table 13.13) are provided for a variety of purposes.

Table 13.13 Miscellaneous Reports

Report Name	Description
Audit Report by Document Number	Use this report to identify discrepancies in document number sequences.
Bank Charges Report	Use the Bank Charges report to list all bank charges entered in the Bank Charges window.
Deposited Cash - Applied Detail	Use this report to help reconcile daily cash transactions and bank statements.
Inter Company Invoices and Receipts Reports	Use this report to verify unposted transactions from one company and applied to another company.

TABLE 13.13 CONTINUED

Report Name	Description
Key Indicators - Daily and Summary	Use this report to compare and measure change in key indicators for two periods.
Supplier Customer Netting Report	This is a report to show the net balance of customers and vendors with exactly the same name, NIF code, or VAT registration.

TROUBLESHOOTING

In summary, the AR application is a subsidiary ledger to the General Ledger, and the application processes revenue transactions, adjustments to billed items, and receipts. In addition, the AR application has a robust set of reports and windows to assist you with collection of open receivable items. It is a relatively complex financial application, and you should consider the following as you work with the setup, transactions, and reports:

- If you have a large number of billing lines, you will want to place indexes on the ra_interface_lines_all table for your Transaction Flexfield columns. Oracle Support can provide your DBA with a performance patch.
- Since AR is a subsidiary ledger to the General Ledger, it will normally maintain an accurate balance among the details in AR and the accounting flexfields in the GL. A small window of vulnerability exists if the journal entry is destroyed in the GL interface before it can be imported and posted to the GL accounts. AR will not let you simply rerun a month-end posting. However, you can get a program from Oracle Support to undo the effects of closing the month, so that you can create a new month-end journal entry.
- To keep the accounts in the AR subsidiary ledger and the General Ledger in balance, always make adjusting entries to the detailed transactions in AR and let AR make the journal entry in the GL.
- Reversing a receipt and starting again is often the fastest way to undo a receipt entry that is causing you problems.
- If the receipt entry programs don't allow you to make adjustments or process customer overpayments and adjustments, check the settings on your profile options and the setup for the transaction type.
- AR reports are date-sensitive and this might affect your ability to balance the subsidiary ledger to the GL at period-end. For example, AR can create an open item trial balance for an earlier date even though some of those items now have been paid off and new open items have been created. To balance properly at the period-end, make sure all of your balancing reports use the period-end date.
- If you implement the multi-org feature (see Chapter 29, "Understanding Multi-Org"), realize that customer records are not partitioned by organization. However, customer addresses and business purposes are partitioned by each of your organizations.

- Most AR reports do not show the Province, County, or the fourth Address Line of the customer record.
- Do not change the Sales Tax Location Flexfield structure after you enter customer addresses or create transactions.
- The customer API does not import Territory Flexfield information.
- You cannot adjust the exchange rate on a foreign currency invoice after it has been posted or after a receipt has been applied. To use a different exchange rate you would have to delete or credit the transaction.

CHAPTER 14

USING ORACLE ASSETS

In this chapter

RELATIONSHIP TO OTHER APPLICATIONS

Oracle Assets (FA) generally receives information from interfaces with either the Oracle Payables (AP) and/or the Oracle Project (PA) module. Oracle Assets can also receive information manually from users who enter it directly into the fixed asset system or upload it from a spreadsheet using ADI (Application Desktop Integrator). In addition, Oracle Assets can receive information from outside feeder systems (non-Oracle applications) through the Mass Addition Interface.

Oracle Payables sends invoices that are charged to an asset clearing account into the Mass Additions table. At various intervals during the month, the mass additions process can be run to transmit the data into the fixed asset module. Construction-in-Progress (CIP) assets can be tracked and analyzed in either the PA or FA module. If Oracle Projects is used, the CIP asset is tracked as defined in the project. After it is completely built, you can send it to Oracle Assets for capitalization. Note that if you are using Oracle Projects for CIP purposes, you will not need to duplicate the effort in Oracle Assets.

Oracle Assets sends fixed asset additions, depreciation, adjustments, transfers, gain/loss, and retirement information in journal entry form to Oracle General Ledger (GL). Oracle's FA relationships to other applications are shown in Figure 14.1.

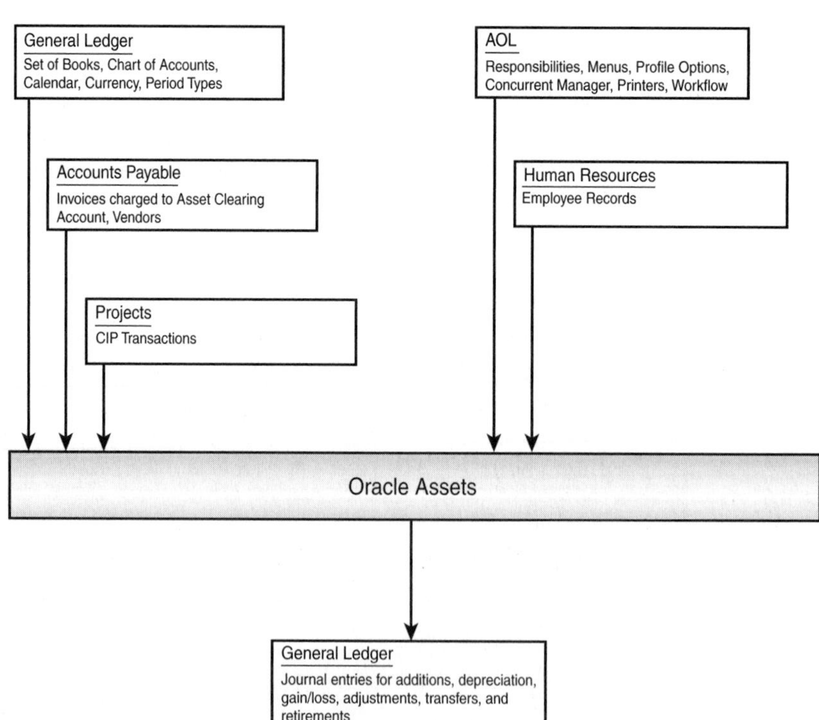

Figure 14.1
This illustrates FA relationships to other applications.

Prior to Release 11*i*, Oracle Assets automatically closed the accounting period after successfully depreciating your assets for the period. Now, running depreciation and closing the accounting period are separate processes. You can run depreciation as many times as desired within a specific period, thus enabling you to make last-minute changes prior to closing the period. For example, say you have already run depreciation when you find out that there is a last-minute cost adjustment to an asset or an asset that you failed to add. You would simply perform a rollback of the depreciation processed earlier for the current open period, make the necessary adjustments to the asset(s), and run depreciation again.

DISCOVERING NEW FEATURES IN RELEASE 11*i*

This section covers the new features found in Oracle Assets release 11*i*. The new version of the software provides more ways to track and analyze asset information.

SECURITY BY BOOK

You can associate a depreciation book to a specific user responsibility in such a way that only users with access to that specific responsibility can view and transact on the assets associated with that particular book. This helps prevent users from inadvertently placing an asset in the wrong set of books, in addition to securing asset data.

ASSET MAINTENANCE

To assist you in the timely maintenance of your assets, Oracle Assets enables you to schedule repair and service events for your long-term capital assets, as shown in Figure 14.2. You can plan to have your assets maintained at appropriate times for your business, such as production shutdowns, or at specified intervals, such as quarterly. As well as scheduling future maintenance events, you can also record the maintenance history of assets.

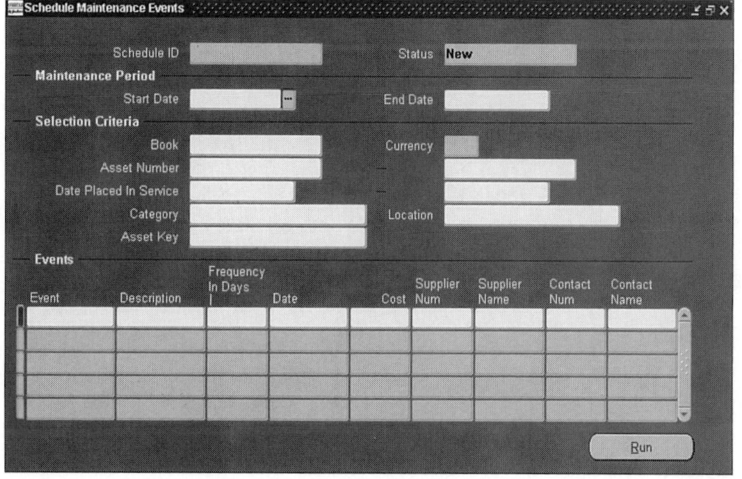

Figure 14.2
Asset Maintenance enables you to schedule repair and service events.

To schedule asset maintenance, navigate to the Schedule Maintenance Events window. Oracle Assets allows you to enter the following criteria:

- **Start and end dates**
- **The depreciation book**—Select the depreciation book containing the assets for which maintenance will be scheduled.
- **Additional selection criteria**—Such as asset numbers, asset category, location, asset key, currency, or date placed in service.
- **An event name and a description**—Please note that both fields are required.
- **Frequency in days**—This field is required if a date is not specified.
- **Date**—Enter the date the maintenance will occur. This field is required if no frequency is specified.
- **Cost**—Enter the cost per event. This field is optional.
- **Supplier number and supplier name**—These fields are optional.
- **Contact number and contact name**—These fields are optional.

Select Run to schedule.

To view a maintenance schedule, navigate to the Maintenance Details window, as shown in Figure 14.3, query the asset you want to review, optionally enter any maintenance changes, and save your work. You can optionally obtain Asset Maintenance information from the Asset Maintenance Report. The Asset Maintenance Report is a standard report that can be used to view assets' maintenance schedules, warranty information, and cost and supplier information. Please note that you must use the Applications Desktop Integrator (ADI) Request center to run this report.

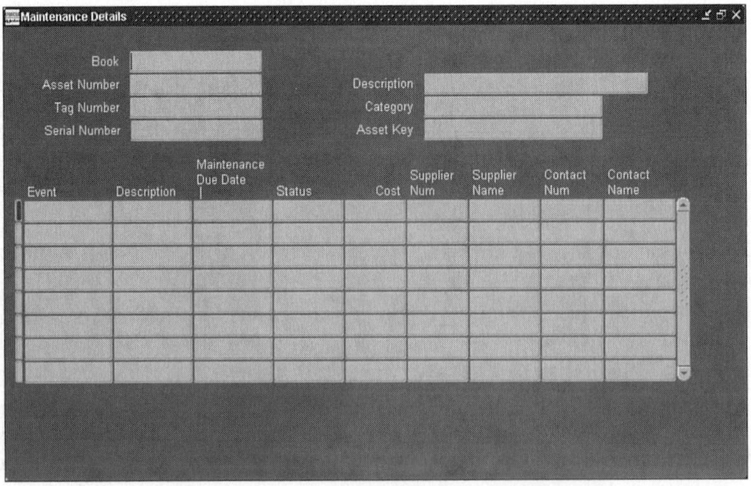

Figure 14.3
Maintenance Details allows you to review and optionally change maintenance details for a particular asset.

MAINTAIN ASSET INSURANCE VALUES

You can manage the risk of loss and damage to your capital assets by tracking their insurance values, thus enabling you to file timely and accurate insurance claims. You can define various insurance categories, such as Fire Insurance and Flood Insurance, and maintain other relevant insurance details, such as the insurance company, the policy number, and the hazard class, as shown in Figure 14.4.

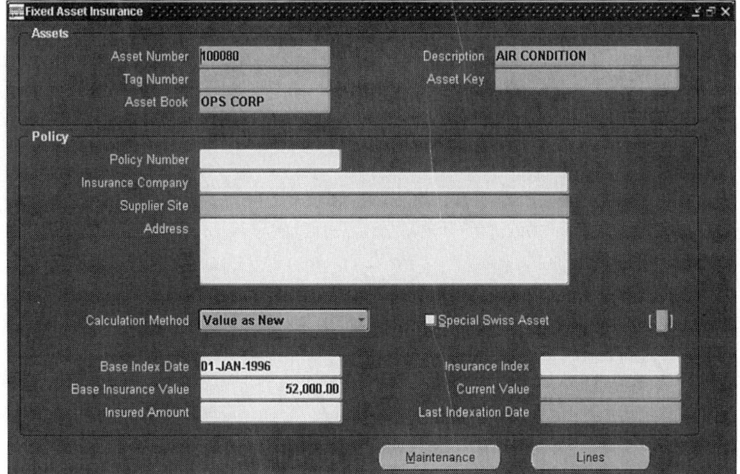

Figure 14.4
Asset Insurance allows you to track insurance values for your assets.

The methods available are

- **Value as New**—The asset's acquisition/production cost is used to determine its insurance value. This value can be indexed annually to calculate the current insurance value. The indexed value can also be incorporated into transactions that affect the assets value.
- **Current Market**—The net book value (NBV), acquisition cost less accumulated depreciation, can be used to determine the asset insurance value.
- **Manual Value**—You can manually enter an insurance value for the asset.

Oracle Assets provides two standard reports for reviewing asset insurance information. You use the Insurance Data Report to review insurance details for assets and verify that the assignments for insurance records are correct. Conversely, you use the Insurance Value Report to review calculations of insurance coverage for selected assets, including insurance values, current insurance amounts, and a calculation of the insurance coverage.

MASS RECLASSIFICATION

You can reclassify a group of assets from one asset category to another based on flexible selection criteria. In addition, you choose whether the newly classified asset inherits the depreciation rules of the new asset category or retains the depreciation rules of the old, as shown in Figure 14.5. This option is available for individual reclassification transactions as well.

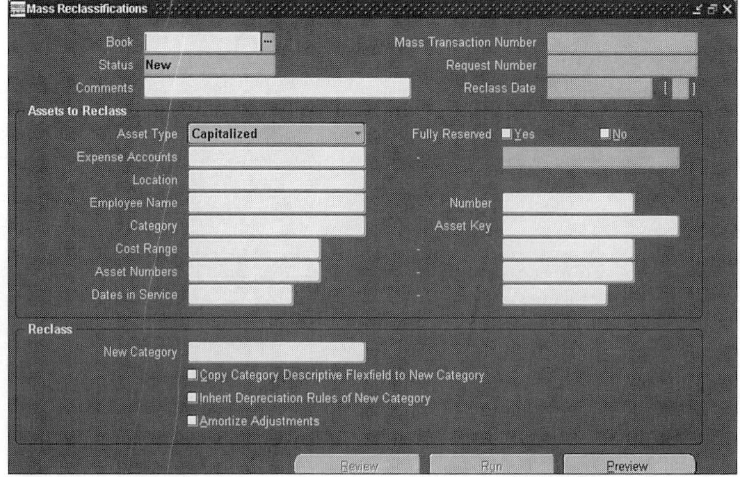

Figure 14.5
Mass Reclassification of Assets enables you to reclassify a group of assets from one asset category to another.

The Mass Reclassification Preview Report shows the before and after states of the assets you are reclassifying before you run the mass reclassification program.

The Mass Reclassification Review Report, on the other hand, shows changes to assets after you run the mass reclassification program.

Mass Transfers

You can take advantage of expanded selection criteria while choosing assets for mass transfer. You can select assets based on the new high-low range capability on the depreciation expense account, cost center, company, and other segments of the accounting flexfield. For example, you can select all assets that belong to a range of cost centers, as shown in Figure 14.6. You also can specify a transfer date in a prior period and Assets will adjust the resulting depreciation expense appropriately.

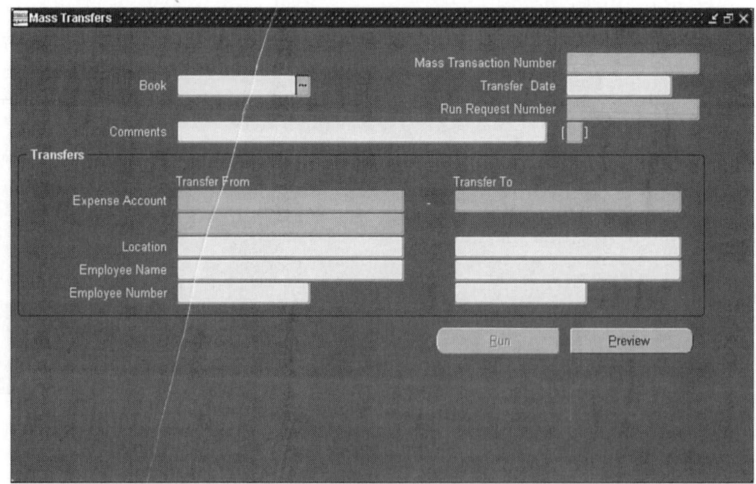

Figure 14.6
Mass Transfers enables you to transfer a group of assets based on selected criteria.

Maintaining CIP Assets in Tax Books

The statutory reporting requirements in Europe and Latin America can be addressed by maintaining CIP assets in tax books. This is optional; it is controlled by rules you define for the tax book and causes Assets to simultaneously add and then later capitalize the CIP assets in the corporate book and all specified tax books.

The Ability to Run Depreciation Multiple Times for a Current Period

When you run depreciation, Oracle Assets now provides you with the option of closing the current period when you run depreciation, by checking the Close Period check box on the Run Depreciation window. If the run depreciation process completes successfully, the current period is closed automatically and the next period is opened for the book. If you do not check the Close Period check box when running depreciation for a book, Oracle Assets does not close the period.

After depreciation is run for the current period, Oracle Assets does not permit transactions for assets successfully depreciated. If you want to make transactions against assets successfully depreciated, the depreciation must be rolled back or the current period closed.

If you have run depreciation for the current period, you can run the Rollback Depreciation to restore the assets to their prior states before running depreciation, provided you did not check the Close Period check box, as shown in Figure 14.7. For example, you might have additional transactions, such as adjustments or additional assets, that you need to process for the period. However, say you have already run depreciation for the period. If the Close Period check box was not checked when you ran depreciation, you could roll back the depreciation and include the missed transactions.

Note that you can roll back depreciation only for the current period. Additionally, to open the next period, you must run depreciation with the Close Period check box checked.

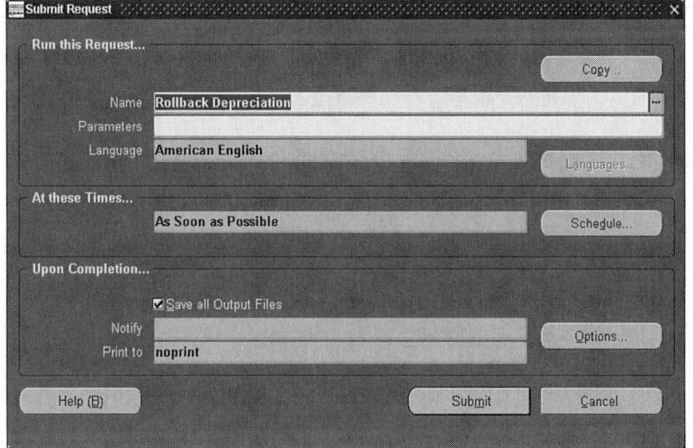

Figure 14.7 Rollback Depreciation enables you to recalculate depreciation for the period.

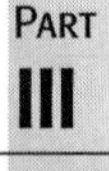

SUPPORT FOR SHORT TAX YEARS

For many companies, a short tax year is a common tax scenario that arises for corporate mergers and acquisitions. Prior to the acquisition/merger, the companies maintain their tax records on different fiscal years, thus when one company adopts the other company's tax year, in accordance with the Internal Revenue Service (IRS), a short tax year occurs. The maximum period of time a tax year can be is 12 months. Using a formula-based depreciation method, accountants are able to calculate the depreciation reporting requirements of a short tax fiscal year for the newly acquired/merged company.

When you add assets in a short tax year, you must identify the asset as a short tax year asset. When you add short tax year assets, you must use either the detail additions process or the mass additions process. You cannot use the quick additions process to add short tax year assets.

You can define custom depreciation formulas to help you properly depreciate the assets acquired for a short tax year, via formula-based depreciation methods.

WHAT-IF DEPRECIATION ANALYSIS ON HYPOTHETICAL ASSETS

Previously in Release 11, you could perform a what-if analysis on your assets by running the What-If Depreciation Analysis Report. The report helped you make depreciation projections based on parameters you entered into the system. However, you could simulate what-if depreciation scenarios only for existing assets using different depreciation rules. Now with Release 11*i*, you can analyze what-if scenarios for assets you plan on acquiring. Thus, you can select an optimal depreciation strategy for your capital assets prior to adding them to Oracle Assets.

The Hypothetical What-if Depreciation Report shows the results of running what-if depreciation on hypothetical assets.

UNPLANNED DEPRECIATION

You can change unplanned depreciation to an asset in the period in which it was added. You can also apply unplanned depreciation to assets using the flat-rate or units-of-production method and the straight-line method.

IMPROVED EXCEPTION-HANDLING DURING DEPRECIATION

Exception-handling within the depreciation process streamlines asset processing during the critical month-end close. The depreciation program processes all valid assets in one operation and flags any exceptions, such as invalid General Ledger code combinations, in the log file. Later, you can review the log file and systemically correct exceptions before rerunning the depreciation program to process the remaining assets. Note, however, that the depreciation program will stop processing assets if certain types of setup or database errors occur.

View Accounting Lines

Oracle Assets enables you to view the underlying accounting entries that are being created by the following three methods:

- **View Accounting Lines window**—You use this to view the detail accounting lines for queried transactions. You can see the account, accounted debit or credit amount, transaction reference, and other relevant accounting information generated behind the scenes by AutoAccounting.
- **T-Accounts window**—You use this to view and print Oracle Assets accounting entries in a graphical T-account format. Use its new, flexible options to customize this window. For example, you can view all the details in a T-account or just the net total. Plus, you can view T-accounts by full accounting flexfield or summarized by account segment.
- **Drill-down from General Ledger**—You can drill down from Oracle General Ledger journal entries to subledger information within Oracle Assets and view the subledger line items and the underlying transactions that make up a General Ledger journal line. You also can drill down to Oracle Assets from the Enter Journals, View Journals, and Account Inquiry windows. If you use Multiple Reporting Currencies (MRC), you can view transactions in the primary functional currency and reporting functional currencies.

MRC Transaction Upgrade Utilities

This provides a flexible solution that accommodates MRC for new and existing customers. If you are an existing Oracle customer, you can continue the accounting life cycle of open business transactions when you begin using MRC. You can run the Assets Upgrade utility to convert open transactions from your primary functional currency to your reporting functional currencies and run other upgrade utilities to perform the same conversion in other Oracle subledgers that support MRC and to initialize General Ledger account balances in your reporting set of books.

Multiple Language Support

Users in the same installation can view seed data in their own languages. When entering QuickCodes (lookups), users enter values in other languages that your site uses.

Critical Implementation Factors

The next section covers some of the items you should consider before setting up your Assets module. Take special note of the critical setup issues.

Issues and Gaps

When you begin to define your implementation process, there are a number of questions that you need to ask yourself. Some of the more important questions are the following:

- What depreciation methods do you use? Are any of these methods unique to your company/industry?

- What prorate conventions do you use? Do all assets in a specific category use the same prorate method?
- What naming convention should be in place for assets? How can naming conventions be used to standardize asset entry and format?
- How do you track assets (using Capital Acquisition Requisition Numbers)? Does this numbering system need to follow through from a feeder system into Oracle Assets?
- How do you handle construction-in-progress (CIP)?
- What will be the feeder system used to populate Oracle Assets?
- Do your corporate and tax books use the same fiscal year?
- How do you categorize assets? To what level do you need to be able to transfer assets (balancing segment, cost center)?
- Do you keep your assets by physical location? Do you assign assets to specific employees?
- Do you need to track assets in different currencies?
- How many tax books do you need? What are they?
- What is the oldest asset that you are tracking?
- What type of asset numbering process is being used? If automatic, what is the last asset number in place?
- What type of security do you need on your asset system?
- Do you tag your assets? Are your tag numbers available in your legacy system? Are any of your tag numbers duplicated in your legacy system?

It is best to set up a database to keep track of issues and gaps that evolve as you enter the setup phase of the project. You might want to segregate your issues by sets of books (corporate and tax).

Reviewing Top Enhancement Requests

Following is a list of the top enhancement requests:

- Ability to run depreciation projections for individual or a range of cost centers
- Ability to transfer an asset(s) from one corporate book to another
- Allow the reinstatement of an asset retired in the previous fiscal year
- Accommodate funds checking for an asset and capital expense charge account
- Ability to run MassCopy for all tax books at one time, instead of individually
- Provide information on assets retired versus active assets on the Asset Workbench
- Permit the retirement of an asset in the same month you add the asset
- Allow the transfer of an asset and its subcomponents at the same time
- Enhance the Property Tax report to include a column for accumulated depreciation

Most of the preceding requests are slated for future releases of Oracle. If you have any questions or additional suggestions, please contact Oracle directly.

RESOLVING CRITICAL SETUP ISSUES

Probably one of the most important issues that needs to be resolved during setup is that of data conversion. Data conversion efforts can take a great deal of time if not planned properly. Experience has shown that many companies are still tracking assets manually on spreadsheets, which can cause difficulties in consistency and form. The other problem with data conversion relates to mapping issues. Many times, the FA module is being configured at the same time or right after the GL module. Given that many companies choose to revise their chart of accounts when setting up GL, this creates mapping issues that need to be addressed in FA.

When setting up legacy data in FA, one trick that I have used in the past is to change your units to be equivalent to your currency total. Typically, an accounting department spends the least amount of time maintaining its FA system. This translates into many old items that are sitting on FA without any meaningful way to determine their location, description, serial number, and so on. For those items, you can set up the units to be equivalent to the dollars of the asset. This provides an easy way to retire portions of those assets over a period of years.

If you discover during data conversion that some assets have been added erroneously, they can be deleted through the Assets Workbench. Find the asset and select the Open button. When you have the asset on the screen, use the delete key (red ×) on the toolbar to delete the asset from the system. This process only works for those assets that have never had depreciation run against them. After you run depreciation, the only way to remove an asset from the system is to retire it.

When setting up this application, keep in mind that the requirements of both the Corporate and Tax departments need to be met. Tax individuals need to be kept in the loop to ensure that all regulatory needs are being fulfilled. It is critical that both areas contribute up front to the setup decisions because some of the setups cannot be changed after they are used.

Table 14.1 describes each setup task and the order in which they must be performed.

TABLE 14.1 SETUP TASKS

Task Number	Optional Setup Step	Description
Step 1	Required	GL Setup: Define chart of accounts, period types, calendars, currencies, and set of books for general ledger
Step 2	Optional	Define unit of measure classes
Step 3	Optional	Define units of measure
Step 4	Optional	Define employees
Step 5	Optional	Define Descriptive flexfield

TABLE 14.1 CONTINUED

Task Number	Optional Setup Step	Description
Step 6	Required with Defaults	Review Account Generator default
Step 7	Required with Defaults	Define additional journal entry sources
Step 8	Required with Defaults	Define additional journal entry categories
Step 9	Optional	Define numbering
Step 10	Optional	Define suppliers
Step 11	Required	Set up Asset Key flexfield
Step 12	Required	Set up Asset Category flexfield
Step 13	Required	Set up Location flexfield
Step 14	Required	Set up system controls
Step 15	Optional	Define locations
Step 16	Optional	Define asset keys
Step 17	Optional	Define standard asset descriptions and other QuickCode values
Step 18	Required	Define fiscal year
Step 19	Required	Define calendars (depreciation and prorate)
Step 20	Optional	Define security
Step 21	Required	Define book controls
Step 22	Required with Defaults	Define additional depreciation methods and rates
Step 23	Optional	Define depreciation ceilings
Step 24	Optional	Define investment tax credits
Step 25	Required	Define prorate and retirement conventions
Step 26	Optional	Define price indexes
Step 27	Required	Define asset categories
Step 28	Optional	Define distribution sets
Step 29	Optional	Define leases
Step 30	Optional	Define warranties
Step 31	Optional	Review default profile options
Step 32	Optional	Define insurance
Step 33	Optional	Define additional responsibilities

Understanding Each Setup Task

Following is a step-by-step description of how to complete each task that needs to be done to configure Oracle Assets. In this chapter, I do not cover in detail the setups that normally occur in other modules. If you need assistance setting up those items, please refer to the specific modules noted for setup procedures.

Creating the General Ledger Set of Books

This step only needs to be done if you have not or will not be using Oracle General Ledger. If Oracle GL is going to be used, this should be completed prior to configuring FA. If Oracle GL is not going to be used, please refer to Chapter 11, "Using Oracle General Ledger," for a detailed description of how to define a set of books, calendar, currency, period types, and chart of accounts.

Defining Units of Measure

Units of measure are typically set up in the Inventory or Purchasing module. If you are not using Oracle Inventory or Purchasing and are planning to use a units of production depreciation method, you can define units of measure in this form. For more information on how to do this, see Chapter 17, "Using Oracle Inventory."

Defining Employees

If you want to assign assets to particular employees, you must define the employees. This is typically done in the Oracle Human Resources, Purchasing, or Payables module. Note that if you are using the Human Resources or Purchasing module, this feature is not accessible from Assets. If you are not using those modules, set up the minimal amount of employee information necessary and save the form. For more detailed information on how to set up employees, see Chapter 23, "Implementing Oracle Human Resources and Oracle Payroll," and Chapter 16, "Using Oracle Purchasing." Please be aware when you set up your employees that you need to take into account any requirements from the modules that share this information (Human Resources, Purchasing, and Payables). Even if you do not plan on implementing them right away, setup decisions made here will impact the future timeline and ease with which these modules can be set up.

Defining Descriptive Flexfields

Descriptive flexfields are used to track information you might need to capture but that is not available on standard forms. Space is available on a specific form for a descriptive flexfield wherever you see a blank white box with brackets around it. Setting up specific descriptive flexfields should be reviewed with your system administrator. Remember that even though you set up a descriptive flexfield, the information will not necessarily print on standard reports, nor will it necessarily carry through to other applications.

One common use for descriptive flexfields is tracking old fixed asset numbers from conversion data. If you are changing your asset-numbering schema and you decide to renumber your old assets, you might need to retain the old numbering information for reference purposes. A descriptive flexfield is an example of how you might accomplish this.

Defining Journal Entry Formats

The journal entry sources are used to identify the types of journal entries being created by Oracle Assets. Oracle comes with many predefined journal entry formats, but additional types can be created if necessary.

Journal entry categories are used to define the type of journal entry being processed. For example, addition, depreciation, adjustment, and retirements are a few types of categories. As with journal entry sources, Oracle comes predefined with many of these values, so unless you have special reporting needs, you will probably not change any of these.

Defining Vendors

Typically, vendors are set up in either Oracle Payables or Oracle Purchasing. If you are not using either of these modules and you want to track vendor information, vendors can be set up in Oracle Assets. Oracle uses the terms *vendors* and *suppliers* interchangeably, and you will find this option under Suppliers in FA.

The only way you can assign an asset to a supplier is if the supplier exists in the vendor file. Note that to use the vendor, Oracle requires setup of at least one pay site for the vendor. The *pay site* is an alternative region reached by clicking the blue box on the left of your screen. For more detailed instructions on how to set up vendors, see Chapter 12, "Using Oracle Payables," and Chapter 16.

Creating the Asset Key Flexfield

This flexfield is used to group assets using nonfinancial information. Examples of an asset key might be a budget-tracking number or a project number. This flexfield has no impact on the financial activities of the asset, but it does come in handy when you want to query up a group of similar assets in the Assets Workbench.

You must define one segment of the asset key even if you decide not to use it. If you do not want to use it, simply set up one segment and uncheck the Displayed and Enabled boxes on the Asset Key Flexfield form. This satisfies the system requirements of having the flexfield set up without causing the users any additional data-entry work. This flexfield can be re-enabled at any time in the future by going back to the form and checking the Displayed and Enabled boxes.

The asset key can be up to 10 segments with a total of 30 characters, including segment separators. Dynamic insertion is also available for this flexfield.

Creating the Asset Category Key Flexfield

Deciding how to set up the category key flexfield is probably one of the most critical setup decisions that needs to be made in FA. Asset categories are what generate most of the accounting entries that are created by FA. The more complex the accounting needs of the company, the more asset categories that will need to be created. Asset categories can be shared by more than one set of books (corporate and tax), but the accounting for each book must be set up separately. For example, the ABC Corp Book can have a category of Software.Oracle (Software is the major category, the period is the segment separator, and Oracle is the minor category). ABC Federal Tax Book can also share the same category, but it will need to have its own series of GL accounts set up for it. Although this is a nice feature if you are using multiple fixed asset books that require different accounting flexfield codes, it can be cumbersome if you have the same accounting rules for multiple sets of FA books.

The category flexfield can accommodate up to seven segments and can be a total of thirty characters wide. Dynamic insertion is *not* allowed for this flexfield. (Dynamic insertion is a feature that allows the system to automatically build valid code combinations based on rules that you provide.) The only requirement when setting up the category flexfield is that you must define at least one major segment. Optionally, you are allowed to define up to six additional minor segments (for a maximum of seven segments total).

Typically, the category flexfield is set up with at least two segments enabled. The segments are usually set up to delineate major and minor category information. To limit the pick list for each major category, you might make your minor category a dependent segment. When planning your category flexfield, think about grouping your segments based on depreciation rules. One note of caution: You cannot have subdependencies. For example, you cannot add a third segment and make it dependent on the second (minor category) segment.

Remember that when you have set up a flexfield and begun using it, any changes could significantly impact the integrity of your existing data. Like the accounting flexfield in GL, you will not want to make changes to this flexfield after it has been established.

Creating the Location Key Flexfield

The location key flexfield is used to track the specific physical location of each asset. Locations can be defined as departments, floor numbers, buildings, counties, cities, states, countries, and so on.

The location flexfield can have up to seven segments and a total of thirty characters (including segment separators). Dynamic insertion can be enabled for this particular flexfield.

Oracle requires that one segment of the location flexfield must be designated as the state qualifier. One purpose for this designator is that it is a parameter in the property tax report. All other segments are optional for this flexfield.

Defining System Controls

To set up the system controls, you must designate the enterprise (company) name; asset numbering scheme (manual or automatic); and key flexfield structures for the category, location, and asset key flexfields that were used. You must also designate the oldest date placed in service for the assets.

Tip

After you assign calendars to a set of depreciation books, you cannot change the Oldest Date Placed in Service. Be very sure that the date you choose reflects the oldest asset you plan on entering.

DEFINING LOCATIONS

If you have elected to use dynamic insertion for the location flexfield, you do not need to do this step. If you have not set dynamic insertion to Yes, you need to define each valid location combination that you want to use. If you have set up dependencies between your location segments, I recommend having the system create the combinations through dynamic insertion. The dependencies serve as a checkpoint and limit the possible errors that can occur with dynamic insertion on. Remember, the dynamic insertion check box can be found on the Key Flexfield Segments form.

One thing to understand about dynamic insertion is that it only enables users to choose values that have been previously defined in the Key Flexfield Values screen. It does not enable users to arbitrarily select any value of their choosing.

CREATING ASSET KEY FLEXFIELD COMBINATIONS

If you have elected to use dynamic insertion for the asset key flexfield, you do not need to do this step. If you have not set dynamic insertion to Yes, you need to define each valid asset key combination. Note that it doesn't matter whether you have elected to assign only one segment to your asset key; you still have to perform this step if dynamic insertion is not enabled.

DEFINING QUICKCODES

There are various types of QuickCodes that you can define additional values for. Some QuickCodes are restricted, and you cannot add new values, but often, you can change the description of the current codes to better suit your needs. QuickCodes generally provide a pick list of values in various forms within the Oracle application. They can be invaluable because they can reduce the amount of typing a user has to do (thus also reducing the potential typing errors that can occur). Table 14.2 lists the Asset QuickCode descriptors, whether they can be changed, existing sample values, and examples of values you might choose to add.

TABLE 14.2 ASSET QUICKCODES

QuickCode Type	Sample QuickCode Values
Asset Description	Some sample values you might want to add include Desktop Computer, Laptop Computer, Chevy Vehicle, Conference Room Table, and so on. Oracle does not come with any asset descriptions predefined.
Journal Entries	You cannot add new codes, but you can change the description of the existing codes to better suit your needs. Examples of existing codes include Addition Cost, Depreciation Expense, Retirement Cost, and Tax Expense. There are 66 predefined Journal Entry QuickCodes.

TABLE 14.2 CONTINUED

QuickCode Type	Sample QuickCode Values
Queue Name	Sample values to add might include Category Hold and Location Flexfield Hold. You cannot change the existing value names.
Property Type	Additional values you might want to add include Long Term Lease, Short Term Lease, Residential, and so on.
Retirement Type	Sample values you might want to add to describe your retirements include Abandonment, Charitable Contribution, and Write Off. The two Oracle predefined values are Extraordinary and Sale.
Asset Category	This is only used if the Asset Category (major category) was set up utilizing table-based validation. (If it was not, you define the categories using the Asset Categories form.)
Asset Subcategory	This is also only used if the Asset Subcategory (minor category) was set up using table-based validation.
Unplanned Depreciation Type	This is used to describe depreciation adjustments that were not planned at the time the asset was added to the system. Examples you might want to add include stolen, accelerated, obsolete, and so on.
Lease Frequency	You cannot enter or alter existing values, but you can change the description of them. Existing values include monthly, quarterly, semiannually, and annually.
Lease Payment Type	Existing sample values include Balloon Payment, Annuity, Bargain Purchase Option, and Bargain Renewal Option. You can add as many additional types as you deem necessary.

DEFINING FISCAL YEARS AND CALENDARS

Fiscal years must be defined beginning with the oldest asset placed in service. You determine the beginning and ending dates of the month. If you are using the standard month (as opposed to a 4-4-5 month), Oracle automatically generates the calendar for the next fiscal year.

Tip

When you are initially setting up your first fiscal years and calendars, fill in the first line and then hit Enter. Oracle automatically generates the next available period for you. You can then edit this line if you have any changes to make. It saves you quite a bit of typing, especially if you are using standard calendar months and years. Remember that you must be sure to include every day in your fiscal calendar. If you miss any dates, you can wreak havoc on your system.

You can set up as many depreciation and prorate calendars as you deem necessary because there is no limit to the number that you can use. I have set up various prorate calendars for special depreciation expense purposes. For example, I was asked to provide a setup to take depreciation based on a flat percentage no matter what the date was that the asset was purchased during the year. I called my prorate calendar "Full Year," and a portion of my setup is shown in Table 14.3.

TABLE 14.3 SAMPLE PRORATE CALENDAR

Convention: FULL YEAR

From Date	To Date	Prorate Date
01-APR-1996	30-APR-1996	01-APR-1996
01-MAY-1996	31-MAY-1996	01-APR-1996
01-JUN-1996	30-JUN-1996	01-APR-1996
01-JUL-1996	31-JUL-1996	01-APR-1996
01-AUG-1996	31-AUG-1996	01-APR-1996
01-SEP-1996	30-SEP-1996	01-APR-1996
01-OCT-1996	31-OCT-1996	01-APR-1996
01-NOV-1996	30-NOV-1996	01-APR-1996
01-DEC-1996	31-DEC-1996	01-APR-1996
01-JAN-1997	31-JAN-1997	01-APR-1996
01-FEB-1997	28-FEB-1997	01-APR-1996
01-MAR-1997	31-MAR-1997	01-APR-1996
01-APR-1997	30-APR-1997	01-APR-1997

The preceding prorate calendar, combined with a special depreciation method, enabled me to take a flat 25% depreciation during year 1, regardless of when the asset was actually purchased.

One other thing to keep in mind with prorate calendars is that there is a check box on the form that enables you to Depreciate when Placed in Service. What this means is that you want your depreciation to be based strictly on the date you set up the asset. This is typically used for assets that are leased such as computer equipment or leasehold improvements. If this box is checked, Oracle begins to depreciate the asset on the date you placed it in service, not the prorate date. For example, if an asset was placed in service on June 1 and your prorate calendar indicated that it should use a prorate date of April 1, it would use June 1 because the check box takes precedence over the prorate date.

It is important to note that your corporate and tax book calendars must have the same fiscal year. If you have different fiscal years (for tax and book purposes), there is no simple, clean way to accommodate this using standard functionality. The only workaround that I have seen involves customization of the Oracle product. You must set up multiple corporate books and calendars and then either develop a script to add mass additions to the second corporate book or reenter the assets manually to each additional corporate book. Remember that one corporate book does not have any relationship to another corporate book in FA. Information cannot be systematically transferred from one corporate book to another using standard functionality.

Defining Book Controls

The book controls are used to set up and direct all the corporate and tax depreciation books that you need. This is where you control whether a particular asset book can post journal entries to the general ledger. Each tax book you define must be associated with a corporate book. To access each of these forms, simply click the blue drop-down box on the left side of the screen.

Calendar Information To set up calendar information, you need to choose one of your previously defined depreciation and prorate calendars. Enter the current open period name for this book. Be sure that you set up the depreciation calendar for *at least* one period before the current period. For the current period, I usually choose a date that corresponds to the last month of the previous fiscal or calendar year. This enables me to run the depreciation process for the data conversion items that will provide a year-end reserve amount for reconciling purposes.

Choose whether to divide depreciation Evenly (evenly each period) or By Days (to divide based on the proportion of days per period). You must also decide whether to depreciate assets that are retired during the first year of life. Oracle Assets automatically updates the Last Depreciation Run Date after you run the depreciation process for the first time.

Accounting Rules This form enables you to tighten or loosen controls for each asset book. For example, you can allow mass changes in your tax book but disallow mass changes in the corporate book. You also designate the minimum amount of time an asset must be held in order to qualify for a capital gain when it is retired and whether you want to allow amortized changes to assets.

The Tax Rules and Allow Mass Copy options are not available to update if you are defining a corporate book. These options are only available if you are defining a tax book.

Natural Accounts In this screen, you enter natural, retirement, intercompany, and depreciation accounts. These can be unique or identical for each set of fixed asset books. Even if you do not want more than one asset book posting entries to your general ledger, you still have to set up accounts for every book you define because these are required fields. I recommend that you use a unique accounting flexfield code combination for the books that have no posting ability in case something happens to go wrong. If you do this, it will be readily apparent to the user where to look if a problem arises.

Journal Categories

This is where you enter the source category that you want to show up in GL when you transfer journal entries from Oracle Assets. Each asset transaction type can have a unique journal category associated with it. I have found that the standard list of categories provided by Oracle is quite extensive, and I use the categories provided. You can, however, decide to set up unique categories if desired.

CONFIGURING ACCOUNT GENERATOR FOR ASSETS

The Account Generator automatically configures itself for each new set of books entered in Oracle Assets; this is where you can customize the accounting entries that are made by each set of books (corporate and tax). In general, Oracle Assets only builds accounting entries based on balancing segment. If you need your entries to include cost center information, you will need to customize Flexbuilder. In case you find yourself in the position of having to customize Account Generator, Table 14.4 provides you with some basic details on what the default information means.

TABLE 14.4 KEY ACCOUNT GENERATOR INFORMATION

Account Generator	Accounting Flexfield Developed
Default CCID (flexfield)	Taken from the Book Controls form
Account CCID (flexfield)	Taken from Asset Categories form
Account Segment (segment)	Taken from the Book Controls or Asset Category form (depending on what account it is trying to build)
Distribution CCID (flexfield)	Taken from Transfer form (expense combination set up in Assets Workbench)

Initial Account Generator settings use the Default CCID for all fields except the natural account. The natural account is generated based on Account Segment, and the balancing segment is taken from the Distribution ID. What this means is that if you have an accounting flexfield with a balancing segment, cost center, and natural account, the default combination would get the balancing segment from your expense combination, the natural account from your GL account, and the cost center from your book controls form. Needless to say, the Account Generator is a very complex product that you would probably want to take a class on before attempting to modify system-generated defaults.

DEFINING DEPRECIATION METHODS

Oracle comes with a considerable number of predefined depreciation methods including Straight line, Sum of the Years Digits, MACRS, and ACRS. If you are using a unique method, you can define your own using one of four different depreciation types: calculated, table-based, units of production, or flat rate. You determine which type you need based on *how* you want Oracle Assets to calculate depreciation.

If you want to depreciate assets over a fixed period of time using specified rates, choose the calculated or table-based depreciation methods. Common examples of this type of depreciation are Double Declining Balance, Sum of the Years Digits, Alternative Minimum Tax, or ACRS.

Units of production depreciate an asset based on usage, not the passage of time. This is especially useful for equipment that is being used on a factory floor or for assets that are used up over time such as oil wells. Note that if you are using this method, you can either maintain your production information manually or track it in another system and import it into FA using the FA_PRODUCTION_INTERFACE table.

A flat rate method is used if you want to allocate a fixed rate over a specified period of time. This method is typically found in use outside the U.S. An example is Japan Declining Balance.

Keep in mind that after you have begun using a particular method, you cannot make any changes to it. If you need to revise it, simply create a new one and assign or mass change it for the assets that need to utilize this method.

An example of the table-based method would be if you require Oracle Assets to depreciate an asset based on a different percentage each year. Table 14.5 illustrates part of the setup if you wanted a method in FA to depreciate based on 25% in year 1, 35% in year 2, and 40% in year 3.

TABLE 14.5 SAMPLE DEPRECIATION METHOD

Name	**SPECIAL**	
Type	TABLE	
Calculation Basis	COST	
Year	Period	Annual Rate
1	1	.25
2	1	.35
3	1	.40
4	1	0
1	2	.25
2	2	.35
3	2	.40
4	2	0
1	3	.25
2	3	.35
3	3	.40
4	3	0

To access the rate table, you have to click the Rates button in the lower-right corner of the screen. Table 14.5 is telling Oracle that any assets purchased in period 1, year 1, should be depreciated at an annual rate of 25%. Year 2 should be depreciated at 35%, year 3 at 40%, and year 4 would have zero depreciation expense. Note, if you indicate to Oracle that you are depreciating an asset for 3 years, it automatically assumes that depreciation will occur over a four-year time frame to take into account the half-year convention. To get around that, use 0% in year 4.

For example, Asset 123 purchased for $10,000 and placed in service in period 3. Using Table 14.5 creates the yearly expense to be taken that is shown in Table 14.6.

TABLE 14.6 ASSET 123 DEPRECIATION EXPENSE SAMPLE

Year	Period(s)	Total Depreciation Expense Taken
1	3–12	$2,500
2	1–12	$3,500
3	1–12	$4,000
4	1–12	$0

The preceding example is based on a prorate calendar that takes depreciation based on a full year.

DEFINING DEPRECIATION CEILINGS

Depreciation expense ceilings are used to limit the amount of depreciation you can take for an asset. This is typically used for tax purposes to limit such things as depreciation on luxury vehicles.

There are also special depreciation cost ceilings that are in effect in some foreign countries. If you use a cost ceiling, Oracle Assets limits the cost basis to the lesser of the asset cost or cost ceiling. Remember that you can only use this option if you have checked the Allow Expense Ceilings and Allow Cost Ceilings boxes in your book controls form. The Depreciation Ceiling box can be found in the default depreciation screen when you are setting up your asset categories.

DEFINING INVESTMENT TAX CREDITS

If your company has investment tax credits, investment tax recapture, or investment tax ceilings, you would enter that information in the ITC forms. There are actually two forms involved: ITC Rates and ITC Recapture Rates. Both forms require virtually identical information except that the IRC Rate Form uses a Basis Reduction Rate where the ITC Recapture Rate form needs a Recapture Rate. These forms also require you to enter the Tax Year, Years and Months (of the Assets Life), and ITC Rate (as a percentage).

Remember that you can only use this option if you have checked the Allow Investment Tax Credits box in your book controls form. The ITC eligible box is found on the default depreciation screen of the asset category form.

DEFINING PRORATE CONVENTIONS

A prorate convention is nothing more than a way to tell Oracle Assets when to depreciate an asset during the first year and last (retirement) year of its useful life. Oracle does not come with any prorate conventions predefined because they are unique to every company.

You can define prorate conventions with prorate dates that have the effect shown in Table 14.7.

TABLE 14.7 PRORATE CONVENTIONS

Convention	What It Means
Actual Months Convention	Takes one month of depreciation in month acquired asset. No depreciation taken in the last month or month you retire the asset.
Half-Year Convention	Takes half-year of depreciation in year acquired asset and last year of asset life. Half-year of depreciation taken in the year that the asset is retired, regardless of date retired.
Standard Modified Half-Year Convention	Takes full year depreciation in year acquired, if acquired during first half of year. No depreciation if asset is acquired in second half of year. For retirement, if retired in first half of year, no depreciation taken. If retired in second half of year, full year depreciation is taken.
Alternate Modified Half-Year Convention	Retirement convention that takes one quarter of a year's depreciation in the year the asset is retired.
Following Month Convention	No depreciation taken in month asset is acquired but takes one month for the last month of the asset's life. As retirement convention, it takes one month's depreciation in the month retired.
ACRS Half-Year Convention	Full-year depreciation in year acquired asset, no depreciation in the last year of the asset's life. As retirement convention, it takes no depreciation in year asset is retired.
Mid-Month Convention	Half a month depreciation taken in month acquired and last month of asset's life. For retirement, takes half of a month's depreciation in the month it is retired.
Mid-Quarter Convention	Half a quarter taken in quarter that asset was acquired and last quarter of the assets life. Same for retirement convention.

One sample prorate calendar was shown in Table 14.3 in the section that discusses setting up calendars and fiscal years. Table 14.8 shows examples of a couple more prorate calendars.

TABLE 14.8 SAMPLE PRORATE CALENDARS

Convention: HALF YEAR

From Date	To Date	Prorate Date
01-APR-1996	30-APR-1996	01-SEP-1996
01-MAY-1996	31-MAY-1996	01-SEP-1996
01-JUN-1996	30-JUN-1996	01-SEP-1996
01-JUL-1996	31-JUL-1996	01-SEP-1996
01-AUG-1996	31-AUG-1996	01-SEP-1996

TABLE 14.8 CONTINUED

Convention: HALF YEAR

From Date	To Date	Prorate Date
01-SEP-1996	30-SEP-1996	01-SEP-1996
01-OCT-1996	31-OCT-1996	01-SEP-1996
01-NOV-1996	30-NOV-1996	01-SEP-1996
01-DEC-1996	31-DEC-1996	01-SEP-1996
01-JAN-1997	31-JAN-1997	01-SEP-1996
01-FEB-1997	28-FEB-1997	01-SEP-1996
01-MAR-1997	31-MAR-1997	01-SEP-1996
01-APR-1997	30-APR-1997	01-SEP-1997
01-MAY-1996	31-MAY-1996	01-SEP-1997
01-JUN-1996	30-JUN-1996	01-SEP-1997
01-JUL-1996	31-JUL-1996	01-SEP-1997

Convention: HALF YEAR

From Date	To Date	Prorate Date
01-APR-1996	31-MAR-1997	01-SEP-1996
01-APR-1997	31-MAR-1998	01-SEP-1997
01-APR-1998	31-MAR-1999	01-SEP-1998
01-APR-1999	31-MAR-2000	01-SEP-1999
01-APR-2000	31-MAR-2001	01-SEP-2000

As you can see, depending on how you handle your accounting, you can set up the prorate calendars to take depreciation based on years, quarters, months, or even days. Note that if you check the Depreciate When Placed in Service box, Oracle Assets begins taking depreciation the month you indicated the asset was placed in service, regardless of the prorate dates chosen.

If you have more than one fiscal year defined, you have to set up more than one prorate calendar. Prorate calendars can be shared, but only if the different books have the same fiscal years.

DEFINING PRICE INDEXES

A price index enables you to calculate gains and losses for retirements using current value instead of historical cost. This feature is most commonly used in countries that require you to base gains and losses on current value rather than historical cost. Oracle Assets enables you to set up price indexes to calculate the gains and losses for your asset upon retirement.

This form is very simple to fill out. You choose a name for your index, enter the value (percentage) that you want Oracle Assets to use for the conversion, and save the form. You can also provide From and To Dates so that the percentage can be changed as you deem necessary.

Oracle Assets enables you to associate a different index for each asset category or use the same index for all categories. To associate an index with an asset category, enter the name of the price index in the Price Index field of the Asset Categories window.

DEFINING ASSET CATEGORIES

Because Asset Categories is the only Asset flexfield not eligible for dynamic insertion, this is the form you have to use to set up each asset category combination. It is where you define asset information that is unique to a particular category such as general ledger accounts, depreciation life, and depreciation method.

One thing to keep in mind here is that you are setting up category *defaults*. There might be times when company policy dictates the use of different choices for a specific category or item. Remember that this change can be made when you actually set up the asset. If you find that you have one category combination that rarely utilizes the default information, you probably should look at adding additional default categories to your system.

The only tricky part about this form is that in order to set up multiple books under a single category combination, you must query up the initial book combination. Navigate down to the lower block where you see "book," and place your cursor on that field. Press the green—on your toolbar to indicate to the system that you are adding information for another book. The lower block of the screen should clear out and enable you to pick another existing book from your list of values (LOV). Choose the additional book and complete the form, including the back screen, where you indicate what the default depreciation information should be.

Note that it is critical this setup step be done correctly. If it is not, errors made in this form can have serious repercussions throughout the application. Mistakes discovered after you have associated an asset with it cannot be changed.

DEFINING FINANCIAL OPTIONS

The financial options would be set up while configuring Oracle General Ledger and Oracle Accounts Payable. If you are not using Oracle GL or AP, please refer to Chapters 11 and 12 for more detailed instructions.

SETTING THE PROFILE OPTIONS

A system administrator generally controls profile options at the system level. Users can change their personal profile options for such things as print parameters. Most of the Oracle Assets profile options are controlled from a responsibility level, and changes should be discussed with your System Administrator.

Note that if you need to set your profile option FA Print Debug to Yes, you might see error messages coming up when you save data in various forms. The message that I have frequently seen is Error: FA_CACHE_RESULTS. Do not be alarmed; this does not harm anything and will stop happening when you change the print debug setting back to No.

CONVERTING DATA FOR MAJOR ENTITIES

This section covers the topics relating to entering your assets into Oracle. It also discusses general maintenance functions.

UNDERSTANDING THE MASS ADDITIONS INTERFACE

Oracle provides an interface table for creating mass additions from outside systems. It is the same table that Oracle uses when transferring assets from Oracle Payables.

Tip

You might want to assign some unique identifier in the table to distinguish the assets set up during data conversion.

When converting assets from an outside system, you can bypass the Create and Prepare part of mass additions by transferring them in with a status of Post.

ADDING ASSETS MANUALLY

Assets can be added using either the Quick or Detail asset forms. Quick is exactly what you would expect: It is a form with limited fields to enter data. Most of the information is set up using predefined system defaults, and most of the default information is derived from the category assignment. The only required fields in the quick form are asset category, assignment to a book, cost, depreciation expense account, location, and asset key (if you made it a required field).

Detail additions enables changes to be made when adding the asset by providing access to the system defaults. If you need to change the category defaults such as life and depreciation method, you want to enter the asset using the detail addition form. Note that there is no way to change the asset cost account and accumulated depreciation account except by changing the asset category assignment.

Assets can be added with a negative cost. If an asset is added as a credit, the journal entry Oracle creates is a credit to monthly depreciation expense and a debit to accumulated depreciation.

ASSIGNING ASSETS TO DEPRECIATION BOOKS

When entering assets, you determine which corporate book they are to be assigned to. Remember that you do not assign assets to Tax books; they are transferred there using the Initial or Periodic Mass Copy function. A specific asset can be assigned to only one corporate book, but it can be assigned to many tax books.

Transferring Assets

Assets can be transferred between employee assignments, expense accounts, and locations. They can be transferred either individually or using the mass transfers form. Individual transfers can be made from the Assets Workbench. Simply query up the asset in question and open it. To transfer between expense accounts and employee assignments, use the Assignments button.

If you want to perform mass transfers, use the mass transfer form (not the Assets Workbench). Provide the To and From fields for locations, expense accounts, or employees. Before you actually commit your transfers, I recommend that you run the Mass Transfer Preview Report. When you are certain the changes are impacting your system the way you want them to, commit the transfer.

The only way to change asset categories is to query the asset up in Assets Workbench. All you need to do is choose the category that you want the asset to be assigned to and save the changes. Oracle Assets creates journal entries to transfer the cost and accumulated depreciation into the new general ledger accounts. Note that it does not reclassify any previously taken depreciation expense. One thing to be aware of, however, is that it will *not* change the default depreciation rules to the default rules of the new category. You must do that manually in the Mass Change window or Books form.

Retiring Assets

To retire a single asset, query up the asset in the Assets Workbench. Choose the Retirements button and then indicate which book you are retiring the asset from. At this point, you can also choose to retire any subcomponents that are associated with the asset. When you are finished indicating your retirement details (such as units retired, retirement type, cost retired, and proceeds of sale), choose the Done button to save your information. Note that Oracle Assets does not enable you to retire an asset added in the current period.

When an asset is retired before it is fully reserved, Oracle FA calculates the gain or loss on the asset retirement. The calculation is based on the following formula: Proceeds of Sale minus Cost of Removal minus NBV Retired plus Revaluation Reserved Retired equals Gain/Loss on Retirement.

Tip

There was a problem that I ran into relative to retirements that I would like to warn you about. It will occur during the testing phase of the process or while you are in production if you begin using the application during a fiscal year. It occurs when you try to retire an asset that has a half-year (or similar) retirement convention. If the date that the system needs to go back to occurs before the first month that you actually ran depreciation within the application, you get an error when running the Gain/Loss Report. The fix is to change the prorate convention assigned to the asset so that it falls in a period where depreciation has been run. The preventative measure is to start your application on the first day of your fiscal year.

MAKING MASS TRANSACTIONS

Most of the Standard Transactions found in Oracle Assets have Mass Transaction counterparts. These functions can save you a tremendous amount of time if your changes have some commonality. Following are the Mass Transaction functions and how they work.

MASS ADDITIONS

The mass addition process is fairly simple. After assets are created in a feeder system (such as Oracle Payables or Projects), run the Create Mass Additions process to send them into the FA Interface table. After they are in FA, review them and make any changes necessary. When they arrive in FA, they have a queue name of NEW.

If you decide to proceed with the additions, add the location, category, assignment, and asset key information. When you are satisfied that they are complete, change the queue name on each one to "post." The next step is to run the Post Mass Additions process. Finally, after you are sure that everything has processed correctly, you use the purge function to clear them back out of the interface table. Note that the purge function can only purge an asset with a queue designation of SPLIT, MERGE, ADJUST, or POSTED.

The available queue names are NEW, SPLIT, MERGE, ADJUST, POST, POSTED or ON HOLD. The queue name changes automatically if you perform a split, merge, or adjustment on the asset. To put an asset on hold, you must click the queue name box and change it yourself. You must also manually change the queue name to POST when the asset is ready to be transferred. When the transfer is complete, Oracle automatically changes the queue name to POSTED.

You can also add costs or invoice lines to an existing asset. The queue name for this type of addition is ADD TO ASSET. If you try to use any other queue name, the Mass Additions process rejects the row because it expects the item to be a new asset.

MASS COPY

The Initial Mass Copy program is used to populate your tax book with assets from a corporate book. The Periodic Mass Copy program can then be run to transfer new additions, adjustments, and retirements into the tax books. Note that the corporate book period must be closed before you can copy information into the related tax book. Whether the mass copy transfers adjustments and retirements is determined when you set up your book controls for each tax book.

Mass copy must be run separately for each tax book that is associated to the corporate book. The assets in the tax books use the category defaults from the tax book that you are copying into.

MASS TRANSFERS

Mass transfers enable you to transfer a group of assets from one employee name, employee number, expense account, or location to another. You enter the value that you want to transfer from and also the value that you want to transfer to. There is also the option of previewing the change before you commit the action.

MASS CHANGE

The Mass Change form enables you to make changes to a group of assets. It is one way to correct or update the financial or depreciation information for a group of assets. Note that after you have run depreciation for an asset, not all fields can be updated.

To initiate a mass change, you choose the Mass Transactions form in Oracle. To change the transfer date, open the box and enter the date on which you want the change to occur. (This date is automatically filled with the system date when you open the form.) You can change the date to any time during the current fiscal year, but you cannot backdate transfers to a previous fiscal year. You also need to indicate which book the change needs to occur in. Next, decide whether you want to preview the changes before you actually make the changes. Then choose Run to actually submit the process.

MASS RETIREMENTS

You can retire assets based on category, key, location, depreciation expense account, employee, asset number range, or the date placed in service range. You can also choose whether you want the subcomponent assets to be retired with the parent assets. Assets can be retired from one book without affecting their status in any other book where they might appear. Note that assets added in the current period cannot be retired.

MASS REVALUATION

Revaluation of assets typically occurs when the book is for a country with a highly inflationary economy. The revaluation is calculated by multiplying the asset cost by the revaluation rate you entered and a cost adjustment is made.

The process provides for review of changes prior to committing them to the system. There are also revaluation reports that can be run to evaluate the changes after committing them. Revaluations do not affect assets added in the current period, CIP assets, assets pending retirement, or fully retired assets.

MASS DEPRECIATION ADJUSTMENT

You can adjust the depreciation taken for one or all assets for a previous fiscal year in a tax book. To adjust the depreciation expense taken for all assets in a tax book, use the Mass Depreciation Adjustments form. Note that some taxing authorities allow you to prorate the depreciation expense you recognize.

To adjust tax book depreciation between minimum and maximum depreciation expense amounts, enter a factor for the calculation. Oracle Assets calculates the minimum and maximum amounts by comparing the accumulated depreciation in your tax book to a control tax book and the associated corporate book.

MASS ADDITIONS PURGING

To delete mass additions from the FA_MASS_ADDITION table, you must run the Delete Mass Additions program. The process automatically removes those assets with queue statuses of Posted, Delete, and Split. If there were any assets added erroneously, all you have to do is change their queue status to Delete.

It might be a good idea to run the Delete Mass Additions Report before running this process. This provides you the opportunity to review those items that will be deleted prior to actually removing them. Note that this process is not reversible, so you will want to be sure that you remove only those items that need to be purged. Purge accessibility should be limited to only those individuals who understand the ramifications of this process.

DATA ARCHIVE AND PURGE

Asset data such as depreciation expense and other transactions can be purged out of the Oracle Assets tables to free up disk space if the information is no longer needed for reports. The Allow Purge option must be set to Yes in the Book Controls form for each book you want to purge. It is generally best to leave it set at No until you are ready to purge to avoid causing an irreversible mistake. Oracle Assets is the only one of the Oracle Applications modules that has Archive *and* restore capability. After you have archived data, it removes it completely from the base tables, but references are made in some archive history tables. So, if you need the information again later, you have the ability to restore. This is generally done by the technical team.

USING CONSTRUCTION IN PROGRESS

Construction in Progress (CIP) is used to track assets that are in the process of being built. Typical examples include large equipment purchases or new leasehold locations that are assembled over a period of time. You can track raw materials, labor, and overhead charges.

Oracle Assets identifies mass additions as CIP-based on the general ledger account they are assigned to in Payables. If they are assigned to a CIP clearing account, they are brought over as CIP assets. You can decide to capitalize them whenever you are ready to place them in service. CIP assets can also be tracked in the Oracle Projects module and transferred to Oracle Assets when they are complete.

Oracle Assets automatically creates the appropriate journal entry transactions when you move an asset from CIP to Asset Additions. At the time when an asset is transferred, you can change the date placed in service. Oracle defaults the depreciation rules to those associated with the asset category. If you need to reverse an asset that was previously capitalized, Oracle changes the asset type back to CIP and creates the adjusting entries.

There are a couple of reports that you will want to use to reconcile your CIP accounts to the general ledger. These reports are the CIP Detail and CIP Summary reports. Both of these reports can be sorted by balancing segment, asset, or CIP account.

Understanding Investment Tax Credits

Investment Tax Credits (ITC) affect assets in the U.S. that were placed in service before 1987. Oracle Assets calculates the ITC amount, depreciable basis, and basis reduction amount.

Note that for an asset to be ITC eligible, ITC must be allowable by both the corporate and the tax book categories. If you are having difficulties, check the default depreciation rules for the category in question.

Understanding Units of Production

The Units of Production method of depreciation is used to allocate the cost of an asset based on usage instead of time. Examples of assets that would be appropriate for the units of production depreciation method might be manufacturing equipment, oil wells, and coal mines. For more detailed information on this topic, please see the section "Defining Depreciation Methods" earlier in this chapter.

Understanding Capital Budgeting

Capital budgets are used to track anticipated asset purchases. To track budget information, a budget book must be created. Budget information can be tracked by full category combination or by major category only. To use this feature, you must have some working knowledge of SQL*Loader, which is used to populate the interface table. Budget information can be changed at any time, but you must delete existing budget information before uploading a new capital budget from a spreadsheet.

Understanding Depreciation

Depreciation is calculated based on the depreciation method, life of the asset, and prorate convention chosen. Also, the salvage value of an item is taken into account when depreciation is calculated. The depreciation process must be run separately for each set of asset books. When you run the depreciation process, Oracle automatically closes your books for the month, so make sure that you have completed all your transactions prior to running this process.

Following is an example of how Oracle calculates depreciation for an asset. For this example, assume that the asset will be set up using the straight-line depreciation method, with an in-service date of September 22, 1999, and the prorate calendar that indicates depreciation in the first year of life will be calculated based on a half-year convention. The company uses a standard calendar year and the prorate date is July 1, 1999. The initial cost is $2,000, and the asset has a four-year depreciable life. Based on this information, the asset will have a total depreciation expense of $250 for calendar year 1999. The calculation is $2,000 divided by four and multiplied by .50 (for the half-year convention indicated by the prorate date of July 1, 1999).

In this scenario, when depreciation is run for the month of September 1999, Oracle will take the $250 and divide it by the six months in the prorate period (July through December), which is $41.67 per month. In September, Oracle will catch up the depreciation expense by booking $125.01. In October, the monthly depreciation expense will revert back to $41.67. By December 31, the total for the year will be $250. Beginning in the second year, Oracle will take $2,000 divided by four and allocate the full $500 (or $41.67 per month) to depreciation for this particular asset.

BALANCING THE SUBLEDGER TO THE GENERAL LEDGER

To reconcile the cost and CIP accounts, use Cost Detail and Cost Summary. Use the CIP Detail and CIP Summary reports to reconcile your CIP cost accounts to your general ledger. To reconcile with Oracle General Ledger, compare the Cost or CIP Summary report with the Account Analysis Report.

Other reports that provide supporting detail include the Asset Additions Report, Cost Adjustments Report, Asset Retirements Report, Asset Reclassifications Reconciliation Report, and Asset Transfer Reconciliation Report. The detail reports are sorted by balancing segment, asset, or CIP cost account, cost center, and asset number, and print totals for each asset or CIP cost center, account, and balancing segment. Both of the summary reports can be sorted by your balancing segment and asset or CIP account.

The Journal Entry Reserve Report can be used to determine how much depreciation expense Oracle Assets charged to a depreciation expense account for any accounting period. The report lists all active (not yet retired) capitalized assets, as well as any assets that you have retired in the period's fiscal year. The report is sorted by balancing segment, expense and reserve accounts, and cost center. It prints totals for each cost center, account, and balancing segment.

Use the Accumulated Depreciation Balance Report to reconcile your reserve accounts to your general ledger.

USING OPEN INTERFACES IN THIS APPLICATION

There are a number of Open Interfaces found in Oracle Assets. You'll find them in the following sections, along with a brief discussion on how they are used.

FIXED ASSET DESKTOP INTEGRATOR

The Fixed Asset Desktop Integrator (ADI) provides a method for you to load information from an Excel spreadsheet directly into the Oracle Assets tables. The two tables it interfaces with are the Mass Addition table and the Physical Inventory table. It also provides a means to download information from Oracle into a spreadsheet in Excel and also a method to print FA reports in various formats including HTML.

The Mass Addition table is generally used in this way during initial data conversion of the system. It provides a place to hold data before transferring it into Oracle Fixed Assets. The Mass Addition table is also used if additions need to be transferred from a system other than Oracle Payables or Oracle Projects.

The Physical Inventory table is used to load information gathered during the physical inventory process through an Excel spreadsheet. This is where you compare inventoried assets to the assets on the books.

IMPORTING ASSETS USING THE MASS ADDITIONS INTERFACE

The database definition of the FA_MASS_ADDITIONS table does not require that you provide values for any columns, but for the Mass Additions Posting program to work properly, make sure you follow the rules in the list of column descriptions. The Mass Additions Posting program uses some of the columns in the FA_MASS_ADDITIONS table, so these columns are marked NULL. Do not import your data into columns marked NULL. You must fill columns marked REQUIRED before you run Mass Additions Post.

The FA_MASS_ADDITIONS table can be loaded directly using SQL*Loader, ADI (Application Desktop Integrator) or another program. If you decide to load the column directly from another system, fill in some values in the Mass Additions window before you post. Columns marked OPTIONAL are for optional asset information that you can track if you want. VARCHAR2 columns are case-sensitive. For columns marked PREP, you can either import information into the column directly or enter it in the Mass Additions window before you post.

Note that if you are using Oracle Payables, the FA_MASS_ADDITIONS table will be populated automatically when you run the Mass Additions Create process in Payables.

USING THE BUDGET INTERFACE

If you maintain your budget information in a spreadsheet, you can upload it to Oracle Assets using the budget interface. You can transfer budget data from any software package that prints to an ASCII file and then use SQL*Loader, ADI, or another program to load the FA_BUDGET_INTERFACE table.

USING THE PRODUCTION INTERFACE

You can enter or update production amounts for assets depreciating under units of production. You can enter production information online, or you can load it automatically from a feeder system using the Upload Periodic Production program. Enter production more than once a period if necessary.

USING THE ADJUSTED CURRENT EARNINGS INTERFACE

You can either have Oracle Assets calculate Adjusted Current Earnings (ACE) information for you or enter it yourself. If you want Oracle Assets to calculate ACE-accumulated depreciation for you, enter historical asset information beginning no later than the last period of fiscal 1989. Start your depreciation books in Oracle Assets before the end of fiscal 1989, and enter asset transactions through the current period.

If you have ACE information from another asset system, you can load it into Oracle Assets using the ACE interface. Define the initial open period of your ACE book as the last period of the last fiscal year you completed on your previous system. Then load the accumulated depreciation for your ACE assets using this interface.

USING THE INV INTERFACE

The physical inventory interface is used to transfer the physical inventory data you have collected. This form and how to utilize it are best tackled by a technical analyst because it requires an understanding of SQL*Loader, ADI, or another program.

UNDERSTANDING KEY REPORTS

Oracle FA reports can be run either singly or by using a request set. A request set enables you to streamline your printing process by grouping reports that you frequently run together. Request sets can be run either in parallel or in sequence. Running in parallel simply means that you do not need them to be run in any particular order, and conversely, running in sequence means that they must be run in a particular order or sequence. The form to set this process up is very self-explanatory and can be used by even the most inexperienced individual.

During the testing phase of your project, it is best to review all available reports in Oracle and run them at least once to determine whether they fulfill any of your reporting needs. Prior to running them, you should make a list of the reports that you use on your current system to compare them against the standard reports. This enables you to develop a list of reporting needs that are not going to be fulfilled with standard reports.

Reports can be run using two different methods. First, you can run them directly from the application using the Submit Requests window. The second method is by running them using the Request Center in ADI. If you choose to use ADI, you can save them in Excel, text, or HTML format. You can then store the output on your hard drive or to a network directory.

In reviewing the reports that Oracle provides, there seem to be five distinct classifications of FA reports. I have grouped these into the following categories: additions, depreciation, mass, reconciling, and other. I will highlight some of the reports that I found to be most helpful and indicate what each one can provide for you.

Probably the most frequently used type of report is the asset addition reports. Oracle comes with about eight reports that provide information on asset additions. Depending on how you want to see them sorted and what parameters are most important to you, there are a variety of standard reports to choose from. When initially configuring your system, you will probably use either the Annual Additions Report or the Asset Additions Report to tie out your cost and accumulated depreciation. The major difference between the two reports is that the Asset Additions Report provides a lot more detail and sort capabilities. If you are looking for more summarized information, use the Annual Additions Report.

There are a few reports that relate to the depreciation expense process. The Journal Entry Reserve Ledger Report and the Gains & Losses Report are actually generated whenever you run the depreciation process in Oracle Assets. In addition to those reports, there are two additional reports that you should be aware of, and they are the Assets Not Assigned to Any Books Listing and the Assets Not Assigned to Any Cost Centers Listing. You should be sure that you run these every month prior to initiating the depreciation expense process. Because the depreciation process aborts when it encounters problems, these reports help alert you to some potential problems that might exist prior to running your depreciation process.

There are also many different predefined Mass reports that come standard with Oracle. You can review mass additions that you created, posted, split, deleted, and purged. You can also print reports that provide mass retirements, transfers, and change information. These reports are very self-explanatory to run and most of them only require date parameters and a book designation to process.

The reports that are most commonly used to reconcile back to the general ledger start with the Unposted Journal Report. This report is generated automatically when you run the depreciation process. If additional copies are desired, it is accessible from the concurrent manager. There are also two drill-down reports available in general ledger called Drill Down Report and the Account Drill Down Report. Both can assist in reviewing entries created by Oracle FA.

To reconcile the cost accounts with GL, you can run the Cost Summary and Cost Detail reports (the CIP Summary and Detail reports to reconcile your CIP cost accounts). The summary report can only be sorted by balancing segment and asset accounts. The detail report can be sorted by balancing segment, cost center, asset number, and asset accounts. If there are any discrepancies, you can also print the asset additions, cost adjustment, asset transfers, and asset retirement reports. These reports provide details to assist you in determining where any balancing problems might have occurred.

Depreciation expense reconciliation can be done using the Journal Entry Reserve Ledger report. This report provides details on all active assets in addition to those assets that you might have retired during the current fiscal year. It is sorted by balancing segment, expense accounts, and cost center. Any assets that have been transferred or adjusted during the fiscal year are shown on the report with a marking to indicate that they have been changed in some way.

There are a vast number of miscellaneous reports that can be used to analyze different types of information. There are many standard tax reports that can be used to provide details for specific tax forms such as Form 4562 Depreciation and Amortization Report and Form 4626 AMT Detail and Summary Report. There are also standard Property Tax Report,

Investment Tax Credit, and Tax Additions reports that specifically target the needs of your tax department. There are also reports to review setup data such as calendars, prorate conventions, asset categories, asset descriptions, asset tags, and price indexes.

One miscellaneous report that will probably be of interest is the Fixed Asset Projection report. This report is not available through the standard report submission; it is found under the depreciation menu path. When you initiate the projections process, it automatically runs the report. The report can be sorted by cost center and provides summary or detailed asset information. You must select the number of periods, start date, and the book that you want the projection to be run against.

SUMMARY

In summary, Oracle Assets is a very powerful tool for managing and keeping track of your assets. The key to success is spending the time up front analyzing your business needs. The program can be set up to accommodate many different requirements, and sometimes the solution might not be readily apparent but is available nonetheless. I hope this chapter has shown some of the ways this can be accomplished.

CHAPTER 15

Using Oracle Projects

In this chapter

INTRODUCTION

The Oracle Projects solution provides a suite of highly integrated applications that give your organization the capability to capitalize on global opportunities. Oracle Projects (formerly known as Project Accounting) enables your organization to set up projects and tasks and assign related expenditures. Costs can be burdened and translated to Revenue, Billing, and Capital items when required. One of the major benefits of using Oracle Projects is the ability for a project-oriented business to manage its projects with a proactive approach.

Although Oracle Projects is a subledger to Oracle General Ledger, it can quickly become the center of your business operations in project-centric business environments. Oracle Projects can be configured to integrate with Oracle Financials, Manufacturing, and HRMS applications or as a standalone application. Using more advanced features enables Oracle Projects to be integrated with project management systems and to extend the existing code to satisfy company-specific business processes.

RELATIONSHIP TO OTHER APPLICATIONS

Oracle Projects integrates with many other Oracle Applications. Figure 15.1 shows the integration points (both to and from Oracle Projects) with Financials, Manufacturing, and HRMS, as well as external systems for validation, input, shared objects, and so forth.

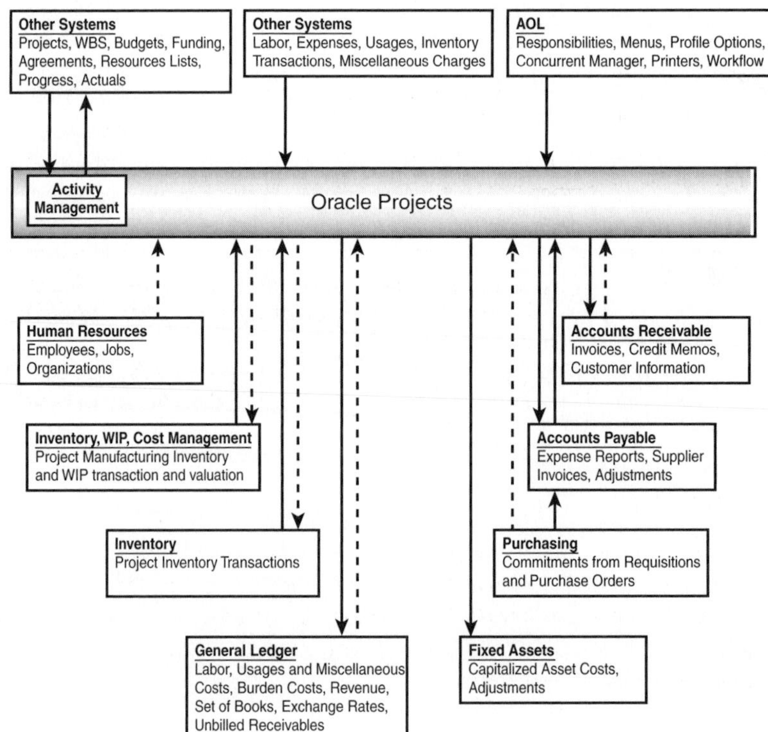

Figure 15.1 Oracle Projects relationship to other applications.

DISCOVERING NEW FEATURES IN RELEASE 11*i*

Established users and consultants who are familiar with Release 11 should be comfortable with the features and functions of Release 11*i* Projects. This section discusses some new features in Release 11*i*.

MULTICURRENCY TRANSACTIONS

In Release 11*i*, Oracle Projects introduces support for multicurrency transactions. This new functionality enables you to enter and maintain transactions in various currencies beyond your functional currency. The following currency attributes are provided:

- **Functional**—The functional currency of the set of books associated with the operating unit into which the transaction is entered.
- **Receipt**—Currency in which the expenditure is incurred.
- **Reimbursement**—Currency in which the employee wants to be reimbursed. The default is functional currency.

The primary area where the multicurrency transactions are most evident is with expense report entry. This functionality enables you to enter expense report receipts as well as receive reimbursement in a currency other than the functional currency. During expense report entry, you can provide the receipt exchange rate. In practice, this rate is based on a rate received from a Bureau of Exchange, a rate on a credit card bill, or a supplied corporate exchange rate.

To use this new functionality, the default currency exchange rate type and date options must be defined. This setup step is accomplished in the Currency tab of the Implementation Options screen. This setup determines the default rate type (for example, Corporate, User, and so on) used when converting transaction currencies into functional currency.

Tip

If you use preapproved batch entry for expense reports, you should define a multicurrency entry folder using Oracle Applications Folder tools. The default screen in preapproved batch entry does not display the currency attributes (Reimbursement Currency, Receipt Currency, Receipt Exchange Rate, and Receipt Amount). These fields should be displayed to support multicurrency transaction entry.

MULTICURRENCY BILLING

Release 11*i* now provides you the ability to invoice customers in any currency. In the Projects Customers and Contacts option screen, you can specify any defined currency as the billing currency along with the appropriate exchange rate type. In addition, you can optionally choose to change and recalculate the billing currency for specific invoice(s) in the invoice review screen using the Recalculate button.

Note

Invoices are transferred to AR in the billing currency.

The billing currency impact is restricted to the invoice itself. Agreements, budgets, events, bill rate schedules, and revenue are all maintained in the functional currency only. Therefore, when billing in a foreign currency, you must first convert the desired foreign currency billing amount/rate into your functional currency for entry into your event/bill rate. During the Generate Draft Invoice process, Oracle Projects converts the functional amount to the billing currency defined on the project.

Tip

You might need to adjust the budget, agreement, and bill rate amounts during the life of your project to account for exchange rate fluctuations between the time of project setup and the time of invoicing.

INTERPROJECT BILLING

Interproject Billing now provides a means for invoicing projects within your company as a standard customer. This allows for greater flexibility where revenue is recognized internal to your company. This new functionality enables you to generate an invoice on one project (the provider project) that will become a supplier invoice on another project (the receiver project).

Interproject Billing enables you to identify a receiver project/task on the provider projects Customers and Contact option screen. The receiving project/task can be either in the same operating unit or in a different operating unit and set of books. Your billing options and methods are otherwise the same. You can use Event-, Work-, or Cost-based billing to generate an invoice in any currency. Your intercompany markup is determined by your billing schedule, burden schedule, or billing extension logic just as it would for any other billable project.

During the Interface to Receivables process, a record is created in the Payables invoice import table. This invoice is imported into Payables and is subsequently transferred onto the receiver project/task in Projects using the standard Payables Transfer to Projects process.

Note

Interproject Billing transactions can cross legal entities and sets of books.

CROSS-CHARGING AND INTERCOMPANY BILLING

Intercompany Billing is similar to Interproject Billing but involves a more centralized approach. Using Intercompany Billing, transactions originating in one operating unit are charged directly to a project owned by a different operating unit. To do this, cross-charging must be explicitly enabled by operating unit.

In the Provider Controls window, you can determine how to handle the cross-charge transactions by using either Borrowed Lent Accounting or Intercompany Billing. Borrowed Lent Accounting creates General Ledger entries from Oracle Projects to account for the shift of revenue/cost dollars between organizations; however, it does not generate any intercompany documents typically required between legal entities. By selecting the Intercompany Billing option, intercompany documents are generated between legal entities to handle the shift of revenue/cost dollars between organizations.

To use this new functionality for Intercompany Billing, you must set up both an Intercompany Billing Project Type and an associated Intercompany Billing Project in each operating unit. This Intercompany Billing Project is specified in the Provider Controls screen and serves as a vehicle for generating intercompany invoices to the operating unit that is being cross-charged.

Note

An intercompany invoice (like an interproject invoice) is recorded in Payables for the cross-charged operating unit. However, this invoice is not a project-related invoice because the cross-charged project has already been charged directly. In this scenario, the project spans sets of books (in other words, transactions from multiple sets of books can exist on a project).

TAX INFORMATION BY RECEIVABLES INVOICE LINES

R11*i* enhances the ability to flag invoice lines as taxable and to automatically assign the proper tax code. Although the tax engine for calculating the amount of tax remains in AR, Oracle Projects has added a similar version of the AR tax hierarchy but has added project-specific options. The Oracle Projects tax hierarchy can be set up to derive the tax code from customer site, customer name, project, event type, expenditure type, retention, client extension, or Oracle Receivables System option.

The Generate Draft Invoice process in Oracle Projects uses this new project-specific tax hierarchy to select the appropriate tax code. Oracle Projects also provides a client extension that is called during this processing to enable you to derive the tax code based on your company-specific business rules. More information about this client extension is provided in the section "Client Extensions," later in this chapter.

Tip

Use of the Tax Code client extension is ideal if you determine your tax calculation based on an attribute of the project, task, or agreement.

As shown in Figure 15.2, Oracle Projects provides output tax code fields that can be entered as defaults when defining expenditure types during system implementation. These default codes can be overridden by the Projects tax hierarchy and the tax code client extension.

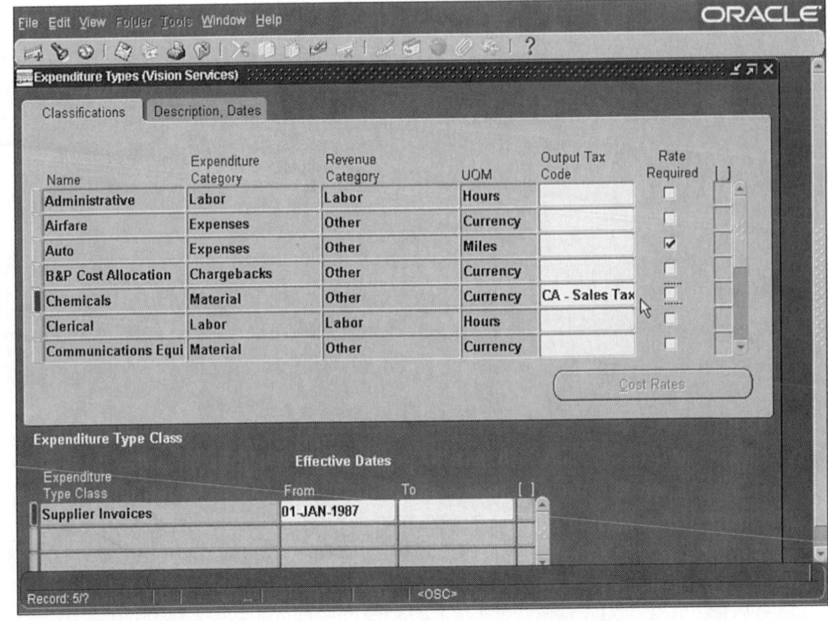

Figure 15.2
Default output tax code can be entered when defining expenditure types.

Note

Oracle Projects does not calculate the tax amount, nor is the tax amount stored on the project. When invoices are interfaced to Receivables, the AutoInvoice program uses the tax code passed from Oracle Projects to find the appropriate tax rate. This tax rate is used by Receivables to derive the appropriate tax account code combination.

PROJECT ALLOCATIONS

Project Allocations in Oracle Projects 11*i* is a new method for distributing costs to project tasks. You can select from several types of allocations, such as the distribution of shared service costs to using projects or the allocation of organization overhead expenses to the projects in that organization. Each allocation you perform is defined as an allocation rule. The system enables you to define as many allocation rules as necessary.

Note

Project Allocations does not replace burdening functionality, nor does it exclude the use of burdening.

Although Project Allocations can be used to distribute overhead expenses to projects, this new feature does not replace the burdening functionality of Oracle Projects. Depending on your business, you might want to implement both of these features to perform different types of cost allocations. The key difference between these two features is that Project Allocations relies on existing cost amounts to allocate to projects, whereas burdening uses estimates of the overhead costs to be allocated. These estimates are stored as percentage rates that are then applied to actual raw cost to derive the burden or allocation amount.

Project Allocations collects costs from a source pool and then distributes this amount to one or more target project tasks, including projects in different operating units. The source cost pool can be derived from any combination of the following:

- A fixed amount entered as part of the Project Allocation setup
- Summarized costs on the source projects and tasks
- GL account balances

Project Allocations distributes the source cost pool amount to target project tasks in either equal or proportional amounts, depending on how the allocation rule is defined. Several methods are available for prorating the source cost pool amount to the target project tasks.

The distributed costs are created as new allocation expenditure items on the target project tasks. In addition to the allocation transactions, your allocation rule can also create reversing expenditure items on the same or another project to offset the allocation transactions.

Oracle Projects provides extreme flexibility in how you define your allocation rules. In addition to the many options available in the standard setup forms, Oracle Projects includes seven new client extensions in Project Allocations. More information about these client extensions is provided in the section "Client Extensions," later in this chapter.

The AutoAllocations feature in Oracle Projects 11*i* enables you to group multiple allocation rules into an AutoAllocation set that can be executed with one concurrent request. AutoAllocations processes allocation rules in parallel or as step-down allocations, depending on how the AutoAllocation set has been defined. An AutoAllocation set can include GL MassAllocations as well as Projects allocation rules.

Enhanced Reporting and Analysis

This section is designed to provide you with some insight into a few of the new reporting and reviewing options now offered within the Projects application.

View Accounting Lines Window

The View Accounting Lines window can be accessed from either the Expenditure Inquiry or Revenue Review window. It is used to view cost, revenue, and cross-charge transactions. Figure 15.3 shows the detailed information provided, such as the account, debit or credit amount, transaction reference, and other relevant accounting information generated behind the scenes by AutoAccounting.

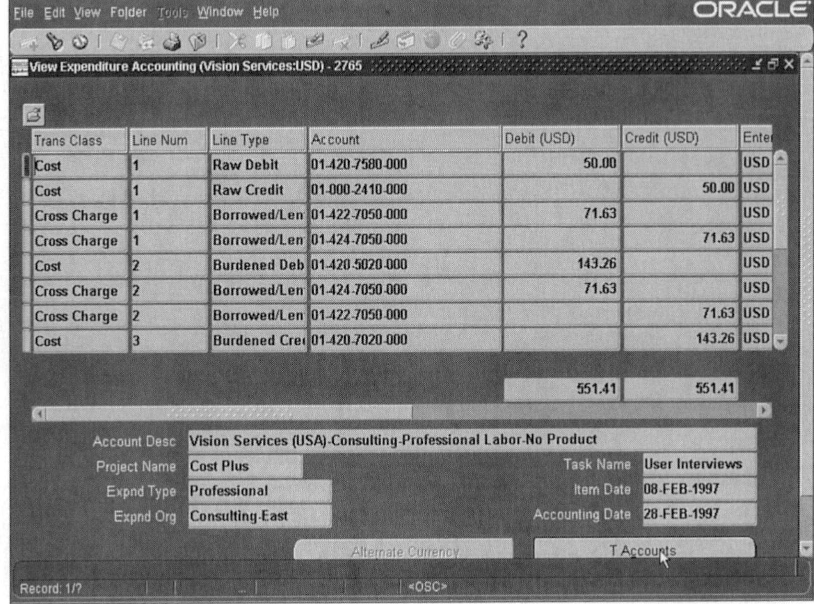

Figure 15.3
The View Accounting Lines window enables you to see detailed transaction information.

T-Accounts Window

The T-Accounts window, shown in Figure 15.4, enables you to view and print Oracle Projects accounting entries in a graphical T-account format. You can access this window from either the Expenditure Inquiry or Revenue Review screen. You can use flexible options to customize this window. For example, you can view all the details in a T-account or just the net total. You can also view T-accounts by full accounting flexfield or summarized by account segment.

Subledger Accounting—Drill Down from GL

R11*i* now enables you to drill down from Oracle General Ledger journal entries to cost and revenue information within Oracle Projects, including transfer price amounts (intercompany billing as well as borrowed and lent). You can view the subledger line items and the underlying transactions that make up a General Ledger journal line. You also can drill down to Oracle Projects from the Enter Journals window, View Journals window, or Account Inquiry window.

The GL drill-down displays the Projects Expenditure Accounting window, as shown in Figure 15.5. From this window, you can view the account, entered and accounted debit/credit, currency and exchange rate information, accounting date, transfer to General Ledger status, transaction class, and total debits and credits.

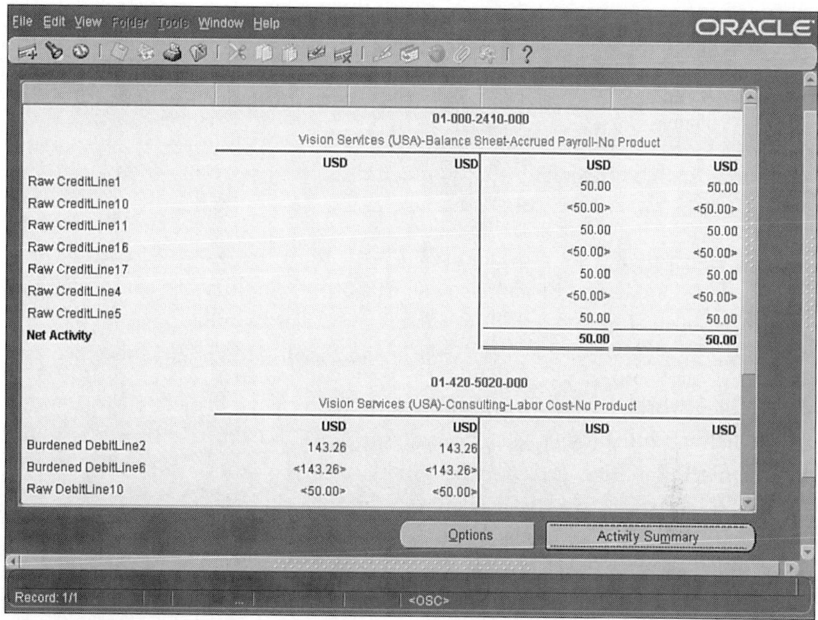

Figure 15.4
The T-Accounts window enables you to view and print accounting entries in graphical format.

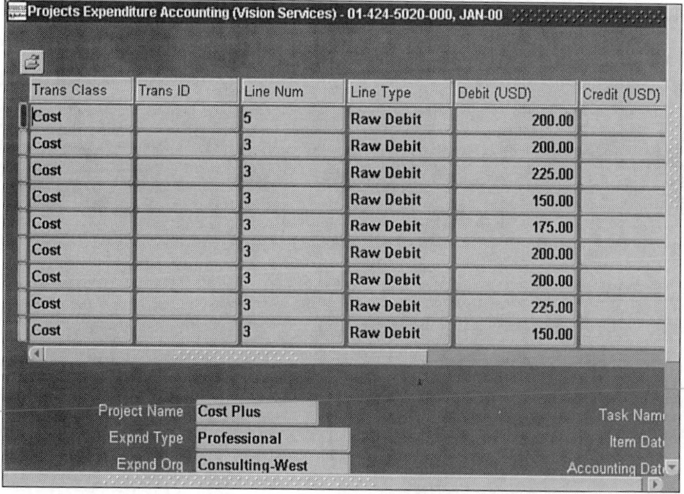

Figure 15.5
You can drill down to project-related information from within General Ledger.

PROJECTS INTELLIGENCE

Oracle now offers the self-service Financials Intelligence product that can be accessed from your Oracle launch page. This section describes the predefined Discoverer workbooks, associated worksheets, and actual reports that are supplied for the Oracle Projects application. These workbooks can be accessed directly from Discoverer or by using the Oracle Business Intelligence system.

Note

Financials Intelligence is licensed separately from Oracle Projects.

For each worksheet, Oracle supplies predefined parameters. These parameters are conditions enabled by default that you can disable by selecting the Conditions option under the Tools menu.

Within worksheets, you can drill down and drill across information to assist you with your business analysis. You can also use this tool to build more extensive queries for analysis, such as labor utilization, cash flow, cash receipts versus billed, and invoice to revenue variance. You can base these advanced queries on the provided worksheets as a starting point.

Three workbooks are supplied by Oracle Projects: Project Cost Analysis, Project Revenue Analysis, and Project Margin Analysis. These workbooks form the foundation of the Projects Intelligence reporting. Many of the columns available in the Project Status Inquiry (PSI) reporting are also available in these workbooks.

Note

The data reported is current as of the latest run of the project summarization process and the designated current reporting period at the time of the run.

The series of reports and charts provided by Projects Intelligence shows project revenue, cost, and margin, as shown in Figure 15.6. Each report enables you to drill down and analyze costs by organization or by class category. You can further drill down from class category to class codes, and from class codes, you can drill down into specific projects. You can also drill into specific projects from organizations.

Workbook—Project Cost Analysis The Project Cost Analysis workbook enables you to analyze project expenses along organizational lines or from a project classification. One worksheet exists in the Project Cost Analysis workbook, Cost Analysis Worksheet.

The Column Dimensions provided by the Project Cost Analysis worksheet include these: ITD Cost, Commitments, Total Cost, ITD Budgeted Cost, ITD Variance, ITD Percentage, Total Budgeted Cost, Total Original Budgeted Cost, and Total Forecasted Budget Cost.

Workbook—Project Margin Analysis The Project Margin Analysis workbook enables you to analyze your projects' margins by customer class for the current reporting period and from your projects' inceptions. In addition, you can compare your actual margins to the current and original budgeted margins. The two worksheets in the Project Margin Analysis workbook are the Period-to-Date (PTD) & Inception-to-Date (ITD) Margin Analysis worksheet and the ITD Actual vs. Budget Margin Analysis worksheet.

The column dimensions provided by the Period-to-Date (PTD) & Inception-to-Date (ITD) Margin Analysis worksheet include PTD Revenue, PTD Cost, PTD Margin, PTD Margin Percentage, ITD Revenue, ITD Cost, ITD Margin, and ITD Margin Percentage.

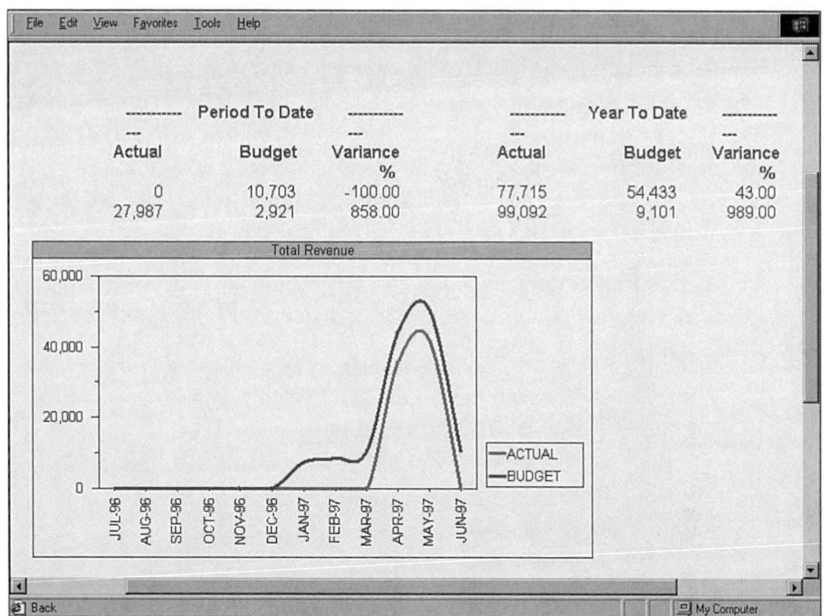

Figure 15.6
Projects Intelligence provides graphical reports and charts with drill-down capability.

The column dimensions provided by the ITD Actual vs. Budget Margin Analysis worksheet include PTD Revenue, PTD Cost, PTD Margin, PTD Margin Percentage, ITD Revenue, ITD Cost, ITD Margin, and ITD Margin Percentage.

Note

In a workbook with multiple worksheets, you can see conditions from both worksheets displayed in a single list.

WORKBOOK—PROJECT REVENUE ANALYSIS The Project Revenue Analysis workbook enables you to analyze your backlog revenue amounts by project class category, class codes, and key members. You can track how much actual revenue is to be earned to meet the total contract value. Only one worksheet exists in this workbook: the Revenue and Backlog Analysis worksheet.

The column dimensions provided by the Project Revenue Analysis worksheet include PTD Revenue, PTD Margin Percentage, ITD Revenue, ITD Margin Percentage, Total Budgeted Revenue, Backlog (defined as total budgeted revenue less ITD Revenue), Percent Backlog, ITD Cost, PTD Burdened Cost, and Over Budget (ITD Revenue less Total Budgeted Revenue).

Caution

The Project Revenue Analysis workbook uses the same security model as the setup for Oracle Projects. The security is based on a user's login ID and on a single organization for the Projects view as defined in the operating unit setup. This also uses Projects security, which is based on the Projects security client extension.

Enhanced Transaction Import

Transaction import in Release 11*i* supports many new features. One of the most important features is the Transaction Import extension. In Release 11*i*, you can write your own PL/SQL procedure and call the stored procedure for each transaction source both before (preprocessing extension) and after (post-processing extension) the Transaction Import process. More information about this client extension is provided in the section "Client Extensions," later in this chapter.

Transaction Import now supports importing cost in any currency, including receipt currency and exchange rate. In addition, cross-charge transactions can be imported from external systems.

Another enhancement to Transaction Import includes validation of descriptive flexfields. You can now validate your descriptive flexfields by using the validation you define while setting up the descriptive flexfield. Furthermore, with Payables supplier invoice costs passing through the transaction import tables, descriptive flexfield information can now be passed from Payables to Projects. If the validation fails in the transaction import tables, the invalid expenditures will be rejected.

With Release 11*i*, you also have the ability to override the default employee organization using the override to organization name column. This feature enables employees to incur and charge expenditures to an organization other than their assigned organizations. Companies now have the option to define the employee organization upon importing transactions. If this option is turned on, you must always interface the employee organization when importing employee-related transactions.

Integration with Other Oracle Applications

One of the strengths provided by Oracle Projects is its tight integration with other applications. Additional integration points in R11*i* are highlighted in this section.

Oracle Internet Time

Oracle Internet Time is a Web-based time-entry vehicle that is fully integrated with Oracle Projects and requires no duplicate setup. Internet Time enables you to

- Quickly enter and approve timecards online from any location where you have access to an Internet browser.
- Activate a workflow process that meets business procedures for approval, correction, and submission routing.
- Bypass the workflow option all together and use auto approval if applicable.
- Save incomplete timecards for later modification and submission.
- View old timecards via Timecard History.
- Copy previous timecards to avoid duplicate entry when creating new timecards.
- Enter or modify timecards on behalf of other employees with the correct security rights.

- Set up aliases for quick entry shortcuts.
- Create timecards in Excel and upload them at a later time (disconnected mode).
- Print a current list of projects and tasks.

ORACLE CASH MANAGEMENT

Oracle Cash Management gives organizations the ability to forecast cash flow by project or range of projects, enabling users to analyze project liquidity. Oracle Cash Management can pull relevant data from the following Oracle modules: Order Entry, Accounts Payables, Projects, Purchasing, and Receivables.

Oracle Cash Management enables users to create forecast templates. These templates provide project-centric organizations with the ability to analyze cash flow from projects across the enterprise as well as specific long-term high-visibility projects. Users also have the ability to forecast in multiple currencies, allowing for the analysis of foreign currency exposure on a project.

Note

A project forecast can be viewed in various currencies. When submitting a cash forecast (select Tools, Submit Forecast), the request form provides a parameter to enter a forecast currency that is different from the project currency.

Cash Management enables you to specify which applications are to be included in the forecasts (Order Entry, Accounts Payable, Accounts Receivable, Purchasing, Projects, and so on). Once specified, the project-related forecasts pull data only from those Oracle products linked to the forecasted projects. Depending on which applications are specified, a forecast could potentially include the following types of inflows and outflows.

Inflows

- Uninvoiced sales orders in Order Entry
- Unreleased project billing events with a billing impact
- Released invoices in Oracle Projects that have not been transferred to Receivables
- Unpaid customer invoices in Receivables

Outflows

- Unordered requisitions in Purchasing
- Uninvoiced purchase orders
- Labor, usages, and miscellaneous transactions in Oracle Projects
- Unpaid supplier invoices and expense report invoices in Payables
- Released Projects expense reports that have not been transferred to Payables or have been transferred to Payables but are still uninvoiced.
- Projects budgeted outflow amounts defined as projected future expenditures from external systems or nonintegrated applications

Tip

When designing your forecast template, you are limited to a maximum of 80 columns for displaying forecast output periods–for example, if the forecast is by GL period, the limitation would be 80 GL periods.

ORACLE ACTIVITY MANAGEMENT GATEWAY RELEASE 11*i*

Note

New features in Release 11*i* for Activity Management Gateway require that the system be at least 11.5.3 with Projects patchset D or higher.

Since version 10.7 (16.1), Oracle Projects has provided a supported option for sharing project information, work breakdown structures, budgets, resource lists, and status information. This bidirectional sharing of data has enabled you to exchange data between external or third-party systems and Oracle Projects without reentry and has been accomplished through the use of tables, views, and stored procedures—Oracle's Activity Management Gateway (AMG). The AMG has provided you the ability to add, update, and delete project headers, task work breakdown structures, budget headers, budget lines, resource lists, and earned value and percent complete information. It also has provided the ability to modify a work breakdown structure, calculate raw and burdened costs on a budget, and baseline the budget from an external system.

Although no major changes to the AMG APIs were made in the base release of 11*i*, several existing APIs have been modified to accommodate interfacing data that would use the new R11*i* Projects functionality.

With the release of 11.5.4 (11.5.3 plus PA patchset D), you now can interface funding and agreement information into Oracle Projects. The new functionality enabled for the AMG is

- Ability to create, update, and delete agreements
- Ability to create, update, and delete funding
- Support of composite data types
- Load-Execute-Fetch support for noncomposite data types
- Validation APIs for checking the ability to delete agreements
- Validation APIs for checking the ability to add, delete, and update funding
- Control Actions for updating and deleting agreements
- Control Actions for adding, updating, and deleting funding
- New views for a list of values validation associated to agreement and funding fields

Oracle Project Connect (for Microsoft Project) Version 2.5

The Oracle Project Connect application integrates Oracle Projects with Microsoft Project using Oracle's AMG. Information shared between Microsoft Project and Oracle Projects includes projects, budgets, resources, progress, and actual costs. In Oracle Projects, you establish the rules for your integrated application to provide controls. You have the ability to disallow modifications from the nonsource system. A full work breakdown structure can be integrated from Microsoft Project, or a less detailed structure can be integrated. This option allows one view for the project management system, whereas Oracle Projects provides a more condensed view of the project.

Release 2.5 enables integration with Oracle Projects R11*i* and with Microsoft Project 2000. New features in Release 2.5 include

- Ability to map additional information received from Oracle Projects resource lists to columns in Microsoft Project
- Elimination of the download of duplicate resource information
- Ability to enable performance tracing on transfer rates between Oracle Projects and Microsoft Project

Critical Implementation Factors

Before undertaking an Oracle Projects implementation, you should consider your business requirements and how current issues and gaps might impact them, as well as how new products might solve specific business needs.

New Products

This section is designed to inform you of new products that are fully integrated with the Oracle Projects Suite. They were (or will be) released post-R11*i*.

Project Resource Management

Project Resource Management (PJRM) is designed to manage the supply and demand for resources across your organization. Oracle's PJRM product helps project managers form project teams and manage resources. This product enables your resource manager to search for resources by skills, competencies, and experience. PJRM builds on the HR foundation, and employees can update their skill sets and nominate themselves for open jobs through self-service. A workflow-driven process requires approval from the employee's manager prior to committing the update. PJRM also provides a resource's confirmed commitments as well as provisions to inform the resource manager of availability.

Oracle Time and Labor

Oracle Time and Labor is Oracle's complete self-service solution to the e-business need for an integrated time management system. All time-related data is entered from this self-service application (or from a set of comprehensive APIs) into a central repository called the *time store*. From there, the data is interfaced to other Oracle applications or external systems as required. The initial integration focuses on Oracle Human Resources, Oracle Payroll, and Oracle Projects.

Timecard configurations include a layout that supports Projects. These configurations are flexible and can be easily tailored to meet your business needs. The integration with Oracle Projects includes complete validation using the Oracle Projects Transaction Controls. To help those workers who are on the road, a disconnected mode is also supported. Also, to help simplify data entry, timecard values can be supplied from the Project Resources Management application. Additional functionality will include the ability to enter hours into flexible time periods, such as semimonthly time entry.

Note

Internet Time will ultimately be replaced by Oracle Time and Labor.

PROJECT CONTRACTS

The new Project Contracts (OKE) application supports the complete contract life cycle. The model starts with a request for information or a proposal and continues through the negotiation phase until the final contract award. Afterward, the system tracks or monitors the execution of the contract and effectively manages the change order process. The integration works well for general contractors who need to interface with both subcontractors and the owner.

On the billing side, OKE fully integrates contracts, contract lines, and funding with Oracle Projects Agreements/Funding. Project Contracts triggers billing activities based on milestone completions, data item deliveries, and product shipments. Additionally, through APIs, it integrates billing events to Oracle Projects. Using a newly introduced project hierarchy, you will be able to map complex contracts and contracts lines to projects and tasks. Project Contracts provides a Deliverables Tracking System (DTS), which enables you to better control contract execution. The billable lines on DTS are controlled by project billing users. Using OKE, you will review the billable line and verify that it is ready to bill. After updating the necessary values, deliverable-based billing events will be interfaced to Oracle Projects.

ENHANCEMENT REQUESTS

This section outlines some of the enhancement requests that have been brought forward to Oracle Development to address issues and gaps in the application. Currently, two focus groups work on providing Oracle Development with system gaps and requirements to enhance the system—the Special Interest Group (SIG) and the Customer Advisory Board (CAB). The SIG sessions meet before the start of every Oracle Applications User Group (OAUG) conference. You are encouraged to take the time to participate in these sessions and become involved. This is your opportunity to engage in the identification of system enhancements. For more information on enhancement requests, please visit the OAUG members Web site.

The following are a few of the business requirements defined for the integration between Oracle Projects, Purchasing, and Payables. These requirements were identified by the AP/PO Projects Integration SIG:

- **Project distributions on purchase orders and requisitions**—When a requisition or purchase order is being approved, the system should validate that the project or task is still valid for charging. If a line is copied on a PO/requisition or a change occurs to the project information, Account Generator should be invoked to modify the accounting segments.
- **Payables should be capable of retaining amounts on Project invoices**—The functionality should be added to retain a portion of the supplier invoice payment until the occurrence of company-defined events. The retained amounts should be accounted for separately.
- **The ability to charge advance and progress payments to Projects should be included**—The functionality should enable you to charge supplier advances and progress payments to projects. The system currently restricts you to an account charge with no project distribution.
- **The project should be charged based on a delivery transaction**—This would enable projects to be charged based on a delivery transaction (receipt), like the General Ledger, and not wait for the supplier invoice. When the supplier invoice is entered and matched to the PO, Payables should only send the variances to Projects.
- **Discount amounts should be interfaced to Projects**—If a project-related invoice has taken the benefit of a discount, this would enable the applicable discounts to be transferred to Projects.
- **Project costs should be accrued at period end**—This would enable the system to accrue project costs at the end of a period in Payables and interface the costs to the General Ledger and Projects.

In addition to the AP/PO Projects Integration SIG, another focus group is devoted to identifying enhancement requirements for the Project Billing module.

CONFIGURING THE APPLICATION

This section describes the setup tasks and sequence required to configure the Oracle Projects application. The tasks should be performed in the sequence listed.

RESOLVING CRITICAL SETUP ISSUES

Oracle Projects can be set up as a standalone application or integrated with the Oracle Application suite. Therefore, when designing your Oracle Projects implementation, it is critical that you consider which applications are going to be integrated with Oracle Projects. The following describes some of the major areas that become key in your setup decisions.

Implementing Oracle Projects as a Standalone Application

When implementing Oracle Projects as a standalone application, certain setups must be completed. When not implementing Oracle Human Resources and Receivables fully, you are required to set up a partial install. Through the Oracle Projects menu, HR organizations, project hierarchies, employees, jobs, and employee assignments can be set up. For Project Costing and Billing, the minimal HR setup is required. Oracle HR offers APIs that enable you to build interfaces from your HR application to the Oracle HR tables. If you are installing Project Billing, critical Receivables fields must also be set up, such as Customer, Payment Terms, and Tax Codes.

A General Ledger set of books, chart of accounts (COA), calendar, and periods must also be defined for your standalone application. If your organization decides not to pass information to the non-Oracle applications, a minimal COA could be defined using one clearing account for all distributed transactions. Implementation options determine whether to interface your costing and revenue transactions to the other applications. For the Project Status Inquiry form, you can incorporate commitments from external systems. This is accomplished through modifications to a view (see the section "Project Status Inquiry," later in this chapter).

Designing Your Chart of Accounts

One of the most time-consuming tasks of an implementation is the designing and acceptance of the chart of account structure in your General Ledger. The Projects integration should be factored into this design process because the Projects module can reduce the COA structure. Companies should consider maintaining their project systems as a subledger, reporting Project P&L statements and details such as product line from the Projects application. With this in mind, a project segment in your General Ledger COA becomes unnecessary and would duplicate information.

Reporting project information from the Projects application can be accomplished through custom reports, data warehouse reports, and standard project reports. Your system should be designed so that your General Ledger provides summary-level reporting, financial statements, and key segment value information for the total company picture. The Projects system is designed to offer your organization a more detailed way of viewing costs and revenues, by Project. Your General Ledger application is designed to review the same information in summary, by account.

A major consideration when designing the setup of the Projects application is the ability to properly populate GL segment values through AutoAccounting and Account Generator. Careful review should be performed for all processes Projects uses to generate account values. Business scenarios must be well thought out when designing AutoAccounting rules. If account values are easily determined, your AutoAccounting process will run more efficiently.

Human Resources Organizations

Human Resources setup design impacts the Projects application because it is heavily integrated with employees, organization assignments, and job titles. HR classifications are used by the Projects application to determine whether an organization is valid for Projects purposes. In the integrated environment, Human Resources is impacted in cases when HR needs to know when an organization should have Projects classifications enabled. Many companies use the pay cost allocation flexfields for linking an organization in HR to the GL segment values. Your HR personnel need to be involved in these decisions because they will most likely be responsible for the setup.

When HR adds new organizations, Projects needs to be informed to ensure the proper HR classification and hierarchy setup. The new organizations must be established on the burden schedule and processes run to compile the multiplier. Job titles must be mapped to the Projects job title and set up in the respective bill rate schedules. With these integration points in mind, your organization should maintain a solid relationship with the HR team.

REPORTING

For information to be reported, it has to be in the system, consistent, and easy to retrieve. The reporting requirements should be fully considered when designing the system setup,as should how the information will flow through the system and reside. Keep in mind the key parameters your company will be reporting from. Oracle Projects offers various fields that can be considered for this purpose, such as class categories, service types, and descriptive flexfields. Standard reports do not support descriptive flexfields information or many of the standard parameter fields.

Your company should define the key reporting fields prior to making setup decisions and plan on writing custom reports through Discoverer, SQL reports, or other reporting tools. Reports are always the last activity to get attention during an implementation. Avoid the stress of missing parameters or key information required for reports by defining the requirements early to ensure that they can be properly reported for your organization.

OTHER IMPACTED APPLICATIONS

Purchasing, Payables, Receivables, Assets, and Manufacturing Modules can all be impacted with the Projects integration. Understanding the flow of information across applications will enhance your system design and setup. The project type set up determines how asset information is passed to Fixed Assets. Payables interfaces information to the Projects application, and Projects interfaces Supplier invoice adjustments to Payables. If AutoAccounting and Account Generator are not designed to produce the same results, your financial information might be misleading. The same holds true for Purchasing Account Generator. Oracle Projects receives customer information from Accounts Receivable, and customer invoices are passed from Projects to AR. If the transaction types are not set up correctly, invoices will be rejected. When looking at the entire integration, setup decisions should be based on the ability to maintain all your systems to ensure smooth integration.

BASIC SETUP TASKS

Table 15.1 shows the tasks required to configure your Oracle Projects application in the order they should be performed. Try not to skip tasks or perform them out of sequence. Many tasks use predecessor tasks for data validation, and you might receive errors if they aren't performed in sequence. After completing these steps, your application will be ready to establish projects and record costs, revenue, and invoicing transactions.

TABLE 15.1 PROJECTS SETUP TASKS

Setup Task Name	Required?
Profile Options	
PA: Licensed to Use Project Billing.	Project Billing
HR: Cross Business Group.	Yes
HR: Enable Security Groups for the Oracle Human Resources application. Required if you are using cross-business group access. DO NOT USE for single-business group access.	No
Set of Books	
Define your set of books.	Yes
Enable currencies you plan to use.	No
Human Resources	
Define locations.	Yes
Define organizations.	Yes
Define organization hierarchies.	Yes
Run Enable Multiple Security Groups. Only run this process if you are using cross-business group access mode.	No
Define security profiles (and global security profiles).	No
Specify a project burdening hierarchy for each business group.	Yes
Define job groups.	Yes
Define jobs.	Yes
Define job mapping.	No
Define employees.	Yes
Receivables	
Define customers.	Project Billing
Set up output tax codes for customer invoices.	No
Set up output tax exemptions for customer invoices.	No

Table 15.1 Continued

Setup Task Name	Required?
Implementation Options and PA Periods	
Define implementation options. ATTENTION: If you have a multiple-organization installation, you must define implementation options for each operating unit. If your system uses cross-business group access, the business group field in the Implementation Options window displays the value All.	Yes
Define PA periods. ATTENTION: If you have a multiple-organization installation, you must repeat this step for each operating unit.	Yes
Expenditure Setups	
Define expenditure categories.	Yes
Define revenue categories.	Yes
Define units.	Yes
Define descriptive flexfields.	No
Define expenditure types.	Yes
Define nonlabor resources. Required if you use usages.	No
Define transaction sources.	No
Nonlabor Costing Setup	
Define cost rates for expenditure types. ATTENTION: If you have a multiple-organization installation, you must repeat this step for each operating unit.	Yes
Define usage cost rate overrides. ATTENTION: If you have a multiple-organization installation, you must repeat this step for each operating unit.	Yes
Labor Costing Setup	
Define compensation rules.	Yes
Define employee cost rates. ATTENTION: If you have a multiple-organization installation, you must repeat this step for each operating unit.	Yes
Define labor cost multipliers.	No
Implement overtime processing.	No

TABLE 15.1 CONTINUED

Setup Task Name	Required?
Burden Costing Setup	
Define cost bases and cost base types.	No
Define burden cost codes.	No
Define burden structures.	No
Define burden schedules. ATTENTION: If you have a multiple-organization installation, you must repeat this step for each operating unit, if the new operating unit is associated with a new business group.	No
Billing Setup	
Define billing cycles.	Project Billing
Define payment terms.	No
Define agreement types.	Project Billing
Define bill rate schedules. ATTENTION: If you have a multiple-organization installation, you must repeat this step for each operating unit.	Project Billing
Define invoice formats.	Project Billing
Define credit types.	Project Billing
Define event types.	No
Budget Setup	
Define budget types.	No
Define budget entry methods.	Yes
Define budget change reasons.	No
Define resource lists. ATTENTION: If you have a multiple-organization installation, you must repeat this step for each operating unit, if the new operating unit is associated with a new business group.	Yes
Project Setup	
Define project statuses.	No
Define class categories and class codes.	No
Define service types.	Yes
Define project role types.	No
Define project customer relationships.	Yes
Define contact types.	No

Table 15.1 Continued

Setup Task Name	Required?
Project Setup	
Define probability lists.	No
Define project types. ATTENTION: If you have a multiple-organization installation, you must repeat this step for each operating unit.	Yes
Define project templates. ATTENTION: If you have a multiple-organization installation, you must repeat this step for each operating unit.	Yes
Project Status Inquiry Setup	
Define derived columns.	No
Define displayed columns.	No
General Setup	
Specify profile option values. ATTENTION: If you have a multiple-organization installation, you must repeat this step for each operating unit.	No
Define request groups for report and process security.	No
Define responsibilities for different functional users.	No
Define frequently used folders.	No
AutoAccounting for Costs	
ATTENTION: If you have a multiple-organization installation, you must repeat these steps for each operating unit. Each setup is required only if using the transaction type. For example, if you are not entering usages, you do not need to complete the Set Up Accounting for Usage Costs step. Additional information on setting up AutoAccounting is provided in the "Advanced Setup Tasks" section of this chapter. Set up accounting for labor costs.	Yes
Set up accounting for expense report costs.	Yes
Set up accounting for usage costs.	Yes
Set up accounting for miscellaneous costs.	Yes
Set up accounting for burden transactions.	Yes
Set up accounting for WIP and Inventory costs, if you are using these expenditure type classes for costs other than those originating in Oracle Manufacturing and Oracle Inventory. See Expenditure Type Classes *(Oracle Projects User Guide)*.	Yes

TABLE 15.1 CONTINUED

Setup Task Name	Required?
AutoAccounting for Costs	
Set up accounting for supplier invoice adjustment costs.	Yes
Set up accounting for total burdened costs.	No
AutoAccounting for Revenue and Billing	
ATTENTION: If you have a multiple-organization installation, you must repeat these steps for each operating unit.	
Set up accounting for labor revenue.	Project Billing
Set up accounting for expense report revenue.	Project Billing
Set up accounting for usage revenue.	Project Billing
Set up accounting for miscellaneous revenue.	Project Billing
Set up accounting for burden transactions revenue.	Project Billing
Set up accounting for inventory revenue.	Project Billing
Set up accounting for work in process revenue.	Project Billing
Set up accounting for supplier invoice revenue.	Project Billing
Set up accounting for event revenue.	Project Billing
Set up accounting for unbilled receivables, unearned revenue, and receivables.	Project Billing
Define Invoice Rounding account.	Project Billing
Set up accounting for invoice write-offs.	Project Billing
Indirect Projects	
Define indirect projects for cost collection, ATTENTION: If you have a multiple-organization installation, you must repeat this step for each operating unit.	No
Contract Projects	
Define contract projects for cost collection. ATTENTION: If you have a multiple-organization installation, you must repeat this step for each operating unit.	Project Billing
Capital Projects	
Define capital projects for cost collection. ATTENTION: If you have a multiple-organization installation, you must repeat this step for each operating unit.	No

No = Optional for both Project Costing and Billing
Yes = Required for both Project Costing and Billing
Project Billing = Required only for Project Billing

UNDERSTANDING EACH SETUP TASK

This section details each setup task in the order it should be performed.

SETTING THE PROFILE OPTION PA: LICENSED TO USE PROJECT BILLING

By default, this profile option is set to No, which means you will be using only Project Costing. You must set this flag to Yes if you will be using Oracle Projects for both costing and billing. This profile option is updateable at the site level.

SETTING THE PROFILE OPTION HR: CROSS BUSINESS GROUP

This profile defines whether single business group access or cross business group access is used in an installation. If this profile option is set to Yes, resources can charge projects belonging to other business groups. If it is set to No, only single business group access is allowed.

SETTING THE PROFILE OPTION HR: ENABLE SECURITY GROUPS

If you're using cross business group access, you must set this profile option. If your company is setting up different responsibilities to restrict access to different business groups, this profile option must be set to No. If the HR setup is securing access to information by the use of security groups, this profile option must be set to Yes.

See Chapter 23, "Implementing Oracle Human Resources and Oracle Payroll," and Chapter 24, "Using Oracle Human Resources," for more information on enabling security groups.

DEFINING YOUR SET OF BOOKS

The Projects application is a subledger to Oracle General Ledger and must be attached to a set of books. The set of books identifies a company that shares a common chart of accounts structure, calendar, and functional currency (the three C's). When you set up Oracle Projects either as a standalone installation or integrated with other Oracle applications, you need to set up one set of books for each set of projects that share a common chart of accounts, calendar, and currency. The following steps are used to define a set of books:

1. Define the Key Accounting Flexfield structure, segments, segment values, and code combinations.
2. Define the fiscal calendar period types and periods.
3. Enable currencies, and define rate types and conversion rates.
4. Create the set of books by assigning a name to a combination of the Key Accounting Flexfield, a calendar, and a currency.
5. Assign the set of books to the site or individual responsibilities.

See Chapter 11, "Using Oracle General Ledger," for more information on configuring a set of books.

ENABLING CURRENCIES YOU PLAN TO USE

When Oracle Projects is installed, it is seeded with the currency of U.S. dollars (USD). If you need to add additional currencies, you must enable them.

See Chapter 11 for more information on currency setups.

DEFINING LOCATIONS

Locations are physical addresses used to identify the location of an employee or organization used in Oracle Projects. The location window allows for several pieces of information, but you are required to provide only a name. You can use location to develop supplemental reporting out of Projects.

See Chapter 23 and Chapter 24 for more information on defining locations.

DEFINING ORGANIZATIONS

Organizations are the key to reporting and assigning ownership to both projects (or tasks) and transactions. The organization you define should match the organizations in your company organization chart. You can control the use of organizations in Projects by assigning the appropriate classifications to the organizations you define.

See Chapter 23 and Chapter 24 for more information on defining locations.

DEFINING ORGANIZATION HIERARCHIES

Organization hierarchies are used to create the relationship between all your organizations. Organization hierarchies are used for reporting and processing purposes and depict the relationship between all your organizations in hierarchical form. You can define many hierarchies and multiple versions of each to satisfy your business requirements. The organization hierarchy is defined in Oracle HR and is used by other applications. For Oracle Projects, you can define which section of the hierarchy will be used. To limit the hierarchy, you must designate the starting organization. That organization and all child organizations in that branch of the hierarchy can be used in Oracle Projects. In addition to defining a starting organization, you also must assign an organization hierarchy version in Projects for each of the following:

- Project/Task Owning Organization Hierarchy Version
- Expenditure/Event Organization Hierarchy Version
- Default Reporting Organization Hierarchy Version
- Project Burdening Hierarchy Version

You must specify each of the hierarchies to each operating unit, except for the Project Burdening Hierarchy. The Project Burdening Hierarchy is assigned to each business group you have defined.

See Chapter 23 and Chapter 24 for more information on defining locations.

Runing the Enable Multiple Security Groups Process

If you have set the profile option HR: Cross Business Group to Yes, you must run the Enable Multiple Security Groups process to ensure that all the cross business group responsibility security features are enabled.

Defining Security Profiles (and Global Security Profiles)

Setting up Security Profiles enables you to limit the view of personal or organizational information by business group. To define this option, you use the Define Security Profile window.

The steps for setting this up are

1. Set up a responsibility that will use the new profile.
2. Create the Security Profile in the Security Profile Form. In Projects, navigate to Setup, Human Resources, Security Profile.
3. Then, run the security list maintenance process from an HR responsibility.
4. Attach the responsibility to the security profile with the HR: Security Profile option.

Specifying a Project Burdening Hierarchy for Each Business Group

Oracle Projects uses the project burdening hierarchy to compile burden groups, and each business group must have only one version of the hierarchy assigned to it.

Here are the steps for setting up the project burdening hierarchy:

1. Select a Projects responsibility that has access to the Organization window for the business group for which you are entering legal entities and operating units.
2. Define the Project Burden Hierarchy using the Organization Hierarchy window.
3. Save your hierarchy version.
4. Navigate to the Define Organizations window, and query the organization you defined as a business group.
5. Click the Others button; then select Project Burdening Hierarchy from the Additional Organization Information list of values.
6. Enter an Org Hierarchy Name and Hierarchy Version Number by clicking anywhere in the Project Burdening Hierarchy field.

Defining Job Groups

Jobs are established in the HR module and assigned to employees. In many cases, these jobs do not suffice on customer invoices and different job titles are required. Job groups enable you to create different lists of jobs in which HR jobs can be mapped to Projects jobs for billing purposes. The two types of job groups are a job group and a master job group. The *master job group* is used as an intermediary mapping group to link the HR and Project jobs.

Keep in mind the master job group can't be used for a bill rate schedule. This mapping feature is explained more in the section "Defining Job Mapping."

See Chapter 23 and Chapter 24 for more information on defining locations.

DEFINING JOBS

The definition of jobs is done in HR (select Work Structure, Jobs, Description). Before you define your jobs, you must do the following as well as define the job groups:

1. Define job flexfield value sets.
2. Define job flexfield segments.
3. Define job flexfield segment values.
4. Define job titles.

See Chapter 23 and Chapter 24 for more information on defining locations.

DEFINING JOB MAPPING

After the jobs are defined, they can be mapped. This is done in the Projects application by selecting Setup, Job Mapping. Typically, the HR job group is mapped to the master job group, and the master job group is mapped to the project job group. This is done in two steps: From HR Job A to Projects Master Job B and from Projects Master Job B to Projects Job C. See Table 15.2 for a graphical explanation.

Jobs that are not master jobs can be mapped to only one master job, whereas multiple non-master jobs can be mapped to the same master job.

TABLE 15.2 DEFINING JOB MAPPING

	HR Job Group	Job Mapping	Master Projects Job Group	Job Mapping	Billing Job Group (Assigned to Bill Rate Schedule)
Job Title	Production Specialist	←	Producer	→	Program Director
	Senior Producer	←	Producer	→	Technical Producer
	Manager, Level 1	→	Project Manager	←	Production Manager
	Manager, Level 2	→	Project Manager	←	Senior Architect

DEFINING EMPLOYEES

Employees must be entered in Oracle HR if that application is installed; otherwise, Oracle Projects can be used. In either case, the setup is the same. The following information is required for defining employees in either HR or Oracle Projects:

- Last name
- First name
- Employee number
- Start date
- Organization
- Job
- Supervisor
- Billing title
- Expense address flag (home or office)

Tip

You might want to consider using the open interface provided in Oracle HRMS for loading employees into the base tables.

See Chapter 23 and Chapter 24 for more information on defining locations.

DEFINING CUSTOMERS

Customers are defined in Receivables and are used by Oracle Projects for billing purposes. The fields required by Oracle Projects are customers, customer addresses, and customer contacts. Each customer must have one primary bill-to address, one primary ship-to address, and one primary bill-to contact. The primary bill-to contact must be entered in the Primary Bill-To Contacts Role window and in the Business Purpose Details window.

Customer data can be entered into the AR application manually or through the customer application program interface (API).

See Chapter 13, "Using Oracle Receivables," for more information on defining customers.

SETTING UP OUTPUT TAX CODES FOR CUSTOMER INVOICES

Oracle Receivables supports two types of revenue-based taxes: VAT and Sales Tax. Both tax types require you to create tax codes and rates. Tax codes can be assigned to customers at all levels of address and bill-to or ship-to business purposes. A tax code can also be assigned to a product and to standard memo lines.

If your system option tax method is VAT, define a code and rate for each tax authority. Declare a default tax code in the system options setup.

See Chapter 13 for more information on defining customers.

SETTING UP OUTPUT TAX EXEMPTIONS FOR CUSTOMER INVOICES

Certain customers and items might be exempt from taxes or exempt from a percent of the tax code rate. Oracle supports exemptions by customer, item, and ranges of items. Users can choose to set up the customer or item exemption either by tax code or by location. Exemptions are entered in AR on the tax exemptions form.

Tip

If a customer, or item, is exempt from all taxes, assign a tax code with a zero rate to the appropriate customer, customer site, or item.

Note

Ensure the desired exception rates options are enabled on the AR System options form.

See Chapter 13 for more information on defining customers.

DEFINING IMPLEMENTATION OPTIONS

The implementation options determine how Oracle projects interface data between other Oracle applications. Implementation options are defined for each operating unit of your organization. The implementation options form contains several tab regions, and the fields on most of these tabs are required.

Table 15.3 highlights the information on the various tab regions.

TABLE 15.3 IMPLEMENTATION OPTIONS TAB REGIONS

Tab	Information
System	Controls the reporting requirements for the Projects application.
Currency	Identifies the functional currency being used for this operating unit.
Project Setup	Specifies which organization hierarchy will be used when assigning project and task ownership and also specifies whether projects will be numbered manually or automatically.
Expnd/Costing	Sets the start day for your expenditure cycle and identifies which expenditures originating in projects will be interfaced to the GL. Identifies the organization hierarchy used to assign ownership of expenditure items in Oracle Projects.
Billing	Controls whether revenue transactions will be posted to the GL as well as the invoice numbering method to be used. Tax defaults are used to determine the output tax for each line on an invoice. You can choose where and how the application will receive the default tax information.
Cross Charge	Used to enable charging to projects owned by different organizations within an operating unit or outside an operating unit.
Internal Billing	Defines internal customers and vendors for interproject or intercompany billings. This tab is optional and used only when you plan to use interproject or intercompany billings.

Defining PA Periods

PA periods are used to track and summarize project transactions and to perform time-phased budgeting. You can set your PA periods to increments of time that are less than your GL periods. You also can define PA periods that span more than one GL period or do not correspond to the last day or cutoff for your GL periods. It is highly recommended that your PA periods have end dates that match the end dates of the GL periods. This makes reconciling your Projects subledger with GL easier.

PA periods can be set to one of the following statuses:

- Never Opened
- Future
- Open
- Pending Close
- Closed
- Permanently Closed

For projects to accept and process transactions, you must have at least one period marked as Open or Future.

Defining Expenditure Categories

Expenditure categories are generally rollups of your expenditure types. They can be used for AutoAccounting your transactions, budgeting, and controlling transactions being charged to a project or task.

Defining Revenue Categories

Revenue categories are rollups of your expenditure types and expenditure categories and are mostly used for reporting purposes. They can also be used for AutoAccounting transactions and project budgeting.

Defining Units

Units are the units of measure for a particular expenditure item. Oracle has predefined Hours and Currency as units, but you can add as many units as necessary to assist in the description of an expenditure item. Some of the more common units of measure besides the predefined two are Tests, Miles, and Each.

Defining Descriptive Flexfields

Descriptive flexfields can be defined and used as a quick and easy way to tailor your application to better fit your business practices. Examples of uses for descriptive flexfields would be to further categorize expenditure items or record pertinent information on projects.

Context-sensitive descriptive flexfields can also be created that prompt you to enter another field of information based on what you entered in your initial flexfield.

DEFINING EXPENDITURE TYPES

Expenditure types are central to the Projects application and provide essential information for both internal reporting and postings to the GL, but also project reporting and billing. You should consider how you will reconcile your projects application to the GL before creating your expenditure types. Expenditure types are assigned a unit of measure, an expenditure category, a revenue category, and at least one expenditure type class. When entering expenditures, you always assign it an expenditure type.

The ability to assign more than one expenditure type class to an expenditure type enables you to use the same expenditure type with several transaction sources or origins. You might enter employee expense reports using self-service applications, but from time to time you might enter them as supplier invoices. This can be accomplished by assigning your travel-related expenditure types to both classes.

DEFINING NONLABOR RESOURCES

Nonlabor resources or usages are uses of assets that are charged and possibly billed to a project. Usages are assigned to an expenditure type that has a Usage expenditure type class. When you define a nonlabor resource, you must assign at least one organization to it. Examples of a nonlabor resource are mileage or computer usage.

DEFINING TRANSACTION SOURCES

Transaction sources are used when importing external data into Projects via Transaction Import. Some of the sources are seeded, whereas others can be defined, but the user is allowed to control the way the data is imported by setting the following attributes: Default Expenditure Type Class, Raw Cost GL Accounted, Import Raw Cost Amounts, Import Burdened Amounts, Import MRC Amounts, Allow Duplicate Reference, Import Employee Organization, Allow Interface Modifications, Purge After Import, Allow Reversals, Allow Adjustments, Process Cross Charge, Pre-Processing Extension, and Post-Processing Extension.

DEFINING COST RATES FOR EXPENDITURE TYPES

You can define cost rates for expenditure types; however, this is not mandatory. If you do want to implement this option, you must make sure the Rate Required box is checked.

> **Note**
>
> If you plan to assign cost rates to usages, you must check this box upon entry because it can't be changed after the expenditure type is set up.

DEFINING USAGE COST RATE OVERRIDES

You can assign a cost rate at the expenditure type level, or you can assign an override at the nonlabor resource level. Assigning the cost to the nonlabor resource is done by organization and overrides the cost rate at the expenditure type level.

Defining Compensation Rules

Compensation rules replicate the pay types your company uses. Examples of compensation rules are exempt and nonexempt, and they define how an employee is paid.

Defining Labor Cost Multipliers

Labor cost multipliers are used to calculate premium overtime rates. An example would be to define an overtime rate of .5 to calculate the premium on time-and-a-half.

Implementing Overtime Processing

If your company has specific overtime calculation policies, the overtime calculation extension enables you to calculate them as they are defined by your business. They can also be transferred to indirect projects.

Defining Cost Bases and Cost Base Types

Cost bases are the mechanism used for grouping raw costs when performing burden calculations. Two cost base types are used when setting up your system for burdening. Burden Cost types are used in the actual burden cost calculations, whereas Other types are used specifically for the grouping of expenditure types (that is, billing extension calculations and reporting).

Defining Burden Cost Codes

Burden cost codes represent the type of recovery burdens you want applied to the organization's raw expenditures. Expenditure types can be assigned to the Burden codes if your organization project-type setup uses the option to account for burden components separately or create separate burden expenditure items.

Defining Burden Structures

The burden structure is the mechanism to link a burden cost code with a burden cost base. After the burden cost codes are linked to the base, you assign expenditure types whose associated expenditure items should be burdened. An expenditure type can be assigned to only one cost base, and if it's not assigned, it will not be burdened. A structure might contain one or all of your cost bases. Depending on the business requirement, your organization might build many burden structures because they can be used differently for project class, organization, costing, or billing purposes.

Burden structures determine whether your burden process should be precedence or additive. *Precedence* burdens and builds your cost base amount from lowest to highest order. *Additive* calculates the burden amount for each cost code based on the raw cost.

Defining Burden Schedules

The burden schedule defines the multiplier rates to be applied to your organization and burden cost code. If your multipliers are built at the highest level of your organization, all of your organizations will be burdened with these rates. The burden logic first looks at the organization level of the expenditure and proceeds up the project burden hierarchy until it finds the burden multipliers. The schedule contains versions, so your organization could have rate changes on a periodic basis.

Note

If you end date a version and start another, the rate changes on the new version apply only to expenditure items within the date range of the version.

Burden schedules are either Firm or Provisional. *Firm* schedules are set and do not anticipate changes for a given period. *Provisional* schedules are normally an estimate and after review are modified to actual burden multiplier rates for reburden adjustments. The start organization of the burden schedule identifies the top level and burdens that organization plus all organizations in the project burden hierarchy that fall below the start organization.

DEFINING BILLING CYCLES

You define a billing cycle to determine and control how invoices are processed. Billing cycles are assigned to contract projects and might be considered during the invoicing process.

DEFINING PAYMENT TERMS

Payment terms are assigned to agreements when you fund a contract project and are used in the invoicing process. They typically are maintained in Receivables and Payables. AR provides two seeded payment terms: 30 Net and Immediate. If you need other terms or offer cash discounts, use the Define Payment Terms form in Oracle Projects to add other choices.

DEFINING AGREEMENT TYPES

Agreement types are used to categorize the various types of contracts you might use when you fund a project. When you enter an agreement type, you have the option of setting a default revenue limit. If you set a hard limit, you will not be able to bill or recognize revenue past the agreement amount.

DEFINING BILL RATE SCHEDULES

Bill rate schedules are set up to account for bill rates or percentage markups on costs in conjunction with billing. They are used for labor and nonlabor items. If you choose a labor schedule type, you can set rates by employee or job. If you use nonlabor, on the other hand, you can enter rates or percentages by nonlabor expenditure items. You can enter as many bill rate schedules as you like, and they are categorized by organization. After they are defined, they can be assigned to the project or task level.

DEFINING INVOICE FORMATS

Invoice formats are defined so that you can control how expenditure lines are summarized on an invoice. You can assign three types of formats: labor, nonlabor, and retention. After they are defined you can attach the invoice formats to your projects to use during the billing process.

DEFINING CREDIT TYPES

Credit types are categorizations that can be defined to recognize employees for revenue. After the credit types are defined, you can assign an employee to a credit type on a project or task level.

DEFINING EVENT TYPES

An event type is a revenue-generating or billing entry that is unrelated to an expenditure item. An event type is assigned to a revenue category and can be classified in one of the following ways:

- **Automatic**—This type of event is automatically created during the invoice or revenue generation if a billing extension is in place.
- **Deferred Revenue**—An invoice-generating event that does not affect revenue.
- **Invoice Reduction**—Reduces an invoice amount without affecting revenue.

Note

An Invoice Reduction entry is entered as a positive number, although it reduces the invoice amount.

- **Manual**—This event can affect revenue or invoice amounts based on the numbers you use.

Note

You can enter different amounts for revenue and invoice if needed.

- **Scheduled Payment**—When you enter a scheduled payment event, it processes the existing expenditure items in chronological order to account for the event amount. This affects invoices only and enables the expenditure detail to be shown on the invoice.

Note

Scheduled Payments are used only for event-based billing.

- **Write-On**—A Write-On event generates a revenue entry for the amount entered and automatically enters the same amount as a corresponding invoice event. With a write-on, the revenue and invoice amount always are equal.
- **Write-Off**—Same as Write-On, but it reduces only the revenue amount. An invoice write-off is entered on the invoice review form.

Note

You enter a positive number in the same way that you do with an invoice reduction.

DEFINING BUDGET TYPES

Budget types enable you to classify budgets, which can be set up for both revenue and cost budgets. Oracle Projects is installed with four seeded budget types: Approved Cost Budget, Approved Revenue Budget, Forecast Cost Budget, and Forecast Revenue Budget. You can add to these values as well as inactivate the types you will not use.

DEFINING BUDGET ENTRY METHODS

Budget entry methods define how you enter the detailed budget information. You can choose an entry level of Project, Top Tasks, Lowest Tasks, or Top and Lowest Tasks. You can categorize the budget by resource (labor or expense), and you can organize the budget by time phase: GL Period, PA Period, Date Range, or None. For cost budgets you can enter quantity, raw cost, or burdened cost detail; for revenue budgets you can enter quantity or revenue values. All these parameters are set when you set up the budget entry methods.

DEFINING BUDGET CHANGE REASONS

When you modify a budget, you can assign a reason for the change. Budget Change reasons are text values that enable you to classify changes in the budget.

DEFINING RESOURCE LISTS

Resource lists are used for budgeting and summarization of actuals for reporting (that is, Project Status Inquiry [PSI]) in Oracle Projects. You can enter resources on two levels. The top level enables you to group resources by revenue category, expenditure category, or organization. The second level enables you to budget or report in more detail by resource (for example, employee, job, or expenditure type). An example would be to group resources by revenue categories of labor, with a detail level by employee or nonlabor, with the ability to drill down to expenditure type detail.

DEFINING PROJECT STATUSES

Project statuses must be assigned to every project to represent the phase of the project. When defining project statuses, you can limit what is processed on a project. The actions you can control are Create New Transactions, Adjust Transactions, Generate Revenue, Generate Invoice, Capitalize Assets, Include in Status Reports, Change Project Probability, and Assign Resources to the Project. The seeded statuses are Unapproved, Submitted, Approved, Rejected, Pending Close, and Closed. These statuses have different settings for controlling the actions and can be used as a base to set up additional project statuses. They can also be deactivated if they are not needed.

DEFINING CLASS CATEGORIES AND CLASS CODES

Class categories enable you to set up a heading (class category) and assign various values (class codes) to the category. An example is a class category of Industry Sector with class codes of High Tech, Transportation, Retail, and so on. You can assign these classifications to projects for use in reporting and can use one classification in your AutoAccounting.

DEFINING SERVICE TYPES

Service types are used to classify your tasks on a project. They can be derived from the project type and are used for reporting and AutoAccounting.

DEFINING PROJECT ROLE TYPES

Project role types are used in the Key Members section of the Project setup. Project Manager is seeded with Oracle Projects. When you define additional project role types, you can also control who can view labor cost data as well as update a project.

DEFINING PROJECT CUSTOMER RELATIONSHIPS

Project customer relationship types explain the relationship a customer has with a project. This is especially helpful when you have more than one customer on a project. Examples of a project customer relationship would be Primary Customer, Secondary Customer, and so on.

DEFINING CONTACT TYPES

Contact types are assigned to individuals on the customer's side who are somehow involved with a project. An example of a customer contact would be defining a Payables contact for invoice purposes. When you assign a customer to a contract project, the billing contact type is required before you can bill.

DEFINING PROBABILITY LISTS

You can define Probability values based on how your company tracks the probability of gaining a project. They are defined as a percentage (for example, 100% Guaranteed, 20% Slim to None, and so on).

DEFINING PROJECT TYPES

The project type is used when projects are created and processed and is also used as a method of classifying your projects. You can define project types with a class of indirect (nonbillable), capital, or contract (billable). When you define project types the information that is required changes based on the project class. For example, when defining a project type with a contract classification, you are required to enter billing information. This is not required for an indirect project type. Project types are used in project templates and predefine several settings and parameters when creating projects.

DEFINING PROJECT TEMPLATES

Project templates are used in project creation and populate several general settings for a new project. You can also define the quick entry fields that enable you to populate additional parameters specific to the project you are creating.

DEFINING DERIVED COLUMNS

A derived column is a PSI column whose value is calculated using a PSI extension that involves one or more SQL statements. These columns are maintained in Oracle Projects at Setup, Project Status Columns.

DEFINING DISPLAYED COLUMNS

PSI is seeded with a default configuration view for the Project, Task, and Resource Status windows. You can add, change, delete, or use the defaults as is. PSI allows for a maximum of 33 columns: 3 text columns for descriptions or comments and 30 numeric columns for ratios, percentages, and amounts. You can use some or all of these available columns.

SPECIFYING PROFILE OPTION VALUES

Profile options are set up by your system administrator to specify default values that affect system processes, system controls, and data entry.

In a multiple-organization environment, you can set up profile options at the responsibility level to control functionality by organization. The profiles to consider are

- PA: Cross-Project Responsibility
- PA: Debug Mode
- PA: Default Expenditure Organization in AP/PO
- PA: Default Public Sector

DEFINING REQUEST GROUPS FOR REPORT AND PROCESS SECURITY

A request group is used at the responsibility level and form level. When it is defined at the responsibility level, it governs what a user operating under that responsibility can select in regards to reporting, request sets, and concurrent programs when operating in the Submit Requests window.

DEFINING RESPONSIBILITIES FOR DIFFERENT FUNCTIONAL USERS

You can create unique responsibilities for your users to limit which menus they can access and which functions they can perform.

DEFINING FREQUENTLY USED FOLDERS

Oracle enables the user to customize her view of frequently used forms. The following windows in Oracle Projects are folder enabled:

- Event Entry and Inquiry
- Expenditure Inquiry
- Expenditure Inquiry Across Projects

- Expenditure Items
- Expenditure Items Across Projects
- Invoice Summary
- Project Status Inquiry
- Projects, Templates Summary
- Review Transactions

Setting Up AutoAccounting

In Oracle Projects, AutoAccounting is used to create accounting transactions at the time that transactions are processed. When these processes are run, AutoAccounting automatically determines the accounting based on the rules you define in your AutoAccounting setup. The following account rules can be assigned:

- Labor Cost Account
- Labor Cost Clearing Account
- Expense Report Cost Account
- Expense Report Liability Account
- Usage Cost Account
- Usage Cost Clearing Account
- Miscellaneous Transaction Cost Account
- Miscellaneous Transaction Clearing Account
- Burden Cost Account
- Burden Cost Clearing Account
- Supplier Invoice Cost Account
- Total Burdened Cost Debit
- Total Burdened Cost Credit
- Labor Revenue Account
- Expense Report Revenue Account
- Usage Revenue Account
- Miscellaneous Transaction Revenue Account
- Burden Cost Revenue Account
- Supplier Invoice Revenue Account
- Event Revenue Account
- Revenue and Invoice Accounts (Receivable Account, Unbilled Receivable Account, Unearned Revenue Account, Rounding Account)
- Borrowed Account
- Lent Account

- Usage Revenue Borrowed Account
- Usage Revenue Lent Account
- Labor Revenue Borrowed Account
- Labor Revenue Lent Account
- Intercompany Invoice Account
- Intercompany Revenue Account
- Provider Cost Reclass Credit Account
- Provider Cost Reclass Debit Account

To set up AutoAccounting, you must define lookup sets, define AutoAccounting rules, and assign AutoAccounting rules. See the section "Setting Up AutoAccounting," later in this chapter, for further information on setting up AutoAccounting.

DEFINING INDIRECT PROJECTS FOR COST COLLECTION

You can define as many indirect projects as you need to record various indirect costs. Indirect class projects can serve many purposes for your company, including the monitoring and tracking of Sales and Marketing, Proposal, Equipment Purchases, Training, Company Initiative, and Administrative expenses. Use the Indirect Project as an extension to the information that is tracked in your General Ledger. For instance, say the IT department budgets one amount for training in the General Ledger budget. In Projects, multiple projects or tasks could be established to track different areas of training for this department. An ERP project is another example of tracking and reporting initiatives throughout the organization that are not tracked in your General Ledger. Using the indirect project enables your organization to burden company costs that are not related to a contract or customer project.

DEFINING CONTRACT PROJECTS FOR COST COLLECTION

This section is designed to guide you through the steps of setting up a contract project.

CREATING A PROJECT TYPE USING THE CLASS CONTRACT To establish a contract to project, you first must create a project type that has the class distinction of contract. Oracle refers to this class of project as Direct in many tables and references. The setup for your project type requires additional invoice and revenue information defined for this class of projects as seen in Figure 15.7. The key regions on the Project Type Setup form are to define the billing information, billing assignments, and distribution rules:

- **Billing Information**—On this form, you define the default billing job group, funding level (task, project, or both), labor and nonlabor bill rate schedules, invoice formats, and invoice cycles.
- **Billing Assignments**—This is used to assign billing client extensions that are specific to this project type.
- **Distribution Rules**—Distribution rules are the mechanism that distinguishes how revenue and invoices should be calculated for your project. The first portion of the rule defines the revenue calculation, whereas the second defines the invoice. Your

project type should have a default distribution rule and can allow all rules enabled or limited. The various types of rules are Work (bill or accrue based on charged expenditures), Cost (bill or accrue based on a calculation), and Event (bill or accrue based on entered milestone).

In addition to the billing information, your costing information defines whether you will be burdening the project, the default burden schedule, and how you will be burdening (same expenditure item, separate expenditure item, or component). Budget control distinguishes the Cost Budget Entry Method, the Revenue Budget Entry Method, and the default resource list for reporting.

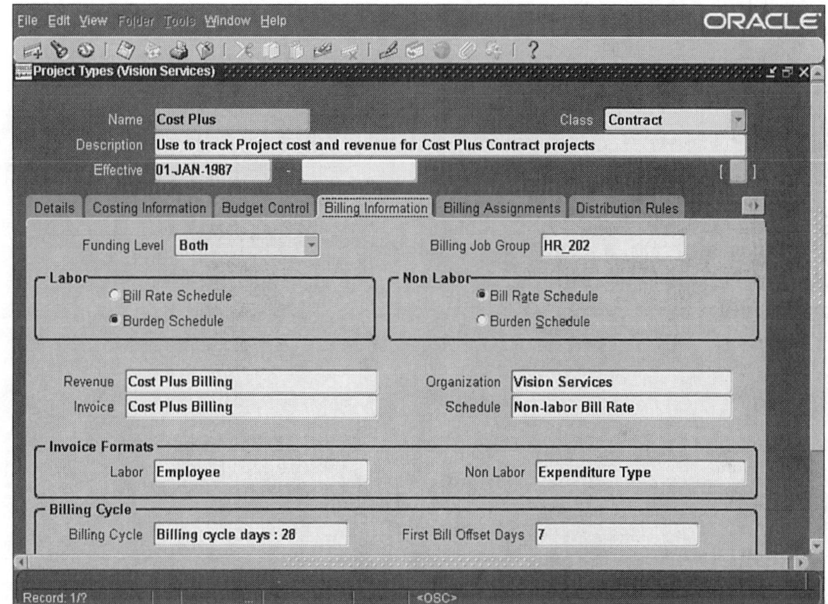

Figure 15.7
Additional revenue and invoicing information is entered for contract project types.

CREATING A PROJECT TEMPLATE USING A CONTRACT PROJECT TYPE After you create a contract project type, you can create project templates. Each of your templates could be designed for a specific distribution rule, burden schedule, or bill rate schedule. Some project users create templates for specific customers or business areas. After the template is created, you can copy it to a project.

CREATING A CONTRACT PROJECT USING A CONTRACT PROJECT TEMPLATE After you create a project template for your contract project, copy the template to a project, proceed with the standard setup, and approve the project. For a contract project, the following items must be entered prior to approving the project:

- **Customer**—Enter your customer information, including the following information:
  - **Address, customer relationship, and contacts**—To generate a bill for a client, a billing contact type must be defined.

  - **Contribution Percentage**—The contribution percentage for each project must equal 100%.
  - **Bill Another Project**—This field is used to identify the project that will be billed when using the Inter-Project Billing feature.
  - **Invoice Currency**—Defines currency information that is used to bill your client. The system defaults to the operating unit functional currency.
- **Project Manager**—Each contract project must have a Key Member type of Project Manager for the project to be approved.

Figure 15.8 shows an example of the information you enter in the Customers and Contacts window.

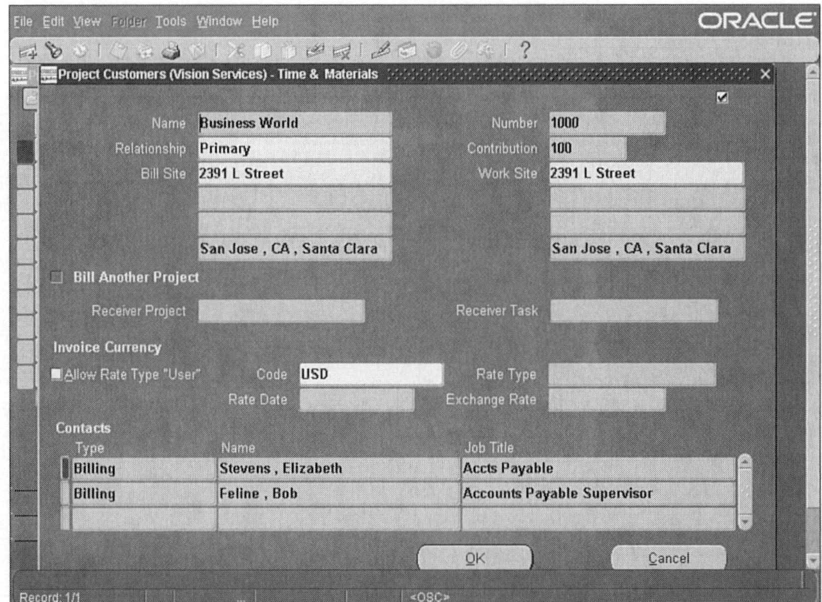

Figure 15.8
Customer and contact information is entered for contract projects.

Your project is now ready for approval, but you might have changes that should be applied to this project from the template or project you copied. On each project and task is the ability to set up burden schedule overrides and bill rate overrides (including employee/job bill rates) and to change the billing schedule that defaulted from the template.

Note

If you modify a bill rate schedule or burden schedule override at the Project level after creating tasks, the change does not cascade down to existing tasks. For the change to be effective at the task level, it must also be made at the task.

APPLYING PROJECT VERSUS TASK OVERRIDES The following logic is used by the Projects application when applying overrides at the project versus task levels:

1. A Bill Rate Override at the task level supersedes the Bill Rate Override at the project level if both the task and project contain overrides.

   Example: On the project, a job bill rate override for Software Engineer is $250. The task level contains a job bill rate override of $325. The system uses $325 to calculate revenue and invoice amounts.

2. If no Bill Rate Override is at the task level, the calculation is taken at the project level.

   Example: Susan Smith has an employee bill rate override at the project level of $350. No overrides exist at the task level. The system therefore uses $350 to calculate revenue and invoice amounts.

Note

> An employee bill rate override always takes precedence over a job bill rate override that has been entered at the project or task level.
>
> For example, Susan Smith has an employee bill rate override at the project level of $350. Susan's job title of Software Engineer has a job bill rate override at the task level of $325. The system uses $350 to calculate revenue and invoice amounts. If the overrides were reversed (and the employee bill rate override was at the task level), the system would still use the employee bill rate override ($350).

3. A discount % at the task level supersedes the discount % at the project level.

   Example: The project discount has a discount rate of 15%, and the task level is null. The system will not use any discount percentage when calculating revenue and invoices. In the same example, task now has a discount of 50% (travel hours). The system therefore uses a discount rate of 50% for this task revenue and invoice calculations.

4. A bill rate override at the task or project level supersedes a discount % at the project and task levels.

   Example: Susan Smith has an employee bill rate override at the project level of $350. Both the project and task levels have a discount of 20%. The system uses $350 to calculate revenue and invoice amounts.

5. Modifications at the project level do not cascade down to the existing tasks.

   For example, the existing tasks contain a discount of 10%. If the project level is modified so the discount is 20%, the system continues to use 10% on existing tasks. To correct this, the new discount % must be entered for every impacted task.

FIXED DATES ON BILL RATE SCHEDULES The ability to enter a fixed date is available at the project and task levels on your bill rate schedule. The purpose for this is that when a bill rate schedule is modified with rate changes that your project or task is using, you can lock in a fixed date for the revenue and invoice calculations.

For example, say your company modifies the standard bill rate schedule with a general rate increase of 15%, effective March 1, 2001. A majority of projects currently using this bill rate schedule are locked into the bill rates that were effective on January 31.

Project A is restricted to use the rates effective on January 1, and Project B is allowed to incur rate increases. The effective rate for a software engineer on January 31 is $225, but on March 1 it increases to $232.

Table 15.4 shows the resulting rate that is used.

TABLE 15.4 FIXED DATES ON BILL RATE SCHEDULES

Project	Fixed Date	Expenditure Item Date	Rate Used
A	January 31	February 5	$225
B	N/A	February 5	$225
A	January 31	March 3	$225
B	N/A	March 3	$232

DEFINING CAPITAL PROJECTS FOR COST COLLECTION

This section is designed to guide you through the steps of setting up a capital project, generating an asset, and interfacing the asset to Fixed Assets.

CREATING A PROJECT TYPE USING THE CLASS CAPITAL To establish a capital project, you first must create a project type that has the class distinction of capital. The setup for your project type requires additional capitalization information defined for this class of projects. The key fields are to define the cost type to use for creating the asset (burdened or raw) and whether your asset requires a complete definition prior to interfacing to Fixed Assets.

The grouping rules, as shown in Figure 15.9, define how to group expenditures for an asset and interface these groupings as separate lines to the Mass Additions Table. A check box is available that enables you to send supplier invoice distribution lines separately to assist you in splitting equipment purchases in mass additions.

CREATE A PROJECT TEMPLATE USING A CAPITAL PROJECT TYPE After you create a capital project type, you can create project templates using the project type—proceed with the standard setup for the project template. You might want to set up default asset information on your template in the Asset Options section.

CREATE A CAPITAL PROJECT USING A CAPITAL PROJECT TEMPLATE After you create a project template for your capital project, copy the template to a chargeable project and proceed with the standard setup and approve the project.

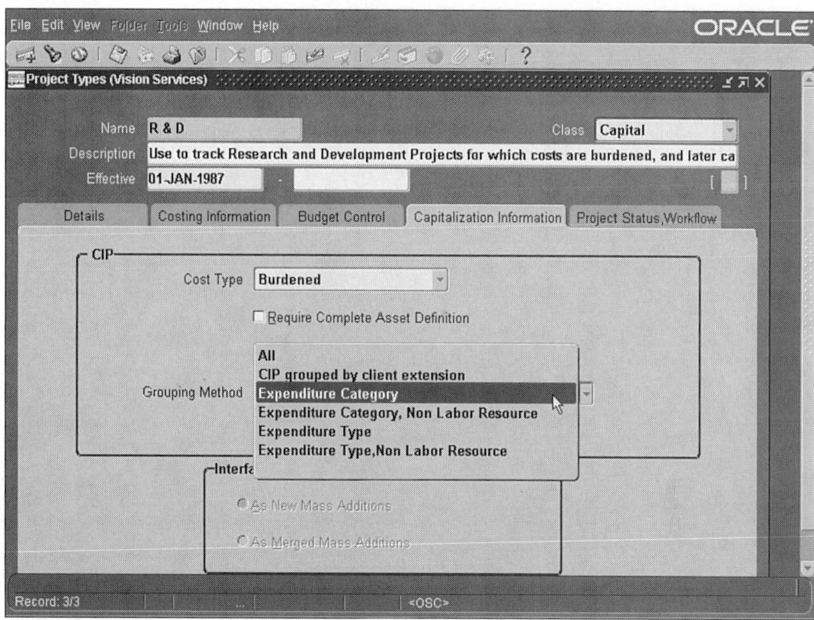

Figure 15.9
You can select a grouping rule to create and interface separate asset lines to Fixed Assets.

DEFINE AN ASSET ON A CAPITAL PROJECT Enter the necessary asset information, such as Asset Name, Estimated In Service Date, Description, Asset Category, Book, Location (can also be populated in Oracle Assets), Units, Employee Name (not required), Depreciate Flag, Amortize Adjustments Flag, Asset Key, and Depreciation Account (Asset Key and Depreciation Account can also be populated in Oracle Assets). When complete, save the asset. Figure 15.10 illustrates the type of information to be entered for assets on a project.

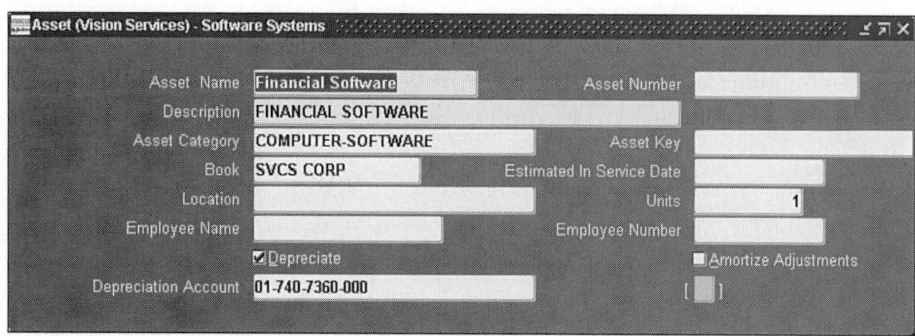

Figure 15.10
Define asset information on your capital projects.

To assign the asset to the project, select the Asset Assignments option. Assign the appropriate assets by clicking the list of values (for some companies there should be only one asset assigned per project).

Note

Assets can be assigned at the task level for a specific project. If you assign assets at the task level, you can't assign them at the project level.

Set the grouping level as shown in Figure 15.11 for the asset as Specific Assets; then, save the record when finished.

Figure 15.11
Set the grouping level for the asset.

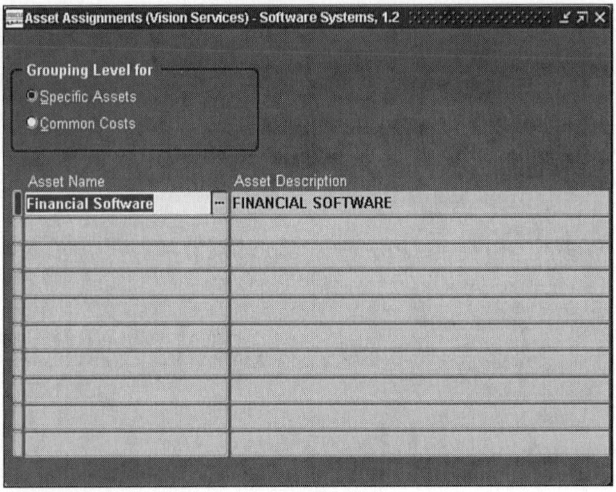

ENABLING ORACLE INTERNET TIME

To set up Oracle Internet Time, follow these steps:

1. Enter Employees. If you are using HR, make sure this has been done before proceeding to the next step. If you are not using HR, this needs to be done in Oracle Projects.
2. Verify that the Timecards responsibility is present using the System Administrator responsibility. You can create a modified responsibility from this original Timecards responsibility to control further access.
3. Assign the Timecards responsibility to every user you want to be able to enter time in Internet Time (see the subsequent steps).
4. Using the System Administrator responsibility, navigate to the Users window, and query the employee using the User Name field.
5. Click the Responsibilities tab, and then assign the Timecards responsibility. The Timecards responsibility gives the user the ability to access timecards.
6. Assign the Workflow responsibility to the employee if you will be using the approval process. The Workflow responsibility gives the user the ability to view notifications and view progress of workflow.
7. Click the Securing Attributes tab, and verify that a line is populated with the `ICX_HR_PERSON_ID` in the Attribute field along with an employee number.
8. Set the profile options. The Internet Time profile options begin with PA, ICX, or MO.

The following Profile options can be set at the user or site level and are required:

- ICX: Date Format Mask
- ICX: Language
- ICX: Limit Connect: User, Site - Required
- ICX: Limit Session Time
- PA Time: Licensed—Must be set to Yes to use Internet Time (site level only)

The following profile options are optional and can be set according to your business's needs (see the *Internet Time User's Guide* for more information):

- PA: Override Approver
- PA Time: Allow Entry of Negative Hours
- PA Time: Timecard Number Prefix
- PA Time: Enable Business Message
- PA: AutoApprove Timesheets
- MO: Operating Unit

To assign users the authority to enter timecards for other employees, follow these steps:

1. Using the System Administrator responsibility, navigate to the Users window, and query the employee using the User Name field.
2. Click the Securing Attributes tab, and enter a line with the ICX_HR_PERSON_ID attribute for every employee the authorized delegate can enter timecards for. Use the list of values in the Value field to select the Person ID.

Tip

You must assign each employee some variation of the Timecards responsibility if he is to have a timecard entered for him—even if he will not access the system. If you do not, you will receive an error. You can, however, place an end date in the effective dates section of the user definition, if you need to restrict use of the system.

ADVANCED CONFIGURATION TASKS AND EXTENSIONS

This section offers more advanced setup steps that take advantage of additional functionality, enhancing the capabilities within Oracle Projects as well as the integrated applications.

ORACLE PROJECTS ADVANCED CONFIGURATION TASKS

After you have the Basic Setup Steps complete, there are several more setup steps (some required, some optional) that might need to be completed. These steps are more involved than the Basic Steps and are explained in the following section.

SETTING UP AUTOACCOUNTING

In Oracle Projects, AutoAccounting is used to create many accounting transactions for Costing, Revenue, and Billing. Your AutoAccounting setup controls how the value of each General Ledger accounting flexfield segment is populated. For each GL segment, you can determine the segment value by identifying a constant. Conversely, you can determine the value by using an intermediate value either for a parameter rule lookup (lookup sets) or for deriving the segment value through a SQL statement. Various Oracle Projects processes generate the debit side of the transaction (distribute or generate processes), whereas other processes generate the credit side (interface processes).

For example, the process Distribute Labor Cost generates the debit side of the labor transaction, whereas the process Interface Labor to General Ledger generates the credit side of the labor transaction.

Note

In the multiple-organization environment, AutoAccounting is defined for each operating unit.

Caution

Not all intermediate parameters are available for each AutoAccounting process. However, the form enables you to select any intermediate parameter when setting up your rules. Assigning an inappropriate intermediate parameter results in a `PA||AA||No Rule Param||` error when processing is run. By running the standard report: IMP: AutoAccounting Functions, you can get a list of intermediate parameter values that are acceptable for each process.

EXAMPLE OF SETTING UP AUTOACCOUNTING For this example, it is assumed that the GL Account Flexfield is defined as Company, Department, and Account. Using this as a base, you will see how to use AutoAccounting options so that Company is a constant, Department is derived from a list of values based on Expenditure Organization (lookup set), and Account is based on Expenditure Type (Descriptive Flexfield: Attribute 1).

DEFINING A RULE TO DETERMINE THE COMPANY USING A CONSTANT In this example, you define an AutoAccounting rule that assigns a constant value to the company segment.

From the Oracle Navigator, select Setup, AutoAccounting, Rules.

For this example, enter the following information into the specified fields:

Name:	AA Company
Description:	Company Code
Intermediate Value Source:	Constant
Constant:	01
Segment Value Source:	Intermediate Value

DEFINING A LOOKUP SET TO DETERMINE THE DEPARTMENT FROM AN INTERMEDIATE VALUE
In this example, you define a lookup set that is used by an AutoAccounting rule to derive the Department segment.

From the Oracle Navigator, select Setup, AutoAccounting, Lookup Sets.

For this example, enter the following information into the specified fields:

Name:	AA LOV DEPARTMENT
Description:	Map the expenditure organization to department

Next, define the segment value lookups by entering expenditure organizations and their associated segment values. Enter the cross-reference information in the lookup set as shown here:

Intermediate Value (Exp. Org.)	Segment Value (Department)
Administration	001
Marketing	002
R&D	003

Tip

You can replace the Lookup Set (as described previously) by using a descriptive flexfield of the Intermediate value. The benefits to this method are as follows:

- An attribute is attached to a field in the application, and you can enforce population of the value prior to saving the record.
- The values to be populated can be linked directly to the GL account segment values, and the user can select only a valid value.
- Lookup tables in Oracle Projects no longer have to be set up, thus eliminating the requirement of duplicate/triplicate entry and the ability of keying in mistakes.

DEFINING A RULE TO DETERMINE THE DEPARTMENT USING AN INTERMEDIATE PARAMETER AND LOOKUP SET In this example, you define an AutoAccounting rule to derive the Department segment using the previously defined lookup set.

From the Oracle Navigator, select Setup, AutoAccounting, Rules.

For this example, enter the following information in the specified fields:

Name:	AA Department
Description:	Department Code
Intermediate Value Source:	Parameter
Parameter Name:	Expenditure Organization Name
Segment Value Source:	Segment Value Lookup Set
Lookup Set:	AA LOV DEPARTMENT

Note

The previous rule is to illustrate using a parameter associated with a rule. The recommended approach when identifying values associated with organizations is to set up the pay cost allocation key flexfields and map GL segment values to your organization. Using this simple SQL, the following department values could be determined (segment2 = department):

Intermediate Value Source: SQL Statement

SQL:

```
SELECT
      ckf.segment2
  FROMpay_cost_allocation_keyflex ckf,
       hr_organization_units o
     WHERE
         ckf.cost_allocation_keyflex_id =
➥o.cost_allocation_keyflex_id
     and o.organization_id           = :1
```

Rule Parameters:

1. Expenditure Organization ID

DEFINING A RULE TO DETERMINE THE ACCOUNT USING A SQL STATEMENT In this example, you define an AutoAccounting rule to derive the Account segment using intermediate parameters and SQL statements.

From the Oracle Navigator, select Setup, AutoAccounting, Rules.

For this example, enter the following information in the specified fields:

Name:	AA Account
Description:	Account Code
Intermediate Value Source:	SQL Statement

SQL Select Statement:	`Select attribute1`
	`from pa_expenditure_types`
	`where expenditure_type = :1`

For the rule parameters, enter the following information:

Sequence:	1
Parameter Name:	Expenditure Type

Note

You need to set up a descriptive flexfield (DFF) on the Pa_expenditure_types table that holds the account value. When setting up the DFF, the values set can be the GL account value set, requiring the user to select a valid value.

Now that you have set up your rules, you can proceed to the assignment section and assign your rules to your functions. Enable the All Supplier Invoices Transaction and Assign Rules:

From the Oracle Navigator, select Setup, AutoAccounting, Rules.

For this example, enter the following information in the specified fields:

Function Name:	Supplier Invoice Cost Account
Transaction Name:	All Supplier Invoices

In the Segment Rule Pairings, enter the following:

Number	Segment Name	Rule Name
0	Company	AA Company
1	Department	AA Department
2	Account	AA Account

Account Generator

Oracle Payables and Oracle Purchasing use Account Generator to define the accounting transactions related to projects. Account Generator uses external client-side software (Workflow Builder) to define these accounting transactions. Project Supplier Invoice Account, Project Expense Report Account, Purchase Order Charge Account, and Requisition Charge Account are examples in which Account Generator derives the GL Accounting Flexfield.

Note

In a multiple-organization environment the Account Generator workflow is shared across operating units.

Tip

Any lookup set defined in Oracle Projects can be used in Workflow Builder to determine an account value.

Segment values for the GL Accounting Flexfield derived by Account Generator can be constants, values from a lookup set, or values derived through a SQL statement to derive the GL Accounting Flexfield. If a SQL statement is used to determine your account segment value, you must register this as a stored procedure that the workflow will call when determining the account.

Note

When setting up your workflow, you set up one step to derive the segment value. However, you also must set up a second step that assigns that value to the appropriate segment.

EXAMPLE OF SETTING UP ACCOUNT GENERATOR This example of setting up Account Generator assumes that the GL Account Flexfield is defined as Company, Department, and Account. In this example, you use Account Generator to derive the GL Account Flexfield such that Company is a constant, Department is derived from a list of values based on the expenditure organization (lookup set), and Account is based on the expenditure type (descriptive flexfield: Attribute 1).

The following example provides the basic setup of the rules mentioned previously in Account Generator. It uses the lookup set defined in the AutoAccounting example for deriving the department segment.

STARTING A BASIC WORKFLOW FOR PROJECT SUPPLIER INVOICE ACCOUNT GENERATION The first step in setting up Account Generator is to open the default workflow provided by Oracle or create a new workflow for the Project Supplier Invoice Account Generation. This workflow should include the following nodes:

- **Node 1 - Start Generating Code Combination**—This standard activity node starts the process.
- **Node 2 - Assign Value to Company Segment Using a Constant**

Name	Value Type	Value	Type
Segment identifier	Constant	Name	Lookup
Segment	Constant	Company	Text
Value	Constant	01	Text
Replace existing value	Constant	True	Lookup

- **Node 3 - Segment Lookup Set Value**

Name	Value Type	Value	Type
Lookup Set Value	Constant	AA LOV DEPARTMENT	Text
Intermediate Value	Item Attribute	Expenditure Organization Name	Text

- **Node 4 - Assign Value to Segment (Success)**—This node assigns the value found in node 4 to the Department and then branches to node 6.
- **Node 5 - Abort Generating Code Combination (Failure)**—This node terminates the process in error.
- **Node 6 - Function to Get Segment Value Using SQL**—This node uses a SQL procedure to derive the value for the Account segment. If the process encounters an error during this step, the function branches to node 5. (Note: You also need to define a new SQL package based on `PAXTMPFB.pls`.)
- **Node 7 - Assign Value to Account Segment After SQL Function**—This node assigns the segment value derived in node 6 to the Account Segment.

- **Node 8 - Validate Code Combination**—This node contains the standard flexfield function for validating a code combination. For this function to work correctly, the attribute value New Code Combinations must be set to True.
- **Node 9 - End Generating Code Combination**—This standard activity node ends the process.

Key activities (nodes) in this workflow will need to be modified to meet your specific needs. The following sections show the modifications to those nodes needed to complete this example.

ASSIGNING A CONSTANT VALUE TO YOUR COMPANY SEGMENT (NODE 2) To assign a constant value to your Company segment, enter the information as shown in Figure 15.12 in the Workflow details.

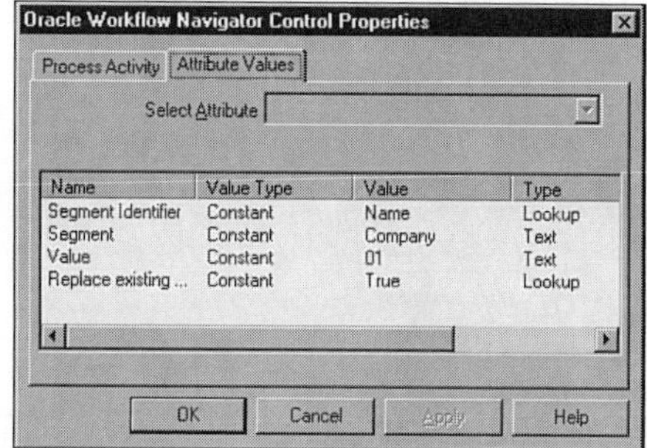

Figure 15.12 Assign a constant value to the Company segment using Workflow.

ASSIGNING A LOOKUP SET TO YOUR DEPARTMENT SEGMENT (NODE 3) To assign a lookup set in Workflow to derive your department segment from a predefined lookup set, enter the information as shown in Figure 15.13 in the Workflow details.

CREATING A WORKFLOW FUNCTION TO CALL YOUR SQL PROCEDURE (NODE 6) To call SQL from Workflow to derive the Account segment, you must create a stored procedure within your database. That procedure is then called by Workflow. The appropriately returned value can be assigned to your segment value.

This example assumes that you have created the procedure XPA_Account in the database DATABASENAME. Enter the information in Workflow as shown in Figure 15.14 to use this procedure for deriving the account segement.

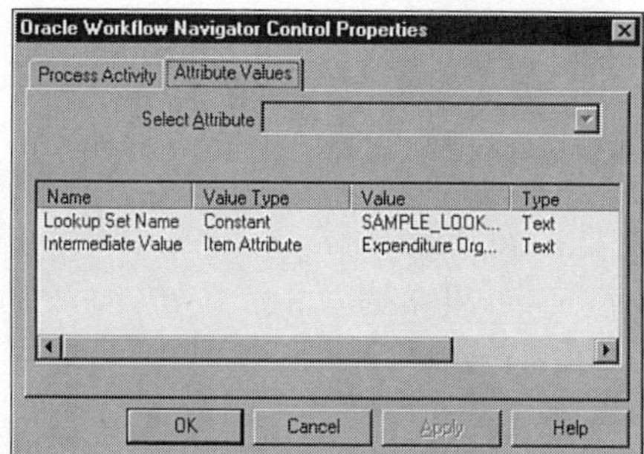

Figure 15.13 Assign a lookup set to derive the Department segment using Workflow.

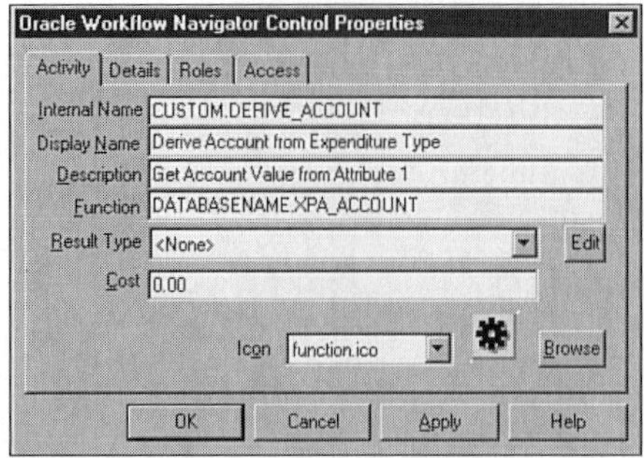

Figure 15.14
Assign a stored procedure to derive the Account segment using Workflow.

FINISHED WORKFLOW EXAMPLE When you have completed the modifications, your workflow should generate your GL Account Flexfield using a constant value for company, a lookup set for Department, and a SQL statement for Account. It should look similar to the workflow in Figure 15.15.

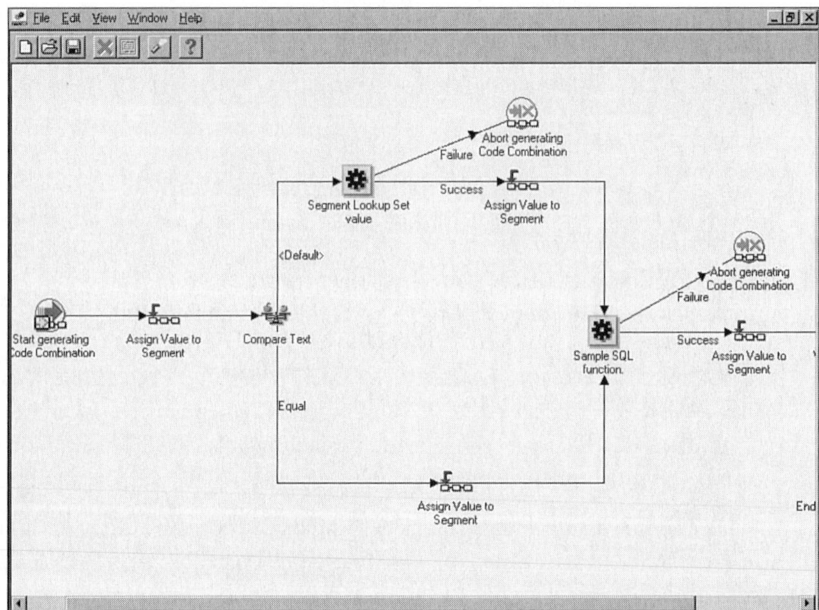

Figure 15.15
Finished sample workflow.

ALLOCATIONS

The following describes the steps required to implement project allocations.

DEFINING AN ALLOCATION RULE This is the first step in implementing any project allocation. You start by specifying a unique allocation rule name for the allocation. When generating allocation transactions, you specify the name of the allocation rule you want executed.

Next, you specify a basis method for the allocation. The basis method determines how amounts are allocated to all the tasks belonging to the target projects. You can choose from the options listed in Table 15.5.

TABLE 15.5 PROJECT ALLOCATIONS BASIS METHODS

Basis Method	Description
Spread Evenly	All the tasks on the target projects that allow allocation transactions will receive an equal portion of the source pool amount.
Prorate	Costs should be allocated to the tasks on the target projects using a prorating formula that you can specify in an Allocation Rule Basis.
Target % and Spread Evenly	Your source pool is first divided among the target projects using percentages you specify for each project. Then, for each project, the percentage of the source pool given to that project is allocated evenly among all the project's eligible tasks.
Target % and Prorate	Similar to Target % and Spread Evenly except that each target project's percentage of the source pool is allocated to its tasks using a prorating formula defined in the Allocation Rule Basis.
Use Client Extension Basis	You can provide your own custom logic for deriving the allocation basis by implementing the Project Allocations Basis Client Extension.

After you have specified a basis method, you choose which allocation method you want to use. You can choose an allocation method of either Full or Incremental.

An allocation method of Full means that each time you generate allocation transactions for this allocation rule, the full amount of the source pool is allocated. You would choose this option if you plan to perform this project allocation only once per period. Otherwise, you would be allocating more than the original source pool amount. For example, if you ran this allocation twice in the current period, you would have allocated 200% of the original source pool amount.

If you plan to generate allocation transactions more than once per period, you should define your allocation rule with an allocation method of Incremental. When the allocation method is set to Incremental, Oracle Projects compares the source pool amount to the sum of any previous executions of your allocation rule for the period and only allocates any new amounts.

The next item specified on an allocation rule is the allocation period type. This option, although required for all allocation rules, has no effect if the source of your allocation pool is a fixed amount. If the allocation is based on accumulated costs on a source project, you need to specify whether you want to use amounts accumulated by PA period or GL period.

Also specified on the allocation rule are the allocation transaction attributes you want Oracle Projects to use when it creates allocation transactions. The end result of Project Allocations is the creation of new expenditure items on your specified target projects. Every expenditure item must have a Project, Task, Expenditure Organization, and Expenditure Type specified. For Project Allocation transactions, the Project and Task references come from your target projects and tasks. The Expenditure Organization and Expenditure Type values, however, must be specified as part of your allocation rule.

Note

Because an Expenditure Type can be linked to more than one Expenditure Type Class, you must also specify the Expenditure Type Class. Oracle Projects uses these values for all destination allocation transactions it generates for this allocation rule. If you want items created with several different Expenditure Organization or Expenditure Type values, you must create separate allocation rules.

DEFINING THE PRORATE BASIS If your basis method involves prorating costs to tasks, you must specify an allocation basis to use. The basis determines how Oracle Projects will prorate the source allocation pool to your target project tasks.

To define a prorate basis, you first specify the basis category you want to use. You can choose to use either summarized project actuals (Actuals) or budget amounts (Budgets) in your prorate basis. If you are using budget amounts for your prorate basis, you can specify which Budget type to use when retrieving budget amounts.

You can limit the amounts selected for use in the prorate basis by listing only those resources you want Oracle Projects to select.

DEFINING THE PROJECT ALLOCATION SOURCES After you have defined an allocation rule, you then specify the Sources for the Project allocation. The Sources definition determines the pool of costs that will be allocated. Sources can be comprised of a fixed source amount, summarized cost amounts on specified source projects and tasks, posted journals in specified GL accounts, or a combination of any of these three.

In the Fixed Source Amount source method, an amount is specified as part of the allocation rule definition. Oracle Projects uses this entered amount to allocate to your target projects and tasks. If this is the only source method you are using on your allocation rule, none of the other fields in the Project Allocation Sources form are relevant, except the Allocation Pool %.

In the Summarized Project Costs source method, you can enter the projects and tasks for which you want costs to be included in the allocation source pool. Note that specifying source projects and tasks is both inclusive and exclusive. For example, you can exclude specific projects or tasks by entering a new Project Source line, specifying the project or task you want to exclude, and ensuring that the Exclude check box is checked.

To limit the source pool to only specific costs on the source projects and tasks, you can specify accumulated amounts by resource that you want to allocate. When you click the Resources button in the Sources screen, you see the Resources window. Here you can list which resource accumulation amounts you want to allocate.

You first select the resource List you want Oracle Projects to use when retrieving summary amounts from the source project. Oracle Projects summarizes costs against each Resource List that has been assigned to the project.

After you've selected the resource List, you can specify which resources in the list you want to be included in the source allocation pool. You can also enter a percentage amount for each resource line.

Note

The entry of specified resources can be both inclusive and exclusive. For exclusions, you must check the Exclude check box. All resources in the resource list that you specified will be included in the source allocation pool except those you've listed with the Exclude check box marked.

In the GL Accounts method, you enter the GL accounts for which you want Oracle Projects to select amounts for inclusion in the allocation source pool. For each account listed, you can specify a percentage amount.

Note

Only the full account name can be entered. You cannot enter ranges of GL accounts in the Project Allocation Sources form.

The Allocation Pool % simply specifies what percentage of the total source pool you want to have allocated to your target projects and tasks. This value defaults to 100, but you can change this. For example, if your total allocation pool amount as specified by your source methods is 100,000, and you enter an allocation pool % of 50, Oracle Projects allocates only 50,000 of the pool amount. This option is useful if you are sharing costs between your source project and the destination projects.

DEFINING THE PROJECT ALLOCATION TARGETS Now that you have defined the amount you want to allocate, you need to specify where you want this amount allocated. The targets of Project Allocations are always projects and tasks, but there are many ways in which you can specify the target projects and tasks.

The most straightforward way is to list each project you want to receive a portion of your allocation source pool. When you list the target projects specifically, you do not need to list the tasks as well. If you do not list any tasks, Oracle Projects either spreads the source amount evenly among all the project tasks or allocates the source amount based on a pro-rate basis, depending on which basis method option you chose for your allocation rule. If you do list a specific task, however, then all of that target project's allocation amount is charged to the task specified, regardless of whether other unlisted chargeable tasks exist on the project.

If your basis method specifies that a target percentage will be used, you can enter percentage amounts for each project listed. Oracle Projects ensures that the sum of all percentages is 100.

Other options are available for specifying your target projects besides listing them. You can specify a project organization and leave the remaining fields blank. This results in Oracle Projects selecting all eligible projects owned by that organization to receive a portion of the allocation source pool. Likewise, you could select all target projects for a specified Project Type, Project Classification, or any combination of these.

If none of these methods works for how you want to identify the target projects, you can implement the Project Allocations Targets Client Extension. If you choose to use the client extension to determine your target projects, you should check the Use Client Extension Targets check box. You then do not have to list any specific projects.

It is also important to remember that your target list can be both inclusive and exclusive. You can exclude specific projects from receiving allocations simply by listing that project in the Targets screen and checking the Exclude check box.

DEFINING PROJECT ALLOCATION OFFSET The last step in defining your Project Allocation is to specify a method and attributes for the offset transaction you want Oracle Projects to create. Typically, whenever you want to perform a project allocation, you want to reduce or offset the amount you've allocated to your target projects on the source project or another project you've created to incur offset transactions.

First, you must specify the Offset method. An Offset method of None means that Oracle Projects will not create any offset allocation transactions for the Project Allocation. Other options include Use Client Extension for Task. This option enables you to derive the Offset Project and Task using your own criteria. You can also enter a specific project and task to use for the Offset.

If you've entered an Offset method other than None, you must specify the Offset transaction attributes you want Oracle Projects to use for the offset transactions it creates. The allocation transaction attributes you specified as part of the allocation rule are used only for the allocation transactions charged to your target projects. The Offset transaction attributes are used for the Offset transactions.

BURDENING

This section illustrates the various accounting and project reporting impact when selecting the three main burden options in Oracle Projects. This is a summary of testing and uses only labor expenditures in the scenarios. The three options test cases clarify and supplement the Oracle documentation to assist in your burden setup decisions.

BURDEN OPTIONS The following three options are offered through Oracle Projects and are designated with the setup of your project type:

- **Option 1**—Burden Cost on Same Expenditure Item
- **Option 2**—Burden Cost on Same Expenditure Item - Account for Burden Cost Components
- **Option 3**—Burden Costs as Separate Expenditure Item

The example provided in this section uses the following values:

Labor hours = 40

Raw Cost rate = $300

The burden schedule used in this example contains the three burden components and rates in the following precedence order:

Precedence	Component	Rate
10	Overhead	.15
20	Fringe	.40
30	G&A	.3

BURDEN COST ON SAME EXPENDITURE ITEM (PROJECT A) This example uses the traditional burden calculations that Oracle Projects provides where the raw expenditure item is burdened and viewing the expenditure item will show the raw cost and total burden cost on the same line (Total Burden Cost = raw cost + burden component calculations). This option was not viewed as flexible by clients and the majority requested that only the burden component piece be posted to the General Ledger or be shown on a separate project. When the total burden costing processes are run, the system creates the burden cost distribution lines and sends to the General Ledger the entire Total Burden Cost. Total Raw cost on this project = $12,000 and Total Burden Cost = $25,116 ($12,000 + $13,116).

If you viewed the Cost Distribution Lines for this expenditure, you would see raw cost entries for $12,000 and burden cost entries for $25,116. See Figure 15.16 for details on how these amounts are derived.

Accounting entries for Raw Costs, Project A:

DR: Payroll 12,000

CR: Payroll Clearing 12,000

Accounting entries for Total Burden Costs, Project A:

DR: Burden Expense 25,116

CR: Burden Recovery 25,116

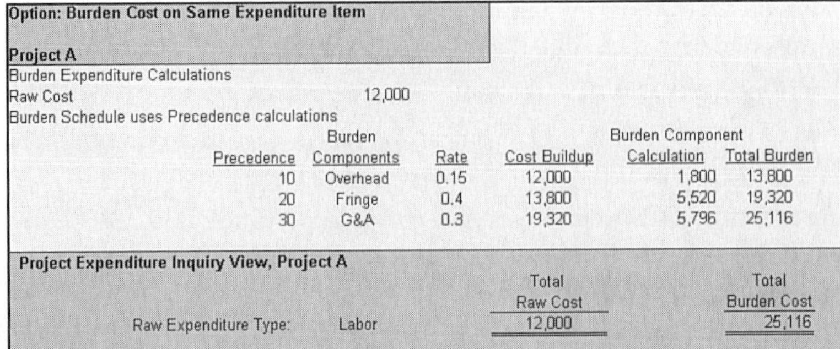

Option: Burden Cost on Same Expenditure Item

Project A
Burden Expenditure Calculations
Raw Cost 12,000
Burden Schedule uses Precedence calculations

Precedence	Burden Components	Rate	Cost Buildup	Burden Component Calculation	Total Burden
10	Overhead	0.15	12,000	1,800	13,800
20	Fringe	0.4	13,800	5,520	19,320
30	G&A	0.3	19,320	5,796	25,116

Project Expenditure Inquiry View, Project A

		Total Raw Cost	Total Burden Cost
Raw Expenditure Type:	Labor	12,000	25,116

Figure 15.16 Burden calculation for burden on same expenditure item.

Project processes use the functions listed in Table 15.6.

TABLE 15.6 BURDEN OPTION SETUP 1: PROJECTS PROCESSES AND AUTOACCOUNTING FUNCTIONS

Process	AutoAccounting Function
Distribute Labor Costs	Creates the raw cost amount and distribution debit line. Calculates the burden amount but creates no burden distribution lines. Debit Account: Labor Cost Account
Interface Labor Costs	Credit Account: Labor Cost Clearing Account
Distribute Total Burden Costs	Creates the debit distribution lines for the burden amounts previously calculated in the burden cost column. Debit Account: Total Burden Cost Account
Interface Total Burden Costs	Creates the credit transfer lines for the burden-calculated amounts. Credit Account: Total Burden Cost Credit Account

Burden Cost on Same Expenditure Item (Project A) - Account for Burden Cost Components (Project Burden) Using the option to account for the burden component on a separate project, you will see the same information as option 1 on the project that incurs the charges (raw cost $12,000, total burden cost $25,116). In both options 1 and 2 the system calculates the Total Burden Costs when running the raw cost distribution processes. The accounting entries for the Total Burden Costs are created and sent to the GL when running the Total Burden Cost Processes.

The main differences with this option are

- You must assign expenditure types to your burden components. These expenditure types must have the expenditure type class assigned of Burden Transaction.

- A project and task must be assigned during the setup of the Project Type to accumulate the Burden Component calculations that are created (Project Burden).
- The burden component calculations are created when running the process Create and Distribute Burden Transactions.
- Companies can view and perform analysis for burden component amounts on a separate project.

The documentation states you can send only the burden component piece to your General Ledger. This is corrected by sending the Total Burden Cost calculated on the original expenditure item to a clearing account.

Note

If expenditure types are not assigned to your burden components or a project or task has not been entered in the Project Type setup to collect the component costs, the process will fail.

Consider this scenario: Your company wants to send only the burden component calculation to the General Ledger. Through AutoAccounting, the setup will send the raw expenditure type burdens to a clearing account and the burden expenditure types parameters to an expense account. See Figure 15.17 for details on how these amounts are derived.

Accounting entries for Raw Costs, Project A:

DR: Payroll 12,000

CR: Payroll Clearing 12,000

Accounting entries for Total Burden Costs, Project A:

DR: Burden Clearing 25,116

CR: Burden Clearing 25,116

Accounting entries for Burden Component calculations Project Burden:

DR: Burden Fringe	5,796		
DR: Burden OH	5,520		
DR: Burden G&A	1,800		
		CR: Burden Recovery Fringe	5,796
		CR: Burden Recovery OH	5,520
		CR: Burden Recovery G&A	1,800

Figure 15.17 Burden calculation for burden on same expenditure item with cost components.

Option: Burden Cost on Same Expenditure Item and Account for Burden Cost Components

*** Burden Cost on Same Expenditure Item, Project A**
*** Account for Burden Cost Components, Project Burden**

Burden Expenditure Calculations
Raw Cost 12,000
Burden Schedule uses Precedence calculations

Precedence	Components	Rate	Cost Buildup	Burden Component Calculation	Total Burden
10	Overhead	0.15	12,000	1,800	13,800
20	Fringe	0.4	13,800	5,520	19,320
30	G&A	0.3	19,320	5,796	25,116

1. Project Expenditure Inquiry View, Project A
***Original Project Charged**

		Total Raw Cost	Total Burden Cost
Raw Expenditure Type:	Labor	12,000	25,116

2. Project Expenditure Inquiry View, Project Burden
***Project for Burden Cost Components - from Project Type**

		Raw Cost	Burden Cost
Burden Expenditure Type:	Overhead	0	1,800
Burden Expenditure Type:	Fringe	0	5,520
Burden Expenditure Type:	G&A	0	5,796
		0	13,116

Project processes use the functions listed in Table 15.7.

TABLE 15.7 BURDEN OPTION SETUP 2: PROJECTS PROCESSES AND AUTOACCOUNTING FUNCTIONS

Process	AutoAccounting Function
Distribute Labor Costs:	Creates the raw cost amount and distribution debit line. Calculates the burden amount but creates no burden distribution lines. Debit Account: Labor Cost Account
Interface Labor Costs:	Credit Account: Labor Cost Clearing Account
Create and Distribute Burden Expenditure Transactions:	Creates the Burden Expenditure Types and amounts, distribution lines that are for the $0 raw amounts and the Burden amount that are shown previously on the Burden Expenditure types. Debit Account: Burden Cost Debit Account
Interface Usage and Miscellaneous Costs:	Creates the distribution credit for $0 raw amounts and the burden credit amount shown on the Burden Expenditure Types previously. Credit Account: Burden Cost Credit Account
Distribute Total Burden Costs:	Creates the debit distribution lines for the burden amounts previously calculated in the burden cost column. Debit Account: Total Burden Cost Account
Interface Total Burden Costs:	Creates the credit transfer lines for the burden-calculated amounts. Credit Account: Total Burden Cost Credit Account

BURDEN COSTS AS SEPARATE EXPENDITURE ITEM (PROJECT A) Using this option the calculations for the burden components are also performed during the process Create and Distribute Burden Transactions. This option differs from the previous two options in that the burden expenditure types will be displayed on the original project charged. See Figure 15.18 for detailed information on how this information is calculated and displayed for this burden option.

In all three options, the following is true:

Total Raw cost = $12,000 and Total Burden Cost = $25,116 ($12,000 + $13,116).

The main functionality with this option is

- When the raw cost distribution processes are run, the burden amount calculated on the Expenditure Item is equal to the raw cost.
- You must assign expenditure types to your burden components. These expenditure types must have the expenditure type class assigned of Burden Transaction.
- The burden component calculations are created when running a new process Create and Distribute Burden Transactions. If expenditure types are not assigned to your burden components, the process will fail.
- Companies have the ability to view and perform analysis for burden component amounts on the project being charged.

Note

The documentation states you can send only the burden component piece to your General Ledger. This is correct, but to accomplish this you should not enable the AutoAccounting rules for Total Burden Cost.

Note

If your company uses WIP accounting and the Cost Accrual accounting extension, the Total Burden Cost AutoAccounting rules can be used to send the burden costs to a WIP account. This holds true for capital class projects as well, sending the Total Burden Cost to a CIP account.

Tip

If using Capital Projects, the Distribute Total Burden process must be run (even if you are not burdening your costs) to successfully generate and interface an asset to Fixed Assets.

Tip

The WIP and CIP concepts can be applied to any of the three burden scenarios. The accounts are determined through your AutoAccounting setup.

Here's another scenario: A company wants to send only the burden component calculation to the General Ledger. By having the raw expenditure types parameters pointing to a clearing account and the burden expenditure types parameters pointing to an expense account, this can be accomplished.

Accounting entries for Raw Costs, Project A:

DR: Payroll 12,000

CR: Payroll Clearing 12,000

If WIP Accounting entries for Total Burden Costs, Project A:

DR: Burden Clearing 12,000

CR: Burden Clearing 12,000

Accounting entries for Burden Component calculations when running Total Burden Costs, Project A:

DR: Burden Fringe	5,796	
DR: Burden OH	5,520	
DR: Burden G&A	1,800	
CR: Burden Recovery Fringe		5,796
CR: Burden Recovery OH		5,520
CR: Burden Recovery G&A		1,800

If WIP or CIP Accounting is used, entries for Total Burden Costs, Project A:

DR: WIP/CIP Clearing 12,000

CR: Expense Recovery 12,000

Figure 15.18
Burden cost calculation as separate expenditure item.

Option: Burden Cost as Separate Expenditure Item

Project A
Burden Expenditure Calculations
Raw Cost 12,000
Burden Schedule uses Precedence calculations

Precedence	Burden Components	Rate	Cost Buildup	Burden Component Calculation	Total Burden
10	Overhead	0.15	12,000	1,800	13,800
20	Fringe	0.4	13,800	5,520	19,320
30	G&A	0.3	19,320	5,796	25,116

Project Expenditure Inquiry View, Project A

		Total Raw Cost	Total Burden Cost
Raw Expenditure Type:	Labor	12,000	12,000
Burden Expenditure Type:	Overhead	0	1,800
Burden Expenditure Type:	Fringe	0	5,520
Burden Expenditure Type:	G&A	0	5,796
		12,000	25,116

PROJECT/BUDGET WORKFLOWS

Oracle Projects has two embedded workflows you can enable to control status changes on projects and budgets. By enabling these workflows, you can specify company-specific approval rules when changing projects from one specific status to another or when changing a draft budget from working to submitted or baselined.

COMMON SETUPS STEPS FOR PROJECT AND BUDGET STATUS WORKFLOWS Both the Project Status Workflow and the Budget Status Workflow are enabled based on project type. To enable a specific project type to use either or both workflows, perform the following steps, as shown in Figure 15.19:

1. Navigation Path PA: Setup, Projects, Project Types.
2. Query the project type for which you want to enable the embedded workflow.
3. Select the Project Status, Workflow tab.
4. Check (select) the options for Use Workflow for Project Status Changes and Use Workflow for Budget Status Changes as appropriate.
5. Save your work.

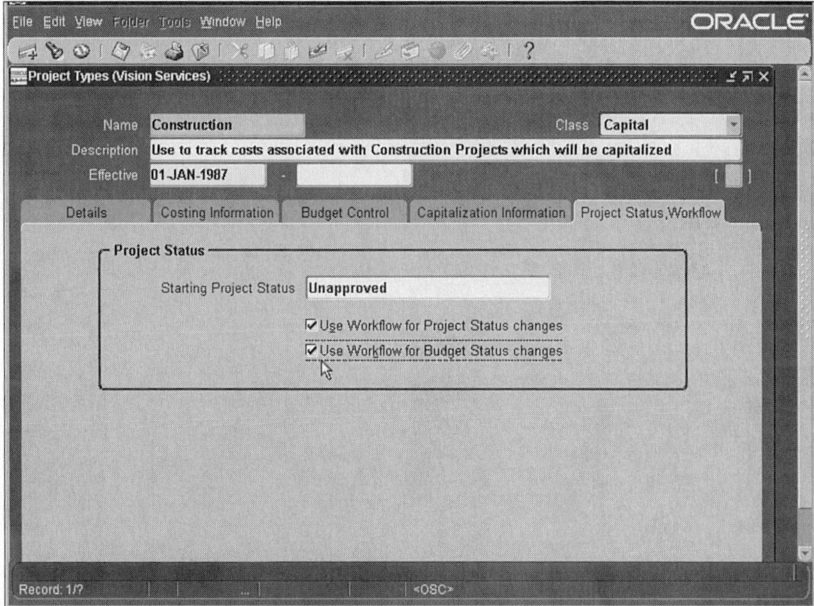

Figure 15.19 Enable Workflow for project and budget status changes on specific project types.

PROJECT STATUS CHANGE WORKFLOW After you have enabled the Project Status Change workflow on the appropriate project types, you must set up the workflow to handle specific changes in Project Statuses. Oracle Projects gives you the flexibility to enable the workflow for only status changes you specify. For example, you can have the Project Status Change workflow enabled when a status is changed from Unapproved to Approved, but not from Unapproved to Submitted.

To enable the Project Status Change workflow for specific status changes, perform the following steps (Figure 15.20 shows how the information looks in the form):

1. Navigation Path PA: Setup, System, Statuses.
2. Query the statuses you need to set up for the workflow.
3. On the Workflow tab, check the Enable Workflow field for the appropriate status that workflow will run when the project status is changed to it. For example, select Approved if the workflow is to be run when the project status is changed to Approved.
4. Select PA Project Workflow for the Item Type field.
5. Select Project for the Process field.
6. Enter a defined status in the Success Status field. This status will be the status of the project if the approval cycle is successful.
7. Enter a defined status in the Failure Status field. This status will be the status of the project if the approval cycle is not successful.
8. Save your work.

Note

The success status does not have to be the status the user requested the project status be changed to.

The failure status does not have to be the project status of the project before the workflow was started.

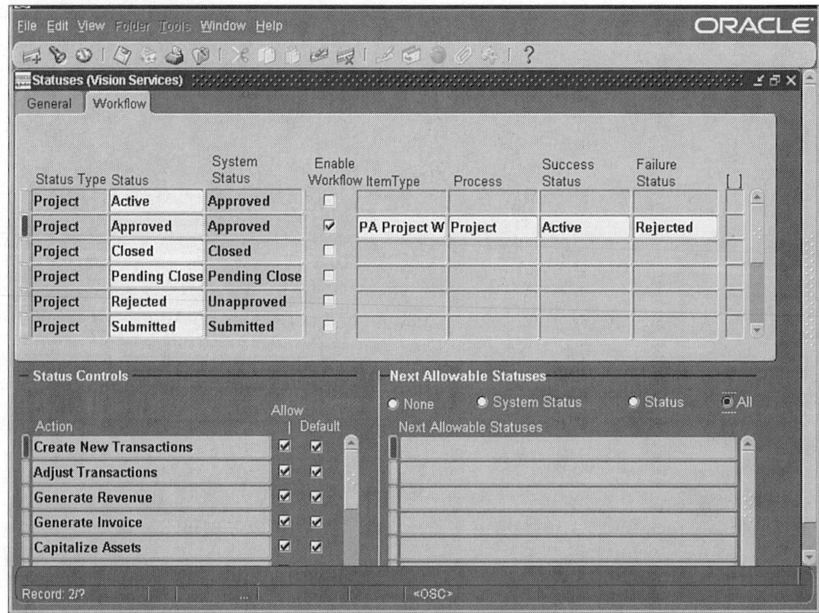

Figure 15.20
Enable and define the Project Status Change Workflow for specific project statuses.

Tip

You can implement multiple approval levels by setting up the success status to be workflow enabled also. This results in a second workflow approval being started.

Budget Status Change Workflow Oracle Projects provides the ability to enable the Budget Status Change workflow not only for specific project types, but also for specific budget types. After you have enabled the Budget Status Change workflow on the appropriate project types, you must enable the Budget Status Change workflow on specific budget types.

To enable the Budget Status Change workflow for specific budget types, as shown in Figure 15.21, do the following:

1. Navigation Path PA: Setup, Budgets, Budget Types.
2. Query the budget types for which you need workflow enabled.
3. Ensure that you are on the record for the appropriate budget type.
4. Check (select) Use Workflow for Budget Status Changes.
5. Save your work.

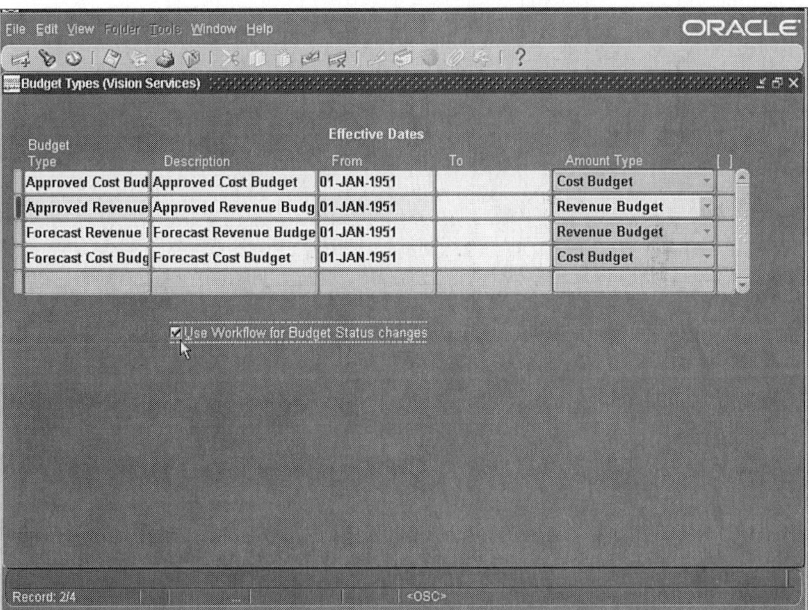

Figure 15.21
Enable budget status change workflows for specific budget types.

Advanced Workflow Setups To provide greater flexibility in using the Project and Budget Status Change workflows, Oracle Projects has provided six client extensions that enable you to further control the workflow functionality. More information on coding client extensions can be found in the section "Client Extensions," later in this chapter.

Note

By default, the Project Status Change and Budget Status Change Workflows send notifications to the manager (as defined in HR) of the person submitting the change.

You can change this routing logic by modifying the Select Budget Approver or the Select Project Approver client extension.

INTERPROJECT BILLING SETUP

Table 15.8 shows the setup steps necessary for implementing Interproject Billing.

TABLE 15.8 PROJECTS INTERPROJECT BILLING SETUP STEPS

Setup Task Name	Once?	Optional?
Define Suppliers for Internal Invoices (AP).	Yes	
Define Separate Expenditure Type for Internal Supplier Invoices (Projects).		Yes
Define Customers for Internal Billing Invoices (AR).	Yes	
Complete Internal Billing Section of Implementation Options for Each Operating Unit (Projects).	Yes	
Define Supplier Site in Each Receiver Operating Unit (AP).	Yes	
Define Customer Site in Each Receiver Operating Unit (AR).	Yes	
Define Receiver Controls in the Provider/Receiver Controls Window (Projects).	Yes	
Define Tax Account Codes for Tax Amounts on Internal Receivables Invoices (AR).	Yes	
Define Tax Codes to Apply Separate Tax Distributions on Internal Payables Invoices (AP).	Yes	
Verify that Receivables and Payables share the same tax codes for tax lines on internal invoices (AR/AP).	Yes	
Ensure that Account Generator creates a proper account for internal invoices (AP).		Yes
Define a Receiver Project and check The Receive Interproject Invoices flag in the Task Details window of the task authorized to receive Interproject Invoices (Projects).		
Define a Provider Project by enabling the Bill another Project flag in the Customer Options screen and identifying the Receiver Project and Task to be billed (Projects).		

MULTICURRENCY SETUP—GENERAL LEDGER

Oracle Projects enables users to enter multiple currency transactions and to generate invoices in currencies other than the operating unit currency. Before this functionality can be enabled, some basic setups need to be completed in the Oracle General Ledger. First, you must ensure the desired currencies are enabled. Next, you validate the predefined Conversion Rate Types and verify that they meet the requirements; additional Conversion Rate Types can be created if desired. Before processing transactions, enter exchange rates for the functional to foreign currency combinations by Conversion Rate Type and Conversion Date. See the General Ledger section for greater detail on defining and maintaining multiple currencies.

MULTICURRENCY SETUP—PROJECTS

After configuring the General Ledger, you must set up multicurrency information in Oracle Projects. On the Implementation Options form, ensure that a default Exchange Rate Date Type and Exchange Rate Type are entered in the Currency and Cross Charge sections. These options provide the defaults Projects will use for foreign currency transactions and translations.

Tip

The Implementations Options form does not require these currency options to be entered. But if they are not entered, users will encounter errors entering foreign currency transactions.

Note

In the current release (11.5.4), project currency = operating unit functional currency.

For projects that will have transactions in multiple currencies, enter the Project Currency Attributes. These attributes are the defaults for the project and can be entered at the project and lowest task level:

- **Default Project Rate Type**—The default exchange rate type to use (for example Corporate, Spot, User)
- **Default Project Rate Date**—A default rate date; optionalAs additional tasks are added to the WBS, the Project Currency Attributes default down to the new subsidiary tasks. If necessary, these attributes can be overridden at transaction entry or import.

Note

Oracle Projects does not require the Project Currency Attributes be entered on the project. If they are not entered, Projects pulls the default from the implementation options, using the following order to select the appropriate attribute:

1. Task
2. Project
3. Currency Implementation Options

Figure 15.22 is an example of a project with a Currency Rate Type of Corporate. When foreign currency transactions are translated, they use the Corporate Exchange Rate stored in the General Ledger.

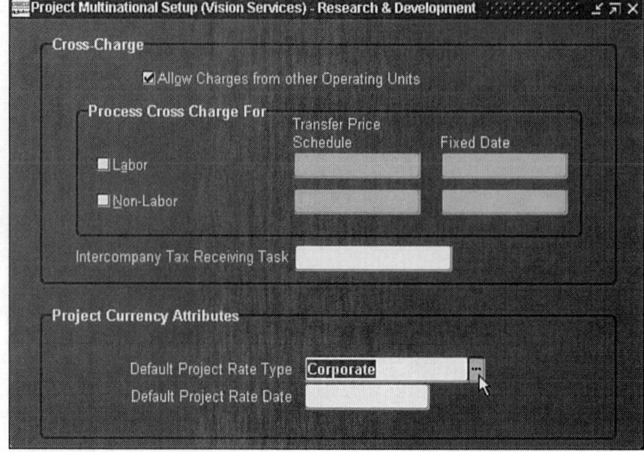

Figure 15.22
Enter your project currency rate type in the cross-charge options section on the project.

Multicurrency Billing Setup

In addition to charging foreign currency transactions to a project, users can bill a customer in any enabled currency. To bill clients in a foreign currency, the project must first be configured for multicurrency transactions.

To configure your project, navigate to the Customers and Contacts option on the Project form. In the Invoice Currency section of the Projects customer form, enter the desired rate options. These options can be changed at any time without impacting existing invoices, write-offs, credit memos, or invoice cancellations:

- **Allow Rate Type "User"**—Check this option to allow a currency rate type of User.
- **Code**—The currency code to default for invoicing this customer.
- **Rate Date**—The Bill Through date is the default date for the exchange rate date. If another default exchange rate date is desired, enter it here.
- **Rate Type**—The default exchange rate type to use (for example Corporate, Spot, User).
- **Exchange Rate**—Default exchange rate. A value can be entered in this field only if the Rate Type is User.

Figure 15.23 shows how this information looks when entered in the Customers and Contacts option of the Projects window.

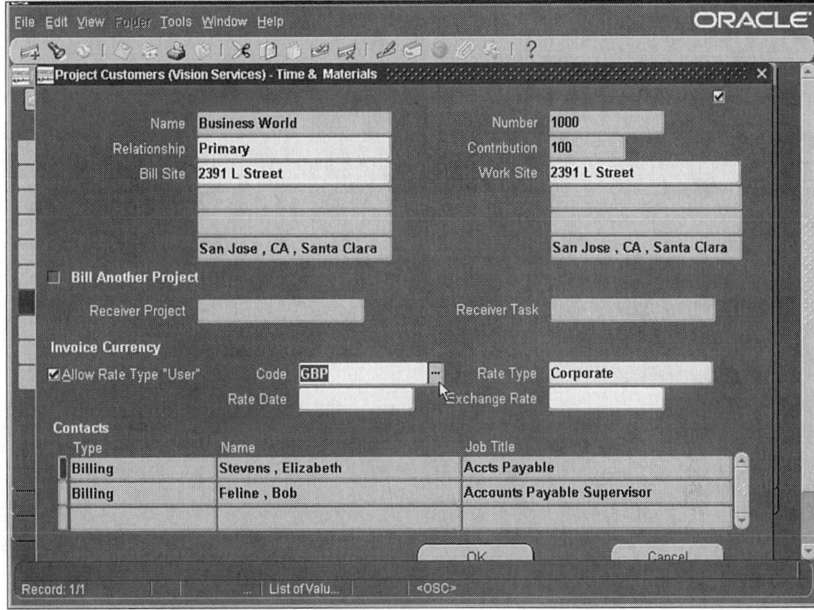

Figure 15.23
Enter multicurrency billing information on the project.

MULTINATIONAL GLOBAL PROJECTS

Release 11*i* offers the ability to establish true multinational global projects. Your company can establish one project that will maintain the customer relationship and provide centralized customer billings. Using the new features, such as Inter-Company Billing, Inter-Project Billing, and Cross Charge, enables you to directly create transactions for all entities performing work against the project. Inter-Company Billings provides legal documentation that will satisfy statutory requirements. Using the global project, transactions can be received in any currency, converted to the project or functional currency of your operating unit, and billed to the customer based on the contract currency.

Note

Although Oracle Projects supports billing a customer based on the contract currency, Agreements will always be in the functional currency of the operating unit.

Consider the following example: A multinational global project is owned by the New York Production organization, and the customer or contract is with a Korean entity. Table 15.9 displays the types of cross-charge transactions that can occur based on the entity performing the work. In this example, the Houston Engineering organization establishes a provider project to create an Inter-Project Billing to the central project.

TABLE 15.9 CROSS-CHARGE CAPABILITY BY OPERATING UNIT

Operating Unit	Operating Unit Currency	Expenditure Organization	Cross-Charge Type	Project Currency	Customer Billing Currency
Germany	DEM	QA	Inter-Company	USD	Korean Won
USA	USD	NY, Engineering	Borrowed & Lent		
Israel	ILS	Manufacturing	Inter-Company		
USA	USD	Houston, Engineering	Inter-Project		

CLIENT EXTENSIONS

Oracle Projects provides numerous places within the code for you to add your own company-specific processing logic. These hooks into the code are called *client extensions*. Unlike customizations (which did not exist in the system as shipped), client extensions are part of the base Oracle Projects code. Each client extension has base default logic (approval extensions return the user's HR-defined manager) and is called during standard processing. An important benefit of client extensions is that they are a supported means for you to modify the logic to meet specific business requirements.

Client extensions are PL/SQL stored packages and procedures that you can modify to include your own custom logic for processing. Client extensions are grouped based on functionality, such as allocations, transaction controls, budget workflow, and so on. Each group represents one stored PL/SQL package. Within this package, each individual client extension constitutes a separate procedure. For example, all Project Allocations client extensions are stored within the package (PA_CLIENT_EXTN_ALLOC). The source extension is a procedure (Source_Extn) within that package.

Client extension package source files are included in the filesystem code shipped from Oracle. They can be found in the `$PA_TOP/admin/sql` directory. Because Oracle Projects calls each client extension regardless of whether you have implemented changes to them, it is important that you retain a copy of the original source code. Therefore, before modifying any client extension file, you should make a copy of the original file in case you have to revert to the standard shipped version.

Here are the steps for implementing client extensions:

1. Determine you business requirements.
2. Determine the logic to achieve the business requirement.
3. Determine client extensions that assist meeting these requirements.
4. Copy the client extension file to a different location and rename it.
5. Code the logic into the client extension package or procedure.
6. Compile the revised package into the database.
7. Test the revised logic.

Note

Be sure to test creation, deletion, and adjustment scenarios as applicable.

Table 15.10 lists the client extensions provided by Oracle Projects in Release 11*i*.

Table 15.10 Client Extensions Available in Release 11i

Procedure Name	Description
Extension: Allocations Extension **Package Name: PA_CLIENT_EXTN_ALLOC** **Files: `PAPALCCS.pls`; `PAPALCCB.pls`**	
Source_Extn	You can use the Source extension to define projects and tasks to include or exclude when creating a source pool. Note that this procedure is called only if the Use Client Extension Sources check box is enabled in the Project Allocation Sources window.
Target_Extn	You can use the target extension to define projects and tasks to include or exclude when allocating costs to target projects and tasks. Note that this procedure is called only if the Use Client Extension Targets check box is enabled in the Project Allocation Targets window.
Offset_Extn	You can use the Offset Projects and Tasks extension to define offset projects and tasks. Note that this procedure is called only if the Use Client Extension for Project and Task check box is enabled in the Project Allocation Offsets window.
Offset_Task_Extn	This Offset Tasks extension is very similar to the Offset Projects and Tasks extension, except this extension is used to define only offset tasks, not both offset projects and tasks. Note that this procedure is called only if the Use Client Extension for Task check box is enabled in the Project Allocation Offsets window.
Basis_Extn	You can use this Basis Extension to use amounts other than target costs when calculating the base rate for target projects and tasks. For example, you can use headcount values for departments as the basis for allocating costs. Note that this procedure is called only if the Use Client Extension Basis check box is enabled in the Allocation Rule window.

TABLE 15.10 CONTINUED

Procedure Name	Description
Txn_Dff_Extn	You can use this Descriptive Flexfields extension to define descriptive flexfield column values to be used for Allocation and Allocation Offset transactions. This extension procedure is called before Oracle Projects creates each transaction.
Check_Dependencies	You can use this Check Dependencies Extension to use amounts other than target costs when calculating the base rate for target projects and tasks. For example, you can use headcount values for departments as the basis for allocating costs. Note that this procedure is called only if the Use Client Extension Basis check box is enabled in the Allocation Rule window.
Extension: AR Transaction Type Extension **Package Name: PA_CLIENT_EXTN_INV_TRANSFER** **Files: `PAXITRXS.pls`; `PAXITRXB.pls`**	
Get_AR_Trx_Type	You can use this extension to determine which Receivables transaction type you want to use when sending invoices from Projects to Receivables.
Extension: Asset Assignment Extension **Package Name: PA_CLIENT_EXTN_GEN_ASSET_LINES** **Files: `PAPGALCS.pls`; `PAPGALCB.pls`**	
Client_Asset_Assignment	You can use this extension to write your own rules for assigning assets the system has marked as Unassigned to specific tasks or asset lines.
Extension: AutoApproval Extension **Package Name: PA_CLIENT_EXTN_PTE** **Files: `PAXPTEES.pls`; `PAXPTEEB.pls`**	
Get_Exp_Autoapproval	You can use this client extension to define your own business-specific rules or conditions for autoapproving expense reports.

Table 15.10 Continued

Procedure Name	Description
Extension: Automatic Invoice Approval and Release Extension **Package Name: PA_CLIENT_EXTN_INV_ACTIONS** **Files: `PAXPIACS.pls`; `PAXPIACB.pls`**	
Approve_Invoice	You can use this extension to define your own custom logic for automatically approving invoices as part of the Generate Draft Invoice process.
Release_Invoice	You can use this extension to define your own custom logic for automatically releasing invoices as part of the Generate Draft Invoice process.
Extension: Billing Cycle Extension **Package Name: PA_CLIENT_EXTN_BILL_CYCLE** **Files: `PAXIBCXS.pls`; `PAXIBCXB.pls`**	
Get_Next_Billing_Date	You can use this extension to derive the next billing date for your project. To use this extension, you must set the billing cycle type to User-Defined for that project. See the section "Defining Contract Projects for Cost Collection," earlier in this chapter.
Extension: Billing Extension **Package Name: User defined** **Files: `PAXITMPS.pls`; `PAXITMPB.pls`**	
User defined	You can use billing extensions to create custom automatic revenue and billing events based on your business rules. Within your user-defined package and procedure(s), you can call several procedures within the package PA_BILLING_PUB, such as insert_event.
Extension: Budget Calculation/Verification Extension **Package Name: PA_CLIENT_EXTN_BUDGET** **Files: `PAXBCECS.pls`; `PAXBCECB.pls`**	
Calc_Raw_Cost	Enables you to define alternate logic for how raw cost is calculated on a budget line. It is called after the quantity is entered. If this extension returns a value, that value is used for the raw cost. Otherwise, the system leaves the value for raw cost blank.
Calc_Burdened_Cost	Enables you to define alternate logic for how the burdened cost is calculated on a budget line. It is called after the quantity is entered. If this extension returns a value, that value will be used for the raw cost. Otherwise, the system leaves the value for raw cost blank.

Table 15.10 Continued

Procedure Name	Description
Calc_Revenue	Enables you to define alternate logic for how revenue is calculated on a revenue budget line. It is called after the quantity is entered. If this extension returns a value, that value will be used for the raw cost. Otherwise, the system will leave the value for revenue blank.
Verify_Budget_rules	Enables you to add additional checks to control budget status changes either to submitted or to baselined.
Extension: Budget Workflow Extension **Package Name: PA_CLIENT_EXTN_BUDGET_WF** **Files: `PAWFBCES.pls`; `PAWFBCEB.pls`**	
budget_wf_is_used	Enables you to add additional checks to determine whether a workflow should be used. For example, you might want to use workflow whenever a specific budget type (Approved Revenue) is used, but not for specific project types.
select_budget_approver	Enables you to change the logic for selecting the default approver for budget status changes.
start_budget_wf	This procedure starts the workflow. It enables you to add additional checks to determine whether the workflow should be started or if you want to change the default workflow that is called.
Verify_Budget_Rules	Enables you to add additional checks to control budget status changes either to submitted or to baselined when workflow is enabled but not for changes that are non-workflow enabled.
Extension: Burden Costing Extension **Package Name: PA_CLIENT_EXTN_BURDEN** **Files: `PAXCCEBS.pls`; `PAXCCEBB.pls`**	
Override_Rate_Rev_Id	You can use this extension to derive a different burden schedule ID than what is used by default.

Table 15.10 Continued

Procedure Name	Description
Extension: Commitment Changes Extension Package Name: PA_CLIENT_EXTN_CHECK_CMT Files: `PACECMTS.pls; PACECMTB.pls`	
Commitments_Changed	You need to use the extension if you have made changes to the PA_COMMITMENT_TXNS_V view (See the section "Understanding Project Commitments," later in this chapter). This extension ensures that the Project Summarization processes look for changes in commitment values based on the changes you made to the view.
Extension: Cost Accrual Billing Extension Package Name: PA_REV_CA Files: `PAXICOSS.pls; PAXICOSB.pls`	
Calc_CA_Amt	This extension enables you to define your own specific business rules for how to handle cost accruals within Oracle Projects.
Get_PSI_Cols	This procedure is called by the PSI Client Extension and is used to get column values for cost accruals.
Verify_Project_Status_CA	This procedure is called by the Project Status Change Extension and checks to see whether your project has cost accrual prerequisites before enabling the project status to be closed.
Check_if_Cost_Accrual	This procedure checks to see whether your project has cost accruals and sets the variables from the appropriate attributes in the billing extension.
Extension: Cost Accrual Identification Extension Package Name: PA_CC_AC Files: `PAICPCAS.pls; PAICPCAB.pls`	
Identify_CA_Projects	You can use this extension to determine which cross-charge projects should use cost accrual during standard revenue generation processing.
Extension: Cost Plus Application Programming Interface Package Name: PA_COST_PLUS Files: `PAXCCPES.pls; PAXCCPEB.pls`	
Get_Burden_Amount	Use this extension to define projects and tasks to include or exclude when creating a source pool. Note that this procedure is only called if the Use Client Extension Sources check box is enabled in the Project Allocation Sources window.

TABLE 15.10 CONTINUED

Procedure Name	Description
Extension: Costing Extension **Package Name: PA_COSTING_CLIENT_EXTNS** **Files: `PAXCHCES.pls`; `PAXCHCEB.pls`**	
Add_Transactions_Hook	This procedure provides the costing client extension hook into the Labor Transaction Extension.
Calc_Raw_Cost_Hook	This procedure provides the costing client extension hook into the Labor Costing Extension.
Extension: Cross-Charging Client Extensions **Package Name: PA_CC_IDENT_CLIENT_EXTN** **Files: `PACCIXTS.pls`; `PAXXIXTB.pls`**	
Override_Prvdr_Recvr	You can use this extension to enforce your business rules regarding the ability to cross-charge between organizations at a level in the organization higher than the level at which you assign projects and resources.
Override_CC_Processing_Method	You can use this extension to change how your cross-charged transactions are processed, such as some transactions being processed as Intercompany Billing while others are processed as Borrowed and Lent. You can also use this extension to exclude certain transactions from being cross-charge processed.
Extension: Descriptive Flexfield Mapping Extension **Package Name: PA_CLIENT_EXTN_DFF_TRANS** **Files: `PAPDFFCS.pls`; `PAPDFFCB.pls`**	
DFF_Map_Segments_PA_and_AP	You can use this extension to modify the attribute category information sent from Payables to Projects, and vice versa.
DFF_Map_Segments_F	You can use this extension to map descriptive flexfields that are sent from Payables to descriptive flexfields defined in Projects, and vice versa.
Extension: Labor Billing Extension **Package Name: PA_CLIENT_EXTN_BILLING** **Files: `PAXICTMS.pls`; `PAXICTMB.pls`**	
Calc_Bill_Amount	You can use this extension to derive billing amounts for individual labor transactions based on your company-specific rules, such as billing overtime to the project at cost.

Table 15.10 Continued

Procedure Name	Description
Extension: Labor Costing Extension **Package Name: PA_CLIENT_EXTN_COSTING** **Files: `PAXCCECS.pls`; `PAXCCECB.pls`**	
Calc_Raw_Cost	This extension enables you to derive the raw cost amount for labor transactions during the costing/distribution process. For example, you can use this extension to calculate a raw cost for employees subject to capped labor rates.
Extension: Labor Transaction Extension **Package Name: PA_CLIENT_EXTN_TXN** **Files: `PAXCCETS.pls`; `PAXCCETB.pls`**	
Add_Transactions	This extension enables you to create additional expenditure items (related items or related transactions) for any original labor transaction. These additional labor transactions are linked to the original transaction, but they can be burdened, billed, and accounted for independently.
CreateRelatedItem	This extension is the procedure you can use to validate and create a Related Transaction from within the Add_Transactions procedure.
UpdateRelatedItem	This extension is the procedure you can use to validate and update a Related Transaction from within the Add_Transactions procedure.
Extension: Organization Change Extension **Package Name: PA_ORG_CLIENT_EXTN** **Files: `PAXORCES.pls`; `PAXORCEB.pls`**	
Verify_Org_Change	You can use this extension to define your company-specific business rules for whether changes can be made to project-owning organizations and task-owning organizations. You can also specify your own error messages if the change is disallowed.
Extension: Output Tax Extension **Package Name: PA_CLIENT_EXTN_OUTPUT_TAX** **Files: `PAXPOTXS.pls`; `PAXPOTXB.pls`**	
Get_Tax_Codes	You can use this extension to define the default output tax code that should be used on invoice lines. This extension is called during Generate Draft Invoices if the system is unable to find a default tax code in the Tax Defaults Hierarchy. See the section "Tax Information by Receivables Invoice Lines," earlier in this chapter for more information on tax hierarchies.

TABLE 15.10 CONTINUED

Procedure Name	Description
Extension: Overtime Calculation Extension **Package Name: PA_CALC_OVERTIME** **Files: `PAXDLCOS.pls`; `PAXDLCOB.pls`**	
Process_Overtime	You can use this extension to define company-specific rules for how overtime is calculated and placed on an indirect project. Included procedures are Calc_Overtime and Calc_Daily_Overtime, which you can use within your custom code to accomplish various overtime calculations.
Extension: Percent Complete Billing Extension **Package Name: PA_BILL_PCT** **Files: `PAXPCTS.pls`; `PAXPCTB.pls`**	
Calc_PCT_Comp_Amt	You can use this extension to define your own company-specific business rules for calculating revenue and invoices based on percent complete accrual. The extension provides default logic you can modify and then register through the billing extensions form. It uses the percent complete information that has been entered against the project or task in the Percent Complete form.
Extension: Project Security Extension **Package Name: PA_SECURITY_EXTN** **Files: `PAPSECXS.pls`; `PAPSECXB.pls`**	
Check_Project_Access	This extension enables you to define business-specific rules regarding users' ability to view project information. Through this client extension, you can enable security, such as only certain responsibilities are enabled to view or update certain project types.
Extension: Project Status Inquiry (PSI) Extension **Package Name: PA_CLIENT_EXTN_STATUS** **Files: `PAXVPS2S.pls`; `PAXVPS2B.pls`**	
Getcols	You can use this extension to set whether the system will use the PSI Column prompts when displaying client extension calculated amounts. If this procedure returns a NULL value, the system uses the prompts from the PSI Columns window.
Get_Totals	You can use this extension to override the totals columns on the PSI screen when using the getcols procedure to determine values. This extension must be modified when using the getcols procedure to use the Totals button.

TABLE 15.10 CONTINUED

Procedure Name	Description
Extension: Project Verification Extension **Package Name: PA_CLIENT_EXTN_PROJ_STATUS** **Files: `PAXPCECS.pls`; `PAXPCECB.pls`**	
Verify_Project_Status_Change	You can use this extension to add your own business requirements for allowing a project status to be changed. For example, you do not want the project status changed until each task has a task manager assigned.
Check_Wf_Enabled	Enables you to add additional checks to determine whether workflow should be enabled. For example, you might want to enable workflow whenever a status is changed from Unapproved to Approved, but not from Submitted to Approved. You can return a disabled response if the old status is Submitted.
Extension: Project Workflow Extension **Package Name: PA_CLIENT_EXTN_PROJ_WF** **Files: `PAWFPCES.pls`; `PAWFPCEB.pls`**	
Select_Project_Approver	Enables you to change the logic for selecting the default approver for project status changes.
Start_Project_Wf	This procedure starts the workflow. It enables you to add additional checks to determine whether the workflow should be started or if you want to change the default workflow that is called.
Extension: Receivables Installation Override Extension **Package Name: PA_OVERRIDE_AR_INST** **Files: `PAPARICS.pls`; `PAPARICB.pls`**	
Get_Installation_Mode	Oracle Projects imports customer data from full installations of Oracle Receivables. However, if you are using an external Receivables system, but want to import customer data from Oracle Receivables, you can use this extension to override the installation value for Receivables from full to shared.
Extension: Transaction Control Extension **Package Name: PATCX** **Files: `PAXTTCXS.pls`; `PAXTTCXB.pls`**	
TC_Extension	You can use the transaction control extension to define business-specific rules regarding whether specific expenditures can be charged to a project or task and whether the items are billable. Note: You cannot set an item on bill-hold through this extension.

TABLE 15.10 CONTINUED

Procedure Name	Description
Extension: Transfer Price Currency Conversion Override Extension **Package Name: PA_MULTI_CURR_CLIENT_EXTN** **Files: `PAPOCACS.pls`; `PAPOCACB.pls`**	
Override_Currency_Conv_Attributes	You can use this extension to change the attributes used to convert the transfer price from the transactional currency to the functional currency for transactions that are cross-charged.
Extension: Transfer Price Determination Extension **Package Name: PA_CC_TP_CLIENT_EXTN** **Files: `PAPTPRCS.pls`; `PAPTPRCB.pls`**	
Determine_Transfer_Price	You can use this extension to derive a transfer price other than that which is computed through standard Oracle Projects for transactions that are cross-charged.
Override_Transfer_Price	You can use this extension to enforce business-specific rules as to whether a derived transfer price should be allowed for cross-charged transactions.

SETTING UP PROJECTS TO INTEGRATE WITH OTHER ORACLE APPLICATIONS

Leveraging the robust functionality of Oracle Projects with the integration of other Oracle applications offers you greater flexibility and enables you to better support project-centric initiatives within your organization.

ADVANCED SETUP TASKS—PROFILE OPTIONS

Table 15.11 shows the profile options that must be set to integrate Oracle Projects with other Oracle Applications (Purchasing, Payables, Receivables, and so on).

TABLE 15.11 ADVANCED PROJECTS SETUP TASKS—PROFILE OPTIONS TO DEFINE FOR INTEGRATION WITH OTHER ORACLE APPLICATIONS

Profile Option	App	Description
PA: Allow Override of PA Distributions in AP/PO	AP/PO	You can set this option to `Yes` to override the accounting code combination generated in Payables and Purchasing.
PA: Default Expenditure Organization in AP/PO	AP/PO	This option enables you to set the expenditure organization that will default to Payables and Purchasing items where Project information is entered.

Table 15.11 Continued

Profile Option	App	Description
PA: Tasks to Display for Expenditure Entry	AP/PO	This option determines which tasks are shown in the list of values when entering requisitions or purchase orders in Purchasing, entering invoices in Payables, or entering expenditures in Projects.
PA: Summarize Expense Report Lines	AP	This option determines whether to summarize expense report lines transferred to Payables, from Projects, by code combination ID.
PA: Receivables Invoice Line UOM	AR	This option provides the default UOM for invoices interfaced to AR. A UOM & UOM class must be defined before this option can be set.
Tax: Allow Ad Hoc Tax Changes	AR	Setting this option to `Yes` allows you to change tax rates and amounts on the Transactions form.
Tax: Allow Override of Customer Exemptions	AR	Setting this option to `Yes` enables you to override the default customer tax exemptions.
Tax: Allow Override of Tax Code	AR	Setting this option to `Yes` allows you to change the default Tax Code on Projects invoice lines.
AR: Use Invoice Accounting for Credit Memos	AR	Projects requires this value be set to `No` to interface Credit Memos and write-offs to AR. Auto Invoice rejects Credit Memos and write-offs from Projects if this value is set to `Yes`.
AR: Transaction Flexfield QuickPick Attribute	AR	In the invoice query form, this attribute defines which transaction attribute can query in the Reference field.
GL: Set of Books Name	GL	Specifies the set of books.
INV: Project Miscellaneous Transaction Type	INV	You should set this to User Entered to select from the list of values of project expenditure types.
PA: AutoApprove Expense Reports	SSE	Set this option to `Yes` to import expense reports from Self-Service Expense to Projects as approved expenditures.
PA: AutoApprove Timesheets	OIT	Set this option to `Yes` to import time sheets from Self-Service Time to Projects as approved expenditures.
PA: Licensed to Use AMG	AMG	Option must be set to `Yes` to use Activity Management Gateway.

PROJECTS INTEGRATION WITH ORACLE PURCHASING

When you integrate Oracle Projects with Oracle Purchasing, you can create distribution lines on a Purchase Order or Requisition that are project related as well as view project commitments through Project Status Inquiry.

To process Purchase Orders and Requisitions that are charged to a project, Account Generator must be set up. The process that needs to be modified is called Purchase Order Charge Account for Purchase Orders and Requisition Charge Account for Requisitions. See the section "Advanced Configuration Tasks and Extensions," earlier in this chapter, for further information.

PROJECTS INTEGRATION WITH ORACLE PAYABLES

The following steps must be performed to integrate Oracle Payables with Oracle Projects. This will allow for interfacing project-related supplier invoices, entering employee expense reports in Payables and interfacing them to Projects, and using Oracle Internet Expenses.

CREATING AN EMPLOYEE AS A SUPPLIER On the Expense report tab of the Payables option form, the options listed in Table 15.12 need to be defined. If the Automatically Create Employee as Supplier box is checked, the options default to the new employee supplier as they are created.

TABLE 15.12 PAYABLES FIELDS—CREATE EMPLOYEE AS SUPPLIER

Option	Description
Payment Terms	The terms used to pay the expense report. Examples include Immediate or Net 10.
Pay Group	Grouping classification used for selecting payments and various reports.
Payment Priority	The way to group suppliers for payment.
Apply Advances	If this option is checked, Payables will apply outstanding advances to new invoices.
Automatically Create Employee as Supplier	Select this option to have Payables automatically create employees as employee suppliers during invoice import.
Hold Unmatched Expense Reports	Requires that the expense report be applied to a purchase order or receipt before being approved.

DEFINING PAYABLES DISTRIBUTION SETS Oracle Payables gives you the ability to speed invoice entry by using Distribution Sets by project information (Project, Task, Expenditure Type, or Organization). A Distribution Set can be assigned to a supplier site so that when an invoice for that supplier and supplier site is created, the distribution set defaults to the invoice.

Setting Up Account Generator for Payables and Expense Reports It is imperative that Account Generator be set up to process supplier invoices or Web expenses that include project-related expenditures. For supplier invoices, the process you need to modify is Project Supplier Invoice Account. If using Internet Expense, you also must modify the process Project Expense Report Account. See the section "Advanced Configuration Tasks and Extensions," earlier in this chapter for further information.

Setting Up and Enabling Oracle Internet Expense Internet Expense enables you to quickly and easily enter expense reports via a standard Web browser. If your company is using Oracle Projects, Internet Expense can be configured to enter project-related expense reports. Internet Expense records project, task, and expenditure information that will be imported into Oracle Projects via Payables. You can set up workflow approvals that are required, or you can set up the system to bypass the approval process altogether.

The following steps must be performed to make Internet Expense project enabled:

1. Oracle Projects profile option for PA: Allow Project Time and Expense Entry is set to `Yes`.
2. Configure the Project Expense Report Account workflow for Account Generator.
3. Define a project-related expense report template in Payables. In the Expense Report Templates window, you must assign valid Oracle Project expenditure types to various Payables expense items.
4. Set the profile option SS Expenses: Enable Projects to `Yes` at the site level.
5. If you want to bypass the projects approval process, set the PA: Auto Approve Expense Reports profile option in Oracle Projects to `Yes`.

Projects Integration with Oracle Receivables

To integrate Oracle Receivables with Oracle Projects, the following steps must be performed.

Setting the Require Salesrep Option If you require sales representative information on your projects and want this information to be transferred to Receivables, you must check the Require Salesrep option box. This option is on the Miscellaneous tab of the Receivables System Options form. When this option is checked, sales representatives must also be defined in the Accounts Receivable application.

Defining Transaction Types for Invoice Processing Oracle Projects passes invoices to the Receivables module. There are two options for this process: Centralized and De-Centralized processing.

Centralized Processing comes with two seeded transaction types: Projects Invoice and Projects Credit Memo.

De-Centralized Processing establishes a standard transaction type and a credit memo transaction type for each organization in HR that has the classification Project Invoice Collection Organization. To create these transaction types, you must run the Oracle Projects process IMP: Create Invoice Organization Transaction Types.

If you process invoices using de-centralized processing, the system traverses the organization hierarchy (from the project organization) until it finds the appropriate invoice organization for the transaction type.

Here are the summarized steps for De-Centralized Invoicing:

1. Determine the organizations that are invoicing organizations, and define the HR classification Project Invoice Collection Enabled for each one.
2. Ensure that the invoice organizations are in the Project/Task Organization Hierarchy.
3. Under Oracle Projects implementation options, disable the Centralized Invoicing box.
4. Run the process IMP: Create Invoice Organization Transaction Types.

DEFINING AUTOMATIC ACCOUNTING IN ORACLE RECEIVABLES Oracle Projects determines the accounts passed to the Receivables application for the standard invoice lines and offset. If you pass taxable invoice lines to Accounts Receivable, the accounting lines for the tax portion of the invoice are calculated using automatic accounting in AR.

You must set up account codes for Auto Invoice Clearing, Revenue, Tax, Freight, Receivable, Unbilled Receivable, and Deferred Revenue within the Receivables application.

SALESREPS AND CREDIT TYPES If you decide to pass Credit Receivers to the Receivables application, you must check the Require Salesrep option box. This option is on the Miscellaneous tab on the Receivables System Options form. Employees must be defined as salespersons in Accounts Receivables. Enter the employee as a salesperson in Oracle Receivables if the employee is eligible for sales commissions or will be a designated project manager.

Note

Use the Oracle Receivables Salespersons window to define salespersons. The name must be entered exactly as it has been created in Human Resources–for example, Adkins, Paul J. The salesperson number should be the same as the employee number, and you must enter a Sales Credit Type of Quota Sales Credit.

SETTING UP INVOICE LINE TAX CODES Tax codes are set up in your Receivables module. In the tax options window, you can choose whether you will be applying sales tax or VAT tax. Sales tax calculations are based on your customer ship to addresses, whereas VAT taxes are based on your tax hierarchy.

The key tax forms to be established are Tax Codes and Rates, Tax Authorities (Locations), Tax Exemptions (assigned to Customers), and Tax Groups (Municipalities). For transactions types, verify in Receivables that the tax-enabled option is checked.

PROJECTS INTEGRATION WITH ORACLE INVENTORY

Oracle Projects provides the ability to interface project expenditure costs from Inventory through a Miscellaneous Issue and to enter project-related costs into Inventory as a Miscellaneous Receipt. Both transactions are generated from the Inventory application and are interfaced into Projects through Transaction Import. Oracle Projects is also fully integrated with the MRP and WIP applications using Project Manufacturing.

To integrate Oracle Inventory with Oracle Projects, the following steps must be performed.

ESTABLISHING TRANSACTION TYPES IN INVENTORY In the Transaction Types setup section of Inventory, you must set up two types of transactions—one for issue to and one for receipt from. The source of an issue transaction type should be Miscellaneous Issue, and the source for a receipt into Inventory should be Miscellaneous Receipt. It is critical that you check the box Project Enabled to allow you to record transactions against a project.

Tip

When setting up transaction types in Inventory for project transactions, ensure that the Project Enabled box is checked.

SETTING PROFILE OPTION AND EXPENDITURE TYPE CLASS The profile option INV: Project Miscellaneous Transaction Type should be set to User Entered to enable you to select a valid Projects expenditure type from the list of values. To see expenditure types when entering an inventory transaction, be sure you assign the expenditure type class of Inventory for each related expenditure type.

Tip

If you are not seeing a list of expenditure types when entering a project-related transaction in Inventory, ensure that the expenditure type class of the expenditure type is set to Inventory.

VERIFYING TRANSACTION SOURCE Oracle Projects provides the transaction source Inventory Misc as the source for interfacing inventory transactions into Projects. You should verify that the source is not end-dated using the navigation under your Projects responsibility: Setup, Expenditures, Transaction Sources. You will notice that the entries are interfaced from Inventory as costed and GL accounted. Projects enables you to adjust these types of Inventory transactions and recost as necessary.

SETTING UP PROJECTS TO INTEGRATE WITH EXTERNAL SYSTEMS VIA ACTIVITY MANAGEMENT GATEWAY

The Activity Management Gateway (AMG) requires several setup steps to use the APIs.

DATABASE SETUPS

Although the APPS schema has all the rights necessary to run the AMG, the APPS schema should not be used as the AMG account. To easily create accounts that have all the appropriate grants and privileges, Oracle provides a script for creating an AMG role. This script is

PACRROLE.sql and can be found on the Application Server in the PA_TOP/admin/sql directory. To create an AMG role, log in to SQL from the directory where the file resides:

```
SQL> @pacrrole.sql &role &un_apps &pw_apps &un_pa &pw_pa
```

For example, to create the role AMG_ROLE in the VISION database, you would type the following:

```
SQL> @pacrrole.sql AMG_ROLE apps apps pa pa
```

After the database role is created, you need to create an Applications user with appropriate Projects responsibilities. This information is used by the AMG to verify security and controls when performing changes, additions, or deletions through the APIs.

After setting up the Applications user, a database user must be created. This database user is created with the script PACRUSER.sql, which can be found on the Application Server in the PA_TOP/admin/sql directory. The database user should be the same as the Applications user who was created previously.

To create an AMG database user, log in to SQL from the directory where the file resides:

```
SQL> @pacruser.sql &role &sys_un &sys_pw &uname &pwd &apps_un &apps_ps
```

For example, to create the database user for the Applications user Services with a password of welcome and the role AMG_ROLE in the VISION database, you would type the following:

```
SQL> @pacruser.sql AMG_ROLE system manager SERVICES WELCOME apps apps
```

Note

If you want to have different users for your integration (for audit purposes or for user-specific security), you should set up multiple database users using the provided script to match your Applications users.

However, database users and Applications users are separate entities with different passwords. Changing the Applications user password does not change the database user password.

Tip

You can use the script PATEMPUS.SQL to set up a large number of database users from existing Applications users (rather than running PACRUSER for each Applications user).

PROJECTS APPLICATION SETUPS

After you have established your database environment, you must set up your integration within the Projects Application. To do this, you must first enable the use of the AMG by setting the profile option PA:Licensed to use AMG to Yes.

Next, you need to register your interface product as a Source Product in Oracle Projects, as shown in Figure 15.24. To do this, perform these steps:

1. Navigation Path PA: Setup, Activity Management Gateway, Source Products.
2. Enter an alphanumeric value in the code field to identify your integration.

3. Enter the full name of your integration in the Meaning field.
4. Enter a description for your integration.
5. Provide appropriate effective dates.
6. Save your work.

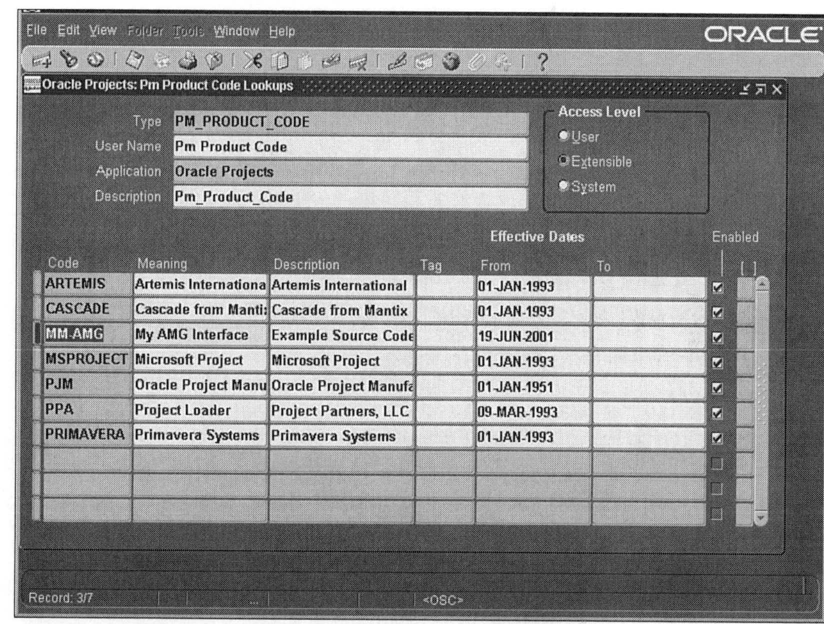

Figure 15.24
Define your source product in Oracle Projects.

Note

The AMG APIs do NOT validate the source product when the APIs are called. Therefore, you can call the APIs and load data into Oracle Projects without having completed this step. However, neither the tasks form nor the budget lines form will work appropriately when trying to display data that has been loaded with a product code that is not marked as effective in the Source Products screen.

SETTING UP SECURITY

One benefit of using the AMG to interface data to Oracle is that it maintains security on several levels. By setting up a database user that matches an Applications user, the integration application can authenticate the user by using the login information to establish a connection with the database. If the connection can't be established, your code can raise an error and not allow the individual to load data.

Furthermore, after a valid username has been established, you can verify that the user has an effective Projects responsibility by using the AMG view PA_USER_RESP_V. If more than one responsibility exists, the user can be given an option to select the appropriate responsibility. This is an important step because user responsibilities can limit what the user is allowed to add, delete, or modify.

Further optional security can be set up through the use of Functional Security and Control Actions.

First, if you want to control which actions can be done via the AMG (control what the integration application can and can't do), you can set up controls through standard Oracle Applications Function Security at the responsibility level.

When calling the AMG APIs, you had to set a global variable for a valid Projects Responsibility. Now, you can set exclusions on that responsibility in Oracle by logging in to the Applications as a System Administration responsibility:

1. Navigation Path SysAdmin: Security; Responsibility; Define.
2. Query the Projects Responsibility.
3. Add various AMG exclusions, such as Add Task or Delete Project.

If the responsibility has the exclusion of AMG: Delete Project, calls to any AMG API that will attempt to delete a project given this responsibility will fail with an error stating that this function is not allowed. Figure 15.25 shows an example of AMG exclusions that can be added to responsibilities.

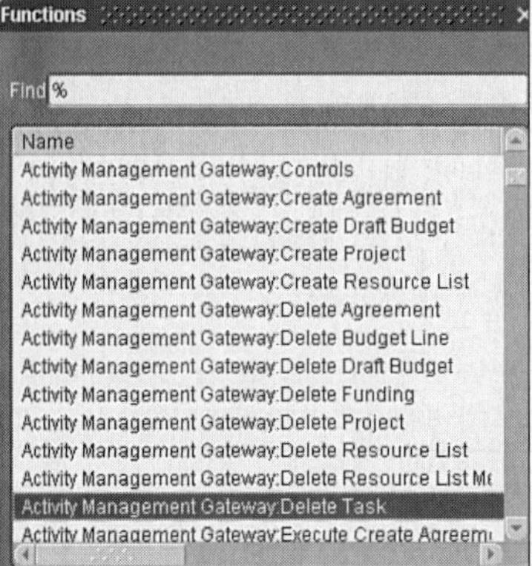

Figure 15.25
Exclude certain actions from being performed through the AMG based on user responsibility.

Using Function Security limits what the AMG is allowed to do, but it does not limit what an Oracle Applications user can do to information from a third-party system. This type of control can be enabled through a feature called Control Actions. Control Actions are defined based on Source Products and limit what can be done in Oracle Projects to information created through that Source Product. To set up Control actions, follow these steps:

1. Navigation Path PA: Setup, Activity Management Gateway, Control Actions.
2. Query your source product.
3. Select an action to be limited.

4. Select a type if appropriate.
5. Set the effective dates as appropriate.
6. Save your work.

Figure 15.26 shows how to set Control Actions so that you can't delete tasks or add funding from within Oracle Projects if the project was created through the My AMG Interface integration. Also, you can't baseline an Approved Revenue budget that originated through the My AMG Interface integration.

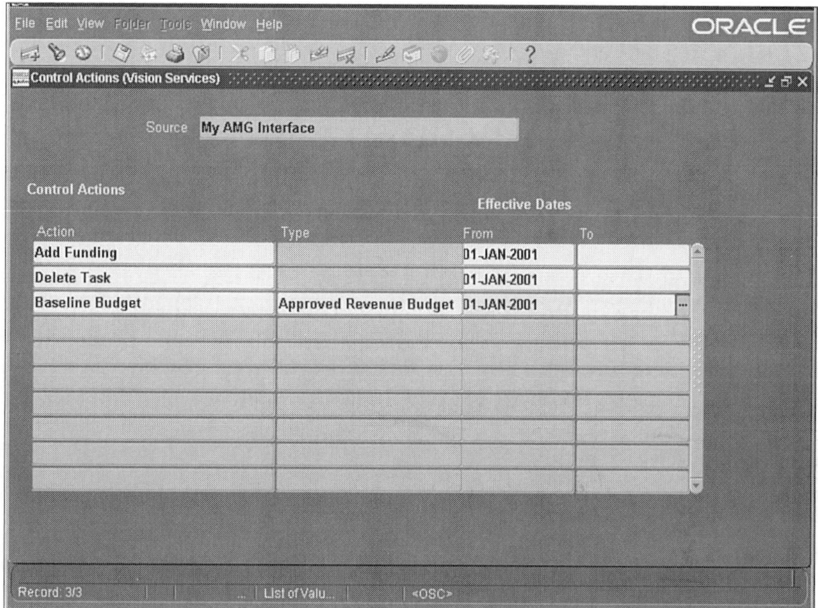

Figure 15.26
Limit what actions can be performed within Oracle Projects on items originating through the AMG with Control Actions.

Implementing Your Interface Code That Calls the Appropriate AMG APIs

The AMG consists of more than 100 views and stored packages, or procedures. Descriptions of these objects can be found in the *Oracle Projects Activity Management Gateway Technical Reference Manual.*

The main workhorses of the AMG are the stored procedures called to load information into Oracle Projects. The APIs have been grouped based on the information that is being loaded—Projects, Budgets, Resources, Status, and General. The packages are

- PA_PROJECT_PUB
- PA_BUDGET_PUB
- PA_RESOURCE_PUB
- PA_STATUS_PUB
- PA_INTERFACE_UTILS_PUB
- PA_AGREEMENT_PUB

Some examples of the procedures in these packages include

ADD_BUDGET_LINE	FETCH_RESOURCE_LIST
ADD_TASK	LOAD_BUDGET_LINE
CHECK_ADD_SUBTASK_OK	LOAD_KEY_MEMBER
CREATE_PROJECT	PA_CUSTOMERS_LOV
DELETE_TASK	PA_SELECT_TEMPLATE
DELETE_PROJECT	UPDATE_BUDGET_LINE
FETCH_BUDGET_LINE	UPDATE_PROJECT

As the names imply, some of these procedures add or update information in Oracle Projects (ADD_TASK, UPDATE_PROJECT), whereas others are used to verify that an action can be performed without violating an Oracle Projects business rule (CHECK_ADD_SUBTASK_OK).

For more information and sample code for writing AMG integration, you can find a detailed white paper ("Close Encounters of the Third-Party Kind") at `http://www.projectp.com`.

EXISTING INTEGRATION BETWEEN ORACLE PROJECTS AND EXTERNAL SYSTEMS

This section showcases what is possible through the use of the AMG and demonstrates how information can be shared between various systems. The examples range from simple integration with Excel spreadsheets (for budgeting) to complex integration with project management systems for tracking earned value information.

INTEGRATION TO PROJECT MANAGEMENT SYSTEMS—COTS SOLUTIONS Advanced Project Management (PM) products offer you a greatly enhanced ability to proactively analyze and control costs, resources, and schedules across your enterprise's business operation. With integration to Oracle Projects via the AMG, you can now see reduced project cost overruns, optimized resource scheduling, improved project life cycle times, and overall improved profitability.

Increasingly, companies today are adopting the disciplines of project management as a business-operation philosophy, and the capabilities of their project management software applications can be a business-critical factor in remaining competitive.

Several project management software packages have integration with Oracle Projects (either through their own software or through a third-party add-on) to help you realize the benefits described here.

ORACLE PROJECTS TO P3E INTEGRATION (RELEASES 11 - 11I) Oracle Projects enhances your enterprise project management capacity by seamlessly integrating with P3e. This integration provides the following features:

- **A usable application**—If the tool was not designed for the intended user, the project manager won't (and can't) benefit from its deployment. Typically, specialized project management software has better application navigation and is designed to reflect a typical workday or work week for the project manager.

- **Highly visual metaphors coupled with very strong reporting capabilities**—Project managers are used to using charts and graphs to manage projects. Also, extremely flexible ad hoc reporting is essential for project analysis.
- **A common data repository**—Resources used by the project manager should be the same resources used in Oracle Projects. Additionally, projects managed by the project managers using a PM tool should be the *same* projects used by Oracle Projects. And lastly, actuals recorded in the PM tool should be the same as those recorded in Oracle Projects. A common data repository that uses the same Oracle technology greatly enhances the sharing of a common data model.

For more information about this project management integration product, visit `http://www.projectp.com`.

PROJECT LOADER (RELEASES 10.7 - R11I) Project Loader is a commercially available software package offered by Project Partners, LLC. Project Loader enables you to interface project-related information into Oracle Projects using a series of interface tables, processes, and Oracle's Activity Management Gateway. Project Loader is designed to help you integrate project management systems, legacy project systems, and even custom budgeting systems with Oracle Projects. This cost-effective, time-saving, batch-oriented approach uses the creation, update, and deletion capabilities of the AMG without requiring additional extensive programming. Data integrity is maintained using the Oracle AMG integrated business rules.

Project Loader provides approximately two-thirds of the code necessary to integrate an external product with Oracle Projects. Customers only need to map data from their external systems to the Project Loader tables. Project Loader already handles processing logic, calling the AMG APIs in appropriate sequences; handles errors; and runs through Oracle's Standard Report Submission, giving you flexibility with scheduling and process prioritization. Furthermore, Project Partners continually monitors the AMG patching to ensure upward compatibility of Project Loader with new Oracle Projects patches and releases.

PROJECT CONNECT (RELEASES 10.7 - R11I) Oracle Corporation provides integration with Microsoft Project and Oracle Project. This application—Project Connect—can be acquired from Oracle.

Oracle Project Connect for Microsoft Project links Microsoft Project and Oracle Projects, so you can work with a project in both applications. The two applications share project information while maintaining the project and function security set up in Oracle Projects. The application uses the AMG to share data.

OTHER APPLICATIONS Other applications that support integration between Oracle Projects and Project Management Software (through Release 11 only) include

- **Artemis**—ProjectView and CostView
- **Mantix**—Cascade

- **Primavera**—Primavera Project Planner, Peak
- **ABT**—Integrator

CONVERTING LEGACY DATA

Many who have experienced converting data from legacy systems are the last to volunteer for future conversion efforts. The quality of the data in the legacy system is normally one of the leading reasons for migrating to a new system in the first place. Oracle Projects provides rich functionality for converting your legacy system information from projects and budgets to transactions, costs, revenue, and billing balances.

PROJECTS, TASKS, AGREEMENTS, FUNDING, AND BUDGETS

Oracle Projects has long supported the ability to import transactional data (time-entry information, expense reports, and usage transactions) through a standard import table. This Transaction Import helped you get transactional data from third-party vendors into Oracle Projects, but the import table worked only for the detailed transaction information and not project setup information. It did not provide a means for importing Project setup values, including the project header, work breakdown structures, key members, project classifications, budgets, funding, and agreements.

Because the Transaction Import Process did not support importing project and budget information, many consultants resorted to writing custom programs or routines that wrote directly to the tables. Some of these programs worked well, but some did not. In writing directly to the tables, you ran the risk of unknowingly violating fundamental Oracle Projects business rules (deleting tasks that had charges against them, placing a subtask under a task that had already incurred expenses, and so on). These violations caused standard Oracle Projects processes, such as distributing costs, generating revenue and invoices, and transferring data to other financial applications, to fail. Sometimes, they even resulted in forms not pulling ANY data for the entire project. Furthermore, Oracle would not support issues arising from writing directly to the tables.

Without writing directly to the tables, how can you get project setup information converted into Oracle Projects?

TOOLS TO LOAD PROJECT SETUP INFORMATION

Because Oracle does not support writing data directly to the Projects tables, you should use a tool that either automates form entry (such as an Excel dataloader) or uses the Activity Management Gateway APIs, such as Project Loader (`http://www.projectp.com`). You can also choose to write your own code to use the AMG APIs. See the section "Setting Up Projects to Integrate with External Systems via Activity Management Gateway," earlier in this chapter, for more information about writing code to use the AMG.

When choosing a tool for converting data, you should take into consideration whether the conversion is one-time or whether the interface will be ongoing. Many companies have legacy systems they need integrated with Oracle Projects but do not plan to eliminate in the near future. This ongoing conversion of data should influence your choice of tools.

Note

Although several companies provide tools to help map information from legacy systems into Oracle tables, these tools still primarily write directly to the tables. Caution should be exercised when using these tools so as not to violate basic Projects business rules.

DATALOADERS Several tools are available that enable you to use an Excel spreadsheet and forms key-mapping to load information directly into the Oracle forms as if you were typing. This option takes a certain amount of setup effort (you must code in each keystroke you would make in the form [tabs, Enters, saves, and so on]) and are sometimes difficult to use when working with forms containing multiple regions. However, after they're set up, they can quickly load large amounts of data.

PROJECT LOADER Project Loader enables you to interface project-related information into Oracle Projects using a series of interface tables, processes, and Oracle's Activity Management Gateway. Project Loader is designed to help you integrate project management systems, legacy project systems, and even custom budgeting systems with Oracle Projects. Project Loader provides interface tables into which you easily can load your data. After the data is in the tables, you submit the appropriate Project Loader process from the Standard Report Submission screen within Oracle Applications. Three processes are included with Project Loader:

- **PPA: Project Loader**—Enables the creation, update, and deletion of projects, tasks, key members, and class categories. It provides the ability to load percent complete information at the time of project loading.
- **PPA: Budget Loader**—Enables the creation, update, and deletion of all types of budgets. Enables the creation, update, and deletion of associated budget lines. It provides the ability to replace existing budgets or create new versions of a budget and enables users to mark budgets as original, revised original, or baselined.
- **PPA: Update Progress**—Enables percent complete and earned value information to be loaded at the task and project levels for accounting, reporting, and enterprise-wide project analysis purposes.

Each process produces an output report indicating successful data loads, as well as a user-friendly exception report in the event of data rejection.

In future releases, Project Loader will also support the integration of agreement and funding data.

ITEMS TO CONSIDER IN CONVERTING PROJECT SETUP INFORMATION

When converting Projects setups (projects, tasks, budgets, agreements, and funding), there are several important considerations. First, do not underestimate the amount of work involved in cleaning up the legacy data. The cleaner the data is, the easier it will be to map.

Second, the availability of the data in the legacy database can't be overlooked. If the data from the legacy systems is limited as a result of storage, prior purging policies, or mapping constraints, this affects the amount of information to be converted.

It is also important to consider how much information you need to convert. Your legacy system might have greater detail than you need in Oracle Projects (such as more detailed work breakdown structures). This is your opportunity to decide whether you can reduce the amount of information being sent.

You should also consider whether this is a one-time conversion or an ongoing conversion of data. Your implementation of Oracle Projects might be replacing a legacy system, so you will need to convert data only once. This can influence the amount of data you choose to convert, as well as the tool you use for conversion. You might have legacy systems (third-party or external) that will not be replaced by Oracle Projects, and the data that is entered in them might need to be sent to Oracle Projects. Again, this potential ongoing conversion of data can be a critical factor in your Oracle Projects data-conversion effort.

Tip

If you're converting data from more than one system, you might want to set up separate Source Products for each legacy system. This allows visibility in Oracle Projects regarding from which system the data was converted.

When using the AMG APIs to load data, you will need to understand the basic business rules within Oracle Projects to ensure proper loading of data. In some cases, you might need to use multiple passes to convert your data as needed. For example, if you have projects that need to be converted with a project status that is not defined as a valid starting status, you must either temporarily change the status to be a starting status or interface the project with a valid starting status and then update the project to the appropriate project status.

Note

If using the AMG APIs to convert legacy project data, you will need to ensure that you have a template setup that allows all the necessary quick entry fields that you will be interfacing. If these fields are not in the template quick entry, that piece of data sent through the APIs will be ignored.

When working with budget information, Oracle Projects provides the ability to track version history. Therefore, if you have this type of history in your legacy system, you might want to interface it. It is important to remember that Oracle Projects will only display baselined budgets in the history. Therefore, to have forms visibility to history, you must baseline a converted budget (manually or through the AMG APIs) before loading your next version.

Note

When using the AMG APIs to baseline revenue budgets, you must first have funding equal to the revenue budget for the baseline to be successful. You can either enter the funding manually in the Agreements and Funding forms or load them through the new Agreement/Funding AMG APIs before submitting your baseline request.

TRANSACTIONS COSTS, REVENUE, AND BILLING

When converting transactions, there are several important considerations. First, do not underestimate the amount of work involved in cleaning up the legacy data. The cleaner the legacy data is, the easier it will be to map.

Second, the availability of the data in the legacy database can't be overlooked. If the data from the legacy systems is limited as a result of storage, prior purging policies, or mapping constraints, the amount of information to be converted will be affected.

After a baseline for converted transactions has been established and transactions have been mapped to the appropriate Project fields, certain decisions must be made in the following areas.

CONVERTED PROJECT COSTS AND THE GENERAL LEDGER

Converted Project costs can be recorded in Projects two ways: via the Transaction Import process or via manual entry in expenditure batches. Data volume normally dictates the feasibility of manual entry.

Various options are available for reconciling Project-related costs and GL amounts. Project-related converted costs either can be interfaced to GL from Projects or are not.

If costs are not interfaced to the GL from Projects, some consideration must be given to reconciling Project and GL balances before converting the data. Also, when costs are not interfaced to the GL from Projects, they can either be brought in to Projects as GL Accounted or not. When they are brought in as GL Accounted, they must include the debit and credit code combination ID. When costs are not accounted prior to import, the Project AutoAccounting rules can derive accounting on converted transactions.

When converted costs are interfaced from Projects to the GL, balance entries will be passed to the GL from Projects.

Note

Projects uses the GL calendar for its periods. You must set up calendars in the General Ledger that correspond to the earliest date of your converted Projects transactions.

A level of detail for converted cost transactions must be determined when considering converting transactions. For instance, conversion costs can be summarized and booked to Expenditure Types reserved for conversion. Alternatively, separate Transaction Sources can be set up for the conversion. This can be important if expenditure type detail needs to be converted. A separate conversion task on the project is yet another vehicle for conversion and facilitates identifying converted transactions from production transactions, when necessary.

Note

If your legacy system does not carry the associated accounting transactions from legacy subsystems, costs can be accounted in projects and still not interfaced to the GL. The Implementation Options can prevent certain cost transactions from interfacing to the GL. That way, AutoAccounting can be used to assign accounting to the transaction. However, you must indicate Allow Adjustments on the Transaction Source for these projects

TRANSACTION IMPORT

The Transaction Import interface table enables you to interface production data and converted data. This provides the best vehicle for converting your legacy cost data. The Transaction Import process performs the necessary validation and loading of the legacy data into the production tables. All transactions interfaced to Projects are imported based on the setup of a Transaction Source.

Tip

Many transaction expenditures that are being converted are for historical reporting purposes only. Consider establishing a transaction source for importing conversion expenditures, marking the source as GL accounted and adjustments not allowed. Import monthly summary expenditures using a clearing account for both the debit and credit accounting lines. By marking the source with adjustments not allowed, you will be unable to modify the converted amounts.

The fields indicated in Table 15.13 show all the potential components of a Transaction Source. The Transaction Sources used for converting legacy data would need to be set up with the appropriate combination of components relative to the legacy data.

TABLE 15.13 MATRIX OF AVAILABLE TRANSACTION SOURCE FIELDS

Field	Description
Transaction Source	Naming convention used for importing transactions. Often relates to the legacy source system. Inventory and Manufacturing transaction sources are predefined.
Default Expenditure Type Class	Defaults the expenditure type class for all transactions coming from this source. Expenditure type class refers to the kind of transactions (expense reports, miscellaneous, usage, straight time, and so on).
Raw Cost GL Accounted	Used for transactions that will not be interfaced to the GL or AP. Used for inventory and manufacturing transactions. When this option is selected, Import Raw Cost Amounts are checked as well.

Table 15.13 Continued

Field	Description
Import Raw Cost Amounts	Indicates whether an item has been costed in the legacy system. This amount is recorded in the Raw Cost column in Projects. The transaction can't incur additional costing, but it can be burdened and interfaced to the GL.
Import Burdened Amounts	Indicates whether an item has been burdened in the legacy system. Import Raw Cost Amount is checked when this option is checked. No burdening can occur in Projects, but the costs can be interfaced to the GL.
Import MRC Amounts	Indicator that the external system provides the functional currency and each associated reporting currency.
Allow Duplicate Reference	Transactions can be uniquely identified to the legacy system. When this option is checked, transactions can carry duplicate references and therefore can't be uniquely identified to the legacy system.
Import Employee Organization	Employees are assigned organizations. For employee-related transactions interfaced, this option allows the use of an organization other than the employee organization to be carried on the transaction.
Allow Interface Modifications	Enables modifications to transactions on the interface table prior to interfacing to Projects.
Purge After Import	All successfully interfaced transactions are purged from the interface table when this option is checked.
Allow Reversals	Allows for the imported transactions or batches to be reversed—this will enable the Allow Adjustments. When required, a corresponding reversal would have to be done in the legacy system.
Allow Adjustments	Enables adjustments functionality to expenditures imported. When not checked, the only means to adjust the items is in the legacy system.
Process Cross Charge	Can indicate that a cross charge occurred in the legacy system and will not be processed in Projects.
Pre Processing Extension	Allows for including an extension before the Transaction Import Process Runs; usually used for loading the interface table.
Post Processing Extension	Allows for including an extension after the Transaction Import Process runs; used for expenditures and expenditure items.

Converting Revenue and Billing Amounts

Unlike the Transaction Import Process, no interface process is available for converted revenue and billing amounts. Here again, you have two options for converting revenue and billing legacy balances. Both involve creating conversion revenue and billing events.

CONVERSION EVENTS

Conversion events can be entered manually or interfaced directly to the tables. Again, data volume normally dictates whether events can be entered manually.

In the case of revenue and billing events, some thought must be given to whether converted revenue is to post to the GL from Projects and whether billings are to be interfaced to AR from Projects and to GL from AR.

In either case, conversion revenue and billing events provide the simplest means to convert your revenue and billing information.

Note

If revenue and billing legacy data are converted manually, funding is required to allow for revenue and billings to generate. This generation means the events are reportable and can interface to AR and GL.

BALANCING THE CONVERSION

After data from the legacy system has been converted, it is important to ensure that the new balances in Oracle balance.

GL BALANCES

When converted data is run through the standard processes, the cost and revenue amounts entered and funded in Projects interface to the GL, based on the AutoAccounting rule definitions. The AR transactions also post to the GL from AR. All transactions post to balanced debit and credit accounts.

Some care needs to be taken that the appropriate periods are opened in the Projects, AR, and GL. If monthly legacy balances are being processed, periods in each module should be opened and closed after transactions have been processed.

If transactions are not posted from Projects but are accounted for in Projects, the Project subledger reports provide the means for comparing converted balances in Projects against converted balances in the GL.

EXTERNAL SYSTEMS

You can use standard reports and forms provided within the Oracle applications to compare balances in Oracle to balances in the legacy system.

When comparing your converted totals with your legacy system, several Project reports can help you. Expenditure reports can provide detail for converted cost balances and billing reports for the converted billing balances.

Online, Project Status Inquiry (PSI) gives you rollups as well as detailed amounts by Project that can assist in checking converted Project balances. Expenditure Item detail provides an online reporting capability for converted data. You can also use the Invoice Review and

Revenue Review forms to provide detailed and summarized information about Project Revenue and Billing totals.

Finally, you can use SQL queries to report against the Oracle tables to display the desired view of the conversion data.

PROCESSING TRANSACTIONS

This section provides you with the steps necessary to enter transactions into Oracle Projects and perform appropriate costing and accounting processing. It also provides the steps necessary to generate revenue and invoices for contract projects, as well as generate asset lines for capital projects. Information is also provided on how to handle adjustments in the system.

CREATING BASIC EXPENDITURE ITEMS

To proceed with this section, you must have a project created from a template. That project must be in an approved status. Also, you must have the required setup steps complete (see the section "Basic Setup Tasks," earlier in this chapter).

To follow the steps for revenue and invoice generation, your project class must be contract.

To follow the steps for generating asset lines, your project class must be capital.

CREATING LABOR TRANSACTIONS

Labor transactions can be entered into the system through Oracle Internet Time or through Pre-Approved Batch.

ORACLE INTERNET TIME You can use the Oracle Internet Time to enter timesheets. If you have been set up as an authorized user, you might be able to enter timesheets for other individuals.

Timesheets can be entered via Oracle Internet Time. To do this, you must log on to Oracle Internet Time (Timecards) from your Oracle Launch page and select Create New Timecard, as shown in Figure 15.27.

Then follow these steps:

1. If you are authorized to enter timecards for multiple people, you will be asked to select the employee name.
2. You should ensure that the week ending date is correct for the timecard that you want to enter.
3. If you are allowed to override the approver, you can select an approver.
4. Add general comments if appropriate in the General Comments field.
5. In the Timecard region, enter project, task, and type information on the line.
6. Enter the appropriate hours for each day of the week.
7. Enter as many different project, task, and type combinations as necessary.

8. Click the Line Details button to add comments to specific time entries.
9. When finished with entering lines on your timesheet, click the Next button. This will provide you with a review form (see Figure 15.28).

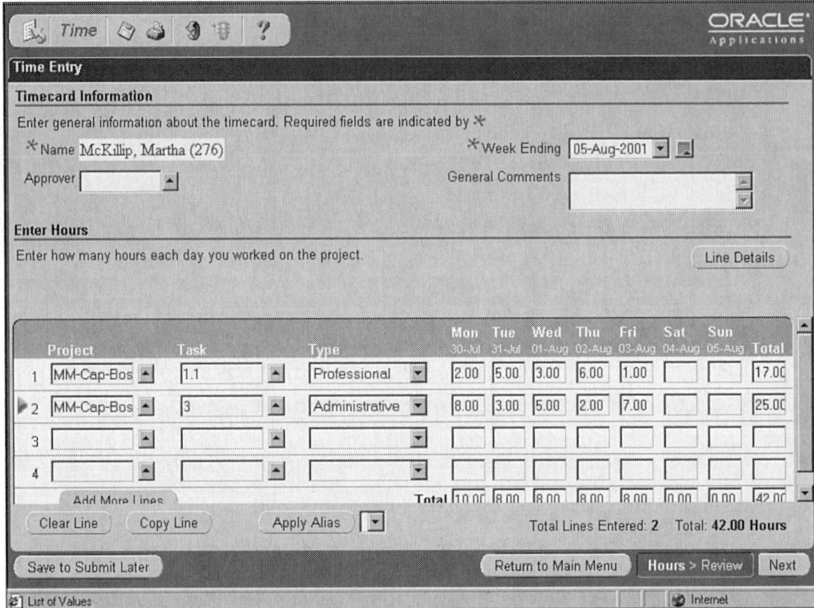

Figure 15.27
Enter your timesheets via Oracle Internet Time.

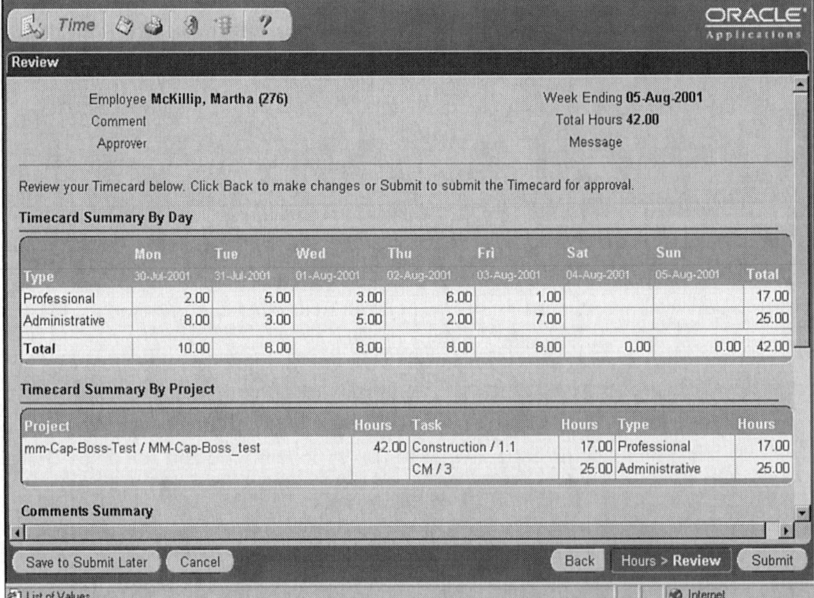

Figure 15.28
After entering your timesheets, you have the opportunity to review before you submit.

At this point, you can go back if you notice errors on the timecard. You also can click Save to Submit Later if you are satisfied with the timecard for now but are not ready to submit it, or you can submit your timecard.

When submitting a timecard, you will be asked whether you are sure you want to submit it. If you respond Yes, your timecard will be submitted. If the profile option for AutoApprove Timecards has not been enabled, a notification will be sent to the appropriate approver for your timecard. After it's approved, the time transactions will show against the projects in Oracle Projects.

PRE-APPROVED BATCH ENTRY OF LABOR You can use the Pre-Approved Batch forms to enter labor hours against multiple employees. As the name implies, there is no additional approval process for items entered through this method. After the batch is released, the labor transactions show on the project.

> **Tip**
>
> If your contract project is classified with a distribution rule of Work/Work, ensure that the job is on your bill rate schedule with an assigned rate.

To enter labor transactions using Pre-Approved Batch (see Figure 15.29), do the following:

1. From an appropriate Projects responsibility, use the following navigation to enter preapproved batches: Expenditures, Pre-Approved Batches, Enter.
2. Enter a batch number and week ending date for the weekly cycle you are recording.
3. Select Timecards in the released, the labor transactions show on class field.
4. Change the description (defaults to class).

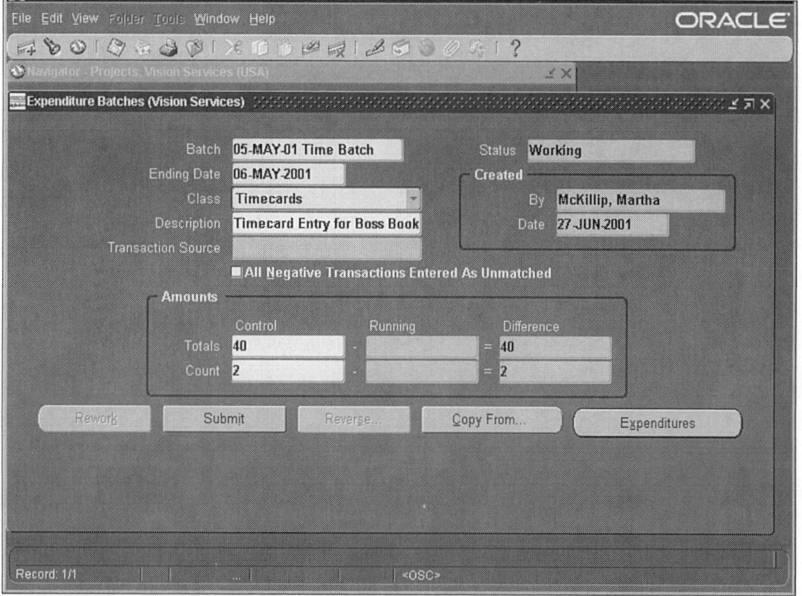

Figure 15.29 Select the type of transaction you want to enter in the Pre-Approved Batch window.

You can optionally enter information in the Control Totals section to cross-check your batch entries for correctness.

Tip

If you have already entered a previous batch that contains similar data to the batch you are about to enter, you can use the Copy From button to create your batch. This functionality is useful for administrative entry where the same employees submit timesheets on a weekly basis.

Next, continue to the Expenditure released, the labor transactions show on Batch window by clicking the Expenditures button. As shown in Figure 15.30, enter the employee name or number. The organization the employee is assigned to will default. Although not required, you might want to enter a control total for this person to provide a cross-check for correctness of entry. Now you are ready to enter transactions for that person:

1. Enter the project, task, expenditure type, and quantity.
2. The UOM (unit of measure) defaults based on the expenditure type.
3. If a description is required, enter this in the Comments field.

Note

More than one employee can be entered per expenditure batch. Save the employee you are working on, and proceed to the field below the first employee.

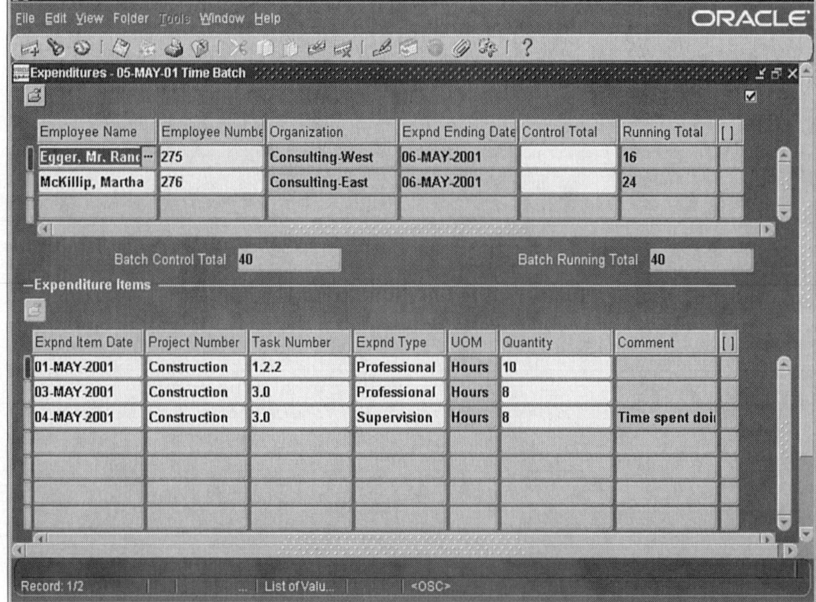

Figure 15.30
Pre-Approved Batch entry enables you to enter timecards for multiple employees.

Tip

When entering labor transactions, only released, the labor transactions show on expenditures can be entered for days in the week-ending cycle.

After the expenditure entry is complete, save your work and return to the batch form. From this form, you can

- Verify that your control totals are correct.
- Submit your batch.
- Release your released, the labor transactions show on batch.

CREATING EXPENSE REPORT TRANSACTIONS

Expense report transactions can released, the labor transactions show on be entered into the system through Oracle Internet Expense (previously Self-Service Expense) or through Pre-Approved Batch.

ORACLE INTERNET EXPENSE ENTRY Expense Reports can be entered via on Oracle Internet Expense. To do this, you must log on to Self-Service Applications (iExpense) and select Create New Expense Report, as shown in Figure 15.31.

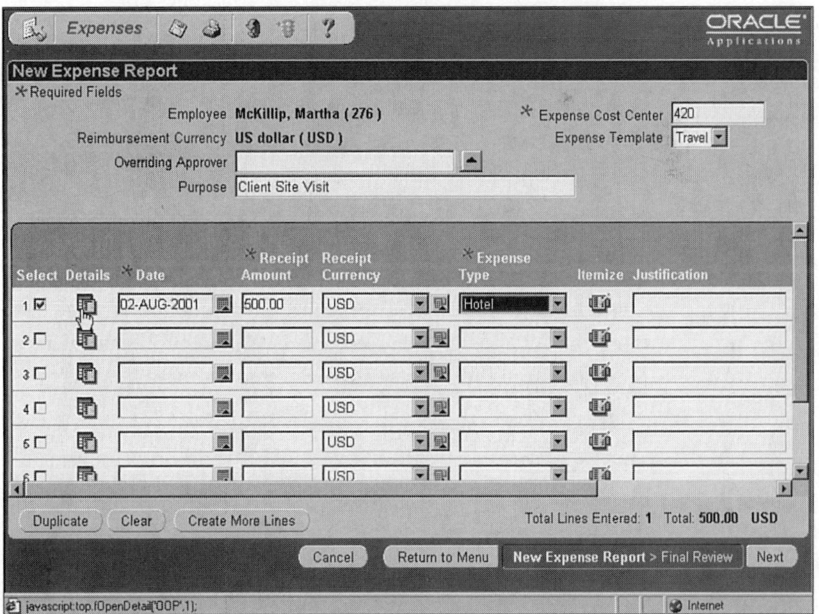

Figure 15.31
Oracle Internet Expense enables you to enter new expense reports.

In the Expense Report header area, select an employee name and expense template. Although the expense cost center is required, it is automatically populated based on the employee.

In the next section, enter the required fields (as shown in Figure 15.32): the date of the expense item, the receipt amount, and the expense type. To enter project information for this expense transaction, click the Details button.

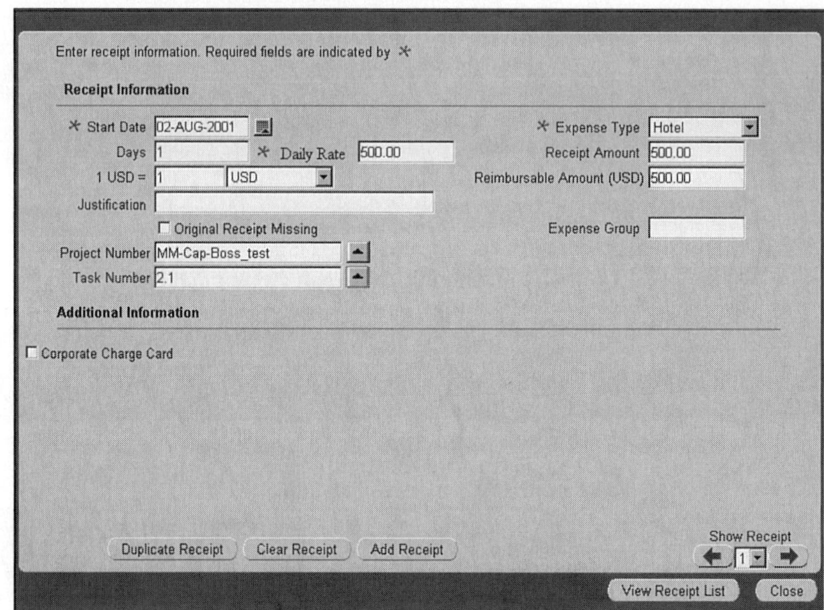

Figure 15.32
Enter your expense report header information for your new expense report.

In the Receipt Detail form, you will notice that several fields are populated from the previous screen: start date, days, daily rate, expense type, receipt amount, and reimbursable amount.

From here, you need to choose the appropriate project and task. When you are finished filling out the receipt detail, click the View Receipt button. This returns you to the original form, and you can enter additional expense transactions as necessary.

After the Expense Report is complete, click Next. You will receive an alert informing you that your expense report is being validated. If an error occurs, a detailed message will display explaining how to resolve the error. If no errors occur, the Review screen will display. At this point you can either submit or save the expense report for future modifications.

If the project approval process is in place, your expense report must be approved via workflow. The expense report is then imported into Payables. After it is approved and processed in Payables, it is interfaced into Projects using the standard processing for Interface Expense Reports from Payables.

PRE-APPROVED BATCH ENTRY EXPENSE REPORTS You can use the Pre-Approved Batch forms to enter expense reports against multiple employees. As the name implies, there is no additional approval process for items entered through this method. After the batch is released, the expense report transactions show on the project.

To enter expense report transactions using pre-approved batch, do the following:

1. From an appropriate Projects responsibility, use the following navigation to enter preapproved batches: Expenditures, Pre-Approved Batches, Enter.
2. Enter a batch number and week-ending date for the weekly cycle you are recording.
3. Select Expenses in the class field.
4. Change the description (defaults to class).

You can optionally enter information in the Control Totals section to cross-check your batch entries for correctness.

Tip

If you have already entered a previous batch that contains similar data to the batch you are about to enter, you can use the Copy From button to create your batch. This functionality is useful for administrative entry where the same employees submit expense reports on a weekly basis.

Next, continue to the Expenditure Batch window by clicking the Expenditures button. Enter the employee name or number. The organization the employee is assigned to will default. Although not required, you might want to enter a control total for this person to provide a cross-check for correctness of entry.

Now you are ready to enter transactions for that person:

1. Enter the project, task, expenditure type.
2. Enter the quantity and amount as appropriate.
3. The UOM defaults based on the expenditure type.
4. If a description is required, enter this in the Comments field.

Note

More than one employee can be entered per expenditure batch. Save the employee you are working on, and proceed to the field below the first employee.

After the expenditure entry is complete, save your work and return to the batch form. From this form, you can

- Verify that your control totals are correct.
- Submit your batch.
- Release your batch.

CREATING USAGE TRANSACTIONS

You enter usage transactions through the Pre-Approved Batch form.

> **Note**
>
> Be sure that you have set up Non-Labor Resources before proceeding with the batch entry. Follow the same path as for the pre-approved time entry or pre-approved expense reports.

To enter usage transactions using a pre-approved batch, follow these steps:

1. From an appropriate Projects responsibility, use the following navigation to enter preapproved batches: Expenditures, Pre-Approved Batches, Enter.
2. Enter a batch number and week-ending date for the weekly cycle you are recording.
3. Select Usages in the class field.
4. Change the description (defaults to class).

You can optionally enter information in the Control Totals section to cross-check your batch entries for correctness.

Next, continue to the Expenditure Batch Form by clicking the Expenditures button:

1. Enter the employee name or number (optional).
2. Enter the organization if no employee is supplied.
3. You can optionally enter a control total for this person or organization to provide you with a cross-check for correctness of entry.

> **Note**
>
> For Usages, an employee is not required but an expenditure organization must be entered. If you enter an employee name or number, the organization defaults from the organization assigned in HR.

Now you are ready to enter transactions for that person, as shown in Figure 15.33:

1. Enter the project, task, and expenditure type.
2. Enter the Non-Labor Resource and Non-Labor Resource Organization.
3. Enter the quantity and amount as appropriate.
4. The UOM defaults based on the expenditure type.
5. If a description is required, enter this in the Comments field.

Note

On the Expenditures Detail window, you will note two additional fields that are required for usages. Both the Non-Labor Resource and Non-Labor Resource Organization are associated with the expenditure type you enter.

Figure 15.33
You can enter non-labor usage transactions in the Pre-Approved Batch window.

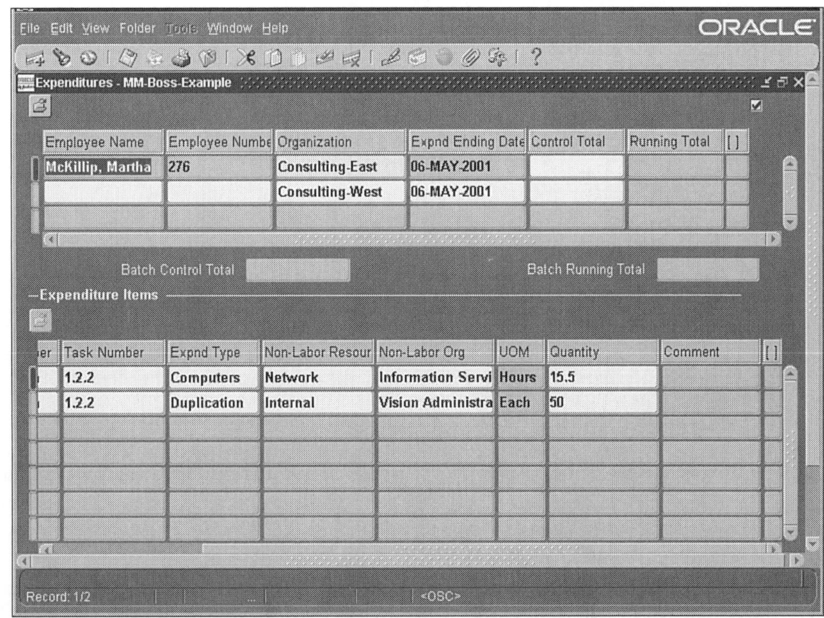

Tip

If you enter an expenditure type and no Non-Labor Resource appears in the LOV, check your Non-Labor Resource setup to ensure that you have set one up for this expenditure type.

After the expenditure entry is complete, save your work and return to the batch form. From this form, you can

- Verify that your control totals are correct.
- Submit your batch.
- Release your batch.

CREATING INVENTORY TRANSACTIONS

Inventory expenditures are created for Projects in the Oracle Inventory module and interfaced through Transaction Import. A predefined transaction source of Inventory Misc has been defined for these transactions.

MISCELLANEOUS PROJECT ISSUES This transaction type enables you to issue items out of an inventory locator to a Project. When you issue an item using this transaction type, the system reduces the inventory quantity by the current average unit cost. If you enter a cost with this transaction line, the system uses the unit cost you have entered versus the current average cost.

Under Type, select Project Miscellaneous Issue. Tab to the Account field, and press Ctrl+L. Then, fill in the required account segment values for the inventory charge.

Click Transaction Lines and enter the following information, as shown in Figure 15.34:

- **Item Number**
- **Sub Inventory**
- **Locator**—Your warehouse location
- **Quantity**—Number of items you are issuing
- **Unit Cost**—If left blank, the system assigns the current average unit cost
- **Account**—Defaults from the header
- **Source Project**—Project you are issuing to
- **Source Task**—Task you are issuing to
- **Expenditure Organization**—Organization incurring the charges

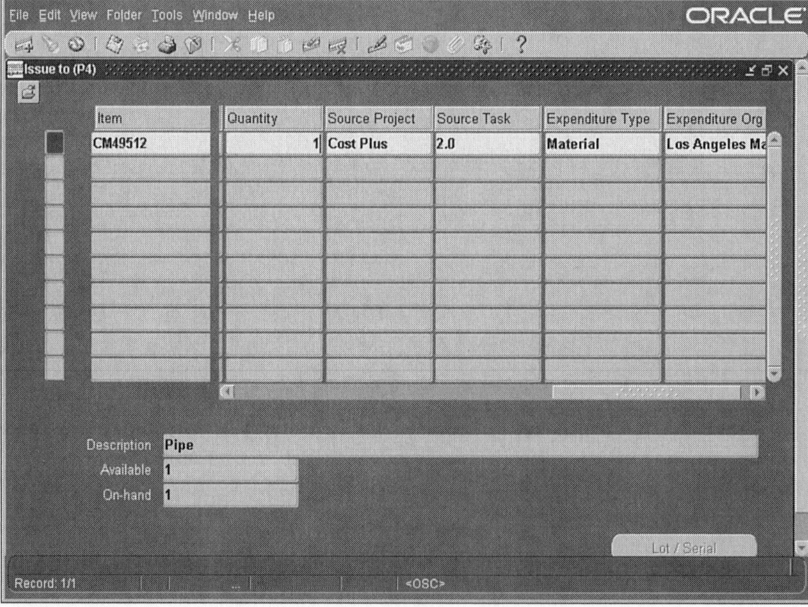

Figure 15.34
You can enter project-related inventory transactions by using one of the predefined project-enabled transaction sources.

Save your work. The inventory system costs the transaction using the cost worker. After being costed, the item(s) can be transferred to Projects.

Tip

To view whether the item is costed, navigate to Transactions, Material Transactions. Under the Reason, Reference tab are two fields to identify the status of the transaction.

Note

When issuing miscellaneous inventory from a project or to a project, the Source Project and Task fields are used to designate the costs being transferred.

RUNNING THE COST COLLECTOR PROCESS To transfer the item to the Projects application, the cost collector process must be run. Figure 15.35 shows the Cost Collector Parameters window where the system asks you for the number of days to leave uncollected or uncosted. Type `0`, and then click OK to submit your request. If this process runs successfully, your costs have been transferred to the Projects interface tables.

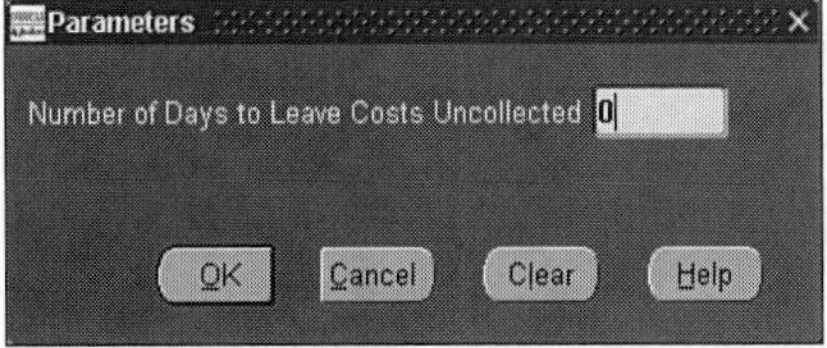

Figure 15.35
Running the cost collector process enables project-related inventory transactions to be transferred to Oracle Projects.

TRANSACTION IMPORT FOR IMPORTING INVENTORY COSTS TO PROJECTS

1. From an appropriate Projects responsibility, use the following navigation: Expenditures, Transaction Import, Import Transactions.
2. Select your transaction source Inventory Misc.
3. Enter a batch name if necessary.
4. Submit your request.

After the process completes successfully, you will be able to review your inventory transaction against your project using the Expenditure Inquiry screen.

Tip

Inventory miscellaneous items are interfaced as costed and burdened, allowing adjustments. If you adjust inventory expenditures, ensure that you have defined your AutoAccounting rules for inventory cost and cost-clearing functions.

DISTRIBUTING COSTS

After you have entered your transactions, you must distribute the costs. Running the distribute cost processes enables the system to calculate raw costs and determine the appropriate accounting debit lines.

DISTRIBUTING LABOR COSTS To distribute labor costs in Oracle Projects, you must run the Distribute Labor Cost process. This process calculates the raw cost for labor transactions and creates appropriate debit accounting transactions based on your system setups. Here's how:

1. From an appropriate Projects responsibility, use the following navigation: Other, Requests, Run.
2. Select PRC: Distribute Labor Costs.
3. Enter the appropriate parameters: Batch Name, Project Number, Employee Name, End Date, and Incurred By Organization.
4. Submit the job.
5. After the job completes, review your report for items that were rejected. Exceptions must be corrected (missing cost rate, AutoAccounting problem, and so on) and resubmitted.
6. Continue with this process until all items are accepted.

Tip

Even though your process completes with a successful status, items might not have to be distributed. You need to review your output files to ensure that your expenditure items processed and were not rejected during processing.

DISTRIBUTING EXPENSE COSTS To distribute expense report costs entered in Oracle Projects, you must run the Distribute Expense Reports Process. This process calculates the raw cost for expense report transactions and creates the appropriate debit accounting lines based on your system setups:

1. From an appropriate Projects responsibility, use the following navigation: Other, Requests, Run.
2. Select PRC: Distribute Expense Report Costs.
3. Enter the appropriate parameters: Expenditure Batch, Project Number, Employee Name, and Through Weekending Date.
4. Submit the job.
5. After the job completes, review your report for items that were rejected. Exceptions must be corrected (missing cost rate, AutoAccounting problem, and so on) and resubmitted.
6. Continue with this process until all items are accepted.

Note

If you are using Internet Expense or entering expense reports in Payables, you do not need to run this process. Cost amounts are interfaced from Payables through the standard interface processes.

Tip

As with any processing, even though your process completes with a successful status, items might not have to be distributed. You must review your output files to ensure that your expenditure items processed and were not rejected during processing.

Distributing Usage Costs To distribute usages and miscellaneous costs entered in Oracle Projects, you must run the Distribute Usage and Miscellaneous Costs process. This process calculates the raw cost for usage and miscellaneous transactions and creates the appropriate debit accounting lines based on your system setups:

1. From an appropriate Projects responsibility, use the following navigation: Other, Requests, Run.
2. Select PRC: Distribute Usage and Miscellaneous Costs.
3. Enter the appropriate parameters: Expenditure Batch, Project Number, Through Date, and Expenditure Type Class.
4. Submit the job.
5. After the job completes, review your report for items that were rejected. Exceptions must be corrected (missing cost rate, AutoAccounting problem, and so on) and resubmitted.
6. Continue with this process until all items are accepted.

Interface Streamline Processes

After distributing costs for your transactions, you must interface the resulting accounting information to the appropriate applications. During the interface processing, the credit side of your accounting transactions is created.

Oracle Projects provides streamline processes that enable you to send transactions to the other applications, import them into the application, and then tie back the transfer to ensure success. All of this is done from within the Projects responsibility (you do not need to log in to GL to run Journal Import, and so on).

Interface Labor Costs to GL

1. From an appropriate Projects responsibility, use the following navigation: Other, Requests, Run.
2. Select PRC: Submit Interface Streamline Processes.
3. For the Streamline Option parameter, select XL: Interface Labor Costs To GL.
4. Submit the job.
5. This process spawns several related processes. After the streamline job completes, review the report for all spawned processes for rejections. Exceptions must be corrected (missing cost rate, AutoAccounting problem, and so on) and resubmitted.
6. Continue with this process until all items are accepted.

Interface Expense Reports to Payables

1. From an appropriate Projects responsibility, use the following navigation: Other, Requests, Run.
2. Select PRC: Submit Interface Streamline Processes.
3. For the Streamline Option parameter, select either of these options:
   - XES: Interface Expense Report Costs to AP (Summarized report)
   - XEU: Interface Expense Report Costs to AP (Unsummarized rpt)
4. Submit the job.
5. This process spawns several related processes. After the streamline job completes, review your report for all spawned processes for rejections. Exceptions must be corrected (missing cost rate, AutoAccounting problem, and so on) and resubmitted.
6. Continue with this process until all items are accepted.

Interface Usage and Miscellaneous Costs to GL

1. From an appropriate Projects responsibility, use the following navigation: Other, Requests, Run.
2. Select PRC: Submit Interface Streamline Processes.
3. For the Streamline Option parameter, select XU: Interface Usage and Miscellaneous Costs to GL.
4. Submit the job.
5. This process spawns several related processes. After the streamline job completes, review your report for all spawned processes for rejections. Exceptions must be corrected (missing cost rate, AutoAccounting problem, and so on) and resubmitted.
6. Continue with this process until all items are accepted.

Transferring Costs from Other Applications

Oracle Projects allows costs to be transferred from other applications into Oracle Projects. Supplier invoice costs from Accounts Payable are such costs. These costs, as well as others, are brought in through the Transaction Import tables.

For the Supplier Invoice costs, a standard standalone process is run through the concurrent manager, as follows:

1. From an appropriate Projects responsibility, use the following navigation: Other, Requests, Run.
2. Select PRC: Interface Supplier Invoices from Payables.
3. Enter the appropriate parameters: Project Number, Batch Name, Through GL Date, and Through Transaction Date.
4. Submit the job.

5. After the job completes, review your report for rejections. Exceptions must be corrected (missing cost rate, AutoAccounting problem, and so on) and resubmitted.
6. Continue with this process until all items are accepted.

Expense Reports entered in Accounts Payable are also costs that are interfaced from another application to the Oracle Projects module. Here's how to bring them into Oracle Projects:

1. From an appropriate Projects responsibility, use the following navigation: Other, Requests, Run.
2. Select PRC: Interface Expense Reports from Payables.
3. Enter the appropriate parameters: Project Number, Batch Name, End GL Date, and End Expenditure Item Date.
4. Submit the job.
5. After the job completes, review your report for rejections. Exceptions must be corrected (missing cost rate, AutoAccounting problem, and so on) and resubmitted.
6. Continue with this process until all items are accepted.

Items that are imported into Oracle Projects via the transaction import tables also require that the Transaction Import process be run (either behind the scenes as is the case with supplier invoices or manually). To run this process manually, do the following:

1. From an appropriate Projects responsibility, use the following navigation: Other, Requests, Run.
2. Select PRC: Transaction Import.
3. Enter the appropriate Transaction Source.
4. Select the batch you want to import.
5. Submit the job.
6. After the job completes, review your report for rejections. Exceptions must be corrected (missing cost rate, AutoAccounting problem, and so on) and resubmitted.
7. Continue with this process until all items are accepted.

PROCESSING ADJUSTMENTS

You can adjust a single expenditure item or multiple expenditure items via the Expenditure Inquiry screen:

1. Use the Find window to limit the selection of transactions by entering fields such as project number, transaction source, batch, time period, billing hold, and so on. Click the Find button.
2. Using your mouse, left-click while holding down the Ctrl key on your keyboard and highlight individual expenditure items to be adjusted. Holding down the Shift key while left-clicking highlights a group of items. The items to be adjusted will be in blue.

3. From the Tools menu, select the adjustment you want to perform (Billable, Non-Billable, Billing Hold, and so on).
4. Fill in any additional information requested to complete the adjustment.

When adjusting expenditure items, the actions in Table 15.14 should be selected along with respective processes to be run.

TABLE 15.14 REQUIRED PROCESSES WHEN ADJUSTING EXPENDITURE ITEMS

Action	Stage	Tools Menu	Processes to Be Run
Items Adjusted - ex: changed from Billable to Non-Billable	Cost Distributed = N	N/A	Costing Processes (Labor, Supplier, Usages, ER)
	Cost Distributed = Y	N/A, note-item has been modified to Cost Distributed =N	Costing Processes (Labor, Supplier, Usages, ER)
	Cost Distributed = N, Revenue Approved = N	N/A, note - item has been modified to Cost Distributed =N	Costing Processes (Labor, Supplier, Usages, ER); Revenue Processes
	Cost Distributed = Y; Revenue Approved = N	N/A, note - item has been modified to Cost Distributed = N	Costing Processes (Labor, Supplier, Usages, ER); Revenue Processes
	Cost Distributed = Y; Revenue Approved = Y	N/A, note - item has been modified to Cost/Revenue Distributed = N	Costing Processes (Labor, Supplier, Usages, ER); Revenue Processes
	Invoice Approved = N; Revenue Approved = Y	N/A, note - item has been modified to Cost/Revenue Distributed = N	Costing Processes (Labor, Supplier, Usages, ER); Revenue Processes; Invoice Processes
Bill Rates modified on Project/Task	Revenue Approved = N; Invoice Approved = N	N/A	Revenue Processes
	Revenue Approved = Y; Invoice Approved = N	Recalculate Revenue	Revenue Processes; Invoice Processes
	Revenue Approved = Y; Invoice Approved = Y	Recalculate Revenue	Revenue Processes; Invoice Processes

Click the Run Request button, and select the processes you want to run. See Figure 15.36 for which processes are available from Expenditure Inquiry.

Tip

At least two processes must be selected when running concurrent processes from the Expenditure Inquiry screen. If you need to run only a single process, exit the form and proceed to the run requests form.

Note

The Through Date on the Streamline Requests is for the week-ending date for labor transactions.

Note

You can also use the Mass Adjust button on the Find Expenditures window to make the same adjustment to several expenditure items. Use the fields on the Find Expenditures window to limit which expenditure items will be mass adjusted.

CONTRACT PROJECTS: REVENUE RECOGNITION AND INVOICING

Revenue and billings are calculated on the expenditures or event transactions that you charge to your project. Before revenue and invoices can be generated, an agreement must be created and funding allocated to your project. An agreement can be funded by multiple projects as long as the project customer is the same as the agreement customer. At this point, a revenue budget is established and baselined, enabling the project to proceed with revenue recognition.

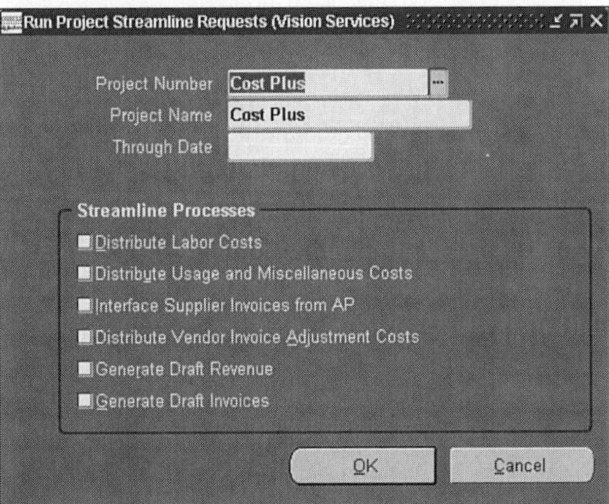

Figure 15.36
After adjusting expenditure items, you can submit the appropriate processes by clicking the Run Requests button.

PREPARING FOR REVENUE AND INVOICE GENERATION To create revenue and generate invoices in Oracle Projects, you first must have appropriate funding on your project. This section discusses how to set up funding and agreements.

ENTERING AGREEMENTS AND FUNDING When a customer agrees to provide a certain amount of money for one or more projects (via a purchase order or other similar contractual document), an agreement needs to be entered in Oracle Projects. To enter an agreement for a customer, do the following:

1. From an appropriate Projects responsibility, use the following navigation: Billing, Agreements.
2. Enter your Customer name and Contract number. The terms might default but can be changed if your contract terms are different.
3. Save your agreement.

Note

A single agreement can fund multiple projects and project-task combinations.

After you have entered your agreement, you need to specify which projects and tasks that agreement is funding. To do this, follow these steps:

1. From the Agreements window where you entered your customer agreement, click the Funding button.
2. Enter the project number, task number, and amount as appropriate.
3. Save your work.

Tip

The total amount entered against your project must equal your project revenue budget in order to baseline your budget. However, the funding does not need to come from a single agreement.

ENTERING REVENUE BUDGETS Now that you have agreements entered and have funded your project, you can create and baseline your revenue budget. To enter your project revenue budget, do the following:

1. From an appropriate Projects responsibility, use the following navigation: Budgets.
2. Enter your project number and budget type (for example, Approved Revenue).
3. A resource name and budget entry method default onto the budget. Change this if necessary.
4. Provide additional header information as desired: Change Reason, Version Name.
5. Click the Details button.

6. Enter the appropriate resource names (based on the resource list selected in step 3) and revenue amounts.
7. Save your work.
8. Return to the main budgets window.
9. Click the Submit button.
10. Click the Baseline button.

Note

The total amount entered on your revenue budget must equal the total amount of funding for the project or tasks to baseline your budget.

Your project is now ready for revenue and invoice processing.

Tip

If you are unable to baseline your budget and the project is funded by multiple agreements, make sure your budget total equals your total funding for all agreements.

CREATING REVENUE AND INVOICE EVENTS Revenue and invoice events are input on the events form and can be entered with both a revenue and an invoice amount or as separate transactions. When entering a revenue event with no associated invoice amount, enter **`$0`** for the invoice event amount. When entering an invoice event with no associated revenue amount, enter **`$0`** for the revenue event amount.

As shown in Figure 15.37, enter revenue and invoice events by following these steps:

1. From an appropriate Projects responsibility, use the following navigation: Billing, Events, Project.
2. Enter your project number and click the New button. Tab to the Event Type, and enter your event type.
3. Populate the event date to coincide with your accounting period. The organization can coincide with the project organization or a valid organization that will be credited for the work.
4. Enter information that is useful for future review and analysis and possibly for printing event descriptions on custom invoice formats.
5. Enter the amount of revenue to be recognized for this event entry.
6. Enter the amount to be billed to the customer that should appear on the invoice for this event.

Note

When entering manual events, an event type of automatic can't be selected.

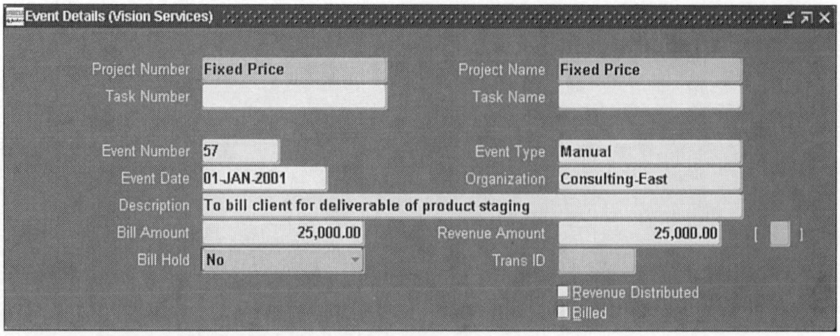

Figure 15.37
Enter revenue and invoice events as needed.

Event Details (Vision Services)

Project Number: Fixed Price — Project Name: Fixed Price
Task Number: — Task Name:
Event Number: 57 — Event Type: Manual
Event Date: 01-JAN-2001 — Organization: Consulting-East
Description: To bill client for deliverable of product staging
Bill Amount: 25,000.00 — Revenue Amount: 25,000.00
Bill Hold: No — Trans ID:
Revenue Distributed
Billed

Revenue and Invoice Distribution Rules To be eligible for revenue and invoicing, each transaction must be billable and the cost distributed for a contract project. The three methods to recognize revenue and bill the Customer are

- As-works occurs (Time and Material)
- Cost-to-cost (percent spent)
- Based on physical percent complete

As-Works Occurs For contract projects that use as-works occurs revenue amount, the potential revenue is simply the sum of the revenue based on the bill rate, markup, or burden schedule. In addition, any events defined are included as project revenues (Manual Event).

The bill rate schedule or burden schedule can be defined at the project or task level.

Cost-to-Cost (Percent Spent) For contract projects using cost-to-cost revenue accrual, the formula is as follows:

((Actual Cost/Budget Cost × (Budget Revenue – Event revenue)) – Previous Revenue

Oracle creates an automatic event using the cost-to-cost billing extension. Standard functionality of the system creates one event for each calculation. Note, because this is a calculated amount based on percentages, employee details (work) do not match the actual revenue calculation.

Tip

Write a custom billing extension to create organization events based on employee work efforts.

Based on Physical Percent Complete With Oracle Projects, you can generate your revenue and invoice based on the percent complete you enter for a project. The formula is as follows:

% Complete (Project or Task level) × Budget Revenue

Oracle uses the Percent Complete Revenue billing extension or Percent Complete Invoicing extension to create an automatic event.

Note

Because this is a calculated amount based on percentages, employee details (work) do not match the actual revenue calculation. The same holds true for the cost-to-cost method.

With Oracle Projects, you associate a distribution rule for revenue accrual and invoicing methods for each project. The distribution rules are listed in Table 15.15.

TABLE 15.15 DISTRIBUTION RULES

Distribution Rule	Description
Work/Work	Accrue revenue and bill as work occurs.
Work/Event	Accrue revenue as work occurs; bill based on events.
Event/Work	Accrue revenue based on events; bill as work occurs.
Event/Event	Accrue revenue and bill based on events.
Cost/Work	Accrue revenue using the ratio of actual cost to budgeted cost (percent spent); bill as work occurs.
Cost/Event	Accrue revenue using the ratio of actual cost to budgeted cost (percent spent); bill based on events.
Cost/Cost	Accrue revenue and bill using the ratio of actual cost to budgeted cost (percent spent).

DISTRIBUTION RULE SCENARIOS The following example illustrates the different calculations that occur against your project based on the distribution rule assigned:

Cost Budget:	$16,000
Revenue Budget:	$40,000
Employee cost rate:	$100/Hr
Employee bill rate:	$200/Hr
Burden rate	.5
Period 1:	40 hours' work, 10% physical complete

Work/Work

When using the work/work distribution rule, the calculations are based on work performed as follows:

Bill Rate Schedule: 40 hr × 200/hr = $8,000 (Revenue and Invoice)

Burden Rate Schedule: 40 hr × 100/hr × 1.5 = $6,000 (Revenue and Invoice)

Work/Event

For this rule, revenue is calculated based on Work; invoice calculation is based on using the Percent Complete Extension:

Revenue - Bill Rate Schedule: 40 hr × 200 = $8,000
Invoice - Percent Complete: 10% × $40,000 = $4,000

Event/Work

Revenue is calculated using the Percent Complete Extension, and invoice generation is calculated based on Work:

Revenue - Percent Complete: 10% × 40,000 = $4,000

Invoice - Burden Rate Schedule: 40 hr × 100 hr × 1.5 = $6,000

Cost/Work

Revenue is calculated using the Cost-to-Cost extension, and invoice generation is calculated based on Work:

Revenue: (40 hr × 100/16,000) × 40,000 = $10,000

Invoice - Bill Rate Schedule: 40 hr × 200 = $8,000

Cost/Event

Revenue is calculated using the Cost-to-Cost extension; invoice is calculated from a Manual Event:

Revenue: (40 hr × 100/16,000) × 40,000 = $10,000

Invoice: Event = $7,500

REVENUE GENERATION PROCESSES The following process generates revenue for your project:

1. From an appropriate Projects responsibility, use the following navigation: Other, Requests, Run.
2. Select PRC: Generate Draft Revenue for a Single Project.
3. Set these parameters: Accrue through Date and Project.
4. Submit the job. After the job completes, review the report for rejects, which must be corrected.

Note

If your project is not generating revenue or an invoice, ensure that an agreement and funding are assigned.

After the revenue generation process is complete, the revenue must be reviewed, approved, and released using the Revenue Review window:

1. From an appropriate Projects responsibility, use the following navigation: Billing, Revenue Review.
2. Enter your project number, and click the Find button. Your revenue amount will appear. If you want to review the revenue lines, click the Lines button.
3. If the revenue is correct, change the status by clicking the Approve button.
4. Save your approval.
5. Once approved, click the Release button.
6. Save your release.

Note

If the mass-generation revenue program is run for a range of projects, the revenues are approved and released during the program.

INVOICE GENERATION PROCESSES This process should be run after costing and revenue processes are complete. The system picks up all eligible items for invoicing including labor, non-labor, and events:

1. From an appropriate Projects responsibility, use the following navigation: Other, Requests, Run.
2. Select PRC: Generate Draft Invoices for a Single Project.
3. Input your bill-through date and project.
4. Click the Submit button.
5. After the job completes, review the report for rejects, which must be corrected.

Note

For work distribution rule type projects, your revenue process must be run before generating invoices because the revenue-generation process calculates bill amounts.

After the invoice generation process is complete, the invoice must be reviewed, approved, and released using the Invoice Review window. Do the following:

1. From an appropriate Projects responsibility, use the following navigation: Billing, Invoice Review.
2. Enter your project number and click the Find button.
3. Click the Lines button to review details, and if taxable, check the Taxable box.
4. Return to the previous form and change the status by clicking the Approve button.
5. Save your approval.

6. Click the Release button.
7. Save your release.

TRANSFERRING REVENUE AND INVOICES TO OTHER APPLICATIONS (STREAMLINE PROCESSES)

After revenues have been released, they can be interfaced to the General Ledger. To do this, follow these steps:

1. From an appropriate Projects responsibility, use the following navigation: Other, Requests, Run.
2. Select PRC: Submit Interface Streamline Processes.
3. For the Streamline Option parameter, select XR: Interface Draft Revenues to GL.
4. Click Submit.
5. After the job completes, review the output reports for rejections and make the necessary corrections. If corrections are made, resubmit the process until all revenues are transferred.

Invoices should now be transferred to your Receivables system by following these steps:

1. From an appropriate Projects responsibility, use the following navigation: Other, Requests, Run.
2. Select PRC: Submit Interface Streamline Processes.
3. For the Streamline Option parameter, select XI: Interface Draft Invoices to AR.
4. Click Submit.
5. After the job completes, review the output reports for rejections and make the necessary corrections. If corrections are made, resubmit the process until all invoices are transferred.

ADJUSTING REVENUE AND INVOICES After you have interfaced your invoice to Oracle Receivables, you might need to perform an adjustment on the invoice or on the expenditures items included on the invoice. The following sections highlight the types of adjustments that can be performed on an invoice.

CREDIT MEMOS If you adjust an expenditure item that has been invoiced, the Projects system automatically creates credit lines for the invoiced expenditures you are adjusting. Adjustments could include marking an item as non-billable, marking an item as billing hold, or changing a bill rate on a bill rate schedule. If you place an item on a bill hold or modify the bill rate, you must mark the item for regenerating revenue.

Note

Credit memo lines are not attached to the original invoice. When a credit memo line is interfaced to the Receivables application, you can apply the line to receipt for the original invoice.

CANCEL/WRITE OFF A RELEASED INVOICE If an invoice is released to Receivables, you can cancel or write off the invoice in Oracle Projects. On the Invoice Review screen, query the invoice you want to cancel or write off. Click Credit and a form will appear, giving you the option to cancel or write off the invoice.

INVOICE CANCEL If you select the option to cancel the invoice, the system credits the full amount of the invoice and leaves the credit in a status of approved. To process this invoice to AR, it must be released. Upon release of the invoice, the system asks for verification of the invoice date. You will also be required to enter an invoice number if you do not have invoice numbers assigned automatically. If an invoice is cancelled, the system marks all related invoice items as eligible for billing and also updates the available funding. The next time an invoice is generated, the system will include the cancelled items of the invoice. To prevent this, the related items should be marked as non-billable or placed on billing hold.

Tip

Events or expenditure items can be placed on a one-time billing hold to exclude items from a current invoice generation.

Note

When canceling an invoice, the system does not allow you to cancel if cash has been applied. In Receivables, un-apply the cash receipt and then cancel the invoice in Projects.

INVOICE WRITE-OFF When you select the Write-Off option, the system enables you to input a write-off amount that is less than the invoice and has the status of Accepted. When using this feature, the system reverses the invoice amount and places it in a write-off expense account you define in AutoAccounting. The items on the original invoice are not marked as eligible for billing because they will not be paid for by your customers.

Note

When processing the write-off of an invoice, the system prevents you from writing off more than the balance due on the invoice.

For further information, see the *Oracle Projects Users Guide*, Chapter 8, "Adjusting Project Invoices."

Changing Invoice Currency

After an invoice has been generated, and before it is released, the exchange rate can be changed, as shown in Figure 15.38. To do this, follow these steps:

1. From an appropriate Projects responsibility, use the following navigation: Billing, Invoice Review.
2. Query the appropriate invoice.

3. Click the Recalculate button to open the Recalculate Invoice currency form.
4. Enter the desired currency, rate type, rate date, and exchange rate. Enter the rate only when using a rate type of User.

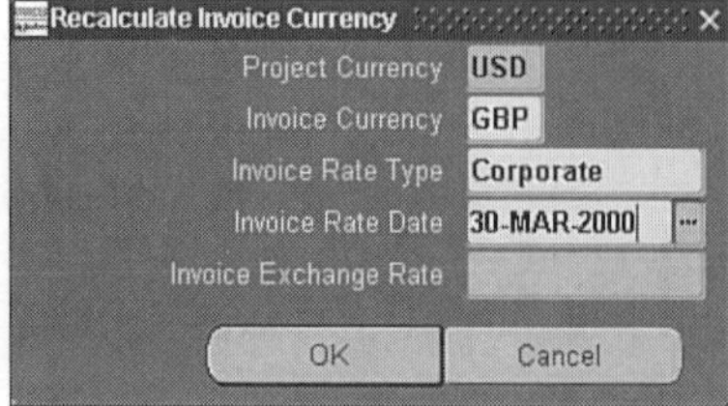

Figure 15.38
You can change the invoice currency after the invoice has been generated but before it has been released.

After accepting the currency changes, re-query to see the new invoice currency and converted invoice amount, as shown in Figure 15.39.

Note

When calculating an invoice in a foreign currency, the system applies the one invoice rate to all transactions. Individual conversion rates can't be applied to expenditure items based on differing expenditure dates.

Capital Projects: Asset Generation

When proceeding to this section, it is assumed that costs have been entered against your capital project and distributed.

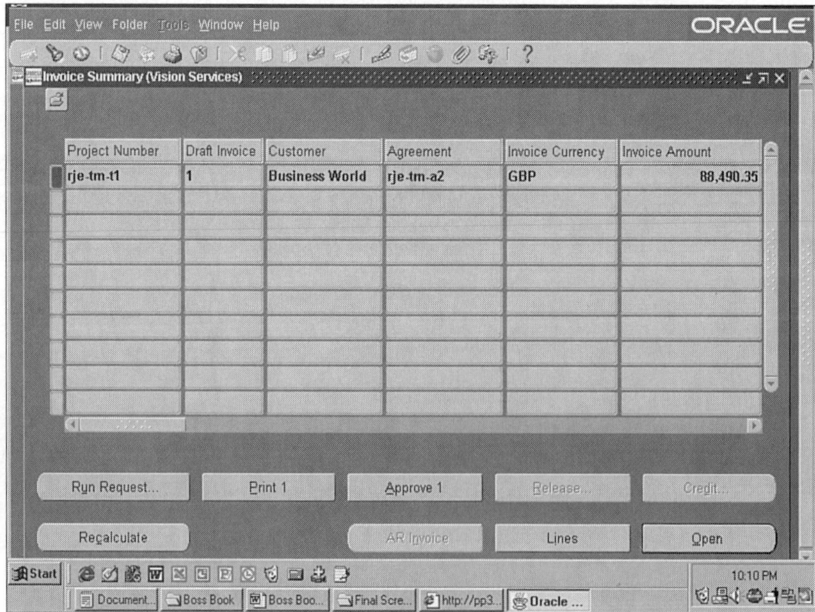

Figure 15.39
Requery your invoice to see the invoice currency change.

Placing an Asset in Service To generate asset lines in Oracle Projects, the assets associated with a project must be placed in service. To do this, follow these steps:

1. From an appropriate Projects responsibility, use the following navigation: Capital Projects.
2. Enter the name or number of the capital project whose asset you want to place in service, and click Find.
3. Click the Assets button.
4. Enter the actual date in service for the asset.
5. Save the record.

Generating Asset Lines and Interfacing Assets to Oracle Assets After the asset has been placed in service, you can begin generating asset lines for that asset. To do this, follow these steps:

1. From an appropriate Projects responsibility, use the following navigation: Capital Projects.
2. Enter the name or number of the capital project for which you want to generate asset lines, and click Find.
3. Select the capital project you want, and click the Generate button.
4. Enter the actual date in service for the asset.
5. Enter the In Service Date Through.
6. Choose whether to include common costs.
7. Click OK to submit the Generate Asset Lines process.
8. After the job completes, review your output reports for rejections. Make any necessary corrections and resubmit as needed.
9. Review your asset lines.

After reviewing the asset lines generated, shown in Figure 15.40, the asset can now be transferred to Oracle Assets:

1. From an appropriate Projects responsibility, use the following navigation: Others, Requests, Run.
2. Select the process PRC: Interface Assets to Oracle Assets.
3. Submit.

After this job completes, you will be able to view the costs in the Mass Additions form in Oracle Assets. At this point, the asset information can be modified if necessary and then generated into an asset in the Oracle Assets system, and depreciation can begin.

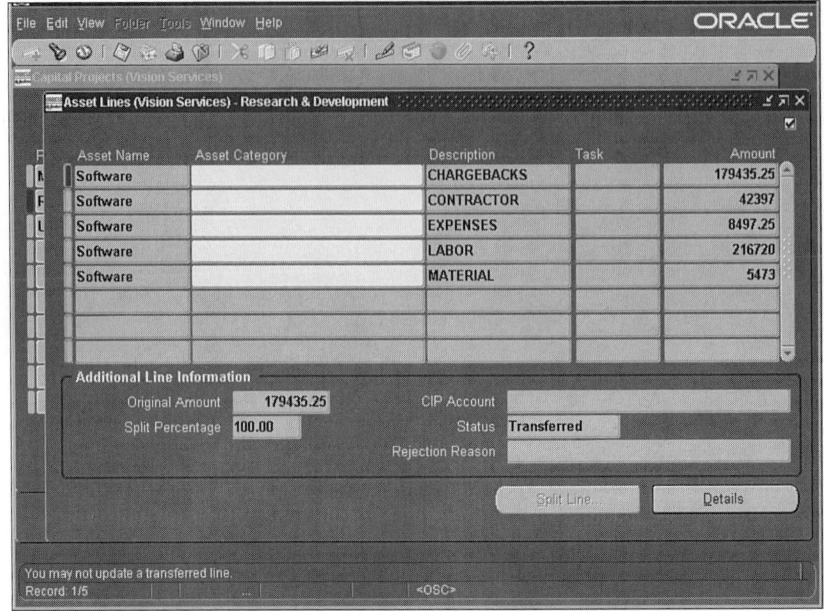

Figure 15.40
Review the asset lines generated for your capital project.

Caution

Before you run the Generate Asset Lines process, you must cost the transactions by running the processes listed here:

- Distribute Labor Costs
- Distribute Expense Report Costs
- Distribute Usage Costs
- Distribute Supplier Invoice Adjustments
- Interface Supplier Invoices to Oracle Projects

You must also run the Update Project Summary Amounts process. It is recommended that the streamline processes be run as well.

Note

Be sure you have an in-service date on your capital project asset prior to running this process; otherwise, no asset lines will be generated.

Tip

If desired, the generate asset lines process can be run from the Oracle Standard Report Submission window and by selecting PRC: Generate Asset Lines (Single or Range of Projects).

Advanced Transactional Features

If you chose to implement any of the advanced transactional features, such as burdening and allocations, you must perform specific processing for those transactions to appear on your projects. This section explains the processing steps required for these features.

Burdening

If you have not chosen to set up burdening, the burden cost amount is set to the raw cost of the expenditure item during the costing processes. However, if you have set up burdening then you must run separate processing for the burden amounts. This process depends on which burden option you have chosen (see the section "Burdening," earlier in this chapter, for additional information).

Burden on the Same Expenditure Items If your project type was set up to burden transactions on the same expenditure items (and you have set up burdening schedules), you must run two processes to create the burden accounting lines and interface burden transactions to your GL. To do this, run the following processes from Oracle's Standard Report Submission screen:

- PRC: Distribute Total Burden Costs (Creates burden accounting lines)
- PRC: Interface Total Burden Costs to your GL (interfaces burden accounting lines to your GL)

Burden on Separate Expenditure Items If your project type was set up to create burden component transactions on the same project or on a different project (and you have set up burdening schedules), you must run two processes to create the burden accounting lines and interface burden transactions to your GL. To do this, run the following processes from Oracle's Standard Report Submission screen:

- PRC: Create and Distribute Burden Expenditure Transactions (creates expenditure items)
- PRC: Interface Usage and Miscellaneous Transactions to your GL (interfaces burden accounting lines to your GL)

Burden Schedule Changes—Compiling a New Version In addition to creating the burden transactions, you might need to make modifications, which can involve modifying your burden schedules. When modifying your provisional schedule to actual rates, you should end-date your provisional revisions and proceed to the Apply Actuals window where final burden multipliers are entered and then compiled. If you modify rates on an existing standard burden schedule, you also must compile the new rates for them to take effect. The compile process marks each expenditure item for recosting that is within the date range of your compiled version.

Note

When compiling a burden schedule revision, the system marks expenditure items for recosting that are within the date ranges of the compiled version.

ALLOCATIONS

The following sections detail how to create allocation transactions if you have chosen to implement the allocations functionality in Oracle Projects.

GENERATING ALLOCATION TRANSACTIONS At any point after you have finished defining your allocation rules, you can begin to generate allocation transactions. To do this, you submit the PRC: Generate Allocations Transactions process.

When you submit this process, you specify the allocation rule for which you want to generate allocations. You also specify a GL or PA Period for which you want source transactions to be selected from. Note that this parameter is mandatory, but if your Project Allocations source is based on a Fixed Amount, this parameter has no impact. The final parameter, Expenditure Item Date, determines the date you want Oracle Projects to use for all Allocation and Offset Transactions generated.

REVIEWING ALLOCATIONS RESULTS Oracle Projects provides the Review Allocation Runs form that enables you to review the results of the PRC: Generate Allocations Transactions process. If you've defined your allocation rule with the Auto Release option disabled, you must approve or release the Project Allocations using this screen before they will appear on your target projects.

If, after reviewing the results of the allocations run, you find problems with the results, you have the opportunity to delete the results instead of releasing them. You can then modify your allocation rule and regenerate your Project Allocations. Note that if you have any Draft Allocations pending release or any Draft Allocations failures, you must delete them in the Review Allocation Runs form before regenerating.

For a successful allocations run, you can drill down to the detail transactions created by clicking the Transactions button. In this screen you can see all Allocations and Offset Transactions created.

RELEASING OR DELETING ALLOCATIONS RESULTS After reviewing your allocation run results, everything appears as expected. Therefore, you can now release the run that will post the allocations transactions to the appropriate projects. After the run has been released, you can then view the transactions on the target and offset projects in the Expenditure Inquiry screen.

Note that for all transactions, both Offset and Allocations, Oracle Projects populates the Comment field with the Allocation Rule Name and Allocations Run ID.

You can't perform any adjustments directly on transactions created by the Project Allocations process. If, after you have released your allocations, you find an error, you must reverse the entire batch of allocations using the Review Allocation Runs screen.

PROJECT REPORTING

Oracle Projects provides numerous ways for you to review the information on your projects.

EXPENDITURE INQUIRY

The Expenditure Inquiry form is very useful to the project and accounting analyst because it displays your project cost details and the revenue and invoice amounts generated against them. In addition, the form offers multiple fields for display, including transaction currency, billable status, costing status, and methods for adjustment.

VIEWING EXPENDITURES—EXPENDITURE INQUIRY FORM

To view expenditure information, use this navigation path: Expenditures, Expenditure Inquiry, Project or All. This displays a Find window in which you can limit the transactions to be queried.

When selecting expenditures for viewing, expenditure item dates can be entered for ranges as well as expenditure type, employee, transaction source, system linkage, and expenditure batch.

Tip

Although the ability to query expenditure items across projects is available, querying one project is more efficient for system performance reasons.

Note

If you want to view specific billing status, processing status, and CIP status, this is available and is very useful when searching for specific transactions. New to 11*i* (see Figure 15.41) is Cross-Charge Information, which can also be used to limit your inquiry.

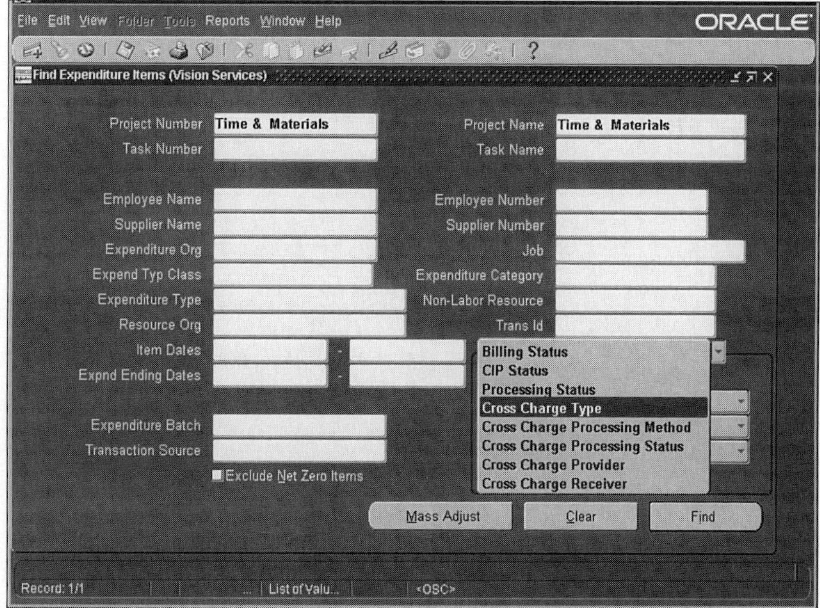

Figure 15.41
You can now search for specific expenditure items by cross-charge information.

Tip

Information being viewed on the Expenditure Inquiry screen can be copied into Excel for additional analysis and formatting. On the main menu, select File, Export. The option is provided to export to Excel.

Folder Tools

The Expenditure Inquiry form offers many additional fields that can be used to view information, as shown in Figure 15.42. From the Folder section, click Show Field. Available fields are displayed and can be used to customize a folder view. Some of the new fields offered are Project Organization, Receiver Operating Unit Information, Receipt Exchange Rate, Transfer Price Information, and many more.

Tip

When saving a custom folder, always reset the query to avoid being locked into the project you are building the query on.

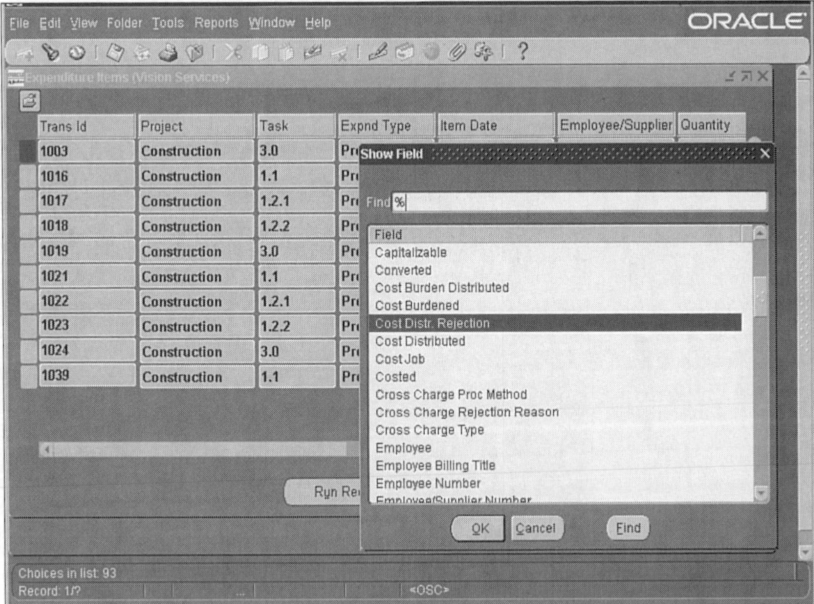

Figure 15.42
Folder tools enable you to change which fields are displayed in Expenditure Inquiry.

Viewing Accounting Lines

In Release 11*i* you now have the ability to view accounting lines for your expenditure item. Place your cursor on the transaction and from Tools; then select View Accounting Lines. The form that opens displays the accounting transactions (debit and credit accounts) for the expenditure item. The option to view T accounts is on the form, and if this is clicked, the entries will be displayed in T account format.

VIEWING ITEM DETAILS

After opening the form with your criteria, you can view additional details. To view the Item Details of this expenditure, the Inquiry Options window is displayed, from which you can select additional information:

- **Cost Distribution Lines**—Displays cost distribution lines for your expenditure, the GL and PA periods, transfer status, and burden amount. If the distribution line is rejected, the reason will be displayed.

Tip

If you have more than one distribution line, place your cursor on the last line to see the GL/PA period and ensure that there are no rejections. One line could be in a previous GL/PA period.

- **Revenue Distribution Lines**—Displays the revenue accounting transactions for your expenditure item, the GL and PA periods, and the transfer status. If rejected, it also displays the reject reason.
- **AP Invoice**—Takes you to the AP invoice overview form in Payables and is available only for Supplier Invoice and Expense Report charges.

UNDERSTANDING PROJECT COMMITMENTS

This section helps you to get a better understanding of what is considered a commitment in Oracle Projects. The Oracle Projects commitment processing is driven from a set of different views. The PA_COMMITMENT_TXNS_V view is the main user-definable view that enables easy customizations to the commitment processing logic. This view contains six underlying view structures that need to be examined for processing:

- PA_PROJ_REQ_DISTRIBUTIONS
- PA_PROJ_PO_DISTRIBUTIONS
- PA_PROJ_AP_INV_DISTRIBUTIONS
- PJM_REQ_COMMITMENTS_V
- PJM_PO_COMMITMENTS_V
- CST_PROJMFG_CMT_VIEW

Views 4–6 are specifically for supporting the integration of Projects and Project Manufacturing.

The summarization process takes information from the PA_COMMITMENT_TXNS_V view and places the detailed results into the PA_COMMITMENT_TXNS base table. From this table, the summarization process summarizes or rolls up three basic values: TOT_CMT_RAW_COST, TOT_CMT_BURDENED_COST, and TOT_CMT_QUANTITY into summarized columns where the To_Date QTY/AMTS are defined by the Current Reporting Period. All amounts are represented in functional currency.

WHAT QUALIFIES AS COMMITMENTS

The following section describes the conditions that report a commitment value in each underlying view. The sum of the values returned from the listed views or queries report as the project commitment.

Requisitions: (pa_proj_req_distributions & pjm_req_commitments_v):

- Does not need to be approved (for example, status can be Incomplete).
- Requisition lines can't be Cancelled or Finally Closed.
- Requisition lines source must be Supplier.
- Requisition header must be type Purchase (not Internal).
- Person receiving the requisition (for example, Requestor) must be active (at the time of commitment reporting).
- Modified by Agent must = N (*).
- Handles destination types of EXPENSE, INVENTORY, and SHOP FLOOR.

Note

For destination EXPENSE, all project-related information must be entered. For INVENTORY and SHOP FLOOR, only the project needs to be identified for the requisition. The view derives the rest of the required project information from the manufacturing tables.

Tip

If your organization wants to include only approved requisitions in the summary tables, add an additional where clause condition to the pa_proj_req_distributions select portion of the union to include requisition approved_flag = 'Y' in the where clause.

Purchase Orders: (pa_proj_po_distributions & pjm_po_commitments_v):

- Does not need to be approved (for example, status can be Incomplete).
- Agent/Buyer needs to be active (at the time of commitment reporting).
- Deliver_to person needs to be active (at the time of commitment reporting).
- PO Header status can't be Closed, Finally Closed, or Cancelled.
- PO Header type can be Standard, Blanket, or Planned.
- Shipments (Line locations) can't be Closed or Finally Closed.
- Release_Num can't be Closed, Finally Closed, or Cancelled.
- Handles destination types of EXPENSE, INVENTORY, and SHOP FLOOR.

Note

For destination EXPENSE, all project-related information must be entered. For INVENTORY and SHOP FLOOR, only the project needs to be identified for the purchase order. The view derives the rest of the required project information from the manufacturing tables.

Tip

If your organization wants to include only approved POs, add an additional where clause condition to the pa_proj_po_distributions select portion of the union to include purchase order approved_flag = 'Y' in the where clause.

Supplier Invoices: (Expense only, pa_proj_ap_inv_distributions):

- Reports all invoices not interfaced to Oracle Projects (approved or unapproved). Invoices must be approved and posted to the GL before Oracle Projects will accept actual costs.
- For invoices that have been matched against a PO, the destination type must be Expense.

Delivered Goods: (Inventory/Wip, cst_projmfg_cmt_view):

- Checks for received/delivered goods into Inventory from both Requisitions and Purchase Orders.
- Checks for received/delivered goods into WIP from Purchase Orders.
- Reports the cost of all items not yet interfaced from Manufacturing (for example, from the Cost Collector) to Oracle Projects.

FORMULAS FOR CALCULATING AMOUNTS AND QUANTITIES

The following represents the formulas used to calculate both Amounts and Quantities.

TOT_CMT_RAW_COST comes from the following sources:

- **pa_proj_req_distributions.AMOUNT**—The basic formula used to calculate this amount comes from po_req_distributions_all, po_requisition_lines_all and is defined as follows:

  Quantity × Price (unit price is represented in functional currency)

  Note that foreign currency is also held at the line level.
- **pa_proj_po_distributions.AMOUNT_OUTSTANDING_INVOICE**—The basic formula used to calculate this amount comes from the po_distributions_all and is defined as follows:

  (Quantity Ordered – Quantity Billed) × Price × Conversion Rate
- **pa_proj_ap_inv_distributions.AMOUNT**—The basic formula used to calculate this amount comes from the ap_invoice_distributions_all and is defined as follows:

  Amount
- **pjm_req_commitments_v.AMOUNT**—The basic formula used to calculate this amount comes from the po_req_distributions_all and is defined as follows:

  Quantity × Price

- **pjm_po_commitments_v.AMOUNT_OUTSTANDING_DELIVERY**—The basic formula used to calculate this amount comes from the po_distributions_all and is defined as follows:

  (Quantity Ordered – Quantity Delivered) × Price × Conversion Rate
- **cst_projmfg_cmt_view.TOT_CMT_RAW_COST**—Has the following amounts:
  - **Inventory**—The basic formula used to calculate this amount comes from mtl_material_transactions and mtl_cst_cost_details and is defined as follows:

    Primary Quantity × Actual Cost
  - **WIP**—The basic formula used to calculate this amount comes from wip_transaction_accounts and is defined as follows:

    Base Transaction Value

TOT_CMT_QUANTITY comes from the following sources:

- **pa_proj_req_distributions.QUANTITY**—The basic formula used to calculate this amount comes from the po_req_distributions_all and is defined as follows:

  Quantity
- **pa_proj_po_distributions.QUANTITY_OUTSTANDING_INVOICE**—The basic formula used to calculate this quantity comes from the po_distributions_all and is defined as follows:

  Quantity Ordered – Quantity Billed
- **pa_proj_ap_inv_distributions.QUANTITY**—The basic formula used to calculate this amount comes from ap_invoice_distributions_all and is defined as follows:

  Quantity
- **pjm_req_commitments_v.QUANTITY**—The basic formula used to calculate this amount comes from the po_req_distributions_all and is defined as follows:

  Quantity
- **pjm_po_commitments_v.QUANTITY_OUTSTANDING_DELIVERY**—The basic formula used to calculate this quantity comes from po_distributions_all and is defined as follows:

  Quantity Ordered – Quantity Delivered
- **cst_projmfg_cmt_view.TOT_CMT_QUANTITY**—Has the following amounts:
  - **Inventory**—The basic formula used to calculate this amount comes from mtl_material_transactions and is defined as follows:

    Primary Quantity
  - **WIP**—The basic formula used to calculate this amount comes from wip_transactions and is defined as follows:

    Primary Quantity

RELIEVING COMMITMENTS

For Supplier Invoices that did not originate from a PO, the invoice amount (unapproved or approved) is treated as a commitment until the invoice is interfaced to Projects. After it's interfaced to Projects, the commitment is relieved. When Supplier Invoices get matched to a PO, the PO portion of the commitment gets relieved. At this point you now have a Supplier Invoice commitment. After the Supplier Invoice gets interfaced to Projects, the commitment is eliminated.

Commitment relief in Manufacturing is dependent on the fact that delivered goods must originate from a Requisition or Purchase Order. When the item is delivered, the commitment amount from the REQ/PO gets reduced.

Note

The commitment amount now gets reported as a costed/delivered item in MFG until the costs get interfaced into Oracle Projects.

PROJECT STATUS INQUIRY

The following section describes the various uses of the Projects Status Inquiry form and how modifications can be made to view information differently based on your organization requirements. This section starts with the basic PSI form and how to use it and proceeds to modifying your PSI columns and the use of the Project Status Inquiry extension.

POPULATING THE SUMMARIZATION TABLES

To view information in the Project Status tables, the process PRC: Update Project Summary Amounts must be run. Oracle Projects requires that costs must be distributed successfully and revenue released for amounts to be summarized. In addition, if you have not set a Reporting Period in your system, Projects will not summarize amounts.

Tip

A company should define a procedure for setting new reporting periods in Projects, and this should be adhered to based on your closing and reporting schedule.

Caution

Summarization occurs for each resource list attached to the project. Having numerous resource lists can degrade system performance. Therefore, you should consider system performance when setting up and assigning resource lists.

SETTING THE REPORTING PERIOD

As shown in Figure 15.43, navigate to the PA Periods form to set a project's reporting period. Inquire your PA Periods and you will see that the Reporting Period is checked. The period that is checked is the period Projects will summarize through. If no reporting period is checked, your system will not summarize amounts. To establish or change your reporting period, click Set Reporting Period. A form will open and identify the current reporting period and suggest the Next reporting period. The Next reporting period is a list of values, and the user can select the reporting period.

Note

If a reporting period is modified to a Prior Period, the PRC: Refresh Project Summary Amounts must be run to correctly restate summarization amounts. The report EXC: Summarization Period Exceptions can be run to identify the impacted projects and enable the user to reduce the number of projects being refreshed.

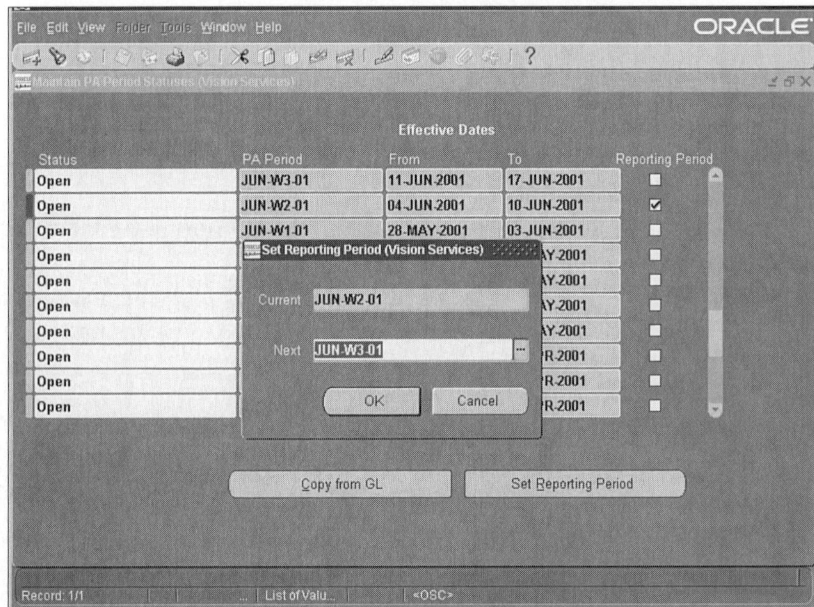

Figure 15.43
Specify the current reporting period to be used by Project Summarization.

VIEWING INFORMATION—PROJECT STATUS INQUIRY FORM

Using the Project Status Inquiry form, you can view summary information and also drill down to details of your expenditures and revenues.

The Find Project Status form enables one to inquiry all projects or limit the selection by Project Number, Project Type, Customer, and Project Member (see Figure 15.44). Additional parameters can be used as viewed on the PSI screen.

Tip

Information being viewed on the Project Status Inquiry screen can be copied into Excel for additional analysis and formatting. On the main menu, select File, Export File. The option will be provided to export to Excel.

PROJECT STATUS SCREEN

The Project Status Summary screen appears after clicking the Find button. This view provides project-level information for your project. Projects summarizes actual amounts based on Prior Period, Current Period, Year To Date, and Inception to Date values. Budgets are summarized the same with additional Total columns for revenue, cost, hours, and original amounts. If you budget your project with a non–time-phased entry method, Projects spreads the budget based on the dates of the budget. If, on the other hand, the budget is for a lump sum amount (no dates), Projects spreads the budget based on the project dates. As an example, say your project spans a three-year period with a total budget of $3 million. If the budget is for the project duration and the current period is December of year two, PSI reporting for budget amounts would be as follows:

PTD Revenue Budget:	83,334
YTD Revenue Budget:	1,000,000
ITD Revenue Budget:	2,000,000
Total Revenue Budget:	3,000,000

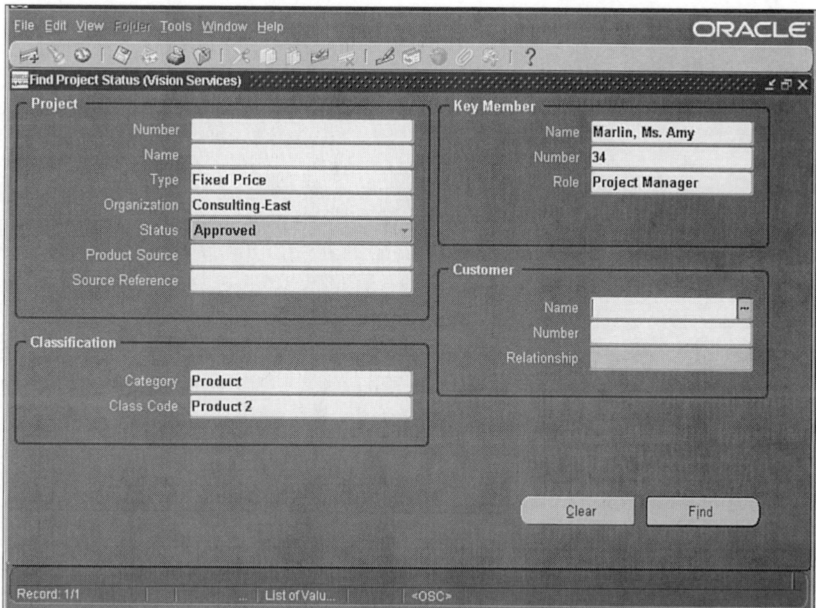

Figure 15.44
The Find Project Status form allows you to pull summarized information based on the parameters you specify.

TASK STATUS

Click the Task Status form; the system provides the same information as the project summary screen but by Top Task. The top task can be exploded into the lowest-level tasks. From the lowest level, actual expenditures can be drilled to and viewed. If you have Revenue

Events at the Task level, they can be viewed from this form (drill down to Events) as well. From each lowest Task level, you can drill to Resource Status, and from there, you can drill down to Actual Expenses.

RESOURCE STATUS

The Resource Status form groups information by your default resource status from the Project Type. From this screen you can not drill down further to Events, Commitments, or Actual Expenditures. A common error on this form is a line with a resource named Unclassified. This problem occurs when the summarization process finds an item (cost/revenue) that does not have a corresponding resource assigned on the resource list. To correct this problem, your resource list must be updated to include the resource type/resource.

Tip

The best method to finding a missing item is to view the Task Status and from there, Resource Status. This navigation path enables you to drill to expenditure items to help determine the cause of the error.

FOLDER TOOLS

The Project, Task Status, and Resource Status forms all provide the option to create your own folder view with folder tools.

VIEWING MULTIPLE BUDGETS AND RESOURCE LISTS

Oracle Projects enables you to budget with multiple budget types and report from multiple resource lists. When you open the PSI form, the system defaults to the Approved Cost/Revenue Budgets and the default Resource List from your project. These can be easily modified using the Tools section. If you're modifying the Cost Budget type, the system opens two forms—one displaying the type currently being viewed and the second displaying all the Cost budget types available and a list of values to select from.

This example modifies a resource list: This form opens with the default resource list Expenditure Category by Employee/Expense Type. From Tools, select Resource Drill-Down List. Note the default list appears in the top corner of the form, and the list of available items on the resource drill-down list form (see Figure 15.45).

By selecting the resource list Expenditure Category by Job Title/Expenditure Type, note the change to the resource lines for the category Labor. In the previous example, the employee is summarized under the Labor category. With the resource list change, the Job is now summarized (see Figure 15.46).

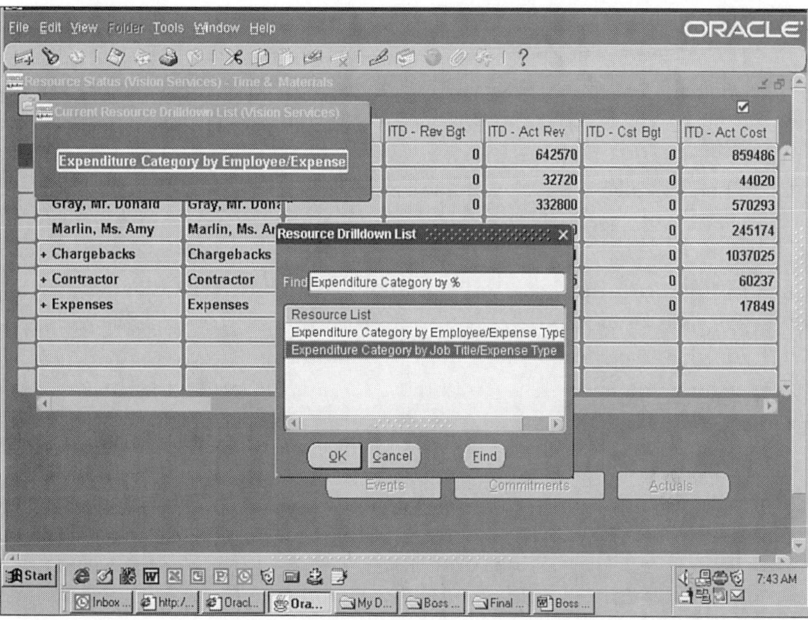

Figure 15.45
You can view summarized project information based on various resource lists.

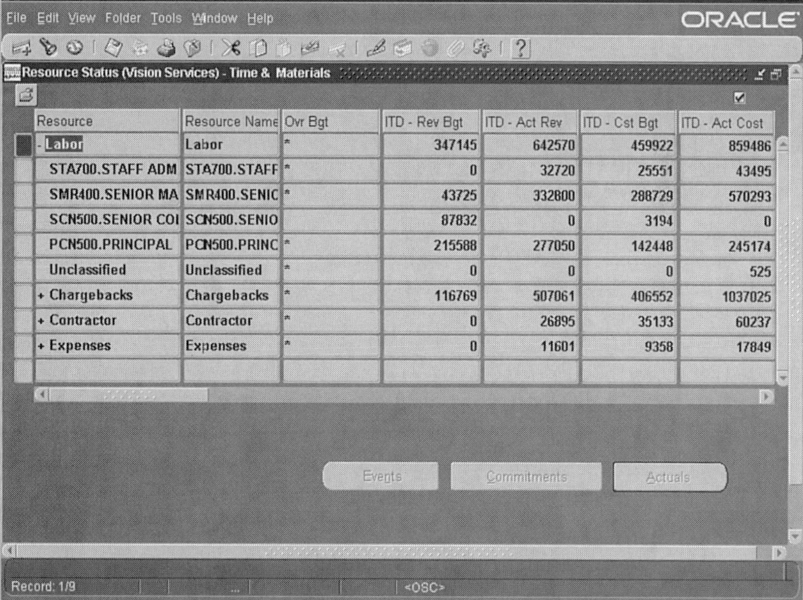

Figure 15.46
Changing the resource list changes how the project information is summarized.

MODIFYING PROJECT STATUS COLUMNS

Oracle Projects is delivered with predefined Project Status Columns. Additional columns are available that do not appear on the standard PSI form, and these can be viewed in the Set Up, Project Status Columns section. Click one of the definitions and the list of values can be opened. A definition can have a type of Text or Numeric, and PSI columns are limited to a maximum of three Text columns. This form can have different columns for Project, Task, and Resource.

MODIFYING COLUMNS TO BE FACTORED BY OR TOTALED Another useful feature is the ability to enable a column to be Factored By or Total. When you check these boxes and regenerate the view, the PSI summarization now allows you to total the columns being viewed and to factor amounts by Tens, Hundreds, Thousands, and so on. To total amounts, click the Totals button on the bottom of the form. To factor amounts, click Tools, Factor By and select the measurement you want to factor amounts by.

CHANGING THE DEFAULT COLUMNS OR ADDING NEW COLUMNS A default column can be modified by adding a new prompt and then selecting a predefined definition on the standard PSI form. Currently, 120 column definitions are provided by Oracle with reference to actual cost and revenue amounts (A), cost budgets , commitments (M), and revenue budgets (R). You can also modify an existing column that was predefined by Oracle. As in any modification, the view must be regenerated after making the change.

In the following example a new column prompt was added called Billable Burd Cost YTD. The definition was predefined and summarized Billable/Capital Burdened Cost Year-To-Date (see Figure 15.47).

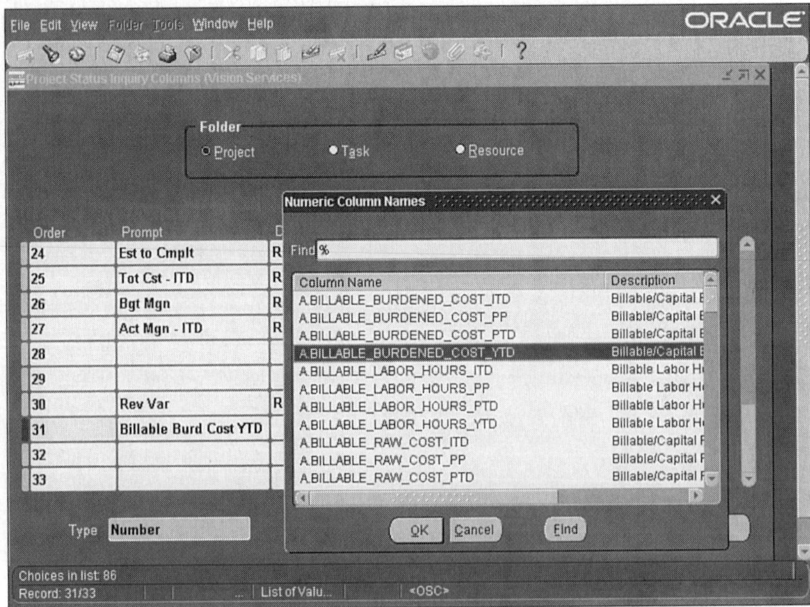

Figure 15.47
You can add more columns, such as Billable Burd Cost YTD, to the PSI form.

ADDING CALCULATIONS TO PREDEFINED DEFINITIONS Standard calculations can be modified with SQL expressions for building custom columns with predefined definitions. SQL Logic can be added for additional information not in the predefined definitions. Your company should be selective in building custom columns because it can impact your product's performance. For further explanation and examples, see Chapter 17 of the *Oracle Projects User Guide*.

In Figure 15.48 a variance column was built for displaying the calculated budgeted ITD labor hours less the actual ITD labor hours. This was accomplished by subtracting the predefined budget ITD labor hour's column from the predefined actual ITD labor hour's column. The view was generated after making the change. Note the prompt name is Labor Hours Variance.

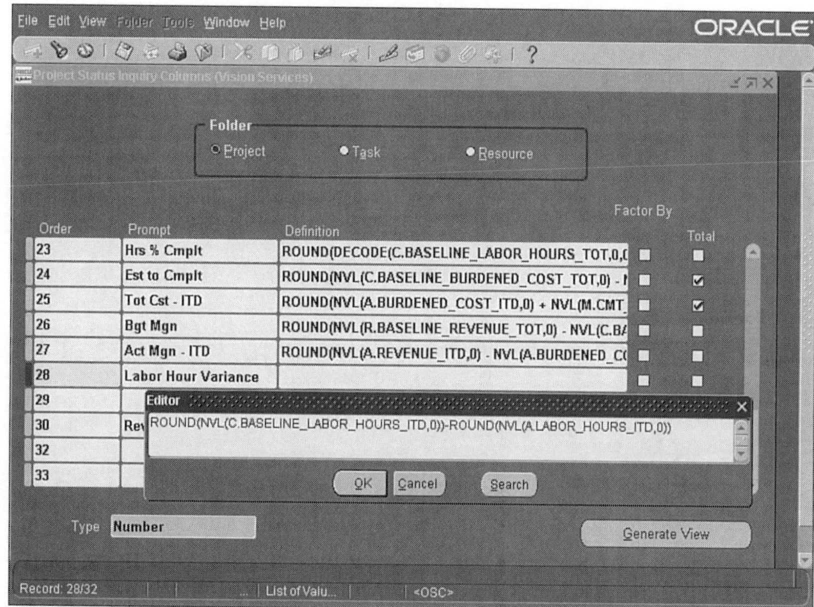

Figure 15.48
You can add columns to PSI that use other PSI columns as part of the calculation.

The Project Status Inquiry screen provides the following results after the form is generated (see Figure 15.49).

PSI CLIENT EXTENSION

Projects offers a PSI client extension that can be used to derive your own column definitions and calculations for the PSI columns. Your extension can be used to override the totals or derive an alternative column value. When building a client extension, you must store the PL/SQL procedure in the database and define the column prompt on the PSI column setup that will use the extension results. More information about these client extensions is provided in the section "Client Extensions," earlier in this chapter.

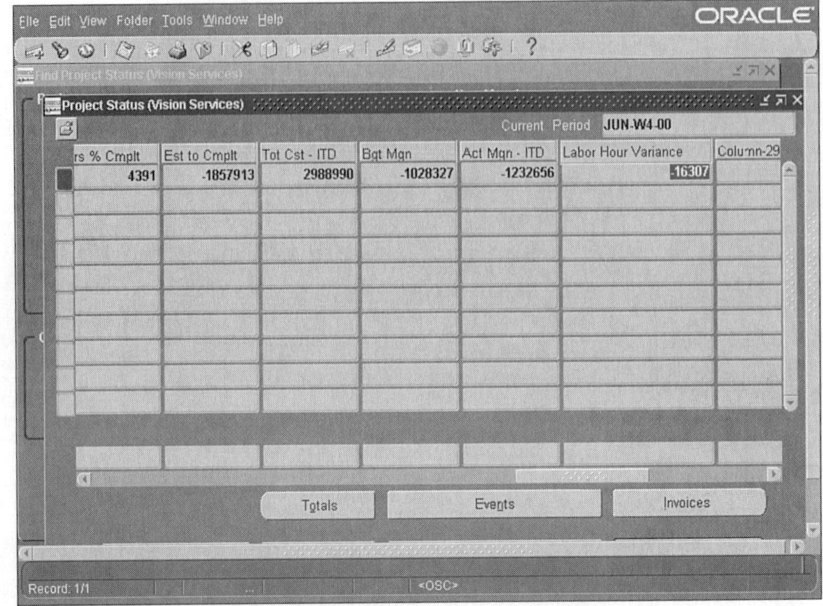

Figure 15.49
New columns are now displayed in the PSI window.

Reconciling Projects to GL

Most companies struggle with reconciling Oracle Projects to their General Ledgers, but it can be simplified. Here are a few suggestions for setup that will make the process smoother as well as some methods to cross-reference detailed information from your General Ledger accounts.

Oracle Projects offers improved reconciliation reports classified as Project Sub Ledger Audit Reports. These reports enable you to drill from a GL account balance to a specific project, range of projects, or expenditure type detail transactions. A useful feature is the ability to drill back from a General Ledger journal line to Project information, providing actual T account information for your transactions.

Account Setup

It can be helpful to set up accounting segment values that are for project-generated entries only. This might not be feasible, but it saves the financial analyst time during the reconciliation process. If he knows specific accounts are related to project WIP or project costs, he knows the actual source. Providing specific accounts per project class (contract, capital, indirect) also is a great way of reducing reconciliation time and enhances your reporting.

Prior to the use of Custom Library, a database trigger could be designed that prevents the end user from entering a project-related account directly. This method would provide an error message upon commit. Custom library enables the same principle and is now the recommended approach.

Tip

A profile option that prevents the user from modifying an account that was generated by Account Generator should be turned on to prevent any modifications to your rules. This option is under PA: Allow override of PA distributions in AP/PO.

Tip

An end user should not be allowed to modify an account in the General Ledger that was generated in a different source system (General Ledger/Set up/Journal Sources, freeze journals).

In your Purchasing and Payables subsystems you might need to require that a project is mandatory when entering invoices or purchase orders (see the following tip). This requirement makes reconciliation between Projects and your GL much more simplified as it ensures the proper account charges based on your Account Generator rules.

Tip

To enforce project entry there are several alternatives to require a project be entered on the Payables or Purchasing distribution lines:

- You can use a mandatory descriptive flexfield to populate the project number and then populate the project field, forcing the user to enter the remaining project information (see `www.projectp.com` for this solution).
- You can use the Custom library and use a database trigger to prevent saving the transaction without a project.
- You can set up Account Generator (Purchasing only) to require a project value to determine the accounts.

How to Find Project Details from Your General Ledger

Frustrating as it might appear, project detail information can be found without too much effort. Reference fields are contained in your journal lines (GL_JE_LINES) that tie back to the projects expenditure cost distribution lines. If you're looking for details that were interfaced specifically from Projects to General Ledger, your journal source name and journal category name identify Projects entries (found on JE_HEADER_ID). To trace back from GL to project details, the reference fields mentioned previously provide useful information.

From GL_JE_LINES_V:

- **Reference_1 = *Batch Name* (Projects)**—This value originates from the BATCH_NAME column in PA's PA_COST_DISTRIBUTION_LINES table.
- **BATCH_NAME**—A concatenation of Liability CCID + GL Date + Concurrent Request ID.

- **Reference_2 = Code Combination ID (for DEBIT transactions only)**—This value originates from the DR_CODE_COMBINATION_ID column in PA's PA_COST_DISTRIBUTION_LINES table.
- **Reference_3**—This equals one of the following:
    - **Cost**—This code identifies the transaction as the DEBIT side of a cost transaction.
    - **Liability**—This code identifies the transaction as the CREDIT side of a cost transaction.

- **Reference_6 = Duplicate of REFERENCE 1.**
- **Reference_2**—Provides the ability to link to the BATCH_NAME in Oracle Projects PA_COST_DISTRIBUTION_LINES_ALL. After linking, this will provide you the details of expenditure item ID, project ID, task ID and amount, and so on. If more information is required the ability is now easy to link further into the PA tables.

TIMING DIFFERENCES—CLOSING CYCLE

Because Oracle Projects does not allow period closure if items remain in the interface table, timing differences have become more manageable. To reduce timing differences, your Payables, Projects, Inventory, and Receivables systems should be closed at the same time. Common problems that can be avoided are ensuring all Inventory transactions are interfaced to Projects after closing Inventory but prior to closing Projects. Project expense reports or Supplier invoice adjustments once transferred to payables should be approved and interfaced to General Ledger prior to closing the Payables period rather than sweeping these costs to the next Payables period.

In Payables, the expenditure item date can be very misleading. As an example, a purchase order is created on June 1, 2001 and the buyer enters an expenditure item date on the purchase order distribution line as June 1, 2001. The item is actually received and invoiced on September 15th of the same year. In Payables, the GL date assigned to the invoice will most likely be 09-2001. When the invoice cost is interfaced to projects, the expenditure item date is June 1, 2001 (purchase order match pulls the date into payables from PO distribution line). The PA period is then determined by the period that the expenditure item date falls into (if open), or the first open period after the expenditure item date. If 08-2001 was the earliest open PA period, this would be the period assigned.

Tip

To alleviate this problem (periods out of sync or even distorted expenditure item dates), most companies add a database trigger in Payables that, upon commit of the Payables distribution line the expenditure item date, is modified. Some companies modify this date to the GL date, invoice date, or even the receipt date.

Based on your organization structure and reporting requirements, you can close your systems within 1–2 days after the period ends. This can be accomplished through streamlining of your company procedures, requiring timely entry of pertinent data, and reviewing and correcting information proactively. Hardware and software stability are critical to the running of timely processes and providing the financial information to the organization. A procedural closing schedule should be published for each closing well in advance so the organization operates with these expectations. This becomes a major change in the philosophy of many companies but can be accomplished through communication, teamwork, and company support.

TROUBLESHOOTING

This section discusses the common errors users encounter and how to correct them while running processes within Oracle Projects.

TROUBLESHOOTING USING CUSTOM FOLDERS WITH EXPENDITURE INQUIRY

The Expenditure Inquiry form offers many folder fields that can be used to troubleshoot or isolate problems. Using the Folder, Show Field option you can view the many options that become available when tracking information. If a project is expected to generate a capital asset, a folder for viewing Capital information could be made available that displays the required process flags against your expenditures. For contract projects where an invoice is not selecting all of your expenditure items, this form can display if the item is billable, revenue was distributed, item is on a billing hold, and so on (see Figure 15.50).

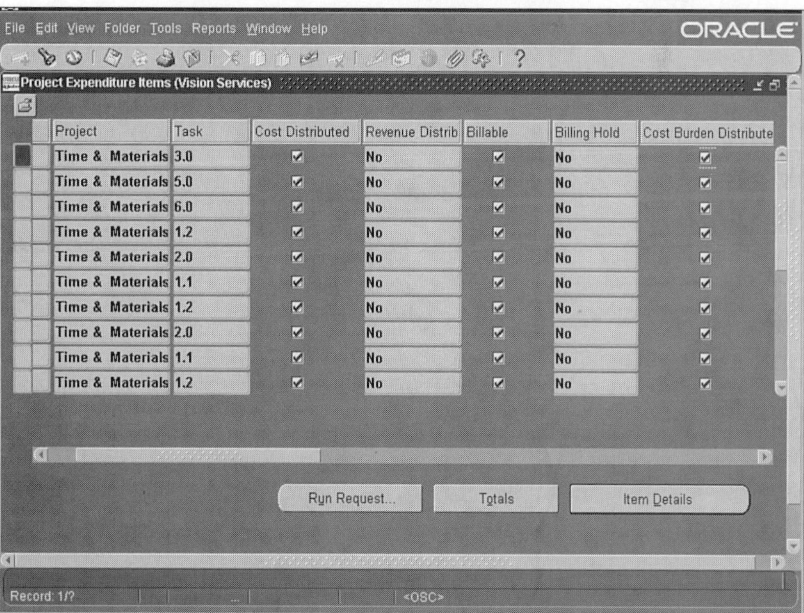

Figure 15.50
Using Folder tools, additional columns can be added to the Expenditure Inquiry screen to aid with troubleshooting problems.

Tip

The Expenditure Inquiry form enables you to reduce your query criteria by limiting items to billing status, processing status, cip status, and cross-charge information.

TROUBLESHOOTING TRANSACTION IMPORT INTEGRATION

If the expenditure date falls outside the project or task active dates, the project or task dates must be extended to include the expenditure item date.

If the employee Assignment is not active, the employee is normally not hired in HR prior to the expenditure date or terminated prior to the expenditure date. If in HR the hire or termination date is within the week cycle for labor, the dates can be shifted in Transaction Import. If it's outside the expenditure cycle, HR should be contacted to resolve the problem. Dates can be modified in either Transaction Import or HR.

If the expenditure organization is not active, in HR, be sure the organization is enabled as a Project Expenditure/Event organization. This error also occurs if a new organization is created and not compiled in the Projects module.

Tip

On the employee assignment, check to see whether the job and organization they are assigned to is active within the expenditure cycle.

Tip

After errors are corrected, the status flag in the import tables needs to be changed from Rejected to Pending. This is done by running an easy SQL script.

LABOR DISTRIBUTION

The following items can be used to help troubleshoot problems in distributing labor costs:

- **Employee is missing cost rate**—In this situation the employee is not assigned a cost rate in Projects. This needs to be assigned in the set up, labor costs rate section.
- **Compiled multiplier is not found**—This refers to a new organization that has been added. Check to see that the organization exists in the Project hierarchy. If not, place it in the hierarchy and then run the process in projects that compiles the burden multiplier for new organizations.
- **Assignment is not active**—Employee might have been terminated after the expenditure was entered but prior to the costing process.
- **AutoAccounting error**—value not found—Check to ensure that your values are populated in either your lookup set or attribute.

Tip

It is important to compile only for new organizations. If the compile process is run for all organizations, the system marks all expenditure items for recosting (within effective date of burden schedule revision).

TROUBLESHOOTING EXPENSE REPORT DISTRIBUTIONS, INTERFACE TO PAYABLES

The following items can be used to help troubleshoot problems in distributing and interfacing expense reports:

- **Compiled multiplier is not found.**
- **Assignment is not active.**
- **Interface - Duplicate Supplier record**—The employee was entered as a Supplier in AP but was not entered as type Employee, and the employee number was not assigned to them. To correct this, change the supplier type to Employee and assign the correct employee number (list of values).
- **Interface - Too many characters in invalid string**—This means that the employee does not have a Home address assigned to her in HR.

Tip

In the HR module, each employee must have a default mailing as Home and an actual address. Ensure that your HR department is entering this information upon hiring an employee.

TROUBLESHOOTING REVENUE PROCESSING

The following items can be used to help troubleshoot problems in revenue processing:

- **No available funding for project**—Ensure that the project is funded and the budget is baselined.
- **Revenue has reached Hard Limit**—If this is a warning, it can be ignored. If it is an error, though, the system will not generate an invoice or a revenue past the hard limit on the agreement screen. To fix this, uncheck the Hard Limit box on the agreement screen or correct the funding and budget amounts.
- **No bill rate or markup was found for this expenditure**—Check the process report because it will place an error message on each item that has no rate. Proceed to the bill rate schedule, and enter the job or expenditure type with a respective bill rate.
- **No eligible events or expenditures were found for processing**—This might be okay, but if you have expenditures or events you feel should have been processed, this requires research.

Tip

Check the enter events and ensure the event has a date assigned within the accrue-through date of your processing. For the expenditures, on the expenditure inquiry screen, check to see that the items are costed and billable.

Note

When processing revenue accrual and multiple periods are open, revenue is assigned to the latest open period if you do not enter an accrue-through date. To prevent this from happening, the revenue should first be generated through the earliest open period and released. The best prevention–although not always possible–is to maintain one open period in your Projects system.

Troubleshooting Invoice Processing

The following items can be used to help troubleshoot problems in invoice processing:

- **No available funding for project**—Ensure that the project is funded and the budget is baselined.
- **Revenue has reached Hard Limit**—If this is a warning, it can be ignored. If it is an error, the system will not generate an invoice or a revenue past the hard limit on the agreement screen. To fix this, uncheck the Hard Limit box on the agreement screen or correct the funding and budget amounts.
- **No bill rate or markup was found for this expenditure**—Check the process report because it will place an error message on each item that has no rate. Proceed to the bill rate schedule, and enter the job or expenditure type with a respective bill rate.
- **No eligible events or expenditures were found for processing**—This might be okay, but if you have expenditures or events you feel should have been processed, this requires research.
- **Check the expenditures on the expenditure inquiry screen and verify that they are costed and revenue has been generated against them (calculated bill amount)**—If not, depending on whether the item is costed, the cost or revenue process should be rerun.

Tip

When first setting up your Oracle Projects application for production use, process a manual revenue and invoice event. If you are able to successfully generate and interface invoice or revenue amounts, you have verified that a majority of the application configuration is on target.

Note

If draft invoices are created using a range of projects, the system will not regenerate the draft in subsequent runs. To pull in new information that is eligible to be invoiced, the single project process should be run.

ADDING NEW ORGANIZATIONS IN ORACLE HUMAN RESOURCES

Creating new organizations requires additional setup information for the organization to be used by Oracle Projects:

- **HR**—Create the organization in Oracle Human Resources. Determine which of the following Organization Classifications should be enabled for the organization (HR should contact Project Accounting personnel):
  - Project/Task Owning Organization (HR Organization = Y)
  - Project Expenditure/Event Organization (HR Organization = Y).
  - Project Invoice Collection Organization (locations only).
  - HR Organization (if employees will be assigned). If enabled, the other section for cost must be filled in. The four fields that require a value are for the Company, Location, Parent Department, and Department. The values will be linked to the General Ledger tables and follow the GL structures.
  - Navigation: Setup/Human Resources/Organizations/Define.
- **HR**—Assign the correct parent organization in the HR hierarchy. (Navigation: Setup/Human Resources/Organizations/Hierarchies.)
- **HR**—Change the organization assignment for employees who should be in the new organization.
- **Projects**—Determine whether any existing projects need to have their organization assignments changed to the new organization. Organization should be changed through the mass update form.
- **Projects**—Organization must be added to the Projects Hierarchy prior to step 6. (Navigation: Setup/Projects/HumanResources/Organizations/Hierarchy.)
- **Projects**—Organization if used as an expenditure organization must be compiled in Oracle projects. *(PRC: Add New Organization Compiled Burden Multipliers.)*
- **Projects**—If the new organization has an organization type of location and the classification Project Invoice Collection Organization is enabled, this organization must be set up as a transaction type in Oracle Receivables. In Oracle Projects run the process *IMP: Create Invoice Organization Transaction Types*.

SUMMARY

As you have seen in this chapter, the Oracle Projects solution provides a suite of highly integrated applications that give your organization the capability to capitalize on global opportunities. Oracle Projects enables your organization to set up projects and tasks and assign related expenditures. Costs can be allocated or burdened and then translated to Revenue, Billing, and Capital items when required. One of the major benefits of using Oracle Projects is the capability for a project-oriented business to manage its projects with a proactive approach.

Although Oracle Projects is a subledger to Oracle General Ledger, it can quickly become the center of your business operations in project-centric business environments. Oracle Projects can be configured to integrate with Oracle Financials, Manufacturing, and HRMS applications or configured as a standalone application. Using more advanced features enables Oracle Projects to be integrated with project management systems and to extend the existing code to satisfy company-specific business processes.

In this chapter, you have been exposed to the tasks necessary to launch a very basic Projects system. As you can see, the Projects implementation is not only dependent on setup steps in other applications, but it also determines many of these setup steps. It is critical that knowledgeable Projects individuals are included in implementation stages for the Oracle Financials and Manufacturing suites.

Do not underestimate the effort to install and configure Oracle Projects. Although Oracle Projects implementations have large technical requirements, you must also incorporate the human and organizational requirements of the company to be successful. In a Projects implementation, three critical user groups exist: the end users who enter time and expenses into Projects; the project managers who are responsible for the creation, scheduling, and deployment of projects; and the accountants who monitor the cost and revenue impact of the projects to the company. You must understand each group's unique requirements and design a solution that satisfies all. You also must properly set these users' expectations of the software and resolve their issues and concerns. Oracle Projects is very flexible and can meet most users' needs. In some cases, however, you might need to help the company redefine certain business processes to take full advantage of Oracle Projects.

During the transition phase of the project, you must train users, convert and load data, and develop the user support infrastructure. After the system goes live, you should audit, maintain, tune, and improve the system as the users take ownership. At that point, Oracle Projects becomes the backbone of your enterprise and the key platform for company growth and competitive advantage.

CHAPTER 16

Using Oracle Purchasing

In this chapter

Oracle Purchasing provides numerous features that enable you to set up your system to reflect your business practices and manage the requisition and purchase of products and services required to run your business. The Purchasing application interfaces with Oracle Payables to assist in bill paying. Through Purchasing, you also interface to Inventory to replenish stock. You also use Purchasing to assist the material planning process in the purchase of goods and services required for the manufacturing schedule.

How Purchasing Relates to Other Applications

Purchasing has relationships to many of the modules in the Oracle application suite. Purchasing shares setup information from General Ledger, Human Resources, Inventory, Payables, and Order Management. The Inventory, General Ledger, Order Entry, Accounts Payable, Accounts Receivable, Fixed Assets, and Cost Management modules share the setup information from Purchasing. Purchasing depends on the Applications Object Library (AOL) for responsibilities, menus, profile options, and other related setups.

Figure 16.1 shows how various modules are related to Purchasing. Each module indicates the information it shares. Arrows show the direction in which the information flows and to which modules the information flows.

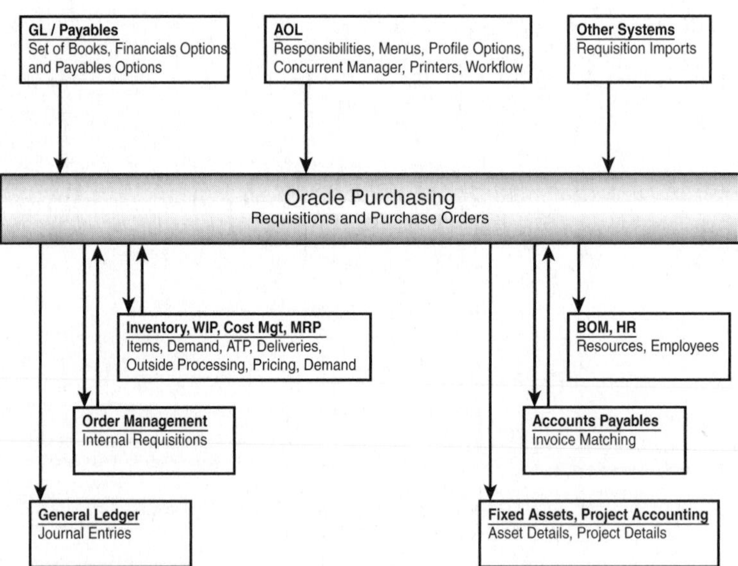

Figure 16.1
A module's relationships to other applications.

Discovering New Features in Release 11*i*

This section briefly describes the new features introduced in Oracle Purchasing 11*i* and some enhancements to existing functions. The important enhancements are in the areas of workflow, approved supplier lists, Purchasing Documents Open Interface, automatic sourcing, Copying PO Documents, capturing additional information, receipt matching, handling customer returns through Purchasing, Electronic Document Delivery, and General Ledger Drill-Down. These important and other enhancements have been briefly discussed below.

ADVANCED WORKFLOW TECHNOLOGY

The advanced workflow technology, starting with Release 11, automates the procurement process through the use of rule-based processes designed for your specific business needs. Employees can use the Web, e-mail, or the applications interface to receive and respond to workflow notifications. Release 11*i* includes new Process Navigator Workflows. Several steps in a business process are linked sequentially into a workflow. At each step, the workflow opens the associated applications window and requires that the related application products be installed. You can complete each step and proceed to the next. You also can leave the process anywhere and return later. You specify a name for each launch of the process workflow, so you can uniquely identify each of the processes you've started.

Figure 16.2 is an example of the new process navigator workflows. This figure shows the procure-to-pay process workflow and its first two activities.

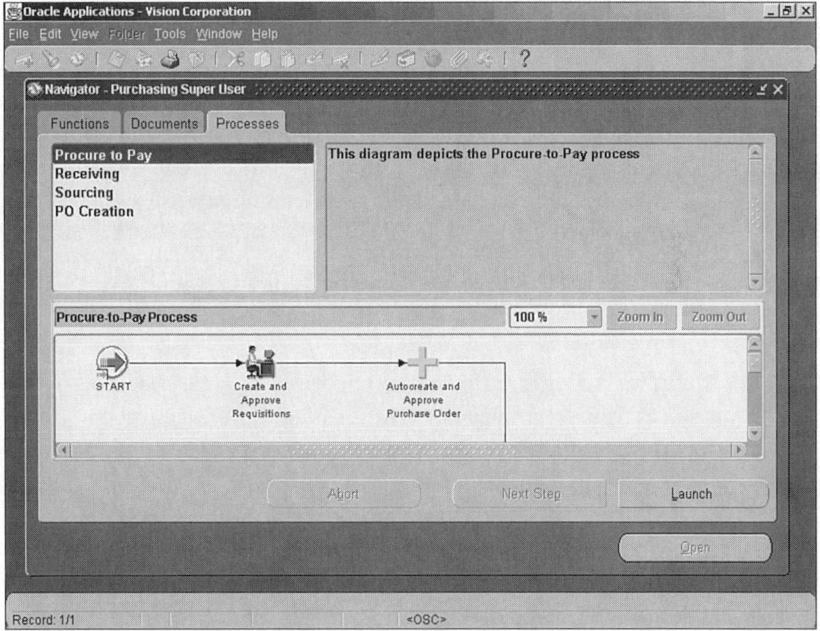

Figure 16.2
The procure-to-pay process workflow and its first two activities.

PROCESS NAVIGATOR WORKFLOWS

Purchasing comes with the following new Procurement Process workflows:

- **PO Creation**—Includes Create and Approve PO, Communicate to Supplier, Acknowledge PO, Change and Re-Approve PO, Communicate Changes to Supplier, and Acknowledge PO Changes.

- **Procure-to-Pay**—Includes Create Req, Autocreate and Approve PO, Communicate PO to Supplier, Confirm Receipt, Create and Approve Invoices, Pay Supplier, and Transfer to GL.
- **Receiving**—Includes Receive Advance Shipment Notice, View Invoice Summary, Create Receipt, Inspect Goods, Reject or Return, and Deliver.
- **Sourcing**—Includes Analyze Commodity, Analyze Suppliers, Create RFQ, Create Quotations, Analyze Quotations, Create Agreement, and Define Sourcing.

Purchasing 11*i* also comes with improved workflow documentation. The documentation now contains more details of built-in workflow processes and gives more details for customization.

IMPROVED NOTIFICATIONS

Requisition Approval and PO Approval workflow notifications in Release 11 had five line restrictions. These have been removed and different programming techniques are now used. Consequently, notification messages now display all lines of the Purchasing document.

APPROVED SUPPLIER LIST

Approved Supplier Lists can now be disabled and reenabled as required. In addition, following are some enhancements made to Approved Supplier Lists and Supply Chain Planning:

- **Capacity constraints in planned orders, with flexible tolerances**—You can now specify capacity constraints on specific items for individual suppliers. You can allocate Planned Orders taking these constraints into account. When the supplier's capacity is insufficient, Supply Chain Planning selects alternative suppliers based on the priorities you have specified.

  You can also specify flexible tolerances for these supplier-item–specific constraints. In other words, you can say that with *n* days advance notice, the capacity can be increased by *x* percentage.
- **Supplier-Specific ordering restrictions**—You can now specify ordering restrictions, such as Minimum Quantity and Minimum Lot Quantity, for a specific supplier and item. You can also specify Lead Time for a specific supplier and item.
- **Delivery calendars**—You can now define delivery dates for a specific supplier and item. Supply Chain Planning adjusts dates on planned orders for valid delivery dates as defined by you.

AUTOMATIC SOURCING

Enhancements made to Automatic Sourcing allow defaulting of sourcing details to purchasing documents. This feature is used in Supply Chain Planning.

Copy Documents

You can use this new function to create new Purchase Orders, Agreements, or Quotations by copying from an existing document. This new function is not available in respect to Requisitions. This function is available under the Tools menu of respective Purchase Order or Quotation forms.

Figure 16.3 shows the Copy Document window. The document type and source document number default based on the document from which this window is invoked. You cannot change them. You must specify a number for target document (the 'copy') and you have the option to copy the attachments from source document.

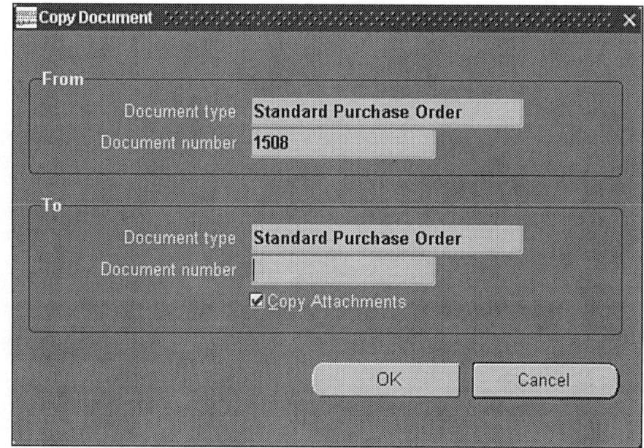

Figure 16.3
Remember that you must enter a number for the target document.

Country of Origin Information

Approved Supplier Lists, Supplier Sites, Standard or Planned Purchase Orders, Release, and Receipts have a new field to capture the country of origin of items. You can track this information through a new field in several reports.

Expiration Date in Blanket Agreements

A new field for Expiration Date in Blanket Agreements enables you to specify a date after which the item can't be ordered.

Electronic Document Delivery

Oracle Purchasing now integrates with CommercePath and RightFAX. If you install this software, it enables you to send documents by automatically faxing them, by e-mail, or over the Internet. Printed Purchase Order Report and Printed Change Orders Report have been enhanced to take a fax number at the time of approval and automatically fax the approved purchase order.

GENERAL LEDGER DRILL-DOWN

Receiving transaction forms have been enhanced with GL integration, which enables drill-down to view accounting information for most receipt transaction types.

INVOICE-TO-RECEIPT MATCHING

This enhancement to Oracle Purchasing and Payables enables you to match a Payables invoice to a purchasing receipt. This enables you to evaluate receiving tolerances better. This also reduces navigation between windows to manage receiving related holds and releases, while trying to approve and pay invoices. Release 11 allowed matching to Purchase Orders Shipments and Distributions only.

MATERIAL SHORTAGE ALERTS

You can enable Inventory Items to display shortage messages on receipt. When you receive an item that's in shortage, the message is displayed with detailed information, so you can make the item available with a high priority.

MULTIPLE REPORTING CURRENCIES

The View Receiving Accounting window has been enhanced to show transactions in entered currency, functional currency from your set of books, and any reporting functional currency.

Purchasing now has MRC Transactions Upgrade Utilities, similar to several other applications. These are scripts you can run to convert open and reversible transactions from the primary functional currency to reporting functional currencies. This enables you to continue the accounting life cycle of open transactions when you switch to Multiple Reporting Currencies.

PAYMENT ON RECEIPT

This function, also called ERS, has several enhancements.

A new profile option (PO: ERS Aging Period) enables you to specify the number of days to wait before Payables automatically generates invoices for purchase receipts.

The Terms and Conditions window for Purchase Orders and Releases includes a new field that allows you to disable Payment on Receipt for individual Purchase Orders and Releases.

You can now change the prefix ERS for invoice numbers generated by Payment on Receipt program. This was the prefix always used in Release 11. It is now the default, and you can change it to something that better indicates your business process.

PURCHASING DOCUMENTS OPEN INTERFACE

The major enhancement to this interface is the capability to import Standard POs. The interface can now process updates to existing purchasing documents, in addition to importing new and replacement documents. Other enhancements include the addition of more fields and import of price/sales catalog information from supplier into Blanket Agreements and Quotations.

A new workflow notification is available for Price Tolerance violations. When you import price/sales catalog information using Purchasing Documents Open Interface, and the revised price exceeds the specified price tolerance, you receive a notification enabling you to accept or reject the price changes.

RECEIPT-BASED EXCHANGE RATE

The Receiving window in 11*i* enables you to capture exchange rate information at the time of receiving. Purchasing automatically recalculates the item price and nonrecoverable tax based on the new exchange rate. Oracle Payables uses this information to calculate exchange rate variations and purchase price variances derived from the standard cost, when you match an invoice to a purchase receipt.

RECEIVING CUSTOMER RETURNS

Purchasing now handles the receipt of sales returns, which was earlier done in Oracle Inventory. You can enter a receipt against a Return Material Authorization (RMA), inspect the return, return the repaired goods, and make receiving corrections.

RECOVERABLE TAXES

Purchasing 11*i* enables you to account for taxes that are fully recoverable, partially recoverable, or not recoverable. You can compute and encumber partially recoverable or nonrecoverable taxes.

A new window titled Tax Code Summary is available from the Tools menu of Requisitions, Purchase Orders, and Releases. This window displays total recoverable and nonrecoverable taxes. Another new window titled Tax Details displays recoverable and nonrecoverable taxes for each line, shipment, and distribution.

CRITICAL IMPLEMENTATION FACTORS

In addition to understanding the factors discussed here, you should identify and understand some key issues underlying a Purchasing implementation. The issues vary depending on the business scenario and requirements. The following common issues apply in all circumstances.

DEFINING YOUR ACCRUAL OPTIONS

The define accrual option allows you to determine whether to accrue expense items upon receipt or at period end. For inventory items, you can only accrue on receipt.

Note

If you use cash basis accounting, the accrual option should be set to Period End. You will not normally run the Receipt Accrual–Period End process.

DEFINING YOUR CONTROL OPTIONS

The define control options allow you to define the percentage by which the autocreated purchase order line cannot exceed the requisition line price. You can also define whether to close a shipment once it has passed inspection, once it has been delivered, or once it has been received. Additionally, you can require the system to notify you when you create a requisition line if a blanket purchase agreement exists for the item. You can also define whether the item description can be updated when a requisition, request for quotation (RFQ), quotation, or purchase order line is created. Through this option, you can prevent the approval of purchase orders created with suppliers that are on hold.

DEFINING YOUR DEFAULT OPTIONS

The define default options allow you to determine how your requisitions imported through the requisition open interface are grouped. You can also determine the currency rate type that is shown on requisitions, purchase orders, RFQs, and quotations. Additionally, you can define the minimum release amount for blanket, contract, and planned purchase orders. You can define what type of invoice matching your organization uses: Two-way matching must match the purchase order and invoice quantities within the tolerance; three-way matching matches the purchase order, receipt, and invoice; and four-way matching matches the purchase order, receipt, inspection, and invoice quantity.

DEFINING YOUR NUMBERING OPTIONS

The define numbering option enables you to determine whether your organization uses automatic or manual numbering.

Note

You can change the method of entering document numbers at any time.

You can also define whether your organization uses numeric or alphanumeric numbering.

Note

If you choose automatic document numbering, you can generate only numeric document numbers. However, you can import either numeric or alphanumeric document numbers.

ISSUES AND GAPS

Purchasing is an extensive module with many capabilities. Although the Review of the Top Enhancement Requests shows some unresolved issues with Purchasing, it is for the most part a fairly complete module for the functions it covers.

REVIEWING TOP ENHANCEMENT REQUESTS

Users have requested that they be allowed to override the supplier and supplier site on approved purchase orders. Sometimes in the dynamics of today's business environment, the supplier or supplier site information might need to change. Also, the fact that a purchase order has been approved does not mean that the purchase order has been printed and executed. Users need the flexibility of last-minute changes.

Users have also requested the capability to change a line type from goods to contracts. This is an important enhancement in that what might begin, for example, as a request for software can turn into a request for contract services. This is another enhancement that provides additional flexibility to the user.

Another enhancement requested by users is that cancelled purchase order lines not be printed on the printed purchase order. Cancelled purchase order lines on a printed purchase can be confusing to both the buyer and the supplier. This confusion can lead to the supplier sending items that have been cancelled.

Users have also requested the ability to enter returns against a cancelled purchase order. A cancelled purchase order might have had activity against the purchase order even though the purchase order had been cancelled.

Also, users have requested the ability to select which changes to a purchase order or requisition require reapproval. This is an enhancement of both flexibility and efficiency. The requirement that the entire requisition must be reapproved slows down the reapproval process and clutters the process.

Oracle Corporation is working on a few other enhancement requests, so you should contact your Support Representative to ascertain the latest position. One example is the Printed Releases Report. Every time you print a Release, it prints the associated Blanket Agreement. Many users have indicated that they should be able to select this.

Another example is the Purchasing Documents Open Interface. This program in 11*i* has been enhanced to import Standard Purchase Orders in addition to Blankets and Contracts. However, the information that can be modified through the interface is limited. Several users have requested enhancements, so that they can modify other information such as line quantity and unit price. The interface also doesn't currently import releases.

CONFIGURING THE APPLICATION

The Purchasing module requires extensive setup for the module to be configured properly to function as advertised. The following section lists all the setup tasks for a Purchasing implementation and briefly describes each task. You should perform the tasks in the order discussed here.

RESOLVING CRITICAL SETUP ISSUES

Prior to setting up Purchasing, you must resolve several critical issues. First, you must determine the set of books and accounting structure. Second, you must set up the organizations, positions, jobs, and users so employees can purchase items.

Table 16.1 shows the setup steps you must consider to configure the Purchasing application.

TABLE 16.1 PURCHASING SETUP CHECKLIST

Step	Requirement
Define set of books	Required with defaults
Define descriptive flexfields	Optional
Define organizations	Required
Define cross-reference types	Optional
Define profile options	Required
Define financials options (part 1)	Required
Define accounting flexfield combinations	Optional
Define tax names	Optional
Define payment terms	Optional
Open and close General Ledger (GL) accounting periods	Required
Open purchasing and inventory accounting periods	Required
Define locations	Required
Define location associations	Optional
Define job flexfield	Required
Define jobs	Required
Define position flexfield	Required
Define positions	Optional
Define position hierarchies	Optional
Enter employee	Required
Define item categories flexfield	Required
Define category	Required
Define category sets	Required
Define default category set	Required
Define control rules and groups	Required
Define position controls	Required

TABLE 16.1 CONTINUED

Step	Requirement
Fill employee hierarchy	Optional
Define usernames	Required
Define purchasing lookup codes	Optional
Define freight carriers	Optional
Define inspection codes	Optional
Define hazard classes	Optional
Define United Nations (UN) numbers	Optional
Define standard notes	Optional
Define unit of measure classes	Required
Define units of measure	Required
Define unit of measure conversions	Required
Define system items flexfield	Required
Define item attribute controls	Required with defaults
Define item templates	Optional
Define item catalog flexfield	Required
Define item catalog groups	Optional
Define buyers	Required
Define item	Optional
Define item relationships	Optional
Define line types	Optional
Define document controls	Required with defaults
Start autosubmit	Required
Define financials options (part 2)	Required
Define purchasing options	Required
Define receiving options	Required
Enter vendors	Required
Define your transactions reasons	Optional
Set up Oracle Workflow	Required
Request your receiving transaction processor	Optional
Define your concurrent process resubmission interval	Optional

UNDERSTANDING EACH SETUP TASK

Setup tasks fall into three categories. First are those setup tasks that the Oracle system requires for the application to operate. In the Purchasing application, you must have employees defined before you can create requisitions. Additionally, you must have buyers defined before purchase orders can be created from requisitions and purchase orders can be processed. Second are those tasks that, although required, contain certain default values which you can allow the system to use. Finally, some steps are completely optional, based on your particular implementation.

DEFINING THE SET OF BOOKS

Before you can implement Oracle Purchasing, you must set up at least one set of books. The set of books defines for the Purchasing application the chart of accounts, the accounting calendar, the functional currency, and the accounting flexfield structure. When defining the set of books, use the setup process described in Chapter 11, "Using Oracle General Ledger." You need not tackle this step if you have already set up the Oracle General Ledger application.

DEFINING DESCRIPTIVE FLEXFIELDS

Oracle Applications have a feature known as descriptive flexfields. Descriptive flexfields place information into the Oracle system that might not be provided otherwise. The descriptive flexfield has global segments that always appear on a flexfield pop-up window of a form and context-sensitive segments that are dependent on other information which appears on the form.

Note

To avoid slowing down data entry, do not set up mandatory descriptive flexfields in the Enter Purchase Orders and Enter Purchase Agreements windows.

DEFINING ORGANIZATIONS

Before you can implement Oracle Purchasing, you must set up the organizations. The organization defines the structure within which the Purchasing application allows employees to buy and receive goods or services. You do not need this step if you have already set up the Oracle Inventory application. When defining organizations, use the setup process described in Chapter 17, "Using Oracle Inventory."

DEFINING CROSS-REFERENCE TYPES

Cross-reference types define the types of relationships between items and other entities. As an example, you can create a relationship to track your old part numbers or to track your customer's part number. You then can assign any number of cross references to items.

Setting the Profile Options

Profile options give you control over the behavior of certain application features. Profile levels are a hierarchy, where user (U) is the highest level of the hierarchy, followed by responsibility (R), application(A), and, at the lowest level, site (S).

Figure 16.4 shows the Personal Profile Values window. Refer to Table 16.2 as you set profile option values.

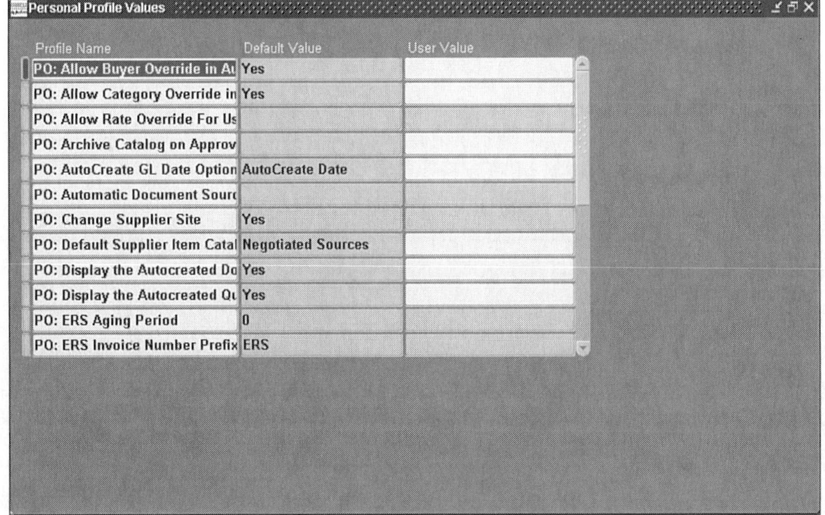

Figure 16.4
Notice that you can enter values for some values and others are disabled.

Table 16.2 Purchasing User/System Productivity Profile Options

Profile Option Name	Required?	Level	Comment
MRP: Default	Yes	SARU	Default PO assignment set sourcing assignment set
HR: Business group	Yes	SAR	Default setup business group
PO: Allow category override in autocreate	Yes	SARU	Default is yes
PO: Allow Rate Override for User	No	SARU	Default is no Rate Type
PO: Archive Catalog on Approval	No	SARU	Default is no
PO: Automatic Document Sourcing	No	SA	Default is no

TABLE 16.2 CONTINUED

Profile Option Name	Required?	Level	Comment
PO: Change supplier name	No	SARU	Yes/no
PO: Default supplier item catalog option	No	SARU	Negotiated sources
PO: Display autocreated quotation	No	SARU	Default is yes
PO: Display find on open catalog	No	SARU	Default is yes
PO: Display the autocreated document	No	SARU	Default is yes
PO: Enable SQL Trace for Receiving	No	SARU	Default is no Processor
PO: ERS Aging Period	No	SAR	Default is 0
PO: ERS Invoice Prefix	No	SAR	Default is ERS-Number
PO: Warn RFQ required before autocreate	No	SARU	Default is no
PO: Item cross-reference warning	No	SARU	Default is disposition
PO: Legal requisition type	No	SARU	Default is both
PO: Price Tolerance (%) for Catalog Updates	No	SARU	No default value
PO: Release during reqimport	No	SARU	Yes/no
PO: Supplier pricing method	No	SARU	Catalog price/last price
PO: Use P-Cards in Purchasing	No	SARU	Default is no
PO: Write Server Output to File	No	SARU	No default value
RCV: Allow routing override	No	SARU	Yes/No
RCV: Print receipt traveler	No	SARU	Yes/No
RCV: Processing	Yes	SARU	Batch/immediate/ online mode

DEFINING FINANCIALS OPTIONS

The financials options are used throughout the Oracle Applications. You define the set of books Purchasing uses as well as defaults to simplify vendor entry, invoice entry, and automatic payments.

Figure 16.5 shows the Financials Options window with its default tab. You can see several other tabs for different information that can be set up here. You do not need this step if you have already set up the Oracle Payables application. When defining financials options, use the setup process described in Chapter 12, "Using Oracle Payables."

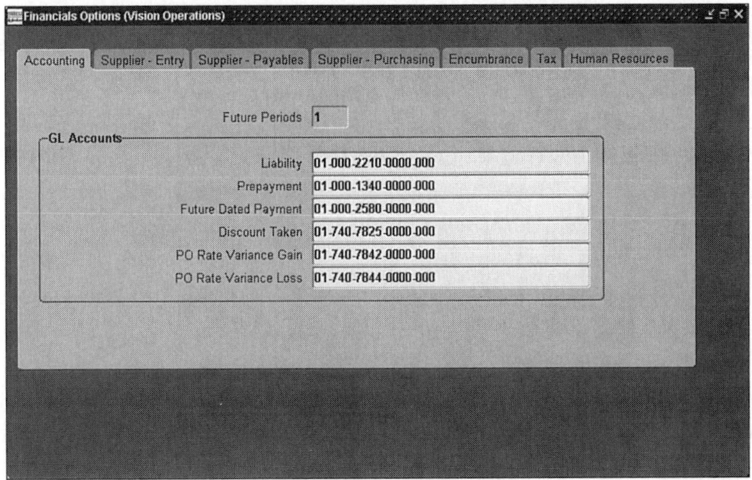

Figure 16.5
Note the default tab here along with the other optional tabs.

Defining Accounting Flexfield Combinations

Your accounting flexfield defines the account structure of your general ledger accounts. The accounting flexfield combinations enable you to take advantage of the applications' flexible tools for recording and reporting accounting information. You must define all acceptable accounting flexfield combinations if dynamic insertion is not allowed. This step is not required if dynamic insertion is allowed. You do not need this step if you have set up the Oracle General Ledger application. When defining accounting flexfield combinations, use the setup process described in Chapter 11.

Defining Tax Names

You must define the taxes you use to record the invoice taxes paid to your vendors. You also define your tax authorities here. You do not need this step if you have set up the Oracle Payables application. When defining tax names, use the setup process described in Chapter 12.

Defining Payment Terms

Define the payment terms that reflect the way you do business. Payment terms are used to calculate the payment schedules for invoices. Payment terms can be defined either as a percentage due or as an amount due. You can also define discounts. There is no limit to the number of payment terms you can define. You do not need this step if you have already set up the Oracle Payables application. When defining payment terms, use the setup process described in Chapter 12.

Opening and Closing Periods in the Accounting Calendar

You must open GL periods to allow posting of accounting entries into the general ledger from a PO. Similarly, you can close a GL accounting period to prevent posting of accounting entries. You do not need this step here if you have already set up the Oracle General Ledger application. When defining opening and closing periods, use the setup process described in Chapter 11.

OPENING AND CLOSING PERIODS IN THE PO AND INV CALENDARS

Purchasing has its own periods that you need to open and close separately from the General Ledger periods. You must open a purchasing period before any transactions can be entered in that period. You can close a purchasing period to prevent transactions in that period. A closed purchasing period can be opened later to allow transactions. However, if a period is permanently closed, you cannot open it again. Use caution before permanently closing a period. A permanent close ideally happens after an annual close when you are sure that there are no more transactions or corrections. You create general ledger journal entries when encumbering requisitions or purchase orders or accruing receipts.

DEFINING LOCATIONS AND LOCATION ASSOCIATIONS

Locations are defined in your organization for where you ship, receive, deliver internally, or bill for goods and services ordered. Additionally, if you group your locations by their Ship To sites, you can have your vendors ship everything to a central receiving location. You can also associate a location with vendors, vendor sites, or inventory organizations.

Note

Define your Ship To locations before defining other locations. Define your vendors before doing any location associations.

Tip

A location can be its own Ship To location. If you want to define a location to be its own Ship To location, do not enter anything in the Ship To field; Purchasing saves the location with the Ship To location as itself.

DEFINING THE JOB FLEXFIELD

Jobs are generic or specific roles within the enterprise. Jobs are independent of organization structures and are generally used where there is flexibility in employee roles. You do not need to perform this step here if you have installed Oracle Human Resources. When defining the job flexfield, use the setup process described in Chapter 24, "Using Oracle Human Resources."

Caution

Proceed carefully and coordinate with human resources if Oracle Human Resources is to be installed.

DEFINING JOBS

You must define the jobs that each employee has. Additionally, you can also define the skills that jobholders require and the grades to which they can be assigned. You do not need this step if you have installed Oracle Human Resources. When defining jobs, use the setup process described in Chapter 24.

Note

You must coordinate the definition of jobs with human resources.

Defining the Position Flexfield

You should use positions to manage fixed establishments of posts that exist independently of the employee assignment. A position is a specific occurrence of one job, fixed within one organization. You do not need to perform this step if you have installed Oracle Human Resources. When defining the position flexfield, use the setup process described in Chapter 24.

Caution

Proceed carefully and coordinate with human resources if you install Oracle Human Resources.

Defining Positions

You do not need to define positions if you have installed Oracle Human Resources. When you define the positions within your organization, you should place them in the organization's position hierarchy. You can also maintain position holders' skills and grades. When defining positions, use the setup process described in Chapter 24.

Note

You must coordinate the definition of positions with human resources.

You cannot change the organization or job once you have saved the definition. You can set up several positions that have the same job in the same organization. Each position name must be unique.

Defining Position Hierarchies

Position hierarchies are much like organization hierarchies. You can set up one primary hierarchy and multiple secondary hierarchies showing reporting lines, including "dotted line" reporting, to control access to information. The Purchasing position hierarchy is defined within a business group. The Purchasing application uses the hierarchy to determine the approval paths for your purchasing documents.

Note

To use position hierarchies for document approval, you must set the Use Approval Hierarchies Profile option to Yes.

ENTERING EMPLOYEES

In Purchasing, an employee can requisition goods and services—but she must first be recognized by the system as a user and she must also be a member of the requisition or purchasing hierarchy. You do not need this step if you have already installed the Oracle Human Resources application. Each employee should be assigned a job and position for document control and approval. When defining employees, use the setup process described in Chapter 24.

DEFINING THE ITEM CATEGORIES FLEXFIELD

You must design and configure your item categories flexfield before you can start defining items. Oracle Applications requires that all items be assigned to categories. You need not tackle this step if you have installed Oracle Inventory. When defining the item categories flexfield, use the setup process described in Chapter 17.

DEFINING ITEM CATEGORIES

A category is a logical classification of items that have similar characteristics. Categories are often the primary sort and/or grouping parameter for major purchasing reports. You do not need this step if you have installed Oracle Inventory. When defining item categories, use the setup process described in Chapter 17.

Tip

You can enter purchase order lines with only a category specified and without an item number. This is useful for one-time items that you do not want to define in your item master. When you define general categories that you can use directly on purchase orders, give them appropriate names to print on the purchase orders.

DEFINING CATEGORY SETS

A category set is a distinct grouping scheme that consists of categories. Category sets are used in reporting for grouping items with similar characteristics. You do not need this step if you have installed Oracle Inventory. When defining category sets, use the setup process described in Chapter 17.

SETTING THE DEFAULT CATEGORY SET

Each item you define must be assigned to a category set. You do not need this step if you have already installed Oracle Inventory. When setting default category sets, use the setup process described in Chapter 17.

Note

The default category set used in Purchasing always enforces the list of valid categories.

Defining Control Rules and Groups

Document control rules set approval limits for your employees for requisitions, purchase orders, and releases. You can assign document controls by the document total, account range, location, item range, or item category range. To approve documents, you must have a document total and account range rule.

Figure 16.6 shows the Approval Groups window. You can give a meaningful name and description to the set of rules. You must then define your rules with a combination of document total, and include and exclude ranges of accounts, commodity codes, and destination locations.

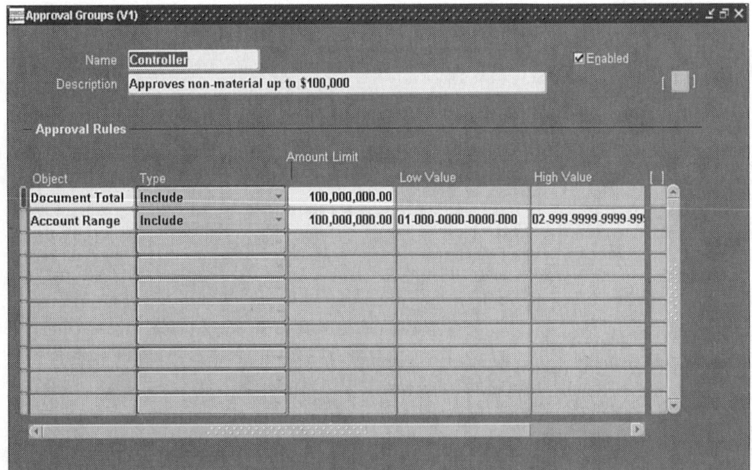

Figure 16.6
Remember to define your rules in the Approval Groups window.

Defining Position Controls or Controls for Jobs

You can assign individual positions or jobs to control groups. The employees assigned the job or position take on the authorization abilities of that job or position. The rules associated with control groups are used as a part of your hierarchy to control the flow of the approval process of your documents.

Filling the Employee Hierarchy

The fill employee hierarchy process creates a direct mapping between the defined position hierarchies and the employees holding the positions in each hierarchy. You must run this process anytime you make a change to the hierarchy for the change to take effect.

Setting Up the Users

You must set up users to assign an employee to a job or position; you do so in the System Administration module. An employee assigned in human resources is matched to the user. You do not need this step if you do not use positional hierarchies for document routing.

Caution

Proceed carefully and coordinate with human resources if Oracle Human Resources is to be installed. If two users are assigned to the same employee, problems with the approval process could occur. Notifications might be sent to the wrong user.

SETTING UP PURCHASING QUICKCODES

Purchasing uses lookup codes to define the lists of values throughout the system. Although there are a large number of lookup codes seeded in Oracle Purchasing, you can add quick-codes that meet your specific business needs.

Note

You cannot change or delete codes once you have added and saved them, but you can change the code descriptions or disable them by entering an end date.

Warning: Before you change the description of a quickcode, you must ensure that you do not run reports that contain previous transactions with the quickcode. Otherwise, any reports generated from the previous transactions can show quickcode descriptions inappropriate for the context.

The safest option is to disable the quickcode you do not want to use and create new quickcodes with appropriate descriptions.

DEFINING FREIGHT CARRIERS

Freight carriers handle internal transfers between organizations and shipments to and from customers and suppliers. You must set up a general ledger account for collecting costs associated with using the carrier. You do not need this step if you have installed Oracle Inventory. When defining freight carriers, use the setup process described in Chapter 17.

DEFINING INSPECTION CODES

You use inspection codes when you receive and inspect items that have been ordered. Each code requires a numerical ranking, which provides an inspection scale. You do not need this step if you have installed Oracle Inventory. When defining inspection codes, use the setup process described in Chapter 17.

DEFINING HAZARD CLASSES

Purchasing places hazardous material information you've defined onto your purchase orders, request for quotes, and receipt travelers.

Note

You can assign a hazard class to multiple UN numbers to identify hazardous items. Follow the next step to define UN numbers.

DEFINING UN NUMBERS

United Nations (UN) numbers provide identification to hazardous materials. UN numbers have descriptions that allow the shipment of hazardous material within the U.S. or internationally.

Note

You can also assign an identification number and a hazard class to each item you define.

DEFINING STANDARD NOTES

You can create attachments for your purchasing documents. The Purchasing module offers the following attachment capabilities:

- Provide unlimited text attachments on your purchasing documents
- Designate the appropriate people who can review the attachments
- Print attachments on your purchase orders and request for quotes for the supplier to review
- Reuse attachments on different documents
- Copy and modify existing attachments to speed up data entry
- Copy attachments from your requisitions to your request for quotes and purchase orders
- Provide standard attachments for an item that you can reference whenever you create a purchasing document for that item

DEFINING UNIT OF MEASURE CLASSES AND UNITS OF MEASURE

Unit of measure classes are groups of units of measure with similar characteristics. Units of measure express the quantity of items. You do not need this step if you have installed Oracle Inventory. When defining units of measure, use the setup process described in Chapter 17.

Tip

Purchasing prints the first four characters of the unit of measure description on the purchase order. Try to make these characters representative of the unit of measure.

DEFINING UNIT OF MEASURE CONVERSIONS

Unit of measure conversions enable you to perform transactions in units other than the primary unit of the item being transacted. You do not need this step if you have installed Oracle Inventory. When defining unit of measure conversions, use the setup process described in Chapter 17.

DEFINING THE SYSTEM ITEMS KEY FLEXFIELD

The system items key flexfield records your item information. You do not need this step if you have installed Oracle Inventory. When defining the system items key flexfield, use the setup process described in Chapter 27, "Administering the Oracle Applications."

DEFINING ITEM ATTRIBUTE CONTROLS

Item attributes are information about an item. Before you can define an item, you must set attribute controls. The control-level attribute type determines whether you have centralized (master level) or decentralized (organization level) control of item attributes. The status control attribute type describes whether certain status attributes have default values that appear when you assign a status code to an item and whether status codes control those attribute values after the defaults are assigned to an item. You do not need this step if you have installed Oracle Inventory. When defining item attribute controls, use the setup process described in Chapter 17.

DEFINING ITEM TEMPLATES

Templates are standard sets of attributes that you can use over and over to create similar items. Templates make item definition easier. You do not need this step if you have installed Oracle Inventory. When defining item templates, use the setup process described in Chapter 17.

DEFINING THE ITEM CATALOG FLEXFIELD

You do not need to define item catalog flexfields if you have installed Oracle Inventory. When you do define them, use the setup process described in Chapter 27.

DEFINING ITEM CATALOG GROUPS

An item catalog group has descriptive elements that are used to describe items. You can group items by these descriptive elements and then use these groupings in reporting. You do not need this step if you have installed Oracle Inventory. When defining item catalog groups, use the setup process described in Chapter 17.

DEFINING BUYERS

Buyers can review all requisitions. Also, only buyers can enter and autocreate purchasing documents. Before you can define buyers, you must define your employees and locations.

DEFINING ITEMS AND ITEM RELATIONSHIPS

Prior to requisitioning anything, you must define your items. In Purchasing, you must create item relationships for items you receive as a substitute for the original item. You do not need this step if you have installed Oracle Inventory. When defining items and item relationships, use the setup process described in Chapter 17.

Defining Line Types

You create line types to reflect the different characteristics for the items you purchase. You might want to define one line type for items you order by quantity and unit price. A second line type might be services you order by hour. A third type might be a line for outside processing operations in Oracle Work In Process.

Note

When the outside processing line type is selected on a document line, you can only enter outside processing items, and the destination type can only be the shop floor.

Before you can define line types, you must define categories and units of measure.

Starting the Autosubmit Program

The autosubmit process is a concurrent program that resubmits itself every 24 hours to purge obsolete notification information from the system. Starting autosubmit is a required step.

Defining Purchasing Options

You define default values and controls used throughout Purchasing through the purchasing options. The categories are

- **Accrual options**—Such as whether to accrue expense items at period end or upon receipt

Note

When using cash basis accounting, you should set this option to Period End, but you will not normally run the Receipt Accrual - Period End process.

- **Control options**—Such as the receipt close point
- **Default options**—Such as the minimum release amount
- **Internal requisition options**—Such as the required order type and order source for internal requisitions
- **Numbering options**—Such as the numbering method, numbering type, and next number for each of your documents

Figure 16.7 shows the Purchasing Options window. Here you see the Default tab when you navigate to the window. You can also see other tabs such as Accrual, Control, Internal Requisition, Numbering, and Tax Defaults options.

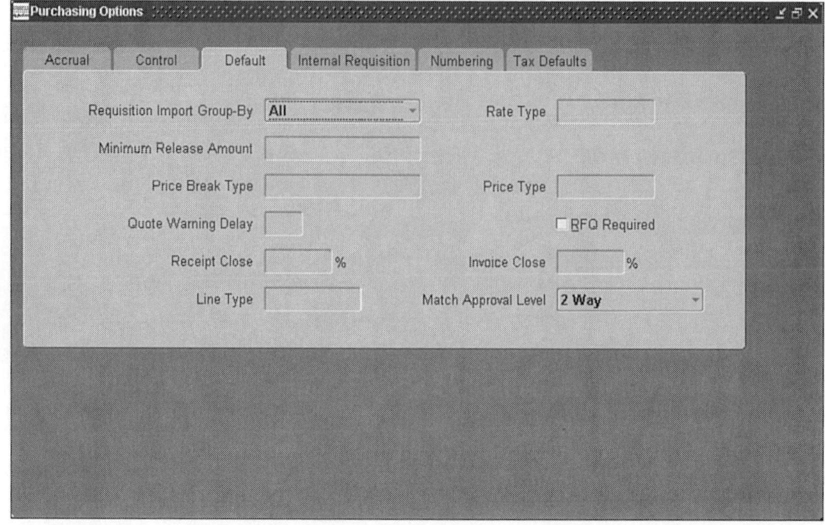

Figure 16.7 Be sure to take a look at the other tabs provided in the Purchasing Options window.

Note

You can override purchasing options when you are creating documents. You can change the method of entering document numbers at any time. If you choose automatic document number entry, you can generate only numeric document numbers.

If you import purchasing documents that reference alphanumeric numbers, you must choose alphanumeric as your number type, regardless of your numbering method. You must set up internal requisitions if Order Entry is installed.

DEFINING RECEIVING OPTIONS

Receiving options govern the receipt of items in your organization. Most of the options set here can be overridden for specific suppliers, items, and purchase orders. You must set up receiving options for each organization.

Figure 16.8 shows the Receiving Options window.

DEFINING TRANSACTION REASONS

Transaction reasons are a standard means of classifying or explaining the reason for a transaction. You do not need this step if you have installed Oracle Inventory. When defining transaction reasons, use the setup process described in Chapter 17.

CONFIGURING FLEXBUILDER

In Release 10, you used flexbuilder to derive the account code combinations in Purchasing. In Release 11*i*, flexbuilder has been replaced by the account generator workflow. Prior to using the account generator in a production environment, you need to define your accounting flexfield structures for each set of books. You also need to define your flexfield segment values and validation rules. Then, you need to set up Oracle Workflow, using the process described in Chapter 28.

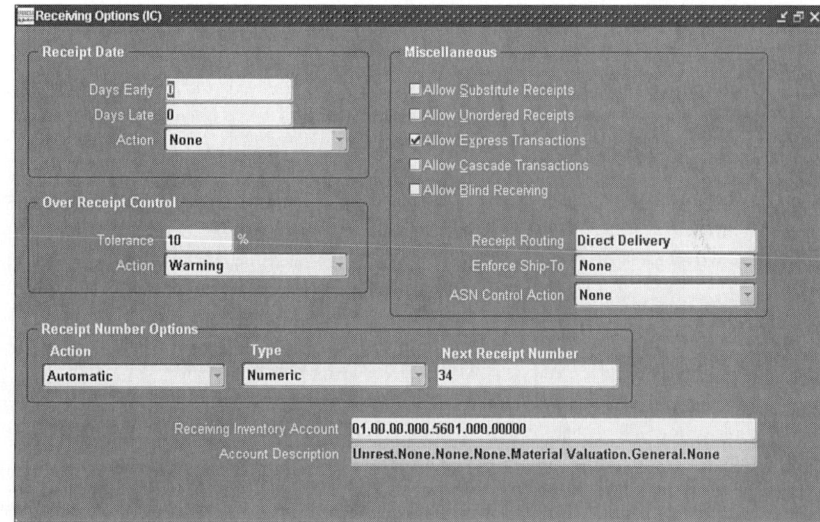

Figure 16.8 Here you see several options logically grouped into various regions according to the functions they impact.

REQUESTING THE RECEIVING TRANSACTION PROCESSOR

If the profile option RCV: Processing Mode is set to Batch, the receiving transaction processor performs the following functions:

- Creates receipt headers for in-transit shipments
- Creates receipt lines for all receipts
- Maintains transaction history information
- Maintains lot and serial transaction history
- Accrues uninvoiced receipt liabilities
- Maintains purchase order quantities
- Closes purchase orders for receiving
- Maintains requisition information
- Maintains supply information
- Maintains inventory information
- Maintains outside processing information

Defining Concurrent Processing Intervals

You define concurrent processing intervals to determine how often certain processes automatically run. Some of the recurring processes are the requisition import used for creating internal sales orders and the receiving transaction processor.

Converting Data for Major Entities

As your organization transitions from its current system to Oracle Purchasing, you will want to move much of the data you've gathered over the years. Currently, importing purchase orders is not supported through the Oracle Applications program interfaces. An organization can enter new and transition purchase orders directly into the applications.

Entering Vendors

Vendors are individuals and companies from whom you purchase goods and services. Employees you reimburse for expense reports can also be entered as vendors. You do not need this step if you have installed Oracle Payables. When entering vendors, use the setup process described in Chapter 12.

Processing Requisitions and Express Requisitions

Processing requisitions online in the Purchasing module is easy and efficient in the Oracle system. Once you set up the requisition hierarchy, the requisition approval cycle makes the flow of requisitions very direct as shown in Figure 16.9. The Purchasing module offers the following features of the online requisition process:

- You can create, edit, and review requisition information online.
- You can review the current status and action history of your requisitions.
- You can route requisitions according to your approval structure.
- You can review and approve requisitions that need your approval.
- You can print requisitions (with status approved, cancelled, rejected, in process, pre-approved, and returned) for offline review and approval.
- You can import requisitions from other systems such as material or distributions requirement planning applications.
- You can perform online funds checking before creating requisitions.
- You can automatically source requisitions from outstanding blanket purchase agreements or quotations you have received from suppliers.
- You can create requisitions quickly and easily for commonly purchased items.
- You can provide attachments as notes on requisition headers and lines.

- You can assign requisition lines to buyers and review buyer assignments for requisition lines.
- You can forward all requisitions awaiting approval from one approver to an alternate approver.
- You can record suggested foreign currency information for each requisition line.

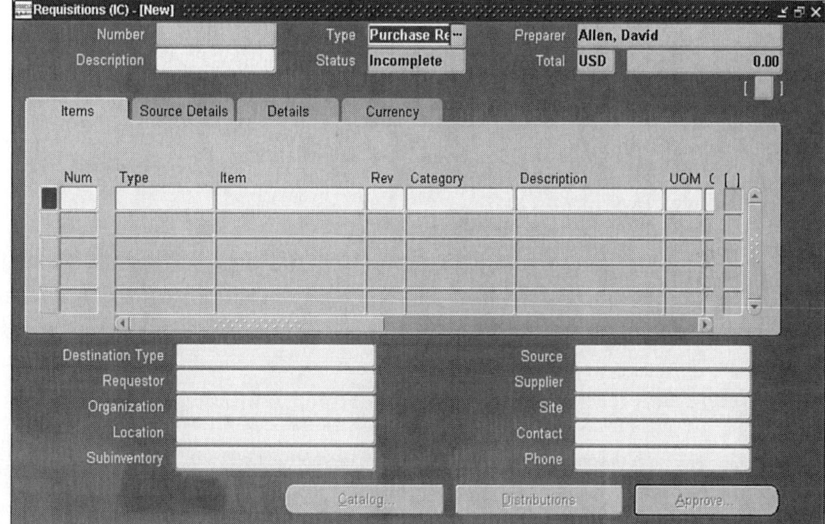

Figure 16.9
The Requisitions window offers several options, such as reviewing, approving, and printing requisitions.

PROCESSING REQUESTS FOR QUOTATION

You can identify requisitions that require supplier quotations and automatically create a request for quotation. You can create a request for quotation with or without approved requisitions so that you can plan ahead for your future procurement requirements. You can record supplier quotations from a catalog, telephone conversation, or response from your request for quotation. You can review, analyze, and approve supplier quotations that you want available to reference on purchase orders and requisitions. You should be able to evaluate your suppliers based on quotation information.

You can receive automatic notification when a quotation or request for quotation approaches expiration. You can review quotation information online when creating purchase orders or requisitions. You can identify a supplier that you want to use only for receiving RFQs and quotations. You can hold all purchasing activity on a supplier at any time. You can create, change, and review supplier information online. You can review the purchase history for a specific item. You can simplify the sourcing of commonly purchased items. You can automatically source the items for which you negotiated purchase agreements.

Processing Purchase Orders

You can review all of your purchases with your suppliers to negotiate better discounts. You can create purchase orders simply by entering a supplier and item details. You can create standard purchase orders and blanket releases from both online and paper requisitions. You can create accurate and detailed accounting information so that you charge purchases to the appropriate departments. You can check your funds availability while creating purchase orders.

You can review the status and history of your purchase orders at any time for all the information you need. You can print purchase orders flexibly by using a number of print options. You can inform your suppliers of your shipment schedule requirements. You can record supplier acceptances of your purchase orders. You can create your purchase orders by providing a quantity and price for each item you are ordering.

Entering Purchase Orders

Figure 16.10 shows the Purchase Orders window. You can enter standard and planned purchase orders as well as blanket and contract purchase agreements. You can enter purchase orders from paper requisitions or without a requisition. You can take approval actions on individual purchase orders and agreements online. You can also enter preference information for purchase order lines, shipments, distributions, and releases.

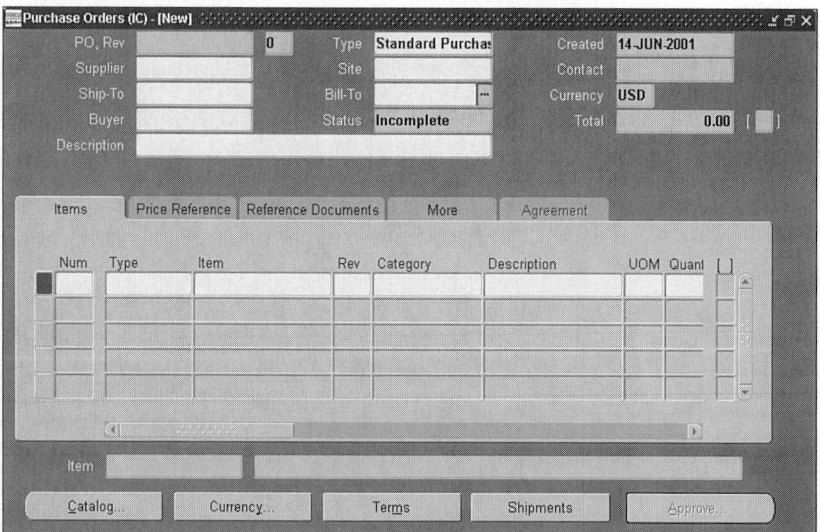

Figure 16.10
The Purchase Orders window allows you to approve current purchases.

Entering Releases

You can create releases for requisition lines if they meet the following criteria:

- The releases are approved and already sourced to an existing blanket release.
- The autosource rule for the item, supplier, and blanket indicates that the release generation method is either automatic release or automatic release/review.

- The requisition line is not already on a purchase order.
- The source blanket is still active, and the release will not put the blanket over the amount limit.
- The item and item revision on the requisition match the item and item revision on the blanket.

Using AutoCreate

Autocreate allows you to create new standard or planned purchase orders, blanket releases, RFQs, and quotations with a minimum number of keystrokes. You can review all approved requisition lines before placing specific requisition lines on a purchase order or RFQ. You can review RFQ headers, lines, and shipments before creating a quotation from a specific RFQ. You can collect all requisition lines that meet a certain set of criteria that you establish.

You can split one requisition line into several PO lines. You can consolidate multiple like requisition lines into single purchase order lines. You can review or change your purchase orders, quotations, or RFQs immediately after creation. You can use document security to control whether buyers can add to certain document types. You can specify foreign currency details during autocreation. You can review requisition lines by currency type.

Figure 16.11 shows the AutoCreate Documents window. You will see here several Requisition Lines that are available for creating purchase orders.

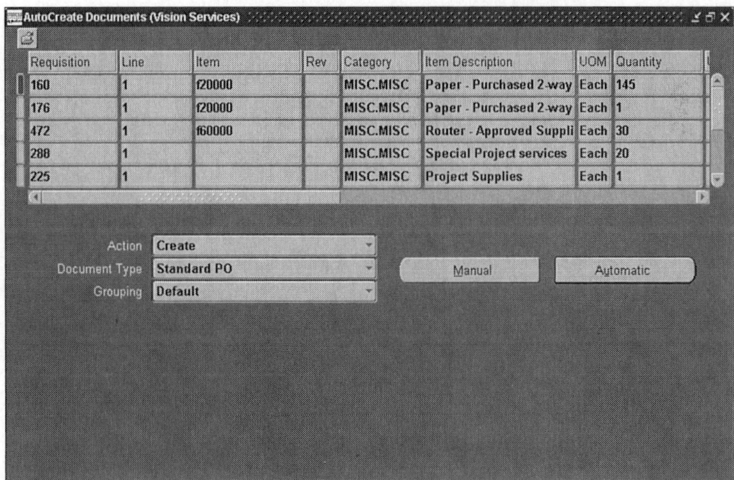

Figure 16.11 With the AutoCreate window you can quickly produce purchasing orders.

Approving and Forwarding Documents

You can change the default forward-from employee for requisitions if Allow Change Forward-From is enabled for the document type in the Document Types window. You can change the default approval hierarchy if Allow Change to Approval Hierarchy is enabled for the document type in the Document Types window. You can change the default forward-to employee if Allow Change to Forward-To is enabled for the document type in the Document Types window. You can enter a brief note to either record information about your approval action or provide instructions for the next approver if your document requires additional authorization. You can launch a print request.

USING MASSCANCEL

You can specify the criteria for canceling groups of requisitions or purchase orders that you no longer want to honor. You can specify a range of accounting flexfields for which to cancel requisitions or purchase orders. You can define multiple ranges of accounting flexfields, including both a low and high value for each key segment.

ENTERING RECEIPTS AND RECEIVING TRANSACTIONS

Figure 16.12 shows the Receipts window. This lists all pending PO Lines that have not been received. You can select all the lines, pertaining to the same supplier, that you're now receiving.

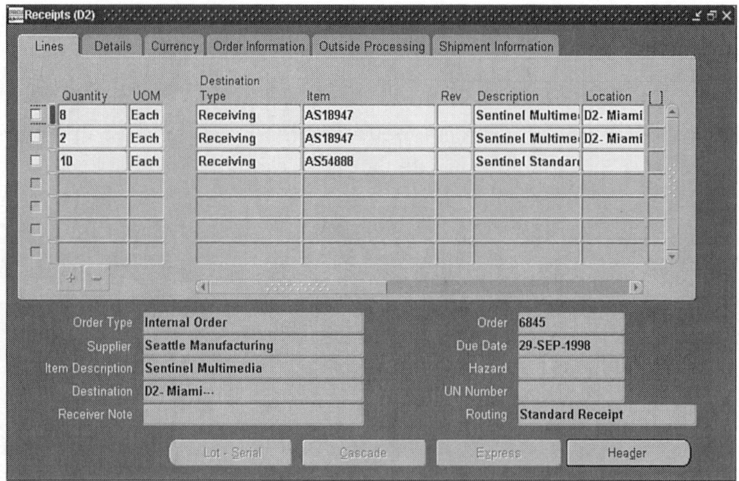

Figure 16.12
Use the Receipts window to quickly see a list of all pending purchase orders.

You can use routing controls at the organization, supplier, item, or order level to enforce material movement through receiving. You can define receiving tolerances at the organization, supplier, item, and order levels, with the lowest level overriding previous levels. You can use blind receiving to improve accuracy in the receiving process. You can use Express Receipt to receive an entire purchase order with a few keystrokes. You can use the Cascade function to distribute a given quantity of an item from a single supplier across multiple shipments and distributions.

You can specify invoice-matching controls. You can print the receiving and inspection documentation you need. You can track, update, and record the receipt of in-transit and inter-organization shipments. You can enter different types of receipt transactions based on your organization's needs. You can record receipt of unordered items based on your item, supplier, or organization defaults. You can record receipt of predefined substitute items if you set your receiving options to allow this feature. You can automatically update related supply information, inventory balances, work in process (WIP) operations, requisition details, and purchase order details while entering a single receiving transaction.

You can record transfers of inventory items from receiving and inspection to inventory or to the shop floor. You can record receipts against services and labor. You can receive services, inventory, expense, and outside processing items using one screen. You can distinguish closed for invoicing from closed for receiving. You can decide how you accrue uninvoiced receipts. You can identify and handle hazardous materials. You can track the quantity and destination of internally delivered items. You can define detailed rules for locator within subinventories for the disposition of inventory receipts.

You can track lot and serially controlled items. You can define which of your items require inspection. You can record returns to suppliers. You can correct receiving transaction errors. You can use flexible search criteria to choose receipts for review. You can view receipts details. You can perform transactions with minimal effort. You can use attachments throughout the receiving process to more completely identify transactions and to inform users of special requirements. You cannot process corrections and returns on an internal order.

Processing Returns to Vendor

You can return delivered items to receiving and return received or delivered externally sourced items to the supplier if the purchase order has neither been cancelled nor finally closed. If the item is controlled, you must specify lot numbers, serial numbers, or locators, as appropriate. When you are entering a return, you must first identify the purchase order number or item that you want to return. You can also return to the supplier unordered receipts that have not been matched.

Writing Off Accruals

Purchasing records an accounts payable liability to an AP accrual account for goods received but not invoiced if the perpetual accrual method is selected. The account is cleared in payables when the invoice is matched and approved.

Purging Purchasing and AP Together

You can purge invoices, purchase orders, suppliers, and related records such as invoice payments and purchase receipts to free space in your database. After a record is purged, the record cannot be queried. The system does maintain summary information to prevent the duplication of invoices or purchase orders.

Importing Requisitions

You can import requisitions from other Oracle Applications or from non-Oracle systems. Requisitions you import can be placed on purchase orders just as you would any other requisition. Requisition import lets you integrate Purchasing with new or existing applications.

REVIEWING TOPICS OF INTEREST

The Purchasing module allows you to maintain control over your purchasing documents and to put into place a flexible approval system designed specifically for your organization. You can allow your employees to enter requisitions online. You can set up an autocreate capability within the Purchasing module. You can also provide a flexible receiving capability within your organization.

USING ORACLE ALERTS AND WORKFLOW

You can establish expiration and release control notification conditions and specify the number of days before the condition is met that you want to be notified.

Amount Not Released alerts let you know that the total planned amount released to date against a planned purchase order, blanket purchase agreement, or contract purchase agreement is insufficient. Amount Released alerts let you know that the total amount released to date against a planned purchase order, blanket purchase agreement, or contract purchase agreement meets or exceeds specified amounts. Expiration alerts let you know that a planned purchase order, blanket purchase agreement, or contract purchase agreement is about to expire. Approved Standard Purchase Orders alerts show the number of approved purchase orders created by each buyer during the past *n* days.

Blanket Notification Expiration alerts show the blanket purchase agreements that are about to expire. Blanket Notification Not Released alerts show the blanket purchase agreements for which an insufficient amount has been released. Blanket Notification Released alerts show the blanket purchase agreements for which the desired amount has been released. Blanket Purchase Releases over Threshold alerts look for blanket purchase releases that exceed a certain dollar amount.

Contract Notification Expiration alerts show the contract purchase agreements that are about to expire. Contract Notification Not Released alerts show the contract purchase agreements for which an insufficient amount has been released. Contract Notification Released alerts show the contract purchase agreements for which the desired amount has been released.

Planned Notification Expiration alerts show the planned purchase orders that are about to expire. Planned Notification Not Released alerts show the planned purchase orders for which an insufficient amount has been released. Planned Notification Released alerts show the planned purchase orders for which the desired amount has been released.

Small Business Suppliers alerts show your suppliers who are identified as small businesses. Standard Purchase Orders over Threshold alerts look for standard purchase orders created in the past *n* days that exceed a certain dollar amount. Suppliers on Hold alerts show the suppliers that you have placed on hold.

UNDERSTANDING KEY REPORTS

The Accrual Reconciliation report is where you analyze the balance of the Accounts Payable (A/P) accrual accounts. The Accrual Write-Off report provides supporting detail for your write-off journal entries. The Backordered Internal Requisitions report details information on your back-ordered internally sourced requisition lines. The Blanket and Planned PO Status report is where you review purchase order transactions for items you buy using blanket purchase agreements and planned purchase orders. The Buyer listing shows the buyer name, default purchasing category, Ship To location, and effective dates of all buyers or a selected set of buyers. The Buyer's Requisition Action Required report identifies all or specific approved requisition lines that buyers have not placed on purchase orders.

The Cancelled Purchase Order report is where you review information on cancelled purchase orders. The Cancelled Requisition report is where you review information on cancelled requisitions. The Contract Status report is where you review the status of your contracts and list purchase order information for each contract. The Create Internal Sales Orders process is where you send requisition information from approved, inventory-sourced requisition lines to the Order Entry interface tables.

The Create Releases process is how you create releases for requisition lines that meet one of the following conditions:

- They are approved.
- The requisition is already sourced to an existing blanket release.
- The autosource release generation method rule for the item, supplier, or blanket release is either automatic release or automatic release/review.
- The requisition line is not already on a purchase order.
- The source blanket is still active, and the release will not put the blanket over the amount limit.

Purchasing 11*i* includes two new reports: Country of Origin Report (by Item) and Country of Origin Report (by Supplier). These two reports list all countries of origin and items sourced, sorted by Item and Supplier, respectively.

The Encumbrance Detail report is where you review requisition and purchase order encumbrances for a range of accounts. The Expected Receipts report is where you review all or specific vendor-sourced expected receipts for a particular date or a range of dates. The Fill Employee Hierarchy process is how you create a direct mapping between the defined position hierarchies and the employees holding positions in each hierarchy. The Financials/Purchasing Options listing is where you review the options set for your system in the Financials Options and Purchasing Options windows. The Internal Requisition Status report is where you print status information for internal requisitions. The Internal Requisitions/Deliveries Discrepancy report is where you list requisition documents with items whose source type is inventory.

The Invoice Price Variance report shows the variance between the invoice price and the purchase price for all inventory and work-in-process related invoice distribution lines. The Invoice Price Variance by Vendor shows the variance between the invoice price and the purchase price for all inventory and work-in-process related invoice distribution lines. The Item Detail listing shows detail information for items defined as purchasing items in the Item window as well as unit of measure conversion, notes, manufacturer part numbers, and dispositions assigned to the item. The Item Summary listing shows the inactive or active status of items.

The Location listing shows internal organization locations and addresses. The Matching Holds by Buyer report is where you review all or selected invoices that Purchasing or your accounts payable system placed on matching hold. The New Vendor Letter report is where you print letters you send to your vendors to ask for information about the nature of their businesses. The Open Purchase Orders by Buyer lists all or specific open purchase orders that relate to buyers. The Open Purchase Orders by Cost Center report reviews all or specific open purchase orders relating to one or more cost centers.

The Overdue Vendor Shipments report is where you follow up with vendors. The Overshipments report lists purchase order receipts with a quantity received greater than the quantity ordered. The Payment on Receipt automatically creates standard, unapproved invoices for payment of goods based on receipt transactions.

The Printed Change Orders report (landscape) and Printed Change Orders report (portrait) print changed purchase orders. The Printed Purchase Order report (landscape) and Printed Purchase Order report (portrait) print purchase orders. The Printed RFQ report (landscape) and Printed RFQ report (portrait) print requests for quotes.

The Printed Requisitions report prints the requisitions that have the status of approved, rejected, in process, pre-approved, or returned. The Purchase Agreement Audit report is where you review purchase order transactions for items you normally buy using blanket purchase agreements. The Purchase Order Commitment by Period report is where you show the monetary value of your purchased commitments for a specified period and the next five periods. The Purchase Order Detail report is where you list all, specific standard, or planned purchase orders. The Purchase Order Distribution Detail report shows account distributions for a range of purchase orders.

The Purchase Order and Releases Detail report shows detail information for your blanket purchase agreements and planned purchase orders. The Purchase Price Variance report shows the variance between the purchase price on the purchase order and standard cost for all items you receive and deliver into inventory and work in process. The Purchase Requisition Status report is where you review the approval status of the requisitions you create. The Purchase Summary Report by Category shows the amount of orders you place with vendors for a given category of item. The Purchasing Activity Register shows purchase order monetary activity carried out for a time interval, such as a day or month.

The Purchasing Database Administration process initiates concurrent processes that purge notifications for RFQs with close dates before the current date, notifications for quotations with expiration dates before the current date, and lot and serial numbers that were entered for receiving transactions that were ultimately not committed. The Quality Code listing shows inspection quality codes. The Quotation Action Required report lists quotations that require follow-up action. The RFQ Action Required report lists RFQs that require follow-up action. The Receipt Accruals - Period End process is how you create period-end accruals for your uninvoiced receipts for Expense distributions.

The Receipt Adjustments report lists purchase order shipments or internal requisition lines with corrections or returns to vendor. The Receipt Traveler facilitates the receiving inspection and delivery of goods within your organization. The Receiving Account Distribution report lists the accounting distributions for your receiving transactions. The Receiving Exceptions report is where you review receipts for which there is a receipt exception. The Receiving Transaction processor processes your pending or unprocessed receiving transactions. The Receiving Transactions Register lists detail information about your receiving transactions.

The Receiving Value report shows item quantity, valuation, and detailed receipt information for your receiving inspection location. The Receiving Value Report by Destination Account lists received items by purchase order destination and distribution account. The ReqExpress Templates listing shows ReqExpress template detail information. The Requisition Activity Register shows requisition activity and monetary values. The Requisition Distribution Detail report lists requisitions, distributions, and charge account information.

The Requisition Import process imports requisitions from other Oracle or non-Oracle systems. The Requisition Import Exceptions report shows errors from the Requisition Import process. The Requisitions on Cancelled Sales Order report shows information on internally sourced requisition lines for which a sales order has been generated and subsequently cancelled. The Reschedule Requisitions process updates requisition information for the rows that Master Scheduling/MRP has inserted into the rescheduling interface table.

The Savings Analysis report (by Buyer) shows buyer performance by purchase order. The Savings Analysis report (by Category) shows buyer performance by category. The Set Flexbuilder Account Flex Structure process assigns an accounting flexfield structure (chart of accounts) to the flexbuilder parameters. The Standard Notes listing shows your standard notes and their start and end dates. The Substitute Receipts report lists all or specific substitute receipts. The Tax Code listing shows the tax authorities and rates that you use when you enter purchase orders or invoices.

The Uninvoiced Receipts report is where you review all or specific uninvoiced receipts for both period end and online accruals. The Unit of Measure Class listing shows the classes of measurement you have defined. The Unit of Measure listing shows the unit conversions you have defined in the Unit of Measure Conversions window. The Unordered Receipts report lists all or selected unordered receipts. The Vendor Affiliated Structure listing shows information about your vendor's parent-child relationships. The Vendor Price Performance Analysis report is where you compare the price of an item from different vendors.

The Vendor Purchase Summary report lists the numbers and amount of orders you have placed with various vendors during a particular period. The Vendor Quality Performance Analysis report is where you review your vendors' quality performance. The Vendor Service Performance Analysis report lists late shipments, early shipments, rejected shipments, and shipments to wrong locations. The Vendor Volume Analysis report shows the dollar value of items you purchase from a vendor. The Vendors on Hold report lists all vendors placed on hold.

TROUBLESHOOTING

The Oracle Purchasing application is at the center of your procurement process. This application is tightly integrated with the planning, inventory, payables, and ledger applications. Consider the following items as you set up and use the Purchasing application:

- Coordinate the way you close purchase orders. If you close documents too early, you can disrupt the payables matching process.
- If you choose automatic document numbering, Oracle can only create numeric document numbers. However, you can still import both numeric or alphanumeric document numbers from a non-Oracle purchasing system.
- Make sure your job/position hierarchy structure supports all the approval levels of your organization.
- The security hierarchy controls which positions have access to certain document types. However, the security system does not grant approval authority.
- When a document is in the approval process, no one can access it from an entry window.
- If the Human Resources application is installed, you must use the Enter Person window in that application to maintain employee information.
- If you customize a workflow, existing documents will not be affected by the change. The change will act only on those documents submitted for approval after the workflow changes.
- You cannot change the supplier after a purchase order is approved because it is a legal document. To change suppliers after approval, you must cancel the existing document and issue a new one to the correct supplier.
- During the fiscal period-end processing, close the Oracle Payables application before closing Oracle Purchasing. Close Oracle Inventory after you close Purchasing.

CHAPTER 17

Using Oracle Inventory

In this chapter

INTRODUCTION

The purpose of the Oracle Inventory application is to assist an organization in defining and tracking inventory items or parts. It helps the organization answer such questions as how many on-hand are there of a particular part and where the parts are located. It provides support for recording the receipt and disbursement of items as well as the physical and cyclical counting of those items. Oracle Inventory also provides for the replenishment of items using either min-max or reorder point planning or replenishment support for items using kanbans.

Inventory items within an organization are stored in locations called subinventories. In these subinventories, you can specify storage locators that can consist of aisles, rows, and bins. You can specify that an item be restricted to specific locators within specific subinventories or that the part can be stored anywhere within the organization. You can specify that an item be lot- or serial-number–controlled or have no controls. In addition, you can indicate that a part be revision controlled.

One of the key tasks in the implementation of the Oracle manufacturing applications is the setup of the Oracle Inventory application. This setup process consists of a number of steps wherein you define such things as the structure of your organization and your inventory items. These setup steps customize the Oracle Inventory application to your unique requirements. This chapter lists the required tasks in order to set up the Oracle Inventory application and points out some of the details for consideration in the key areas of the setup process.

In addition to the setup tasks, this chapter also highlights some of the key Oracle Inventory transactions with important considerations for use of these transactions.

ORACLE INVENTORY RELATIONSHIPS TO OTHER APPLICATIONS

The Oracle Inventory application is the foundation for all the other Oracle manufacturing applications. The inventory item definition and the associated on-hand inventory balance of an item are used by the other Oracle applications. Figure 17.1 indicates the interrelationships that Oracle Inventory has with the other Oracle application products.

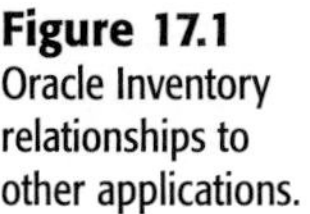

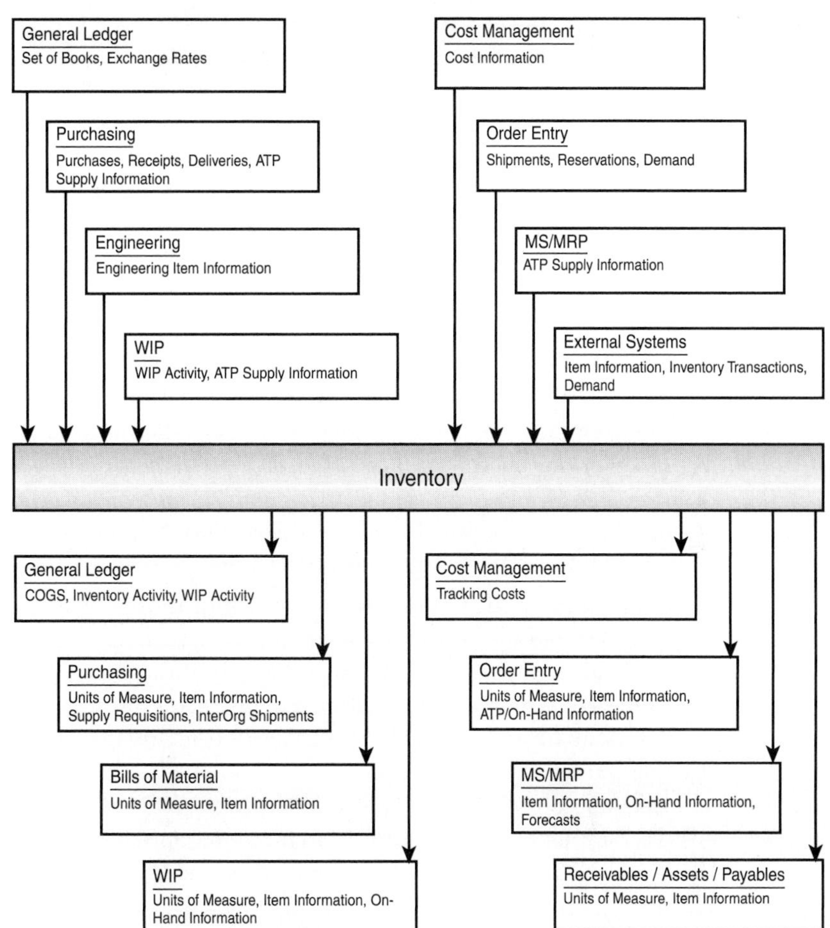

Figure 17.1
Oracle Inventory relationships to other applications.

DISCOVERING NEW FEATURES IN RELEASE 11*i*

Following are the features in the Oracle Inventory application that are new to release 11*i* of the product. Also included is a brief description of the new functionality:

- **Cycle Count Open Interface**—A new interface routine has been added that allows you to export your scheduled cycle count requests into a newly created interface table, MTL_CC_ENTRIES_INTERFACE. After your count records have been exported into this table, you can then transfer this information into external recording systems to conduct the physical counting activity. Any count records collated through external devices can then be written back into the interface table, where standard APIs can be called to import the information back into the Oracle Inventory module where further processing is performed using standard cycle count functionality. The interface routine supports count requests generated by external systems as well as those scheduled using the standard Oracle cycle count functionality. Any imported requests that do not correlate to an Oracle cycle count schedule will be processed as an unscheduled count request.

- **Material Move Orders**—To provide greater visibility and segregation between physical inventory movements originating through materials management/planning activities and those generated through operational processes, Oracle has added new functionality to cater to move orders. Move orders enable planners and production controllers to request the movement of material within a warehouse for the purpose of fulfilling replenishment requirements, relocating material stockholdings, or facilitating quality controls and handling. Move orders can be generated either automatically or manually depending on the transaction type that is used, and they incorporate workflow procedures to allow for the enforcement of appropriate authorization and notification requirements. Move orders can be utilized only for transactions within individual organizations—any interorganization transfers must be processed using the existing internal requisition process in Oracle Purchasing.
- **Material Shortage Alerts and Workflow Notifications**—This new functionality has been added to allow for timely recognition and subsequent routing of inventory receipts that might cover any material shortages that exist throughout your inventory organizations. Oracle Inventory automatically performs checks during specific inventory receipt transactions to determine whether the material being received is more urgently needed elsewhere within the organization. If such a shortage does exist, the system transmits a notification using either alerts or workflow processes. This functionality is linked to the following receipt transaction forms: Inventory Receipts, Miscellaneous Transactions, WIP Material Transactions, WIP Completions, and Work-Orderless Completions.
- **Serial Item Genealogy**—Oracle Inventory offers enhanced visibility of the composition and transactional history of any serial controlled item through the View Genealogy functionality that has been added to the Serial Items form. This functionality provides a graphical display of all transactional and component activity—from assembly through to finished good completion and subsequent order placement—of all serial controlled items.
- **Reservations Open Interface**—The functionality formerly provided by the demand open interface is no longer available in Release 11*i*. External demand for items should now be created using the functionality available in the Oracle Advanced Supply Chain Planning module. Reservations against external demand are now allocated using a combination of new Sales Order APIs and the Reservations Open Interface. MTL_ RESERVATIONS is a new table that has been created in Release 11*i* and is coupled with a synchronization routine that maintains this table in parallel with the MTL_DEMAND table. Consequently, any interfacing of material reservations or allocations is now performed using the Reservation Interface form instead of the Demand Interface form.

- **Model/Unit Effectivity**—New fields have been added to the Find Serials, Serial Numbers, Inter-Organization Transfer, and Master/Organization Item forms to enable you to capture and query on the end model/unit numbers assigned to your component inventory items when using Oracle Project Manufacturing.
- **New Transaction Types for Project Manufacturing**—Three new transaction types have been added to allow for more flexible allocation of inventory item movements between projects. These new transaction types are Inter-Project Borrow, Inter-Project Payback, and Inter-Project Transfer.
- **New Kanban Card Replenishment Types**—An Intra-Organization replenishment card has been added to allow for the initiation of Material Move orders when material transfers are required from a central stocking location into a production line stocking location. Production cards have also been implemented to initiate discrete jobs, repetitive schedules, or flow schedules from the appropriate kanban replenishment signals.
- **Intrastat Movement Statistics Enhancements**—Intrastat is the system for collecting statistics on the trade of goods between members of the European Union. Oracle has enhanced its Intrastat functionality to automatically create the movement statistic records for any interorganization material transfers. The Movement Statistics Processor is used to compile the movement statistics for a user-nominated period; these statistics can then be used to create the appropriate Intrastat and Extrastat records.

Critical Implementation Factors

A number of factors contribute to the successful implementation of any manufacturing planning and execution system. Among the most important are the following:

- High-level executive commitment to the project
- Good user involvement and support of the project
- Availability of application product and process expertise
- Adequate information technology resources, including hardware and system personnel
- Good fit of the application product to the manufacturing process
- Keeping the number and size of modifications to the application product minimal

Successfully implementing an application package such as Oracle Inventory also requires several key activities:

- Educating users to ensure the application product is set up to accurately reflect the manufacturing environment
- Providing good user procedures and training to ensure the successful operation of the system
- Comprehensively testing the application product and making any necessary modifications to ensure the product performs as required to support the manufacturing process and to ensure users can perform the appropriate application transactions

In addition to the factors and activities listed here, another consideration that contributes to the rapid and successful deployment of Oracle Inventory is the philosophy of simplicity. For instance, when setting up Oracle Inventory, you can make a number of choices between many alternatives. Often, the best choice is the simplest one. The simplest choice can be easily understood and tested. Often, the simplest choice requires less user input and reduces the chance for errors.

An example might be managing tool room inventory. To start, the users might want to simply be able to control the issuing and receiving of tool room inventory and know how many tools are available. This might mean starting with item records for the tools and a subinventory for the tool room. Issues and receipts could be handled with miscellaneous inventory receipt and issue transactions, perhaps with account aliases to ensure the correct accounts are charged.

When users get more familiar and confident with the system, they could add slightly more advanced techniques, such as performing cycle counts or physical inventories of the tool room items using the standard system processes. You could implement the simple technique of min-max planning for the replenishment of the tool room inventory. If you have enough data and confidence in the system, you could consider more advanced techniques such as reorder point planning.

Using the simplest alternatives often leads to the quickest and most successful implementation of a system.

Reviewing Top Enhancement Requests

Oracle Corporation attempts to continually enhance its application products. Following are some of the top potential enhancements to the Oracle Inventory application that might be included in future releases:

- Provide an option to include the on-hand quantity on the cycle count listing report and allow a cycle count frequency of less than one count per year
- Provide an option to open accounting periods in all organizations with a single command or process
- Provide the capability of item on-hand balances to be transacted into negative quantities at the subinventory level
- Provide the capability to transfer all material in a specific stock locator to a new locator in a single transaction
- Print all category segments on Inventory reports
- Provide the capability to generate Min-Max purchase requisitions based on the Supplier unit of measure

- Provide the capability to view the on-hand quantity for an item in a unit of measure other than the primary unit of measure
- Support cycle counting of zero on-hand items without requiring item-subinventory relationship definitions
- Provide the ability to use the same locator code in different subinventories
- Provide an excess inventory report
- Provide a data-archiving option for Inventory data

CONFIGURING THE APPLICATION

The setup process for Oracle Inventory consists of a number of steps whereby you define such characteristics as the structure of your organization and your inventory items. These setup steps customize the Oracle Inventory application to your unique requirements. You must, however, perform a simple preliminary step before you can set up Oracle Inventory. You need to set up an Oracle Applications System Administrator responsibility. Consult the Oracle Applications Systems Administrator's Guide for information on how to perform this step. Following are all of the remaining setup steps. This chapter describes these setup steps in considerable detail. The specific steps that are required and not optional are noted accordingly.

REQUIRED SETUP TASKS

The following are the required setup tasks:

- Create a set of books (required).
- Define the system items key flexfield (required).
- Define the item categories key flexfield (required).
- Define the item catalog group key flexfield (required).
- Define the stock locators key flexfield (required).
- Define the account aliases key flexfield (required).
- Define the sales orders key flexfield (required).
- Define locations (optional).
- Define employees (optional).
- Define the organization calendar and exceptions (required).
- Define organizations (required).
- Define organization inventory parameters (required).
- Change to a valid inventory books organization (required).

- Define intercompany relationships (required).
- Define receiving options (optional).
- Define picking rules (optional).
- Define available to promise(ATP) rules (optional).
- Define planners (optional).
- Define unit of measure classes and units of measure (required).
- Define unit of measure conversions and interclass conversions (optional).
- Define subinventories (required).
- Define stock locators (optional).
- Define item books attribute controls (required).
- Define categories (required).
- Define category sets (required).
- Define default category sets (required).
- Define statuses (required).
- Define item catalog groups (optional).
- Define item types (optional).
- Define item templates (optional).
- Define items (optional).
- Define cross-reference types (optional).
- Define item delete constraints (optional).
- Define cost types (required).
- Define cost activities (optional).
- Define books material subelements (optional).
- Define material overheads (optional).
- Define default material overhead rates (optional).
- Define freight carriers (optional).
- Define organization shipping network (optional).
- Define shipping methods (optional).
- Define economic zones (optional).
- Define movement statistics parameters (optional).
- Define account aliases (optional).
- Define transaction source types (optional).
- Define transaction types (optional).

- Define transaction reasons (optional).
- Define purchasing options (optional).
- Open accounting books periods (required).
- Start material and cost interface managers (optional).
- Set profile options (required).
- Define container types (optional).
- Define commodity codes (optional).
- Define customer items (optional).
- Define customer item cross-references (optional).
- Define notification lists (optional).
- Define shortage parameters (optional).
- Define kanban pull books sequences (optional).

Creating a Set of Books

The set of books defines for all of the Oracle Application modules the accounting flexfield structure (chart of accounts), the fiscal calendar, and the functional currency.

You must define the set of books before you can perform any of the other setup steps. When you define a set of books, use the setup process described in Chapter 11, "Using Oracle General Ledger."

The tasks in this process are

- Define the key accounting flexfield structure, segments, segment values, and code combinations.
- Define the fiscal calendar period types and periods.
- Enable currencies, and define rate types and conversion rates.
- Create the set of books by assigning a name to a combination of the key accounting flexfield, a calendar, and a currency.
- Assign the set of books to the site or individual responsibilities.

Defining the System Items Key Flexfield

The systems items key flexfield is sometimes called the item flexfield. This flexfield is an Oracle Application key flexfield that contains the structure definition of your item or part number field. You need to define whether your item number is a single segment or multi-segmented field and the length of each individual segment. If your part number is more than one segment, you also need to specify the order of the segments and the segment separator.

All Oracle Application products that reference items share the item flexfield definition and support multi-segmented implementations. Every item defined requires this item number, which is also required to transact and report item information. You need to define the system items key flexfield before you can define any items.

Note

An increasing number of manufacturing enterprises use a single segment (field) non-meaningful item number. The capability of the Oracle application software to retrieve item information by a number of different methods, including item catalogs, manufacturer's part numbers, and item cross-references, has reduced the requirement for the use of a meaningful multi-segmented item number key.

To define the system items flexfield, you need to provide the following information:

- How many separate segments your item number has
- The length of each one of the separate segments and their sequence as well as the segment separator (the character used to separate segments, such as a period or dash)
- Whether any of the segments will be validated

In addition to the structure of the flexfield, you need to define any applicable value sets to be used in validating the flexfield segments, and finally, you need to freeze and compile the flexfield.

Tip

In some installs you might want to create a database sequence that can be used to default a system-generated numerical sequence number to each newly created item. To perform this you must do the following:

1. Create a database sequence via sqlplus (DBA assistance might be required) using the following syntax:

   ```
   create sequence apps.<sequence_name>
   start with <number_you_want_to_start_with>
   ```

2. Create a value set for the appropriate item flexfield segment. The format type can be either `number` or `character`, and the validation type must be set to `none`.
3. Open the value set and enter **`SQL Statement`** in the Default Type field. In the Default Value field, the following statement must be entered:

   ```
   select <sequence_name> .nextval from dual
   ```

4. Freeze and recompile the System Items Flexfield.

For help in defining this flexfield, you can reference the *Oracle Flexfields User's Guide*.

Defining the Item Categories Key Flexfield

A category is a logical classification of items that have similar characteristics. A category set is a way of grouping categories. In Oracle, you can define various item categories and category sets to facilitate retrieval and reporting to meet your unique requirements. For any report or inquiry that allows you to specify a range or list of items, you can also specify a category set and range of categories. This capability is one of the most important and powerful features of the Oracle application products.

You must design and configure your item categories flexfield before you start defining items because all items must be assigned to categories. The tasks to define item categories are as follows:

1. Define the flexfield structures for the item categories flexfield.
2. Define categories. See the section "Defining Categories" later in this chapter.
3. Define category sets. See the section "Defining Category Sets" later in this chapter.
4. Assign default category sets for each functional area. When you install Oracle Inventory, you must assign a default category set for each of the following applications areas: Inventory, Purchasing, Order Management, Costing, Engineering, and Planning. The default category set can be the same or different for each application area. As you add new items, Oracle Inventory automatically assigns them to the default category sets with a default category value. See the section "Defining Default Category Sets" later in this chapter for additional detail on defining default category sets.

To define the flexfield structure of an item category, you need to provide the following information:

- How many separate segments your item category has
- The length of each one of the separate segments and their sequence and segment separator
- Whether any of the segments will be validated

In addition, you can specify the prompts for entering the data in each of these segments, as well as the values for any of the value sets that will be used in validating the categories. You also need to freeze and compile the flexfield.

You can define multiple structures for your Item Categories Flexfield, with each structure corresponding to the various grouping schemes you might want to adopt within your organization. You can then associate each one these structures to the appropriate categories and category sets that are to be defined.

For help in defining this flexfield, you can reference the *Oracle Flexfields User's Guide*.

Note

One of the best ways to understand the process and various individual steps in defining item categories, their flexfield structures, and values is to look at a sample. When you install Oracle Inventory or Oracle Purchasing, Oracle provides two category flexfield structures by default: item categories and PO item category. Examining these two category structures and their definitions can be educational and informative.

You can use item categories to do the following:

- Summarize a history of demand and generate forecasts for all items in a selected item category.
- Perform min-max and reorder point planning for a range of item categories.
- Select items from requisitions to be automatically created into purchase orders by purchasing item category.
- Run reports and inquiries for a single item category or range of item categories.
- Assign material overhead rates by item category.

Defining the Item Catalog Group Key Flexfield

Oracle Inventory enables you to create multiple catalog groups to aid in item classification. Each catalog group can have its own set of item characteristics, called descriptive elements. You can define as many descriptive elements as necessary to describe your items and specify whether an entry for the element is optional. Once you have cataloged your items, you can search on one or more descriptive elements to assist in locating items for order entry or group technology purposes.

To define the item catalog group flexfield, you need to indicate how many separate segments are contained in your flexfield, how long each segment is, and whether you want to validate any of the values that you assign to the segments. After defining the structure of your flexfield and any applicable value sets, you need to freeze and compile your flexfield definition to enable the Item Catalog Group Flexfield pop-up window.

Note

Even if you decide not to use item catalogs, you still must enable at least one segment in the item catalog flexfield and then compile the flexfield before you can define any items.

Defining the Stock Locators Key Flexfield

A stock locator is a physical area within a subinventory where you store material (such as a combination of row, aisle, bin, or shelf).

To define the stock locator flexfield, you need to provide the following information:

- How many separate segments your stock locator has
- The length of each one of the separate segments
- Whether any of the segments will be validated

In addition to the structure of the flexfield, you need to define any applicable value sets for validation of the flexfield, and then you need to freeze and compile the flexfield.

For help in defining this flexfield, you can reference the *Oracle Flexfields User's Guide*.

Tip

The stock locators key flexfield definition is global across all of the subinventories in an organization. This means that you can't have the same locator (such as Aisle 1, Row 1, Bin 1) in two different subinventories. If you have the requirement to use the same locator in several subinventories, you can make the locator unique by putting the subinventory identification in the first segment of the locator flexfield definition.

Note

Even if you will not be using locator controls, you still need to compile and freeze the stock locators flexfield because all of the Oracle Inventory transactions and reports require a frozen flexfield definition. You don't, however, have to configure the flexfield in any specific way.

Defining the Account Alias Key Flexfield

The account alias flexfield is a key flexfield that allows you to use a shorthand label for a general ledger account number combination when entering Inventory transactions. This can reduce keystroke entries as well as the chance of entering the wrong account numbers for your inventory transactions.

To configure your account alias flexfield, you need to indicate the number of separate segments your flexfield has, how many characters each segment has, and whether you want to validate the segments. In addition to defining the structure of your flexfield and any applicable value sets, you need to freeze and compile the flexfield definition. This compilation enables the Account Aliases Flexfield pop-up window.

Note

Even if you decide not to use account aliases, you still need to compile and freeze the account aliases flexfield. All of the Oracle Inventory transaction inquiries and reports require a frozen flexfield definition. However, you don't need to configure the flexfield in any specific way.

Defining the Sales Order Key Flexfield

The sales order flexfield is a key flexfield used by Oracle Inventory to uniquely identify sales order transactions that Oracle Order Management interfaces to Oracle Inventory. If you are using Oracle OM, you should define this sales order flexfield as order number, order type, and order source. This combination makes sure that each order management transaction interfaced to Inventory is unique.

Note

Even if you don't ship items against sales orders, you still need to compile and freeze the sales order flexfield because all the Oracle Inventory transaction inquiries and reports require a frozen flexfield definition. You don't, however, have to configure the flexfield in any specific way.

Tip

You must assign a value to the profile option OM: Source Code to determine the source code that will be used to populate the third segment of this flexfield. Oracle Inventory defaults the value of this profile option to `Order Management`.

When enabling the Sales Order Flexfield segments, set the Required field in the Validation Information region to `Yes`; this will improve performance when updating existing demand or inventory reservations.

Defining Locations

You should define the names and addresses for the locations you use within your organization as well as for the location of your inventory organization itself. A number of Oracle Applications, including Inventory, use locations for requisitions, receiving, billing, shipping, and employee assignments.

For each location that you are going to use, enter the following information: name, organization, description, address style (such as United States), contact, and all of the address data lines and fields such as city, state, and ZIP. You also need to indicate, by way of check boxes, whether the location is a ship-to site, office site, receiving site, bill-to site, and internal site.

Tip

The standard Oracle Purchasing purchase order print program prints the bill-to and ship-to locations you have defined for your organization in the bill-to and ship-to lines on your purchase order. It does not print a company or organization name in the first line of this location address. Therefore, you probably want to include your company name as the first line of the location definition that you will be associating with your inventory organization.

Defining Employees

Oracle Applications use defined employees as the list of values source for employee fields in the applications. Within Oracle Inventory, employee information is used primarily to record the employees who perform cycle count and physical inventory count transactions.

You need to enter the names, addresses, and other pertinent information for all of the employees who will be performing these inventory count transactions. See Chapter 24, "Using Oracle Human Resources," for additional information on defining an employee.

Defining the Organization Calendar and the Calendar Exceptions

A workday calendar defines the valid working days for a manufacturing organization and consists of a pattern of repeating days on and off and exceptions to that pattern. You specify the start and end dates and the weekend schedule for each calendar. You can define any number of workday calendars and assign them to any number of organizations, and any number of organizations can share a calendar.

You can apply exceptions to the workday calendar by specifying individual days, loading them from an exception template, or copying a set of exceptions from another calendar.

For any workday calendar, you can also specify any number of shifts. Each shift can have a different weekend schedule and a list of specific work interval start and end times. Shifts inherit workday exceptions and workday patterns from the base calendar. You can specify shift exceptions that can either override or add to those of the base calendar. A calendar must have, at a minimum, one shift and one workday calendar defined.

For each organization, you specify the calendar to use. If you intend to perform inventory forecasting, reorder point planning, perform available to promise analysis, or use shortage messages or cycle counting, you are required to define a workday calendar. All scheduling functions use the calendar's available workdays to plan and schedule activities. For additional details on defining the organization calendar and the calendar exceptions, see Chapter 19, "Using Oracle Engineering and Bills of Material."

Tip

Any calendar created should span at least a two-year period to ensure that all associated manufacturing functionality performs correctly. This information will be entered in the Calendar Date Range fields shown in Figure 17.2.

When the calendar is initially created or each time subsequent modifications are made, the calendar must be rebuilt by selecting Tools and then Build from the menu bar. The calendar or modifications to it will not be visible to other Manufacturing modules until the build process has completed successfully.

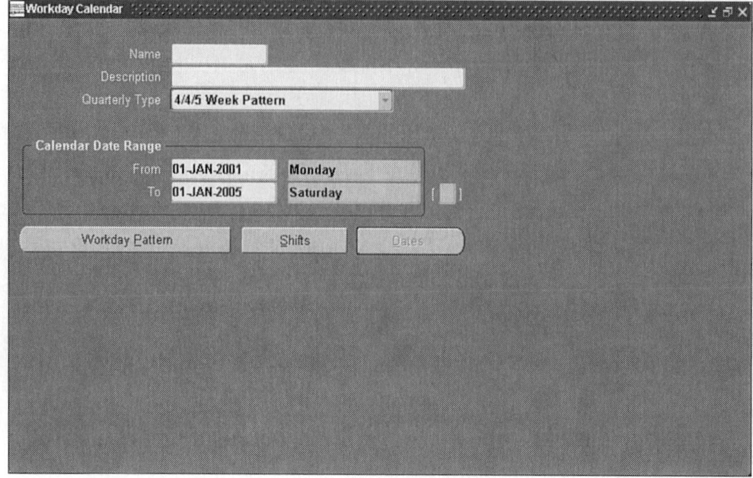

Figure 17.2
To define a calendar, select Setup, Organizations, Calendars.

DEFINING ORGANIZATIONS

An inventory organization is an organization for which you track inventory transactions and on-hand balances and that manufactures or distributes parts and products. Some examples of organizations are manufacturing plants, warehouses, distribution centers, and sales offices. In a number of the Oracle Applications, information is secured by the inventory organization. You need to select an organization that has been classified as an inventory organization in order to run any of the following applications: Oracle Inventory, Bills of Material, Engineering, Work In Process, Master Scheduling/MRP, Capacity, and the receiving functions in Purchasing.

Before defining organizations, you need to understand the item definition process in Oracle Inventory. You define items in a single organization sometimes referred to as the item master organization. Other organizations (child organizations) refer to the item master for item definition. Once an item has been defined in the master organization, it can be enabled or assigned to any of the other organizations.

Note

It is possible to define and operate the Oracle Inventory application with a single inventory organization. However, this is not recommended. The primary reason is that it limits future application flexibility and growth. It is recommended that you define, at a minimum, a separate master and child inventory organization even if you only have a single organization presently.

To define an inventory organization, you need to specify the organization name, the organization type, and a three-character abbreviation for the organization. This unique code is used to identify the organization with which you want to work. In addition, because Oracle Inventory allows you to create multiple inventory organizations that relate to differing sets of books, you need to specify which set of books the organization will be tied to.

Note

In a multiorganization install, for any inventory organization you define, you MUST allocate it to the appropriate Operating Unit.

Defining Organization Inventory Parameters

A number of inventory, costing, control, and movement parameters are associated with an inventory organization. This section outlines some of the areas and associated parameter data you need to specify for an inventory organization.

You must provide the following default inventory parameters:

- The master organization where items will be initially defined.
- The workday calendar for planning, scheduling, and determining days to perform cycle counts.
- The process organization that is applicable, if any, to the new organization.
- Optionally, you can specify the demand class to be used in forecast consumption, shipment, and production relief.
- The number of days that a move order requisition will wait for the required approval action. The move order workflow approval process uses the value entered here to determine the intervals at which to forward a reminder notification to the selected approver and, if the reminder is not acted upon, when to automatically approve or reject the move order.
- The desired action to be taken when the move order approval process reaches the second timeout phase based on the interval set in the previous step. The available options are to Approve Automatically or Reject Automatically.

Note

To bypass the move order approval process and have any move order requisitions automatically approved, you should set the Move Order Timeout Period to 0 days and select Approve Automatically in the Move Order Timeout Action field.

- The level of locator control for the inventory organization. Select from the following settings for the locator control option:
  - **None**—Locators not required anywhere in this organization for inventory transactions.
  - **Prespecified Only**—All transactions require a valid, predefined locator for each item.
  - **Dynamic Entry Allowed**—All transactions require a locator for each item, but the locator can be either predefined or dynamically entered at the time of transaction.
  - **Determined at Subinventory Level**—Transactions use locator controls defined at the subinventory level.
- Indicate whether negative inventory balances will be allowed.

Note

There is an Inventory profile option called INV: Override Neg for Backflush. If you specify Yes for this option, Oracle WIP, when it backflushes components with assembly or operation pull, ignores the preceding setting and drive inventory negative if there is not enough inventory on-hand in the supply subinventory specified on the bill of material.

- Enter the default capacity load weight and unit of measure.
- Enter the default capacity load volume and unit of measure.

These parameters are shown in Figure 17.3.

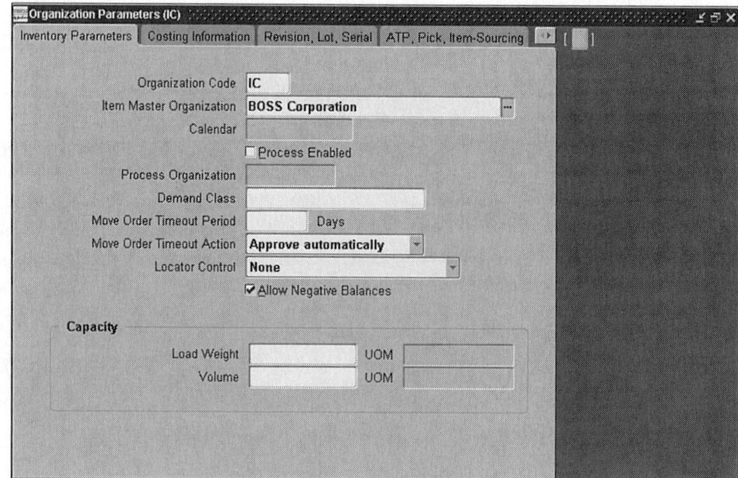

Figure 17.3 Defining organization inventory parameters.

You must specify the following costing information, as shown in Figure 17.4:

- The costing organization can be either the current organization or the item master organization.
- The costing method can be standard or average.
- When the costing method is set to average, select the appropriate Average Rates Cost type.
- Indicate whether all GL transactions are posted in detail.
- Indicate whether to reverse encumbrance entry upon receipt into inventory.
- See Chapter 20, "Using Oracle Cost Management," for further detail on defining the default material subelement and the other cost information organization parameters.

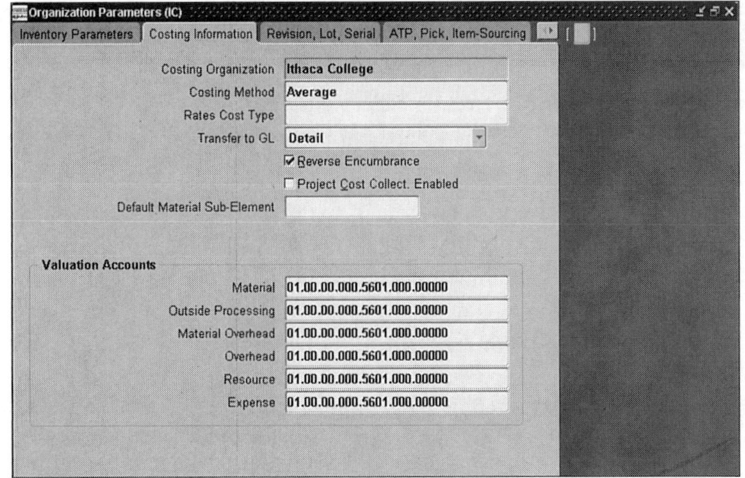

Figure 17.4 Defining organization costing parameters.

You need to specify default valuation accounts for the organization. This organization, in turn, will be the default account for the subinventories, for which you define the following:

- **Material**—An asset account that tracks material cost
- **Material Overhead**—An asset account that tracks material overhead cost
- **Resource**—An asset account that tracks resource cost
- **Overhead**—An asset account that tracks resource and outside processing overheads
- **Outside Processing**—An asset account that tracks outside processing cost
- **Expense**—The expense account for tracking a nonasset item

You must specify the following default general ledger accounts to be associated with this organization (using the Other Accounts tab):

- Sales
- Cost of Goods Sold
- Purchase Price Variance
- Inventory A/P Accrual
- Invoice Price Variance
- Encumbrance
- Project Clearance
- Average Cost Variance

For the revision, lot, and serial number parameters, specify information in the following areas:

- **Starting Revision**—Enter a starting revision to be the default for every new item.
- **Lot Number Uniqueness**—Select either None where unique lot numbers are not required or Across Items where unique lot numbers for items are required across all organizations.
- **Lot Number Generation**—Select At Item Level when you will specify a starting lot number prefix and starting lot number when you define the item; User Defined when you will enter a lot number when you receive the item; or At Organization Level when you will define the starting prefix and lot number in the following fields (the lot number will be generated by the system and be assigned to the item when it is received):
    - **Zero Pad Suffix**—Indicate whether to add zeroes to right-justify the numeric portion of lot numbers.
    - **Prefix**—Optionally, enter an alphanumeric lot number prefix to be used for system-generated lot numbers.
    - **Length**—Optionally, enter a maximum total length for the prefix and number that WIP will validate if the WIP parameter for lot number is based on inventory rules.
- **Serial Number Uniqueness**—Select either Within Inventory Items when you want unique serial numbers within an inventory item; Within Organization for unique serial numbers within the current organization; or Across Organizations for unique serial numbers across all organizations.
- **Serial Number Generation**—Select At Item Level when you will specify a starting serial number prefix and starting serial number when you define the item or At Organization Level when you will define the starting prefix and serial number in the following fields:
    - **Prefix**—Optionally, enter an alphanumeric serial number prefix to use for system-generated serial numbers.
    - **Starting Serial Number**—Enter a starting serial number to use for system-generated serial numbers.

You must supply the following ATP, pick, and item sourcing parameters:

- Select a default ATP rule. If you use Order Management, the default is the ATP rule for the master organization.
- Select a default picking rule.
- Enter a default subinventory picking order. The value here displays when you define a subinventory.
- Enter a default locator picking order. The value here displays when you define a locator.

- Check the Pick Confirmation Required check box if you require your inventory pickers to manually pick confirm orders fulfilled from this organization. If you do not check the box, the pick confirm process will be triggered automatically.
- Select an item sourcing replenishment type. Select None for no default source for item replenishment; select Supplier if you will be replenishing items from suppliers; or select Inventory if you will replenish items from another subinventory in this or another organization. If you specify Inventory, you need to specify an organization in the following organization field and a subinventory in the subinventory field if you specify the current organization in the organization field.

You must provide inter-org information parameters to correctly transfer charges between organizations when items are moved between organizations:

- **Inter-Organization Transfer Charge Option**—Specify None if you don't want to add transfer charges to a material transfer between organizations; Predefined Percent to automatically add a predefined percent of the transaction value for inter-organization transfers (and also enter that percent); Requested Value to add a discrete value for inter-organization transfers; or Requested Percent to add a discrete percent of the transaction value when performing an inter-organization transfer.
- **Inter-Organization Transfer Accounts**—Enter the default inter-organization cost accounts, which will appear by default in the Inter-Organization Shipping Networks window when you set up shipping information between organizations.

If Oracle Project Manufacturing is installed, you need to specify additional organizational information regarding projects:

- Check whether Project Reference Enabled will be activated.
- Check whether Project Cost Collection Enabled will be activated.
- Select the project control level: project or task.

Changing to a Valid Organization

Normally, when you sign in to an Oracle Inventory transaction session, the system requires you to select an organization. Oracle then associates your session with this inventory organization. However, when you first set up the inventory application, no inventory organizations are defined. To associate the following setup steps with the correct organization, you need to either log off and then log back in and select your organization or perform the Change Organization transaction that is available on the menu list.

Defining Intercompany Relations

If you are configuring a multiorganization environment and expect to perform sales transactions across operating units, this form can be used to designate the appropriate shipping and receiving customers to be used for intercompany invoicing.

Intercompany sales orders often involve orders that are entered in one specific operating unit that will ultimately be shipped out of a warehouse that is associated to a different operating unit. These operating units might or might not belong to separate sets of books. The accounting transactions generated are such that after the order is shipped, the inventory asset account for the shipping organization is credited and the cost of goods sold account debited. On the other hand, the sales revenue is recognized in the order entry organization. Because the two organizations belong to different operating units than the appropriate intercompany revenue, receivables and payables entries are also generated.

To define these relationships, you must specify the following:

- The shipping operating unit.
- The selling operating unit.
- The customer name or number that represents the selling organization customer from the perspective of the shipping operating unit.
- The selling organization customer location.
- The transaction type to be used for entries of this nature.
- The supplier name and, if available, the supplier site that represents the shipping organization vendor from the perspective of the selling operating unit.
- The appropriate freight account.
- The Revalue Average box. Check this if you are using average costing.

Note

Oracle Inventory and Receivables must be installed before any intercompany relationships can be successfully created. If Oracle Payables is not installed then the fields in the AP Invoicing for Selling region are not required.

Defining Receiving Options

You need to specify which receiving options are applicable when you are receiving items from other organizations. If Oracle Purchasing is installed, you can also receive purchased items into inventory using these options. Some of the options that you can specify include

- The action to take when an item is received early or late
- The action to take if more than the quantity ordered has been received
- One of the following three options for how items will be received into inventory:
    - **Direct**—If items will be received directly into their inventory location with a single step transaction
    - **Standard**—If items will first be received and then in a second step delivered to their inventory location
    - **Inspection**—If items will first be received, then inspected, and in a third step delivered to their inventory location

- An indication if unordered items can be received or if substitute items can be received
- Specifications for the processing of receipt numbers, express receipts, cascade transactions, blind receiving, and Advance Shipping Notice (ASN) control

These options are the default receiving options for the organization. However, most of these receiving options can be overridden at the supplier, purchase order, or item level. For additional details on specifying the receiving options for an organization, see Chapter 16, "Using Oracle Purchasing."

DEFINING PICKING RULES

When you use Oracle Inventory and Oracle Shipping Execution to ship items against customer sales orders, you need to define picking rules. You assign a picking rule to an item to define the priorities that Inventory uses to pick units of that item for a sales order. You specify the sources and prioritization for subinventories, lots, revisions, and locators to be used when the item is pick-released. You can specify None for any of the criterion fields, and Inventory will ignore that criterion when picking. You can define a unique picking rule for each item or use a generic picking rule for the organization.

If the subinventory, lot, or revision is assigned before pick release, the assignment is used rather than the picking rule. For example, if a subinventory is assigned on a lot-controlled item before pick release but the lot isn't assigned, the picking rule is used to assign the lot.

Note

A picking order of 1 on a subinventory or locator means that Order Management will pick items from that subinventory or locator before others with a higher number such as 2, 3, or 4.

DEFINING AVAILABLE-TO-PROMISE RULES

ATP (Available-to-Promise) rules define supply and demand sources, time fence parameters, and available-to-promise calculation methods. You can give the ATP rule a meaningful name. You assign an ATP rule to an item to define the options that Inventory uses to calculate the available quantity of an item on a requested date or the first date on which a requested quantity is available for an item. If there is no ATP rule for the item, Order Management/Shipping uses the default ATP rule for the organization.

The *Oracle Inventory User's Guide* has several good examples to illustrate the effect on ATP of picking various options in the ATP rules.

Note

To perform standard Available-to-Promise calculations from Order Management in 11*i*, you don't have to have Oracle Advanced Planning and Scheduling installed. You do, however, need to perform some setup steps that typically are associated with the Advanced Planning and Scheduling module; refer to the *Oracle Order Management User's Guide* for further detail. Specifically, the profile option INV: Capable to Promise must be set to Enable PL/SQL based ATP without Planning Output, and the Data Collection concurrent process must be periodically run from within the Order Management module.

DEFINING PLANNERS

You can specify a material planner code for every item defined. The Oracle Master Scheduling/MRP and Supply Chain Planning applications use this planner code to group items for planning and reporting purposes. For example, you can specify when using the planner workbench that you only want to work on items associated with a single planner code. Several material planning reports can be sorted by a single or range of planner codes. You need to define your planner codes first before they can be assigned to items. To define a planner code, you just need to specify up to 10 characters for the planner code and enter a description for the planner code. See Chapter 21, "Using Oracle Planning Applications," for additional details on using planner codes.

DEFINING UNIT OF MEASURE CLASSES, UNITS OF MEASURE, UNIT OF MEASURE CONVERSIONS, AND INTERCLASS CONVERSIONS

Oracle Inventory provides a flexible way of defining and transacting items in their units of measure. The process of defining units of measure to use in Oracle Inventory involves several steps:

1. Define unit of measure classes and the base unit of measure (UOM) for each class.
2. Define multiple units of measure for each unit of measure class.
3. Define conversions between units of measure of the same and of different classes.

For example, you might want two classes of UOM for quantity and weight. The base UOM for quantity might be "each" and weight might be "pound". You might want additional quantity class units of measure to be "dozen" and weight class units of measure to be "kilogram". For each unit of measure, you must specify a label or code such as EA, DZ, LB, or KG. The following steps outline the process for defining the sample information:

1. Define the two UOM classes of Quantity and Weight and identify their base UOM of EA and LB.
2. Define the additional UOM of DZ in the class Quantity and the UOM of KG in the class Weight.
3. Specify the conversion between EA and DZ to be 1DZ=12EA and the conversion between LB and KG to be 1KG=2.2LB.

Table 17.1 shows the results of the preceding definition process.

TABLE 17.1 DEFINING UNITS OF MEASURE

UOM Class	Class Description	Base UOM	UOM Description	Other UOM	UOM Description	Conversion
Quantity	Quantity	EA	Each	DZ	Dozen	1DZ=12EA
Weight	Weight	LB	Pound	KG	Kilogram	1KG=2.2LB

When you define an item, you indicate its primary unit of measure, such as each (EA), which is the item's stocking unit of measure.

If you require, you can also specify an item-specific unit of measure conversion. For instance, you could specify that 1EA of this item = 5LB. Then, you could transact in pounds, and Inventory would convert a transaction of 50LB back into the primary unit of measure of quantity of 10EA for the item.

An entire chapter in the manual *Oracle Inventory User's Guide* describes in detail the process of defining units of measure.

Note

Units of measure in Oracle are global, which means they are used by all organizations and they only need to be defined once.

Oracle supplies no seeded values for units of measure. This means that you have to define at least one unit of measure class and its base unit of measure. This also means that you need to define all the rest of the unit of measure classes and units of measure that you think that you will require.

Tip

You can change almost any item attribute on an inventory item. About the only exception is the item's unit of measure. Once an item has been created and saved, you cannot change its unit of measure. Therefore, when you are creating inventory items, you need to be careful to define the correct unit of measure. If you do happen to create an item with an incorrect unit of measure, see the Tip in this chapter in the section "Setting the Profile Options," later in this chapter, to recover the item record.

DEFINING SUBINVENTORIES

A subinventory is a subdivision of an organization, representing either a physical area or a logical grouping of items (such as a storeroom, receiving dock, or discrepant material area). All inventory transaction activity must reference a subinventory, and all material within an organization must be stored in a subinventory. It is therefore required that you define at least one subinventory. For each subinventory, you need to define both inventory and accounting information.

Some of the inventory information you need to provide when defining a subinventory includes

- A subinventory name
- Whether the inventory is quantity tracked
- Whether items are tracked on the Balance Sheet as assets
- A depreciable check box that has been added in 11*i* to provide for specific Network Logistics functionality in future releases
- Whether items in this subinventory will be used in ATP calculations
- Whether items will be used in available to reserve calculations
- Whether to include on-hand item quantities in the planning process (Nettable)

If you specified that the locator control is Determined at Subinventory Level when you defined your organization, you have to specify a type of locator control for the subinventory:

- **None**—No locator information is required for transactions in this subinventory.
- **Prespecified**—Inventory transactions require a valid prespecified locator for each item.
- **Dynamic Entry**—Inventory transactions require you to enter a valid predefined locator, or you can define a locator dynamically at the time of the inventory transaction.
- **Item Level**—Locator control information for inventory transactions is defined at the item level.

Select Inventory, Supplier, or Subinventory as the source type for replenishment in this subinventory. If you select Supplier, it means you plan to replenish items from a supplier. If you select Inventory, it means you plan to replenish items from a subinventory in another organization. Or alternatively, you can select Subinventory if you want to replenish items internally, from another subinventory within the same organization. You have to additionally specify the organization used to replenish items and the subinventory if you specify sourcing from another organization.

You can optionally provide the following additional inventory information when defining a subinventory:

- You can select a picking order value that indicates the priority of picking from this subinventory relative to another subinventory. Note: A picking order priority value of 1 means that Order Management will pick from this subinventory before other subinventories with a higher value.
- If you are using min-max planning at the subinventory level, you can enter preprocessing, processing, and postprocessing lead times for items in the subinventory.

You need to specify the following general ledger accounts to accumulate the following types of costs for items in this subinventory:

- Material
- Outside processing

- Material overhead
- Overhead
- Resource
- Expense
- Encumbrance (if using in Oracle Purchasing)

Note

> The general ledger accounts listed here for each of the subinventories will default from the organization definition, and they only need to be overridden if they are different from the organization accounts.
>
> After you define the subinventory, you can specify the stock locators for this subinventory. (Click the Locators button.) You can also assign items to this subinventory. (Click the Item/Subinventory button.)

The notify field is new to 11*i* and allows for selection of a specific notification list, from which workflow notifications can be triggered to individual users when using the new Move Order functionality to transact items to and from this subinventory.

DEFINING STOCK LOCATORS

A stock locator is a physical area within a subinventory where you store material (such as a row, rack, aisle, bin, or shelf). You can turn on locator control for the whole organization, for a specific subinventory, or for a particular item. Item quantities can be tracked by locator. You can restrict an item to a specific locator.

You must first define the structure of the stock locator flexfield before you can define any specific stock locators. See the section "Defining the Stock Locators Key Flexfield" earlier in this chapter for guidance on this task. The tasks in the process to define a specific stock locator are

1. Enter the locator and its description.
2. Enter the subinventory where the locator resides. (Optionally, you can specify the stock locator/subinventory relationship using the Define Subinventory screen.)
3. Optionally, enter a picking order value for Order Management picking priority. (A priority of 1 gets picked before 2, 3, and so on.)
4. You can also optionally enter capacity constraint information such as maximum weight, volume, or number of items that can be stored in this locator. This information is captured for informative purposes only and has no direct impact on performing any inventory transactions into the specific locators.

Note

Using locators in Oracle Inventory has advantages and disadvantages. Some of the advantages are the following:

- You can restrict an item to a specific locator if required.
- You can locate items by locator within a subinventory, which should make it easier to locate the item in a large subinventory.

The disadvantages of using locators are as follows:

- Every transaction into a locator-controlled subinventory requires not only the keying of the subinventory but also the keying of the locator.
- You must set up and maintain the list of locators for each item restricted to a prespecified list of locators, and the item can't be stored anywhere in the system until this maintenance has been performed. In addition, if you want to store this item in another locator, you must add the locator to the prespecified list before you can store it there.

DEFINING ITEM ATTRIBUTE CONTROLS

Each item has a number of item attributes such as lead time, cost, unit of measure, item status, revision control, and so on. You need to specify for each of these attributes the level at which Oracle Inventory will maintain the item attribute, at the item master level or at the item/organization level (see Figure 17.5). This means that you can choose between centralized or decentralized control of your item attributes.

You can specify that a particular item attribute, such as unit of measure, be maintained at the item master level. This means that Oracle Inventory will maintain this value at the item master level, the value will be the same in every organization where this item has been enabled, and the value cannot be updated at the item/organization level. For another item attribute such as lead time, you can specify that the value be maintained at the item/organization level. This means that each organization can have the same or a different lead time for obtaining the same item.

When you define item attribute controls, you specify only the level at which the item attribute is controlled, master level or org level, and not the value of the attribute. Some attributes can only be set at a specific level, and in those cases, you have only one option.

There are eight specific item status attributes. You can set all eight of these attributes for an item with a status code. For each of these item status attributes, in addition to specifying the control level of master or org level, you also need to specify the status setting of Defaults Value, Not Used, or Sets Value. This status setting determines whether a particular attribute can be set by the status code and, if so, whether it can be changed. See the section "Defining Statuses" later in this chapter for additional detail regarding these status attributes and their status settings.

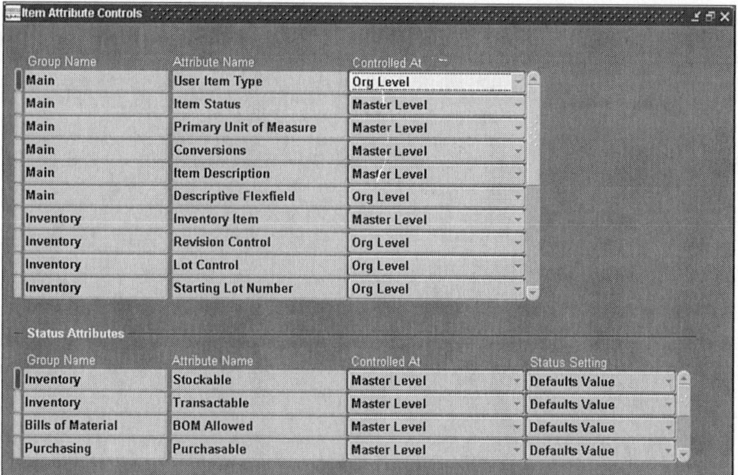

Figure 17.5
Maintaining item attributes.

Defining Categories

One of the key strengths of the Oracle Inventory application is the capability to allow the user to attach several user-defined categories to an item and inquire and report on the items using these categories.

After you define the item categories key flexfield, the next step in the category definition process is the definition of the names for each one of the categories. To define a new category, you have to specify both the category flexfield structure name and a unique category name.

Defining Category Sets

After defining both the item categories key flexfield and the categories, the next step in the category definition process is the definition of category sets.

To define a category set, you must provide the following information:

- A unique category set name.
- A category flexfield structure.
- A control level of Master Level if you want items assigned to this category set to have the same value in all of the organizations to which the item is assigned or Org Level if you want items assigned to this category set to be able to have a different value in each of the organizations to which this item is assigned.
- A default category, which is the value that Oracle Inventory allocates to an item when it is initially assigned to the category set. You can override this default category with an appropriate category immediately after assigning the item to the set.

- Indication of whether to enforce a list of valid categories. If you turn on this feature, you can only assign an item to those categories that you define as valid categories for this category set. If this option is not selected then you will be able to assign an item to any category that uses the same flexfield structure as this category set.
- A list of valid categories. If you indicate that you want a list of valid categories enforced, you enter the list of valid categories.

Defining Default Category Sets

The last step in the definition process for categories is the assignment of default category sets for each application functional area. You need to assign a default category set for each of the following application areas: Inventory, Purchasing, Order Management, Costing, Engineering, and Planning. The default category set can be the same or different for each of these application areas.

As you add new items and enable them for use by specific functional areas, Oracle Inventory automatically assigns the items to the default category set for each functional area and allocates it the appropriate default category value. You can override the category sets default category, and in addition, you can manually assign an item to additional category sets.

The concept behind default category sets is to ensure that all items enabled for use in specific functional areas are, at a minimum, assigned to one common category set. Therefore, when selecting this default category set for reporting purposes, the user can be assured that all items allocated for use in the specific functional area will be returned for analysis. You can change a functional area's default category set under certain conditions; however, when doing so you should ensure that every item within the functional area belongs to the new default category set. Otherwise, the concept of default category sets will be compromised. You should never change the default Purchasing category set after you have started creating requisition or purchase order lines using the categories.

Note

It is recommended that you pick a value for the default category of a category set that allows you to determine that an item has not had a category assigned to it. For example, if you choose a default value of Unassigned or Unknown and the user forgets to override the default category with a valid item category, it is easy to identify those items that have not had a valid category assigned to them.

Tip

Prior to Release 11.5.3, the Inventory module restricted items to being assigned to only one category within a category set. In Release 11.5.3 and beyond, the Category Sets form now shows a check box labeled Allow Multiple Item Category Assignments, which when checked allows more than one category within a category set to be allocated to an individual item. This functionality is not backported to prior releases.

Defining Statuses

Eight key controlling item attributes, called *status control attributes*, are flags that exist for each functional area and control whether items are available for use within that particular area. They are highlighted in the item attribute list in the section "Item Definition" later in this chapter and also listed here:

- BOM Allowed
- Build in WIP
- Customer Orders Enabled
- Internal Orders Enabled
- Invoice Enabled
- Transactable
- Purchasable
- Stockable

You can set all eight of these attributes with a user-defined item status. For each of the status attributes, you can specify whether the value of the attribute should be Yes or No. You specify these values with the Define Item Status Codes screen. For instance, you might want to define a status code of Production and give a value of Yes to all of the attributes. Another status you might choose to define is Preannounce with all of the attributes Yes except Customer Orders Enabled. This allows you to apply this status code to a new part and start purchasing and making the part and putting it into inventory without taking orders for the part yet. After announcement of the product, you can update the part with a status of Production and start taking customer orders.

In addition to specifying the status value of Yes or No for each of the status attributes, you can also specify a status setting for each of the status attributes. The status settings are

- **Defaults Value**—The status value will be set by the status code and can be changed later.
- **None**—The value is not set by the status code.
- **Sets Value**—The status value will be set by the status code and it cannot be changed.

You define these status settings at the Item Attribute Controls screen. See the section "Defining Item Attribute Controls" earlier in this chapter for further details on this activity.

Defining Item Catalog Groups

Item catalogs group items that share similar descriptive elements. Oracle Inventory lets you create multiple catalog groups to aid in item classification. Each catalog group can have its own set of item characteristics, called descriptive elements. You can define as many descriptive elements as necessary to describe your items and specify whether an entry for the element is optional. Once you catalog your items, you can search on one or more descriptive elements to assist in locating items for order entry or group technology purposes.

To define catalogs, you set up as many catalog groups as you need. Each group has characteristics called descriptive elements that describe items belonging to the group. The steps involved in setting up item catalogs follow:

1. You must first define the structure of the item catalog group key flexfield. See the section "Defining the Item Catalog Group Key Flexfield" earlier in this chapter for guidance.
2. Define item catalog groups.
3. Define descriptive elements within each group.
4. Optionally, define aliases for items in the catalog group.
5. Optionally, specify recommended categories associated with the group.
6. Assign items to groups and enter descriptive element values.
7. Optionally, you can update an item's description with concatenated catalog group information.

To define an item catalog group, you need to

1. Use the Item Catalog Groups screen.
2. Enter a unique name for the catalog group.
3. Enter a description of the catalog group.

To define descriptive elements for the catalog group, follow these steps:

1. Click the Details button on the Item Catalog Groups screen when defining the catalog group or query the catalog group on the screen and select Details.
2. Select the descriptive elements tabbed region.
3. Enter a sequence number.
4. Name the descriptive element such as size, speed, or color.
5. Specify whether the descriptive element is required.
6. Specify whether the descriptive element will be automatically used to create the catalog description. When you define a descriptive element for a catalog group, you can specify that this element be concatenated with other descriptive elements and used to update the description of the item.

To assign an item to a catalog, follow these steps:

1. Use the Master Items Summary window and select an item. Select Catalog on the Tools menu.

Note

Item catalog information is created and maintained at the master level and not at the organization level. This feature prevents conflicting values in different organizations.

2. On the Item Catalog window that appears, enter a catalog group. The descriptive elements for this catalog group display in the Name field.
3. Enter a specific value for each of the descriptive elements that pertain to the item.
4. Indicate whether to include a descriptive element in a catalog-derived item description.
5. Save your work and select Update Description if you want the item description updated with the descriptive element values you defined.

DEFINING ITEM TYPES

An item type is a user-defined field that you can attach to every item. After you define an item type, it appears in the list of values for the user item type attribute. You can use the item type field to assist in the retrieval of items. However, Oracle applications do not print or group any of their reports by the item type field. Oracle has already predefined some item types that you can use, and you can add your own. Some examples of item types that have already been predefined are purchased item, finished good, subassembly, kit, and outside processing item.

Note

You can specify the item type with an item template. A number of customers use the item type to indicate which template was used to define an item. Oracle also uses this convention in the creation of its sample items.

Note

Remember, Oracle applications do not use the item type field to group items for reports. The item category field is used for this purpose. If you require reports grouped by item type, you need to create your own custom reports in addition to those already provided by Oracle.

DEFINING ITEM TEMPLATES

When you define an item, you can specify more than 150 item attributes about the item. To simplify this process, you can use item templates. An item template is a set of item attributes that you can use over and over to assist in defining similar types of items.

After you define an item template, you can use it to create an item, and then you only have to specify the item attributes not already supplied by the item template. You can apply the same or different templates to an item multiple times. The most recent attribute values (from the last template applied) override previous values, unless the previous value is non-updateable (for example, the primary unit of measure, which is never updateable).

Oracle Inventory provides a number of predefined item templates that you can use to assist in creating items. Some examples of item templates already predefined are purchased item, finished good, subassembly, kit, and outside processing item. For additional details regarding the item attributes specified in each one of these supplied templates, refer to the *Oracle Inventory User's Guide*. Alternatively, you can print the supplied Inventory report entitled Item Template listing.

Note

It is highly recommended that you use either the predefined templates supplied by Oracle or those you define yourself to assist in the process of item creation. When creating items, using templates can reduce keystroke entries as well as the chance of entering incorrect data.

DEFINING ITEMS

You use the Master Item form to define and update items and the attributes associated to them. This exercise can be performed long-hand, or you can use some of the techniques already mentioned, such as item templates, to expedite this process.

DEFINING CROSS-REFERENCE TYPES

You can use cross-references in Oracle Inventory to retrieve an item by attributes other than its part number. For instance, you might want to retrieve an item by its old part number or by its blueprint number. To be able to do this, you first must define the cross-reference types such as Old Part Number or Blue Print Number. You do this by giving each cross-reference type a name and description with the Cross-Reference Types window. Then, you assign the cross-references to items using the Cross References List of Value under the Tools menu when defining the item using the Master Items or Organization Items definition window. You can make the cross-reference assignment to an item applicable to all organizations or to just a specific organization. The item assignment process can also be performed from the Cross-Reference Types window, by selecting the appropriate Cross-Reference and clicking the Assign button.

You can assign multiple cross-references to an item. For example, you might want to assign an Old Part Number of OLD123 to an item and a Blue Print Number of B1234 as well. This allows you to retrieve this item by using either reference with the Item Search window. You can also look up this reference information at any time within either the Master or Organization Item definition windows by looking under Cross References on the Tools menu.

DEFINING ITEM DELETE CONSTRAINTS

Oracle Inventory predefines a number of item delete constraints to check for conditions that should prevent you from deleting an item. For instance, several of the delete constraints prevent the deletion of an item if there are jobs, repetitive schedules, purchase orders, or sales orders referencing the item. You can specify additional delete constraints to supplement the standard item delete constraints.

Note

You don't normally need to specify any additional item delete constraints unless you have additional tables or fields in your system that reference items the Oracle Inventory application is not aware of. If you do have this condition, see the section on creating custom delete constraints in the *Oracle Bills of Materials User's Guide*.

Defining Cost Types

Before you can enter item costs, you need to define cost types. A cost type is a set of costs used for future, current, historical, or simulation purposes. Oracle Inventory comes predefined with three cost types: frozen, average, and pending.

If you use standard costing in your organization, Oracle uses the frozen cost for all transactions at the time of the transaction. You can update frozen costs by running a standard cost update. If you use average costing, Oracle uses the average cost type and updates your average costs after the appropriate transactions.

You can also define cost types for your own use such as for simulation or historical purposes. Many of the cost reports can be submitted based on the cost type that you specify. For details regarding the definition of cost types, see Chapter 20.

Defining Cost Activities

In addition to cost types, you can also optionally define cost activities. Cost activities are processes or procedures that consume costs and time. Some organizations use activity-based costing to more accurately identify their product costs, particularly in the area of indirect costs. The definition of cost activities is described in more detail in Chapter 20.

Defining Material Subelements

Cost subelements are a smaller classification of cost elements. You can optionally define material subelements if you want further cost breakdowns for your material costs. For each material subelement, you need to indicate the method of allocating the cost to the subelement (basis type). See Chapter 20 for further details on defining material subelements.

Defining Material Overheads

You need to define material overheads if you want to keep track of overhead rates. If you are using standard costing, you can optionally define a material overhead for things such as purchasing or freight. Each overhead is charged when an item is received into inventory. See Chapter 20 for further details.

Defining Default Material Overhead Rates

If you have decided to use material overheads, you can optionally enter default rates for your organization or categories. Then when you define your items, Oracle Inventory automatically uses the defaults. See Chapter 20 for further details.

DEFINING FREIGHT CARRIERS

A freight carrier is an organization or company that provides item transportation services between your organization and your customers, between your suppliers and your organization, and between several of your organizations for an inter-organization item transfer. To define a freight carrier, you need to provide a unique name for the carrier and the carrier description. You also need to specify a general ledger distribution account for the carrier that collects costs associated with using that carrier.

DEFINING THE ORGANIZATION SHIPPING NETWORK

You can use the Shipping Networks screen to define the accounting information and the relationships that exist between shipping and destination organizations (see Figure 17.6). When you define a new organization relationship, the shipping information you specified in the Organization parameters appears by default on the Shipping Networks screen. For each organization relationship, you specify for an organization whether it is a shipping organization, a destination organization, or both.

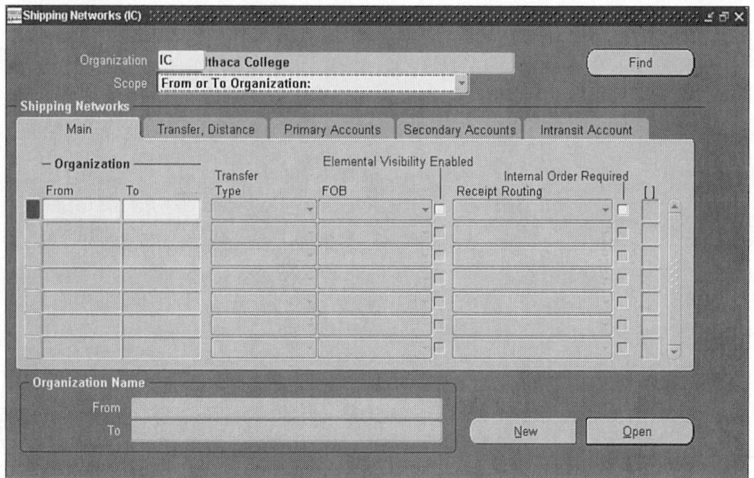

Figure 17.6
Defining organization shipping relationships.

You also specify for each organization relationship whether the shipping transfer type is direct or in-transit. You normally use the direct type if the shipping time is small and the in-transit type if the time to transfer between the organizations is significant. When you move items between organizations with a transfer type of in-transit, Oracle moves material to in-transit inventory before it reaches the destination organization. If you specify the in-transit transfer type, you also need to indicate which organization owns the material while it is in-transit. You also need to indicate the type of receipt routing that is performed (direct, standard, or inspection) at the destination organization when the material is transferred in-transit.

You need to indicate whether internal requisitions are required from the destination organization when you perform inter-organization transfers of items, if internal requisitions are deemed to be required you will not be able to perform an interorganization inventory transfer using the Transfer Between Organizations form to that organization. You also need to define an inter-organization charge type. You can specify to automatically add a predefined percentage to the transaction value, not add any transfer charges, add a discrete value, or add a discrete percentage to the transaction value. You can specify different discrete values or percentages for each of the organizational shipping relationships that you have defined.

You have to provide general ledger account codes to record charges associated with an inter-organization transfer. You can also optionally specify shipping methods and lead times associated with the shipping methods. The lead times are used by MRP when planning inter-organization supply.

Note

The definition of the organization shipping network is not bidirectional. If you have to move goods from a sending organization to a receiving organization and also move goods from the receiving organization back to the sending organization, you need to define two interorganizational relationships.

Defining Shipping Methods

The shipping method code is used to represent the specific shipping methods that are available to each of the inventory organizations. It is recommended that shipping method codes be created to represent all possible combinations of freight carriers and service levels—for example, UPS 1 Day, FedEx 1 Day, UPS 2 Days, and so on. The shipping methods and the appropriate freight carriers can then be tied together for each organization or warehouse that will use them via the Carrier Ship Methods form. These setups become relevant for the Order Management and Shipping Execution modules.

Defining Economic Zones

Economic zones can be defined for the purpose of capturing inventory movement statistics for the specific global zones within which you conduct business. To define an economic zone, you enter a zone code, name for the specific zone, and description; finally, you must assign the specific country names that fall within this designated region to your zone code. As an example, Oracle Inventory comes seeded with a zone code for the European Union, to which you can add the appropriate country names.

Defining Movement Statistics Parameters

If you intend to capture and report on inventory movement statistics, you must use the Movement Statistics Parameters window to define the parameters and legal entity relationships that will determine how these statistics are collated. Statistics can be gathered for transactions internal to or external from specific economic zones within legal entities. This functionality is primarily delivered for the specific intrastat and extrastat reporting requirements imposed on members of the European Economic Union.

Defining Account Aliases

An account alias is a shorthand label for a general ledger account-number combination that you can use when entering inventory transactions such as miscellaneous issues or receipt transactions. When you enter an inventory transaction, you can enter the account alias instead of the multi-segmented account number. Using account aliases can reduce the number of keystroke entries as well as the chance of entering the wrong account number for your inventory transactions. In addition to a user-friendly reference to a particular account number, an account alias is also a transaction source type of its own. This means you can query and report on transactions using the account aliases.

To set up account aliases, you first need to define the account aliases key flexfield as detailed in an earlier section in this chapter. You then use the Account Aliases window to define an account alias and its associated general ledger account number.

Defining Transaction Source Types

Transaction source types enable you to classify transactions according to their origins, such as a purchase order or physical inventory. When you perform a transaction, you specify a transaction type and a source. For example, for a PO receipt, the transaction source type is Purchase Order and the actual purchase order number is the source.

Oracle Inventory provides a number of predefined transaction source types, including purchase order, sales order, account, job or schedule, internal requisition, internal order, cycle count, account alias, physical inventory, standard cost update, RMA, and inventory. In addition to these predefined source types, you can define your own source types. You can also associate a list of valid sources with your transaction source type.

You can define additional transaction source types in the Transaction Source Types window. This window also allows for the specification of a list of valid sources. You can then use these user-defined source types along with predefined transaction actions to define a new transaction type.

Defining Transaction Types

Oracle Inventory provides transaction reporting and querying capabilities by transaction type. A transaction type is the combination of a transaction source type and a transaction action. Oracle Inventory provides for a number of predefined transaction types. In addition to those transaction types provided by Oracle, you can use the Transaction Types window to define additional transaction types. A user-defined transaction type is a combination of a user-defined transaction source type and any one of the six predefined inventory transaction actions, which include issue from stores, subinventory transfer, direct organization transfer, intransit shipment, cost update, and receipt into stores.

Defining Transaction Reasons

A transaction reason is a way of classifying or explaining the reason for a transaction. Oracle Inventory provides for transaction reporting and inquiring by transaction reason. You can define your own transaction reason codes that you can enter when you perform an inventory transaction. To define a transaction reason, you use the Transaction Reasons window.

An example is that you want to take a number of your new low-cost, high-quality material items to a trade show for display and then give the items away at the show to customers. You can create a transaction reason of Trade Show and use this reason for all material issues for the show. You can later report on all of the items issued for the show by this transaction reason.

Defining Purchasing Options

If you will be using inter-organization shipments with in-transit inventory, you need to use the Enter Receipts transaction to receive items into the destination organization. To perform this transaction effectively, you should define certain default control options in the Purchasing Options window to save you time when you create your receipts. Refer to Chapter 16 for further details.

Opening Accounting Periods

Oracle Inventory uses accounting periods to group material and work-in-process transactions for accounting purposes. An accounting period must be open for you to be able to perform an inventory transaction. That means that the inventory transaction date must fall within the beginning and ending dates of the open accounting period. You first need to define your accounting periods in Oracle General Ledger. Then before you can enter transactions in Oracle Inventory, you need to open an accounting period. You use the Inventory Accounting Periods window to perform this function. Oracle Inventory enables you to have more than one inventory accounting period open at one time. However, after an inventory accounting period is closed, it cannot be reopened. The period open and close process must be performed for each inventory organization that is enabled.

Starting the Material and Cost Interface Concurrent Managers

Transaction managers in Oracle execute a number of processes, including material transaction, demand reservation, move transaction, resource cost transaction, remote procedure call, and material cost transaction. These managers run at periodic intervals that you specify. You can also specify the number of transaction workers and the number of transactions processed by each worker during each interval. You need to start the material transaction and material cost interface managers if you want to perform transactions in the background or in concurrent processing mode or if you use custom forms and data collection devices to enter transactions. The move transaction processor should be started to allow assemblies received from outside processing suppliers to be moved on to the next operation in the manufacturing process. You can use the Interface Managers window to view the status of the transaction managers, and from the Tools menu you can launch the transaction manager that you have highlighted.

You do not have to launch these transaction managers if you decide to process all of your transactions online and if you do not use the transaction interface.

SETTING THE PROFILE OPTIONS

Each of the Oracle Applications has a set of profile options that allow you to indicate how the application should access and process information. The Oracle Inventory profile options all have an indicator of INV. In Oracle Inventory, you can indicate what the application uses when creating, processing, or transacting an inventory item. For example, you can specify with profile options what the default unit of measure for an item should be or what the default item status should be.

You can also indicate the processing control that the Inventory application uses for transacting items. The profile option labeled TP:INV Transaction Processing Mode allows you to specify for all inventory transactions that the processing control should be via background processing, concurrent processing, or online processing. You select online processing if you want your transactions processed immediately. You select the other processing options if you want your transactions processed after you save your work, freeing your terminal to allow you to continue with other tasks. You can also specify form-level processing, which allows you to specify for each type of inventory transaction the type of processing control you want.

For additional information on the various profile options and the choices that you can make for each of these options, see the Oracle manual *Oracle Inventory User's Guide*.

Tip

A profile option called INV:Updatable Item Name defaults to a value of No and generally should be left with this value. However, you might have created an item record with bad data in it that can't be corrected; for example, units of measure on an item cannot be modified once entered. You want to be able to reuse this item number and rekey in the correct data. You can update the INV:Updatable Item Name profile option to Yes, change the bad part's item number to some obsolete number, and then recreate the item with correct data. Remember to change this profile option back to No so that you don't inadvertently update an item number key by mistake.

DEFINING CONTAINER TYPES

An item can be defined as a container within the Physical Item Attributes region on the define items form, for use in the Shipping module. A container can be considered to be anything that is used to hold items that are to be shipped—for example, pallets, boxes, bags, and so on. To perform this process, container types must be configured using the Container Types form, where the container type and description must be entered.

DEFINING COMMODITY CODES

Commodity codes are used to group customer items in much the same manner as category codes are used to group inventory items. The business functionality and meaning of these codes are user defined and must be entered via the Customer Item Commodity Codes window.

DEFINING AND CROSS-REFERENCING CUSTOMER ITEMS

You might want to enter customer item codes into your Oracle Inventory system so as to enable cross-referencing of your item codes with the appropriate customer item numbers. By cross-referencing customer items with your own inventory items, you might be able to achieve faster order processing and shipments by allowing customers to place orders using their own specific customer item numbers. These functions are performed via the Customer Items and Customer Item Cross Reference windows.

DEFINING NOTIFICATION LISTS

If you want to have inventory planners automatically notified of any move order approvals that relate to inventory being transferred into or out of the respective subinventories under their control, you must define a list of individuals who should receive such notifications.

DEFINING SHORTAGE PARAMETERS

Your can configure Oracle Inventory to automatically send material shortage alerts and notifications when a material shortage occurs within an inventory organization. A material shortage is deemed to have occurred when unsatisfied demand for a specific item exceeds the available quantity of any incoming supply of that same item. Oracle Inventory automatically performs checks during specific inventory receipt transactions to determine whether the material being received is more urgently needed elsewhere within the organization. If such a shortage exists, a shortage alert appears in the transaction window that gives you the option to navigate directly to the View Potential Shortages form, which identifies where demand exists for this item within the organization. Workflow-based notifications can also be directed to prespecified individuals alerting them of this condition.

Oracle Inventory always considers WIP jobs, WIP schedules, and any sales order lines that have been pick-released and detailed but not fully sourced as sources of demand. Any transaction type that uses a transaction action of one of the following can be configured as supply types that will trigger these shortage alerts:

- Receipt into stores
- Intransit receipt
- Direct organization transfer
- Assembly completion
- Negative component issue

This condition must be set up from within the Define Transaction Types window.

The Define Shortage Parameters window shown in Figure 17.7 must be used to configure how Oracle Inventory will determine what is deemed to be demand and supply, along with which functional groups are to be notified when a shortage is detected.

The items for which these shortage parameters are to be enforced must be nominated using the Define Items window, by enabling the Check Material Shortage check box from within the Inventory tab.

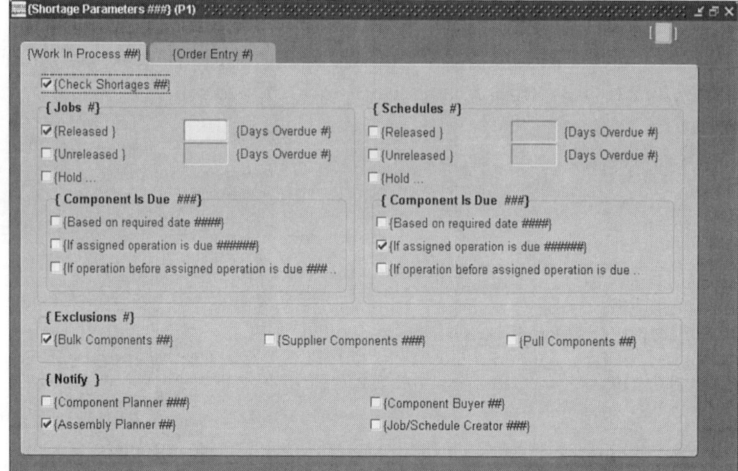

Figure 17.7 Defining material shortage parameters.

DEFINING KANBAN PULL SEQUENCES

Oracle Inventory provides support for *kanbans*, which are pull-based replenishment signals designed to initiate shorter lead times and reduced inventory levels. You can generate kanban cards for an item, a subinventory, or a locator. Functionality is provided, via a callable API, to read these kanban cards and trigger a replenishment signal from external devices such as bar code readers. These replenishment signals can be one of the following:

- **Supplier sourced**—Generates a purchase request
- **Inter-org sourced**—Results in an interorganization transfer
- **Intra-org sourced**—Triggers predefined material move orders from subinventories within the same organization
- **Production sourced**—Initiates discrete jobs, repetitive schedules, or flow schedules for the specific items

Kanbans are generally replenishable and cycle through the system from full to empty, remaining active until they are withdrawn. One-time signals, called *non-replenishable kanbans*, can be used to manage sudden spikes in demand. To replenish an item using kanbans, you must first define a pull sequence for each item. An item can have multiple pull sequences, termed a *kanban chain*, which models the replenishment network on the shop floor—for example, production line to stores and then stores to supplier. A pull sequence is used to calculate either the number of or the quantity in each kanban container at the specific kanban locations, which can be either subinventories or locations.

You must use the Pull Sequences window to view, update, and define the source of replenishment for a kanban-planned item in a kanban location. Figure 17.8 highlights the following information that must be entered in this form to successfully define a pull sequence:

- The item and subinventory for which the sequence is being defined. If either the item or subinventory is under locator control then the stock locator must be entered as well.
- The source type of the replenishment activity and the appropriate sourcing entities:
    - **Inter-Org**—The source organization warehouse and subinventory, and possibly the relevant stock locator.
    - **Intra-Org**—The source subinventory, and optionally the stock locator.
    - **Production**—The production line code.
    - **Supplier**—The supplier and supplier site. If you do not nominate these values in the pull sequence, Oracle Purchasing chooses the supplier based on the appropriate sourcing rules when it creates the purchase order or blanket release.
- In the Kanban tabbed region, you must nominate the calculation method and the relevant parameters for the chosen method:
    - **Do Not Calculate**—Enter a value for the Size and Number of Cards fields.
    - **Kanban Size**—Enter a value in the Number of Cards field and optionally a value for Minimum Order Quantity.
    - **Number of Cards**—Enter a value in the Size field and optionally a value for Minimum Order Quantity.
- In the Planning tabbed region, enter the lead time for this location. Also, optionally enter the allocation percent (percentage of independent demand for this item that is to be sourced from this sequence), lot multiplier, and the number of safety stock days.

Tip

The subinventory and locator specified in the first pull sequence for a replenishment chain must equal the subinventory and locator on either the material control region of all bills of material using this kanban location or the WIP supply location on the Organization Item Master. If the values do not match exactly, the kanban planning for the item will fail.

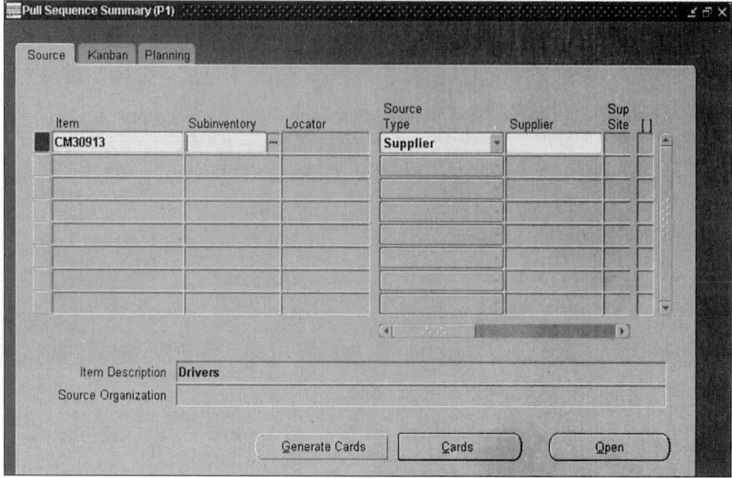

Figure 17.8
Defining Kanban pull sequences.

Loading System Items

Oracle Inventory provides for two different methods of loading inventory items. One method uses online windows described later in the section "Item Definition." This method is appropriate for loading new items and for the initial creation of inventory items when the number of items is relatively small (several thousand or less). When an organization has a large number of inventory items to load (in the tens of thousands or more), it becomes advantageous to load these items in a more automated manner.

Oracle Inventory provides for the mass creation of items through the use of an item interface. Before you use the item interface, you need to write and run a custom program that extracts item information from your legacy system, formats this information, and inserts it into the `MTL_SYSTEM_ITEM_INTERFACE` table. If you will be using item revisions, you also need to insert the revision detail into `MTL_ITEMS_REVISIONS_INTERFACE` table. You then run the item interface to import the data. The item interface validates your data and imports the new items. You need to first import your items into the item master organization before you can import your items into any specific organization or into all the children organizations. In addition to item attributes and revision details, you can also import item material cost and material overhead through the item interface.

Tip

The system items open interface can be a very resource-intensive process. To assist in optimizing the time taken to load items, you might want to split the total number of items to be loaded into manageable batch sizes and also use the set_process_id field to split the batch load across multiple processes. You can allocate a specific value to the set_process_id for differing batches and then run a multiple number of item load processes at the same time, one for each set_process_id.

PROCESSING TRANSACTIONS

Oracle Inventory provides a number of online transactions to support the tracking of inventory items. Following are some of these transactions.

ENTERING RECEIPTS AND RECEIVING TRANSACTIONS

Oracle Purchasing and Oracle Inventory both allow for the receipt processing of purchased material. You can also use the Enter Receipts window to receive items shipped in-transit between organizations. This processing includes the receipt, inspection, and delivery of incoming material. For a detailed explanation of the transactions that support the receiving process, see Chapter 16.

ENTERING RETURNS AND ADJUSTMENTS

In addition to being able to receive incoming purchased material, it is sometimes necessary to correct or adjust a receiving transaction and to return a purchased item to the vendor. The Oracle Inventory and Purchasing modules both allow for returns and adjustments of received materials. For additional details regarding these transactions, see Chapter 16.

TRANSFERRING MATERIAL BETWEEN SUBINVENTORIES

To transfer an item from one subinventory to another, or from one locator within a subinventory to another locator within the same or a different subinventory, you use the Subinventory Transfer window. This transaction also allows for material transfers between asset and expense subinventories and from tracked to nontracked subinventories. It also allows you to use a user-defined transaction type when performing the subinventory transfer.

To perform a subinventory transfer, you navigate to the Subinventory Transfer window and then enter the following information:

- **Date and time of the transaction**—The present date and time appears by default on the screen. However, depending on the setting of the profile option INV:Transaction Date Validation, you can override this with an earlier date and time.
- **Transaction type**—Specify either a predefined transaction type or one that you have defined.
- **Transaction type**—Optionally, enter the source of the transaction type and whether inventory information should be defaulted from the serial number.

Then, to enter the item to transfer, you select Transaction Lines and enter the following information, as shown in Figure 17.9:

- The inventory item to transfer or serial number if you specified default inventory information from serial number.
- The revision of the item (optional).
- Subinventories from and to which to transfer the item.

- The locators from and to which to transfer the item (optional). You must enter locators here if you specified the item or subinventory is under locator control.
- A lot number for the item (optional).
- A unit of measure. Inventory defaults the primary unit of measure for the item, but you can enter an alternate unit of measure if desired.
- The quantity of item to transfer based on the unit of measure specified.
- A reason code for the transaction and up to 240 characters of text to describe the transaction (optional).
- Lot or serial number information. Click the Lot/Serial button and enter the lot or serial number information for the item to be transferred.

After entering the information for the item to be transferred, remember to save your work.

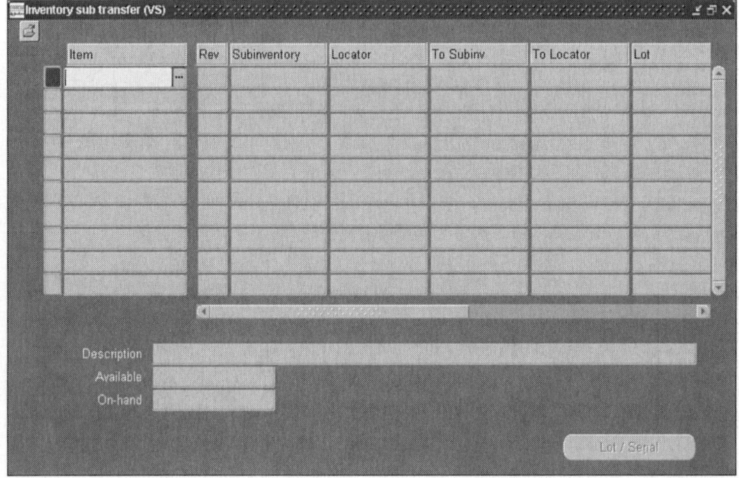

Figure 17.9
Subinventory transfer line details.

TRANSFERRING MATERIAL USING MOVE ORDERS

A Move Order is new functionality in 11*i* that represents a request for movement of material within a single organization. This request is fulfilled by the initiation of either a subinventory transfer or an account issue transaction. Move Orders enable planners and facility managers to request the movement of material within the warehouse or facility for replenishment, material storage relocations, and quality handling purposes.

Three Move Order source types are available to the user, and each type refers to the entity that created the move order:

- **Move Order Requisitions**—Manually generated requests for Move Orders, they are available for both subinventory and account transfers. You can use a workflow-based approval process to convert these requisitions into authorized move orders. If no approval process is used, the requisition becomes a move order immediately.

- **Replenishment Move Orders**—Move order requests that are generated via the varying replenishment and planning functions available within Oracle Inventory. These processes can be configured to generate move orders if the inventory is to be sourced from another inventory location within the transacting organization. The sources of replenishment move orders are Min-Max Planning, Replenishment Counting, and Kanban Replenishment. For Min-Max and Replenishment planning, you can set the subinventory source type at the Master/Org Items, Subinventory, or Item/Subinventory level. For Kanban replenishment, you set the subinventory source type at the Pull Sequence level. Replenishment move orders are generated as preapproved and ready to be transacted.
- **Pick Wave Move Orders**—Move order requests that are generated by either sales order picking or internal sales order picking. The new Shipping Execution pick release process generates move orders to bring material from its source location in inventory to a staging subinventory in the dispatch area. Pick Wave move orders are also generated as preapproved and ready to be transacted.

The basic process flow required to generate and complete move orders is as follows:

1. Create a move order for the required material. You can manually create the requisition or have it automatically generated by Pick Release, Kanban Replenishment, Min-Max, or Replenishment Counting.
2. Approve the move order if required. A seeded workflow is provided with 11*i* that manages Work Order Approvals. If approval is required then the item planner must approve the move order lines.
3. Detail the move order. Detailing is the process that uses Oracle Inventory picking rules to determine where to source the material required to fulfill the specific request lines. The detailing process fills in the move order line details with the actual transactions to be performed and allocates the material to the move order.

Tip

You should not detail a move order too soon in the business process because the detailing process for a move order creates pending transactions and removes the appropriate inventory quantities from being available. Detailing should not be done until you are ready to print a pick slip and actually move the material.

4. Print a pick slip if desired, or push the move order line details to mobile devices for transacting through the relevant Move Order APIs.
5. You are now ready to transact the move order. You can transact all the order lines at once or one detail line at a time as the items are moved. If you transact less than the requested quantity, the move order stays open until the total quantity is transacted or the move order is closed or cancelled.

For the detailed transactional steps and data entry required to complete a full move order transaction, you should refer to the *Oracle Inventory User's Guide*. Figure 17.10 provides a visual example of what the Move Order screen in 11*i* looks like.

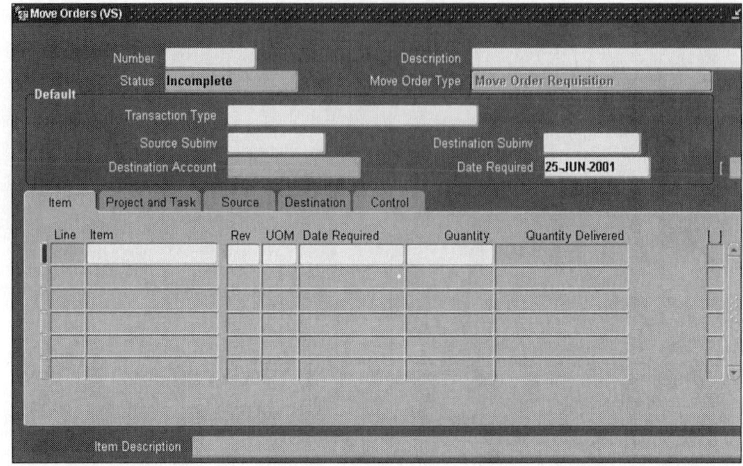

Figure 17.10
Definition form for move orders.

Transferring Material Between Organizations

To move inventory items from one organization to another, you can use either a direct or in-transit shipment. You normally use a direct transfer if the time to move items between the organizations is small. In this type of transfer, the item goes directly in a single transaction (Inter-organization Transfer window) from a subinventory in one organization to a subinventory in another organization.

If the transportation time between two organization is significant, you transfer material from a subinventory in the shipping organization to in-transit inventory using the Inter-organization Transfer window. Then when the material reaches its destination, you use the Enter Receipts window to receive the material into a subinventory in the destination organization. The Free On Board (FOB) point defined in the Shipping Networks window determines the ownership of the material while it is in-transit. If the FOB point is set to Shipment, the destination organization owns the material immediately when the shipping organization ships it and whilst it remains in-transit. If the FOB point is set to Receipt, the shipping organization owns the shipment until it is received in the destination organization.

To transfer material from your current organization to another organization or to in-transit inventory, you use the Inter-organization Transfer window and enter the following information:

- **The date of the transaction**—The present date appears by default on the screen. However, depending on the setting of the profile option INV:Transaction Date Validation, you can override this with an earlier date.

- **The organization into which to transfer the material**—The selected organization must first have been defined as a valid organization into which to receive material from your current organization (Define InterOrganization Shipping Networks).
- **The transaction type**—Specify either a predefined transaction type or one that you have defined.
- **The source of the transaction type**—You also enter whether inventory information should be defaulted from the serial number (optional).
- **Shipping information**—Such as shipment number (required if the To Org uses in-transit inventory), freight carrier, waybill number, and so on (optional).

Then, to enter the items to transfer, you select Transaction Lines and enter the following information, as shown in Figure 17.11:

- **The inventory item to transfer**—You can specify the same item more than once if you want to transfer the item to different subinventories or locators.
- **A revision that is common to the item in both organizations**—You enter this for a direct transfer, if the item is under revision control in either organization.
- **The subinventory the item is from.**
- **The subinventory the item is going to**—This is optional only for in-transit transfers.
- **The locators**—If you specified locator control for the item, enter from and to locators.
- **The lot number**—If the item is under lot control, enter lot number for the item. If there are multiple lots to transfer, complete the remaining steps and then click the Lot/Serial button to display the Lot Entry window.
- **The unit of measure**—The primary unit of measure for the item appears by default but can be replaced with any valid alternate unit of measure.
- **The quantity of the item to transfer.**
- **A reason code and up to 240 characters of text in the reference field to describe the transaction**—This is optional.

You can also enter transfer charges to assign to the To organization, freight costs and GL account numbers to charge to the From organization, and lot and serial numbers for each one of the items being transferred.

Remember to save your work to process the interorganization transfer transaction.

MAINTAINING SHIPMENTS

You can use the Maintain Shipments window to find, view, and update inventory in-transit shipping information. You can also use the Maintain Shipments window to view or cancel Advanced Shipment Notices (ASNs). Some of the information you can view or update includes the packing slip and bill of lading numbers, ship-to location, number of containers, receipt routing, and reason code.

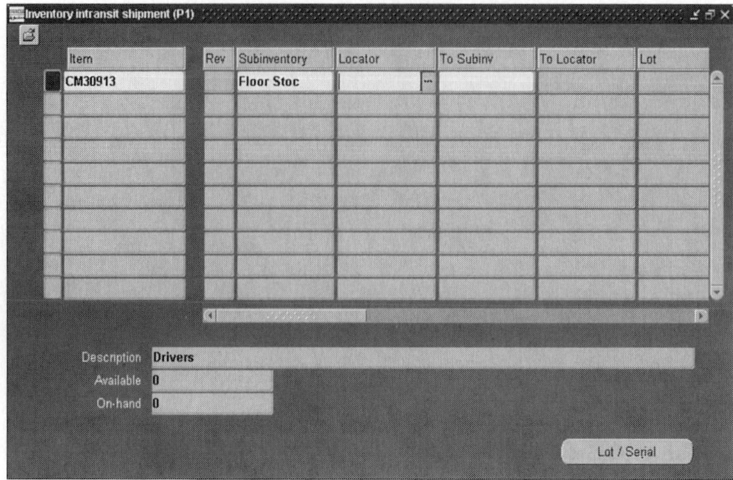

Figure 17.11 Interorganization transfer lines.

MISCELLANEOUS TRANSACTIONS

The miscellaneous transaction in Oracle Inventory is one of the most powerful and flexible transactions in the system. It allows you to receive and issue material that is not a normal purchasing/receiving, work-in-process, or order management/shipping transaction. You can use this transaction to

- Issue items and charge the material issue to a department such as marketing, charge to a special expense account such as scrap, or charge to a project.
- Make manual adjustments to the general ledger by receiving material from one GL account to inventory and then issuing the material from inventory to another GL account.
- Receive items into inventory other than from a purchase order from a supplier. For example, you might discover some items hiding in an out-of-the-way place that need to be put into a subinventory and charged to an inventory adjustment account.
- Initially load quantity on-hand information for items when you start to implement Oracle Inventory.

To perform a miscellaneous transaction, follow these steps:

1. Select the Miscellaneous Transaction screen.
2. Enter the date and time of the transaction. The present date appears by default onscreen. However, depending on the setting of the profile option INV:Transaction Date Validation, you can override this with an earlier date and time.
3. Enter a miscellaneous transaction type for the transaction. This can be a system-defined transaction type such as Miscellaneous Issue or Account Alias Issue or a user-defined transaction type.

4. You can optionally enter the following information:
    - The source of the transaction type
    - The general ledger account number to which the material is issued or received
    - An indication of whether item information should be defaulted from the serial number

Next, click the Transaction Lines button in the Miscellaneous Transaction window to enter the item information you want to issue or receive. This step opens the Transaction Lines Detail folder window, shown in Figure 17.12, where you can enter such information as

- An item number that you want to issue or receive and a revision number if required.
- The subinventory, locator, and lot number, if required.
- The unit of measure. You can replace the default.
- The quantity of the inventory item to issue or receive.

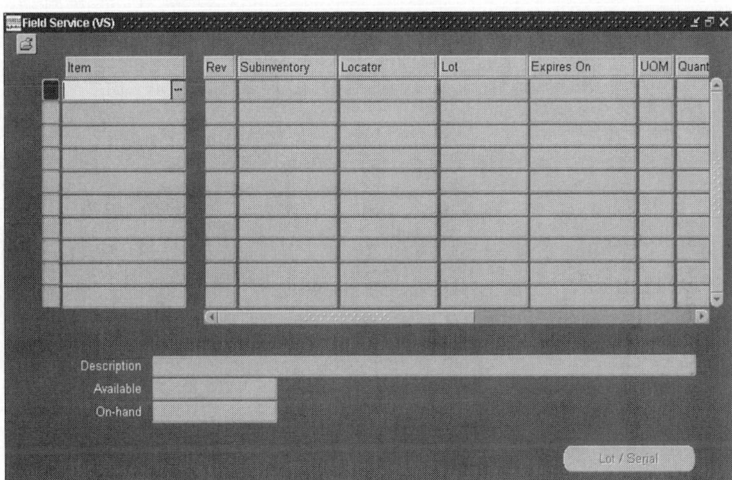

Figure 17.12 Miscellaneous transaction lines.

You can enter additional information for the transaction, such as a reason code, an additional 240 characters of free text, a different GL account for the item than entered on the header screen, and the unit cost of an item if using average costing. If you have additional items to transact against the same miscellaneous transaction criteria entered on the header screen, you can continue to enter additional lines for those items on the same screen. Remember to save your work so that Oracle Inventory will process your miscellaneous transaction.

RECEIVING AND INSPECTING CUSTOMER RETURNS

If a customer wants to return an item that has been ordered from your organization, you must first enter a return material authorization (RMA) in Oracle Order Management. The next step in the customer item return process is to determine whether the item needs to be inspected before internal delivery of the item to the appropriate subinventory can be performed. You specify this with the item attribute of RMA Inspection Status. A status of Inspection Required means that you must first perform an inspection of the returned items before you can complete the RMA Receipt transaction and put the items back into inventory. Even if you have specified Inspection not required, you can optionally perform the inspection step.

To perform the inspection process on a customer return, you must first find the appropriate transaction line via the Receiving Transactions window (under the Customer tab) and then click the Inspect button. To find the relevant line, you can enter a number of differing search criteria, including the RMA number and line. To process the inspection, you must specify whether you are accepting or rejecting the items being transacted, the quantity and unit of measure of the item, a quality and reason code, along with the inspection date and any comments you want to record. Accept means you have successfully inspected the items, and the next step to perform is the RMA Delivery transaction to put the items into inventory. Reject means you are either returning the items to the customer or scrapping the items entirely. For those items you are rejecting with Return, you then need to cancel the return line in Oracle Order Management.

After the successful inspection of the customer return, if it is required, your next step is to perform an RMA Delivery transaction. You need to provide the following information: the RMA number, the line item of the RMA, the quantity of the item to be received, and the subinventory into which to receive the material. You can also let the unit of measure of the item being returned default from the RMA, or you can override it. Optionally, you might want to override the transaction date or enter a reason code for this transaction under the Details tab in this window.

RETURNING ITEMS TO CUSTOMER

If you have the requirement to return repaired or substituted items to your customer after the customer has sent them to you, you would accomplish this within the Returns transaction window. Before you can return items to a customer, you must first receive the items with the RMA Receipt transaction described previously. The information required to perform the RMA Return transaction is the date and time of the transaction (which can default from the system), RMA number for the item to be returned, the inventory item number, the line item number of the RMA, the subinventory from which to return the item, a unit of measure (which will default from the RMA and can be overridden), and the quantity of the item to return. You might also have to specify the locator for the subinventory and the lot or serial numbers of the items being returned. You can also optionally enter a reason for this transaction.

PURGING TRANSACTIONS

Oracle Inventory provides for the capability to purge transaction history and associated accounting information.

Note

You should use this transaction purge capability with a great deal of caution because once the information is removed, you can no longer query or report on this information. For example, the accrual reconciliation report, or transaction register can no longer retrieve purged transaction information and report on it.

To purge transactions, you specify Transaction Purge in the Name field of the Purge Transactions or All Reports window and then specify a name for the purge and a purge through date. The date specified must be in a closed period.

RESERVING INVENTORY

You can set aside inventory of an item to reserve it for an account, an account alias, or a user-defined source such as a particular type of customer order. Reservations prevent the issue of the inventory that is set aside to anything other than that reservation's source type. To reserve an item, navigate to the Item Reservation window. When the Find Reservations window appears, click New and enter the following information:

- In the Default Demand Source block, select the appropriate source type for the reservation:
    - **Sales Order**—Enter a sales order number and line number that identifies the quantity to reserve.
    - **Inventory**—Enter the source against which you want to make the reservation.
    - **Account**—Enter the organization code and account number for which the reservation relates.
    - **Account Alias**—Enter the organization code and account number for which the reservation relates.
- In the Demand tabbed region, shown in Figure 17.13, enter the following:
    - The organization code for the organization with demand.
    - Item number for the item in demand.
    - The Demand source, if different from the default.
    - A user-defined name to reference the reservation.
    - The header number associated with the demand source—in other words, the sales order number.
    - The line number that identifies the item quantity to reserve—in other words, the sales order line.

    - The need by date.
    - The unit of measure.
    - The reservation quantity. This must be greater than 0 and less than or equal to the available quantity.
- In the Supply tabbed region enter the following:
    - The Supply source type for the item
    - A user-defined name to reference the reservation
    - The applicable revision for the item, if revision tracking is enabled
    - The lot number of the item to reserve, if lot control is enabled for the item
    - The subinventory from which to reserve the item
    - The locator from which to reserve the item if the item is under locator control

Save your work to reserve the specified quantity of inventory of the item.

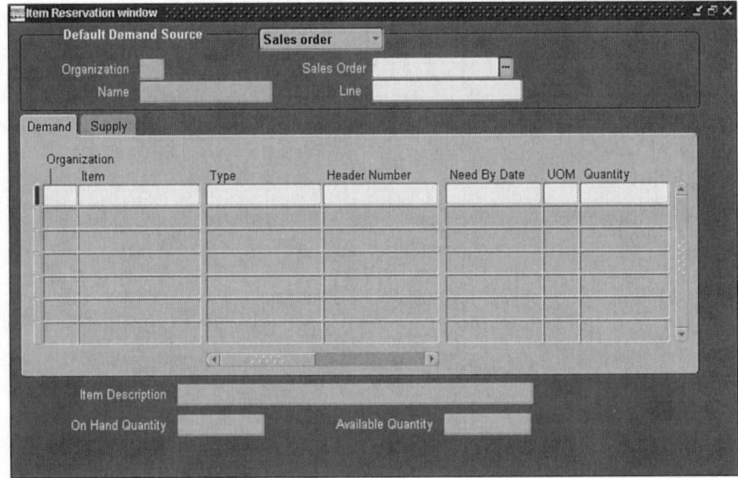

Figure 17.13 Entering demand detail for item reservations.

Note

Be cautious in reserving inventory for a specific requirement that is far into the future. This could prevent you from issuing the reserved material for a different near-in requirement even though in the future, a supply of inventory might arrive and meet the inventory needs of your far-out requirement.

ENTERING STATISTICS

Oracle Inventory features a capability to gather, review, and report statistical data associated with material movements. This capability has been primarily developed to assist in the Intrastat reporting requirements of the European Union. If you have the requirement to meet these reporting requirements, you should consult the *Oracle Inventory User's Guide* for additional detailed information regarding this capability.

Item Definition

The steps to defining an item are as follows:

1. Key in the item key or part number and the item description.
2. Use templates or existing items (copy items) to define items in the master organization.
3. Enter values for item attributes that were not set by templates or copying items.
4. Enter values for item categories and catalogs.
5. Enable the item in the organizations where you will be using the item.
6. Update organization-level item attributes that are different for each one of the organizations; examples are the lead time of the item or planner code or WIP supply subinventory.

To define an inventory item, you always must enter at least two pieces of information: the item key or part number and the item description. All of the other item information can default, such as the unit of measure and item status with the attributes associated with the item status. In addition, you can individually specify each one of the item attributes. You don't need to specify any of the item attributes that don't apply to the item.

Oracle Inventory has an extensive list of item attributes to help you describe and control how your items are used. For ease in data entry, these item attributes are separated into application areas. Table 17.2 lists item attributes by application area. The eight key controlling item attributes called status control attributes appear in bold.

Table 17.2 Attributes for an Inventory Item

Application Area	Item Attribute
Bill of Materials	Base Model
Bill of Materials	**BOM Allowed**
Bill of Materials	BOM Item Type
Bill of Materials	Engineering Date
Bill of Materials	Effectivity Control
Costing	Cost of Goods Sold Account
Costing	Costing Enabled
Costing	Include in Rollup
Costing	Inventory Asset Value
Costing	Standard Lot Size
General Planning	Carrying Cost Percent
General Planning	Fixed Days Supply

TABLE 17.2 CONTINUED

Application Area	Item Attribute
General Planning	Fixed Lot Size Multiplier
General Planning	Fixed Order Quantity
General Planning	Inventory Planning Method
General Planning	Make or Buy
General Planning	Maximum Order Quantity
General Planning	Min-Max Maximum Quantity
General Planning	Min-Max Minimum Quantity
General Planning	Minimum Order Quantity
General Planning	Order Cost
General Planning	Planner
General Planning	Source Type (Replenishment)
General Planning	Safety Stock Method
General Planning	Safety Stock Bucket Days
General Planning	Safety Stock Percent
General Planning	Source Organization
General Planning	Source Subinventory
Inventory	Cycle Count Enabled
Inventory	Inventory Item
Inventory	Locator Control
Inventory	Lot Control
Inventory	Lot Expiration (Shelf Life)
Inventory	Neg Measurement Error
Inventory	Pos Measurement Error
Inventory	Reservable
Inventory	Restrict Locators
Inventory	Restrict Subinventories
Inventory	Revision Control
Inventory	Serial Generation
Inventory	Shelf Life Days
Inventory	Starting Lot Number
Inventory	Starting Lot Prefix
Inventory	Starting Serial Number

TABLE 17.2 CONTINUED

Application Area	**Item Attribute**
Inventory	Starting Serial Prefix
Inventory	**Stockable**
Inventory	**Transactable**
Inventory	Check Material Shortage
Invoicing	Accounting Rule
Invoicing	**Invoice Enabled**
Invoicing	Invoiceable Item
Invoicing	Invoicing Rule
Invoicing	Payment Terms
Invoicing	Sales Account
Invoicing	Tax Code
Lead Times	Cum Manufacturing Lead Time
Lead Times	Cumulative Total Lead Time
Lead Times	Fixed Lead Time
Lead Times	Lead Time Lot Size
Lead Times	Postprocessing Lead Time
Lead Times	Preprocessing Lead Time
Lead Times	Processing Lead Time
Lead Times	Variable Lead Time
Main	Conversions
Main	Descriptive Flexfield
Main	Item Description
Main	Item Status
Main	Primary Unit of Measure
Main	User Item Type
MPS/MRP Planning	Acceptable Early Days
MPS/MRP Planning	Acceptable Rate Decrease
MPS/MRP Planning	Acceptable Rate Increase
MPS/MRP Planning	Calculate ATP
MPS/MRP Planning	Demand Time Fence
MPS/MRP Planning	Demand Time Fence Days
MPS/MRP Planning	Forecast Control

Table 17.2 Continued

Application Area	Item Attribute
MPS/MRP Planning	MRP Planning Method
MPS/MRP Planning	Overrun Percentage
MPS/MRP Planning	Pegging
MPS/MRP Planning	Planning Exception Set
MPS/MRP Planning	Planning Time Fence
MPS/MRP Planning	Planning Time Fence Days
MPS/MRP Planning	Reduce MPS
MPS/MRP Planning	Release Time Fence
MPS/MRP Planning	Release Time Fence Days
MPS/MRP Planning	Repetitive Planning
MPS/MRP Planning	Rounding Control
MPS/MRP Planning	Shrinkage Rate
Order Management	Assemble to Order
Order Management	ATP Components
Order Management	ATP Rule
Order Management	Check ATP
Order Management	Customer Ordered Item
Order Management	**Customer Orders Enabled**
Order Management	Default Shipping Organization
Order Management	Internal Ordered Item
Order Management	**Internal Orders Enabled**
Order Management	OE Transactable
Order Management	Over Return Tolerance
Order Management	Over Shipment Tolerance
Order Management	Pick Components
Order Management	Picking Rule
Order Management	Returnable
Order Management	RMA Inspection Required
Order Management	Ship Model Complete
Order Management	Shippable Item
Order Management	Under Return Tolerance
Order Management	Under Shipment Tolerance

TABLE 17.2 CONTINUED

Application Area	Item Attribute
Physical Attributes	Container
Physical Attributes	Container Type
Physical Attributes	Internal Volume
Physical Attributes	Max Load Weight
Physical Attributes	Min Fill Percentage
Physical Attributes	Unit Volume
Physical Attributes	Unit Weight
Physical Attributes	Vehicle
Physical Attributes	Volume Unit of Measure
Physical Attributes	Weight Unit of Measure
Purchasing	Allow Description Update
Purchasing	Asset Category
Purchasing	Default Buyer
Purchasing	Encumbrance Account
Purchasing	Expense Account
Purchasing	Hazard Class
Purchasing	Invoice Close Tolerance
Purchasing	List Price
Purchasing	Market Price
Purchasing	Outside Processing Item
Purchasing	Outside Processing Unit Type
Purchasing	Price Tolerance
Purchasing	**Purchasable**
Purchasing	Purchased Item
Purchasing	Receipt Required (3 Way Inv.)
Purchasing	Inspection Rqd. (4 Way Inv.)
Purchasing	Receipt Close Tolerance
Purchasing	RFQ Required
Purchasing	Rounding Factor
Purchasing	Taxable Item
Purchasing	UN Number
Purchasing	Unit of Issue

TABLE 17.2 CONTINUED

Application Area	Item Attribute
Purchasing	Use Approved Supplier
Receiving	Allow Express Transactions
Receiving	Allow Substitute Receipts
Receiving	Allow Unordered Receipts
Receiving	Receipt Days Early
Receiving	Receipt Days Late
Receiving	Enforce Ship-To Location
Receiving	Over Receipt Qty Action
Receiving	Over Receipt Qty Tolerance
Receiving	Receipt Date Action
Receiving	Receipt Routing
Service	Serviceable Product
Service	Support Service
Service	Warranty
Service	Coverage
Service	Service Duration
Service	Billing Type
Service	Service Starting Delay
Work In Process	**Build in WIP**
Work In Process	WIP Supply Locator
Work In Process	WIP Supply Subinventory
Work In Process	WIP Supply Type
Work In Process	Overcompletion Tolerance Type
Work In Process	Overcompletion Tolerance Value

You can set all eight of the status control attributes with a user-defined item status. See the section "Defining Statuses" earlier in this chapter for additional detail regarding defining item status control.

To assist in the item definition process, you can copy existing items. You can also use predefined or custom templates that attach a whole list of attributes to your items rather than require you to enter each item attribute individually.

Note

When you copy an item, Oracle does not copy all of the data associated with the item. Categories, organization assignments, catalog group information, and costs are not copied from one item to another.

Defining Lot and Serial Number Information

You can assign either lot or serial number information to your inventory items. For those items you have specified that you want to be under lot control, when you enter receipt or issue transactions, you need to specify the lot control information for those items so that the system will assist you in tracking the lots associated with the items. Likewise, if you have specified serial number control for any of your items, you need to specify the serial numbers for those items when you transact those items into and out of inventory.

You can specify for each of your inventory items that you want the item to be lot-controlled, to be serial-number–controlled, or to have no lot- or serial-number–control. When you use Oracle Work In Process, you cannot specify that an item be both lot-controlled and serial-number–controlled.

For an item to be defined as lot-controlled, there can be no on-hand quantity of the item. When you specify that you want an item to be lot-controlled, you can also specify a starting lot prefix to be used when you define a lot number for the item. You can also specify a starting lot-number suffix. Afterwards, this number will be incremented for each succeeding lot. For every item that you specify that you would like to be lot-controlled, you also need to specify the type of lot-expiration (shelf-life) control: for no shelf-life control, "No control"; for a specific number of days for all lots of this item, "Shelf-life days"; and to specify an expiration date as you receive each lot, "User-defined." For items with shelf-life days control you need to specify the number of days each lot is to be active.

For an item that you want to be serial-number–controlled, you need to specify whether the serial numbers for the item will be created and assigned when you receive the item ("At inventory receipt"), created and assigned when you ship the item ("At sales order issue"), or assigned predefined serial numbers when you receive the item ("Predefined"). For all the serial numbers that you define, you can specify a starting alpha prefix and a starting serial-number suffix to be used when generating the serial numbers for the item.

Defining Item and Subinventory Information

You use the item/subinventory relationship to specify a number of different pieces of information about the item and the subinventory. You can restrict an inventory item to a list of subinventories with the Restrict Subinventories attribute on the item. Then you can assign a list of subinventories to an item. You can specify valid subinventories for zero quantity cycle counts for an item. You can also specify items for an ABC analysis at the subinventory level.

If you want to perform min-max planning and replenishment processing for an item at the subinventory level rather than the organization level, you can specify planning information and locators for the item in its assigned subinventories.

To specify item/subinventory relationship information, you can specify the item on the Master Items or Organization Items Summary window, then select Item Subinventories from the Tools menu, and then enter the subinventories for the item.

Alternatively, you can specify the subinventory on the Subinventories Summary window and then click the Item/Subinventory button to enter the items associated with this subinventory on the Item Subinventories window. For each of the item/subinventory relationships specified, you can also specify whether you would like to min-max plan this item in this subinventory and the min and max quantities for the item. You can also specify order modifiers to be used for the item in this subinventory including minimum order or repetitive rate, maximum order or repetitive rate, and fixed lot multiple quantity or repetitive rate. You can enter lead-time information for the item in the subinventory. You can also specify sourcing information for the item in the subinventory. You specify Supplier if you want to fill requisition requests for this item in this subinventory from a supplier, specify Inventory and the organization if you want to fill requests by internal requisitions from existing inventory, or alternatively specify subinventory to fulfill requests for this item from the specified subinventory via move orders.

If you want to also restrict an item to specific locators, you specify the Restrict Locators attribute on the item, and you enter the locators to which to assign the item in the subinventory in the Locators block on the Item Subinventory window, as shown in Figure 17.14.

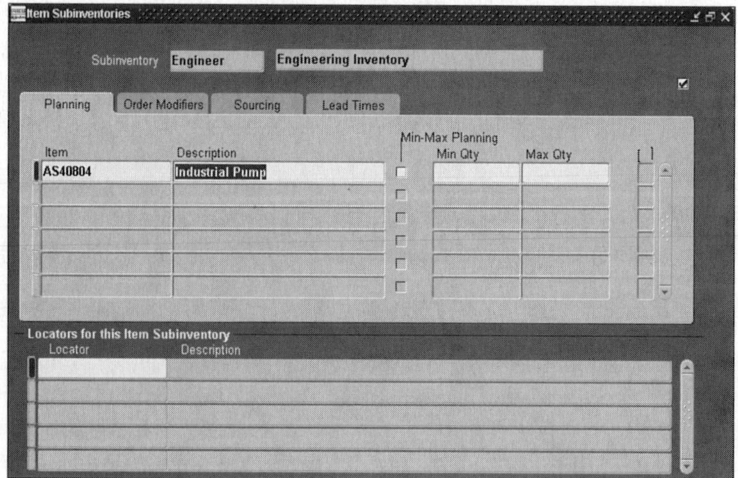

Figure 17.14
Restricting items to specific subinventory and locators.

DEFINING ITEM RELATIONSHIPS, CROSS-REFERENCES, AND MANUFACTURER PART NUMBERS

Oracle Inventory allows you to establish several different ways to report and inquire on an item. You can define relationships for an item, you can establish cross-references for an item, and you can specify manufacturer part numbers for an item.

You can establish for any item rules that relate it to any other item. You do this by using the Item Relationships window and specifying the item that is the From part of the relationship and a different item that is the To part of the relationship. In addition, you specify the type of relationship: Related just means the two parts are related in a nonspecific way, and Substitute means one item is a substitute for the other. You also indicate whether the relationship is Reciprocal. A substitute relationship that is reciprocal means that you can use the From item as a substitute for the To item, and vice versa. Figure 17.15 shows the layout of the Item Relationships form.

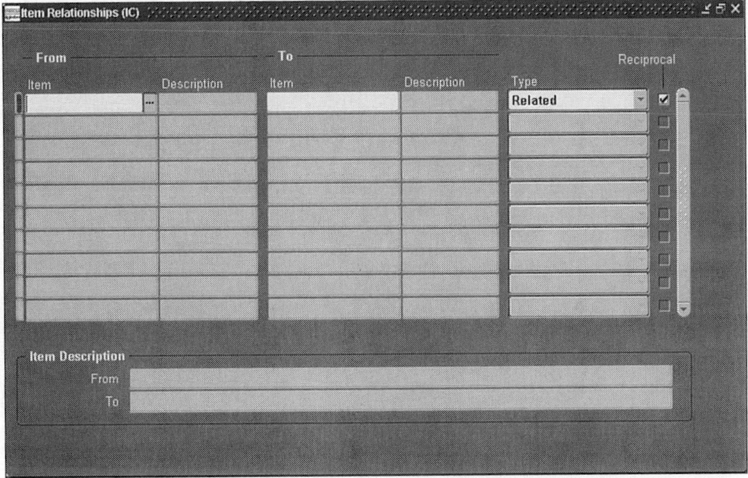

Figure 17.15 Establishing item relationships.

Note

Item relationships can normally only be used for inquiry and reporting purposes. However, in Oracle Purchasing, once you define a substitute item for an item, you can receive the substitute item in place of the originally ordered item. You need to make sure that the ordered item and the substitute item share the same base unit of measure.

To establish a cross-reference for an item, you must first define the cross-reference types you want to use, such as Old Part Number or Blue Print Number as defined in the section "Defining Cross-Reference Types" earlier in this chapter. You can then assign these cross-references to items by using the Cross-References Types screen or select Cross References from the Tools menu when you are using the Master Items Summary screen. After you select the item and the cross-reference type, you need to indicate whether this cross-reference will apply to all organizations or just to a specific organization. You then enter the cross-reference value. For example, this is the actual value for the Old Part Number for the item.

In addition to cross-references and item relationships, you can also specify manufacturer part numbers for an item. You can use the manufacturer part number for reporting purposes and for searching for an item. You do this first by defining the manufacturers in the Manufacturers window. Then, you enter the manufacturer part number and the item. You can assign the same item to multiple manufacturer part numbers.

Defining Item Transaction Default Subinventories and Locators

You can define a default shipping, receiving, and move order receipt subinventory and locator for an item. Oracle Order Management displays the default shipping information when you ship the item. Oracle Purchasing and Inventory display the default receiving information when you receive the item. Oracle Inventory displays the default move order receipt information when you are transacting a move order for this item. You use the Item Transaction Defaults screen shown in Figure 17.16 to specify the item, the subinventory, and whether this is to be the default shipping, receiving, or move order receipt subinventory. If you are using locators for the item, on the same Transaction Defaults screen in the Locators alternative region, you can also specify a default locator to be used in addition to the subinventory.

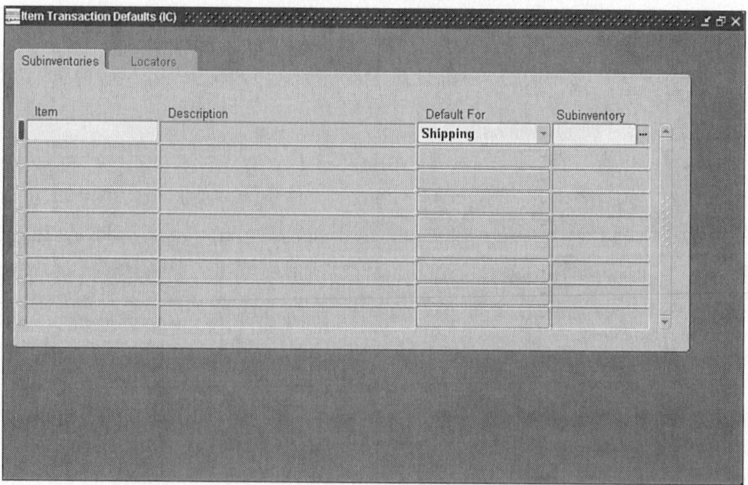

Figure 17.16 Defaulting subinventories and locators.

ADDITIONAL APPLICATION FUNCTIONS

The primary purpose of this chapter has been to assist in the configuring of the Oracle Inventory application by describing how to perform the setup of the Oracle Inventory application. In addition, a few of the basic inventory transactions have been described. There are a number of additional application functions included in the Oracle Inventory application module. Following are some of these additional application functions and a short description of these functions:

- **Item inquiry**—There are a number of online inquiry functions provided for items including on-hand inventory, lot and serial numbers, available-to-promise inventory, item cost, item attributes, and status. The supply and demand for an item can be viewed online. Searches for items can be performed by item number, description, catalog, category, status, and item cross-references.
- **Inventory transaction inquiry**—Inventory transactions can be reviewed online. The transactions can be viewed in detail or summarized by date, item, subinventory, locator, category, or transaction type.
- **Planning and replenishment**—Support is provided for planning of inventory items using min-max, reorder point, and kanban planning. When inventory planned items get below a minimum or reorder point, an inventory planning function generates purchase requisitions for purchased items and jobs for manufactured items. Support is also provided to calculate safety stocks and to develop forecasts. Also provided is a means to support replenishment of items when doing manual replenishment counts from a non-tracked subinventory. Also available is the kanban system of pull-based replenishment. Support is provided to read kanban cards and trigger a replenishment signal.
- **Counting**—There are a number of transactions and reports provided to support the counting of inventory items. The functions of taking a physical inventory and cycle counting are both supported. ABC analysis can be performed to determine the high-volume items so that faster-moving items can be counted more frequently than slower-moving items.
- **Interface to Accounting**—All the inventory transactions generate general ledger accounting transactions. There is support provided to transfer summary or detailed inventory transactions for a given period to the General Ledger.
- **Reports**—Inventory reports are included in the areas of transactions, items, costing, ABC analysis, counting, planning, forecasting, receiving, safety stock, and application setups.

SUMMARY

The Oracle Inventory application helps you to define and track the inventory items for your organization. The application can be used to perform these tasks for a simple, one-subinventory warehouse. Oracle Inventory can also be used as the base for a complex, multi-organizational, material planning and supply system fully integrated with a complete financial accounting system. To efficiently and accurately perform these tasks, it is necessary to customize the application to fit your requirements. This customization process is called application setup. The purpose of this chapter has been to assist the application implementation team in the application setup process. Descriptions of some of the basic Inventory transactions have also been provided.

A reminder for a successful implementation of Oracle Inventory is to start with the simplest approach whenever possible, educate and train the users, and test rigorously. When these suggestions are used along with good management support and a dedicated implementation team, success can almost be assured.

CHAPTER 18

Using Oracle Order Management

In this chapter

INTRODUCTION

Oracle Order Management (OM) is a group of products that provide the facility to capture sales orders, compute the price of items on order line, complete the order by shipping the items, and passing the information to an accounts receivable system. The core products in this group include

- Order Management
- Shipping Execution (SE)
- Basic Pricing

Additional products that integrate with OM are Oracle Advanced Pricing, Oracle Configurator, Oracle Accounts Receivable, and Oracle Advanced Planning and Scheduling.

RELATIONSHIP TO OTHER APPLICATIONS

Oracle Order Management provides features that allow the user to set up the application to reflect an organization's order fulfillment business practices and manage the order capture and shipment of its products (see Figure 18.1). Other applications that support Oracle Order Management are

- Oracle Inventory
- Oracle Accounts Receivable
- Oracle Work In Process
- Oracle Purchasing
- Customer Relationship Management Suite
- External Systems

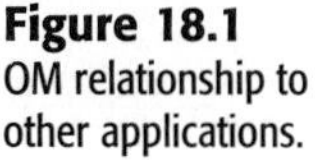

Figure 18.1
OM relationship to other applications.

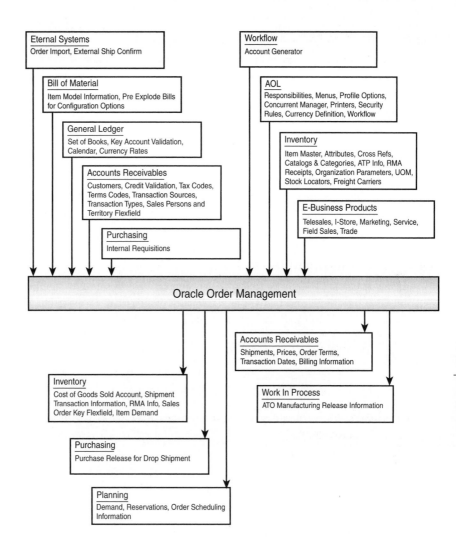

DISCOVERING NEW FEATURES IN RELEASE 11*i*

Oracle Order Management is a new product that replaces the Oracle Order Entry and Shipping product. It now has features that enable the application to function in the e-business environment. While it preserves the functionality of the Order Entry/Shipping module, the new features in OM significantly enhance its ability to include Internet selling and order fulfillment. This section highlights some of the new features introduced in Release 11*i*.

ORDER MANAGEMENT AS A FULFILLMENT ENGINE

The fulfillment engine facility enables you to define as many order types as needed by your business, with each order type having its unique set of processing steps within its own unique sequence. This facility enables you to process business-to-consumer order transactions, which normally require credit card processing with payment approval from the credit card issuer. It also facilitates business-to-business transactions, which usually require credit checks to be made against the organization's receivables system.

ORDER CAPTURE FROM ANY SOURCE

This facility enables you to integrate order management functionality with Oracle Telesales, Oracle iStore, Oracle Marketing, Oracle Service, Oracle Field Sales, and Oracle Trade Promotion.

ORDER IMPORT ENHANCEMENTS

New edits and validation and error- handling capabilities have been added to Order Import. Online viewing of orders that did not import due to errors is available. You can review and fix those errors using the same forms and then re-import the orders. Order Import can be run in validation-only mode without importing the data. This allows for viewing the data and correcting problems in the interface table before the base Order Management tables are updated. Certain enhancements have been made in response to requests by the EDI trading community. Now, if there are differences in the system-calculated price and the price provided by the user on an inbound order (850/ORDERS), Order Import will return a warning message. If there are differences in the system-generated payment terms and the payment terms provided by the user, Order Import will return a warning message.

ITEM CROSS-REFERENCE

This facility enables customers to order in their internal, customer-specific item numbers, or your internal item numbers. The following commonly used generic identifiers are available:

- UPC (Universal Product Code)
- EAN (European Article Number)
- JAN (Japanese Article Number)
- CLEI (Common Language Equipment Identifier)
- ISBN (International Standard Book Number)

Decimal Quantity Handling

Standard items order quantities can be specified as decimal quantities. At item setup you can specify whether decimal quantities are allowed for an item.

Over/Under Shipment

You can now define tolerances for both over- and under-shipments. This enables you to avoid the work of adjusting small quantity differences that can be acceptable to your customer.

Returns Enhancements

The enhanced Returns functionality enables users to mix returns and shipments on the same order. Acknowledgment documents can now be printed. The Depot Repair process enables you to track goods returned for repair.

Order Changes

By using role-based Processing Constraints you can control which users have permission to make changes. Specific users, through responsibilities, can be assigned authority to make updates, cancellations, and deletions of orders. There is functionality to inform an authorized user when a user with less authority attempts to make an unauthorized change.

Order Cancellations

You now have the ability to cancel a sales order line with or without a reason code entry after the order has been booked. The Change Order History function enables you to record and track changes in order quantity for historical and analytical purposes after the order is booked. Multiline selection during order line cancellation is now permitted. Now when you cancel lines even after Pick Release, Oracle Shipping Execution will have visibility to the changed quantities. Order Import too has been enhanced to process cancellation requests.

Order Copy

The following enhancements have been incorporated in Order Copy:

- Copy orders at original prices
- Copy directly from sales forms
- Copy lines from orders to returns
- Access newly copied orders
- Append lines to existing orders
- Copy selected lines only to an order
- Reprice a copied order

CREDIT CHECKING

Enhancements in credit checking functionality enable you to specify a maximum number of days due for invoices for determining and imposing credit holds. Also, tax is now included as part of the balance in the credit exposure calculation. Multiple bill-to locations can be assigned to the same order and in this case the bill-to credit limits will be separately evaluated for the value of the order assigned to each bill-to location.

HOLDS AND RELEASES

Holds and releases can now be applied directly from the Sales Order form or through the new Order Summary window. The system can also be requested to send FYI notifications to specific users when a hold is applied.

ERROR MESSAGE HANDLING WINDOW

Error messages can be viewed from processes such as online mass changes, copying orders, and other concurrent programs using the standardized Message window. The messages can be saved for viewing later or you can discard the messages. While you are viewing the messages, you can also send text message notification to other users.

FREIGHT AND SPECIAL CHARGES

A set of APIs has been provided in Oracle Order Management that can capture, store, update, and view costs associated with a shipment, order, container, or delivery. Customer written program logic can be attached to these APIs to allow these costs to be converted to charges that are added to the order. You then have the option to either itemize or summarize such charges on your orders. Customer charges will be passed to Oracle Accounts Receivable for invoicing.

INVOICING

Oracle Order Management passes detailed discount and promotional information to Oracle Accounts Receivable. Freight and other information will also be passed to receivables. Now you have the option to pass a customer item description from OM to Oracle Accounts Receivable for invoice printing for item records where the description is available. You now have the ability to select whether to invoice the quantity ordered or quantity shipped where an over-shipment has occurred.

ORDER NUMBERING

Oracle Order management provides much needed flexibility for order numbering that is frequently required by users. Some of the new capabilities included are

- Users can select separate number sequence by order type. The system will validate that the combination of order type and order number is unique.
- Enables users to specify that a set of order numbers should be gapless, in order to meet requirements in certain legal jurisdictions. Gapless number sequenced orders cannot be deleted after entry; however, they can be cancelled.

DEFAULTING

The new defaulting framework in Oracle Order Management has the capability for defaulting of more order and line attributes from various sources than was possible in the Order Entry module. You can base the default value for a field on other fields, such as values previously entered for the order, the customer, or the order type.

LINE SETS

Oracle Order Management has added new functionality to enable you to group order lines into arrival line sets. When order lines are grouped in this manner, all order lines in the set are scheduled so that they can be delivered to the same destination at the same time.

ORDER WORKBENCH ENHANCEMENTS

The Order Organizer has been given a tree structure and also contains order summary information. You can also define your own folders in the Order Organizer, Order Pad, and Find windows.

ENHANCED PLANNING AND RESERVATION LOGIC

In Oracle Order Management users now have the option to check Available-to-Promise (ATP) or display availability as soon as they enter a line. They can also choose to reserve the inventory at the time of order entry, if the request date is within a user-specified time frame. If, however, the request date is farther in the future, an automatic Workflow process performs the reservation as the requested ship date moves within the Allocation window.

CONFIGURING THE APPLICATION

The following section of this chapter describes the setup tasks and sequences required to configure the OM application. The tasks should be performed in the sequence listed. The module requires extensive setups for it to be configured accurately to function as advertised. The setup process involves setting up other related applications, which include Oracle General Ledger, Oracle Receivables, and Oracle Inventory. Some of the setup steps are optional, depending on whether you have the related applications installed and whether you use the related features. As an example, if your business requires you to provide drop shipment capability, you will also need to set up Oracle Purchasing. If your business supplies models and kits, you must set up Oracle Bill of Material and Oracle Selling Point Configurator.

RESOLVING CRITICAL SETUP ISSUES

Before delving into setting up Oracle Order Management, several critical items must be addressed. First, the Set of Books and Accounting structure must be determined. Second, the Organizations from which the Customer can order products must be set up. Finally, before a customer can order any items, they must be set up in the Inventory application.

SETUP TASKS

Table 18.1 shows the tasks required to set up the OM Application in the order that they should be performed. Try not to skip tasks or perform them out of sequence because many tasks use predecessor tasks for data validation and you might receive error messages.

TABLE 18.1 OM SETUP TASKS

Setup Task Name	Required?
Define Set of Books	Required with defaults
Define Flexfields	Required with defaults
Multiple Organization	Optional
Inventory Organizations	Required
Profile Options	Required
Parameters	Required
Invoicing	Required with defaults
Salespersons	Required
Tax	Required
Quick Codes	Required with defaults
Workflow	Required
Document Sequence	Required
Order Import Sources	Optional
Units of Measure	Required
Item Information	Required
Items	Required
Configurations	Optional
Pricing Formulas	Required with defaults
Price Lists	Required
Customer Class	Required with defaults
Customers	Required
Item Cross-Reference	Optional
Sourcing	Optional
Agreements	Required with defaults
Transaction Types	Required
Cost of Goods Sold (COGS)	Required with defaults
Modifier and Freight Charges	Required with defaults

TABLE 18.1 CONTINUED

Setup Task Name	Required?
Processing Constraints	Required with defaults
Defaulting Rules	Required with defaults
Credit Checking	Optional
Holds	Optional
Attachments	Optional
Shipping Setup	Required

UNDERSTANDING EACH SETUP TASK

Setup tasks fall into three categories. First, there are those setup tasks that the Oracle system requires for the application to operate. In the Oracle Order Management application, you must have Items defined before you can place orders. Additionally, you must have Customers defined before you can ship any items. Second, there are those tasks that, although required, contain certain default values that you can allow the system to default in. Finally, there are steps that are completely optional, based on your particular implementation needs. The following sections describe each setup task in detail.

DEFINING A SET OF BOOKS

Before Oracle Order Management can be implemented, you must set up at least one Set of Books. The Set of Books defines for the Order Management application, the Chart of Accounts, the Accounting Calendar, the Functional Currency, and the Accounting Flexfield Structure. When defining the Set of Books, use the setup process described in Chapter 11, "Using Oracle General Ledger."

DEFINING KEY FLEXFIELDS

Oracle Applications share Key Flexfields. Key Flexfields are a major feature of the Oracle Applications as a whole and provide a mechanism for the Oracle Applications to provide you a flexible way to define how the Oracle Applications should represent objects such as accounting codes and part numbers. Key Flexfields can be set up from any application. The Key Flexfields are usually established during the setup of Financial and Manufacturing modules implementation. Key Flexfields in General Ledger, Inventory, and Accounts Receivable should be set up before setting up Order Management.

DEFINING THE STOCK LOCATORS FLEXFIELD

The Stock Locators Flexfield is used to capture more specific stock location information about your inventory such as aisle, row, and bin item information. This Flexfield is set up in the Inventory application implementation. See Chapter 17, "Using Oracle Inventory," for a detailed description of this process.

DEFINING THE SALES ORDER FLEXFIELD

The Sales Order Flexfield is set up in the Inventory application and is used by the Order Management interfaces to Inventory. This Flexfield must be set up prior to placing demand or making reservations in Order Management. See Chapter 17 for a detailed description of this process.

DEFINING THE ITEM FLEXFIELD

The System Items Flexfield is required for the transacting and reporting of item information. This Flexfield is defined during the Inventory application implementation. See Chapter 17 for a detailed description of this process.

DEFINING THE TERRITORY FLEXFIELD

The Territory Flexfield is owned by the Accounts Receivable application and is an optional step in the Accounts Receivable implementation. The Territory Flexfield is used in reporting and is only required if you have salespersons, invoicing, or customer purposes business requirements. See Chapter 13, "Using Oracle Receivables," for a detailed description of this process.

DEFINING THE SALES TAX LOCATION FLEXFIELD

The Sales Tax Location Flexfield is owned by the Accounts Receivable application and is an optional step in the Accounts Receivable implementation. The Sales Tax Location Flexfield is used in establishing the sales tax for your customers based on their shipping address. See Chapter 13 for a detailed description of this process.

DEFINING ITEM CATEGORIES FLEXFIELD

The Item Categories Flexfield is owned by the Inventory application and is a required setup in the Inventory implementation. See Chapter 17 for a detailed description of this process.

DEFINING ITEM CATALOG GROUP FLEXFIELD

The Item Catalog Group Flexfield is owned by the Inventory application and is a required setup with defaults in the Inventory implementation. See Chapter 17 for a detailed description of this process.

DEFINING INVENTORY ORGANIZATIONS, ORGANIZATION PARAMETERS, SUBINVENTORIES, AND PICKING RULES

Inventory Organizations, Organization Parameters, Subinventories, and Picking Rules are owned by the Inventory application, and defining them is a required step in the Inventory implementation. Organizations are distinct distribution entities, which are also referred to as warehouses. You must also define the control options, account defaults, Set of Books, and Master and Costing Organizations associated with this organization. At least one subinventory is required with each organization. A subinventory is a physical or logical grouping of your inventory. Finally, you must define the priorities that Oracle Inventory uses to pick items for a sales order. See Chapter 17 for a detailed description of this process.

DEFINING PROFILE OPTIONS

Setting Profile options is a required and important task. Many OM programs use profile options to determine fundamental logic in the way that they process transactions. Table 18.2 shows the profile options in OM that can affect user and system productivity.

Tip

Don't skip a profile option simply because it is optional. Some of the profile options can improve your corporate controls over cash and enhance user productivity.

TABLE 18.2 OM PROFILE OPTIONS

Profile Option Name	Required?	Level*	Comment
AR: Use Invoice Accounting for Credit Memos	Yes	URAS	Default is No
BOM: Check for Duplicate Configuration	Optional	S	Default is No
BOM: Component Item Sequence Increment	Optional	URAS	Default 10
BOM: Configurator URL of UI Manager	Yes	URAS	
BOM: Default Bill of Material Levels	Optional	URAS	1
Journals: Display Inverse Rate	Optional	URAS	Default is No
OM: Administer Public Queries	Yes	URAS	
OM: Apply Automatic Attachments	Optional	RAS	Default is Yes
OM: Autoschedule	Optional	RS	Default is Null
OM: Auto Push Group Date	Optional	RS	Default is Null
OM: Charging Privilege		URAS	
OM: Context Responsibility for Upgraded Orders		R	
OM: Credit Card Privileges	Optional	RAS	Default is None
OM: Credit Memo Transaction Type	Yes	S	
OM: Cust Item Shows Matches	Yes	URS	Default is No

TABLE 18.2 CONTINUED

Profile Option Name	Required?	Level*	Comment
OM: Customer Relationships	Obsolete		
OM: Debug Level	Optional	URAS	3
OM: Discounting Privileges	Optional	URAS	Default is Full
OM: Estimated Authorization Validity Period	Yes	URAS	21 Days
OM: GSA Discount Violation Action	Optional	S	Default is Warning
OM: Included Item FreezeMethod	Yes	S	Default is Booking
OM: Invoice Numbering Freeze Method	Yes	US	Default is Automatic
OM: Invoice Source	Yes	S	
OM: Invoice Transaction Type	Yes	S	
OM: Inventory Source Location	**Obsolete**		
OM: Item Flexfield	Yes	S	
OM: Log Directory for Generated Packages	**Obsolete**		
OM: Negative Pricing	Optional	RAS	
OM: Non-Delivery Invoice Source	Yes	S	
OM: Notification Approver		URAS	
OM: Order Purge per Commit		S	Default is 100
OM: Over Return Tolerance	Yes	S	Default is 0 (zero)
OM: Over Shipment Tolerance	Yes	S	Default is 0 (zero)
OM: Over Shipment Invoice Basis	Yes	RAS	Default is Shipped
OM: Payment Method for Transactions	Optional	URAS	Credit Card
OM: Reservation Time Fence	Optional	RS	Default is Null

TABLE 18.2 CONTINUED

Profile Option Name	Required?	Level*	Comment
OM: Return Item Mismatch Action	Yes	URAS	Default is Allow
OM: Return Unfulfilled Reference Line Action	Yes	RS	Default is Allow
OM: Risk Factor Threshold for Electronic Payments	Optional	RS	Default is 50
OM: Set of Books	Obsolete		
OM: Schedule Line on Hold	Optional	RS	Default is Null
OM: Show Discount Details on Invoice	Yes	RAS	Default is No
OM: Show Line Details	Optional	URAS	Default is No
OM: Source Code	Yes	S	ORDER ENTRY
OM: Use Configurator	Optional	S	Default is No
OM: Under Return Tolerance	Yes	S	Default is 0 (zero)
OM: Under Shipment Tolerance	Yes	S	Default is 0 (zero)
QP: Accrual UOM Class	Optional	AS	
QP: Blind Discount Option	Yes	AS	Default is Yes
QP: Bypass the Pricing Engine	Yes	RAS	Default is No
QP: Item Validation Organization	Yes	R	No Default
QP: Line Volume UOM Code	Optional	AS	No Default
QP: Line Weight UOM Code	Optional	AS	Default is No
QP: Negative Pricing	Yes	AS	No Default
QP: Source System Code	Yes	AS	No Default
QP: Unit Price Precision Type	Yes	AS	Default is Standard
QP: Verify GSA	Yes	S	Default is No
Sequence Numbering	Yes	RAS	
Tax: Allow Ad Hoc Tax Changes	Yes	URAS	Default is Yes

TABLE 18.2 CONTINUED

Profile Option Name	Required?	Level*	Comment
Tax: Allow Override of Customer Exemptions	Yes	URAS	Default is Yes
Tax: Allow Override of Tax Code	Yes	URAS	Default is Yes
Tax: Calculate Tax on Credit Memos	Optional	RAS	Default is No
Tax: Inventory Item for Freight	Optional	URAS	No Default
Tax: Invoice Freight as Revenue	Optional	URAS	Default is No
Tax: Use Tax Vendor	Yes	RAS	Default is No

**Levels can be User, Responsibility, Application, or Site. The system administrator sets most profile options. Legend: U = User; R = Responsibility; (A) = Application; S = Site*

DEFINING ITEM VALIDATION ORGANIZATION PARAMETER

The Item Validation Organization parameter in Order Management determines the manufacturing organization against which your items are validated. This field usually holds the value of your Master Inventory organization. In Order Management, organization is synonymous with warehouse. Note, you cannot have any open orders when performing updates to Order Management Parameters. After it finds open orders, a warning message will display. You will need to click the OK button to ignore the warning or click the Cancel button to not commit the changes.

DEFINING INVOICING INFORMATION

Invoicing information is defined in the Accounts Receivable implementation. Payment terms, invoicing and accounting rules, autoaccounting parameters, territories, and invoice sources are defined during Accounts Receivable implementation. See Chapter 13 for a detailed description of this process.

DEFINING SALESPERSONS

Sales Credit is assigned to a salesperson when you enter orders and returns. A salesperson is assigned to one or more territories, and each salesperson has a revenue, freight, and receivables account assigned to him. You can also designate whether a salesperson receives quota or nonquota sales credits. Salespersons are defined during Accounts Receivable implementation. See Chapter 13 for a detailed description of this process. Figure 18.2 shows the Salesforce screen for capturing salesperson information.

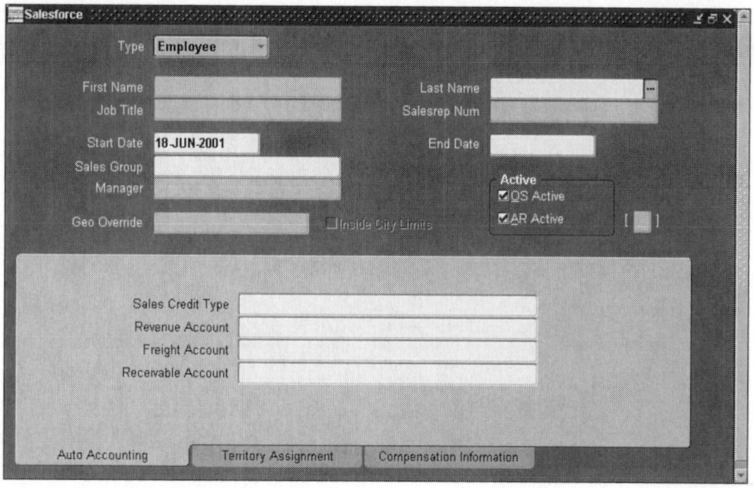

Figure 18.2
Salesforce.

DEFINING TAX

Order Management allows you to quote an estimated tax for your orders at the time of entering the order. These tax estimates can be based on the tax status such as address information, and VAT (Value Added Tax) codes assigned to items, sites, and customers. However, the actual tax amount on the customer's invoice might vary. Tax codes are defined during Accounts Receivable implementation. See Chapter 13 for a detailed description of this process. Figure 18.3 shows the Tax Codes and Rates screen for capturing tax information; Figure 18.4 shows the Tax Exemption screen used for tax exemption information.

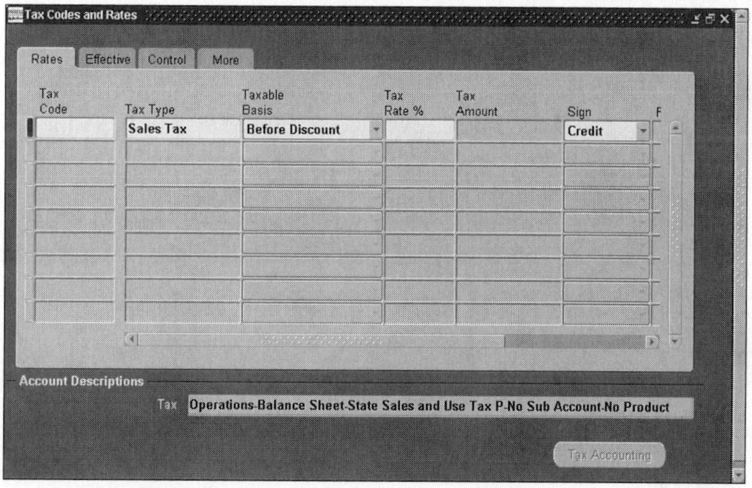

Figure 18.3
Tax codes and rates.

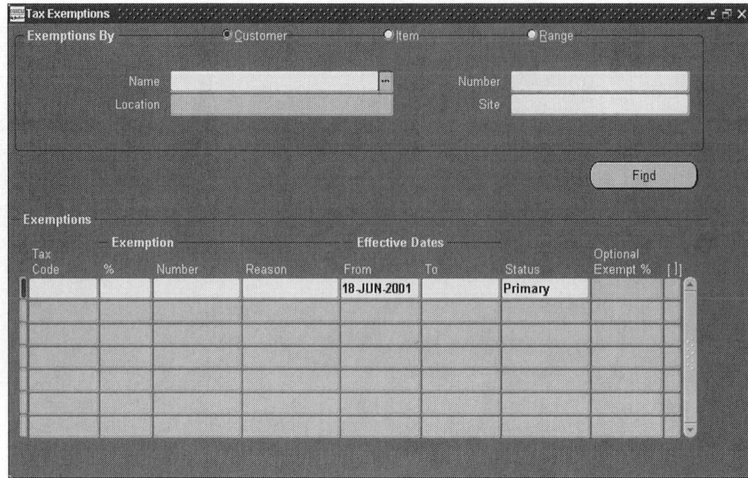

Figure 18.4
Tax exemptions.

DEFINING QUICK CODES

Order Management enables you to define Quick Codes that provide user supplied values for many list of values throughout the OM application. Quick Code types that you can set up include

- Cancellation Codes
- Credit Cards
- Freight Terms
- Hold Types
- Note Usage Formats
- Release Reasons
- Sales Channels
- Shipment Priorities

You can create as many quickcodes as your business requires. You can also inactivate quickcodes. Figure 18.5 shows the Oracle Order Management Lookups screen for setting up quickcodes information.

DEFINING WORKFLOW

Order Management enables you to use the Oracle Workflow module to give you control over the sequence of events that should take place in processing of orders, returns, order lines, and return lines. Order Management gives you the flexibility to pattern your organization's processes in terms of generic order processes. You can pattern your business process by copying and editing seeded process or model your business processes by using a combination of seeded and custom components. You can use workflow processes to establish the order processing events for different types of orders.

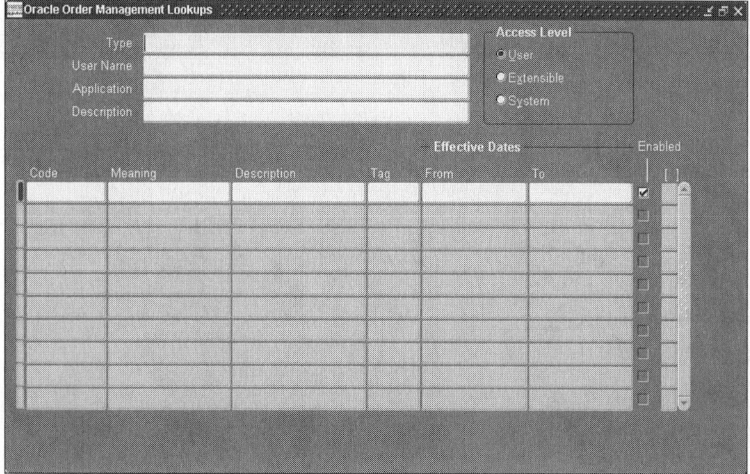

Figure 18.5
Order management lookups.

DEFINING DOCUMENT SEQUENCES (ORDER NUMBERING)

Order Management uses AOL Document Sequence functionality for order numbering. This enables you to define document sequences that automatically generate numbers for your orders and returns as they are entered. Define a single document sequence to assign unique consecutive numbers to all orders and returns, or define multiple document sequences that are assigned to different order types. If gapless order numbers are required, you can set up document sequences as gapless in the Define Documents Sequences window. If you choose to use gapless numbering, be sure to save your changes frequently to minimize record lock contention problems. Order Management also enables you to manually enter the order numbers for certain types of orders. To do this, define a document sequence as manual and assign it to a desired order type. Figure 18.6 shows the Document Sequences screen for capturing document sequencing information.

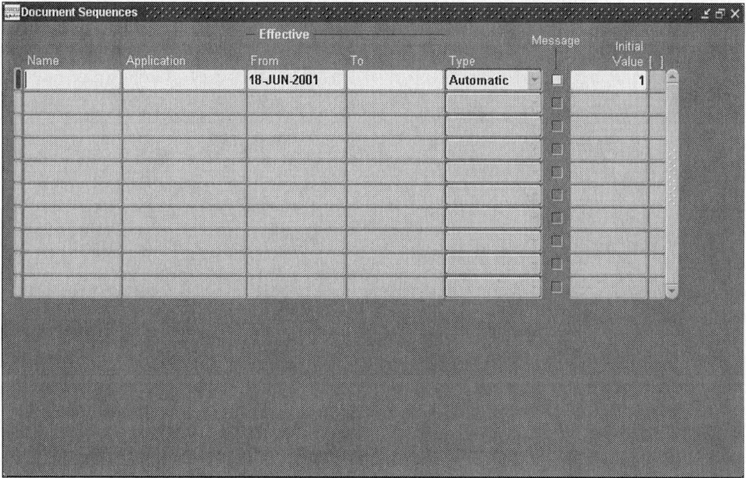

Figure 18.6
Document sequences.

Note

Set the profile option Sequential Numbering to Always Used at the Order Management Application level. Set the document sequences to Automatic, Gapless, or Manual.

DEFINING ORDER IMPORT SOURCES

Order Management enables you to import order information from historical orders, orders from other quote and sales systems, and changes to orders. It is a good practice to define a unique name for each source of order information you will be using. You can execute Order Import for multiple sources at one time. Figure 18.7 shows the Order Import Sources screen for capturing order import source information.

Note

If you want to import internal sales orders from Oracle Purchasing, be sure to define an Order Import source to be used when you transfer the internal requisition data from Oracle Purchasing to create an internal sales order in Order Management.

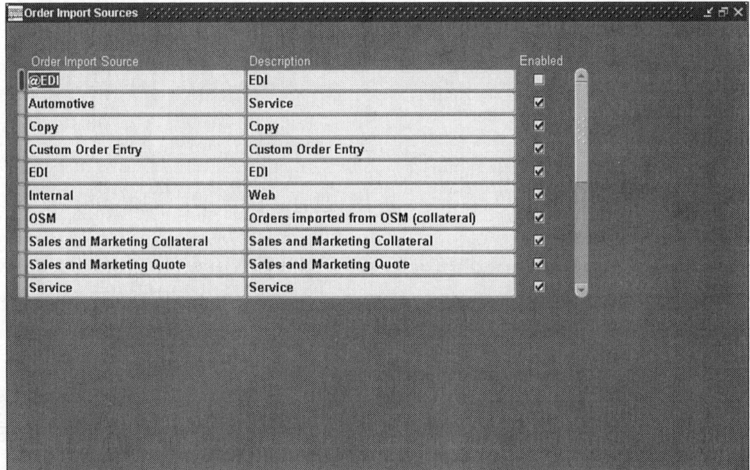

Order Import Source	Description	Enabled
@EDI	EDI	☐
Automotive	Service	☑
Copy	Copy	☑
Custom Order Entry	Custom Order Entry	☑
EDI	EDI	☑
Internal	Web	☑
OSM	Orders imported from OSM (collateral)	☑
Sales and Marketing Collateral	Sales and Marketing Collateral	☑
Sales and Marketing Quote	Sales and Marketing Quote	☑
Service	Service	☑

Figure 18.7
Order import sources.

DEFINING UNITS OF MEASURE

Units of Measure are defined in the Manufacturing Application Implementation. Units of Measure are used for tracking, counting, sorting, weighing, and moving items. Each item that is defined must have a primary Unit of Measure, and each line of an order must have a Unit of Measure associated with the quantity of the item.

DEFINING ITEM INFORMATION

Items are defined in the Oracle Financials or Manufacturing Implementation. Items must be set up before Order Management can function. Orders cannot be placed for items that have not been defined.

DEFINING ITEM CONFIGURATIONS

Item configurations are set up using Oracle Bills of Material's configuration functionality. Each model, option class, option item, standard component, and included items must be defined as an item. To provide your customers the capability to order unique configurations of a model, you must define model and option class Bills of Material.

MANAGING PRICING

Order Management provides you with a robust capability to enable you great flexibility in managing your pricing to reflect your pricing policies. You can define a single master price list, or you can have any number of price lists. You can also use standard value rule sets to default prices into an order from your agreements, customers, or order types. To support sales to foreign countries, you can assign a currency to each price list.

Order Management has numerous streamlining and maintenance reducing features to assist you in managing your price lists. You can easily update pricing by a percentage or fixed amount for an entire price list or a subset of items in a price list. You can readily create new price lists using the copy feature in Order Management. It enables you to copy an entire price list or a subset of items from a price list. Inventory items can be added to a price list by item category, by item status, or from a range of items. When items are added, they might carry no price or the inventory cost as the price. Order Management enables you to create groups of items that can be added to the price list as a group with effective start and end dates. You can create pricing formulas for your price list that can change prices of other items based on price fluctuations of a particular item. Should your pricing policy result in a rules change, Order Management will automatically recalculate the prices. Finally, you can easily create customized discount programs, prorated discounts, and GSA discounts.

To set up pricing, you must first define your Pricing Attributes Descriptive Flexfield, which is used to modify the price of an item. Next, you need to enable your parameters for the pricing components that are used in your pricing rules. Then, you define your pricing rules to support your pricing policy. Finally, you define your price list to include all orderable inventory items.

MANAGING CUSTOMERS, CUSTOMER PROFILES, AND CUSTOMER RELATIONSHIPS

Customers are set up in the Accounts Receivable Implementation. See Chapter 13 for details on the implementation of Customer, Customer Profiles, and Customer Relationships.

To speed up the order-entry process, it is recommended that when you set up your customers, define the primary customer address, contact, and telephone. You should also enter information such as the order type, sales channel, and price list associated with the particular customer.

When you set up your customers, each one is assigned a profile class. These profiles are used in credit checking to set tolerance percentages, total limits, and per order limits. Finally, you need to define one-way and reciprocal customer relationships. You can use these relationships to restrict addresses, agreements, and commitments that appear, as well as to allow payment application for related customers.

ENTERING CUSTOMER AGREEMENTS

In Order Management, you can define binding and nonbinding agreements. Agreements are referred to during the entry of an order to get relevant default values for a particular customer, such as assigned pricing, accounting, invoicing, and payment terms. Additionally, when pricing, the pricing engine will ignore qualifiers attached to a price list associated with an agreement if the agreement is chosen at the time of entering the order. The pricing engine will, however, still check for product and pricing attributes in the price list associated with the agreement. Agreements let you do the following:

- Define your agreement using customer part numbers and inventory item numbers.
- Make revisions to the original terms and maintain these changes and their reasons under separate revision numbers.
- Attach an already existing price list to an agreement or define new prices.
- Assign optional price breaks by quantity.
- Set effective dates for agreement terms.
- Set payment terms including invoice and accounting rules.
- Set freight terms including the freight carrier.
- Apply agreement terms to sales orders by reference agreements.

DEFINING TRANSACTION TYPES

Order Management enables you to define transaction types that help you categorize your orders and returns. For your different order types you can assign a default price list, defaulting rules, order lines, return lines, line types, workflow assignments, payment, and freight terms.

DEFINING COST OF GOODS SOLD

The Inventory Interface determines the Cost of Goods Sold (COGS) account for each transaction. Each COGS account is validated against the chart of accounts associated with the Set of Books profile. If the generated COGS account is valid for the rules for the set of books, the transaction is interfaced. If the COGS account is not valid, the transaction is rejected.

DEFINING DEFAULTING RULES

Order Management enables you to define and modify defaulting rules that help the efficiency and accuracy of the order-entry process. In defining the rules you can establish the source and prioritization for defaulting order information to reduce the amount of data you must enter manually in the Sales Order window.

DEFINING CREDIT CHECKING

A customer's outstanding balance is calculated through the use of credit-checking rules. You can define as many different rules as your business needs require. Order Management uses the currency of the order to determine credit limits.

When credit-checking rules are defined, you can implement the automatic credit checking of your orders. With this feature you can check credit at order time, shipment time, or both, thus preventing the shipment of products to customers with unacceptable outstanding credit exposure.

To activate automatic credit checking, you must first define your credit-checking rules. Second, you assign the credit-checking rules to an order type. Third, in the customer profile class, you enable credit checking and set individual order limits, the customer's outstanding credit balance limit, the percentage by which a customer can exceed his order limit or total limit, and the currency used for his orders. Finally, you create a customer profile to implement credit limits for individual customers or customer sites.

Note

Credit checking does not occur on an order if the credit limit is not defined in the same currency as the order uses.

Credit checking does not occur on any orders for the customer or site, regardless of other credit-checking parameters, unless credit check is set to Yes on the Customer Profile.

Credit checking does not occur on an order using payment terms unless Credit Check is set to Yes on the Customer Profile.

Defining Holds

You can stop an order, an order line, a return, or a return line from continuing to process through the Workflow by using a hold. You can apply holds manually, such as an individual-order hold, or automatically based on a set of criteria you define, such as credit-check hold. These holds can be applied at specific processing steps in your Workflow or to a customer or item at any step in the Workflow.

The General Services Administration (GSA) hold is used to ensure that a specific group of customers always receives the best pricing. If an order is placed for a customer not in the group but is given the same level of discount as the group, that order is automatically placed on hold until a review is completed.

With the credit-check hold, you can limit a customer's orders to preset limits, for either all orders or individual orders. Using the credit limits and credit rules you define, Order Management performs an automatic credit check on your customers. Additionally, you can exclude certain customers, types of orders, or payment terms from credit checking.

Another type of hold uses hold sources to apply a particular hold to a group of existing orders, returns, or their lines and to new orders that meet your hold criteria. The key feature of hold sources is that you can hold all current and future orders for an unreleased item. You can take orders for an item, recognize the demand, and yet hold the order line until the item is ready. When the item is available, the hold source is removed, and the individual order lines can be released. Figure 18.8 shows the Holds screen for setting up holds information.

You control who can define, apply, and remove holds through the use of responsibilities.

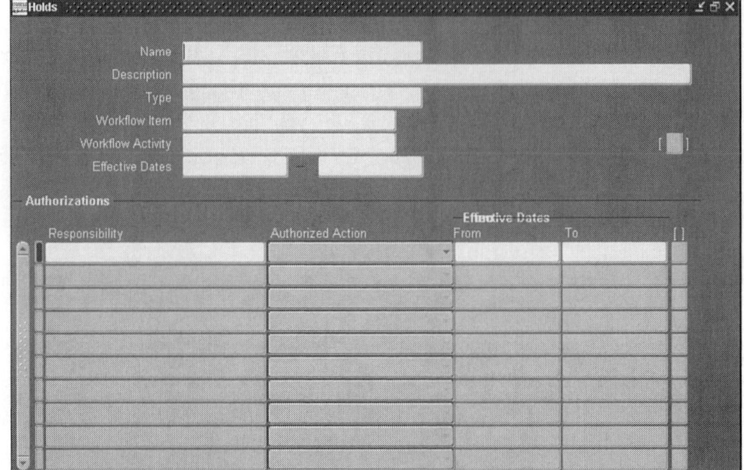

Figure 18.8
Holds.

DEFINING ATTACHMENTS

Order Management enables you to automatically apply attachments to orders and returns based on the attachment addition rules you define. The attachments feature provides for standard documents, adding free-form text to order, order lines, returns, and return lines. You can attach different types of attachments, which could be graphics, free-form text and HTML pages. It also supports multilingual support for translation purposes. When creating the order or order line through Order Import, automatic attachments are applied if the profile option OM: Apply Automatic Attachment is set to Yes.

DEFINING FREIGHT CHARGES

Order Management enables you to define your allowable freight charges used in your business. Freight charges are assigned to shipments during shipping conformation. You can have multiple freight charges assigned to a shipment, and you can override the suggested freight amount at shipping confirmation. You can use either your functional currency or the order's foreign currency, depending on your business needs. The freight and special charge costs can be estimates or final. The actual costs are captured at shipping confirmation and can be converted to charges based on freight terms and other rules you have defined. Different freight costs are set up in Shipping Execution.

DEFINING FREIGHT CARRIERS

Freight Carriers are defined in Shipping Execution Implementation. Freight Carriers are used to identify all the carriers that you use to ship items from your organization to internal and external customers, and inter-organizational transfers.

Note

Freight Carriers must be defined in each Inventory Organization.

DEFINING SHIPPING TOLERANCES

Order Management enables you to capture shipping tolerance levels for over- and under-shipments during shipping confirmation. This feature enables you to define a different tolerance level for ordered and expected return quantities. Using this information Order Management automatically fulfills an order line within the shipping tolerances you had defined.

PROVIDING DATA FOR MAJOR ENTITIES

The following sections describe how to provide data for major entities.

RELEASING ORDERS TO MANUFACTURING

The Manufacturing Release process releases demanded order lines or line details for Assemble-to-Order (ATO) items and configurations to Oracle Manufacturing for processing by Oracle Work In Process if the order lines have successfully completed all prerequisite cycle actions.

Note

Only items with the Assemble-to-Order item attribute set to Yes are processed by Manufacturing Release.

SENDING SHIPMENTS TO ORACLE ACCOUNTS RECEIVABLE FOR INVOICING

The Receivables Interface transfers shipped item information to Oracle Accounts Receivable. This includes quantities, selling prices, payment terms, and transaction dates. You can also process credit memos and credits on accounts created from returns.

IMPORTING ORDER INFORMATION INTO ORDER MANAGEMENT

You can use Order Import to import sales orders from external sales order systems or to import internal orders created from internal requisitions in Oracle Purchasing.

With Order Import, you can import order-entry data from both Oracle and non-Oracle systems. You can import order-entry data from your legacy order-entry system, thus making the transition to Order Management as smooth as possible. Figure 18.9 shows the Order Import Request screen.

The following profile options affect Order Import:

- **OM: Included Item Freeze Method**—Controls when included items are determined for a configuration's bill of material.
- **OM: Item Validation Organization**—The organization used for validating items and bill of material structures.

- **OM: Reservation Time Fence**—Controls the number of days out that inventory will be reserved when scheduling an order line.
- **OM: Apply Automatic Attachments**—Determines whether rule-based attachments are applied without user intervention.

Items must be defined for them to be orderable for using Order Import. Bills of material also need to be defined for models if you have any complex items that customers can order in various configurations.

Holds are automatically applied to imported orders and order lines that meet the hold criteria.

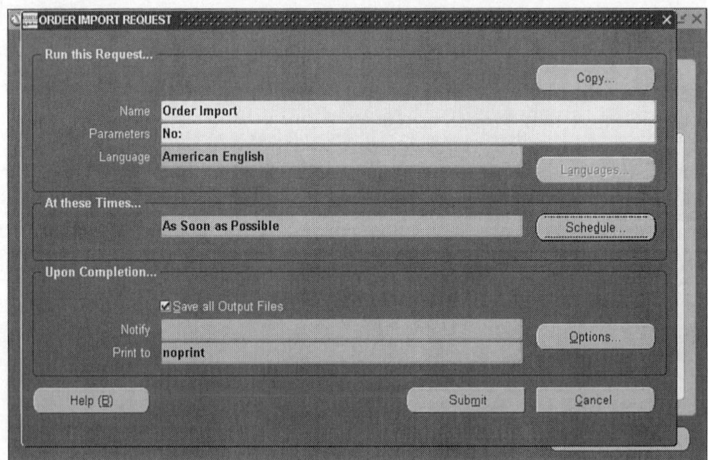

Figure 18.9
Order import request.

USING THE DEMAND INTERFACE

The Demand Interface places demand for shipments. The Manufacturing applications use this information for forecasting and product planning and schedule requirements.

The OM: Source Code profile option affects the operation of the Demand Interface.

Only holds that specify the Demand Interface in the Cycle Action field prevent the Demand Interface from processing the records. The Demand Interface ignores all other holds, including those for credit checking.

USING THE INVENTORY INTERFACE

The Inventory Interface transfers information on the shipped picking lines for any eligible order lines. If an order line item is non-shippable but has shippable included items, the shipped included items are interfaced when the order line is eligible.

The Inventory Interface determines the Cost Of Goods Sold (COGS) account for each transaction.

Note

You must remove any unreleased holds that specify no cycle action or a cycle action of Inventory Interface on orders or order lines that you want to interface to Oracle Inventory.

USING THE RMA INTERFACE

The Return Material Authorization (RMA) Interface transfers authorized return information to Inventory and obtains receipt information from Inventory. The profile option OM: Source Code is used by the RMA Interface to uniquely identify each return transaction.

To process a return line, an item must be Returnable, Shippable, Stockable, and Transactable.

USING THE SHIP CONFIRM OPEN INTERFACE

The Ship Confirm Open Interface loads externally derived shipping data into picking tables and closes the pick slip without using Confirm Shipments. The Ship Confirm Open Interface takes data loaded into three interface tables; validates the information contained within the interface tables; loads the valid data into the picking header, picking line details, and freight charges tables; and closes the pick slip.

PROCESSING TRANSACTIONS

Order Management provides you the ability to manage and control your sales order process. It has functionality that lets you enter sales orders, copy sales orders, import orders and returns, schedule orders, cancel orders and returns, apply hold, release holds, and close orders.

The Sales Order form in Oracle Order Management enables you to organize, enter, view, and update your order information. Line-level independence gives you the ability to capture regular orders as well as returns using the same form. The Sales Order form offers an entry point for creating and editing information as well as for reviewing summary information from other systems such as Shipping, Receivables, Purchasing, and so on, and status of orders.

ORDER PROCESSING

The following sections describe the order processing functionality.

SALES ORDER WORKBENCH

The Sales Order Workbench is composed of the following windows: Find Orders, Order Organizer, Sales Orders, Order Mass Change, and Line Mass Change. These windows give you access to a number of operations you can perform on orders and returns.

ENTERING SALES ORDERS

The Sales Order window lets order you enter, view, and update sales orders. You can also enter returns, order standard items (both shippable and nonshippable), and set configurations using this window. You can also adjust pricing, assign sales credits, record payment information, attach notes, schedule shipments, query item availability, and make reservations (including selection of subinventory).

COPYING SALES ORDERS

This feature enables you to create a new order or return by copying data from any exiting order or return. You can determine how much information you want to copy from an exiting order or return.

Note

When copying cancelled lines to a new order or return, the lines carry over the original ordered quantity.

SCHEDULING ORDERS

You can schedule orders at order entry through the use of the Sales Order window. However, if you have a special department that schedules orders, you can separate the functions and use the Schedule Orders Workbench.

CANCELING ORDERS AND RETURNS

When you cancel sales orders, order lines, returns, and return lines, Order Management automatically adjusts reservations for cancelled lines.

Note

When canceling an entire order, you must do so before any of the order lines are shipped or invoiced. When canceling an entire return you must do so before you run RMA Interface or Invoicing Activity on any of the return lines. Figure 18.10 shows the Find Orders screen for finding the order to be cancelled.

APPLYING MASS CHANGES

You can apply Mass Changes to several orders, returns, order lines, or return lines in a single transaction. You must multiselect the orders you want to apply mass change to and select the Mass Change option from the Tool menu. In the Order and Line Mass Change windows, you can multiselect orders and various other selection criteria.

Figure 18.10
Finding orders.

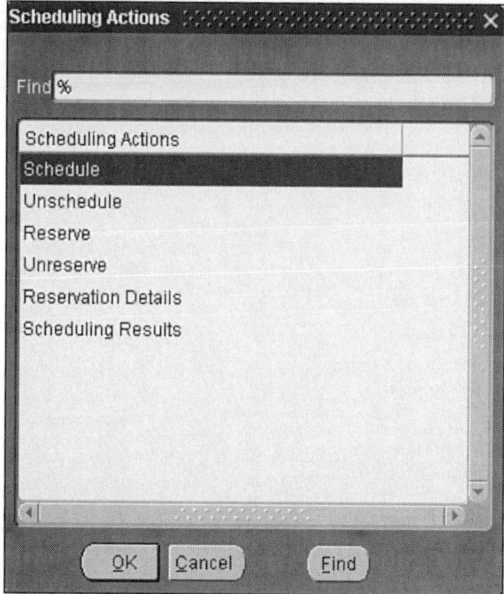

APPLYING AND RELEASING HOLDS

You can apply holds to orders, returns, and lines in the Sales Order window. You also can apply holds to be effective immediately. To apply holds to specific orders, returns, order lines, or return lines, use the Order Organizer window to identify them individually. After you have created a hold source, you can release it from the Sales Order window or Order Organizer. Figures 18.11 and 18.12 show screens for finding orders and applying holds.

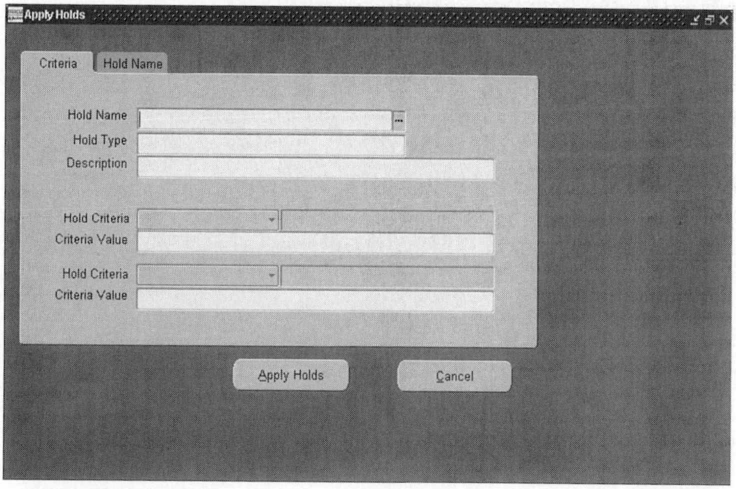

Figure 18.11
Applying holds.

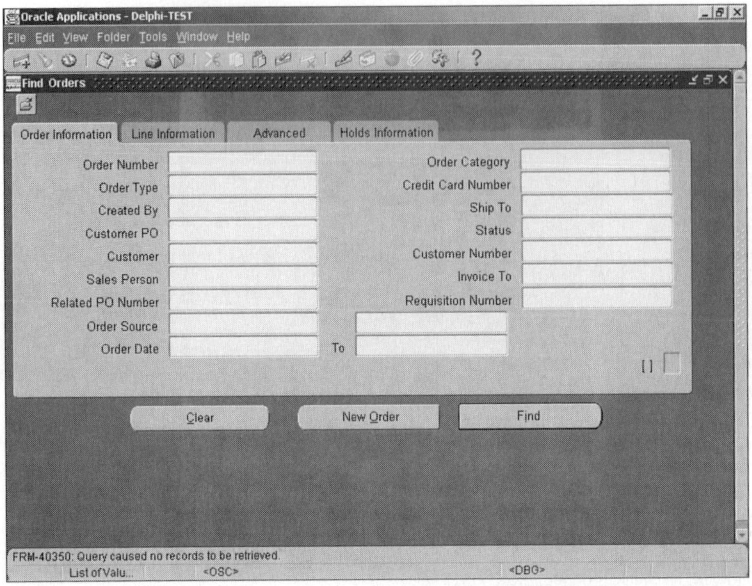

Figure 18.12
Finding orders.

CLOSING ORDERS

Workflow can be used to close lines and orders. Order Management provides seeded close line and close order workflow subprocesses to close the order header and lines. After an order is closed, no lines can be added. At the end of every month, Order Management checks to see all the lines associated with closed orders are in closed status. It closes the order header if it finds that all the lines are closed.

UNDERSTANDING PRICING FUNCTIONS

Pricing adds features to Order Management that enable you to execute pricing and promotional calculations for Oracle Order Management as well as other Oracle Applications. The features available in Pricing enable you to efficiently set up your pricing information, and build your complex data relationships that determine the correct price for your items. The pricing engine which is invoked by Order Management enables you to perform the following functions:

- Set a list price for an item or item hierarchy.
- Set a list price based on volume breaks.
- Calculate price based on usage brackets for usage pricing and counterpricing.
- Point break (all quantity in one bracket).
- Range break (quantity in each bracket gets the price of that bracket).

- Set a list price or discounts at multiple levels of flattened hierarchies and usages.
- Set the precedence to select the correct price or discount.
- Dynamically calculate the price based on a simple or complex formula.
- Define a formula to create a price relation (price of item A is Price of Item B + $20).
- Set up GSA prices.
- Define pricing agreements.
- Get a price or discount from an external source (my price = competitor's price 5%).
- Set a percent, fixed, or lump sum discount or surcharge.
- Figure N-Dimensional pricing (if width is between 2 and 4 and thickness is between 1 and 3, multiply the price by 0.3).
- Set the benefit or surcharge based on total volume of multiple order lines of the same order.
- Set up deals and promotions.
- Set up buy one get one free.
- Set up coupon issue (buy over $10,000 and get a coupon of $250 for future purchase).
- Issue gift-certificates.
- Set up other item discount (Buy X and Y, get 25% off on Z).
- Set up item upgrade (for the price of 2oz. Cologne get 3.4oz. Cologne).
- Set up terms upgrade (buy over $5000 and get upgraded to Next Day Delivery).
- Set discounts as "to be accrued".
- Set up freight and special charges.
- Mark discounts as exclusive or incompatible to each other.
- Set up cascading discounts (discounts to be applied on subtotals).
- Create your own eligibility conditions by grouping the qualifiers.
- Define your own qualifier and qualifier sourcing rules (if today = Full Moon, give 10% discount).

The pricing engine looks for answers to the following questions to determines a price:

- Who qualifies for prices and benefits?
- What is the product hierarchy and what pricing attributes pertain to this item or service?
- How should it adjust the order price or order line price?

Note

Oracle Pricing is licensed as Oracle Advanced Pricing.

Understanding How Credit Checking Works

The credit-checking feature in Order Management enables users to validate orders against user-defined rules to ensure that the customer has the necessary credit established with your organization to allow the order to be processed and shipped prior to receiving payment. The credit-checking feature includes validating orders to verify sufficient customer credit is available to let it flow through the workflow process, sending appropriate notification to parties of orders on credit holds, providing a method to release holds and approve the order, and providing reporting and query tools to allow your credit department to perform its function efficiently. Order Management allows you to automatically place orders on hold that do not satisfy your credit rules. You control which orders need to go through the credit check and which can be exempt by specifying order types and customer classes and other criteria that you might want to enforce. You might need to establish different credit-checking rules at different points in the order process flow. Separate credit-checking rules can be assigned at the time of booking and shipping when setting up the order type. You can also block the processing of a line or group of lines, which do not meet your business rules that control exposure and cash flow.

Understanding Shipping Tolerances

Order Management enables you to capture shipping tolerance levels for over- and under-shipment at ship confirmation. The feature enables you to define different shipping tolerance levels for ordered and expected return quantities. At the time when Oracle Shipping Execution tries to over-ship an order, Order Management processes the order based on the shipping tolerances you define. For Order Management to perform an over-shipment, it determines if the ship quantity is within the over-shipment tolerance level defined, notifies the responsible personnel when an over-shipment is above the established shipping tolerance, issues the material for any unpicked or unreserved quantity and rolls back ship quantity with a process error message. You can review the Over Shipment Report for shipping tolerances. The report shows shipping tolerance data based on the customer, site, item, warehouse, ship date, and order type.

Processing Returned Material

Order Management enables you to use the Sales Orders window to enter, view, and update return materials authorizations (RMAs) and assign credit orders for your customers to authorize them to return goods to you. The authorizations can be for replacement, as well as returns with or without credit. If your business practice requires that items be returned for credit, Order Management can block customer credits from being issued until the items have been inspected and accepted by your company. Attachments can also be applied to provide additional information for your returns. You can set up different types of credit orders by specifying the order and line types. You can tailor your order types and RMA line types to suit your business needs. Then each order and line type can be associated with a workflow process. Credit order types must have an order type category of Return. If your business requires, you can have a Mixed order type which can contain both sales order and return lines. It is worth noting that you cannot enter return lines into an order with an order type of Regular.

Understanding Order Import

Order Import in Order Management is an open interface that is composed of interface tables and a set of APIs. The Order Import feature can be used to import new, changed, and completed sales orders or returns from external applications. Orders might come from different sources such as internal orders for internal requisitions created in Oracle Purchasing or as EDI transactions that are prepared by the Oracle e-Commerce Gateway. The import process in Order Management verifies all the data in the import process to ensure its validity within the Order Management application. The valid transactions are then passed as orders with lines, price adjustments, reservations, and sales credits into the Order Management tables. The Order Import Correction window provides a facility to examine the order data and correct information that fails the import process. The Order Import process generates summary information that lets you know of the total number of transactions Order Import evaluates, and succeeded or failed transactions.

Understanding Invoicing Activity

In Order Management the Invoicing workflow activity is used to transfer shipped item data that includes quantities, selling price, payment terms, and transaction dates to Oracle Accounts Receivable. The Receivable module uses this information to create invoices and accounts for revenue. This process also enables you to process credit memos and credit on accounts generated from returns. When the Invoicing workflow activity is completed, you can run AutoInvoice from Oracle Accounts Receivable to import invoice and credit information into Oracle Receivables.

The following profile options affect the operation of the Invoicing Interface:

- **OM: Invoice Numbering Method**—This option determines whether or not the Invoicing activity should generate invoice numbers based on the delivery name. If this is set to Delivery Name, invoice numbers for shippable lines are generated based on delivery name while invoice numbers for nonshippable lines and RMA lines are created automatically based on the selected Non-Delivery Invoice Source profile.
- **OM: Show Discount Details on Invoice**—This option determines whether you want detailed discount information and extended amounts to print on the invoice.
- **OM: Invoice Source**—This profile option value is passed to Receivables if no value is entered for the transaction type.
- **OM: Non-delivery Invoice Source**—This profile option value is passed to Receivables if the OM: Invoice Numbering Method profile option is set to Delivery and the order line is nonshippable.

Understanding Order Purge

It is a good practice to purge old data from your Order Management system. This helps to create space in the database and significantly improves performance for transaction processing and maintenance. Order Management provides this functionality in the Order Purge Selection and Order Purge programs. It enables you to select and purge orders based on criteria you specify. The orders that you want to purge must be in closed status and no open demand must exist for these orders. There must not be any open work orders, open invoices, open returns, or open requisitions for these orders to be successfully purged. Figures 18.13 and 18.14 show screens used in the purge process. The following selection criteria are available:

- Order Number (enter range)
- Order Date (enter range)
- Creation Date (enter range)
- Order Category (enter range)
- Order Type (enter range)
- Customer

Note

If the selection criteria have orders that do not meet the purge restrictions mentioned previously or if the purge process encounters locked records, process errors will occur.

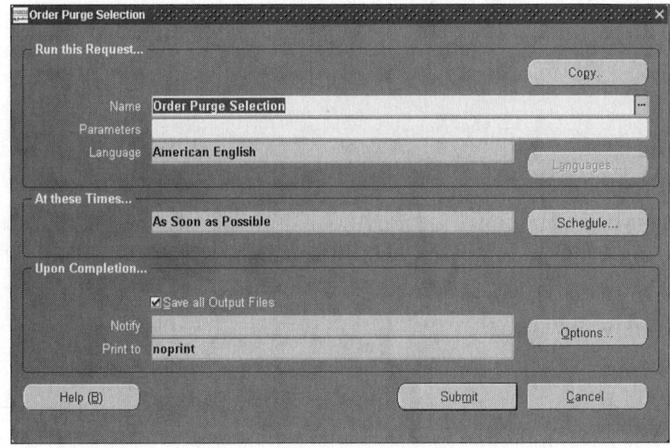

Figure 18.13
Order purge selection.

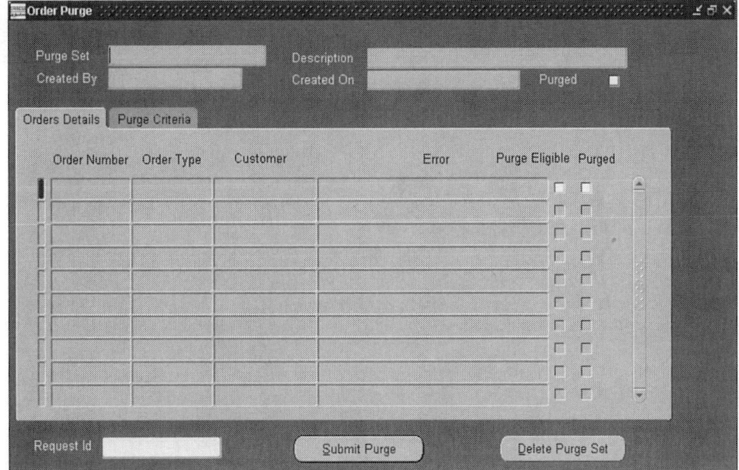

Figure 18.14
Order purge.

UNDERSTANDING KEY REPORTS

Order Management provides a number of standard reports to help manage your business and improve productivity. Table 18.3 lists the key reports that will be especially helpful in your operations.

TABLE 18.3 OM REPORTS

Report Name	Description
Comprehensive Order Detail Report	The Comprehensive Order Detail Report provides a detailed, comprehensive listing of information about each order, including sales credits, price adjustments, shipping, cancellation, and schedule details.
Order/Invoice Detail Report	The Order/Invoice Detail Report provides detailed invoice information for orders that have been invoiced.
Sales Order Acknowledgment	The Sales Order Acknowledgment informs your customers about the items, prices, delivery dates, service, and installation details for orders they place with you.
Credit Orders Detail Report	The Credit Orders Detail Report shows returned lines for a specific credit order type, line type, specific item, date range, order number, and salesperson.
Credit Orders Summary Report	The Credit Orders Summary Report shows all return lines in an order.
Returns By Reason Report	The Returns By Reason Report shows all return material authorizations for various return reasons.

Table 18.3 Continued

Report Name	Description
Hold Source Activity Report	The Hold Source Activity Report shows holds placed and removed under a hold source during the time period you specify.
Internal Order and Purchasing Requisition Discrepancy Report	The Internal Order and Purchasing Requisition Discrepancy Report provides the differences between the purchasing requisition entered and the actual items ordered during order entry.
Order Discount Detail Report	The Order Discount Detail Report shows discounts applied to orders by order line detail.
Order Discount Summary Report	The Order Discount Summary Report shows discounts applied to orders.
Orders on Credit Check Hold Report	The Orders On Credit Check Hold Report shows all the credit holds currently outstanding for a customer within a date range, or identifies why a particular order is on hold.
Outstanding Holds Report	The Outstanding Holds Report shows order holds for the customer or customers you choose.
Sales Order and Purchase Order Discrepancy Report	The Sales Order and Purchase Order Discrepancy Report shows differences between the sales orders and purchase orders for a drop shipment so that you can identify where manual changes must be made.
Unbooked Orders Report	The Unbooked Orders Report shows orders you have entered but not booked.
Cancelled Orders Report	The Cancelled Orders Report shows all orders that have been cancelled.
Cancelled Orders Reasons Detail Report	The Cancelled Orders Reasons Detail Report shows the reasons for the cancelled lines and who entered the cancellation.
Order/Invoice Summary Report	The Order/Invoice Summary Report shows summary invoice information about orders that have invoiced, including ordered amount, invoiced amount, adjusted receivables, and balance due.
Orders By Item Report	The Orders By Item Report shows all sales for a particular item or group of items.
Salesperson Order Summary Report	The Salesperson Order Summary Report shows orders for one or more salespeople.
Workflow Assignments Report	The Workflow Assignments Report shows the header and line flow combinations and item types for order workflows.

TROUBLESHOOTING

In summary, the Order Management application is completely new software in 11*i*, and it is just now stabilizing to the point where users can consider using it in a business production situation. Almost certainly you'll face many challenges as you implement OM. Consider the following techniques for dealing with those challenges:

- Read the chapter titled "Working with Oracle Support," on this book's Web site, to understand how to effectively and efficiently use Oracle Support to resolve bugs and problems with the software.
- Don't try to implement anything earlier than maintenance pack 11.5.4.
- Many known interface issues exist with OM and INV and OM and AR. You must perform several integration tests in a conference room pilot to prove that OM works satisfactorily in your business environment.
- Budget extra implementation time for this module.
- Watch for periodic updates on the support site, called MetaLink. Changes are made often, and you need to stay current.
- Network with other users of Order Management through groups such as the Oracle Applications User Group to learn about others' experiences with this module.

CHAPTER 19

USING ORACLE ENGINEERING AND BILLS OF MATERIAL

In this chapter

USING ORACLE ENGINEERING

Oracle Engineering provides a means to control item revisions and Bill of Material changes using Engineering Change Orders (ECOs). It also provides an environment to manage Engineering prototype information and to smooth the transition of this information to Manufacturing when it is required.

Figure 19.1 shows the major relationships between Oracle Engineering and the other Oracle Applications. These relationships affect the setup and operation of the Oracle Engineering application.

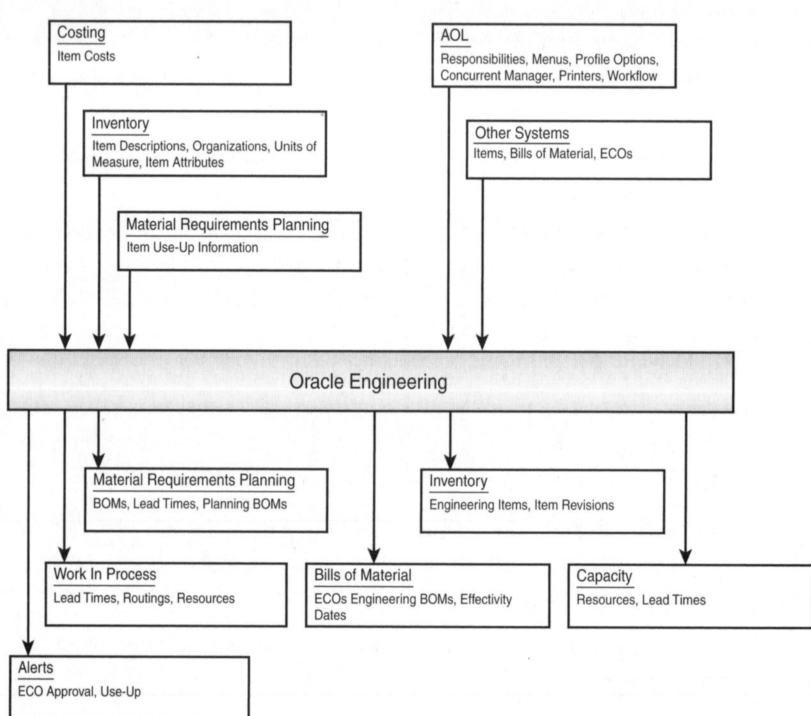

Figure 19.1
How the Oracle Engineering application interacts with the other Oracle Applications.

DISCOVERING NEW FEATURES IN RELEASE 11*i*

If you have had experience implementing earlier releases of Oracle Engineering, much of what you see in Release 11*i* will be familiar; however, some features and revised tables have been added.

Oracle Workflow came into being with later releases of the 10.7 Applications. If you are implementing or upgrading to Release 11*i*, it is important to have some understanding of its operation. It is particularly important within Oracle Engineering because it provides the facility to control an Engineering Change Order (ECO) approval cycle using a Workflow.

Oracle Workflow is dealt with in detail in Chapter 28, "Using Oracle Workflow."

Like Release 11, Release 11*i* also provides an ECO open interface. This interface allows for ECO information to be imported to the Oracle Engineering application from an external source.

CRITICAL IMPLEMENTATION FACTORS

The following factors should be considered before undertaking an implementation or upgrade of the Oracle Engineering application.

ISSUES AND GAPS

There have been a number of enhancements identified for Oracle Engineering that would improve functionality. Although these might not necessarily be seen in future releases, there has been consensus among users that these potential changes are important. These are some of the opportunities:

- In the Define ECO window, you cannot currently see the Purchase Orders and Discrete Jobs that relate to the revised items.
- Transferring an Engineering BOM from Engineering to Manufacturing involves transferring each subassembly level independently. There is no global transfer function for an Engineering BOM.
- ECO revision tracking is a manual process. There is no link between changes made to an ECO and the ECO's revision level.
- The capability to record costs associated with an ECO is available for information only. There is no automated process to collect implementation cost information for ECOs.
- Item revisions in Oracle Manufacturing must follow an ASCII sequence. There is currently no capability to create a "user-defined" revision sequence.

CONFIGURING THE APPLICATION

The following section describes the setup tasks and sequence to configure Oracle Engineering. The tasks should be performed in the sequence listed.

In Release 11 and on into Release 11*i* of the Oracle Applications, a new tool called the Oracle Applications Implementation Wizard was made available. Its purpose is to improve the way in which the setup and configuration of the applications are managed. It is particularly useful for ensuring that conflicts do not arise with setup steps that overlap two or more applications. The wizard technology is built on Oracle Workflow.

RESOLVING CRITICAL SETUP ISSUES

Before setting up the Oracle Engineering application, some thought needs to be given to the existing processes for controlling changes and prototyping activity:

- Decide whether Oracle Engineering will be the primary mechanism for controlling engineering changes within your organization. You can manage changes outside Oracle and keep only a record of the changes within the system.

- Carefully consider the approval process you want to use for changes. Oracle Engineering provides a number of options, with Oracle Workflow providing the most flexibility for creating and managing an approval process.
- Decide how much control you need over access to change order information. There are several Profile Options and Security Functions that can be set for each user that determine which pieces of data can be changed.
- Determine whether you will use Engineering Items and BOMs. If you choose to, you need to also decide how you will manage the transition of this information to manufacturing.

Table 19.1 shows the sequence of tasks involved in setting up Oracle Engineering and whether they are required.

TABLE 19.1 ORACLE ENGINEERING SETUP TASKS

Setup Task Name	Required?
Set Profile Options	Yes
Enter Employees	Yes
Define Change Order Types	No
Define ECO Departments	No
Define Autonumbering	No
Define Approval Lists	No
Define Reasons	No
Define Priorities	No
Start AutoImplement Manager	No

UNDERSTANDING EACH SETUP TASK

This section provides detail on each of the setup tasks and the order in which they should be performed.

SETTING THE PROFILE OPTIONS Table 19.2 shows the profile options that directly affect the operation of the Oracle Engineering application.

TABLE 19.2 ENGINEERING PROFILE OPTIONS

Profile Option Name	Required?	Level*	Comment
ENG: Change Order Autonumbering-System Administrator Access	Yes	SARU	Default is No
ENG: ECO Department	No	SARU	
ENG: ECO Revision Warning	No	S	Default is No

TABLE 19.2 CONTINUED

Profile Option Name	Required?	Level*	Comment
ENG: Engineering Item Change Order Access	No	SARU	Default is Yes
ENG: Mandatory ECO Departments	No	S	Default is No
ENG: Model Item Change Order Access	No	SARU	Default is Yes
ENG: Planning Item Change Order Access	No	SARU	Default is No
ENG: Require Revised Item New Revision	No	SA	Default is No
ENG: Standard Item Change Order Access	No	SARU	Default is Yes

**Levels can be Site, Application, Responsibility, or User. The system administrator sets most profile options.*

ENTERING EMPLOYEES To use Oracle Engineering, you must enter employees. These will be used to create and approve changes. If you have not installed Oracle Human Resources Management Systems, the installer will create the employee tables for you. Figure 19.2 displays the People screen, where you can enter the employees. You can't access the employee screen if Oracle Human Resources has not been installed.

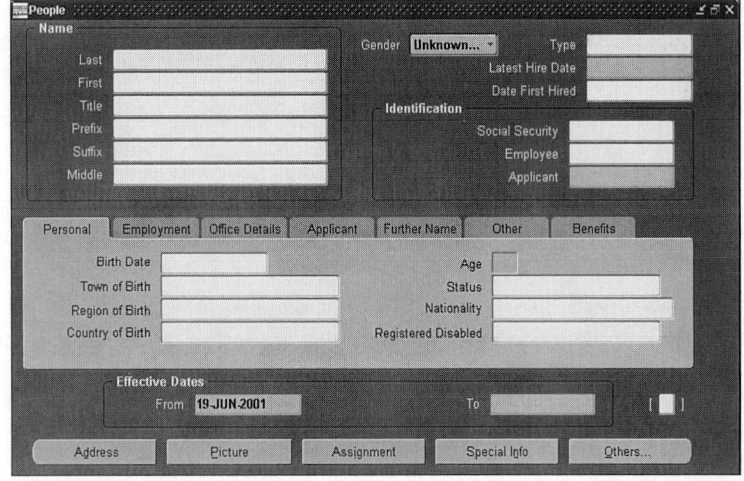

Figure 19.2
The People screen.

DEFINING CHANGE ORDER TYPES You can define a number of change order types to facilitate easy identification of your ECOs. A typical application would be the creation of an ECO type for manufacturing items only and a separate type for ECOs that affect both manufacturing and engineering items and assemblies. Figure 19.3 shows the form for creating such ECO types.

You can associate a change order type with an ECO approval workflow (see Chapter 28). You can optionally assign a priority to the change order type (see the following section). If this is the case, Oracle Workflow takes control of the approval process based on the business rules you have associated with the approval flow. If the type and priority have not been linked to a workflow, Oracle Engineering automatically designates the ECO as Approved.

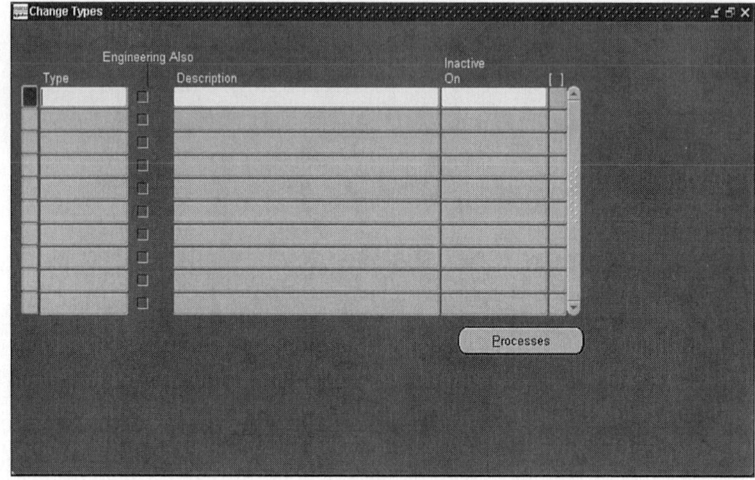

Figure 19.3
Use this screen to define your Engineering Change Order Types.

Tip

Consider creating a change order type for temporary deviations or waivers. If you are using workflows, you can create a separate workflow for these changes. They typically require different approvals to regular ECOs.

Defining Engineering Change Order Departments Oracle Engineering provides access control for ECOs by enabling you to group employees into departments. Figure 19.4 displays the form where any ECO created can be assigned to a department, and the department ownership can then be changed to move the ECO between departments. An example would be moving an ECO from a Design/Development Engineering department to a Manufacturing Engineering department. To apply this control, the ENG: ECO Department profile must be set for the user to ensure that each user is associated with an ECO department. You can require a responsible department to be assigned to all ECOs by setting the profile option ENG: Mandatory ECO Departments to Yes.

Defining Autonumbering You can choose to number your engineering changes manually or have the application create the numbers for you following a sequence. Change numbers can be assigned a prefix, which will become part of the number suggested by Oracle.

The use of prefixes can be controlled across your business. You can choose to specify prefixes by any of the following:

- Specific user in the current organization
- Specific user across all organizations
- All users in the current organization
- All users across all organizations

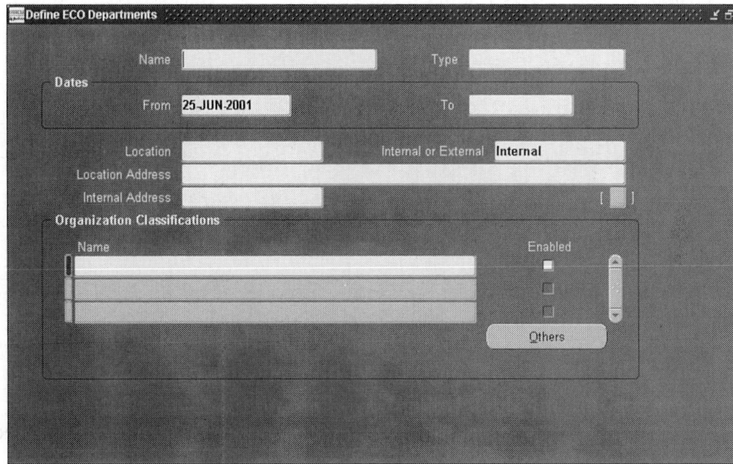

Figure 19.4
With this screen, you can define ECO Departments and specify locations and organization classifications.

This feature will be useful to businesses with decentralized engineering functions where change tracability is important. Different prefixes can be assigned depending on the origin of the change. It will also be useful if there is a centralized engineering function with multiple manufacturing entities. The same prefix can be enforced across all organizations.

Even if autonumbering is active, you can assign a number manually. Be aware that Oracle will consider that suggested change number to be used and will offer the next one in the sequence when you define the next engineering change.

Defining Approval Lists Apart from using Oracle Workflow to control the approval process, Oracle Engineering also provides basic ECO approval using Oracle Alert. This function is available in releases prior to Release 11*i*. To use the approval function, you must create approval lists using the employee names of the approvers. Figure 19.5 shows all the necessary fields to enter your list of approvers.

Defining Reasons To assist you in categorizing your changes, Oracle Engineering supports the creation of ECO Reasons. If you have been using ECOs with a legacy system, these probably exist. Typical reasons would be Customer Requested Change, Product Safety Change, Cost Reduction, and so on.

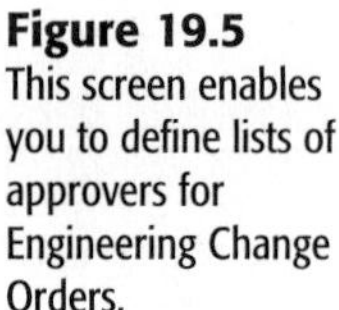

Figure 19.5
This screen enables you to define lists of approvers for Engineering Change Orders.

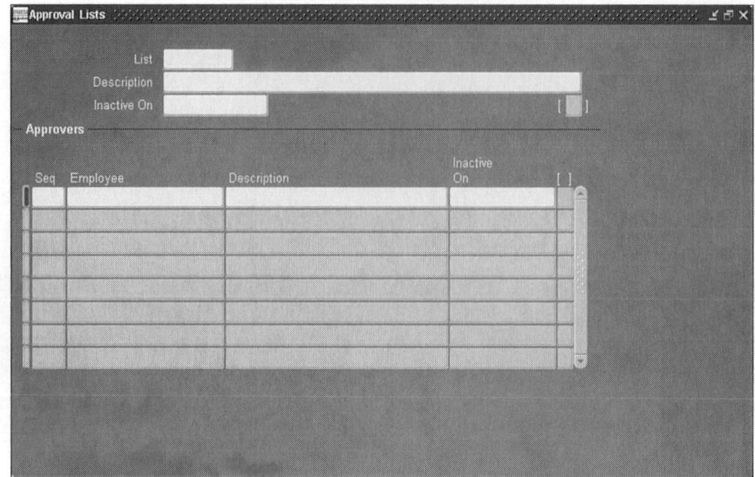

DEFINING PRIORITIES You can define priorities that can be assigned to your changes. Again, these are for your own information only. Typical priorities would be Mandatory, Production Convenience, Urgent, Immediate, and so on.

RUNNING THE AUTOIMPLEMENT CONCURRENT MANAGER PROGRAM Oracle Engineering provides functionality to automatically implement ECOs based on the effective dates assigned to the change. If you choose to use this functionality, you must run the AutoImplement Concurrent Manager Program. It automatically implements any change that has an effective date less than or equal to the current date and a status of Scheduled. You must specify the frequency at which this program should be run.

CONVERTING DATA FOR MAJOR ENTITIES

With Release 11*i* of the Oracle Engineering application, an ECO open interface is provided. This simplifies the process of importing historical ECO information from legacy systems. Details of the open interface tables are provided in the *Oracle Manufacturing, Distribution, Sales and Service Open Interfaces Manual.*

If you are converting data from a legacy system, you can use the Oracle Bills of Material Open Interfaces to populate Engineering data. These interfaces can also be used to import Manufacturing BOM data. The conversion process is described later.

You can use these interfaces to import primary and alternate Engineering BOMs and Engineering Routings.

Engineering item data can be imported using the Open Items Interface. This interface is also used to import Manufacturing item data (see Chapter 17, "Using Oracle Inventory").

The data to be converted from a legacy system must first be extracted and formatted for use in the interface tables. These tables are the following:

- MTL_SYSTEMS_ITEM_INTERFACE
- MTL_ITEM_REVISIONS_INTERFACE

Oracle maintains a third table to record errors resulting from the import process (MTL_INTERFACE_ERRORS). All records being imported are validated against the setup parameters that have been defined in Oracle Inventory.

Processing Transactions

The following sections deal with the operation of the Oracle Engineering application and the transactions that are involved.

Maintaining Engineering Change Orders

Change orders are created and updated using the Engineering Change Orders window.

Defining, Implementing, Mass Changing, and Purge Engineering Change Orders

The following sections explain the transactions that are involved in creating and managing an ECO.

Defining an Engineering Change Order When you create the ECO using the Engineering Change Orders window, you must enter the ECO identifier. If you have selected Autonumbering in the setup steps, the next available number defaults. You then need to select the ECO type. Figure 19.6 shows how to select the ECO type. Depending on how the ENG: Engineering Item Change Order Access profile option has been set, you can allow or deny access to Engineering items and BOMs. This profile option needs to be set for each User, and it only affects ECO types that change Engineering items.

You can choose to enter a responsible department for the ECO. As discussed in the setup steps, this information can protect ECOs from updates by Users outside the specified department. It can be particularly useful if you need to transfer ownership for a change between departments—for example, from Design Engineering to Manufacturing Engineering.

Tip

If you do not set the ENG: ECO Department profile option for a particular User, users then have access to *all* ECOs. If no department has been specified on the ECO, any User with the correct responsibility also has full access to this ECO. If this is of concern to you, be sure to set the profile option *and* ensure that the correct department is specified on the ECO. You should set the profile option ENG: Mandatory ECO Departments to Yes.

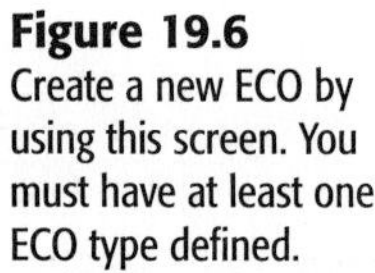

Figure 19.6
Create a new ECO by using this screen. You must have at least one ECO type defined.

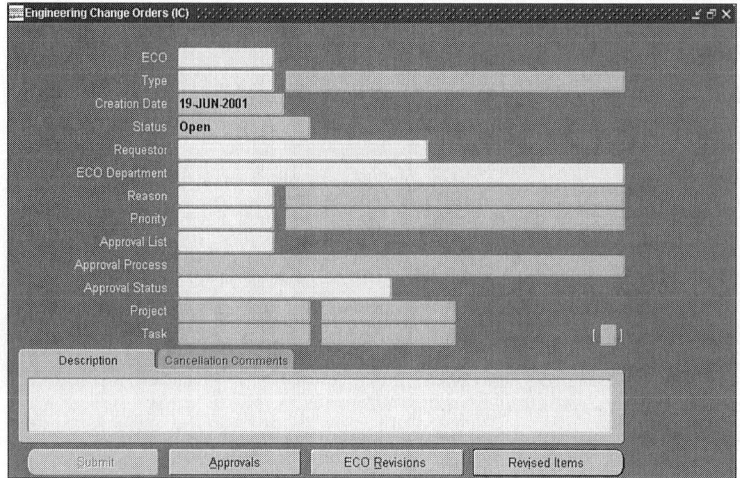

You can then select your ECO reason and priority for the change. As discussed in the setup steps, Oracle Engineering evaluates the ECO type/priority combination if it has been assigned to a Workflow and then passes control of the approval cycle to that Workflow. If you are not using Oracle Workflow to manage the approval cycle, you can select an approval list that was defined in your setup. This approval list is used with an Oracle Alert, which is discussed later in the section "Using Engineering Alerts." If you do not select an approval list and you are not using a Workflow for approval, your ECO approval status defaults to Approved.

Tip

Consider carefully the level of control you need over your ECOs. Oracle Engineering provides numerous options to restrict access to changes and to control the approval cycle. Do you really want your changes to have a default approval status of Approved? If you currently have a paper-based approval process, this might not seem like an issue. If you truly want to benefit from the functions Oracle Engineering provides, you might want to reconsider this.

If your ECOs are likely to go through numerous changes during their life cycle, you might choose to assign a revision to the ECO and continue to update this as you make subsequent changes.

You can enter the implementation costs associated with your ECO. Currently, this information is only used for reference and is not derived from Inventory, Planning, Purchase Order, or Costing information.

Your Engineering Change Orders can be applied to items or BOMs. These are termed *Revised Items*. You can choose to use Oracle Engineering to control the release and update of items. In this case, you can also control the revision of the item using your ECO. The profile option ENG: Require Revised Item New Revision can be set to Yes to force a new item revision each time a change is created.

If you are changing an existing BOM, you can also choose an alternate BOM as the revised item. If a BOM does not currently exist and your ECO is creating the BOM through the change, you can add the BOM parent item as the revised item and then add the components using the Revised Components window.

Tip

If you are using Oracle Engineering and Oracle Bills of Material together, you should consider using an ECO to create and release *all* new BOMs and their component items. This process provides traceability to the original ECO through Oracle Bills of Material.

When the revised items are being entered, you need to assign the effective dates that will be used for the items and any components that might exist. You can choose to assign the date and implement the change regardless of on-hand inventory balances, or you can make the change dependent on a "use-up" date. This date is calculated by the Material Requirements Planning (MRP) process for all items. It is based on the date by which the on-hand quantity will be completely depleted by existing gross requirements. If the use-up date changes as a result of on-hand quantity or if requirements change, you can have an alert send the ECO Requestor a message (see the section "Using Engineering Alerts" later in this chapter). Obviously, this only impacts changes that have not yet been implemented.

Tip

Oracle does not consider any material supply (for example, Purchase Orders or Discrete Jobs) in the calculation of the use-up date. It is based solely on on-hand inventory and gross requirements. Your Planners and Buyers have to review pending changes to ensure that the supply is cancelled or rescheduled as necessary.

You can make your change dependent on the use-up date for the revised item or for any of the revised components. You can also indicate whether the change to the revised item should be MRP Active. If it is active, MRP considers the pending change in its requirement calculations. If you have made the change dependent on the use-up date for a revised component and its use-up date changes, MRP suggests a revised effective date. However, it continues to use the current effective date in planning component requirements.

Tip

The only case where MRP makes use of a revised effectivity date is when the use-up component is the revised item itself.

You can determine whether the component requirements on unreleased WIP discrete jobs or repetitive schedules should be updated when your change becomes effective. The component requirements on jobs and schedules that have already been released will not be affected by an ECO.

If you need to add disposition information for the revised items and components, Oracle Engineering provides scrap, rework, and use-up dispositions that can be applied to WIP and Inventory. These are for information only.

When entering the revised component information, you must specify whether the ECO is going to add, change (modify), or disable the component. If you are modifying component information, Oracle enables updates to quantity and other parameters associated with the component usage on the BOM.

Release 11*i* provides the capability to attach files to your ECO. These can be text, spreadsheet, or graphics files. You might find it useful to attach copies of part or assembly drawings to your changes.

Finally, you need to submit your ECO for approval. As discussed previously, how this happens depends on the process you have chosen to use. If you are using Workflow, you can submit the ECO to the approval workflow as soon as it has been created. If you are using approval lists, an alert is forwarded to the individuals on the list requesting their approval. If you use neither of these methods, your ECO defaults to Approved status.

IMPLEMENTING ENGINEERING CHANGE ORDERS To implement the ECO, the approval status must be Approved. Implementation can be either manual or automatic. The changes to revised items on an ECO can be scheduled concurrently or can have different effectivity dates. Oracle marks implemented changes and updates the implemented date. When all your changes on an ECO have been implemented, Oracle marks the ECO as implemented. You cannot change ECO information for a revised item that has been implemented.

Using the manual implementation process, you implement all or individual revised items. The effective date for all components of a revised item is updated to reflect the implemented date, and status of the component item is now implemented. Even if the revised component has a future effective date, Oracle Engineering modifies this when the change has been implemented.

To use the automated implementation process, you must change the revised item status to Scheduled. Oracle Engineering now uses the revised item effective date to manage the change for you.

Tip

Nothing happens until the AutoImplement Concurrent Manager Program runs. You must schedule this program as discussed in the setup steps.

Mass Changes Using Engineering Change Orders The mass change function, shown in Figure 19.7, enables you to make changes to several BOMs simultaneously (add, disable, or modify components). When used with Oracle Bills of Material alone, this function can be used to make the changes immediately. If you are also using Oracle Engineering, you can use the mass change function to create an ECO. You can then approve and implement the ECO or any part of it, as discussed previously.

Figure 19.7
The Mass Change Bills screen enables you to mass change your engineering or manufacturing bills of material.

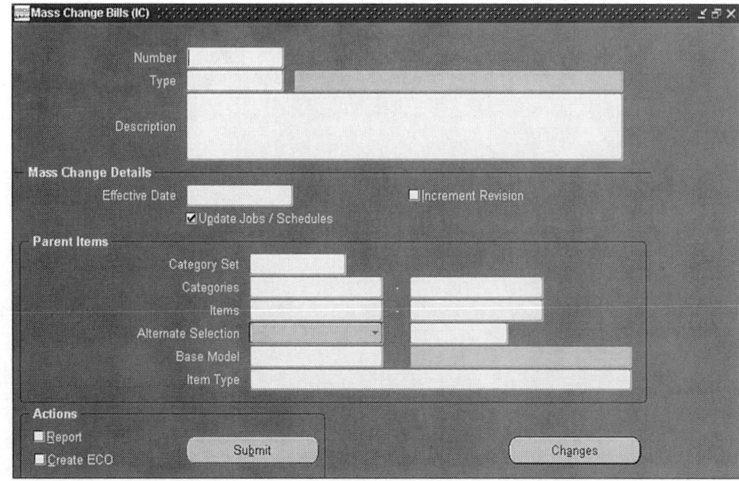

There is further discussion of the mass change functionality in the section "Using Oracle Bills of Material."

Purging Engineering Change Orders Over time, you might end up with a substantial number of implemented ECOs. Oracle Engineering provides a Purge function to enable you to remove ECO information that is no longer required. Purging ECOs removes all the information apart from the revision information already stored with items and BOMs.

Tip

If you really do not need to retain the ECO information within Oracle Engineering, ensure that you have some other appropriate means of storing and retrieving historical ECO data.

Managing Engineering Prototypes

Oracle Engineering provides an environment for managing Engineering prototype information, shown in Figure 19.8 and Figure 19.9. This information includes Engineering items, Engineering BOMs, and routings. This information is stored alongside the Manufacturing data. The items, BOMs, and routings can be transferred to Manufacturing when the Engineering activities are complete.

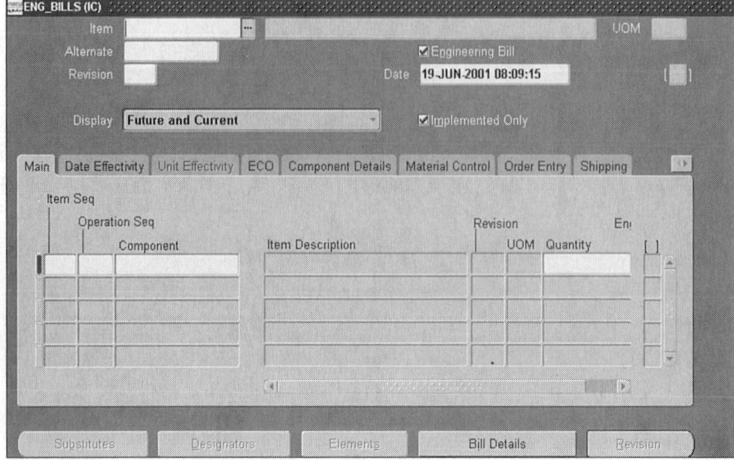

Figure 19.8
This screen enables you to create an engineering bill of materials.

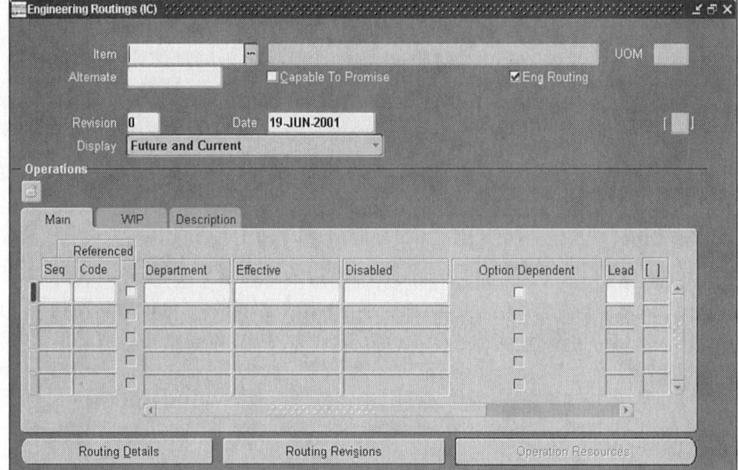

Figure 19.9
This screen enables you to define the required operations, sequences, and resources.

All the functions that can be performed with Manufacturing items, BOMs, and routings can also be used with their Engineering counterparts. This includes planning, purchasing, costing, selling, WIP transactions, inventory transactions, and revision control. The use of these functions for an Engineering item is controlled through the item attribute values set for the item. A full explanation of the use of item attributes can be found in Chapter 17.

If you want to control your Engineering items as they move through a development cycle, you can use item statuses to do this. You should create item statuses that reflect the level of control you need at each stage of the development cycle. Certain item attributes can be placed under status control and their values predetermined for that status. This could be used, for example, to prevent prototype assemblies from being sold to customers but to allow for the purchase of their components. Item statuses are discussed in detail in Chapter 17.

To prevent the proliferation of item numbers, Oracle Engineering also enables you to use item catalogs to attach characteristics to your items. Design or Development Engineers can use this feature to search for existing item numbers based on certain characteristics. The creation of item catalogs is discussed in Chapter 17.

An added feature to Oracle Engineering is the model/unit number effectivity support. This feature enables you to associate end item model and or unit numbers with items. You will notice new fields within Oracle Engineering windows. This is a new feature for Release 11*i* and did not exist in Release 11 of Oracle Engineering.

DEFINING AN ENGINEERING ITEM AND REVISIONS Engineering items are created in the same way as Manufacturing items (see Chapter 17 for information on how to define an item). Setting the Engineering item attribute to Yes differentiates these items from Manufacturing items. You should also set the BOM Allowed attribute to Yes (Chapter 17 explains the use of Item Attributes).

Revision control operates in the same way as for Manufacturing items. You can manually assign and track revisions, or you can use Oracle Engineering to manage the revisions using ECOs, as described earlier.

DEFINING AN ENGINEERING BOM AND ROUTING Engineering BOMs are created in the same way as Manufacturing BOMs. Both the Engineering Item attribute and the BOM Allowed attributes must be set to Yes. Depending on how the BOM will be used, you must also set the BOM Item Type item attribute (see the section "Using Oracle Bills of Material" later in this chapter).

One application would be the creation of an alternate Engineering BOM for an existing Manufacturing BOM to enable prototyping of changes to take place. The use of alternate BOMs is discussed in the Oracle Bills of Material section of this chapter.

A similar situation exists for Routings. In much the same way as Manufacturing Routings, you can create an Engineering Routing that can be used to prototype new or modified process flows. Another option is to create an alternate Engineering routing for an existing Manufacturing routing. The creation and use of routings is discussed in the Oracle Bills of Material section.

DEFINING ITEM/ORGANIZATION ATTRIBUTES Having created an Engineering item, you must set the item and item/organization attributes. The assignment of item attributes is covered in detail in Chapter 17.

TRANSFERRING ENGINEERING DATA When the development and prototyping activity is complete, you can transfer or copy the Engineering item, BOM, or routing to Manufacturing.

You cannot transfer an item or BOM that already exists in Manufacturing, and you can only transfer or copy Engineering data within the same inventory organization.

If you copy an Engineering item, you must assign a new name and description because the original information remains in Engineering.

If you are transferring an Engineering BOM, the component items must already have been transferred, or you can transfer them at the same time as the BOM. The copy function copies BOM and component information simultaneously.

Tip

Oracle only transfers components on the first level of an Engineering BOM. If you are transferring a multilevel BOM, you need to transfer each of the subassemblies separately, starting with the lowest-level assembly.

If there is an Engineering Routing associated with the Engineering BOM, you can transfer both together. All the components on the BOM will continue to be associated with the relevant operations on the routing. If you don't transfer the routing, you lose this relationship.

USING OPEN INTERFACES IN THIS APPLICATION

Open interfaces were mentioned earlier in this chapter in relation to converting data. These interfaces can also be used to allow data from external sources to be incorporated into the Oracle Engineering application.

Release 11*i* of Oracle Engineering continues to provide an ECO open interface. This allows you to import ECO information from an external application or data source.

Bills and components can be created, updated, or deleted using the Open Bills of Material Interface. Routings can be created, updated, or deleted in a similar manner using the Open Routing Interface. These interfaces can have applications in your organization when design-related data is created and maintained externally to Oracle Engineering—for example, in a Product Data Management (PDM) system. You could create your Engineering BOMs or routings using these interfaces and then use Oracle Engineering to manage the transfer of the BOMs and routings to Manufacturing.

Full details of the operation of the interfaces can be found in the Oracle reference manual *Oracle Manufacturing, Distribution, Sales and Service Open Interfaces Manual, Release 11*i.

IMPORTING ITEM INFORMATION

The Open Item Interface was discussed in the section "Converting Data for Major Entities" and in Chapter 17. This interface would also have an application in the creation of new item data based on imported data from an external system.

USING ENGINEERING ALERTS

Oracle Engineering comes with two standard alerts:

- **ECO Approval Notification**—In the discussion of ECO approval, one of the processes available uses an approval list to route an ECO for approval. This alert sends a message to each individual defined on the approval list, letting her know that an ECO requires her approval.
- **ECO Use-Up Date**—When a revised item's effectivity date is based on the use-up date of another item, this alert sends a message to the ECO requestor if the use-up date becomes different from the effectivity date.

These alerts need to be enabled, and alert-checking needs to be scheduled if you intend to use them.

UNDERSTANDING KEY REPORTS

Table 19.3 lists the standard reports provided with the Oracle Engineering application and a short description of each.

TABLE 19.3 ORACLE ENGINEERING REPORTS

Report Name	Description
Engineering Change Order Approval List Report	Lists the approvers for ECOs based on defined approval lists.
Engineering Change Order	Reports on Engineering Detail Report with the changes option to include changed component information.
Engineering Change Order Priorities Report	Reports the change order priorities that have been defined for use with Oracle Engineering.
Engineering Change Order Reasons Report	Lists the change order reasons that have been defined for use with Oracle Engineering.
Engineering Change Order Schedule Report	Reports on schedule information for pending ECOs up to a specified date.
Engineering Change Order Types Report	Lists the change order types that you have created.

USING ORACLE BILLS OF MATERIAL

Oracle Bills of Material provides the tools required to create and manage product structures and the manufacturing processes that are related to them. It includes the capability to create and manage complex product configurations to satisfy unique customer requirements, and with Release 11*i*, it includes tools to implement flow-manufacturing concepts in your business.

It has relationships with the Costing, Purchasing, Inventory, Order Management, MRP, WIP, Engineering, and Capacity applications (see Figure 19.10).

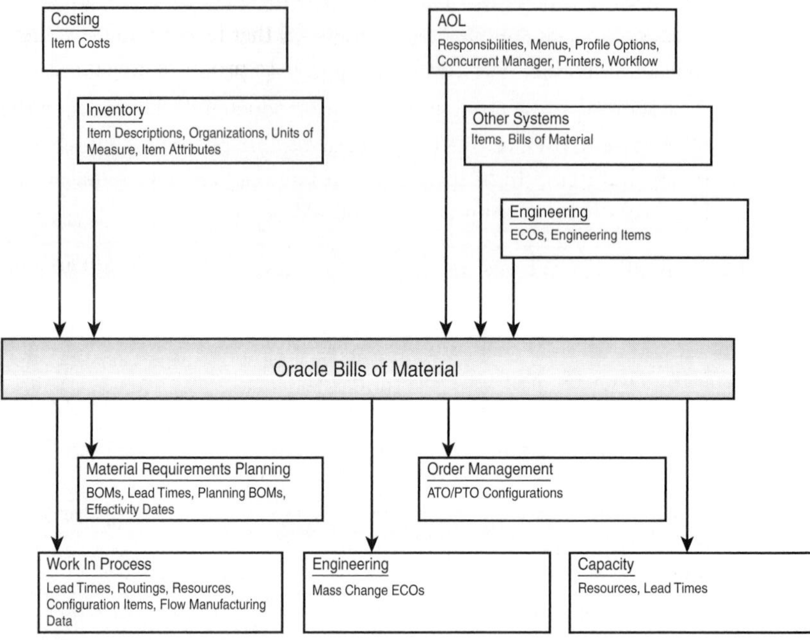

Figure 19.10
The major relationships between Oracle Bills of Material and the other applications.

DISCOVERING NEW FEATURES IN RELEASE 11*i*

With the introduction of Release 11 Oracle has added significant Just-In-Time (JIT) functionality. The most important feature is the introduction of Flow Manufacturing functionality. This has a number of impacts on Oracle Bills of Material. Flow Manufacturing continues to evolve within Oracle Bills of Material with ATO flow enhancements specific to Release 11*i*. This new feature enables you to create product families that are similar in resource usage, design and development, and manufacturing process for planning at a group level.

Although Flow Manufacturing is not based on new concepts, the fact that it has now been integrated into the applications is recognition of the benefits that it can provide in a modern manufacturing environment.

Flow Manufacturing is based on *pull* concepts:

- Customer demand pulls product through manufacturing rather than driving a production schedule based on anticipated demand.
- Raw materials are pulled through the manufacturing process (starting with the supplier) instead of being pushed onto discrete jobs.
- Material is back-flushed to relieve inventory when assemblies have completed manufacturing.
- Production lines are arranged by families of similar products rather than by process flow.

Some of the basic concepts of Flow Manufacturing are the following:

- Products and parts are grouped into product families. These product families can be created similar in resource usage, design, and manufacturing process.
- Product families are made up of products that have similar product synchronization (sync). The processes used to produce these products are similar.
- Product sync is assigning processes to product and then defining the sequence in which they are carried out.
- Production lines must be defined for parts and product families.
- You can define standard processes to be used with flow manufacturing.
- A *Flow Routing* is used to create product sync. This is similar to a regular routing in that it includes processes and resources.
- A new feature added in Release 11*i* is the Routing Network Designer. This graphical tool is used to define a product routing network as a visual network of operations and flows. This functionality enables you to sequence processes and line operations and perform load balancing. The tabular Routing Network window is replaced by the Routing Network Designer, which has a new window.
- In Release 11*i*, the Flow Manufacturing functionality has added the ability to switch existing/alternative routings. Essentially, this enables you to switch a new alternate flow routing with the existing primary routing. This robust functionality also enables you to create a new traditional alternate routing and switch it with the primary routing.
- A *Mixed Model Map* is used to assist in the design of the manufacturing line. Flow manufacturing is concerned with the balancing of manufacturing lines against a forecasted daily rate. This tool calculates several pieces of information to assist with the balancing task. You can regroup “events” (similar to operations on a routing) and regenerate the map to ensure that the line is balanced.
- Model/Unit Number Effectivity Support is a new feature for Release 11*i*. The model/unit number effectivity enables you to associate end item model/unit numbers with items. New fields have been added to several windows in Bills of Material and Engineering to support this feature.

Critical Implementation Factors

Although most manufacturing operations already use Bills of Material, some of the functionality available within the Oracle application does require careful consideration.

Attempting major changes in manufacturing technologies while implementing Oracle Bills of Material might not be too successful. Consider waiting until you have a stable business system implemented before moving towards flow manufacturing or a configure-to-order environment (unless these are already part of your business processes).

ISSUES AND GAPS

Although Oracle Bills of Material does provide adequate functionality for most businesses, there are always opportunities to improve.

Some of the enhancements to the Oracle Bills of Material product that users have suggested might make their way into future releases of the product:

- The capability to perform mass changes to routings. This is currently available for BOMs.
- Sorting the BOM Structure report by item number. It can currently be sorted by item sequence or operation sequence only.
- The capability to view reference designators in a BOM comparison.
- Being able to view costing, where-used, and routing information from the Indented BOM inquiry window.
- The capability to view usage of substitute components in the where-used inquiry window.

CONFIGURING THE APPLICATION

The following section describes the setup tasks and their sequence to configure Oracle Bills of Material. Because some tasks are dependent on others, you should perform them in the sequence shown.

As mentioned in the section on Oracle Engineering, the Oracle Applications Implementation Wizard is available with Release 11*i* of the applications. Consider using this to ensure that the setup steps are managed properly.

RESOLVING CRITICAL SETUP ISSUES

Access to create and update Bills of Material is a consideration. Oracle Bills of Material does provide some control through the Profile Options listed in the setup. You can allow access to certain BOM item types by setting these profiles at the User or Responsibility level.

Table 19.4 lists the tasks involved in setting up Oracle Bills of Material.

TABLE 19.4 BOM SETUP TASKS

Setup Task Name	Required?
Set Profile Options	Yes
Define Exception Templates	No
Assign Workday Calendar to Organization	Yes
Define Bills of Material Parameters	Yes
Define Department Classes	No
Define Resources	No
Define Resources Groups	No

Table 19.4 Continued

Setup Task Name	Required?
Define Simulation Sets	No
Define Locations	No
Define Departments	No
Assign Resources and Resources Shifts to Departments	No
Define Overheads	No
Associate Overheads with Departments	No
Define Alternates	No
Define Standard Bills of Material Comments	No
Define Standard Instructions	No
Define Change Order Types	No
Define Delete Constraints	No
Define and Build Workday Calendar	Yes

Understanding Each Setup Task

This section provides details on each of the setup tasks for Oracle Bills of Material and the order in which they should be performed.

Setting the Profile Options Table 19.5 shows the profile options that directly affect the operation of the Oracle Bills of Material application.

Table 19.5 Bills of Material Profile Options

Profile Option Name	Required?	Level*	Comment
BOM: Check for Duplicate Configuration	No	S	Default is No
BOM: Component Item Sequence Increment	No	SARU	Default is 10
BOM: Configuration Item Delimiter	No	S	Default is No
BOM: Configuration Item Type	No	S	Default is No
BOM: Days Past Before Starting Cutoff of Order Entry Bills	No	S	Default is 0
BOM: Default Bills of Material Levels	No	SARU	Default is 1
BOM: Default WIP Supply Values for Components	No	S	Default is Yes

TABLE 19.5 CONTINUED

Profile Option Name	Required?	Level*	Comment
BOM: Hour UOM	No	S	Set to the hour UOM you will be using
BOM: Inherit Option Class Operation Sequence Number	No	S	Default is No
BOM: Model Item Access	No	SARU	Default is Yes
BOM: Perform Lead Time Calculations	No	S	Default is No
BOM: Planning Item Access	No	SARU	Default is Yes
BOM: Standard Item Access	No	SARU	Default is Yes
BOM: Update Resource UOM	No	S	Default is No

**Levels can be Site, Application, Responsibility, or User. The system administrator sets most profile options.*

DEFINING EXCEPTION TEMPLATES Exception Templates are used to indicate nonworking day exceptions and shifts within the Workday Calendar. Typically, these are used for national holidays, shutdowns, and so on. The process for creating these is described in Chapter 17.

DEFINING AND BUILDING THE WORKDAY CALENDAR The Workday Calendar is usually created as part of the Oracle Inventory setup and can be seen in Figure 19.11 (see Chapter 17). It holds information on the organization's working patterns, including nonworking days and/or shifts.

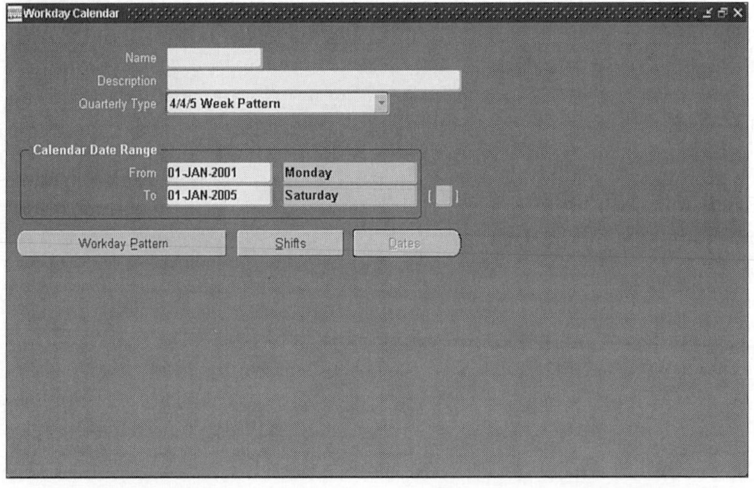

Figure 19.11
You can define shift information and workday patterns using the Workday Calendar form displayed here.

Tip

If you choose to set up your workday calendar from within Oracle Bills of Material, you should be aware that effective use of Oracle Master Scheduling/MRP requires you to define a 445 or 544 weekly quarter pattern. If you use calendar months or a 13-period calendar, your MRP resolution goes to monthly buckets only (which is not necessarily a good thing if you are a Master Scheduler).

Assigning a Calendar to an Organization When the calendar has been created, it must be assigned to an inventory organization. If you are creating more than one organization, you should assign a calendar to each. One calendar can be shared across multiple organizations.

Defining Bills of Material Parameters Figure 19.12 displays the BOM parameters that must be set for each organization that you are creating. The BOM parameters window enables you to set the BOM level and configuration item options. Set the maximum number of BOM levels to be used for explosions, implosions, and loop checking. This should be considered along with the BOM: Default Bills of Material Levels profile option. Oracle Bills of Material allows a maximum of 60 levels. This should be more than adequate for most implementations!

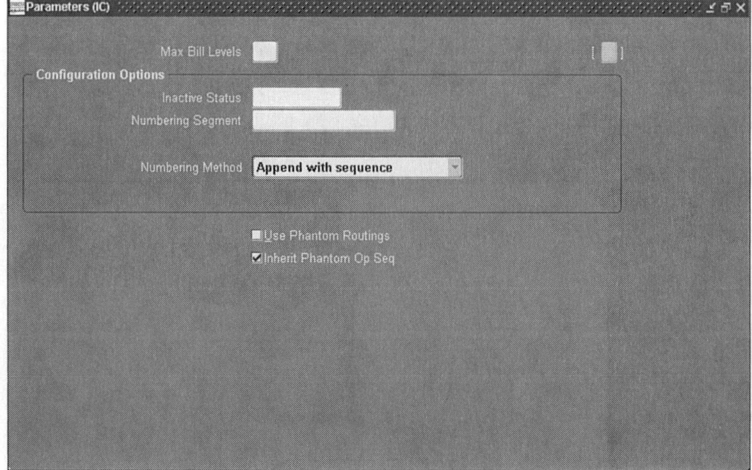

Figure 19.12 Define your bills of material parameters for each organization using the Parameters screen.

Tip

If you are converting legacy data, this would be an appropriate time to consider the depth of existing BOMs.

If you will be using configure-to-order, you can also set a number of BOM defaults using this window. An inactive status can be set and used to tag completed configuration items. In a configure-to-order environment, Oracle enables you to specify the numbering segment to be used in creating configuration item numbers. This assumes that you have created a numbering segment in the System Items flexfield (see Chapter 17).

For configure-to-order, you can also define one of three numbering methods to be used for your configuration items:

- **Append a sequence**—A sequence number internally generated by Oracle is appended to the numbering segment that was previously assigned.
- **Replace with sequence**—The numbering segment is replaced with the internally generated sequence number.
- **Replace with Order, Line Number**—The Sales Order number and line number are substituted for the item segment.

DEFINING DEPARTMENT CLASSES Department classes are used for reporting purposes only. If you need to group departments for shop floor scheduling or control reports, this can be done with the Department Classes window.

DEFINING RESOURCES AND RESOURCES GROUPS Resources are required to enable shop floor scheduling and collection of cost information when routings are used. Resources are also required if you intend to use Outside Processing functionality. Figure 19.13 shows the Resources definition screen, which allows you to assign these resources to departments and shifts.

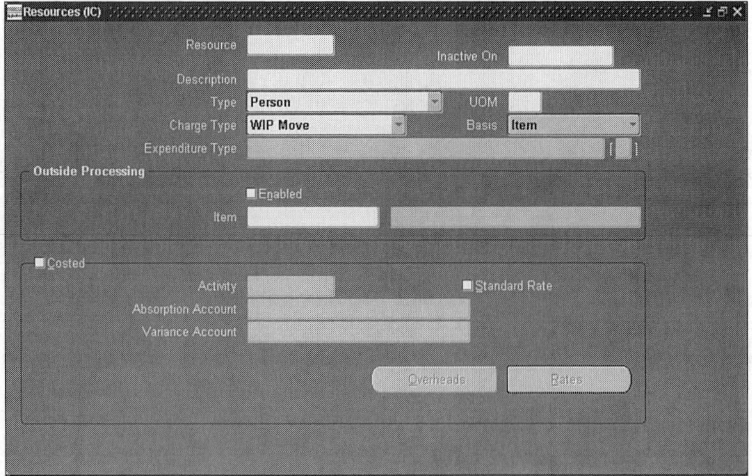

Figure 19.13 This shows you where to define your resources, such as employees, machines, and outside processes.

Oracle enables you to create resources to account for most things used in a manufacturing operation, including people, equipment, cash, outside processing services, and floor space.

To correctly use routings, you need to assign the required resources to departments and then assign the departments to operations, including the resources and usage you require.

There are two prerequisites before you can define resources:

- You must set up the units of measure to be used and any conversions that will be required. This is part of the Inventory setup (see Chapter 17).
- A site-level profile option (BOM: Hour UOM) must be set to the unit of measure (UOM) that will be used to represent one hour. Resources can only be scheduled when their UOM is the same as this setting or if there is a UOM conversion defined for it.

Each department resource can also be assigned to a resources group. Figure 19.14 shows where to create lookup codes for your resources groups. This allows for the creation of bills of resources, which are used in Oracle Capacity (see Chapter 21, "Using Oracle Planning Applications").

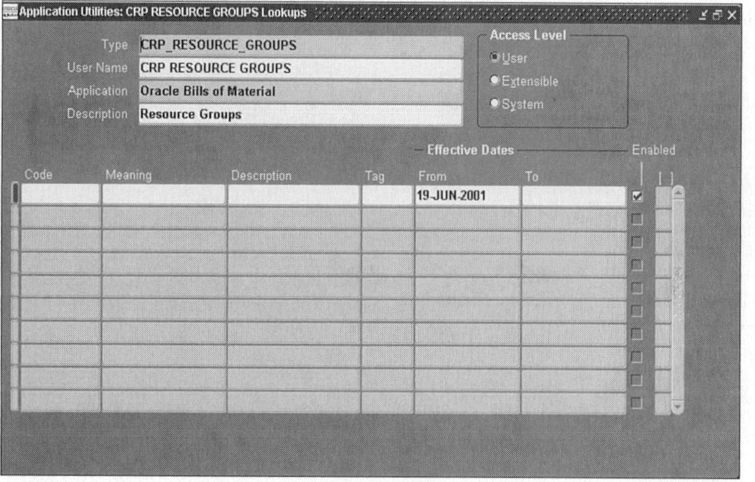

Figure 19.14 This screen enables you to define lookup codes for resource groups.

PART III CH 19

DEFINING SIMULATION SETS This is an optional setup step. Simulation sets are used with Oracle Capacity. They enable you to define modifications to available capacity for your routing-based resources (see Chapter 21). Notice in Figure 19.15 that you can indicate the simulation set to be used in scheduling.

DEFINING LOCATIONS You must define delivery locations if you have defined departments with Outside Processing resources (see Chapter 16, "Using Oracle Purchasing"). Figure 19.16 shows location name, address, and shipping details. Locations can also be defined in Oracle Purchasing or Oracle Human Resources.

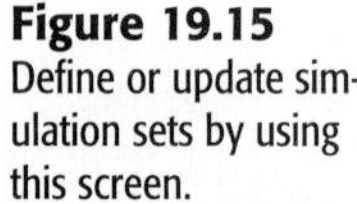

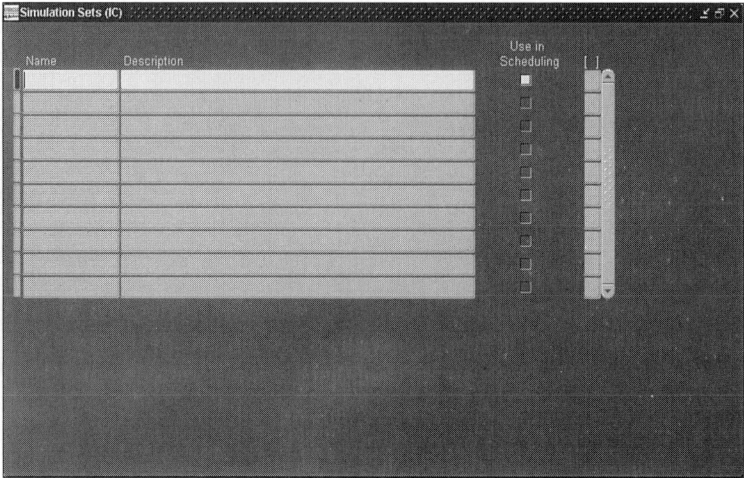

Figure 19.15
Define or update simulation sets by using this screen.

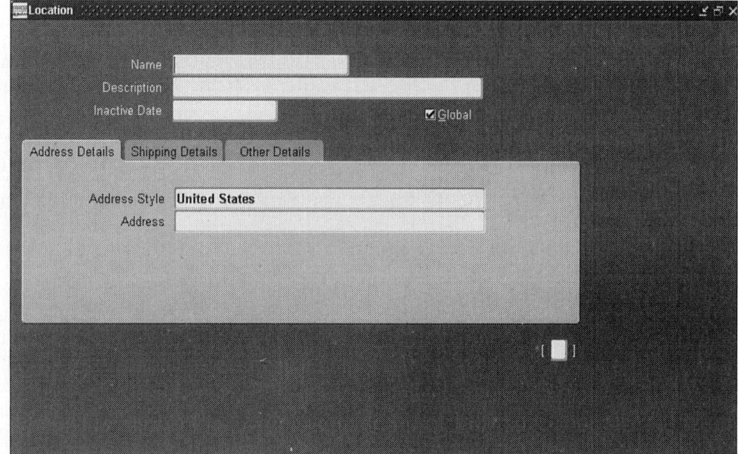

Figure 19.16
Use the Location screen to define specific locations.

DEFINING DEPARTMENTS Departments are required if you will be using routing-based manufacturing. Figure 19.17 shows the screen to define departments within your organization. A department consists of one or more people, suppliers, or machines. You can also indicate where you want to collect cost and apply overhead.

ASSIGNING RESOURCES AND SHIFTS TO DEPARTMENTS If you are using routing-based manufacturing, you need to assign your resources to a department. You can also assign shifts to these resources.

If you plan on using Oracle Capacity, you can group the department's resources by resources group and then assign simulation sets for each resources shift.

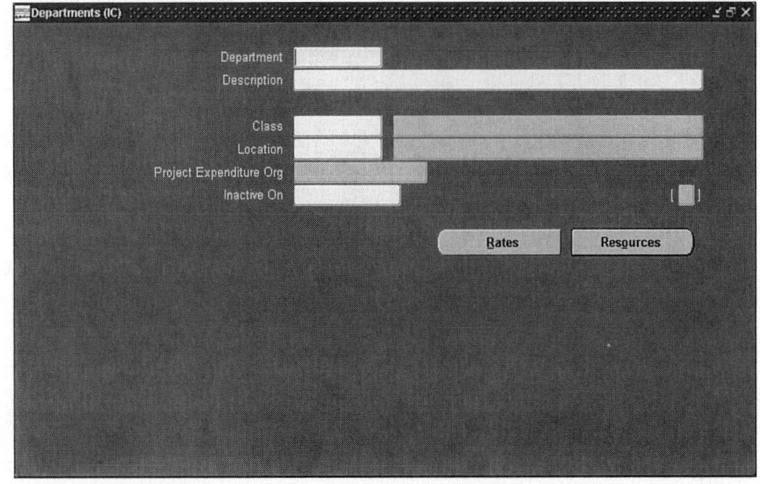

Figure 19.17 Define your departments using this screen. This form also allows you to assign your rates and resources to departments.

DEFINING OVERHEADS AND ASSOCIATING OVERHEADS WITH DEPARTMENTS As part of the department setup, you define any overhead costs that might be related to the department and then associate these overheads with the department.

DEFINING ALTERNATES An alternate BOM is a separate list of items that can be used to produce an assembly. Although there is still only one assembly item, one or more alternate BOMs can be associated with the assembly. Some applications could be the following:

- Manual and automated processes for producing the same assembly require different component items. The components might differ because of packaging or for other reasons.
- An assembly might be built using different key component items based on availability. Alternate BOMs would be applicable here if the choice of other components varied based on the choice of the key component.

You create the alternate names using the alternate window. The name chosen can be alphanumeric, but ensure that it relates in some way to its function.

Tip

You may reuse the same alternate name on any number of assemblies. The relationship between BOM and alternate is unique to a particular assembly item number. So, an alternate name of "MANUAL" can be used on several assemblies with different components being used each time.

DEFINING STANDARD BOM COMMENTS You can define standard BOM comments that can then be assigned to any BOM you create.

DEFINING STANDARD INSTRUCTIONS Standard instructions can be created and then used with any routing operation or standard operation.

DEFINING CHANGE ORDER TYPES You can define change order types that can be used to tag mass changes to your Bills of Material. If you will be using Oracle Engineering, you might want to define these as part of that setup. Figure 19.18 shows the form to create your change types, which enable reclassification to changed items.

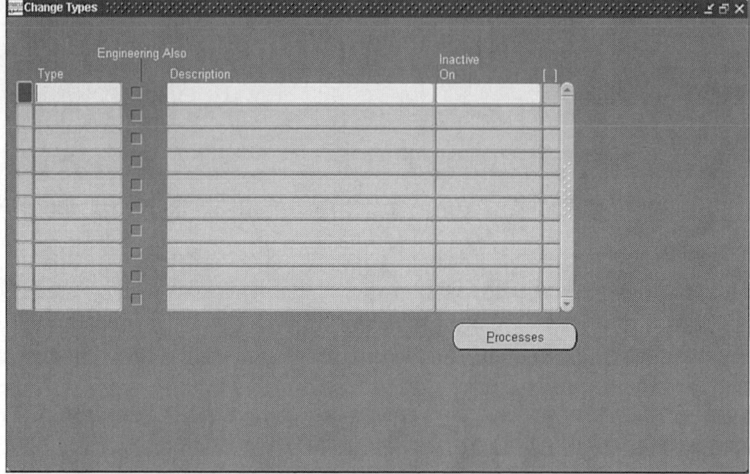

Figure 19.18
This screen enables you to create your engineering change order types.

DEFINING DELETE CONSTRAINTS Deleting a BOM or routing could have huge implications for your organization. Figure 19.19 shows the form that enables you to create specific business rules that govern deletion. Oracle Bills of Material comes with a set of predefined deletion constraints. These should prevent you from doing the unthinkable. However, operational requirements vary from business to business, and the Define Deletion Constraints window enables you to specify customized constraints. This same mechanism can be used to specify constraints for the deletion of items, bills, components, routings, and operations.

You must enter your criteria in the form of a SQL select statement specifying whether to delete if rows are found.

Tip

To specify custom delete constraints, you should have a thorough understanding of the Oracle Application database tables and the relationships between them. For most organizations, the default constraints provided are adequate.

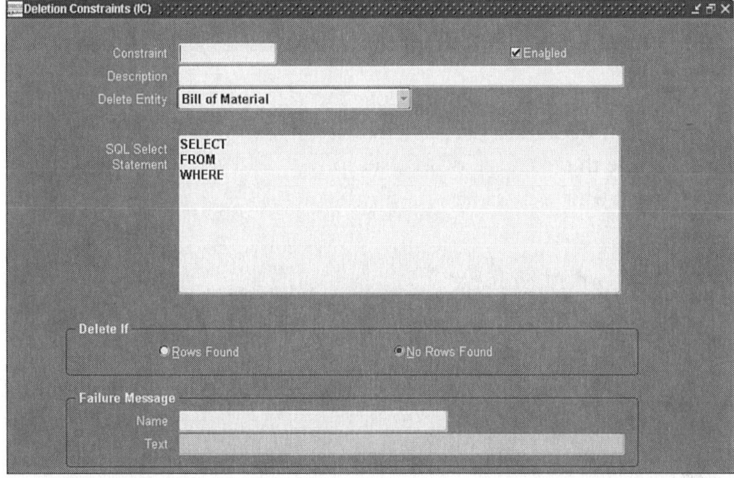

Figure 19.19
Create your delete constraints using this screen.

CONVERTING DATA FOR MAJOR ENTITIES

Oracle provides two tools with the Oracle BOM application that provide for conversion of legacy data:

- Open Bills of Material Interface
- Open Routing Interface

The operation of these interfaces is fully described in the Oracle documentation.

There are some basics that you need to consider. If you are fortunate to be in a "green field" situation, conversion of legacy data is not a concern. For most people, there is legacy data to contend with. Using the open interfaces requires some programming to extract the data from the legacy system, format it correctly, and then insert it in the interface tables. You should consider the amount of effort required to develop and test the extract programs compared to the volume of data to be converted. If there are a small number of BOMs and routings and if the number of items per BOM is small, manually entering the data could be an option.

In most cases, manually entering your BOMs and routings is not a viable option.

Tip

Before attempting to populate the interface tables, ensure that the following have been done:

- All required inventory items (parent items, component items, planning items, and so on) have already been loaded.
- All required BOM setup tasks have been completed.

Oracle provides full validation of the data being loaded through the open interfaces. You will save yourself time and effort in identifying and correcting errors if both these steps are complete.

If you choose to use the open interface program to convert your BOMs and Routings, use the following process:

- Extract your data from the legacy system.
- Populate the interface tables.
- Run the BOM/Routing import program using the "Import Bills and Routings form."
- Review any errors in the interface tables using SQL*Plus or a custom developed report. (The Process_Flag is not set for any rows that have errored.)
- Correct the problems associated with any failing rows.

The Open Bills of Material Interface tables are the following:

- BOM_BILL_OF_MTLS_INTERFACE
- BOM_INVENTORY_COMPS_INTERFACE
- BOM_REF_DESGS_INTERFACE
- BOM_SUB_COMPS_INTERFACE
- MTL_ITEM_REVISIONS_INTERFACE

The Open Routing Interface tables are:

- BOM_OP_ROUTINGS_INTERFACE
- BOM_OP_SEQUENCES_INTERFACE
- BOM_OP_RESOURCES_INTERFACE
- MTL_RTG_ITEM_REVS_INTERFACE

PROCESSING TRANSACTIONS

The following sections cover the transactions that are involved in the operation of the Oracle Bills of Material application.

MAINTAINING BILLS OF MATERIAL

Oracle Bills of Material provides for five distinct types of bill:

- **Standard Bill of Material**—Is the most commonly used type. Lists components and usage quantities.
- **Model Bill of Material**—Is used to configure to order. Defines options and option classes.
- **Option Class Bill of Material**—Groups optional components on a BOM. Becomes a component of the Model Bill of Material.
- **Planning Bill of Material**—Is used with Oracle Master Scheduling. Planning percentages can be assigned to components.

- **Engineering Bill of Material**—An Engineering BOM can be defined as an alternate to a manufacturing BOM. It provides for Engineers to prototype variations of a product without affecting the manufacturing BOM.

Bills of Material are created, maintained, and viewed using the same Bills of Material window.

DEFINING A BILL The three prerequisites to defining a BOM are as follows:

- The parent item and all components must already be defined as inventory items.
- The BOM Allowed item attribute must be set to Yes for the parent item and components.
- The parent item BOM Item Type attribute must be set to model, option class, planning, or standard. This depends on the function of the BOM.

To define a Bill, navigate to the Bills of Material window and enter the assembly item number. Figure 19.20 displays the Bills of Material definition screen. This form enables you to create a manufacturing or engineering bill, copy an existing bill, or make reference to a common bill. If you want to create an alternate BOM, you should choose the alternate name from the list created in the earlier setup steps. If you choose to use revision control for your Bills, you should also enter the revision BOM and revision date.

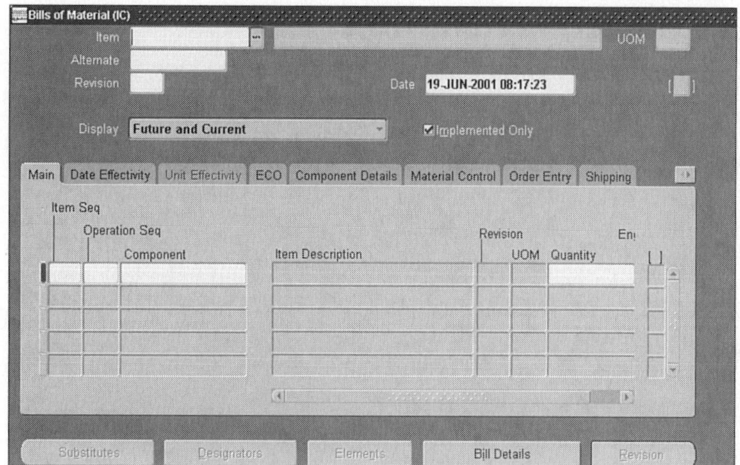

Figure 19.20
Create your Bills of Material using this screen.

In the Components region of the window, enter the item sequence number (which can be used to dictate the sort order of components when printing the BOM), the operation sequence number (which is used in conjunction with a routing), and the component item number.

In the Main region of the window, enter the quantity of the component required for the assembly.

There are other regions available to enter additional information for the component and assembly combination:

- **Effectivity**—Enter the in and out BOM effectivity dates that apply to this component. This is optional when creating a new BOM.
- **Component Details**—Enter the planning percentage (if this is applicable), the yield factor (used in MRP, 1=100% 0.9=90%), and whether the component should be included in cost rollups (the material cost, not the routing cost, is used).
- **Material Control**—You can choose to specify the Supply Type for the component on this particular assembly rather than use the Supply Type specified for the component item. The available types are Assembly Pull, Bulk, Operation Pull, Phantom, Push, or Supplier. These are described in detail in Chapter 22, "Using Oracle Work In Process." If you set the profile option BOM: Default WIP Supply Values for Components to Yes, Oracle Bills of Material defaults the component values for Supply Type from the item master. In this region, you can also specify the supply subinventory to be used for this component and the locator if the subinventory is under locator control.
- **Order Management**—If the BOM BOM is a model, option class, or kit, you can enter min and max order quantities to be used with Oracle Order Entry. You can also specify whether Available-to-Promise (ATP) should be checked for the component. You must set the Check Component ATP item attribute to Yes for the assembly if you want to do this. The component can be set to Optional or Mandatory. The Mutually Exclusive field applies to option class BOMs and determines whether the option should be the only one available for selection or part of a list. The Basis field affects the way in which the quantity of the component is treated. If it is set to Option Class, it is not possible to override the quantity for the option when entering a sales order. (Oracle uses the component quantity × the option class extended quantity.)
- **Shipping**—You can specify whether the component is shippable. The value defaults from the component item attributes. If you want to have this component show on the shipping documentation, you can set Include on Ship Docs to Yes. The Required to Ship field affects Pick to Order (PTO) items only. The item must be available to allow shipment of the order. The BOM Required for Revenue field affects Receivables. If the component has this field set to Yes, an invoice cannot be created for the parent item until the component has shipped.

To speed up the creation of a Bill for an assembly that is similar to another, Oracle provides a BOM copy function. When creating the BOM, you can simply specify the assembly that's the BOM you want to copy. The components, usage quantities, and other characteristics can be modified as required when the BOM has been copied. Any revision of a BOM can be copied. A similar function is available for use with routings.

Tip

The copy function operates on a single BOM level *only*. It does not copy the components of assemblies below the first level of the BOM you are copying.

If you are copying the BOM from another Inventory Organization, you must ensure that the components of the BOM exist in the destination organization. You can only copy from another BOM organization that shares the same item master as the destination.

Tip

The copy function is particularly useful if you are creating *alternate* BOMs. These are typically very similar to the primary BOM with only minor modifications.

Oracle Bills of Material enables sharing of BOM information across organizations using a Common Bill of Material. This is useful if the same assembly structure and components are to be used in more than one organization and you want to administer the BOM from one central location.

Before you reference a common BOM, you must ensure the following:

- The BOM you are referencing BOM as a common BOM cannot reference another BOM as a common BOM.
- If you reference an alternate BOM as a common BOM, both must share the same alternate name.
- If the BOM you are creating is a manufacturing BOM, the common BOM referenced must also be a manufacturing BOM.

Tip

Your current Inventory Organization and the one in which the Common BOM resides must share the same Item Master organization. If there are components already assigned to your new BOM, you cannot reference a Common BOM.

If you are referencing a Common BOM in an Inventory Organization other than the one in which you are creating BOM the new BOM, all the components must exist in the current organization.

Common Routings can be referenced in a similar manner.

For Model and Option Class BOMs, you can enter item catalog descriptive elements that can be used in conjunction with Order Entry to select options based on description. Item Catalogs are described in Chapter 17.

Oracle Bills of Material provides for the use of reference designators. These enable references to be made on the BOM to written instructions or drawings that, for example, indicate the location of a component. The reference designators are assigned to the component when it is added to the BOM. To speed up data entry, Oracle can append prefixes and suffixes to your designators. You can choose to have Oracle require separate designators for each component usage (for example, a quantity of five per assembly of a component requires five separate designators), or BOM you can choose to add as many as you need.

Tip

If you intend to share the reference designator information with a Computer Aided Manufacturing (CAM) system or to share the reference designators from a Computer Aided Design (CAD) system, please ensure that you are consistent in the formats being used when creating BOMs.

Substitute components can be added to any component on a standard BOM. More than one substitute component can be assigned per component on the BOM. The usage quantity of the substitute can be different from that of the original component, and there are no restrictions BOM on using the same substitute for several components on the same BOM.

Tip

The use of substitute components can confuse people. Although they will appear on some of the Oracle Master Scheduling/MRP reports, they are only there as a *reference*. Oracle assumes that when you are aware of an issue with the standard component, you will use the substitute information to take whatever action you need to. *Unfortunately, nothing will happen automatically!*

With Release 11*i* of Oracle Bills of Material, you can attach files to any BOM or routing you create. This opens up the possibility to include text files, drawings, spreadsheets, graphics, and so on.

Oracle provides a loop-checking facility when you have created and saved a new BOM. BOM loops occur when the parent assembly includes itself as a component. The loop can be created through any subassembly, not just on the first level of the BOM. BOM loops cause serious problems with MRP and Cost rollups. As well as having loop-checking available when a BOM is created, Oracle Bills of Material provides a concurrent program to check for BOM loops on a range BOM of assemblies.

Tip

If you are importing BOMs and components from a legacy system, take extra care to ensure that BOM loops are not created inadvertently.

MASS CHANGING SEVERAL BILLS The Mass Change functionality enables you to apply changes to a BOM number of BOMs based on parameters you specify. Changes can be made to add, delete, or replace components. In addition, you can change a component quantity, yield factor, or other information for a component of a BOM.

If you are using Oracle Bills of Material on its own, you can generate and execute the change directly. Oracle only allows you to make future changes on Engineering BOMs in this way. If you are also using Oracle Engineering, you can use the Mass Change functionality to create an Engineering Change Order (ECO) that can be implemented using a future effectivity. This type of change can be applied to both Manufacturing and Engineering BOMs.

In executing your Mass Change, Oracle enables you to specify limits for the assemblies to be affected. There might be reasons why you would want to apply a change to *all* assemblies, but in most cases, you will want to operate with a subset of your assemblies. You can specify a range based on item number, item category, or item type.

Tip

Consider creating an item category that groups your assemblies by product family. This enables you to use BOM and ECO functions limited to a particular product family. The creation of item categories is discussed in Chapter 17.

Caution

Mass Changes can be drastic measures. This is a powerful function that could affect every single assembly in your database. Consider carefully the desired end result and even more carefully the limits you specify for the assemblies to be affected.

Tip

In the unlikely event that a Mass Change is made in error, it is possible to create another mass change (using the same limits) to undo the damage.

Deleting Item Information In the section on setups, I discussed the creation of deletion criteria. Oracle Bills of Material comes with a set of predefined deletion criteria to control the deletion of BOM, routing, and item information. These constraints are described in detail in the Oracle documentation but include checks for the following conditions:

- Open Sales Orders for the assembly
- Open Work Orders for the assembly
- Repetitive Schedules referencing the assembly
- Demand exists for the assembly

You can begin to see that the deletion of BOM, routing, or item information could wreak havoc in your database if the information is already being used or referenced elsewhere.

From the Deletion Groups window, you can specify the type of deletion you want to perform. The type of deletion you can perform depends on the modules you have installed. In a typical manufacturing environment with Oracle Inventory and Oracle Bills of Material installed, you can delete items, bills, components, and routings from this window. You can choose to archive BOM and Routing information for future reference. You need to specify a name for the deletion group.

Tip

Resist the temptation to name your groups "AA", "AB", and so on. Over time, the number of groups will build up, and it will be difficult to remember what exactly you were doing. Make the names meaningful.

There are two ways to operate the delete function:

- You can specify the BOMs, routings, or items you want to delete and perform a CHECK. Oracle reports any error conditions that would occur if you continue with the delete process, giving you an opportunity to take whatever action you need to.
- If you have checked the deletion and are happy with the results, you can go ahead and execute it.

DEFINING ROUTINGS AND STANDARD OPERATIONS

Routings list the sequence of operations required to manufacture a product. Figure 19.21 shows the screen to define your operational information. As with Bills of Material, Oracle enables you to define alternate routing names. These can be used to describe alternate process flows to be used when manufacturing an assembly. You can also create an Engineering routing as an alternate to a Manufacturing routing and use it for prototyping an alternate process flow. You can share any alternate labels you create between your BOMs and routings. If you do create an alternate BOM with the same label as an alternate routing, the components are added to the operations on the alternate routing.

Figure 19.21
Create your routing using this screen.

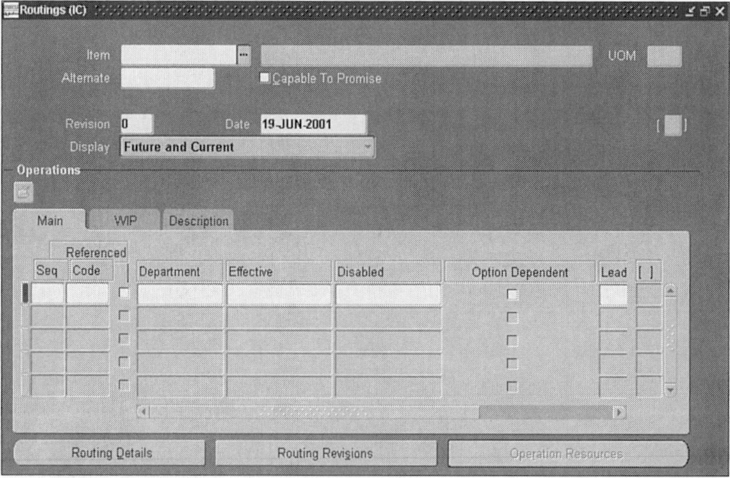

When you create a Bill of Material that is associated with a routing, you can choose the operation sequence number to which a component should be issued. This flexibility provides for components to be issued only to the operations where they are required. You can choose to issue *all* material to the first operation of the routing if you want.

Oracle Work In Process provides for the back-flush (inventory relief) of components in the process as assemblies are completed. When a routing is being created, you have the option to specify at which operations the back-flush transaction can happen.

If the routing is being created for model or option class items, you can specify the operations that are required for that particular model or option. This allows a customized routing to be created when a particular option is selected in a configuration.

Resources are associated with the operations on a routing. You can select one or more resources for each operation. For each resource being assigned to an operation, you have the choice to include the resource in scheduling and lead-time calculations. If the resource has been defined as cost, you can also collect the cost information using the routing.

Resource usage can be specified as lot-based or item-based. A lot-based usage can be useful for tasks related to the setup of a manufacturing operation. Item-based usages vary depending on the number of items being processed.

Resources can be scheduled based on resource units per item or item units per resource, depending on the resource and how it is being used. The costs associated with a resource can be manually charged or automatically charged, based on move transactions or Purchase Order receipts in the case of outside processing items.

You can specify a completion subinventory to be used with the routing. The Routing Details button, when selected, enables you to indicate a completion subinventory (see Figure 19.21). This is the default subinventory used by Oracle Work In Process when the assembly is being completed.

In defining a routing, you can also define how move transactions are recorded and resources are consumed using the Autocharge and Count Point fields. Their usage is described in the *Oracle Bills of Material User's Guide, Release 11*i.

A Standard Operation is an operation that is created as a template to be used repeatedly on routings. Figure 19.22 shows you the form to create standard operations. It is created in much the same way as any other operation. When the Standard Operation has been set up, it can be copied into a new operation on any routing you are creating. You can change any of the detail copied to the new operation to suit your needs.

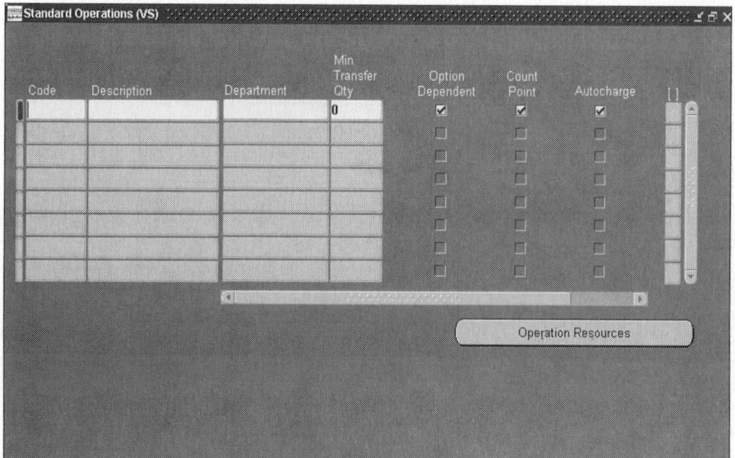

Figure 19.22
This enables you to define your standard operations.

CALCULATING LEAD TIMES

Lead times play an important part in the planning process and in the calculation of Available-to-Promise (ATP) dates.

You can calculate lead times for manufactured items using Oracle Bills of Material. There are two types of lead time calculated:

- **Cumulative Manufacturing Lead Time**—This is the total time it would take to manufacture an item if all the components were on-hand but all the subassemblies had to be manufactured level by level.
- **Cumulative Total Lead Time**—This is the total time it would take to manufacture the assembly if there were no components on-hand. The calculation assumes that all components have to be purchased and all subassemblies are to be manufactured level by level.

Item categories (see Chapter 17) can be used to limit the manufacturing items that are affected by the recalculation programs. There might be groups of items whose lead times you want to manage manually.

If you modify a routing by adding or deleting operations or by changing resource usage, you need to recalculate the lead times for the assemblies using the routing.

Also, changes to the BOM structure or individual-component lead times can affect the assembly-cumulative lead times. These should be rolled up after BOM changes.

UNDERSTANDING CONFIGURE TO ORDER

For many products, customers are demanding a greater degree of customization. Oracle Bills of Material provides the tools required to support customizations of this kind.

The Configure To Order tools allow options to be defined that can be grouped into unique product configurations to satisfy a customer requirement.

There are two ways in which this can be done:

- **Assemble to Order**—A unique configuration to satisfy the customer order is created from Assemble to Order (ATO) models and options that are defined through BOMs, manufactured, and then shipped to the customer. The ATO Flow enhancement feature enables you to create product families similar in resource usage, design, and manufacturing process for planning.
- **Pick to Order**—The customers' order is made up of Pick to Order (PTO) Models and option classes, which are picked from stock and then shipped to the customer.

The distinction between both methods blurs because of the flexibility Oracle Bills of Material provides in structuring model and option class BOMs. Various combinations of ATO and PTO models and options are possible to support many business scenarios. These BOMs can also include purchased items, phantom assemblies, and standard BOMs as part of their structure.

In the section on defining a BOM, I discussed models and option classes. To define an ATO Model, the Assemble to Order item attribute must be set to Yes. The BOM Item Type attribute will be set to Model. ATO option classes also require the Assemble to Order item attribute to be set to Yes, but the BOM Item Type will be Option Class. PTO models and options have the Pick Components item attribute set to Yes. The use of item attributes is discussed in Chapter 17.

Tip

ATO models can only have ATO option classes structured to them. Similarly, PTO models can only have PTO options structured. It is possible to combine elements of ATO and PTO items on a BOM. Set the Pick Components attribute for the parent model to Yes and add ATO models to the BOM as components.

You can make the components of your model optional or mandatory. This enables you to specify items that must always be included as part of a configuration. The use of the Mutually Exclusive field was covered in the section on defining a BOM. When used with the Optional field, you can force the selection of one or more options, or no options if you want.

BOMs made up of multiple levels of PTO and ATO models and options can become complex and can make planning an interesting activity. You can assign planning percentages to your models and options. In this way, you can use forecast or historical usage to predict the mix of options that are likely to be used in your configurations. Master Scheduling uses this information to derive planned orders and suggest reschedules of existing orders for the components required to support this.

If your company will have multiple inventory organizations, you can use Common Bills of Material to share models and options across the organizations. In this way, it is possible to have a remote site take complete Engineering responsibility for a product and have the other sites that are building the product reference it as a Common Bill. Your ECOs will only have to be applied in the organization that owns the common BOM.

Note

As with all usage of common BOMs, all the organizations must share a common Item Master Organization. Your models and options will have to be defined in that organization and then assigned to the other organizations.

Available-to-Promise (ATP) checking can be used at Order Entry time. Oracle evaluates the earliest date that an item will be available to satisfy an order requirement. To enable ATP checking, you use two item attributes:

- **Check ATP**—An ATP check can be performed on this item.
- **ATP Components**—There are components of this item that require ATP checking.

In this way, ATP can navigate through your model and option BOM structure, evaluating only the components that you have selected for checking.

With ATO configurations, the order-entry and manufacturing process is more complex. When entering the order, you have to choose from the options that are available on the model being ordered. This unique configuration must be released to manufacturing to allow it to be built (Manufacturing Release). This configuration remains linked to the sales order. To identify the unique configuration, you can choose to autocreate a configuration item. Oracle creates the item and assigns a BOM and routing. How the configuration item number looks depends on the options you selected for the configuration item numbering method when you set the BOM parameters (see the BOM Parameter setup step earlier in this section). Oracle Bills of Material do a cost rollup for the single-level bill of the configuration item.

When the configuration has been released to manufacturing, the Production Planner or Scheduler can use the AutoCreate Final Assembly Orders process to create a discrete job for the configuration. Creating the job establishes a reservation from the sales order to the job. When you complete a quantity from the final assembly order to inventory, you also create a reservation from the job to the finished goods inventory. As quantities are completed to inventory, the reservation on the discrete job is relieved.

Note

If there are multiple sales orders linked to a discrete job, you should be careful to specify which one the completion is for. Otherwise, Oracle picks the sales order with the earliest ship date and uses that for the relief.

To ensure that all items on a configuration are available to ship, order entry does not allow pick release of the order if there are discrete jobs for configuration components linked to the sales order that are still in process. If you have multiples of the configuration on the sales order, you can pick release quantities as they arrive in your finished goods inventory.

Over time, you will accumulate configuration items for all the unique configurations you have manufactured. In the setup section, I discussed the Inactive Status for configuration items. This was part of the BOM parameter setup. Using the Deactivate Configuration Items concurrent program, you can apply this status configuration to items that have zero on-hand inventory or where there have been no recent sales orders for the item. Use the item delete process to purge these items from your system when the status has been updated.

USING OPEN INTERFACES IN THIS APPLICATION

Apart from their application in converting legacy data, the same open interfaces can be used to import BOM data from external systems.

USING THE BILL AND ROUTING IMPORT INTERFACE

In a manufacturing environment, a typical application using the open interfaces would be the import of product data from a Product Data Management (PDM) system or a Computer Aided Design (CAD) system. The interfaces can be used to create, update, and delete BOMs and Routings. The function being performed through the open interfaces is dependent on the value set in the TRANSACTION_TYPE column (Create, Update, or Delete). Full details of the operation of the Open Interfaces can be found in the *Oracle Manufacturing, Distribution, Sales, and Service Open Interfaces Manual, Release 11.*

Tip

If you are in a multiple site situation and are not able to run the application's multi-org in a single database instance, you should consider using the open interfaces to move critical BOM data between databases.

Understanding Key Reports

Oracle Bills of Material provides a comprehensive set of reports that will support most business needs. Before you consider these in detail, it is worth mentioning that there are some powerful online inquiries that eliminate the need to run some printed reports.

The Indented Bills of Material inquiry window provides a useful tool. It has applications for Design/Development Engineers, Manufacturing Engineers, Materials Professionals, Manufacturing Management, and Cost Accountants. Enter the assembly item number, the BOM alternate name (if applicable), and the revision and effectivity information. You also need to specify the number of levels of the bill that you want to explode. This value defaults based on the profile option BOM: Default Bills of Material Levels. You can also specify whether you want to see costing, material control, and lead-time information. When the bill is exploded, you can view the entire BOM structure with component effectivity information and choose to view material control, costing, and lead-time information. You can choose to expand and collapse BOM levels to suit your needs.

Another extremely useful inquiry window is the Bill Components Comparison. This can be used to compare any two bills. Typical applications would be comparing primary and alternate BOMs or comparing the BOMs for the same assembly across two inventory organizations. You can choose to view the differences only or to view all components of both BOMs. The differences will be tagged within the window.

The third inquiry window to consider is the Item Where Used. This implodes the BOM structure, following the usage of a component upward through all the using assemblies in the structure. You can specify how many levels you want to implode. The window provides an indented view of the structure that can be expanded or collapsed as required.

Table 19.6 provides an overview of the reports provided with Oracle Bills of Material and a summary of their functions.

Table 19.6 Oracle Bills of Material Reports

Report Name	Description
Bills of Material Comparison Report	Similar to the inquiry screen. Compares two bills to highlight differences.
Bills of Material Listing	Reports on Engineering or Manufacturing bills but without component or routing details.

TABLE 19.6 CONTINUED

Report Name	Description
Bills of Material Loop Report	Checks an assembly or range of assemblies for BOM loops. Reports No Data Found if there are no loops.
Bills of Material Structure Report	Shows the detailed structure for an assembly or range of assemblies. You can choose how many levels to explode.
Bills of Material Parameters Report	Shows the values set for the BOM parameters. Useful when setting up Oracle Bills of Material.
Consolidated Bills of Material Report	Summarizes component usage from all levels of a bill.
Delete Items Report	Shows the deletion history for items, components, BOMs, operations, and routings.
Department Classes Report	Shows department classes and the departments that belong to these.
Department Report	Provides detail of department and overhead information.
Item Where Used Report	Similar to the Online Inquiry, this report provides information on the using assemblies for a component.
Resources Report	Provides details of resources cost and overhead information.
Resources Where Used Report	Similar to the Item Where Used report. Shows the routings that use the selected resources.
Routing Report	Shows detailed information on routings based on the items specified.
Standard Comments Report	Reports all standard comments that have been defined.
Standard Instructions Report	Reports all standard instructions that have been defined.
Standard Operations Report	Provides information on Standard Operations that have been created. You can choose to display resource information.
Workday Exception Sets Report	Shows all workday exception sets that have been defined to be used with the workday calendar.

TROUBLESHOOTING

- If you choose to use Oracle Engineering to manage your ECO approval process, you can use an Oracle Alert or a workflow to do this. Alerts have been available in previous releases of the applications and are still of value. An ECO approval workflow provides more complete functionality in describing your process by allowing conditional branching. The trend in the development of the Oracle Applications is to increase the integration of workflow technology. If you wish to "future-proof" your implementation, you should consider using a workflow for the approval process (see Chapter 28).

- The Autoimplement Manager is a critical part of your ECO process if you choose to have Oracle Engineering manage the implementation of your engineering changes. Make sure that this concurrent program is running at all times and is scheduled to run daily at a minimum. You should monitor this concurrent program to ensure that it does not fail.
- ECOs can affect discrete jobs and repetitive schedules that are created in the Work In Process application. You need to coordinate your change activity with the users in your organization that are responsible for planning and scheduling (see Chapters 21 and 22).
- Although it is covered earlier in this chapter, it is worth mentioning again that the Mass Change functionality is a very powerful tool. You should use it carefully. Although it is possible to undo changes that go wrong, it is better to avoid having to do this.

CHAPTER 20

USING ORACLE COST MANAGEMENT

In this chapter

UNDERSTANDING THE STRUCTURE OF THE COST MANAGEMENT APPLICATION

The Oracle Cost Management application provides an organization with a full-absorption, perpetual cost system for purchasing, inventory, work in process, and order management transactions. This application provides comprehensive valuation and variance reporting and supports activity-based costing. It also provides extensive cost simulation, copying, and editing capabilities. Cost Management supports the perpetual costing methods of standard and average costing along with the newly available periodic costing method.

The application is built around five predefined cost elements: material, material overhead, resource, overhead, and outside processing. Product costs are the sum of the elements used. If you use manufacturing costing, you can define an unlimited number of cost sub-elements.

UNDERSTANDING DEFINITIONS OF COST ELEMENTS

Cost elements and sub-elements are defined as follows:

- **Material**—The Material Cost Element is the raw material or component cost at the lowest level of the bill of material. It is determined from the unit cost of the component item.
- **Material Sub-Element**—These elements are used for detailed classification of material costs, such as plastic, steel, or aluminum. The material sub-elements are used to determine the default basis type (allocation charge method) for the cost and assign the appropriate amounts to the costed items.
- **Material Overhead**—Use the Material Overhead Cost Element for the overhead cost of material, calculated as a percentage of the total cost, or as a fixed charge per item, lot, or activity. If you use the Work In Process application, you can apply material overhead at the assembly level, and you can use several allocation methods.
- **Material Overhead Sub-Elements**—You can define and assign Material Overhead Sub-Elements to item costs to further categorize material overhead. For example, this assignment can include purchasing, freight, duty, or handling cost.
- **Resources**—The Resources Cost Element is used for direct costs required to manufacture products. It is calculated as the standard resource rate times the standard units on the routing, per operation, or as a fixed charge per item or lot passing through an operation. Resources can be people, machines, space, or miscellaneous charges.
- **Resources Sub-Elements**—Use resource sub-elements to identify specific machines, people (labor), floor spaces, and so forth. Each resource you define will be classified as a resource sub-element. See Chapter 19, "Using Oracle Engineering and Bills of Material," for additional information.
- **Overhead**—The Overhead Cost Element is used to record overhead costs of resources and outside processing. This cost element is calculated as a percentage of the resources or outside processing cost, as a fixed amount per resources unit, or as a fixed charge per item or lot passing through an operation. You can define multiple overhead

sub-elements to cover both fixed and variable overhead. Each sub-element can have its own rate. You can assign multiple overheads to a single department.

- **Overhead Sub-Elements**—Overhead sub-elements are usually applied in the routing and represent a detail breakdown of production overhead.
- **Outside Processing**—This cost element is the cost of processing purchased from an outside supplier. It can be a fixed charge per unit or the standard resources rate times the standard units on the routing operation. To implement outside processing costs, you must define a routing operation in the Bills of Material application and use an outside processing resource.
- **Outside Processing Sub-Elements**—These sub-elements are associated with the outside processing cost element and are used to represent services suppliers provide. They can be configured to charge at actual or standard cost rates and can be set up to generate a purchase price variance when charged.

ACTIVITIES

Activities are an action or task you perform in a business that uses a resource or incurs cost. You can associate all product costs to activities, and you can define activities and assign them to any sub-element. You can also assign costs to your activities and build your item costs based on activities.

BASIS TYPES

Costs are assigned to an item using basis types to establish a cost allocation formula. Each sub-element cost must be assigned a basis type; thus enabling each sub-element cost to be then allocated to the appropriate items. Predefined basis types in the Cost Management application are as follows:

- **Item**—Use the item basis type with material and material overhead sub-elements to assign a fixed amount of cost per item. This basis type is usually used for purchased components. This basis type is used with resource, outside processing, and overhead sub-elements to charge a fixed amount per item moved through an operation.
- **Lot**—The lot basis type is used to assign a fixed lot charge to items or operations. The cost per item is calculated by dividing the fixed cost by the item's standard lot size for material and material overhead sub-elements. For routing steps, the cost per item is calculated by dividing the fixed cost by the standard lot quantity moved through the operation associated with a resource, outside processing, or overhead sub-element.
- **Resource Value**—Use the resource value basis type to apply overhead to an item, based on the resource value earned in the routing operation. This basis type is used with the overhead sub-element only.
- **Resource Units**—The resource units basis type is used to apply overhead to an item, based on the number of resource units earned in the routing operation. This basis type is used with the overhead sub-element only.

- **Total Value**—You can use the total value basis type to assign material overhead to an item, based on the total value of the item. This basis type is used with the material overhead sub-element only.
- **Activity**—The activity basis type is used to directly assign the activity cost to an item. You can use this basis type only with the material overhead sub-element.

COST MANAGEMENT'S RELATIONSHIP TO OTHER APPLICATIONS

The Cost Management application is tightly integrated with many Oracle applications that define products or create transactions for products. See Figure 20.1 for a diagram that shows which applications are related to the Cost Management application. Directional arrows show the flow of transactions or source data to or from the Oracle Cost Management application.

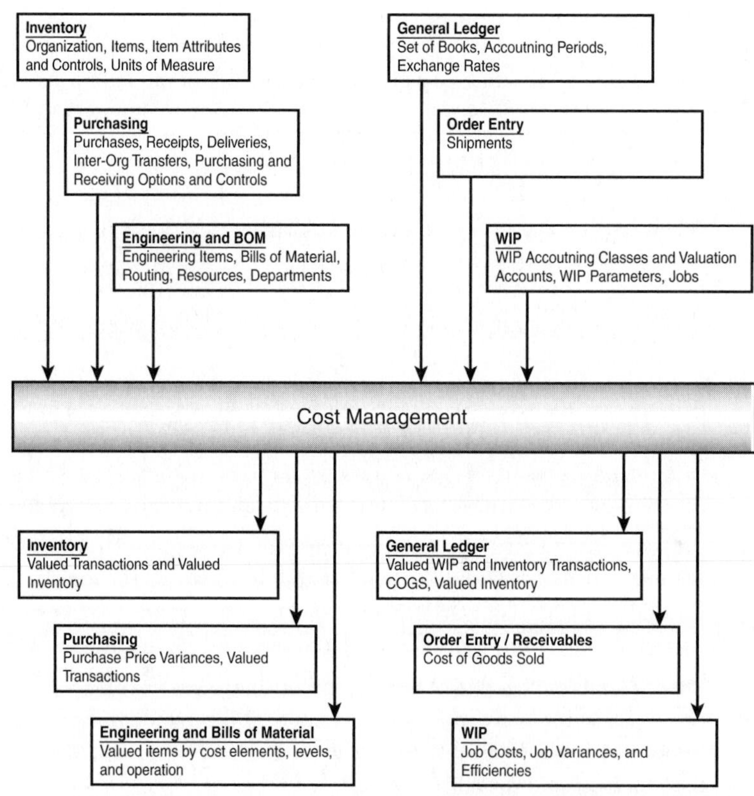

Figure 20.1
Cost Management relationships to other applications.

DISCOVERING NEW FEATURES IN RELEASE 11*i*

Following are the features in the Oracle Cost Management application that are new to Release 11*i* of the product. Also included is a brief description of the new functionality:

- **Support for periodic costing methods**—In addition to the mandatory perpetual costing options of Standard and Average costing, Oracle Cost Management now supports two additional periodic costing methods: Periodic Average Costing and Periodic Incremental LIFO (Last-In-First-Out) Costing. Periodic costing is a method that enables you to capture item costs and value your inventory on a periodic basis. It can be used to provide the following levels of cost granularity:
    - **Ability to capture actual acquisition costs based on supplier invoiced amounts, plus any other direct procurement charges that might be deemed relevant (that is freight, customs, or insurance charges)**—If no invoices are matched to valid receipts at the time the periodic cost processor is run, the purchase order price is substituted. Functionality is provided to enable identification and correction of item costs where PO substitution is used.
    - **Ability to capture actual manufacturing transaction costs using fully absorbed resource and overhead rates.**
    - **Ability to provide average inventory costs over a predefined period as opposed to averaging costs on a transactional basis.**
- **The option to capture cost records for each organization using either or both of the periodic costing methods in addition to your selected perpetual method**—You can choose whether or not to create Periodic Costing distributions and send them to the general ledger after a periodic costing run. You can also disable the perpetual costing general ledger transfer and opt instead to produce accounting entries only after each periodic costing run.
- **The Cost Management module maintains the perpetual and periodic costing systems separately**—To accommodate this, a series of new reports have been provided for the management of the periodic costing system. A copy-cost program has also been incorporated that enables the copying of costs across cost types. For example, you can copy your periodic costs into any cost type associated with your perpetual methods—that is you might want to annually reset your standards based on the prior periods periodic average cost. A periodic cost open interface has also been provided, so if you have been using periodic costing in a proprietary system, you have a supported mechanism under which to import quantities and costs to use for your initial period opening periodic balances.
- **Support for resubmitting errored material costing transactions**—Cost transactions that have failed to process, including project cost transactions, can now be resubmitted through the View Material Transactions window.

- **Support for various average costing enhancements**—The new enhancements for average costing are as follows:
  - During interorganization transfers, you can now either transfer costs using the sending organization's elemental costs or choose to have them summarized into the material element.
  - You can capture variances created by negative cost movements when WIP Final Completion transactions are transacted.
  - You can return assemblies to WIP at the average cost for the particular job.
  - You can view a graphical representation of the history of an item's cost from the Item Cost History Inquiry window. You also can view the item cost as a specific date by selecting from various points on the graph.
  - You have the option to transfer Invoice Price Variance directly to inventory rather than expense.
- **Support for various WIP standard and average costing enhancements**—These are the new enhancements available:
  - You can now scrap a flow schedule assembly at any operation, which results in the components that are required at that operation and preceding operations to be automatically issued and expensed from inventory. Assemblies that have been scrapped can subsequently be returned, thus placing the issue components back into inventory.
  - Phantom resource and overhead costs can now be used in addition to phantom material costs.
  - The costing module can now appropriately handle WIP assembly over-completions. If you complete more assemblies without changing the job quantity, on assemblies that are associated with lot-based resources and overhead, the resource and overhead are over-relieved from WIP inventory.
- **Support for elemental summarization of standard cost ledger postings**—A new profile option, CST:Account Summarization, has been added that enables you to choose between summarizing elemental accounts or maintaining elemental account visibility in the general ledger.

Critical Implementation Factors

Because the Oracle Cost Management application is tightly integrated with several manufacturing applications that define and value the company's products and business transactions, a project team that works closely together produces best results. Don't treat the Cost Management module as simply an accounting responsibility. Consider the following:

- **Get commitment from all levels and departments in your organization**—Accounting, engineering, purchasing, inventory management, and information technology must work together to implement the Cost Management application.

- **Make sure your company's engineering function is involved and understands the requirements of the Cost Management module**—Certain costs and variances required by the accounting and reporting functions can impact the structure of the bills of material and routings.
- **You should have your cost accountant involved in the configuration and testing of the BOM, WIP, and Inventory applications.**

CONFIGURING THE APPLICATION

To ensure that the application works correctly for you, it must be configured to suit your business needs. There are many setup steps in the Oracle Inventory, Bills of Material, Work In Process, and Purchasing applications that must be configured before Cost Management, and these steps have a large impact on the Cost Management application. After you complete the required setup tasks in the other applications, there are eleven setup steps (some required, others optional) in the Cost Management application.

REQUIRED SETUP TASKS

If you are responsible for configuring Oracle Cost Management, make sure you understand how the following items are configured in the other applications:

- General Ledger
    - Define a set of books
    - Define daily and period rates
- Inventory
    - Define organizations and organization parameters
    - Define units of measure
    - Define subinventories
    - Define categories, category sets, and default category sets
    - Define accounting periods
    - Define items and item attributes and controls
    - Define account aliases
    - Launch the transaction managers
- Purchasing
    - Define receiving options and controls
    - Define purchasing options
- Bills of Material
    - Define Bills of Material parameters
    - Define resources
    - Define departments

- Associate resources with departments
- Define overheads and assign them to departments
- Control overheads by resource
- Define and review routing and Bills of Material structures

- Work In Process
    - Define WIP accounting classes and valuation accounts
    - Define WIP parameters

After you configure the required items in the other applications, you can set up the Oracle Cost Management module. There are eleven setup steps in Cost Management (see Table 20.1 later in this chapter for the full list), and four are required as follows:

- Set Profile Options
- Set Security Functions
- Define Cost Types
- Define Material Sub-Elements

RESOLVING CRITICAL SETUP ISSUES

Please see Chapters 16, "Using Oracle Purchasing"; 17, "Using Oracle Inventory"; 19, "Using Oracle Engineering and Bills of Material"; and 22, "Using Oracle Work In Process," for more details about how to set up the configuration steps owned by those applications. The following topics are presented here because they are especially important to the Cost Management application:

- Costing Organization Parameters
- Default Interorganization Information
- Inventory or Manufacturing Costing
- WIP Accounting Classes

COSTING ORGANIZATION PARAMETERS

The definition of organizations is a central concept for Oracle Applications. Because organizations must be defined early in the configuration of the Inventory application and Inventory usually precedes Cost Management in the implementation schedule, you should try to identify the Cost Management business requirements before setting up the Inventory application. When you define the Costing Organization parameters in the Inventory application, consider carefully the following items:

- The costing organization can be either the current organization or the Item Master Organization.

- Select your perpetual costing method: standard or average costing:
    - **Standard costing**—Uses predefined costs for valuing inventory, WIP, and interorganization transactions. Variances are recorded for differences between standard and actual costs. When you use work in process, each organization is required to maintain its own item costs.
    - **Average costing**—Uses the average weighted value of all receipts of the purchased items. For manufactured items, this method uses a weighted average of all resources and materials consumed. You cannot share costs between organizations in an average costing organization, and average costs are maintained separately in each organization.

Note

You cannot change the costing method after transactions have been performed.

- Indicate whether GL transactions will be posted in detail.

Note

If you post in detail, the system creates large journal entries to post a line for each transaction. It is often better to post journal entries in summary, keep the detail out of the general ledger, and use subledger reports for detailed analysis.

- Indicate whether to reverse an encumbrance entry upon receipt into inventory.
- Indicate whether you want to collect Project Cost information.
- Select a default material sub-element to be used when you define item standard costs. This default enables faster entry of item costs.
- Specify Default Valuation Accounts for the organization. These Default Valuation Accounts will be the default accounts for the organization's subinventories. There are six default accounts to define:
    - **Material**—An asset account for material cost.
    - **Material Overhead**—An asset account for material overhead cost.
    - **Resources**—An asset account for resources cost.
    - **Overhead**—An asset account for resources and outside processing overheads.
    - **Outside Processing**—An asset account for outside processing cost.
    - **Expense**—An expense account for nonasset items.
- You should specify the following general ledger accounts that will be the default values associated with the inventory organization:
    - **Sales**—Enter an income statement account to be used as the default revenue account.

- **Cost of Goods Sold**—Use an income statement account for the default cost of goods sold entries.
- **Purchase Price Variance**—Enter a variance account that will be used to record the difference between purchase order price and standard cost. (This account is not used with average costing.)
- **Inventory A/P Accrual**—Enter a liability account to represent all purchase order receipts that are not matched in Accounts Payable.
- **Invoice Price Variance**—Nominate a variance account that will be used to record the difference between the purchase order price and the actual invoice price.
- **Encumbrance**—Enter an expense account that will be used to recognize the reservation of funds when a purchase order is approved. This entry is only used if you use encumbrance accounting.
- **Project Clearance Account**—When performing miscellaneous issues to capital projects, the project clearance account is used to post the distributions.
- **Average Cost Variance**—If you use average costing, and allow negative quantity balances, this account will represent the inventory valuation error caused by issuing your inventory before your receipts.

DEFINING DEFAULT INTERORGANIZATION INFORMATION

If you have multiple locations or organizations, the following setup steps are important to your material movement activities. Accounting rules are designed to govern intercompany shipments and receipts. You can implement those accounting rules when you configure the required interorganization information; a sample screen layout of this detail is provided in Figure 20.2.

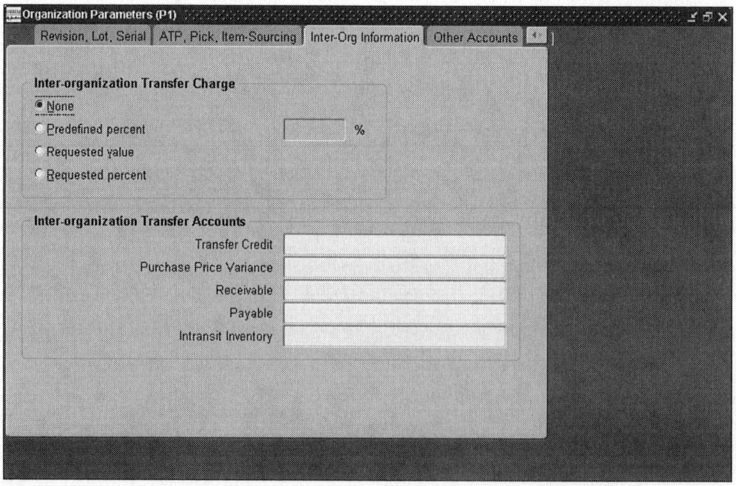

Figure 20.2
To set up interorganization defaults, select Setup, Organization, Parameters.

DEFAULT INTERORGANIZATION OPTIONS When you determine the Default Inter-Organization options, you configure how you charge your internal cost to transfer material between organizations. For example, this cost transfer could be a handling or paperwork charge. The options are as follows:

- **No transfer charges**—Self-explanatory.
- **Predefined percent of transaction value**—A default percentage is defined in Define Organization Parameters.
- **Requested added value**—The system requests a discrete value that is added to the material transfer at the time of the transaction.
- **Requested percent of transaction value**—The system requests, at the time of the transaction, a percentage of the transfer value to add to the material transfer.

DEFAULT INTERORGANIZATION TRANSFER ACCOUNTS The Default Inter-Organization Transfer Accounts are default general ledger accounts that are defined for each organization. The appropriate accounts from each organization are used when you define an interorganizational relationship. The accounts are described as follows:

- **Inter-Inventory Transfer Credit**—This account collects the transfer charge cost. These charges reduce expenses for the sending organization.
- **Inter-Organization Payable**—Set this account to the clearing account used by the receiving organization. It represents an intercompany payable liability.
- **Intransit Inventory**—This account represents the value of transferred inventory that has not arrived at the receiving organization. This is an asset account, and for organizations using average costing, this account is the default material account.
- **Inter-Organization Receivable**—Use this account to represent the clearing account for the shipping organization. It represents an intercompany receivable asset.
- **Inter-Organization PPV**—When you use the standard cost method, the receiving organization uses this account to recognize the difference (price variance) between the standard cost of the shipping organization and the standard cost of the receiving organization.

INVENTORY OR MANUFACTURING COSTING

Inventory and manufacturing costing are broad terms used by Oracle to describe costing functionality that has been expanded and improved from Release 11.0 on. Both the standard and average costing methods have been made available to manufacturing organizations, so it is important for you to determine whether you are a distribution or manufacturing organization and whether you will use the standard or average cost method.

Inventory costing is specific to distribution organizations that do not use Work In Process but might use Purchasing, Order Management/Shipping, and Bills of Material. Manufacturing costing is applicable to organizations that specifically use the Work In Process application but might also use other applications.

Consider the following standard costing scenarios:

- If you use standard costing in a distribution organization, the costing method is standard, and all transactions are valued at the frozen standard costs. Two cost elements are used: material and material overhead.
- If you use standard costing in a distribution organization with bills of material, the costing method is standard, and all five cost elements are used if costs are rolled up.
- When a manufacturing organization uses standard costing, the costing method is standard, and all five cost elements are used.

Consider the following average costing scenarios:

- If you use average costing in a distribution organization, the costing method is set to average, and all five cost elements are used.
- If you use average costing in a manufacturing organization, the costing method is set to average, and all five cost elements are used. In this scenario the CST:Average Costing profile option will be automatically set to Inventory and Work In Process.

If you are upgrading from Release 10 to Release 11*i*, Oracle includes the Release 10 cost processor for backward compatibility. However, if you want to change cost scenarios at the same time you upgrade, you will begin using the new Release 11*i* average cost processor, and that event will be inconsistent with your ending inventory balances. For example, if you use manufacturing standard cost in Release 10 and you want to begin using manufacturing average costing after the upgrade to Release 11*i*, you have a complex upgrade. To keep the system's perpetual records in balance, you will have to proceed carefully.

DEFINING WIP ACCOUNTING CLASSES

WIP Accounting Classes are defined in the Work In Process application. These classes control the accounting distributions for work in process activities and the details of costing information from production that you receive in the general ledger.

TYPES OF DISCRETE PRODUCTION You can define accounting classes for three types of discrete production: standard discrete, asset nonstandard discrete, and expense nonstandard discrete.

Standard Discrete You can define accounting classes for standard discrete jobs and use these accounting classes to group job costs. By using different accounting classes, you can separately value and report the costs associated with subassembly and finished goods production.

When you create jobs using the Planner Workbench, you can specify the discrete WIP Accounting Class. The way you select the WIP Accounting Class determines the account distribution for the job and could give you various cost breakdown scenarios. If you do not specify an accounting class, the system uses the accounting class defined by the Default Discrete Class parameter.

The account codes associated with the WIP Accounting Classes are used to make accounting entries throughout the production cycle. The valuation accounts are charged when material is issued to a job. When a job is closed, final costs and variances are calculated and posted to the variance and valuation accounts associated with the job. When the accounting period is closed, these journal entries are automatically posted to the General Ledger application.

Nonstandard Discrete You can use nonstandard discrete accounting classes to group and report transactions for various types of nonstandard production. For example, field service repair or engineering projects could use nonstandard discrete accounting classes.

For recurring expenses that you are tracking using nonstandard jobs, such as machine maintenance or engineering projects, define your accounting class with a type of expense nonstandard. The valuation accounts carry the costs incurred on expense jobs as an asset during the period and automatically write them off to the variance accounts when the period closes.

For nonstandard production activities that you want to carry as an asset, define your accounting class with a type of asset nonstandard job. Asset nonstandard discrete jobs are costed the same as standard discrete jobs. Valuation accounts are charged when material is issued to a job, and final costs and variances are calculated and posted to the appropriate variance and valuation accounts when the job is closed.

REPETITIVE ACCOUNTING CLASSES You must define accounting classes for each repetitive line/assembly association that you create. The schedule for an assembly and line association uses accounts from the Repetitive Accounting Class, and whenever you transact against the line/assembly association, those accounts are charged.

If you use a different accounting class for every line/assembly association, you will achieve detailed cost management reporting. However, you can use accounting classes to group production costs. For example, you can analyze repetitive manufacturing costs by assembly regardless of the line on which the assembly was manufactured by using the same accounting class for all lines that build the assembly. Alternatively, you can use the same class for all assemblies on a line to do line-based cost reporting.

WIP ACCOUNTING CLASS ELEMENTAL ACCOUNTS You can enter separate accounting codes by cost element and by WIP accounting class. You can also share accounts across elements and classes to summarize an account distribution detail.

If you use the standard costing method, the accounts are debited at the standard cost when material is issued and resources are charged to a job or schedule. Outside processing is debited when the items are received into the job or schedule from the Purchasing application. Account codes are credited or relieved at the standard cost when you complete assemblies from a job or schedule, close a job, or close an accounting period.

If you use the average costing method, the accounts are debited at the average cost in effect at the time of the issue transaction. The accounts are credited when you complete assemblies from a job.

You can define the following elemental accounts or valuation accounts for WIP accounting classes:

- Material
- Material overhead
- Resource
- Outside processing
- Overhead

There are cost differences (called variances) when the actual costs charged to a valuation account do not equal the credits to the account when assemblies are completed from a job or schedule. The following variance accounts are supported in Work In Process:

- Material variance
- Resource variance
- Outside processing variance
- Overhead variance
- Standard cost adjustment variance
- Bridging variance
- Expense variance

For more information on the setup of these accounts, see Chapter 22.

SETUP TASKS

Table 20.1 shows the setup tasks to be completed for the Cost Management application. The tasks are influenced by the type of costing methods, standard or average, inventory or manufacturing, that you use.

TABLE 20.1 ORACLE COST MANAGEMENT SETUP TASKS

Set Up Task Name	Required?
Set Profile Options	Yes
Set Security Functions	Yes
Define Cost Types	Yes
Define Activities and Activity Costs	No
Define Cost Groups (Project Manufacturing Costing only)	No
Define Material Sub-Elements	Yes

Table 20.1 Continued

Set Up Task Name	Required?
Define Overheads	No
Define Material Overhead Defaults	No
Associate Expenditure Types with Cost Elements (Project Manufacturing Costing only)	No
Define Category Accounts	No
Associate WIP Account Classes with Category Accounts	No

Understanding Each Setup Task

This section describes the tasks that must be performed and some of the decisions that you will need to make.

Setting Profile Options

The profile options that directly affect the operation of the Cost Management application are listed in Table 20.2.

Table 20.2 Cost Management Profile Options

Profile Option Name	Required?	Level*	Comment
CST:Account Summarization	Yes	S	Default is Yes
CST:Cost Rollup wait for Table Lock	Yes	SAR	Default is None
CST:Cost Update Debug Level	Yes	SARU	Default is None
CST:Exchange Rate Type	Yes	S	Default is None
CST:View Cost Privilege	Yes	SARU	Default is None

**Levels can be Site, Application, Responsibility, or User. The system administrator sets most profile options.*

CST: Account Summarization For Standard Costing only, the value of this profile option indicates whether elemental costs are summarized before being transferred to the General Ledger. If this option is set to No, elemental account visibility is maintained. The system administrator sets this option at the site level.

CST: Cost Rollup—Wait for Table Lock This indicates whether the cost rollup waits until the desired information is available or ends with an error after 10 attempts. The system administrator can update this option.

CST: COST UPDATE DEBUG LEVEL The cost update program creates a log file, and this profile option determines the level and type of messages to print in the cost update log file. This option should be defined as Regular at the site level because that is the least level of detail. Consider defining it to Extended or Full at the application, responsibility, or user level. The system administrator can update this profile option at all levels. The effect of each option is as follows:

- **Regular**—Log every subroutine.
- **Extended**—Log every SQL statement.
- **Full**—Log every SQL statement and keep any temporary data in the database.

CST: EXCHANGE RATE TYPE This profile option indicates whether to convert foreign currency using the end-of-period or period-average rate. The system administrator can update this option at the site level. Use this profile to control the exchange rate type used for the Margin Analysis Report, Material Distribution Report, and WIP Distribution Report.

SETTING THE SECURITY FUNCTIONS

During implementation, the system administrator sets up security functions. Because many organizations consider cost information to be highly sensitive and confidential, the administrator might give privileges to add, update, delete, or view costs. Privileges are implemented with function security, and the function names are listed in parenthesis.

PRIVILEGE TO VIEW COST (CST_VIEW_COST_INFORMATION) The privilege to view cost information determines whether a specific user can see costing information. The Resources, Departments, and Indented Bills of Material windows are governed by this function.

> **Tip**
>
> If you exclude the privilege to maintain costs from a user, you can allow that user to print reports, but not change any costs, by leaving the Privilege to View Cost function as part of the user's responsibility.

PRIVILEGE TO MAINTAIN COST (CST_MAINTAIN_COST_INFORMATION) The Privilege to Maintain Cost function determines whether costing information can be created, updated, or deleted. This function affects the Bills of Material and the Routing windows. Because a cost rollup will save costs in the database, the Privilege to Maintain Cost function must be included as part of the responsibility for those users who perform rollups.

OTHER PRIVILEGES THAT MIGHT BE IMPLEMENTED WITH SECURITY FUNCTIONS The functions shown in Table 20.3 determine whether costing information can be created, updated, or deleted from various windows.

TABLE 20.3 PRIVILEGES AND FUNCTION SECURITY

Privilege	Function Name	Window
Maintain Cost Groups	CST_CSTFDCGA_MAINTAIN	Cost Groups
Maintain Activities	CST_CSTFDATY_MAINTAIN	Activities
Maintain Cost Types	CST_CSTFDCTP_MAINTAIN	Cost Types
Maintain Item Costs	CST_CSTFITCT_MAINTAIN	Item Costs
Material Sub-Elements	CST_CSTFDMSE_MAINTAIN	Material Sub-Elements
Overheads	CST_CSTFDOVH_MAINTAIN	Overheads

DEFINING COST TYPES

A cost type is a group of costs with a specific name. You can define and update an unlimited number of simulation or unimplemented cost types. For example, you might want to create a cost type called Lower of Cost or Market. Figure 20.3 provides an example of the fields required when defining cost types in Release 11*i*. The Cost Management application has three predefined cost types:

- **Frozen standard costs**—The Frozen cost type is used to value transactions and inventory balances for organizations that use the standard cost method. This cost type is not available for organizations using average costing.
- **Average costs**—The Average cost type is used to value transactions and inventory balances for organizations that use the average cost method. It holds the average unit cost of items on-hand. This cost type is not available for organizations using standard costing.
- **Pending and all types you define**—You can use all other cost types for any purpose. For example, you can create a cost history, perform a product cost simulation, or develop future frozen costs. Because these cost types are not implemented (frozen), you can create and update them at will. If you use the standard cost method, you can transfer costs from pending and all other cost types to update the frozen cost type.

If you are using the average cost method, you must also define at least one Average Rates cost type to hold sub-element rates or amounts. Select this Average Rates cost type when you define the Average Rates Cost Type parameter in the Organization Parameters window of the Inventory application. The Average Rates cost type is not used by organizations that use the standard cost method.

DEFINING ACTIVITIES AND ACTIVITY COSTS

Use activities to assign indirect costs to items based on the effort expended to obtain or produce the item. In your business, activities are processes that consume costs and time. Figure 20.4 shows an example of how these activities are defined within the cost application.

In addition to cost elements and sub-elements, you can associate costs with an activity by clicking the Activity Costs button on the Setup Activities screen and populating the relevant fields into the Activity Costs form (see Figure 20.5). Activities can be directly related to producing items, such as runtime or setup time, or, activities might be indirect in nature, such as engineering efforts.

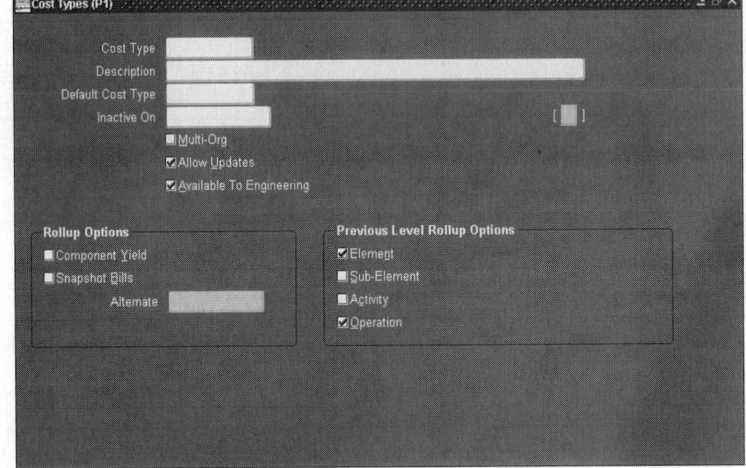

Figure 20.3
To define cost types, select Setup, Cost Types.

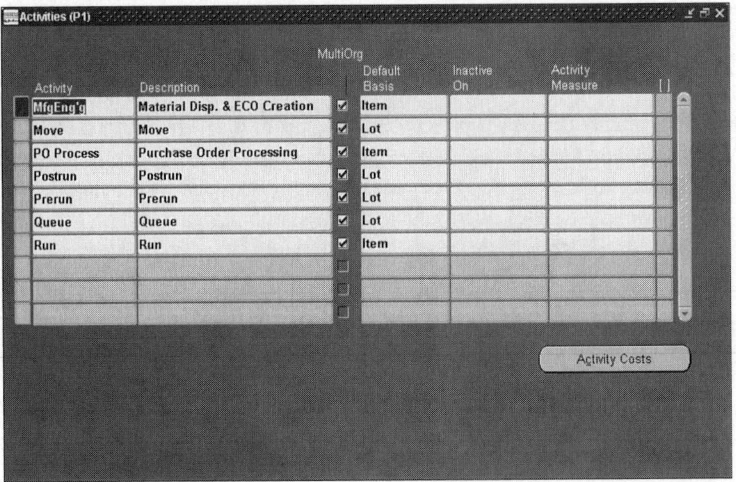

Figure 20.4
To set up activities, select Setup, Activities.

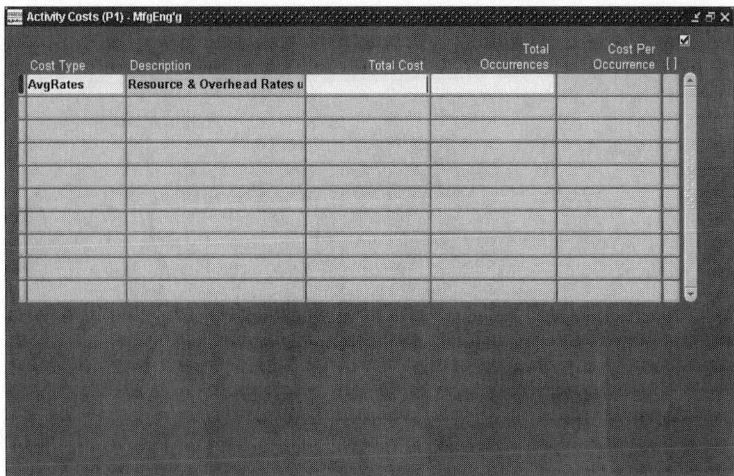

Figure 20.5
Assigining costs to activities.

DEFINING COST GROUPS

You can define, and subsequently use, project cost groups if the Project Cost Collector Enabled parameter was checked in the Define Organization Parameters window when configuring the Oracle Inventory module. Project cost groups are used to segregate project-related costs. The Cost Management module comes seeded with a Common cost group, and enables any number of user-defined cost groups to be created. Each project can then be associated with a project cost group. If you do not specifically assign a project to a user-defined cost group, costs for that project are derived using the Common cost group. For each project cost group, you must define the elemental valuation and borrow/payback variance accounts that are used to capture the ledger activity for the cost group. The borrow/payback variance represents the difference between current average cost and the original borrowing cost for any inventory temporarily loaned to other projects. The cost groups can also be assigned to WIP accounting classes.

DEFINING MATERIAL SUB-ELEMENTS

Material sub-elements are used to classify your material costs, such as plastic, steel, or aluminum. You can define material sub-elements, determine the basis type (allocation charge method) for the cost, and assign an appropriate amount. A material sub-element has a default activity and a default basis type assigned to it. The form used to define material cost sub-elements is shown in Figure 20.6.

If the Project Cost Collection Enabled parameter in the Define Organization Parameters window is set, you must also associate a project expenditure type with each sub-element by selecting the Project Expenditure tab and defining the appropriate association (see Figure 20.6).

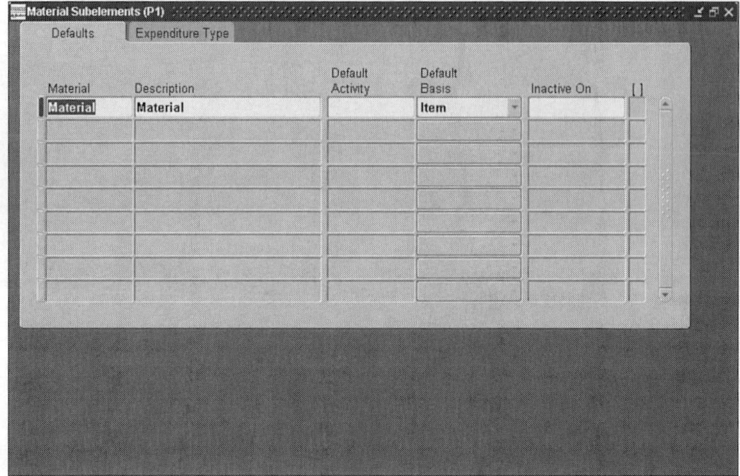

Figure 20.6
Defining material cost sub-elements.

Defining Overhead and Overhead Cost Sub-Elements

You use material overhead and overhead cost sub-elements to add indirect costs to item costs. You can add cost on a percentage basis or as a fixed amount. The Cost Management application enables you to separate overhead costs associated with materials from other overhead costs:

- **Material Overhead Sub-Elements**—Define material overhead sub-elements and assign them to item costs (see Figure 20.7). To control the cost allocation, determine the basis type for the cost and define an appropriate rate or amount. For example, you might use a sub-element such as purchasing, freight, or material handling.
- **Overhead Sub-Elements**—Define overhead sub-elements and assign them to your item costs. Determine the basis type for the cost and define an appropriate rate or amount. Overhead sub-elements are applied in the routing and usually represent production overhead. You can define overheads based on the number of units or the lot amount moved through an operation, or based on the number of resource units or the value charged in the operation.

Tip

Each overhead sub-element has a default basis, a default activity, and an absorption account. Set up a pool of cost accounts in the general ledger and use the overhead absorption account as an offset account.

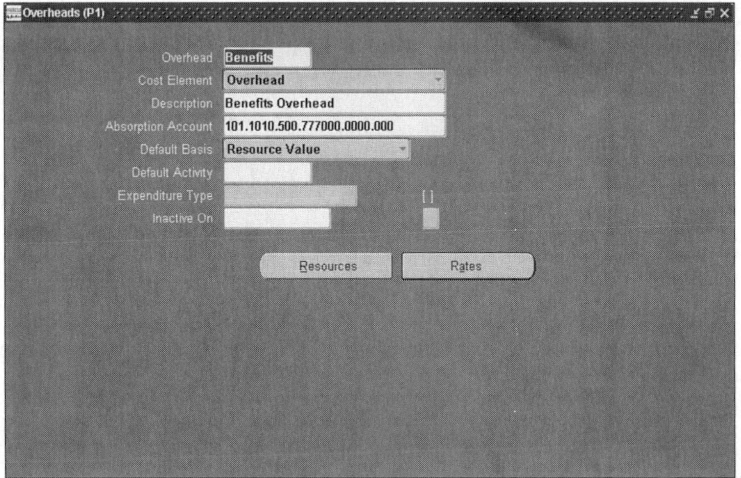

Figure 20.7 Defining material overhead sub-elements and assigning them to item costs.

To earn either material overheads or overheads based on resource units or value, you must associate resources to the overhead sub-elements for the relevant cost types. To do this, click the Resources button shown in Figure 20.7 to open the Resources Overhead Associations window.

To associate department and overhead combinations with a cost type, click the Rates button to open the Overhead Rates window and complete the details in the Rates window (see Figure 20.8). The Rates button is available when defining overhead sub-elements only.

You can apply each of these sub-elements using different allocation methods or basis types. Material overhead is absorbed when an item is received into inventory or is completed from work in process. Resources overhead is absorbed as the assembly moves through routed steps in work in process.

Note

When you use the Bills of Material application, you must configure the bills of material parameters before you can use the overhead cost element in the Overhead window.

Defining Resources Use the Define Resources window in the Bills of Material application to define the time an assembly spends at an operation and the cost of the operation. A resource can be anything that is required in your production process. For example, resources can be employees, machines, outside processing services, or physical space. The routing requires a resource and usage rate for all scheduled activities. Resources are defined in the Bills of Material application. For more information on defining resources see Chapter 19.

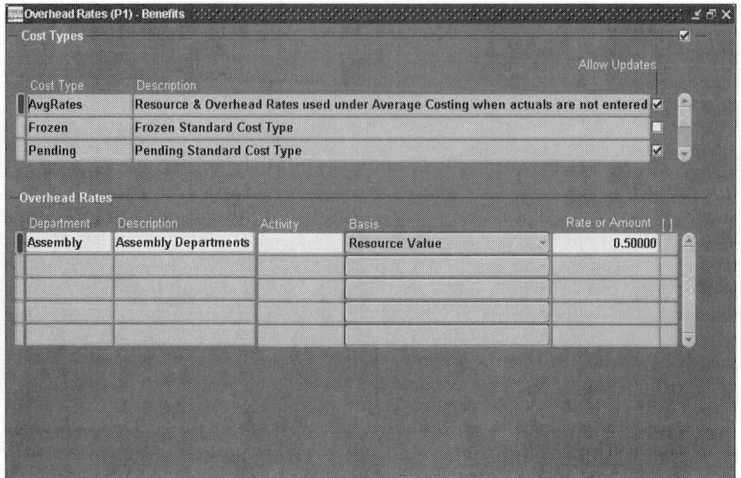

Figure 20.8
Associating department and overhead combinations with a cost type.

When you define a resource, you can enable the Costed check box in the Resources window to collect and assign costs to the resource. If the resource is costed, use the Standard Rate check box to indicate whether to charge jobs and repetitive schedules based on a standard rate. Figure 20.9 shows how these fields appear on the Define Resources form.

If the resource is costed, enter an absorption account that is used to offset resource charges in work in process. Also, enter a variance account to collect resource rate variances for a job or repetitive schedule.

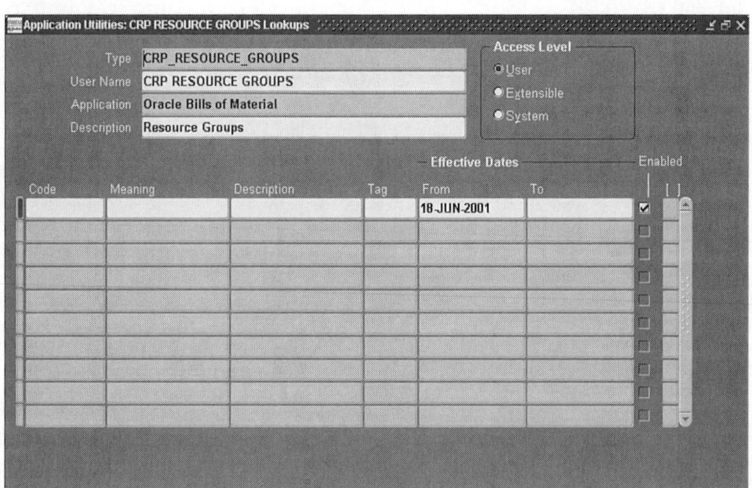

Figure 20.9
The Define Resources form.

In the Resource Overhead Associations window, you can attach overhead sub-elements to the resource, choose a cost type, and enter a rate based on the resource unit of measure.

Tip

If you are defining an outside processing resource that interacts with the Purchasing application, do not change the accounts that default into these fields because Purchasing controls your receiving valuation account.

ENTERING EMPLOYEES AND EMPLOYEE LABOR RATES If you have defined people resources and want to collect labor costs, you must define the employees and their labor rates. If you have installed the Oracle Human Resources Management application, you can define the employees through that application; otherwise, the Work In Process application provides a window to enter the employees and the rates. See Chapter 22 for more information.

DEFINING MATERIAL OVERHEAD DEFAULTS

To help speed up your data entry when you define items, you can define and update default material overhead sub-elements and rates. When you define items, the system enters these default values for you into the frozen costs if you are using the standard cost method or into the average rates if you are using the average cost method.

For items that you purchase, enter the material costs. For items that you produce, enter the rolled-up costs. You can specify a default inventory organization and category for the same material overhead sub-element. If you have more than one default for a sub-element, the category default takes precedent over the organization default. If you have two category level defaults, the default that matches the item's planning code takes precedence.

Tip

You must define material overhead defaults from the master cost organization.

ASSOCIATING EXPENDITURE TYPES WITH COST ELEMENTS

If you plan to transfer project costs to Oracle Projects, you must associate expenditure types with the appropriate cost elements. This enables project transfers and project-related costs associated with miscellaneous transactions to be properly processed after they are transferred to the Projects module.

DEFINING CATEGORY ACCOUNTS AND ASSOCIATING CATEGORY ACCOUNTS WITH WIP ACCOUNTING CLASSES

If you use the product line accounting setup, Cost Management enables you to use categories to drive the selection of WIP Accounting Classes. You can use product line accounting when you use either the standard or average cost method. See Chapter 17 for more information on categories. The setup for product line accounting is a four-step process:

1. Create categories for each of your product lines and associate them with the default product line category set.

2. Enter general ledger accounts for each category and subinventory combination in the Category Accounts Summary window. If you don't enter a subinventory, the accounts will apply to all subinventories that use the category. You can enter accounts to accumulate costs for material, outside processing, material overhead, overhead, resources, encumbrance, analytical invoice price variance, analytical purchase mirror, noninvoiced sales order, noninvoiced revenue, analytical revenue mirror, analytical margins of cost of goods sold, and average cost variance.
3. Create definitions for the WIP Accounting Classes that will be used as your default WIP Accounting Classes.
4. Make associations of the WIP Accounting Classes with the product line categories. Use the Default WIP Accounting Classes for Categories window to make the associations.

Tip

If you use the standard cost method, you can define WIP accounting classes at the category level for each organization. If you use the average cost method, you define WIP accounting classes at the cost group/category level for the organization, as shown in Figure 20.10.

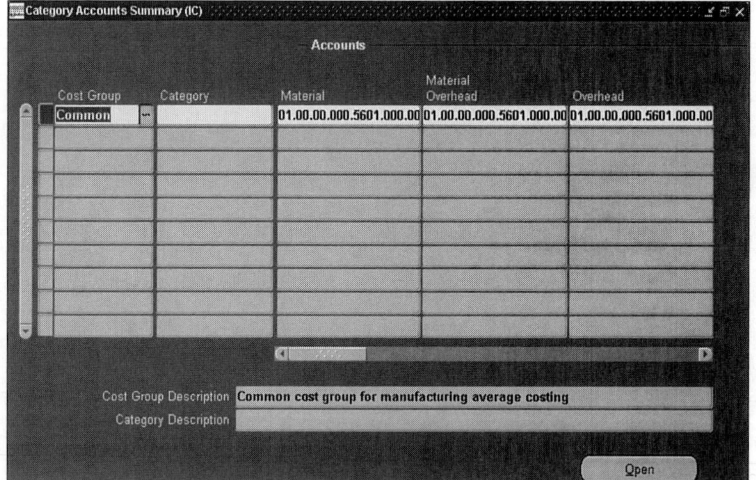

Figure 20.10 Defining WIP accounting classes at the cost group/category level for the organization.

PROCESSING TRANSACTIONS

Cost Management information can be viewed, defined, rolled up, updated, copied, purged, and so forth. This section describes the following transaction processes:

- Defining Item Costs
- Copying and Mass Editing Items and Accounts

- Roll Up Assembly Costs
- Updating Standard and Average Costs
- Maintaining Accounting Periods
- Closing Discrete Jobs
- Purging Cost Information
- Purging Margin Analysis Load Run
- Purging Standard Cost Update History

DEFINING ITEM COSTS

If you use the standard cost method in the Item Costs window, you can enter costs for purchased items or enter additional costs for products with costs generated from the cost rollup.

If you share costs among organizations, you can only define costs in the master organization. When you define a new item, Cost Management determines your costing method (standard or average) and creates a frozen or average cost type record, respectively, using the format shown in Figure 20.11. If no inventory transactions have occurred, you can modify the frozen cost type record. This feature enables you to directly set the frozen standard cost for the item. However, if inventory transactions have occurred for this item, the system has a set of perpetual records that are already valued at the old item costs. To revalue the perpetual balances, you must define a cost in a cost type other than frozen and then perform a cost update to adjust the perpetual values and load a new frozen cost for the item. Although you can use any cost type you have defined, many companies use the pending cost type as the staging area for changes to item standard costs.

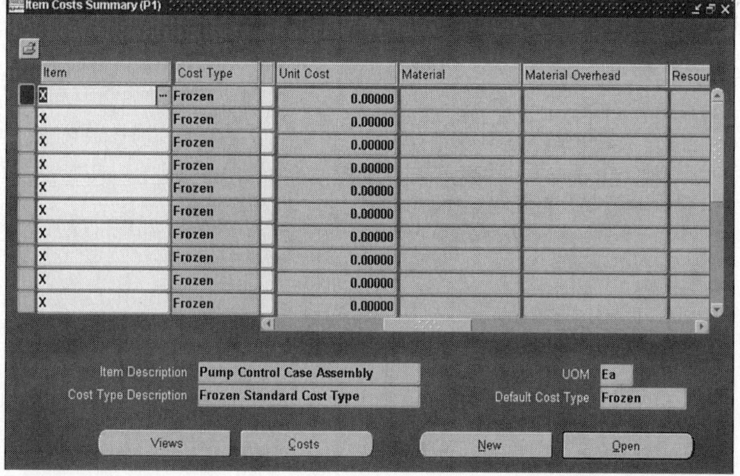

Figure 20.11
Format for creating a frozen or an average cost type record.

Note

If you use the average cost method, you cannot edit average costs in the Item Costs window as described previously. Instead, use the Update Average Costs window to perform maintenance on average costs.

If you use the Bills of Material application, you can run the Costed Bills of Material Explosion Reports for any cost type to see the effect of pending cost changes on an item. If you want to use the resources, outside processing, and overhead cost elements when you define item costs, you should define the Bills of Material parameters first so you will have access to the material and material overhead cost elements. See Chapter 19 for details.

COPYING AND MASS EDITING ITEM COSTS AND ACCOUNTS

Because most companies that use the Cost Management application have thousands of items stored in the database, maintenance of costs and account values could be difficult if each record had to be updated individually. Cost Management provides two utilities to perform mass edits on item costs and item accounts.

MASS EDITING ITEM COSTS

When you use the Mass Edit Cost Information window, you can apply mass edits for the following elements of cost information:

- You can apply new activity rates to item costs.
- You can change item shrinkage rates to a specified rate, or you can copy percentages from your planning shrinkage rates.
- You can use mass edits to make new costs and change existing costs by a percentage or an absolute amount.
- You can create new costs by averaging data from purchase orders or payables transactions.

You must plan carefully and develop a strategy to restrict mass edits to sub-elements with similar basis types. Do not mix rate-based and amount-based sub-elements in the same mass edit because the basis formulas calculate differently, and the values you enter in the Fixed Rate and Change Amount fields will be plugged into the formulas in drastically different ways. For example, if you enter 5.00 in the Fixed Rate field, an amount-based sub-element will increase by 5 units of your currency. However, a rate-based sub-element will multiply the cost by 5.

There are five types of mass edits available in Release 11*i*. You select the request name in the Mass Edit Cost Information window. These edits are named as follows:

- The Apply Last Activity Rates name is used to update item costs after you change rates on activities.
- Use the mass edit name called Change Cost Shrinkage Rates to change cost shrinkage rates for items.

- Select the name Mass Edit Actual Material Costs to create costs for your items from actual purchasing or accounts payable transactions or documents.
- The Mass Edit Material Costs request can be used to update material sub-element costs by a fixed amount or percentage as determined by the basis type.
- Use Mass Edit Material Overhead Costs request to change material overhead sub-elements by a fixed amount or percentage as determined by the basis type.

MASS EDITING ITEM ACCOUNTS

You can perform mass edits on account assignments for selected items in the Mass Edit Item Accounts window. You can edit the following accounts:

- Cost of Goods Sold
- Encumbrance
- Expense
- Sales

Although you can share standard costs among organizations, Cost Management does not share the item accounts. If you must change your accounts, you must make the change in each organization.

Tip

Because you edit account assignments for all items, a category of items, or a specific item, categories are essential to mass editing item accounts. If you can't use categories, your options to mass edit are limited to a single item or all items.

COPYING COST BETWEEN TWO COST TYPES

You can copy from one cost type to another and specify an item or category range. For example, you could initialize a new cost type by copying from the frozen cost type. Because the copy does not perform a cost update, you cannot copy to the frozen or average cost type. You can copy item costs within an organization or across organizations. If you are copying within an organization, you can also copy activity costs, resources and overhead costs, or resources and overhead associations.

The three copying options that control how the copy is made are as follows:

- **If you select Merge and Update Existing Costs, costs that exist in the source are created when they don't exist in the target cost type**—Costs that exist in the target but are not found in the source cost type are left unchanged. Where items exist in both cost types, the target is updated with the cost of the source item.
- **Use the Copy Over New Information Only option to add item costs in the source cost type to the target cost type**—Items that exist in both cost types or that exist only in the target cost type are left undisturbed.

- **The option Remove and Replace All Cost Information simply replaces all item costs from the source cost type in the target cost type**—If an item cost existed in the target cost type that was not in the source cost type, it will be deleted from the target.

Tip

The cost rollup function can also be used to copy costs for rollup items (assemblies). When the assembly does not exist in the cost type being rolled up, the cost rollup program automatically copies the assembly cost information from the default cost type that is allocated to the cost type being rolled.

Rollup Assembly Costs

If you use the Bills of Material application, you can perform either a full cost rollup or a single-level cost rollup from the Assembly Cost Rollup window. A full cost rollup explodes the complete bills of material for assemblies. The rollup process starts at the lowest level of the bills of material and builds the cost of each assembly. The rollup follows the hierarchy of the bills of material structure and calculates the costs for higher-level assemblies. The full rollup uses the most current bills of material structure and component costs to make all calculations.

You can optionally select a single-level rollup if you want to calculate costs only at the first level of the bill structure for each assembly. This rollup method does not reflect changes in the bills of material structure or cost changes that have occurred at a level below the first level of your assemblies. A good use of the single-level rollup is to quickly assign costs to new assemblies without changing the costs on existing subassemblies.

You can control the reports that come from the rollup program, and you have the option to print the Consolidated Bills of Material Cost Report, the Indented Bills of Material Cost Report, or no report.

Tip

A loop in a bill of material is caused when a bill is assigned as a component to itself. Because a bill loop can cause rollup errors, before performing a full rollup, you should verify the structure of the bills of material. Run the Bills of Material Loop Report for the range of items in your rollup to quickly get a list of assemblies with problems.

Updating Standard and Average Costs

Use the standard cost update process to define and roll up pending costs and then roll over pending costs to the frozen standard cost type. The cost update program is a batch program that you launch from a concurrent request submission. The update program waits on jobs that perform a period close, a job close, or a transfer to the General Ledger application. The update delays processing of accounting transactions until the cost update completes.

Note

If you want a standard cost of zero for an item, you must set it to zero. If you simply don't define a cost in the pending cost type, the update does not update the frozen cost to zero for those items.

Cost Management produces a journal entry to revalue the general ledger accounts for perpetual inventory balances to the new standard costs. The update revalues the on-hand balances in the organizations that share the updated costs. If you use the Work In Process application, the cost update revalues any discrete job balances.

Tip

To accurately reflect standard cost variances in the current period, try to run your cost update at the beginning of the accounting period before inventory transactions are processed.

Tip

Due to the type of processing the Standard Cost update program performs, it cannot be run simultaneously for the same inventory organization. If this occurs, the later submitted process errors out. To help manage this occurrence, it might be warranted to make the Standard Cost update program incompatible with itself; forcing the conflict resolution manager to process scheduled cost updates individually, and waiting for any currently running updates to complete before starting another.

Note, however, that making the standard cost update program incompatible with itself causes the program to execute these requests sequentially across the entire instance—meaning that one organization's standard cost update is forced to wait for another organization's standard cost update to complete.

If you use the average cost method, you can update the average cost of items to include additional costs, such as job variances, freight, or invoice price variances. Navigate to the Update Average Costs window to perform the cost maintenance. You can implement a total cost change (prorated proportionately across all elements), a percentage change to selected elements and levels, a new average cost for selected elements and levels, or a value change to increment or decrement on-hand inventory balances.

When using average costing you also have the option of automatically transferring variances between purchase order price and invoice price back to your inventory item costs. This process is driven from a user-nominated adjustment account. More often than not, this account is the Invoice Price Variance account. This process gives you the ability to value your inventory at costs as close to actual as possible. This transfer process picks up only invoices that have been posted to the General Ledger to ensure that the invoices are approved for payment and validates the appropriateness for any variances to be added back into inventory.

You can run this transfer process for only one organization at a time—specifying the individual adjustment account to be processed at runtime. Any invoice variance transfer adjustments that are made to item costs are recorded as an average cost update transaction in the Item Cost History or View Material Transaction inquiry form. To initiate this process, you must submit the Transfer Invoice Variance to Inventory Valuation request from the standard request submission form. If the automatic update option is selected during submission, the process automatically updates the inventory values. If you do not select Automatic Uupdate, the process creates records in the cost update open interface table—from where you can run the Inventory Transaction Open Interface manager to report on any potential updates using the Invoice Transfer to Inventory report prior to committing the updates.

REPORTING PENDING ADJUSTMENTS You can simulate the effects of a pending cost adjustment by running specific reports. Navigate to the Report Pending Cost Adjustments window and enter the cost type for the cost update in the parameters field. This concurrent process launches two jobs: one to simulate a cost update from the cost type you specify to the frozen cost type and the other to launch the Inventory, Intransit, and WIP Standard Cost Adjustment Reports. From these reports you can analyze the revaluation changes the standard cost update would perform for current inventory balances.

REPORTING COST UPDATE ADJUSTMENTS Cost Management enables you to optionally save cost update history records. You can print Historical Inventory and Intransit Standard Cost Adjustment Reports, and if you use the Work In Process application, you can print the Historical WIP Standard Cost Update Report. These reports show the adjustments made by the cost update to inventory and work in process perpetual balances.

PERIODIC COSTING

The Cost Management application now enables periodic costing techniques to be adopted in conjunction with the use of the previously available perpetual costing methods. Cost Management in 11*i* provides support for two distinct methods of periodic costing: Periodic Average Costing (PAC) and Periodic Incremental Last-In-First-Out (LIFO). Periodic costing enables you to cost items from one or more inventory organizations based on invoice price (if the invoice price is available); otherwise, the purchase price is used. For manufactured items, periodic costing balances represent the sum of the actual cost of resources and materials consumed.

Sharing Periodic Costs across a group of inventory organizations belonging to the same legal entity is possible. The perpetual costing method for those same organizations within the legal entity can be a mixture of both Standard and Average costing. You can use either or both periodic methods to cost the inventory transactions for a given period, and use either method to view the results and produce inventory valuation reports. You can also manually change the Periodic Cost of an item by performing a periodic cost update.

MAINTAINING ACCOUNTING PERIODS

Cost Management uses the same periods, fiscal calendar, and other financial information that is found in the General Ledger application. See Chapter 11, "Using Oracle General Ledger," for more details about the general ledger. Because each inventory organization opens and closes periods in its fiscal calendar independently, this feature provides flexibility in financial controls and scheduling the fiscal closing for each organization. You must open a period before inventory, work in process, or costing transactions can be processed, but it is not necessary to close one period before opening the next.

You might get messages as you begin the period close process in the Inventory application. These messages can be caused by unprocessed transactions. Because these transactions will never process after their period is closed, you must examine and repair these transactions before continuing the close.

Tip

Check the transaction interfaces each week and fix any records that the interface cannot process. If you keep the transaction interface clear, the month-end period close will go more smoothly. The number of these problematic transactions can be easily seen by clicking the Pending button on the Inventory Accounting Periods form.

When you close the period, you accomplish several tasks:

- **The system closes the open period for inventory and work in process transactions**—When a period is closed, it cannot be reopened.
- **The system automatically creates inventory and work in process accounting journal entries in the general ledger interface**—You can perform a general ledger transfer at any time during an open period without closing the period. Interim transfers enable you to reconcile and transfer information weekly or more frequently so there will be less work during the month-end processing cycle.
- **Cost Management calculates all the subinventory values for the end of the period.**

Follow these steps to properly close and process all your inventory and work in process transactions:

1. Make sure everyone in your organization has completed entering all inventory and work in process transactions.
2. Verify that there are no transactions hung up in the inventory and work in process transaction interfaces.
3. Check the transaction cost manager process in the concurrent manager. If you use the Work In Process application, perform the same check on the resource transaction cost manager.

4. Verify that the Order Management application has transferred all shipment details to Inventory.
5. Run the Material Account Distribution Report for the period and audit the contents for abnormally high transaction volumes or quantities. Also, perform a sanity check that you have made the right accounting distributions.
6. Verify that the perpetual inventory value at the end of the period matches the value you report in the general ledger.
7. If you use the Work In Process application, verify that the inventory balances with the WIP Account Distribution Detail Report.
8. Close the Payables and Purchasing applications before closing the Inventory and Work In Process applications.
9. Close the accounting period in the Inventory application. The system automatically closes the Work In Process application and transfers the accounting entries to the general ledger interface.
10. Import and post the journal entry in the General Ledger application.

Tip

It's often easier to make a correction in the subledger before you close the fiscal period than it is to make a reconciliation in the general ledger and then make an adjusting journal entry.

Closing Discrete Jobs

Job closures are an important event for the Cost Management application. Until you close a job or change the status of the job to Complete—No Charges, you can make material, resource, and scrap charges to the job. Closing a discrete job prevents any further activity on the job. If you use the standard cost method, the Work In Process application recognizes variances when you close a job. The job closure process writes off any balances in any cost elements to the variance accounts. Using the Work In Process application, you can select which jobs to close or unclose. Choose Close or Unclose from the Special Menu to submit the request. The status of jobs submitted for close changes to Pending Close until the close process completes. If for some reason you have an abnormal termination of a request to close jobs, the status might be Pending Close. To clear the process, these jobs must be manually resubmitted.

The close process runs the Discrete Job Value Report for the standard and nonstandard asset jobs after job variances are computed.

Tip

Run the Discrete Job Value Report before closing a job so that you can fix any inaccuracies.

COSTING REPETITIVE SCHEDULE PERIOD CLOSE TRANSACTIONS

You do not close a repetitive schedule. The closing of the accounting period causes the system to zero WIP accounting balances and recognize variances. Use the Repetitive Value Report to check your transactions and balances before you close an accounting period.

If you have positive balances in the repetitive schedules when the period closes, the system debits the WIP Accounting Class variance accounts and credits the WIP Accounting Class valuation accounts.

For more information about closing jobs, see Chapter 22.

PURGING COST INFORMATION

You cannot purge frozen costs if you are using the standard cost method or average costs if you are using average costing. However, you can purge other cost types and all or part of the costs within the cost type. For example, you might want to purge only purchased items from a cost type. Use the Purge Cost Information window to initiate a purge. This program removes the selected cost information permanently from the database, and these records are not retrievable after you run the purge. If you disable the Allow Updates check box when you define a cost type, you can prevent accidental loss of data through purging.

PURGING MARGIN ANALYSIS LOAD RUN

If you use the Receivables, Inventory, and Order Management, applications, you can use the Margin Analysis Report. Before running this report, you must run the Margin Analysis Load Run, which, based on your parameters, creates temporary data in tables that are used by the report program. When they are no longer needed, you can purge the temporary data from previous margin analysis load runs by navigating to the Purge Margin Analysis Run window.

PURGING STANDARD COST UPDATE HISTORY

When you update costs, the system enables you to save the details for historical reporting and to rerun adjustment reports. When you no longer need such information, use the Purge Standard Cost History window to purge it.

UNDERSTANDING KEY REPORTS FROM COST MANAGEMENT

There are many reports available to help monitor your costs. Table 20.4 describes some of the major reports.

TABLE 20.4 ORACLE COST MANAGEMENT REPORTS

Report Name	Description
Cost Type Comparison Report	Use the Cost Type Comparison Report to show the differences in item costs for two cost types. You can compare by cost element, activity, sub-element, department, this/previous level, or operation.
Elemental Cost Report	Use the Elemental Cost Report to report and summarize item costs by cost element.
Indented Bills of Material Cost Report	This report shows item costs by bills of material level. The report lists the detailed assembly costs by sub-element to the lowest level of the bill.
Intransit Value Report	Use the Intransit Value Report to report the value and quantity of items in the intransit inventory.
Inventory Value Report	Use the Inventory Value Report to show quantity, valuation, and detailed item information for each subinventory.
Margin Analysis Report	If you have the AR, OM, and INV applications, the Margin Analysis Report is a major analysis tool. The report shows revenue, cost of goods sold, and gross margin information for each item shipped or invoiced within a date range. This report can show summary or detail information by customer, order, and line number.
Invoice Transfer to Inventory Report	The Invoice Transfer to Inventory report lists all charges transferred to inventory during a specific time period for each inventory item.

TROUBLESHOOTING

The Cost Management application can be difficult to set up because it is dependent on the configuration of four other applications: Inventory, Work In Process, Purchasing, and Bills of Material. In addition, this application doesn't get much respect from the implementation team because it is viewed as a minor application or assigned second-class status. Consider the following as you configure and use the Cost Management application:

- Make sure a cost accountant is involved in the parts of the configuration of the four applications that precede the Cost Management setup.
- Understand the business requirements of your organization for Cost Management before you configure the Inventory, Work In Process, or Bills of Material applications.
- Try to perform cost updates at the beginning of a month before transactions start in the new month.

- Don't include a mix of rate-based and amount-based basis types in a mass edit.
- Perform the fiscal month-end closing on the applications in the following order: Payables, Purchasing, and Inventory/WIP.
- Do not create journal entries in detail unless you have very low transaction volumes.
- Make sure you follow good job closure procedures to recognize variances on discrete jobs. If you have a lot of jobs to close, consider performing that action during off-peak hours.
- Transfer inventory transactions to the general ledger periodically to minimize processing at month end.
- Verify that inventory transactions are not getting hung up in the transaction processing interfaces. Do this regularly. Make sure the transaction interfaces are clear before closing the fiscal period.

CHAPTER 21

Using Oracle Planning Applications

In this chapter

INTRODUCTION

This chapter covers the setup and use of the Oracle Planning Applications. The Planning functionality in this chapter includes Master Demand Scheduling (MDS), Master Production Scheduling (MPS), Material Requirements Planning (MRP), Supply Chain Management, and Capacity Requirements Planning (CRP).

USING ORACLE MASTER SCHEDULING/MRP

The Oracle Master Scheduling/MRP Applications provides a capable forecasting and planning solution for most organizations. When used with the Supply Chain Planning functionality and Oracle Capacity, these capabilities can extend to support a multi-site/multi-organization manufacturing and distribution planning process.

Figure 21.1 shows the major relationships between Oracle Master Scheduling/MRP and the other Oracle applications. The relationships affect the setup and operation of the Oracle Master Scheduling/MRP Applications.

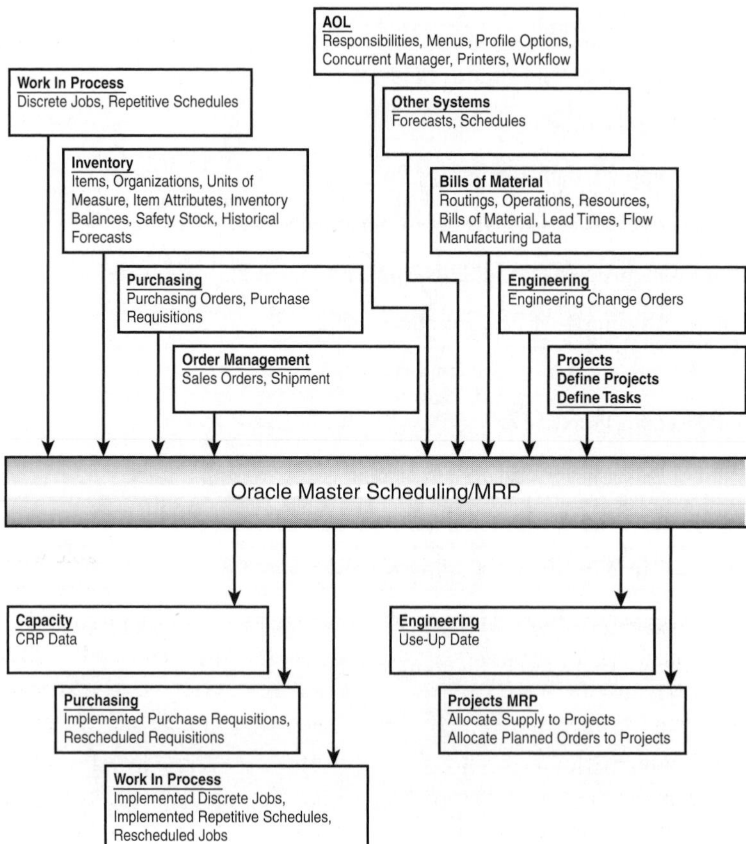

Figure 21.1
This is how the Oracle Master Scheduling/MRP Applications interacts with the other Oracle Applications.

DISCOVERING NEW FEATURES IN RELEASE 11*i*

Release 11*i* introduces new features that enhance the operation of the Oracle Master Scheduling/MRP Applications:

- **Deliver Frequency Calendars**—Delivery dates, which define the dates an organization can receive an item, can be established for each supplier or supplier/item combination.
- **Tolerance Fences**—Capacity tolerance percentages can be established for each of your suppliers, which enables you to see your suppliers' ability to increase capacity upon your notification within a time frame.
- **Redefinition of Rank and Allocation Percent**—Rank and allocation percent for sourcing are redefined during the upgrade process. AutoInstall upgrades the new sourcing rules with the new sourcing logic and maintains the original definitions.
- **Supplier Capacity Constraints**—By specifying time-phased capacity constraints for each supplier and by linking planned orders to a specific supplier (based on capacity), Planning will attempt to source the planned order from the primary supplier. However, if the capacity is not available, it will source the requirement from an alternate source.
- **Historical Allocation**—Planning will recognize all the historical allocations for each source, organization, or supplier when recommending sources for new planned orders.
- **Supplier Order Lead Times and Order Modifiers**—Supplier specific lead times and order modifiers can be established for each item/supplier combination to ensure orders are placed in the necessary time frame for your supplier to react.
- **Line Scheduling Workbench**—The workbench is used to simulate work orders to the production line. Some of the capabilities of the Scheduling Workbench are
    - Availability of components
    - Creating and completing flow schedules
    - Rolling flow schedules forward
    - Creating flow schedules from parent lines
    - Deleting flow schedules
    - Viewing unscheduled orders
    - Viewing the resources load as related to capacity
- **Workflow Messages**—Exception messages are now available which will enable the process to be automated for quicker corrective action. The recipients of the exception messages are not only internal employees, but also suppliers and customers. Planning calculates the expected performance of your plan, and the BIS (Business Intelligence) corrective action workflow compares the predicted performance to the target values and generates an exception message when the performance is off target.
- **Project Manufacturing Supported by Planning Modules—**The Planning modules support the end item model/unit effectivity of Project Manufacturing by which the system explodes the bills of material based on the model and unit number specified in the demand orders. Schedule entries can be done model/unit and create demand and planned orders with the unit number specified.

- **New Supply and Demand Types**—In support of Project Manufacturing, borrow and payback types have been added. The system recognizes a payback as a supply for the lending project and a demand for the borrowing project. Also, a new demand type has been added to the kanban calculation to calculate average daily demand. The demand type enables you to calculate the kanban size and quantity based on flow schedules, repetitive schedules, and work orders.
- **Flow Manufacturing New Windows**—Schedulers use the Line Scheduling Workbench to create and manage flow schedules and to simulate work assignments to production lines by using the following new windows:
    - Unscheduled Orders
    - Flow Schedule Details
    - Flow Schedule Summary

Critical Implementation Factors

You should consider the following factors before you undertake an implementation or upgrade of the Oracle Master Scheduling/MRP Applications.

Companies implementing and using the Master Scheduling/MRP Applications have identified some areas that require enhancement. These are some of the enhancements that have been submitted to Oracle Applications Development:

- A fixed amount of safety stock should be added to the Planning Detail report.
- The MRP Planning report should be able to be costed as an option.
- Notes that are created in the Planners Workbench should be passed to Purchasing (buyers).

Configuring the Application

The following section describes the setup tasks required to configure the Oracle Master Scheduling/MRP Applications. If you are implementing Release 11*i* of the applications, you can use the Oracle Applications Implementation Wizard to manage the setup tasks.

Resolving Critical Setup Issues

Before you begin the setup of the Oracle Master Scheduling/MRP Applications, there are some key issues that should be considered.

MPS Versus MRP Planning for Items

If you are converting data from a legacy system, you will probably have already decided on whether items should be MPS planned or MRP planned. If not, you need to consider at what level you want to plan items.

Traditionally, MPS planning was reserved for items that required close attention and manual intervention to manage supply quantities. In many organizations, this would include items that are manufactured and some purchased items on allocation or with long lead times. MPS planning within the Oracle Master Scheduling/MRP Applications provides for this level of control.

The decision should be based on how closely you want to manage an item. When you know which direction you want to take for an item, you need to set the Planning Method item attribute appropriately (see Chapter 17, "Using Oracle Inventory," for an explanation of item attributes). If you are converting legacy data, you can set this attribute when importing data through the Open Item Interface (see the section "Converting Data for Major Entities).

DETERMINING THE PLANNING PROCESS FOR YOUR ORGANIZATION

Before getting your team involved in the setup of the Master Scheduling/MRP Applications, you need to understand how the planning processes currently operate within your business. Thess applications provide a lot of capabilities to address the needs of a wide range of organizations.

The Forecasting, Master Scheduling, MRP, and Supply Chain Planning tools are complex by themselves. When you start to put them together to build a planning process for an enterprise that consists of a number of organizations, the task might seem daunting.

There is no one way to structure a planning process. As you prototype the planning process, pay particular attention to the options available for loading forecasts, loading schedules, and managing relief/consumption. There will be some degree of trial and error involved before you arrive at a process that works for you.

ORACLE MASTER SCHEDULING/MRP SETUP TASKS

Before you proceed with setting up the Oracle Master Scheduling/MRP Applications, you should complete the setup of the following applications:

- Oracle Inventory
- Oracle Purchasing
- Oracle Bills of Material
- Oracle Work In Process
- Oracle Capacity (if used)
- Oracle Project Manufacturing (if used)
- Oracle Workflow

Table 21.1 identifies the steps required to set up the Oracle Master Scheduling/MRP Applications. Because there are dependencies between steps, they should be completed in the sequence listed. An asterisk (*) indicates the steps that apply only if Supply Chain Planning is used.

TABLE 21.1 ORACLE MASTER SCHEDULING/MRP SETUP TASKS

Setup Tasks	Required
Establishing System Administrator Tasks	Yes
Defining Key Flexfields	Yes (part of Inv module setup)
Establishing Set of Books	Yes (part of Inventory module setup)
Defining Supplier Planned Inventories*	No
Defining Deliver-to Locations	Yes
Defining Employees	Yes
Defining Master Scheduling/MRP Planning Parameters	Yes
Defining Planning Exception Sets	No
Defining Demand Classes	No
Defining Planners	No
Establishing Planner Workbench	Yes
Defining Profile Options	Yes (Required with Defaults)
Defining Forecast Sets	No
Defining MDS Names	No
Defining MPS Names and Options	No
Defining MRP Names and Options	No
Identifying Workflow Options	No
Identifying Shipping Methods*	No
Defining In-Transit Lead Times*	No
Establishing Assignments Sets	No
Defining Sourcing Rules and Bills of Distribution	No (but recommended)
Defining Inter-Organization Shipping Network*	No
Defining DRP Names and Options*	No
Starting the Planning Manager	Yes
Running Information Audit	No (but recommended)

UNDERSTANDING EACH SETUP TASK

This section provides detail on each of the setup tasks and the order in which they should be performed.

ESTABLISHING SYSTEM ADMINISTRATION

Define responsibilities (required) and set up printers (optional). Set the number of processes for the Standard Manager (which runs the MRP planning processes) per the formula:

[4 + (2* number of snapshot workers defined in profile option)]

DEFINING KEY FLEXFIELDS

Coordinating the setting of Flexfields with other modules (inventory and human resources) is very important before setting up Planning because once established, Key Flexfields are usually not changed.

Tip

You can select a specific category set to be assigned to planning functions. This controls which categories you can use to query records in the Planner Workbench, so give this category set some thought.

ESTABLISHING A SET OF BOOKS

If your Calendars, currencies, and set of books have previously been set up, you can go to the next setup task. However, if you are implementing the Planning Applications in a multi-org environment, you have the opportunity to set up more than one Calendar, more than one currency, and more than one set of books (see Chapter 29, "Understanding Multi-Org").

DEFINING SUPPLIER-PLANNED INVENTORIES

If you are using supply-chain planning, you have the option to assign an inventory organization to a supplier. In this way, you can integrate the supplier organization into your planning process. You must first define a supplier, create a supplier organization, and then assign an inventory organization to that supplier.

In the same way, you can also assign an inventory organization to a customer, which enables integration of this organization into your supply chain.

Tip

If you establish a customer inventory organization, consider how you want to set the value of the profile option MRP: Use Ship Arrived Flag. This profile option tells the planning process how to identify which sales orders already shipped from internal organizations to customers have arrived.

Note

You must enter safety stock information for individual inventory items before MPS/MRP will calculate a safety stock for the item.

DEFINING DELIVER-TO LOCATIONS

If you will be creating purchase requisitions from planned orders, you must define at least one deliver-to location. This will be used in the creation of a purchase order from the requisition. If you are implementing Oracle Purchasing, you can define the deliver-to location while setting up that application.

DEFINING EMPLOYEES

Employees need to be set up to allow the creation of purchase requisitions from planned orders. These requisitions are imported into Oracle Purchasing to create Purchase Orders. You must define individuals who will create requisitions, create purchase orders, approve purchases, and perform receipt transactions.

Note

Only employees are allowed to release planned orders from the Planner Workbench, so be sure to define all planners as employees and link their employee names to their user logon names.

If you have installed Oracle HRMS, you can use this application to set up your employees. Otherwise, you can use the Enter Employee form provided with the Master Scheduling/MRP Applications.

DEFINING PLANNING PARAMETERS

Figure 21.2 shows the Planning Parameters screen, which is used to set default values for the planning module. When you work with this window, consider checking the Snapshot Lock Tables box to ensure data consistency of on-hand quantities and order quantities during a planning run. Select the system execution defaults, and enter repetitive planning parameters as required. These values default into plan options, but they can be changed for each individual plan. They must be defined for any inventory organization in which MRP will be run.

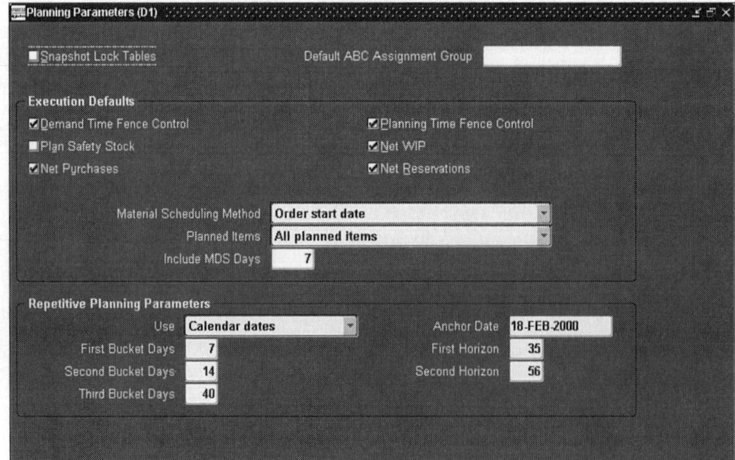

Figure 21.2
Planning Parameters screen.

The planning parameters determine the basic defaults to be used in the planning process:

- **Snapshot Lock Tables**—Setting this parameter tells the planning process to lock tables when gathering on-hand order quantity information for the snapshot. If you set this parameter, you prevent certain transactions from taking place while the snapshot processes are running. The benefit is that you obtain more accurate order and inventory information for the planning process. With the memory-based planning engine, locking tables during the planning run is unlikely to have a significant impact on users performing transactions. How long the tables remain locked is determined by the value of the profile option MRP: Snapshot Pause for Lock (Minutes).
- **Default ABC Assignment Group**—This is not required, however, some organizations choose to implement their plans based on item ABC assignments.
- **Demand Time Fence Control**—You can determine whether demand time fences are honored in the planning process. If they are, forecast demand within the time is not considered. Sales order demand is still valid within the demand time fence.
- **Plan Safety Stock**—This tells the planning process to calculate safety stock for items when the plan is run. You must specify the safety stock parameters for your items if you need this planned.
- **Net Purchases**—You can choose to have your plan consider all purchases as supply. If you do not choose to net purchases, there will be no reschedule messages for your requisitions/orders, and the planning process will generate new planned orders to meet supply requirements. This may result in oversupply.
- **Planning Time Fence Control**—This determines whether planning time fences are honored in the planning process. If this parameter is set and you have time fences specified for items, the planning process will not suggest new orders within the time fence or provide reschedule-in suggestions for existing orders. You will still receive reschedule-out suggestions. If the parameter is not set, the planning process will plan new orders and create reschedule suggestions regardless of how the planning time fence is set for your items. (There are several new profile options that affect the behavior of the planning process within the planning time fence.)
- **Net WIP**—If this parameter is set, the planning process will consider existing discrete jobs and repetitive schedules as supply for an item. If the parameter is not set, there will be no reschedule suggestions for existing jobs, and new jobs will be planned to meet supply requirements. If not checked, this may result in oversupply.
- **Net Reservations**—This determines whether existing reservations are netted off on-hand quantities when the plan is run. If this parameter is not set, the planning process will consider the on-hand quantity as being available regardless of reservations.

- **Material Scheduling Method**—Two options exist for this parameter. Operation Start Date schedules material to be available to meet the start date for a particular WIP operation. Order Start Date schedules material to be available for the start date of a discrete job. Use Operation Start Date if there is a lengthy interval between steps on your routings and you do not wish to have material available until the routing operation is due to start.
- **Planned Items**—You can specify whether the planning process considers all planned items, demand schedule items, or supply schedule items.

Tip

Although Oracle Master Scheduling/MRP provides these options, you will probably want to select All Planned Items for this parameter. This way, you include all possible sources of demand in your plan. If you want to exclude certain items from the planning process on an individual basis, you can set the MRP Planning Method attribute for these items to Not Planned. See Chapter 17 for an explanation of the item attributes.

- **Include MDS Days**—You can optionally specify a number of days of past due MDS demand to include in the planning process. If you enter no value, the process will consider all MDS entries. A value of zero means that no past due MDS entries will be considered. If you will be using repetitive schedules, you must also define default parameters at this step.
- **Work dates or Calendar dates**—You can specify whether the dates for your repetitive schedules will be based on work dates or calendar dates. Using work dates forces your repetitive planning periods to follow the workday calendar. Choosing calendar dates enables your planning periods to include dates that are not part of the workday calendar.
- **Anchor Date**—You can specify the date from which the repetitive planning periods start. You can anchor subsequent planning runs to this date or choose a new one.
- **First Bucket Days, First Horizon, Second Bucket Days, Second Horizon, and Third Bucket Days**—You use *buckets* to define three time periods for your repetitive plans. This enables you to obtain better control of repetitive schedules in the near term, and monitor overall changes in requirements further out. The periods are specified by selecting a bucket size (in days), which will be used as the basis for suggested schedules. The periods are bounded by the horizon, which is specified in days. The third period is bounded by the planning horizon you specify when you execute the plan.

Tip

The bucket days used in the first and second periods should be small to enable more finite control of suggested schedules. Consider using a higher number of bucket days for the third period, where an overall picture of supply and demand is required.

DEFINING PLANNING EXCEPTION SETS

Planning exception sets enable you to structure the way in which you view and implement planning exceptions related to items, orders, and resources. An exception set must be assigned to an item using the Exception Set item attribute (see Chapter 17 for an explanation of item attributes). Use of a planning exception set enables the following additional exception messages (which do not otherwise appear in the Planner Workbench):

- **Excess Quantities**—When the projected on-hand quantity exceeds zero or the safety stock for the item by more than the excess quantity you specify.
- **Repetitive Variance Exceptions**—When the suggested repetitive schedule exceeds the current schedule by more than the percentage you specify.
- **Resource Shortage**—When the capacity for a resource is overutilized by more than the percentage you specify.
- **Resource Excess**—When the capacity for a resource is underutilized by more than the percentage you specify.
- **Overpromised Exceptions**—When the available-to-promise quantity falls below zero or the safety stock for the item.
- **Shortage Exceptions**—When the projected on-hand quantity falls below zero or the safety stock value you have specified for an item within the time fence for the item.

The exceptions are based on choosing a time period within which the exception condition is tested. The periods to choose from are

- **Cumulative Manufacturing Lead Time**—This lead time can be calculated by Oracle Bills of Material and is based on raw materials being in stock, but requiring subassemblies to be manufactured.
- **Cumulative Total Lead Time**—This lead time can also be calculated by Oracle Bills of Material, but is based on raw materials being purchased and all subassemblies being manufactured.
- **Planning Time Fence**—This is based on the planning time fence defined for an item.
- **Total Lead Time**—This is the fixed lead time plus [variable lead time multiplied by the order quantity].
- **User-Defined Time Fence**—You can enter a number of days to be used as a user-defined time fence for exception reporting.

Tip

You can create a number of exception sets with different sensitivities that you can apply to different types of items. To do this, you can add the exception set name in an organization level item template (or update an existing template) and then apply the template when you create an item. Item templates are explained in Chapter 17. Although you can define multiple exception sets, only one set can be applied to an item at a time.

DEFINING DEMAND CLASSES

Demand classes enable you to group similar types of demand together. A typical application is the creation of separate demand classes for a particular group of customers (for example, separate classes for retail customers and distributors).

Demand classes provide significant flexibility in the planning process:

- **Forecast Consumption**—You can assign a demand class to a forecast. This affects how forecast consumption operates for the forecast. Sales orders can also have a demand class associated with them, and the planning manager uses this as part of the consumption logic.
- **Order Entry**—You can associate a demand class with an order type or with the ship-to address for a customer. When an order is entered, the relevant demand class is associated with the order.
- **Organization Demand Class**—A demand class can be associated with an organization. This has implications for forecast consumption and schedule relief if you are using supply-chain planning.
- **Master Schedules**—You can assign a demand class to an MDS or MPS. Sales orders with a demand class matching that of an MDS relieve it. Discrete jobs with a demand class matching that of an MPS relieve it.
- **Planning**—If a demand class is associated with an MPS, you can control the way jobs, schedules, and reservations are netted in the planning process by assigning demand classes to these entities.

DEFINING PLANNERS

Using the Planners window, you can define the planners for your organization. This enables you to group items by planner within planning reports and on the planner workbench. To assign a planner code to an item, you must update the planner item attribute (see Chapter 17). Planner codes must be defined at the organization level, Item Master.

SETTING UP THE PLANNER WORKBENCH

The *planner workbench* is the basic tool that most organizations use to review and implement recommendations from the planning process. It is a common interface that is used with both Master Scheduling/MRP and Supply Chain Planning. Some prerequisites to using the planner workbench are

- **Define Employees to Enable You to Load Purchase Orders**—This step should already be complete. Only employees can release planned orders from the planner workbench.
- **Define a Deliver-to Location to Enable New Requisitions to be Loaded**—This step should also be complete.
- **Assign Purchasing Categories and List Prices**—The categories and list prices are assigned in the Oracle Inventory setup (see Chapter 17). Make sure that the Item

Master has a zero in the list price field if no PO list price is defined. Otherwise, Requisition Import will fail for buy items released from the planner workbench.

- **Set Requisition Numbers to be Automatically Assigned**—This is part of the Oracle Purchasing setup (see Chapter 16, "Using Oracle Purchasing") and is a prerequisite to implement planned orders as purchase requisitions from the workbench.

You can customize the display of information on the planner workbench by setting parameters for the horizontal plan and horizontal capacity views. You can also set some defaults to be used:

- **Supply/Demand Alternate Region**—You can assign a cutoff date to be used when displaying new orders and reschedule recommendations. You can also enter a default job class to be assigned to discrete jobs created from the workbench (see Chapter 22, "Using Oracle Work In Process," for an explanation of job classes). You can assign a load group to be used when creating purchase requisitions from the workbench. The options are to group by buyer, item, category, supplier, individual requisitions per planned order, or all planned orders on one requisition.
- **Horizontal Material Plan Alternate Region**—You can define Display Bucket Type, Display Factor, Decimal Places, Field Width, Independent Demand Type, and, optionally, Source List to define the way data is displayed in the Horizontal Plan window. You can check each type of plan information you want displayed in your horizontal plan.
- **Horizontal Capacity Plan Alternate Region**—You can indicate the type of information you want included in the Horizontal Capacity Plan display.

SETTING THE PROFILE OPTIONS

Table 21.2 shows the profile options that directly affect the operation of the Oracle Master Scheduling/MRP application.

TABLE 21.2 ORACLE MASTER SCHEDULING/MRP PROFILE OPTIONS

Profile Option Name	Level*	Comment
MRP:Plan Revenue Discount	S	No default.
MRP:Plan Revenue Price List	S	No default.
MRP:ATP Assignment Set	S	No Default.
MRP:Calculate Excess Exceptions	S	Default is No on Time Fence.
MRP:Calculate Suggested Repetitive Schedules	S	No default.
MRP:Compute Sales Order Changes	S	Default is Yes.
MRP:Consume Forecast	S	Default is Yes.
MRP:Consume Forecast Set Summary	SARU	No default.

TABLE 21.2 CONTINUED

Profile Option Name	Level*	Comment
MRP:Consume MDS	S	Default is Yes.
MRP:Consume MPS	S	Default is Yes.
MRP:Cutoff Date Offset Months	SU	Default is 12 months.
MRP:Debug Mode	SARU	Default is No.
MRP:Default DRP Plan Name	S	No Default.
MRP:Default Forecast Date	SARU	Default is Yes.
MRP:Default Forecast Name	U	No Default.
MRP:Default Plan Name	U	No Default.
MRP:Default Schedule Name	U	No Default.
MRP:Default Sourcing Assignment Set		No Default.
MRP:Demand Time Fence Days	S	No Default.
MRP:Environment variable to set path for MRP files	S	No Default set for Profile. System will put the files in $MRP_TOP/$APPLOUT by default.
MRP:Firm Planned Order Time Fence	S	Default is Yes.
MRP:Firm Requisitions Within Time Fence	S	No Default.
MRP:Include Scheduled Receipts in Use-up Calculation	S	Default is No.
MRP:Interface Table History Days	S	Default is five days.
MRP:Maintain Original Schedule Version	S	Default is No.
MRP:MPS Relief Direction	SAR	Default is Backward, then Forward. Stop and restart the planning manager if this profile is changed.
MRP:Perform Planning Manager Function in Loads	S	Default is Yes.
MRP:Planning Manager Batch Size	S	Default is 250.
MRP:MRP Planning Manager Max Workers	S	Default is 10.
MRP:MRP Purchasing By Revision	S	No Default.
MRP:MRP Purge Batch Size	S	Default is 25000.
MRP:MRP Requisition Load Group Option	SRU	Default is Supplier.
MRP:Retain Dates within Calendar Boundary	S	Default is Yes.

TABLE 21.2 CONTINUED

Profile Option Name	Level*	Comment
MRP:Snapshot Pause for Lock (Minutes)	S	Default is five minutes.
MRP:Snapshot Workers	S	Default is 5.
MRP:Sourcing Rule Category Set	SU	No Default.
MRP:Time Fence Warning	SARU	Default is Yes.
MRP:Trace Mode	SARU	Default is No.
MRP:Use Direct Load Option	SARU	Default is No.
MRP:Use Ship Arrived Flag	SARU	Default is No.
Concurrent:Sequential Requests	S	Should be set to No.
MRP:Activate OLP	S	No [For upgrade from 10.7 to 11.5].
MRP:Combine Sugg Repetitive Schedules	S	No.
MRP:New Planner Backward Compatibility	S	Y [if upgrading from 10.7 to 11*i*].
MRP:Repetitive Past Due Supply Days	SA	[upgrade from 10.7 to 11.5].
MRP:Old Sales Orders Cutoff Days	S	For upgrade from 10.7 or 1103 to 11.5. This profile option is added by Patch 1518877 and causes the Planning Manager to ignore sales orders with a due date before the value entered into the profile option. This fixes a problem with the Planning Manager hanging during sales order consumption after the upgrade.

**Levels can be Site, Application, Responsibility, or User. The system administrator sets most profile options.*

Note

You might see 40 additional profile options relating to the i2 Factory Planner and RHYTHM software packages. These were created during a period when Oracle Planning and i2 were to be integrated, but this integration has been cancelled, and these profile options are not active.

A value must be set for a profile option where a default is specified. The default may be accepted without change. New profile options can be added by patches, but you should always review profile options after applying any megapatch and contact Oracle Support if information is required to set the correct value.

DEFINING FORECAST SETS

Figure 21.3 shows the Forecast Sets screen, which is used to group individual forecasts into a forecast set. Sets can be useful for combining forecast information that comes from related sources. An example would be to create a forecast set that consists of individual regional sales forecasts. At least one forecast set must be defined before an individual forecast is defined. There is no restriction on how many sets that can be defined.

When you define a forecast set, you must select a "bucket" type to be used as the default for entering forecast information. Buckets can be days, weeks, or accounting periods. You must also indicate the level at which the forecast and consumption process will operate. If you are using Oracle Order Entry and Oracle Receivables, you have the option to define the forecast set at the customer, bill-to, or ship-to level. This option determines the sales orders that consume the forecast set. There is also an option to define the forecast set at the item level. If you do not have Oracle Order Entry or Oracle Accounts Receivable installed, this is the default.

For each forecast set (assuming you will use forecast consumption), you must specify the forward and backward consumption days that will be used (forecast consumption is discussed later in this chapter).

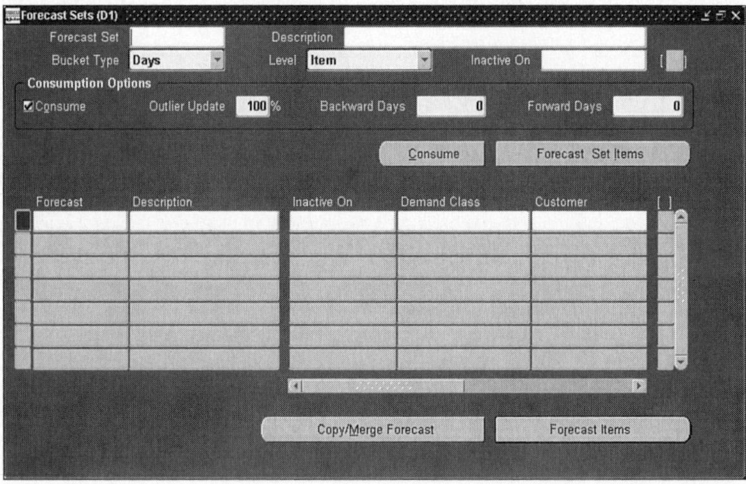

Figure 21.3
Forecast Sets screen.

DEFINING THE MASTER DEMAND SCHEDULE

Figure 21.4 shows the Master Demand Schedules (MDS) screen, which contains the demand for products supplied by your organization. Typically, the MDS consist of Sales Order and Forecast information. You can optionally associate an MDS with a demand class. Demand classes (discussed later) enable you to group similar demand types (for example, by customer).

The MDS can be relieved by sales order shipments. To allow this, you must set the MDS Relief option to Yes in the Define MDS Names form.

Note

MDS relief occurs only if the MRP:Consume MDS profile option is set to Yes and if you check the MDS Relief box in the MDS Names form.

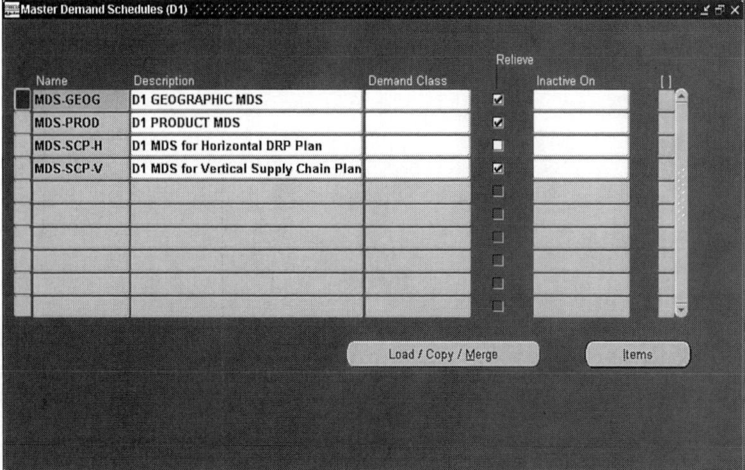

Figure 21.4
Master Demand Schedules screen.

DEFINING THE MASTER PRODUCTION SCHEDULE AND OPTIONS

The Master Production Schedule (MPS) contains the build schedule for your organization. This can consist of discrete quantities or build rates if you are using repetitive scheduling.

As with the MDS, you can choose to associate a demand class with the MPS. This ensures that only discrete jobs associated with the demand class can relieve the MPS. If you choose the Inventory ATP option, your MPS will be considered as supply in any ATP calculations carried out by Oracle Inventory.

Tip

The supply will be visible in the Inventory Supply/Demand inquiry form. For this reason, you should check this box for only one plan at a time; otherwise, you will be overstating available supply.

The Feedback option enables the Planner/Scheduler to see how much of a planned order has been implemented by comparing the Snapshot to the current value in the Horizontal Material Plan. When defining the MPS, you can choose the Production option to allow autorelease of planned orders against the schedule for those items with the Release Time Fence attribute set in the Item Master.

You can define multiple master production schedules, each with a unique name. However, only one MPS plan at a time should be active. Enter a date in the Inactive On field to inactivate a plan. You can easily reactivate a plan if necessary by deleting the date in this field.

The MPS relief option allows the original MPS quantities to be reduced when discrete jobs, inter-organization shipments, purchase orders, or purchase requisitions are created. This prevents overstating requirements if Material Requirements Planning (MRP) is run between MPS runs. There is no MPS relief for repetitive items between MPS runs.

Before you can launch an MPS plan, you must define the options for the plan. You can see only plan names in the launch form for which options have been defined. These options default from the parameters defined during organization setup, but they can be changed.

Tip

For MPS relief to happen, the profile option MRP:Consume MPS must be set to Yes and the relieve box must be checked in the Define MPS Names form.

Defining Material Requirements Plan and Options

In the Material Requirements Planning (MRP) process, net requirements for material are calculated. The MRP contains planned orders/schedules to support the net requirements as well as recommendations for rescheduling or canceling existing orders. Any number of material requirements plan names can be defined. This enables you to generate multiple MRP plans, each with a unique name. However, only one MRP plan at a time should be active. You can inactivate a plan by entering a date in the Inactive On field in the MRP Names form. You also can easily reactivate the plan by removing the date in this field.

As with the MPS, you can select the feedback option to enable a Planner to check the quantity of a planned order that has been implemented by comparing the Snapshot to the current value in the Horizontal Material Plan. You can also choose the Production option to enable autorelease of planned orders against the plan schedule for those items with the Release Time Fence attribute set in the Item Master.

Before you can launch an MRP plan, you must define the options for the plan, as shown in Figure 21.5. You can see only plan names in the launch form for which options have been defined. These options default from the parameters defined during organization setup, but they can be changed.

Identifying Workflow Options

Enable Exception Messages to send messages to predefined contacts for specific jobs to fix problems. You must use Workflow Builder to perform this task. You can also modify the seeded workflows to tailor the notification process to your business needs.

Defining Shipping Methods and In-Transit Lead Times

You can define shipping methods as QuickCodes to be used with interorganization transfers. These could be a specific carrier or a description of a method (air, sea, and so on).

For use with supply-chain planning, you might want to associate a lead time to be used with each shipping method. This lead time can be defined when creating the interorganization shipping network. This step is also typically part of the Oracle Inventory setup (see Chapter 17).

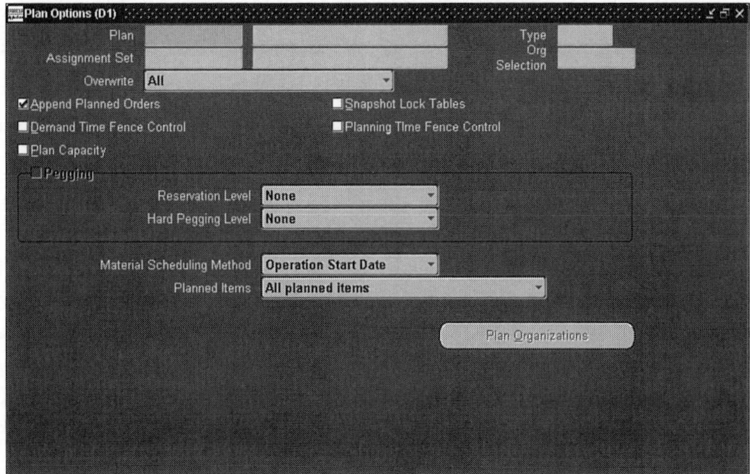

Figure 21.5
Plan Options screen.

DEFINING SOURCING RULES AND BILLS OF DISTRIBUTION

Sourcing rules and bills of distribution are associated with the operation of supply-chain planning. *Sourcing rules* define how an item will be replenished within a single organization or across all organizations. *Bills of distribution*, on the other hand, can define replenishment across an entire enterprise, which includes supplier organizations, distribution centers or hubs, and manufacturing operations.

The operation of supply-chain planning is discussed later in this chapter.

ESTABLISHING ASSIGNMENT SETS

When the sourcing rules and bills of distribution have been defined, they must be assigned to an assignment set. You have several options for assigning these:

- An item across all your organizations
- A single item in an organization
- All items in an organization
- A category or categories of items
- Categories of items in an organization
- All organizations

Assigning the sourcing rules and bills of distribution enables you to define the supply chain for your enterprise. After you have created the assignment set, you must enter its name in the profile option: MRP:Default Sourcing Assignment Set.

DEFINING INTERORGANIZATION SHIPPING NETWORK

In this setup step, you define how transfers of items between inventory organizations will operate. An organization can be a shipping organization, destination organization, or both.

You can also decide whether you will use in-transit inventory. Part of the setup involves the assignment of accounting information to be used in recording charges associated with the transfer of items.

This setup step is typically completed in Oracle Inventory (see Chapter 17) and must be completed if you're using supply-chain planning.

DEFINING THE DISTRIBUTION REQUIREMENTS PLAN

Define any number of distribution requirements plans names. This enables you to generate multiple DRP plans, each with a unique name. The Distribution Requirements Plan (DRP) contains similar information to a material requirements plan, but it is based on the material requirements to support a distribution network (considering suppliers, manufacturing locations, warehouses, distribution centers, and customer locations).

The same setup options apply to a DRP and MRP.

STARTING THE PLANNING MANAGER

The planning manager process is responsible for the maintenance of a number of planning tasks including the following:

- Consumption of forecasts by Sales Orders
- Relief of the MDS by Sales Order shipments
- Relief of the MPS by the creation of Purchase Orders and Discrete Jobs
- Support of the MRP open interface routines

Although the planning manager is initiated from the Planning Manager window, it runs as a concurrent process based on the processing interval you specify. You can also check the status of the Planning Manager from this window.

Tip

The default of 30 seconds for the processing interval seems to work well in most circumstances. In some situations, though, the planning manager process will fail. If users are vigilant, they will notice this through inconsistencies in the consumption or relief processes. However, it would be wise to create an Oracle Alert to monitor the status of the planning manager and notify an administrator if it fails. You should also note that the processing interval is calculated based on the start time of the previous request.

RUNNING INFORMATION AUDIT

Oracle Master Scheduling/MRP provides an audit report to enable you to check the integrity of the data that will be used in the planning process. A series of predefined audit statements are provided to check for potential errors in the database (for example, items that are planned as buy but are not purchasable).

If you are converting data as part of your implementation, this report should be run after the conversion process has completed.

CONVERTING DATA FOR MAJOR ENTITIES

If you are implementing Oracle Master Scheduling/MRP and want to move data from a legacy system, it needs to be converted. A number of open interfaces are provided with the applications that can assist with the conversion process.

Tip

Before converting any data using the open interfaces, ensure that all the setup steps in the relevant applications are complete. Data imported through the interfaces will be validated against your setups.

The open interfaces directly relevant to Oracle Master Scheduling/MRP are the following:

- Open Forecast Interface
- Open Master Schedule Interface
- Supply/Demand Interface API [new in 11.5]
- Sourcing Rules API [new in 11.5]

These interfaces are discussed in the section "Using Open Interfaces in This Application," later in this chapter.

You should also consider the conversion of Items and Bills of Material, particularly because many planning parameters are associated with item attributes or BOM structures. Conversion of item and BOM data is covered in Chapter 17 and Chapter 19, "Using Oracle Engineering and Bills of Material."

Tip

If you're converting bills of material that reference subinventories (in the Material Control section), be sure you have set a value for the profile option INV: Expense to Asset Transfer. The value does not matter, but if no value is set, the import process will fail.

As with all conversions, you need to assess the costs involved in developing programs to extract data from your legacy system and insert it in the relevant interface tables. In some cases, it might be more economical to create forecast and master schedule data using the Master Scheduling/MRP Applications, particularly if the volume is small.

PROCESSING TRANSACTIONS

The following section covers the main transactions involved in using Oracle Master Scheduling/Material Requirements Planning.

Maintaining Forecasts

Estimating or forecasting future demand is a critical activity in the planning process. Oracle Master Scheduling/MRP provides for manual entry of a forecast or for the creation of forecasts based on historical data. Forecasts are consumed each time you receive a sales order from your customers. You can group complementary forecasts into forecast sets.

After you have created a forecast set with at least one forecast, you can create detail entries for a forecast.

Manual Forecast Entry

To create a manual forecast entry, you need to select one of your previously defined forecasts. The forecast information is entered by item number, as shown in Figure 21.6. Each forecast entry is valid for a particular bucket. The buckets can be days, weeks, or accounting periods. The bucket type defaults from the information entered when the forecast set was created.

Tip

To speed up the entry and maintenance of forecast information, you can choose to enter a bucket type, a start date and end date for the forecast, and a quantity. This is useful if you have multiple identical forecast quantities over a number of identical periods (for example, 10,000 per week for ten weeks). The bucket type is copied into the MDS or MPS if loaded from the forecast and is not easily changed, so give some thought to how you set these up when creating the forecast.

For each forecast entry, you can also specify a confidence percentage that will be applied to the forecast. This percentage is used to anticipate requirements when the forecast is loaded into an MDS or MPS. A percentage less than 100% reduces anticipated requirements when the forecast is loaded into an MDS or MPS.

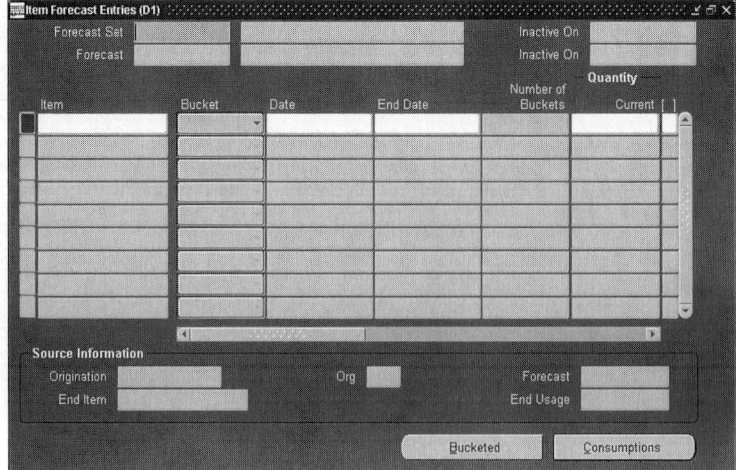

Figure 21.6
Item Forecast Entries screen.

FORECASTING BASED ON HISTORICAL DATA

In conjunction with Oracle Inventory, you can create a forecast rule, which can be used to generate forecasts based on historical data. Two methods are provided:

- **Focus Forecasting**—Produces a forecast for a single period only by applying five models to historical data, averaging the results, and selecting the model with the lowest error percentage to create the forecast.
- **Statistical Forecasting**—Can be used for any number of periods and uses a mathematical model to predict future demand based on historical data.

You define forecast rules in Oracle Inventory (see Chapter 17). To do this, you must define a name for the rule and the bucket type to use. You must then specify which historical information should be considered in creating the forecast:

- Sales order shipments
- Issues to WIP
- Miscellaneous issues
- Inter-organization transfers

You must also select the forecasting method that the rule will use. If you choose focus forecasting, the application will use focus forecasting algorithms to choose a best-fit forecast based on historical transactions.

If you choose statistical forecasting, you can specify the following:

- The maximum number of historical periods to be considered in the calculations.
- The smoothing (alpha) factor.
- Use a trend model. You can also specify the amount of smoothing to be used in this model.
- Use a seasonality model. You can specify a smoothing factor to be used with the seasonality indexes. You can use both trend and seasonality models together.
- If you choose to use a seasonality model, you can enter a seasonality index by period.

When you create the forecast, you can choose to apply the forecast rule to all items, a specific item, a category of item, or all items in a category set (see Chapter 17 for an explanation of category sets).

Tip

It is unlikely that you would want to apply a forecast rule to *all* items in an organization. If you plan on using historical forecasting, consider creating item categories that will enable you to segregate the items that would benefit this method of creating forecasts.

You need to specify an overwrite option when generating a forecast using a forecast rule. This is explained in the next section.

COPYING AND MERGING FORECASTS

While maintaining separate forecasts for business reasons (by region and by customer), you might need to combine forecasts into one to be used in a subsequent planning operation. It might also be useful to copy an existing forecast (rather than manually re-create it) and then modify it to simulate a particular scenario.

Oracle Master Scheduling/MRP provides a tool to accomplish this. There are some critical parameters in the copy/merge process that you should consider:

- **Overwrite Option**—Selecting an incorrect option can cause problems that are difficult to undo. All Entries causes any existing forecast entries in the destination forecast to be *deleted* and replaced with the source forecast information. The No option means that any existing entries in the destination forecast are left as-is, and the source forecast data is *appended*. Same Source Only means that any existing forecast entries that had previously been loaded from the same source forecast will be *deleted* and the newly copied or merged forecast entries will be added to the forecast.

Tip

When a forecast or MDS is overwritten, the item quantity and date details are removed from the Entries form. However, the items themselves are still shown in the Items form until the Planning Manager Once-A-Day worker is launched (usually right after the system date changes) by the Planning Manager. This worker removes any items with no dates or quantities from the Items form. This is often confusing to users who do not expect to see the overwritten items in the Items form. After performing the copy and overwrite, you can manually launch the Once-A-Day worker to clean up the Items form without waiting for the Planning Manager's midnight run.

- **Start and Cutoff Dates**—You can choose how much of a forecast should be merged or copied. Forecast entries outside of this date range will not be merged or copied. The system date defaults into the start date field, but it can be changed to a different date if desired.
- **Explode**—If you are forecasting using planning bills of material), you can use this function to create a forecast for the components of those bills of material. To do this, copy the forecast containing the planning items into another forecast with the Explode option enabled. The destination forecast will now contain forecast entries for the components. See Chapter 19 for an explanation of planning bills of material.
- **Current/Original Quantities and the Consume Option**—See the next section of this chapter for a discussion of consumption.
- **Modification Percent**—You can choose to modify *all* entries in the source forecast by a percentage as they are merged or copied into the destination.

- **Carry Forward Days**—You can shift the dates on the source forecast entries by a number of days as they are merged or copied. This can be a positive number (shift forward) or a negative number (shift backward).

Caution

The carryforward method does not work when the manufacturing calendar quarterly type is calendar months or 13 periods and the forecast bucket type is periods. Use a 4/4/5 or 5/4/4 calendar quarterly type.

THE FORECAST CONSUMPTION PROCESS

Oracle Master Scheduling/MRP provides forecast consumption to replace forecasts with sales order demand as the sales orders are loaded. This prevents situations from arising where sales order plus forecast quantities overstate the true requirements. Consumption is enabled for a forecast set and applies to all forecasts within the set.

Note

If you enter customer information but do not specify the correct forecast level, the forecast consumption ignores the customer information.

Other parameters associated with the forecast set affect the way that consumption operates:

- **Outlier Update Percent**—This is the maximum percentage of the original forecast quantity that a single sales order can consume. This prevents an unusually large or unanticipated sales order from consuming all the available forecast.
- **Forward and Backward Consumption Days**—These parameters tell the planning manager the number of days to look forward and backward from the sales order schedule date when locating forecast entries to consume. The planning manager will first look backward (if backward consumption days is greater than zero) and then forward (if forward consumption days is greater than zero) for a forecast to consume.

Caution

Consumption results might not be as expected when the calendar quarterly type is calendar months or 13 periods. Use a 4/4/5 or 5/4/4 calendar quarterly type.

Tip

Forward and backward consumption days work with the bucket size you specify for your forecast entries. Choose the combination carefully! If you enter your entire forecast for a month with a bucket size of Day or Week and make the entry for one day or one week, this seriously reduces the chances of the planning manager finding a valid forecast to consume. You run the risk of overstating the demand when you load the forecast into an MDS along with sales orders. You should choose the combination of consumption days and bucket size that works best for your business.

If you associate a demand class with a forecast, this also affects consumption. When a sales order is entered with an associated demand class, the planning manager looks for a forecast entry with the same demand class to consume. If it does not find one, it looks for a forecast with *no* demand class, and failing that, it overconsumes.

Overconsumption is a mechanism that provides feedback that the planning manager could not find adequate forecast quantities to consume. This process cannot physically consume more forecast than exists; however, it records the fact as Overconsumption. This entry shows as a zero original quantity and a negative current quantity.

Tip

You can create an alert to notify the planner whenever a forecasted item is overconsumed.

You should also be aware of how consumption appears when you query a forecast. When a forecast entry is created, the quantity entered becomes the current quantity. This quantity also populates the original and total fields. When a sales order is loaded that consumes the forecast entry, querying the forecast shows that the current and original fields now reflect the fact that consumption has occurred. The current field is reduced by the quantity of the consuming sales order. The original field still shows the original forecast quantity.

Unconsumption is the process by which forecast consumption is reversed if there is a change in the sales order quantity or in the sales order schedule date.

To further complicate the way in which consumption occurs, you have the option to consume forecasts as you use the forecast copy/merge process.

Tip

There are a lot of options available to manage forecast consumption. Ultimately, you will want to load forecast information into a master schedule. If this will be an MDS, you might also want to load sales orders. Using any or all of the options available (consuming forecast sets or consuming forecasts while copying or merging), you will need to get to a forecast that will represent anticipated demand for your products. In this way, you can be sure that adding sales orders to the MDS will not cause demand to be overstated.

MAINTAINING MASTER SCHEDULES

In the setup, you will have defined master schedule names. As described earlier, you can define Master Demand Schedules and Master Production Schedules. A Master Demand Schedule (MDS) contains all sources of demand, including anticipated shipments. The Master Production Schedule (MPS) contains the supply to meet the demand in the MDS. A Master Schedule can include discrete and repetitive items.

The Master Demand Schedule is used to

- Demand management
- Schedule the production schedule

- Validate the production schedule
- Manage the production schedule

LOADING A MASTER SCHEDULE

You can load a master schedule from internal sources or with data from external sources through the Open Master Schedule Interface (see the section "Using Open Interfaces in this Application").

You can choose from a number of internal sources when loading a master schedule:

- **A Forecast**—You can select a forecast to be used.
- **Interorganization Planned Orders**—These can be loaded from one or more of the organizations that are defined.
- **Sales Orders Only**—This can be all sales orders or only sales orders with scheduled dates from the load date forward.
- **Another MDS or MPS**—As with the forecast load process, you can apply a modification percentage to all entries in the source schedule when it is being loaded. You can also use carry-forward days (positive or negative) to shift the source schedule dates forward or backward by a specified number of days.
- **Source Lists**—These are described in the setup steps.

Some of the other options available when loading a schedule are the following:

- **Sales Order Demand Class**—You can limit the load to include sales orders with a specific demand class associated.
- **Demand Time Fence**—This gives you control over the loading of forecast and sales order entries using the demand time fence defined for an item (see the Material Requirements Planning section for a description of time fences).
- **Overwrite**—The overwrite options work in the same way as for merging and copying forecasts. The same warnings apply.
- **Start and Cutoff Date**—You can limit which forecast entries to load by specifying these dates.
- **Explode**—This determines whether the load process should explode items in an MDS. The level of explosion is set by the Max Bill Levels parameter in Oracle Bills of Material. This can be modified if you create manual MDS entries.
- **Consume, Backward Consumption Days, Forward Consumption Days, Outlier Percent, and Quantity Type (original or current)**—These options are related to the consumption of forecast during the load process. If you are loading sales orders and forecast, you can choose to consume during the load process or consume the forecast set and load the forecast with the consume option set to No.

Note

The Planning Modules support Project Manufacturing's end item model/unit effectivity, which enables you to enter schedules by model/unit, create demand, and generate planned orders with unit number specified.

MANUAL MASTER SCHEDULE ENTRIES

In every business situation, there will be exceptional requirements that are not driven by dependent demand. Typical examples would be the planning of spares requirements or manufacturing/engineering prototypes. In these cases, you have the option to load the demand into a forecast, or alternatively, you can create a manual master schedule entry (MDS or MPS). Such items must have the MRP Planning attribute set to MPS Planned.

Tip

Take care when using manual master schedule entries. If you create manual entries and then subsequently reload the schedule from forecasts/sales orders, there is a risk that you could overwrite the original manual entries. If this is not what you intend, choose the Overwrite option Same Source Only, which protects your entries with a manual source. Alternatively, you could keep your manual entries in a separate schedule and subsequently load them into the schedule you intend to use for planning.

SCHEDULE RELIEF

Schedule relief operates in a similar way to forecast consumption and is also controlled by the Planning Manager process. You control whether schedules should be relieved by setting the Relief flag when you define the schedule name.

An MDS is relieved when sales order shipments occur. This prevents doubling-up of demand when sales orders are included in the MDS and it is used in a subsequent planning process. Every time a sales order shipment occurs, the planning manager relieves (reduces) the relevant MDS entry and flags it as having been relieved.

An MPS is relieved when a discrete job, inter-organization shipment, purchase order, or purchase requisition is created. In the same way, this process prevents the MPS from overstating supply.

It is possible to stop the relief process by using the profile options MRP:Consume MDS and MRP:Consume MPS. By setting these profiles to No, you can temporarily prevent schedule relief from happening.

The MRP:MPS Relief Direction also affects the way in which MPS relief happens. The default on installation is Backward, then Forward. This means that the planning manager searches backward from the discrete job or purchase order date for the earliest quantity to relieve and then moves forward. You can change this profile to Forward Only, preventing earlier MPS entries from being relieved.

Tip

If you change this profile option, you need to stop the planning manager and restart it for the new profile setting to take effect.

Reducing MPS

One additional tool to help maintain the MPS where purchase orders or work orders are not used is the Reduce MPS item attribute, which assists with keeping the MPS quantities current. Do not check this attribute if you create purchase orders or work orders—these will also relieve the MPS.

This attribute value is set in Oracle Inventory with the following values:

- **None**—The MPS is not reduced.
- **Past Due**—This reduces the MPS quantity to zero when the entry becomes past due.
- **Planning Time Fence**—This reduces the MPS quantity to zero if an entry violates the planning time fence set for the item.
- **Demand Time Fence**—This reduces the MPS quantity to zero if an entry violates the demand time fence set for the item.

Generating an MPS Plan

You can use an MDS or MPS as the source for an MPS planning run. The planning process uses the requirements in the source MPS/MDS to calculate the required supply. The output is an MPS plan with order and reschedule recommendations.

Tip

The Planning Manager must be running to get a truly consistent picture of demand. The load Master Schedule process does not include demand automatically. The running of the Planning Manager picks up all of the demand.

The process and options for generating an MPS plan are similar to those used for an MRP plan and are covered in the next section.

Material Requirements Planning

The MRP planning process calculates net material requirements from gross requirements. The gross requirements can be obtained from an MPS or an MDS. As mentioned earlier in this chapter, you might not require an MPS as part of your planning process if demand is stable and you do not need to manually control a production schedule. In this case, you can use an MDS as the source of requirements for the MRP planning process.

Deriving the time-phased net requirements in the MRP planning process involves considering on-hand quantities and scheduled receipts on a just-in-time basis. The planning process also considers Master Scheduling/MRP item attributes and the BOM structure. The output from the planning process is an MRP plan containing planned orders, repetitive schedule suggestions, reschedule/cancellation recommendations for existing orders, and rate change suggestions for existing schedules.

Note

The Master Scheduling/MRP planning process assumes infinite capacity is available to meet the requirements of the material plan. You can use Capacity Requirements Planning (CRP) to determine the existing capacity available to support the material plan. CRP is discussed later in this chapter.

GENERATING AN MRP

Use the Launch MRP or Launch MPS window to start the planning process. By default, the current date is displayed as the Anchor Date for repetitive item planning. You can select an earlier date to be used as the start of the repetitive planning periods. You can also choose a date for the plan horizon. By default, this date is derived using the number of months specified in the MRP:Cutoff Date Offset Months profile option. You can change this if you want.

You can set options that affect how the MRP planning (and MPS planning) process operates:

- **Overwrite**—You can choose All to generate a completely new plan. In this case, all firm planned orders and MPS entries are overwritten. If you choose None, firm planned orders are not overwritten. The third option is Outside Planning Time Fence, which overwrites firm planned orders outside the time fence for an item in an MRP plan. For an MPS plan, this option overwrites all MPS entries outside the planning time fence. Time fences are discussed in the next section.
- **Append Planned Orders**—This option has a significant effect on how much control is passed to the planning process to make recommendations. It works together with the Overwrite option. When you plan an MPS and choose not to overwrite entries, selecting Append Planned Orders does not generate reschedule recommendations or planned orders before the last date in the source schedule. You should only use this combination if you intend to manually manage the master schedule. In the case of MRP, this combination creates new planned orders but takes into account any firm planned orders that exist.

  If you choose the overwrite option to be All and select Append Planned Orders for an MPS or MRP plan, everything in the previous plan is deleted and replaced with new recommendations.

  Using the overwrite option Outside Planning Time Fence and selecting append planned orders means that the new plan only deletes planned entries beyond the planning time fence and replaces these with new recommendations.

  If you select None as the overwrite option and do not select append planned orders, the planning process does not generate new orders. With this combination, you decide how to best manage the MRP or MPS.

- **Demand Time Fence Control**—Select this option if you need to consider the demand time fence for items when generating the plan.
- **Net WIP**—Using this option enables you to consider discrete jobs or schedules in the planning process.
- **Net Reservations**—Selecting this option enables you to consider the planning process inventory that has been reserved for orders.
- **Snapshot Lock Tables**—See the section "Defining Planning Parameters." You can override the default here.
- **Planning Time Fence Control**—If you choose this option, the planning process uses the planning time fences specified for items to control new order suggestions and reschedule recommendations.
- **Net Purchases**—Use this option to tell the planning process to consider existing purchase orders and requisitions when generating the plan.
- **Plan Safety Stock**—If you have set safety stock levels for your items and the stock will be MRP planned, you can choose this option to plan safety stock in the planning process. Item safety stock is controlled using the Safety Stock Method item attribute. It is either MRP planned as a percentage of gross requirements or is manually specified through Oracle Inventory (non-MRP planned).

Tip

If there is no demand, MRP will not calculate any safety stock with the attribute set to MRP Planned. If you want to have safety stock on-hand even in periods of no demand, consider using non-MRP planned safety stock and enter the required quantities in the Inventory Safety Stock form.

- **Plan Capacity**—You can choose this option to generate a capacity plan. If you need to generate an RCCP capacity plan, you can also specify the bill of resources to be used and a simulation set (if you have created one). See the section "Using Oracle Capacity" later in this chapter.
- **Pegging**—If you need to use the graphical pegging features, select this option. The planning process generates the information required to peg supply back to the top-level demand.
- **Material Scheduling Method**—See the section "Defining Planning Parameters." You can override the default here.
- **Planned Items**—See the section "Defining Planning Parameters." You can override the default here.

Order modifiers also affect how the planning process generates planned orders. By default, the planning process uses lot for lot sizing. This means that you get a single planned order to satisfy the net requirements for each day. Your business might already have planning policies established that dictate how orders should be created. Oracle Master Scheduling/MRP provides the following order modifiers to use in the planning process (which are set as item attributes; see Chapter 17:

- **Fixed Order Quantity**—You can manually assign an order quantity that will always be used for an item. If requirements on a single day fall short of this quantity, an order for the fixed quantity will be planned. If requirements on a single day are greater that the fixed quantity, two or more orders will be planned. You can use this attribute to set a fixed production rate for repetitive planned items.
- **Fixed Lot Multiplier**—You can assign a multiplier that will be used to create a single planned order. Requirements greater than or less than the multiplier will be rounded up to the next nearest multiple. This is useful when Purchasing buys in cases, but the items are stocked in eaches.
- **Minimum and Maximum Order Quantity**—You can use these attributes separately or together. With a minimum specified, when requirements are less than the minimum, a planned order is created for the minimum quantity. When requirements are greater than the maximum quantity on a single day, two or more orders are created with each order not exceeding the maximum quantity. For repetitive planned items, these attributes affect the daily rate.
- **Fixed Days Supply**—When a number of days is specified for this attribute, the planning process aggregates requirements for this number of days into a single planned order.
- **Round Order Quantities**—If you have fractional usage quantities for items, it is likely that the planning process will create planned orders with fractional quantities. By setting this attribute to Yes, the planning process will suggest a planned order quantity with next largest whole number.

CONTROLLING THE PLAN

To assist with managing the planning process and reducing the amount of maintenance that is required, the Oracle Master Scheduling/MRP Applications include some control options:

- **Acceptable Early Days**—This control is set as an item attribute. You can specify a number of days that an order can be delivered before it is required. The planning process checks the value of this attribute and does not generate a reschedule-out recommendation if the early delivery date meets the value set in this attribute. Using this attribute, you can decide whether it is better to hold some extra inventory rather than continually review and implement reschedule recommendations.
- **Time Fences**—Time fences enable you to protect portions of your plans based on policies you define. You specify time fences using item attributes. The time fence item attributes describe the limit of the time fence as being the plan date plus one of the following: cumulative manufacturing lead time, cumulative total lead time, total lead time, or a user defined number of days (see the section "Defining Planning Exception Sets" for a description of what these lead times mean). If you specify User Defined for

a time fence, you must also specify the number of days using the time fence days attributes. There are three types of time fences available:

- **Demand Time Fence**—When you generate a plan and enable demand time fence control, the planning process only considers actual demand with the time fence. Forecast that falls within the time fence is ignored.
- **Planning Time Fence**—When planning time fence control is enabled, the planning process does not plan orders or make reschedule-in recommendations inside the planning time fence. You still receive reschedule-out recommendations.
- **Release Time Fence**—You can choose to have the planning process automatically release planned orders based on a release time fence. Within the time fence, purchase requirements are released as purchase requisitions and make requirements are released as discrete jobs. This process does not automatically release repetitive schedules.

■ **Firm Order Planning**—To further protect planned orders and actual orders, you can *firm* them. Firming an order fixes the quantity and date and, in most cases, prevents reschedule recommendations. Oracle Master Scheduling/MRP supports three types of firm order:

- **Firm Planned Order**—This is a planned order where the Firm flag set has been set using the planner workbench (see the section "Using the Planner Workbench"). When using firm planned orders, you can use the overwrite options during plan generation to prevent them from being overwritten. You do not receive reschedule recommendations for these orders if you rerun the planning process. By default, there is no time fence associated with firm planned orders. If you want to create a time fence for these types of orders, you should set the MRP:Firm Planned Order profile option to Yes.
- **Firm MRP Implemented Order**—When you use the planner workbench to implement planned orders as discrete jobs or purchase requisitions, you can choose to firm them without releasing them. If you rerun the planning process, you get reschedule recommendations for these orders until you release them.
- **Firm Scheduled Receipt**—When you release a firm implemented order, it becomes a firm scheduled receipt. Firm scheduled receipts cannot be affected by the overwrite options chosen when running the planning process. You do not receive reschedule recommendations for these orders if you rerun the planning process.

  Although you can firm purchase requisitions and discrete jobs through the planner workbench, you can also do this using the Oracle Purchasing and Oracle Work In Process applications.

Caution

The setting of the profile option MRP:Firm Planned Order Time Fence affects the behavior of the planning process within the planning time fence. If the profile option is set to "yes" (the default value), then all planned orders for items with existing firmed purchase orders or work orders will be scheduled for after the date of the firmed purchase order or work order, even if actually required earlier.

If you are using Oracle Engineering, Engineering Change Orders (ECOs) can also affect the planning process. See Chapter 19 for an explanation of effective dates and use-up dates.

COPYING MPS AND MRP PLANS

You can copy MPS and MRP plans using the Copy Plan window. This provides you the flexibility to take a copy of a plan, modify it, and replan it while still maintaining the original. Using this approach, you can see the impact of changes to your plan and continue to modify it until you are satisfied with the results without changing the original.

Before copying a plan, be sure the following are done:

- Define an MPS or MRP name and run the plan that will be the source plan.
- Define an MPS or MRP name the same type as the source plan that will be the destination plan.
- The same organization must own both plans: source and destination.
- Log in to the same organization that owns the plans.
- The responsibility of the user has to be the same for both plans.
- All plan options and flags are copied from the source plan to the destination. Do not define options for the destination plan. The copy plan process works only for plans with no defined options.

USING THE PLANNER WORKBENCH

The planner workbench, as shown in Figure 21.7, is provided with the Oracle Master Scheduling/MRP Applications to assist in the review of plan information and the implementation of plan recommendations.

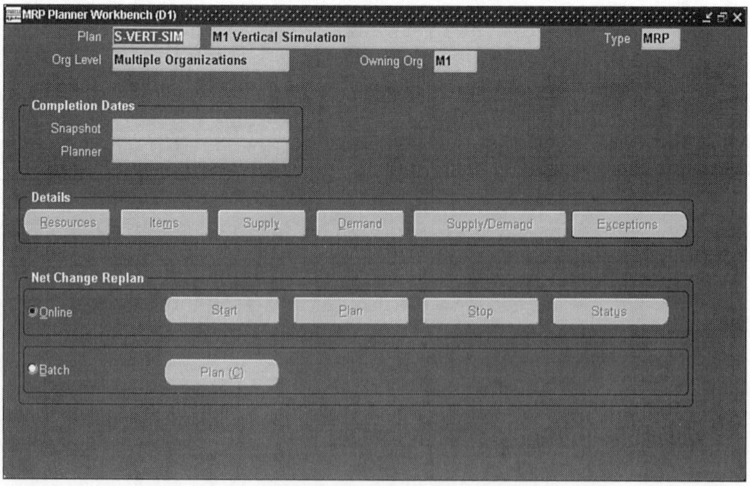

Figure 21.7
MRP Planner Workbench screen.

REVIEWING PLAN INFORMATION

You can review the following plan information using the planner workbench:

- **Resources**—You can review a plan's resources information by department or line.
- **Item On-Hand Quantities**—You can verify the quantities on-hand for an item including nettable/non-nettable quantities and subinventory detail.
- **Item Supply/Demand**—With this view, you can see detailed supply and demand information generated for your plan.
- **Horizontal Plan View**—You can use this view to review your planning information in a horizontal format.
- **Enterprise Plan View**—The enterprise plan view provides an overview of all supply and demand for your items.
- **Graphical View**—You can graphically review supply and demand for items. You have the option to review supply and demand together or separately.
- **Snapshot Versus Current**—When using the horizontal plan view, enterprise plan view, or graphical view, you can choose to use snapshot or current data. Snapshot data was valid at the time when the plan was generated. You can choose the current view option to see the effect of changes you have made since the plan was generated.

Note

You must check the Feedback option in the MPS Names or MRP Names form to have this functionality.

- **Planning Exceptions**—You can review a summary of exceptions created during the plan generation. Optionally, you can review detailed exceptions for items, orders, and resources. Some exceptions are only generated if an item has an exception set assigned. See the section "Defining Planning Exception Sets" for an explanation.
- **Graphical Pegging**—If you selected the pegging option when generating the plan, you trace the relationship between supply and demand, and vice versa.
- **Available-To-Promise (ATP)**—When you use the horizontal plan view, you can review ATP information for items, as shown in Figure 21.8. ATP is calculated for each item as: on-hand inventory + supply – committed demand.

Note

This information is only calculated if the Calculate ATP item attribute is set to Yes for an item. The ATP information provided through Oracle Master Scheduling/MRP should be used for guidance only. It does not take account of any ATP rules that have been defined in Oracle Inventory and applied to an item (see Chapter 17). This ATP information is also available on the Planning Detail Report.

Figure 21.8
Items screen.

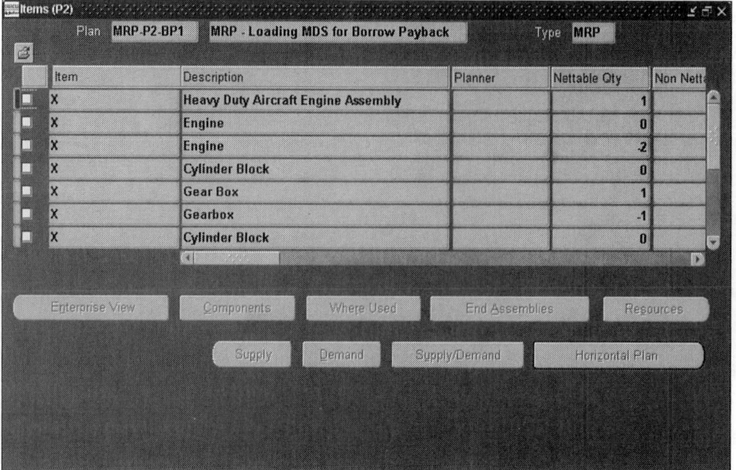

- **Capable To Promise (CTP)**—CTP extends ATP by adding the availability of capacity to its calculation. You can review CTP information in your plan if you set the INV: Capable To Promise profile option in Oracle Inventory. You must also specify at the item level whether to check material and resource availability using the Check ATP item attribute. The item must also have a routing that specifies CTP.

NET CHANGE REPLAN

With the planner workbench, you also have the facility to replan changes to orders without generating a completely new MRP or MPS. This is called Net Change Replan. Oracle Master Scheduling/MRP offers two methods of doing this:

- **Batch Mode Planner**—This enables you to make all your changes and submit them for replanning as a batch. The advantage with this method is that while you are carrying out replanning, other users still have access to the plan information.
- **Online Planner**—The online planner enables you to replan changes by loading all plan data into memory while the session is active. Although this reduces the number of reads from the database tables during the session, it also prevents other users from accessing the plan data until you are finished.

Tip

The Net Change Replan process makes changes only to released orders; therefore, until you release the order or schedule, the Net Change Replan changes the item status back to the status in effect as of the last planning run.

Implementing Recommendations

This section on the planner workbench has mostly concentrated on reviewing plan information. Most users spend the majority of their time doing this. When you are happy with the information in the plan, you can start to release orders, schedules, and implement reschedule recommendations:

- **Firming Planned Orders**—You can use the workbench to firm planned orders. Order firming is discussed in the section "Generating an MRP." MPS Planned items are also visible in the MRP Planner Workbench and are always firmed. This is because dates and quantities for MPS planned items can be changed only in the MPS Planner Workbench, and not in the MRP Planner Workbench.
- **Implementing a Planned Order**—Depending on how the Make or Buy item attribute is set, you can implement the order as a purchase requisition or discrete job. Planned orders for make items that are also purchasable can be implemented as discrete jobs or purchase requisitions, and vice versa. You select planned orders using the Supply/Demand window. For orders that are being implemented as discrete jobs, you can also modify the build sequence, schedule group, alternative BOM/routing, and demand class. The implemented orders can then be released using the Release Window.
- **Implementing Repetitive Schedules**—You can use the planner workbench to review suggested repetitive schedules and implement and release them. When selecting schedules to implement, you can modify the first and last unit completions dates, total schedule quantity, daily rate, and processing days. As you modify any of these values, the other values are automatically recalculated.
- **Releasing a Job or Schedule as Firm**—When releasing jobs or schedules, you can choose the firm option.
- **Rescheduling Scheduled Receipts**—During a planning run, there might be recommendations to reschedule existing purchase requisitions or discrete jobs. The reschedule recommendations are reschedule in, reschedule out, and cancel. Use the supply/demand window to select rescheduled jobs and requisitions for release. You cannot reschedule purchase order receipts from the planner workbench. This must be done in the Oracle Purchasing application (see Chapter 16). You can use the Order Reschedule Report to review purchase order reschedule recommendations.

Using Supply Chain Planning

For organizations that consist of multiple manufacturing and distribution locations, Supply Chain Planning provides the capability to integrate planning across the entire enterprise.

With Supply Chain Planning, you can choose to generate plans for all organizations in the enterprise through one single planning run. You can optionally choose to have parts of the enterprise remain autonomous in the planning process.

Demand schedules for a supply chain plan can include the Master Demand Schedules from all organizations. This incorporates all types of supply that are valid for an MDS (sales orders, forecasts, and so on). Supply schedules in a supply chain plan include Master Productions Schedules, Material Requirement Plans, and Distribution Requirement Plans from any or all organizations.

As mentioned earlier in the setup section, you can create organizations to represent your customers and suppliers. In this way, supplier and customer organizations can be modeled and integrated in your supply chain. In the setup, you will also have considered the interorganization shipping network and the shipping methods. These affect how material moves between organizations within the supply chain. Supply-chain planning also provides sourcing rules and bills of distribution to define how replenishment takes place within the supply chain.

SOURCING RULES AND BILLS OF DISTRIBUTION

This section explains the use of sourcing rules and bills of distribution. These are used to describe the operation of your supply chain.

ENHANCED SOURCING IN R11*i*

New sourcing logic in R11*i* has been enhanced in several ways:

- Supplier constraints at the supplier site (such as capacity, processing, lead time, and delivery pattern) are now factored into the planning process to provide more accurate sourcing of demand to suppliers.
- You can now allocate planned orders to sources taking historical allocations into account. Planning uses purchasing history to determine the current allocations necessary to achieve your targeted allocations.
- In previous versions of Oracle MRP sourcing logic (R10.7 and R11), the time period that is considered by planning was the plan horizon, and only planned orders were considered in the allocation process. In the enhanced sourcing logic available in R11*i*, the effective period of the sourcing rule is the time period Planning considers for the calculation of the split (unless the end date is beyond the plan horizon, in which case the end date of the plan horizon is used). Both planned orders and historical purchases are considered in the allocation process.
- In addition, the interaction of planned orders and sourcing rules has changed in the planning process itself. Previously, planned orders were generated using the item level order modifiers as part of the supply creation process. Sourcing was then performed on these newly created planned orders. The R11*i* enhanced sourcing requires planned order sourcing to be done inline with the planned order creation process since vendor capacity, order modifiers, historical information, and lead times are now taken into account.

Sourcing Rules

Sourcing rules, as shown in Figure 21.9, define how replenishment takes place in one organization or in all organizations. They can be used in standard MRP planning for a single organization as well as for supply-chain planning. The replenishment source takes the form of one of the following:

- **Transfer From**—The item is sourced through an inter-organization transfer from a specified organization.
- **Make At**—The item is manufactured at the organization.
- **Buy From**—The item is purchased from a supplier.

You can apply effective dates to the rule, but in the case of sourcing rules, this can only apply to the shipping organizations. Ranking can be used with sourcing rules to determine priorities. You can also assign an allocation percentage to be used when items are sourced from multiple organizations or suppliers. Time phasing can also be used to switch an item from make to buy within a sourcing rule. This is useful if you need to buy in or transfer an item from another organization while manufacturing is being started in the receiving organization.

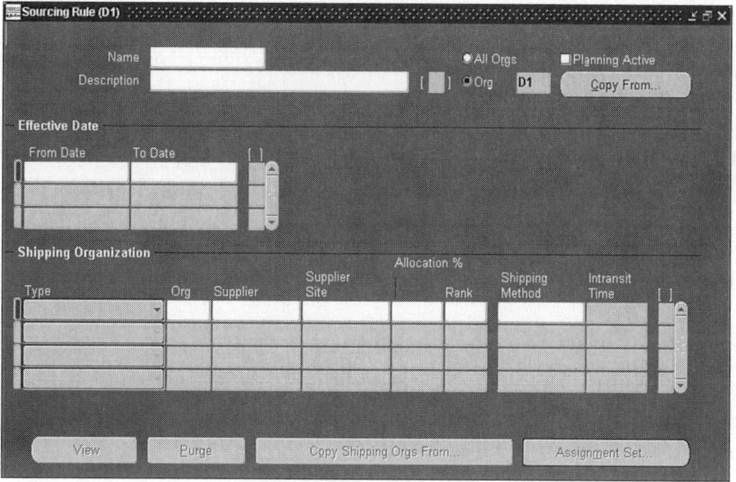

Figure 21.9
Sourcing Rule screen.

Bills of Distribution

Bills of distribution, as shown in Figure 21.10, are used in supply-chain planning and represent a combination of individual sourcing strategies that can be used across all organizations in the supply chain. Unlike sourcing rules, the sourcing strategies defined in bills of distribution can apply to different organizations at different times. As with sourcing rules, you can assign allocation percentages and rankings within a bill of distribution.

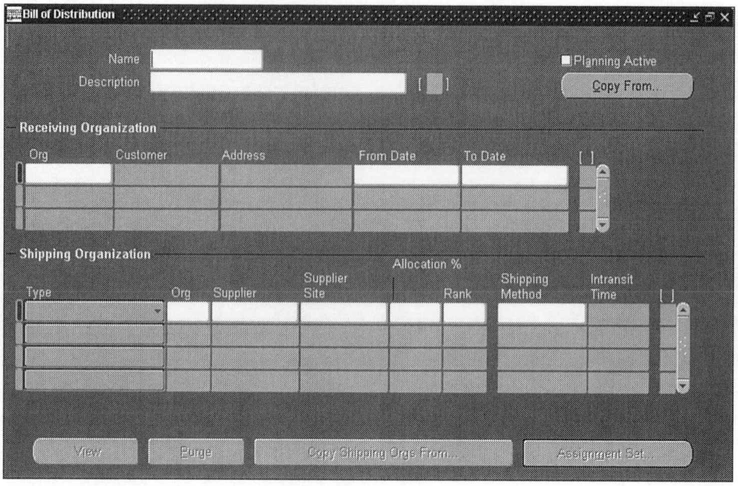

Figure 21.10
Bill of Distribution screen.

ASSIGNING SOURCING RULES AND BILLS OF DISTRIBUTION

To use sourcing rules and bills of distribution, you must create assignment sets to assign the rules to organizations and/or items in the organizations. Creating assignment sets is discussed in the section "Understanding Each Setup Task" at the start of this chapter. You also must select one assignment set and enter its name in the profile option MRP:Default Sourcing Assignment Set.

Note

The sum of the sourcing rules and bills of distribution must equal 100% before they can be applied. Also, the rules and bills will not take effect until assigned to an item or a range of items.

GRAPHICAL VIEW

You can review assignment sets using an inquiry window. You can also view the indented where-used information and indented supply-chain bills for an item. This provides a graphical representation of the supply chain for an item.

MASTER SCHEDULING

Supply chain master scheduling works in a similar way to the master scheduling process described earlier in this chapter. You can load a supply chain MDS with multiple sources of demand from across the supply chain. You can use source lists (described in the setup section) to specify the sources of data to be loaded into the supply chain MDS.

A supply chain MPS represents the supply required to meet the demand in a supply chain MDS or another MPS. When you define a supply chain MPS, you can specify whether it will be used to plan all organizations or specific organizations.

Supply chain MPS plan generation works in a similar way to MRP/MPS plan generation. For the supply chain MPS, you can specify organization-specific plan options if the plan covers multiple organizations.

MATERIAL REQUIREMENTS PLANNING AND DISTRIBUTION REQUIREMENTS PLANNING

The planning method for items is specified using the Planning Method item attribute (see Chapter 17). For any item, this enables you to specify whether it is any of the following:

- MRP Planned
- MPS Planned
- MRP/DRP Planned
- MPS/DRP Planned
- DRP Planned

When you define a supply chain MRP or a DRP (see the setup section), you can specify whether these plans apply to all organizations or specific organizations. As with supply chain MPS generation, you can specify plan options that are specific to certain organizations. See the section "Material Requirements Planning" for a description of plan options.

SUPPLY CHAIN PLANNER WORKBENCH

When using supply chain planning, the planner workbench provides you with additional options. Most of the information described in the section "Using the Planner Workbench" can be reviewed across all organizations, including the following:

- Horizontal Plan View
- Enterprise View
- Graphical Pegging

When implementing planned orders, suggested schedules, or reschedule recommendations, you can choose to do this across multiple organizations.

USING ORACLE ALERTS WITH THIS APPLICATION

Oracle Master Scheduling/MRP comes with two associated Oracle alerts. These alerts check forecast overconsumption based on a predetermined schedule. The alerts send an e-mail message to a specified recipient or list of recipients when an overconsumption exception occurs.

You can use the Forecast Overconsumption—Summary alert to send a summary message or the Forecast Overconsumption—Detail alert to send detail information on the sales orders that caused the overconsumption.

To use either alert, it must be enabled and the alert scheduler must be running. Your System Administrator can assist with the alert setup.

Tip

You should consider creating an additional alert to monitor the Planning Manager concurrent process. If this process fails, forecast consumption and schedule reliefs will not function. Although this was mentioned in the setup section, it is important to repeat it here.

USING OPEN INTERFACES IN THIS APPLICATION

There are five open interfaces provided to work with the Oracle Master Scheduling/MRP Applications:

- **Open Forecast Interface**—You can import forecast entries from an external system into Oracle Master Scheduling/MRP using this interface. The entries are validated using your current setup.
- **Open Master Schedule Interface**—Master Schedule data can be imported into Oracle Master Scheduling/MRP using this interface. Again, the entries are validated using your current setup.
- **Open Forecast Entries Applications Program Interface**—This differs from the Open Forecast Interface in that it allows an external system to insert, update, or delete entries in an existing forecast.
- **Open Supply/Demand Applications Program Interface**—This interface permits supply and demand information from external systems to be imported into Oracle. This is a new API in Release 11.5.
- **Sourcing Rules Application Program Interface**—This interface permits sourcing rules to be imported from an external source into Oracle.

As with all other open interfaces provided with the Oracle applications, you might need to write programs to do the following:

- Extract data from the external system
- Format it as required for use in the open interface tables
- Insert the data in the interface tables

Full details of the operation of the interfaces can be found in the Oracle reference *Oracle Manufacturing, Distribution, Sales and Service Open Interfaces Manual.*

TAKING ADVANTAGE OF BEST PRACTICES

In many organizations, master scheduling and material requirement planning generates a lot of information. Sometimes, this can become too much for a Planner to review and analyze. There is always the risk that an important piece of information will be overlooked.

To minimize the effect of information overload, you should leverage some of the tools provided in the Oracle Master Scheduling/MRP application:

- **Planner Workbench**—Apart from the productivity benefit of being able to review and implement recommendations through a single common interface, the workbench also provides the capability to filter information using "finds." You should also consider placing items with common planning requirements under unique planner codes. The planner code does not have to be a person; it can be used to represent any particular grouping that you might need. You should also consider the planning horizon being used in plan generation. If it extends too far, there is a risk that too much data will be generated, and the information might also be unreliable.
- **Folders**—Folder queries can be constructed and saved to make querying data in the Planner Workbench much more efficient. Some examples are querying by make or buy code, by planner, by order type, or by suggested order start date. Folders can be used to reorganize the display of columns in the Planner by hiding or showing columns and changing their sequences and widths.
- **Exception Sets**—You can minimize the volume of data to be reviewed in the planner workbench by creating and assigning exception sets. You can use the exception messages to search through the plan data to find exceptions that need to be dealt with as a priority.
- **Planning Reports**—Many of the planning reports provided with the application are most useful if you need to see detail for a particular forecast, schedule, plan, or item. The Planned Order report and Order Reschedule Report provide similar information to that presented on the planner workbench. You can use the report parameters to limit the volume of data to be reviewed. For example, use the Out Days and In Days filters to limit orders being displayed on the Order Reschedule Report. Do you really need to see all orders that are being rescheduled out by one day?

Note

Only one plan should be active at one time; otherwise, you could be using plans that contradict one another and thereby be relying on bad planning information.

MRP: UNDERSTANDING KEY REPORTS

Table 21.3 lists the reports provided with the Oracle Master Scheduling/MRP Applications.

TABLE 21.3 ORACLE MASTER SCHEDULING/MRP REPORTS

Report Name	Description
Audit Information Report	Shows exceptions generated when predefined audit criteria are applied to your data. See the setup section.
Current Projected On-Hand vs. Projected Available Graphical Report Report*	Use this report to produce a graphical display of the current projected on hand vs. projected available inventory. You can use this report for MPS, MRP, and DRP plans.
Demand vs. Replenishment Graphical Report*	Shows a graphical summary of material availability for MPS, MRP, or DRP plans.

PART III CH 21

Table 21.3 Continued

Report Name	Description
Financial Analysis Report*	Provides a costed summary of a DRP or MRP plan. Plans the monetary resources required to fulfill the DRP or MRP plan.
Forecast Comparison Report	Use this report to compare forecasts based on quantities or quantities and costs.
Forecast Detail Report	Shows the forecast detail for an individual forecast or a forecast set. You can display this report in a horizontal or vertical format.
Late Order Report*	This report shows planned or actual orders, including in-transit shipments, that are past due in a specified plan.
Master Schedule Comparison Report	Use this report to compare master schedules based on quantities or quantities and costs.
Master Schedule Detail Report	Provides a horizontal or vertical view of the detail within a master schedule.
Master Schedule Status Report*	Shows shipping activity for an MDS or production activity for an MPS.
Order Reschedule Report*	Use this report to view reschedule recommendations generated by an MPS, MRP, or DRP plan for discrete jobs, purchase orders, and purchase requisitions.
Planned Order Report*	This report shows new planned orders recommended during plan generation.
Planning Detail Report*	Shows the detailed information related to an MPS, MRP, or DRP plan. You can choose to view this information in a horizontal or vertical format.
Planning Exception Sets Report	Lists the planning exception sets that you have defined.
Planning Manager Worker (once-a-day tasks)	Manually submits the planning manager worker. The planning manager also automatically submits this process.
Planning Parameters Report	Prints your planning parameters.
Roll Flow Schedule	Adds undercompletions quantities to the schedule and subtracts overcompletions quantities from the schedule for simulation purposes only.
CRP Reports	You can submit the following capacity reports from Oracle Master Scheduling/MRP: • CRP Rate Based Report • CRP Routing Based Report • RCCP Rate Based Report • RCCP Routing Based Report

** These reports are also available as supply chain versions.*

MRP: FROM HERE

When implementing the Oracle Master Scheduling/MRP Applications, you should also review the material in the following sections or chapters:

- "Using Oracle Capacity" (the next section of this chapter)
- Chapter 17
- Chapter 16
- Chapter 19
- Chapter 22

USING ORACLE CAPACITY

Oracle Capacity provides the functionality to ensure you have sufficient resources (labor and machines) to satisfy your production requirements. Oracle Capacity calculates your load capacity by resource or by production line. Two methods of performing capacity calculations (RCCP and CRP) are discussed in the following section.

DISCOVERING NEW FEATURES IN RELEASE 11*i*

Release 11*i* introduces several new features that enhance the functionality of the Oracle Capacity module:

- **Date Effective Routings**—You can now plan changes in the manufacturing process by effective dates and disable dates on routings. Planning uses these dates when calculating the resources requirements.
- **Efficiency and Utilization**—You can specify efficiency and utilization rates in calculating capacity to plan based on rates or calculated capacity available.
- **Phantom Routing**—Phantom assemblies are now included in generating the resources requirements for planned orders.
- **Term Changes**—The following term changes are new:
    - Low Utilization Percent changed to Resource Underloaded
    - High Utilization Percent changed to Resource Overloaded
    - Utilization changed to Load Ratio
    - Line Speed changed to Production Rate

The Oracle Capacity application provides methods to enable you to monitor the utilization of available capacity. You can do this using the following:

- **Rough Cut Capacity Planning (RCCP)**—This is used in conjunction with your master schedules. RCCP is typically used to check the utilization of critical resources over a long period.

- **Capacity Requirements Planning (CRP)**—This is used with material requirements plans to check the utilization of resources. CRP considers scheduled receipts and on-hand inventory when calculating capacity requirements. It is typically used for reviewing capacity utilization in the near term.

For both RCCP and CRP, you can choose to plan capacity based on scheduled resources that have been assigned to operations on routings (routing-based) or by production lines (rate-based). Capacity for routing-based plans is in hours per resource per week. Capacity for rate-based plans is stated as production rate per week per production line.

Figure 21.11 shows the major relationships between Oracle Capacity and the other Oracle applications. The relationships affect the setup and operation of the Oracle Capacity application.

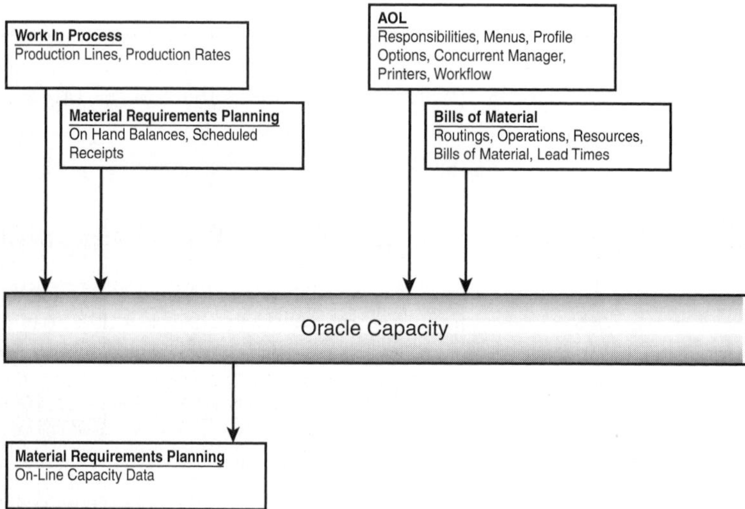

Figure 21.11
Capacity relationship to other applications.

Configuring the Application

The following section describes the setup tasks required to configure the Oracle Capacity application. If you are implementing Release 11*i* of the applications, you can use the Oracle Applications Implementation Wizard to manage the setup tasks.

This section provides detail on each of the setup tasks and the order in which they should be performed.

To use Oracle Capacity, you must first complete the setup for the following:

- **Oracle Inventory**—All required setups must be completed.
- **Oracle Bills of Material**—You should complete all the required setup steps. Define your Bills of Material and routings. You should also calculate the routing lead times.

- **Oracle Master Scheduling**—You should complete all the required setup steps to enable you to launch MPS or MRP planning. Capacity planning is performed only in conjunction with MPS or MRP planning.

Tip

Completing the setup of these applications enables you to run some of the Oracle Capacity reports and use some of the online inquiries. To use all the available analysis tools, you should continue to complete the setup steps that follow.

UNDERSTANDING EACH SETUP TASK

The following sections describe each setup task in detail.

DEFINING RESOURCES GROUPS (OPTIONAL)

You can create resources groups, as shown in Figure 21.12, and assign resources to these groups in Oracle Bills of Material (see Chapter 19). Because resources groups can be used when loading a bill of resources to subsequently create an RCCP, you should group resources based on the way you intend to generate or use your capacity plans.

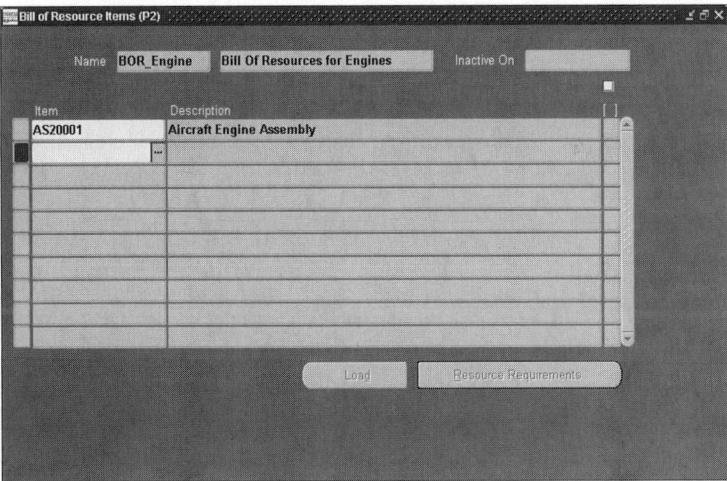

Figure 21.12
Resources screen.

DEFINING SIMULATION SETS (OPTIONAL)

Simulation sets enable you to model the effect of resource changes on your plans by grouping the changes. When you have defined a set, you use it when assigning resources for a department in Oracle Bills of Material. You have the option to define capacity changes at this time. These can be the following:

- Add or delete a day
- Add or delete capacity for a shift

Capacity modifications are always changes to existing capacity. While making these changes, you can select a simulation set to associate with the capacity change. This simulation set can then be used when reviewing RCCP and CRP plans. You can also specify the simulation set when generating an MRP or MPS plan if you choose the Plan Capacity option. Simulations should be used for short-term capacity changes only. If the change will be permanent, you should modify department, resources, and shift information accordingly in Oracle Bills of Material.

You can use the capacity modifications associated with the Simulation Set in the Work In Process module by checking the Use in Scheduling box.

Note

Rate-based items can't be included in simulation sets; this is for discrete manufactured items only.

DEFINING AND LOADING BILLS OF RESOURCES (OPTIONAL)

A bill of resources is a consolidation of all resources necessary to build an item. This is used for RCCP capacity planning. The resources requirements can be for discrete production (department/resources combinations) or for repetitive planning (production lines).

DEFINING MULTIDEPARTMENT RESOURCES (OPTIONAL)

When setting up resources in Oracle Bills of Material, you can assign a resource across multiple departments. When you generate an RCCP or CRP, you can choose to aggregate the resource usage across all departments using the resource. See Chapter 19 for information on defining resources.

HORIZONTAL PLAN DISPLAY OPTIONS

Options are available to control the way in which the horizontal plan display works for both CRP and RCCP. You can define the options using the Preferences window under View RCCP or View CRP.

SETTING PROFILE OPTIONS

The following profile options can be set for Oracle Capacity:

- **CRP:Default Bill of Resources Set Name**—This profile can be set at the site, applications, responsibility, or user level. You can enter a bill of resources set name that will default for the users any time they use a bill of resources window. This is an optional profile for which there is no default value.
- **CRP:Spread Discrete Requirements**—You can select to have the discrete job load placed on the first day of an operation or spread over the total length of the operation. This profile is set at the site level. The default value for this profile option is No upon system installation. Your System Administrator typically maintains profile option settings.

PROCESSING TRANSACTIONS

The following section covers the main transactions involved in using Oracle Capacity.

ROUGH CUT CAPACITY PLANNING

As explained earlier, the intention of Rough Cut Capacity Planning (RCCP) is to provide an overall picture of capacity utilization for critical resources. Unlike CRP, it does not include scheduled receipts and on-hand quantities when calculating capacity.

CREATING BILLS OF RESOURCES (OPTIONAL)

To gather resources requirements for RCCP, you must create a bill of resources. The bill of resources shows all resources required to manufacture a particular item. Bills of resources apply to both rate-based and routing-based capacity planning. You can choose to load the bill of resources automatically or add the items manually. The automatic process explodes through the BOM structure for an item and gathers all resources requirements. When using the load process, only current resources are considered.

The load process can be initiated for a single item or a range of items. If you have defined product families in Oracle Bills of Material, you can use these to load a bill of resources. The resources requirements for each of the family members is rolled up in the bill. You can then review capacity for the product family and the product family members.

You can use resources groups to limit the resources loaded into the bill to those that belong to a particular group.

ROUTING-BASED RCCP

Routing-based RCCP capacity utilization is calculated as follows:

Capacity utilization = Required Hours/Available Hours

The bill of resources information and the details for the master schedule entry are used to establish the required hours. Available hours are calculated using the resources information defined in Oracle Bills of Material (capacity units, availability, efficiency, and utilization) as follows:

Available hours = capacity units * shift hours per day * workdays per week * efficiency * utilization

For 24-hour resources, the formula is:

Available hours = capacity units * 24 hours per day * workdays per week * efficiency * utilization

The efficiency and utilization factors are the new factors in R11*i*.

RATE-BASED RCCP

Rate-based RCCP capacity utilization is calculated as follows:

Capacity Utilization = Required Rate/Available Rate

Bill of resources information and the repetitive schedule allocation process are used to allocate the master schedule rate to production lines to arrive at a required rate. The available rate is calculated using the production line information set up in Oracle Work In Process (maximum hourly rate and line availability).

VIEWING RCCP

You can view RCCP capacity requirements for a selected master schedule. You can also use the simulation sets described earlier to see the effect of capacity changes for the schedule. If you choose the routing-based view, you can enter a resource and view its capacity utilization for the selected master schedule, as shown later in Figure 21.13. Choosing the rate-based view enables you to specify a production line and view its capacity utilization for the selected master schedule. You can also view this information graphically by exporting the data to Excel.

USING RCCP DATA

When you review the data for rate-based or routing-based RCCP, you can determine situations where resources or production lines are underloaded or overloaded. You can use this information to balance capacity by modifying the usage of resources, adding additional resources, adding shifts, adding production lines, increasing production line rates, and so on.

CAPACITY REQUIREMENTS PLANNING

Capacity Requirements Planning (CRP) analyzes capacity utilization for short-term requirements, taking into account scheduled receipts and on-hand inventory balances.

ROUTING-BASED CRP

Routing-based CRP utilization is calculated as follows:

> Capacity Utilization = Required Hours/Available Hours

The required hours are calculated using dates and quantities generated by the planning process for planned orders, discrete jobs, and repetitive schedules. The available hours are calculated based on the resources availability information defined in Oracle Bills of Material.

> Available hours = capacity units * shift hours per day * shift days per week * efficiency * utilization

For 24-hour resources, the formula is

> Available hours = capacity units * 24 hours per day * workdays per week * efficiency * utilization

The efficiency and utilization factors are the new factors in R11*i*.

RATE-BASED CRP

Rate-Based CRP utilization is calculated as follows:

> Capacity Utilization = Required Rate/Available Rate

The required rate is calculated using actual rate information created by the planning process. The available rate uses the production line information that was defined in Oracle Bills of Material (maximum hourly rate and production line availability).

VIEWING CRP

Before you can review CRP data, you must generate a plan with the Plan Capacity option selected. When generating a plan, you can also choose to apply a simulation set. See the section "Generating an MRP" in "Using Oracle Master Scheduling/MRP."

The view options are similar to those used for RCCP (see Figure 21.13). You can view information for resources utilization using the routing-based option and production line utilization using the rate-based option.

As with RCCP data, you can export your CRP data to Excel to view it graphically.

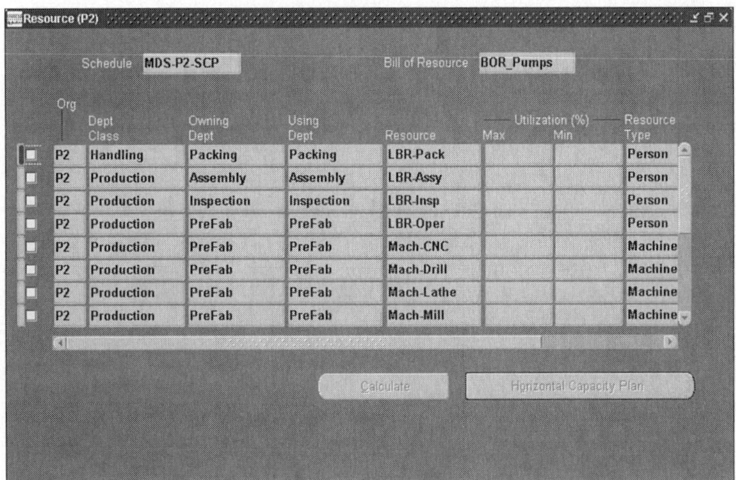

Figure 21.13
Resource Availabilty screen.

ORACLE CAPACITY: UNDERSTANDING KEY REPORTS

Table 21.4 lists the reports provided with the Oracle Capacity application.

TABLE 21.4 ORACLE CAPACITY REPORTS

Report Name	Description
Bill of Resources Report	Prints your Bills of Resources.
CRP Rate-Based Report	Shows detailed capacity information for repetitively planned items that are manufactured on rate-based production lines for a selected material requirements plan.
CRP Routing-Based Report	Shows the detailed capacity plan and resources availability information for a selected material requirements plan.

TABLE 21.4 CONTINUED

Report Name	Description
RCCP Rate-Based Report	Prints a rough cut capacity plan for repetitively planned items that are manufactured on rate-based production lines for a selected master schedule and bill of resources.
RCCP Routing-Based Report	Shows the rough cut capacity plan and resource availability information for a selected master schedule.

ORACLE CAPACITY: FROM HERE

When implementing the Oracle Capacity application, you should also review the material in the following section and chapter:

- "Using Oracle Master Scheduling/MRP" (the first section of this chapter)
- Chapter 19

TROUBLESHOOTING ORACLE PLANNING APPLICATIONS

- The memory-based planning engine can be problematic to set up and keep running consistently. It is worth the effort because it offers significant improvement in processing time over the standard planning engine, even with modest computing power. If you need assistance, Oracle Support can provide additional documentation to help with the configuration. Check the Oracle MetaLink Web site.
- If you are experiencing inconsistencies in master schedule relief or forecast consumption, you should verify that the Planning Manager is running. If not, you should investigate any errors and restart the Planning Manager.
- The Planning Manager performs vital maintenance activities for Master Scheduling/MRP Applications, and it is therefore critical for it to be running. However, sometimes it might run for only a short amount of time, which makes it difficult for you to know whether it is running. To ensure the Planning Manager is running, check the concurrent log file and make sure it is active.
- Open interface concurrent programs validate the data in the interface tables during the processing. This validation process flags rows with errors and leaves them in the interface table. You must research and correct these errors in a timely manner; otherwise, data inconsistencies will exit. Inquires and reports track the errors.

CHAPTER 22

USING ORACLE WORK IN PROCESS

In this chapter

Oracle Work In Process provides a comprehensive set of tools to enable most organizations to manage their manufacturing operations. Over time, Oracle has expanded the capabilities of this application to provide support for "mixed mode" manufacturing. This enables organizations to continue to operate traditional discrete manufacturing (where appropriate) but also to incorporate elements of repetitive and flow manufacturing.

Figure 22.1 shows how Oracle Work In Process relates to the other Oracle Applications. These relationships affect the setup and operation of the Oracle Work In Process application.

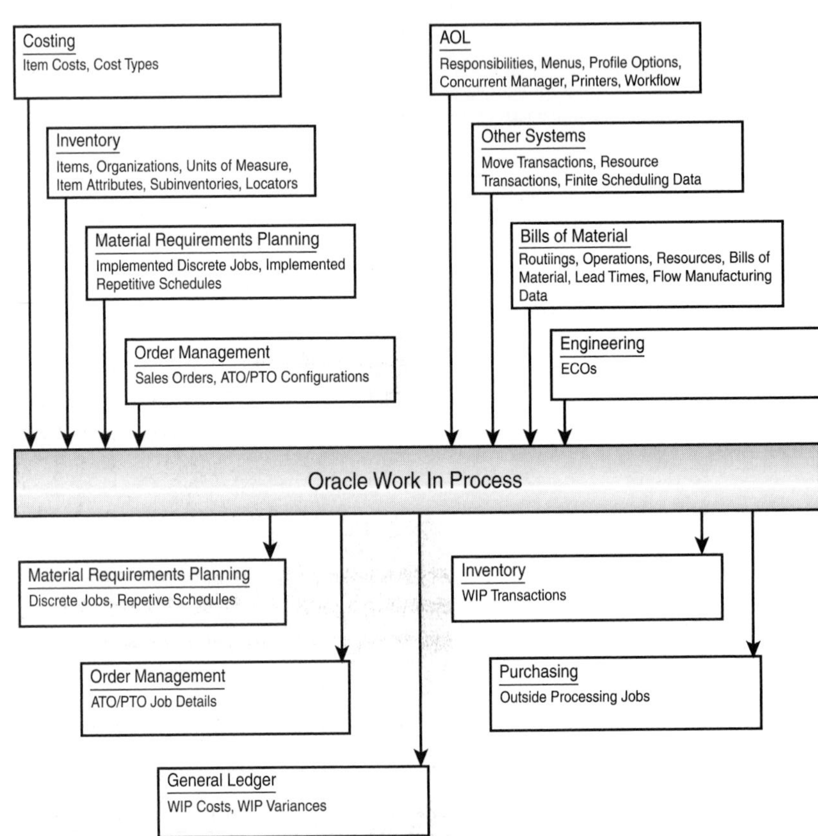

Figure 22.1
This is how the Oracle Work In Process application interacts with the other Oracle Applications.

DISCOVERING NEW FEATURES IN RELEASE 11 AND RELEASE 11*i*

The following is a list of features in Release 11 and new features added for Release 11*i*:

- **Integration with Projects and Tasks Set Up in Oracle Projects**—If you operate in a project-manufacturing environment, the application now enables you to define, track, and cost jobs by project. Projects and tasks are set up in Oracle Projects.

- **Average Costing in a Manufacturing Implementation**—Average costing for manufacturing transactions is available (see Chapter 20, "Using Oracle Cost Management").
- **Flow Manufacturing**—With Release 11, Oracle has introduced tools to support flow manufacturing concepts. Oracle Release 11*i* has also enhanced the flow manufacturing functionality. Flow manufacturing is based on "pulling" the product and material through the manufacturing operation. To ensure flexibility, manufacturing lines are created and balanced to support a changing mix of product. Manufacturing is organized by grouping products into families that require similar manufacturing processes. There is further discussion of flow manufacturing in Chapter 19, "Using Oracle Engineering and Bills of Material."

  To support this approach, Oracle has made available Work Order–less Completions. Rather than creating discrete jobs or repetitive schedules, you can base product manufacturing on a forecasted daily production rate and use work order–less completions to manage the backflush of pull *and* push components. (WIP supply types are discussed later in this chapter.) Any resource and overhead costs associated with the assembly can be collected from the flow routing when the backflush transaction occurs.
- **Saving Simulated Discrete Jobs**—In previous releases of Oracle Work In Process, you had the capability to simulate discrete jobs. Unfortunately, after the simulation was complete, the discrete job had to be created from scratch. In Release 11, WIP now provides a facility to create discrete jobs from your simulations.

Release 11*i* enhancements to flow manufacturing include

- **Ability to select from a list of schedules that are to be completed on a particular day**—You can do this after completing assemblies. This is an enhancement to flow schedules.
- **For assembly scrap, the ability to scrap or return from scrap any unscheduled assemblies and assemblies being built on flow schedules.**
- **Ability to create requisitions for outside processing when the job or schedule is released**—You can also do this when moving assemblies into an outside processing operation. The option exists where you can require purchase requisitions to be created manually.
- **Ability to place the item revision number for an outside processing item on the requisition**—This occurs when a purchase requisition is created for any outside processing of an assembly component. The Bill of Material revision number is used if the item is the assembly being built.
- **Assemblies can be automatically completed into inventory when received from the outside processing supplier**—This can be done during the last operation on the routing of an outside processing operation that has PO Move resources attached to it.
- **Sales orders can be linked to flow schedules and unscheduled flow assembly completions**—This allows you to reserve completed assemblies to the associated sales order.

- **Viewing ATP Status of Discrete Job Component Requirements**—A facility is now available to check component ATP information when creating, simulating, or viewing a discrete job. In previous releases, checking of on-hand balances was available, but this did not provide any visibility of quantities that were allocated to other jobs and schedules.
- **Job Details Can Be Viewed Online as Jobs Are Defined**—It is now possible to view component material requirements, operations, and resource requirements from the same window that is used to define and update jobs.
- **View Pending Job Transactions**—You can view pending discrete job transactions that could prevent you from purging, closing, or changing the status of a discrete job. Until now, the WIP application only provided a warning that there were pending transactions.
- **Restricted Delete on Outside Processing Resources when a PO Has Been Created**—WIP will prevent you from deleting resources in use at outside processing operations if a purchase requisition or purchase order has been created.
- **WIP Scheduling Interface**—An open interface has been added to allow information from external systems to schedule discrete jobs. This is discussed later in this chapter.
- **Improved Material Transaction Processing**—A number of improvements have been made to the way WIP material transactions work.

The following are new features added to Release 11*i*:

- **Production Kanban**—You can use kanban indicators to create repetitive schedules, discrete jobs, or flow schedules. Upon completion, it automatically changes the supply status of the kanban card to full, which notifies you that the order has been fulfilled.
- **Discrete Workstation**—This enables you to access critical production information and perform common shop floor transactions from a single window without having to return to the navigator window.
- **Completion Transaction Integration with Oracle Quality**—You can make quality results collection mandatory or have it run as a background process as assemblies are completed or returned on discrete jobs or repetitive schedules.
- **Model/Unit Number Effectivity**—This enables you to associate end item model/unit number with items in addition to interacting with Oracle Projects.
- **Workflow-Based Alerts and Intelligent Messaging**—This is a trigger to send an alert to users. This is primarily for users who move items into inventory during WIP completion and component return transactions, which notifies them of shortages in an inventory location or on a sales order. When shortages are found, users can be notified.

Here are the new enhancements to Release 11*i*:

- **Over-Completion**—Without additional steps, you can over-complete assemblies on jobs and schedules with established tolerance limits. This results in moving more assemblies and then exiting at a particular routing operation.

- **Sales Order Reservations for Standard Items on Discrete Jobs**—You can use existing reservations functionality for assemblies more frequently because sales orders are linked to jobs without having to define the assembly as an ATO item.
- **Phantom**—The new BOM parameters (BOM: Use Phantom Routings and BOM: Inherit Phantom Operation Seq) give you control inheritance of a parent assembly operation sequence and specify whether resources and overhead on phantom routings are recognized for costing and capacity planning purposes.
- **Scrap**—You can scrap assemblies on a discrete job in which all assembly pull components are required at or before the operation. The scrap can be fully costed and automatically charged to the job.
- **Completion**—Repetitive schedules and job statuses are automatically updated to Complete when the total number of assemblies completed and scrapped on a job or repetitive schedule is greater than or equal to the required quantity.
- **Outside Processing for Manufacturing Collaboration**—This coordinates production activities, scheduling, and the communication of information between you and your outside processing suppliers.
- **Outside Processing and the Need by Date**—The need by date can be determined based on the start date of the operation following the outside processing operation.
- **Outside Processing for Supplier Management Portal Integration**—Outside processing suppliers can use this enhancement to view outside processing purchase orders and access WIP job or schedule instructions.

This is the new form for Release 11*i*:

- **Discrete Workstation (WIPPCBDW)**—This new form contains the Discrete Workstation window located on the Work in Process main menu.

The following is the changed form for Release 11*i*:

- **Operations (WIPOPMDF)**—Select the Tools menu and select the Update Need By Date menu to open the Update Need By Date window.

Critical Implementation Factors

Before embarking on an implementation of Work In Process, the topics addressed in the following sections should be given consideration.

Issues and Gaps

Companies implementing and using WIP have identified some issues and gaps with the application. With Release 11*i*, Oracle has incorporated additional functionality that addresses some of the gaps. Perhaps notable is the introduction of functionality to allow organizations to use flow manufacturing techniques. In addition, the capability of WIP to interact with Oracle Projects offers useful functionality.

REVIEWING TOP ENHANCEMENT REQUESTS

Some of the concerns that are being addressed through the Oracle Applications User Group (OAUG) include

- There is no physical inventory facility available to use with Oracle Work In Process. This makes it tedious to count components and assemblies in a discrete manufacturing environment.
- It is not possible to create inventory reservations for WIP component requirements.
- Outside processing jobs do not complete or close automatically when assemblies are received from the supplier.
- There is currently no warning provided by the WIP application if assemblies are over-completed on a discrete job. It is still possible to monitor the status of job completions using standard or custom developed reports. However, this requires frequent review by the Planner or Scheduler.
- The WIP application does not automatically consider substitute components when there is not adequate stock available of the primary component.
- If there are "pull" components on an assembly, there is no automated check of the on-hand quantities before it is released. The Scheduler or Planner must review the balances on-hand through an online inquiry.
- In an Assemble to Order (ATO) manufacturing environment, there is a significant amount of manual maintenance required to keep Sales Orders and Discrete Jobs synchronized.

REQUIRED SETUP TASKS

The following section describes the tasks required to set up the Work In Process application.

CONFIGURING THE APPLICATION

To ensure that the application works correctly for your business, it must be configured to suit your needs. Before configuring Work In Process, you should complete the required setup steps for Inventory, Bills of Material, Engineering, Cost Management, Projects and MRP.

RESOLVING CRITICAL SETUP ISSUES

To set up the Work In Process application, you need to carefully consider the manufacturing approaches that exist in your organization. The Oracle WIP application will support the following:

- Discrete Manufacturing
- Repetitive Manufacturing

- Project Manufacturing
- Assemble To Order Manufacturing
- Flow Manufacturing

To further complicate things, WIP can also support combinations of these manufacturing approaches. The implementation team needs to find the best fit from these approaches and plan the setup accordingly.

The WIP application is tightly integrated with the Oracle Inventory and Oracle Cost Management applications. It is essential that there is adequate Cost Accounting input to the setup of this application.

Table Showing Setup Tasks

Table 22.1 outlines the setup tasks to be completed for Oracle Work In Process.

Table 22.1 Oracle Work In Process Setup Tasks

Setup Task Name	Required?
Define Work In Process Parameters	Yes
Define WIP Accounting Classes	Yes
Set WIP Profile Options	Yes
Define Production Lines	No
Associate Lines and Assemblies	No
Define Schedule Groups	No
Define Employees	No
Define Labor Rates	No
Define Shop Floor Statuses	No
Define Job and Schedule Documents	No
Define Operation Documents	No

Tip

Some of these steps are conditionally required based on the manufacturing approach that you decide to use. Further information on the dependencies is provided in the sections that follow.

Understanding Each Setup Task

This section describes in detail the tasks that need to be performed and some of the key decisions that you will need to make. Because of dependencies between setup steps, these need to be completed in the sequence outlined in the following sections.

DEFINING WORK IN PROCESS PARAMETERS

The selections made for the WIP parameters depend very much on how your organization runs its manufacturing operations.

For discrete manufacturing (for example, building product in batches or lots), the following need to be defined:

- **Default Discrete Class**—You can specify a WIP accounting class that will default when you create a discrete job without choosing a specific class. To set this value, you must first create the WIP accounting class you want to use as the default. The creation of WIP accounting classes is discussed in a subsequent setup step. This is the one case where you need to skip to a later step to complete the setup properly.
- **Default Lot Number Type Parameter**—If you are using lot numbers in association with your WIP jobs, you can specify how the lot number is determined. It can either be based on the job name or use the lot number rules that have been defined in Oracle Inventory (see Chapter 17, "Using Oracle Inventory").
- **Respond to Sales Orders**—This parameter works in conjunction with Assemble to Order (ATO) functionality. Sales Orders for Assemble to Order configurations are linked with discrete jobs. You can set this parameter to determine how your jobs will be affected by changes to the sales orders they are linked to:
  - **Never**—Jobs will not be affected.
  - **Always**—Unreleased jobs will be placed on hold if there are changes made to the sales order configuration.
  - **When Linked 1 to 1**—Changes to the sales order configuration will place the discrete job on hold, but only if the sales order–to–discrete job relationship is unique.

For Repetitive Schedules, you need to set the following parameters:

- **Recognize Period Variances**—You can determine which schedules qualify for having cost variances posted to the General Ledger. This can either be all repetitive schedules or just those that have a status of "Cancelled" or "Complete - No charges."
- **Autorelease Days**—This sets the timeframe that WIP uses to search for a schedule to automatically release when the previous schedule is completed.

If you will be using Available To Promise (ATP) checking for components, you should select the component ATP rule to be used. These rules are set up in Oracle Inventory (see Chapter 17).

If you have defined your inventory organization as an "Average Costing" organization (see Chapter 20), you can set some additional WIP parameters:

- **Default Completion Cost Source**—This parameter determines how resource costs will be charged when assemblies are completed from a job into their completion inventory. This can be System Calculated, which is dependent on the setting of System Option (see the next parameter), or User Defined. User Defined enables you to choose a cost type that you have created. The value for this parameter is determined by the Cost Type parameter, which is explained later.

- **System Option**—If you have chosen System Calculated for Default Completion Cost Source, you must choose one of the following:
    - **Use Actual Resources**—The resource costs are calculated based on actual costs.
    - **Use Predefined Resources**—The resource costs are calculated based on predefined resource costs.
- **Cost Type**—If you have chosen User Defined for the Default Completion Cost Source, you need to select a cost type for this parameter. For an explanation of how to define a Cost Type, see Chapter 20.
- **Auto Compute Final Completion**—Setting this parameter to Yes sets the default for the WIP completion transaction. When the last assembly on a job is completed, choosing this option ensures that there is no positive cost balance left on the job. The default can be changed when the WIP transaction is being processed.

The following parameters also affect the way in which Move Transactions are processed:

- **Shop Floor Status for PO Move Resources**—This parameter affects the behavior of transactions for jobs with outside processing operations. You can assign a "no move" status to ensure that the only way assemblies can be moved from the queue of an outside processing operation is with a Purchase Order receipt. This ensures that quantities moved into and out of the queue step will match.
- **Require Scrap Account**—By setting this parameter to Yes, you can force the user to provide an account to be charged for scrap transactions from your discrete jobs. If you do not set this parameter, it becomes optional for the user to provide an account number.

Tip

If you process a scrap transaction without specifying an account, the value of the transaction will be associated with the job. You will have to treat this as a variance when the job is closed or at the end of an accounting period.

- **Allow Creation of New Operations**—You can determine whether additional operations can be added for a discrete job when a move transaction is being processed.
- **Allow Moves Over No Move Shop Floor Transactions**—You can prevent users from processing moves between "no move" intraoperation steps. The "Move Transactions: Allow Skipping Over No Move Statuses" security function can also be set for an individual user.

Backflush transactions will be affected by the settings of these parameters:

- **Supply Subinventory**—You can specify the default WIP supply subinventory to be used for backflush transactions.
- **Supply Locator**—This parameter applies to a subinventory that is under locator control (see Chapter 17). The same considerations apply as when setting up a default WIP supply subinventory.

Tip

Oracle Manufacturing provides a number of ways to specify the default WIP supply subinventory to be used. It can be set at the WIP application level, on the Bill of Material, or in the Item attributes. Consider carefully at which level you will set the default. In some cases, it might be appropriate to have all material pulled from one subinventory for a particular assembly, and this can be set on the BOM. In other cases, you might want to default the subinventory based on the type of component, and this can be set with the item attributes (see Chapters 17 and 19).

- **Lot Selection Method**—If you are using lot control for items (see Chapter 17), you can determine how a backflush transaction will select the component lot to process. This can be manual, based on the lot expiration date, or First In First Out, using the receipt date.
- **Lot Verification**—Lots can be verified when backflushing to ensure that the lots being selected are the ones that were actually used during the manufacturing process. This can be done for *all* lots, or you can choose to verify the *exceptions* only and assign lots to these manually.

You can set the intraoperation steps to be enabled for use in WIP. The "Queue" step is always enabled.

Tip

Regardless of how you set this parameter, the "To Move" step will be enabled at the last operation in a routing to allow completion of assemblies to inventory.

DEFINING WIP ACCOUNTING CLASSES

To collect job or schedule cost information and any cost variances that might arise during manufacture, you can create WIP accounting classes.

The classes themselves should be based on some logical grouping that makes sense in your business—for example, product families, subassemblies, final assemblies, and so on. These enable you to specify the valuation and variance accounts that should be used for a particular job or schedule. See Figure 22.2 for clarification on how you assign a WIP accounting class to all discrete jobs. As discussed previously, you can assign a default WIP accounting class to be used for discrete jobs. This can be changed when the job is being created.

Tip

In Release 11*i* of Oracle Work In Process, you can use Product Line Accounting to link a default WIP accounting class with a product line category set. In this way, you can ensure that specific valuation and variance accounts are used when discrete jobs or schedules are created for a particular product line. For more information on this feature see Chapter 20.

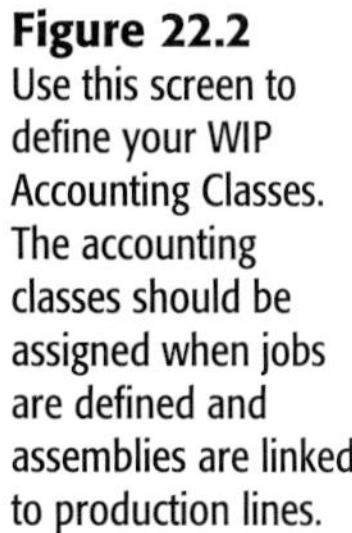

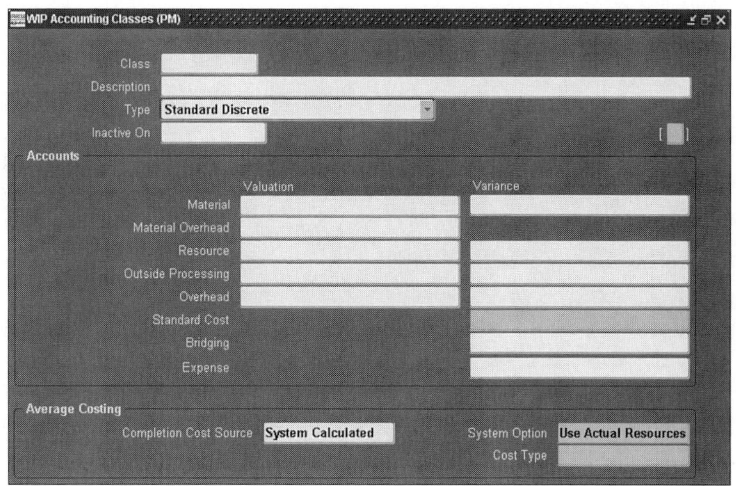

Figure 22.2
Use this screen to define your WIP Accounting Classes. The accounting classes should be assigned when jobs are defined and assemblies are linked to production lines.

Tip

You should complete the setup of WIP accounting classes with the assistance of a Cost Accountant. This step has significant implications for the operation of Oracle Cost Management.

WIP accounting classes use the following Valuation Accounts:

- **Material**—If you have set up a standard costing organization, this account will record WIP material transactions at standard cost. If your organization uses average costing, material transactions will be charged to this account based on the current average cost.
- **Material Overhead**—Using standard costing, this account will be charged based on standard cost when material with an associated overhead is issued to a schedule or job. With average costing, the current average cost will be used.
- **Resource**—This account is debited when resources are charged to a job or schedule and is credited when assemblies are completed. With standard costing, resources are charged based on the standard cost. If you are using average costing, they are charged based on the current resource rate.
- **Outside Processing**—In a standard costing organization, outside processing costs are charged to this account based on the purchase order price or the standard cost, depending on how you have set up outside processing. For average costing organizations, the current resource rate or the PO cost is used.
- **Overhead**—Any overhead costs associated with a resource or department are charged to this account. It is charged at standard cost when resources are used on a job or schedule and is credited when assemblies are completed from a job.

You also define variance accounts to track the cost differences that arise when costs charged to a valuation account do not match the credits to that account when assemblies are completed from a job or schedule. Oracle WIP supports variance accounts for the following:

- Material
- Resource
- Outside Processing
- Overhead
- Standard Cost

SETTING THE PROFILE OPTIONS

Table 22.2 shows the profile options that directly affect the operation of the Oracle Work In Process.

TABLE 22.2 ORACLE WORK IN PROCESS PROFILE OPTIONS

Profile Option Name	Required?	Manufacturing Approach*	Level**	Comment
TP:WIP Background Shop Floor Material Processing	Yes	ALL	SARU	Default is Online Processing.
TP:WIP Completion Material Processing	Yes	Dis, Rep, Prj	SARU	Default is Online Processing.
TP:WIP Completion Transaction Form	Yes	Dis, Rep, Prj	SARU	Default is Online Processing.
TP:WIP Completion Transactions First Field	Yes	Dis, Rep, Prj	SARU	Default is Job.
TP:WIP Concurrent Message Level	Yes	Dis, Rep, Prj	SARU	Default is Message Level 0.
TP:WIP Material Transaction Form	Yes	Dis, Rep, Prj	SARU	Default is Online Processing.
TP:WIP Material Transactions First Field	Yes	Dis, Rep, Prj	SARU	Default is Job.
TP:WIP Move Transaction	Yes	Dis, Rep, Prj	SARU	Default is Online Processing.

Table 22.2 Continued

Profile Option Name	Required?	Manufacturing Approach*	Level**	Comment
TP:WIP Move Transactions First Field	Yes	Dis, Rep, Prj	SARU	Default is Job.
TP:WIP Move Transaction Quantity Default	Yes	Dis, Rep, Prj	SARU	Default is None.
TP:WIP Operation Backflush Setup	Yes	Dis, Rep, Prj	SARU	Default is Online Processing.
TP:WIP Resource Transactions First Field	Yes	ALL	SARU	Default is Job.
TP:WIP Shop Floor Material Processing	Yes	ALL	SARU	Default is Online Processing.
TP:WIP: Workorder-less Completion Default	Yes	WO	SARU	Default is Unscheduled. This profile option does not work with R11. It will be used in future releases.
WIP:Default Job Start Date	Yes	Dis, Prj	SARU	Default is No.
WIP:Define Discrete Job Form	Yes	Dis, Prj	SARU	Default is Interactive Definition.
WIP:Discrete Job Prefix	Yes	Dis, Prj, WO	SARU	Default is None.
WIP:Exclude Open ECOs	Yes	ALL	SARU	Default is Yes.
WIP:Job Name Updateable	Yes	Dis, Prj	SARU	Default is Yes. An individual user can't set this option himself. It can be set by the System Administrator for a specific user.

TABLE 22.2 CONTINUED

Profile Option Name	Required?	Manufacturing Approach*	Level**	Comment
WIP:Move Completion Default	Yes	Dis, Rep, Prj	SARU	Default is No.
WIP:Requirement Nettable Option	Yes	ALL	SARU	Default is View all subinventories.
WIP:See Engineering Items	Yes	ALL	SARU	Default is Yes.
WIP: Enable Outside Processing Workflows	No	ALL	S	Optional.

* *Manufacturing Approach—Discrete, Repetitive, Project, WorkOrder–less.*
** *Levels can be Site, Application, Responsibility, or User. The system administrator sets most profile options.*

DEFINING PRODUCTION LINES

A production line represents a unique collection of departments, operations and/or manufacturing cells used to manufacture your products. Oracle WIP enables you to create production lines and then link them with repetitive schedules, discrete jobs, and work order–less completions.

The specifics of defining a production line to be used with repetitive schedules are covered later in this chapter.

Note

Production lines can be assigned when you create a discrete job. This facility is available for information purposes only.

DEFINING REPETITIVE ASSEMBLIES

If you plan on using repetitive manufacturing, you must identify the repetitive assemblies and then assign them to one or more production lines. This is discussed later in this chapter.

Tip

If you have installed Oracle Master Scheduling/MRP, you must set the Repetitive Planning item attribute to Yes in Oracle Inventory for your repetitive assemblies. This forces the planning process to plan your assemblies based on daily production rates rather than discrete quantities. Item attributes are discussed in Chapter 17, and repetitive planning is discussed in Chapter 21, "Using Oracle Planning Applications."

DEFINING SCHEDULE GROUPS

You can create Schedule groups, which can be assigned to discrete jobs. Figure 22.3 shows that you are able to create a Schedule group for your jobs. Schedule groups can be a useful way to associate similar jobs with each other—for example, jobs being built to satisfy orders for a particular customer.

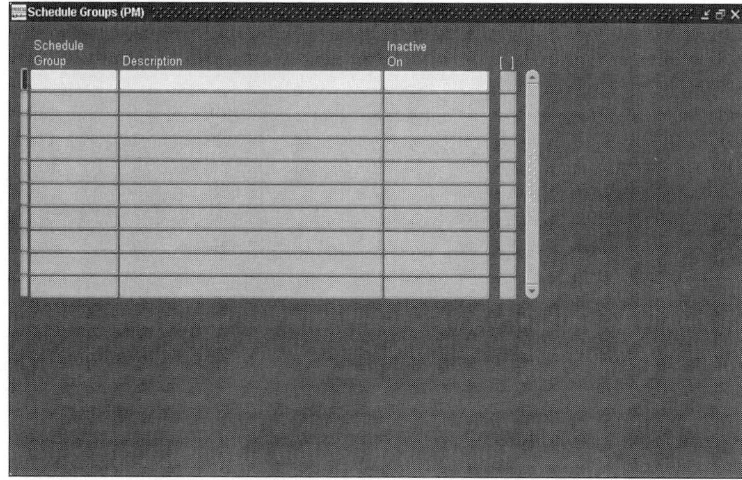

Figure 22.3
Define your schedule groups using this screen.

> **Note**
>
> Schedule groups also have an application in Build Sequencing, which is available in Release 11*i* of Oracle WIP. You can set a sequence for jobs that have been associated with a particular schedule group. One application would be to create a schedule group for jobs related to a customer and then use sequencing to prioritize the completion of these jobs.

DEFINING EMPLOYEES

If you need to collect labor costs based on "person" resources, you must define the employees. If you have installed Oracle Human Resources Management Systems, you can define the employees through that application; otherwise, Oracle WIP provides a form to do this (see Figure 22.4).

DEFINING LABOR RATES

For each employee that you define, you can enter an hourly labor rate. Figure 22.5 indicates that you can assign labor rates to employees. In fact, you can assign several hourly rates per employee with different effectivity dates. When you use actual costing, Oracle WIP uses the current rate when costing your "person" resource transactions.

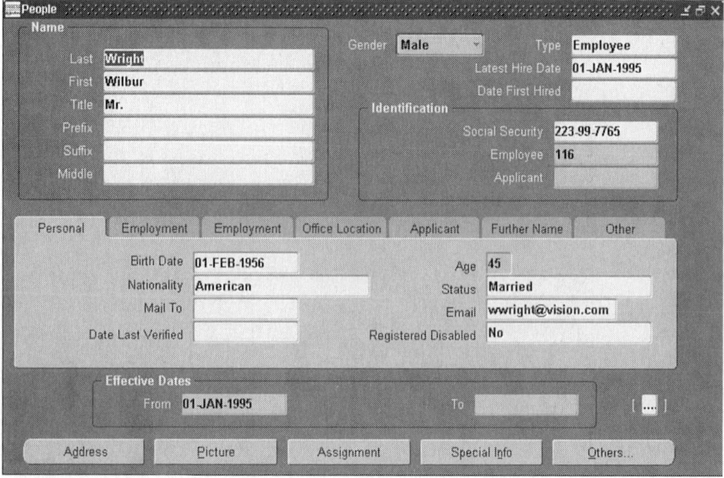

Figure 22.4
Use this to define your employees. This screen is not accessible if Oracle Human Resources has been installed.

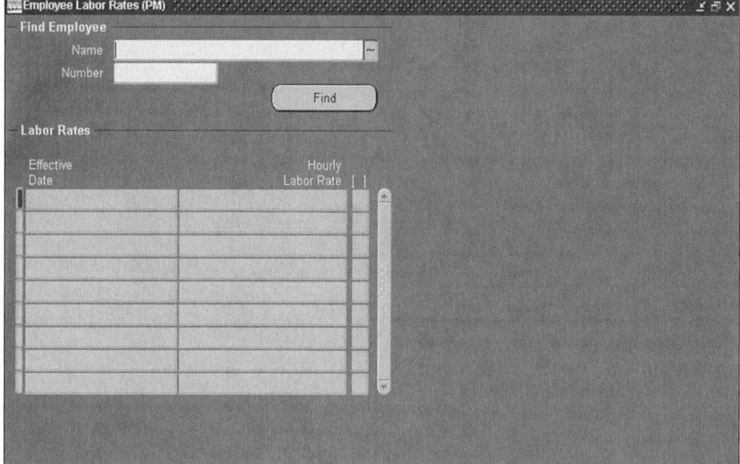

Figure 22.5
Use this screen to assign labor rates to employees.

Defining Shop Floor Statuses

Shop Floor Statuses can be created and used to control move transactions within your manufacturing operation. Figure 22.6 shows how you can define a shop floor status and choose to allow movement. These statuses can be assigned to the intraoperation steps of a routing. A typical application would be to create a “Quality Hold” status. You can decide whether you want to prevent move transactions when this status is assigned or you want to use it for information only.

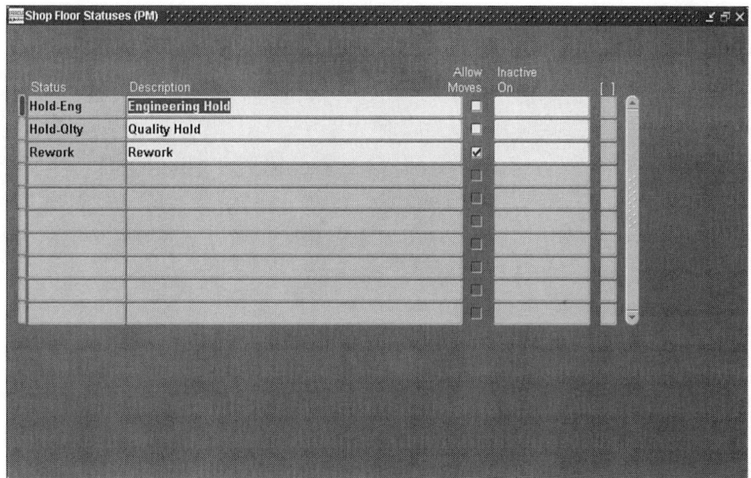

Figure 22.6
Use this screen to define shop floor statuses.

Defining Job and Schedule Documents

Release 11*i* of Oracle WIP provides the facility to attach a variety of file types to your discrete jobs and repetitive schedules. These could be drawings, images, flowcharts, manuals, and so on.

You also have the option to create a "catalog" of standard documents that you can choose from when defining a job or schedule. If these exist, you can assign them at this setup step.

Defining Operation Documents

As with Job and Schedule Documents, you can assign documents to Operations. At this setup step, you can define standard documents that you can choose from when defining an operation. Figure 22.7 also shows how to set your documents as standard, template, or one time. A typical application would be assigning operation instructions for a piece of equipment or a manual process that could be reused on several operations.

Defining Report Sets

Concurrent programs and reports can be developed into request groups and request sets. A *request group* is a collection of reports or concurrent programs. A *request set* defines the run and print options.

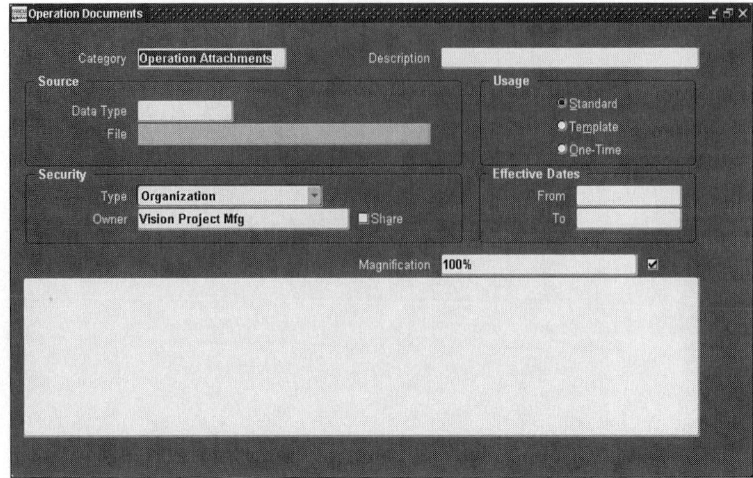

Figure 22.7 Define your operation documents, which can be attached to work in process routing operations, using this screen.

CONVERTING DATA FOR MAJOR ENTITIES

If you are implementing Oracle Work In Process and have been using another ERP system, you need to consider the conversion of your legacy data.

Oracle provides the basic tools to provide conversion of legacy data through the Oracle Manufacturing, Distribution, Sales, and Service Open Interfaces. The Oracle reference documentation explains the operation of the interfaces in detail.

Item and Bill of Material data are required to support your Work In Process implementation. There are two interfaces available to facilitate importing this data:

- **Open Item Interface**—Used for the import of Item Master data. This is covered in Chapter 17.
- **Open Bills of Material Interface**—Used for the import of BOM information. This is covered in Chapter 19.

Additionally, if you have existing routing information, this can be imported through the Open Routing Interface (see Chapter 19).

For importing Discrete Job and Repetitive Schedule information, Oracle provides an Open Job and Schedule Interface. Although this is designed to interface with other scheduling systems, it has applications in the conversion of WIP data from a legacy system. The WIP Mass Load concurrent program reads data from the interface table and creates the discrete jobs and repetitive schedule.

The use of these interfaces requires development of programs to extract data from the legacy system, format it based on the open interface guidelines, and then insert rows in the interface tables. When the import programs are run, Oracle validates the data in the interface tables based on the current setup of the relevant application (Inventory, Bills of Material, or WIP).

Tip

> Before you run any import program, ensure that *all* setup steps are complete. This will save you a lot of time in not having to manually sort through errors that have occurred because of an incomplete setup.

As with any data conversion effort, you need to assess the costs involved in developing custom software to extract and format your legacy data. With Items, Bills of Material, and Routings, the development cost will probably be justified. In many cases, it might be more cost-effective to create your discrete jobs and schedules manually at the time of conversion. Of course, this depends on the nature of your business.

PROCESSING TRANSACTIONS

This section covers the normal transaction activity that occurs within the Work In Process application.

WORK IN PROCESS TRANSACTIONS

The following sections cover the transactions that are involved in the operation of the Oracle Work In Process application.

PROCESSING SHOP FLOOR TRANSACTIONS

The shop floor transactions in WIP are typically related to routing-based manufacturing. Details of the creation of a routing are covered in Chapter 19.

INTRAOPERATION STEPS Routings consist of operations that define the flow that an assembly will follow in manufacturing. For each of these operations, you can assign intraoperation steps that you can use to control transaction processing.

A summary of these steps is as follows:

- **Queue**—Assemblies in this step are typically awaiting processing.
- **Run**—Assemblies in this step are in process.
- **To Move**—Assemblies in this step have completed processing and are waiting for subsequent processing. If the assemblies are in the "to move" step of the last operation on a routing, they are available for completion.
- **Scrap**—Assemblies in this step are not considered available, but from a costing point of view, WIP considers them complete at the operation. Scrapping of assemblies is discussed later in this chapter. If you do succeed in salvaging assemblies at this step, you can move them to another step at this operation or to another operation.
- **Reject**—Assemblies in this step are not considered available. As with the "scrap" step, WIP does consider them complete at the operation. You can use this step to hold rejected assemblies that either require disposition or are awaiting rework. When you

are sure what you need to do with these assemblies, you can move them to another intraoperation step at this operation or move them to another operation.

ADDING, UPDATING, AND DELETING OPERATIONS To maintain flexibility, you can add operations to your jobs and schedules. You can do this even if a routing does not exist. Discrete jobs must have a status of unreleased, released, on-hold, or complete. You can only add operations to repetitive schedules that are unreleased. Typically, this would enable you to add a temporary unplanned operation to a job or schedule.

Tip

WIP (depending on your security settings) will also allow the creation of "ad hoc" operations for discrete jobs while processing move transactions. This might be useful in creating temporary operations to allow processing of rework while a job is running.

You can also update operations on a job or schedule. An example would be the inclusion of revised work instructions that might be linked to an operation. Operations can be updated for discrete jobs with statuses of unreleased, released, on-hold, and complete. Operations on a repetitive schedule can be updated; they have a status of released, on-hold, or complete. There must be only one active schedule for the assembly/line combination when the update happens.

Operations can also be deleted from a job or schedule if required. You cannot delete operations if there has been completion, move, or resource charging activity at that operation.

RESOURCES Resources are "things" that are required to perform an operation. These could include labor, equipment, outside processing services, and so on. Creating and assigning resources is discussed in Chapter 19.

When you create resources, you can define them to be automatically charged to a job or schedule when move or completion activity takes place either within WIP or as a result of outside processing PO activity. If required, resources can also be manually charged when moves take place or at any other time—for example, on completion of a job or schedule.

Resources can be added or updated while you are adding or updating operations (using the "Operations" window). It is possible to add a resource to a job or schedule that does not have any operations assigned. If you are adding a resource to a job or schedule that does have operations assigned, you must add the resource to the department that the operation is linked to (see Chapter 19).

If you delete an operation, the related resources are also deleted. You can delete resources while updating operations. Both transactions are carried out from the Operations window. WIP does not enable you to delete resources when there has been transaction activity on the schedule or job that has used the resources.

Move Transactions When using routings with operations assigned, product is moved through the sequence of operations using the Move Transactions window. There are two ways in which assemblies can move:

- **Intraoperation Moves**—Where assemblies move between the enabled intraoperation steps assigned within an operation (see Intraoperation Steps).
- **Interoperation Moves**—Where assemblies move between an intraoperation step of one operation and an intraoperation step of another operation.

Typically, product will move from the "to move" step of an operation to the "queue" step of a subsequent operation. In the case of rework and scrap, assemblies can move back to a previous step or indeed a prior operation.

The move transaction can also be used to perform a completion if the assemblies are at the "to move" step of the final operation (see the section "WIP Completion Transactions").

The effect of move transactions on material is discussed in the next section.

Shop Floor Statuses Within the WIP application, you can set up any number of shop floor statuses that can be applied to the intraoperation steps used on a job or schedule. These statuses are used to prevent move transactions from taking place. In most organizations, this level of control is used to enforce a quality hold on a job or schedule. The statuses are defined and maintained using the Assign Shop Floor Statuses window.

Tip

Shop floor statuses are assigned to a specific discrete job or assembly/production line combination.

You cannot assign the same status to more than one intraoperation step at the same operation on a job. You can assign multiple statuses to the same step if this is required.

Tip

Oracle WIP provides additional controls for move transactions using the WIP parameter Allow Moves Over No Move Shop Floor Statuses (see the setup steps earlier in this chapter).

Job and Repetitive Schedule Statuses Statuses can be assigned and maintained for jobs and schedules. These can be used to control the way in which the job is processed, and in some cases WIP automatically updates the status.

Tip

These statuses are not directly related to shop floor statuses, although in some cases they can have a similar effect.

The following is a summary of some of the more important statuses:

- **Unreleased**—The job or schedule has not yet been released for production. No transactions can be processed, although the job or schedule can be updated.
- **Released**—The job or schedule is available for production. Transactions can be made. This status is updated using the Discrete Jobs or Repetitive Schedules window.
- **Complete**—The total quantity on the job or schedule has been completed. WIP updates a job to this status automatically when the original job quantity has been completed. Transactions can still be processed against a job with this status, so it is possible to over-complete (see WIP Completion Transactions). How this status updates for repetitive schedules depends on the setting of the Autorelease Days parameter and the availability of an unreleased schedule (see the section "Autorelease of a Schedule").
- **Complete-No Charges**—The total quantity on the job or schedule has been completed. No further transactions can be processed on jobs or schedules with this status. Because this status is manually assigned by updating a job or schedule, you can use it to prevent any further transaction activity. For repetitive schedules, WIP can update a schedule to this status automatically (see the section "Autorelease of a Schedule").
- **On Hold**—The job or schedule can be updated, but no transactions are possible.
- **Cancelled**—The job or schedule has been cancelled, and no further update or transaction activity is possible. You can, however, change the status back to Released if necessary.
- **Closed**—This applies to a discrete job. The discrete job close process has been run, and no further update, transaction, or status change activity is possible. Closed does not apply to repetitive schedules because any costs and variances are posted to the general ledger as the financial period closes.

PROCESSING MATERIAL TRANSACTIONS

The following sections explain how typical material transactions are processed within the Work In Process application.

SUPPLY TYPES Oracle uses supply types to determine how material is planned, supplied through the Work In Process application, and costed. You can set the supply type at the item level or on a particular Bill of Material.

Tip

> The choice of setting the supply type at the item or Bill of Material level depends on how you want to manage the material flow through production. If it is likely that an item will have one supply type regardless of the assembly it is used on, setting this at the item level is adequate. However, if the supply of material changes depending on the assembly an item is used on, you must set the supply type on the BOM.

The following is a summary of the supply types from a WIP perspective:

- **Assembly Pull**—Component requirements are relieved from the supply subinventory when the assembly is completed.

Tip

Default supply subinventories are discussed in the setup section. You can assign the supply subinventory to a component on a Bill of Material, or it can be assigned at the item level (see Chapters 17 and 19).

- **Operation Pull**—Component requirements are relieved from the supply subinventory when the assembly completes a backflush operation.
- **Push**—Component requirements must be issued to the job or schedule.
- **Bulk**—Components with this supply type are not typically issued to jobs or schedules. The bulk designation is normally used for components that are expensed on receipt or on issue.
- **Supplier**—WIP creates requirements for components with this supply type when you create a job or schedule. They are not typically transacted.
- **Phantom**—This supply type is unique to phantom assemblies and has a significant impact on the planning process. When used as a subassembly within a BOM structure, phantom assemblies become transparent, and only their components are seen in the planning process. It is possible to treat a phantom assembly as a top level assembly and build it in WIP.
- **Based on Bill**—This is not a true supply type, but an indication that the supply type set on the Bill of Material will be used. For discrete jobs and repetitive schedules, this is the default supply type and can be changed when a discrete job is being created or when repetitive assemblies are being associated with production lines.

ISSUING/RETURNING MATERIAL How Oracle WIP handles the issue and return of material depends on the supply type set for the components:

- **Issuing and returning specific components**—Using the "WIP Material Transactions" window, you can issue or return components of a job or schedule regardless of the supply type. This includes items with a supply type of bulk, supplier, and phantom. You must select the "specific component" option to do this. For jobs or schedules that have a routing, you can perform these transactions against components at any operation.
- **Issuing and returning all push components**—To simplify the issue or return of the push component requirements on a job or schedule, you can choose the All Material option. All push components can then be either issued or returned with one transaction.

Tip

WIP enables you to transact "ad hoc" components to a job or schedule. These are component requirements that are not currently associated with the job or schedule. This option could save you the bother of having to update the material requirements on a job or schedule if a "one-off" component is required.

The following transactions perform a backflush where the component requirements are deducted from the supply subinventory automatically. This eliminates the need for multiple transactions to issue the components to the job or schedule:

- **Completing assemblies to inventory using the Completion transaction**—Components with a supply-type of assembly pull are issued from the supply subinventory when the completion transaction takes place (backflush).
- **Moving and completing assemblies to inventory using the Move transaction**—This transaction is carried out using the Move Transaction window. Completing or moving assemblies to inventory causes components with a supply-type of assembly pull or operation pull to be relieved from the supply subinventory (backflush). You can determine when operation-pull components will be backflushed by assigning them to a particular operation when the Bill of Material is defined (see Chapter 19).
- **Completing assemblies at an operation**—Using the Move Transaction window, you can move assemblies through an operation. If there are components that have a supply type of operation pull and they are assigned to the operation, they will be relieved from the supply subinventory (backflush).
- **Receiving assemblies from outside processing operations**—This applies to outside processing assemblies that have pull components. When a Purchase Order receipt is performed, any pull components are relieved from the supply subinventory (backflush)

Tip

If the Allow Negative Inventory Balances parameter is set to Yes in Oracle Inventory, WIP enables you to process transactions that could drive an inventory location negative. You will receive a warning that this will happen. Even if this parameter is set to No, WIP will drive inventory locations negative for a backflush transaction if the on-hand balance is not sufficient. See Chapter 17 for information on setting the organization parameters.

If you need to undo a backflush transaction that was processed in error, WIP provides a reverse backflush transaction. This can be processed from the Completion Transaction and Move Transaction windows. The assembly quantity in the completion subinventory is reduced and the balances of the component subinventories are increased based on the usage.

Oracle WIP enables you to replenish supply subinventories using the WIP Material Transactions window. This replenishment is based on the discrete job name or the repetitive schedule. You can also use a completion transaction to feed subassemblies to the supply subinventory of the next using assembly.

SCRAPPING MATERIAL/ASSEMBLIES How you manage component and assembly scrap using WIP depends on a number of factors.

If you are using routings, then you can enable the Scrap intraoperation step for any operation at which you anticipate scrapping. When you move assemblies to the scrap step of an operation, you can optionally enter an account code to collect the scrap cost. If you do not enter an account, the cost stays with the schedule or job until the accounting period closes or you close the job. For standard discrete jobs, MPS/MRP planning does not see any quantities in the scrap step as supply and replans accordingly. Scrap on repetitive schedules and nonstandard jobs is not netted from the supply quantity.

Tip

If an assembly has operation or assembly pull components and you attempt to move assemblies into the scrap step before a pending backflush has completed, you receive a warning. You risk a situation where the on-hand quantities will not reconcile when the backflush transaction eventually completes. You can get around this problem by pushing the assembly pull or operation pull components onto the job or schedule to ensure that the subinventory balances remain correct.

In the absence of a routing, you can transact the assemblies to be scrapped to a completion subinventory and then scrap the assemblies using a miscellaneous issue to a scrap account. (See Chapter 17 for an explanation of miscellaneous transactions.)

Scrapping partially completed assemblies always causes a dilemma. Depending on the percentage of the assembly completed, you can choose to scrap the components only or to scrap the assembly and deal with any unused components as you see fit.

Scrapping assembly and operation pull components does not normally pose a problem. If there has not been a backflush transaction, you can scrap these components from the supply subinventory using a miscellaneous issue transaction.

Scrapping push components requires the return of the components to a subinventory (which could be any subinventory) where they can be scrapped using a miscellaneous issue transaction.

ADDING/UPDATING AND DELETING MATERIAL REQUIREMENTS The material requirements on a discrete job or repetitive schedule can be updated if the status is released, unreleased, on-hold, or complete. You can add components, change quantities, change supply type, and supply subinventories using the Material Requirements window. This provides for flexibility in the manufacturing process when additional material is required to complete a specific job or schedule or when substitutions need to be made.

Tip

Although some organizations might prefer to control the material requirements through updating a job or schedule, WIP also enables you to issue "ad hoc" components (see the section "Issuing/Returning Material").

For nonstandard discrete jobs, you can use the Material Requirements window to add components and assemblies to your job. A typical use would be adding an assembly for rework and components that will be used in the rework.

There are no restrictions on deleting material requirements from jobs or schedules that have a status of unreleased. If the job or schedule has a status of released, on-hold, or complete, you can delete requirements that have not yet been transacted.

WIP Completion Transactions

The topic of completion transactions is also discussed in the section "Issuing/Returning Material." Depending on the manufacturing approach you are taking, WIP provides different options for the completion of assemblies to inventory:

- **WIP completion for jobs and schedules with routings**—You need to ensure that the assemblies to be completed are in the "to move" step of the last operation. The completion transaction can either be done with the Completion Transactions window, shown in Figure 22.8, or the Move Transactions window. If you need to return assemblies from the completion subinventory to the job or schedule, you can do this using the "return" transaction type. This moves the assemblies back to the "to move" step of the last operation and reduces the completed quantity on the job or schedule. You cannot "over-complete" quantities on a job or schedule that has a routing without adjusting the job or schedule quantity.

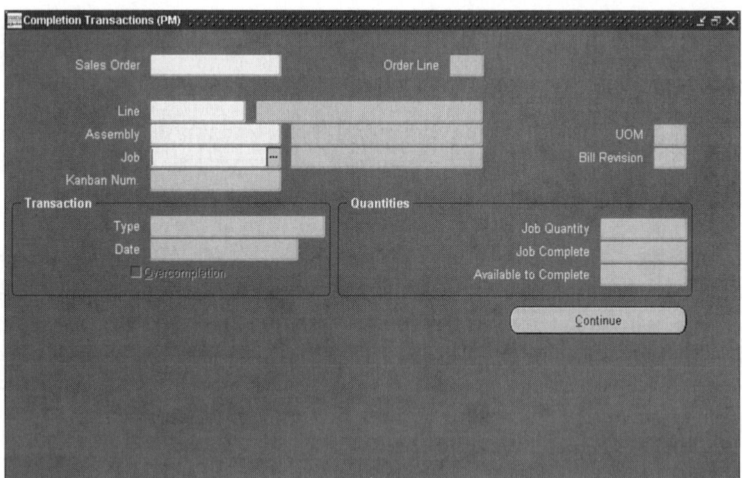

Figure 22.8
This screen is used for processing your completion transactions.

- **WIP completion for jobs and schedules without routings**—These are completed using the Completion Transactions window. As with jobs and schedules that have routings, you can use the "return" transaction type to move assemblies back from inventory to the job or schedule. You can "over-complete" assemblies when there is no routing. This enables you to accommodate production overruns.

Tip

Completions and returns for repetitive schedules ensure that schedules are selected on a first-in, first-out basis.

Tip

Over-completions are not always a good thing. If you do not want to have quantities completed greater than the job or schedule quantity, you will need to monitor your jobs and schedules closely. You can use the Complete - No Charges status to prevent further completions on a job.

- **Work Order–less completions**—If you are using flow manufacturing methods, you can use work order–less completions to complete assemblies to inventory without the creation of a discrete job or repetitive schedule.

Purging Jobs and Schedules

Oracle Work In Process provides a concurrent process to purge jobs and schedules that are no longer required. To be considered valid for purging, a discrete job must be closed in an accounting period that is also closed. Repetitive schedules can be purged if they have a status of Cancelled or Complete - No Charges and are also in an accounting period that has been closed.

You can review the jobs and schedules that would qualify for purging by choosing the Report Only option before proceeding with a purge.

Tip

When you purge discrete jobs and schedules using this program, *all* related data is removed from the database. If you need to retain information on jobs and schedules that you are about to purge, ensure that you have made alternative arrangements to store it.

Managing Discrete Jobs

This section covers the tasks associated with the creation and maintenance of discrete jobs. The Discrete Job form is shown in Figure 22.9.

Discrete Job Types

Oracle Work In Process provides for two types of discrete jobs:

- **Standard**—This is the most typical job type used in manufacturing. It provides for material requirements to be specified referencing a Bill of Material and to associate a routing with the job that will provide information on the operations and resources required to build the assembly.

- **Nonstandard**—This job type is typically used to deal with exceptions in the normal manufacturing process. If necessary, you can add material requirements to a nonstandard job, or you can choose to use it to collect cost information for work performed only. Some applications for a nonstandard job could be rework, repair, prototypes, or project-related work.

DEFINING DISCRETE JOBS

When defining a standard discrete job (see Figure 22.9), you need to consider the following:

- The Job Name can be defaulted based on an internally generated sequence. If you have set a prefix using the WIP: Discrete Job Prefix profile option, this is used.

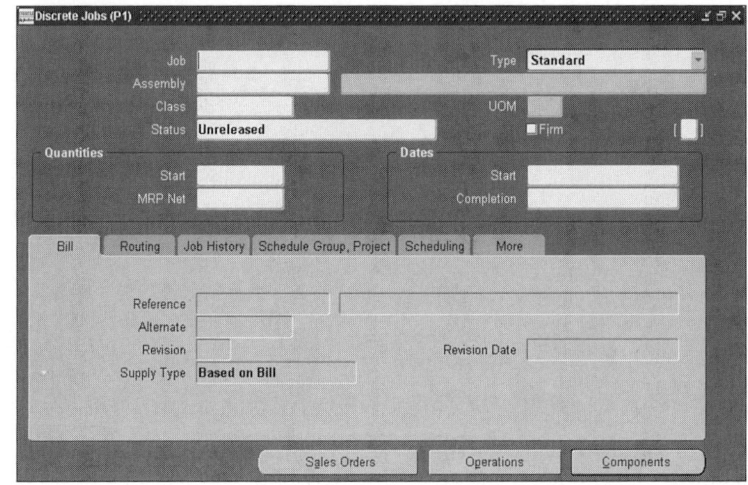

Figure 22.9
This screen enables you to define your Discrete Jobs for manufacturing orders.

Tip

WIP uses an ASCII sequence for the job names if you take the default. You might need to choose a starting sequence number that allows for proper sorting in reports. You need a DBA to assist with setting the starting sequence.

- WIP defaults the assembly's primary BOM and routing if they exist. You can choose an alternate for either the BOM or routing if one exists.
- If you have set up a default WIP accounting class, it defaults on your job (see the setup steps earlier in this chapter). You can override the default if you need to.
- The job status defaults to Unreleased. If you need to change it to a released or hold status, you can do this when you are defining the job. This depends on how you want to control your manufacturing operation (see the section "Processing Shop Floor Transactions").
- There might be situations where you do not want to receive reschedule suggestions for a discrete job, and in this case, you should choose the firm option. Setting the firm

option means that MRP planning does *not* create reschedule suggestions for your discrete job if there are changes in supply or demand. MRP creates additional planned orders if more supply is required.

- Use the MRP Net Quantity with care. For standard discrete jobs, MPS and MRP consider any quantities scrapped off a job as being a reduction in the total supply. If you try to use the MRP Net Quantity to account for process yield losses and subsequently scrap assemblies, MRP over-plans.
- If you associate a routing with a standard discrete job, you can enter either a start or completion date, and WIP forward schedules or backward schedules the job using the routing.
- If you are not using a routing, you can enter the start or completion date, and WIP schedules the job based on the fixed and/or variable lead times for the assembly.

When you are defining nonstandard discrete jobs, you should consider the following points:

- The use of an assembly with a nonstandard job is optional; however, if you are going to use a routing, you have to select an assembly.
- Nonstandard jobs cannot be firmed.
- You can use the MRP Net Quantity field to account for yield loss on nonstandard jobs. The MPS and MRP planning processes don't consider scrap on nonstandard jobs when calculating the supply.
- If you have not assigned a routing reference to the nonstandard job, you must specify both the start and completion dates and times.

Both standard and nonstandard discrete jobs can be associated with projects. This enables you to track material and resource costs specific to a project.

Tip

You can only relate discrete jobs to projects if the Project References Enabled org parameter has been set to Yes in Oracle Inventory.

Discrete jobs can be linked to Sales Orders manually for Assemble to Order items. For Configure to Order Sales Orders, Final Assembly orders can also be created automatically (see Chapter 19 for a discussion of the Assemble to Order process).

Using the Planner Workbench with Discrete Jobs

In the case of standard discrete jobs, WIP also enables you to create discrete jobs from the Planner Workbench. When the MPS and MRP planning processes are run, planned orders and reschedule suggestions are available through the Planner Workbench. This is part of the Oracle Master Scheduling/MRP application.

In a discrete manufacturing environment, using the Planner Workbench eliminates a lot of the tedious work involved in reviewing reschedule and planned order reports and then making the required changes by individually creating jobs or revising them.

There are two actions that would typically be carried out using the workbench:

- **Implement Planned Orders**—Using this function, you can convert any or all of the planned orders into discrete jobs. The workbench can default the job name and WIP accounting class (if you have selected these to default in your setup). The job start date and the job quantity default to the MPS/MRP recommendation. These can be overwritten if you want. The job status defaults to "unreleased". This can also be changed to "released" or "hold" from the workbench. Oracle uses the WIP Mass Load process to create discrete jobs from your selections on the workbench.
- **Reschedule Scheduled Receipts**—This function enables you to execute reschedule recommendations for your discrete jobs. You can view and reschedule existing discrete jobs based on push-out, pull-in, and cancel recommendations. Again, changes are implemented using the WIP Mass Load process.

SIMULATING A DISCRETE JOB

Simulating a discrete job, as shown in Figure 22.10, enables you to determine which materials, operations, and operation resources are necessary for a specific job. Also, you can simulate a discrete job to analyze any of the following:

- The effects of start and completion date changes.
- Variations in on-hand and available-to-promise component quantities.
- Changing the Bill of Materials or individual components being used.

In Release 11*i*, you now also have the option to create a discrete job directly when you are happy with the simulation.

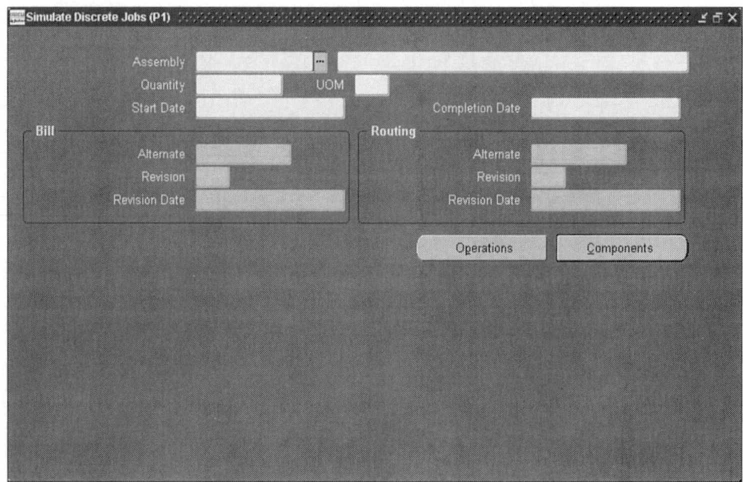

Figure 22.10
You can use this screen to define a discrete job simulation, complete with operations and components.

Updating a Discrete Job

By querying an existing discrete job, WIP enables you to change certain information, depending on the status of the job:

- **Job Name**—If the WIP: Job Name Updateable profile option is set to Yes.
- **Job quantity**—There are no restrictions on changes for unreleased jobs; however, the quantity cannot be changed to less than the quantity that is in process. If the job is linked to a sales order, you cannot change the quantity to less than is on the sales order.
- **Schedule Dates**—You can change the start or completion dates and times.
- **Operations**—These can be added, changed, or deleted.
- **Resources**—These can be added, changed, or deleted.
- **Material Requirements**—These can be added, changed, or deleted.

Managing Repetitive Schedules

This section covers the tasks that are associated with the creation and maintenance of repetitive schedules.

Defining a Production Line

As mentioned in the setup section, you must define production lines if you plan on using repetitive scheduling (see Figure 22.11). You should give some thought to the following pieces of information that are required:

- **Hourly Rates**—A min and max rate should be specified. This information is used in scheduling.
- **Start and Stop Times**—This is used to calculate the availability of the production line. Making the start and stop times the same means that it has 24-hour availability.
- **Lead Time Basis**—This can either be fixed or routing-based. If the line has a fixed lead time basis (all assemblies take the same amount of time to run through the line), you need to specify in hours how long it will take to process the first assembly through the line. If the lead time varies on the line depending on the assembly you are building, you can specify that a routing-based lead time is used. In this case, Oracle uses the assembly routing to calculate the lead time.

Assigning an Assembly to a Production Line

After you have created a production line, shown previously in Figure 22.11, you can associate your repetitive assemblies with it. Various combinations of production lines and repetitive assemblies are possible—for example, one assembly built on multiple lines or many assemblies built on one line.

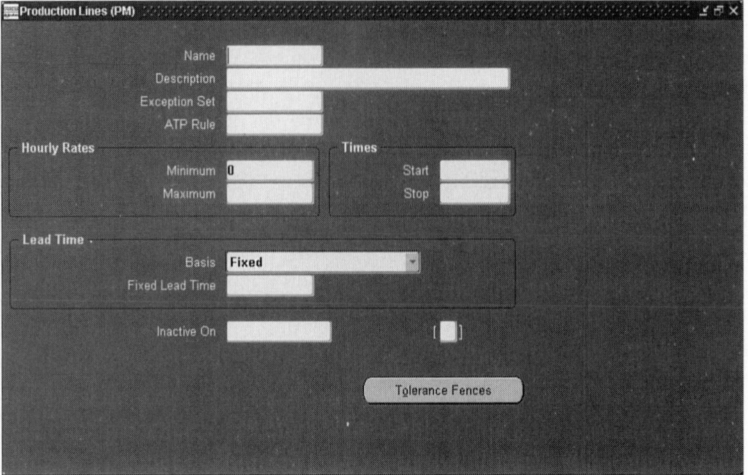

Figure 22.11 Use this screen to define your production lines. Here, you can describe a specific set of operations, departments, and manufacturing cells that produce one or more products.

When assigning a repetitive assembly to a production line, you need to consider the following:

- **Completion Subinventory**—You can assign a completion subinventory to be used for a particular production line and assembly combination. If the assembly has a routing assignment, the completion subinventory defaults from the routing. You need to set a value for this field if you will use Move transactions to complete assemblies.
- **WIP Supply Type**—The value here defaults to Based on Bill but can be overridden. See the section "Processing Material Transactions" for an explanation of supply types.
- **Accounting Class**—This can be defaulted based on the default accounting class associated with the Item (see the setup section "Define WIP Accounting Classes"), or you can assign your own.
- **Line Priority**—You have to set a priority for the production line in each assembly/line combination you create. Master Scheduling/MRP uses this to select the lines for which to create repetitive schedules. It starts with priority 1 and works its way through other line priorities if additional lines are required.
- **Hourly Production Rate**—This defaults to the maximum rate that was defined for the production line when it was created. If you change this value, it must be less than the maximum value that has been set for the line.
- **Lead Time Line**—You can optionally select a line to be used in the calculation of lead time for a repetitive assembly. Oracle Master Scheduling/MRP uses the lead time to plan the repetitive schedules. If you do not select a line and you perform a lead time rollup, no lead time is assigned to your assembly.

Defining a Repetitive Schedule

Repetitive schedules can either be created from planned schedules (using the Planner Workbench) or can be manually defined. You manually define repetitive schedules using the Repetitive Schedules window, as shown in Figure 22.12. Here, you can enter the line and assembly information as well as details of the daily quantity and the start and completion dates. Depending on whether the assembly has a routing or a fixed lead time has been assigned to the production line, WIP calculates the start and completion dates.

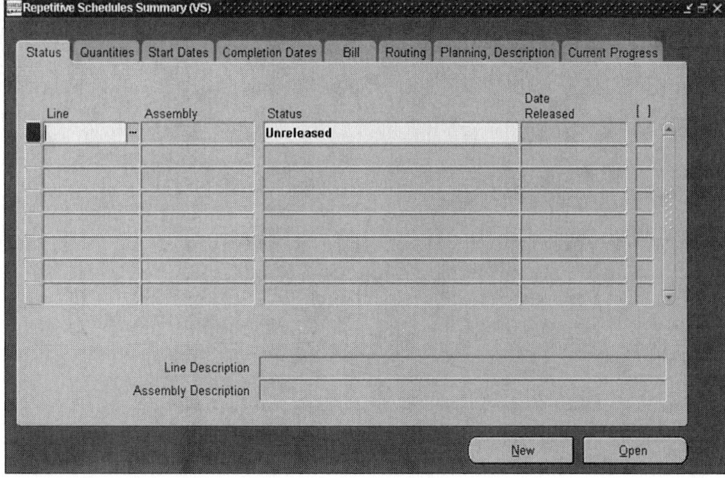

Figure 22.12
Use this screen to define your Repetitive Schedule.

Using the Planner Workbench

As with discrete jobs, the Planner Workbench provides a useful tool to implement your repetitive schedules. The most significant differences are the following:

- Master Scheduling/MRP does not provide reschedule recommendations for repetitive schedules. Instead, it creates new repetitive schedules to match increases in requirements for a repetitive assembly.
- You cannot "firm" a repetitive schedule from the workbench. You have to query the schedule using the Repetitive Schedules window and then firm it from there.
- When you implement repetitive schedules from the Planner Workbench, their status will be set to Pending - Mass Loaded. Before you can start building with these schedules, you must update their status to Released. You can do this in the Repetitive Schedules window, or you can use the Change Status option to update the status for a selected range of schedules.

Updating Repetitive Schedules

Using the Repetitive Schedules window, you can make changes to existing schedules. These changes can include the following:

- Modifying the status of the schedule—for example, from Unreleased to Released for a manually defined schedule.
- Changing the total schedule quantity, daily quantity, or number of processing days.

- Changing the schedule dates. How this works depends on whether the assembly has a routing or the production line has a fixed lead time assigned. Depending on the dates being modified, you might have the option to select the *reschedule point*, which is the date WIP uses as the basis for rescheduling.

Tip

The mass change feature enables you to perform a status update on a range of schedules—for example, from Pending - Mass Loaded to Released.

PRODUCTION RATES AND CAPACITY

The WIP application provides you with a number of ways of permanently or temporarily adjusting repetitive scheduling to cope with capacity issues:

- You can increase the daily quantity on a repetitive schedule to account for overtime or an increase in resources on a line.
- Define an additional schedule to run on another line.
- For more permanent changes, you can change the start and stop times for a line, add more days to the workday calendar, or increase the production rate on a line.

Tip

If you need to protect your repetitive schedules from unrealistic changes in production rates, you can define a planning time fence and set acceptable rate increases and decreases using item attributes (see Chapter 17 for an explanation of Item Attributes).

AUTORELEASE OF A SCHEDULE

As discussed in the setup steps, it is possible to specify a window that WIP will use to look for schedules to release when the current schedule is completed. When this happens, the current schedule status is changed to Complete - No Charges and the next schedule within the autorelease timeframe is released.

If WIP cannot find a schedule within the autorelease timeframe, the current schedule status is changed to Complete, enabling further transactions and charges to occur on the schedule.

BALANCING THE SUBLEDGER TO THE GENERAL LEDGER

Every time a job or schedule is charged, relieved, or closed, WIP creates journal entries. You can choose to post these journal entries at the close of a financial period or post them more frequently (weekly, daily, and so on). Depending on your Inventory setup, these transactions are posted in summary, or the detail of every job or schedule related transaction can be posted (see Chapter 17).

Use the WIP Value Report to report the value of Work In Process inventory for an accounting period. Use the WIP Account Distribution and Inventory Account Distribution reports to reconcile the three reports to the General Ledger.

USING OPEN INTERFACES IN THIS APPLICATION

Oracle provides four open interfaces that can be used with the Work In Process application. These are explained in the *Oracle Manufacturing, Distribution, Sales and Service Open Interface Manual*:

- **Open Job and Schedule Interface**—Enables you to import job and schedule information from a variety of sources. A typical application would be the import of data from an external finite scheduling tool. The interface treats the data entered as planned orders, repetitive schedule suggestions, or update and reschedule recommendations. When data is imported through the interface, Oracle creates discrete jobs, creates repetitive schedules, or updates existing jobs and schedules.
- **Open Move Transaction Interface**—Provides for the import of move, completion, and return data. Typical sources of this data would be external shop floor control systems, test systems, or computer-integrated manufacturing (CIM) systems. When the transactions are imported through this interface, Oracle processes the relevant move, completion, or return transactions.
- **Open Resource Transaction Interface**—Enables the import of resource-related transactions from external systems. This data could be obtained from non-Oracle payroll or attendance recording systems. When data is imported through this interface, Oracle processes the relevant resource and overhead transactions.
- **WIP Scheduling Interface**—Enables detailed scheduling information for discrete jobs to be imported. This interface is designed to be used with third-party finite scheduling tools.
- **Import Scheduling Information (WIPSILDW)**—Another new feature of Oracle Work In Process for Release 11*i*. This enables you to exchange data between Oracle WIP and third-party finite scheduling systems. You can copy schedules from other programs or applications into an interface table and import them into Work In Process.

Note

You must ensure that *all* setup steps are complete before using any of the open interfaces. Oracle validates transactions created through the interfaces against the current system defaults and parameters.

UNDERSTANDING KEY REPORTS

In Release 11*i*, WIP now provides online inquiries from many transaction screens. This eliminates the need to run some reports or jump between windows to verify data. For example, job details can be viewed (material requirements, operations, and resources) when a job is being created.

Table 22.3 provides a summary of the standard reports and concurrent programs provided with the Work In Process application.

TABLE 22.3 ORACLE WORK IN PROCESS REPORTS

Report Name	Description
AutoCreate Final Assembly Orders	Is a concurrent program that is used to automatically create final assembly orders for assemble-to-order items (see Chapter 19).
Close Discrete Jobs	Is a concurrent program that can be scheduled to close jobs based on job number, class, or job status.
Discrete Job Data Report	Provides all job details including quantities, schedule, material requirements, operations, and resources.
Discrete Job Dispatch Report	Lists all jobs to be completed with a status of Released, Complete, and On Hold.
Discrete Job Listing Report	Lists all jobs, regardless of status. Can be run for all jobs with a status of Unreleased to show candidates for release.
Discrete Job Pick List Report	Is used to create a pick list of all components required to supply a job or range of jobs. Requirements are sorted by supply type.
Discrete Job Routing Sheet	Produces a listing of the operations and material requirments for a job or range of jobs. Can be used as a "traveler" to move with the job through the manufacturing process.
Discrete Job Shortage Report	Has two uses: • It shows jobs with open material requirements (parts still to be issued). • It shows jobs with component shortages. Please note that this report only reports shortages based on existing discrete jobs. Planned orders and reschedule recommenda tions from the planning process are not taken into account.
Discrete Job Value Report—Standard Costing	Shows variances and charges for discrete jobs in a standard costing organization. The report is automatically submitted when you close standard discrete jobs.
Discrete Job Packet	This report provides a convenient way to request the Discrete Job Pick List, Discrete Job Routing Sheet, and Discrete Job Shortage Report as a set.
Employee Rates Listing	Reports on employees and their hourly rates.
Expense Job Value Report	Shows summarized charge transaction information for expense jobs.
Import Jobs and Schedules	Submits the WIP Mass Load program to load transactions from the Open Job and Schedule Interface (see the section "Using Open Interfaces in this Application").
Job Lot Composition Report	Reports on the lot numbers assigned to components and assemblies on any discrete job.

Table 22.3 Continued

Report Name	Description
Job and Schedule Interface Report	Is submitted when the WIP Mass Load program is run from the Import Jobs and Schedules screen. It produces a listing of jobs created, schedules created, and discrete jobs that were updated by the mass load. Information on failed transactions is included. This report also includes the new Kanban Number field for discrete jobs.
Move Transaction Report	Provides information on move transactions that can optionally include transaction details.
Production Line Report	Shows information on the production lines that have been defined, including the assemblies assigned.
Purge Jobs and Schedules	Is a concurrent program that purges jobs and schedules (see the section "Purge Jobs and Schedules").
Purge Report	Reports the results of a discrete job and/or repetitive schedule purge.
Repetitive Line Report	Shows the repetitive schedules that are assigned to a line or group of lines. Effective and pending schedules can be reported.
Repetitive Pick List Report	Similar to the Discrete Job Pick List Report. Reports on the component requirements for a schedule or range of schedules.
Repetitive Routing Sheet	Shows the operations, material requirements, and resources for schedules.
Repetitive Schedule Data Report	Lists complete information for repetitive schedules including schedule dates, quantities, material requirements, operations, and so on.
Repetitive Schedule Shortage Report	As with the equivalent report for discrete jobs, this lists either open material requirements or shortages based on available material.
Repetitive Shop Packet	Runs a group of four reports: • Repetitive Pick List Report • Repetitive Routing Sheet • Repetitive Schedule Shortage Report • Repetitive Line Report
Repetitive Value Report	Reports a summary of the charge transactions associated with a schedule or group of schedules.
Resource Performance Report	Shows resource efficiency by department.
Resource Transaction Report	Reports resource transactions for discrete jobs and schedules.
Shop Floor Statuses Report	Shows the detail of shop floor statuses that you have created.
Schedule Group Listing	Provides information on any schedule groups that have been defined.
WIP Account Distribution Report	Provides detailed account information for WIP cost transactions that are not material-related. There is a similar report in Oracle Inventory to provide information on the material cost transactions.

Table 22.3 Continued

Report Name	Description
WIP Account Summary Report	Provides summary information on any WIP cost transactions. As with the previous report, this excludes material cost transactions that can be reported using an Oracle Inventory report.
WIP Accounting Classes Report	Reports on the WIP accounting classes that have been defined.
WIP Location Report	For jobs and schedules with associated routings, this report shows the location of the assemblies by operation.
WIP Offsetting Account Report	Lists WIP cost transaction detail by offsetting account.
WIP Outside Processing Report	Reports information for jobs and schedules that have outside processing resources.
WIP Parameters Report	Shows all WIP parameters with their values. This is useful in verifying the setup of Work In Process.
WIP Value Report	Reports in detail on the value of WIP inventory for a specified financial period.
*New Reports Added to Release 11*i	
Performance to MPS	Displays scheduled versus actual production aggregated across the enterprise for given date range.
Production Efficiency	Displays efficiency of resources for a given date range.
Production Per Employee	Displays production value per employee.
Product Quality	Displays yield percent and scrap percent for a given date range.
Scrap by Reason	Displays pie graph of scrapped quantity and reason codes by organization.
WIP Inventory Trend	Displays line graph of the value for work in progress by organization.

Troubleshooting

- Engineering Change Orders (ECOs) can have an impact on your jobs and schedules. By default, ECOs which have a status of Release, Schedule, or Implement, will update discrete jobs with a status of Unreleased. Repetitive schedules that have a status of Unreleased, Released, or On Hold will also be updated by these ECOs. You can optionally choose to have ECOs with a status of Open, update your jobs and schedules (by changing the profile option WIP: Exclude Open ECOs to No).
- If there is a significant level of ECO activity in your organization, you should be cautious about releasing large numbers of jobs and schedules with future dates.

- Some organizations find the planner workbench to be of limited use in its current form. Oracle plans to make this a more intuitive tool in future releases of the applications. In the meantime, your users may choose to use the Planned Order Report and Order Reschedule Report within the MRP application to manage Discrete Jobs or to supplement the workbench.
- Many users find the shortage reporting capabilities of the Work In Process application to be limited. While the reports within the WIP application will take account of actual jobs and schedules, they do not account for planned activity. You should consider using Planning Exception sets and the Shortage Exception to provide better visibility of requirements arising from actual and planned activity. Planning Exception Sets are discussed in Chapter 21.

CHAPTER 23

IMPLEMENTING ORACLE HUMAN RESOURCES AND ORACLE PAYROLL

In this chapter

If you are reading this chapter, you have likely decided to take on the challenge of implementing a new Human Resources Management System. This chapter presents an overview of issues to consider for such an implementation. Common issues affecting both HR and Payroll are addressed. Finally, a description of many of the steps required for configuration of the Oracle HR/Payroll application is included. There are separate chapters regarding implementation of HR or Payroll (Chapter 24, "Using Oracle Human Resources," and Chapter 25, "Using Oracle Payroll") relating specifically to each module independently. Notes on Oracle Time Management are included with the Payroll chapter. Additionally, related HRMS information appears in Chapter 26, "Using Oracle Advanced Benefits."

Another important note to consider when reading this chapter involves Human Resources and Payroll systems in general. Many of the issues addressed are not unique to Oracle and should certainly be considered for other HRMS package software such as SAP and PeopleSoft. For instance, consider the following:

- Human Resources departments are loaded with government legislative and compliance reporting. Setup of an HRMS application directly affects the structure and content of data produced by these reports.
- Payroll departments are required to transmit benefit files to and from third-party benefit administrators. These must be created based on the specific requirements of each administrator.
- Historical data conversion and various approaches to conversion of HR/Payroll data have many common issues when dealing with packaged software.
- Payroll systems that go live mid-year must have some mechanism for converting month to date, quarter to date and year to date balances. Many employers must also consider the conversion of fiscal month, quarter, and year to date balances.
- Integration testing and parallel testing requirements are certainly not unique requirements to Oracle.

Critical HRMS Implementation Factors

This section addresses a number of critical implementation factors that should be addressed when implementing an Oracle HR/Payroll system. If you have already implemented Oracle Financials, some of these HR/Payroll issues will be common. However, beware. Human Resources and Payroll systems are quite different from Financial systems. Your success implementing a Financial system might not translate into a successful HR/Payroll implementation.

The Initial Phase

A detailed requirements analysis must be performed along with a high-level gaps analysis. This must occur early in the project to obtain good estimates of the expected project duration. This issue is closely tied to the next critical implementation factor of resources in that at least one experienced Oracle HR/Payroll resource should be involved. A solid project plan that identifies expected workload and assigns client resources to as many of the tasks that are reasonable should result from the requirements and gaps analysis. If this analysis is neglected, unpleasant surprises almost certainly will arise later in the project. The time to implement an HR/Payroll implementation (regardless of whether it is Oracle, SAP, or PeopleSoft) is often underestimated by a client.

Resources

It is important to have a mix of functional and technical Oracle consultants as well as functional and technical personnel from the client. There is no perfect number of consultants. The scope of the project, number of employees, complexity of the client's business, time allotted before go-live date, and knowledge base of the users all factor into how many project-dedicated personnel are required.

Interaction between technical and functional project team members is necessary for project success. Although it might be important to have separate technical and functional teams, there should not be a permanent dividing line between these teams. Having good communication and cooperation between the technical and the functional personnel increases the chances of having a successful project and producing good results for the client.

Functional Consultants

The Oracle HRMS product is very flexible and highly configurable. Because of the greater the flexibility of a product, the greater the number of decisions that must be made during the project. It is recommended that functional consultants in both Human Resources and Payroll be used, although this expertise might be achieved with one person. At least one consultant should have experience with the Oracle HR/Payroll products themselves. Again, this product is highly configurable. Experience with Human Resources and Payroll systems in general is not sufficient. The user community might have to live with setup decisions for years to come. The number of decision points is high. The cost of wrong or less-than-optimal decisions is high.

Technical Consultants

The Oracle HRMS database is somewhat complex. Two mistakes commonly made on projects are (1) assuming that experienced Oracle Financials technical consultants will easily translate into effective Oracle HR/Payroll technical consultants, and (2) assuming that the client IT staff can handle these tasks without outside assistance. These issues are not about aptitude or potential. The issue is about experience.

An Oracle Financials consultant can be trained on Oracle HR/Payroll and certainly become effective. The mistake is to assume that the learning curve for the Oracle HR/Payroll database is the same as that of Oracle General Ledger. The result of this mistake is to significantly increase project duration, resulting in higher project costs possibly causing important deadlines to be missed.

The client IT staff must be represented and participate on the project. However, be careful not to assume that this staff will quickly master the Oracle HR/Payroll database. They will rely heavily on the experience of technical Oracle HR/Payroll consultants. If the learning curve for an experienced Oracle Financials consultant (who might already know the Oracle Tools of Forms and Reports) is high, the learning curve for an IT staff not previously exposed to Oracle will be higher.

It truly is a matter of spending the time and money to bring in experienced resources to help do the job right. The alternative is the increased price for bad, hastily made, or incomplete decisions.

Finally, the emphasis here has been on bringing in experienced functional and technical leadership. However, this leadership should not work in a vacuum. The user must be able to maintain the system after it goes live. Thus, it is imperative that clients have full-time functional and technical staff to work on the project. This staff must become the experts so that dependence on consultants is not necessary for a long-term basis after the new systems go into production.

Executive Sponsorship

A vital component of the HR/Payroll implementation is the involvement and support of upper management. It is important for the team personnel to be able to rely on the support of management. The management team must be available to answer questions, make decisions, and communicate to other client management on the progress and impediments of the project.

This can be vitally important when the user community has used the same HR/Payroll systems for many years. Old habits die hard, and some users might refuse to assume tasks that they consider to not be their jobs. The new Oracle HRMS system brings much opportunity but also introduces potential frustrations as employees' roles might need to change. Upper management must remain involved to make decisions that affect employees' future responsibilities.

Part of this support by management is financial. Management needs to stay informed on where the project stands in relation to project timelines and allotted budget. The best consultants can resolve almost any business requirement. However, time and money add up. Management must be prepared to step in and make decisions and change business requirements or identify requirements of lower priority that can be solved in a future phase of implementation.

Documentation

The user should keep thorough, accurate, and complete documents of processes, procedures, and decisions made during the project. If done correctly, this documentation can lead to enhancements and further refinement by client personnel (not consultants) after the project has completed and the new HR/Payroll system is live. Training manuals should be developed and constantly updated as testing is performed and changes are made to the system. Documents should be developed for the following categories:

User documentation

Solution design

Technical specifications

Training

It can be frustrating and frightening for a user to need to make changes to the system without sufficient documentation. The user might not fully understand why the system was set up in its current state. Thus, project documentation can provide not only the understanding of why the system was set up in the way that it was, but also what steps were necessary to provide the solution.

Documentation must be clear, concise, and accurate. It should be reviewed by the client during the project implementation. Proper documentation provides the road map to make new system decisions. Sticky notes posted on a wall do not stand the test of time.

PARALLEL TESTING

After rigorous system testing has occurred, parallel testing should occur on Oracle Payroll implementations. First, I'll define parallel testing. *Parallel testing* involves duplicating operations between the legacy system and the Oracle Payroll system. However, duplicate operations do not imply duplicate results. Duplicate results are certainly the goal. The parallel test is necessary to identify test results that do not match the results produced by the legacy system. Also, the parallel test is necessary to provide hands-on training for the actual users who will operate the eventual production system.

If sufficient payroll testing or conference room pilot testing has already occurred, parallel testing would not be necessary. This is true, but the key word is sufficient. Some items can slip through rigorous payroll testing.

For example, a data conversion for tax information might have been tested for many employees. However, you will never really know whether the correct federal, state, and local taxes are being withheld until every employee has been tested. Various states have reciprocity laws for employees who work in one state but live in another. Because of these many combinations, parallel testing ensures that every combination has been met. Moreover, the tax information calculated during the parallel test might not match because Oracle Payroll calculates differently from the legacy system. Usually, the discrepancies are a result of incorrect legacy system calculations. However, nothing should be taken for granted.

The parallel test should be performed primarily by the actual end users who will be operating the future production system. This gives the users hands-on, real-world scenario training to reinforce any user training classes that have been conducted. Certainly, this effort causes a burden on client staff because they are being asked to perform two jobs at once.

Some users simply do not have the manpower to handle data entry in two systems to run a true parallel of the one system and the new Oracle system. A good alternative to this is to use some kind of auditing tool. There are several tools of this kind on the market. The Implementation Team Leader would designate a Test Coordinator for each day that testing is being conducted. Having a Test Coordinator designated by day provides greater flexibility of scheduling, particularly if work is being done on more than a regular eight-hour day and through weekend and holiday time.

The role of the Test Coordinator is to prepare the testing document, hand out assignments to the testing team, assist individual team members with assignments, and log the results of the testing. The Test Coordinator gives problems identified by category to individuals knowledgeable in the area to resolve the problems. After a designated number of problems are found on one issue, no further testing on that function is done until the problem or problems are resolved. This eliminates valuable testing time being wasted on an already known problem. At the end of the testing period, the Test Coordinator documents the results of the test items and presents the findings to the Implementation Team Leader. It is recommended to have Subject Matter Experts from the various areas (Benefits, Compensation, Payroll, and so on) on hand to assist as members of the testing team and to answer questions regarding their areas of expertise. Support from the Technical function and DBAs is crucial.

How long should you parallel test? This answer varies from project to project. As a general rule, consider three full parallel runs over a three-month period. Essentially, you spend the first couple of weeks of each month performing the parallel test and the second couple of weeks of each month resolving problems and issues from the previous parallel test and preparing the system for the next parallel test.

How should you structure and prepare for each parallel test? First, your DBA must establish a clean test database environment. Then, the DBA must prepare this environment to mimic a specific point in time that will correspond to the payroll period to be tested. The pay period to be paralleled does not have to be the current pay period. It can be a period back in time; however, this requires advance planning to ensure that the DBA has the appropriate production system backups and the client has the correct legacy system data backups prior to the desired payroll period dates. This is accomplished differently for different projects.

Some clients might already have a production Oracle system with Financials live. These same clients might have already converted some of their HR data into the Oracle production system prior to the official go-live date for HR/Payroll. In this situation, the DBA should perform a complete backup of code and data from the production system and refresh this information onto the test environment as of a specific point in time. Then, any other data conversions or migrations that are planned for the future HR/Payroll system must be performed. For example, the Oracle production system might already have employees, addresses, and assignments loaded in addition to the existence of other Oracle Application modules. After this information is refreshed into the test environment, other HR/Payroll scripts (or data entry) must occur (for example: Personal Payment Methods, Salary, and Element Entries). If a mid-year conversion is planned, the Balance Initialization routines must be initiated.

The Balance Initialization process should be elaborated on. On the first parallel test, the balance initialization might not provide as much value as it will on the future parallel tests. The first parallel test is likely to have many test results that are inaccurate. One small mistake can affect the results for numerous employees. These mistakes are often a result of user errors. Remember, this is a training exercise for the actual end users and provides an excellent learning experience for users without the risk of error to a real paycheck.

Other mistakes that can affect numerous employees involve data conversions. For example, one data conversion routine for benefits might have *operated* correctly to load employee bonuses; however, the correct operation might have been using an incorrect source data file for bonuses from another pay period. Another example could be a data conversion routine that incorrectly loaded pretax deductions for only one element. This one element causes the taxes and net pay to be incorrect for a large population of employees.

Thus, having correct balances prior to the first parallel test might not have improved the test results significantly. However, the Balance Initialization should seriously be considered by the time of the second parallel test.

After the parallel test has completed and after the project team has corrected programs, procedures, and so on, you are ready for the next parallel test. It might be unlikely that you can reuse the same test environment. Thus, the DBA must again refresh this environment to mimic the specific point in time that will correspond to the payroll period to be tested. As you approach the second and third parallel tests, you might have the opportunity to attempt back-to-back payroll period parallels without a refresh. This has an added advantage by allowing you to test month-to-date balances that are sometimes required in interface programs to third-party administrators.

If you want confidence when the new Oracle HR/Payroll system is ready to go live, you should have it after conducting parallel tests.

Celebrating Successes

An HR/Payroll implementation takes a significant amount of time to complete. The stress level will get high and it is vital to have a cohesive, productively functioning team. The difficulty is that there is only one finish line. The finish line is to successfully go live. However, this might be many months or even more than one year away. The team must recognize accomplishments along the way. There is no magical formula, but there are numerous small and large things that can be done to help the team feel motivated to continue its drive for success.

Common Unrealistic Project Expectations

One of the most common responses observed after a company purchases any new software package is the expectation that the new system will finally do everything it always wanted. It will also do all these tasks faster, simpler, and automatically. One of the hardest tasks a project manager must accomplish is to properly manage these expectations. This section will outline some of the more common surprises that can surface while implementing Oracle HR/Payroll.

HR/Payroll Is Just Another Oracle Application

This is generally the initial reaction of companies who have already implemented Oracle Financials and are preparing to implement HR/Payroll. They expect that the knowledge they have gained from the other applications will automatically transfer to the HR/Payroll modules. They also expect that any external resources they used for implementing the Financial modules will be equally experienced in implementing HR/Payroll.

You will quickly discover that the only areas that remain consistent in HR/Payroll are in constructing Key Flexfields and defining responsibilities and task flows. From there, the module takes on a life of its own. The HR/Payroll module was developed by a completely different development group located in the United Kingdom. Some of their unique terms show up every now and then, such as cheque and spinal points. The underlying HR/Payroll database table structures are very complex. At some implementations, we have developed SQL scripts to retrieve payroll results that required SQL Joins to 22 different tables.

Some companies plan to modify Oracle Payroll's Check Writer to conform to their own payroll check design. This is usually because they have been successful in completing this same task on their AP check form and do not expect any problems. Oracle Accounts Payable provides hooks in their check writing process that enable companies to insert the necessary escape sequences for the MICR coding. These same hooks do not appear in the Payroll Check Writer process. A simple task in AP can become a major modification in Payroll.

As stated before, successful Oracle Financials implementers do not automatically make successful Oracle HR/Payroll implementers. Many projects have missed implementation dates and exceeded budgets because the learning curve for HR/Payroll was grossly underestimated.

Vertex Will Handle All My Taxing Issues

One of the key selling points of Oracle HR/Payroll is its tight integration with Vertex. Vertex refers to the payroll tax engine product produced by Vertex Corporation that is bundled with Oracle Payroll. Indeed, there is minimal setup required to have the proper taxes withheld in a normal payroll run. Vertex automatically recognizes the proper taxes to withhold based on the ZIP code of the employee's primary address and work location. Vertex also recognizes all full and partial reciprocity laws between states when employees work in one state and live in another.

Initially, this is a blessing to many payroll departments because they will no longer have to keep up with all the changing tax laws in all their jurisdictions. Some companies are surprised to discover that their legacy systems were not withholding all the proper taxes from their employees. For employers located in only one state, this occurs at the local and school district levels. For employers located in multiple states, this also occurs at the state level. The initial reaction is to turn the tax off and continue to tax in the same manner as the legacy system. Oracle does provide methods to conform the tax withholding rules to your legacy system. Although Oracle provides the users with this flexibility, you should seriously consider your legal obligations to the jurisdictions in which you do business before making these options part of your implementation strategy.

The next area of frustration with the Vertex integration occurs when a tax has been withheld in error. This generally happens when an employee's primary address or work location was entered incorrectly or late and the problem was not discovered until the employee received his check. Oracle does not provide an easy method to return this amount back to the employee. You must make a balance adjustment to remove the withheld balance, as well as the Subject To tax balance. These adjustments can be complex and might cause problems later during the quarterly and year-end closes. The actual money can be refunded to the employee through another payroll "non-payroll" element, an AP check, or petty cash. If you want to research additional information regarding the creation of these balance adjustment elements, Oracle has published a white paper called "Balance Adjustment Procedures," which can be found on its MetaLink Web site. BOSS Corporation has also written a white paper, "Creating Easy-to-Use Adjustment and Refund Elements," which can be found on its Web site (`www.BOSSCorporation.com`).

No More Manual Wage Attachment Calculations

Oracle HRMS provides an easy setup process to establish involuntary deduction elements for all the different wage attachments. The federal and state laws concerning wage attachments are complex, and Oracle HR/Payroll is designed to support all these laws. Once again, this is a blessing to the payroll department due to the complexity of these laws. Oracle uses a series of tables and fast formulas to determine the amount to be withheld from the employee's payroll. The user can view—and in some cases modify—the tables used to calculate the withholding and fee amounts. It is worthwhile to note that Oracle uses the employee's work location to determine the rules to be used when calculating the withholding and fee amounts.

Note

Although the table for a specific state might support a rule that is different from the Federal Consumer Credit Protection Act, the programs within Oracle are intelligent enough to determine which calculation (state or federal), when applied to the employee's earnings, provides the greater benefit to the employee and will withhold accordingly.

There are many stories where companies complete a parallel run and discover that the child-support and garnishment calculations do not agree. After a detailed and time-consuming investigation, it has been discovered that court orders have been issued in violation of the law for the employee's work state and the judges needed to issue new orders. Oracle (out of the box) does not support the legislative requirements for withholding of state and local tax levies; however, this can be accomplished with the proper setup of the individual state and local tax levy elements.

Because of the ever-changing tax laws, there are many associated patches for wage attachments. As you go through your testing phase, do not assume that the Oracle calculation is always correct. You might need to contact Oracle Worldwide Support to discover that a missing patch is causing the calculations to be incorrect.

UPDATING THE FIT TAXABLE BALANCE IS STRAIGHTFORWARD

One of the first tasks in preparing an implementation plan is to decide on a target implementation date. The easiest date to begin any new payroll system is the first paycheck of a new calendar year. All year-to-date totals start at zero on January 1, and there is no need to load balances from your legacy system. However, this is generally the busiest time of the year for a payroll department. Also, many companies want to phase different locations into the new system throughout the year. For many reasons, some companies have to transfer payroll balances from the legacy payroll system into Oracle Payroll.

Many companies assume that this will be a straightforward and simple task. They quickly discover, however, that their legacy tax balances do not map easily to the many components of the tax balances in Oracle. The FIT Taxable balance within Oracle Payroll is a good example of this challenge. To calculate the FIT Taxable balance, you must load in the following balances:

- Gross Earnings
- Supplemental Earnings for FIT
- Supplemental Earnings for NWFIT
- Def Comp 401K
- Section 125

Clearly, there is not a one-to-one correlation between the balances in the legacy system and in Oracle Payroll. Do not underestimate the time it will take to prepare the numbers that Oracle requires for a balance load. I recommend that you simulate a quarterly and year-end close during your testing of the balance loads. Many mistakes that are made during the balance load do not surface until you attempt to create the necessary quarterly and year-end files and reports. Corrections to these balances can be complicated and time consuming.

WHEN WE ARE ON ORACLE, PAYROLL SHOULD RUN MUCH MORE QUICKLY

This is a very delicate issue and there are no universal answers or predictions on how long a payroll will run in Oracle. One of the most powerful features of Oracle Payroll is that balances are not explicitly stored. Whenever a balance is referenced, Oracle dynamically calculates the balance by adding up all payroll run results for the requested period. This enables you to query on a year-to-date based on any date in the past through the power of DateTracking. Although this is a powerful feature not found in many payroll systems, it can have a negative effect on the processing times.

Because the early implementers of Oracle Payroll were unsatisfied about the processing times, Oracle instituted a process of storing the latest balances in tables to improve performance. This has improved processing times, but other performance-tuning might be necessary. One of the reasons I previously stressed the importance of performing complete parallel runs is to discover whether there will be any performance issues.

Some performance tips to try if you experience unsatisfactory run-times include the following:

- **Summarize timecards**—Instead of processing five timecards at 8 hours each, summarize this to one timecard of 40 hours.
- **Experiment with the THREADS parameter of the PAY_PROCESSING_PARAMETERS table**—The general rule of thumb is two threads per CPU.
- **Any balances that are referenced in a FastFormula are updated in the latest balances table**—If you suspect that your processing times are spent calculating a particular balance, place a reference to this balance in a FastFormula that will execute for every employee.

These are just a few of the more common techniques for improving performance. You might need to work closely with your DBA and IT staff for any hardware performance solutions.

When Oracle Is Implemented, We Will Not Have to Rely on IT Support Anymore

This comment comes from both the user and IT departments. Most legacy systems require heavy IT involvement to keep the system in compliance with tax laws. There is usually a backlog of enhancement requests from Payroll and Human Resources as well. Many companies elect to purchase these systems to lessen the burden on in-house resources.

During the marketing phase, Oracle stresses the flexibility of FastFormulas and the availability of easy-to-use reporting tools. Unfortunately, this is often interpreted to mean that an end user will be able to write her own reports or modify a FastFormula. Granted, the tools being referenced are very easy to use. The problem centers on the complex structure of the Oracle HR/Payroll table design and detailed programming logic incorporated in the FastFormulas.

As mentioned previously, a simple SQL query to retrieve a list of all employees with a United Way deduction might result in a complicated table join. At some implementations, we have observed complex Oracle Payroll joins through SQL requiring access to 22 tables. DateTracking also complicates simple queries because there can be multiple records in a table for the same employee. Clearly, preparing reports from payroll results requires some extremely intense knowledge of table structures and SQL coding techniques.

The entire gross to net calculation in Oracle Payroll is accomplished with the use of FastFormulas. One of the strongest assets of Oracle Payroll is that you can control this process by modifying or writing your own FastFormulas. However, one look at an existing formula reveals that the everyday end user lacks the necessary skills needed to properly change a calculation.

IT involvement during the implementation process is essential to the success of the project. This is especially important if you are using external consultants. IT must be able to step in and support the system when it is time to let the consultants go. It is unwise to allow all of the knowledge gained from implementing your system to leave with the consultants when they walk out your door.

These are some of the recurring issues when implementing Oracle HR/Payroll. This section is not intended to scare you. Its purpose is to keep you from making some of the more common incorrect assumptions while you implement your system. Careful planning and constant testing yield a powerful and important tool in achieving the goals stated in your enterprise's mission statement.

HISTORICAL DATA CONVERSION APPROACHES

Conversion of legacy data is a major step in nearly all system implementation projects. With HR/Payroll systems, core employee data must be transferred from the current system to the new one. There are a few acceptable methods of accomplishing this with Oracle's HRMS. These will be outlined in the following sections along with advantages and disadvantages of each. Caution: Notice that none of the options in this overview suggests writing programs to load data directly into the application database tables. This is because the table structure and table interdependencies are quite complex due to a high level of normalization. Many tables can be impacted with the entry of a single record type. Using the application screens and/or available APIs guarantees that all appropriate tables are updated in the proper manner. Furthermore, direct table loading might void your Oracle Support agreement.

MANUAL ENTRY

With this approach, users actually key the data into the application windows. This is a very non-technical method, but for some implementations, it might be the most preferred. If the current system contains a smaller, manageable number of records and technical resources are low or unavailable, manual data entry might be the way to go. Additionally, if a large user community were available for the task, it might take less time than you might expect, and it would be a great training exercise for those involved. Sometimes large record volumes in major implementation projects make this option unacceptable. Fortunately, there are other options.

SCREEN LOADER

A Visual Basic for Applications (VBA) script can be run to transfer data from a Microsoft Excel spreadsheet to GUI forms. This is an acceptable option if the conversion volumes are too large for actual manual entry and the user would prefer a semi-automated approach. It works by selecting certain data from the legacy system and importing it to an Excel spreadsheet. It can then be formatted in proper entry order with the required control commands and automatically written to the Oracle forms via the VBA script. The script includes looping logic to keep the process going until all data has been loaded. Think of this as robotic data entry. You can even watch the entry process on the PC screen as if a user were actually typing the information. The setup of the format can be tricky because you must consider all system responses and handle them in the controls. Field order and cursor movement must match the form exactly. Another caution is the load speed, which can be controlled. The PC can run the load script faster than the Oracle Application can respond in some cases, causing error conditions when fields get overwritten accidentally. Also, large volumes of records loaded in this fashion can tend to use a lot of PC memory resources, occasionally causing system lockups. It is best to run the loads in batches. For very large implementations, this option might not be the best. There are still two remaining methods for dealing with large volumes of data.

ORACLE APIs

Oracle provides callable Application Program Interfaces (APIs) that can be used to load the legacy data properly. An API is a stored PL/SQL Program/Package that resides in the database. This method works by developing PL/SQL scripts that call the appropriate APIs. In this script, additional business rules and validation can be written into premanipulate data prior to the API usage. Exception handling can be tailored to provide reporting on the progress and issues in the load. The appropriate data from the legacy system is selected and loaded to a temporary table that will be processed by a program that calls the APIs using data from the temporary table. The API handles loading the data into the appropriate database tables in the same way the data would be loaded if it were entered manually through the Oracle HRMS GUI forms. The APIs deal with much the same data as the forms, meaning that the data is grouped and loaded as if by form type (People, Assignment, and so on). This method is ideal for large numbers of records, but it requires technical resources with PL/SQL programming skills. Great care must be taken in testing the results of the load in a non-production environment because the records loaded cannot be rolled back or undone. Updating for corrections is possible, however. Additionally, you must also know the internal code designations for items that are loaded. Simply loading the user-readable value is not acceptable. The final method provides the added benefit of rolling back an unsatisfactory load.

DATA PUMP

This method uses the same APIs that you can call directly, but it requires less technical knowledge to operate. PL/SQL programs are provided (generated by running a process called the Meta Mapper) that will load data into the Data Pump tables. (You must still populate temporary tables with legacy data as a starting point.) When the Data Pump tables have been populated, you can then run the Data Pump to load the data into the application database tables. There are a number of advantages to using the Data Pump. First of all, it permits running in validation mode so that you can check for errors before actually running the load. If you discover errors after an actual load, you can rerun the Data Pump to correct the errors. The Data Pump process takes advantage of multithread environments, meaning that if you specified a multithread option for payroll processes, the Data Pump engine processes in the same manner. This means the Data Pump load process could potentially run many times faster than the normal API process. Another nice feature is the ability to load user values instead of internal code values. Data Pump handles the translation of the value to the code internally. The Data Pump process is submitted through Submit Reports & Processes like many other normal processes, so it is simpler to use for less technical individuals.

As you can see, there are a number of options available for loading legacy data into the Oracle HRMS. Each implementation project has its own unique parameters and constraints. These should be considered when making the decision on how to load legacy data. No single method is right for every implementation, but enough options exist to provide for a choice of the one that is the best fit.

OTHER DATA CONVERSION CONSIDERATIONS

Now that you have an understanding of the approaches to Oracle HRMS data conversion, there are other issues to consider. This section focuses on issues regarding the types of data that you need to migrate into the new system.

FINDING ORACLE'S APPLICATION PROGRAM INTERFACES

APIs were introduced earlier. If you consider using APIs for data conversion, you will want to obtain a list of the APIs available within Oracle HR/Payroll. The name and type of the API and the PL/SQL code are stored in Oracle tables. By querying the tables, you can easily get the name, code, or type of an API.

Following are the relevant Oracle tables:

- USER_SOURCE—All Database Objects created for the users
- DBA_SOURCE—All Database Objects created for the DBA
- ALL_SOURCE—All Database Objects

Table 24.1 shows the table structure.

TABLE 24.1 TABLE STRUCTURE

Table Name	Column Name	Data Type	Description
USER_SOURCE	Name	Varchar2 (30)	Name of the API
	Type*	Varchar2 (12)	Type (procedure/package)
	Line	Number	Line Number (Each line of the PL/SQL code is stored as one record.)
	Text	Varchar2 (4000)	PL/SQL code
DBA_SOURCE	Owner	Varchar2 (30)	Owner name
	Name	Varchar2 (30)	Name of the API

Table 24.1 Continued

Table Name	Column Name	Data Type	Description
	Type*	Varchar2 (12)	Type (procedure/package)
	Line	Number	Line number (Each line of the PL/SQL code is stored as one record.)
	Text	Varchar2 (4000)	PL/SQL code
ALL_SOURCE	Owner	Varchar2 (30)	Owner name
	Name	Varchar2 (30)	Name of the API
	Type*	Varchar2 (12)	Type (procedure/package)
	Line	Number	Line number (Each line of the PL/SQL code is stored as one record.)
	Text	Varchar2 (4000)	PL/SQL code

* *Packages are stored as* PACKAGE *and* PACKAGE BODY, *where* PACKAGE *is the specification of the program and* PACKAGE BODY *is the actual program.*

To identify the Oracle HR APIs, perform the following. In SQL*Plus, connect to the Oracle database as the APPS user and then issue the following query to find out the name of an API:

```
Select distinct NAME
From USER_SOURCE
Where NAME like 'HR_%'     (identifies packages starting with
HR_)
And Type = 'PACKAGE';      (This is optional; use either
'PACKAGE BODY'OR 'PACKAGE')
```

After performing the previous query, you should be able to identify the name of all APIs. Next, you will want to find out detailed information about specific APIs that can potentially be used by your data conversion team. You can use the following query to obtain a copy of the PL/SQL source code for any desired API. This query produces an output file named api.txt that contains a description of the API and corresponding comments retrieved from the API. This output file can be viewed in any text editor. The following is the PL/SQL code to produce this file:

```
SQL> Spool api.txt
SQL> Select TEXT
    from USER_SOURCE
    Where NAME = '{Name of the API}';
SQL> Spool off;
```

Note

You can change the way you find an API name from the database. Here, we are talking about retrieving a distinct name from the database. Although it doesn't take much time (thanks to higher server sizing and configuration), it is an overhead to the database. Instead, you can get the name of all the APIs from the database by using the following SQL:

```
SQL> Select OBJECT_NAME
     From    ALL_OBJECTS
     Where OBJECT_NAME like 'HR%'
     And    OBJECT_TYPE = 'PACKAGE';
```

The following is another SQL statement that is useful for retrieving the PL/SQL code from the database based on API names achieved in the previous statement. The query processes quickly because you have identified an exact API name without using the `LIKE` statement.

Consider this API-related tip when interacting with Oracle Worldwide Support on TARs. At times, the API version is required to help the Oracle Support personnel. The following SQL statement obtains the version of the `HR POSITION` API:

```
SQL> Select TEXT
     From    USER_SOURCE
     Where NAME = 'HR_POSITION_API'
     And    line = 2;
```

Oracle 11*i* HRMS API Conversion

The following information will help technical project team members during data migration and conversion. This information should help you understand the 11*i* Application Program Interfaces available within the Oracle HRMS product suite.

Assumptions:

- The term *globally* refers to the ability to use Oracle's application program interfaces (APIs) for multiple countries in version 11*i*. Depending on the API, a procedure within the API can be used for any country (WW) or have a specific procedure for that country. A localized country API contains validation rules specific to that country. Review the API's procedure headers within the package before using it to ensure the correct validation is being applied.
- An API can have multiple purposes. Therefore, one or many calls to an API might be required, depending on the processing need. A process could appear at different steps in the conversion. For this document, showing multiple calls of an API will be reflected only when it is used in another step. Within a step, the API could be called more than once for different procedures contained in that API.

- The API steps shown here are a sample but are not inclusive of all possible HRMS conversion steps. Business requirements will determine API use beyond the steps shown here. For 11*i*, more than 600 APIs are available, and around half are available for Benefit Administration.
- In the following sample API processing descriptions, Creating Employer Data APIs, API 1 or 2, or both, must be performed.
- In the Creating Employee Data API, the APIs are in the order used to create an employee. Address precedes Assignment for Payroll/Tax purposes. An exception occurs if the APIs are not done in this order.
- Optional API calls are dependent on data availability and business decisions.

Creating Employer Data:

1. `hr_job_api`—Used globally for creating jobs after the job key flexfield has been set up
2. `hr_position_api`—Used globally for creating jobs after the position key flexfield has been set up
3. `hr_valid_grade_api`—Used globally for combining a job to grades

Creating Employee Data:

- `hr_employee_api`—Used globally for creating the information associated to the People form hire and rehire process (employee number, name, hire/rehire date, and so on). It also initializes other tables with a predefined default record (such as assignment, employee address, and so on).
- `hr_person_address_api`—Used globally for creating and updating address information for an employee, and also contacts later in the conversion. Oracle needs the employee address process completed second due to the relationship with the Payroll and Tax processes.
- `hr_assignment_api`—Used globally for updating the initialized record created in step 1 for employee assignment information generally associated to the Assignment form. This process establishes a connection between the employee and the employer through updating the employee for organizational information (organization, job, position, location, salary basis, GRE, and so on). It also will create a second assignment if required.
- `hr_maintain_proposal_api`—Used globally to create and update the salary process associated with the Salary form. This process performs salary approval, next salary review period, and so on.

Optional API Calls:

- `hr_ex_employee_api`—Used globally to create termination records in the process of terminating employment. This process is in association with the end employment form and updates information in various other tables for other forms. The person has to be created as an employee prior to running this API, whether through conversion or manual entry.

Note

When using this process, the procedure final_process_emp should be used only when no other processes need to be performed on an employee. This process prevents any other transactions from occurring on an employee, such as payroll, AP expenses, or benefit processing. A final process can be reversed if rehire or other processing needs to occur.

- `hr_contact_api`—Used globally to create, update, or delete "contact" type.
- `hr_sit_api`—Used globally to create and update special information types (SIT).

Conversion Options: What History Should You Migrate to Oracle HRMS?

It is a common desire to convert as much information from your legacy system as possible into the Oracle HRMS system. However, practicality is necessary in addressing this issue. There are restrictions and data validation options with Oracle HRMS that might not have been met by your legacy system. Note that the method of conversion is addressed in the previous section. Following are a few of the types of data that you might want to convert:

- **Conversion of Employees**—This refers to much of the basic information of an employee such as Name, Birth Date, Date of Hire, and so on. This is usually a good candidate for data conversion. I generally recommend that you convert only the most recent demographic information as opposed to the entire history. For instance, if a female employee has been married over the past few years, you should only concern yourself with her current last name. Otherwise, you will encounter date-tracking complications in converting the history of every date and name change that has occurred for this employee.
- **Conversion of Addresses**—This is another good candidate for conversion; however, the conversion process is more involved than most people expect. Oracle Payroll requires an accurate county and ZIP code for each employee. This is required due to the impact an employee's residence has on Payroll taxation. Many legacy systems do not retain County information. Thus, your conversion must first derive the correct county for each employee. When more than one valid county exists for a given city, state, and ZIP code, you must contact your employees to determine the correct county. This is not a concern if you are not installing Oracle Payroll or using the Vertex tables.
- **Conversion of Assignments**—This is a typical goal but one you must repeatedly review based on the various components of the employee assignment (organization, position, grade, and so on). For instance, many companies desire to convert job history into the Oracle HR assignment records. However, during your Oracle HRMS system design and configuration, you might have reengineered your job-naming strategy. Thus, there might not be a one-to-one correlation between old job names and new job names. Moreover, if old job titles became obsolete but you still wanted to convert this job history information, you would first need to create the obsolete job title as a valid selection in Oracle before converting the jobs and subsequently end-dating the obsolete job names.

  This same logic holds true for conversion of organizations. Due to buyouts, consolidation, restructuring, and so on, organization history might be difficult to convert. You would need to create all obsolete organizations before the conversion could succeed.

Thus, a more practical approach might be necessary. Consider converting assignment *history* into Special Information Types and converting only the latest information into the employee assignment. If your legacy system only has sufficient information to convert the employee's organization, payroll, and salary basis, prepare to update other information such as jobs and grades manually.

- **Conversion of Salary**—This is usually a good candidate for conversion. Note that you must first convert an employee's assignment with a valid salary basis before attempting conversion of salary. Also, it is common to convert salary history using effective dates of each salary for each employee.
- **Conversion of Tax Information**—Earlier releases of Oracle HRMS did not offer APIs for tax information. This was usually accomplished by screen keystroke emulation described earlier in this chapter. Now that APIs have become available, Tax Information is a good candidate for conversion.
- **Conversion of Earnings and Deductions**—Consider using Batch Element Entry to accommodate this type of conversion, where you focus on one compensation or benefit element at a time. You can create batches by converting your information from the legacy system and then invoking the Oracle HRMS process to convert this information into the Element Entries tables.
- **Year to Date Balance Conversion**—If you bring your new system live in the middle of a calendar year, this process is a must. Please see the section "Year To Date Balance Conversion" in Chapter 25 for details to approaching this process.

UPGRADING TO 11*i*

When upgrading to Release 11*i*, you can expect downtime! Oracle does provide an Upgrade Timing Spreadsheet to assist you in calculating the expected downtime. Refer to the *Oracle Applications Pre-Upgrade Guide*, which provides extensive details for upgrading to 11*i*. Following are a few of the critical issues for your HR and Payroll support team.

Because Oracle view names have changed, and with them many of the database names used in FastFormulas, it is critical that you review your custom formulas and change the names where appropriate.

The way dates are stored in the system has changed from DD-MON-YYYY to YYYY-MM-DD HH24:MI:SS. You should modify all custom processes or FastFormulas that use dates.

Your Paid Time Off (PTO) accrual plans need to be revisited. 11*i* uses FastFormulas to support PTO accruals. This makes PTO accruals much more flexible than in previous releases. Oracle added two new input values to the elements: Entry Effective Date and Expiration Date. Following the upgrade, the Expiration Date uses a default year equal to the Entry Effective Date. If you do not change the Expiration Date, when you run the Carry Over process, your results will be zero.

COMPLETE REINSTALL OF 11*i*

Some existing 10.7 and 11.0.x users have decided to create a new install of the Oracle Applications Release 11*i* and use existing APIs to move their data into this new instance. This strategy was born out of the early frustration of using the upgrade scripts Oracle offered for 11*i* migration. These scripts were taking an exorbitant amount of time to complete, and some organizations could not afford to be down for the time necessary to complete the migration. Therefore, they completely established a new 11*i* instance and rebuilt all their elements and structures using all the new functionality, including benefits. At go-live time, they used the standard APIs and moved existing data into this new instance. This strategy is very similar to the one they might have used when they implemented Oracle for the first time.

Using this strategy implies that you are performing your 11*i* migration and benefits redesign at the same time. You will be redesigning all your benefit plans using the new functionality Oracle brings with Standard and Advanced Benefits. You will also need to map your current employees' benefit elections to this new structure and use the delivered APIs to enroll them at go-live time. See Chapter 26 for additional details.

There are pros and cons for using this strategy. Performing a complete reinstall enables organizations to take advantage of the knowledge they've gained by using Oracle Applications over a number of years. How many times have you said, "I would have done this differently had I known how it really worked?" Now you have the chance to implement Oracle the way you intended back on your initial implementation project. To use a golfing metaphor, you are taking a mulligan on your original Oracle implementation!

This strategy has many drawbacks, though. Bringing over all history transactions using APIs is difficult. And, retaining history through Oracle HRMS DateTrack, is a huge long-term issue for most Oracle HRMS customers. Resources might not allow you to keep two versions of the applications going until you complete your migration. It also might be difficult to link the old solution to the new one when reporting on history transactions. This strategy should be carefully studied before going down this path. Additionally, Oracle's 11*i* migration scripts might become more efficient in the future.

No matter the option you choose, always test, test, and test again!

DATETRACK INFORMATION

DateTrack is an Oracle HRMS feature that enables you to view the system (employee, organizations, benefits, and so on) based on any desired snapshot in time. DateTrack enables you to establish an effective date to either enter information that takes effect on your effective date (which could be a past, present, or future date) and to review HRMS information as of the effective date. DateTracking is Oracle's method of maintaining a continuous history of key information on employees such as salary, assignments, and benefits. This tracking can begin with the date the applicant is first interviewed, continuing with the hire date, tracking all events of the employee's work history, and culminating with the employee's retirement or termination.

DateTracking is one of the most helpful tools Oracle provides for tracking employee information. The DateTrack feature provides a means of knowing when records were changed by using DateTrack History. To access DateTrack History, choose the DateTrack icon from the Windows toolbar. This opens the Summary window with rows that show what employee information was changed and the date. You can use the option of a full history by clicking the Full History button in the DateTrack Window. This gives you a folder menu from which you can select specific information for review. It is also possible to customize this folder to fit individual user needs.

DateTracking is used when making additions, changes, or corrections to data. It is not used on all forms. Forms (such as Grades, Grade Rates, Jobs, People, and Position) opened directly from the Navigator Menu (sometimes referred to as top-level forms) access a common DateTracking date. This date remains in place until changed by the user. Forms opened from these forms (subsidiary forms) such as address, assignment, and element entries, have override ability from the top-level form. This allows different DateTracking dates to apply only while in these subsidiary forms. On returning to the higher-level form, the DateTracked date reverts to the date on the top-level form.

For example, consider a situation where you were viewing Organizations from the Organization form. Assume now that you have changed your effective date to 01-JAN-2002 so that you can view the current organization definitions as of this date. Next, if you navigate to the Person form, your session date remains at 01-JAN-2002. You are not able to view information on an employee who was hired on or after 02-JAN-2002. This is because the employee does not exist as of your effective date. Now, assume that you have navigated to the Element Entries form for an employee. However, you desire to view the employee's element entries as of an earlier date such as 01-NOV-2001. You can change the system effective date to view these element entries. When this form is closed and you return to the Person or Assignment form, the system date changes back to 01-JAN-2002. This is because you changed the effective date while on a subsidiary (or child) form as opposed to changing the effective date on the top-level form (Person, Job, Organization, and so on).

The power of DateTracking can be observed during benefits enrollment time. Use of the DateTrack feature enables you to put in the new rates and coverage before year-end. For example, if the current day of the year is 01-DEC-2001, you can change your effective date to 01-JAN-2002 to allow entry of employee benefit changes scheduled to take place at the beginning of the next calendar year. Entry of these future changes will not affect payroll results from 01-DEC-2001 (assuming your payroll calendar does not have 01-DEC-2001 and 01-JAN-2002 within the same payroll period).

When logging on to Oracle HRMS, the effective date always defaults to today's date. When you have changed the DateTrack date to a past or future date and completed your transaction, you should reset the altered effective date. Not doing so could result in incorrect data for other transactions you enter. The following choices listed should be investigated thoroughly and the action to be changed should be analyzed closely to make the correct decision.

DATE TRACK PROFILE OPTIONS

There are profile options for Date Track that can be configured for your specific implementation. The security options for DateTrack are usually set by the System Administrator, who would have knowledge of the user's level of proficiency.

Tip

As you establish a strategy for the following security options, consider starting with allowing users very limited ability to change DateTracked information; then, as the user becomes more confident and knowledgeable, allow her to control this function by giving her unlimited ability to do so.

Options available from DateTrack security using the user profile option of DateTrack:Date Security include the following:

- **All**—Allows the user to access past, present, and future dates (most typical selection).
- **Past**—Allows the user to only access past dates.
- **Present**—Allows the user to only access current date.
- **Future**—Allows the user to only access future dates.

Reminder options are the following:

- **Always**—Causes pop-up dialog box reminder to the user of the current session date each time a top-level form is invoked from the Oracle HRMS Navigator.
- **Never**—Does not require user acknowledgment of pop-up dialog box reminder for current session date.
- **Not Today**—Causes pop-up dialog box reminder to the user of the current session date, if the current session date is not today, each time a top-level form is invoked from the Oracle HRMS Navigator.

DATE TRACK USER DECISIONS

The user will encounter several types of DateTrack decisions while inserting, updating, and deleting records. Here are some of the situations a user may encounter.

Typical options for deleting records consist of the following:

- **End Date**—The user wants to establish a final date for the existence of the current record without actually deleting the history of the record itself. In essence the user wants to maintain history of the information up until the date of deletion.
- **Purge**—The user wants to totally remove this record from the database without retaining the history of the record.

Deleting options when future records exist are as follows:

- **All**—The user has requested to delete a record even though future dated records exist. The user wants to delete all occurrences of future records.
- **Next**—The user has requested to delete a record even though future dated records exist. The user *only* wants to delete the next occurrence of this record without deleting further future occurrences of the record that exist after the next occurrence.

Typical options for modifying records include the following:

- **Update**—The user wants the new record to add to, not destroy, historical records that exist. The new record becomes the active record as of the current DateTrack session date.
- **Correction**—The user wants the new record to overwrite and destroy the current record that is displayed. (Note that multiple changes within the same day must always be a Correction.)

Modifying records when future records exist are as follows:

- **Insert**—Insert the current record while retaining the future records. This causes the currently inserted record to remain active from the current session date until the date of the next future record.
- **Replace**—Delete future records and replace those records with the current record.

REQUIRED ORACLE HRMS SETUP STEPS

Configuring the Oracle Human Resources, Payroll, and Advanced Benefits modules requires *analysis* of the various setup steps in a different order than is required for actual *configuration* of your production environment. For instance, the first few setup steps involve the creation of Key Flexfields. Until a detailed requirements analysis has occurred, the structures of these Key Flexfields cannot be established. One of the real assets of the Oracle system is its flexibility; this Oracle asset can be one of your biggest headaches if not implemented properly.

It is common to address certain details of this type of requirement analysis in a test database environment. During this phase of the implementation, it is not uncommon to jump between implementation steps. This enables the user to test out the implications of setup decisions. Then, after the user is comfortable with the *requirements* for all setup steps, the actual setup steps can be followed in order in the production database. The following sections contain issues and strategies to consider with certain HRMS implementation steps. Oracle Corporation has documented overall implementation steps in the *Oracle HRMS Implementation Guide*.

DEFINING KEY FLEXFIELDS

Analysis for defining the Key Flexfields within Oracle HR and Payroll requires different timing depending on the Flexfield in question. The analysis for Job, Position, and Grade Key Flexfields typically occurs very early during the project implementation. The Cost Allocation Key Flexfield analysis occurs fairly early (sometime before Compensation and Benefits analysis). Note that the Cost Allocation Key Flexfield must contain the segments required to support the Oracle General Ledger Accounting Key Flexfield but can contain additional segments to support other interfaces or payroll requirements. The People Group and Special Information Type Key Flexfield definition can occur any time within the project. Often, the People Group gets defined as you are defining your element links. People Group is one way to "group" employees eligible for specific elements.

Each Flexfield with Oracle HR/Payroll must be set up via `SYSADMIN` responsibility. For each Key Flexfield, the following steps are required:

- Value Sets must first be created for each Flexfield segment where a predefined set of choices should be made available to the user.
- Value Set Values must be created to establish the specific predefined set of choices available to the user.
- Segments are created for each Flexfield. Generally, Dynamic Inserts should be set to Yes. If a predefined set of choices should be established for a given segment, Value Sets must be attached.
- Cross Validation Rules can be established to control the combination of segment values that a user can enter when selecting the values for all segments.
- Aliases can be established for providing shorthand user selections, which, in turn, imply a combination of values for several segments.
- Freeze and compile the Flexfields after all segments have been defined.
- Database items can be created to allow access of individual segment values as opposed to only having access to the entire Flexfield (combination of all segments).

DEFINING DESCRIPTIVE FLEXFIELDS

Defining Descriptive Flexfields (DFFs) can occur any time within the project. The actual setup steps are similar to those of Key Flexfields. Note that each segment within a Descriptive Flexfield is generally viewed independently of the other segments. This is similar to the People Group Key Flexfield. In essence, a Descriptive Flexfield is generally not interpreted as a combination of values to establish one entity. By contrast, a Job Key Flexfield is interpreted as one job name regardless of the number of segments that were combined to create the job name.

Descriptive Flexfields also have another characteristic that can be both a blessing and a curse. DFFs can be "context" sensitive (that's the blessing); however, if you make them "context" sensitive, you can't use them in FastFormulas (that's the curse). It is important that you evaluate how you want to use this information when you make the decision to make your DFF context sensitive or not.

DEFINING EXTRA INFORMATION TYPES

Extra Information Types (EITs) are extensions to Descriptive Flexfields. They provide the client with a virtually unlimited number of information types. EITs can also be secured. Also, you must set up Responsibility access to your EITs.

ENABLING CURRENCIES

Enabling currencies might be necessary prior to setting up the Business Group organization. With 11*i* multiple currencies can be set up for an individual Business Group. Confirm through the `SYSADMIN` responsibility that the desired currencies have been enabled.

DEFINING USERS

Defining users occurs later in the project when Oracle HRMS Security is implemented. For United States implementations, Oracle is seeded with default responsibilities US HRMS Manager, US HR Manager, and US Payroll Manager. These responsibilities are sufficient during the early phases of an implementation. At the time when salaries and compensation and benefits are loaded into the database and testing has been completed, other security responsibilities should be defined based on job responsibilities.

PUBLIC SYNONYMS AND GRANT PERMISSIONS TO ROLES

The Database Administrator must create public synonyms and run the process Grant Permissions to Roles. This process must be run before running the process Generate Secure Users, which becomes necessary when Security has been implemented later in the project.

DEFINING APPLICATION UTILITIES LOOKUP TABLES

Application Utilities Lookup Tables are set up at various times throughout the project depending on specific user needs. For example, an Application Utilities Lookup Table exists for organization types. This table is not required and can be set up at any time. Many other Application Utilities Lookup Tables are predefined. Application Utilities Lookup Tables can be set up as System, Extensible, or User. Both System and Extensible QuickCodes have seeded values. Both Extensible and User Application Utilities Lookup Tables can have values added by the user.

DEFINING LOCATIONS

Locations within Oracle HR are physical sites with unique mailing addresses. Oracle Payroll uses these locations to establish payroll taxation requirements. When an employee is assigned to work at a specific location, Oracle Payroll uses the address of that location to determine taxation rules and rates.

Consider the situation where a company has several buildings next to each other. If Postal Service mail generally arrives separately at each of these buildings, it is likely that each building will need to be set up as a separate location. Conversely, if the Postal Service generally delivers to one location, only one location will be required within Oracle Payroll.

Keep in mind that other Oracle modules share Locations with HR/Payroll. Thus, it might be necessary to define more locations than are required by Payroll. If the same Oracle Locations are to be used by Oracle Payroll and any other module, these locations should be defined within Oracle HR/Payroll to ensure that the address is set up with the appropriate payroll validation.

DEFINING BUSINESS GROUP ORGANIZATION

A Business Group is a special type of organization. Each Business Group has one government legislation. Thus, to pay employees from more than one country, multiple Business Groups are generally set up. An exception to this approach involves significant customization. Although Oracle Payroll is capable of paying different currencies for employees from other countries, the legislation that drives taxation must be overwritten using FastFormula. The Business Group identifies the specific Key Flexfields that will be used. Also, the Business Group identifies how employee numbering occurs. Employee numbering can be manual entry, automatic system generation, or automatic use of the national identifier.

Oracle HRMS (HR, Payroll, Advanced Benefits) comes delivered with a Setup Business Group. This Business Group can be reused. In this case, the name of the organization must be changed from Setup Business Group to a name corresponding to the company's top organization.

Tip

A word of warning: The name of your Business Group does print on many of your legislative reports, and you do not want "Setup Business Group" printed on these reports. If HR is being implemented after other Oracle modules (such as Financials), it is critical that you inform your system and database administrators that you need to change the name of the "Setup Business Group." When the name changes, so does the underlying Business Group ID within the various Oracle database tables! You will need to make changes to all the modules that point to this ID.

When you navigate to a Business Group organization, you will notice that the Others button has several choices. Work Day defaults can be established for the typical working day within the company. These defaults can be overwritten at lower levels for individual employees. Reporting Categories and Statuses can be enabled for the Business Group. Seeded Reporting Categories include Fulltime - Regular, Fulltime - Temporary, Parttime - Regular, and Parttime - Temporary.

DEFINING VIEW ALL ACCESS TO BUSINESS GROUP

This is a `SYSADMIN` function. Navigate to the System Profile options and select the default responsibility (for example, US HRMS Manager). Ensure that the HR:Business Group option is set to the desired Business Group. By default, this is set to the Setup Business Group. Also, on this window, review the HR:User Type. For the responsibility US HRMS Manager, the HR:User Type should be set to HR with Payroll User. Also, if a Business

Group is being used other than the Setup Business Group, this affects other Oracle modules. Within Accounts Payable, the Business Group must be set up within the Financials System Parameters. If there are no AP vendor employees or buyer employees already entered, modify the table `FINANCIALS_SYSTEM_PARAMETERS.BUSINESS_GROUP_ID`.

Defining Human Resources Organizations

Human Resources Organizations have an organization classification of HR Organization. These are the actual organizations to which employees are assigned. When determining the requirements for defining HR organizations, there are generally these competing agendas:

- General Ledger Costing
- Security and access to the HR/Payroll system
- Management Reporting
- Government Reporting (particularly AAP Reports)
- Other Oracle modules (Projects, Purchasing, and so on)

Most clients take HR organizations as far down as the GL Cost Centers require. For other management reporting, you might need to take the organizations down further. Next, look at security requirements as far as who needs to access information. You might find that you have a satellite office where the HR manager should view or update employees from that site only. The organization hierarchy must be organized to enable this. Government Reporting (AAP, EEO-1, VETS-100, and so on) is the next challenge, particularly with AAP reports. Finally, consider what other Oracle modules share this information and how you can incorporate their requirements within HR.

Defining Government Reporting Entity Organizations

At least one Government Reporting Entity (GRE) organization must be defined. The number of GREs required is based on the number of federal identification numbers within the company. Information that can be entered for a GRE includes the following:

- Employer Identification Number
- Government reporting information for EEO-1, VETS 100, and new hire reporting
- Federal tax rules
- State tax rules
- Local tax rules
- State Quarterly Wage Listings
- W-2 reporting
- Multiple Worksite reporting

Also keep in mind that organizations with multiple GREs can define a Tax Group when necessary for reporting as a Common Paymaster.

DEFINING OTHER ORGANIZATIONS

Oracle HR offers numerous other classifications for organizations that might require additional organization setup. The following organization classifications can be defined:

- Reporting Establishment
- Corporate Headquarters
- AAP Organization
- Benefits Carrier
- Workers Compensation Carrier
- Beneficiary Organization
- Payee Organization

DEFINING BENEFIT CARRIERS

You can establish benefit carriers and associate them with your imputed earnings or pretax or voluntary deductions. The first step is to establish the address of the carrier in the Location window. You then set up the carrier in the Organization window using the location you just established. Make sure you use the classification Benefits Carrier. Navigate to the Element Description window for each of your benefits elements; then, click the Further Information button and select your carrier in the field Benefits Carrier.

DEFINING ORGANIZATION HIERARCHIES

Organization hierarchies are fairly straightforward to implement within Oracle HRMS. You can define one primary hierarchy and as many secondary hierarchies as desired. Because organization hierarchies are date-tracked, you can maintain a history of what your company looked like at any point in time. The main items that influence the structure of your organization hierarchies are the following:

- HRMS security requirements
- Management reporting requirements
- Government reporting requirements

It can be easier to maintain your system if the previously stated goals for organization hierarchies are combined into one hierarchy; however, there is no significant disadvantage to creating multiple hierarchies. Review each of the hierarchical goals first in isolation, and then determine whether there are common goals between different hierarchies that will allow consolidation of multiple hierarchies.

DEFINING JOBS

Jobs are designed to be generic roles an employee can fill at a company. A given job name determines whether employees holding the job title are eligible for paid overtime. The job can be for either exempt employees or nonexempt employees but not both. The FLSA code will establish this status.

When setting up jobs, think carefully about government reporting requirements such as EEO-1, AAP, and VETS-100. Jobs within the United States can be associated with an Equal Employment Opportunity (EEO-1) Category. Oracle Human Resources has 10 seeded EEO-1 Categories that can be selected. Jobs can also be associated with job groups within an Affirmative Action Plan (AAP). The AAP codes are user-definable Quick Codes. Additional items to associate with a job include line of progression (which establishes the relationship from one job group to another) and Salary Code.

Management reporting requirements should also be considered when defining a job. This is often a major influence on the number of Key Flexfield segments that are established for a job. Each job name is a concatenation of each of the Job Key Flexfield segments. For example, if you desire to perform reports on all employees who are accountants regardless of whether they are cost accountants, senior accountants, tax accountants, and so on, the role of Accountant can be established as one segment, and the description or level of accountant (Cost, Senior, Tax, and so on) can be established as a preceding segment.

Although jobs are designed as generic roles within an organization, many organizations define Oracle HR jobs as if they are positions. Positions are discussed later. The reason for this strategy within implementation is because jobs are flexible. Whenever the organization restructures, jobs do not necessarily need to change. Positions must be changed within Oracle HR when the organizations change.

Finally, keep in mind that jobs are shared with other modules, such as Oracle Purchasing. Purchasing must establish its purchasing approvals using either jobs or positions. Thus, the setup of Oracle HR jobs must not be made in isolation by the Human Resources department.

Defining Positions

A position is a distinct job within an organization. Like jobs, each position name is a concatenation of each of the Position Key Flexfield segments. Positions offer more features than jobs within Oracle but also have reduced flexibility.

A key feature of positions is the ability to define a position hierarchy. Another feature of positions involves vacancy management. When vacancies occur at a particular position, they must be filled by another employee with similar skills within the organization. Remember that a position is a specific job within a specific organization. One way to fill the vacancy is to review all other positions that exist for associated jobs. In essence, this is a review of employees in other organizations throughout the company that contain the same job.

Oracle HRMS security can be based on the position hierarchy. Thus, the use of positions adds more functionality than the use of jobs alone. The reverse argument in whether this security functionality is necessary involves whether organizations and the organization hierarchy can sufficiently meet security needs.

Positions are shared with other Oracle modules, such as Purchasing. Purchasing must establish its purchasing approvals using either jobs or positions.

DEFINING POSITION REPORTING HIERARCHIES

If positions have been defined, a position hierarchy almost certainly will be defined. Recall that most of the key reasons for defining positions involve the position hierarchy. In addition to the ability to define HRMS security using the position hierarchy, Oracle Purchasing often uses the same hierarchy to establish lines of approval.

Multiple position hierarchies can be defined, although one hierarchy must be the primary reporting hierarchy. Any position can exist in more than one hierarchy, but a position can appear only once within a given hierarchy. (This is the same case as with organization hierarchies.)

DEFINING CAREER PATHS FOR JOBS AND POSITIONS

A career path maps employee progression within the company from one job or position to another job or position. Note that career paths cannot be mixed between jobs and positions. An employee progresses from one job to another job or one position to another position but not from a job to a position.

When defining career paths based on positions, use the position hierarchy. Remember that multiple hierarchies can be created if multiple career paths are desired.

When defining career paths based on jobs, navigate to the career path window to define career path names. Next, define the jobs that are associated with each career path name. Finally, define lines of progression to show the relationship from one career path name to another. These lines of progression are used by AAP reports.

DEFINING GRADES

Grades are designed to establish relative compensation and benefits analysis among different employees within the company. Like jobs and positions, a Grade Name is the concatenation of each of the segments within the Grade Key Flexfield. Also, grades can be established as being valid for only certain jobs or positions.

DEFINING GRADE RATES

After establishing the Grade Names, you can associate values to each grade. These are called grade rates. The rates can be either a fixed value or a range of values. These grade rates can then be used to validate salary proposals. Oracle HR warns you if you attempt to assign an employee a salary that falls outside the parameters you established in your grade rates. Grade rates are date-tracked, which means you can keep a history of these rates. You can also enter values at a future date without affecting current values. If your organization desires to associate different grade rates to employees based on what region of the country in which they reside, you must set up distinctly different grades for each region. In this case, you could consider setup of your Grade Key Flexfield to have the first few segments the same for each region with a final segment indicating the region as the only difference from one grade name to the next.

Defining Pay Scales

You can also use pay scales to establish values for your grade names. Pay scales are very common when pay levels are negotiated, as with union groups. These scales are a series of grade steps or points with specific values of pay for each step. You have the flexibility to establish different pay scales for different unions or one single set of pay points for all your employees. When established, employees are placed on a step within their grade. Employees move up the steps through an incrementing process. Note that pay scales are not tied to salary administration. For a detailed discussion of pay scales and progression point values, see the topic "Pay Scales and Pay Progression" in Chapter 24.

Defining Progression Point Values

The next step in the process is to assign rates to each of the progression points in the pay scale. Unlike grade rates, you must enter a fixed value for each point. These values are also date-tracked so that you can keep a history and enter future values. The rates are normally defined in monetary units, but they can also be defined as integers, days, or hours. An example of the use of hours would be to define a point value to signify the maximum number of overtime hours that can be worked in a week.

Defining Grade Steps and Points

The final step in the process is to associate a subset of the progression points to each grade. Each point in the grade is considered a step. The steps of pay scales are normally followed in sequence; however, this window allows certain grades to be established where employees can skip the normal steps of a particular pay scale and jump several steps to the next step defined for the grade. Note within Oracle HR the fact that a grade can only be associated with one pay scale. Thus, each unique pay scale identified within your organization will require setup of a unique grade.

Defining Payment Methods

Payment methods define how an employee or third party is paid. There are three types: check, NACHA (direct deposit), and cash (which is rarely used). You can define as many payment methods as needed for each of these types. For example, you might have multiple payroll bank accounts throughout your organization. Each bank account would be set up as a separate payment method. You must select one of these methods as the default method for each of your payrolls.

Defining Consolidation Sets

Some of the post-payroll run processes can utilize consolidation sets, which group similar payrolls together. These processes include NACHA, Check Writer, Costing, and several of the standard payroll reports. This enables you to produce one NACHA file for all the payrolls in a consolidation set. Generally, these payrolls should have similar calendars to facilitate the scheduling of the processes. Consolidation sets are simply a list of payrolls that can be processed together after the payroll gross-to-net calculation has occurred for each payroll.

Defining Payrolls

You must define payrolls to pay your employees in Oracle HR/Payroll. Employees are assigned to payrolls on their assignment window. Payrolls can also be used to group like employees together for reporting purposes. Payrolls can be defined to limit employee eligibility to certain earnings, deductions, and benefit plans. Security definitions can be established based on payrolls to limit access to various windows within the Oracle HRMS product suite for certain groups of users. Normally, you define payrolls to establish different payment frequencies, such as your monthly payroll, your weekly payroll, your biweekly payroll, and so on. During the payroll definition, you must supply the first pay period ending date, day offsets from this date for cutoff, scheduled run and payment dates, and the default payment method. Other items established at payroll definition include the default consolidation set, NACHA bank information, valid payment methods, and costing information. Oracle Payroll then generates a payroll calendar. After the payroll calendar has been generated, the user can modify the calendar to reflect changes for holiday processing.

Defining Earnings

Earning elements are used to represent compensation types such as salary, wages, and bonuses. Several salary elements are generated automatically by Oracle Payroll. They are Regular Salary, Regular Wages, Overtime, Time Entry Wages, Shift Pay, GTL Imputed Income, and Company Car. Oracle's US Payroll provides the users with an earnings template that can be used to generate custom earnings elements. The earnings template generates several of the required objects needed to make an element function correctly within the system. Four classifications can be chosen during the earning definition process. These classifications determine how the element will be used by the system. They are as follows:

Earnings

Supplemental Earnings

Imputed Earnings

Non-Payroll Payments

The Earnings classification generally represents earnings for time worked such as salary and hourly wages. Supplemental Earnings include a variety of special earnings paid to employees, such as bonuses and sick pay. Imputed Earnings are for non-cash compensation such as personal use of a company car and company paid premiums for group term life insurance. Non-Payroll Payments are for payments to the employee that are not subject to tax reporting, such as expense reimbursement.

Each classification is further broken down by categories. These categories determine how the element is to be subjected to tax withholding. You will see references to these categories as "Tax Categories." Oracle provides a wide range of tax categories that cover the majority of taxing requirements for most organizations. However, occasionally you need to create a new tax category. Tax categories can be added via the Application Utilities Lookup Tables (QuickCode tables, if you're using a release prior to 11*i*) types US_EARNINGS, US_IMPUTED_EARNINGS, US_SUPPLEMENTAL_EARNINGS, and US_PAYMENT.

The calculation rule is the link to the creation of the FastFormula that will support the element. Here, the user has the option of Flat Amount, Percentage of Regular Earnings, Hours times Rate, or Hours times Rate multiple.

DEFINING DEDUCTION AND BENEFIT ELEMENTS

Oracle's US Payroll provides the users with a deductions template that can be used to generate custom deduction or benefit elements. Similar to the earnings template, the deductions template generates several of the required objects needed to make the element function correctly within the system, saving the client the need to create each of these objects separately.

Deduction elements fall into three main classifications. They are the following:

Pre-Tax Deductions

Involuntary Deductions

Voluntary Deductions

Pre-Tax Deductions are further defined by category. The categories for Pre-Tax Deductions are Deferred Comp 401k, Deferred Comp 403b, Deferred Comp 457 (403b and 457 categories were added with 11*i*), Health Care 125, and Dependent Care 125. It is very important to use the correct category when establishing your pre-tax deductions. The category determines how your pre-tax deduction will be processed by the various federal, state, and local taxing authorities.

Involuntary Deductions are also further defined by category. Again, the category determines how the deduction will be processed. Involuntary deductions are highly structured and tightly controlled by various federal and state laws. The categories for Involuntary Deductions are Alimony, Child Support, Spousal Support, Bankruptcy, Credit Debt, Garnishment, Educational Loan, Employee Requested, and Tax Levy.

Oracle provides seeded involuntary deductions that can be used if your company employs the services of a third party to support your involuntary withholding.

Voluntary Deductions can also be further defined by categories, but unlike the other two classifications, categories are not required. Voluntary deductions generally capture employee-requested deductions, such as United Way or any post-tax benefit plan elections.

All deductions must have an amount rule to instruct Oracle Payroll on how to calculate the deduction. The rules are as follows:

Flat Amount

% of Earnings

Payroll Table

Benefits Table

The Flat Amount rule is the simplest. The generated element includes an input value called Amount, which gives the formula the deduction amount. The % of Earnings rule includes an input value called Percentage. This value gives the formula the percentage to use. The default formula uses the Regular Earnings balance as the base amount to apply the percentage. The rule Payroll Table enables you to look up the deduction amount in a preestablished payroll table. This table must be defined in the Table Structure window.

The final amount rule for deductions is the Benefits Table used for Oracle Basic Benefits. These tables are based on coverage levels to determine the amounts of employees' and employers' contributions toward a benefit plan. You establish the various coverage levels by updating the Applications Utilities Lookup type US_BENEFIT_COVERAGE. When you have defined your deduction element for the benefit plan, use the Benefits Contributions window to populate the employee and employer contributions. Do not use the Table Structure window to establish the benefits table.

DEFINING EMPLOYER LIABILITY ELEMENTS

Oracle Payroll automatically generates employer liability elements that are used to capture the employer contribution amounts for medical and dental benefit plans. All the employer tax liability elements are also automatically generated through the tight integration with Vertex. You might need to establish some additional employer liability elements for 401k; like employer contributions; or other employer costs associated with required employee safety equipment, tools, and so on. These elements are established using the Element Description window. Create these elements using the classification called Employer Liabilities.

DEFINING INFORMATION ELEMENTS

Oracle HRMS provides an element classification called Information that enables you to hold almost any kind of information items issued to employees such as cellular phones, company cars, laptop computers, or identification badges. Generally, these elements are not processed during a payroll run, but they could be referenced in any FastFormula.

Other uses for Information elements include accumulating hours for absence management and PTO (Paid Time Off) plans. Vertex uses information elements to feed various tax balances that appear in inquiry windows and on reports.

You define Information elements with the Element Description window using the classification called Information. The actual information being stored is defined in the Input Values, which you must also define.

DEFINING BENEFIT PLANS

Oracle 11*i* provides the clients with a comprehensive method of defining all your organization's employee benefits from the basic to the complex. Eligibility, employer contributions, and employee withholdings are rules-based. This is a good time to review your company's policies to ensure accurate reporting and withholding (see Chapter 26).

Defining Taxability Rules for Tax Categories

Oracle Payroll enables you to control the rules that Vertex will use when taxing the various earnings and deductions. The installation process populates these rules for a number of categories of supplemental earnings and imputed earnings. It also completes the rules for three of the pretax deduction categories. You should review these rules for all your taxing authorities including state, county, city, and school district. Vertex uses these rules to drive its tax calculations. You can add your own categories for supplemental earnings, imputed earnings, and pretax deductions to handle any unique tax requirements. This is also the place to maintain rules regarding the inclusion of categories of supplemental and imputed earnings in a state's payroll exposure to Workers Compensation. All these rules are maintained on the Taxability Rules window.

Defining Input Values for Elements

Oracle Payroll automatically creates the necessary Input Values for earnings and deductions based on the calculation and amount rules you select on the Earnings and Deductions definition windows. There are times, however, when you want to maintain some additional information on these elements or you have created your own Information element for a particular purpose. You can create your own input values through the Element Description window. You must add these values before linking and adding the element to any employees. When the element is in use, Oracle Payroll does not enable you to add or change characteristics of input values after an element has been linked or contains balances.

During the definition process of input values, enter a name for the input value and select a unit of measure (money, hours, character, date, number, or time). You can enter a number in the Sequence field to control the order in which the Element Entries window displays the input values. You can also require an entry for the value and/or restrict the values allowed by selecting an Application Utilities Lookup Table to act as a lookup for the input value. FastFormulas can also be used to validate the entries as outlined in the following section.

Defining Validation Formulas

Oracle FastFormulas are powerful tools that can control the actual gross-to-net calculation of a payroll. They can also be used to validate entries into input values during the entry of an element in an employee's Element Entries window. For example, a formula could check an employee's length of service or salary before an amount is allowed to be entered into a bonus earning element. You must write the formula before you define the element and the corresponding input values.

Validation formulas are entered in the Formulas window using the formula type Element Input Validation. You must observe the following rules:

The formula must have one input value called entry_value.

The formula must set and return a local variable called formula_status. It must have the value of s for success or e for error.

The formula can return a text variable called formula_message that contains a text message. It can be used with either an s or e formula_status.

The formula cannot return any other values.

You cannot reference any other input value from another element in the formula.

You cannot return a value to any other input value.

Defining Element Links for Earnings, Deductions, and Benefits

When the element has been defined, input values established, and all validation rules applied, you are now ready to define eligibility and costing. You use the Link window to determine the groups of employees eligible for the element. You must also define a separate link for every costing combination for this element. The Link window can also be used to enter qualifying conditions such as age or length of service. You can also establish defaults, minimums, and maximums for each of your input values at the link level.

Obviously, you can create multiple links for the same element, but Oracle HR/Payroll enforces the rule that an employee cannot be eligible for an element more than once. The following is a list of components you can use to define eligibility:

Payroll

Salary Basis

Employment Category

Organization

Location

Job

Grade

People Group

Position

Defining Taxation and Other Elements

Oracle Payroll comes with all the necessary elements and calculations for tax deductions, tax credits, and employer liabilities already in place through its tight integration with Vertex, Inc. You must establish a separate support agreement with Vertex when you purchase Oracle Payroll. This enables you to receive monthly updates for any tax changes. These elements do require links to establish the costing matrix for your taxes. These links must be in place before you attempt your first pay run.

Oracle also includes several Workers Compensation elements (Workers Compensation, Workers Compensation2 ER, Workers Compensation3 ER, Workers Compensation EE, Workers Compensation2 EE, and Workers Compensation Information) that also require links. These elements are created automatically by the installation process. The Workers Compensation and other WC ER elements store the amount of the employer's liability for each employee's WC premium. The Workers Compensation Information element stores the

Mod 1 Surcharge, Post Exp Mod 2 Surcharge, Post Prem Disc 1 Surcharge, and employee's payroll exposure. The Workers Compensation EE elements store the employee withholding amounts.

You must also define the following tax information at the GRE level:

- Federal-level supplemental withholding calculation method and any common paymaster for the GRE's employee
- Identify whether the state and local taxes will be withheld for all states and localities or only those defined by the client
- Self-adjust methods in use at the federal and state levels
- State-level rates needed for calculation of SUI (state unemployment insurance)
- Identifiers used at the state and local levels

Defining Payroll Balances

Oracle Payroll automatically creates balances for you when you define an earning or deduction. The name of the balance is the same as the name of the element. Oracle also creates all the necessary tax balances needed to support the Vertex integration.

There might be some special balances needed to support unique requirements that are specific to your enterprise. One of the most common user-defined balances is one to store pension eligible earnings. You define this balance through the Balance Window.

The definition process includes three steps. The first step is to uniquely name your balance. You also can supply a reporting name for your balance. This name will be used on reports and the statement of earnings.

The second step involves entering all the balance feeds for this balance. Here, you select one or more individual elements that feed the balance. You can only use those elements whose input values have the same unit of measure as the balance. Normally, this is the run result (Pay Value) of the element.

The final step is to list all the desired dimensions for this balance. Dimensions generally include Assignment Within GRE Year to Date, Assignment Within GRE Month to Date, and so on.

Note that if your company uses fiscal balances for benefits or bonus calculations, the fiscal dimensions must be added to the balances. Oracle does not provide the fiscal dimensions for any balances.

Defining User Tables

You can define your own tables within Oracle Payroll that store information such as wage codes, shift differentials, or any other amounts for your earnings and deductions. These tables are *not* created through SQL, but with the Table Structure window. Oracle FastFormula can access these tables through the `GET_TABLE_VALUE` statement. Do not use the Table Structure window to store rates for your medical and dental benefit plans. Oracle Payroll provides a special table for this purpose. Use the Benefits Contributions window to enter these rates.

After you define your rows and columns of the user table with the Table Structure window, use the Table Value window to enter values into the table.

You can also set up tables to support deductions that were defined with the amount rule Payroll Tables. The formula for the deduction uses a row type to help determine which row of the table to use to retrieve the deduction amount. There are three predefined row types:

Age Range

Salary Range

Job Class

You can set up any additional types you require.

DEFINING PAYROLL FORMULAS

Oracle Payroll automatically creates a formula for every earning and deduction element you define through the Earnings and Deductions windows. Note that elements created from the Element Description window do not automatically create an associated formula. You can modify these formulas through the Write Formulas window. Remember to thoroughly test any changes you made to the generated formula.

Formulas can generate different types of run results. Direct Results normally update the input value Pay Value of the element containing the formula. You can only have one direct result per formula. The formula can also generate many indirect results. These results are passed to input values of other elements that will process further in the pay run. Formula results are covered in the next section.

DEFINING PAYROLL FORMULA RESULTS

As stated in the preceding section, formulas generate formula results. These results are defined in the Formula Results window. The different types of formula results include the following:

- **Direct Results**—Only one per formula, normally passed to the Pay Value input value of the element containing the formula.
- **Indirect Results**—Results that are passed to the input values of nonrecurring elements that will process later in the pay run. The priority number of the element that will receive this indirect result must be higher than the element that is passing the results.
- **Update**—Results that are passed to recurring elements that will process later in the pay run. Like indirect results, the priority number of the receiving element must be higher than the passing element.

- **Message**—Text message that you can pass from the formula to the Payroll Message report. You define on the Formula Results window whether the message is a warning or fatal error.
- **Stop**—The formula can send stops to the calling element or other elements to prevent their processing in the run.

Defining Salary Basis

The salary basis is used to define how the salary is entered, such as hourly, monthly, or annually. For example, you can state an employee's salary in monthly terms but place her in a biweekly payroll. The salary basis does not have to match the pay periods.

Oracle Payroll generally expects you to use the basis of Monthly Salary for the seeded element Regular Salary and the basis of Hourly Salary for the seeded element Regular Wages. However, do not be deceived by the Input Value named Monthly Salary on the Regular Salary element. In actuality, you can associate any Salary Basis with this element. When you observe the element entries for an employee, the amount stored in the Monthly Salary input value might not actually be a monthly amount. However, Oracle has designed the Regular Salary formula to properly interpret this amount based on the employee's assigned salary basis.

Additionally, you can establish your own salary elements and associate any salary basis with them. Make sure you thoroughly test these elements with all your salary administration scenarios.

The salary basis is defined in the Salary Basis window. As stated previously, you associate a salary element with the salary basis. When you enter a salary proposal through the Salary Administration window, Oracle HR automatically updates the appropriate input value of the salary element. If you associate a grade rate with the salary basis, Oracle HR uses the grade rate to validate the salary proposals.

Enabling Salary Approvals

After you have defined your salary basis for each of your salary elements, you need to determine who can enter salary proposals and who can approve them. Salaries for new employees are automatically approved. However, all future salary changes must be approved after they have been entered. You can separate the approval process from the entry process by only adding the approval function to the menu of responsibilities for users who are authorized to perform approvals.

Defining Proposal Reasons and Performance Ratings

Oracle comes seeded with default proposal reasons and performance ratings. You should review the Application Utilities Lookup Tables for `PROPOSAL_REASONS` and `PERFORMANCE_RATING` for completeness. You can add other entries to these types to incorporate you own reasons and ratings.

Oracle HR enables you to break down a salary proposal into multiple components. For example, an employee might receive a raise that includes a 6 percent cost of living increase with a 10 percent performance increase. If you need to expand the salary components to include your proposal reasons, the system administrator must update the view for the Salary Management folder.

DEFINING BENEFIT COVERAGES

Benefit coverages are defined in the Application Utilities Lookup Table `US_BENEFIT_COVERAGE`. You establish the default employee and employer contribution amounts for the health care benefit plans using the Benefits Contributions window. Query the benefit plan, which is the element name for this plan. In the Coverage field, select from the pick list each of the coverages valid for this plan. For each coverage level, enter the employee and employer contribution amounts. If either component has no contribution, enter zero.

DEFINING ELEMENT SETS

Element sets are simply a collection of element names. Oracle HRMS uses element sets to enable you to restrict the elements that can be entered or viewed on a customized version of the Element Entries window. This is used to limit the elements that are processed by a particular payroll run. Finally, element sets can be used to define the elements over which the costs of other elements are to be distributed.

Element sets are defined with the Element and Distribution Set window. Enter a unique name and select the type: Distribution, Run, or Customization. Distribution sets are used for cost distribution, run sets for payroll runs, and customization sets for customizing the Element Entries window. You can select your elements by classification, like Pre-Tax deductions, or by individual element name.

DEFINING PERSON TYPES

Person types are used to identify different groups of people. You might want to capture different types of information for different groups of people. You can also restrict access to certain sensitive groups of people. Person types can be used to accomplish these goals.

There are three main types of people you can maintain in your system. They are Employee, Applicants, and External. Oracle HR defines a special category of External called contact. These are people who are associated with employees or applicants, such as dependents.

Oracle HR comes seeded with default person types. These can be modified or added to. Use the Person Types window to make these modifications. During the definition process, you determine the name of the person type and the associated system name. The system name is used to define how Oracle should treat this person type.

Defining Assignment Statuses

Assignment statuses are used to record employee and applicant current statuses within the enterprise. You can use assignment statuses to track permanent or temporary separation from your company, such as paid or unpaid medical leave, family leave, or military service. There are four main system statuses for employees. They are the following:

Active

Suspend

Terminate

End

You assign your own names to these statuses through the Assignment Status window. Each system status can have several user statuses related to it.

Employee assignment statuses are used to control payroll processing. Each status has a payroll status of Process or Do Not Process assigned to it. You can also have different formulas execute for an employee when her status changes.

Defining Special Information Type Key Flexfield

Oracle HR delivers a Key Flexfield called Special Information Types, which enables you to store special personal information that is unique within your organization. Each type of information is a separate structure of the flexfield. Companies use this flexfield to store information such as skill requirements for jobs, pension-related information, and additional retiree information. Oracle delivers some of these structures automatically. They include ADA Disabilities, ADA Disability Accommodations, and OSHA Reportable Incidents.

Define your structures in the same manner as all your other Key Flexfields. When defined, you must enable your Special Information Type for the Business Group through the Special Information Types window. You use this window to define how the structure will be used. Make sure you check Other if you want to use this structure at the employee level.

One downside to Special Information Types is that you cannot create database items for this flexfield. Therefore, Oracle FastFormulas cannot access data stored in these flexfields. If your FastFormulas must reference this data, consider using either the People Group flexfield or one of the supported (non-context sensitive) descriptive flexfields.

Defining Workers Compensation Codes and Rates

Workers Compensation is only valid for sites with Oracle Payroll installed. Each state has a workers' compensation program that provides insurance for employees with work-related injuries. The first step in the process is to define each of your Workers Compensation carriers through the Organization window. Make sure you use the Workers Compensation Carrier classification. At the GRE level, associate these carriers to each state through the State Tax Rules window. You also enter the Experience Modification rate and the Employer's Liability and Premium Discount rates, if applicable. Next, verify that the Taxability Rules for your Imputed and Supplemental Earnings properly represent earnings included in the employee's payroll exposure.

You must next define the WC codes and rates for each carrier and location in the state through the WC Codes and Rates window. This window enables you to query each state and carrier. If you leave the location field blank, the codes and rates you enter will be used for all locations in that state for that carrier. If you want to enter rates for a particular location, you must also query the location.

Defining Workers Compensation Job Codes

When you have defined all your Workers Compensation codes and rates, you must associate these codes to each of your jobs. At this time you also enter the Executive Weekly maximum (if one exists for this state), the state's rules regarding inclusion of overtime earnings in the payroll exposure, and any standard surcharges in use in this state.

Use the Workers Compensation Job Codes window to query each of the states. For each state, you must select the job titles and assign the corresponding Workers Compensation code. One of the most common error messages on the Payroll Message report is the dreaded `Cannot determine Workers Compensation rate for this employee`. Generally, this means that you have not associated a Workers' Compensation code for this employee's job title in the work state for this employee.

Defining Absence and Paid Time Off Accrual Plans

Paid Time Off Accruals are important in tracking such benefit policies as vacation and sick time available for employees. Within Oracle HRMS, you must first set up one separate Hours Taken element for each accrual plan you create. For each accrual plan, you must establish a start rule for when the accrual should begin accruing for an employee. For each accrual plan, you must establish a period of ineligibility to identify when an employee is allowed to begin taking vacation/sick leave using the amount she has accrued. You must also establish bands identifying the accrual rates associated with each length of service.

Oracle provides several seeded FastFormulas to support PTO accruals and eligibility/ineligibility. You might choose to modify these formulas or write your own. Batch Element Entry refers to the ineligibility rules/FastFormulas when adding the nonrecurring absence element to the employee record.

Defining Human Resources Budgets

Human Resources budgets are a mechanism for monitoring workload requirements and work vacancy information throughout the year. Oracle HR can be set up to enable you to determine budget variances between budgeted and actual requirements for organizations, jobs, positions, and grades. To define budgets, navigate to the Budgets window. For each Budget Name you define, you must identify what Oracle Work Structure (jobs, grades, and so on) that this budget is based on. Then, you must establish target goals for each Work Structure item within each period of time throughout the calendar year.

TROUBLESHOOTING

If you are planning to implement Oracle HR/Payroll/Advanced Benefits, you are likely to obtain an excellent long-term solution. However, over the short-term, you are facing quite a challenge. Earlier in this chapter, there were numerous tips.

The earlier sections on Critical Implementation Factors and Unrealistic Project Expectations contain many tips. The biggest message from this chapter is that Oracle HR/Payroll and Advanced Benefits are likely the most challenging to implement of the Oracle Applications. An experienced Oracle Financials consultant is usually *not* sufficient to meet the needs of an Oracle HR/Payroll project. It is highly advisable to establish project team members with specific experience on Oracle HR/Payroll. Your current project success and the likelihood of optimal long-term solutions will be greatly influenced by your decision.

CHAPTER 24

Using Oracle Human Resources

In this chapter

The Oracle Human Resources (HR) Application is the foundational module for the Oracle Human Resources Management Systems (HRMS) product suite. Other Oracle HRMS modules that are built based on HR include Oracle Payroll, Training Administration, Time Management, and Advanced Benefits. This chapter focuses primarily on Oracle HR-specific issues. Before looking into specific Oracle HR issues, consider the following background as to why an organization might want to implement an HRMS system using Oracle HR.

In today's competitive business environment, many companies are recognizing that Human Resources management is vital. Although much attention has been given over the past decade to improving computer system productivity in financial and manufacturing systems, most top organizations are beginning to turn attention to an overlooked area: management of their employees. Employees are not listed on a balance sheet; however, the truly top organizations recognize that employees are a vital asset. Companies might ask simple questions such as the following:

Why aren't we able to retain top quality employees?

Are our salary and benefit plans sufficient to attract top quality employees?

Are our employees trained properly to play an optimal role in the creation or delivery of the products or services we provide?

Are there potential employees with a skill set that could improve our productivity or even revolutionize our current business? If so, how can we obtain this skill set or these employees?

With this perspective in mind, examine the issues in implementing the Oracle HRMS product suite, beginning with current features.

DISCOVERING NEW FEATURES IN RELEASE 11*i*

Release 11*i* HR has the following new features:

- Employee and Manager Self-Service.
- Self-Service Benefit Enrollment.
- Grievance Tracking.
- EEO-4 and EEO-5 Equal Employment Opportunity Reporting. EEO-4 is for State and Local Governments, and EEO-5 is for K-12 School Systems.
- Premium Reconciliation Reporting.
- U.S. record-keeping for continuing benefits payments and family support orders (QDROs).
- Enhanced Salary Planning capabilities—Salary Surveys. (APIs will exist for uploading of third-party survey data for jobs.)
- 403b and 457 pre-tax annuities support.
- Flexible dates, meaning employers can use different date formats, such as MM/DD/YY.

- Extended Pay for organizations that require the option to pay an annual salary over a 9- or 10-month year, as well as over the standard 12-month year.
- Position Management and Position Control that integrate with Public Sector Budgeting, Oracle Payroll, and Oracle General Ledger.
- Forms Configurator and People Management templates.
- Tenure Tracking.
- Collective Agreements.
- FYI Notifications.
- Global Competencies.
- Medical Assessments.
- ADP and Ceridian Payroll Interfaces Delivered with Oracle HR.
- Communication Delivery Methods window.
- Configurable Transaction Business Rules.
- Visa detail-enhanced data capture.
- Tenure Tracking.
- Job Groups.
- PayMIX/ BEE Functionality merged—BEE Enhancements.
- Position Date Tracking.
- VERTEX Geocodes for HR-Only Installations.
- Generic Third-Party Payroll Backfeed.
- Generic Payroll Interface toolkit.
- Third-party administrator data export/import, which is configurable and provides for the run and rerun of processes to generate interface files.
- Java versions of Hierarchy Diagrammers.
- SkillScape Integration.
- Absence Enhancements.
- Standard Benefits (not to be confused with Advanced Benefits discussed in Chapter 26, "Using Oracle Advanced Benefits") provides for extended flexibility when defining employment benefit plan coverage, eligibility, and amounts.

Note

If you are upgrading from a previous version, Basic Benefits are still available. Only when Standard or Advanced Benefits have been thoroughly tested and implemented should the Basic Benefits be discontinued.

- Bargaining Unit/Contract Information.
- Person Types (for Benefits, multiple concurrent person types will be allowed; new seeded person types have been added).

Paid Time Off accrual enhancements include the following:

- In addition to increased delivered input values/forms, the use of FastFormulas has been added to increase flexibility when determining eligibility and accrual rates.
- Flexible definition of plan start dates (not just January 1).
- Flexible calculation of the rate of accrual.
- Prorating of accruals for part-time employees.
- Suspension rules for issues such as leave of absence.
- Rules can be defined for accrual (for example, accruals can be defined based on hours worked).
- Adjusted service dates to credit service for rehired employees or to identify grandfathered benefits from mergers and acquisitions that will be recognized.
- One set of Element Links for each plan. (In previous releases, several elements were created for each accrual plan, including Carry Over Element, Residual Element, and more.)

GLOBALIZATION SUPPORT

For additional assistance with database configuration, please refer to the following Oracle documents:

- "Oracle8 National Language Support" (White Paper - June, 1997)
- *Oracle Applications Concepts*

National Language Support brings with it several features that support the localization of the Oracle database and applications. Among these are local language, national identifiers, monetary symbols, date and time configurations, numeric settings, and calendar conventions. Reports and forms can be viewed in the language and formats familiar to the user. This is particularly important with the implementation of self-service.

Note

Translation tables (table names ending with _TL) must be populated.

Oracle is delivered with American English for language and cultural environment defaults. You can change any or all of the default settings. The locale-specific data (NLSDATA) is identified and loaded at runtime. The NLS_LANG parameter sets the default language, territory, and character set used by the database.

It is important to note that the character set chosen to support the server can accommodate the character set used for the client. If you fail to select an adequate character set, you will lose data in the translation. When properly configured, when a client application character set is different from the database character set, the data conversion becomes transparent to the user.

Note

Character sets can't be changed without re-creating the database. If several character sets are needed to support the client application, the database character set chosen must be equal to—or a superset of—all possible client character sets. UTF8 is a superset of all other character sets.

In addition to the user being able to view the information in her own language and familiar formats, SQL functions used by FastFormulas can override the NLSDATA parameters passed to the system. An example of this follows:

```
To_Date('DEC-30-01','MON-DD-YY','NLS_DATE_LANGUAGE = American')
```

This might be used in an environment in which your French organization needs to report information to the head office in the United States.

Many of the APIs also include language/culture parameters that aid the international business organization.

HUMAN RESOURCES SELF SERVICE

Through the Self Service Human Resources (SSHR) application, employees and managers can view and update appropriate information via a Web-based application (see Figure 24.1). If you have been looking for real returns on investment in an attempt to cost-justify your HRMS implementation, this is your module! By permitting the person responsible for the information to update that information, you have eliminated several time-consuming processes. For example, a simple address change currently requires that an employee complete an Address Change Form (or similar document). The form is passed to the employee's manager or administrative support person who must prepare it for delivery to Human Resources, via the mailroom or postal system, where the information either is entered or prepared for input to the system. As you can see from Figure 24.2, direct input saves time and money and reduces the risk of error and lost information. One entry to the Oracle database and all appropriate modules and outbound interfaces have the correct information. By allowing employees and managers to view their information online, you provide improved service and reduce the need for many paper reports and phone inquiries to your Human Resources and Payroll departments.

With the multilinguistic enhancements available in Release 11*i*, managers and employees can view the information in their own languages and familiar formats. So, while your server might be using German as its language base and formatting rules, your employees in the United Kingdom can view their information in English (where cheque is spelled correctly).

SSHR is delivered with Employee and Manager views as starting points for configuring your self-service environment.

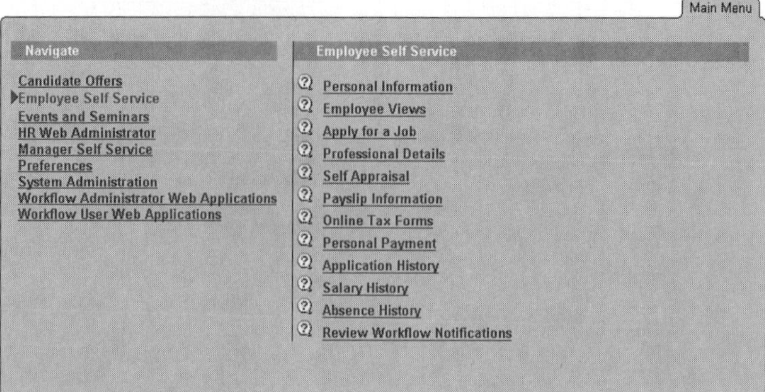

Figure 24.1
Preparing to invoke Self Service HR.

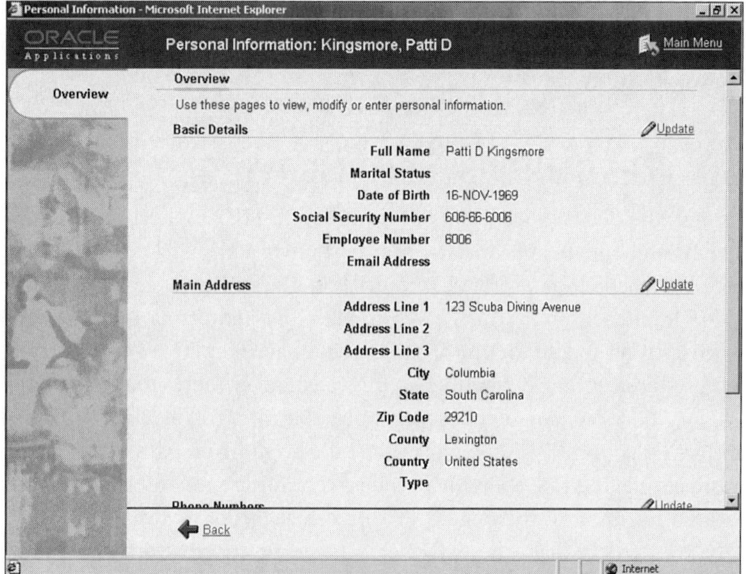

Figure 24.2
The employee updates personal HR information.

Candidate Offers is an example Self Service Recruitment workflow process that enables hiring managers to submit candidates for vacancies in the enterprise (see Figure 24.3). Using Self Service, the manager can add personal data, including an electronic copy of a resume and offer data, which can be routed for approvals. The candidate is added to the database as an applicant. The process contains offer details and a standard offer letter.

User Help is configurable and can be enhanced to include reminders, or *ticklers*, to assist the user with the next step or additional considerations. For example, when an employee completes a name change, the tickler response might include the following prompts: `Change your W4 information`, `Change of Address`, `Change of Insurance Coverage`, `Change Beneficiaries`, and `Change Contact Information`.

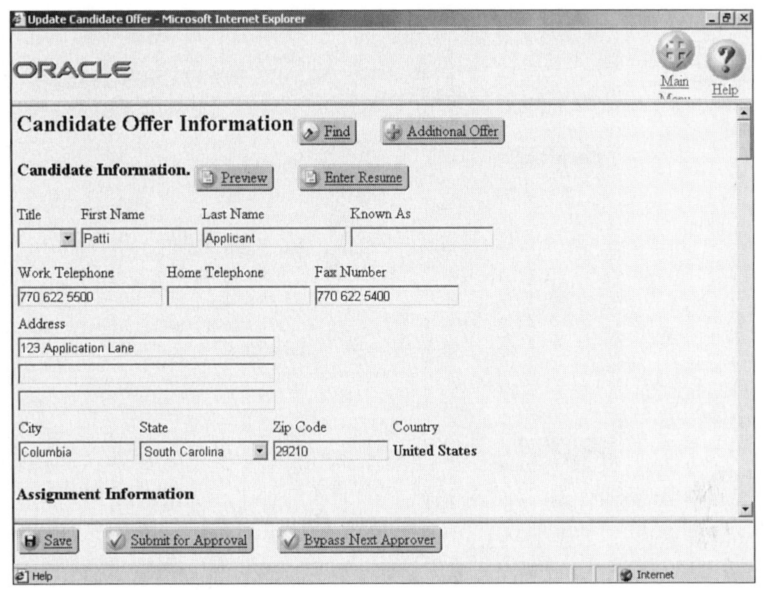

Figure 24.3
The manager updates candidate offer information.

SSHR uses Workflow to manage information between Human Resources professionals, management, and employees. This enables the manager to enter a salary increase for an employee and have the system notify the appropriate level of management that a salary change is pending approval. The salary change is approved and applied to the employee's record, and notifications are sent to the manager and the employee.

HR TIPS

This section contains various suggestions and tips to consider when implementing Oracle HR.

FORMS CONFIGURATOR

The Forms Configurator tool, also referred to as Quick Hire or People Management Configurator, is a great addition to the HRMS applications. With the seemingly endless number of fields of data you can capture about your employees, often many of the form fields represent data either you do not capture or that seem to be in the way when you are trying to enter a new employee.

This enhancement allows you to easily design your own forms. With almost every field available to you through the normal People and Assignment forms, a functional user can construct forms that meet his business requirements. Figure 24.4 provides an example of a new hire window created by the Forms Configurator.

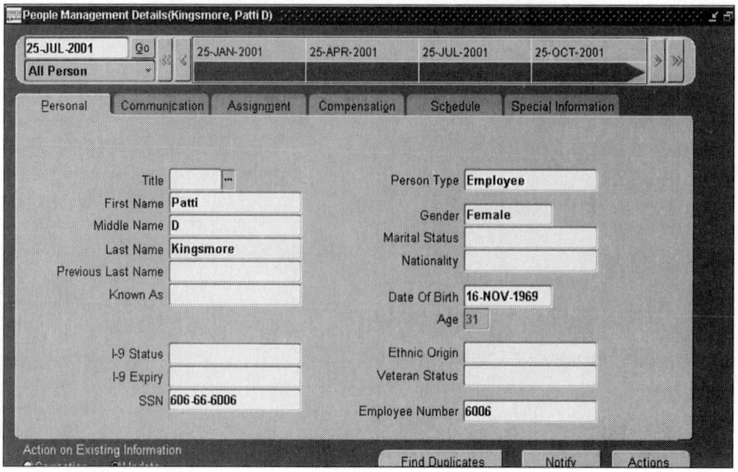

Figure 24.4
The Forms Configurator adds efficiency to the new hire process.

The tool used to build your forms is Forms Configurator. Oracle also provides templates as starting points to configure your forms. The sample templates are referred to as People Management Templates and include Hire Applicants, Enter Employees, Maintain Employees, and Visa Details.

The windows available are as follows:

- **Summary**—What HR data do you want to see at a glance about your employees? This form enables you to configure the form to display the most important data to you about an employee.
- **Maintenance**—This window enables you to enter data. You can configure forms to maintain data on current employees, to enter data on applicants or new hires, or to perform specialized data entry for specific high-volume data you maintain. Date track functionality also is available. The configurable form might include several tabs for inputting data. You select the fields you want to see, which are required, and which are updateable.
- **Find**—The configurable Find window allows for both simple and advanced searches of employees and applicants.

New Hire Reporting

Employees now must be reported in most states and Canada within the various regulated times (5–35 days), depending on the local legislation. All states at a minimum require the following:

- Employee full name
- Social Security number
- Hire date

Additionally, some states require

- Employee address
- Date of birth
- Job
- Salary
- Hours normally worked per week
- Category of full- or part-time employment
- Indicator as to whether health care is available to employee and dependents
- Any existing child support obligations

New Hire Reports are submitted by Government Reporting Entity (GRE) Numbers and must include the following information:

- GRE legal name and address
- Federal Identification Number (IRS issued) or State Unemployment Insurance (SUI) Identification Number (some states require both numbers)
- Contact person's (person responsible for compilation of report) name, job, and work telephone number

New hire reporting was established due to national concerns over child welfare and fraud in state programs such as workers compensation and unemployment insurance. Based on each state's requirements, exclusions to this report are employees with age, wages, or hours less than the state minimum. The Oracle-delivered New Hire Report is designed to meet the various formatting and data requirements of each state. The only state as of this writing that does not accept the Oracle New Hire Report as printed is Tennessee. Tennessee has its own form and the information must be copied onto that form. See Tennessee State Law for more details.

In most cases, the Payroll Department is the contact point for information on child support and other obligations of this type, and it therefore is usually responsible for submitting the New Hire Reports (one for each state in which employees are hired and one for each GRE).

Employee Hire Process

The new hire process consists of entering an employee into the system in order to pay the employee and to record information on the employee relevant to your enterprise's business requirements. Employee name and person type at the minimum must be entered.

One way to handle this task is through the Applicant Method of entering prospective new hires as Applicants during the interviewing process and then converting their person type to Employee with the appropriate effective date or date of hire (DOH). Using Oracle's Recruitment and Applicant Tracking functionality, you can record vacancies or openings in your enterprise, advertise those openings using Self Service HR, and maintain data on recruitment activities. When someone applies for the opening, you record both personal and applicant assignment information and any other relevant data you use to select prospective employees, such as qualifications or competencies.

When entering a new employee, basic personal data that is usually recorded includes address information, contacts, beneficiaries, and telephone numbers (work and home). The flexibility of Oracle HR enables you to capture any data you want to about your enterprise's personnel assets. You can enter an employee's picture, her qualifications, and schools and colleges attended. You also can enter an employee's competencies using proficiency levels and rating scales. In addition, you can use Special Information Types and Extra Information Types to create structures to capture any additional information you require that is not provided as standard Oracle HR fields.

Former employees can also be rehired and classified as new hires. Caution should be exercised when entering the new "hire date" to maintain the integrity of the existing records. If the rehire is to receive credit for previous employment, you must enter both the original hire date and the adjusted service date.

Note

An employee can't be rehired unless the termination for the employee's previous period of service includes a Final Process Date.

If the employee has been entered in error, there is an option to Cancel. There are limitations on this function, though, and they should be reviewed carefully. These limitations exist if any of the following have occurred:

- Employee has been processed in a payroll run.
- Employee type has changed.
- New assignment has been made. (Giving an employee a new assignment creates a date tracked record and should not be deleted.)

The complexity of entering new hires is dictated by the amount of information a company maintains on its employees and the mode of data entry used. This function can be time-consuming to the new user but after gaining some proficiency becomes less cumbersome. The suggested method is to enter the company's necessary information before the employee's first day of employment and then enter the employee specific information (Ethnic Origin, I-9 status, Veteran Status, and so on) on the employee's first day at work from the documents the employee fills out. With the aid of People Management templates, Manager Self Service, and Employee Self Service, 11*i* has eased the burden placed on the HR staff to key in data on new employees.

The new employee's national identifier, person type, birthday, gender, and address must be entered before the employee can be processed in Oracle Payroll. An employee can have only one primary address but can have multiple secondary addresses. The multiple addresses feature is helpful in organizations such as those in the public sector that hire large numbers of students. This feature is also helpful in industries that hire seasonal help. The first address you enter is listed by default as Primary. Enterprises using Oracle Payroll must note that the employee's primary address is used to support federal, state, and local tax rules. Thus, to have taxes calculated correctly, each employee must have a valid address. Additionally, Oracle HR provides numerous country address styles to enable all necessary address information to be entered based on each specific country's address requirements.

Now that personal data has been entered for the new hire, her "relationship" to your enterprise is represented using Oracle's assignment. The employee assignment function in Oracle is a mandatory component for paying the employee using Oracle Payroll or the supported interfaces with ADP and Ceridian payroll services. Components that must be present are the following:

- GRE (Government Reporting Entity)
- Organization and Location with a physical street address—not a post office box
- Payroll
- Employment Category, such as full-time or part-time status
- W4 and other tax information as appropriate (this requires valid employee and work location addresses that include county name; therefore, Vertex is required)
- Salary Basis
- Approved Salary (all first time entry of salaries are automatically approved)

Other common assignment information is entered for a new hire. Each employee is given a job or position (see Chapter 23, "Implementing Oracle Human Resources and Oracle Payroll," for discussion on the uses of jobs versus positions). The employee job influences issues such as government reporting (Equal Employment Opportunity and Workers Compensation) and whether an employee's job is eligible for overtime pay. Employees are often assigned grades to establish a relative basis of comparison of their salary to other employees in the same grade. The People Group functionality is commonly used on the assignment based on each customer's specific requirements. People Group Key Flexfield segments work independently from each other, providing specific methods of identifying employees that cannot be easily identified elsewhere in the application.

Salary is the next item that should be entered for a new hire. As previously mentioned, to pay and report employee information, it is necessary for an employee to have an approved salary and a salary basis as a component of the employee assignment. Oracle has designed the salary function to automatically approve the initial salary entered for the new hire. All future salary entries after that are established as proposed salaries and must be approved before becoming effective. Some enterprises restrict the approval of salaries to higher management and/or Human Resources or Payroll personnel.

Tax information must also be entered for a new hire. Oracle provides a method for capturing federal, state, and local taxes, including tax credits and employer taxes that the company must pay and report on. Before an employee can be paid, it is necessary to have at least the Federal and State tax forms completed. Local, township, and school district taxes should be completed according to the laws in place for the locality. Earlier in the new hire discussion about addresses, the importance of having a correct primary address for each employee was stressed. This is imperative to ensure that the Vertex calculations for taxes and tax balances will be correct. The employee's home (primary) address and work location on her assignment establish the state and locality tax information valid for the employee. In the event that there is an error in the taxes and tax balances, Oracle provides a means to make a manual adjustment (see "Tax Balance Adjustments" in Chapter 25, "Using Oracle Payroll").

To pay a new hire, a Personal Payment Method is required. Oracle Payroll enables the enterprise to pay employees using the following methods:

- Check
- Direct Deposit (NACHA)
- Combination of both Direct Deposit and Check

Oracle Payroll functionality provides for any combination that the enterprise policy demands. Any employee not having a Personal Payment Method is paid by the default method, usually by check. Earlier information on setting up new hire assignments stressed that each employee must have a valid GRE to be paid using any of these methods.

Finally, new hires should be enrolled in benefits and assigned any recurring elements that represent continuing earnings or deductions. If you are using Basic Benefits, this is accomplished through element entries. Oracle HR/Payroll uses elements as a means of holding information on employees for compensation, deductions, benefits, employee absences, and other items distributed to employees, such as company cars. Although most element entries are created by manual entry in the Element Entries window, some element entries can be automatically generated based on the existence of other earnings, deductions, or employer liabilities. If you use Standard or Advanced Benefits, any enrollment elections can automatically be created in the employee's element entries.

EMPLOYEE TERMINATION

When an employee ends employment, you terminate her from Oracle HR (see Figure 24.5). Oracle HR then establishes an end date to the employee's current period of service. To terminate an employee, keep in mind the following:

- If the employee is deceased, the Oracle system requires that you select Deceased in the Reason for Leaving field to provide for proper recording on the W2 Wage and Tax Statement.
- Actual Date is the only field required, and this is generally the last day worked and the date when the employee's person type changes to ex-employee.
- Notified and Projected dates are informational and can be used by the user depending on the level of reporting required on terminations.

- Final Process Date is the date after which no further processing can occur. This is an optional field, but this date is required if the employee is ever rehired. See the section "New Hire Reporting" earlier in the chapter. Setting this date past the Actual Date enables further payroll processing for additional or late payments.
- Last Standard Process Date is new with 11*i*. This field is required if you use Oracle Payroll. The field defaults to the next payroll period end date for the employee and represents the last date for normal payroll processing.

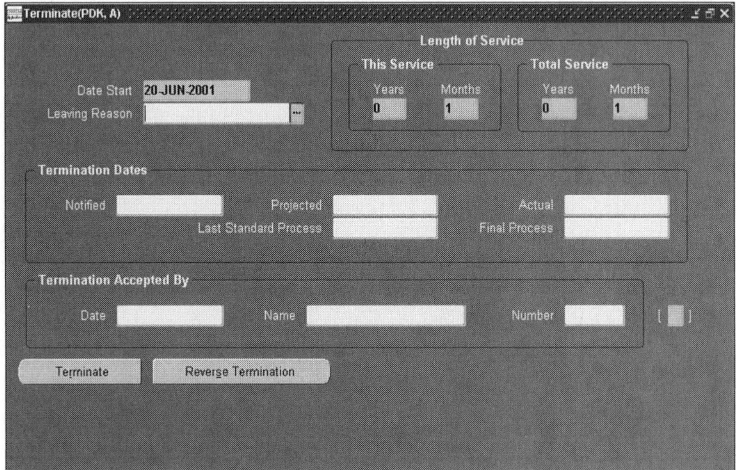

Figure 24.5
Terminating an employee.

A termination can be cancelled by selecting Reverse Termination if the employee decides not to leave or if the date of termination changes, as is often the case. Oracle HR accommodates this by changing the Person Type back to Employee.

Oracle HR has provided a Termination Report that lists all the terminations and the employees' reasons for leaving. The report can be run for any time period. Recruiting and other HR functions find this report very useful in analyzing turnover and retention. The accuracy of this report depends, of course, on the care used when choosing the leaving reasons. The user can add to the list of reasons for leaving by modifying the Application Utility Lookup Table LEAV_REAS. To realize optimum use of the leave reasons, the user should add those that will provide the most accurate description relating to her particular industry and business.

MANAGING EMPLOYEE ABSENCES

Human Resources departments must track employees' absences from work. They need to identify the types of absences that are allowable, track the dates and reasons for the absence, and group related absences for reporting and analysis. They must also work closely with Payroll so that the employee is properly credited for paid time off. Oracle offers an absence management tool that is included with the base Human Resources module. This section describes its setup and use.

Oracle manages absence information at multiple levels. The top of this structure is called *absence category*. This enables you to group your related absences. Examples of absence categories are the following:

- Medical Leave
- Family Leave
- Personal Leave
- Professional Leave

Within each of these categories, you establish *absence types*. For example, you can set up the following absence types under the category of Family Leave:

- Paid Maternity/Paternity
- Unpaid Maternity/Paternity
- Dependent Care

Finally, you can state a reason at the time you record the actual absence. For example, you can establish reasons such as Birth of a Child or Adoption of a Child as valid reasons. These reasons are established in the Application Utility Lookup Table ABSENCE_REASON.

The key setup steps for Absence Management are covered fairly well in the *Oracle Human Resources U.S. User's Guide*. There are a few things to keep in mind while you are completing the setup.

You set up a different nonrecurring absence element for each of your absence types. We recommend that you name the element the same as the absence type for clarity. Remember to set the Termination Rule to *Actual Termination*. Check the Multiple Entries Allowed box so that you can record multiple occurrences of this absence type in a pay period.

Note

Do not select the Process in Run box if this element will be used in a Paid Time Off (PTO) accrual plan.

There must be at least one input value on this element. Generally, this input value will capture the hours associated with this absence type. If you plan to make entries to this element via Batch Element Entry (BEE), you must also define an input value named Date Earned.

If only certain employees are eligible for certain absence types, use the Link window for this element to restrict this eligibility. For example, you can offer Paid Family Leave to only your full-time employees by utilizing the employment category on the Link window.

Oracle HR functionality to further manage employee absences exists with Paid Time Off (PTO) Accrual plans. Many companies require their employees to earn vacation and sick time through accruals. Oracle HR provides a standard mechanism that enables employees to accrue vacation and sick time on a pay-period or other basis. You can configure rules for accrual rates, carryover of time, bought or sold time, and any unused accruals. PTO functionality in 11*i* is much more robust than in Release 10.7. An excellent white paper, "Oracle HRMS Documentation Update for Patch 865749 Absences and PTO Accrual Plans," can be downloaded from Oracle's MetaLink Web site.

Position Management and Position Control

Public sector and higher education institutions have long awaited the functionality released in 11*i*.

The initial release of 11*i* introduced DateTracking for positions in addition to more available standard fields to capture position information. In addition to defining the organization and job underlying the position, you can capture hiring information such as FTE and Headcount, Working Terms, and Additional Details such as comments or ad copy. With Release 11*i* minipack C, Position Management and Position Control were released.

Position Management enables you to configure your business rules to control the creation of new positions, control transactions for existing positions, or changes to position data. The capability now exists to route and approve new positions using Oracle Workflow before the database is updated. You have the option to use the position hierarchy, use the supervisor hierarchy, or create a routing list to approve and notify others of updates to your positions.

Position Control Budgeting enables you to create budgets at many levels in HRMS, including job, organization, position, grade, or a combination of these work structures. You can create budgets based on full-time equivalency, headcount, or money. When you link budgets to employees' pay via payroll element pay values, you can report budget versus actual values. You also can compare budgeted versus committed values. The same routing and approval discussed with position management also applies.

Position Control is integrated with Oracle Payroll, General Ledger, and Public Sector Budgeting. Thus, the usefulness of these new features is enhanced in other Oracle Application modules.

Position Management and Control also introduces business rule functionality. Predefined rules exist to validate position transactions and budgets. You can set the status level for each rule as ignore, warning, or error. Oracle delivers a limited number of rules that might apply to your organization. Fortunately, FastFormulas are made available that further extend this functionality.

Standard Benefits

See Chapter 26 for information on Advanced Benefits and additional discussion of Standard Benefits.

Note

Both Standard and Advanced Benefits can be used with Self Service HR. However, only Advanced Benefits allows for changes to enrollment based on life events. If Standard Benefits is used, the Benefits Staff must manually control the availability of the SSHR Enrollment forms to the employees (in essence, the open enrollment period). When open enrollment has ended, the appropriate staff rather than the employee would complete changes to the employee's benefits.

Typically, if you use a third party to administer your plans and you do not offer a flex credit program, Standard Benefits should meet your business requirements. However, if you want to use Life Event Management, you will need the Advanced Benefits product discussed in Chapter 26.

In addition to the multiple forms provided by Oracle to support benefit eligibility, coverage rules, employee withholding amounts, and employer liability amounts, Oracle allows the use of FastFormulas to further expand the flexibility to meet your company's business requirements.

Note

After you have defined your benefit elements, you must link the elements. You do not need to enter eligibility requirements, though. Use an open link. With Basic Benefits, you must use eligibility rules at the link level, often resulting in employees' benefit elements being end-dated when a change occurs, even though they are still eligible for the benefit. This will not happen with Standard or Advanced Benefits, if you use the open link.

Government Reporting

The requirement on organizations by the United States government for employee reporting is an important responsibility of a Human Resources department. As more and more government reporting requirements are placed on U.S. companies, the need for purchasing packaged HR software such as Oracle Human Resources increases. Many companies realize that they will need to continue paying the costs of maintaining and reporting on this type of information. Thus, many of the HR package software purchases in the upcoming millennium will probably be influenced by the desire to remain compliant with government regulatory bodies.

The Oracle HR product has been designed to handle this reporting necessity with as much flexibility as possible. The reports that can be produced with use of Oracle HR satisfy government reporting requirements and provide the information necessary for an enterprise to review its practices and progress internally.

There are five main areas and reports to focus on:

- **EEO**—Equal Employment Opportunity
- **AAP**—Affirmative Action Plans

- **VETS-100**—Federal Contractor Veterans Employment
- **ADA**—American with Disabilities Act
- **OSHA**—Occupational Safety and Health Act

The EEO and AAP reports are government-mandated reports that measure employment and advancement of employees by gender and ethnic origin within the enterprise base. With 11*i*, Oracle HR has expanded its previous functionality of EEO-1 reporting to now include EEO-4 and EEO-5 reports.

The VETS-100 Report reports on the employment and advancement of Veterans in the categories of disabled and Vietnam-era.

ADA Reports represent those employees with disabilities and helps to monitor that employers are making reasonable accommodations for those employees identified as having discernable disabilities.

OSHA Reports records and reports workplace injuries and illnesses, including the number and severity of each.

All these reports should provide two things: compliance with government regulations and a means for enterprises to review their internal practices for fairness and safety. The first is required and the second recommended. This chapter will provide no in-depth discussion of the definitions and compliance-issues that encompass these items, but it will offer an overview of the functionality that Oracle HR provides to produce these reports and provide a tool to the enterprise to use in monitoring these functions.

When planning all these reports, please read and make sure you understand how the Government Reporting Entity (GRE) Numbers factor into this reporting. The *Oracle HR User's Guide* gives detailed information on the reporting hierarchy. The reporting requirements for each company require customer-specific setup according to how their information should be reported. Before running these reports, the enterprise must set up its reporting establishments, including Corporate headquarters and AAP Organizations along with the hierarchy and overrides for any individual employees as indicated.

Additionally, to support government reports, particularly EEO and AAP, care must be given to the creation of Jobs and Grades within Oracle HR. Creating Job Groups and Lines of Career Progression is a functional issue that must be resolved by each company before the Oracle system can be set up and before you can ever hope to produce some of the government-mandated reports.

EEO Reporting Setup Steps

Follow these steps to set up EEO Reporting:

1. For each Business Group and GRE, enter the information necessary for submission of the report, including EEOC and EEO-1 Identification Number. Select whether you are submitting EEO-1, EEO-4, or EEO-5 reports.
2. Enter an EEO category for each job.

3. Ensure each employee has the following recorded:

   Gender.

   Ethnic origin.

   GRE.

   Job.

   For EEO-4 reporting, salary and EEO function are also required.

   For EEO-5 reporting, the employment category is also required.

4. Identify types of EEO reporting to be submitted:

   Individual Establishment Report

   Headquarters Report

   Establishment Employment Listing

5. Identify and define reporting organizations.
6. Build establishment hierarchies.
7. Enter any necessary overrides for employees who should be counted differently.
8. Run the EEO Report.

AAP REPORT SETUP STEPS

AAP Reports show the relative position of ethnic minorities compensation and comparison in a job line of progression. Follow these steps to set up AAP Reporting:

1. Ensure that each employee has the following:

   Gender

   Ethnic origin

   GRE

   Job

2. Determine salary codes for jobs by selecting grades to represent each salary.
3. Define lines of progression for your jobs using Affirmative Action standards.
4. Determine job groups that jobs belong to.
5. Associate each job.
6. Define an AAP Organization to represent each Plan.
7. Determine the AAP hierarchy.
8. Run the AAP Reports, which include AAP-Workforce Analysis and AAP-Job Group Analysis.

VETS-100 SETUP STEPS

Follow these steps to set up VETS-100 Reporting:

1. Register Reporting Categories and Reporting Statuses for the Business Group.
2. Enter information necessary for submission of VETS-100, such as the Department of Labor company number. If you do not submit EEO reports, enter the GRE Employer Identification Number and Standard Industrial Classification.
3. Record EEO categories for jobs.
4. All employees with a qualifying Veteran status have been assigned to the following:

   Job

   Employment Category

   GRE
5. Identify and define the reporting organizations necessary.
6. Build establishment hierarchies.
7. Enter any necessary overrides at the employee level.
8. Run VETS-100 Report. Based on the number of hiring locations for your enterprise, run either the single-establishment hierarchy report or the multiple-establishment reports, including the Headquarters Report, Hiring Location Report, and Consolidated Report.

ADA

The approach for setting up for ADA reports is similar to the preceding reports except the emphasis is placed on identifying those employees who have disabilities and entering any pertinent information about their disabilities and any accommodation requests. Indicating an employee as disabled is accomplished by checking the Disabled Box when entering personal employee information. Oracle HR comes delivered with two predefined Special Information Types for recording ADA information and accommodation requests.

OSHA

Again, the setup and data capture for this report follows similar standards as for the others with focus on work-related illnesses and injuries that must be entered. Oracle HR comes delivered with a predefined Special Information Type for recording OSHA reportable incidents.

The flexibility of the Oracle HR functionality to support government reporting is demonstrated in the establishment of a correct reporting organizational hierarchy for one of these reports. When you have defined the organizational hierarchy for one report, you might have done the majority of the work for the others. This avoids repeating work and puts you on the road toward having correct, viable reports in a government-mandated format ready to be submitted with a minimum of effort required. Moreover, as the U.S. government institutes new reporting requirements, the Oracle HR system enables you to have a foundation so you can meet these new requirements more promptly and with less cost. If you speak with Compliance Officers for large corporations, you will quickly recognize the worth of these system-driven reports.

PAY SCALES AND PAY PROGRESSION

The use of Pay Scales is a common need when addressing union contracts. It is common to have an HR policy where various jobs have prenegotiated rates of pay based on duration of employee service. For example, after 6 months, the employee is paid $X, after 12 months, $Y, and so on.

There are two main obstacles to overcome in solving this problem via Oracle HR. First, Pay Scales are not tied to Salary Administration. Second, Oracle's implementation of automatic progression (how an employee's rate of pay is advanced from one step of the pay scale to the next) is not flexible. Automatic progression is not based on each individual employee's hire date, nor is it based on the amount of time an employee has occupied a specific step on a pay scale.

The following has not been implemented but is a proposed solution for these two issues. The solution uses Oracle Pay Scales for data storage only. The automatic processes within Oracle HR will *not* be used to allow employee advancement to a new progression step. Custom processes are written to handle these situations. These custom processes, in turn, use the supported Salary Administration API to generate new salary proposals.

Consider a two-part solution. One solution solves the issue when an employee becomes eligible to advance to the next step on a pay scale. The second solution addresses the issue when there is an annual pay increase for all steps on a given pay scale.

The first solution addresses the advancement of an employee from one step to the next in a pay scale. The custom process performs the following activities:

1. Read the employee's records for assignment and underlying grade step point placement. Determine the employee's current *pay scale*, *step*, and *date* at that step. Note: A Descriptive Flexfield segment on the assignment form should be created to contain a Grade Step Override Date. This override date exists to handle issues such as unpaid leave. If a date value exists in this field, the program should ignore the effective date in the Grade Step form and use this override date (regardless of whether the override date is before or after the Grade Step's effective date).
2. Based on the employee's pay scale, read the table corresponding to the Grade Step Placement window to determine whether the employee is already at the *ceiling*. If so, stop.
3. Read the table corresponding to the Pay Scale window to determine the *frequency* at which an employee should progress to the next step.
4. Based on the date from step 1 and the frequency from step 3, if the employee is not eligible to advance to the next step, stop. If the employee is eligible to advance to the next step, write a SQL statement to update the table (no API is currently available) to place the employee at the next available step for the Progression Point Placement window.

Caution

There is significant risk in writing directly to database tables. We do not recommend this as a general practice. Because Oracle does not offer an API for this item, the only other alternative involves use of a report followed by a manual process. It is recommended that extensive testing occur on this step.

5. Clear the segment Grade Step Override Date from the employee assignment Descriptive Flexfield.
6. Generate a salary proposal using the Salary Administration API.
7. The HR Manager must approve the proposed salary changes through the Oracle HR application.

The second solution addresses the issue when there is a pay increase (usually annual) for all steps on a given pay scale. The custom process performs the following activities:

1. Determine whether a new date tracked record exists in the progression point values table.
2. If a new entry is identified, search the employee assignment Grade Step Placement database table to find all employees who are at that specific progression-point step on that specific pay scale.
3. Write a SQL statement to update the table (no API is available) to reflect that the employee's current progression point step has a new rate of pay. This step might not be required. The fact that the employees are already assigned to the step should automatically point them to the correct new rate of pay.
4 Generate a salary proposal using the Salary Administration API.
5. The HR Manager must approve the proposed salary changes through the Oracle HR application.

When naming the points to a pay scale, be descriptive. Instead of referring to pay scale points generically as 1, 2, 3, 4, and so on, use names such as 6 months, 12 months, 18 months, Temp Supervisor, Temp Maintenance, Temp Foreman, Temp Mechanic, and so on.

One last thing to help make things more confusing: If you begin looking at the database tables through SQL, you'll discover the terminology of *spines*. Progression points on the application windows are called *spinal points* in the database. Pay scales on the application windows are called *parent spines*.

Setting Up Collective Agreements

With Release 11*i*, Oracle provides two additional forms to assist you with managing agreements with Collective Bargaining Units. Note that the basic functionality of salary administration remains the same. You must complete the following tasks prior to setting up your Collective Agreements:

1. Define the Bargaining Unit Organizations.
2. Define the Employer Organization(s).
3. Define your Grades and Grade Descriptions.

After these steps have been defined, you can create your Collective Agreements. You can attach the actual agreement using the attachment feature within Oracle.

You tie the Collective Agreements and Grades together with the Collective Agreements and Grade Structures form.

BENEFICIARIES WITH ORACLE HR

During the benefit enrollment process, employees can name beneficiaries for benefits in these classifications:

- AD&D (insurance coverage for accidental death or dismemberment)
- Life Insurance
- 401(k)
- Pension
- Profit Sharing
- Stock Purchase

The beneficiaries are normally individuals who are entered into Oracle HR as contacts or organizations. When the beneficiary is set up, you can attach her to an employee's benefit element via the Beneficiaries window if you are using Basic Benefits or via Designations during enrollment if you are using Standard or Advanced Benefits.

Regardless of which benefit model you use, the first step in the process is to set up the beneficiary. If the beneficiary is an individual, navigate to the Person window of the employee to whom this beneficiary is to be associated (Navigation path: People, Enter and Maintain). Click the Others button and select Contact. Make sure you are date-tracked to the date the person becomes a beneficiary of the employee. Complete the window, making sure you include the name, gender, birth date, Social Security number, and address (if different from employee). If the beneficiary is an organization, such as an alumni association or local foundation, navigate to the Organization window (Navigation path: Work Structures, Organization, Description). As with all organizations, you must set up a Location record for the address of the organization before navigating to the organization window. Verify that you have set up the organization with the classification as *Beneficiary Organization*.

BATCH ELEMENT ENTRY USES

Batch Element Entry (BEE) is a means of entering mass information for elements for numerous employees (see Figure 24.6).

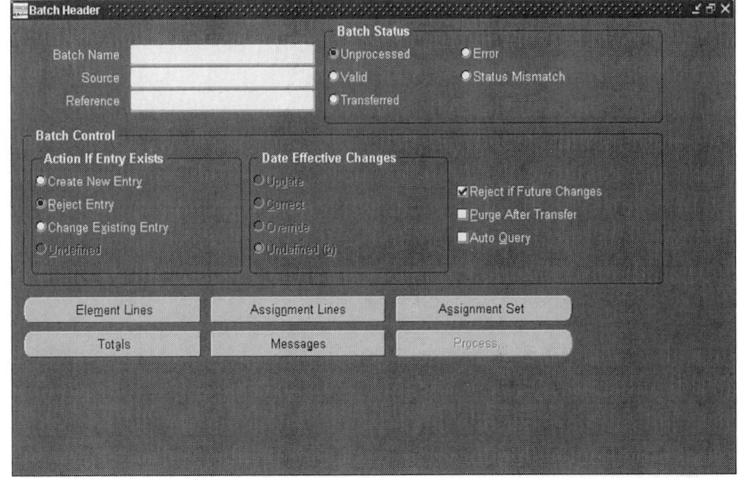

Figure 24.6
Preparing to create a batch of elements.

BEE is used by many enterprises to accomplish the following Payroll functions:

- Record timecard data
- Enter special nonrecurring earnings or deductions, such as Bonuses
- Enter one-time changes to normal recurring earnings or deductions

BEE can be used for the following nonpayroll tasks:

- Absence Management
- Benefits Administration for Basic Benefits
- Salary Administration

To enter batch headers and control totals, do the following:

1. Set the effective date desired.
2. Enter a name, reference number, and source of the batch.
3. Select the action to be taken if a batch line ends up matching an existing Element Entry. Actions are the following:

   Create new entry

   Reject entry

   Change existing entry

4. If Change entry is selected, indicate what type of change should be made to the existing Element Entry:

   Update

   Correct

   Override

5. If Reject is selected, you cannot select override.
6. If Purged after Transfer is desired, select this check box.
7. Choose the Totals button to validate the batch before transfer.

Enter Batch Lines by doing the following:

1. Choose the Line button and select the HR/Payroll element to which you want to make entries.
2. Choose the Default button to allow the default window to display the input values.
3. Enter default values.
4. Uncheck the Display check box for any field you do not want to display in the Lines window.
5. In the Lines window, enter data required for the batch.
6. Save your entries.
7. Batch lines can be retrieved and you can update a batch before you transfer it

Note also that Batch Element Entry can be used in interfaces to provide for the automated load of element entries. The interface needs to write to the following tables:

- PAY_BATCH_HEADERS
- PAY_BATCH_LINES
- PAY_BATCH_CONTROL_TOTALS

After a batch has been created, you validate it. See Table 24.1 for the various statuses a batch can have.

TABLE 24.1 BATCH STATUSES

Valid	Transferred	Unprocessed	Error	Status Mismatch
All headers, lines, and control totals are valid.	All headers and lines have been transferred to Element Entries.	One line, at a minimum, is unprocessed.	One line, at a minimum, is in error.	Combination of statuses in the batch, lines are not consistent.

APPLICATION DATA EXPORT

Application Data Export (ADE) is a powerful data extract tool specific to Oracle's HRMS application. Many users are not aware of what ADE is and what benefits it can provide. A common misunderstanding of ADE is that it is a separate program, possibly even a non-Oracle product, when in fact it is an Oracle product and is tightly integrated with the application. This misunderstanding is probably due to the fact that the program is not documented in the Human Resources or Payroll user manuals.

ADE can be used from within the application by selecting the ADE button on the application toolbar at the appropriate time, or it can be run in standalone mode without the application running at the time. Most Human Resources and Payroll professionals know that they have unique needs for data, perhaps unlike any other groups in an organization. These people know that they receive many questions and are required to provide analysis on the organization's employee population and associated data. Employee lists, phone number listings, and birthday lists are just a few of the most basic requests. ADE puts power into their hands by providing them access to data without having to request a formal report from the MIS department. The users are not totally independent from MIS because technical skills are required to set up the ADE environment, but from that point the users can then generate data on their own.

The following are various topics and tips to consider when using ADE:

- **Running ADE from within Oracle HRMS**—On most forms, the user is permitted to supply a value in a field and perform a query that returns matching data to that form. For example, one might go to the People form and query on all those employees with names beginning with "A" ("A%" in the Last field). When the data is returned, the user can invoke ADE by clicking the Data Export button on the toolbar (furthest button to the right). ADE starts and enables the user to fetch the data and place it into a program on his desktop (for example, MS Word, MS Excel). All fields associated with that form are exported to the specified destination. All the folders within the application allow for ADE to be selected, exporting the contents of the folder to a selected destination. As you might imagine, when ADE is run in this manner, the data exported is limited to the data that can be viewed onscreen. Often, additional fields are required. In these cases, it is possible to run ADE in standalone mode.
- **Running ADE Standalone**—ADE works by running established queries against the database and enables the user to place that extracted data into a program that he can use to further analyze or utilize the data. Microsoft Excel spreadsheets can be created as well as Microsoft Word documents. From that point, any sort of reports, graphics, form letters, or printed labels can be generated. The queries that ADE runs are based on database views. The views can be further refined with styles.
    - **Views**—Views are simply saved SQL statements that are normally created by MIS. SQL statements can be quite complex, joining many tables within the application. Most requests for information can be satisfied with a small number of well-designed views. These views can be further refined in ADE by creating Styles.
    - **Styles**—Styles can also be created by MIS, but they also can be created by HR or Payroll personnel who have some technical aptitude. A style can specify a subset of columns that are available in the view.

  To run an ADE query in standalone mode, the user simply selects a style and specifies constraints at runtime to limit the query if necessary. At that point, ADE fetches the data and returns the results to a window for display. The user can then export the contents to another program if desired.

- **Other ADE Features**—Security in ADE is controlled by application security. When using ADE, you select a responsibility the same way as within the application. Also, if configured to do so, ADE can be used to upload data to the application database. For example, the application provides for exporting of salary information and uploading of salary changes. This is actually accomplished using ADE, although it might not be immediately apparent to the user. The same holds true for some of the letter-generation capabilities of the application (recruitment letters). ADE can also be used in conjunction with organization and position hierarchy diagrammers.

PRODUCING MS WORD DOCUMENTS USING ADE

Oracle HRMS provides a number of methods of automatically creating MS Word documents such as form letters or labelsz from Oracle data using ADE. It also enables creation of MS Excel spreadsheets, but because that is a more straightforward process and is well documented in other places, it is not covered in this discussion. Creation of MS Word documents is somewhat more involved and requires more setup.

There are four ways to produce Word documents using Oracle/ADE. They are as follows:

1. Use the recruitment letter form. This method enables you to place individuals into a form who are to receive letters. This is a fine choice for small numbers of recipients. This method can include functionality that would produce letters based on certain types of status changes of applicants. The database views that you base your letters on must contain certain columns for this method to work.
2. Generate letters with an export from a form. This method limits your person selection to queries that can be run on a form and columns that are available to that form. It is not a very flexible approach and therefore not recommended.
3. Generate letters using the MS Word Letter Request form. This method will be discontinued in future releases of Oracle HRMS (post 10.7).
4. Generate letters/labels using standalone ADE. This method is most flexible and is the recommended approach in most cases.

The remainder of this discussion contains detailsz on the setup and processing of method 4.

RECOMMENDED SOLUTION

To use this method, you must modify an existing Style or create a new Style in ADE. To do this, you must have System Administrator rights to ADE, and you might need an available view that contains the data you need. The Styles you use are based on views or application forms. If you want to create a view, remember the naming convention "HRV_" should precede any view name that will be used by ADE. An MS Word merge document must be created and placed in the proper directory. The demonstration in the following section details a simple address label creation based on an existing view of all active employees. It shows how to use criteria to limit results of the process.

SETUP STEPS

The following stepsuse an existing view of all employees to create a simple address label:

1. Create or modify a Style.

   Start up ADE in standalone mode and sign in as system administrator. Select the Style tab and enter the following settings:

   - **Form:** GENERAL—Tells the system that this style is not based on a form.
   - **View:** HRV_CURRENT_EMPLOYEES_US—You can use or create any view that contains the data you want to include in your document. The name of the view *must* begin with HRV_.
   - **Document:** Address.doc—This is the actual name of the Word document that will be used. It should exist in the \APPLICATIONS\HRIO\LETTERS subdirectory of the drive on which ADE is installed. See step 2 for instructions to create the document.

2. Create a Word document. You do this by performing the following steps in the order listed here:

   - Go back to Paths tab in ADE. Click the Test button and select the style that you created in the prior step.
   - Click OK, and MS Word is launched. A document is created with merge fields that equate to fields from the style. You can create the labels using these merge fields. Then create merge options by selecting Tools, Mail Merge menu options from within Word.
   - Click the Create button, select the type of merge document (Mailing Labels, in this case) desired, and select Active Window.
   - Click the Get Data button. Select Open Data Source. Use the Windows File Select facility to locate HRIO.XLS (usually in \APPLICATIONS\TEMP in the directory that ADE is installed in). Respond Entire Worksheet when the system prompts you for a range to include.
   - Click the Setup button to select formatting options for your labels. Select the type of labels you want to use (5160 - Address, for this example). Then create the layout of your label by inserting merge fields in the way you want them to appear.
   - Click OK. The layout of your document changes to reflect the appearance of your labels.
   - Close the Merge Helper form and save the file using the same name that you specified in the "Document" setting for your style. Be certain to save the file in the \APPLICATIONS\HRIO\LETTERS subdirectory of the drive that ADE is installed in.

3. Run ADE query. You do this by performing the following steps in the order listed here:

   - Start ADE in standalone mode and choose the Style that was modified in the Query Details box.

- You can narrow the results of a query by selecting a field in the Criteria box and then clicking and dragging the button to the right of that box down to the Selection Details area. You are prompted to input your selection criteria. In this example, you want to see only those employees whose location begins with the number 951. Enter this value and click OK.
- Then click the Fetch button to execute the query. The system runs the query and displays results in a spreadsheet-type format. Click the Word button to initiate the merge.
- This launches MS Word with the data selected by the query formatted within the document that was created earlier.
- You can print this document immediately or save it under a different name for later printing.

Please note that this final process might take several minutes to run depending upon the size of your query. Also, the seeded `HRV_CURRENT_EMPLOYEES_US` view, on which this example is based, contains a flaw that sends the County data to the State field.

IMPLEMENTING HR AFTER FINANCIALS

Many companies are faced with a situation in which they desire to implement Oracle HR/Payroll after they have previously implemented Oracle Financials. Because of shared data between HRMS and Financials, there are often changes required to the Financial modules to accommodate the requirements of HRMS.

From an Oracle Payroll perspective, things are fairly easy. Generally, you should map segments of the Payroll Cost Allocation Key Flexfield to the corresponding segments of the Oracle General Ledger Accounting Key Flexfield. In essence, it is usually better if GL is implemented before Payroll.

When looking at issues affecting Oracle Human Resources, the issues are more challenges. The following areas of shared data must be addressed:

- **Organizations**—Because these are used by Oracle Projects and other modules, you should prepare for additions and likely changes to organizations due to different HRMS security, costing, and reporting requirements. Note that it is not a requirement that HR use the exact same organizations that have been set up for the other modules. However, it does make good sense when a common organization is being represented.
- **Locations**—If the same locations that were set up for Financials are planned for use by HRMS, you should assure that each location has an address. Moreover, prepare each address to obtain the appropriate Vertex validation by opening and saving each location from within HRMS. Otherwise, employees cannot be assigned and paid using this location.
- **Jobs/Positions**—Oracle HR nearly always requires changes to jobs and positions that have been set up for use in Oracle Financials. This is because of management and government reporting requirements. In particular, implementers of Oracle Purchasing

require either jobs or positions to identify buyers. However, if a position has been set up with one segment titled "Buyer," the HR department will almost assuredly require this to be changed.

- **People/Assignments**—Some data within the underlying tables might need to be altered, depending on exactly how your data has been stored by Oracle Financials. These are usually more minor issues when compared to the other items of shared data. For instance, the last name and first name of employees might have been entered in uppercase. Because this is not as desirable for HR reports or Payroll checks, you might want to change items such as this.
- **Addresses**—Employee addresses set up for use by Oracle AP require attention because AP does not establish the appropriate Vertex validations required by Payroll. You will likely need to write SQL scripts or prepare to delete and reenter certain addresses.

TROUBLESHOOTING

If you are planning to implement Oracle HR, consider that much of your upcoming challenge is an art. Sure, there are technical (or scientific) issues, such as the section earlier in this chapter discussing implementing Oracle HRMS after financials. Because Human Resources processes are often an art, most companies might never know whether they are obtaining a "good" implementation of Oracle HR. Troubleshooting HR processes and HR software implementation is thus generally not focused on getting the "right" answer. This is because there are often numerous answers with some degree of "correctness." The focus should be on whether you obtain solutions that make optimal use of the functionality of your Oracle Human Resources system.

At BOSS, we believe your best chances of obtaining optimal solutions are to work with heavily experienced individuals who know Oracle HR functionality thoroughly but who are not confined from creative thinking so that nonstandard solutions can be created based on your specific needs.

CHAPTER 25

Using Oracle Payroll

In this chapter

DISCOVERING NEW FEATURES IN RELEASE 11*i*

Release 11*i* Payroll new features include the following:

Oracle Cash Management integration provides for payroll check reconciliation.

Vertex Quantum Tax Engine is written in C, not Microfocus Cobol.

Category is expanded for 403(b) and 457.

Benefits enhancement support for OAB module.

Legislative payroll hooks enable you to enter extra Fast Formula checking in the Gross to Net calculation.

PayMIX and Batch Element Entry are consolidated. PayMIX is a U.S.-specific interface prior to Release 11*i*. The PayMIX and Batch Element Entry windows are merged in 11*i* and are referred to as Batch Element Entry, or BEE.

Performance is improved in the Transfer to GL process.

Performance is improved in Direct Deposit Advice process.

Performance is improved in various reports.

The payroll iterative engine aids in gross ups and pretax arrearage; note that these iterations occur in memory and do not result in additional run results in the database. The actual payroll process still creates the same number of Run Results as it does currently.

Oracle Time Management provides global support.

Business Intelligence System 1.3 is a cross-application function for issues such as revenue reporting.

A note if you are an Oracle Advanced Benefit (OAB) customer: Even though OAB takes a different approach to benefits enrollment/eligibility, your current HRMS setups for Elements, Element Links, and Element Entries will not be interrupted. You can continue to process Oracle Payroll as you have before. In fact, OAB makes extensive use of Elements and Element Entries. Note that there is no planned built-in migration of HR Element Links to OAB Benefits Enrollment/Eligibility for those customers who desire to convert their elements to the new OAB mechanisms for enrollment.

PAYROLL PROCESSING (FROM BATCH ELEMENT ENTRY TO CHECKWRITER TO GL)

There are several operations that take place during a typical payroll process within Oracle Payroll:

- **BEE**—Timecards are entered or are transferred from a timekeeping system.
- **Payroll Process**—Calculation engine for Oracle Payroll.
- **Prepayments**—Identifies payments as either check or direct deposit. It also prepares payments to third-party organizations for wage attachments.

- **Check Writer**—Prepares file for printing payroll checks and any third-party payments.
- **NACHA**—Prepares file for transfer to National Automated Clearing House.
- **Deposit Advice**—Prepares file for printing deposit advices for employees receiving direct deposit.
- **Costing**—Generates costing data to be transferred to General Ledger. It also prepares summarized costing reports based on actual payroll data.
- **Void Payments**—Allows payments to be voided.
- **Transfer to GL**—Transfers the costing data previously generated to the General Ledger.

PAYROLL PROCESSING: BEE

Prior to 11*i*, PayMIX and Batch Element Entry were separate functions for entering elements. These functions have been combined and enhanced and are now referred to as Batch Element Entry.

BEE (Batch Element Entry) provides for rapid entry of data batches, including timecard data, one-time earnings or deductions, and one-time changes to existing earnings or deductions. BEE is the interface that receives timecards from Oracle Time Management. Additionally, BEE is the interface used for receiving timecards in the United States from time and attendance systems (see the section titled "Time and Attendance Integration with BEE").

The existence of timecards within BEE has no effect on payroll processing. These timecards must be validated and transferred to the Element Entries tables before they can be processed.

The Batch Header form, shown in Figure 25.1, is where all batch entry and processing must start. The batch is identified and located for additional entry by the name entered in Batch Name. The processing status of the batch is also displayed on the Header screen.

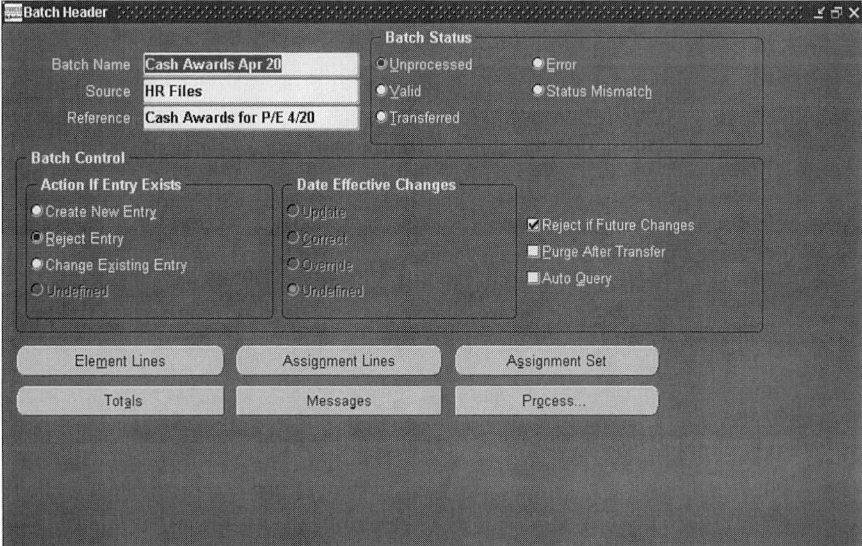

Figure 25.1
Header screen for a batch before any processing.

The batch status values are

- **Unprocessed**—The batch has not been validated or transferred.
- **Valid**—The batch header and lines have been verified and no errors have been found.
- **Error**—There is an error in either the batch header or the batch line items.
- **Transferred**—The batch line items have been transferred to the Entries table. Note that the transfer process performs both a validation and a transfer.

After information has been saved in BEE, run the BEE Validation process to ensure that the entries are correct. Investigate and correct any that show errors. This process verifies the following:

The employee's assignment number exists in the database.

The employee is eligible for the earning or deduction.

Earnings or deduction element exists to receive the data entered.

Where values are entered as override, the original value is there to accept the override.

That no discrepancies exist with system-generated BEE batch totals.

When a batch is *not* in Transferred mode, you can still make additions and corrections to the batch. When the batch has been transferred, you can no longer change or delete the information in the batch.

Note

A new function added for 11*i* is the capability to roll back a batch transfer after it has been successfully completed. This process may only be run if the batch has not been deleted after the original transfer is completed. If the batch has been deleted, no rollback is possible.

The rollback process, submitted from the Submit Requests window, has an option for completing the process even if the elements transferred have existing run results from payroll processing. The payroll interlock rule, which prevents rolling back a payroll process that has had further processing, is not invoked for BEE rollback. This option should be used with extreme caution.

Payroll Processing: Payroll Processing

The Payroll Process is the primary calculation engine for Oracle Payroll. It processes all earnings, deductions, employer liabilities, and other payments that exist on an employee's Element Entries. When submitting the payroll process, you have the option to select the payroll period ending date and date of payment for a specifically define payroll. (Note that a payroll is a group of employees designed to process together on a set frequency.) At times, you might want to submit subsets of employees for special payroll processing. Assignment Sets are a useful tool to help achieve this. Also, keep in mind that the QuickPay process is available when payroll processing is desired for only one employee at a time.

Payroll Processing: Processing Prepayments

The Prepayments process is run after the payroll is complete. The Prepayments process distributes the money in all the methods the user has defined. (Generally, this separates checks from direct deposits.) It also separates any third-party payments that were generated by wage attachments. Actual processing of payments is covered in the following section.

Payroll Processing: Payments Processing

The payments process consists of running three processes for paying employees: Check Writer, NACHA, and Deposit Advice. These are fairly straightforward processes. Check Writer produces checks to match each employee's Statement of Earnings (SOE). It also generates checks to third-party organizations for wage attachments. One drawback on third-party checks is that Oracle Payroll does not consolidate paychecks from multiple employees even when they have a common third-party organization. Oracle generates one check per employee. Many companies choose not to use this function for that reason. NACHA prepares an output file so that you can send money to the various banks and credit unions. Deposit Advice produces a file containing the Statement of Earnings from those employees using Direct Deposit.

Note that Oracle Employee Self Service now provides an online statement to the employee in addition to, or in place of, a printed statement. More users are investigating this means of making advice notices available to employees. Federal guidelines permit this but each state law needs to be investigated thoroughly if the user chooses an online method. Employees should be given ample notice that a new payroll system has been chosen, a sample copy of the SOE, and, if online, information on how to access the SOE. Recommendation is for a detailed memo with a sample copy of the SOE to include a telephone number and contact name to call if questions or concerns regarding their paycheck or direct deposit choice arise. If using an outside vendor to process paychecks, it is recommended that a backup payment source be identified. Identify either an in-house printer or another outside source. This information is usually included in a disaster recovery plan.

Payroll Processing: Voiding Payments Process

Oracle provides a method to void checks that were printed and need to be cancelled. This process can be useful in the case of printing errors, last minute terminations, or other reasons that necessitate the check being cancelled.

Payroll Processing: Costing

The Costing process coverts the results from a payroll run into the appropriate debits and credits. This process is an important prerequisite to the Transfer to GL process. Even if payroll processing has already occurred for a payroll period, the costing data from the Element Links windows can be changed to apply to any payroll transactions that have not already been costed. Thus, running the Costing process provides verification of accurate costing before it is received by GL.

Many users are disturbed by the fact the Costing reports only show the costing side of the journal entry without showing the balancing side of the journal entry. If you want to see both the costing and balancing sides of the journal entry, you must develop your own report from the data stored in the payroll costing tables.

PAYROLL PROCESSING: TRANSFERRING TO GL

The Transfer to GL process is initiated after you have verified that payroll costing is correct. This information is transferred to the GL_INTERFACE table and is, in turn, imported by users of Oracle General Ledger. Some clients desire additional manipulation of payroll costing data at this point. If so, carefully define your business rules and prepare to manipulate the payroll data in the GL_INTERFACE table prior to its import into GL.

QUICKPAY PROCESSING

The QuickPay process is a useful tool for calculating payroll payments outside of the normal payroll cycle. The process can be initiated at any time and processes pay for individual employees within a few minutes. The process is especially useful for processing payments for employees who have been paid incorrectly or for processing final payments for terminating employees residing in states requiring that final wages be paid within a specific time period. During implementation, QuickPay runs are an excellent method of testing earnings, deductions, and tax calculations.

The QuickPay process is initiated from the employee Assignment window. Identify the employee for which you will be processing a QuickPay. Navigate to the Assignment window. Select Others and then QuickPay. Figure 25.2 shows the entries required to start a QuickPay. Enter the Date Paid, the check date, and the Date Earned, which must be within a valid pay period.

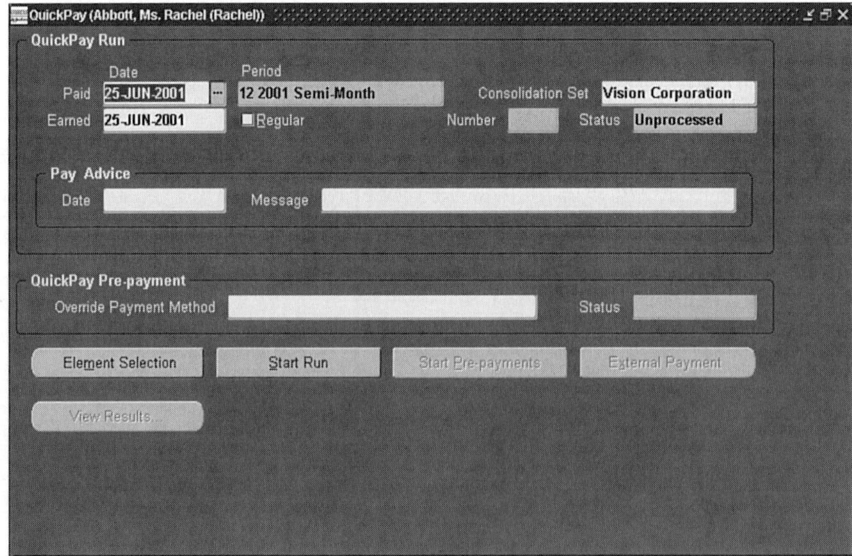

Figure 25.2
Click the Start Run button to process the QuickPay.

QuickPay runs accomplish the same results as the normal Oracle Payroll process submitted through Submit Processes and Reports. QuickPay runs calculate earnings, taxes, and deductions just as the normal payroll process runs. QuickPay runs can be specified as either regular or supplemental runs just as the normal payroll process runs. The distinction is that the QuickPay run is convenient and efficient for processing one employee. To process one employee through the normal payroll process runs, an Assignment Set of one employee needs to be created. Then, the Assignment Set needs to be referenced when submitting the payroll process through Submit Processes and Reports. Clearly, the QuickPay is less cumbersome than the normal payroll process.

When the QuickPay process is completed, the results can be reviewed immediately. This provides for the determination of the accuracy of the QuickPay run. The following review options are available from the View Results button:

View Run Messages

Run Results

SOE Report

Tax Balances

Earning and Deduction Balances

View Run Messages displays system messages (warning or error) that occurred during the QuickPay run.

Run Results lists each element containing a Pay Value that was processed for the employee. This is particularly useful for viewing payroll elements that are not displayed on the employee's Statement of Earnings, such as Employer Liability elements.

SOE Report opens the Employee Statement of Earnings window to provide a view of all earnings and deductions and the resulting net pay that would be included on a paycheck.

Tax Balances displays federal, state, and local taxes. This is useful in viewing quarter-to-date and year-to-date tax balances for the employee.

Earning and Deduction Balances is similar to the Tax Balances button. This selection provides a review of employee balances of earnings and deductions for nontax elements.

If the payroll run results are satisfactory, a manual check can be issued, or the QuickPay can be included in the next scheduled Prepayments run. QuickPay gives the user the capability to override the employee's default payment method (Check or NACHA). After Prepayments has completed, the External/Manual Payments window can be invoked to establish the check number for the manual check.

Overriding Tax Information

Some individuals, including highly compensated employees, request to withhold supplemental taxes at a higher rate than legally required. The Oracle Payroll System provides a method to do this at the state and federal levels. The user can enter separate rates for state and federal in the employee tax information.

The three following conditions must be met to use a supplemental tax override rate:

The GRE must have flat percentage override selection as a calculation method.

A nonzero override rate must be specified.

A supplemental, not regular, payroll must be run.

The default withholding method is used if the three preceding conditions listed are not met.

To specify a Federal Income Tax (FIT) override, you select FIT override and enter the percentage in the Rate field. To withhold a Fixed FIT each period with no tax calculations occurring, enter the fixed amount. For Supplemental tax override, you enter a percentage in the Rate field to override the regular rate. The same procedure is used for State Income Tax override.

For state supplemental tax override, you must first specify a flat rate calculation method for the employer's GRE. Select the supplemental state withholding tax calculation method to be used for employees of this GRE.

Another note to consider when overriding tax information is the duration intended for the tax override. If the override is only intended for one pay period, you must remember to change the employee's W4 tax information back to its original values after the payroll run has been processed.

Other issues can arise requiring the override of tax information within Oracle Payroll due to tax rules when an employee works in one state and lives in another state. Similarly, these tax rules apply within certain states when an employee lives within one locality but works in another locality. In these situations, Oracle Payroll creates multiple tax records (multiple state tax records, multiple county tax records, or multiple locality tax records). If the user desires to force the taxation to be solely from one state, county, or locality, the user can set the employee's tax information to 100% in the desired tax jurisdiction and 0% in the other tax jurisdiction record. A note of caution is necessary here.

Caution

Oracle Payroll is extremely flexible in the area of tax information to accommodate numerous issues, including sudden tax law changes. You should carefully research all relevant tax laws before overriding the defaults supplied by Oracle Payroll.

PROCESSING STATE QUARTERLY WAGE LISTINGS

One of the most important features of an automated payroll application is the ability to produce tax reports. Oracle HRMS provides for the production of required tax reporting. U.S. states require quarterly filings that give employment level and wage information for that employer within the state. The result of the process is a summary report and an associated electronic file that can be written to magnetic media and submitted to the state.

Running this process is simple. It is submitted for processing to the concurrent manager through the Submit Reports and Processes window, just like any other report or process. If the report ends in error, it can be rolled back using the standard Rollback process. If the report does err, it is most likely due to the fact that a balance adjustment has been made at some point that causes a balance to carry a negative value. The Request Log of the job in error contains an ASSIGNMENT_ID that enables you to identify the individual who is causing the error condition. Another balance adjustment can be made at that point to correct the negative condition. The SQWL job can then be run again. Oracle offers a Negative Balance Report that identifies potential problems. It is advisable to run this report just prior to running SQWLs.

SQWL SETUP

Before successfully running the SQWLs, a number of parameters need to be set up. You need to identify any GREs in a state as a transmitter of the wage listing file and provide setup data. This information, as shown in Figure 25.3, is set up at the Organization level under the GRE/Legal Entity Organization Classification. There are four different groups of parameters there: SQWL Employer Rules (1), SQWL Employer Rules (2), SQWL Generic Transmitter Rules, and SQWL State Transmitter Rules. You need to be familiar with the format requirements of the states with which you file and set those parameters accordingly. You also need to set up employer identification and contact information.

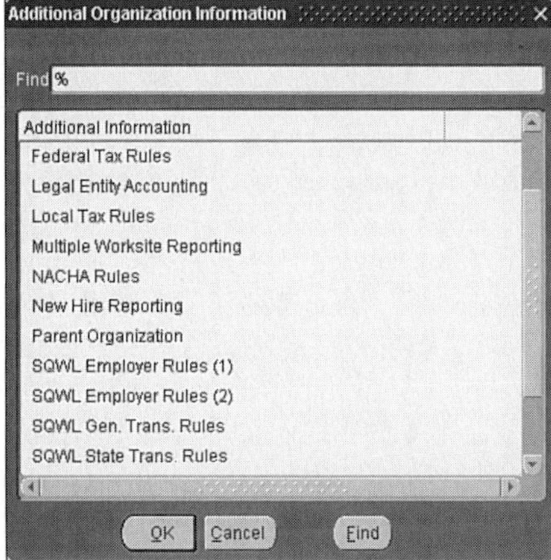

Figure 25.3
Click the SQWL rule to open the entry form.

A few states (Alaska, California, and Missouri) request parameters to be set at the employee level. These are set in the alternative region of the person's Assignment window called GREs and Other Data.

SQWL Running

The SQWL jobs (called State Quarterly Wage Listing) are submitted individually by state. Parameters requested at runtime include state, quarter, format, and transmitter GRE. A summary page is produced that shows amounts that can be balanced to other reports for verification.

W-2 Year-End Processing

One of the most important tasks that must be completed by the payroll department is the preparation of W-2s and the supporting magnetic media. This section outlines the various steps to guide you in making the year-end process run smoothly.

Early in December each year, representatives from HR, Payroll, and MIS should meet to review the end-of-year schedule. During this meeting, members must map out the last payroll runs of the year and schedule the processing of year-end balance adjustments. Generally, these adjustments are for items such as relocation expenses, personal use of company cars, and education assistance. After the completion of the meeting, you should have a detailed calendar of all the year-end events.

Oracle strongly recommends that you run a series of year-end reports to validate the employees before beginning the year-end process. They are the following:

- **Taxable Balance Verification Report**—This report identifies incorrectly withheld amounts for Social Security, Medicare, FUTA, SUI, and SDI Taxes. This report is especially helpful if there were balance loads performed sometime during the year.
- **Invalid Address Report**—This report lists people with invalid primary addresses.
- **GRE Totals Report**—This report helps you balance W-2s. It lists totals for either selected GREs or all GREs. You should be able to balance this report with the year-to-date registers.
- **Negative Balances**—This report lists negative year-to-date and/or quarter-to-date amounts in several tax balances. This can be very helpful if any of the tax balances were incorrectly loaded during an initial balance load procedure.

To demonstrate how you would correct a problem identified by one of the reports, assume that the Negative Balances Report listed negative amounts in the Excess balance for SUI ER in Massachusetts. According to the Tax Withholding rules, Section 125 deductions are subject to SUI. However, assume that you loaded the balances as if Section 125 deductions were not subject to SUI. The SUI ER Subj Whable balance was understated by the Section 125 amounts, and the SUI ER 125 Redns balance should have been zero. For this example, assume the YTD Section 125 amount was $56.10. Therefore, you needed to add 56.10 to the SUI ER Subj Whable balance and subtract 56.10 from the SUI ER 125 Redns balance.

The first step in the process is to determine what element to use to make the balance adjustment. During the initial balance load, Oracle generates elements to be used in balance initialization. These are created with the SRS process called Initial Balance Structure Creation. You can also use these elements to make balance adjustments. Navigate to the Balance window (navigation path: Compensation and Benefits, Balance) and query the name of the balance that needs to be adjusted. In this case, you need to adjust balances for SUI ER Subj Whable and SUI ER 125 Redns. Click the Initial Feed button and note the name of the element and input value. Table 25.1 outlines possible Initial Value Feeds for your balances.

TABLE 25.1 SUI ER BALANCE FEEDS

Balance	Initial Feed	Input Value
SUI ER Subj Whable	Initial_Value_Element_202_2_1	3
SUI ER 125 Redns	Initial_Value_Element_202_2_1	6

Now, you can create the balance adjustments. Navigate to the Adjust Balance window for the subject employee (navigation path: People, Enter and Maintain, Assignments, Other, Adjust Balance). Make sure you are date-tracked to the effective date of the balance adjustment. Select from the pick list the element Initial_Value_Element_202_2_1, and type **-56.10** in input value 3 and **56.10** in input value 6. Save your work. Other balance adjustments are performed in a similar manner.

The next step in the year-end process is to create the balance feeds for the various W-2 boxes. In the following example, assume that you plan to use W-2 Box 13C (cost of group-term life insurance over $50,000), W-2 Box 13D (elective deferrals to a section 401(k) cash or deferred arrangement), and the Pension Plan and Deferred Comp boxes in region 15. Table 25.2 contains possible balance feeds that need to be established.

TABLE 25.2 W-2 EXAMPLE BALANCE FEEDS

W-2 Box	Balance Feed	Input Value
W-2 Box 13C	Dependent Life Imputed.	Pay Value
	Employee Life Imputed.	Pay Value
W-2 Box 13D	401(k) Pretax.	Pay Value
W-2 Pension Plan	All Pension Earnings.	Pay Value
Def Comp	This box is automatically checked if W-2 Box 13D is defined.	

The name in the Balance Feed column is the name of the element you created to calculate the earning or deduction. The phrase All Pension Earnings means that you add a balance feed for every earning element that should be included in pension-eligible earnings.

Now you are ready to run the first step of the year-end process, called the Year-End Pre-Process. The Year-End Pre-Process is the Oracle Payroll utility that archives the employee balances for a specific year and GRE. When archived, this data is available for end-of-year reporting. If an employee's record has changed after running the Year-End Pre-Process, you can retry the process for that employee. It is not necessary to rerun the entire process. In instances where multiple employee balances are changed, it might be easier to roll back the entire Year-End Pre-Process and rerun again from scratch. If you have generated any of the following reports, you must first roll them back (use the Rollback Process) prior to retrying the Year-End Pre-Process:

Federal W-2 Magnetic Media

State W-2 Magnetic Media

Federal 1099-R Magnetic Media

State 1099-R Magnetic Media

To retry selected employees in the Year-End Pre-Process, use the Retry Payroll Process *(not the Retry US Payroll Process)*. To roll back the entire Year-End Pre-Process, use the Rollback Process.

When the Year-End Pre-Process is completed, you can then print the W-2 Register. This report can be printed in either detail or summary. This report prints the contents of each box for every employee (if the detail option is selected) and totals for the entire GRE. Balance these totals to the GRE Totals report and any year-to-date registers.

After performing the necessary balance adjustments, running the Year-End Pre-Process, and balancing the totals to the various registers, you are now ready to print the W-2 statements. Run the Employee W-2 report from the Submit Requests window. You can print W-2s for the entire GRE population or for a single organization, location, or employee. You can also sort the output by Employee Name, Social Security Number, Organization, Location, Termination Reason, or ZIP Code. Form W-2s are printed four copies per page, in accordance with the Evergreen #5206N preprinted laser form. This process is totally rerunnable and does not require you to retry the employee in the Year-End Pre-Process (unless you changed a balance).

The final step in year-end processing is to create the necessary magnetic tapes for the various federal and state agencies. These tapes contain the annual wage and tax statements of employee earnings and tax withholding for your enterprise. You must successfully run the Year-End Pre-Process for each GRE before running a federal or state magnetic W-2 report.

You run the Federal Magnetic W-2 Report from the Submit Requests window. In the Name field, select Federal W-2 Magnetic Media from the list of values. In the Year field, enter the tax year for the report. In the Transmitter GRE field, select the name of the GRE that functions as the transmitter of the W-2 report. This process creates the W-2 records for *all* GREs on one tape. It creates a file on the server that MIS needs to copy over to a tape.

The State Magnetic report is run in a similar manner. Once again, this process is run from the Submit Requests window. In the Name field, select State W-2 Magnetic Media from the list of values. In the State field, select the desired state. In the Year field, enter the tax year for the report. This process also creates State W-2 records for all GREs. MIS also has to copy the server file to a tape.

This completes the synopsis of year-end processing. Clearly, the hardest part was performing the necessary balance adjustments and balancing the totals to the expected results. Some companies perform this task after every quarter in an effort to streamline the year-end process. They copy their production database instance to a test instance and balance the current YTD amounts to their quarterly reports. They also run the reports listed previously to catch any problems before they get to the crunch of year-end.

Regular Versus Supplemental Pay Runs

Oracle offers two types of payroll runs to use when processing employee's earnings and deductions. They are the following:

- **Regular**—Is used to process employees' regular earnings along with their usual deductions. By definition, regular earnings are earnings for time worked, such as salary and overtime. Normally, you process only one regular run per pay period.
- **Supplemental**—Is used to process supplemental earnings such as bonuses, awards, sick pay, and any other special, one-time earnings. You can run as many supplemental payroll runs as necessary in a pay period.

The first step in understanding the ramifications of regular versus supplemental pay runs is to understand how these pay runs are structured. Regular runs process for each employee all recurring earnings and deductions not yet processed in the period. It also includes all nonrecurring earnings and deductions that currently exist in an employee's element entries that have not been processed. In both of these cases, regular runs process *supplemental* earnings that exist in the element entries and have yet to be processed. Oracle Payroll only allows one regular run per employee per period (with the exception described later in this section).

Supplemental runs process all supplemental earnings for an employee with unprocessed entries for the period. All deductions, whether recurring or nonrecurring, that have their processing type set to All are also processed in supplemental runs. Finally, supplemental runs process all unprocessed recurring earnings (regular or supplemental) and deductions for employees with a status of Terminated, for whom final pay has not yet been processed.

When you understand which elements are processed by regular and supplemental runs, you can turn your attention to tax withholding issues. The default income tax withholding method for regular runs is Regular withholding (also called Percentage or Annualized Wages withholding). Regular runs, by default, process any supplemental earnings with regular withholding rates. If you want to process supplemental earnings that exist in regular runs at supplemental rates, you must mark these earnings as Tax Separately. You accomplish this task by setting the input value called Tax Separately on the supplemental earnings to Yes. Note that when an element is marked as Tax Separately, the element cannot be processed in a QuickPay, and the Payroll process must be used.

The default withholding method for supplemental runs is Supplemental Withholding. However, these runs apply regular withholding rates to any regular earnings included in final payments.

One other method that you can utilize is called Cumulative Withholding. This method applies to employees whose earnings occur unevenly during the year. Regular and supplemental runs both use this method for the regular earnings and commissions of those employees who qualify for and have requested it. Navigate to the Tax Information window of the requested employee and check the Cumulative Taxation box to turn on this method.

As mentioned previously, you can, in certain situations, process more than one regular run in a pay period for an employee. Generally, this is necessary when you have completed the normal pay process for a period and a stray timecard that must be processed arrives late. Assume also that the checks have been printed and the NACHA file has already been sent. Below are the steps to follow to process this additional check as a regular run in the same period:

Enter the timecard in the requested period either through BEE or directly to the employee's Element Entry window.

Navigate to the QuickPay window for this employee. Make sure to mark the pay run as a regular run.

Click the Element Selection button and mark all the elements you want to process. This enables you to schedule the specific deductions you want to process with this additional timecard. Generally, any deduction that is calculated on a percent-of-earnings basis (such as a 401(k)) should be included, but flat amount deductions (such as medical and dental) should not be deducted again.

Run the QuickPay and any associated post-payroll processing.

COSTING OF EARNINGS

Oracle Payroll is extremely flexible when it comes to costing of earnings. Cost information can be obtained at several levels within the Cost Allocation Key Flexfield: Payroll, Organization, Element Link, Assignment, Element Entry, and BEE. The valid cost levels are established when defining Flexfield Qualifiers for each segment of the Cost Allocation Key Flexfield.

Understanding how qualifiers are used is critical to understanding why your costing entries are behaving the way they are. You are given the opportunity to apply any or all of the qualifiers to each segment. If a qualifier is not enabled for a segment at the specific level, the segment does not appear on the form.

TABLE 25.3 FLEXFIELD QUALIFIERS USED FOR COST ALLOCATION KEY FLEXFIELD

Qualifier	Impact on Costing
Payroll	If enabled and no other entry is made for the same segment from the other levels, Costing uses the segment entered at the Payroll Description window. If each of your organizations/companies has a different payroll, you may wish to consider enabling the qualifier for Company. Typically, Payrolls are used across companies and no costing segments include this qualifier. This results in no costing entries generated based on the Payroll Description—except the suspense account. However, qualifiers do not have any effect on the Suspense Account string.
Organization	If enabled and no other entry is made for the same segment from the Element Link Costing window, Assignment Costing window, or the element Entry window (or BEE), Costing uses the segment entered at the Organization Description window. Organization will override any costing segments entered at the Payroll Description Costing window. Typically, Company, Division, or Cost Center segments are enabled at this level. This enables Human Resources users to assign employees to an organization without requiring knowledge of the GL number for company, division, or cost center. These numbers are automatically associated with the employees' GL records based on the organization assigned.
Link	If enabled and no other entry is made for the same segment from the Assignment Costing window or the Element Entry window (or BEE), Costing will use the segment entered at the Element Link window. Typically, organizations will use Fixed Costing for deductions and tax with holding elements. To provide for Fixed Costing, all segments must include the Link qualifier. If an element is identified as Fixed Costing, the costing segments will not be overridden from any level.
Assignment	If enabled and no other entry is made for the same segment from the Element Entry window (or BEE), Costing will use the segment entered at the Assignment Costing window. Typically, only exception entries are made at this level. For example, an employee is assigned to a special project for an extended period of time, and you wish to have the wages for this employee charged to another Cost Center or Wage Account other than the default established for this employee's organization. You would enter these values in the Costing window within the Assignment Form. Another example might be an Administrative Assistant that divides his time between two cost centers. His Assignment Costing window would include either cost centers at 50% each, or other percentage so that the combined percentages would equal 100%.
Entry	If enabled, Costing will use the segment entered at the Element Entries window or entered via BEE. This is the last level, and entries made to costing at this level will override entries made at any other level. Typically, short-term overrides are made at this level. Segments such as Project, Department, Job, or Task commonly use this qualifier. You must consider what types of overrides your company allows from a Time Card type of entry. If an employee works between cost centers within pay periods, you may want to consider enabling this qualifier for cost center.

TABLE 25.3 CONTINUED

Qualifier	Impact on Costing
Balancing	All segments that will be transferred to the GL must have this qualifier enabled; otherwise, an invalid Costing String is created and the record errors when imported to GL. The values entered for balancing segments occur on the Element Link window.

Note

All segments that are mapped to the GL must have the qualifier enabled at the Link and Balance levels if you are interfacing to the Oracle General Ledger System. Not entering all the segments will result in errors during the Transfer to GL process.

When preparing for the implementation of HR Organizations, it is recommended that you keep the GL requirements in mind. Costing defaults for all of your elements can be established based on HR Organizations. This aids in the future maintenance of employee information. The HR department does not have to concern itself with the GL cost segment values. The HR department merely needs to assign an employee to the correct organization. These costing defaults are particularly beneficial when an employee's earnings are costed the same way every pay period. Keep in mind that these costing defaults for an organization are flexible and can be overwritten during payroll processing. If Oracle Payroll retrieves costing information at a lower level, such as Element Entries, it overrides the defaults from the employee's organization.

Oracle Payroll is very flexible in dynamically changing a cost segment value from one payroll period to the next. Timecard records can be entered into BEE using different cost segment values for each record. Consider a maintenance employee who works four hours at a cost center, two hours at another cost center, and still two more hours at a third cost center. The next day, this same employee works at other cost centers. For more details about the integration of cost data into BEE, please see the section of this chapter titled "Time and Attendance Integration with BEE."

What about cost defaults for groups of employees where the organizations of the employees do not apply? This is where the People Group Key Flexfield becomes particularly beneficial. Consider a situation where you want to separately obtain cost account information for employee Regular Salary using a distinction between executive and administration employees. In this example, executive and administration employees might be scattered throughout numerous organizations. You could set up a People Group Key Flexfield segment to distinguish these two groups and then establish two Element Links for Regular Salary based on the People Group segment value.

Here are a few thoughts that might influence your transfer of costing information for balancing/offsetting entries to the GL. At BOSS Corporation, we have observed that balancing segments behave as if they are fixed-costed even if the earnings element is defined as Costed. Consider setting up the Element Link with a fully qualified balancing segment. This works if you are balancing to only one account for cash. If you have multiple cash accounts, you need another solution. If you are too far into your implementation and cannot change your Element Links, be prepared for another solution. You need a customized process that is invoked after you have run the Transfer to GL process. You need to create a preprocess program that alters the data before the GL performs its import.

Costing of Overtime

Many times, companies want to separate out the premium portion of overtime to one GL account and the straight time portion to the normal straight time GL account. This allows the cost accountants to focus on the premium labor costs when overtime is required to complete a certain project or task.

This poses a problem for Oracle HR/Payroll because costing is performed at the element level. The standard Overtime element calculates the total overtime payment, including the straight time and the premium time. How can you separate this out to the two different GL accounts?

The key to the solution is to use two of the most powerful tools that Oracle gives you when implementing HR/Payroll: Fast Formulas and Indirect Formula Results. The first step in the solution is to create your own Overtime element because Oracle does not enable you to modify the seeded elements. Define the element with a Classification as Earnings and a Category as Overtime. Select HOURS_X_RATE_MULT_RECUR_V2 as the Calculation Rule. Oracle generates a formula called XXXXXXX_HOUR_X_RATE_MULT, where XXXXXXX is the name you gave your new Overtime element. You now need to make a copy of the formula used on the Overtime element and paste it into the generated formula. Make sure that you change all references of Overtime to XXXXXXX in the formula.

Study this new formula, and you will notice that Oracle has already separated out the straight time portion of the Overtime calculation into a variable called straight_OT. You only need to add a new statement that subtracts straight_OT from OT_pay to yield a new variable called premium_OT.

Oracle already sends the straight time portion of the overtime calculation to an Information element called Straight Time Overtime. Oracle uses this element for its Workers Compensation calculations. You need to create a new Information element called Premium Time Overtime, using the Oracle example as a guide.

Now navigate to the Formula Results Rules window and select from the pick list the name of the seeded Overtime element. Make note of the Formula Results region of the window. You need to set up your Overtime element exactly like the one you see here. Now select from the pick list your Overtime element, delete the Standard line in the Processing Rules region of the window, and save your work. Add the Standard line back in and make sure you specify the name of your formula. Down in the Formula Results region, add variable names exactly like the seeded Overtime element. Finally, add one more line using the premium_OT variable as an indirect result to the Information element you created previously.

The final step is to set up the Costing. The key to the solution is *not* to cost the Overtime element you created, but to cost the two Information elements. This enables you to specify different account numbers for each portion of the Overtime calculation.

There is one drawback to this solution that you must keep in mind. As stated previously, you establish the costing on the Element Link windows for the Information elements and not the Overtime element. There might be an occasion where you need to override this costing at element entry time. If you enter an override account number on the element entry for your overtime element, either through BEE or on the Element Entry window, the formula overrides both the straight time portion and the premium time portion with this override account. Oracle has stated that this is expected behavior and requires an enhancement request to modify it.

OVERTIME FLSA COMPLIANCE

Release 11*i* of Oracle Payroll is still not Fair Labor Standards Act (FLSA)–compliant in the calculation of overtime. The seeded Oracle Payroll earning for Overtime does not properly calculate the adjusted overtime base rate of pay when the payroll frequency is greater than one week. The seeded Overtime earning calculates an average rate based on the entire payroll period, not on a separate week-by-week basis. Note that this implies that FLSA compliance can be met within the product if you define your payrolls with a frequency of weekly.

As an example, assume a biweekly payroll period from 01-DEC through 14-DEC for an employee making $10/hour (see Table 25.4). Note in this example that the earning Sales Commission was created with Overtime Base checked on the Earnings Form.

TABLE 25.4 ELEMENT ENTRIES

Date	Earning Element	Hrs	Multiple	Amt
Week 1				
07-DEC	Time Entry Wages	40	1	$400
07-DEC	Sales Commission			$200
07-DEC	Overtime	10	1.5	
Week 2				
14-DEC	Time Entry Wages	40	1	$400
14-DEC	Overtime	1	1.5	

FLSA guidelines expect this overtime calculation:

Week 1 ($400 + $200) / 40 hours = $15/hour

$15/hour * 10 hours OT * 1.5 multiple = $225

Week 2 ($400) / 40 hours = $10/hour

$10/hour * 1 hour OT * 1.5 multiple = $15

FLSA Overtime = $225 + $15 = $240

Oracle Payroll calculates:

($400 + $200 + $400) / (40 hours + 40 hours) = $1,000 / 80 hours = $12.50/hour

$12.50/hour * 11 hrs OT * 1.5 multiple =

Oracle Payroll Overtime = $206.25

Thus: Employee is underpaid for the current payroll period by $33.75.

There are three different approaches to solving FLSA overtime-compliance calculations. Two of these solutions involve the use of Oracle BEE. These solutions involve the entry of an adjusted rate of pay into BEE for each overtime record. Approach #1 involves calculating the adjusted overtime rate before a record is inserted into BEE. Approach #2 involves calculating the adjusted overtime rate after records already exist in BEE. Approach #1 can only be used if you have an external Time & Attendance system. The integration program from Time & Attendance to BEE can include all the overtime rules. If you are using Oracle Time Management, you need to use Approach #2. If Approach #2 is used, it is vitally important that the BEE Transfer process, which transfers BEE batches to the Element Entries window, is not run before the overtime adjustment process is run.

Questions you must ask in implementing an adjusted overtime calculation are the following:

- Which earnings (Commission, Bonus, and so on) can influence an adjusted overtime rate of pay?
- Where do these adjustment earnings reside?
- Does the integration program have access to all earnings for the current pay period at the time that the integration is being run?

Some earnings can be set up in Oracle as recurring earnings. If so, the overtime calculation program must read an employee's Element Entries to determine whether the specific recurring earnings exist. Other earnings, such as commissions, might have been previously fed through a different process into BEE. Thus, the overtime calculation program must read BEE to determine whether the specific nonrecurring earnings exist. The integration gets complicated and is very rules-based, but the FLSA deficiency can be solved.

Approach #3 for solving FLSA overtime issues involves Fast Formula customization, careful setup of your Earnings elements, and careful procedures for how these elements are used. Instead of using the seeded elements for Time Entry Wages and Overtime, create your own

Earnings elements such as Week 1 Wages, Week 2 Wages, Week 1 Overtime, and Week 2 Overtime. Any earnings that should be used to influence the adjusted overtime base rate of pay must be created in the same manner such as Week 1 Bonus and Week 2 Bonus.

Prepare to modify the formulas for Week 1 Overtime and Week 2 Overtime. Week 1 Overtime must calculate its adjusted overtime base rate based on the existence of Week 1 Wages, Week 1 Bonus, and so on, within the current pay period. The formula for Week 2 Overtime must use similar logic.

Finally, if you use approach #3, be sure that interfaces between the time-entry system and BEE are analyzed. The interface program must be customized to split week 1–related elements from week 2 if the source data from the time-keeping system does not have these items already split.

Regardless of the current solution you choose, if the Oracle Payroll product is ever upgraded to become FLSA-compliant using the seeded Overtime element, take these steps to be prepared. All other earnings elements (Commission, Bonus, and so on) must be created carefully. On the Earnings window, select the appropriate check boxes for FLSA Hours and Overtime Base. Remember that if you fail to check these boxes appropriately, you cannot change the earnings' definitions later. In the meantime, your custom process to calculate an adjusted overtime-base rate of pay can use this information in establishing its rules for calculation.

401(K) CALCULATIONS/COMPANY MATCH

Oracle Payroll is now delivered to provide for the automatic creation through the Deductions window of a 401(k) company match element. However, earlier versions of the product did not have this functionality. The following discussion is still a useful learning tool regarding the flexibility and power of Fast Formula.

One of the most common benefit plans that companies offer employees is a 401(k) savings plan that usually includes a company match. This section outlines how at BOSS Corporation we used standard Oracle features to implement a typical 401(k) plan. The features we used include the following:

- Balance Definitions
- Global Values
- Fast Formulas
- Formula Results

The sample 401(k) plan has the following rules. Employees can elect to contribute up to 15% of their eligible earnings to the plan. The company matches 50 cents to every dollar, up to 10% of the eligible earnings. The deductions should stop when employees reach the IRS maximum amount allowed for 401(k) plans.

The first task is to set up a balance that will define eligible earnings. Use the Balance window,displayed in Figure 25.4, to define this new balance (navigation path: Total Compensation, Basic, Balance). In this example, name the balance Earnings 401k. After completing the initial window, click the Feeds button and select from the pick list all the earnings that should be used when calculating the pretax deductions. Click the Dimensions button and select from the pick list the desired dimensions. Use Assignment within GRE Run in the formula. This balance will be used to calculate both the actual deduction and the company match.

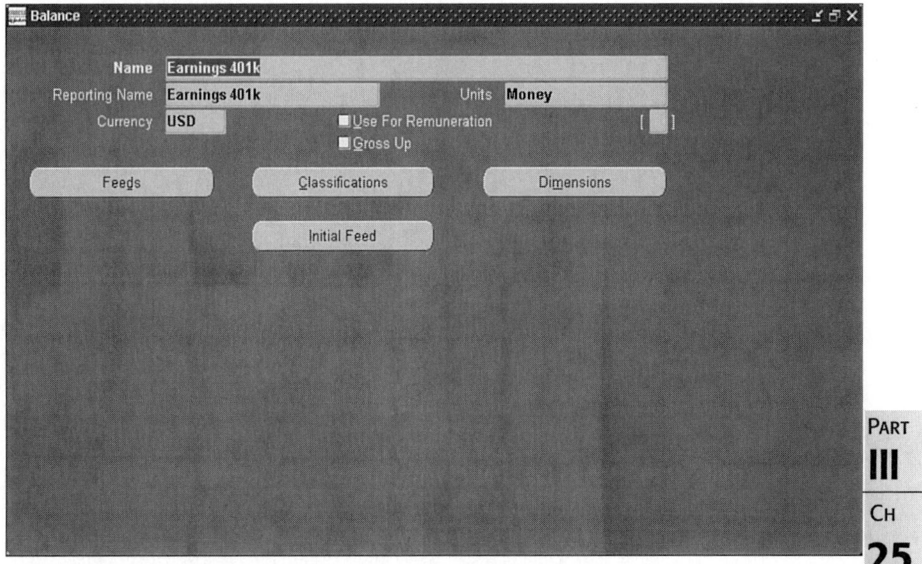

Figure 25.4 Creating a new balance.

Next, define a Global Value that will store the maximum year-to-date deduction allowed under the IRS rules. Navigate to the Global Values window (navigation path: Total Compensation, Basic , Global Values) and define this amount. The 2001 amount is $10,500. Each year you can update this value using this window. In this example, name this value Pre_Tax_401K_MAX. Figure 25.5 shows the result of this update.

Now define the Pre-Tax deduction. Navigate to the Deduction window (navigation path: Total Compensation, Basic , Deductions) to set up this deduction. Use Pre-Tax Deduction as the classification and Deferred 401(k) as the category. In this example use Percent of Earnings as the Calculation Rule. This enables Oracle to generate a default formula that you can modify for your use.

Next, define the element that will store the company match portion of the 401(k) plan. Navigate to the Element Description (navigation path: Total Compensation, Basic, Element Description) and set up this element as an Employer Liability. The formula passes the calculation results to this element.

Now make changes to the generated formula to calculate both the deduction and the company match. Navigate to the Write Formula window (navigation path: Total Compensation, Basic, Write Formulas), and query the formula that Oracle created. Normally, the name of the formula is XXXXX_PERCENT_OF_EARNINGS, where XXXXX is the name of the deduction definedpreviously in the example. Click the Edit button to bring up the Edit window. Scroll down to the section where the actual deduction is calculated. Oracle inserts a comment right before the logic that instructs users where to put their custom modifications. The default formula uses the Regular Earnings balance. As the formula comments suggest, you want to replace the Regular Earnings balance with the one you created previously. Create a separate validation formula to validate the maximum 15% rule. You can also use the Maximum field on the Input Value to control the maximum allowed for the percentage.

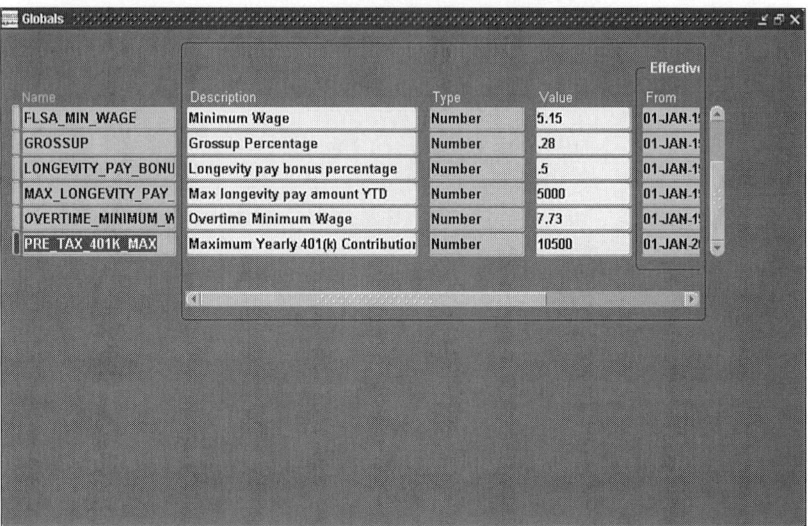

Figure 25.5
Enter a meaningful description for the Global Value.

The key modification to this formula is to include logic that calculates the company match. The results of this calculation should be stored in a variable that is included on the Return statement. This enables you to pass this result to the Employer Liability element you created previously. To do this, navigate to the Formula Results window (navigation path: Total Compensation, Basic, Formula Results), and select from the pick list the Pre-Tax deduction for our 401(k) plan. With the cursor down in the Formula Results region of the window, click the New Record icon to open up a new line. Select from the pick list the name of the variable that stored the result of the company match. In this example, use EMPL_CONTR. This automatically passes the results of the formula to the Employer Liability element.

After keying in the necessary links for each element, you are now ready to enroll people into the plan. You only have to add one element, the Pre-Tax deduction element, to Element Entries of participating employees. Enter the desired percentage in the corresponding input value. The formula handles the rest.

By using standard Oracle features, we were able to administer a typical 401(k) plan that can enforce IRS rules, calculate the company match, and enforce any special plan rules.

403(B) AND 457 DEFERRED COMPENSATION ELEMENTS

In 11*i*, Oracle has added some pre-tax element types in addition to 401(k): 457 Deferred Compensation and 403(b) tax-sheltered annuity. All of these pre-tax elements may have the company match element automatically created when the original deduction is created.

Oracle has also added some new functionality for these pre-tax elements.

For 401(k), 403(b), and 457, an after-tax option has been added. This enables employees to continue having this deduction taken, as an after-tax amount, when the plans pre-tax contribution limit has been reached. This option, like the employer match option, automatically creates an after-tax element.

The elements for the employer match and after-tax options are created when the deduction element is created. The name of the additional element is the same as the original deduction with two letters added to the end—AT for the after-tax element and ER for the matching element. These two elements must be linked, along with the original deduction, if they are to be assigned to employees.

The 403(b) and 457 deductions also include a catch-up provision. This provision will automatically change an eligible employee's maximum pre-tax contribution limit. Once this provision is set on, the employee's deduction amount can be changed to meet the catch-up amount.

The catch-up provision is set for an element, as shown in Figure 25.6, by going to the employee's Element Entries window—select People, Enter and Maintain, Assignment, Element Entries, and select the element to be changed. Click the Entry Values button and select the appropriate value from the List of Values in the Catchup Type field.

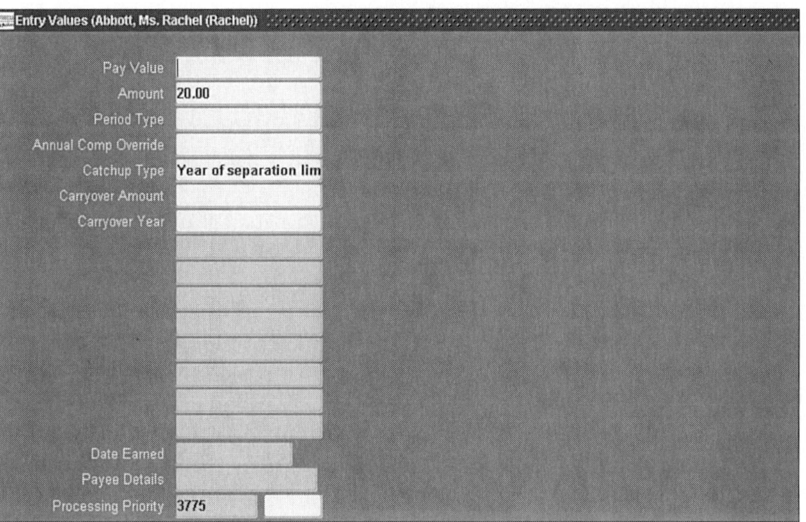

Figure 25.6
Adding 403(b) and 457 Catchup data.

Using Special Inputs Elements

Oracle has designed a method of making one-time changes to recurring earnings or deduction elements called Special Inputs. Special Inputs elements are automatically created for the earnings and deductions elements the user creates. These elements prevent the need to make manual calculations and to change recurring amounts. Moreover, if the recurring amounts themselves had to be changed, the user would need to remember to change the permanent amounts back.

Special Inputs elements enable you to do the following:

- Replace the normally calculated amount with another amount (using the Input Value: Replacement Amount)
- Provide a number to add to or subtract from the calculated amount (using the Input Value: Additional Amount)

Special Inputs elements can be entered either through BEE or through direct entry into the Element Entries window. The Special Inputs are named the same as their corresponding recurring element except that Special Inputs is added after the name. For example, a recurring element named Academic Housing Allowance would have a corresponding Special Inputs element named Academic Housing Allowance Special Inputs.

It is also possible to adjust arrearage balances for deductions when using Special Inputs. Special Inputs elements that are set up to allow for arrearage have an extra Input Value called Special Input Adjust Arrears. This makes it very easy for the user to correct an arrearage amount without requiring manual work and having to keep tally sheets of money owed to the employee or employer.

Generating Arrears for Nonrecurring Elements (via Recurring Zero Dollar Elements)

Standard functionality of Oracle Payroll only enables arrears processing to occur on recurring elements. This can be set up on the Deductions window. There are check boxes for both Arrears and Partial Deduction that affect how Oracle Payroll handles insufficient funds.

Arrears occur on a deduction when an employee fails to have sufficient earnings within a particular pay period to satisfy all his required deductions. Oracle Payroll automatically transfers the unsatisfied deduction amount from one payroll period to the next. If the next period generates sufficient earnings to cover current pay period deductions, Oracle Payroll determines whether an arrears balance has been carried forward from a previous pay period.

This functionality is very powerful, but consider the situation where an organization wants to have Oracle Payroll automatically handle arrears processing for nonrecurring deduction elements. Unfortunately, arrears cannot occur unless the element is recurring. Thus, you must fake out the system.

Your requirements can be met by first setting up a recurring deduction and ensuring that the check box for arrears (and partial deductions, if desired) is checked. Then assign this deduction element to an employee's Element Entries. In the Element Entry Input Value for Amount (assuming this is a Flat Amount deduction), enter a value of zero.

If nothing else occurs after this point, Oracle Payroll attempts to process a zero dollar deduction, which fortunately has no effect on pay. Moreover, the resulting paycheck does not show the existence of this deduction.

Now, when the employee incurs a pay period where a one-time deduction amount should be assigned, use the corresponding Special Inputs element for that deduction. By feeding an Additional Amount to the Special Inputs element, the deduction itself changes from zero to this additional amount. Then, if there are insufficient funds within the pay period, the recurring deduction goes into arrears and attempts to satisfy itself in the next pay period.

What is the business case for such a scenario? Consider an organization that has a company store where employees can purchase its products. If an employee makes a purchase from the store, the company might have a policy to allow the amount of purchase to be deducted from the employee's next paycheck. This nonrecurring transaction can be fed to Oracle Payroll as the Special Inputs element described previously. After that, Oracle Payroll ensures that the money is recouped either in the next pay period or in a future pay period due to arrears processing.

RETRO PAY

The Retro Pay Process is used to adjust earnings or deductions in the current period for changes that should have taken place in the past (retroactively). Retro processing is usually required when items do not reach the payroll department in a timely fashion. Union negotiations sometimes result in a retroactive situation as well as changes in benefit tables. The effective date of the retroactive changes is crucial. After the effective date and affected employees are identified, you run the retroactive pay process and then run the current payroll.

Retroactive processing is usually not a result of payroll or management errors but changes to original entries such as those items listed previously. The system calculates the difference between the original entry and the retroactive entry and makes the adjustment. This eliminates manual calculation by payroll personnel and greatly reduces the margin for error.

A new Retro Pay option has been added in 11*i*—the *Retro Pay by Run process*. This enables you to see the results of the Retro Pay calculations for each Payroll process that is included within the beginning and ending date parameters. For example, if an employee receives an increase in June that should be backdated to March, Retro Pay by Run would create modified process statements for all Payroll processes in March, April, May, and June. The standard Retro Pay run, which is called Retro Pay by Aggregate in the documentation, processes the previous example the same as the by Run method, but the results are a single amount and entry to the Retro Pay element.

Additional information on Retro Pay process follows:

The process recognizes partial pay periods for salaried employees.

Pay changes apply to all hours entered after start date for hourly employees.

Calculation is based on balance differences, not run result.

Use of YTD balance in Retro Set could cause problems when crossing year-end.

Adjustments that cross year-end are recognized in the current pay period.

Overtime for hourly employees is recognized by the process.

Deductions can be adjusted retroactively.

Make the End Date value at least one day into the current pay period when submitting the Retro Pay process.

Input values on retro pay element are extremely important.

Retro Pay setup steps are as follow:

1. Navigate to Total Compensation, Basic, Earnings.
2. Date-track to effective date of earning.
3. Create a Retro Pay Earning with the following element attributes:
   - 3.1. Classification: Earning
   - 3.2. Category: Regular, Nonrecurring
   - 3.3. Calculation Rule: Flat Amount
4. Save and close form.
5. Navigate to Total Compensation, Basic, Element Description.
6. Query the Earning you just created. Verify Process in Run and Multiple Entries allowed. Navigate to Input Values.
7. Create two new input values: Start Date and End Date, with date format for units of measure. Save and close window.
8. Navigate to Total Compensation, Basic, Link.
9. Link the Retro Pay Earning, save, and close.
10. Navigate to Payroll, Retro Pay Set.
11. Date-track to date of created earning.
12. Name the retro pay set, navigate to the lower part of the form, choose Gross Earnings_ASG_LTD for the balance, the retro pay element, and Pay Value as the input value, and save.
13. Navigate to Payroll, Assignment Set.
14. Create the name of the assignment set and the payroll for the employees who will receive retro pay and save.

15. Select the Amendment button and include all the people who need retro pay. Save and close.
16. Navigate to People, Enter and Maintain, and locate your person.
17. Navigate to the Salary Window, create a new record, and enter the new salary with the date it became effective. Save your record.
18. Navigate to Processes and Reports, Submit Processes and Reports.
19. Choose the Retro Pay or Retro Pay by Run Process and fill in the parameters with the name of the assignment set, retro pay set, and the start and end dates (start date should be when the increase occurred—end date should be period end date of the next unpaid payroll). Submit.
20. After the process is complete, you will be able to view the employees' entries and see the retro pay element with the retro amount.
21. Process the next payroll and see the retro pay paid to the employee.

Tax Balance Adjustments

There are several occurrences that necessitate that Tax Balances be adjusted. For example, an employee might receive imputed income, such as stock options or relocation expenses outside of a regular payroll run. This would make it necessary to adjust tax balances including the Gross Earnings Subject to Tax Balance. Oracle Payroll has provided a means to adjust both of these Tax Balances through the Tax Balance Window.

To make adjustments to an employee's Gross Earnings Subject to Tax balance, you do the following:

Select the name of the earnings type.

Enter the gross amount of the change.

The system then locates the applicable balances and makes the adjustment.

To make adjustments to taxes withheld, you handle it in the same manner as listed previously. If you have defined the Tax Rules for the GRE to use the Self Adjust method, the calculation of employee withholding for Social Security, Medicare, State Unemployment Insurance, or State Disability Insurance is corrected with the next payroll run. This also corrects the Employer Liability balances for the same taxes.

It is important to have fully tested the operations of the Tax Balance window so that you do not endanger the accuracy of your tax balances.

Another common use for the Oracle Payroll Adjust Tax Balance window involves manual checks. Often, a company quickly hand-calculates the amount of tax required when preparing a manual check for an employee. Thus, these exact tax amounts must be entered along with the amount of gross pay through the Adjust Tax Balance window. If the tax amounts were manually calculated incorrectly, they might self-adjust during the next pay period as described earlier.

Tax Balance Adjustments Example

The following is a sample procedure for entering Stock Options for employees, where the taxes were paid externally to Oracle Payroll. You will use the Adjust Tax Balance to accomplish this task.

Note that a very simple process exists that makes auditing these adjustments at a later date much easier. Print screen shots of all the adjusting entries made and of the balances before and after the adjustments are completed. This will give you the entire record of the transaction.

For this example, assume that an employee exercised a stock option and the corresponding taxes were either paid by the employee or were "grossed up" in the payment check. Following is the breakdown of the example:

Gain on Stock Option exercise:	\$5,295.62
FIT Taxes Withheld	\$1,482.77
State Taxes Withheld	\$317.74
Medicare Taxes Withheld	\$76.79
Net Amount of exercise	\$3,418.32

Assume that you have already created an Imputed Earning element called Stock Options that will record the gross amount of the option.

The first step in entering the adjustment is to navigate to the employee's Adjust Tax Balance window (navigation path: People, Enter and Maintain, Assignment, Other, Adjust Tax Balances). Make sure you are date-tracked to the date when this adjustment occurred.

Select the earning named Stock Options and then fill in each of the dollar values as indicated previously.

The Work Address region of this window is completed automatically by the system. In this case, assume that the employee has already reached the limit for Social Security. Save your work. The system automatically creates balance adjustments for all the affected balances. You can review these adjustments in the Payroll Process Results window (navigation path: View, Payroll Process Results). Normally, this is all you need to record the event.

However, there previously existed a bug in Oracle Payroll that caused the Medicare EE Taxable, Medicare ER Taxable, and the SUI ER Taxable balances to be incorrect. Therefore, you needed to make some additional balance adjustments to correct this situation.

During the initial balance load of the YTD amounts, Oracle automatically created the necessary balance adjustment elements that you will use to fix this bug. You can determine the name of these elements by querying the balance via the Balance window (navigation path: Compensation and Benefits, Balance) and clicking the Initial Feed button. They are outlined in Table 25.5.

Table 25.5 Initial Balance Feeds

Balance Name	Element Name	Input Value Name
Medicare EE Taxable	Initial_Value_Element_202_0_1	11
Medicare ER Taxable	Initial_Value_Element_202_0_1	14
SUI ER Taxable	Initial_Value_Element_202_2_1	7

Navigate to the employee's Adjust Balance window (navigation path: People, Enter and Maintain, Assignment, Others, Adjust Balance). Select from the pick list the first element name from Table 25.5 (Initial_Value_Element_202_0_1). Tab over to the 11 input value name and key the Gross amount that was entered on the Adjust Tax Balance window. Put the same number in input value name 14. This adjustment adds the gross amount to the two Medicare taxable balances. Save your work.

The Status radio button should change to Completed. Click the New Record icon (the big green cross) and select from the pick list the next element name from Table 25.5 (Initial_Value_Element_202_2_1). Tab over to the input value name 7 and key the negative of the gross amount (–5295.62). This example assumes that the employee has already reached the SUI limit for his state. The Oracle bug assumes that all of this gross should be in the Taxable balance for SUI. This adjustment removes the gross. You also need to key the Jurisdiction code for the employee's work state. If it were Georgia, the Jurisdiction code would be 11-000-0000.

The Status radio button should change to Completed. This completes the process. You can review the results of this adjustment by reviewing the Tax Balance window for this employee (navigation path: View, Tax Information, Tax Balances).

Tax Only Earnings

Note that a side-effect exists when using Tax Only on the definition of earnings. There will be confusion as you review payroll results from the online Statement of Earnings (SOE) window. For each earning marked as Tax Only, Oracle Payroll displays a separate window on the SOE for the given pay period. This can get confusing because each individual SOE does not show all the tax deductions. However, the combination of all SOEs for the current payroll run, when added together, have the correct tax and deduction calculations. Fortunately, at the time of processing CheckWriter or NACHA, these items will be combined into one check or deposit advice (assuming that each earning has been defined without a requested Separate Check).

COSTING AND TRANSFER TO GENERAL LEDGER

Throughout this chapter, I have discussed various ways to set up your costing matrix for earnings and deductions. When this matrix is established and you have entered all your cost codes (at the Organization, Element Link, Assignment, or Element Entry level), you are ready to run the costing process.

The first step in running Costing is to decide how often you plan to send the costing data to GL. Some companies transfer costing data to GL after every payroll run, whereas others wait and transfer the data all at once at the end of the month. When you run the Costing process, you specify a starting and ending date and either a Payroll or Consolidation Set. The process then scans the payroll run results of the selected payroll or consolidation set and generates costing data for any run result within the date span that has not yet been costed. When the costing process has completed, you can run either of the two supplied cost summary reports. As noted in other sections of this chapter, these reports only show the costing side of the journal entry and do not show the balancing side entry.

After running the Costing process, if you discover that some of the cost codes were set up incorrectly, you can correct the codes at the Organization, Element Link, or Assignment level and retry the costing process for the affected employees. There is no need to rerun the corresponding payroll process. If you need to correct the coding at the Element Entry level, you need to roll back the costing process and rerun the payroll process of the affected employees. When this is completed, you then rerun the costing process.

The Transfer to GL process works in a similar manner. You specify a date range and either a payroll or consolidation set. The process scans the costing tables. It then transfers any costing records within the span and for the desired payroll or consolidation set that has not yet been transferred. All records are inserted into the GL interface table GL_INTERFACE. Oracle GL users then import the journal entries through the normal import process. You cannot retry individual employees on the Transfer to GL process. You can only roll back the entire run, make your corrections, and rerun the process.

Some companies must manipulate this data before it eventually lands in GL. Other companies still use legacy GL systems instead of Oracle GL. In either case, you can write customized code that accesses the data in either the costing tables in Payroll or the interface tables from Oracle GL. Do not modify the records in the costing tables because Oracle tightly controls the interactive action locks between the various payroll processes. You might want to create your own interface tables that would contain the modified tables. Currently, Oracle only supports an automated interface directly to Oracle GL. If you want to import payroll costing data to any other Oracle module, such as Project Accounting, you must write this interface yourself.

GL FLEXFIELD CHANGES: STEPS TO CHANGE PAYROLL COST ALLOCATION

What should you do if new costing requirements force changes to the structure of segments of the Oracle General Ledger Accounting Key Flexfield? For example, what if the old cost center was five digits and now it will be seven digits? Note that in this discussion, this is not merely referring to adding additional Value Set values to a Value Set for a given flexfield segment. The requirement is to change the structure of, or add segments to, the Cost Allocation Key Flexfield. Although there is much more thorough testing that should be conducted, consider following these steps to begin the process:

1. Change Cost Allocation Key Flexfield Value Sets to point to new GL value sets.
2. Ensure that the Oracle Payroll window GL Flexfield Map is now only referencing the newly desired Cost Allocation Key Flexfield segments. This implies that some of the previously used segments might no longer be used.
3. Change Oracle HR/Payroll Organizations, Element Links, and Payrolls for every organization and element to ensure that the new GL costing values are selected.
4. Change Cost Allocation Key Flexfield Qualifiers.
5. Change Cost Allocation Key Flexfield displayable segments.
6. Confirm that Oracle HR/Payroll Organizations, Element Links, appear okay when you query them. In essence, confirm that there are no Form errors and that you can save simple changes to the records.
7. Run the Payroll process for one employee or small group of employees.
8. Run the Costing process.
9. Run the Transfer to GL process.
10. Analyze the GL_INTERFACE table.
11. Have General Ledger team import records to further identify problems.

Laser Printing of Payroll Checks

The standard delivered solution for printing payroll checks is to spool the results of the Check Writer process to a printer that is mounted with preprinted forms. The user is responsible for providing the mechanism for getting this done. The easiest solution is to purchase the preprinted forms from an Oracle supported vendor, such as Evergreen. This solution, however, requires the user to match up the check numbers preprinted on the form with the check numbers generated by Check Writer. If the printer "eats" one of the forms, the check numbers can very easily get out of sync. Because it is undesirable to preprint signatures on the check form, you also have the issue of how to turn these unsigned checks into valid cashable documents.

At BOSS Corporation, we have observed several solutions to this problem. These solutions did not attempt to modify the results from the Oracle Check Writer process. Instead, processes were introduced that took the standard results from Check Writer and inserted the needed information.

The first solution uses the macro features of Microsoft Excel. If you are familiar with Excel, you can follow along. Make a bit-mapped image of the check signature and store it on a controlled PC. Next, create an FTP script that prompts the user to key in the concurrent request ID of the Check Writer process. This script then copies the output file from the

Unix server to the controlled PC. The user then starts Microsoft Excel and executes the specially designed macro. This macro steps through the copied file and inserts the signature into the appropriate spot. The final step is to spool the resultant spreadsheet to the laser printer where the Evergreen forms are already loaded. You still might have the problem of keeping the check numbers in sync. However, you have the advantage of not having to run the checks through a check signer.

This solution is easy to implement and uses tools that probably already exist. It does have its drawbacks. First, Excel can only handle approximately 450 checks in one spreadsheet at a time (memory constraint). The FTP process must recognize this limit and requires you to break up the Check Writer file into multiple import files. Each file has to be processed through the macro and printed separately. Obviously, this solution is unthinkable for check runs that number into the thousands. Additionally, it does not address the check number syncing issue.

The second solution provides a much cleaner approach to the problem. Again, we did not attempt to modify the standard Check Writer process. This time we used a third-party product called Optio DCS (Document Customization Server) from Optio Software. This product is designed to receive output files and enable users to manipulate the results. By using this product, we totally redesigned the look and feel of the check document. Normally, the actual check prints at the top of the form, followed by the Statement of Earnings. Our client wanted to flip this around and print the actual check on the bottom of the form. We also inserted the company logo and signature. The biggest gain was that we were able to print the check number in the MICR format at the bottom of the check document. This enabled us to use standard printer stock and not preprinted forms.

We were surprised with the ease of use of this product. It does require the use of a laser printer with the special MICR cartridge. There are also obvious control issues because this solution is very easy to implement. Most printers provide some hardware-locking features that enable you to physically control the use of the MICR cartridge.

Another solution also involves the use of a laser printer with a MICR cartridge. Evergreen, an approved Oracle vendor, has a program that reads the CheckWriter output file and prints the check on its unprinted check stock. Everything printed on the check is output from the program, including a company logo and a signature if requested. The check stock it supplies is the folding sealed check that can be handed out without stuffing it in an envelope. When the Evergreen program was used, the only layout for the check was the standard Oracle check, which is exactly the same as what is in the CheckWriter output file. Evergreen may have added reformatting capabilities. The advantage of using the Oracle format is that the check stub looks just like the online SOE window.

ORACLE FAST FORMULA

Throughout this chapter, I have demonstrated the power of Fast Formulas and its capability to solve your special payroll calculation challenges. This section summarizes some recommendations for Fast Formulas.

The biggest advantage of Fast Formulas is the capability to access Database Items when performing payroll calculations. Database Items are pieces of information that Oracle automatically maintains for you. Examples of useful database items include the following:

Year-to-date 401(k) deduction amount

Total Regular Earnings for current pay run

An input value on another element

Global Values

Segments from a Key Flexfield

My first recommendation uses the last example from the preceding list. Many times, Oracle HR/Payroll users must decide where to store needed information. Do you use the People Group Flexfield, or should you use Special Information Types? If you need the information in a Fast Formula, use the People Group Flexfield. At the time of this writing, Oracle HR does not create a database item for information stored in a Special Information Type.

Several of our solutions at BOSS Corporation use the power of Indirect Results. This is where the results of one formula can be passed on to another element. When using this powerful feature, make sure that the receiving element processes *after* the generating element. You accomplish this task by assigning the receiving element a higher priority number than the generating element. We have used this feature to calculate imputed income and deduction amounts in the same formula and pass the results to the corresponding element. When doing this, do not forget to handle the situation when there is insufficient pay to cover a deduction.

Many times, we have created Table Structures to store necessary rates for payroll calculations. The Fast Formula statement GET_TABLE_VALUE can be used to retrieve these rates. We have used this feature when rates are different based on either a location or a value from one of the People Group Flexfield segments.

Year-to-Date Balance Conversion

During initial conversion and implementation, companies are faced with the decision of whether to implement in the middle of a calendar year or to wait until January 1. Clearly, the job is easier when you can wait until the start of a new calendar year. However, this is generally the busiest time of the year for a payroll department. Also, many companies want to phase different locations into the new system throughout the year. For many reasons, some companies have to transfer period balances from the current payroll system into Oracle.

One of the most unique features of Oracle Payroll is that it does not explicitly store year-to-date, quarter-to-date, and month-to-date balances. These numbers are automatically derived by calculating the balances as they would have appeared at the current session date. This date can be arbitrarily set by using a feature called date-tracking. You can literally see year-to-date, quarter-to-date, and month-to-date results for any date in the past, as long as the Oracle Payroll system was active on that date.

Although this feature is very powerful, it complicates mid-year conversions. Oracle needs to have a starting point to begin these calculations. Therefore, you must perform an initial balance load to establish this starting point. A good recommendation is to coincide the implementation date with the start of a quarter. This enables you to only need to provide the year-to-date balances as of the starting date. If the implementation date is not at the start of a quarter, you have to load quarter-to-date values additionally. Moreover, if your implementation date is not at the beginning of a month, you need to load month-to-date values.

Balance loads can be broken down into two parts. The first part is the easiest. This involves loading a balance for each earning and deduction element you defined in Oracle. Strangely enough, this part is not required. Oracle does not use any of these balances when calculating taxes or preparing the end-of-year W-2s.

The second and most difficult part requires that the tax balances must be addressed next. Oracle Payroll maintains many tax-related balances with its tight integration to Vertex. (For definition and description of Vertex, see the section "Vertex Will Handle All My Taxing Issues" in Chapter 23, "Implementing Oracle Human Resources and Oracle Payroll.") Because Vertex has no knowledge on how taxes were calculated in the legacy system, you must manually provide the numbers to populate the Vertex required balances. Following is a partial list of all the balances required just to calculate State Unemployment Insurance (SUI):

SUI EE Gross

SUI ER Gross

SUI ER Subj Whable

SUI ER Taxable

SUI ER Liability

There are many other tax bodies that must be loaded in a similar fashion. For companies with sites in different states, there might be different rules on what earnings should go in each balance.

How do you go about determining what should go in each balance? Oracle has published a white paper titled "Oracle HRMS TRM Supplement: US Legislative Balance Initialization" that lists the required balances. You must determine what numbers should go in each balance. Start with the Taxability Rules window to drive this process. This window (navigation path: Compensation and Benefits, Taxability Rules) outlines which earnings are taxable for each tax body. It also outlines which pretax deductions should be subject to each tax body. Use these rules to determine which earnings and deductions make up each balance. It is generally a good idea to produce a spreadsheet that explicitly provides a road map that a legacy programmer can use to prepare a file of these balances.

The next step is to load these numbers into the Oracle-provided interface tables. These tables are described in the *Oracle HRMS Implementation Guide*. When loaded, you must first run the Initial Balance Structure Creation process from the application. This process creates the necessary initial balance feed elements and links. When completed, the next step is to validate the table load by running the Initial Balance Load Process using the Validate option. This verifies that the interface table was loaded properly. When verified, rerun the Initial Balance Load Process with the Transfer option. This actually performs the balance load. You have the option to undo the entire process if you need to start from scratch.

When the load is completed, you can review the balances online using the Employee Balance window. (This functionality actually did not work for us at our last client site. Oracle has stated that this has since been fixed.) The final task is to do a test parallel payroll run. Do this because many of the tax calculations are self-adjusting. This allows problems with the balance load to "stick out like a sore thumb." For example, if you understated the subject wages for SUI, Vertex tries to self-adjust the SUI liability down using negative numbers. Likewise, if you did not properly load the Medicare Withheld balance, Vertex tries to catch up all of the deductions with one large deduction. Both of these deductions really do stick out.

Because of the complex nature of Oracle tax balances and the possibility of each state having unique subject tax rules, the balance load process is very complicated. It is also a very iterative process requiring many attempts before all the problems are ironed out. Do not underestimate the task involved, and prepare for significant payroll testing.

THIRD-PARTY ADMINISTRATOR TRANSFERS (PRO-C, PL/SQL)

Most organizations use outside administrators to handle the record keeping and processing of certain company benefits. Examples of these types of benefit plans include 401(k), Pension, Medical, Dental, and Supplemental Life Insurance.

Do not underestimate the time required to create these interface programs. First, every third-party vendor has a unique file format they require for receiving payroll data. The Oracle Payroll database is complex, so careful time must be taken to extract each item of information required by the vendor.

Regardless of whether the third-party administrator interface is written in Pro-C or PL/SQL, you must allow time for each interface for analysis, design, coding, unit testing, and integration testing. Depending on your number of interfaces, this can become a project in and of itself. Do not underestimate it.

However, in your desire to get a head start on third-party interfaces, be aware that full design and coding cannot be completed until after many system setup decisions have been made regarding your Compensation and Benefit elements. For example, a 401(k) interface might need to know how much of an employee's 401(k) loan was repaid during the current pay period. Thus, the interface must be designed to identify the 401(k) deduction element and the 401(k) loan element.

Another example of this involves medical deductions. Most large companies offer several medical plans (PPO, HMO, and so on). Your third-party interface requirements for each medical plan must be designed to identify one medical plan element from another.

TIME AND ATTENDANCE INTEGRATION WITH BEE

Prior to Release 11*i*, an external Time and Attendance (T&A) system can be integrated with Oracle Payroll via BEE. To begin this process, an analysis must be done to map Oracle Payroll earnings to appropriate earning codes from the T&A system. Although it would be ideal for the T&A system earning codes to be named exactly the same as the earning elements in Oracle Payroll, this is often unrealistic. For example, the T&A system might have limitations on the number of characters allowed in an earnings code name.

The characteristics of the application program interface (API) from the T&A system can influence this mapping analysis. Consider a T&A API where a single output record contains hours and time worked. In this example, consider a record containing 12 hours worked from 10 p.m. to 10 a.m. The 12 hours worked might need to be split within Oracle as 8 hours Time Entry Wages and 4 hours Overtime. Moreover, a nighttime shift differential record might be necessary in Oracle for all, or a portion, of those 12 hours. Thus, one record from the T&A system could produce 3 records within Oracle BEE, as demonstrated in Table 25.6.

TABLE 25.6 EXAMPLE OF TIME WORKED

Oracle Earning Element	Hours
Time Entry Wages	8
Overtime	4
Shift Differential	8

Mapping can be affected by costing requirements. Within Oracle BEE, the costing on a single record cannot be split. Consider a variation from the previous example where the 12 hours should have been split evenly across two cost centers. This might cause a need for 6 records within BEE, as demonstrated in Table 25.7.

TABLE 25.7 EXAMPLE OF SPLIT COSTING

Oracle Earning Element	Hours	Cost Center
Time Entry Wages	4	100
Time Entry Wages	4	200
Overtime	2	100
Overtime	2	200
Shift Differential	6	100
Shift Differential	6	200

The frequency of data transfer should be considered. Determine how often batches should automatically be transferred into BEE. Over the course of a payroll period, it is not necessary to transfer data from the T&A system every minute. A transfer once per day is too infrequent. Consider an hourly transfer. This should be frequent enough, even during the final day of payroll close. Ensure that you have a manual capability to transfer batches into BEE. Determine when other network traffic (unrelated to payroll) occurs. Carefully coordinate the scheduled time for payroll transfers. If there is typically a peak of network traffic at the top of each hour, establish your automatic transfer at 15 minutes after each hour.

To organize BEE batches, determine who will review batches and establish a batch-naming convention for the Reference Name of a batch. Consider grouping batches weekly and by location to facilitate sorting for user access and for reporting. Table 25.8 shows the breakdown of a sample naming convention: YMMDDLLRRRRRR.

TABLE 25.8 SUGGESTED BEE BATCH NAMING CONVENTION

Item	Description
Y	Year, expressed as only one digit (0 for 2000, 1 for 2001, and so on) to allow more text to be visible in the Reference field on the BEE Batch Information window
MM	Month
DD	Day
LL	Location
RR	Reference number identifying the original source of the data from the legacy system

Other issues for grouping of batches should be considered. BEE is designed so that separate batches exist for flat amount (Earnings) batches versus rate × time (Time) batches. You might want to create separate batches that are dedicated to exceptions (such as reduction in pay to recurring elements using Special Inputs elements).

The integration into BEE involves insertion into these primary tables:

PAY_BATCH_HEADERS
PAY_BATCH_LINES
PAY_BATCH_CHECKS

If dynamic costing information is included in this integration, the integration accesses these tables:

FND_ID_FLEX_SEGMENTS
FND_FLEX_VALUES
PAY_COST_ALLOCATIONS_F
PAY_COST_ALLOCATION_ KEYFLEX

First, identify which cost segments (such as location and cost center) can dynamically change from one payment period to the next. There will be other segments, such as a cost account, which will probably not change. In this example, assume that cost center and location are segments 1 and 2, respectively. Also assume that these are the only segments that can dynamically change. For each time-entry record, verify that the values actually exist in the value set for segments 1 and 2 by accessing the following tables:

FND_ID_FLEX_SEGMENTS

FND_FLEX_VALUES

Second, now you know that each of the segment values is a valid value, but now you need to determine whether the code combination is valid. Determine whether the code combination exists for the business group within the following tables:

PAY_COST_ALLOCATIONS_F

PAY_COST_ALLOCATION_ KEYFLEX.

If the code combination exists, retrieve cost_allocation_keyflex_id. If it does not exist, insert into these tables using the PYCSKFLI package and retrieve the newly created cost_allocation_keyflex_id.

Consider one final note on the integration from T&A to BEE. Keep in mind that Oracle Payroll is not Fair Labor Standards Act (FLSA)–compliant. The integration can be written to accommodate FLSA rules such that each overtime record within BEE can have an adjusted overtime rate.

OTHER INTERFACES

In this chapter, I have discussed various interfaces including interfaces to BEE (timecards), Oracle General Ledger (costing information), and Third Party Administrators (benefits information). Within payroll, this covers the most common interfaces that are required by an Oracle Payroll implementation.

However, other interfaces might be required. If Oracle Projects is being implemented, you might need to transfer payroll cost information to the Oracle Project Accounting modules. This is a customized interface and is usually designed to process during the Transfer to GL process.

Some implementations of Oracle HR/Payroll occur without the presence of the Oracle General Ledger module. In this case, a customized interface to a third-party GL system is required. This custom interface is usually implemented as a process to be run after the Oracle Payroll Costing process.

Interfaces for Benefits Enrollment and Salary Administration are discussed in Chapter 24, "Using Oracle Human Resources."

ESTABLISHING LATEST BALANCES

To improve performance when referencing a balance amount, the Oracle HRMS application balance call function is designed to first check for the presence of a figure in a table of latest balances and use it before dynamically generating the balance amount from historical detail. If the balance amount does not exist in the latest balance table, the balance must be generated. All balances that are referenced in Fast Formulas used in pay runs are automatically entered into the latest balances tables (PAY_ASSIGNMENT_LATEST_BALANCES, PAY_PERSON_LATEST_BALANCES). If a user runs a report that references many balances that are not present in the latest balances table, the report could require significant processing time because the report must cause each of the latest balances to first be generated. To help alleviate this problem, references to the required balances can be placed in a Fast Formula so that entries to the latest balances tables are created by the system. When dealing with balances that are related to tax jurisdictions (states, cities, and counties), a jurisdiction code must be supplied as an input value for the fast formula. The following setup shows the steps required to enable this functionality.

The first step is to create an element by navigating to the Total Compensation, Basic, Element Description window. Create a nonrecurring element with Classification of Information. Turn on the check boxes for Multiple Entries Allowed, Process in Run, and Indirect Results.

Note

The Priority should be set so that the element processes after the VERTEX element, which normally has a priority of 4250.

Add an input value for the jurisdiction code by clicking the Input Values button. This Input Value should be defined with Name = Jurisdiction, Units = Character, and Sequence = 1. Also, be sure that the check boxes for User Enterable and Database Item have been checked.

Next, create your Element Link by navigating to the Total Compensation, Basic, Link window. Remember to date-track to the appropriate start date for your implementation.

After linking the element, create a Fast Formula by navigating to the Total Compensation, Basic, Write Formulas window. Include all appropriate balance names. Don't forget the Inputs Are and Return statements. The Fast Formula should look like this:

```
Inputs are jurisdiction (text)

LB1  = CITY_SUBJ_WHABLE_ASG_JD_GRE_QTD
LB2  = CITY_SUBJ_WHABLE_ASG_JD_GRE_RUN
LB3  = CITY_SUBJ_WHABLE_ASG_JD_GRE_YTD
LB4  = CITY_WITHHELD_ASG_JD_GRE_QTD
LB5  = CITY_WITHHELD_ASG_JD_GRE_RUN
LB6  = CITY_WITHHELD_ASG_JD_GRE_YTD
LB7  = COUNTY_SUBJ_WHABLE_ASG_JD_GRE_QTD
LB8  = COUNTY_SUBJ_WHABLE_ASG_JD_GRE_RUN
LB9  = COUNTY_SUBJ_WHABLE_ASG_JD_GRE_YTD
LB10 = COUNTY_WITHHELD_ASG_JD_GRE_QTD
.
.
.
LB47 = MEDICARE_ER_TAXABLE_ASG_GRE_RUN
LB48 = MEDICARE_ER_TAXABLE_ASG_GRE_YTD
LB49 = REGULAR_EARNINGS_ASG_GRE_QTD
LB50 = REGULAR_EARNINGS_ASG_GRE_YTD
Return
```

Now that you have created the Fast Formula, you must associate your element with your Fast Formula. This can be accomplished by navigating to the Total Compensation, Basic, Formula Results window. After saving your work, remain on the same window because you must feed the jurisdiction code to your custom element. Select the VERTEX element and add a formula result row that feeds Jurisdiction to your new element's input value, called Jurisdiction. Note that the Jurisdiction formula result from the VERTEX element now feeds both your new element and any other VERTEX elements that were previously associated with the VERTEX element.

How It Works

Because your elements are information-type elements and are indirectly fed by another element (VERTEX) to which everyone will automatically be assigned, you do not have to explicitly assign your elements to employees. The element has been created with a priority level such that it will always be processed after the VERTEX element from which the jurisdiction code originates. Fast Formulas currently have a limitation of allowing no more that 64,000 characters, meaning if you have a lot of balances that you need to reference, you need to break up the references into more than one Fast Formula and element. This is not a problem. Simply be certain to include a jurisdiction code feed to each additional element as well.

In the preceding example, the jurisdiction code passed to the new element is the code for the employee's residence. It might be necessary to create an additional element attached to another Fast Formula that references the same jurisdiction-related balances but passes the jurisdiction of the work location to this element to establish balances for that particular jurisdiction. The work location jurisdiction code can be found in the VERTEX element as well (LOC_ADR_GEOCODE).

Compensation Approaches

The main objective of a payroll system is to pay your employees with accurate and timely paychecks that includes regular pay, any special pay, retro payments, and supplemental pay. For each of these pay types, the following sections explore some issues that need to be considered when setting up the Oracle HR/Payroll System. There might be other questions that pertain to your business, but these are the major ones. The Oracle system provides a method for handling most of these, but as is true with any system, it cannot provide a means for every pay factor for every client.

Compensation Approaches: Regular Pay Increases

Regular pay increases are those that occur for merit increases, cost of living increases, recognized performance, and other company-specific reasons. Regular increases normally are submitted by the employee's manager with proper higher management approval with sufficient time to process them in a regular pay run on the effective date of the increase.

Some important factors to consider are the following:

Who can approve regular pay increases? Management, what level of management, human resources, payroll, administration, or a combination of these?

Are mid–pay period increases allowed?

Are all increases effective on the first day of the pay period?

Are there any manual processes that will continue to be manual after the new Oracle system goes live?

Are there any functions being performed by your current system that will not be available with Oracle that will require manual workarounds?

Are pay increases annual, across-the-board, or on employee anniversary dates?

Are there any special considerations for overtime, double-time, and holiday pay?

COMPENSATION APPROACHES: ALLOWANCES/SPECIAL TYPES OF PAY

Special types of pay include items such as Housing Allowances, Relocation Allowances, Longevity Bonuses, and so on. These types of pay can be short-term, one to two months, or ongoing for an unlimited amount of time.

Consider these points when planning how your Oracle system will be used to pay employees for these items:

If the user has allowances or special types of pay, do you create one element to handle all allowances or types or individual elements for each different allowance or type?

Are these pay types a percentage, a flat amount, or a combination of both?

Is your calculation of overtime a factor?

COMPENSATION APPROACHES: RETRO PAYMENTS

In a perfect payroll environment, there would be no retro payments because all increases would be received in Payroll with sufficient lead-time to include in the correct paycheck. Consultants and Human Resources and Payroll personnel know this is often not the case. Clients with unions often spend long amounts of time negotiating new contracts, usually after the present contract has expired. This would most likely result in retro payments for increased salary, deductions for increased benefits, and other negotiated items that would result in retro payments. Documents (both online and paper) to authorize increases often get delayed. Although it is not an easy issue to resolve, it is best to be realistic and plan for retro payments in the most efficient method possible. The Oracle system is designed to assist in this endeavor.

Listed following are some of the decisions that must be made when planning your Retro Pay Elements:

Are retro salary increases allowed, and if so, how will they be handled?

What level of approval is needed?

Are retro allowances and special pay types allowed?

How will overtime be handled in regards to retro payments?

Will manual work be involved?

How will retro payments affect costing?

For additional information on how to configure Oracle Payroll to allow for Retro Pay processing, see the section in this chapter titled "Retro Pay."

Compensation Approaches: Supplemental

Supplemental payments are those items that are not a part of the regular pay given to employees. Supplemental pay is usually items above the normal salary. It is best to consult your Tax Advisor on whether items should be taxed as supplemental. The following list of questions to consider is not an exhaustive, complete list, but it should provide a head start:

What items (tuition, executive training, and so on) are considered supplemental wages and therefore subject to supplemental taxes?

Are supplemental wages to be issued in a separate check?

What is your company's policy regarding supplemental wages? Does it need to be revisited? Is compliance with tax regulations an issue?

Compensation Approaches: Summary

When planning your pay system using Oracle Payroll, it is recommended to review your pay policies for fairness and address any issues where compliance with federal, state, or local regulations is involved.

Understanding Key Reports

Oracle delivers standard key reports to document the Payroll process. This section discusses the use of each of these reports. They include the following:

Payroll Message Report

Gross to Net Summary Report

Payroll Register Report

Element Result Listing

Employee Deductions Taken

Employee Deductions Not Taken

NACHA Report

Federal, State, and Local Tax Remittance Reports

Costing Breakdown Summary reports

Before discussing these reports, you need to understand a feature of Oracle that causes great confusion throughout the Oracle Payroll world. When you define a Payroll during your initial implementation setup, you must state the first pay period ending date and a series of offsets from this date. These offsets are used to build a payroll calendar of dates and period names. For example, if during setup you stated that your first period end date was Sunday, December 26, 1999, your frequency was Weekly and your check offset was 5, this means that all your period ending dates will be Sundays and your payment dates will be Fridays. Oracle generates a calendar with all the dates completed for each of the years you specified in the Number of Years box. Also note that Oracle assigns a period name for each period. Generally, these are named 1 2000 Weekly for the first period, 2 2000 Weekly for the second period, and so on.

The feature occurs for companies that have payment dates greater than the period ending date (for example, the check offset is greater than zero). When you run a payroll, the Payroll Process requires that you state the period ending date and the check date. Assume that you want to run the payroll with a period ending date of 09-JAN-2000 and a check date of 14-JAN-2000. You would expect Oracle to assign this payroll run to the period named 2 2000 Weekly because this is the second payment date in 2000. (This assumes payments in 2000 on 07-JAN and 14-JAN; it also assumes that a previous payment on 31-DEC-1999 was associated with the payroll calendar of the previous year.) However, when reviewing the results of this payroll on the Payroll Run Results window, Oracle assigns this payroll run to 3 2000 Weekly! Apparently, Oracle takes the payment date, scans the calendar, finds the period in which this payment date falls between the period start date and the period end date, and assigns this period name to the payroll run. Because 14-JAN-2000 falls between 10-JAN-2000 and 16-JAN-2000, Oracle assigns 3 2000 Weekly to the payroll run in this example.

All the standard Oracle reports that list period names and dates use this confusing period name in their headings. You must use this name when running the standard Payroll reports, or you get erroneous results. Keep this in mind when you run the reports that require the period name in the selection window. This does not affect the actual checks, direct deposits, and NACHA files. It also has no negative effects on the State Quarterly reports or the Year End Processing. Oracle users have complained about this feature at user group meetings. Oracle has recognized the problem and has indicated plans to change this process in a future release.

After the successful completion of a payroll run, you should navigate to the Payroll Processing Results window and note the period name Oracle Payroll has assigned this run. Now, you are ready to run your reports. All these are run from the Submit Requests window. Generally, you run the reports in the following order:

- **Payroll Message Report**—This report lists any errors, warnings, or informational messages that were logged during the pay run. Use this report to locate employees with missing timecards, employees with no earnings, deductions that were automatically stopped by reaching a "towards owed" balance, or any other error situations that might arise during the gross-to-net calculation. Do not proceed to any other postprocessing steps until you are satisfied that all messages have been resolved or acknowledged.

- **Gross to Net Report**—Use this report to balance to any expected totals. It lists totals of each earning, deduction, and other elements of pay, including hours. One processing quirk is that you must be date-tracked to a date that is equal to or greater than the payment date before the pick list will include the period name you want to process. Remember to use the period name that Oracle Payroll assigned to this pay run. There have been several patches associated with this report. Your version of the report might not include all these patches. Some of the problems include the following:
    - Missing totals for involuntary deductions
    - Missing totals for wage attachment fees (no resolution at press time)

  If you experience problems with this report, make sure you contact Oracle Support to receive the latest version of this useful report.
- **Payroll Registers**—One of the most important reports out of a payroll run is a detail listing of the gross to net calculation for each employee. Originally, Oracle Payroll did not include a detail report by employee, assuming that companies would use the online review of a Statement of Earnings to resolve any problems. However, the user community consistently placed this report high on the desired list of enhancements. Therefore, Oracle responded by introducing their version of the detailed Payroll Register Report. It lists for each employee in the pay run the detailed gross-to-net calculation. It can also list year-to-date totals for these elements. There were performance problems with earlier versions of this report. Also, companies did not like the format of the report that lists one employee per page. Many companies have produced their own custom version of the payroll register.

The other two payroll registers that Oracle produces were the predecessors of the existing detailed report. They only list payment totals by employee and do not show the actual gross-to-net calculation. However, these reports are helpful for payroll check bank reconciliation:

- **Element Result Listing**—When reviewing the Gross to Net report, you might need to know which employees have had payroll results for a particular earning or deduction total. The Element Result Listing is a very helpful report that lists every assignment that has the selected element in its run results. Use the payment date of the payroll run as the beginning and ending dates. Select a sort order that conforms to any source documents that you will use to reconcile the totals. The total listed for the selected element should match exactly to the total on the Gross to Net report.
- **Employee Deductions Taken**—There is a summary and detail version of this report. It lists, for each employee, the deductions taken in a period together with a year-to-date balance for each deduction. The summary version of the report presents totals only. Remember to use the period name that Oracle assigned to the payroll run.
- **Employee Deductions Not Taken**—These reports (summary and detail versions) are similar to the Employee Deductions Taken reports but also report on deduction amounts that went into arrears due to insufficient earnings. Use these reports to track arrears processing for deductions.

- **NACHA Report**—After you have run the Prepayments process and the NACHA process, you can run the NACHA report. This is the only Oracle Payroll-supplied report that lists all the NACHA Payments by employee. The totals on the NACHA file should balance to the totals on this report.
- **Federal and State Tax Remittance Report/Local Tax Remittance Report**—These reports are recent additions to Oracle's standard reports. They are replacements to the Tax Summary Listings that many companies had problems processing. Most of the problems were performance issues. These are the only Oracle Payroll-supplied reports you can use to pay the various taxes after each pay run. You select a check date range to process and, optionally, a GRE. If you leave the GRE blank, the report processes assignments for all GREs within the specified date range. You can also request MTD, QTD, or YTD totals along with the Check to Date totals.

One drawback to these new reports is that you cannot receive totals by payroll within a GRE. The previous Tax Summary listings did provide selection criteria by payroll.

- **Costing Breakdown Summary Reports**—After you have run the Costing process, you can run the two Costing Breakdown Summary reports. One report enables you to select results by a date range (Cost Breakdown Report for Date Range), whereas the other enables you to select by costing runs (Cost Breakdown Report by Costing Run). They both show summarized totals from the select costing runs. As stated before, these reports only show the costing side of the journal entry. All the balancing entries do not show on these reports. Therefore, the report might not balance. Many companies design their own costing reports that show the complete balanced journal entry. Remember that any run results that could not be properly costed automatically end up in the suspense account that you established on your payroll definition window.

Oracle Time Management: Tables and Policies

Oracle Time Management (OTM) is designed to collect time and attendance data for processing through Oracle HRMS and Payroll. The ultimate goal of OTM is to produce timecards into Oracle Payroll. The use of OTM usually enables you to avoid a custom interface of timecards into Oracle Payroll's BEE (Batch Element Entry).

Within OTM, Time and Attendance can be collected via one or a combination of the following methods: Autogen, Manual Entry, and Interfaces from time clocks. The Autogen method is the most efficient of the three. To utilize the Autogen process within OTM, the following tables need to defined:

- **Holiday Calendar**—The Holiday Calendar defines paid and unpaid holidays. For a person to be paid for a holiday, the Holiday Calendar must be created, maintained, and assigned to an Earning Policy that has been assigned to the employee. The employee must have time entry created for the pay period containing the holiday, and the information must be sent to BEE. If time worked is entered on a holiday or a holiday is entered on a date not listed on the Holiday Calendar, the system generates warnings during the Validate Timecards process.

- **Shifts**—Shifts are defined based on standard Start and Stop work times. Shifts are used in defining Work Plans. Work Plans, in turn, are used in defining Rotation Plans. Thus, Shifts must be created prior to setting up Work or Rotation Plans.
- **Work Plans**—Work Plans identify the applicable shifts for each day of the week. Each Rotation Plan consists of at least one Work Plan. Work Plans are also used for the calculation of Off Shift Premiums and Shift Differential Overrides.
- **Rotation Plans**—Rotation Plans are used to indicate dates when an employee moves from one Work Plan to another. If the employee does not change Work Plans, a Rotation Plan for the single Work Plan needs to be defined. The Rotation Plan is used for the Autogen process and calculates Off Shift Premiums and Shift Differential Overrides. *All employees are assigned to a Rotation Plan, even if the Rotation Plan consists of a single Work Plan.*
- **Project Accounts**—Project Accounts are used to input time and/or dollar estimates for tasks or projects. This form applies only to manually input time.
- **Variance**—Variance tables are used to define high and low levels of hours per period or hours by Organization, Location, or Earning.
- **Earnings Groups**—Earnings Groups are used to group Earnings for reporting purposes and for the accumulation of hours to be used in calculating weekly overtime caps on the Earning Policy.

The following Policies might be defined for OTM and assigned to the employee at the assignment level:

- **Hour Deduction**—Used for the automatic deduction of hours for meals or breaks.
- **Shift Differential**—Used to define the start and stop times and the corresponding premium to be calculated.
- **Premium Eligibility**—Used to define the authorized premium associated with each Premium Eligibility Policy.
- **Premium Interaction**—Used to define how Premiums relate to each other.
- **Timecard Approver**—Can be set at either the Organization level or Supervisor level. This must be defined for OTM.
- **Earnings**—Defines daily/weekly base, overtime rules, holiday calendar, and premium policy assigned to each employee. Please note that it is not necessary to set up the Policies in the order listed. However, all other policies must be defined prior to defining Earning Policies.

Table 25.9 lists the Direct Links between an Oracle Time Management Table or Policy and the form it is assigned to.

TABLE 25.9 OTM TABLE/FORM RELATIONSHIPS

Table/Policy	Forms			
OTM Table/Policy	**HRMS Person Assignment**	**OTM Earning Policy**	**OTM Work Plan**	**OTM Rotation Plan**
Holiday Calendar		D		
Work Plan				D
Rotation Plan	D			
Shift			D	
Earning Group		D		
Earning Policy	D			
Hour Deduction	D			
Shift Differential	D			
Premium Eligibility		D		
Premium Interaction		D		

Prior to setup, the various policies and inventory of your needs must be completed to ensure all areas have been considered and to avoid duplication.

TROUBLESHOOTING

This chapter has been loaded with various tips and techniques associated with implementing and using Oracle Payroll. In many cases, the specific solutions I have documented can be directly used by your implementation. However, the more important thing you should retain is the *approaches* I have taken to various solutions. It is quite likely that your implementation will require similar customer-specific solutions.

Oracle Payroll is considered by many consultants to be the most complex Application produced by Oracle Corporation. Do not underestimate the complexity of implementing any payroll system. If you have not read Chapter 23, you would be wise to do so. There are a number of important items in Chapter 23 that should influence your expectations of implementing Oracle Payroll. At BOSS Corporation, we have many customers who are both happy with the Oracle Payroll product and satisfied with our approach to implementation of this complex module.

CHAPTER 26

Using Oracle Advanced Benefits

In this chapter

INTRODUCTION

The most exciting enhancement released from Oracle HRMS in recent time has been the introduction of the new benefits model. Oracle has completely revamped the way benefits are defined and processed with 11*i*. These enhancements have added many new tools to the HRMS workbench, but also created some confusion to the user community. What is the best implementation approach to convert to the new benefits model? Do I need to license the new Advanced Benefits module? Can I use our existing benefit deduction elements with the new benefits model? Before any of these questions can be answered, you must explore the alternatives that Oracle offers with 11*i* with respect to benefits. 11*i* now offers three versions of benefits and each is discussed in the following sections.

ORACLE BASIC BENEFITS

The first version is the one that is most familiar with current Oracle HRMS users. Basic Benefits is the version that was part of the core HRMS family for Releases 10.7 and 11.*x*. It is still available with 11*i*. In this version, all benefits are controlled by elements, and eligibility is determined by element links. This version is very payroll-centric, meaning that premium calculations are not performed until a payroll is run. Basic Benefits has many shortcomings, which spawned the need for the new model. Most existing users of Oracle HRMS developed "bolt-on" modifications to handle these shortcomings, such as open enrollment and life event management. Not many users realize, however, that this version will still work in 11*i*. This means that you might want to phase in your benefits implementation after you have safely migrated to 11*i*. This strategy will be discussed later in this chapter.

ORACLE STANDARD BENEFITS

Standard Benefits (OSB) is now part of the core HRMS product with the introduction of 11*i*. This version is much more powerful than Basic Benefits and addresses many of its deficiencies. Premium calculations are now made by Standard Benefits and passed as flat amounts to Oracle Payroll. Eligibility is now handled with flexible and configurable eligibility profiles. Enrollment forms are used to capture election information from participants. All users who either purchase or upgrade to 11*i* receive Standard Benefits along with the core HRMS functionality. OSB is not back ported to either 11.03 or 10.7.

ORACLE ADVANCED BENEFITS

Advanced Benefits (OAB) is an extension of Standard Benefits and contains much of the needed functionality for managing a full benefits offering in-house. Some of the main features found only in Advanced Benefits include

- Life Event Management
- Flex Credit Management for cafeteria style benefit plans
- Managing reimbursement requests for Flexible Spending Accounts
- Communication kits for open enrollment and life event processing
- What-if functionality to assist with enrollment elections

Advanced Benefits is a separate licensed module and must be purchased. When existing 10.7 and 11.*x* users purchase 11*i* they must also purchase this module to gain its additional functionality. You do not have to purchase Oracle Payroll to use Advanced Benefits. Therefore, Oracle users must make a very important decision when they implement their 11*i* strategy. Does Standard Benefits offer enough functionality for your situation, or do you have to purchase Advanced Benefits? Following are some key decision factors to use when making this decision.

OAB Key Decision Factors

The two most important features of Advanced Benefits that are not available in either Basic or Standard Benefits are Life Event Management and Flex Credit Management. Many organizations are offering more comprehensive benefits programs to attract qualified employees in this competitive job market. The most frequent modifications to Basic Benefits provided these features for current 10.7 and 11.*x* users. If your benefit program provides enrollment opportunities based on certain life events, such as marriage or the birth of a child, and these events have been difficult to manage, then you should seriously consider Advanced Benefits. OAB can automatically detect life events by monitoring changes made to the HRMS database. You can set enrollment restrictions and time limits for each life event to ensure that you are following the rules set out in your Benefits Summary Plan Documents. These life events can trigger an automatic communication to the employee notifying him of his opportunity to change his benefit elections. If the user has implemented Self Service, the Web site can now automatically be available to the employee so that he can record his new elections. Only employees who experience life events will be able to make elections using Self Service.

Some early adapters of Standard Benefits are beginning to realize some of the disadvantages of not having life event management. When employees are terminated, Standard Benefits does not automatically de-enroll them from their selected benefit programs. You must go to the Non-Flex Program window, select the terminated employee, and then save the record. The point here is that all life event management in Standard Benefits must be done manually. This includes changes in coverage and rates for any benefit plan based on compensation and/or age.

Flex Credit Management allows organizations to offer credits to their benefit participants to be used to purchase benefit elections. These credits are automatically calculated by OAB and awarded to eligible participants. OAB tracks the use of these credits and can allocate the excess amounts based on rules that you establish. Excess credits can be paid out to participants as cash or rolled over to a default plan such as a healthcare reimbursement account. Once again, organizations that offer a cafeteria-style benefits plan should strongly consider OAB during implementation. Otherwise, they will have to manage flex credits with bolt-on modifications to Standard Benefits.

Implementation Strategies

Current 11.*x* and 10.7 users have a huge upgrade task when they decide to implement 11*i*. The task is complex enough without having to completely redesign benefit management. Because Basic Benefits still functions under 11*i*, users should seriously consider postponing this benefit redesign until they have completed the migration to 11*i*. This will allow time to resolve all 11*i* issues before undertaking this complex project. It might also allow the new benefit options to mature, as there are some initial quality issues. There will also be more resources to draw from when you need assistance with your implementation. This includes resources that come cost-free such as list servers and user groups. Standard and Advanced Benefits offer many choices and decisions that should be studied carefully without the pressure of completing an 11*i* upgrade project.

Assume that you are now ready to begin your task of implementing benefits using the new functionality that Oracle offers. There are several implementation strategies that you can use to migrate your existing benefits to the new structures. Each one will be discussed in the following sections.

Complete Reinstall of 11*i*

Some existing 10.7 and 11.*x* users have decided to create a new install of the Oracle Applications Release 11*i* and use existing APIs to move their data into this new instance. This strategy is discussed in Chapter 23, "Implementing Oracle Human Resources and Oracle Payroll." This strategy will allow you to rebuild all your existing elements and structures using new benefits functionality.

Conversion Versus Process New Elections

As discussed previously, the benefit models in 11*i* are significantly different from previous releases. There are really no upgrade scripts available that will take current benefit data in Oracle and automatically create your programs and plans in 11*i*. Therefore, you must rebuild your benefit programs with this new functionality. After this process is complete, you still have some big decisions to make on how to get your current employee base into this new model. There is an excellent white paper on Oracle Corporation's Metalink Web site that addresses this process. It is titled "Implementing Oracle Benefits in Release 11*i*" and can be found in the Technical Libraries section. This should be considered required reading for anyone who is implementing any of the new benefit models. This includes new Oracle clients on 11*i* as well as clients migrating from a previous release. The remainder of this section will highlight the main topics of this paper.

Oracle delivers a series of APIs that will allow you to load current and historical elections directly into the benefit tables. This assumes that you have already built and tested your benefit programs in 11*i*. You must first decide if it is necessary to load any historical election information into 11*i*. This might be necessary if you want to default new elections based on historical elections. Certain enrollment requirements might also be driven from historical election. This is common in dental and vision plans, which might require a minimum enrollment period before changes are allowed. U.S. customers are now required to produce HIPAA certifications to prove coverage history. OSB/OAB would not be able to produce this information until at least 18 months of history have been accumulated in these modules.

Loading historical information can be complex and very time-consuming. You must map your legacy data to the new Oracle definitions and write the necessary code to load this into the APIs. You might want to shorten this process by loading in only the current elections. Clearly, the advantages of having this information at your go-live date must be weighed against the time and effort it will take to load this information.

The second approach is to use open enrollment to load in current enrollment information. Every participant must re-enroll in the new benefit programs using either Self Service, or by completing new election forms to be entered by benefits personnel. This will allow participants to "clean up" their benefit elections, including dependent and beneficiary designations. This approach is simpler and should be considered for users who are on very tight implementation schedules. There is no need to perform any data mapping from the legacy data to the new benefit definitions.

The drawbacks to this second approach are many. No current elections can be defaulted, because there is no current enrollment information in the system. You will not be able to enforce any election rules based on current enrollment either, because OSB/OAB will not know the current enrollment information. As stated previously, HIPPA certifications will have to be completed outside of the system until enough history has been processed in OSB/OAB.

The task of implementing either Standard or Advanced Benefits is a major component of your 11*i* upgrade or install. Make sure you explore all your options before making the best decision for your enterprise.

COMPENSATION OBJECTS

Compensation objects are the building blocks of benefits. Navigating down the compensation object hierarchy, programs are at the highest level, followed by plan types, plans, and options. Similar to other Oracle Applications, you build from the bottom up. In the case of Benefits, you are working your way up the compensation object hierarchy. During implementation you will begin by configuring the options available to your employees. For example, your medical coverage might include Employee Plus Family or your savings plan might offer certain funds for investments. The highest level in the hierarchy is the program. This would include all plans for a similar benefits offering and have similar eligibility requirements and the same enrollment periods.

After the compensation objects are defined and you have completed some of the basic setup steps such as defining your program/plan years, you begin to expand on the configuration of your benefit offerings. Attach eligibility profiles for both participant and dependent coverage to limit which people are eligible for your offerings. You configure life event functionality to determine what changes to a person's HR record create potential enrollment opportunities or changes to current elections both during open enrollment and during the plan year. You define communications to be sent to participants. You configure variable rate profiles and standard rates that can be automatically sent to Oracle Payroll for processing. If your program offers flex credits such as a cafeteria style offering, define the amount of flex credits provided and how a participant can spend those flex credits.

Many of the configurations or settings available for definition at the lower levels of the compensation object hierarchy are also available at higher levels. Definitions at the higher levels cascade to the lower levels. This is true not only for the compensation objects but also the enrollment requirements defined at the program and plan levels. Unless the requirements are different at the lower level, your setup will be a lot cleaner and easier to manage if you set the rules at the highest level. For example, Participation Eligibility can be defined at the program level, the plan type in program level, the plan in program level, the plan level, and the option in plan level. A check box for Participation Eligibility Override Allowed is available on many different forms. If your requirements are the same for the majority of your program; for example, if you are eligible for the program you are eligible for all the plans in the program; it would be redundant to attach the eligibility profiles to the program and to each of the plans. The result would be the same if you only attached the profiles to the program and your maintenance would be greatly simplified. If there were additional or different participant eligibility profiles for one of the plans, simply attach the different profiles to that one plan. The configuration at the lower level overrides the setup at the program level.

During implementation as you start building at the lowest levels, you will be very tempted to check every check box and fill in every field on every form you navigate to. Before you DateTrack on the first form and begin setup, spend a little time reviewing the forms and the functionality available at the different levels of the compensation object hierarchy.

As you are building your compensation objects, the View Program Structures offers a great way to review your compensation objects setup. This form allows you to view your entire compensation object hierarchy structure and navigate directly to the object of interest by pressing the traffic light icon. You can view by program, by plan type, by plan, or by option. Starting by option, expand the navigation branch, select an option, and you can see which plans the option is defined in. Selecting by program, you can expand the branches and see all programs defined, the plans in those programs, and the options available in those plans.

PROGRAMS

Programs are the highest level in the compensation object hierarchy and therefore the last compensation object configured. Programs group plans that have similar eligibility requirements and the same enrollment periods for participants to enroll in. It is the umbrella for your benefit offerings. Some of the types of programs you can set up include Core, COBRA, and Flex Credit programs. At the program level, you set the currency, define the activity reference period, frequencies for enrollment and rates, and the periods your program covers. You can configure whether or not participation eligibility override is allowed. For example, if a person is found ineligible for the program, you can manually override the results of the participation process and enroll the person in the program. Determine if you want to use all assignments for eligibility and for rates. Determine whether or not you want to track ineligible persons.

At the program level, you define which plans and plan types are included in the program. For example, your medical plan could be included in both your main benefit offering and in the COBRA Program. The same plan can be used in both programs. It will be the plan in program configurations that differentiate the eligibility, rates, and so on, for the occurrence of the plans and options.

Define the participation start and end dates, any waiting period that exists for the program, and any maximum enrollment periods for each program. There might be a six-month waiting period for your benefit program you offer to eligible employees and a maximum enrollment period for the COBRA program. These definitions can be overridden at lower levels by the occurrence of life events.

Attach participant eligibility profiles or rules to determine which of your employees are eligible to participate. For example, your employees might be required to be full-time regular employees or part-time regular employees with at least 1000 hours worked to be eligible for the program.

You can attach life events that determine whether the occurrence of that life event causes a participant to be eligible or ineligible to participate. For example, the life event Termination would cause you to be ineligible for the regular employee program offered but eligible for the COBRA program.

Program Enrollment Requirements

For each program you define, you must also set up the enrollment requirements. The process of determining a person's electable choices is based on the requirements you define for programs and at the plan levels, if different. Although participation eligibility has already been defined for the program, it is the enrollment requirements that create electable choices by defining the rules associated with enrolling in a program or changing current elections.

You define the enrollment method (either automatic or explicit), enrollment code, coverage dates, and rate start and end dates. Enrollment codes determine the choices current and new participants can elect. For example, current participants can keep, choose, or lose elections. Also, you determine whether or not the program allows unrestricted enrollment, default enrollments, and automatic enrollments.

You can also define limitations for the minimum and maximum number of plans in a plan type within a program that a participant can enroll in and any required period of enrollment. Also, configure default enrollment codes for those participants that fail to respond to an active life event in a certain time period. For example, if you are currently enrolled in the plan type Medical, and you fail to make any changes to your elections, your resulting default enrollment could be Same Enrollment and Rates, Defaults as configured in your program, or Nothing.

You must also define the timing related to enrolling in a program. For open enrollment, define the start and end dates for enrollment and changes to current elections, when to close enrollment, and the coverage and rate start and end dates. For each life event that affects the program, define the period of enrollment or window of time the employee has to elect or make changes to his enrollment.

In addition to the timing of enrollments, you can define restrictions related to enrolling in the program. Based on life events that occur, you can restrict the elections the employee can change. Also, if the employee doesn't respond, you can set default enrollments. At the plan type and plan levels, you can select what enrollment changes the employee can make based on the life event. For example, if an employee gets married, you set whether the employee can change the option and not the plan or can change both the plan and the option.

Finally, you can set the dependent coverage designations at the program or plan type level, any certifications such as Social Security number or date of birth needed for the dependent, dependent eligibility profiles, and changes you can make to dependent coverage based on a given life event.

Plan Types

Plan types group similar plan offerings. Examples include medical, dental, flexible spending accounts, and life insurance. These plan classifications allow you to define the types of options a participant can elect and the minimum and/or maximum number of plans a participant can enroll in concurrently.

Plans

Plans are the individual offerings available to employees if they meet the enrollment requirements. Plans can be either in a program or a separate offering, termed plan not in program. Examples include a medical plan offered in a program or a savings plan that is independent of any program offering.

Information you can define for each plan includes which plan type it belongs to, general definitions such as a COBRA payment date, and the primary funding method. If different from the program level, configure whether or not participation eligibility override is allowed, if you want to use all assignments for eligibility and for rates, and whether or not you want to track ineligible persons. Also, determine whether participation can be waived.

Define any restrictions associated with the plan, imputed income implications, and for plans not in a program, the currency, the activity reference period, and frequencies for enrollment and rates. Also for each plan, set plan periods, reporting groups, and any regulations such as Section 125 or COBRA.

If the plan eligibility for a plan in program is different from the requirements configured at the program level, attach eligibility profiles or rules to determine which of your employees are eligible to participate. Also, if different, you attach life events that determine whether the occurrence of that life event causes a participant to be eligible or ineligible to participate in the plan.

Further, define waive participation reasons and the certifications needed for an employee to waive coverage in the plan. For example, a Plan Waiving Participation Reason could be that the participant is covered by another plan. An example of a certificate is a Proof of External Coverage.

Set up the options that are available in the plan. The list is based on the plan type you defined for the options. For each option in plan, attach life events that determine whether the occurrence of that life event causes a participant to be eligible or ineligible to select that option in the plan. For example, marriage would make an employee eligible to select EE (employee) and Spouse option while a divorce would make her ineligible for the same option.

Oracle supports flexible spending account plans such as Dependent Care Reimbursement. Define the dates you accept a claim request through, the types of goods and services that can be reimbursed, and the relationship types an employee can make claims for.

Plan Enrollment Requirements

Plan enrollment requirements are very similar to the configuration available for programs. In addition to the enrollment requirements discussed for a program, you can define limitations for the number of options an employee can elect within a plan. For example, a participant should not be able to enroll in both the Employee Only and Employee and Family options for the medical plan. However, a participant might not be limited to the number of options he can select in a retirement plan.

For plans that you offer, you can define enrollment certifications such as proof of good health. At the plan or option in plan level, you could require enrollment certifications for life events. Also, define actions required by an employee such as designating a dependent or beneficiary to complete enrollment in the plan.

Configure designation requirements if different from the ones described at the option level. You can also set the dependent coverage designations, any certifications needed for the dependent, the dependent eligibility profiles, and changes you can make to dependent coverage based on a given life event if not defined or different from the program level.

Options

Options represent the choices your employees have for coverages or elections within the plans they enroll in. For each option, define which plan types, and therefore plans, the option is available for. By defining Participant plus Family, an employee can elect to cover himself and his family under the medical plan or defining Six Units would allow an employee to select a level of employee life insurance coverage.

In addition to defining which plan types the options are available for, you can configure the designation requirements for each option. Based on an employee's contact records, for example, spouse and children, define the personal relationships that are required to select the contact during enrollment. The contact relationship in an employee's contact record must have the Personal Relationship field checked to be available in the list of dependents or beneficiaries to designate. In addition to specifying which relationship types are available, you also enter the minimum and maximum numbers required. If you do not define the designation requirements, there are no restrictions on who can be designated.

Options are reusable; the same option could be used for both medical and dental plan types. The basic definition of an option includes the name, the plan types the option is available to, and the designation requirements. Consider using the term *Individual* or *Participant* instead of Employee if the option could be used in multiple situations. For example, the option name EE Only is not appropriate for a COBRA plan. Using Individual allows you to use the same option for both plans and keeps you from having to set up multiple options that represent coverage for one person. Options are linked to individual plans on the Plans form. Once attached, you can determine eligibility profiles and life event eligibility for the existence of the option in that specific plan. An example of an option in plan life event eligibility would be the life events Marriage and Divorce. The life event Marriage would make you eligible for the EE Plus Spouse option in the Medical (or any other) plan. The life event Divorce would make you ineligible for the same option in plan.

Enrollment requirements, defaults, limitations, required certifications, and designation requirements can also be defined at the option in plan level on the Plan Enrollment Requirements form. Based on the configuration of Program Enrollment Requirements for plan types and plans, you can determine whether or not a participant can change his options (and or plans) based on the occurrence of a life event.

Life Events

Life events transform Oracle Benefits from a static data capture device into a responsive, proactive benefits management tool. By configuring the database triggers, the application will tell you when a participant is eligible to enroll in a program or plan or change his or her current elections during the benefit year and when to send communications to the participant.

Used along with the new Self-Service Human Resources, employees update their own HR record, for example their marital status or the birth of a child. The system can automatically detect the life event and process the life event to determine eligibility and electability. Also, the Line Manager functionality allows supervisors to change an employee's record such as employment category and compensation level that could also trigger a potential life event.

Using Life Events

Life events are defined as any changes to a person's human resources data that could affect eligibility and electability for the benefits your enterprise offers. Life events are categorized as explicit, temporal, or scheduled. Explicit life event reasons include the life event reasons you define as changes in a person's human resources record that are triggers for potential impact on compensation object eligibility. Examples include Divorce, Change in Assignment Status, or Change in Personal Residence. Temporal life events result from the passage of time. An example would be a dependent reaching age 19. Scheduled life events are defined enrollment opportunities by the employer. For example, yearly open enrollments are scheduled life events.

The impact of life event functionality is a key part in the management and processing of a benefit program. Life events can control enrollment eligibility for compensation objects, rates for benefit elections, coverage provided, and communications sent to participants. Life events are reusable. They are set up independently and can be associated with programs, options in plans, and rates.

Life events and participant and dependent eligibility profiles work together to determine eligibility for compensation objects. A participant might be eligible for an Employee and Spouse option based on the life event Marriage. However, the dependent eligibility profiles must also cover the spouse and be attached to this same compensation object. Also, the designation requirements must be defined in order to actually designate the participant's spouse during enrollment.

After a life event has been processed by the system, you can view both active and potential life events for a participant. The status listed for each life event indicates the processing completed by the system. Detected indicates the potential person change has been detected but not processed. If you create a life event manually, it is initially given the status of Unprocessed. The status will change to detected when processed. A Started status indicates the participation process has evaluated the life event and the participant has electable choices. When the status is Started, you can enroll or change the current elections for a participant. To view the enrollment opportunities based on the life event, navigate to the enrollment opportunities and then electable choices forms. A wide range of data is available including the flex credits available to the participant, limitations for enrolling, and possible certifications required.

As meticulous as you might be in configuring the life event functionality, there might be times where a potential life event should be voided or the system did not detect a potential life event. Functionality exists to manually create and to manually void life events.

CONFIGURING LIFE EVENTS

Configuring life events begins with defining the person changes or the underlying database triggers that drive life event functionality. Use descriptive names, such as "Hire an Employee Asg Type Any Value to EE Asg" or "Divorce -EE Marital Status Any Value to Divorced." For each person change, define the database changes that allow Advanced Benefits to detect a potential life event.

The person changes are based on certain HRMS tables and columns and the old and new values that you specify. The tables available hold data about the people (PER_ALL_PEOPLE_F), assignments (PER_ALL_ASSIGNMENTS_F), and contacts (PER_CONTACT_RELATIONSHIPS). Other tables hold data relating to ending employment, absences, addresses, budget values, and benefit balances. For example, for the person change event Birth of Child Contact Type No to Child Value, define the table name as PER_CONTACT_RELATIONSHIPS, the column name CONTACT_TYPE, the old value as No Value and the new value as Child.

The next step is to define the Life Event Reasons. Oracle provides some seeded life event reasons mainly used in the derived factors in eligibility profiles and for COBRA. You will need to set up additional life events based on the way your HRMS system is configured and the applicable business rules for your enterprise. Some of the categories of qualifying life events are changes in marital status, changes in the number of dependents, changes in employment status, changes in residence, and changes in dependent status. Life events such as Ending a Qualified Domestic Partner Relationship, Birth of a Child, Termination of Employment, Change in Residence, and Change in Worksite Location can be set up.

Setup includes defining the type of life event—for example, personal or work; any timeliness evaluations, and the occurred date determination, such as the date the event occurred or the date the event was recorded. If the life event such as Hire an Employee or Death of Employee should be processed regardless of any other life events detected, check the Override check box. The next step is to link the person changes created in the previous step to the appropriate Life Event Reason.

Now that the life event has been defined, the work begins. The next logical step in the setup is to define Collapsing Life Events. When more than one life event occurs in the same period, usually one day, the system needs to know which one to process. An example that you may run into during testing is Hire an Employee, Change in Residence, and Change in Worksite Location. This will occur if you have not defined any of these as the overriding, or winning life event. Using conditional logic, determine which life event takes priority when two or more events occur during the tolerance days. During the participation process, the system detects all potential life events and based on the collapsing rules and the override flag on the life event reason definition, the system is able to determine which life event to process.

Life Events can be used to determine participation eligibility for programs, plan types in programs, plans in programs, plans, and options in plans. The occurrence of a life event can cause a person to become eligible or ineligible for the compensation object. For example, Termination can cause a former employee to be ineligible for the enterprise's benefit program. At the same time, the life event can also cause the former employee to be eligible for the COBRA program. Although the navigation is different, the concept and appearance of the form are similar for options. On the Life Event Reason Impact on Eligibility for an option in a plan, define the life events that impact a participant's eligibility for an option. An example would be the life event Adopt a Child that would qualify a participant to select Family Coverage for the medical or dental plan. Divorce would cause the participant to be ineligible for the Participant Plus Spouse option.

Although designation requirements and dependent eligibility profiles are not specifically a part of life event configuration, it is a good time to review some basic setups. The designation requirements plus dependent eligibility profiles determine who can be designated during a participant's enrollment. Designation requirements are used to create the list of dependents or beneficiaries a participant can designate during enrollment. Dependent Eligibility Profiles, as the name implies, determine eligibility for a participant's contacts. These configurations are important for testing your setup of life events.

At this point in the configuration of life event functionality, a participant might be eligible for a compensation object based on the occurrence of a life event. However, the system has not created electable choices for the participant. If you try to enroll an employee, there are no enrollment opportunities available. For the system to create electable choices, you must define the enrollment requirements for the life events. Enrollment requirements can be defined at the program and plan levels and represent when a participant can enroll and restrictions on the enrollment or enrollment change.

Using the Timing tab and Life Event tab on the Enrollment Requirements form, establish when a participant can enroll or change her current elections based on the occurrence of each of the life events. Set up the enrollment period start and end dates for the life event and the number of days after the enrollment period for ineligibility.

Using the Life Event tab on the Enrollment Requirements forms, determine what changes the participant can make based on her current enrollment. You can define the requirements at the following levels: program, plan type, plan in program, or option in plan. For example, the current enrollment could preclude changes or the participant might still be eligible but not able to change her enrollment. On the plan type and plan tabs, if the life event allows for an employee to make changes to her elections, select whether the employee can change the option but not the plan, or the plan but not the option, or both.

To configure the dependent coverage changes a participant can make based on a given life event, use the Dependent Coverage tab on the Program or Plan Enrollment Requirements forms. Navigate to the Dependent Change of Life Event form. For each life event that might affect dependents, select the life event and the code for the changes allowed. For example, for the life event Birth of a Child, the change dependent coverage code should be May Add Dependents. Be sure to set up the open enrollment life event and the code that applies, May Either Add or Remove Dependents.

LIFE EVENT PROCESSING

During daily HRMS processing, the database triggers or person changes that cause life events you defined are loaded into the Person in Life Event Reason table. Initially, the potential life event is given the status of detected.

The next step is to run the Participation Process. These four concurrent programs, based on the parameters you select, determine the dates, people, programs, and so on, that you want to process. The concurrent program determines each participant's eligibility and electability for enrollment or changes to current enrollment elections. You should determine the scheduling of these processes based on the size of your enterprise and the amount of benefit activity you expect. It can be set to run nightly or weekly or even on demand during the day. The Participation Processes detect, and if necessary, create potential life events. Then the Participation Process selects the life events to process, establishes participant eligibility, determines electable choices, and processes changes to enrollment results. There are four Participation Processes. The Life Event batch process selects all people with potential life events, whereas the Scheduled batch process is used for open enrollments and other scheduled life events based on the enrollment period dates. The Temporal batch process, based on the parameters and effective date range you enter, selects all persons who meet your parameters. Finally, the Selection batch process selects the people and compensation objects based on the effective date parameter. It determines eligibility but does not create electable choices.

After the potential life events have been identified, the participation process selects the life event to process. There might be more than one potential life event for a person but only one life event can be active and process. Based on the rules and other setup choices you make, the life events are evaluated against the collapsing rules that exist and against the override flag on the life event reason to select a winning life event to process. If there are still multiple life events and the system cannot determine which one to process, the program stops and errors. If this part of the process is successful, one life event will be selected to process and the other potential life events will be voided. The system then checks for potential related person's life events based on the winning life event and creates any potential life events for related persons.

Based on the winning life event, the process then establishes the participant's eligibility for the compensation objects selected in the parameters. The process evaluates derived factors and eligibility profiles, checks the eligibility defined on compensation objects such as the Life Event Reason Impact on Eligibility for an option in a plan, checks for override flags on compensation objects, and evaluates waiting periods and other enrollment requirements. The system determines whether a person is eligible and creates or updates the eligibility status. If a currently enrolled participant is found to be ineligible, the process de-enrolls the participant from the compensation object. A participant can be de-enrolled from the Employee Plus Spouse option resulting from a divorce life event or even from the program if the employee is no longer eligible. If a person is found to be ineligible either for the first time or still ineligible for a compensation object, the process ends. If the Track Ineligible Persons check box is flagged, the ineligibility is updated to the database.

The process has established which people are eligible for the compensation objects. Next it determines electable choices for the people. Based on the life events and enrollment requirements you defined, the system evaluates electable choices. This part of the process is based on the configuration of the Program Enrollment Requirements and the Plan Enrollment Requirements forms. Designation requirements for dependents and beneficiaries are examined, as well as any required certifications. If all these conditions are met, electable choices are created. Also, at this point, flex credits and imputed income are evaluated. If either is found to be applicable, data is created to hold the shell plans in a participant's record. Based on all the processing so far, coverage, rates, and eligible dependents are also determined.

Finally, the Participation Process can make changes to enrollment results. Any automatic enrollment rules are updated to the participants benefit record. If the participant has no electable choices, the database is updated accordingly. For example, if the life event did not create electable choices or changes for the participant, the status of the life event is set to Processed. If a person is no longer eligible, the enrollment results are updated accordingly.

For those participants who are eligible and have electable choices created, the system sets the life event status to Started. To view the active life events, navigate to the Person Life Events form. To begin enrollment or make changes to a participant's elections, navigate to either the Flex Program Enrollment form or the appropriate enrollment form depending on the type of program or plan.

ELIGIBILITY PROFILES AND DERIVED FACTORS

After the compensation objects have been defined and the life events functionality has been configured, you must control who can enroll in the benefits you offer. If there are no eligibility profiles attached to your program, everyone is eligible. By attaching an eligibility profile to a compensation object, you restrict who can enroll. The profiles can be attached to a program, plan type in program, plan in program, plan, and option in plan. The profiles are reusable. If an employee is eligible for all plans in the program, simply define the eligibility requirements once at the program level because eligibility cascades down the compensation object hierarchy.

Eligibility profiles work with life events (Advanced Benefits) and enrollment requirements to create electable choices for the benefit package your enterprise offers. Eligibility is determined during the Participation Process for Advanced Benefit users. For Standard Benefits, eligibility is determined when a person is queried on the enrollment form.

Similar to the functionality that element links provide in Basic Benefits, Benefit Eligibility Profiles restrict the employees and their dependents that can be covered. Just as an element link can restrict which employee can receive an earning element based on her people group or salary basis, an eligibility profile can limit the options an employee can elect based on the same fields. However, in addition to defining eligibility for a compensation object, you can also use the same profiles to determine ineligibility. By checking the Exclude check box on the profile for the value FullTime - Temporary for the criteria Full/Part Time on the Employment Tab, any employee working on a full-time temporary basis would be excluded from receiving the benefit. The values for this parameter are from the pick list you configure for an employee's employment category on their assignment.

Another significant difference from element links is the large quantity of human resources data on which you can base your profile configuration. You can use personal, employment, derived factors, related coverages, and other predefined criteria. You can also define a rule. The Display All tab on the Eligibility Profile form is an easy way to display all of the criteria you have defined for a particular profile.

Derived benefit eligibility factors offer a systematic way to establish when a person is eligible for benefit offerings. The criteria you can select from include compensation level, hours worked, percent full-time, age, length of service, and combined age and length of service. By defining the thresholds required for your requirements, the system can alert you to a potential eligible participant. Hours worked in a period can be used to define the number of actual hours an employee must attain before becoming eligible. You define the minimum or maximum number of hours for the factor. You could use the defined balance Regular Hours Worked to determine the number of regular hours an employee worked. This should not be confused with the Scheduled Hours criteria available on the Employment tab. The scheduled hours criteria look at the hours on an employee's assignment standard conditions. Scheduled hours would be 40 hours per week or 1000 hours per year. This field does not allow you to define greater than or less than criteria. If you set an eligibility requirement based on scheduled hours equal to 1000, any employee who is scheduled for 1001 hours would not be eligible. Another derived eligibility factor is the Full Time Equivalent. This factor uses an employee's assignment budget value. You could build an eligibility profile that requires an employee to be at least 50% full-time equivalent.

The derived factor age is useful in configuring Dependent Eligibility Profiles. Dependent profiles, similar to Participant Profiles, restrict coverage for eligible dependents. Many enterprises define qualifying dependents as spouses, domestic partners, unmarried children under the age of 19, unmarried children between the ages of 19 and 25 who are full-time students, or disabled dependents. To define eligible children using Oracle's Dependent Eligibility Profiles, it is simply a matter of defining three profiles. The criteria for the first definition is relationship type of Child, marital status of Single Status, and derived age of Under 19). The second profile would use the same relationship and marital status but with a derived age of 19–25 and Student status as Full-Time Student. The criteria for the third profile would be based on the dependent's disabled status.

Tip

One thing to watch for is on the add contact record, the marital status, student, and disabled information is not available. You must ensure these fields are entered on the People Enter and Maintain form for the dependents to be found eligible. Also, designation requirements must be defined before the eligible dependent can be selected by name for coverage. For a dependent to be found eligible for coverage, she is only required to meet one of the profiles. This functionality is attained when the profiles are attached to the compensation object(s).

When attaching profiles for both participant and dependents to compensation objects, select whether or not the profile is required. The rule of thumb is that each profile marked as required is mandatory and at least one of the optional profiles must be met. In the previous dependent eligibility example, all three would be listed as optional. Another situation would be where only one eligibility profile is attached. In this situation, the results are the same regardless of whether or not the required box is checked.

After you have set up eligibility for participants and their dependents you can configure the life events (Advanced Benefits) to trigger a change in enrollment for a participant whose dependents are no longer qualifying dependents and therefore ineligible for coverage. For example, a dependent that has not aged out of coverage gets married. By creating a related person life event and configuring the program or plan enrollment requirements, a change in enrollment opportunity for the participant who has family coverage potentially exists. Enrollment could be opened to allow the participant to choose less coverage. To process dependents who age out of qualifying status, run the Maintain Designee Eligibility concurrent process.

Benefit Program Setup Example

Both Standard and Advanced Benefits provide many new features and flexibility that did not exist in previous releases. It would be difficult, if not impossible, to explain each of these in just one chapter. Probably the best way to introduce you to this new functionality is to step through a very simple benefit program setup process. You will see how each of the compensation objects is defined and how they interact with each other. This demonstration should provide a starting point for your understanding of this complex module. We will not cover every needed step but introduce you to the major ones.

We will define a simple benefit program that includes medical, dental, and long-term disability (LTD) benefits. It also provides flex credits that can be used to purchase various options within these plan types. Following is a breakdown of our demonstration benefit program:

Program Name	Acme Benefit Program
Medical Plans	Coyote HMO Roadrunner PPO
Dental Plan	Painless Dental
LTD Options	50% of salary 60% of salary

For the Medical and Dental plans, we offer the following coverage options:

- Employee Only
- Employee and Spouse
- Employee and Children
- Family

You will set eligibility at the program level. All full-time employees and any part-time employees who work 1000 hours a year will be eligible. You will also define dependent eligibility.

The rates are listed in Table 26.1.

TABLE 26.1 RATES FOR THE ACME BENEFIT PROGRAM

Plan Type	Plan Name	Employee Only	Employee and Spouse	Employee and Children	Family
Medical	Coyote HMO	$2,800	$4,200	$4,100	$5,000
Medical	Roadrunner PPO	$3,100	$5,700	$5,300	$6,800
Dental	Painless Dental	$290	$540	$620	$770
LTD 50%		$82			
LTD 60%		$164			

This plan awards $2,800 of medical flex credits, $290 of dental flex credits, and $164 of LTD flex credits.

Okay, Let's get started!!

This setup example follows the recommended setup steps outlined in the Oracle Metalink document id 1081587.6.

STEP 1: DEFINE PROGRAM/PLAN YEAR PERIODS

This screen (not shown) is used to establish your plan years. Enter the start and end dates for each of your plan years; you must include a record for every plan year. You can set up within year periods for programs that start in the middle of a plan year. Period Types are either Calendar or Fiscal.

STEP 2: DEFINE LIFE EVENT REASONS

Figure 26.1 is used to set up any life events that are necessary to drive enrollment opportunities. Several come seeded. In this example, you set up a life event called Divorce. The Type is set to Personal, meaning the event is tied to the participant's personal data, as opposed to being work related. The Occurred Date Determination defines when the life event is recognized. Other choices include Day After Event Occurred Date, Date Event Recorded, Later of Day After Occurred Event Date or Event Recorded Date, and Later of Event Occurred Date or Recorded Date.

Click the Person Changes button and then the Define Person Change button to define the person change associated with this life event. Complete the screen as shown in Figure 26.2.

Figure 26.2 displays how you define what data has to change for this life event to fire. You must be familiar with the database schema to properly define life events. This example shows that the Marital_Status field in the PER_ALL_PEOPLE_F table must change from any value to Divorced for this life event to occur. Return to the Person Changes Cause Life Events screen and picklist this person change you just created. Your screen should look similar to Figure 26.3.

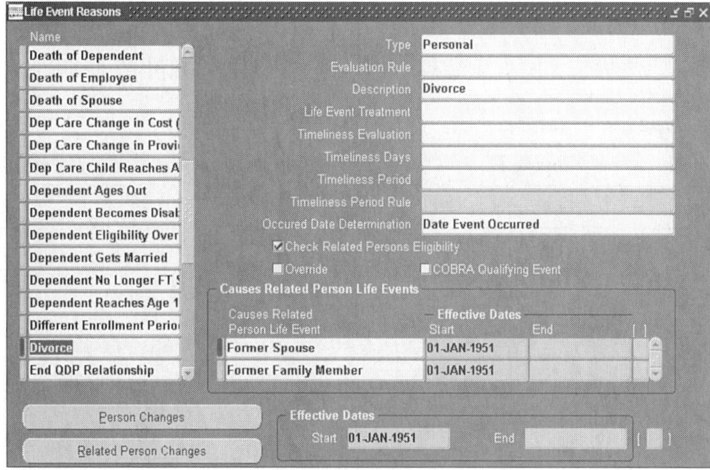

Figure 26.1
Life event reasons showing Divorce.

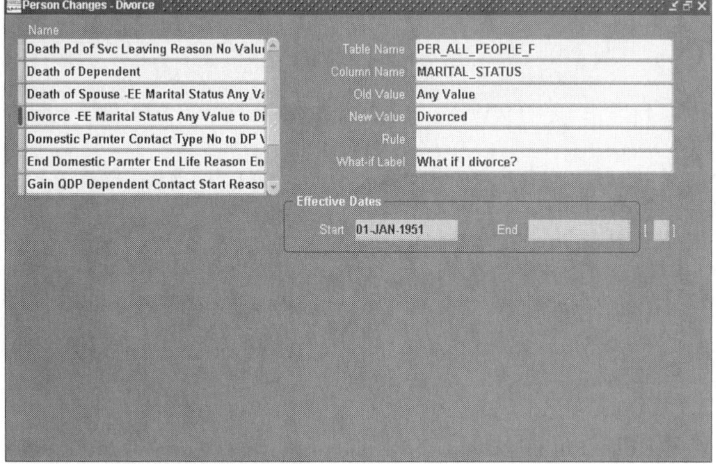

Figure 26.2
Person Changes screen showing Divorce setup.

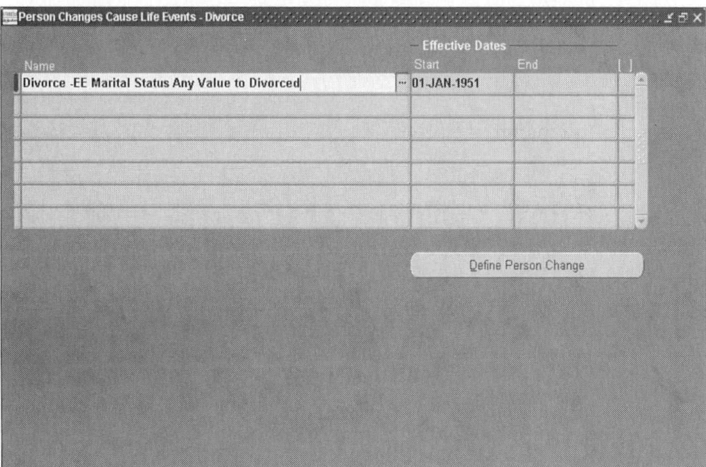

Figure 26.3
Person Changes Cause Life Events screen showing the Divorce person change.

STEP 3: DEFINE PARTICIPANT ELIGIBILITY PROFILES

Now you begin to define the eligibility profile for participants. Figure 26.4 outlines the eligible person types.

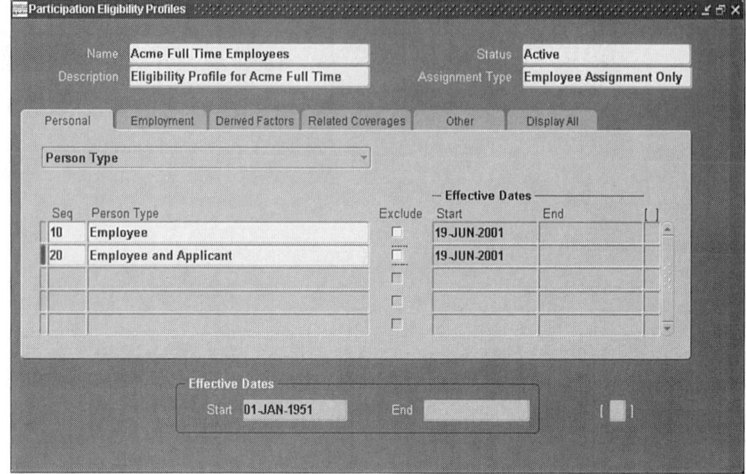

Figure 26.4
Participation eligibility profiles for full-time employees.

Next, select the Employment tab and complete the screen as shown in Figure 26.5.

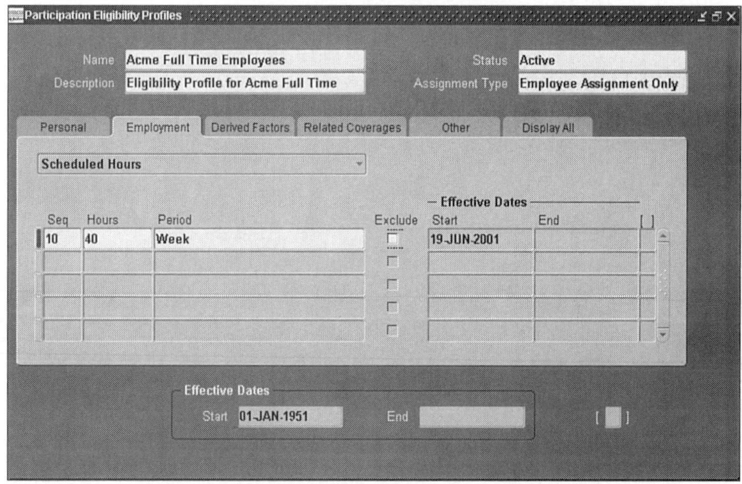

Figure 26.5
Participation eligibility profiles showing scheduled hours.

Figure 26.5 demonstrates how to describe attributes related to a participant's employment. Here you are stating that an eligible employee must be scheduled to work 40 hours per week. Other data items that can be set on this tab include Assignment Set, Bargaining Unit, Assignment Status, Full/Part Time, Grade, Hourly/Salaried, Job, Legal Entity, Organization, Pay Basis, Payroll, People Group, and Work Location.

When you select the Display All tab, you get a nice recap of the complete eligibility profile, as shown in Figure 26.6.

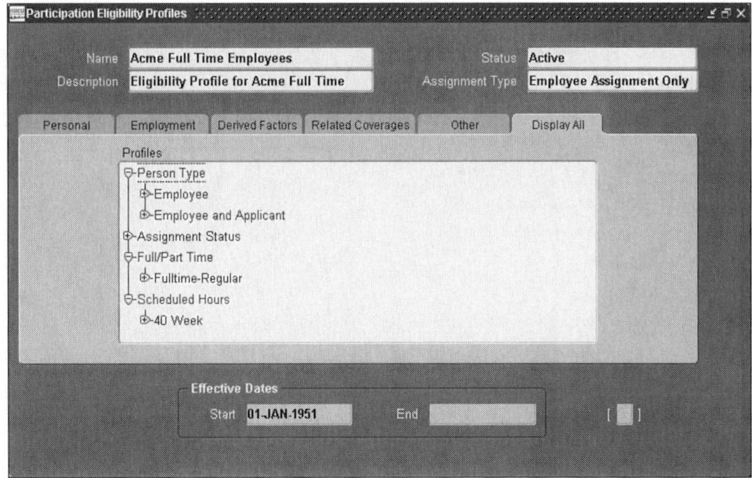

Figure 26.6 Participation eligibility profiles showing all attributes.

The part-time eligibility profile is similar to this one. Next, you will define a dependent eligibility profile.

STEP 4: DEFINE DEPENDENT ELIGIBILITY PROFILE

We will demonstrate one of the dependent profiles here. You can create as many as necessary to properly define dependents who can be covered under the various benefit plans. Figure 26.7 shows a profile for dependents who are younger than 19.

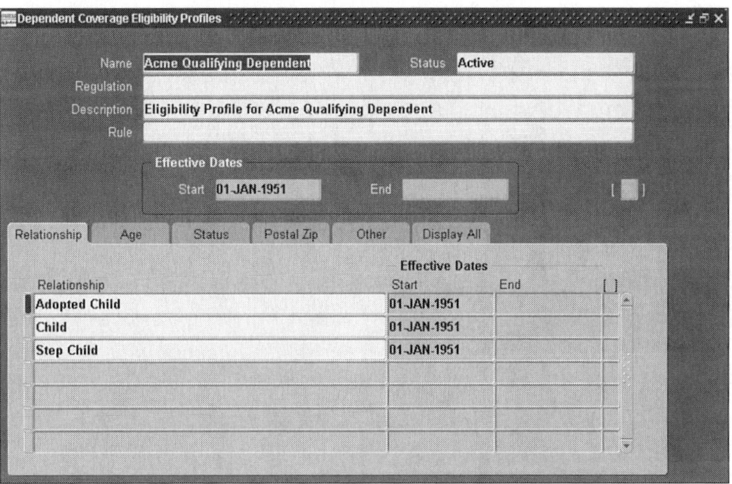

Figure 26.7 Dependent coverage eligibility profiles showing valid relationships.

Figure 26.7 defines the valid relationships for a qualifying dependent. You can select any of the defined relationships from the contact screen.

Select the Age tab to define the Age rules shown in Figure 26.8.

Figure 26.8
Dependent coverage eligibility profiles showing age requirements.

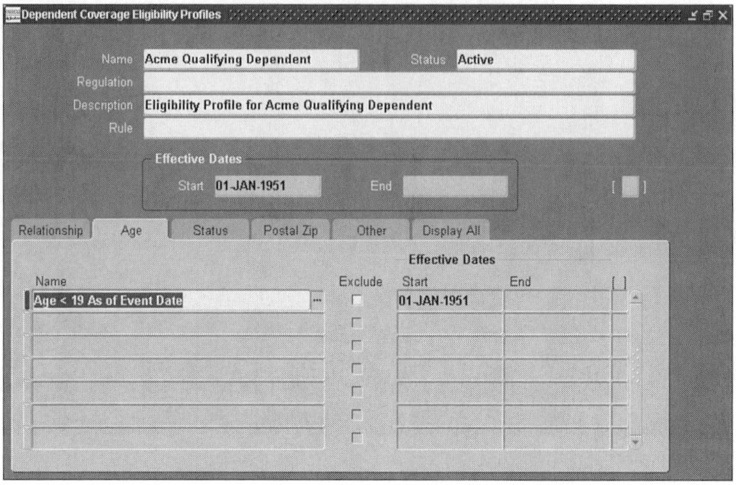

Set any other necessary attributes, and select the Display All tab to see a recap.

As stated before, you can define other profiles to cover spouses and full-time students who are between 19 and 25.

Step 5: Define Plan Types

Use this screen (not shown) to define each of your plan types. The option type is used to classify the options you want to associate with this plan type. The Compensation category can be used in system extracts, which is a new feature with OSB/OAB that creates the necessary files that are sent to your benefit carriers. The Self Service display controls whether the plans in this type are displayed vertically or horizontally—Horizontal is the default. Use Minimum and Maximum to control how many plans an eligible person can belong to simultaneously in this plan type.

Step 6: Define Options

Figure 26.9 displays the option for Employee and Spouse coverage. If this option was a Waived option, you would check the Waive Option box. If your plan requires that a person must stay enrolled in this option for a period of time, complete the Required Period of Enrollment region of this screen. In the Plan Type region, define which plan types will use this option.

Next, click the Designation Requirements button to define which contact relationships are valid with this option.

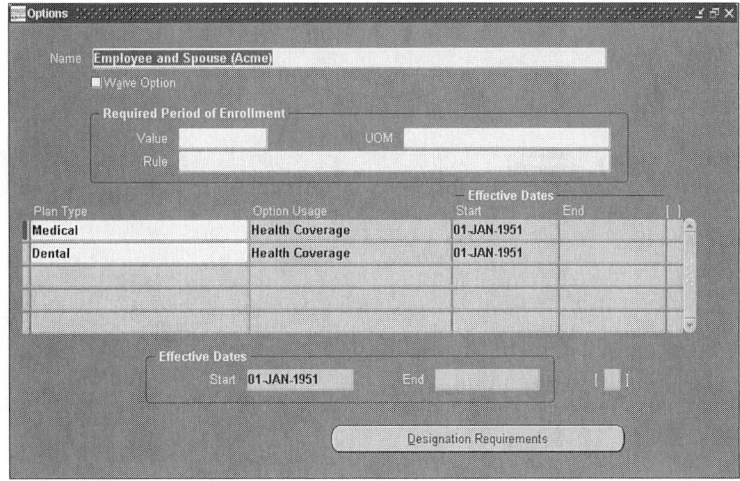

Figure 26.9 Options screen showing an Employee and Spouse option.

Figure 26.10 demonstrates how to ensure that only one spouse can be covered in this plan type. Other options, such as Employee and Family, would include this definition as well as one for children.

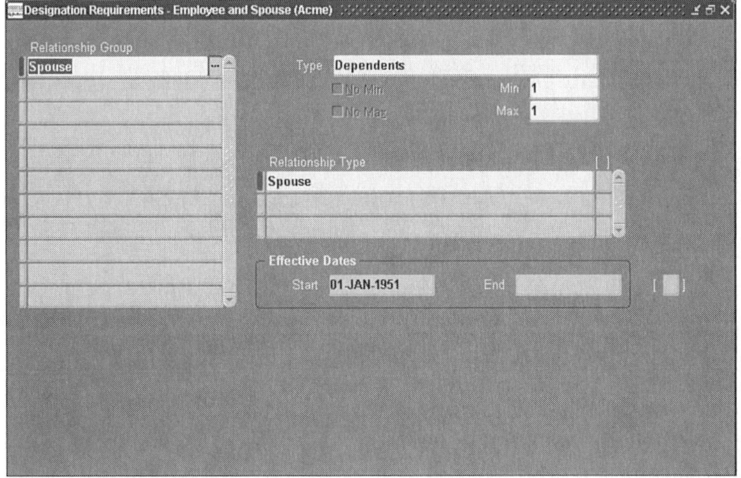

Figure 26.10 Spouse definition using designation requirements.

You also would define options for your LTD plan called 50% of Base Pay and 60% of Base Pay. Because LTD is an employee-only plan, set the designation requirements to No Designees. Select Dependents in the Type field, and set the Minimum and Maximum to 0.

STEP 7: DEFINE BASIC PLAN INFORMATION

Now you will start piecing together all your compensation objects. Figure 26.11 defines the plan.

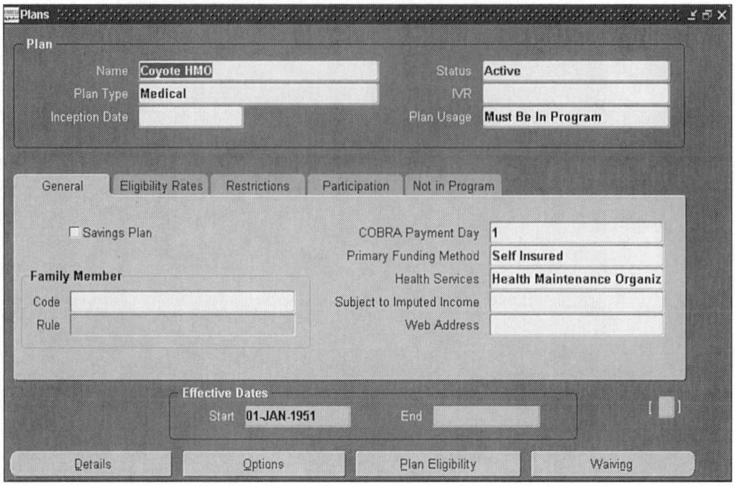

Figure 26.11
Plan screen showing Coyote HMO setup.

You will put many of your rules at the program level, so Figure 26.10 shows that you will leave many of the fields blank down at the plan level. Some of the fields you will fill out here include

- **Status**—Choices are Active, Closed, Inactive, and Pending.
- **COBRA Payment Day**—This is when the COBRA payment check is due.
- **Primary Funding Method**—Your choices are Self-Insured, Fully Insured, Split, and Trust.
- **Health Services**—Identifies which type of medical plan it is (HMO, PPO, and so on).
- **Family Member**—This section is used to determine whether you should check for designation requirements. You set this at the program level.

The items under the other tabs are discussed when you get to the program level. The Details button is used to set plan years, reporting groups, goods and services, government regulations, and organizations. Click the Options button to include all the valid options for this plan (see Figure 26.12).

You need to complete a plan definition for each of your benefit plans. One additional plan that is necessary in your example is a placeholder for your flexible credits. It is set up just like your other plans. No options are associated with it, but you must remember to mark this plan as a placeholder for the flex credits. You do this by clicking the Restrictions tab and marking the box as shown in Figure 26.13. See the section titled "Flex Credits and Benefit Pools" for a further discussion on flex credit setup.

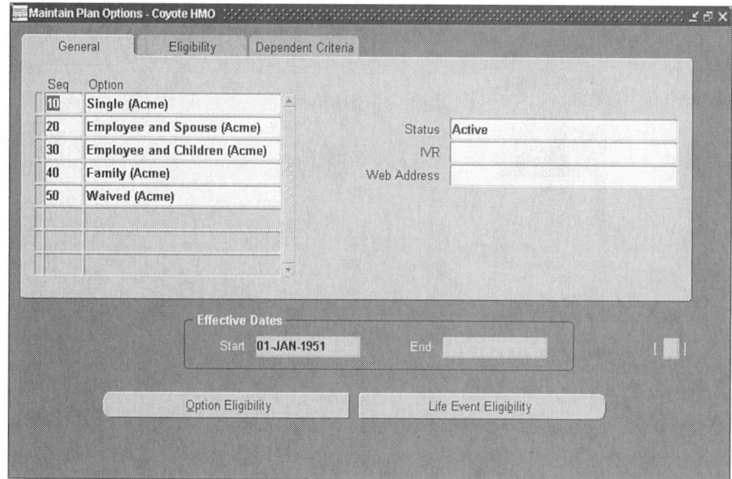

Figure 26.12
List of valid options for Coyote HMO.

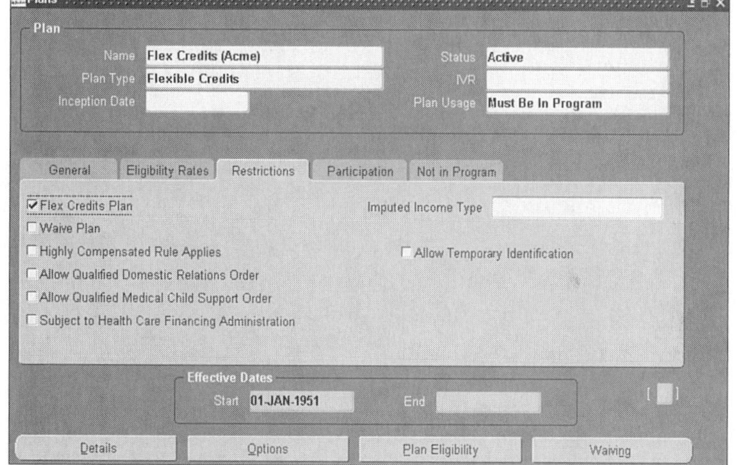

Figure 26.13
Plan screen showing Flex Credits setup.

Step 8: Define Program

Now you will begin to combine more of your compensation objects into a program. Some key items shown in Figure 26.14 include

- **Activity Reference Period**—Defines how the system will express activity rates for plans in this program
- **Enrollment Rate/Frequency**—Defines how rates will be communicated to employees
- **Family Member region**—States that you will check for designation requirements for all plans in this program

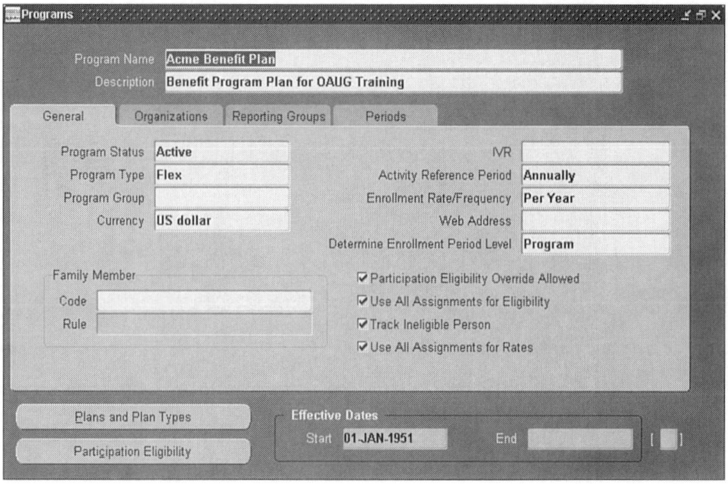

Figure 26.14
Programs screen showing Acme Benefit setup.

You add the plan and plan type information by clicking the Plan and Plan Types button. These screens are fairly self-explanatory and are not listed here. Next, you must attach your eligibility profiles to the plan. Click the Participation Eligibility button to get to the following screen (see Figure 26.15).

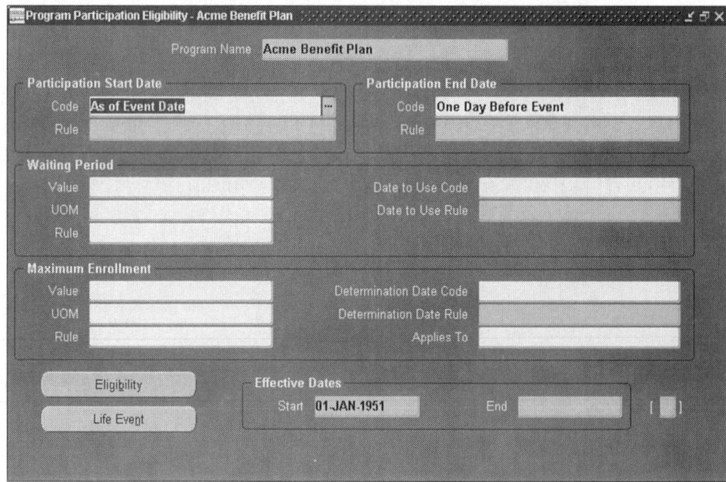

Figure 26.15
Program Participation Eligibility screen.

You can control things such as participation start date, waiting period, and maximum enrollment on this screen. Next, click the Eligibility button to add your profiles.

Figure 26.16 lists all the participation profiles you created previously.

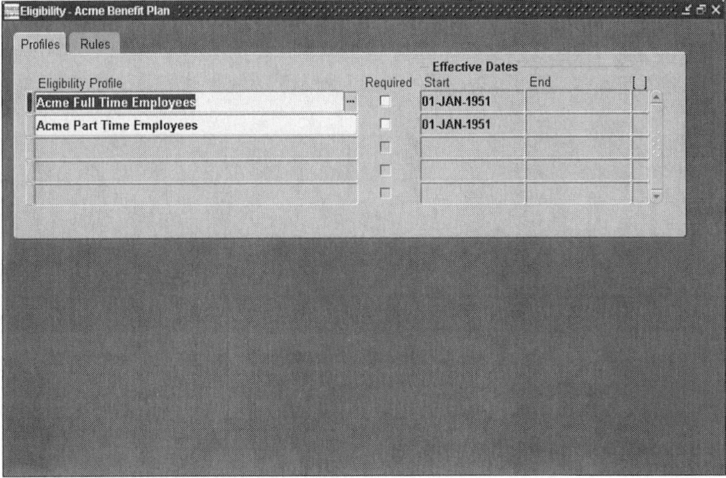

Figure 26.16 Participant Eligibility screen showing eligibility profiles.

Step 9: Define Program Enrollment Requirements

The Method field determines how the enrollment will be accomplished. Figure 26.17 states the employee will explicitly make his elections.

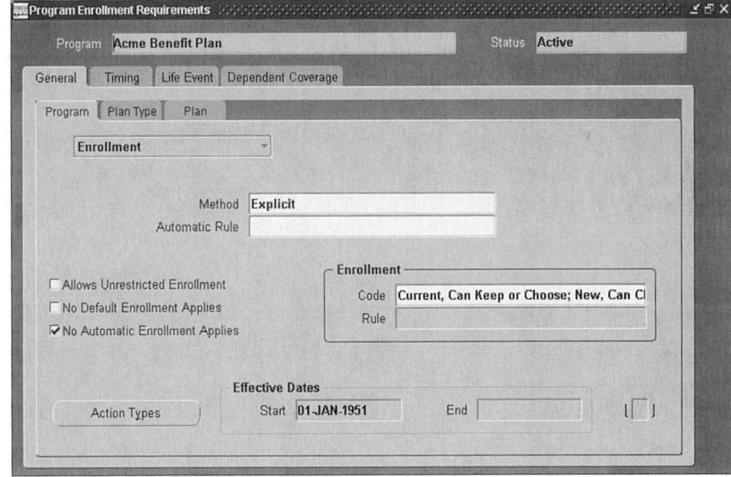

Figure 26.17 Program enrollment requirements for Acme Benefits.

The Enrollment Code states what the employee can do during enrollment. In this case, current employees can keep their current elections or choose new ones, but new employees must choose new elections.

Other tabs under the General tab enable you to define when coverage should begin, when new rates should take effect, plan type limitations, and default elections employees will receive if they fail to make their choices during enrollment. Next, select the Timing tab to establish dates and time limits for enrollment.

Figure 26.18 shows the open enrollment dates for each selected plan year. You can also state enrollment periods for each life event that can trigger an enrollment opportunity. You enter these by selecting the Life Event tab next to the Scheduled tab.

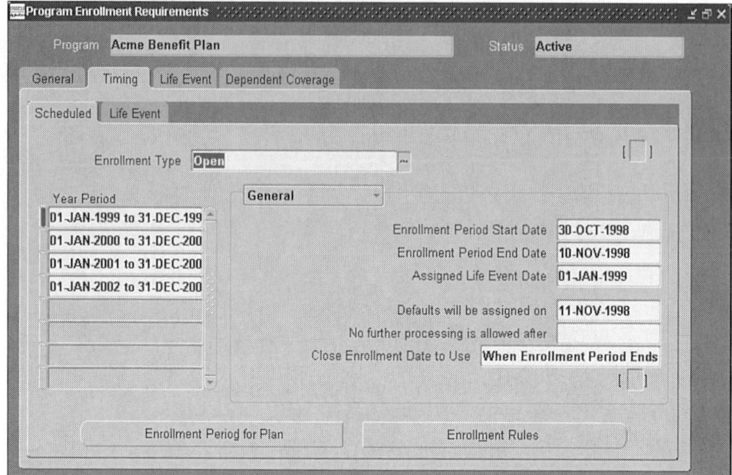

Figure 26.18
Timing information for scheduled open enrollments.

The Life Event tab next to the Timing tab is used to define life event requirements for a program, plan type, or plan. Next, attach your Dependent Eligibility profiles to your program. Select the Dependent Coverage tab to get the screen shown in Figure 26.19.

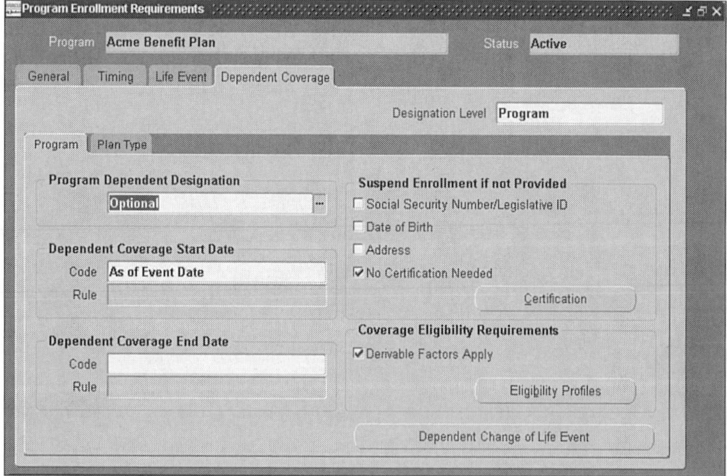

Figure 26.19
Dependent coverage definitions under Program Enrollment Requirements.

Here you can set start and end dates for dependent coverage, and also state the certifications necessary to provide coverage. Click the Eligibility Profiles button to attach your profiles.

Figure 26.20 displays the list of profiles you created in the previous step. Only contacts that satisfy any of these profiles are allowed to be listed as covered dependents. Return to the previous screen, and click the Dependent Change of Life Event button. This screen enables you to select which life events will trigger an opportunity to change covered dependents.

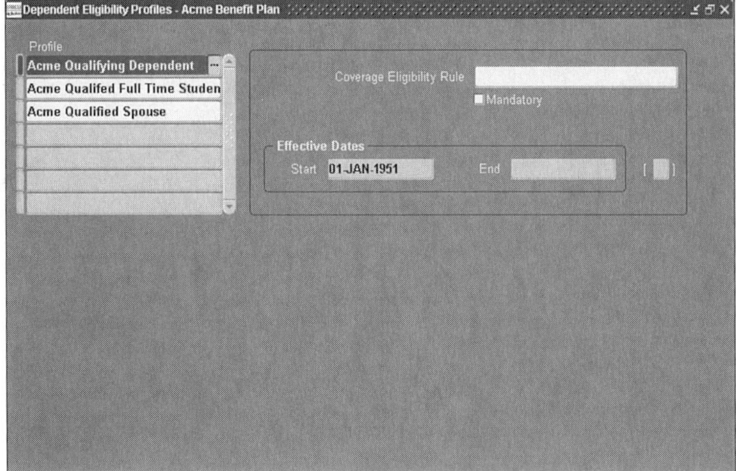

Figure 26.20
Listing of valid dependent eligibility profiles.

Step 10: Define Standard Rate Calculations

You must create a standard rate for each option in each of your plans. The screen shown in Figure 26.21 also connects this option to the appropriate payroll element in Oracle Payroll. Obviously, this element must be set up beforehand. Yours is defined as a pre-tax deduction with a flat amount processing rule. The Calculation Method tab is used to define this processing rule and to state the flat amount.

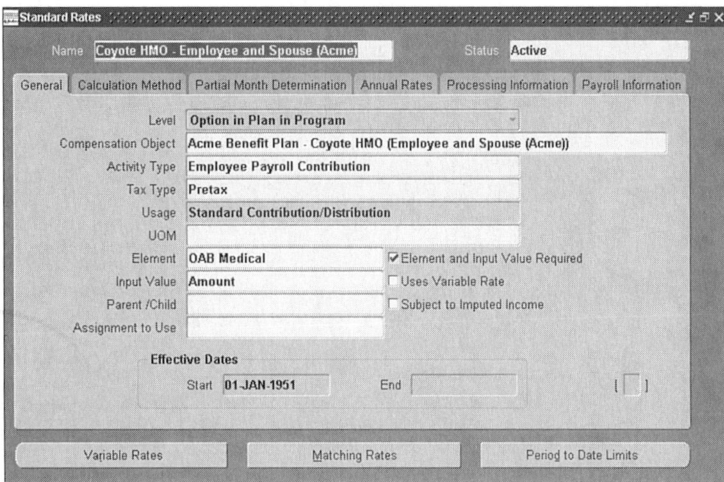

Figure 26.21
Example of a standard rate for an employee and spouse option.

You also must create a standard rate for your flex credits. Figure 26.22 demonstrates this requirement.

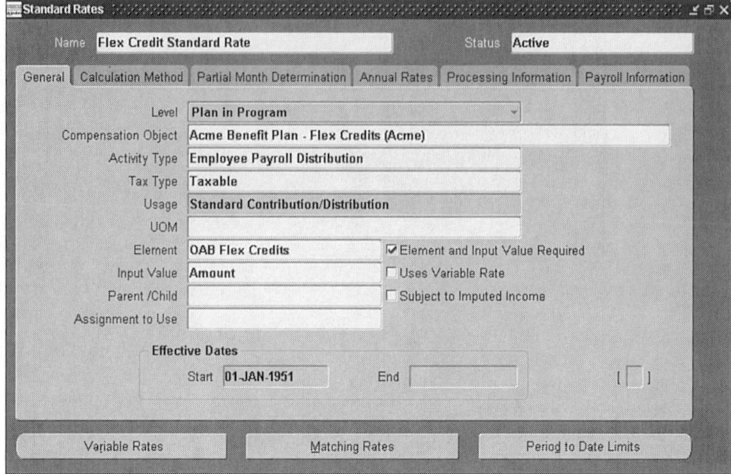

Figure 26.22
Example of a flex credit standard rate.

The remaining setup steps for flex credits are covered in the "Flex Credits and Benefit Pools" section and will not be repeated here. As stated at the beginning of this exercise, many options and screens are involved in setting up a benefit program. Hopefully, this simplified exercise gets you started on your trip to understand this important and complex module in the Oracle HRMS suite of modules.

Imputed Income for Domestic Partner Benefits

The next example demonstrates the setup steps to compute imputed income for domestic partners in a medical plan. IRS dictates that the employer cost of providing benefits to domestic partners must be included in a participant's taxable income. This example assumes that this annual amount is $2,400. This example also demonstrates pre- and post-tax standard rates. The pre-tax deduction represents the employee cost of the benefit coverage for the participant, whereas the post-tax deduction represents the employee cost of the benefit coverage for the domestic partner.

Although many of these steps fall under the various implementation steps for Advanced Benefits, the following will present the setup of imputed income from start to finish. These procedures presume some basic setup of programs and other related setups have already been completed. Also assumed is the fact that Oracle Payroll will be used.

The first step is to set up a plan type for imputed income. Navigate to Total Compensation, Programs and Plans, Plan Types, and set the effective date. Name the plan type and give it the option type of Other. Figure 26.23 shows the plan type for the Imputed Income Shell Plan you will use in a subsequent step.

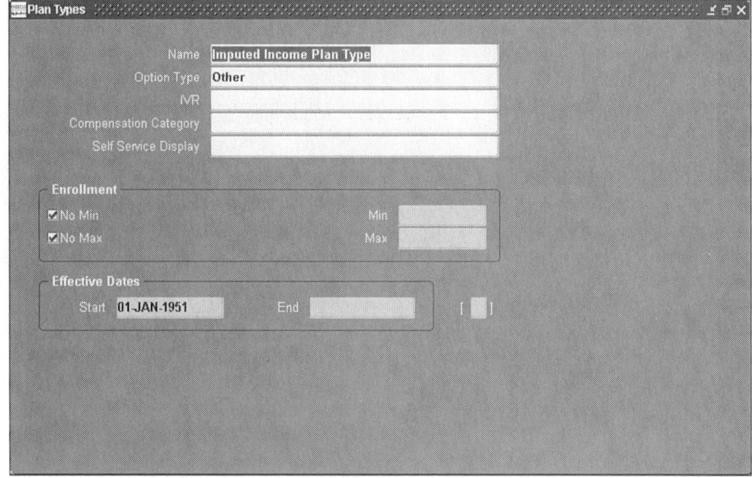

Figure 26.23 Plan type showing imputed income.

The next step is to set up the option EE and Qualified Domestic Partner and designate (limit) which contacts can be selected for this option. Navigate to Total Compensation, Programs and Plans, Options, and set your effective date. Give the option a descriptive name and select the plan types (and therefore plans) to which this option is available (see Figure 26.24).

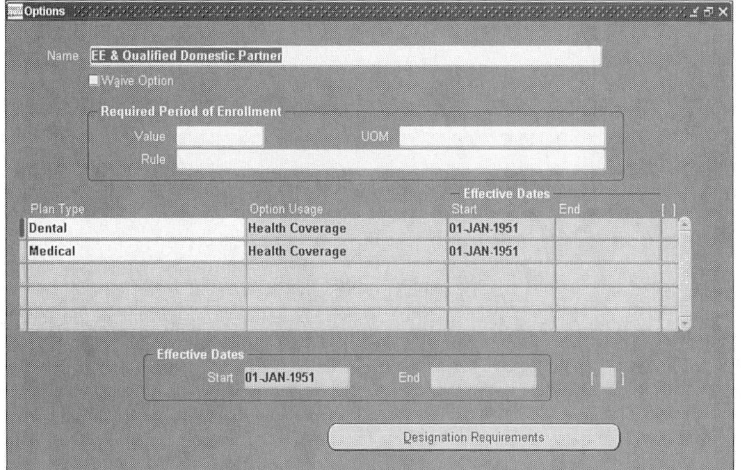

Figure 26.24 Options screen showing Domestic Partner setup.

Designation Requirements limit which type of an employee's contacts or personal relationships that can be selected when an option is chosen. Clicking the Designation Requirements button on the Options form accesses the form shown in Figure 26.25. Select the Domestic Partner Relationship Group. Select Dependents as the type of designees you are defining, and set both the minimum and maximum number of dependents to 1. Select the Domestic

Partner Relationship Type. The contact relationship in an employee's contact record must have the personal relationship field checked to be available. For Domestic Partner, this flag must be manually checked. If the designation requirements are not met, the option is not displayed during enrollment.

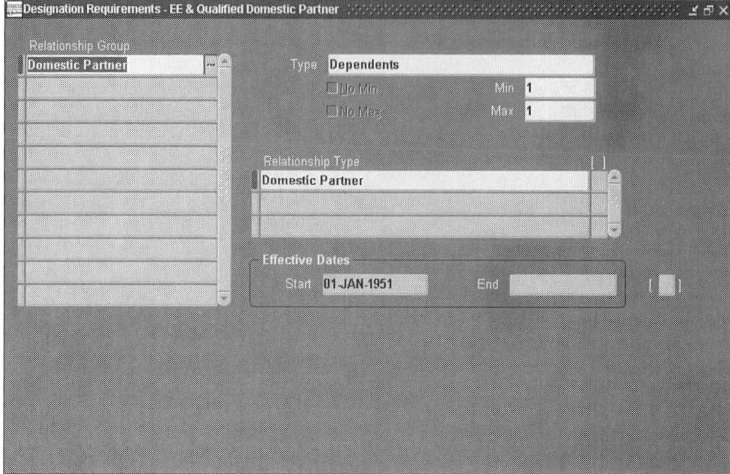

Figure 26.25 Designation Requirements showing Domestic Partner.

The next step is to define the plans required to record imputed income for a domestic partner benefit. Figure 26.26 shows an example of the imputed income shell plan. The Imputed Income Shell Plan will not be visible when enrolling an employee in the program. It is used to hold the imputed income calculations. You are limited to one shell plan per business group.

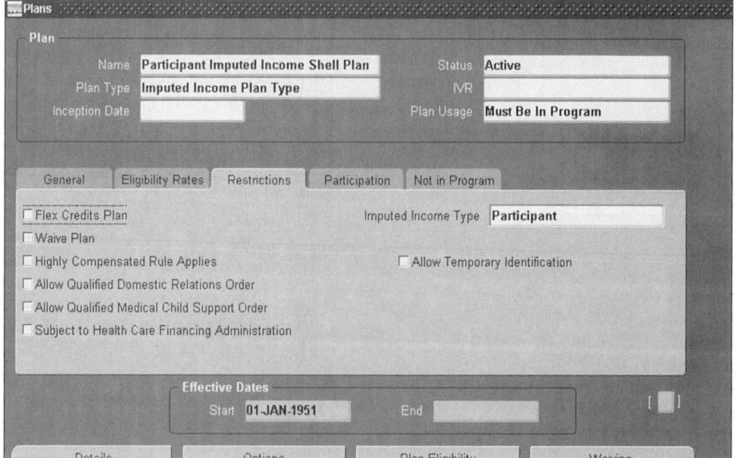

Figure 26.26 Plan screen showing imputed income shell plan.

Navigate to Total Compensation, Programs and Plans, Plans, and set the effective date. Name the plan and give it an Active Status. The Plan Type is Imputed Income Plan Type defined in the previous setup step. The Plan Usage is Must Be in Program. Select the Restrictions tab, and select Participant as the Imputed Income type.

After the imputed income plan is defined, you define each of the plans for the program. Figure 26.27 shows the medical plan for this program. The difference for a plan that covers domestic partners is to select Dependent as Subject to Imputed Income on the General tab of the Plan.

Figure 26.27
Plans screen shows a medical plan setup.

Plans
Plan
Name HealthNow POS
Status Active
Plan Type Medical
IVR
Inception Date
Plan Usage Must Be In Program
General | Eligibility Rates | Restrictions | Participation | Not in Program
Savings Plan
COBRA Payment Day 1
Primary Funding Method Self Insured
Family Member
Health Services Other
Code
Subject to Imputed Income Dependent
Rule
Web Address
Effective Dates
Start 01-JAN-1951
End
Details | Options | Plan Eligibility | Waiving

Click the Options button on the Plan form to enter the EE and Qualified Domestic Partner option. Set the Status to Active, as shown in Figure 26.28.

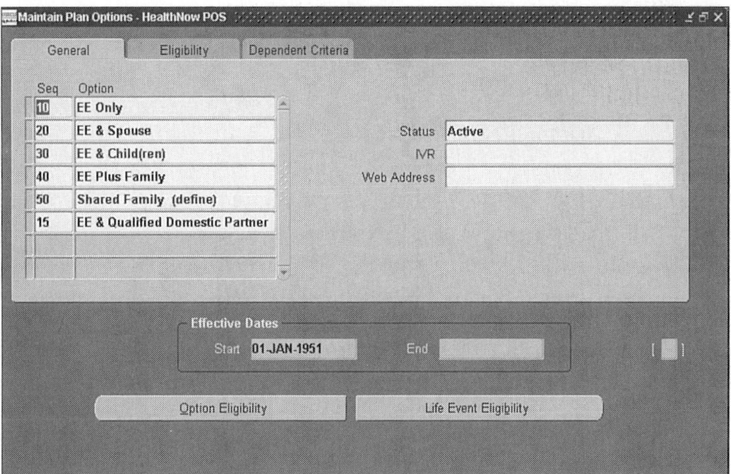

Figure 26.28
Medical plan with domestic partner option.

Click the Life Event Eligibility button to add the life events that qualify the employee to be eligible or ineligible to select this option. These life events were defined in a previous step.

Select the life event Start QDP Relationship to enable the employee to be eligible to select this option, or select the life event End QDP Relationship to make the employee ineligible for this option.

Although not pictured, add the Imputed Income Plan Type and Imputed Income Shell Plan to your program. Navigate to Total Compensation, Programs and Plans, Programs; then query the name of your program. Click the Plans and Plan Types button to enter this information. Also, a Dependent Eligibility Profile, which includes the relationship Domestic Partner, should be attached to the program on the Program Enrollment Requirements form.

The next step is to create a Variable Rate Profile for Imputed Income. In this example, you have used a simple formula of one flat amount. You also could create variable rate profiles if the rate varies based on the age of the participant. Navigate to Total Compensation, Rate/Coverage Definitions, Variable Rates, and set your effective date. Name the Variable Rate Profile—use a descriptive name such as Variable Rate Imputed Income HealthNow EE Plus DP. Figure 26.29 shows a generic setup of a variable rate profile.

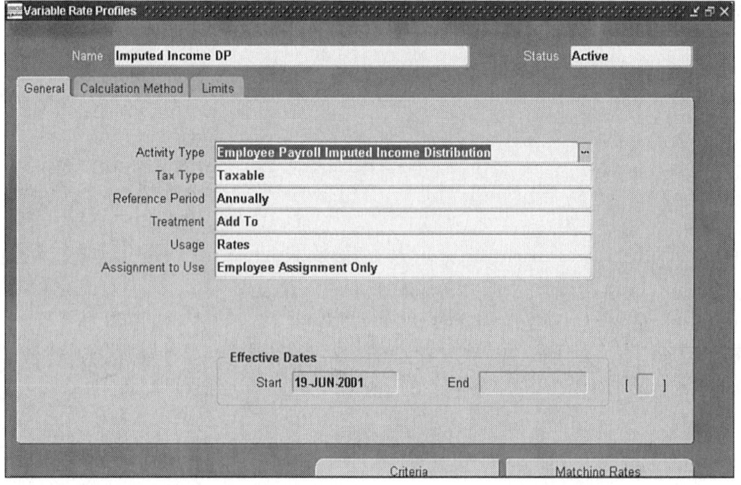

Figure 26.29
Variable rate profile for domestic partner imputed income.

On the General tab, set the Activity Type to Employee Payroll Imputed Income Distribution; then set the Tax Type to Taxable. The Reference Period is Annually, which tells the system how you state your rates. The Treatment is Add To, and the Usage is Rates, which enables you to attach the profile to the imputed income calculation.

On the Calculation Method tab, select Flat Amount as the method and enter **$2,400** as the Flat Amount. This amount should be updated annually. Figure 26.30 shows the completed screen—the flat amount of $2,400 is from the example. Your rate will probably be different.

Next, set up the Imputed Income. Navigate to Total Compensation, Rate/Coverage Definitions, Imputed Income, and set your effective date. Name the Imputed Income calculation and associate it with the Participant Imputed Income Shell Plan. The Activity Type is

Employee Payroll Imputed Income Distribution, the Source is Payroll, (which tells the system that Oracle Payroll will process the earning), and the Status is Active. Check the box labeled Select to Process Each Pay Period to do just that. Figure 26.31 shows the completed screen.

Figure 26.30
Variable rate profile showing the calculation method.

Variable Rate Profiles

Name: Imputed Income DP
Status: Active

General | Calculation Method | Limits

Calculation Method: Flat Amount

☐ Value Entered At Enrollment
Flat Amount: 2400
Min
Max
Increment
Default
Annual Max
Annual Min

Operator
Coverage Operator
Compensation Factor
Value Rule
Rounding Code
Rounding Rule

☐ Always Sum All Coverage
☐ Always Count All Participants

Criteria | Matching Rates

Figure 26.31
Imputed Income screen showing domestic partner setup.

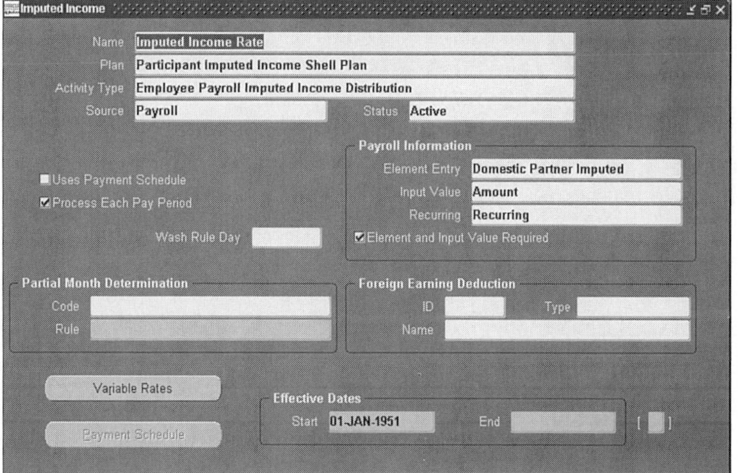

Imputed Income

Name: Imputed Income Rate
Plan: Participant Imputed Income Shell Plan
Activity Type: Employee Payroll Imputed Income Distribution
Source: Payroll
Status: Active

☐ Uses Payment Schedule
☑ Process Each Pay Period
Wash Rule Day

Payroll Information
Element Entry: Domestic Partner Imputed
Input Value: Amount
Recurring: Recurring
☑ Element and Input Value Required

Partial Month Determination
Code
Rule

Foreign Earning Deduction
ID
Type
Name

Variable Rates
Payment Schedule

Effective Dates
Start: 01-JAN-1951
End

The Payroll Information section on this form tells Oracle how to process the imputed income earning in a payroll process. Select the element Domestic Partner Imputed, select the Input Value Amount, and select Recurring for Recurring. Also, make sure the Element and Input Value Required check box is checked. This setup assumes that you have already created this earning element in Oracle Payroll.

Figure 26.32 shows how you attached the Variable Rate to the Imputed Income calculation. Click the Variable Rates button, and select the Variable Rate defined earlier.

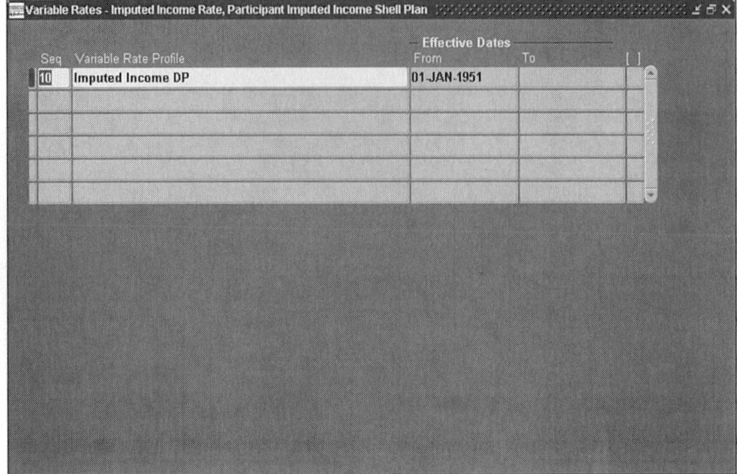

Figure 26.32
Linking the variable rate profile to the variable rate.

The next step is to set up a shell rate. Similar to Flex Credits, you have to set up a standard rate with a $0.00 amount to enable the imputed income calculation to be passed to an employee's element entries for payroll processing. For this example, this passes the $2,400 to the earning element.

Navigate to Total Compensation, Rate/Coverage Definitions, Standard Rates, and set your effective date. The Status is Active. On the General tab, the Level is Option in Plan in Program. The Compensation Object is the program, plan, option combination Individual Choice—HealthNow POS (EE & Qualified Domestic Partner) where Individual Choice is the name of your program. The Activity Type is Employee Payroll Imputed Income Distribution, and the Tax Type is Taxable. Select the element Domestic Partner Imputed, and the Input Value Amount. Also, make sure the Element and Input Value Required check box and the Uses Variable Rate check box are checked. Now when an employee elects Domestic Partner coverage when enrolling, this shell or shadow rate (element entry) is passed to the employee's element entries. Figure 26.33 shows the completed screen.

On the Calculation Method tab (not shown), select Flat Amount as the Calculation Method. Check the Calculate for Enrollment check box, and enter the Flat Amount `0`.

On the Processing Information tab (not shown), check both the Assign on Enrollment and Process Each Pay Period Default boxes. Then, select Payroll as the Source and Recurring in the Recurring field.

Next, set up the Standard Rates for an employee enrolling in the EE & Qualified Domestic Partner option in the HealthNow POS plan. Set up both a pre-tax and an after-tax standard rate (deduction). Navigate to Total Compensation, Rate/Coverage Definitions, Standard Rates, and set your effective date.

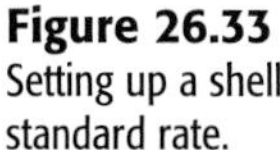

Figure 26.33
Setting up a shell standard rate.

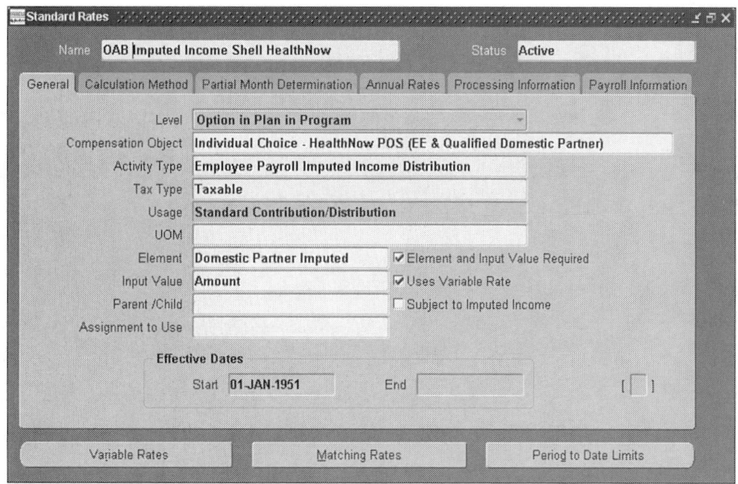

Beginning with the pre-tax deduction, name the rate. The pre-tax deduction is the benefit cost to the participant; the Status is Active. On the General tab, the Level is Option in Plan in Program. The Compensation Object is Individual Choice—HealthNow POS (EE & Qualified Domestic Partner). The Activity Type is Employee Payroll Contribution, and the Tax Type is Pretax. Select the element OAB Medical and the Input Value Amount. Also, make sure the Element and Input Value Required and Subject to Imputed Income check boxes are checked.

On the Calculation Method tab (not shown), select Flat Amount as the Calculation Method. Check the Calculate for Enrollment check box, and enter the Flat Amount `4,200`, which represents the annual pre-tax cost to an employee for the coverage.

On the Processing Information tab (not shown), check the Assign on Enrollment, Display on Enrollment, and Process Each Pay Period Default check boxes. Select Payroll as the Processing Source, and Recurring for Recurring. Figure 26.34 shows the completed screen for the pre-tax standard rate.

The after-tax portion of the cost (deduction) is set up similarly. The after-tax portion is the additional cost to the employee for domestic partner coverage and is not necessarily related to the employer cost you set up on the imputed income rate. The difference is the Tax Type After-tax, and the element would be Medical Post Tax. The Flat Amount on the Calculation Method Tab would be 2,400.

Because your program offers Flex Credits, you need to add the pre-tax Individual Choice—HealthNow POS (EE & Qualified Domestic Partner) standard rate to the Benefit Pools. Assume that this Benefit Pool has already been set up; then, navigate to Total Compensation, Rate/Coverage Definitions, Benefit Pools, and set your effective date. Query the Benefit Pool for your program, Individual Choice, and add the line shown in Figure 26.35.

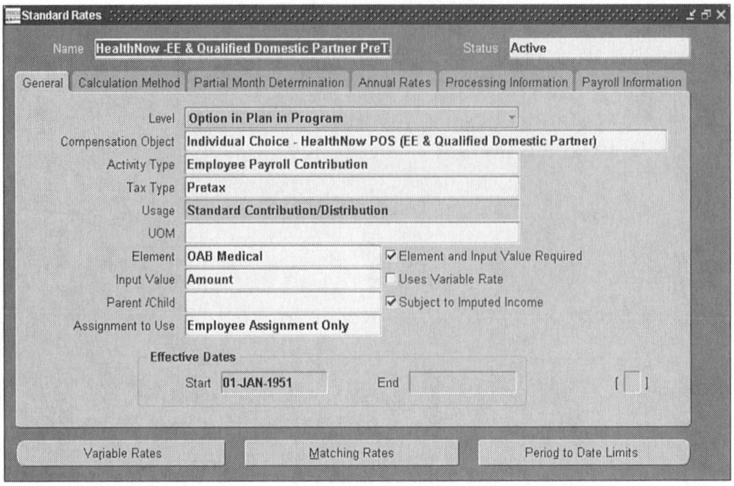

Figure 26.34
Standard rate for the medical plan deduction.

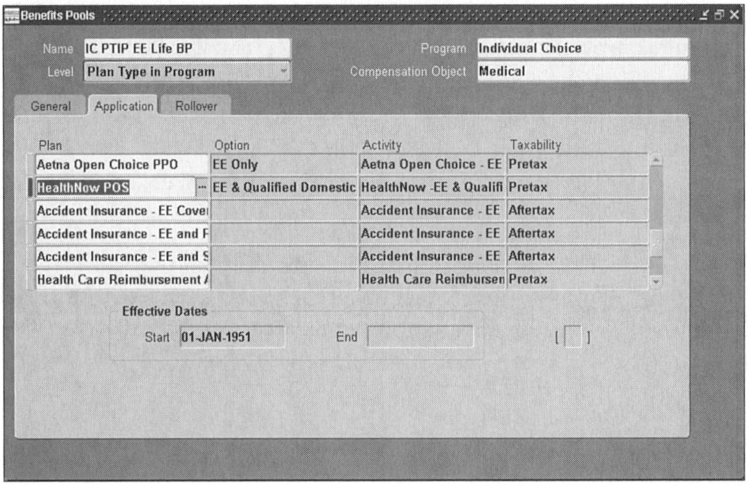

Standard Rates

Name: HealthNow -EE & Qualified Domestic Partner PreT | Status: Active

General | Calculation Method | Partial Month Determination | Annual Rates | Processing Information | Payroll Information

Level: Option in Plan in Program
Compensation Object: Individual Choice - HealthNow POS (EE & Qualified Domestic Partner)
Activity Type: Employee Payroll Contribution
Tax Type: Pretax
Usage: Standard Contribution/Distribution
UOM:
Element: OAB Medical — ☑ Element and Input Value Required
Input Value: Amount — ☐ Uses Variable Rate
Parent /Child: — ☑ Subject to Imputed Income
Assignment to Use: Employee Assignment Only

Effective Dates
Start: 01-JAN-1951 End:

Variable Rates | Matching Rates | Period to Date Limits

Figure 26.35
Changes to the Benefits Pool to support domestic partners.

Benefits Pools

Name: IC PTIP EE Life BP | Program: Individual Choice
Level: Plan Type in Program | Compensation Object: Medical

General | Application | Rollover

Plan	Option	Activity	Taxability
Aetna Open Choice PPO	EE Only	Aetna Open Choice - EE	Pretax
HealthNow POS	EE & Qualified Domestic	HealthNow -EE & Qualifi	Pretax
Accident Insurance - EE Cove		Accident Insurance - EE	Aftertax
Accident Insurance - EE and F		Accident Insurance - EE	Aftertax
Accident Insurance - EE and S		Accident Insurance - EE	Aftertax
Health Care Reimbursement /		Health Care Reimbursen	Pretax

Effective Dates
Start: 01-JAN-1951 End:

The setup for Imputed Income for Domestic Partner Benefits is now complete. The next section demonstrates the use of imputed income.

USING IMPUTED INCOME FOR DOMESTIC PARTNER BENEFITS

This section demonstrates the use of the Imputed Income for Domestic Partner setup you completed in the previous section. This demonstration assumes that Advanced Benefits is installed and you have a defined life event called Start QDP Relationship. In this example, you are processing a new hire who has identified a domestic partner as a contact. Because more than one life event is triggered by hiring a new employee, your collapsing life event rules have determined that the new hire life event is the winning event.

The employee, S. PK, has been added as a new hire to the Oracle HR system. She has been assigned to the IC Semi-Monthly payroll. Navigate to the Contact form from the People, Enter and Maintain form. Click the Others button, and select Contacts. Enter a contact with the Contact Relationship as Domestic Partner. This generates the potential life event of Start QDP Relationship based on the Person Change that is defined based on this field. As mentioned previously, the new hire life event also is generated. Complete the remainder of the record (row), being sure to check the Personal Relationship check box. Oracle Benefits uses this field—not the grayed Benefits check boxes—to determine when a contact can be selected as a Designee during an employee's enrollment. Figure 26.36 shows the completed Contact screen.

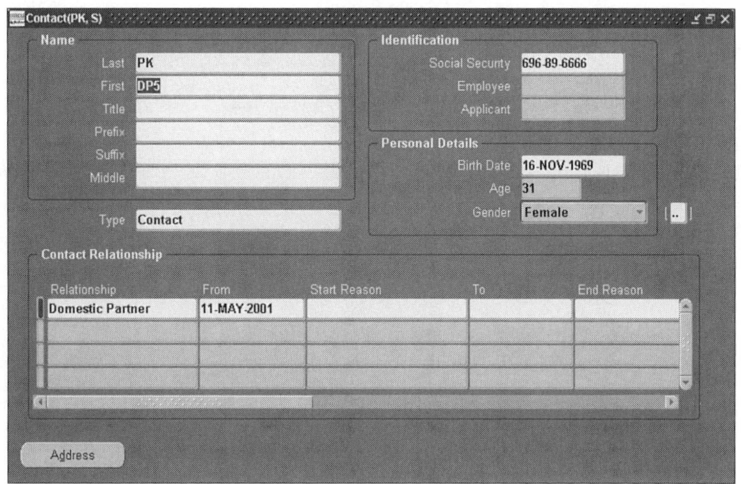

Figure 26.36
Contact screen showing domestic partner for sample employee.

After your new hire has been entered and her domestic partner identified, the potential life events New Hire and Start QDP Relationship have a status of Detected. Run the Participation Process to process the life event to determine eligibility and electability. Figure 26.37 demonstrates the process that was run in Life Event mode with restrictive parameters to detect only the sample employee. Navigate to Processes and Reports, Submit Requests to run the concurrent process. Select the Participation Process: Life Event. In addition to the parameters listed, set the Audit Log parameter to Yes. This generates a log you can review to help resolve any errors that might occur. This is very helpful when first testing your benefits setup.

Based on tour benefits setup, the Participation Process has changed the new hire life event status from Detected to Started. Now it is time to enroll the sample employee in the program. Navigate to the Flex Program Enrollment form (select People, Total Comp Enrollment, Benefits Enrollment, Flex Program). Query PK, S, who has been found eligible for the Individual Choice Program (your program from the previous section). Enroll her in the HealthNow POS EE & Qualified Domestic Partner plan and option (see Figure 26.38).

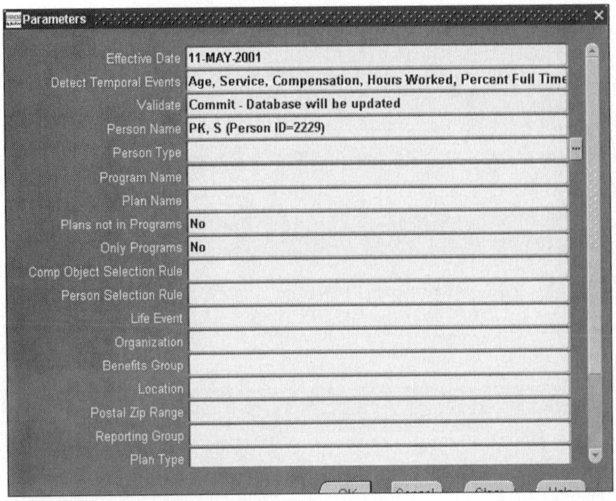

Parameters

Effective Date: 11-MAY-2001
Detect Temporal Events: Age, Service, Compensation, Hours Worked, Percent Full Time
Validate: Commit - Database will be updated
Person Name: PK, S (Person ID=2229)
Person Type
Program Name
Plan Name
Plans not in Programs: No
Only Programs: No
Comp Object Selection Rule
Person Selection Rule
Life Event
Organization
Benefits Group
Location
Postal Zip Range
Reporting Group
Plan Type

Figure 26.37
Completed parameter screen for the Participation Process: Life Event.

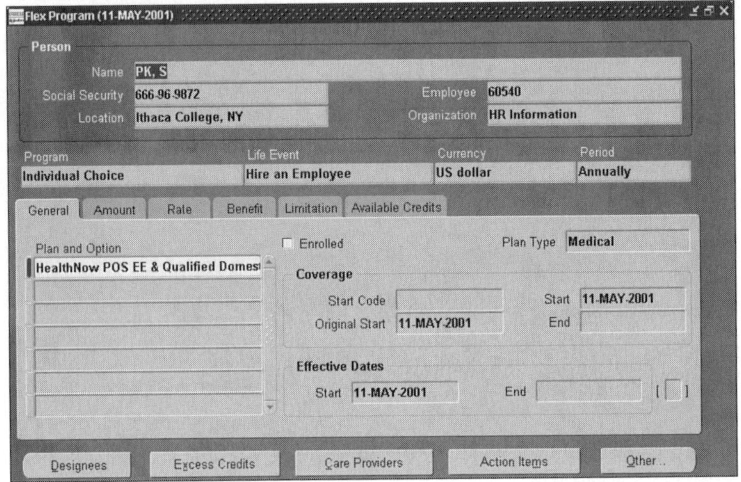

Figure 26.38
Flex Program enrollment screen for sample employee.

Click the Designees button to designate her domestic partner. On the Designate Dependents tab, select PK, DP5 and check the Covered check box. Figure 26.39 shows a summary of the employee's covered dependents and the plans they are covered under.

After the enrollment is saved, Oracle Benefits automatically creates the element entries on S. PK's record. To view, navigate to People, Enter and Maintain, Assignment, Elements. The element Domestic Partner Imputed with the input value amount is displayed in Figure 26.40. The amount of 100.00 represents the imputed income for one pay period. Because your sample payroll is a semi-monthly payroll, there are 24 periods in the year. This balances to the total annual amount of $2,400 established in the previous section.

Figure 26.39
Designating the domestic partner.

Dependent/Beneficiary Designation
Person
Name PK, S
Social Security 666-96-9872
Employee 60540
Location Ithaca College, NY
Organization HR Information
View Dependents
Designate Dependents
Designate Beneficiaries
Plan: Option
HealthNow POS: EE & Qualified Domestic Partner
Seq
Covered Dependents
Relationship
Employee
Start
Through
5
PK, DP5
Domestic Partne
11-MAY-2001
Effective Dates
Start 11-MAY-2001
End
Certifications
Care Providers

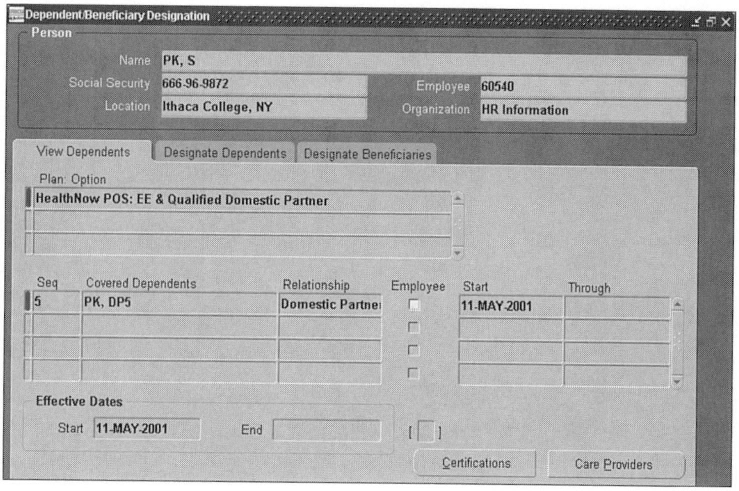

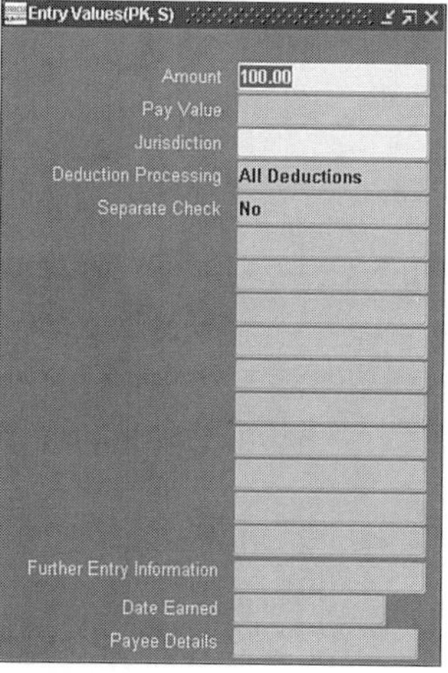

Figure 26.40
Element entry values for Domestic Partner Imputed.

Entry Values(PK, S)
Amount 100.00
Pay Value
Jurisdiction
Deduction Processing All Deductions
Separate Check No
Further Entry Information
Date Earned
Payee Details

The results from a payroll are shown in Figure 26.41. The imputed income is $100.00, which is the $2,400 annual variable rate for imputed income divided by the 24 pay periods. The OAB Medical deduction is $175.00, which is the $4,200 annual pre-tax standard rate for this coverage. The Medical Post deduction represents the after-tax employee cost for the domestic partner coverage.

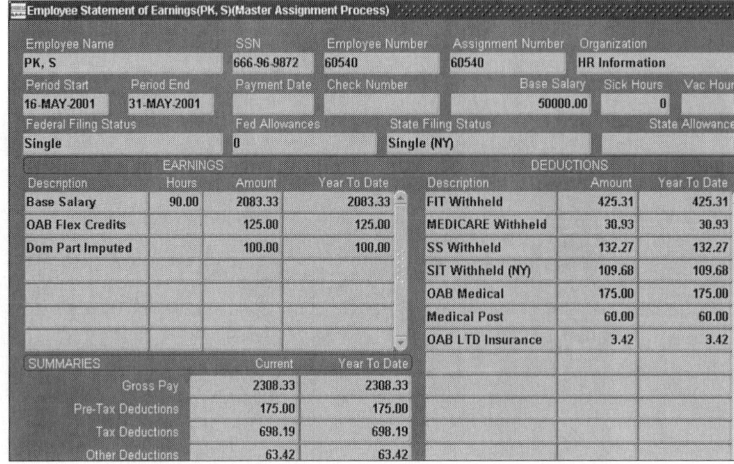

Figure 26.41
Statement of earnings after a payroll has been run.

Flex Credits and Benefit Pools

Many enterprises offer a cafeteria-style benefits program to their employees. By providing a calculated number of benefits flex credits to eligible employees, the employees are able to select from the available selections, options, and coverages to create their own personalized benefits package. The concept of creating a flex credit program includes calculating the credits available to each employee, how the employees can spend the flex credits, how excess and deficit credits are handled, the structure of the program including the plans and options offered to employees, and the configuration of the payroll elements to process the employees' elections during the payroll cycle.

Although the configuration steps fall under the various implementation steps for Advanced Benefits, the following will present the setup and use of a flex credit program. These procedures presume some basic setup of programs has already been completed. This example also assumes that Oracle Payroll is being used.

Step 1: Define Flex Credit Plan Type

The first step is to set up a plan type for flexible credits. Name the plan type and give it the option type of Other. This step creates the plan type for the Flex Credit Shell Plan that will be set up in a following step. Figure 26.42 demonstrates this setup.

Step 2: Define Flex Credit Plan

The next step is to define a shell plan for our flex credits. The Flex Credit Shell Plan will not be visible to an employee enrolling in the program. It is used to hold the flex credit calculations.

Name the plan and give it an Active Status. The Plan Type is Flexible Credits defined in the previous setup step. The Plan Usage is Must Be in Program. Select the Restrictions tab and check the Flex Credits Plan. Also, set up the plan periods for the plan. You access the plan periods screen by clicking the Details button. Figure 26.43 shows this setup.

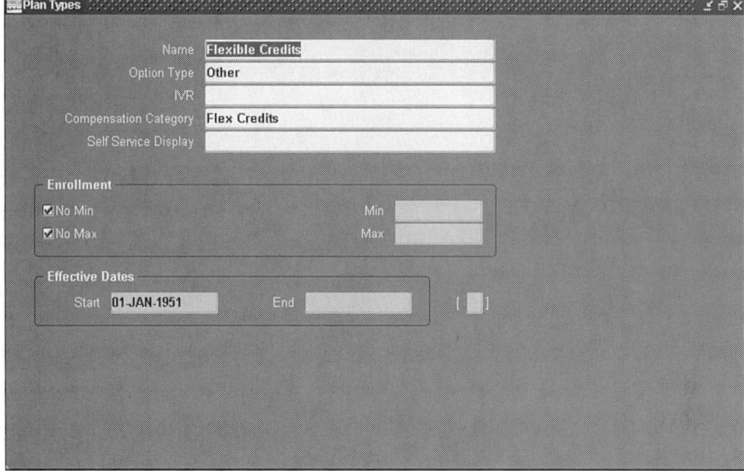

Figure 26.42
Setup of flexible credits plan type.

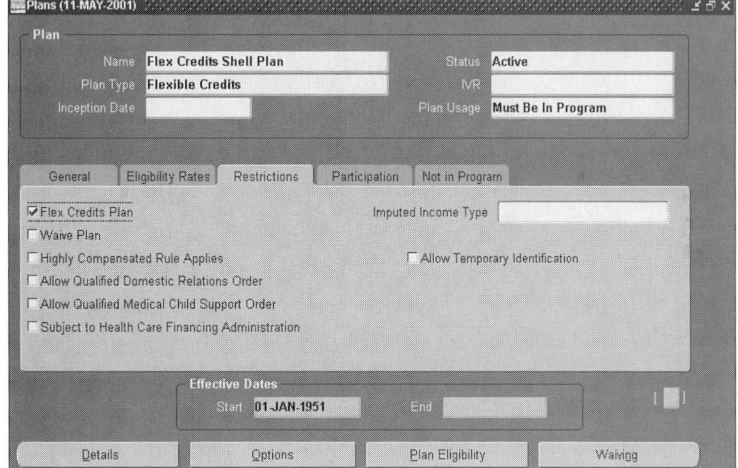

Figure 26.43
Setup of flex credits shell plan.

STEP 3: DEFINE THE PROGRAM

Figure 26.44 shows the definition of the Flexible Credit Program. The important information to note on the setup is the Program Type value of Flex or Flex Plus Core. By setting the Activity Reference Period to Annually, the definitions of flex credits and benefit costs are stated on an annual basis.

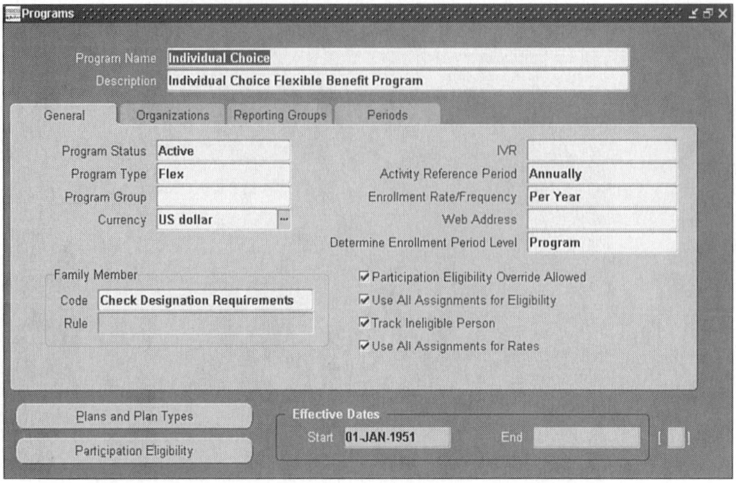

Figure 26.44
Program setup for the sample program.

Include the Flex Credits Shell Plan in the program (see Figure 26.45).

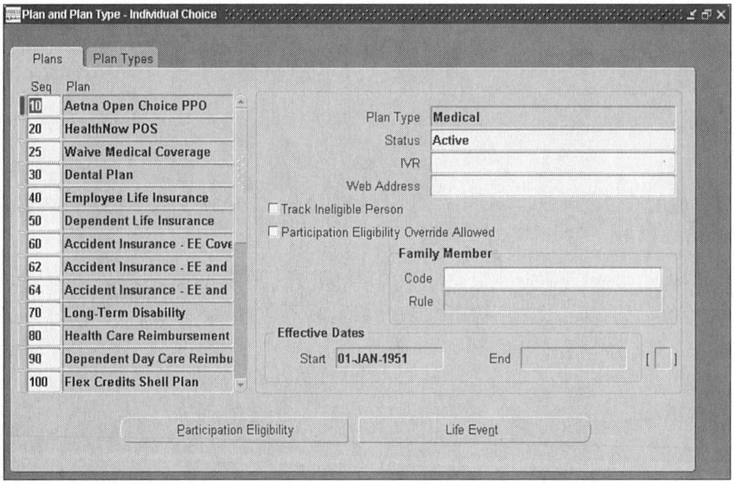

Figure 26.45
List of all the plans in the program.

STEP 4: DEFINE FLEX CREDITS

Figure 26.46 shows the definition of the flex credits the enterprise provides to the employees. There are a variety of ways to configure flex credits. The following example defines flex credits at the plan type in program level. A more clear-cut way could be to set up flex credits at the program level by defining one flex credit and provide a flat amount of credits. You can also create a Fast Formula rule to compute the total flex credits. In this example, by defining the flex credits at the plan type in program level, you can accommodate within the application, the various calculations required to compute total flex credits available to participants. Also, this enables you to control how the employees are able to spend the flex credits when setting up the benefit pools.

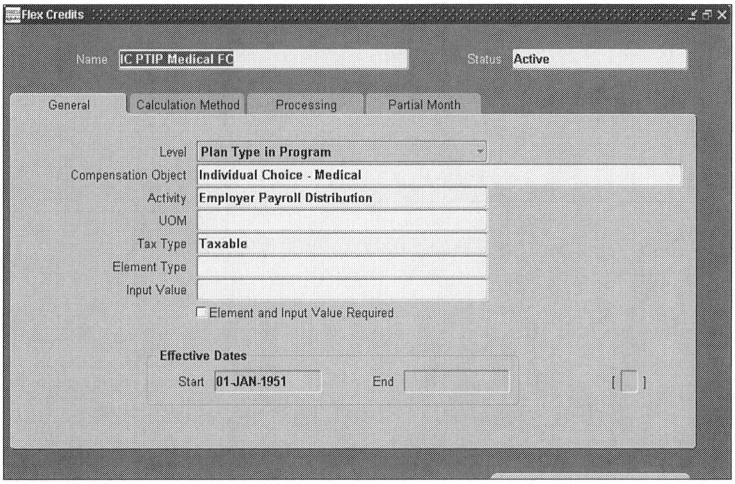

Figure 26.46
Definition of flex credits.

The setup begins with naming the flex credits. For this example the level is plan type in program and the related compensation object should be selected. The activity is Employer Payroll Distribution, which signifies the credits are provided by the employer during the payroll process. The Tax Type should be defined as taxable.

On the Calculation Method tab, define how the flex credits are calculated. In this example, you are providing a flat amount of $3,000 for medical flex credits. Other calculation methods include multiple of compensation or a rule that calculates the flex credits. Depending on the calculation method chosen, various fields are enabled and should be defined to configure the calculation. Figure 26.47 shows the completion of this screen.

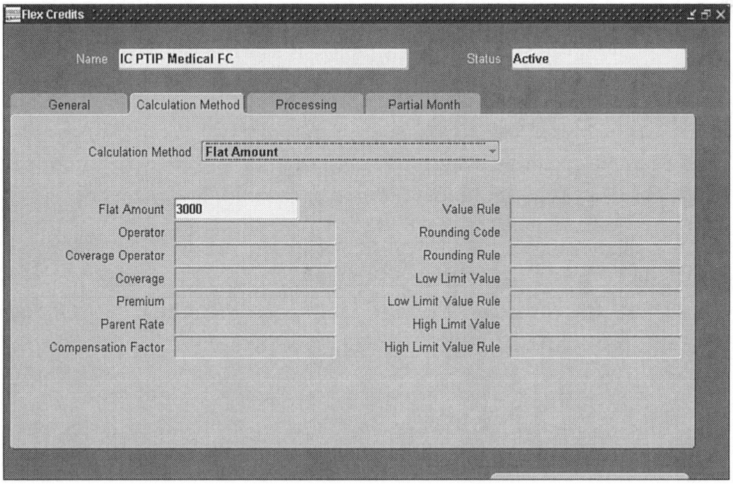

Figure 26.47
Calculation tab on flex credits definition.

Figure 26.48 shows the processing rules for the flex credits. By defining the source as Oracle Payroll and as a Recurring entry, and to process each pay period, the flex credit, if provided to the employee, will be divided evenly over the number of periods in the payroll and included in each pay run.

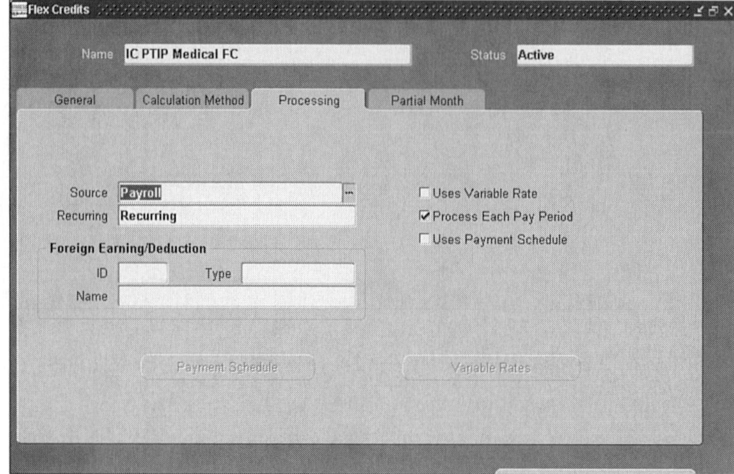

Figure 26.48
Processing tab on the flex credits definition.

Similar setup steps would be followed for each flex credit defined for the plan types in programs. Although not pictured here, IC PTIP Dental FC, IC PTIP EE Life FC, and IC PTIP LTD FC were defined.

STEP 5: DEFINE FLEX CREDIT STANDARD RATE

The next step is required to define the shadow or shell standard rate definition that will provide the flex credit information to a participant's element entries and therefore to Oracle Payroll for payroll processing.

The shell rate is created at the plan in program level. The Activity Type is Employer Payroll Distribution, which signifies the employer provides the credits during the payroll process. The Tax Type should be defined as taxable.

Select the element you have set up to process the flex credits during the pay run. Also, make sure the Element and Input Value Required check box is checked. The OAB Flex Credit earning element was defined the same way any earning element is defined to process in Oracle Payroll. Figure 26.49 shows the completed screen.

Figure 26.50 shows the Calculation Method tab for the standard rate. Select Flat Amount as the Calculation Method, check the Calculate for Enrollment check box, and enter the Flat Amount `0`. The actual amount will be passed from the flex credit definitions set up in the previous step.

Figure 26.49
Standard rate setup for flex credits.

Standard Rates
Name OAB Flex Credit Shell
Status Active
General | Calculation Method | Partial Month Determination | Annual Rates | Processing Information | Payroll Information
Level Plan in Program
Compensation Object Individual Choice - Flex Credits Shell Plan
Activity Type Employer Payroll Distribution
Tax Type Taxable
Usage Standard Contribution/Distribution
UOM
Element OAB Flex Credits
Element and Input Value Required
Input Value Amount
Uses Variable Rate
Parent /Child
Subject to Imputed Income
Assignment to Use Employee Assignment Only
Effective Dates
Start 01-JAN-1951
End
Variable Rates
Matching Rates
Period to Date Limits

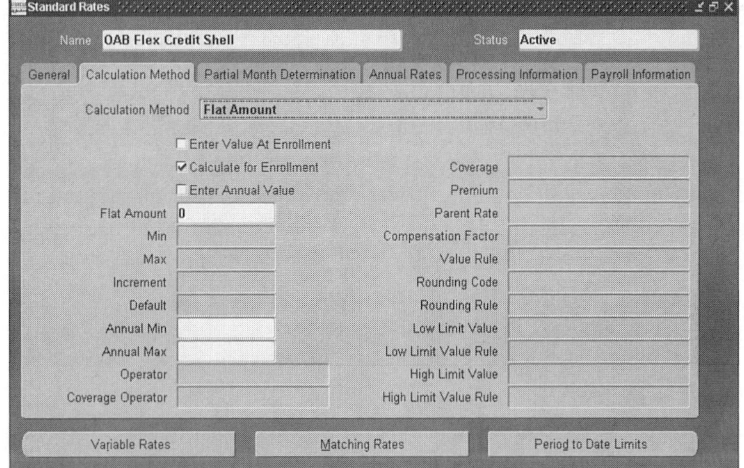

Figure 26.50
Calculation Method tab on standard rate.

On the Processing Information tab, check Assign on Enrollment, check Process each Pay Period Default, select Payroll as the Processing Source, and Recurring for Recurring. By defining the source as (Oracle) Payroll and as a Recurring entry, and to process each pay period, the flex credit, if provided to the employee, will be divided evenly over the number of periods in the payroll and included in each pay run. Figure 26.51 shows the completed screen.

STEP 6: DEFINE BENEFIT POOLS

Configure benefit pools to manage the use of flex credits by participants. Benefit pools control how the participants in the flex credit program can spend the flex credits provided to them and any rules relating to the treatment of excess credits.

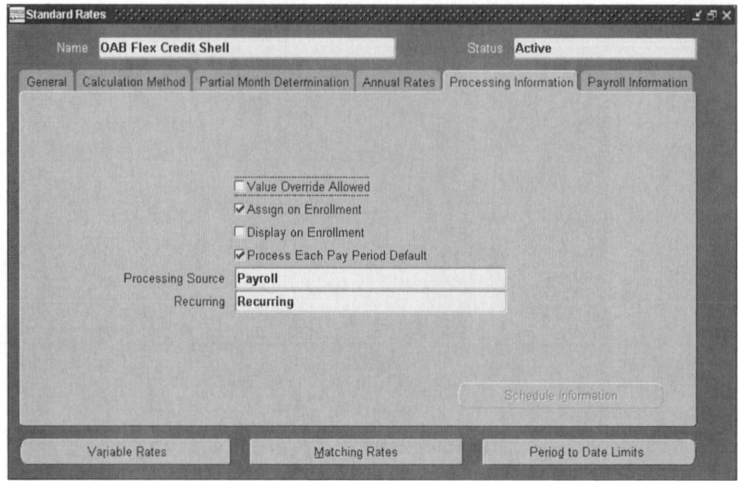

Figure 26.51
Standard Rate Processing Information tab.

You define one benefit pool for each flex credit defined earlier. In this example you need benefit pools for the Medical, Dental, EE Life, and LTD flex credits you defined for the plan types in program. If you set up one flex credit at the program level, you only need one pool.

By using descriptive names, you will be able to determine the source of the credits when enrolling a participant in the flex credit program. Define the level of the benefit pool equivalent to the flex credit defined and the related compensation objects. On the General tab, check to include program flex credits. For the system to automatically allocate excess credits, be sure to check the Automatically Allocate Excess check box. Define the excess treatment required by your enterprise, for example, receive as cash or roll to another program. Define the default excess treatment order. Also define any restrictions on the benefit pool. Figure 26.52 shows the completed benefit pool setup.

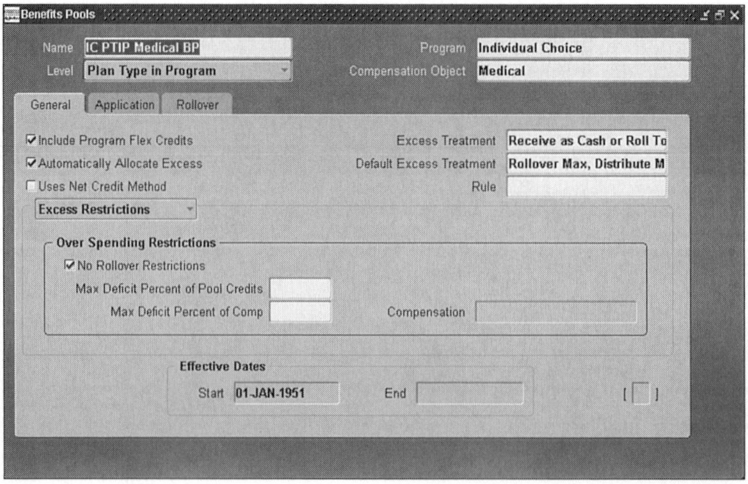

Figure 26.52
Setup of benefit pools.

Figure 26.53 shows the Application tab for your benefit pool. On the Application tab, picklist all the plan and option combinations on which your employees can spend the flex credits provided by the benefit pool. If the plan and option are not defined here, an employee will not be able to use flex credits when enrolling in that plan. On the other hand, when an employee enrolls in one of these plans and options, the flex credits will be applied to the selection.

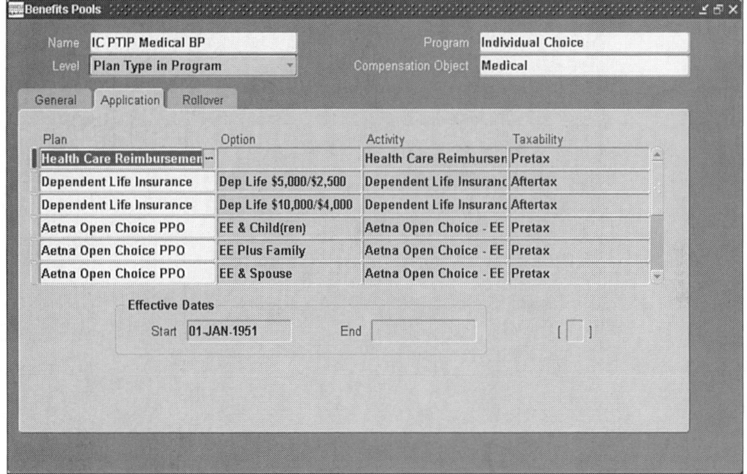

Figure 26.53
Application tab on benefit pool setup.

USING FLEX CREDITS

Run the Participation Process: Life Event to allow Advanced Benefits to determine eligibility, electability, and so on, for the potential life events for participants in the flex credit program. Figure 26.54 shows the parameters to use to run the process for one test employee.

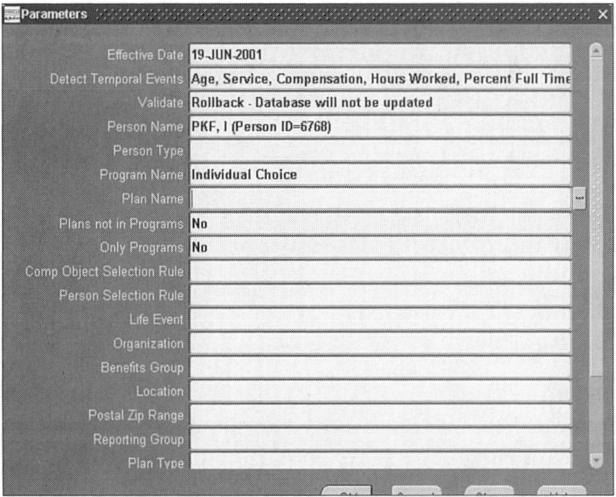

Figure 26.54
Parameters for running the Participation Process: Life Event.

On the Flex Program Enrollment form, you can access the available credits for a participant enrolling in the flex credit program. Figure 26.55 shows the available credits from the enrollment form. You access this screen by clicking the Others button and selecting Available Credits. Based on the configuration performed, the four benefit pools are available to the participant.

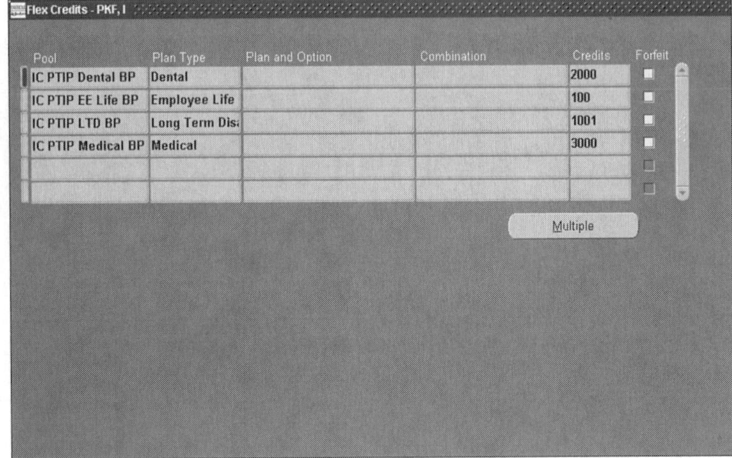

Figure 26.55
Available flex credits during enrollment.

Figure 26.56 shows the Flex Program Enrollment form for your sample employee. This is similar to the examples you did in the eariler sections.

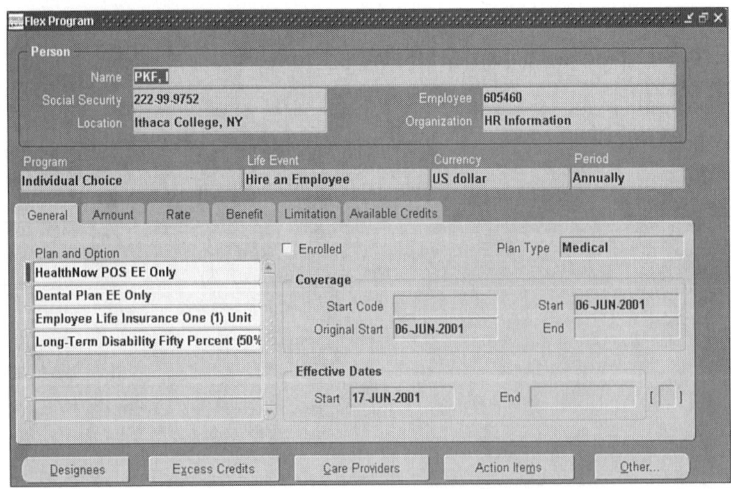

Figure 26.56
Flex Program Enrollment form for sample employee.

Figure 26.57 shows the element entries for your sample employee after the enrollment was completed. The amount shown is the pay period amount for the total annual amount awarded.

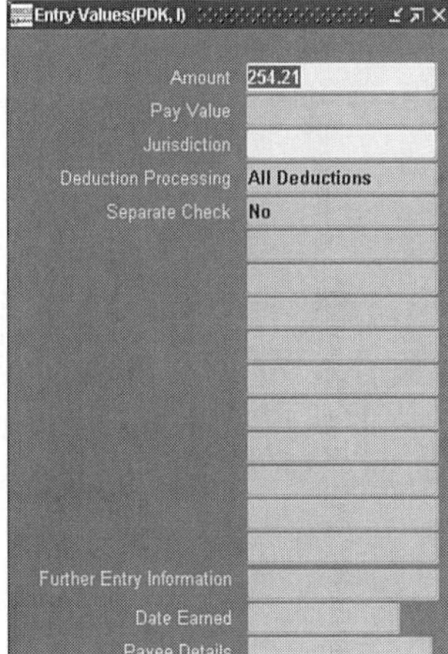

Figure 26.57
Element Entries for sample employee.

SUMMARY

As you can now appreciate, the new benefits functionality that Oracle provides with 11*i* is robust and complex. It is impossible to describe every feature available in one volume, let alone one chapter. Hopefully, our discussions and examples will help you overcome the huge learning curve ahead of you. Before long, you will realize, as we have, that this new feature of 11*i* might be the most important addition to the Oracle HRMS suite of modules.

CHAPTER 27

Administering the Oracle Applications

In this chapter

As an Oracle Application system administrator, you hold the keys to the application. Whereas a database administrator is responsible for maintaining the engine and workings of the application, the system administrator governs user access to your system. Without such a role, your users would have free reign of your applications.

As an Oracle Applications system administrator, you are responsible for defining and maintaining the following:

- The users of the system
- Users' responsibilities
- Reports and report sets a user can run
- System and user profiles
- Concurrent processes and processing
- Printers

In this chapter, you will study the setup and functionality of the Oracle Systems Administration module.

RELEASE 11*i* CHANGES

System administration functionality has changed relatively little with the release of Oracle Applications 11*i*. User interface enhancements, look and feel improvements, and updated help features comprise the majority of changes to this release.

System administration–specific enhancements with Oracle Applications Release 11*i* include

- Improved Release Management features are now available.
- Attachment/Export functionality can now include references to Document Management Systems.
- Advanced concurrent request scheduling now allows schedules based on external calendars.
- Request Set submission APIs now support programmatic submission of concurrent request sets.
- Improved application patching features are now available.

UNDERSTANDING SECURITY

As the Oracle Applications system administrator, you define the users of Oracle Applications. Additionally, you assign each user one or more responsibilities that grant the user access to the Application functions that are appropriate to his or her roles in the organization.

Through the proper planning, creation, and maintenance of these application responsibilities security is achieved.

This section introduces you to the various components of Oracle Applications security.

RESPONSIBILITIES

A *responsibility* is the level of authority you provide a user to give him access only to the data and functions appropriate to his roles in the organization (see Figure 27.1). Each responsibility provides access to

- A specific application or applications
- A set of books or an organization
- A restricted list of windows to which a user can navigate
- A restricted list of functions a user can perform
- Reports in a specific application

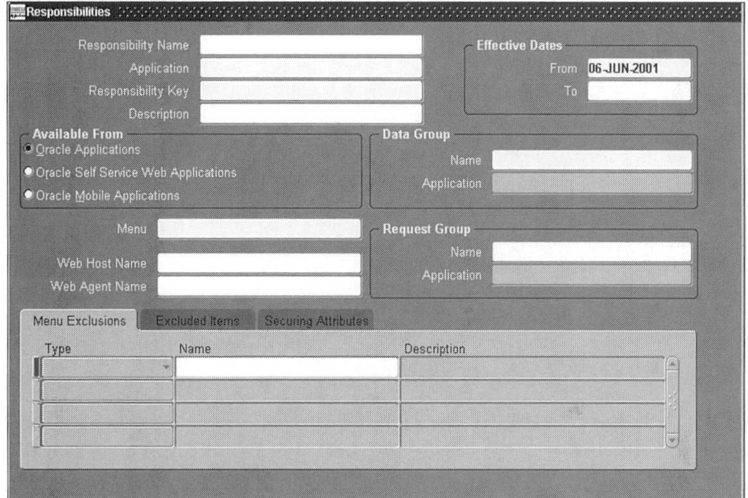

Figure 27.1
Define and maintain responsibilities using the define responsibilities form.

Oracle Applications are delivered with a variety of predefined responsibilities. Often referred to as *super-user* responsibilities, these predefined responsibilities typically grant users full access to application functionality. Your applications implementation team will often use these responsibilities for setting up and configuring the applications. Therefore, you should create custom responsibilities that grant access only to the business functions your users require.

Each user should be granted at least one responsibility. For example, an Accounts Payable clerk might be assigned to a responsibility that limits her access to entering invoices. Check payments or invoice adjustments might require a different responsibility assigned to a Payables supervisor.

In addition, a user can have more than one responsibility. Using the previous example, your same Accounts Payable clerk might also be given a General Ledger Inquiry responsibility that allows her to look up account balances in the ledger. There is no limit to the number of responsibilities that can be granted to a user.

Just as one user can have multiple responsibilities, one responsibility can have multiple users. You might have several Accounts Payable clerks who all require invoice entry functionality. In this case, you can assign the same Payable responsibility to all clerks.

Note

It is strongly advised that you limit access to predelivered super-user responsibilities because they possess the capability to change your application setups.

DEFINING A RESPONSIBILITY

Figure 27.1, earlier in this chapter, is an example of the define responsibility form. When you define a custom responsibility, you assign some or all of the following components:

- Data Group
- Request Group
- Menu
- Menu Exclusions
- Excluded Items and Securing Attributes

Each of these components is discussed in greater depth in the following sections.

DATA GROUP

A *data group* determines to which Oracle database accounts a responsibility's forms, concurrent programs, and reports connect. In essence, you are telling Oracle to which grouping of data you want this responsibility to have access.

Every Oracle Application carries an internal application ID that uniquely identifies it to the database. This ID is created automatically during the installation process. The paring of this internal Oracle ID and the application itself define a data group.

If a custom application is created, you can assign an Oracle ID, registered with the applications, and include it in a data group as seen in Figure 27.2. This process enables a responsibility to have access to the data stored in custom applications.

Note

Oracle Applications transaction managers run requests based on data groups. If you create custom data groups, you will need to create new transaction managers for applications that require the use of transaction managers.

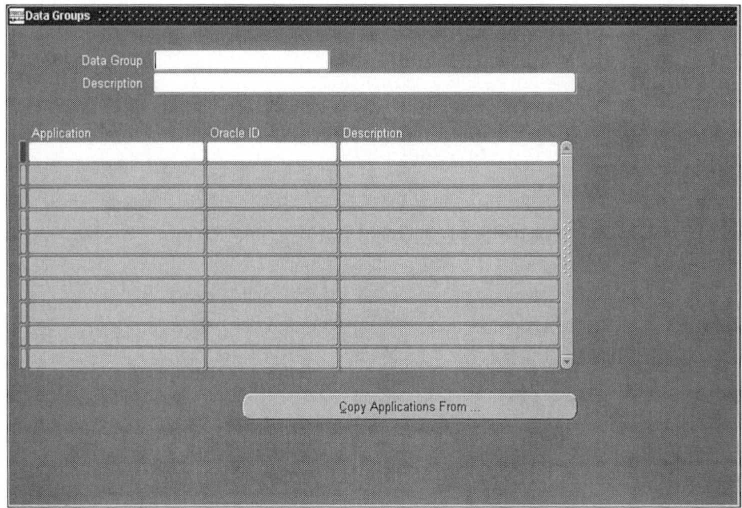

Figure 27.2
Data groups are defined using the define data group form.

REQUEST GROUP

A *request group* defines the concurrent programs, including requests and request sets that an application user can run under a particular responsibility. You grant users of a responsibility access to reporting through the request group as illustrated in Figure 27.3.

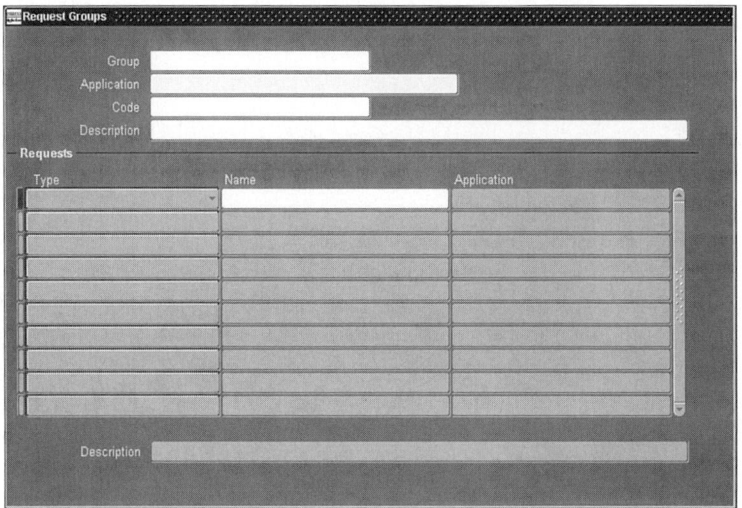

Figure 27.3
Grant users access to reporting by using the request groups form.

A responsibility can have only one request group. Therefore, you must create one responsibility for every unique request group. For example, lets assume you have two General Ledger users, user A and user B. Both should be allowed to create journal entries, inquire on accounts, and run reports. User A should be allowed to run journal reports, whereas user B should have access to all financial reports.

In this scenario, users A and B will not be able to share the same responsibility because they require access to different concurrent requests.

Note

If you do not assign a request group to a responsibility, users working under that responsibility can't run any reports, request sets, or other concurrent programs from a standard submission form.

MENUS

A *menu* is a hierarchical arrangement of functions and submenus of functions. A menu is assigned to each responsibility. Menus are defined and modified using the define menu form as seen in Figure 27.4.

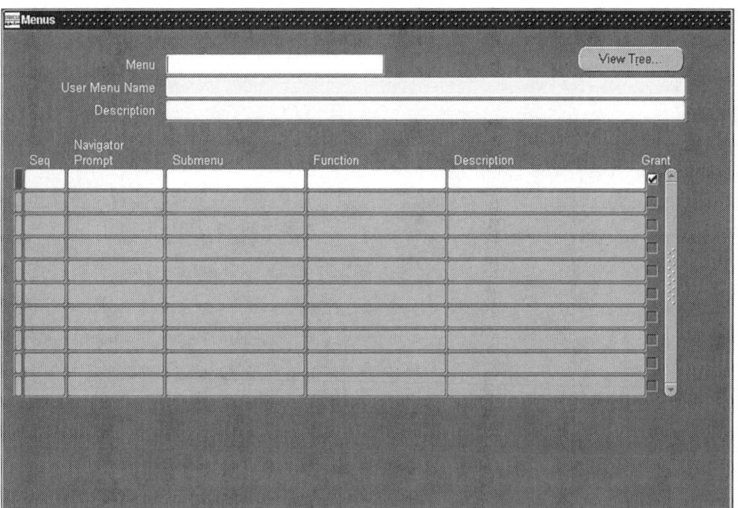

Figure 27.4
Create or modify application menus using the define menu form.

Each Oracle Applications product has a "full access" responsibility with a menu that includes all the functions associated with that application. When you create a new responsibility, you can restrict the functionality of the responsibility by defining rules to exclude specific functions or menus of functions of the full access menu.

Note

Oracle recommends that you restrict a full access menu to certain responsibilities.

Analyzing the Menu Reports

The menu report documents the structure of character mode menus. This report is useful when defining new or editing existing character-based menus. You can use a hardcopy of this report to document your customized menus before upgrading your Oracle Applications.

The function security menu report set documents the structure of the menus you are using. This report set is useful when defining new menus. If you are upgrading from a prior release, use the report set to document your existing menus. You can use a hardcopy of the output of this report set to document your customized menus before upgrading your Oracle Applications.

The function security menu report set consists of the function security functions report, the function security menu report, and the function security navigator report.

Protecting Yourself During an Upgrade

To preserve your custom menus during an upgrade of the Oracle Applications, you should use unique names for your custom menus. As an example, you can start your custom menus' names with the three-letter code of your organization, such as XYZ_General_Ledger_Super_User.

Note

Oracle Applications standard menus might be overwritten when the Oracle Applications are upgraded to a newer version.

Modifying Existing Menus

You can modify an existing user-defined menu by either adding or eliminating functions and subfunctions from the menu hierarchy.

Note

It is recommended that you do not modify a standard menu delivered with the Oracle Applications because these menus can be overwritten when Oracle Applications are upgraded.

Combining Pieces of Several Menus You can create a new menu through combining other menus or submenus. You attach the menus you want to reuse to the new menu you are creating.

Menu Exclusions

The Menu Exclusions tab region enables you to restrict access to specific menus or functions within a responsibility. By selecting a name in this region, you are excluding that menu or function from all users of that given responsibility.

Note

When you exclude a menu from a responsibility, all functions nested within that menu are also excluded.

When you exclude a function from a responsibility, all occurrences of that function throughout the entire menu structure of that responsibility are excluded.

EXCLUDED ITEMS AND SECURING ATTRIBUTES

You identify excluded items and securing attributes when you want to exclude functions from Oracle Self-Service Applications. Functions are excluded by selecting them from a list of valid functions associated with that responsibility.

USERS

To log on to Oracle Applications, you need an Oracle Applications username and password. This logon is different from the username and password you use to log on to your computer or computer network. It is also different from any Oracle database IDs you might have. Your Oracle Applications logon connects you to your responsibilities, which controls your access to the Oracle applications, functions, reports, and data.

DEFINING A USER

An authorized user of Oracle Applications is known as an applications user identified by an applications username. A new applications user uses the applications username to log on to Oracle Applications and access data through Oracle Applications windows. Users are defined and modified via the define user form as seen in Figure 27.5.

Figure 27.5
Create and modify users of the application via the define user form.

Users
User Name
Description
Password
Password Expiration
Days
Accesses
None
Person
Customer
Supplier
E-Mail
Fax
Effective Dates
From 06-JUN-2001
To
Responsibilities
Securing Attributes

Responsibility	Application	Security Group	Effective Dates From	To

Consider the following items as you define your application users:

- An application user can work with only one responsibility at a time.
- The username must not contain more than one word.
- You should use only alphanumeric characters (A–Z and 0–9) in the username.
- You must limit your username to the set of characters that your operating system supports for filenames.
- Usernames can be issued start and stop dates.
- Usernames can't be deleted from the system after they're created. Username inactivation is handled through the use of stop dates.
- A password must be at least 5 characters and can extend up to 100 characters.
- A password can be set to automatically expire after a given number of days or logons.
- You should use alphanumeric characters (A–Z and 0–9) in a password. All other characters are invalid.

Note

It is recommended that you define meaningful usernames, such as the employee's first initial followed by her last name.

In addition to granting a user access to the applications, a user ID can also be linked to an employee ID or person. Employee IDs, which typically are defined in the Oracle HMRS application, differ from application IDs in that employee IDs carry such information as a user's job and position, organization location, and reporting hierarchy. See Chapter 23, "Implementing Oracle Human Resources and Oracle Payroll," for more information on defining employees.

Auditing Users

As the Applications system administrator, you have the ability to monitor application users and the changes they make to data. This ability can be extremely useful in a highly distributed environment where your users might be spread over several locations, states, or even countries.

System administrators can monitor user activity through the use of Sign-On audit features and through the use of the AuditTrail feature.

Sign-On Auditing Through the use of the Sign-On audit feature in Figure 27.6, you can monitor user sign-on activity at the following levels:

- **User**—Use this level to monitor who is signed in to the applications, his sign-in time, and his session duration, as well as which terminal he has signed in to.

- **Responsibility**—In addition to monitoring all the previously mentioned items, this level also tracks which responsibility the user is using.
- **Form**—This level tracks all the previously mentioned items and provides information about which application form the user is currently using.

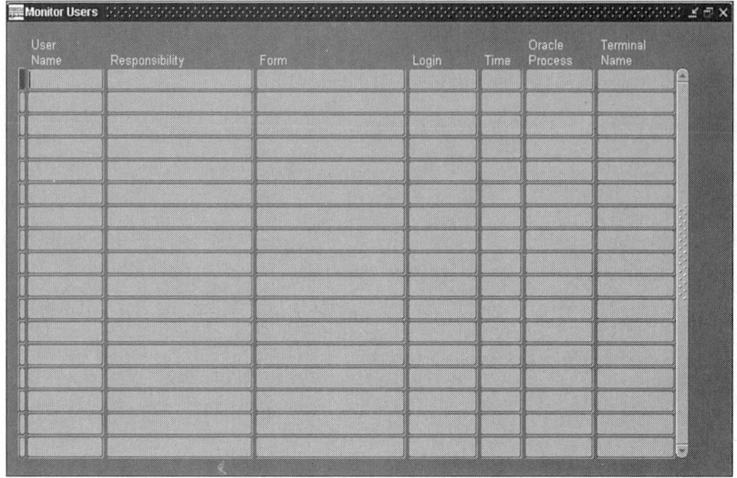

Figure 27.6
Monitor application users via the monitor users form.

In addition to the form-based auditing features, Oracle Applications provides a variety of sign-on audit reports for the System administrator.

Note

You define your level of Sign-On auditing via the Application System Profile options.

AUDITTRAIL Whereas Sign-On audit features help the system administrator track who is currently signed in to the system, AuditTrail features help determine what data changes those users are making. AuditTrail can track data changes at both a row or column level in the underlying database tables.

AuditTrail tracks who made a change, when it was made, and what was changed.

The six steps in setting up the AuditTrail feature are as follows:

1. Identify the tables and columns to be audited.
2. Create an audit group.
3. Specify the columns you want to audit.
4. Identify the Oracle IDs or data elements you want to audit.
5. Run AuditTrail Update Table reports.
6. Develop auditing reports.

MAINTAINING PROFILE OPTIONS

Oracle Applications uses profile options to manage the way the applications look and behave. By changing key profile options, the system administrator has the ability to modify functionality at various levels throughout the application. Therefore, you should carefully evaluate and test any changes made to user profiles before implementing in a production environment.

You can set profile options for your user community through the System Profile window. If you change a user's profile option value, that change takes effect as soon as the user logs on again or changes responsibilities.

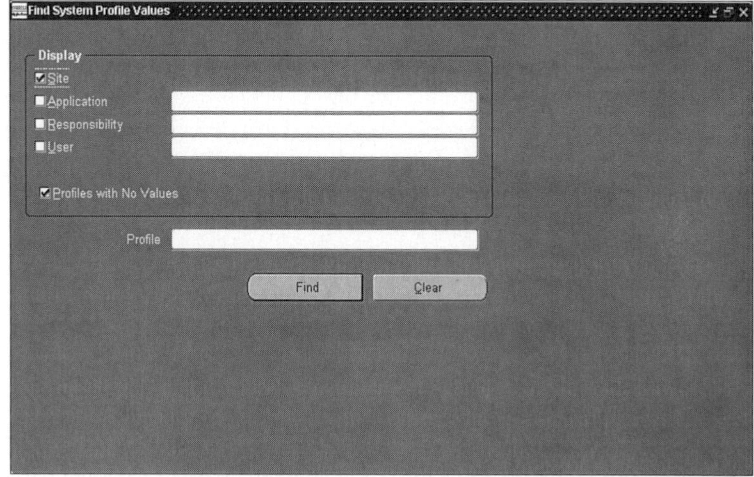

Figure 27.7 Modify profile values via the system profile option form.

As seen in Figure 27.7, profiles have four levels:

Site	Option settings pertain to all users at an installation site.
Application	Option settings pertain to all users of any responsibility associated with the application.
Responsibility	Option settings pertain to all users currently logged on under the responsibility.
User	Option settings pertain to an individual user, identified by his application username.

The values that you set at each level provide the runtime values for each user's profile. When a profile option is set at more than one level, the site profile has the lowest priority. The site profile is superseded by the application profile. The application profile is superseded by the responsibility profile. The user profile has the highest priority.

Note

You should set site-level option values before specifying profile options at the other three levels after installing Oracle Applications. The options specified at the site level work as defaults until the same options are specified at the other levels.

UNDERSTANDING CONCURRENT PROCESSING

In Oracle Applications, online operations run simultaneously with programs that run in the background. This capability is known as concurrent processing. The system administrator manages when programs are run and how many operating-system processes are devoted to running programs in the background.

When a user runs a report, a request to run that report is inserted into a database table, and a unique identifier known as a request ID is assigned to the request. A concurrent manager reads requests from this table and runs the request if the manager's definition is satisfied about how many operating-system processes it can devote to running requests.

The following determines when a concurrent program actually starts running:

- When it is scheduled to start
- Whether it is placed on hold
- Whether it is incompatible (it cannot run) with other programs
- Its request priority

SETTING UP WORKERS AND SCHEDULES

You can activate and restart managers individually. A restart of a concurrent manager forces the internal concurrent manager to reread that concurrent manager's definition. Activating a manager allows the internal concurrent manager to start that manager when its work shift starts.

You should restart an individual manager for the following reasons:

- When you modify its work shift assignments
- When you modify a work shift's target number of processes
- When you modify its specialization rules
- When you change a concurrent program's incompatibility rules

When you shut down an individual manager, if you choose to deactivate the manager, all requests that are currently running are allowed to complete. If, on the other hand, you terminate the requests and deactivate the individual manager, all requests that are currently running are immediately stopped and marked for resubmission when the manager is later activated. See Figure 27.8 for an example of the Administer Concurrent Managers form.

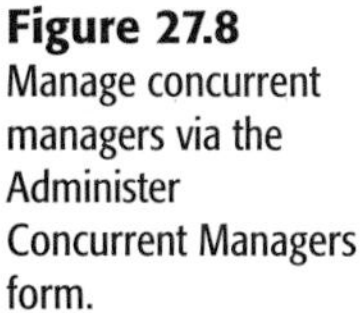

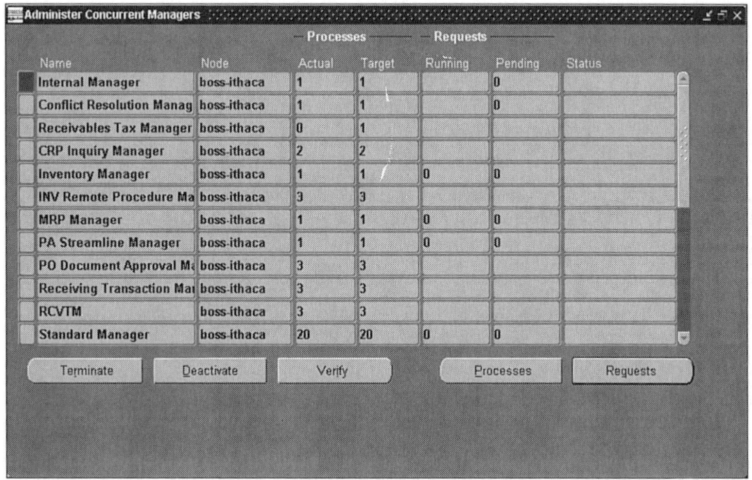

Administer Concurrent Managers

Name	Node	Processes: Actual	Processes: Target	Requests: Running	Requests: Pending	Status
Internal Manager	boss-ithaca	1	1		0	
Conflict Resolution Manag	boss-ithaca	1	1		0	
Receivables Tax Manager	boss-ithaca	0	1			
CRP Inquiry Manager	boss-ithaca	2	2			
Inventory Manager	boss-ithaca	1	1	0	0	
INV Remote Procedure Ma	boss-ithaca	3	3			
MRP Manager	boss-ithaca	1	1	0	0	
PA Streamline Manager	boss-ithaca	1	1	0	0	
PO Document Approval Ma	boss-ithaca	3	3			
Receiving Transaction Mai	boss-ithaca	3	3			
RCVTM	boss-ithaca	3	3			
Standard Manager	boss-ithaca	20	20	0	0	

Terminate | Deactivate | Verify | Processes | Requests

Figure 27.8
Manage concurrent managers via the Administer Concurrent Managers form.

Note

You can also create a specialized concurrent manager for running all of your recurring periodic batch jobs.

You should never modify the standard manager because it is designed to pick up any jobs that are not sent to the specialized processor.

In some instances you might need to have the concurrent manager(s) restarted from the operating-system level. Reasons for this can include an inability to successfully shut down or restart the managers internally, runaway concurrent jobs, or any other number of reasons. In this event you should contact your database administrator. She will have scripts—similar to the following—that can start and stop the concurrent managers from the operating system.

The following is an example of a script that can be used to start the concurrent managers:

```
$FND_TOP/bin/startmgr sysmgr="DATABASE NAME" mgrname=MANAGER NAME
```

The following is an example of a script that can be used to stop the concurrent managers:

```
$FND_TOP/bin/CONCSUB applsys/password SYSADMIN 'System Administrator'
SYSADMIN CONCURRENT FND SHUTDOWN
```


Concurrent Programs and Reports

A concurrent program is a program that does not require continued interaction to perform a specific task. A concurrent program can be a report or a process such as the batch posting of journal entries to the general ledger.

Oracle Applications-specific information can be organized and presented in what is known as a report. You can print reports or view them online. Reports can be as simple as summary information or as complex as a complete detailed listing.

You can group reports into a collection known as a request set. A request set submits all of the reports and programs as a single transaction. The individual reports and programs in a request set can be run serially or in parallel.

A report or request set provides different information each time it is run through report parameters. If the report or request set has parameters associated with it, the user is requested to provide input each time the report or request set is requested.

Additionally, you can set up a report or request set to resubmit itself on a regular basis. This feature is useful if you have a process that runs on a periodic basis and requires no parameters or static type parameters.

DEFINING AND REGISTERING EXECUTABLES

You are required to define a concurrent program executable for each executable source file used with concurrent programs. This concurrent program executable links the source file with the concurrent request users can submit. Program executables are defined using the define applications form as seen in Figure 27.9.

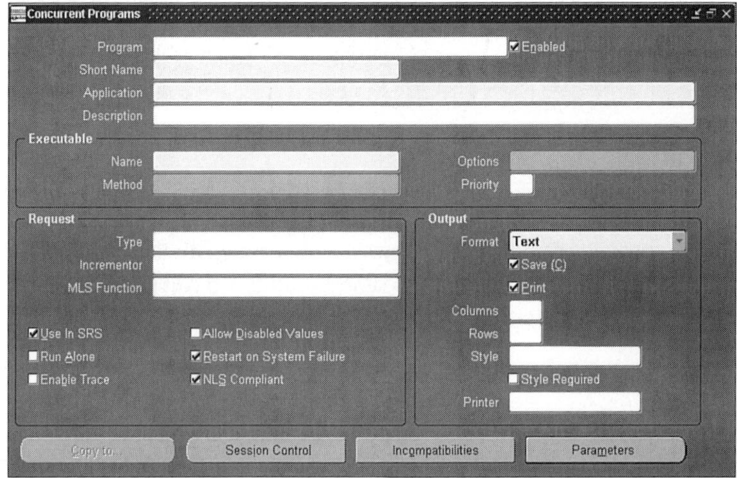

Figure 27.9
Define application programs using the define applications form.

Note

You cannot add new immediate programs to a concurrent manager program library. Oracle recommends that you use spawned concurrent programs instead.

The combination of application name plus program name uniquely identifies your concurrent program executable.

The concurrent managers use the application to determine in which directory structure to look for your execution file.

You cannot change the execution method once the concurrent program executable has been assigned to one or more concurrent programs in the Concurrent Programs window.

The maximum size of an execution filename is 30 characters.

DEFINING SETS

A request set lets you run several reports or concurrent programs conveniently and quickly. If you want to run the same report or process more than once with different parameters, you can include that report or process in the request set multiple times. Request sets are defined in the define request set form as seen in Figure 27.10

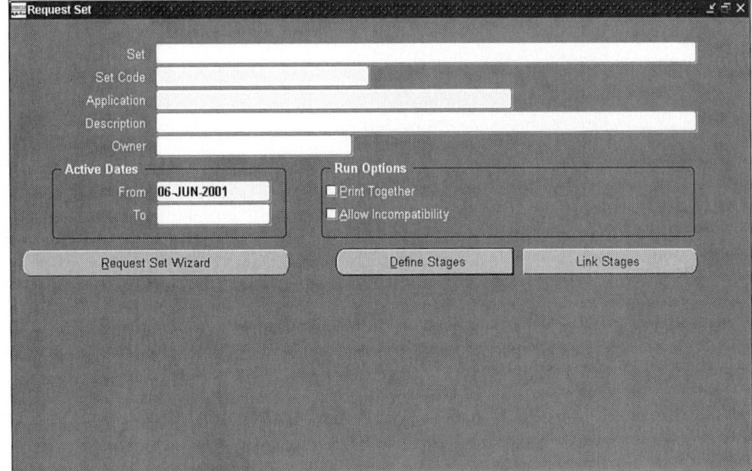

Figure 27.10 Group reports or programs using the define request set form.

You can also run the reports and processes in a report set in a sequential or parallel order. If you create a request set where a report depends on the results of a prior report, then run the reports in the request set in sequential order. You can also specify whether to stop processing if there is an error in any of the reports in the sequential request set.

You can select your printer options for a request set on a report-by-report basis. You can select a different printer for each report or any combination, including the same printer for all reports.

Note

All concurrent programs that run request sets are titled Request Set <name of request set>.

MANAGING CONCURRENT REQUESTS

A concurrent manager is responsible for running all processes assigned to it within the applications. As an application's system administrator, one of your duties is to manage these processing activities. Your primary tool for accomplishing this is the View Concurrent Requests form.

From the form in Figure 27.11 you can monitor any given process through its four phases:

- **Inactive**—Indicates the request can't be run at this time
- **Pending**—Indicates the request is waiting to run
- **Running**—Indicates the process is currently running
- **Completed**—Indicates the process has finished execution

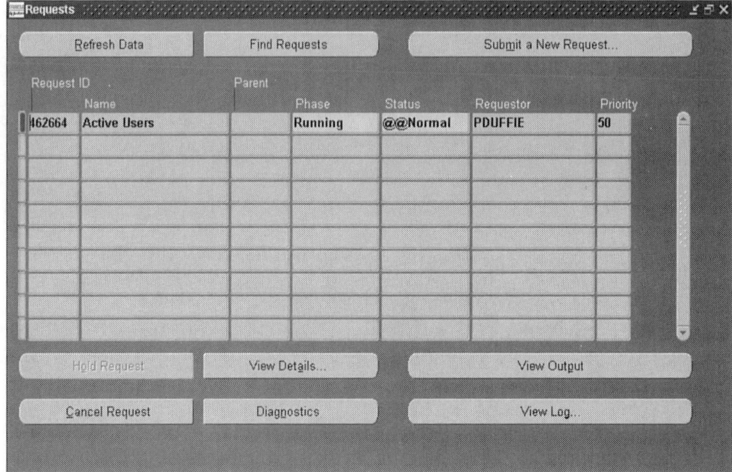

Figure 27.11 Monitor requests using the find requests form.

Within each of these phases, a concurrent request can report any number of statuses. In a sense, a *phase* can tell you what a concurrent request is doing, whereas a *status* tells you how that request is doing.

Inactive Stage Statuses

Within the Inactive phase you will find that your request will have one the following statuses:

- **Disabled**—Indicates the concurrent program has not been enabled for execution
- **On Hold**—Indicates the request has been placed on hold
- **No Manager**—Indicates no manager is assigned to the request or that the manager is down

Pending Stage Statuses

Within the pending phase, your request has one the following statuses:

- **Normal**—Indicates the request is waiting for an available manager
- **Waiting**—Indicates this is a child request waiting for a parent to mark it as ready to run

- **Standby**—Indicates that this request is waiting for an incompatible program to complete
- **Scheduled**—Indicates that this request is scheduled to begin execution at a specified time

RUNNING STAGE STATUSES

Within the running phase, your request has one the following statuses:

- **Normal**—Indicates the concurrent program is in progress
- **Paused**—Indicates this is a parent process that is waiting for a child process to complete
- **Resuming**—Indicates a parent process is continuing after the completion of a child process
- **Terminating**—Indicates the process has been terminated

COMPLETED STAGE STATUSES

Within the completed phase, your request has one the following statuses:

- **Normal**—Indicates the concurrent program completed normally
- **Warning**—Indicates the process completed normally but with messages
- **Error**—Indicates the process was incapable of completing
- **Terminated**—Indicates the process has been terminated
- **Canceled**—Indicates the process was canceled before it started

Note

Although a system administrator's privileges extend beyond those of the average user, she does not possess the ability to view the output of another user's requests.

A system administrator possesses only the ability to view manager output and log files from other users.

UNDERSTANDING THE `concsub` SYNTAX

You use the `concsub` utility to submit a concurrent request from the operating system prompt.

The syntax for the `concsub` utility follows:

```
CONCSUB applsys/pwd 'Responsibility application shortname'
 'Responsibility name' 'Username' [WAIT={Y|N|n}] CONCURRENT
 'Program application shortname' PROGRAM
```

The parameters associated with the `concsub` utility follow:

`applsys/pwd`	The Oracle username and password that connects to Oracle Application Object Library data.

`Responsibility application shortname`	The application shortname of the responsibility. For the system administrator responsibility, the application shortname is `SYSADMIN`.
`Responsibility name`	The name of the responsibility. For the system administrator responsibility, the responsibility name is `System Administrator`.
`Username`	The application username of the person who submits the request. For example, `SYSADMIN` is the username of the system administrator.
`WAIT={Y|N|n}`	Set `WAIT` to `Y` if you want `concsub` to wait until the request you submit completes before `concsub` returns you to the operating system prompt. Set `WAIT` to `N` (the default value) if you do not want `concsub` to wait. You can also enter an integer value of `n` seconds for `concsub` to wait before it exits. When used, `WAIT` must be entered before `CONCURRENT`.
`Program application shortname`	The application shortname of the program. For the `deactivate`, `abort`, and `verify` programs, the application shortname is `FND`.
`PROGRAM`	To submit the Shutdown All Managers concurrent request, use the program `deactivate`. To submit the Shutdown Abort Managers concurrent request, use the program `abort`. To submit the Verify All Managers Status concurrent request, use the program `verify`.

You can hide the password when using `concsub`. If you supply only the username (no `/pwd` in the first argument), the system prompts you for the password. You can also put the password in a file and then redirect the password to standard input (`stdin`).

UNDERSTANDING PRINTERS

When you run a report in Oracle Applications, a report is generated and the output is formatted. As a user, you have the choice to publish this report online or direct the output to a printer.

As a system administrator, you are responsible for identifying printers to be used for output and registering them with the application.

Two choices are available to you with regard to registering your printer with the applications. The first is to register a printer that has already been predefined by the applications. Oracle Applications delivers a list of these predefined printers from which you can choose. However, if your printer is not in the predefined list of printer choices, you must build a custom printer definition to register.

The four stages to defining a custom printer in Oracle Applications are

- Defining a new printer driver
- Defining a new printer style
- Defining a new printer type
- Registering the printer

DEFINING A NEW PRINTER DRIVER

A *printer driver* delivers commands to the operating system that tell the printer how to output the specified print style. The printer driver consists of a string of escape sequences, such as follows. Printer drivers are defined using the define printer drivers form as seen in Figure 27.12.

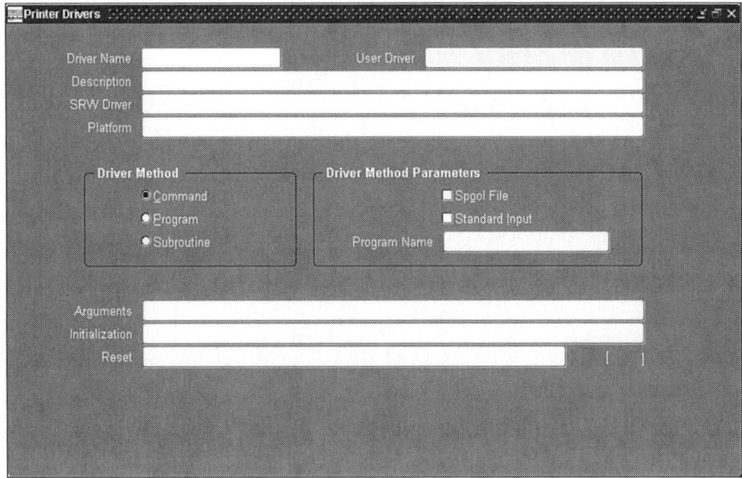

Figure 27.12
Define custom printer drivers using the define printer drivers form.

The following escape codes define the A4 initialization:

```
/eE/e&l1026a5.25C/e(s0t0p12h8.5V
    /eE        Esc E    Reset Printer
    /e&l1O     Landscape
    /e&l26A     A4 Paper
    /e&l#C     VMI(#/26")
    /e(s0T     Typeface
    /e(s0P     Fixed Font
    /e(s12H     12 cpi
    /e(s#V     Font Size (# points)
```

This escape sequence sets up the landscape initialization:

```
/eE/e&l1o2a5.25C/e(s0t0p12h8.5V
```

Use these escape codes to define the landwide initialization:

```
/eE/e&k2G/e&l7h1o2a5.45C/e(s0p16.66H/e&k6.75H
```

The following escape codes define the portrait initialization:

```
/eE/e&l0o2a7C/e(s0t0p11H/e&a5L/e&k2G
```

To configure a printer for a 132-column landscape, use the following escape codes:

```
/eE/e&l1O/e&l1E/e(oN/e(s0P/e(s8.5V/e(s0S/e(s0B/e(s0T/e
(s11H/e&k10H/e&l5.5C/e&k2G
```

To set up a portrait printout with 80 columns and 66 rows, use these escape codes:

```
/eE/e&l0O/e&l1E/e&a6L/e(0N/e(s0P/e(s8.5V/e(s0S/e(s0B/e(s0T/e
(s11H/e&k10H/e&l6D/e
```

You can set up a dynamic portrait printer with 80 columns and 66 rows with these escape codes:

```
/eE/e&l0O/e&l1E/e&a6L/e(0N/e(s0P/e(s8.5V/e(s0S/e(s0B/e(s0T/e
(s11H/e&k10H/e&l6D/e&k2G
```

Finally, you can use the following codes to configure a compressed print line of 180 characters per line in landscape orientation:

```
/eE/e&l1O/e&l1E/e(0N/e(s0P/e(s8.5V/e(s0S/e(s0B/e(s0T/e(s14H/e&l5.5C/e&k2G
```

Using Escape Codes

When using PCL, any commands that use the same prefix can be strung together after the prefix. The concatenation is ended when a command ends in a capital letter.

The following highlights common HP LaserJet printer PCL commands:

Command	Description
/eE	Reset
/e&l0S	Simplex print operation
/e&l1S	Duplex print long-edge binding
/e&l0H	Eject page
/e&l2A	Letter
/e&l3A	Legal
/e&l#P	# of lines (5–128)
/e&l0O	Portrait
/e&l1O	Landscape
/e&l#E	Top margin, # of lines
/e&l#F	Text length, # of lines
/e&a#L	Left margin, # of columns
/e&a#M	Right margin, # of columns
/e&l1D	One line/inch
/e&l2D	Two lines/inch
/e&a#R	# of rows

Command	Description
/e&a#C	# of columns
/e(s#V	# of points
/e(s1S	Italic
/e(s4S	Condensed
/e(s3B	Bold
/e(s4099T	Courier

Note

Always consult your printer's documentation to obtain the most current list of escape code sequences.

Most printer vendors offer Web sites that contain machine-specific escape code sequences.

DEFINING A NEW PRINTER STYLE

The look of the printed output depends on the print style. Additionally, your ability to print a report in a particular print style depends on the type of printer. A printer driver specific to the particular printer and the operating system is also required (in addition to the print style) for a report to properly print. Define your print styles using the define print styles form as seen in Figure 27.13.

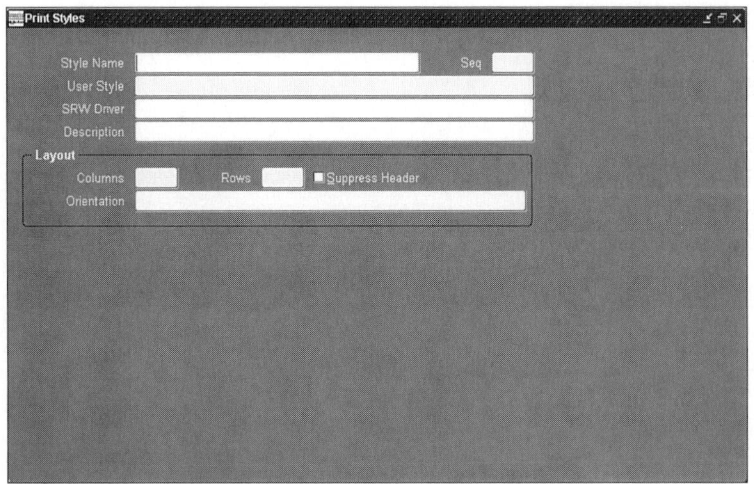

Figure 27.13 Define print styles using the define print styles form.

Table 27.1 shows the standard printer styles available with the Oracle Applications. The column SRW refers to the name of the Oracle Reports printer driver (Oracle Reports used to be called SQL*ReportWriter), and the values in this column are names of print driver files for print styles such as portrait and landscape.

TABLE 27.1 PRINT STYLES

Name	Username	Cols	Rows	Orientation	SRW
PORTRAIT	Portrait	80	65	Portrait	P
LANDSCAPE	Landscape	132	60	Landscape	L
LANDWIDE	Landwide	180	45	Landscape	W
DYNAMIC	Dynamic	0	0		
DYNAMIC PORTRAIT	Dynamic Portrait	80	66	Portrait	PD

The concurrent manager sends completed reports to the operating system. The operating system in turn issues a print command or calls a custom print program that issues an operating system print command.

The handling of page breaks, carriage returns, line feeds, bold text, and underlined text instructions normally is provided by the SRW file.

If you want to issue any page breaks, carriage returns, or line feed instructions before the output file is to be printed or after the output file is printed, you must enter the information in the printer driver's initialization or reset string.

The dimensions of a report are determined by the columns and rows values in the print style and override the width and height values provided in the SRW driver file.

DEFINING A NEW PRINTER TYPE

A *printer type* is simply a grouping of printer styles and printer drivers. Each printer type can have one or more of these pairings. Printer types are defined using the define printer type form as seen in Figure 27.14.

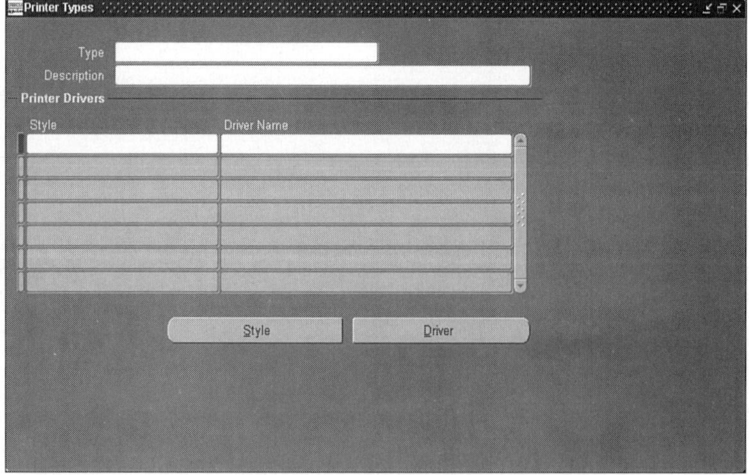

Figure 27.14
Define printer types using the define printer types form.

Note

Be sure to include all styles that you intend to use with a printer in the printer type definition.

REGISTERING A PRINTER

You must register all printers with the Oracle Applications before the printer can be recognized by the system and output can be generated. Printers are registered using the define printer form as seen in Figure 27.15

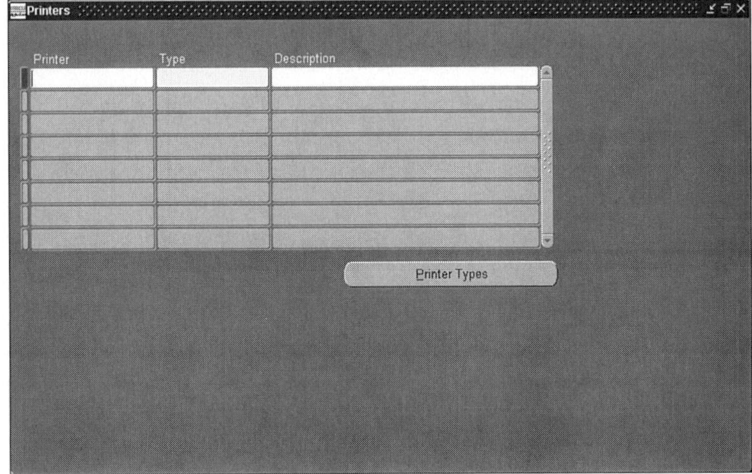

Figure 27.15
Define printers using the define printer form.

You register the individual printers by specifying the printer's operating system name, which is unique. You then must indicate the kind of printer it is by selecting a printer type.

Note

Consult with your database administrator or operating system administrator before defining the name of your Oracle Applications printer.

Note

Anytime you make a change to the printer driver, printer type, or printer definition, you should restart the concurrent manager for the changes to take effect.

TROUBLESHOOTING

System administration for the Oracle Applications is not difficult, but the work is not like other personal computer applications. The system administrator works with users, operating system administrators (Unix or NT), database administrators, and network administrators to establish and secure the computing environment.

Consider the following items to administer the Oracle Applications effectively:

- **Oracle Support can be very helpful**—Through use of both its phone support and Web-oriented self-service applications (`www.oracle.com/support`), a wealth of knowledge is available to you.
- **Do not modify program definitions for Oracle concurrent programs**—Copy the program, rename it, and make modifications to definitions for the copy.
- **Be careful when marking program definitions with the run alone attribute**—This program definition might block the transaction processors and cause the transactions to build up in the interfaces until the run alone program finishes.
- **A concurrent report might finish completely but with a status of Warning when it failed to print**—Check the end of the concurrent request log to see whether you should be working on a printer problem or a report problem. If necessary, contact your operating system administrator or DBA.
- **Do not alter the definition of the standard concurrent manager unless you are certain you have defined other concurrent managers to accept your requests.**
- **Changing passwords in the applications is tricky**—If you change the password for the applsys user, you must not change passwords for any other usernames at the same time. You should log out and log on between changes.
- **Printer definitions are cached in memory when the concurrent managers start up**—If you change definitions, restart the concurrent managers to complete the change.
- **Only the system administrator can create a new country code**—Other responsibilities in the applications can access the countries but cannot create new records.

CHAPTER 28

USING ORACLE WORKFLOW

In this chapter

Oracle Workflow is a quasi-technical tool that enables users to graphically define rules to automate processes. The underlying PL/SQL statements enable the workflow module to translate the defined rules into automated activities.

Workflow enables you to define several business activities as PL/SQL procedures (or an external program that it calls) and notifications. You can use conditions and routing rules to join these activities as processes and subprocesses. A workflow process can branch to different activities based on rules and notification responses. Examples of standard rules that can be used are And/Or Activities, Comparison Activities, Wait Activity, Loop Counter Activity, Voting Yes/No Activity, and Master/Detail Coordination Activities.

Workflow is especially useful for business processes that cannot be fully automated, that require human interaction, or have too complex of a business that can't be handled by other tools like Alerts.

SKILLS REQUIRED TO USE WORKFLOW

To work with Oracle Workflow, there are two distinct skill sets required. The skill sets are the end-user skill set and the technical skill set. It is best if the users have a combination of these two skill sets. If not, two or more users should work together to ensure the process flows realistically.

Caution

No matter what the user's skill level, *always* back up the Oracle supplied workflow processes before making *any* changes. You can do this by saving the workflow as a .wft file, using the workflow builder.

You can find .wft files of all Oracle shipped standard workflows on the server. You can copy these to your windows environment so users can use them and not directly affect the database copy.

USER SKILL SET

The user skill set requires that the users be able to define a business process graphically. This includes the activities within the process, data attributes, and expected results of the process. All this can be done in a passive, offline, environment using the flat file component of Oracle Workflow.

TECHNICAL SKILL SET

The technical user assigned to Oracle Workflow must be proficient in PL/SQL and be able to transform user requirements into PL/SQL code.

Both skill sets can be easily learned at the Oracle education classes. The Workflow class is not a PL/SQL class; an introductory class to PL/SQL is required.

TARGET USERS

Oracle Workflow is useful to various types of users involved in design, development, and implementation of a business solution. Following are some examples of how workflow can be used in various stages of a solution development.

FUNCTIONAL DESIGNERS

Functional users who have a basic understanding of technical aspects (programming not required) can represent their business processes as workflow diagrams instead of paragraphs of text. Doing so not only presents the picture graphically, but it also eliminates the need to translate the text into a flowchart for use by technical members.

TECHNICAL DESIGNERS

Technical users can present a workflow diagram as a design deliverable instead of flowcharts or other technical documents. A workflow diagram is better understood than flowcharts or technical documents when presented to the functional users. However, workflow diagram is not a replacement for detailed design documentation.

PROJECT MANAGERS/PRESENTERS

Workflow diagram can be used as a proof of concept for a solution being designed. The solution can be presented in various levels of detail (high-level process and subprocesses). Such presentation has more clarity and impact on an audience in a presentation, as opposed to text or bullet points.

NON-APPS USERS

Workflow can be installed and used with Oracle Databases without Oracle Applications. The workflow product is available independently of Applications and can be installed and used independently of Applications for other complex business solutions.

DISCOVERING NEW FEATURES IN RELEASE 11*i*

Oracle Workflow 2.5 (Release 11*i*) is more robust than its counterpart: version 2.0 for Release 11. The changes and additions to Oracle Workflow 2.5 are highlighted in the following sections.

PROCESS WORKFLOWS

Several Oracle Applications now include process workflows. A new tab on the navigator window called Processes lists all process workflows available for the application.

Figure 28.1 shows the Procure-to-Pay process workflow in Purchasing. This enables you to go through each step—from requisition in Purchasing to payment in AP. At each step, the workflow opens the associated applications window and requires that the related application products are installed (in this example, AP). You can complete each step and proceed to the next. You can leave the process anywhere and return later. You will specify a name for each launch of the process workflow so that you can uniquely identify each of the processes you've started.

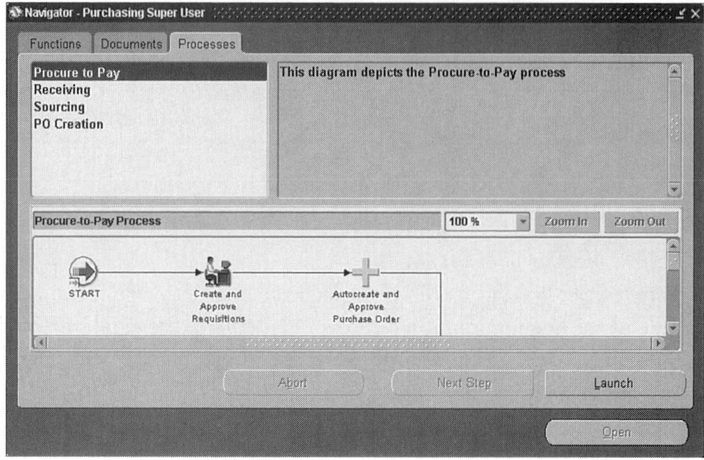

Figure 28.1
Procure-to-Pay Process Navigator Workflow.

Document Management Integration

Workflow 2.5 provides open integration with Document Management systems. This is accomplished through a set of PL/SQL procedures to initiate common document management functions in the supported document management systems.

Support for Forced Synchronous Processes

Workflow Engine in version 2.5 supports forced synchronous processes. This accelerates the execution speed. The restrictions on using forced synchronous processes are explained later in this chapter.

Web Pages to Manage Preferences

Workflow 2.5 has two new Web pages: User Preferences and Global Preferences. Figure 28.2 shows the Global Workflow Preferences Web page, which enables the Workflow Administrator to set global defaults for workflow preferences.

Figure 28.3 shows the General Preferences Web page. This Web page allows setting workflow preferences for individual users, such as notification formats and so on.

Although these two Web pages are available to system administrators and Workflow administrators, a Self-Service responsibility is also available that can be assigned to individual users. The responsibility is called Preferences, and it enables users to set their own preferences.

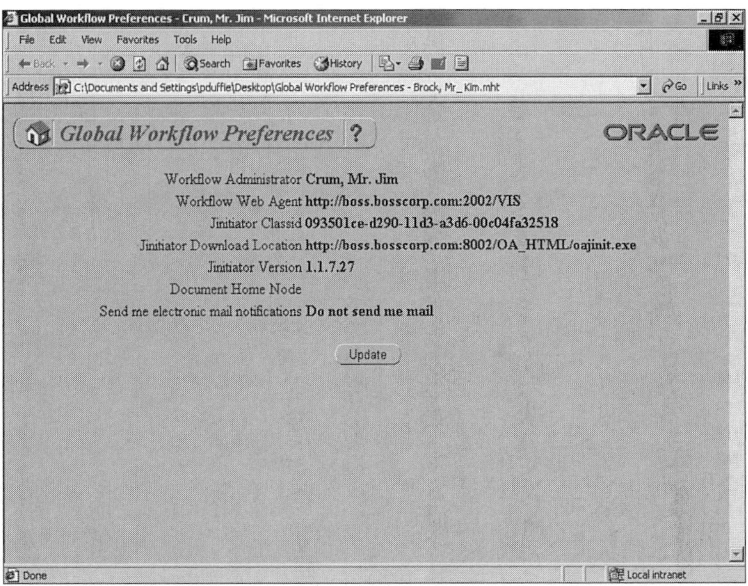

Figure 28.2
The Global Workflow Preferences Web page.

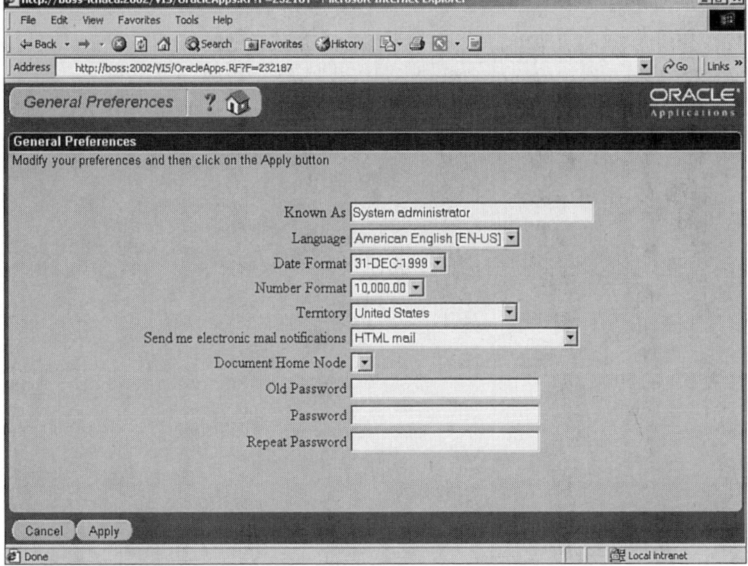

Figure 28.3
The General Preferences Web page.

By default, SYSADMIN is the Workflow administrator. As part of your workflow setup, you must log on as SYSADMIN and specify Workflow administrator as a user or responsibility so you can allow others to perform this role.

Caution

During initial testing, set the Send Me Electronic Mail Notifications option to Do Not Send Me Mail. This enables testing of the workflows without being complicated by potential errors in the setup of the notification mailer.

Advanced Queues Integration

Workflow always allowed both online and deferred activities, which will be executed later by the background engine. Workflow 2.5 takes advantage of Oracle 8 Advanced Queues processing to enhance performance and efficiency and also enable callouts to external systems. The external function, on completion, must return appropriate return information in the inbound queue.

Launch Process Web Page

Testing is a repetitive task performed several times during the development of a workflow. This task is a lot easier in Workflow 2.5 using the new Launch Processes Web page.

Figure 28.4 shows the Launch Processes Web page. After you open this page in your Web browser, you must specify the workflow item type, item key, process to be tested, and default values for item attributes if so desired.

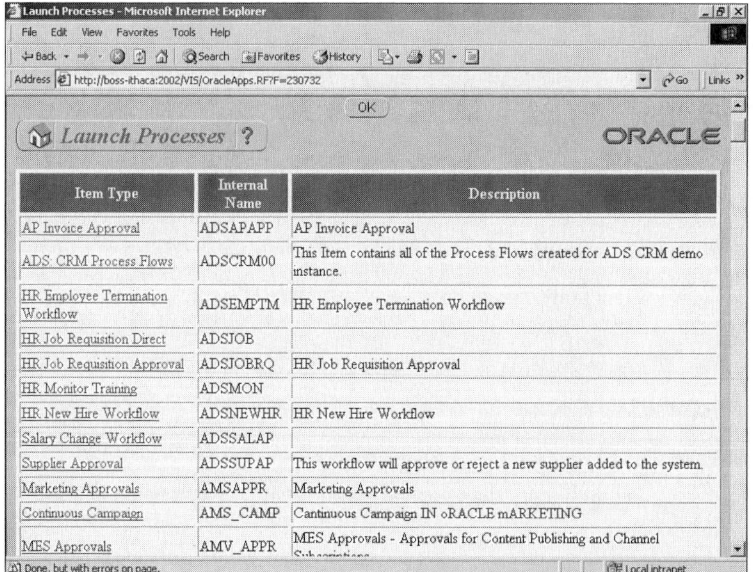

Figure 28.4
The Launch Processes Web page.

Quick Start Wizard

Quick Start Wizard, a new feature of Workflow Builder, uses a standard design template. When you select Quick Start Wizard either from the File menu or the toolbar of Workflow Builder, you first need to enter internal and display names for the item type and the default process. The wizard automatically creates a new workflow with your default process and start and end activities. The Quick Start Wizard also attaches the Standard Item Type to your workflow so that the standard objects can be easily used in your workflow.

This is a major enhancement to the way you can build a workflow. In earlier versions, you first had to define individual components and add them to the workflow by dragging and dropping them onto the process canvas. With version 2.5, you can start with a clean process and create new components as you add them to the process. In other words, you can now build a workflow as a top-down design.

ENHANCED NOTIFICATION RULES

Workflow 2.5 allows you to reassign notifications for a specified period of time or to automatically respond to notifications with a specific response.

ENHANCEMENTS

Workflow 2.5 includes many enhancements in all areas, including APIs, notification mailer, notification Web page, Workflow Builder, Workflow Definition Loader, Workflow Engine, Workflow Monitor, and Workflow Process Design.

The general stability and error handling of workflow has been improved. In many situations, where the workflow would have earlier stopped with a STUCK status, it now gives better error messages that enable users to understand why it is stuck. Some changes in the WF Engine and Workflow Process Design improve performance. Between versions 2.0.1, 2.0.2, and 2.0.3 (corresponding with Applications Releases 11.0, 11.02, and 11.03) defunct and redundant data were in the workflow tables. All such data have been removed from the tables.

APIs

Notification APIs include a new transfer function in addition to the existing forward function. Whereas the forward function delegates the notification to another role and retails the ownership, the new transfer function transfers the activity ownership as well.

Following are some important enhancements:

- **WF Directory APIs**—Include a set of new APIs to manage ad hoc users and roles. To support this, a new column, Expiration_Date, has been added to WF_USERS and WF_ROLES tables.
- **WF Engine**—Includes new APIs to support Document Management integration. Certain WF Engine APIs also support Java Interface. The new Java APIs reference the existing PL/SQL APIs.
- **WF Monitor**—Includes a new API, GetAdvancedEnvelopeURL, for returning a URL with an attached access key to display the Activities List.
- **WF Preferences APIs**—Include a new function that retrieves the value of a user preference for a specific user.

- **WF Purge APIs**—Have been enhanced with new functions for more flexibility in purging.
- **WF Queues APIs**—Are new and support integration with Oracle8's Advanced Queues.

NOTIFICATIONS

Workflow 2.5 enables you to associate a post-notification PL/SQL procedure, which executes in RESPOND, TRANSFER, or FORWARD mode.

Workflow 2.5 notification mailer supports HTML message body. Other APIs related to notifications have been enhanced to support the HTML format.

All validated fields on the notification Web pages include a list of values. The Find Notifications and Worklist pages have been enhanced with additional search criteria.

Notification mailer now fully supports MIME-encoded messages. A new e-mail notification format, MAILATTH (plain text with attachments), is now available in addition to MAILTEXT and MAILTHTML. If your preference is set to MAILTHTML, you can now respond by clicking the appropriate button, which will automatically create an indirect response e-mail with correct response code. However, Workflow now supports only indirect response e-mail notifications; whereas earlier versions support both direct and indirect response. This means that you must include the response template in your e-mail and edit the response values embedded between double quotes (" ").

WORKFLOW ADMINISTRATION

Workflow 2.5 includes several new scripts and features for better administration.

New administration scripts exist that enable you to clean up workflow queues in the system tables, and scripts exist that enable you to check for process definition errors, errors resulting from various versions of the same process definition, and invalid hanging foreign keys.

Workflow scripts now include several scripts that enable you to change internal names of workflow objects such as item types, activities, activity attributes, lookup types, lookup codes, messages, and message attributes. These scripts not only update the internal name in the appropriate WF table, but all are references to that object in all related tables.

Just the ability to assign a workflow administrator through a screen in System Administrator is a big plus. You used to have to assign users to a group within the Web server, and the password could not be hidden adequately.

Caution

These scripts have caused problems on some occasions. Always back up your workflow before attempting to run any of these scripts. After you run the scripts, test the workflow many times with all possible combinations of transactions.

Workflow Engine

Workflow Engine is enhanced to execute from non-savepoint environments (for example, database triggers). It automatically traps `Savepoint not allowed` errors and defers execution to the background engine.

Workflow client components are enhanced to check versions of the workflow server components to avoid version mismatch between server and client components.

Standard workflow activities include some new activities that give users more flexibility, such as Compare Execution Time activity, Defer Thread activity, Launch Process activity, and Notify activity.

A new set of concurrent process activities enables users to submit concurrent requests from workflow in two ways. One way is to submit a concurrent request and continue with workflow execution; another way is to execute a concurrent request and wait for its completion.

Tip

fndwfaol.wft is the item type that contains the Concurrent Process activities. To use these activities, you must open this item type and copy the functions into the workflow where they will be used.

Workflow Home Page

Workflow home page is enhanced to include a worklist of notifications in addition to all the links to Oracle Workflow's Web-based features.

Workflow Monitor

Workflow monitor is enhanced to give workflow administrators direct access to the notification details page for any open notification.

User Key

Workflow processes now have a key called User Key. As opposed to the Item Key normally used to identify items, you can now set user-friendly values to the User Key, such as PO Number. The Find Processes Web page has a field User Key, and you can search workflow items by the User Key you assign to the process.

Understanding the Major Components of Workflow

The major components of Oracle Workflow are the Oracle Workflow Builder, the Workflow Engine, the Workflow Definitions Loader, the notification system, and the Workflow Monitor. Each is defined briefly here:

- **Oracle Workflow Builder**—A tool that runs on MS-Windows and is used to graphically create and modify workflow processes.
- **Oracle Workflow Engine**—A large PL/SQL package that has the necessary workflow procedures to create and run workflow processes.
- **Workflow Definitions Loader**—Enables the users to go from a flat file to the database and back again.
- **Notification System**—Begins with a notification from the Workflow Engine, and then sends a message to users defined by roles. Any responses received from the notification recipients are validated and the engine is notified to resume processing according to the responses.
- **Workflow Monitor**—A system-administration tool that monitors processes. It can be a great tool for maintaining and troubleshooting workflows after they are deployed.

Workflow Builder

Oracle Workflow Builder is where the users create, view, and modify business process definitions. Using a navigator window, the users define the activities and underlying components of business processes (see Figure 28.5). The users then graphically create a process diagram by assembling the activities in the process window.

Workflow Builder allows the users to save a process diagram to a database or a flat file. When saving the process, Workflow Builder will perform some basic validations. In order to run the process, the users must save the process to the database.

Workflow Engine

The Workflow Engine is embedded in the Oracle server. It monitors workflow status and coordinates the routing of activities for a process. Calls to the Workflow Engine notify the engine of initiation and completion of workflow processes or of changes in the state of these processes.

The Workflow Engine determines the eligibility of activities to run. If it determines that an activity is eligible, it then runs the activity. The Workflow Engine supports sophisticated workflow rules, including looping, results-based branching, parallel flows, rendezvous, voting, timeouts, and subprocesses.

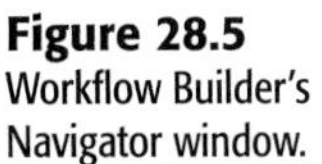

Figure 28.5
Workflow Builder's Navigator window.

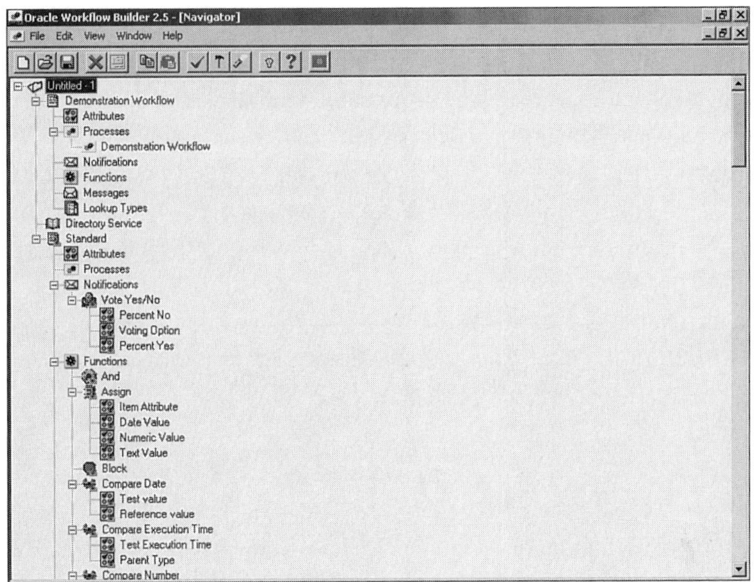

WORKFLOW DEFINITIONS LOADER

The Oracle Workflow Definitions Loader is a utility program that allows the users to transfer process definitions between a database and a flat file. The utility runs on the server. Because the Definitions Loader allows the users to source control process definitions in a flat file, they do not have to be online to work.

NOTIFICATION SYSTEM

The Oracle Workflow notification system enables users to receive and respond to notifications using e-mail or a Web browser. In this way, activities that cannot be automated (requiring human interaction), such as requisition approvals, can be handled within the workflow process. Since Web functionality is available, all users with access to the Internet can be included in the workflow process.

The notification system routes electronic notifications to a user role. The role can encompass a single user or a group of users. Drill-down capability to Oracle application forms is also available through the notification system if the users have appropriate security access.

Each notification includes a detailed message to ensure that the users have all the information needed to make an informed decision. Included in all notifications requiring a response are the response buttons—one for each response. This ensures that the response provided is understood by Workflow, thus allowing the process to continue to the next activity.

Workflow Monitor

The Workflow Monitor is a Java applet that allows users to graphically view the status of a single workflow process. The process can be displayed in detail or users can display the status of a specific activity of a process.

When the process or activity is viewed, Workflow places a box around the activity that is currently running. Green process connector lines indicate completed processes. Black connector lines have not been executed. If an error occurs in an activity, a red box appears around that activity's icon.

Tip

The system will appear to lock up after users tell the Workflow Monitor to retrieve a process. Have patience, it takes time for the process to load!

Workflow Item Types and Items

A workflow definition or design you create is known as an item type. Examples are the Oracle-supplied Requisition Approval and PO Approval item types.

When you execute your workflow item type, each run or instance is called an *item*. From the previous example, if you execute the PO Approval item type for several POs, each one is called an item.

As you create and run many items of an item type, each item is identified by a unique identifier, called the *item key*. By specifying the item type and item key, you uniquely identify an item. This is useful especially when you have to examine a workflow item from the Workflow Monitor.

Using the Workflow Engine

Oracle's Workflow Engine is implemented in server-side PL/SQL. When a call is issued to one of its PL/SQL APIs, the Workflow Engine is executed. The Workflow Engine can run in real-time, or, if this is too costly, it can send the activity to the background engine to be run as a background task.

The Workflow Engine serves the client application by:

- Managing the status of all activities for an item
- Determining which new activity to transition to whenever an activity completes
- Executing function activities automatically, whether real-time or through a background engine
- Calling the Notifications System to send notifications
- Maintaining an audit history of an activity's status
- Detecting error conditions and executing error processes

Additionally, the Oracle Workflow Engine supports results-based branches, parallel branches, rendezvous, loops, and subprocesses.

Initiating a Workflow Process

Caution

Users can *add* processes and activities to an Oracle standard workflow but should *never delete or skip any standard activity*! If processes or activities are deleted (or skipped), the standard Oracle application functionality could be impaired!

Tha basic problem when you skip or delete an activity is that any attribute values that it is setting or any database updates it is doing will not be done. You must carefully do this in your custom activities.

A workflow process is initiated when an application executes a procedure that calls the `WF_ENGINE.CreateProcess` and `WF_ENGINE.StartProcess` APIs. These APIs are embedded in the application's code.

The application makes a call to the `CreateProcess()` API to create an instance of a Workflow process. The creation of the instance triggers the Workflow Engine. After an item is created, calls must be made to APIs to set necessary item attribute values (`SetItemAttrText()`, `SetItemAttrNumber()`, and others).

A call to the `StartProcess()` API starts the workflow process instance. Once the `StartProcess()` is started, the Workflow Engine identifies and executes the `Start` activity. It then follows the process to determine the next activity to transition to after completing each activity. This process continues until the Workflow Engine comes to a notification or blocking activity. If a notification activity is encountered, the notification system is called upon to notify the performer. Where a response is expected from the notification, the workflow execution branches according to the transition defined for the specific response. Where no response is expected from the notification, the workflow execution continues with the next activity in the process. The Workflow Engine continues following the workflow process until it encounters an `End` activity.

As the process runs, a savepoint is set for each completed function activity. When the commit process is initiated, all completed activities are saved as part of one commit cycle. If an error occurs during the commit process, the database can be set back to any previous save point.

Activity Status

At the time an activity is executed, its state is updated by the Workflow Engine to one of the following status types:

- **Active**—The activity is in the process of being executed.
- **Complete**—The activity executed successfully and is complete.
- **Deferred**—The activity has been moved to the background engine to be run.

- **Error**—The activity has encountered an error during execution.
- **Notified**—The activity is waiting for a response to a notification or from an external program.
- **Suspend**—The activity is placed on hold until released by the system administrator.
- **Waiting**—The activity is waiting for other activities to complete in order to continue processing.

Note

Only the workflow administrator can suspend a process. If a notification has been sent and is responded to while the process is suspended, the response will be saved and held until the system administrator removes the process from suspended mode.

CALLING THE WORKFLOW ENGINE

The Workflow Engine manages processes and applies Workflow Engine APIs to function activities. The engine must be informed when an activity completes. The `WF_ENGINE.CompleteActivity()` API automatically calls the engine when process, notification, and function activities complete.

If a response is required from a notification activity, users must be sure that the form or Web page calls the `WF_ENGINE.CompleteActivity()` API when the transaction is completed by the user's response. Also, if the function's activity calls an external program, be sure to code that program to call the engine when its processing completes.

WORKFLOW PROGRAM INTERFACES

Oracle APIs are grouped logically based on function. For example, WF_ENGINE APIs start or run processes, communicate attribute information, and state changes that take place. Each item is uniquely identified by its item type and key and is passed to subsequent API calls for each specific process.

Following is a list of PL/SQL packages that contain workflow APIs (procedures/functions):

WF_CORE

WF_DIRECTORY

WF_ENGINE

WF_MONITOR

WF_NOTIFICATIONS

WF_PREF

WF_PURGE

WF_QUEUE

FND_DOCUMENT_MANAGEMENT

UNDERSTANDING THE BACKGROUND ENGINE

The background engine is a set of PL/SQL procedures within the package WF_ENGINE. The background engine runs processes and activities that are too costly to run in real-time and runs them in a batch process. All deferred or timed-out activities that satisfy the arguments of the procedure at the time the procedure is invoked are executed using the background engine. If new processes and activities are deferred or timed-out, they are held until the next time the background engine is initiated. The background engine can be run for a specific item type or all item types, for deferred activities, for timed-out activities, or for both.

Tip

11.5.4 (or the iProcurement patch to 11.5.3) introduces a new parameter to the Background Engine program called Stuck Activities. After this patch is applied, all scheduled executions of the background engine error out and have to be restarted.

The users must start at least one background engine if any deferred processes or activities have been defined. This process is available from the System Administrator responsibility.

Tip

If the users set up only one background engine, be sure it is set to handle deferred, timed-out and stuck processes for all item types.

DEFERRED PROCESSES

The Oracle Workflow Engine uses threshold and activity costs to determine which activities are deferred and which are run in real-time. The default threshold of the Workflow Engine is set at 50. The cost has no bearing on time or money but is an arbitrary scale defined by Oracle with 0 being the minimum and 100 being the maximum. The cost of individual activities is, by default, 0.

Given the default threshold of the Workflow Engine at 50, if an activity's cost is 50 or lower, the Workflow Engine determines that the activity is a real-time activity and processes it as such. If the activity's cost is specified to be more than 50, the activity is deferred to be run by the background engine.

There are two ways to defer an activity. Because the default cost of individual activities is 0, the threshold of the Workflow Engine can be set to less than 0 (say, -1) so that any activity started after that will be deferred. You must remember to immediately reset the threshold to the default value. Alternatively, the cost of an individual activity must be specified to be a higher value (say, 100). In this case, you don't need to reset the value of default threshold after starting the activity.

TIMED-OUT PROCESSES

When an activity times out, the Workflow Engine calls on the notification system to deliver the notification. The activity's status is then updated to *notified*. The background engine assigned to timed-out processing monitors the system for activities having the notified status. If the activity's timeout values have been exceeded, it is marked as having timed out. The Workflow Engine is called to follow the timeout transition.

USING THE WORKFLOW DIRECTORY SERVICES

Oracle Workflow Directory Services enable Workflow users to define who users are and what roles they play in the process. The user creates a directory repository that is referenced by Oracle Workflow and that contains user and role information. The user repository is made up of three database tables with the following views: `WF_ROLES`, `WF_USERS`, and `WF_USER_ROLES`. Each view contains required information about a user or role.

An understanding of workflow terms enables the user to better understand workflow configuration:

- **Role**—One or more users who share a common bond such as a common responsibility.
- **Directory Repository**—A set of database tables and views that contains user information.
- **`WF_ROLES`**—Roles, responsibilities, or positions referenced in a directory repository. Currently maps to `WF_USERS`, Oracle HRMS positions, Oracle Applications responsibilities, Oracle engineering approval lists, and `WF_LOCAL_ROLES`.
- **`WF_USERS`**—Actual users of the system. Currently maps to Oracle HRMS employees, Oracle receivables, customer contacts, and `WF_LOCAL_USERS`.
- **`WF_USER_ROLES`**—Combines `WF_ROLES` and `WF_USERS`.

Three local tables are used when the Oracle Workflow cartridge is installed. They can be used to add information about users and roles that is not included in the existing directory repository. These local tables are `WF_LOCAL_USERS`, `WF_LOCAL_ROLES`, and `WF_LOCAL_USER_ROLES`.

Tip

Local tables are optional and are generally used when utilizing Workflow as a standalone system with applications other than Oracle applications. In order to enter data into the `WF_LOCAL` tables, users must use SQL*PLUS or create a custom application interface.

CREATING A WORKFLOW PROCESS

A workflow process is made up of the following six components:

- **Item type**—A group of workflow components that must be associated with a specific item type.
- **Item type attribute**—A component of an item type that can be referenced by an activity.

- **Process activity**—The graphical diagram of a business process including function, notification, and process activities.
- **Function activity**—Actual automated running of a process as defined in a PL/SQL stored procedure.
- **Notification activity**—Activity that sends a message to a user and may require the user to respond.
- **Lookup type**—List of values.

USING THE WORKFLOW BUILDER

The Workflow Builder consists of a navigation tree containing a list of all process components needed to develop a workflow diagram. The users can drag and drop process, notification, and function activities from the navigation tree into a process window.

PLANNING THE PROCESS

The process should be planned thoroughly on paper before using Workflow Builder to create and diagram the process. Always look at a process as a work in progress and design it to be flexible to encompass future changes.

With Workflow 2.5, you can actually do this planning using Workflow Builder. Because you can now build top-down designs, your starting point is the top process. Therefore, you start adding subprocesses, activities, notifications, and other components as you go.

Tip

A process should be broken into key components in order to make modification easier.

When a process is being run by Workflow and changes are made to that process, the changes are not recognized until the process starts anew. If the users break the process into components, it then can be modified while the process is running and inserted before it reaches that point in the process. This will ensure the change is recognized during the current process run. Process planning steps should include the following:

1. Identify the business needs that the process encompasses.
2. Determine the activities needed for the process.
3. Determine how the process will be triggered. Is it triggered by a completed transaction or some other condition?
4. Identify the expected results of the process and define the possible results as lookup codes in a lookup type.

PROCESS ACTIVITIES

Process activities produce an expected result that users can then define as a lookup type. An example of this is the Employee Requisition Approval process, which can be completed with an approved or rejected result. Both codes, approved and rejected, are defined in the lookup type.

FUNCTION ACTIVITIES

Function activities return a result that determines the next transition in the Workflow process. The users define the result as a lookup code. For example, in the Employee Requisition Approval process, the function that finds an approver returns TRUE or FALSE. The workflow process branches differently depending on whether an approver is found.

NOTIFICATION ACTIVITIES

Notification activities can be just an informational note or they can require a response from the recipient.

If the message sent by the notification activity is informational only, a response is not required. The users should create and include `Send` message attributes in the message.

If the message requires a response, users must create `Send` message attributes that provide adequate information so that the recipient can make a decision and respond. The user also creates `Respond` message attributes that prompt the user to respond. If the message requires a response, a particular response generally will define the route that the notification activity will take. This is called *branching activity*. The Workflow Builder automatically creates an attribute with the internal name `RESULT`. `RESULT`, therefore, is a reserved word and can't be used as an internal name for any other attributes. You must specify a display name and lookup type for this attribute.

DEFINING THE ITEM TYPE

Item types are defined in the data store or the workspace using the Item Type Properties page.

When defining a new item type, Workflow requires that the users give it a unique internal name. The internal name must be all uppercase and cannot have any spaces or colons. The maximum length is eight characters. Internal names are used by Oracle Workflow APIs, SQL scripts, and PL/SQL procedures to identify an attribute. If the user deletes an item type, the user also deletes the internal name.

The user next must assign a display name and optional description to the item type. The display name will appear in the navigator tree.

The item type selector/callback function is a PL/SQL procedure that the Workflow Engine can call prior to executing an activity. It enables an item type to have multiple workflow processes associated with it. Based on the selector callback/function, an item type can determine the correct process to run. The command for this is RUN. It can also be used to reset (SET_CTX) or test (TEST_CTX) context information for an item type prior to running an activity.

With previous versions of Workflow it was not possible to change the internal name of an item type. The only workaround was to copy the item type, paste it in the navigator, and then give it a new internal name. Workflow 2.5 includes a SQL script on the server to change the internal name of an item type. You should make a backup copy of your item type before running this script. After you change the internal name using this script, test the workflow several times with all combinations of transactions.

Defining Item Type Attributes

Item type attributes determine what values are valid and how the attribute is used. The following attribute types define the characteristics of your items:

- **Text**—Alpha text that has a specified character length.
- **Number**—A number can have an optional format mask.
- **Date**—A date can have an optional format mask.
- **Lookup**—One of the lookup values associated with a lookup type.
- **Role**—A role name from the list of role names defined in the directory service.
- **Attribute**—A reference of the name of an existing item type attribute used in a process in which the user wants to maintain references.
- **URL**—A Uniform Resource Locator, which is an address to a network location. Allows users to access this address from the notifications Web page.
- **Form**—This includes the internal function name and optional form parameters of an Oracle applications form. Users might have access to these parameters from the Notification Viewer form.
- **Document**—This is an attached document defined by a document type. It includes the name of the document management system and a document reference.

Defining Lookup Types and Codes

Within a process, lookup types provide a predefined list of values when referenced by activities, attributes, and notifications.

Although a lookup type must be associated with an item type, it can be referenced by components of other item types. Usually, lookup types are referenced as results types.

The lookup code is the internal name associated with the lookup type. Once an internal name is defined, the lookup code cannot be changed.

An example of a lookup type is the Approval lookup type included in the Standard item type that comes installed with Workflow. It has two lookup codes: APPROVE and REJECT.

Defining Messages and Message Attributes

Messages must be created separately in the navigator and then associated with a notification. When creating a message, the user provides an internal name, a display name, and a description of the message. The user also must specify the priority of the message. Each message has its own priority.

Tip

Oracle defaults the message sort based on priority. This functionality is available when the recipient uses the notifications summary or browser but is not accessible by e-mail.

The Body Property page is where users define the message subject and text. Once a message is defined, users can assign message attributes.

Tip

Within the same data store, messages are not shared by item types. Lookup sets are shared by item types.

Linking an item attribute correctly is critical to your workflow performance.

Tip

When defining item attributes, users must specify that they will be used elsewhere, such as in message notifications. If they aren't defined in item type attributes, they can't be called by the message notification system.

Message Attributes

Whenever the users create a message attribute, it must be associated with a message. A message attribute behaves differently depending on how the user defines the message source. A source of `Send` allows the users to reference a constant or the runtime value of an item type attribute. A source of `Respond` prompts the recipient to respond to the message. The notification system uses a message's `Respond` attributes to generate the response section of a notification. A message can have multiple `Respond` attributes.

Tip

When you need to create a message attribute that references an item attribute, the easiest way to create it is to copy the item attribute and paste it in the message. Workflow Builder automatically creates the link.

Tip

To distinguish `Send` attributes from `Respond` attributes, Oracle has overlaid a red question mark on the Send icon to create the Respond icon.

If the users require a particular response to be the result of a notification activity, they must specify a display name and lookup type for the `Respond` attribute. This attribute is automatically created by Workflow Builder with an internal name of `RESULT`. `RESULT`, therefore, is a reserved word and can't be used as an internal name for any other attributes.

DEFINING A FUNCTION ACTIVITY

Function activities are normally used to fully automate steps in a process and return a completion result. The function activity calls on a PL/SQL stored procedure to execute this activity. Each function activity must have a cost assigned to it (default cost is 0).

ASSIGNING A COST TO A FUNCTION ACTIVITY

The cost of an activity determines whether a process is deferred to the background engine for processing, or processed in real-time. Generally if a function activity requires a large amount of processing time or resources, users should assign a high cost to the activity.

Oracle's predefined threshold for activity cost is 50. If an activity is assigned a cost of 50 or less, the activity is performed in real-time. If the cost is over 50, the activity is deferred to the background engine for processing.

HANDLING EXCEPTIONS

When creating a process, the users should always model the exception handling process. This will enable Workflow to handle all defined exceptions automatically. When an exception is raised, Workflow automatically captures the SQL error in the error stack. You must capture any error condition, set the context, and raise an exception. The APIs in the `WF_CORE` package can be used to accomplish this. The context and error stack is displayed when you view the workflow status through Workflow Monitor.

DEFINING A PROCESS ACTIVITY

Process activities must be defined before the users can diagram them. All process activities must be associated with an item type.

When defining the process activity, users must indicate whether the process is runnable, meaning a process whose instance can be created and started using `CreateProcess()` and `StartProcess()` APIs. A runnable process is indicated by a check mark in the Runnable box on the Control Properties screen under the Activities tab. Each item type must have at least one runnable process and can have more than one runnable process if necessary.

Non-runnable processes can be called only within other processes. They are referred to as *subprocesses*.

Looping allows an activity to be visited more than once. When setting up a process activity, if the Loop Reset box is checked, the loop will continue to execute until a specific result is returned. If the loop reset button is unchecked and the activity is visited more than once, the specified activity is ignored by the process.

Tip

For the majority of process activities, you can leave the loop reset button CHECKED.

DIAGRAMMING THE WORKFLOW PROCESS

Diagramming is the last step in a bottom-up design. At this point, diagramming a process entails no more than taking the activities the users have previously defined and using the icons to draw the process. However, in a top-down design, the process diagramming is where you start, and you define various components as you go along.

If your notifications use roles, before diagramming the process you must load all roles from the Oracle Workflow directory into Oracle Workflow Builder. Specific roles can also be determined dynamically. To do so, you must have a text attribute for the role and then set its value through one of the function activities using the `SetItemAttrText()` API. The default value for Performer in the notification must refer to this attribute.

Note

A node is a single activity in a diagram. An activity may be repeated several times in a diagram and each iteration is considered a node.

DRAWING THE DIAGRAM

To open an existing workflow diagram, open it from the database or flat file, expand the item type processes by clicking the plus signs (+), and then double-click the process activity.

To create a new diagram, select Quick Start Wizard from the File menu of Workflow Builder, and then specify an internal name and display name for both the item type and default runnable process activity. The Quick Start Wizard will automatically create the item type and default process from the template.

To draw a diagram, simply drag and drop the activity icons from navigator into the process window. An easier way is to right-click the whitespace in the process diagram and select a new activity (process, function, or notification). Each icon is considered a node of the process.

To create transitions, simply click and hold the right mouse button while moving the cursor from the source activity to the destination activity. The transition will follow the direction of the mouse.

Each process must have at least one start and one end node. These have the activity type set to Start and End, as opposed to Normal. When you use Quick Start Wizard, it automatically creates these two activities for the default process activity. When you add new start and end activities in other processes, you must go into the Node tab of the activity properties and change the activity type to Start or End from the default value of Normal.

Editing a Transition

A transition can be edited in several ways as follows:

- **Reposition a transition label**—Simply click the label and drag it to the new position.
- **Hide transition label**—Place the cursor on the transition, click the right mouse button, and select Hidden Label.
- **Bend a transition**—Click the transition and hold the left mouse button down. Drag the transition into the shape as required. This will create a vertex point in the transition. The user can reposition the vertex point to get the desired bend.
- **Loop transition back to its original activity**—Bend the transition as described previously. At the vertex point, select the transition arrowhead and, while holding down the right mouse button, drag it back to the original activity.
- **Remove a vertex point**—Select the vertex point and simply drag it to another vertex in the transition to combine the two points.
- **Straighten a transition**—Select the transition to be straightened and click the right mouse button. Select Straighten from the menu.
- **Alter transition result**—Select the transition and, using the right mouse button, select Results. (Used only when a transition has a result assigned to it.)
- **Lock a transition from further edits**—Select the transition and, using the right mouse button, select Locked from the menu. Be aware that any user with access to editing a diagram can release the lock.
- **Delete a transition**—Select the transition and, using the right mouse button, select Delete Transition from the menu.

Customizing a Node

The user can customize a node within a process by going into the Process Activity property page. Once the user customizes a node, its label name will be appended with an `-N` to identify it as a unique instance. You must select Show Instance Labels from the View menu of Workflow Builder to show these.

Setting Activity Attribute Values

An activity can be used many times within a process and the value of the activity attribute can vary from node to node. The user can change the attributes assigned to that activity in the Attribute Values control page.

REFERENCING STANDARD ACTIVITIES

Oracle Workflow provides a group of standard activities. Definitions of these standard activities follow:

- **Start**—Does not perform an action. Used as a designator to indicate the start of the process.
- **End**—Does not perform an action. Used as a designator to indicate the end of the process.
- **Noop**—Does not perform an action. Used as a placeholder in a process.
- **And/Or**—Used to converge branches of activities once those activities have completed.
- **Compare (Date, Number, or Text)**—When provided with a date, number, or text, compares the values in an item type attribute with the data provided.
- **Wait**—Pauses the process for the time period specified.
- **Block**—Pauses the process until a manual step or external process completes.
- **Wait for Flow**—Pauses a process until a designated process completes a specified activity.
- **Continue Flow**—Restarts the process paused by a Wait for Flow activity.
- **Role Resolution**—Determines a single user from a role that is comprised of many users.
- **Loop Counter**—Counts the number of times an activity has been visited or has looped.
- **Assign**—Assigns a value to an item attribute.
- **Get Monitor URL**—Gets and stores the Workflow Monitor URL in an item attribute.
- **Vote Yes/No**—Sends a notification to the users in a role and then tallies the Yes/No answers.

CREATING NOTIFICATION ACTIVITIES

A notification activity must be associated with an item type. Notification activities link the notification with the type of response expected. Notification activities also send notifications to all users who fit the role type.

When creating a notification activity, the default setup is to allow multiple users to be notified. Once a single user responds with a result, the notification is removed from all the other recipients' notification lists.

If voting is required, the Expand Roles box must be checked when setting up the notification activity. Voting requires all the recipients to respond to the message. The result is determined based on a user-defined formula and the process activity continues based on the result returned.

E-MAIL

If a notification is sent to the users via e-mail, the `Respond` attribute is written into the text of the e-mail message.

Tip

When users respond to a message, they must be careful to use the exact response allowed or the response will error.

NOTIFICATIONS WEB PAGE

Notification via the Notifications Web page enables users to respond by clicking one of the response buttons. Links to other Web pages can be provided within the notification as well. Figure 28.6 shows a notification in the Notifications Web page.

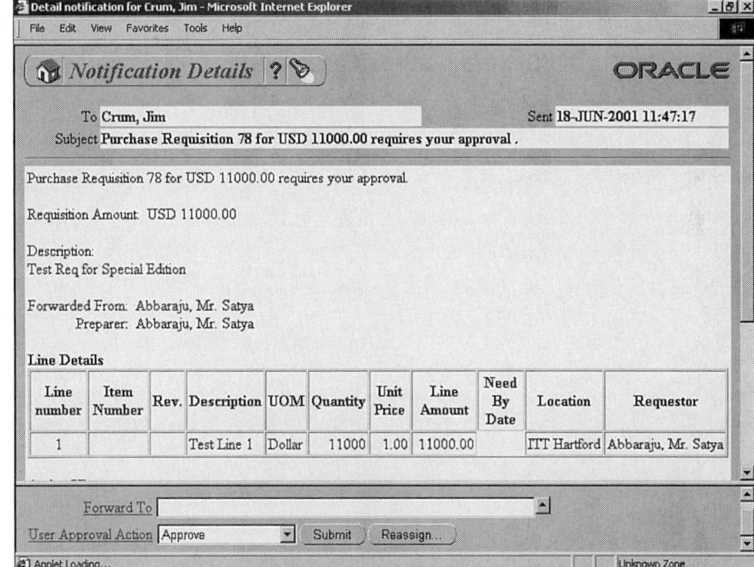

Figure 28.6 The Notifications Web page.

NOTIFICATION VIEWER

The Notification Viewer provides the lookup type pick list so the recipient can respond to a notification. It also enables drill-down capability so users can view Oracle application's forms.

AUTOMATIC PROCESSING RULES

The users can define rules for automatic notification handling. Each rule is specific to a role and can apply to any or all messages of a specific item type or message name. A rule can perform any one of the following actions: forward, respond, or no action.

Each time the notification system sends or reassigns a notification to a role, the automatic notification handler tests the notification against that role's list of rules to find the most specific match.

MONITORING WORKFLOW PROCESSES

Oracle Workflow allows users to check the status of a process using the Status form or using the Java-based Workflow Monitor.

Using the Workflow Monitor is the best choice, when available, because it provides significantly more information regarding process status.

WORKFLOW STATUS FORM

The Workflow status form is a standard Oracle applications form that displays process status information. Oracle has developed this form as a folder form so that users can adapt the displayed information to suit their individual needs.

The form can be called from any Oracle application form by using `FND_FUNCTION.EXECUTE`. The developer form name is `FNDWFIAS` and the function name is `FND_FNDWFIAS`.

Users must provide the following parameter information in order to tell Oracle Workflow which process they want to review:

```
ITEM_TYPE=<item_type> And ITEM_KEY=<item_key>
```

The Workflow status form provides information about the process' activity, type, status, result, start date, and so on. All information is in character, not graphical, format.

Figure 28.7 shows a workflow item status in the Notifications List Web page. You can drill down into the item to see details for each activity.

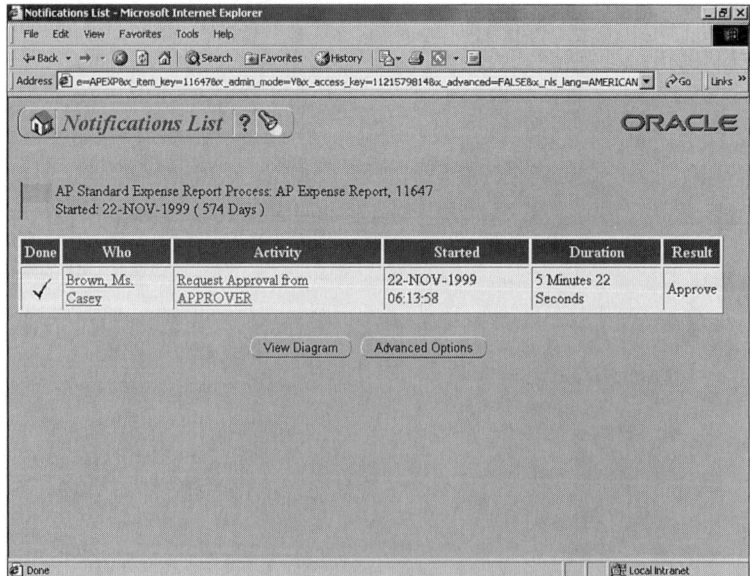

Figure 28.7
The Notifications List Web page.

USING THE WORKFLOW ADMINISTRATOR

The Workflow Administrator graphically displays the called process. The users get detailed information about the process' or individual activity's status.

Figure 28.8 shows Workflow Administrator. You will see the process control path marked in green; you can also see the details of currently highlighted activity.

Figure 28.8
The Workflow Administrator.

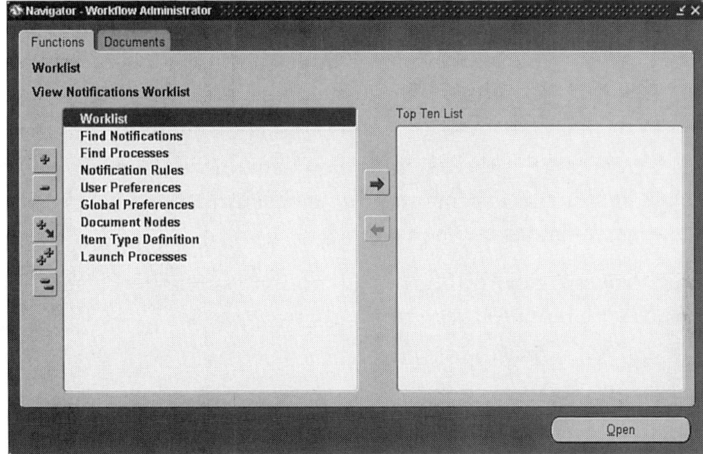

The form is divided into four areas—process title, process diagram window, detail tab window, and administration buttons—in order to give the users the most detail.

The process title provides the process name, item key, and user key that identifies the process the user is monitoring. The user can drill down to the subprocess level and the process title field will change to display the subprocess name.

The process diagram window graphically displays the process the user is monitoring. This is a read-only window, so there is no possibility of accidentally modifying the process from this form.

Oracle uses colored boxes to indicate the state of a process. Red means the activity has erred, green means the activity is in process or active, and yellow means the activity is suspended. A process can be suspended only using workflow administrator access and the user must be in administrator mode.

The transition arrows between the activities are color coded as well. A thick green line indicates that a transition path has been traveled, whereas a black line indicates it has not.

To receive more detail on an activity, you simply click the icon in the detail tab window. By clicking an empty space in the diagram, you can deselect any activity that was previously selected.

To drill down to the subprocesses, double-click an activity. The subprocess is then displayed and its information appears in the detail tab window.

The detail tab window provides detailed information about the process or activity. There are five tabs in which information may reside. They are as follows:

- **Definition**—Contains information about the processor activity's properties.
- **Usage**—Same as the definition but displays properties as a node in the process.
- **Status**—Shows status, result, and error information.
- **Notification**—Displays notification details if applicable for the activity.
- **Item**—Contains item type and attribute information.

The final section contains the administration buttons, which appear only when the user runs Workflow Administrator in administrator mode. Each button makes API calls when selected. The following six buttons may be available:

- **Abort Process**—Aborts the selected process, cancels any outstanding notifications, and prompts for a result to assign to the aborted process.
- **Suspend Process**—Suspends the selected process.
- **Resume Process**—Activates a suspended process.
- **Reassign**—Reassigns the notification to a different performer and requires the entry of a role name.
- **Expedite**—Enables users to roll back a process that has erred. It provides two choices: Skip the activity and assign it a specified result or try to execute the activity again.
- **Attribute**—Enables users to change an item attribute's value.

Reviewing the Process List

The process list allows the users to find specific process instances based on search criteria. All processes listed are in ascending order by item type, and then item key. Each process instance is summarized.

Reviewing the Notifications List

The notifications list displays all processes that have been sent to a role and require a response.

If an error occurs because of a notification, you can click the Result column to get more details about the error.

You can select the user link in the WHO column to send e-mail directly to the role that the notification was assigned to.

The Advanced Options button takes the users to the Activities List Web page, where they can specify filtering criteria to view other activities.

The View Diagram button brings the users to the Workflow Administrator to view the process diagram. This button can be used only when in administrator mode.

FILTERING THE ACTIVITIES LIST

The users can set up criteria to view specific process activities in the current process instance. The user can search by activity status—active, complete, error, or suspended—as well as by activity type—response notifications, FYI notifications, functions, and standard workflow items.

CONSIDERATIONS IN SETTING UP WORKFLOW

You should define and schedule at least one background engine to handle deferred and timed-out activities. You also must determine where notifications will be sent. All notifications can go to e-mail, which does not determine whose notification goes where. Additional considerations follow.

DEFINING THE `WF_RESOURCES` ENVIRONMENT VARIABLE

Be aware that if you are using the Workflow cartridge, you must customize the directory service views during setup. Workflow cartridge is installed when Workflow is a standalone system and is not being used with Oracle applications. The `WF_RESOURCES` environment variable is set up only when the user is using Workflow cartridge.

DEFINING A WEB AGENT

You cannot define a Web agent until you have installed Oracle Web Application Server. If you plan to use HTML statements, the Web agent is needed by the notifications mailer. The Web agent is also used by Oracle Workflow Web components.

ASSIGNING THE ADMINISTRATOR TO A ROLE

When assigning the Workflow Administrator to a role, you should map all users that will be given administration access into one group. This group should then be assigned to a single role in Oracle Workflow Directory Services.

CUSTOMIZING WEB PAGES

Oracle Workflow allows you to modify the Workflow's Web page to display the company's unique custom logo.

SECURING WEB PAGES

Securing the Web page when Oracle Workflow is embedded in Oracle applications is completed using the Oracle self-service Web applications security setup. This security is set up when completing the Release 11*i* installation. These setup steps do not require the purchase of Oracle self-service Web applications.

If the user is using the Oracle Workflow cartridge, secure the user Web pages with the authentication feature contained within Oracle Web Application Server.

USING NOTIFICATION MAILER

The Notification Mailer sends e-mail messages and processes responses for the workflow notification system.

The Notification Mailer scans the database for messages to be sent. It then reconciles the recipient role with the e-mail address, which is generally an e-mail distribution list. To encompass multi-language processing, Notification Mailer changes its database session to the preferred language of the role using the role and territory settings. When compiling the message, it selects information based on the message attributes. It then creates the message using a message template. The message is then sent using the Oracle InterOffice, Unix Sendmail, or a MAPI-compliant mail application. Responses are returned to a response account and the Notification Mailer calls the appropriate Notification API to complete the notification process.

SETTING UP MAIL ACCOUNTS

The user must have at least one mail account to send and receive responses. If preferred, the user can set up separate `Send` and `Respond` mail accounts.

Private folders should be set up in the `Response` account and named according to the value set for the `discard`, `process`, and `unprocess` Notification Mailer arguments. The process folder contains all processed responses; the unprocess folder contains unprocessed responses; and the discard folder contains discarded responses.

Note

Note that the Notification Mailer remains running unless there is a database failure or unless the PL/SQL package state changes for the session.

SETTING UP MESSAGE TEMPLATES

Templates are defined in the System: Mailer item type. The Notification Mailer has six predefined message templates, as follows:

- **Open Mail**—Used for notifications that require a response.
- **Open FYI Mail**—Used for notifications that do not require a response.
- **Canceled Mail**—Used when a notification is canceled. It sends a message of cancellation to the recipient.
- **Invalid Mail**—Notifies appropriate recipients that their response is invalid.
- **Closed Mail**—Used when a notification is closed. It sends a message to the recipients informing them that the notification is now closed.

- **Summary Mail**—holds notification summaries.
- **Warning Mail**—informs recipients of unsolicited mail they have sent.

Establishing Access Protection

Access protection does not provide security, per se. Workflow access protection prevents a user of a workflow definition from modifying seed data objects. Access protection enables users to control access to all workflow definitions except lookup codes, function attributes, and message attributes.

Oracle Workflow uses defined access levels as follows:

- Levels 0–9 are reserved for the Oracle internal workflow team.
- Levels 10–19 are reserved for the Oracle internal application object team.
- Levels 20–99 are reserved for Oracle applications and other Oracle product teams.
- Levels 100–999 are reserved for Oracle customers. On installation of Workflow Builder, the user is given a default access level of 100.
- Level 1000 is used for public access.

To protect an object from customization, the user assigns the object an access protection level equal to the user's current access level. If the user assigns the object an access level lower than the user's, the user will not be able to modify it. A level higher than the user's access level means another user can modify the object.

An object protected against customization is considered seed data.

Tip

A small lock appears on an object's icon to indicate that the object is read-only.

Workflow Definitions Loader

The Workflow Definitions Loader allows the user to transfer files between the database and a flat file (but don't tell your supervisor unless you want to bring work home!).

Use the loader to back up definitions prior to a database upgrade. Workflow Definition files have the .WFT extension.

The Workflow Definitions Loader involves a concurrent process that can be run in one of four modes: upgrade, upload, force, and download:

- The upgrade mode upgrades definitions from an input file and preserves customizations by using the access level defined in the input file.
- The upload mode uploads definitions from an input file while overwriting customizations using the default access code.

- The force mode uploads definitions from an input file disregarding access levels.
- The download mode downloads specified item type definitions to a flat file.

SETTING UP A DATA STORE

Setting up a data store is not difficult. It is critical that you build the data store step-by-step in the most logical manner. The version of Workflow in 11*i* enables workflows to be designed either top-down or bottom-up. Outlines for both types of design are included here.

The following outline gives you the appropriate step-by-step bottom up process to follow to ensure that all components of a data store have been configured in the correct order. Following are the steps:

1. Set Up Item Types
    - 1.1. Internal Name (eight characters or fewer, no spaces)
    - 1.2. Display Name
    - 1.3. Selector (if needed)
        - 1.3.1. Set Up Attributes
        - 1.3.2. Internal Name (column name in an Oracle table)
        - 1.3.3. Display Name
        - 1.3.4. Type (text, number, URL, and so on)
    - 1.4. Set Up Lookup Types
        - 1.4.1. Internal Name
        - 1.4.2. Display Name
        - 1.4.3. Lookup Code (the expected results)
    - 1.5. Set Up Messages
        - 1.5.1. Internal Name
        - 1.5.2. Display Name
        - 1.5.3. Subject
        - 1.5.4. Body (text and attributes)
        - 1.5.5. Drag Down Necessary Item Attributes and Create Message Attributes Out of Them
            - 1.5.5.1. Send/Respond
            - 1.5.5.2. Lookup Type
            - 1.5.5.3. Default Value (item attribute)
                - 1.5.5.3.1. If Source Is Respond, the User Must Create a `RESULT` Item Attribute
                - 1.5.5.3.2. Send/Respond
                - 1.5.5.3.3. Lookup Type

1.5.5.3.4. Default Value (a constant)

1.5.5.3.5. Set Up a `RESULT` for Every Message the User Needs a Response on

1.5.6. Priority (set on properties of message)

1.6. Set Up Notifications

1.6.1. Internal Name

1.6.2. Display Name

1.6.3. Result Type

1.6.4. Message

1.6.5. Timeouts

1.6.6. Expand Roles (used in voting or FYI to more than one person)

1.6.7. Change Icon

1.7. Set Up Functions

1.7.1. Internal Name

1.7.2. Display Name

1.7.3. Result Type

1.7.4. Cost (determines whether the user will defer an activity; if cost is above 50, the user must set up a background engine)

1.7.5. Error Process/Timeout Process

1.7.6. Loop Reset

1.8. Set Up Processes

1.8.1. Internal Name

1.8.2. Display Name

1.8.3. Result Type

1.8.4. Runnable?

2. Drag and Drop Icons from Navigator to Process Window
3. Draw Transitions
4. Customize Nodes (recipients for notifications, start and end nodes)

The following outline is for top-down design and gives you the appropriate step-by-step process to follow to ensure that all components of a data store have been configured in the correct order:

1. Invoke the QuickStart Wizard that Creates a New Item Type

1.1. Internal Name (eight characters or fewer, no spaces)

1.2. Display Name

1.3. Persistence Type

1.4. Number of Days (if Persistence Type = Temporary)

1.5. New Process Internal Name

1.6. New Process Display Name

2. Diagram Process

2.1 Set Up Lookup Types

2.1.1. Internal Name

2.1.2. Display Name

2.1.3. Description

2.1.4. Lookup Code (the expected results)—minimum two per Lookup Type

2.1.4.1. Internal Name

2.1.4.2. Display Name

2.1.4.3. Description

2.2. Set Up Activities (Notification, Function, Process)

2.2.1. Internal Name

2.2.2. Display Name

2.2.3. Description

2.2.4. Result Type (if want more than one branch from an activity)

2.3. Draw Transitions

2.3.1. Indicate Results

3. Add Details

3.1. Set Up Attributes

3.1.1. Internal Name

3.1.2. Display Name

3.1.3. Description

3.1.4. Type (Text, Number, URL, Date, Form, Document, Lookup, or Role

3.1.5. Length (Text) or Format (Number or Date) or Lookup Type (Lookup) or Frame Target (URL or Document)

3.1.6. Default Type (optional)

3.1.7. Default Value (optional)

3.2. Set Up Messages

3.2.1. From Message Tab

3.2.1.1. Internal Name

3.2.1.2. Display Name

3.2.1.3. Description

3.2.1.4. Priority

3.2.2. From Body Tab

3.2.2.1. Subject

3.2.2.2. Body

3.2.3. From Result Tab (if message requires response)

3.2.3.1. Display Name

3.2.3.2. Description

3.2.3.3. Lookup Type (must be the same as assigned to the Notification Result Type for which this message is designated)

3.2.3.4. Default Type (optional)

3.2.3.5. Default Value (optional)

3.2.4. Drag Down Necessary Item Attributes (automatically fills in all fields except Send/Respond and links back to item attribute)

3.2.4.1. Send/Respond

3.3. Finish Configuring Processes (must right-click each Process in the Navigator Tree and choose Properties)

3.3.1. From Activities Tab

3.3.1.1. Result Type

3.3.1.2. Icon (for all processes, the icon should be the yellow box with gears, as is the default)

3.3.2. From Details Tab

3.3.2.1. Error Process

3.4 Finish Configuring Notifications (must right-click each notification in the Diagrammer window and choose Properties)

3.4.1. From Activity Tab

3.4.1.1. Message

3.4.1.2. Icon (optional)

3.4.1.3. Expand Roles

3.4.2. From Details Tab

3.4.2.1. Error Process

3.4.2.2. On Revisit (Loop Reset)

3.4.3. From Node Tab

3.4.3.1. Timeout

3.4.3.2. Priority

3.4.3.3. Performer

3.5. Finish Configuring Functions (must right-click each notification in the Diagrammer window and choose Properties)

3.5.1. From Activity Tab

3.5.1.1. Function Name

3.5.1.2. Function Type

3.5.1.3. Icon

3.5.1.4. Cost

3.5.2. From Details Tab

3.5.2.1. Error Process

3.5.2.2. On Revisit (Loop Reset)

3.5.3. From Node Tab

3.5.3.1. Timeout

3.5.3.2. Performer

3.6. Configure End Nodes

3.6.1. Set Start/End to End

3.6.2. Result

PREDEFINED WORKFLOWS EMBEDDED IN ORACLE APPLICATIONS

Table 28.1 describes the areas where Oracle has embedded the workflow functionality. Additional workflow processes can be developed as custom workflows and linked appropriately. This list is sorted by alphabetical order for ease.

TABLE 28.1 PREDEFINED WORKFLOWS EMBEDDED IN ORACLE APPLICATIONS

Oracle Application	Workflow Process	Description
Application Implementation Wizard	Workflow is used throughout Wizard.	A set of Workflow processes that walks users through the implementation and setup of Oracle applications.
Applications Object Library	Standard item type.	The Standard item type has reusable workflow components that can be plugged into any of your workflow processes.
Internet Procurement (previously called Self Service Purchasing)	Receipt Confirmation Process.	Enables the users to confirm receipts on the Web.
Internet Procurement (previously called Self-Service Purchasing)	Requisition Approval Process.	An employee requisition is submitted through the appropriate manager approval hierarchy. The status of the requisition is also updated.

TABLE 28.1 CONTINUED

Oracle Application	Workflow Process	Description
Oracle Engineering	Engineering Change Orders.	Submits an engineering change order to the appropriate people for approval.
Oracle Federal HR	GHR Personnel Action Process.	Enables routing of Request for Personnel Action form for data entry, signature, and review.
Oracle Federal HR	GHR Position Description.	Enables routing of Position Description form for data entry, signature, and review.
Oracle Federal HR	GHR Within Grade Increase Process.	Enables automatic processing of Within Grade Increase actions without manual intervention.
Oracle General Ledger	Global InterCompany System (previously called CENTRA).	Notification and approval of intercompany journals over a set threshold, between sender and receiver companies.
Oracle General Ledger	Journal Approval Process.	Using an approval hierarchy and authorization limits, enables journal entries to be approved online prior to posting.
Oracle General Ledger	Step-Down Allocation.	Initiates the GL Allocation Process and directs the batch to the GL Mass Allocation Process or the GL Recurring Journals Process.
Oracle HR	Task Flow Item Type.	A predefined item type you can use to set up your task flows.
Oracle Order Entry	ATO Change Order Management.	Oracle Order Entry/Shipping Process Navigator flow.
Oracle Payables	AP Open Interface Import Process.	Based on setup, can verify and validate account code combinations in the open interface table. Used when importing invoice information from an outside system.
Oracle Payables	Credit Card Transaction Employee Workflow.	After the Credit Card Transaction Validation and Exception Report has been run, Workflow notifies users of transactions against their credit cards and enables them to review and respond to charges.
Oracle Payables	Credit Card Transaction Manager Workflow.	When the Credit Card Transaction Employee Workflow executes, Workflow also sends notification to the employee's manager for review and approval of the credit card charges.

TABLE 28.1 CONTINUED

Oracle Application	Workflow Process	Description
Oracle Payables	Expense Reporting Workflow.	Review and management approval process of employee expense reports. Used by both Web employees and Oracle payables.
Oracle Planning	Planning Exception Message.	Notification to suppliers, customer con-contacts, or internal personnel inform-ing them of planning exceptions and enabling corrective action.
Oracle Process Manufacturing	Item Activation.	Notifies an approver to approve a newly created item. The items are inactive until approved.
Oracle Process Manufacturing	Lot Expire and Lot Reset.	Notifies when a lot or sublot is expiring or is ready for retesting.
Oracle Process Manufacturing	QC Assay Testing.	Notifies QC analyst to perform tests on newly created samples.
Oracle Process Manufacturing	QC Sample Acceptance.	Notifies QC analysts to perform tests on newly created samples and manages testing results for acceptance.
Oracle Process Manufacturing	QC Sample Creation Notification.	Notifies and prompts a valid user to enter QA samples.
Oracle Project Manufacturing	Contract Project Definition.	Project Manufacturing Navigator Process flow.
Oracle Project Manufacturing	Indirect/Capital Project Definition.	Project Manufacturing Navigator Process flow.
Oracle Projects	Budget Approval Process.	Using the appropriate hierarchy, the project budget is routed to the correct managers for approvals and baselining of budget.
Oracle Projects	Project Approval and Status Change Process.	Using the appropriate hierarchy, the project is routed to the correct managers for approvals and notification of status changes.
Oracle Purchasing	Automatic Document Creation Process.	Automatically creates standard purchase orders or releases against blanket agreements using approved purchase requisition lines, but only if the requisition lines have the required sourcing information.
Oracle Purchasing	Change Orders Process.	Controls which change order documents must be reapproved. Routes appropriate change orders through the management approval process.

TABLE 28.1 CONTINUED

Oracle Application	Workflow Process	Description
Oracle Purchasing	Document Approval Process.	Performs all approval-related activities that exist in Oracle purchasing based on the appropriate approval hierarchies and authorization limits.
Oracle Purchasing	Price/Sales Catalog Notification.	This workflow sends a notification to the buyer when Price/Sales Catalog updates sent through Purchasing Documents Open Interface exceed the tolerance you predefine.
Oracle Purchasing	Procurement Workflow.	Allows transaction processing. This workflow enables you to perform all the steps in the procurement process. It includes Document Approval, Automatic Document Creation, Change Orders, Account Generation, Send Notifications, Price/Sales Catalog Notification, and Receipt Confirmation Workflows.
Oracle Purchasing	Send Notification.	This is a document maintenance workflow that identifies documents that are incomplete, rejected, or in need of approval, and it notifies respective users.
Oracle Receivables	Credit Memo Request Approval.	Routes a credit memo request for approval using an organization's internal management hierarchy and approval rules defined.
Oracle Service	Field Service Dispatch.	Inserts or updates service request data into the interface table and sends a notification to the field service engineer with dispatch information.
Oracle Service	Service Request Actions and Dispatch Process.	Routes a service request action to individuals in the organization for resolution. Also notifies, with instructions, the appropriate service personnel who need to be dispatched to a field site.
Oracle Service	Service Request Process.	Routes a service request to individuals in the organization for resolution.
Oracle Web Customers	Customer Self-Service Registration Approval Process.	Enables customers to receive authority, which consists of a username and password, for access to shipping information over the Web.
Oracle Web Customers	Order Entry Review Process.	Enables orders to be reviewed and approved or rejected online. Notifies salesperson and customer of approval or rejection decision.

TABLE 28.1 CONTINUED

Oracle Application	Workflow Process	Description
Oracle Web Employees	360 Degree Assessment Process.	Sends notifications to a group of people that they are to perform an assessment as a group. Responses from the group are also handled by this workflow.
Oracle Web Employees	Candidate Offer Approval Process.	Flows an employment offer through management approval hierarchy.
Oracle Web Employee	Career Management Reviews Process.	Sends notifications to reviewers for appraisals and assessments.
Oracle Web Employees	Employee Direct Access.	Enables employees to review personnel data as well as make limited changes, such as marital status and address changes.
Oracle Web Employees	Expense Reporting Workflow.	Review and management approval process of employee expense reports. Used by both Web employees and Oracle payables.
Oracle Web Employees	Person Search Process.	Controls navigation for entering search criteria and producing lists of people.
Oracle Web Employees	Person Suitability Match Process.	Enables entering of matching criteria for search purposes. Provides a list of employees who match criteria and produces a bar chart representing their skill sets.
Oracle Web Suppliers	Supplier Self-Service Registration Approval Process.	Enables a supplier to receive authority, which consists of a username and password, for access to account and shipping information over the Web.
Process Manufacturing Intelligence	Process Manufacturing Inventory Turns.	Sends notifications whenever the actual values of the inventory fall outside the target values defined.

TROUBLESHOOTING

My Workflow process is stuck! What's wrong?

This is a common occurrence when transition is ambiguous. Workflow Builder verifies that you have drawn a transition for every lookup code. When a function activity returns a value that doesn't match with one of the lookup codes, Workflow is confused with the transition. In all such situations, the workflow is just stuck! Therefore it is a good practice to have a `<default>` transition for every result.

Certain errors in PL/SQL procedures do not raise exceptions or do not return proper error codes. In such situations, the workflow is also stuck. The only way to overcome this is to test your PL/SQL code thoroughly for exception handling before plugging it into the workflow.

If this is happening with every run of the workflow even after fixing the previous two problems, it may be helpful if you loaded the workflow again. Before loading the workflow again, delete the existing workflow from the database using one of the supplied SQL scripts or the WFLOAD utility. Then load a clean copy from your Workflow Building or using WFLOAD utility.

My Workflow process is forced-out (terminated) with a TIMEOUT result! What's wrong?

This happens especially when the background engine executes a workflow process and encounters unhandled exceptions. When your PL/SQL code encounters certain database errors, but doesn't capture exceptions, this situation arises. To troubleshoot these situations, change your background engine parameters to include only DEFERRED processes, but not TIMEDOUT processes. The Workflow Engine will then show the actual errors that it encountered instead of the forced TIMEOUT error.

What does the check box Expand Roles do?

The Expand Roles check box, when checked, sends a notification to every user assigned to that role. Each user then gets to respond to the notification. This is critical for voting or FYI notifications. The Expand Roles check box, when unchecked, sends a single notification to all users assigned to that role, but when one user responds, the notification is closed to all other users responses.

Is there any debugging capability in workflow?

Workflow currently does not debug PL/SQL activity functions. Future additions of workflow should have some debugging capability. To debug a workflow, make sure all function activities are working correctly before linking them into the process. If you continue to get error messages, you can always insert `dbms_output.put_line` to see more specifically what logic is being executed.

My process does not loop where it's supposed to; what's wrong?

Verify that the Loop Reset is checked in the check box. The definition for each workflow activity includes a property called Loop Reset which is a check box on the Details property page for the Activity definition. This box should always remain checked unless you are a workflow expert. The Loop Reset property controls how the Workflow Engine behaves when it transitions back to part of a process that has already been executed. When a process transitions back over itself, it is called a loop.

CHAPTER 29

UNDERSTANDING MULTI-ORG

In this chapter

Oracle multi-org functionality enables you to have multiple sets of books, subledgers, and transaction organizations in one instance of an applications database. By using multi-org technology, an enterprise can gain the following benefits:

- You can use a single installation of the Oracle Applications to support any number of business organizations using multiple sets of books.
- You can define different organization models.
- You can have any number of legal entities within a single installation of the Applications.
- You can implement organization security by responsibility so that information is available only to users linked to an organization.
- You can automatically make intercompany transactions across sets of books and legal entities.

Oracle Applications and Multiple Organizations

Oracle Applications that are directly impacted by the Multiple Organizational process are Oracle Cash Management, Order Management, Payables, Projects, Purchasing, Receivables, Sales Compensation, Sales and Marketing, and Service.

Understanding the Key Tables

The multiple organization structure simply partitions key tables to provide for an ORG_ID number per row. This, in turn, is used to provide security and data segregation. Criteria used to partition tables include the following:

- The table contains a GL Account Code (code combination ID).
- There is a business reason for the table to be partitioned (for example, the entity should not be shared).
- The table contains transaction data.
- The table is an interface table where data being loaded is partitioned.
- The table includes a foreign key to a partitioned table and is accessed independently (in other words, not just as a child of a partitioned table).

The following Oracle Applications modules that are discussed in this book contain database tables that are secured by multi-org operating units:

- **Oracle Payables**—Chapter 12, "Using Oracle Payables"
- **Oracle Projects**—Chapter 15, "Using Oracle Projects"
- **Oracle Purchasing**—Chapter 16, "Using Oracle Purchasing"
- **Oracle Receivables**—Chapter 13, "Using Oracle Receivables"
- **Oracle Order Management**—Chapter 18, "Using Oracle Order Management"

In addition to the previous applications, the Oracle Cash Management, Sales and Marketing, and Services use the multi-org data structures.

CRITICAL IMPLEMENTATION FACTORS

The key to the implementation of a successful multiple organizational environment is in the planning. Organizational structure, responsibilities, security, and data replication are critical factors that must be taken into account.

UNDERSTANDING ORGANIZATION STRUCTURES

There are actually several dimensions at play within the multi-org structure.

Nine types of organizations are supported by the Oracle Applications, and you can define these organizations and the relationships among them:

- **Set of Books**—A reporting organization that uses a common chart of accounts, functional currency, and fiscal calendar. See Chapter 11, "Using Oracle General Ledger," for more information about sets of books.
- **Business Group**—The highest level in the organization structure is usually used to represent the entire enterprise or a major division. The business group secures the human resources information. Several sets of books can share the same business group, or a business group can have several sets of books.
- **Legal Entity**—A legal company for fiscal or tax reporting purposes. Several legal entities can share the same set of books.
- **Balancing Entity**—A segment in the key accounting flexfield and a logical divider for preparation of financial statements. The balancing entity is usually the company segment in the chart of accounts represented by the key accounting flexfield.
- **Operating Unit**—Associated with a legal entity and represents the basic unit of organizational security in Oracle multi-org. By choosing a responsibility, each user can access information for only their operating unit associated with that responsibility.
- **Inventory Organization**—Processes transactions and holds balances for a manufacturer or distributor of items.
- **HR Organization**—Usually represents a basic management or reporting group and exists within a business group.
- **Project Organizations**—Hierarchies that are defined in the Oracle Projects Application. These hierarchies are assigned to operating units.
- **Asset organizations**—Used to perform asset-related transactions in the Oracle Assets Application.

The human resources dimension consists of the business group and the human resources organizations.

The business group is the consolidated enterprise, a major division, or an operating company. It's the highest level human resources organization and holds all employees of the enterprise. You need more than one business group only if you segregate employees on an enterprise-by-enterprise basis. Oracle provides you with your first business group, which it has named Setup Business Group. You can change the name to be consistent with your company's naming conventions.

Under the business group are the Human Resources Organizations. These are used by the Human Resources module to segregate employees into reporting groups at levels lower than the business group, such as location or department. Refer to Figure 29.1 for a sample Business Group structure.

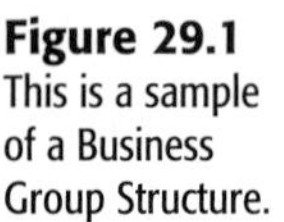

Figure 29.1 This is a sample of a Business Group Structure.

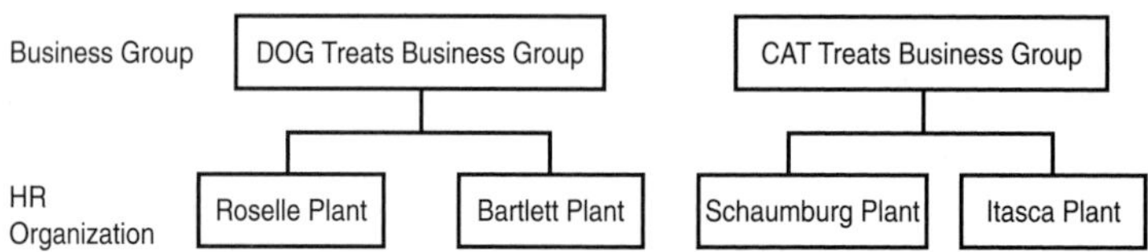

Tip

Lay out your organizational structure before beginning setup in the system.

The next dimension of the multi-org structure is the set of books, legal entity, operating unit, and inventory organizations. The first step to modeling your organization inside the Oracle Applications is to determine how many sets of books your company requires. A set of books is defined by the three Cs: Calendar, Currency, and Chart of Accounts. Generally, if the three Cs are the same for each company you are setting up, they can share a set of books. If any one of the three Cs is different, you must have separate sets of books for each company that is different.

Security can be set up to ensure that each company's data integrity is maintained if multiple groups of users in several companies share a set of books. Implementing security can be done by setting up security rules based on the balancing segment within the key accounting flexfield.

The next step to designing your organization structures is to define one or more legal entities. Oracle's definition of a legal entity is that it represents a legal company for which you prepare fiscal or tax reports, *but*—and this is a big but—the organizational legal entity currently within the multi-org structure only supports automatic intercompany invoicing and movement statistics within the financials. Legal entity is used extensively for the Oracle Human Resources Management System. You will explore some issues with this concept shortly. Legal entities are assigned to a set of books.

Finally, the operating unit is under the legal entity organization. The operating unit is an organization that uses any or all of the following applications: Oracle Payables, Receivables, Purchasing, Projects, Order Management, Sales Compensation, Sales and Marketing, Service, and Cash Management. Information is secured by operating unit, and each user sees information for only her own operating unit. A sample structure appears in Figure 29.2.

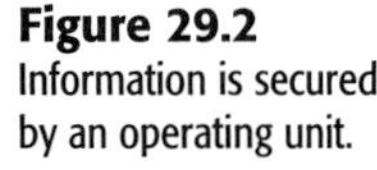

Figure 29.2
Information is secured by an operating unit.

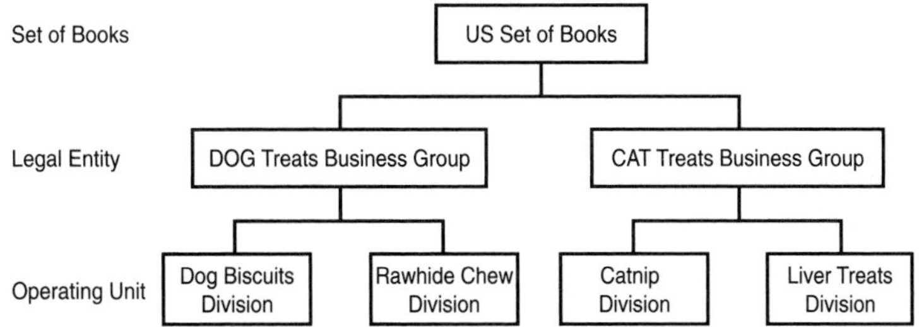

Within the operating unit are the inventory organizations. These organizations track inventory transactions, maintain inventory balances, and can manufacture or distribute products. You can have multiple inventory organizations that report to one or more operating units within the same set of books. Inventory Organizations have been inserted into the organizational structure in Figure 29.3.

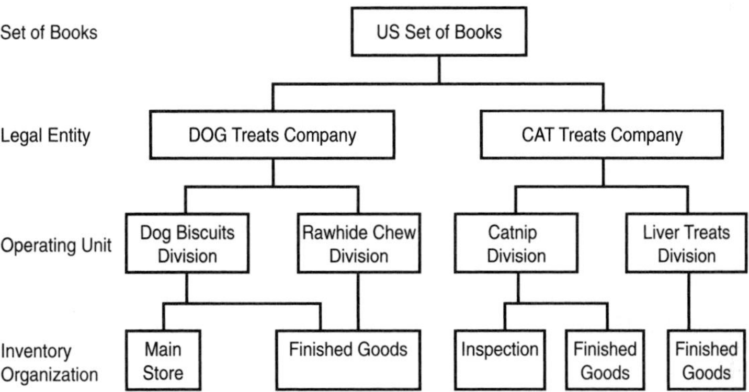

Figure 29.3
A legal entity can have multiple operating units, but an operating unit can have one, and only one, legal entity.

Here's an example to illustrate how this works. If both the Dog Biscuit Division and the Rawhide Chew Division share the same tax ID number, they can be separate operating units under the legal entity. Figure 29.3 is an example of this type of structure.

If they do not share the same tax identification number, you logically separate the legal entities into two separate legal entities. An example of this is provided in Figure 29.4.

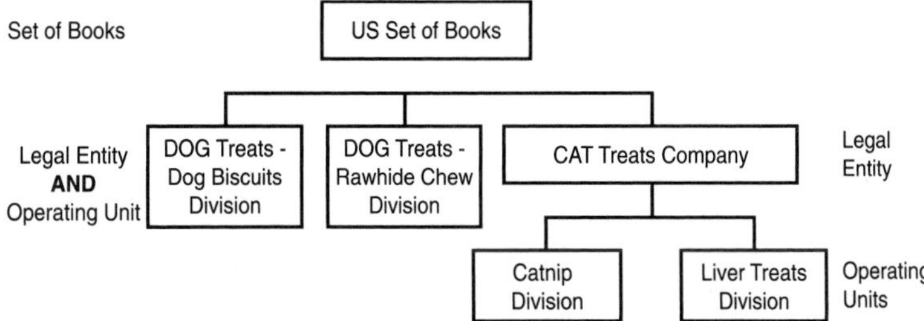

Figure 29.4
Each legal entity has its own unique tax identification number.

CENTRALIZED TRANSACTION PROCESSING WITHIN ORACLE APPLICATIONS

What about the company that wants centralized processing across legal companies? The solution is to create a single legal entity with one operating unit. Remember: Oracle uses the legal entity organization for automatic intercompany invoicing and movement statistics only. Tax reporting by each legal company can still be maintained separately for general ledger reports and subledger purposes by using the balancing segment in your chart of accounts as your legal company designator. Oracle defines the balancing segment as an entity for which you provide a balance sheet.

Therefore, if you centralize processing, you can use your balancing segment within your chart of accounts to separate legal entity data within the ledger. To report and process 1099s in Payables, Oracle provides a mapping for tax identification numbers to balancing segments under the Payables menu path: Setup, Taxes, Reporting Entities. See Figure 29.5 for an example of centralized and decentralized organizational structures.

> **Tip**
>
> **The key to setting up an effective multi-org structure is to determine whether you will have centralized or decentralized processing.**

DECENTRALIZED TRANSACTION PROCESSING WITHIN ORACLE APPLICATIONS

If you decentralize processing, you must have an Operating Unit and, if necessary for taxing purposes, a legal entity for each group that processes any or all of the following: Payables, Receivables, Purchasing, Projects, Order Management, and Cash Management. See Figure 29.5 for an example of centralized and decentralized organizational structures.

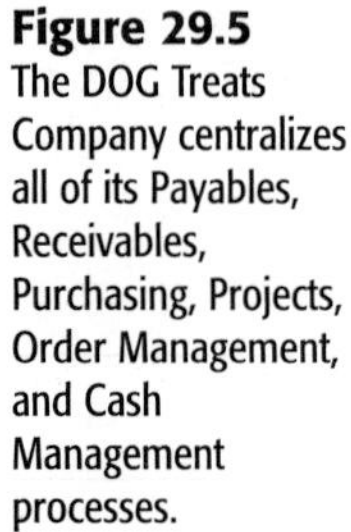

Figure 29.5
The DOG Treats Company centralizes all of its Payables, Receivables, Purchasing, Projects, Order Management, and Cash Management processes.

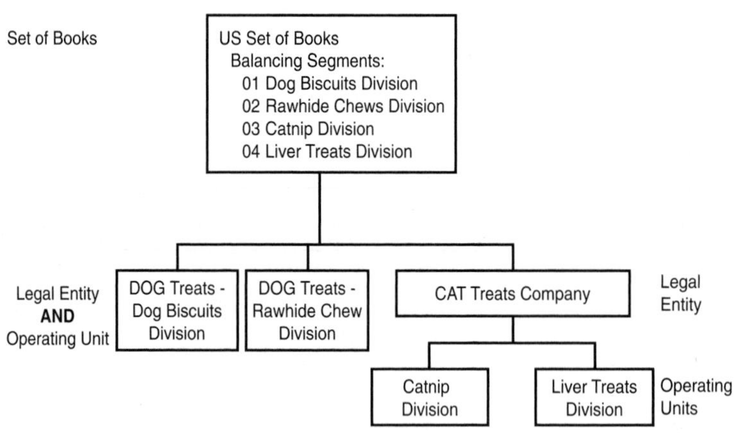

Limitations on Centralization/Decentralization Support

Except for a few Payables and Receivables reports mentioned later in this chapter, Oracle does not support a combination of centralized and decentralized processes at this time. If you set up multi-org as a decentralized structure, you can give your users access to all responsibilities that represent all organizations to create a centralized capability in a decentralized environment. The users must switch from responsibility to responsibility to gain access to each operating unit for transactions and reporting.

You can set up a quasi-centralized/decentralized environment. An example would be a centralized payables department and decentralized purchasing department where the Payables Department handles all supplier invoices and payments and the Purchasing Departments are split among the various operating units.

The users for the Dog Treat Company would be given the responsibilities listed in Table 29.1.

Table 29.1 Sample User Responsibilities

User Type	Responsibility
Centralized Payables User	
Payables Clerk1	AP Clerk—Dog Biscuit
	AP Clerk—Rawhide Chew
Decentralized Purchasing Users	
Buyer1	Buyer—Dog Biscuits
Buyer2	Buyer—Rawhide Chew

This enables the payables clerk access to all accounts payable information by switching responsibilities to access the needed operating unit.

Linking the Organizational Structures

You currently have a human resources structure and a legal entity structure. You now create the link between the two dimensions. This link is created within the system administration responsibility and involves setting up responsibilities and system profile options for each operating unit. A responsibility defines what functionality of an application is available and a responsibility is assigned to users. Each responsibility is assigned a set of system profile options. The system profile options link a responsibility to a business group, set of books, and operating unit.

Tip

Understand the link between your organizational structures and user responsibilities before beginning setup in your system.

Security

Data can be secured in several ways using responsibilities within the Oracle multi-org structure.

Each responsibility is linked to a set of books, a business group, and an operating unit. Each responsibility also can have its own unique menu structure to allow access to only those areas of the menu tree applicable to the user's job requirements. To provide the most flexibility, the responsibility is where data security is assigned.

Responsibilities can also be limited as to which inventory organizations they can view and enter data into. When the user goes to the Choose Inventory Organization window, she sees only those inventory organizations to which she has security access.

With few reporting exceptions described in the following list, Oracle multi-org structures do not allow viewing data across operating units. You must create custom reports to view this data.

Seed Data Replication

Data is replicated to multiple operating units when one of the following occurs:

1. When an installation or upgrade creates new seed data, the replication process is run as part of the setup procedures.
2. When a new operating unit is created and saved, the seed data replication program runs automatically to replicate seed data in the new operating unit.
3. The AutoInstall adadmin option, Convert to Multiple Organization architecture, is manually run as a concurrent process.

Configuring the Application

Before beginning system configuration and to ensure that your multi-org setup works as expected, you should always draw your organizational structure on paper before beginning setup. Add and revise components until it meets your company's present and projected needs.

Setup Steps

The following steps represent the required setup sequence for multi-org functionality:

1. Develop the Organization Structure. When developing your organizational structure, run through different process scenarios on paper before entering setup data in the system. Consider your business groups, requirements for accounting sets of books, operating units, and inventory organizations.

2. Define your sets of books. Each set of books you define requires that an accounting calendar, a chart of accounts consisting of your key accounting flexfield structure, and an active currency be set up prior to defining the set of books. Be sure to set up values for your retained earnings and intercompany accounts if you are using them because these will be required to complete your set of books' configuration. Make sure your choice of the balancing segment in the chart of accounts fits your organization's reporting, security, and intercompany transaction requirements.
3. Define your locations (names and addresses) for legal entities and inventory organizations in the Define Location window.
4. Define at least one business group. This task is optional because Oracle provides a predefined business group. You may modify the predefined business group. You should define all your business groups before defining any other type of organization.
5. Next, associate responsibilities with business groups. If you have several business groups, you associate each responsibility with only one business group. You may have to create many new responsibilities to implement the security and partitioning of your design.
6. Define the rest of your organizations. Be sure to use the correct responsibility for each organization when proceeding with the remaining setup.
7. Set up all your legal entities and then finally your operating units. By defining all of your organizations at this step, you help to ensure a streamlined configuration process when you define organizational relationships.
8. Define Organization Relationships. Remember that business groups and legal entities are separate structures. Business groups and legal entities are linked through responsibilities using the system profile options. Legal entities and inventory organizations are linked by a set of books.
9. Define responsibilities using the Define Responsibilities window as system administrator. Responsibilities define what functionality of an application is available to a user.
10. Set the operating unit profile option for each responsibility. The profile option is "MO: Operating Unit."
11. Convert to Multiple Organization Architecture. When your setup is complete, have your database administrator run the AutoInstall utility adadmin. Be sure to choose the option to convert to multi-org. This process should only take a few minutes to run.
12. Set the profile option "OM: Item Validation Organization" if you have a different item validation organization.
13. Set profile options specific to your operating units. For each responsibility, set the following:
    - HR: Business Group
    - HR: User Type

- GL: Set of Books Name
- OM: Item Validation Organization
- INV: Intercompany Currency Conversion
- TAX: Allow Override of Tax Code
- TAX: Invoice Freight as Revenue
- TAX: Inventory Item for Freight
- Sequential Numbering

14. Define Inventory Organization Security (optional). You can restrict your inventory users to selected inventory organizations by defining security based on responsibility.
15. Configure each application for each operating unit.
16. Use the Define Security Rule window to create various rules that secure data entry by balancing each segment of the key accounting flexfield for each legal entity. Each security rule specifies a range of values to include or exclude from the rule.
17. Run the Multi-Org Setup Validation report. This report will help you identify setup issues. Use the System Administrator Responsibility to run the report. This report gives you information on specific attributes on customers and suppliers and verifies that you have set up consistent profile option values for all your responsibilities.
18. Implement document sequencing if you wish to use this feature of the Oracle Applications. For each application that supports document sequences, make the configuration at the set of books level.
19. If you use the Multiple Organization Intercompany Invoicing function, define your intercompany relations.
20. Set the profile option MO: Top Reporting Level. The default is the most restrictive and is set for the operating unit.
21. Configure the conflict domains for each operating unit if you need to run two or more incompatible concurrent programs simultaneously. Incompatible concurrent programs from different conflict domains can run simultaneously. This step is optional.

Reporting

Multi-org is essentially a security system and tends to fragment the enterprise view so that members of an organization can only see and report on data within their own organization. For those enterprises with many organizations and some centralized business functions, multi-org in version 10.7 caused reporting difficulties because it was impossible to get an enterprise view of the data. Oracle has solved this problem by providing several key reports and profile options to enable reporting access to more than one organization at a time.

The profile option is called MO: Top Reporting Level, and it can be set to one of three levels at the responsibility level. To run reports across organizations, set the profile option for the set of books or legal entity level:

- Set of books level
- Legal entity level
- Operating unit level

Oracle Payables

The following reports can be run from any of the three levels and will therefore support some enterprises with centralized payables functions:

- Accounts Payable Trial Balance
- Payables Accounting Entries Report
- Payables Account Analysis Report

Oracle Receivables

The following reports can be run from any of the three levels and will therefore support some enterprises with centralized receivables functions:

- Aging - 4 Buckets Report
- Aging - 7 Buckets Report
- Aging - 7 Buckets by Salesperson Report
- Aging - 7 Buckets by Collector Report
- Aging - 7 Buckets by Account Report
- Credit Hold Report
- Customer Credit Snapshot

Troubleshooting

If in doubt, call Oracle Support. Once in a while the multi-org functionality will not replicate setup data no matter what you do. Oracle Support should be able to help you out.

If user responsibilities suddenly begin to point to the wrong organization, check your site-level profile options using the System Administration responsibility. If someone has changed the site level MO:Operating Unit value, and the responsibility level value has not been assigned, you will have this problem.

Never rearrange your organizational structure by reassigning operating units to different legal entities or business groups. Set up new operating units and new responsibilities pointing to them. Your historical data will remain available in the old organization, new data in the new organization.

PART IV

APPENDIXES

APPENDIX

Employment Market

In this appendix

INTRODUCTION

The employment market for skilled Oracle professionals has been quite robust throughout the 1990s and early 2000s. To understand the Oracle market, you must first understand what the varied skills that establish a person as an Oracle professional are. It is interesting to see how the demands for Oracle professionals have changed over time.

Recall that Oracle Corporation changed information system departments within corporate America, and throughout the world, by creating superior relational database products and tools. Many companies, such as SAP and PeopleSoft, approached the information technology market by building solid HRMS, Manufacturing, and Financial applications that were built on a relational database. The relational database of choice was often Oracle.

Thus, there were heavy technical "roots" in the early Oracle professionals. These individuals often were known for strong database administration skills. They had to understand how to manage the intense database system requirements of products that were created by companies such as SAP and PeopleSoft. In addition, strong data architecting (modeling skills) were needed for customizations to these products.

Next, Oracle Corporation began to make an aggressive push into the applications market, most notably in the financial area. Based on the success of Oracle Financial applications, Oracle began creating Manufacturing and Projects applications and finally Human Resources Management System (HRMS) applications.

This push by Oracle into the packaged application solutions market created new opportunities for IT professionals. A new need arose for functional consultants who understood the business issues of a financial institution. For instance, accounting professionals were needed to help provide advice regarding the configuration of the Oracle Financial products. Technical consultants were needed to prepare customizations, write reports, and write trigger code at the form and database levels for specific Oracle Applications. These technical consultants became proficient in SQL (structured query language), PL/SQL (procedural SQL), and SQL*Loader.

This new Oracle Applications software market created a new distinction in identifying skills for an "Oracle professional." The skills of the functional accountant are fairly easy to distinguish from the skills of a technical database administrator (DBA). However, there was now a new classification of technical skills that had arisen to use technical experts who had obtained a thorough understanding of the exact tables and table relationships within and among the various Oracle Application modules. The DBA was no longer the only type of technical Oracle professional. Whereas the DBA might often have had the technical expertise to become a strong technical Oracle Applications professional, the DBA often found that she did not have time to become an expert of both disciplines. Thus, technical Application experts emerged.

The problem-solving products most commonly used by the technical Application experts were Oracle Forms and Oracle Reports. Many technical application specialists took their knowledge of the Oracle tools and transitioned fairly easily in problem solving between the various Oracle Financial modules. Additionally, the database schemas among the various Oracle Financial modules were very similar. It was, and still is, common for a strong Oracle Accounts Receivable or Fixed Asset expert to become proficient on Oracle General Ledger or Accounts Payable in a short amount of time.

During the second half of the '90s, Oracle Corporation threw a curve ball at the packaged applications industry with the creation of the Oracle Human Resources Management Suite (HRMS). This is described as a curve ball because the intricacy of the database design was more complex than the Oracle Financial modules. The emergence of Oracle HRMS created two new types of experts: functional HRMS professionals and technical HRMS professionals. In the early 2000s, Oracle has expanded to numerous new Applications, such as Advanced Benefits (OAB) and the Customer Relationship Management (CRM) Applications. Thus, at this point, it would be fair to classify the primary different types of Oracle Professionals as follows:

Database Administrators

Technical Financial/Project Accounting /Manufacturing Experts

Technical Human Resources Management System Experts

Functional Manufacturing Experts

Functional Financial Experts

Functional Project Accounting Experts

Functional Human Resources Management System Experts

The question often arises, why is Oracle HRMS (Human Resources, Payroll, Advanced Benefits, Time Capture/Time Management, and Training Administration) so much more complex? For starters, the Oracle HRMS development group created a new approach to interfaces for data conversion and migration. Previous Oracle Applications used "Interface" tables to receive and provide import for data. The Oracle HRMS Applications included numerous (more than 60) application program interfaces (APIs).

However, the HRMS technical complexity did not stop there. Understanding the Oracle HR tables is not overly difficult, but understanding the Oracle Payroll tables is. Many strong technical Oracle Financial developers discovered that a significant learning curve exists in Oracle HRMS, primarily due to Oracle Payroll complexity.

Throughout this discussion of the development market, other skills became important. The tools mentioned earlier, such as Oracle Forms and Oracle Reports, did not have to be used only on Oracle Applications. Custom software applications can be created with these Oracle tools used for user interface and data retrieval. Thus, some Oracle technical experts were skilled with Oracle tools but had no exposure to database administration nor to the Oracle Applications.

Oracle Forms did not overwhelm various business professionals as a user interface. The standards within the Oracle Forms product were usually not CUA (Common User Access) compliant. Recall that CUA was established in the 1980s primarily because of the influence of Microsoft with its Windows Operating System and IBM with its OS/2 Presentation Manager Operating System. Oracle Forms was far less robust and user-friendly than Presentation Manager, Windows, and even PowerBuilder. Thus, the demand for Oracle tools experts did not become overwhelmingly high if these professionals did not have associated Oracle Applications experience. The demand did exist, but not to the extent of the functional and technical disciplines addressed earlier. But the Oracle Forms *6i* product has been introduced with Release 11*i* of the Applications. Forms *6i* has a more consistent touch and feel—similar to using a standard Internet browser.

As the late '90s and early 2000s arrived, still new technical experts were required. These professionals included Web experts. The Oracle Applications are now Web-enabled, requiring new training and new disciplines even for Oracle Applications technical specialists. For example, the necessity for implementing Oracle Workflow in support of the various Oracle Self-Service modules has introduced a new set of technical disciplines.

I have certainly left out numerous other skills and employment opportunities that were influenced by the Oracle market. Consider the following.

Programmers were necessary. Managers, designers, developers, and testers were necessary to create each of the Oracle products. As the Oracle products (from the database to the tools to the applications) became more popular, Oracle needed to greatly expand its Sales and Marketing staffs. Moreover, as the various Oracle products gained industry momentum, the need for experienced consultants grew. Thus, skilled recruiters found significant work in locating and matching talented consultants with clients in need of assistance for their implementations.

Skills Needed to Become a Consultant

The high demands for skilled consultants often inspire individuals to ask, "What must I do to become an Oracle Consultant?" First, as you read the section in this chapter on how the Oracle market developed, you must first identify what type of Oracle professional you want to be. The disciplines that can be pursued are functional, technical, and project management.

Technical Consultants

A technical consultant must have a strong knowledge of relational database concepts (for example, operational primitives, functional dependencies, normalization forms) and the Oracle tools (particularly Oracle Reports). A technical understanding of Oracle Workflow is a growing need that is based on the explosion of Oracle's Self-Service Applications. If the technical consultant desires to be a DBA, there are specific relational database skills related to sizing a database and tuning a database that must be learned. If the technical consultant desires to assist with implementations of the Oracle Applications, he needs to master the database model for the appropriate models desired. Other technical consultants must gain proficiency with creating blocks of program logic in PL/SQL and Java that can be stored in database packages, procedures, and triggers.

Functional Consultants

A functional consultant must have a strong knowledge of the business discipline associated with a particular Oracle Application. For instance, a Payroll professional must fully learn how Oracle Payroll performs its calculations. The Payroll professional should establish a solid understanding of tax rules and laws within the various government legislative bodies where the professional desires to implement Oracle Payroll.

Also, the functional consultant generally must obtain some moderate technical understanding of Oracle. A basic understanding of SQL is helpful to the functional consultant. Even if you have no plans to write intricate SQL scripts, it is helpful to understand basic methods for extracting or reviewing data that exists in the database.

One of the most overlooked skills of aspiring functional consultants is the need to be a problem solver. Technical consultants are generally trained to continually solve new problems. This is not always the case for functional professionals. For example, consider a solid accounting professional with 15 years of Accounts Receivable and Accounts Payable experience. This professional certainly understands many overall AR and AP issues. However, if this professional has worked for only one corporation during these years, it is possible that this professional has not been required to solve different industry approaches to paying or receiving payment from customers. Every new Oracle Application implementation offers some new variation of business problem solving.

Project Management

Another important discipline needed in some consultants is project management skills. Being a good functional consultant or a good technical consultant does not necessarily make the consultant a candidate to be a good project manager. Although project management techniques are a separate discipline, it is generally advisable for an aspiring Oracle project manager to also establish either a strong technical or functional background with various Oracle modules.

Database Administrator

Solid database administration is crucial for the operation of Oracle Applications. The database administrator must become an expert in the overall understanding of relational databases. The DBA should be responsible for installation, configuration, backup/recovery, fault tolerance, performance, and troubleshooting problems. The DBA must learn advanced SQL to help tune the database. The DBA, or other properly trained technical consultants, should be involved with the design review of any customizations, as they may affect database performance.

The DBA must be well organized to prepare strategies for system backup and restore. The nature of the assignments for a DBA requires an individual who can often work off-hours on a regular basis. To install new patches or perform backups and restores to an Oracle database, the DBA must minimize the business impact to users. Time left out of the system for a user can mean money lost for the business. The DBA's requirement for off-hours work is added to by the emergency needs of a system during the normal business day. If the Oracle system is not responding, the DBA must be available to bring the system back up as efficiently as possible.

A good DBA is easy to justify because an excellent one can easily improve performance and reliability of an ERP system by three to five percent. If you have 100 users on the system and they are three percent more efficient because you have a good administrator, that is the equivalent savings of three full-time employees.

Character Traits of a Good Consultant

Character traits might seem like an insignificant issue when dealing with the complex world of Oracle technology. There are many quality people in this world who do not have qualities to be a good Oracle applications consultant. Clearly, a good consultant must have solid Oracle skills. However, good skills alone are generally not sufficient to be a good long-term consultant. In the consulting industry, you basically have no assets (unless you are selling a product). The main thing that a consultant has is her reputation.

Here are some suggested character traits that you might want to consider if you desire to establish an excellent long-term reputation as a quality consultant:

- Clarity
- Accuracy
- Passion for the Product or Service
- Genuine Concern for the Client

Clarity implies good communication skills. Can you clearly communicate your suggested solutions to the client? Can you clearly understand the business needs being expressed to you by your client? Can you clearly communicate with written documentation to allow future employees of your client to understand how you solved their problem?

Accuracy is primarily built upon both knowledge and an honest communication of that knowledge. To be accurate about a subject, you must first fully understand the subject. When you understand the subject, you must communicate the correct answers to your client and not just the easy answer or the answer that you believe the customer wants to hear.

A passion for the service you are providing might not be necessary on a short-term basis. However, if you do not have a strong belief (or passion) that the service you are providing will bring significant value to your client, you will have difficulty maintaining a high motivation level long-term. If you do not have a passion believing that the products you are implementing are good, you will not maintain a high motivation long-term. Not every client will be excited about his Oracle implementation. It will often be necessary for the consultant to bring some enthusiasm and excitement to a project that is not superficial.

A concern for the client might seem obvious, but it still should be addressed. If you do not genuinely have a concern for your client, it will be difficult for you to maintain a high motivation level throughout a long implementation project. Moreover, it will be difficult for you to maintain a cohesive environment for project decision-making. It is really important to understand and actually care about the needs, emotions, and concerns of your client. An Oracle implementation can be overwhelming for many clients who have grown accustomed to doing business in only one fashion for their entire career. It can be challenging for a heavily experienced consultant, who "knows" the best answer based on her many implementations, to remain patient and accept that the best answer might not be chosen by your client. Without a genuine concern for your client, you find it difficult to be patient when you feel your experienced solutions are not being properly received and accepted.

Consulting Advantages

There are many advantages that consulting can offer. The challenging lifestyle of a consultant is worth a premium total compensation package. The most visible monetary advantage of consulting is the salary. Consultants tend to make higher salaries than they would in full-time operational jobs. The financial advantages of consulting often extend well beyond the higher salaries. If the consulting engagement requires travel, you can build up frequent-flyer miles quickly. Cashing in frequent-flyer miles to an airline for free travel is real money savings to the consultant. Frequent guest programs at hotels offer similar financial advantages. Other financial advantages to travel involve expense reimbursement. If the consultant worked in his hometown, he would have to incur a cost to eat anyway. With expenses being reimbursed, this is a cost savings to the consultant, which further improves his financial situation.

Perhaps the greatest advantage to consulting is that the job rarely becomes stagnant. If a person is a problem solver, consulting offers the potential to continually solve new problems at the next consulting assignment. The consultant has the opportunity to avoid maintenance mode of a system. While the client obtains a production system with procedures to handle the normal repetitive business, the consultant leaves to a fresh, new engagement. It is less typical for a consultant to become bored from a repetitive job.

There is another advantage to avoiding maintenance mode on a system. After the consultant leaves the project, he does not have to continually live with poor implementation decisions that were made by the client (although he might have to live with knowledge of any poor decisions that he personally made). The consultant gets to leave and tackle new challenges. If the consultant made mistakes on the previous job, as any human will do, he has the opportunity to learn in these mistakes and do an even better overall job on the next project. Every person will observe business-world decisions that he disagrees with. If a poor, or less than optimal, solution is made by the client, the consultant will not have to spend years in maintenance mode being reminded of a decision that was made against his recommendation. He simply moves on and solves new challenges on the next implementation.

The consultant often has the advantage of retaining expert knowledge. As you continually solve new problems for new businesses, you should learn from your successes and mistakes. As you implement Oracle systems, you will continually see the changing technology. This will allow you to stay current with new Oracle technology and further help you to remain an expert in your area of operation.

There are lifestyle advantages that a consultant can observe. The hotel lifestyle can offer many nice conveniences including a freshly cleaned room everyday. The hotel is often located near the client's place of business; so long commutes to the office are not necessary. The opportunity to see new places is a big advantage. Every area of the world has its own unique features and personality. Many times you cannot truly appreciate the region of the country or of the world until you have had an opportunity to spend time there.

Consulting Disadvantages

There are disadvantages to accepting a job in consulting. The biggest disadvantage is the impact on families. When consulting requires travel, there is less time to build those vital relationships with family members. Even when the consultant does not travel, long hours are often required on projects. If the in-town consultant comes home late from the project every night, a similar strain occurs on the family. All the advantages listed earlier will not equal the pain encountered if a marriage suffers. If you are considering a consulting job that requires extensive travel and you are married, make this a team decision. Here are a few suggestions to ease this lifestyle:

- **Communicate by calling home**—Stay in communication regularly (preferably daily) with your spouse and family.
- **Communicate and don't put things off**—Communicate with your family just as you would if you were at home. If there are important family subjects, don't wait for the weekend to address everything face to face. Otherwise, you will spend the entire weekend problem solving.
- **Maximize the quality of time together**—Because the weekend is your only time with your family, make sure it is quality time.
- **Remember the long hours**—Many non-consulting jobs or in-town consulting jobs require long hours. Remember that even if you've remained in town, you might often be working long hours anyway. Thus, the quantity of your lost time together might not be as much as you think.
- **Go on vacation**—You are building up frequent-flyer miles and frequent hotel stays. Let your family be the recipient of these benefits. Travel for free, and allow the family to look forward to these vacations!

Another disadvantage to consulting is the overwhelming pressure to perform. The client looks to the consultants as the experts. There are many project challenges that require detailed investigation and creative solutions. Being an expert consultant is not as simple as memorizing a book or memorizing a few implementation steps. There is pressure not only to come up with a solution for difficult challenges, but also to determine whether this is the best solution available. And if this were not enough, there is pressure to produce these solutions in a timely manner. The client pays dearly for your time, and you will want them to feel the value of their investment.

Burnout is another disadvantage of consulting. The high energy and hard work required to solve a client's problems do not subside when the project is over. It all starts over again. Many people only do one ERP implementation in a lifetime and barely survive. I know consultants who have done two projects a year for five years and are still alive to tell about it. This work pattern, combined with the other disadvantages mentioned in this section, can wear a person down. Many consultants will experience burnout and need to take a break.

Other disadvantages exist in consulting. Your consulting job requires enormous flexibility. Airport delays can't be easily planned for. At each new client, you are continually required to learn a new business and new business culture. You will not remain settled in because you always feel as if you are changing jobs. If a business culture allows for numerous competing agendas, you must be prepared that your issues might be neglected. This is difficult for a problem-solving consultant to accept; however, it is vital for the consultant to remain mature and adept in whatever environment exists. The work environment might not always be optimal and can impact your performance. You simply have to learn to deal with it. You have accepted this high-powered job as a problem-solver and should do so to the best of your abilities based on the constraints of the project. Remember, if a particular project has a poor work environment, you get to leave when the project is over.

Support Jobs

The Oracle Applications market has created the need for product support specialists. Some developers and consultants choose to work for Oracle Worldwide Support. There are several advantages to this type of position. Travel requirements are minimal. The opportunity for fresh problem-solving activities exists. Working for Oracle Worldwide Support allows employees to keep up with current releases of the Oracle products. In some ways, a support specialist is like a consultant because they are both solving customer-specific problems. The support personnel will often need to re-create the customer's scenarios on their own systems before recommending a course of action for correction.

There are some difficulties in playing a support role for any product, and Oracle is no different. The problems logged in by clients are often some of the more difficult ones that the client has encountered. These can be issues where the client and consultants have not identified a solution that is acceptable to the client. Other problems called in by the clients are often product deficiencies or bugs. Identifying bugs to the client is not usually a glamorous position. Tension can be high when the client calls Oracle WWS to have a bug addressed. The client wants things fixed and wants them fixed right away. It is not as simple as looking up the error message in a reference manual and telling the client how to fix it. If the errors are due to bugs, support personnel can be caught in the middle of tension between the development group and the client. The development group might require significant time to design an appropriate long-term solution for the bug that meets the needs of all clients. Sometimes, the development group will review the issue as being lower priority than other development issues. These are difficult issues to communicate to a client, and they add challenge to the job of Oracle support specialists.

Product Development Jobs

"Creating a better mousetrap." That is the goal of most software developers. There are many software development opportunities available at Oracle, software companies, consulting firms, and your own IT department. Developers are needed to create new products and to prepare upgraded functionality to existing products. Seeing the latest and greatest functionality can be very appealing. Moreover, being able to influence the direction of technology and product functionality can be even more appealing.

Oracle Corporation has been very innovative with creating new products and expanding functionality of existing products. This challenge should continue to create new jobs for top-notch developers. A successful product development effort also requires good management and solid quality assurance (QA) testing. Thus, project manager jobs are necessary to support product development.

Product development jobs are not limited to Oracle Corporation. Some companies review Oracle product functionality and focus on a particular area where they feel the product is deficient. These companies hire developers to create their own products, which can be interfaced to the Oracle products. Thus, new product development and consulting jobs can be created from third-party organizations. See the chapter titled "Finding Additional Compatible Solutions," on this book's Web site, for a list of other companies that make Oracle-compatible software products.

Sales/Marketing Jobs

What good is a superior product if no one knows about it? Oracle Corporation does an effective job of heavily promoting its products to new and existing clients through the Sales and Marketing staff. These jobs are available to people with good marketing skills. However, these jobs also require a desire to understand and learn the various Oracle products.

Sales and marketing are important in the consulting world, particularly for large-scale implementations. Rather than market the merits of the Oracle products, a third-party organization must be able to market its services. These companies must be able to demonstrate how they will add value to implementations through product expertise, implementation methodology, and many other distinguishing factors.

RECRUITING JOBS

The wide variety of Oracle-related job opportunities that have been described in this chapter creates the need for recruiters who are industry specialists. Recruiters must learn which of the particular skills (technical consulting, functional consulting, sales, and so on) are needed by Oracle Corporation, consulting organizations, and end-clients of Oracle. Then, the recruiters must identify where the best talent exists. Many companies do not have the time to keep an Oracle industry-specific expert employed who knows instantly where to find the best talent. Thus, recruiting jobs are an offset of the Oracle product growth.

WORKING FOR ORACLE CORPORATION

One way of keeping up with the latest Oracle-related technology is to work for Oracle Corporation itself. Oracle offers a wide variety of job opportunities similar to those that have been discussed earlier in this chapter.

Oracle Corporation employees have access to training classes that are generally offered prior to the public availability to outside companies. This provides Oracle employees (sales staff, consultants, support staff, and so on) with the most current technological information. Although having this advanced technological knowledge prior to the outside world is usually short-lived, the advantage should not be overlooked. There is always excitement and certainly value in having an up-front look at technology in any industry.

Oracle Corporation developers actually have the opportunity to shape future project direction. This is an intriguing opportunity that is worth consideration of top software developers.

Perhaps one of the biggest disadvantages in working at Oracle involves the overall company size. With corporate success comes growth, and Oracle has certainly grown at an impressive rate. However, growth causes problems at many large organizations, including Oracle. Large companies usually have added bureaucracy, which can hinder responsive decision-making. Other advantages and disadvantages can be reviewed in Appendix B, "Consulting Market," in the section "Larger Diversified Consulting Firms."

WORKING FOR ORACLE CUSTOMERS

One way to gain access to Oracle technology is to work for a client company that has implemented Oracle products. Numerous companies have installed Oracle databases. Many of these companies also use Oracle technologies for custom Reports and Forms development. Many other companies have installed various Oracle Applications on top of the Oracle database.

What are the advantages in working for a customer of Oracle? First, as stated previously, you have the opportunity to work with state-of-art technologies. You have the opportunity to monitor upcoming releases of the various Oracle products to help ensure that your organization is maintaining a competitive advantage in the marketplace. You can participate in enormous user groups through the Oracle Application's Users Group (OAUG, `www.oaug.org`).

Avoiding travel is another advantage. Many Oracle experts (whether they are Oracle Corporation employees or third-party consultants) have a requirement for a high level of travel. Some Oracle experts choose to work for clients of Oracle so that they can avoid the burnout of a prolonged travel schedule.

Job stability is also an advantage of working for a client of Oracle. The job responsibilities and assignments are more likely to be consistent from one day to the next when compared to typical job responsibilities of a consultant. Also, many clients realize their dependence on Oracle-trained employees and this brings longer-term stability. Most clients desire to keep their top Oracle-trained employees happy to avoid the costs of higher-paid outside consultants.

There are disadvantages in working for Oracle customers. For starters, not every Oracle customer desires to stay current on all of the latest Oracle products. Of course, this might not be a disadvantage to some people who prefer to avoid the headaches associated with bleeding-edge technologies. Another disadvantage involves the potential for monotonous routine. Many Oracle professionals desire new problem-solving opportunities on a regular basis. However, Oracle clients are involved or will eventually be involved in a maintenance mode. Maintenance mode of any system can become monotonous.

Another disadvantage involves the likelihood of less compensation. The value of a consultant trained on state-of-the-art Oracle technologies is heavily inflated over the typical value of an IT staff member responsible for maintaining an Oracle system or any other system. The Oracle client company must justify and balance the salaries paid to its Oracle-trained employees to the overall salary structure and policies of the organization.

WHAT HAPPENED IN THE EARLY 2000S?

Before understanding current Oracle employment trends in the 2000s, first consider a few issues that influence Oracle product demand and, in turn, Oracle-related jobs. Packaged software from companies such as Oracle, PeopleSoft, and SAP were selected in the late 1990s and are selected in the 2000s for many reasons. Companies such as Oracle can devote numerous man-years of effort to developing applications that they believe will meet the needs of the vast majority of their customers. Not every company has the ongoing budget to spend on many man-years worth of development. Moreover, even if companies have the budget, they must hire and retain a sufficient number of properly trained employees if they desire a high quality in their homegrown systems. They must hire sufficient numbers of people to cover both ongoing maintenance of the existing systems and future software development.

The issue of maintenance and upgrade of a company's existing systems should be discussed further. Legislative issues must be kept up to date. Suppose that the government establishes new reporting requirements for Human Resources reports for Equal Employment Opportunity or Affirmative Action Planning. These must be created in the homegrown system. However, if you owned Oracle HR, you could expect that Oracle will create a solution in a future release. Consider sales tax and payroll tax changes. If a company owns Oracle Financials and Payroll, it can expect that the Oracle product suite, through its relationships with Vertex, will include the latest tax legislation.

The point is that there are significant reasons why companies purchase Oracle products in the 2000s. Consider further that there is a competitive fear that many companies will experience within their respective industries. No company wants to lose ground to the competition or be less flexible in responding to the continually changing needs of its customers. If a company knows that its key competitors have installed the latest technologies from Oracle, it can influence the company to consider the same. Just because your competition makes a decision to purchase Oracle products, does not mean that it is the best decision for you. However, any successful company will monitor the actions and directions of its competitors and will desire to avoid being at a competitive disadvantage in any area of its business. For example, has your competition reduced costs by using software to make its supply chain more efficient?

In early 2000, many clients anxiously awaited the release of Oracle Applications Release 11*i*. When it was finally released to the public in May–June 2000, many clients were prepared to consider implementing the new exciting products, but, based on delays from previously announced release dates, they had believed that the release 11*i* products would be more stable.

I often recommend to our clients to delay using a new major product release for at least six months after its release to the public. However, an interesting thing occurred six months after release 11*i* hit the streets. Late in 2000, many segments of the U.S. economy had encountered major slowdowns and even recession. Later, Oracle Corporation agreed to extend its de-support dates for Release 10.7 of the Applications through December 2002. These two issues (economy and de-support date changes) gave many companies room to delay IT spending.

These factors have slowed implementation and upgrade plans of IT departments through 2001. However, the lure of the features or Oracle's Release 11*i* products is expected to fuel an increase in demand for Oracle jobs in 2002. In essence, the need for successful corporations to remain competitive with their technologies will fuel this increased demand.

It is my expectation that future demand will be very solid for Oracle products, and thus, future Oracle-related jobs should be plentiful. The Oracle market will probably not grow as explosively as it did in the mid-90s but probably will not remain as slow as it was in 1999–2001.

Upgrades to R11*i*, R12

Companies will choose to upgrade for a variety of reasons. New technological improvements at the database level could inspire clients to want to increase the processing speeds of reports and processes. New functionality for Oracle Applications that targets specific business industries such as public sector, higher education, and other vertical markets might influence existing customers to want to upgrade their Applications. New legislative product releases or changes to the Oracle products to accommodate new legislative changes will also influence many clients to need to upgrade. The major opportunity to reduce costs and streamline business processes by utilizing Oracle's Self-Service Applications will inspire clients to purchase Release 11*i*.

The message here is that Oracle database and application specialists will be needed over the upcoming years to assist clients with upgrades to Applications Release 11*i* and, eventually, Release 12. As the existing installed base of Oracle products grows, the market for upgrades to existing installations will also grow.

Phase II Applications/Functionality

There will be other Oracle employment opportunities that arise from current Oracle clients. Many new Oracle implementations have focused, and will continue to focus, on implementing core and "necessary" functionality. There might be many desired functions that have been identified during a requirements analysis that will need to be implemented in the future.

This desire for Phase II functionality or Phase II secondary applications constitutes a demand for skilled Oracle professionals. This demand is not likely to create as many new job opportunities as have other Oracle employment opportunities. However, the demand still exists and will create employment and other consulting opportunities. The Phase II project team sizes are likely to be a subset of the sizes of the original project teams as a general rule.

Many companies will attempt to solve Phase II issues using existing company staff that has worked on the initial implementation of the products. This is because the paradigm shift of learning new technology will be less of a hurdle. For example, consider a client that had identified many Phase II issues associated with desired reports. During Phase I, this existing client staff might have successfully learned the tools for Oracle Reports and the appropriate database model (AP, AR, and so on) from which the reports should be created. For more complex features and truly new features, there should still be need for outside consulting assistance to augment client staff, depending on the complexity of requirements.

Oracle Corporation Is an Engine of Growth

It is worth noting that there will be Oracle-influenced employment opportunities in areas not discussed in this chapter. Oracle Corporation can be viewed as an engine of growth. As the volume of Oracle product sales continues to grow, there will continue to be demand for more industry experts to satisfy that demand. As Oracle creates new products, there will be need for new product specialists.

APPENDIX 

Consulting Market

In this appendix

The consulting market for Oracle opportunities has experienced explosive growth in recent years. Solid opportunities still exist over the upcoming years. The nature of these opportunities will differ based on the type of consulting organization involved. The following includes an in-depth analysis of the types of consulting firms who specialize in Oracle expertise. This analysis reviews independent consultants; smaller, more specialized consulting companies; larger, diversified consulting companies; and Oracle Corporation consulting. The following analysis reviews advantages and disadvantages to consultants at each of these different types of consulting arrangements. The analysis also addresses advantages and disadvantages to the employing organizations that desire to hire Oracle-skilled consultants.

INDEPENDENT CONSULTING

Some heavily Oracle-experienced consultants choose to work independently of other consulting firms. In certain cases, these consultants are some of the most heavily experienced consultants available. This opportunity can be really appealing to the consultant who desires to maximize his earnings potential. These consultants tend to be quite confident and willing to take risks. In return, they have the opportunity to make more money than other nonindependent consultants with similar skills do because there are no middlemen in their own corporation sharing in the revenues they generate.

INDEPENDENT CONSULTING: ADVANTAGES TO CONSULTANT

There are advantages for consultants who desire to remain or become independent. As mentioned in the introduction, money is a big motivator. If the consultant is confident that she can continually find new work, she will likely be able to make more money. An end client can pay the consultant much less than it pays a larger firm. Yet, the individual consultant can make more because there are no marketing costs or corporate overheard. Additionally, there is no intercompany revenue sharing, and so on, to be satisfied.

Independent consultants have the advantage of significant freedom. They are not weighed down by corporate politics. They are free to move from one project to the next based on their own timing. They are free to research job opportunities anywhere in the world. Some independent consultants enjoy the opportunity to relocate for a project to minimize travel requirements.

Independent consultants have tremendous flexibility for vacations. It is not uncommon for a consultant who has finished a long-term project to desire a longer-term vacation. The independent consultant has no vacation requests or approvals needed from her own company.

Independent consultants have flexibility of work environment. There are some consultants who do not work well in teams; however, these same consultants might have a wealth of knowledge about a particular Oracle product. It can be their desire to deliver the absolute best services available with no one looking over their shoulders and micromanaging their efforts. If these types of consultants remain independent, they do not have to deal with the same coworkers from project to project. Moreover, they do not have to deal with the same managers and supervisors from project to project. These consultants have great flexibility in making their own project decisions. Then, when the project is over, they can leave and not have to deal with the same coworkers or team members on a longer-term basis.

Independent Consulting: Advantages to Employing Company

The greatest advantage to a company that chooses to offer contracts to independent consultants is financial. The opportunity exists to find the most heavily qualified individual consultant at the absolute lowest price. This can be very tempting for companies that are overwhelmed by the typical consulting rates charged by larger consulting organizations. Another advantage to the employing company is that it receives just-in-time help on projects, using consultants who are experts in the specific functional and technical areas required by the company.

Independent Consulting: Risks to Consultant

There are considerable risks to a consultant who works independently. First, the consultant has no other marketing department following up on other Oracle consulting opportunities. Thus, there is little or no opportunity to establish a backlog of work. His company does not have other existing projects in progress where the consultant could choose between one of these at the completion of the current project.

Another risk of independent consulting involves project duration. It is always more desirable to obtain a longer-term project as opposed to a shorter-term project. However, if a consultant is between assignments and out of work, he can accept a short-term assignment even though he did not want to. The bills still have to be paid. The problem with the short-term assignment is that the consultant needs to spend time searching and interviewing for new job opportunities. This is a difficult thing to do if you have made a commitment to your current short-term employer to deliver a high-quality level of service. It is difficult to remain focused on your current client if you know you must almost immediately search for another job.

There is a timing risk due to unexpected project terminations. In this day and age where mergers and acquisitions are common, the independent can be caught in the middle. Many companies proceed through an Oracle, PeopleSoft, or SAP implementation and suddenly terminate the entire project. Sometimes, this is due to a buyout or merger. Sometimes, it is due to an internal power struggle. Sometimes, it is because the company is enduring new financial pressures from industry that affect its budget. If the project abruptly stops, the independent consultant might have had zero time to be prepared.

Independent consultants face risks to their individual reputation. If a project does not go well, it cannot be blamed on their firm. The consultants receive full blame, regardless of whether they agree with the assessment.

The other reputation issue deals with project completion and short-term project extensions. Consider the situation where the consultant has signed a six-month project. Assume that the consultant has delivered top-quality service during these six months. When the six months nears its end, the consultant must look for other work. The problem exists when the existing client desires an extension. If the extension is longer-term, the decision to stay remains fairly easy.

However, what if the existing client only needs three or four more weeks of support, while a new prospective client offers a one-year project? Here is the dilemma. From a legal perspective, the consultant has completed his term and does not have to stay. From a short-term or medium-term job stability perspective, the new opportunity is difficult to turn down (particularly in a market where consulting opportunities have become scarce). What if leaving the existing client puts its business in jeopardy? How important is it to take the client all the way to the finish line? Clearly, if the consultant chooses to leave, the existing client can become quite upset. The consultant might have lost any opportunity for future, repeat business or, most importantly, the opportunity to have a good client reference.

Maintaining skills through adequate personal training is another risk to the independent consultant. The Oracle technologies are rapidly changing. It is difficult for the independent consultant to schedule regular training due to responsibilities from his current project. The consultant must maintain the full burden of off-hours training or training in between projects.

Independent Consulting: Risks to Employing Companies

Employing companies face many risks when attempting to employ independent consultants. The first risk involves knowing whether you have found the best available consultant. Did you have the time to research numerous consultants and check references? Moreover, did the reference checking include actual end clients who have had to live with the work after the consultant left their project? Making sure that the reference checks are not simply old consulting friends who might not be objective is advisable. It takes time to research and find good consultants. Keep in mind that a consultant is only going to provide her good references.

Employing companies have risks using independent consultants due to inconsistent project standards and methods. The employing company must take full responsibility for project management without the assistance of an experienced consulting manager who is backed by others in a consulting firm. An independent consultant often has loose-cannon project methods and desires to operate as a free spirit. Thus, the client management must rigorously monitor quality assurance and project controls. By contrast, many consulting firms offer standard project methods that are understood by all its consultants who are sent to your project.

Loyalty from the independent consultant is a big risk. If an independent consultant is motivated primarily by money, how will she react if another firm offers her more money to do the same thing she is currently doing? Some independent consultants can resist this urge. Others cannot. The example in the previous section is worth noting here also. What if your implementation was only expected to cover a six-month period? When you offered the contract to the consultant, there was no way of knowing every variable and risk that the project faced. Thus, six months was only an estimate of need. What if you near the end of six months and determine that you desperately need three or four more weeks' effort? Will the consultant remain loyal to you if another company offers her more money with a one-year contract?

Related to the loyalty issue are the client's best interests in general. The independent consultants are in business to make money for themselves and not for their firm. Some independent consultants might want to protect their best interests and minimize the level of assistance and support they provide to fellow team members with similar skill levels. The client should monitor reactions by in-house team members and other consultants to determine whether the independent consultant is a prima donna as described in the chapter titled "Working with Consultants" on this book's Web site. Establishing the best team players in this type environment is difficult for the employing company and requires careful management by the client.

Finally, consider that the independent consultant is also her own marketing department. Her attention will lose focus at times because she must continually search for her next project.

SMALLER, SPECIALIZED CONSULTING FIRMS

Many heavily Oracle-experienced consultants choose to work for smaller, specialized consulting firms. These consultants often share similarities to independent consultants in that they desire to make more money than they can at larger, more bureaucratic organizations. Many consultants at these firms are often quite entrepreneurial in nature and desire to avoid the largest consulting organizations. However, they know that to grow a successful business, they need a team working for their same goals, so they do not want to work as independent consultants. These consultants also prefer the idea of a smaller team where their individual success can influence the success and direction of the company.

SMALLER, SPECIALIZED CONSULTING FIRMS: ADVANTAGES TO CONSULTANT

As is the case for independent consultants, money is a big motivator for consultants who work for smaller consulting firms. The smaller company has fewer layers of management, less corporate administration, and smaller overall marketing staff. Thus, there are fewer numbers of people who must share in the profits being generated by each consultant. This allows for significantly higher salaries. Yet, along with these higher salaries, there is a greater stability of income.

Consultants of smaller firms do not share the same level of anxiety near the end of a project that an independent consultant experiences. The consultant at these firms has an easier opportunity to accept short-term extensions at the end of a project. The consultant can continue to work on project completion until the client is satisfied without wondering whether he will have a job when the project is over. The consultant does not need to worry about the financial impact of missing other long-term opportunities because there are usually other heavily experienced consultants within the firm to satisfy other opportunities.

Minimal corporate bureaucracy is a huge reason why many consultants prefer smaller consulting firms. The red tape and political infighting that can occur in large organizations can sap the creative energy of a consultant. A top-notch consultant usually prefers exerting energy to solve client business issues. These consultants often state they do not desire to exert energy related to internal fighting between various regional or vertical business units within a large consulting firm.

Visibility is a big advantage to consultants at smaller specialized consulting firms. It is unlikely for a consultant's good deeds to get lost in the shuffle. The best performers in any type of business want to be recognized and made to feel that contributions are genuinely important. Greater corporate visibility makes these types of firms attractive to some of the most heavily experienced consultants.

Smaller, Specialized Consulting Firms: Advantages to Employing Company

Many firms that have hired consultants to assist with implementations believe the best value exists with smaller, specialized consulting organizations. These firms tend to offer some of the most heavily experienced consultants at rates cheaper than the largest consulting companies, yet with greater stability than can be obtained with independent companies.

The smaller, specialized consulting firms tend to have the most experienced consultants for the reasons stated in the previous section. It is worth noting again that the primary reason is because these firms can afford to pay their employees more than larger, more bureaucratic organizations. Many of these consultants have been trained in implementation methods from previous employment experiences at the larger consulting firms.

By definition, a specialized consulting firm is specialized. Thus, it tends to focus its energies on a specific discipline or niche. There is usually some consulting company that happens to specialize in the exact product or service desired by the employing company. Consider a company that specializes primarily or exclusively in providing Oracle-skilled functional and technical consultants. This company does not exert energy trying to market and support numerous other ERP products. This smaller, specialized company does not hire COBOL programmers to assist organizations in outsourcing or fixing old legacy systems. The old saying, "Jack of all trades, master of none," applies here. Being a master of more than one trade is possible, but the greater the diversity of product/service offerings, the more challenging it is for a firm to master your Oracle needs. The smaller, specialized consulting firm cannot meet all business needs. However, its energies and business can be focused on exactly what the employing company needs to succeed with an Oracle implementation.

The costs of contracting with smaller company consultants are usually cheaper when comparing comparable talent at the Big 5 or Oracle. This is a big advantage to the employing company.

Smaller, Specialized Consulting Firms: Disadvantages to Consultant

There are disadvantages to consultants who choose to work for smaller, more specialized consulting firms. These consultants cannot maintain the same comfort zone that a larger company such as the Big 5 or Oracle can offer. These consultants are less able to put their jobs into "cruise control" as they can at the larger companies. Because the organization is smaller, there are fewer overall consultants who can help pick up the slack.

Related to this issue is the fact that a consultant's weaknesses can be more easily exposed. The consultant can no longer sit back and hope that someone else within the organization can solve the big problems. Consultants at these smaller firms must usually take more responsibility and be more flexible in solving the needs of their clients.

The smaller organization might not be the best choice for the younger, less-experienced consultant. The smaller firm might provide less of a career path or ability to set up a mentoring relationship. For those who are just beginning their careers or those who are on "partner track," the small firm's flat hierarchy might be a negative. The smaller, specialized consulting firm is a flatter organization, and this could be a problem for someone who feels the need to climb a corporate ladder.

There can be less job stability in some specialized consulting firms. If the market slows in the area where the company has established its specialty, the company can come under greater pressure to survive. Some companies will not be able to overcome this situation due to a lack of diversity in other product and service offerings.

Related to the job stability issue is the quality of the management at the smaller, specialized consulting organization. You should thoroughly research the reputation and quality of management of a smaller firm. Because there are fewer layers of corporate management and bureaucracy, there are fewer places to hide poor management with poor market vision.

Smaller, Specialized Consulting Firms: Disadvantages to Employing Company

Smaller consulting firms can pose disadvantages to companies employing Oracle-skilled consultants. Sure, these consulting companies can usually offer higher-experienced consultants at a less expensive price. However, what kind of backup plan can the consulting firm offer if something negative happens to top-quality consultants who have been offered to the employing company? Does the smaller firm have the presence within the industry to respond with the same level of quality and experience with future consultants? Does the smaller firm have a suitable implementation method, or is it more of a body shop? As a result, checking out references should be imperative for the employing company.

Smaller consulting firms desire to grow. The desire for growth can inspire some companies to sell you services in related, but newly established product/service areas. For instance, a company with a historical track record of helping companies implement Oracle Financials from both a functional and technical perspective might attempt to translate that "Oracle" experience into future implementations of Oracle HR/Payroll. In this example, the company's past Oracle implementation successes could deceive the employing company into believing that the new Oracle modules are simply an extension of their previous experience. In reality, the functional and technical issues of Oracle HR/Payroll are dramatically different from Oracle Financials. Issues such as this have burned many hiring organizations.

A further example involves the assumption that a good Oracle Manufacturing technical consultant quickly translates into a good Oracle Manufacturing functional consultant. This, too, is often incorrect. The message is that a hiring company must be prepared to shop around more than once depending on the exact, particular disciplines it needs to solve its specific business issues. Shopping around takes time.

Another disadvantage to using smaller consulting firms involves project team size. If your project has the potential to grow quite large, research to determine the breadth of experience that the consulting firm can offer.

Finally, there is a disadvantage for an employing organization in that it must expend more effort to shop around to find the best-specialized firm to meet each of its various Oracle product implementation needs. By definition, a specialized consulting firm is distinguished in one or a few areas but not in every area needed to meet all the business needs of the client.

LARGER, DIVERSIFIED CONSULTING FIRMS

Many consultants learn and develop solid skills and business practices at larger, diversified consulting organizations. Examples of companies referred to here include the Big 5 firms, Oracle Corporation, EDS, CSC, and other large, diversified service providers. These and other similar large firms offer many employment opportunities to Oracle-skilled professionals.

LARGER, DIVERSIFIED CONSULTING FIRMS: ADVANTAGES TO CONSULTANT

Consultants who choose to work for larger, diversified consulting firms obtain a number of positive factors. These larger firms already have a large account base. The Big 5 already has a large number of relationships based on years of accounting relationships. The larger companies have better brand recognition than do smaller firms. Because the larger firms are by definition larger, they are better able to win large consulting contracts that employ many consultants. When these firms arrive at a prospective client, they have less need to introduce themselves simply to prove to the prospective client that they are a credible organization. This brand recognition can bring greater job security to Oracle-skilled consultants.

Larger consulting firms have the opportunity to support more-extensive training programs. This can be particularly attractive to younger, developing consultants who have great potential but need more experience and training. When Oracle Corporation creates new training courses, it is common for the Big 5 and similar corporations to send some consultants to these classes.

Consultants often gain good habits when working for the Big 5 and other diversified consulting companies. Most of the companies have well-documented implementation methods. If the consultant works on a project where the organization is actually making good use of the methods, there is a tremendous opportunity to learn. A younger consultant can learn proper documentation standards and proper project estimation/tracking methods. The advantage to the consultant is usually not the specific method being used, but the fact that a thorough, organized series of methods is being followed. These types of methods and the requirement for meticulous organization will be invaluable as the consultant progresses through his career.

Finally, the opportunity for local work is a little higher. Most consultants are required to travel, and this remains the case for large consulting firms. However, if the big consulting company has a larger number of Oracle-related projects than does a smaller company, then statistically, the odds are in greater favor that one of these projects will be in the hometown of the consultant.

Larger, Diversified Consulting Firms: Advantages to Employing Company

A company that is considering an ERP system implementation has good reasons to consider employing the Big 5 and other large, diversified consulting organizations. Larger consulting companies offer financial stability. There is less likelihood that the consulting firm being engaged will go out of business before the project is complete.

Larger, diversified consulting firms usually bring local executive account management. Some hiring organizations feel more secure when they know they can drive across town to speak to a partner or principal of the organization. Sure, a hiring firm of a smaller, more specialized consulting organization could have the opportunity to pick up a phone or send an e-mail. However, there is a tangible security to some people when they feel they can meet face-to-face that same day with an executive who has the power and influence to make changes when a project has begun seeing difficult times.

Larger consulting firms often bring solid project methods that are designed to help maintain control of larger projects. Moreover, these methodologies have often been used with many other clients. Even in cases where the method has been somewhat inferior for other clients, the larger consulting firm has had opportunities to document and learn from critical mistakes. The method does not ensure project success, but it offers a higher probability of success.

Related to the methods is project management in general. The Big 5 and similarly sized organizations often have senior project managers who have direct experience managing large-scale implementations.

Larger consulting organizations have more historical documentation and best-practices information that can potentially be used by the consultants to benefit the employing company. This can be an advantage, although it often becomes a more neutral factor than it should be. If the large consulting firm does not have a truly centralized mechanism for sharing information across its various regional and vertical business lines, the client will never benefit from this past project information. Certainly, this issue is not a negative factor to the employing organization and, at worst, is a nonissue. The question is whether these potential advantages for the client can be actually realized due to the consulting company's internal organizational structure.

Larger consulting firms offer the potential for one-stop shopping for solving the entire setup software needs of a client. They have access to more resources in more product areas than do smaller firms. However, although this is definitely an advantage, the advantage might not be as large as it seems. No firm has the time or the resources to properly research the best solution for every business need. Even though the employing organization might not obtain the *best* solution in the arrangement, the odds are greater that a *good* solution will still be recommended.

Finally, larger consulting firms, by definition, have more employees. If a sizable number of these employees have direct, hands-on skills in the particular Oracle discipline, the hiring firm has a little more project stability. Turnover can be high when dealing with experienced IT professionals and particularly when the professionals have high-demand Oracle-related skills. If your project were to lose key consultants before completion, the larger consulting firms have a chance to be well equipped to provide a suitable replacement.

Larger, Diversified Consulting Firms: Disadvantages to Consultant

There are disadvantages to consultants who choose to work for larger, diversified consulting companies. Working for any large company involves a much higher incidence of company politics. Playing company politics has enabled many professionals to advance their careers more quickly when compared with consultants and other professionals who did not want to "play the game."

There are other political issues that are often influenced and exaggerated by the internal structure of a large firm. To satisfy numerous types of clients, large consulting firms will often align business services based on regional or industry-specific vertical markets. Although this is a good goal for certain disciplines (such as COBOL or C programmers), it can produce problems in disciplines (such as Oracle) where there are not excessive numbers of highly skilled professionals. For example, the firm as a whole might have a sufficient number of Oracle Projects consultants, but this might not help a regional manager who might have few or no Oracle Projects consultants within his region.

For instance, it might make great strategic sense for the organization as a whole to attempt to meet the needs of a particular higher education institution that is implementing an Oracle ERP system. However, assume that the large consulting firm has a business line or service line designed to exclusively work with higher education accounts. Now assume that the university desires to implement Oracle Human Resources. It might happen that most of the skilled HR consultants report to different private sector regions of the country or the world. The managers of these regional consultants often resist "giving" their skilled consultants to another internal branch unless they can obtain the full revenue that they would observe in the open market. On the other hand, the higher education vertical-market executive might scoff at the idea of paying high interbranch rates for using these consultants. The higher education vertical-market executive in this example can be faced with the dilemma: "Do I forego revenue and pay the high interbranch rate, or do I attempt to train someone who really does not have the appropriate experience so that I can make my profit margin?" Even executives and managers who desire to work well together between business units will face disincentives to do so because of the financial incentives of the business structure.

What is the message? In this example, a consultant with all the necessary skills might live in the exact same town where the business opportunity exists; however, because the consultant "belongs" to a different region or vertical unit, she might miss the opportunity for an assignment that is both exciting and local. This can leave a real sour taste in the mouth of a consultant who missed opportunities simply due to organizational politics.

Related to the politics issue is the issue of the overall bureaucracy of larger consulting organizations. A consultant can experience frustration when attempting to accomplish certain tasks because of the red tape and number of approvals necessary to ensure that all company policies have been satisfied. Because many business policies are firmly entrenched, the consultant has much less opportunity to make changes to business philosophy and direction. There is less visibility, which can influence opportunities for advancement. Certainly, there are more numerous corporate levels required to advance through to get near the top of this type of company.

Finally, less pay is the biggest disadvantage to consultants working at larger consulting firms. Because of the greater number of levels of management and the much higher corporate overhead, it is more difficult for the highest salaries to trickle down to the actual consultant. As the consultant becomes more and more experienced, there is a much greater financial temptation to consider working for smaller, more specialized firms that focus on her particular type of skill.

LARGER, DIVERSIFIED CONSULTING FIRMS: DISADVANTAGES TO EMPLOYING COMPANY

Disadvantages exist to employing companies that choose to contract the services of larger, diversified consulting firms. There is a general perception that bigger implies better. Although this can be true on the management front, it is often not true from the perspective of experience levels supplied by the consulting organization.

Consider the disincentives for the best Oracle-skilled consultants to remain with the large consulting organization. These disincentive issues were discussed in the preceding section and include issues such as lack of top salaries, less corporate visibility, and higher corporate politics and bureaucracy. If you were a consultant and felt that you could make more money, endure less corporate bureaucracy, and still do the exact same Oracle-related work at a smaller, more specialized firm, how long would you continue to work under your existing arrangement? Now that you are a hiring manager who is about to employ the services of a large firm, what indications (separate from the sales ability of your sales representative) do you have that the actual consultants who are coming to your project are actually some of the most highly skilled in the industry?

There are occasions when this environment can be turned into a positive by the large, diversified consulting organizations. Most of these firms believe that they have good management and good methods; however, they inwardly know that they do not have enough of the most highly skilled and experienced resources. Many of their consultants have been groomed through solid internal training programs, yet they might still be younger with less experience.

There are large consulting organizations that solve this issue by subcontracting Oracle-specific work either to independent consultants or to smaller, more specialized firms. This enables the larger consulting company to bring in the most experienced talent, yet still take advantage of the corporate methods they already have in place. If the large consulting firm is resistant to this type of subcontracting business arrangement, it still has the potential to create good project teams. However, the risk to the client is tremendously higher than usually expected.

It is recommended that the hiring organization do more than simply check the overall references of the large consulting firm. References should be checked based on the individual project team members assigned to a particular client. This keeps pressure on the large consulting organization to supply a higher quality and greater experienced level of talent. It is recommended that references be checked for most resumes that are being proposed for the project. After all, are you purchasing the name of a firm or purchasing the skills of the individual consultants that you will see on a daily basis?

The final disadvantage is the higher cost of big-company consultants, although this issue can be exaggerated. Overall, it costs an employing company more to hire equivalently trained consultants at a large organization than at a small organization. This is usually the case over the short term. However, this cost can be exaggerated in the long term. If the larger firm brings the overall management and experience to increase the probability of project success, the higher cost of consultants can be justified.

ORACLE CORPORATION CONSULTING

A large number of consultants choose to work for Oracle Corporation itself. Oracle Corporation consultants can be found all over the world. As can be expected, these consultants usually focus exclusively on consulting related to products produced by Oracle Corporation.

ORACLE CORPORATION CONSULTING: ADVANTAGES TO CONSULTANT

Advantages for consultants at Oracle Corporation are significant. Perhaps the biggest advantage that Oracle Corporation can offer its consultants is state-of-the-art training. Oracle Corporation is continually creating new and more exciting products. Consultants at Oracle often get to hear about the products before they are officially released to the public. Oracle Corporation invests significantly to keep its consultants well trained on functionality of relevant Oracle products. A consultant has the advantage in some cases to stay ahead of industry peers regarding exposure and training to the latest and greatest products.

The number of consultants who are trained on any given Oracle product is usually higher at Oracle Corporation than at any other company in the world. Because there are more trained consultants on a particular Oracle module, there are more in-house contacts for an Oracle Corporation consultant to contact when she experiences challenges and problems on a project. However, this advantage can be exaggerated. On some occasions, there can be so many consultants asking so many internal questions that an overload occurs. The strongest consultants with the most knowledge to answer these questions can only answer so many questions in a week while still providing adequate value to their own clients. Nevertheless, this communication environment is still an advantage.

Because Oracle Corporation Consulting has assisted in many past projects, a great deal of project documentation and white papers exist. This can be particularly helpful to less-experienced consultants who desire to learn from the experiences from past projects within the firm.

Consultants at Oracle Corporation have the ability to learn a method that is tailored specifically for implementing Oracle Applications. Oracle AIM (Application Implementation Method) is the standard used by most Oracle Corporation consultants. Knowledge of this method is particularly advantageous to less-experienced consultants who are learning proper project standards and techniques. AIM can help guide a less-experienced consultant who has not yet obtained much industry experience through the steps of an implementation project. (See a similar discussion in the section "Larger, Diversified Consulting Firms: Advantages to Consultant.")

Finally, because of the large number of consulting projects being implemented by Oracle, there might be an opportunity for the consultant to find work that is closer to home. Most consultants have 100% travel requirements, but the chances are at least a little higher that local work can be obtained.

Oracle Corporation Consulting: Advantages to Employing Company

Companies that choose to employ Oracle Corporation consultants have the potential for several advantages. First is the potential pipeline of information to the product development groups and to other Oracle Corporation employees. If there is a critical decision that needs to be made on a project, the Oracle Corporation consultant is likely to have the best access to an internal decision-maker at Oracle.

The use of Oracle's Application Implementation Method is an advantage to employing companies. It is critical that a client uses a structured and methodical approach to increase the chances of long-term project success. Most Oracle Corporation consultants are trained on this method and bring this knowledge to their clients.

A more subtle advantage to employing companies who choose to use Oracle Corporation consultants involves the overall negotiation of product purchases. Depending on the number of products being purchased and many other factors, a company facing an upcoming implementation can sometimes use this as bargaining power with Oracle Corporation. The potential for moderately discounted consulting rates might be obtained in exchange for agreement for a full-scale product suite purchase.

Employing companies generally obtain consultants from Oracle Corporation who have been trained on the critical Oracle products required for the project. This level of training is advantageous particularly when new product versions arrive. The Oracle Corporation consultants have the potential to be well informed from a training class on all the latest and greatest product features.

Oracle Corporation Consulting: Disadvantages to Consultant

Disadvantages exist for consultants who choose to work for Oracle Corporation. For starters, corporate bureaucracy at Oracle Corporation can cause much inefficiency. Note the write-up in the section "Larger, Diversified Consulting Firms: Disadvantages to Consultant." There is an example of a skilled Oracle HR expert who is forced to miss a fabulous local opportunity due to big company politics. Oracle Corporation is very similar to these other big companies when dealing with the political infighting of various regional and vertically aligned business units. A consultant can find her personal goals compromised and ignored due to this type of bureaucracy.

For equivalent skills and experience, many Oracle Corporation consultants observe lower pay in relation to other Oracle-skilled consultants. This disadvantage to the consultant is very much similar to the issues discussed with larger, diversified consulting firms. There is simply a great deal of corporate overhead and many layers of management who have their hands in the bucket and must share in the profits generated by each consultant.

Oracle Corporation consultants sometimes observe disadvantages in the project environment because they work for Oracle. Many clients find some Oracle Application product area that they perceive to be deficient within the particular Oracle products that they have purchased. The client will often desire the consultant to pressure Oracle to "fix" problems with the product. Although the Oracle Corporation consultant was not responsible for creating the products herself, the client will expect her to put pressure on others within Oracle to improve or fix the product. This implied responsibility and pressure on the consultant could be counterproductive. The consultant would be better utilized designing new solutions to meet the specific customer's needs instead of trying to defend her organization on the merits of the product.

Another disadvantage that influences the growth of Oracle Corporation consultants involves objectivity in decision-making. Although Oracle products tend to be very reputable in the marketplace, not every item created by Oracle is superior in every single niche. A consultant at Oracle might feel implied pressure to "sing the company tune" and promote products with an Oracle brand name even when competing products exist that might better serve her client. This does not mean that a consultant at Oracle will compromise her client's best interests. The message is that there is certainly pressure and challenges that must be overcome to obtain true objectivity. Further, Oracle Corporation might discourage the consultant from making a creative and appropriate extension or modification to the basic product. This can stifle the experienced consultant and create frustration when unable to do the right thing to meet client requirements.

Related to this issue is that Oracle Corporation consultants might lose out on the opportunity to learn about new non-Oracle products. Regardless of the merits of the following products, it would take extremely unusual circumstances for an Oracle Corporation consultant to be allowed to spend significant consulting time assisting with PeopleSoft HR/Payroll, SAP General Ledger, Microsoft SQL Server, and so on. Thus, the Oracle Corporation consultant might not be developing the most diversified industry skills.

Oracle Corporation Consulting: Disadvantages to Employing Company

Companies that choose to employ Oracle Corporation consultants often observe disadvantages. Many clients feel that they pay higher consulting rates for lower levels of Oracle product experience. The client initially assumes that the most heavily Oracle-experienced consultants should logically come from Oracle itself. This is not necessarily the case.

The client might actually receive more junior consultants in some cases who are fresh out of an Oracle training program. Thus, the consultants are well trained but not necessarily well experienced. This situation can occur for several reasons. First, some of the best Oracle Corporation consultants might be engaged in long-term projects with existing customers. These consultants who have gained the most hands-on experience are not available to leave their current client in the middle of the project. Others of the most heavily experienced consultants leave the company because of big-company politics or other issues. These consultants can usually obtain more money doing the same work with a specialized, smaller consulting firm. As a result, some clients observe higher costs for equivalent, or even lower, levels of experience.

Finally, corporations who choose to use Oracle Corporation consultants sometimes lose the opportunity to receive objective and optimal solutions. In particular, if their consultants continue to be trained on only Oracle products, what other non-Oracle solutions might best meet the client's needs? In many cases, out-of-the-box solutions using the Oracle products are the best choice. However, are the particular Oracle Corporation consultants assigned to each project always equipped to recommend or design the best industry solution? Similarly, do you think that an Oracle Corporation consultant will be encouraged to objectively acknowledge that a particular product from Microsoft, PeopleSoft, or SAP might actually be good?

Summary

Each of the types of consulting alternatives described in this chapter can offer special opportunity to consultants depending on where you are in your career and what your specific needs are. You should not focus too much on any one section in this chapter. All should be considered together to help have a more objective assessment of the industry as a whole. It can be easy to overlook the various disadvantages discussed. Yet, the disadvantages are real, and every type of consulting opportunity has a downside.

APPENDIX

IMPLEMENTATION CHECKLIST

In this appendix

The purpose of this appendix is to provide a checklist of things that typically occur during an Oracle Applications implementation. Each implementation is unique, and you will want to adapt this list to your own project requirements.

PLAN AND INITIATE THE PROJECT

Every implementation requires substantial planning prior to beginning the implementation process. It is critical to know the scope, resources, timeline, and final objectives for your project. You should consider allocating between three and five percent of your total budget to planning activities. However, don't look at that budget allocation as a cost or overhead to the project. If you don't plan well, you will surely lose three to five percent in project team efficiency. Create a realistic project plan that will ultimately result in a successful, timely implementation. Use this phase of the project to establish the plan, controls, and procedures.

MANAGEMENT COMMITMENT

The most important thing you must do is make sure that your top level management is engaged and involved with the implementation project:

- Realize that the decision of your company's owners or CEO to purchase a new system is not the end, but instead the beginning of their involvement.
- Top management must display visible commitment to the new system and demonstrate involvement by attending education sessions, demanding progress reports, participating in setting policies, and so on.
- This implementation process should be given a number two priority—second only to running the business.

PLANNING

This list shows items you might want to consider as you prepare the software implementation project plans:

- Evaluate various implementation methods, such as rapid, preconfigured, phased, big-bang, reengineered, customized, and program office.
- Establish a formal project organization including a steering committee, a project team, and a project manager.
- Develop a high-level project work plan. Don't lock in your detailed project plan until you finish the analysis phase of the project. Don't let a project sponsor or steering committee lock in a budget until the analysis phase is complete.
- Determine time and cost criteria for the project. Try not to lock into a firm production date until you complete the analysis phase.
- Determine and document the assumptions that are in effect at the time the project is initiated.
- Create a risk assessment deliverable and a plan to mitigate risks.

- Document anything that is out of scope for the project.
- Conduct a high-level review of business requirements.
- Review data conversion methods available and determine which method is best for each module.
- Determine test plans and the degree of effort required.
- Develop a high-level reporting strategy. Estimate the volume of custom reports to be written for each module.
- Define transition policies after reviewing business constraints.
- Estimate the time required to complete tasks. Decompose tasks longer than four days into shorter subtasks.
- Load the implementation plan into the Project Management software tool.
- Establish a working budget and understand the planned return on investment.
- The project plan remains a living document as revisions are made, new tasks are added, tasks are deleted, and resources are added or deleted.

STAFFING

Staffing your project is the process of bringing resources and skills to the project team. Most companies must form an implementation team of functional, technical, managerial, and consulting resources and skills. Consider the following:

- Identify the project manager, internal sponsors, steering committee, and managers, both technical and functional.
- Identify internal technical and functional resources for each module. Form a project team. Establish an organization chart for the implementation team and end users.
- Determine the technical and functional skill sets needed by members of the project team.
- Make sure project team members can make decisions about business processes, requirements, and policies.
- Identify technical and functional external resources.
- Select at least one database administrator and system administrator.
- Develop an education plan for the project team. Analyze educational needs for internal resources and identify the classes each team member will attend.

CONTROLS

Project controls are the procedures, practices, and policies you use to govern the software implementation activities. Tight controls can stifle and delay the work. However, a lack of control is almost always expensive and risky. Project controls include the following:

- Define scope, goals, and terms for the project.
- If you think you need it, develop a project quality plan. If you don't think you need it, think again.

- Establish an issue tracking and resolution process.
- Define policy and justification criteria for modifications to the Oracle applications.
- Define custom report policy and justification criteria.
- Define a policy and justification for custom interfaces.
- Define acceptance criteria for the Oracle Applications software.
- Define a policy for implementation of non-core business requirements.
- Define the policies and procedures for the activities that fall outside the software. This activity often takes a back seat to the other activities of the project, but these policies and procedure are equally important in running the business.
- Document the policies and procedures in a standardized and consistent manner.
- Determine the impact of other corporate projects and initiatives on the Oracle Applications project.
- Define a policy and justification for creation of custom reports.

Communication

When a small implementation team makes enterprise-wide decisions about future business processes, communication helps the organization accept the change to the new software. Following are aspects of communication to consider:

- Review project goals, scope, and deliverables with the project team.
- Tell the project team, the project sponsor, and the steering committee about your implementation strategy.
- Obtain a sign-off of the project plan by project team members.
- Determine communication methods for project stakeholders.
- Create a companywide communication plan regarding the project's goals, objectives, timelines, and status.
- Determine the frequency and locations of project status meetings for the project teams, project managers, and steering committee.
- Schedule and conduct a kickoff meeting for the project team.

Logistics

The implementation project will last from four months to more than a year. Take the time at the beginning to set up a decent work area and make the team comfortable, efficient, and productive:

- Obtain workspace, equipment, and supplies needed for the project team.
- Set up a project war room. Ensure everything necessary is present to make the implementation team efficient.

ANALYZE THE BUSINESS AND THE TECHNOLOGY

You need to define high-level business requirements during the planning and initiation phase of the project for planning purposes. However, when the project has started, it is critical to perform an in-depth analysis of the business requirements to ensure that all the details of the requirement are understood and documented. When the detailed analysis has been performed, you should have an accurate definition of the scope. Project scope and the work plan will continue to change until the analysis is complete.

The following list shows many of the activities of the analysis phase of the implementation project:

- Document current business operating processes, policies, and requirements.
- Determine special business requirements for transition to new systems.
- Inventory the current technical architecture.
- Identify discussion materials needed for review during analysis meetings. Gather copies of all current reports.
- Define all integration points among Oracle modules.
- Determine the fit between Oracle Applications and non-Oracle systems at all integration points.
- Define and estimate the scope of custom interfaces.
- Obtain file specifications for all interfaces.
- Design custom interface programs.
- Determine future business processes and detailed requirements.
- Determine future technical architecture requirements.
- Document contingency plans and requirements.
- Gather information about processing volumes and frequencies.
- Assess risks and variables affecting system performance, fault tolerance, availability, and response time.
- Establish policies and procedures for working with Oracle Support. Create a TAR tracking log.
- Define and document all setup information choices. Define Key and Descriptive Flexfields.
- Perform detailed analysis of legacy reports. Construct a matrix to compare Oracle and legacy reports.
- Design custom reports.
- Design conversion programs for legacy data.
- Document gaps and the proposed resolution for each.
- Define and estimate the cost of custom extensions to the applications.
- Document any policy changes.

- Define all data loads for each module.
- Verify accuracy of all legacy data that will be loaded into the Oracle Applications.
- Identify any balance loads.
- Define test plans.
- Review transaction volumes and frequencies.
- Complete the estimating spreadsheet for hardware sizing.
- Review system-sizing estimates from the planning phase of the project to ensure original estimates were accurate. Adjust if necessary.
- Determine security requirements.
- Determine Responsibilities and User Profiles.
- Determine audit and control requirements.
- Update the project plan to reflect changes.
- Audit your project for red flags.
- Define and confirm new business policies and procedures.

Build and Configure Your System

At this stage of the project, the installation process should be complete and development/test instances will be created. When the business requirements have been clearly defined, the process of building, configuring, and testing the system can begin:

- Create responsibilities and users.
- Configure the system from setup documents completed during business analysis. Make sure to document any changes or fine-tuning of the configuration parameters.
- Map business requirements to Oracle Application function points.
- Load data manually and through open interfaces into the test instance.
- Map legacy data to be converted to Oracle Application Program Interfaces (APIs).
- Build, balance, and unit test legacy data conversions, initializations, and loads.
- Code and test custom reports.
- Code and unit test custom interfaces.
- Use the Optimal Flexible Architecture (OFA) when you install the applications.
- Implement a backup, recovery, and fault tolerance strategy.
- Conduct a conference room pilot test of the fully integrated system. Document a test plan, verify results, and repeat until results meet business requirements.
- Configure the production system when you have determined the freeze point for Oracle patches and integration tests.
- Always analyze build activities and decisions for their impact on future upgrades.
- Make sure you document all spontaneous changes in the setup documents.

TRANSITION TO THE NEW SYSTEM

When the system has been configured, built, and tested, the next step toward final implementation is to perform transition tasks. These tasks prepare the system for production use by the users:

- Prepare training materials.
- Create user procedure and system operation manuals.
- Identify end users for training and schedule classes.
- Conduct user-training classes.
- Load data and beginning balances into the production database manually or programmatically through open interfaces.
- Enable end-user support capability.
- Make sure project documentation reflects the system as built.
- Audit your project for red flags.
- Achieve a team consensus on the go/no-go decision.

SUPPORT THE PRODUCTION SYSTEMS

The production Oracle system requires administration and support. There might be a formal handoff from the implementation team to the support organization, or some of the project team members might remain involved as power users and administration staff. When the system stabilizes, start improving and refining the system to keep moving forward.

This list shows supporting activities required for Oracle ERP systems after users begin making production transactions:

- Make sure the system is fault-tolerant and the database backups are reliable.
- Verify that end users are capable of operating the system. Conduct additional training and support as required.
- Apply patches carefully after testing. Test everything you get from Oracle before applying it to your production system.
- Monitor the use of free space within the database.
- Monitor system response time and tune concurrent processes that consume the most system resources.
- Identify disk I/O hot spots and redistribute I/O across the physical disk drives.
- Conduct a post implementation audit to verify that business requirements were met, measure user satisfaction, and create the basis for continuous process improvement based on the new applications.

Many of the items mentioned previously require the preciseness of science, but others require the creativity of art. Both preciseness and creativity are inherent in the implementation of your Oracle Application software. Implementation is making things happen. The scientist and the artist both want to make things happen; each uses different means to reach an end. To achieve a successful implementation at your company, use both the traits of a scientist and of an artist. Be precise and creative in order to be successful.

INDEX

Symbols

A

C

D

E

F

G

N

O

P

Q

R

S

T

U

V

Y

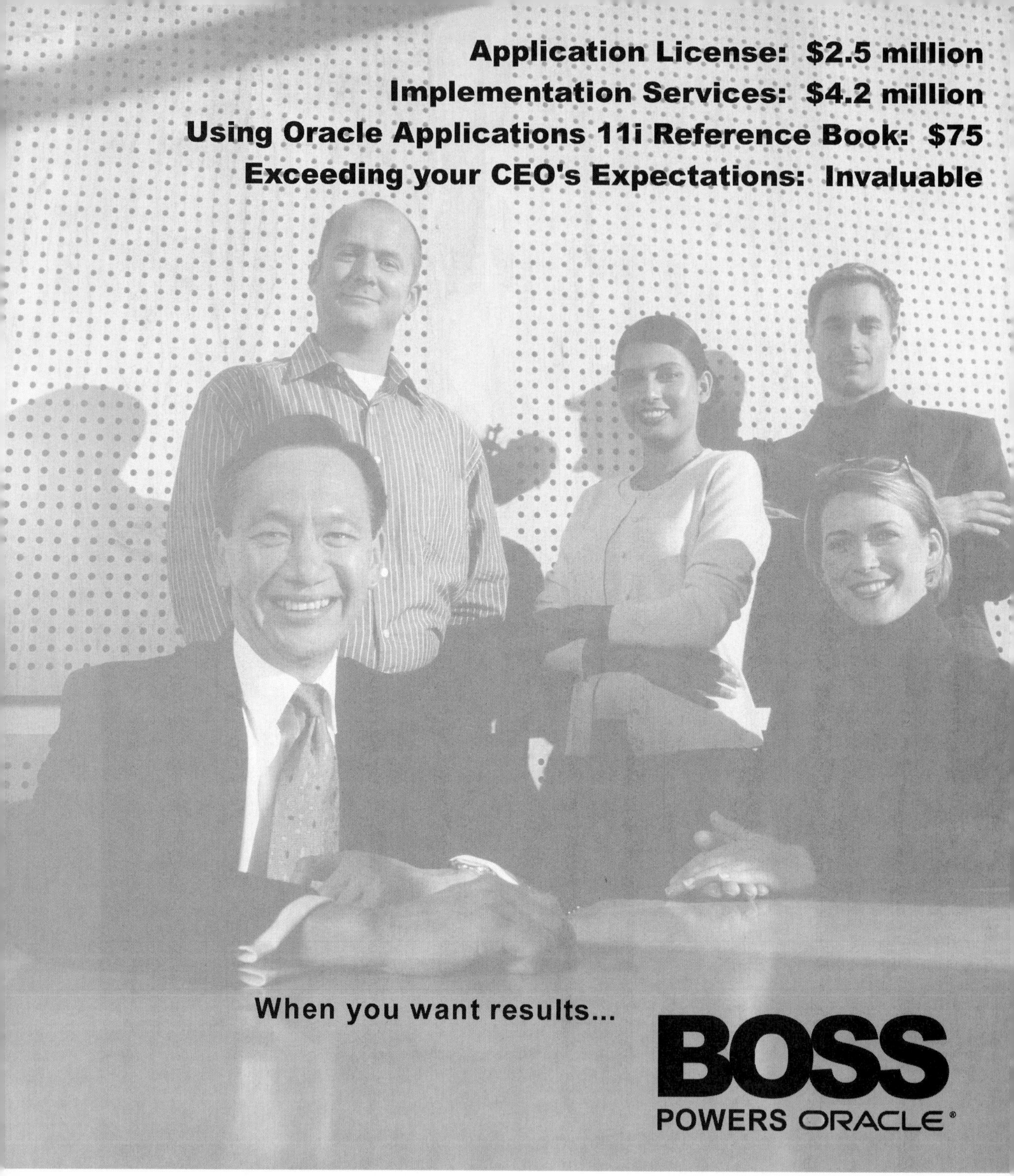
Application License: $2.5 million
Implementation Services: $4.2 million
Using Oracle Applications 11i Reference Book: $75
Exceeding your CEO's Expectations: Invaluable
When you want results...
BOSS
POWERS ORACLE®

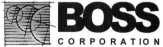